Glencoe Accounting

P9-BJE-864

Log on to the Online Learning Center glencoeaccounting.glencoe.com

Improved Technology

Learn software with instruction integrated right into the book

- Peachtree®
- QuickBooks®
- Microsoft® Excel

New Student Edition Features

Connect to the real world of business

- Standard & Poor's Personal Finance Q&A
- WebQuest Internet Projects
- Working in the *Real World*
- Winning Competitive Events
- International Accounting

Reading and Academic Integration

Reinforce reading and academic skills

- Reading Strategies
- Connect to…Academics
- Do the Math

First-Year Course

GLENCOE
Accounting
Real-World Applications & Connections

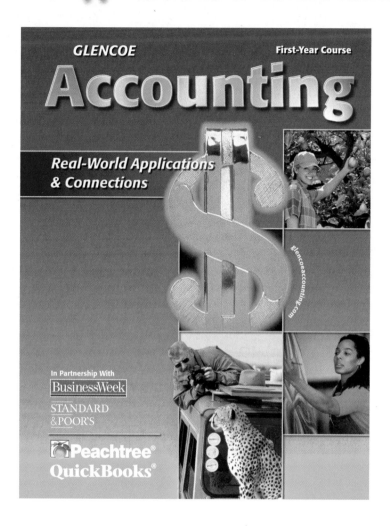

Donald J. Guerrieri
Norwin High School,
Retired
North Huntingdon,
Pennsylvania

F. Barry Haber
Fayetteville State
University, Retired
Fayetteville,
North Carolina

William B. Hoyt
Wilton High School
Wilton, Connecticut

Robert E. Turner
Northwestern State
University
Natchitoches,
Louisiana

Glencoe

New York, New York   Columbus, Ohio   Chicago, Illinois   Peoria, Illinois   Woodland Hills, California

Notice. Information on featured companies, organizations, and their products and services is included for educational purposes only and does not present or imply endorsement of the *Glencoe Accounting* program. Permission to use all business logos has been granted by the businesses represented in this text.

Glencoe

The **McGraw-Hill** Companies

Send all inquiries to:
Glencoe/McGraw-Hill
21600 Oxnard Street, Suite 500
Woodland Hills, CA 91367

ISBN-13: 978-0-07-868829-4   (Student Edition)
ISBN-10: 0-07-868829-9   (Student Edition)

ISBN-13: 978-0-07-873985-9   (Teacher Wraparound Edition)
ISBN-10: 0-07-873985-3   (Teacher Wraparound Edition)

4 5 6 7 8 9   079   10 09 08

Donald J. Guerrieri

Donald J. Guerrieri has taught accounting at both the secondary and college levels. His work for a firm of certified public accountants gave him hands-on experience in working with real-world clients. Dr. Guerrieri has written numerous articles about teaching accounting for a number of educational journals. Now retired from his position as Accounting Instructor at Norwin High School, North Huntingdon, Pennsylvania, he is a program speaker at business education seminars and conferences.

F. Barry Haber

F. Barry Haber has taught accounting principles courses to literally thousands of students for more than 40 years. Dr. Haber is a certified public accountant and has served on the Minority Doctoral Fellows Committee of the American Institute of Certified Public Accountants (AICPA). In addition to teaching accounting principles, Dr. Haber has authored three other textbooks in addition to a number of articles and accounting cases. He is retired from his position as Professor of Accounting at Fayetteville State University, Fayetteville, North Carolina.

William B. Hoyt

William B. Hoyt is an Accounting Instructor at Wilton High School, Wilton, Connecticut. He has been a force in accounting curriculum development for many years and served as a member of the writing task force for the National Standards for Business Education. The author of various articles in professional journals, Mr. Hoyt was named Connecticut's Outstanding Business Educator of the Year in 1996, and in 1997 the National Business Education Association named him National Secondary Teacher of the Year.

Robert E. Turner

Robert E. Turner is an Assistant Professor in the College of Business at Northwestern State University, Natchitoches, Louisiana. Previously, he served as Vice President for Business Affairs at McNeese State University, Lake Charles, Louisiana, and at the University of Louisiana at Monroe. Mr. Turner's broad experience includes teaching accounting and other business subjects at the high school and college levels. He is a frequent speaker at educational conferences, seminars, and workshops around the country.

Introducing Glencoe's Business Partners

STANDARD &POOR'S

Standard & Poor's is the world's leading provider of independent investment research, indexes, and ratings. Financial decision makers around the world use S&P's widely recognized investment data and analysis to help create growth and manage wealth. Among its many products are the S&P 1200, the premier global equity performance benchmark; the S&P 500, the premier U.S. portfolio index; and credit ratings on more than 220,000 securities and funds worldwide.

BusinessWeek

BusinessWeek is the leading global resource of ground-breaking news and analysis in a fast-changing business world. Across print, television, and on-line media, *BusinessWeek* offers essential insight that provides a competitive edge. *BusinessWeek* is the world's most widely read business magazine, with more than 8 million readers, including online and television viewers.

Peachtree®

Peachtree is a line of home, education, and business application software with emphasis on accounting products. Having sold more than a million packages of its software, Peachtree is recognized as a leader in the small business accounting market.

Robert Half International Inc.

Robert Half International Inc. is the world's first and largest staffing service specializing in accounting, finance, banking, and technology systems. With more than 300 offices internationally, Robert Half provides services for both full-time and temporary professionals.

AICPA

The American Institute of Certified Public Accountants is a national professional organization for Certified Public Accountants in the United States. With more than 200,000 members, the AICPA provides resources and information to its members, enabling them to provide valuable services to employers, clients, and the public.

Contributing Editors

Cynthia A. Ash
Davenport University
Granger, Indiana

Louann Cummings
The University of Findlay
Findlay, Ohio

Patrick C. Hale
Angelina College
Lufkin, Texas

Sandra S. Lang
McKendree College
Lebanon, Illinois

Alice Sineath
Forsyth Technical Community College
Winston-Salem, North Carolina

Kimberly D. Smith
County College of Morris
Randolph, New Jersey

Educational Reviewers

Jayne Abernathy
Accounting Teacher
Centerville High School
Centerville, Ohio

Barbara A. Berg
Vocational Business Teacher
Carey High School
Carey, Idaho

Sibyl Cole-Olfzewski
Computer Tech. Teacher
Medina High School
Medina, Ohio

Naomi Crane
Accounting Teacher
Southwest High School
Fort Worth, Texas

Johnsie Crawford
Accounting Teacher
Brandon High School
Brandon, Florida

Carrie Davis
Business Teacher
Yoncalla High School
Yoncalla, Oregon

Melinda G. Dibenedetto
Business Department Chair
Shades Valley High School
Birmingham, Alabama

Christine Fink
Business Teacher
Cocalico High School
Denver, Pennsylvania

Patricia Kay Fordham
Business Teacher
Central High School
Salt Lake City, Utah

Patsy A. Frost
Business Department Chair
Scituate High School
North Scituate, Rhode Island

Ruby Garr
Business Department Head
I.H. Kempner High School
Sugar Land, Texas

Karen King Gilliland
Business Department Chair
Winchester Community High School
Winchester, Indiana

Norma C. Isassi
Accounting Teacher
H.M. King High School
Kingsville, Texas

Karen LaClair
Business Department Chair
Simsbury High School
Simsbury, Connecticut

Chris Mendez
Accounting Teacher
Bel Air High School
El Paso, Texas

Regena Morris
Business Education Teacher
Arlington Heights High School
Fort Worth, Texas

Jeff Noyes
Business Education Teacher
Minnetonka High School
Minnetonka, Minnesota

Karen Poidomani
Business Teacher
William Floyd High School
Mastic Beach, New York

Martha Ramirez
Business Teacher
McCallum High School
Austin, Texas

William Sinai
Computerized Accounting Dept.
Chair
West Valley Occupational Center
Woodland Hills, California

Violet Snell
Business Department Chair
MacArthur High School
San Antonio, Texas

Alfonso Vargas
Accounting Teacher
Hueneme High School
Oxnard, California

Karen Wood
Accounting Teacher
Centerville High School
Centerville, Ohio

Dianne L. Young
Dean of Students
Wilmington High School
Wilmington, Delaware

We wish to acknowledge the contributions of the following:

Jayne Abernathy, Xenia, OH
Jim Adams, New Albany, IN
G. Armstrong, Bath, NY
Ron Baldini, Pulaski, WI
Alan Balog, Ravenna, OH
B. A. Banks-Burke, Hudson, OH
Denise M. Barbaris, West Milford, NJ
E. Patricia Barnes, Evansville, IN
Lou Ellen Bass, Four Oaks, NC
Linda Becker, Cary, NC
Perry Beckerman, Brooklyn, NY
Kathleen Beetar, Houston, TX
Scott Behnke, Wales, WI
Len C. Bigler, Grand Rapids, MI
Jackie Billings, McAllen, TX
Lee Birnbaum, Farmingdale, NJ
Cheryl Birx, Canandaigua, NY
Linda J. Black, Mt. Airy, GA
Elbert F. Black, Hastings, MI
Cindi Blansfield, Auburn, WA
Josephine Bliss, Merced, CA
D. Bogataj, Flat Rock, MI
Kelly Brock, Columbus, GA
William A. Brogdon, German Town, TN
Rachelle Brown, Morocco, IN
Jessie Broxmeyer, Long Beach, NY
Margaret Broyles, Forest Park, OH
Gus Buchttolz, Wyoming, MI
Ronda K. Budd, Grove City, OH
Pete Bush, Leesburg, FL
Michelle Cardoza, Tulare, CA
Walter Carlson, Torrance, CA
Marisa Charles, Houston, TX
Bill Christianson, Spokane, WA
Jodi S. Clark, Warner Robins, GA
Anthony Paul Corbisiero, West New York, NJ
Ron Craig, Anaheim, CA
Lynn Crawford, Cudahy, WI
Claudia Cullari, Fair Lawn, NJ
Jo Damron, Abilene, TX
Jan Davis, Port Neches, TX
Toni DeFuria, Old Tappan, NJ
Denise Deltondo, Girard, OH
Carolyn Deshler, Moorpark, CA
Diane DeWitt, Freeport, IL
Wanda Drake, Jackson, TN
Buzz Drake, Barrington, IL
Ray Dunavant, Denison, TX
Tearle Dwiggins, Pendleton, IN

Susan España, Rocklin, CA
Morris P. Fair, Sr., Jackson, TN
Glenn Fong, Sacramento, CA
Julie Fox, Wisconsin Rapids, WI
Carolyn Francis, Baytown, TX
Cherilynn Frost, Livonia, MI
Patricia T. Gardella, Vineland, NJ
Robert D. Garrison, Belleview, FL
Kimberly Morris Gehres, Adrian, MI
JoAnn Gipson, Garland, TX
Nancy Glavic, New Concord, OH
Joyce Greemon, Gastonin, NC
Sheree Green, Teaneck, NJ
Andrea Gross, Vidor, TX
Guzzeta, Plant City, FL
Ronald L. Hainds, Jacksonville, IL
Kellie Hair, Kennesaw, GA
Sheryl J. Hane, Norco, CA
Janice Hanes, Fort Worth, TX
Marion Hanneld, Omaha, NE
Farolyn Hanscom, Riverside, CA
Wanda Harris, Eden, NC
Tammy Hatfield, Tullahoma, TN
Felicia S. Hatten, Detroit, MI
Debra R. Hauser, Shrub Oak, NY
Richard Heim, Latham, NY
Audrey M. Hendry, Huntington Beach, CA
John Hodgins, Marysville, WA
Helen Hogan, Lithonia, GA
Betty L. Holloway, Maplewood, NJ
Carol Huprich, Dover, OH
Antoinette Hutchings, Slate Hill, NY
David Ifkovic, Wilton, CT
Steve Ingmire, Indianapolis, IN
Waydene C. Jackson, Stone Mountain, GA
M. Jackson, Houston, TX
Irma D. James, Dayton, OH
Carol Jekel, Flushing, MI
Lori Jepson, Montclair, CA
Kay Jernigan, Vanceboro, NC
Glenn Johnson, Mukwonago, WI
Judy Jones, Amarillo, TX
Mary K. Jones, Neenah, WI
Ted Juske, Mundelein, IL
Beverly Kaeser, Appleton, WI
Linda Keats, Stevens Point, WI
Sue Kelley, Hubbard, OH
Mary Kay King, Dickson, TN
Carol Kinney, Eau Claire, WI

Ann Klingelsmith, Greenville, MI
Tammy Koch, Minocqua, WI
Patrick Kubeny, Rhinelander, WI
Cheryl M. Lagan, Ossining, NY
Amelia Lard, Memphis, TN
Marianna Larkin, Waxahachie, TX
Becky Larsen, Irvine, CA
Sharon Larson, Crystal Lake, IL
Inez Lauerman, Shingle Springs, CA
Annette Laughlin, Oswego, IL
Steve Leighton, Brooklyn, NY
James Leonard, Palos Hills, IL
Sue Lewis, Littlerock, CA
Stan Lewis, Champaign, IL
Donna Lewis, Morehead City, NC
Theresa Lueras, Daly City, CA
Sherry Lund, Port Angeles, WA
Linda Lupi, West Bloomfield, MI
A. Mallette, New York, NY
John Matera, Kenosha, WI
Alice Matthews, Artesia, CA
Sarah McBride, Hickory, NC
Rebecca McKnight, Gainesville, FL
Pam Meyer, The Woodlands, TX
J. Miller, Madison, OH
Gloria Morris, Fort Worth, TX
Karen Mozingo, Greenville, NC
Ralph A. Muro, Binghamton, NY
Dianne Murphy, Rancho Cucamonga, CA
Jill N. Murphy-Totten, Middletown, OH
John Murray, Fraser, MI
Karen Neuman, Parma, OH
William Nitch, Niles, OH
Bonnie N. Nute, Munford, TN
Betty O'Dell, Escondido, CA
Deborah Ottmers, San Antonio, TX
Donna Owens, Missouri City, TX
RaeNell Parker, Menomonie, WI
Ronda Patrick, Kirkland, WA
Diane Personett, Rushville, IN
Hank Petite, Bloomfield, NJ
Glenn Philpott, Belleville, IL
Kip Pichel, Auburn Hills, MI
Patti Pletcher, Bristol, IN
Mark G. Pretz, Harlingen, TX
Diane A. Prom, Oak Creek, WI
Lydia Quinones, Dunwoody GA
Mary C. Rabb, Winchester, TN
Margaret Ralph, Portland, IN
Glenda Razor, Santa Ana, CA

Tom Reach, Aliso Viejo, CA
C. Redmond, Lakewood, CA
Suzanne Reisert, Floral Park, NY
Edlyn Reneau, Corpus Christi, TX
Ruth Riley, Poland, OH
Melanie Rodges, Keller, TX
Rosalinda Rodriguez, McAllen, TX
Mary R. Roth, Warner Robins, GA
Frank Rudnesky, Pine Hill, NJ
Joyce Sadd, Hastings, NE
Lawrence Sakalas, Southgate, MI
Gary L. Schepf, Irving, TX
Donna M. Scheuerer, Farmingdale, NY
Jerry Schlecher, Hartland, MI
Sue Smith, Whittier, CA
Pete Smith, Mishawaka, IN
James Smith, Greensboro, NC
Linda Songer, Orange Park, FL
Linda Spellich, Belleville, MI
Carolyn R. Spencer, East St. Louis, IL
Camille Sroka, Toms River, NJ
Will Stauske, Cedarburg, WI
Beverly Stergeos, Fort Worth, TX
Linda Stevens, Houston, TX
Anne Stewart, Clearwater, FL
Geoffrey Strauss, Endicott, NY
Amy C. Strickland, Columbus, GA
Debbie Stuebbe, Bakersfield, CA
Ken Swiergosz, Toledo, OH
Bonnie Toone, Evansville, IN
Robert Torres, Anaheim, CA
Jeff VanArsdel, West Lafayette, IN
Jill Vicino, Darien, IL
Lina Volesky, West Bend, WI
Sandy Wainio, Durham, NC
David D. Weaver, Palmdale, CA
Irene Webb, Hackensack, NJ
Kathy Webb, Garland, TX
Gloria Wein, Aberdeen, NJ
Victoria Wenke, Burlington, WI
Donna Wheeler, Madison, IN
Patricia Williams, Tampa, FL
June Winkel, Plymouth, WI
Ann Wittmer, Waco, TX
Karen M. Wolf, West Carrollton, OH
William W. Wunrow, Green Bay, WI
Thomas F. YingLing, St. Marys, OH
Carol Young, Yorba Linda, CA
Cy Young, Garden Grove, CA
Cheri Zuccarelli, Phelan, CA

TABLE OF CONTENTS

TABLE OF CONTENTS

TABLE OF CONTENTS

Unit 3   Accounting for a Payroll System   306

Symantec
Corporation

Underground
Station

TABLE OF CONTENTS

TABLE OF CONTENTS

TABLE OF CONTENTS

TABLE OF CONTENTS

The Structure of This Book

Your textbook contains 29 chapters that are logically organized in six units. Each chapter consists of two or three sections. This structure presents your accounting lessons clearly and simply. Your book also contains a wide variety of features to clarify the lessons and tie them to real-life situations.

Units

Each unit introduces a major aspect of accounting. The photo and features in the unit opener are organized around a common theme that indicates how people in the real world use accounting.

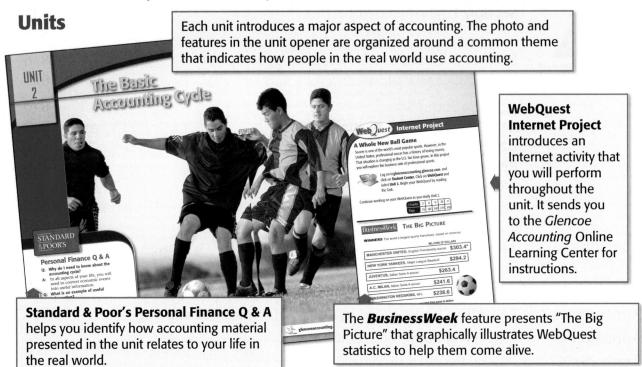

WebQuest Internet Project introduces an Internet activity that you will perform throughout the unit. It sends you to the *Glencoe Accounting* Online Learning Center for instructions.

Standard & Poor's Personal Finance Q & A helps you identify how accounting material presented in the unit relates to your life in the real world.

The *BusinessWeek* feature presents "The Big Picture" that graphically illustrates WebQuest statistics to help them come alive.

Chapters

Reading strategies throughout the chapter guide you before you read each chapter, as you read it, and after you have read it. They highlight the most important concepts in the chapter before you read. As you read, these strategies prompt you to identify how accounting concepts affect your daily life right now, recognize similarities and differences in concepts, recall previously introduced ideas and apply them to new material, identify key concepts, and restate concepts in your own words. After You Read strategies suggest activities to organize what you have learned.

What You'll Learn introduces the chapter topics.

Why It's Important sets the stage and shows how chapter materials are relevant to the business world.

Exploring the *Real World* of Business spotlights a successful, well-known company to illustrate an accounting topic discussed in the chapter.

Working in the *Real World* establishes a bridge between the chapter's content and the real-world workplace.

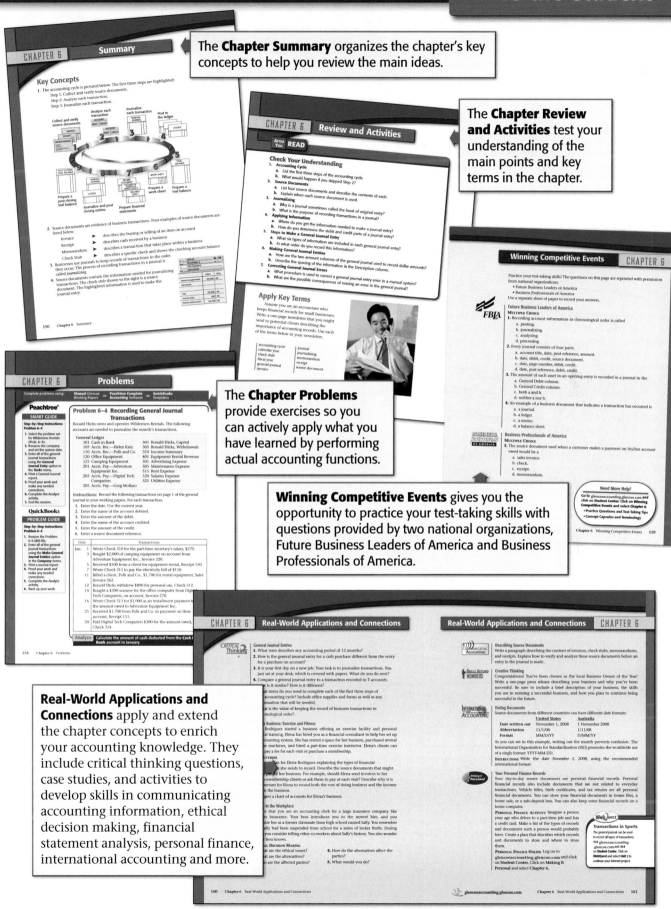

The **Chapter Summary** organizes the chapter's key concepts to help you review the main ideas.

The **Chapter Review and Activities** test your understanding of the main points and key terms in the chapter.

The **Chapter Problems** provide exercises so you can actively apply what you have learned by performing actual accounting functions.

Winning Competitive Events gives you the opportunity to practice your test-taking skills with questions provided by two national organizations, Future Business Leaders of America and Business Professionals of America.

Real-World Applications and Connections apply and extend the chapter concepts to enrich your accounting knowledge. They include critical thinking questions, case studies, and activities to develop skills in communicating accounting information, ethical decision making, financial statement analysis, personal finance, international accounting and more.

Sections

Each section opens with the **Main Idea** of the section; **Read to Learn...**, which lists the major topics and their page numbers; and **Key Terms** that you will learn in that section.

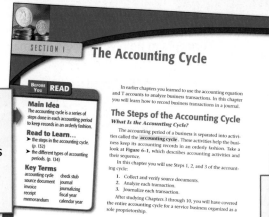

Figures aid your visual learning of key concepts, relationships, and accounting forms and documents.

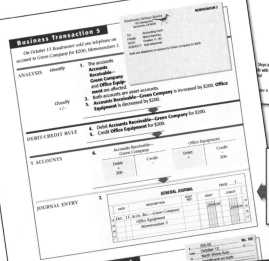

Each **Business Transaction model** is a step-by-step process for you to use in analyzing activities that affect a business.

The section **Assessment** helps you reinforce the section's main idea by creating a visual organizer. **After You Read** helps you organize materials you learned in the section. A **Do the Math** activity sharpens your math skills. **Problems** check your understanding of the materials introduced. Answers to section assesment problems are provided in Appendix H.

Features

Connect to... LANGUAGE ARTS

In accounting *capital* refers to money used to start up or grow a new business. The term comes from the Latin word for head–*caput.* In ancient times nomadic herdsmen measured their wealth by the number of animals they had. They got this number by counting heads.

The **Connect to...** feature links accounting concepts to other subjects, such as history, science, and language arts.

The **Math Hints** feature with savvy tips and instructions will help you understand and perform math functions related to accounting activities.

+/- MATH HINTS

Using Algebra The basic accounting equation is in the form $a = b + c$.
- To find b, rewrite the equation as $b = a - c$.
- To find c, rewrite the equation as $c = a - b$.

CULTURAL Diversity

Business Practices
Giving business gifts internationally can be tricky. Some cultures attach meaning to certain gifts and colors. For example, in Japan, white chrysanthemums are used only for funerals.

The **Cultural Diversity** feature gives you information about practices and customs in other countries and cultures.

Accounting Careers in Focus

VICE PRESIDENT, FINANCE
3E Company, Carlsbad, California
Trish Lady

Tips from ... Robert Half International Inc.
On average, companies interview six candidates for each job opening. Distinguish yourself from the competition by rehearsing your answers to potential questions with a friend or family member. During the meeting you will come across as informed, prepared, and confident.

Q: What does 3E Company do?
A: We help businesses meet their environmental, health, and safety responsibilities.

Q: Why did you choose an accounting career?
A: I knew I had a strong aptitude in mathematics but I didn't know how to turn that into a career. Luckily, I had an algebra teacher in high school who steered me toward a practical application for my math skills: accounting.

Q: What are some factors that have been key to your success?
A: Being open to opportunities has definitely helped me. For example, I was working as a chief financial officer for a real estate firm. I then took a different career path to focus on business development, helping companies reach their long-term goals. The skills I learned from that experience gave me a better background to draw from in my current role.

Q: What do you like most about your job?
A: I like the variety of responsibilities and the intellectual challenge it presents.

Q: What skills are needed to become a vice president of finance?
A: You need a strong background in accounting. It's also important to know how to allocate time, money, and other resources. You must be able to shift your focus from day-to-day accounting procedures to ways you can help your company achieve its long-term goals.

CAREER FACTS
- Nature of the Work: Ensure that the company follows state and federal laws, research and recommend investment opportunities, organize and manage the budget process.
- Training or Education Needed: A master's degree in finance or business administration; at least 10 years of experience in a public accounting firm or in finance. Many companies require a CPA license.
- Aptitudes, Abilities, and Skills: Long-term planning skills, negotiation skills, communication skills, and management skills. Management is the process of deciding how best to use the resources of a business.
- Salary Range: $70,000 and up, depending on experience, location, and company revenues.
- Career Path: Gain experience in a public accounting firm, and gradually assume roles of increasing responsibility.

Thinking Critically What attributes can make a compa...

The individuals featured in the **Accounting Careers in Focus** introduce you to a wide range of interesting and attainable career choices in the field of accounting.

Computerized Accounting CHAPTER 6

General Journal Entries

Making the Transition from a Manual to a Computerized System

Task	Manual Methods	Computerized Methods
Recording general journal entries	• Analyze the source document to determine which accounts are affected. • Using a general journal form, enter the details of the transaction. • Check for equality of debits and credits.	• Analyze the source document to determine which accounts are affected. • Enter the transaction details in the general journal using the account numbers for each ledger account. • The software will calculate the equality of debits and credits.

Peachtree® Q & A

Peachtree Question	Answer
How do I enter general journal entries in Peachtree?	1. From the *Tasks* menu, select General Journal Entry. 2. Enter the date of the transaction. 3. Enter the source document reference. 4. Enter the account number to be debited. 5. Enter a brief description of the transaction. 6. Enter the debit amount. 7. Enter the account number to be credited. 8. Enter the credit amount. 9. Click Save.

QuickBooks Q & A

QuickBooks Question	Answer
How do I enter general journal entries in QuickBooks?	1. From the *Company* menu, select Make General Journal Entries. 2. Enter the date of the transaction. 3. Enter the account to be debited. 4. Enter the debit amount, source document reference, and description. 5. Enter the account to be credited. 6. Enter the credit amount, source document reference, and description. 7. Click Save & Close.

The **Computerized Accounting** feature helps you move from a manual accounting system to a computerized system using the Peachtree and QuickBooks accounting software programs.

...uctions, see your Glencoe Accounting Chapter Study Guides and Working Papers.

Glencoe's Reading Strategies

Use this menu for strategies to get the most from your reading.

Before You Read

Set a Purpose
- How does the subject of the section relate to your life?
- How could you use what you learn in your own life?

Preview
- Read the chapter and section titles to preview the topics.
- Read the headings and questions related to them to learn more about the topic being introduced.
- Skim the figures, photos, forms, charts, and graphs. How do they support the topic?
- Look for key terms that are boldfaced. How are they defined?

Draw from Your Background
- What have you read or heard concerning new information on the topic?
- How is the new information different from what you already know?
- How will the information that you already know help you understand the new information?

As You Read

Predict
- Predict events or outcomes by using clues and information that you already know.
- Change your predictions as you read and gather new information.

Connect
- Think about people, places, and events in your own life. Do you see any similarities with those in your textbook?
- Can you relate the textbook information to other areas of your life?

Question
- What is the main idea?
- How do the figures, photos, forms, charts, and graphs support the main idea?

Visualize
- Pay careful attention to details and descriptions.
- Create graphic organizers to show relationships that you find in the information.

Notice Compare and Contrast Sentences
- Look for clue words and phrases that signal comparison, such as *similarly, just as, both, in common, also,* and *too.*
- Look for clue words and phrases that signal contrast, such as *on the other hand, in contrast to, however, different, instead of, rather than, but,* and *unlike.*

Notice Cause-and-Effect Sentences
- Look for clue words and phrases, such as *because, as a result, therefore, that is why, since, so, for this reason,* and *consequently.*

Notice Chronological Sentences
- Look for clue words and phrases, such as *after, before, first, next, last, during, finally, earlier, later, since,* and *then.*

After You Read

Summarize
- Describe the main idea and how the details support it.
- Use your own words to explain what you have read.

Assess
- What was the main idea?
- Did the text clearly support the main idea?

- Did you learn anything new from the material?
- Can you use this new information in other school subjects or in your personal life?
- What other sources could you use to find more information about the topic?

Be an Active Reader!

Glencoe's Top 10 Reasons to Become a Better Reader

10. Give yourself more choices in life. Reading well opens the door to a wider variety of interesting career options.

9. Empower yourself through the written word. Teach yourself sailing, computer skills, the latest techniques in skateboarding. Discover how to create your own Web site.

8. Improve your chances of getting into and graduating from an institution of higher learning. On the average, a person who gets a postsecondary education makes three times more money than a high-school dropout!

7. Increase your chances of getting a job when you look for one. That's important, considering that the average person will hold 11 different jobs over his or her lifetime.

6. Advance more quickly in your chosen career. In many positions, people with strong reading skills are 10 times as likely to receive training from their employer as those with limited reading skills.

5. Make the country economically stronger. More people reading well means more people contributing to the progress and prosperity of the country.

4. Save money and gain confidence. For example, you'll be able to pass your driver's test and read the lease for your first apartment.

3. Be more civic minded. People who read well are more likely to vote and to participate in democratic elections and in civic life.

2. Once learned, never forgotten. Reading is a lifelong skill, like riding a bicycle—once you learn, you'll never forget!

1. Enjoy life more! Reading not only helps you get ahead and stay ahead in life—but also, it's fun!

Introduction to Accounting

Personal Finance Q & A

Q: Why is accounting important to me?

A: Learning accounting can help you to keep track of your personal finances or to start your own business. You may even find that an accounting career is a good fit for your talents and personal interests.

Q: What do I need to know if I go into business for myself?

A: You will need to know procedures and standards. Accounting procedures help you keep track of your money. Accounting standards provide rules for preparing financial reports. You need financial reports to get bank loans or to get other people to invest in your business.

THINK IT OVER

Have you ever seen financial information about a company? Where have you seen it? Did you understand what it reported?

WebQuest Internet Project

Risks and Rewards

An *entrepreneur* takes an idea and turns it into a business. This involves risks, but those risks can turn into big rewards. The chart shows the trend of risk-takers' confidence over nine quarters. You may wonder what chance you have to become a successful entrepreneur. After you complete this project, you may have the answer.

Log on to **glencoeaccounting.glencoe.com** and click on **Student Center.** Click on **WebQuest** and select **Unit 1.** Begin your WebQuest by reading the Task.

Continue working on your WebQuest as you study Unit 1.

Chapter	1	2
Page	25	45

BusinessWeek THE BIG PICTURE

HAPPY DAYS Entrepreneurs' confidence in the economy over time.

Confidence

Q1 Q2 Q3 Q4 Q5 Q6 Q7 Q8 Q9

Data: vFinance Investments Inc.   *Source*: Reprinted by permission from *BusinessWeek*.

You and the World of Accounting

What You'll Learn

1. Describe how personal skills, values, and lifestyle goals affect career decisions.

2. Find information about a variety of careers.

3. Set career goals.

4. Identify career opportunities in the accounting field.

5. Describe the types of businesses and organizations that hire accountants.

6. Compare for-profit businesses and not-for-profit organizations.

7. Define the accounting terms introduced in this chapter.

Why It's Important

► To find out if an accounting career might be right for you, you need to get to know yourself and learn about different opportunities.

BEFORE YOU READ

Predict

1. What does the chapter title tell you?
2. What do you already know about this subject from personal experience?
3. What gaps exist in your knowledge of this subject?

Exploring the *Real World* of Business

THINKING ABOUT A CAREER

National Geographic Society

Have you ever dreamed about hiking to a remote village in Costa Rica or boating to an untouched tropical island? Writers and photographers from *National Geographic* magazine may have done it. Millions worldwide read *National Geographic* for images and stories of cultures, nature, science, and technology. It is the jewel of the **National Geographic Society**—the world's largest nonprofit scientific and educational organization.

The **National Geographic Society** makes films, books, maps, and radio programs in addition to running a cable TV channel and an award-winning Web site. In any given week, you might find the organization sponsoring a fossil dig in Africa or a study of sharks off the California coast. Producers and accountants work together to fund these projects. The **Society** employs more than 1,300 people who have a common interest in expanding our vision of the world.

What Do You Think?

What type of job opportunities do you think exist at the **National Geographic Society**?

Working in the *Real World*

APPLYING YOUR ACCOUNTING KNOWLEDGE

It's tough to figure out what you want to do with the rest of your life! Career counselors say that most people will have six to seven different careers throughout their lives. Some of us change careers entirely—from archeologist to teacher, or from freelance writer to photographer. Others stay within the same industry, but change specialties—from book designer to Web site designer, or from pediatrician to emergency care physician.

Personal Connection

1. What type job do you have now or have you had in the past? Is it in a field you might continue to work in?
2. Imagine yourself in five years. What type of job do you have? Where are you living? What skills are you using?

Online Connection

Go to glencoeaccounting.glencoe.com and click on **Student Center.** Click on **Working in the Real World** and select **Chapter 1.**

Exploring Careers

BEFORE YOU READ

Main Idea
A successful career choice begins with learning about yourself.

Read to Learn...
➤ the importance of choosing a career. (p. 6)
➤ how to assess yourself in terms of a career. (p. 7)
➤ the resources that are available to help you make career decisions. (p. 10)

Key Terms
skills
values
lifestyle
personality
personal interest tests
networking

Film producer? Animator? Web site designer? History teacher? Pediatrician? Financial analyst? Environmental consultant? Who—me?

Choosing a Career
What Do You Want to Do?

Let's face it: Not many of us know what we want to do with the rest of our lives, especially when we're still in high school. You may be thinking, "I'll just take some liberal arts courses in college and something will come up" or "I'll just work for a while to make some money and then fall into a career." You know what? Something may come up, and you may just fall into a career; but if you ask people who really love what they do, odds are that they took some time to really get to know themselves and what turned them on.

Danielle and Steve have been friends since their freshman year. Like most students, they've been too wrapped up with classes, homework, and activities to think about what their lives will be like after high school. This all changed at the start of their senior year. Steve sees it as the end of a long haul, but Danielle sees it as the beginning of a whole new life.

> *Closing his locker door with his elbow, Steve turns to see Danielle smiling at him.*
> *"Hey Dani! How's it going?"*
> *"Great," says Danielle, holding up her class schedule. "They say the last year in high school is always the best."*
> *"What are you taking?"*
> *"Let's see. I have chemistry, literature, algebra, speech, and accounting."*
> *"Ouch, tough schedule! Did you say accounting? I would have never guessed you to be a number cruncher."*
> *"I don't think I want to just 'crunch numbers.' I've always aced math, so I figured if I take accounting now, I'll know if I really like it enough to study it as a career. Besides, there are tons of ads in the paper for accounting jobs. If you're good at it, you can write your own ticket. Think about it: Companies*

need employees who know how to run their businesses. Plus it's not just sitting at a desk crunching numbers. My aunt is a financial advisor. She loves her job and travels all over the world."

"Slow down, Dani, it's only your senior year in high school. Don't you think it's a bit too soon to be playing career woman?"

"The sooner the better, Steve!"

"Maybe you're onto something here."

Unlike a job, which is simply work for pay, a career is built on a foundation of interest, knowledge, training, and experience. Have you thought of what you may want your career to be? If not, you are not alone.

Assess Yourself in Terms of a Career Vision

Who Are You?

Before choosing a career, you'll want to do a little soul-searching. The more you know about yourself, the easier it will be to make career choices.

- What are your personal interests and skills?
- What are your values, and how will they affect your career?
- What lifestyle interests you?
- How will your personality affect a career choice?

You have the answers to the questions but just don't know it yet!

SKILLS & TRAITS	CAREER EXAMPLE
Creative thinking	Fine arts and humanities careers, such as actor, artist, or musician
Knowing how to learn	Training or teaching careers, such as business consultant or training coordinator
Responsibility	Health-related careers, such as surgeon, dental hygienist, or home health aide
Friendliness	Hospitality and recreation careers, including cruise director, hotel manager, or park ranger
Honesty	Child-care workers, veterinarians, and other family and consumer science workers
Decision making	Financial planners, accountants, and other business and office careers
Analytical	Construction careers, including surveyors, general contractors, or electricians
Adaptability	Any of the public service careers, such as teaching, fire fighting, or serving in the armed forces
Self-control	Entrepreneur or manager
Self-esteem	Communications and media occupations, such as computer artist or book editor

As You READ

In Your Experience

Achieving Success
Describe a time when you made a special effort to achieve a goal. How might this experience help you be successful in your career?

Your Interests, Skills, and Traits

You're more likely to enjoy a career that uses your interests, **skills**, and traits. Skills are activities that you do well. Consider John King. When John was a kid, he built an elaborate fort in his yard. As a teen he studied major metropolitan architecture. When he finished high school, he worked at a graphics company making calendars. The pay was good, but John lost interest and enrolled in school to study his true passion, architecture. Today John is a partner in a successful Los Angeles architecture firm and loves his job.

Are you good at math? Do you write well? Are you creative? Do you like to meet lots of new people, or like John, do you enjoy building things? Everyone has different skills and abilities—it's the combination that gives you a unique selling point. The chart on page 7 lists some skills and traits that employers have identified as being valuable. Although these skills and traits are useful in various situations, the chart shows examples of careers that require them.

How many of these traits do you have? Make a list. It will come in handy when you begin to consider careers that interest you.

Values

One way to get to know yourself better is to examine your values. **Values** are the principles you live by and the beliefs that are important to you. Values are really about actions, not words. If you like to spend your free time volunteering at a local hospital or senior center, one of your values might be helping others.

What you value and believe may change as you get older. Most people, though, have a basic set of values that they follow throughout their life.

As you read this section, think about your personal beliefs. Remember, values are actions, not aspirations. Which values are important to you? Can you think of careers that would benefit from these values?

Responsibility. Being responsible means being dependable and taking positive actions, such as showing up on time to take a friend to an appointment or honoring a commitment. If you value responsibility, you might think about a career as a supervisor or manager.

Achievement. You value achievement if you try to be successful in whatever you do. I know, you're thinking, "Who doesn't want to be a success?" The truth is that wanting and achieving are two different things. For example, if you take action to train outside of regular practices to make first string on the basketball team, you value achieving goals.

Relationships. If you especially value interacting with your friends and family, relationships are important to you. After all, sharing the joy of your accomplishments is half the fun. Those who value these types of connections might avoid occupations that require a lot of travel and might base their career decisions on the ability to live close to family and friends.

Compassion. Do you care deeply about people, animals, or special causes? For you, a career that allows you to show your compassion may outweigh all the money in the world. For example, if you love being around animals, you might enjoy a career in veterinary medicine or the marine sciences.

Courage. Courage is not just being brave in the face of physical danger. Courage is also about overcoming other fears. For example, it takes courage to make a speech to the whole school, even if you are fearful or nervous. If you can put your beliefs on the line, you may be headed for a career in politics or law.

Recognition. If receiving acknowledgement and appreciation of your work is important to you, then you value recognition. You might consider a career as a novelist or a television news reporter.

Many people share the same values, but how they apply them is unique to each person. To some, courage may be accepting the challenge of a job they know little about. To others, it may be turning down the big money to do something they really love. Think about your values. What can you learn from your values that will help you narrow your career choices?

Lifestyle Goals

Your **lifestyle** is the way you use your time, energy, and resources. For example, many people devote themselves to work, earn lots of money, and put off the benefits of free time until they're older. Others accept smaller paychecks and work fewer hours to spend more time with family and friends now. If you want to work as a business manager or accountant for a professional sports team, you'll have to live in a city that has such a team, even if the weather's bad! If you want to be an actor, get ready for life on the road.

- What's really important to you?
- Do you want to go for the big bucks?
- Do you want to live in a big city with endless activities or a small town where everyone knows your name?
- Do you want to collaborate with a group of people or to work solo?

Make a list of how you'd like to spend your time, energy, and resources. These are your lifestyle goals. Try to focus on careers that closely match them.

Personality Traits

Imagine what it would be like if all your friends had the same personality. What if they were all shy or serious? Even worse, what if they all had the same sense of humor? It's a good thing we each have our own **personality**—a set of unique qualities that makes us different from all other people.

What is your personality? Are you confident, dependable, funny, friendly, sympathetic? Be honest. Do you prefer being with people or spending your time with things, such as reading books or working with computers? You probably wonder what this has to do with accounting. Well, your personality affects your preferences for working with data, people, or things.

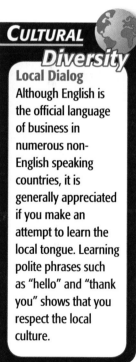

CULTURAL Diversity

Local Dialog
Although English is the official language of business in numerous non-English speaking countries, it is generally appreciated if you make an attempt to learn the local tongue. Learning polite phrases such as "hello" and "thank you" shows that you respect the local culture.

As you collect information about yourself, you'll want to complete a personal career profile such as the one shown in **Figure 1–1**. Use this profile to help you evaluate whether the careers you're considering match your skills, interests, values, and personality.

Making Career Decisions
Where Do You Go from Here?

Once you have a clear vision of yourself and how you want to live, you are ready to research careers and set goals.

Research the Possibilities

How do you find the right career for you? Here are some places to start:
Guidance Counselors. School counselors do a lot more than just show you the quickest way to get from your homeroom to the cafeteria. They can help you identify the things you like to do. One way they accomplish this is through testing, called **personal interest tests**, which help you identify your preferences.

Figure 1–1 Personal
Career Profile Form

PERSONAL CAREER PROFILE FORM

Name Darla Johnson	Date December 12	Career Marketing Manager, Music Industry

Your Values I believe in equal opportunities for all people. I like to be creative.	**Career Values** All kinds of people work in the music industry. As a marketing manager, I would be able to use my creativity, as well as work with other creative people.
Your Interests I have a large collection of jazz and blues CDs and keep up with up-and-coming artists that are featured on independent labels. I love getting together with friends and having parties.	**Career Duties and Responsibilities** As a marketing manager, I would make contacts with music stores and distributors, labels, and artists. I might send out press releases, arrange for artist appearances, and map out company marketing strategies to increase profits.
Your Personality I am very outgoing and get bored with sitting in class or reading. I have a great imagination and love group discussions.	**Personality Type Needed** A marketing manager must work well with people. Sharp communications skills and attention to details are important.
Skills and Aptitudes My best subject is history, and I am president of my school's debate team. I am not big on writing letters or grammar but love to communicate in person.	**Skills and Aptitudes Required** Good verbal communication skills are essential for a marketing professional. Although history may not be particularly important, good perceptions of what works and what doesn't work might be important.
Education/Training Acceptable I would be interested in learning more about getting a business degree, but also believe that if I could get in on the ground level in the music industry and learn the ropes, I could be successful as well.	**Education/Training Required** I suppose a degree in marketing might open a lot of doors for me. A knowledge of how marketing and accounting fits into the big picture of a music corporation would definitely help.

Contacts. Networking is making contacts with people to share information and advice. Find out about specific careers through networking.

Library. Print materials on every career imaginable can be found in your public library. Try books on careers or magazines that focus on your interests like *House & Garden, Metropolitan Home,* or *BusinessWeek.*

Internet. The Internet is a great source of educational and career information. Check out ideas for putting together the perfect résumé or browse through job opportunities at Paramount Pictures!

Organizations. Professional organizations are groups of people who have common career interests. You can learn about interesting careers by getting to know the American Institute of Certified Public Accountants (AICPA) and the Institute of Management Accountants (IMA).

As You READ

It's Not What It Seems

Network A television *network* is a group of linked stations. In your personal life, a *network* is the people you know or can get to know.

Set Career Goals

Once you have a clear vision of your interests and the types of careers you want to pursue, it's time to put a plan into action.

Map Out a Plan. For starters you'll need to make a list of the careers you've researched and compare possibilities. The easiest way to do this is to make a chart. List the careers you're interested in along the top and list your personal information along one side. Where they meet, X marks the spot.

After selecting the career choices that look the most promising, decide which one you'll pursue. Reaching your ultimate career goal is not going to happen overnight. There are many intermediate goals to achieve along the way. Here are some steps to help you achieve your career goals:

1. Decide on a long-term goal. Learn as much as you can about careers that interest you. Visit job fairs to obtain information.
2. Identify actions that will lead to the long-term goal. What skills, education, or training will you need? Make plans early.
3. Take action! Make your plans and put them to work.
4. Diversify your skills. Experience different work environments.
5. Realize your long-term goal. Setting and implementing these steps will help you achieve a career that you desire.

Education. Most careers require some education or training beyond high school. Unfortunately, deciding to further your education and finding the cash to pay for it are two different things. For ideas on help in paying tuition, you can turn to many of the same places you turned to for career information: books, the Internet, and your friend, the guidance counselor.

On-the-Job Training. Imagine taking only your favorite school subject and getting paid for it! That's how on-the-job training works. Suppose you're thinking about eventually opening your own accounting firm. While in school, you might work as an office assistant at a local accounting firm to learn how accounting services are provided. It's a great way to find out if accounting is the career for you, and you'll be paid for your efforts.

Internships. Another way to obtain career experience is to work as an intern. Many companies offer summer or longer internships to students. Some offer modest pay. Successful interns are often offered positions in the company once their internships are completed. The key is to become so valuable that they miss you when you're gone!

READ

Reinforce the Main Idea

Draw a diagram like the one shown here. Show how people your age may benefit in their careers by first learning about themselves. Add answer circles as needed.

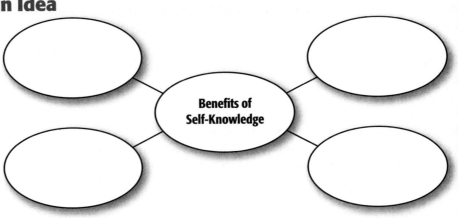

Benefits of Self-Knowledge

 ## Do the Math

Congratulations! The good news is that you've decided to attend a local community college after high school. The bad news is that tuition for an 18-week semester is $1,820. You estimate travel expenses of $20 per week and $300 for books and supplies. You plan to work 20 hours a week, earning $6.75 per hour, and you will apply all your paychecks toward college expenses. Social Security and income taxes will take about 15 percent of your earnings.

1. What is the total cost for a semester?
2. Assume that you have already saved $300 toward your first semester's costs. Approximately how long will it take to save enough to cover your tuition and books for one semester?

 ## Problem 1–1 **Studying Yourself**

Instructions Think about the things you like to do and your particular skills. Make a list of at least five personal interests or skills. After you complete your list, use the career resource materials described in this section to identify one or more careers that match each interest or skill. Choose one career and write a one-page description of how your skills and interests fit this career.

Problem 1–2 **Gathering Career Resources**

Instructions Use the personal career profile form in **Figure 1–1** as a guide, and compare three careers that you find interesting. Use the resources mentioned in this section to gather information: guidance counselors, networking, print materials, the Internet, and professional organizations. You may find other references in your school or local public library. After completing your comparison, write a brief summary; identify which of your choices you prefer and explain why.

Accounting Careers: The Possibilities Are Endless!

Some people believe accounting is boring. There, we said it. It's a pretty safe bet that you didn't enroll in an accounting course because you thought it would lead to a career in the spotlight. How often do you see Brad Pitt starring in an action thriller about a jet-setting accountant? Exactly. However, who do you think develops and approves the budget for his films to go into production? Who do you think advises Mr. Pitt how to invest the hefty salary he makes? You got it—someone just like you, who is good with accounting concepts and knows how to handle money.

The point is: Accounting can be a lot of things you would never have imagined. So, if an accounting career matches up with some of your interests and goals, hang in there. We promise there is a lot more to it than crunching numbers!

The Changing Horizon
Is Accounting More Than Arithmetic?

Sure, some careers in accounting can be a little dry, but there are many more that are dynamic and exciting. Think of any business—Warner Music, Nike, the Hard Rock Cafe. They all look to accountants to help run their businesses. Think of your favorite celebrities—maybe Will Smith or Natalie Portman. Most have financial advisors. Movie producers hire accountants to track production costs. Publishers of magazines, such as *PC World* and *Sports Illustrated,* depend on accountants to work with national advertisers to keep things running smoothly. In this chapter you will identify career opportunities in the accounting field.

Accounting is not just adding and subtracting. An **accountant** handles a broad range of responsibilities, makes business decisions, and prepares and interprets financial reports. These are skills that successful businesses cannot do without. If you are good, the sky is the limit.

Types of Organizations
What Career Opportunities Exist in Accounting?

If you still picture accountants huddled over pages of numbers in back offices, the following scenarios should set you straight.

For-Profit Businesses

"Okay, everybody. Show time in five minutes." The announcement comes as the members of the band adjust guitar straps and prepare to go out on stage. A crowd of 30,000 fans, dropping thirty-five bucks a head, waits

BEFORE YOU READ

Main Idea
If you learn accounting, you can choose from a wide variety of careers.

Read to Learn...
➤ how accounting careers can be exciting. (p. 13)
➤ the different organizations that hire accountants. (p. 13)

Key Terms
accountant
accounting clerk
for-profit business
not-for-profit organization
public accounting firm
audit
certified public accountant (CPA)

As You READ

Key Point

Where Accountants Work
• For-profit businesses
• Not-for-profit organizations
• Public accounting firms

for their entrance. Drew Taylor jokes with the band just offstage and then watches as they head out to the fans' applause.

Drew gets a rush being backstage amid all the excitement of a live show. As the financial assistant to the band's business manager, he often spends time at the performances. For Drew, working with numbers came as naturally as his love for music. He studied accounting throughout high school and college, and in his spare time he dabbled with the guitar and hung around recording studios with friends who were in the music business.

It wasn't long before Drew started working as an accounting clerk at a studio. An **accounting clerk** is an entry-level job that can vary from specializing in one part of the system to doing a wide range of tasks. Drew's accounting clerk experience and networking efforts landed him a position with one of the music industry's top business managers. Drew still dreams of recording his own music one day, but for now, he's quite content helping orchestrate the financial security of his music idols.

Entertainers perform to earn a profit. **For-profit businesses** operate to earn money for their owners. The majority of businesses in the United States are for-profit businesses.

Today, computers handle much of the basic accounting work, freeing accountants to do more planning for future operations. Computer technology means that accountants are no longer tied to a desk or an office. If you worked for artists such as Alicia Keys, Maroon5, or Modest Mouse, you would probably spend part of your time traveling. Laptop computers and modems can connect you to your work as you travel to other cities and countries.

In order to explore accounting career opportunities, you need to compare the various types of business organizations. Not all organizations are for-profit businesses.

Not-For-Profit Organizations

"Listen up, folks! Here's the draft of the news release we're sending out tomorrow," shouts Darin Korman, waving a stack of papers in the air. "We need to get our position before the public while Congress is still considering the environmental legislation. Questions?"

"What else are we doing to alert voters to the potential value of this legislation?" a team member asks from the back of the room.

Darin, the team leader, opens a folder. "Here's our total plan. We begin filming a TV spot tomorrow. Next week, the art for our magazine ads will be finished, and they'll run in six different magazines. We'll also post a call-to-action on our Web site asking visitors for their support. We can all thank Maya for putting together a budget for the media campaign."

Maya Cruz beams as her boss Darin describes a typical campaign put together for a group—like Sierra Club or Audubon Society—that works to protect and preserve the environment. Such groups operate as **not-for-profit organizations**, also known as *nonprofit organizations*. These organizations operate for purposes other than making a profit. When Maya was very young, her parents founded a similar group dedicated to cleaning up the local waterways. Maya helped her parents in the difficult task of soliciting donations within their community. As she grew older, Maya pursued the study of accounting with the sole purpose of continuing her involvement in environmental causes.

It is important to identify the various accounting functions involved with each type of business organization. Most not-for-profit organizations have the goal of balancing their income with expenses rather than earning a profit for owners or investors. Some not-for-profit organizations, like United Way or Boy Scouts of America, get their income from donations. Other organizations get income through tax dollars. Government agencies, such as your school or a federal agency, fall under this category.

There are thousands of opportunities in the not-for-profit arena. Like Maya did, you may prefer to combine your interest in accounting with a cause that you hold close to your heart.

As You READ

Compare and Contrast

For-Profits and Not-for-Profits What are the similarities in the work done by accountants at a for-profit business and those employed by a not-for-profit organization? How are their tasks different?

Public Accounting Firms

"It seems like all the ducks are in a row." Jana Passeno takes another look at the Whitley Company accounting reports on her desk.

"Yes, we have identified the last few questions we need to go over with Whitley's accounting manager," Greg Hally says as he finalizes a short list.

Jana and Greg work for the public accounting firm Radcliff & Pratt. **Public accounting firms** provide clients a variety of accounting services including the independent audit. An **audit** is the review of a company's accounting systems and financial statements to confirm that they follow generally accepted accounting principles.

An *independent audit* is not done by company employees. For example, the accountants who work at Whitley cannot do an independent audit. Instead, it is done by certified public accountants who work for public accounting firms. A **certified public accountant (CPA)** is an accountant who has met certain education and experience requirements and passed a national test. Like doctors and lawyers, CPAs are licensed by the states.

Radcliff & Pratt is a small firm, but many certified public accountants work for the four largest accounting firms known as "The Big Four": Ernst & Young, Deloitte & Touche, KPMG, and PricewaterhouseCoopers.

Jana feels pride in her job. When companies such as Coca-Cola or General Electric sell their stock on a U.S. stock exchange, potential buyers depend on audited financial statements to make decisions. Once Jana signs off on the financial statements of a company, the public has greater assurance that the information is correct.

Public accounting firms have many job opportunities besides auditing. Possibilities include financial planning and preparing tax returns. You might be interested in a job as a forensic accountant. *Forensic accountants* take cases that involve issues like fraud or employee theft. Did you know that since 9/11, forensic accountants have played a major role in tracking down suspected terrorists?

From entertainment to health care, conservation to entrepreneurship, the career possibilities in accounting are endless!

As You READ

In Your Own Words

Certified Explain the significance of being a "certified" public accountant.

Reinforce the Main Idea

Create an organizer like the one shown here. List at least three accounting career opportunities in each type of organization.

Career Opportunities		
For-Profit Businesses	Not-for-Profit Organizations	Public Accounting Firms

 ## Do the Math

Assume that the federal government pays new accountants without a master's degree an annual salary of approximately $23,500. The starting salary for new accountants with a master's degree is approximately $35,500. If you spent $21,000 to attend graduate school, how many months would you work at a new job in the federal government before the difference in salary pays for your graduate school expenses?

 ## Problem 1–3 Checking Out Accounting Careers

Instructions Using the resources described in Section 1, research possible careers for people with accounting degrees. List at least five different careers and the formal training and work experience needed for each. Choose one career as your preference and write a paragraph describing why this career appeals to you.

 ## Problem 1–4 Matching Interests and Careers

Instructions Using the three career examples described in this section, make a list of the personal interests and skills of the accountants described in each situation. Compare the list to your own interests and skills. Then think of three types of businesses (or actual companies) for which you might want to work. How would you learn about accounting career opportunities in those companies? Aside from pursuing needed training or education, what else would you do to prepare to work in that career? Share your ideas in class.

 ## Problem 1–5 Researching Public Accounting Firms

Instructions Surf the Internet or conduct research in your library to find information about "The Big Four" accounting firms. Create a table of information about each firm and the services the firm provides.

 ## Problem 1–6 Interviewing Accountants

Instructions Interview members of the accounting field to investigate entry-level job requirements, career tracks for the profession, and projected trends for the future. Write a short report about your findings.

Accounting Careers in Focus

ACCOUNTING MANAGER
Keytroller, Inc., Tampa, Florida
Mandy Martensen

Q: Why did you choose an accounting career?

A: In college, I was majoring in a different subject and had to take an accounting class as one of my requirements. I fell in love with accounting as soon as I took that first course. I enjoy math and problem solving.

Q: What are some factors that have been key to your success?

A: I'm a quick learner and willing to try anything at least once. I'm not afraid to ask questions or to try my hand at something new. If you want to go far in the accounting field, you must be open to new things.

Q: What do you find most challenging about your job?

A: Working in a team-based environment is especially stimulating. In today's world you can't work alone. You usually work with others as a group, especially on large projects. But you also need to learn how to step in and be a leader when necessary.

Q: What advice do you have for accounting students just beginning their careers?

A: You have to like what you do or you won't get very far. If you aren't sure what path you want to follow, consider earning a degree in business; you'll take at least one class in every area and something you really enjoy will stand out.

> **Tips from . . .**
>
> **RHI Robert Half International Inc.**
>
> In business, success is usually a team effort. Help the group get ahead by lending co-workers a hand. You will not only show initiative but also gain allies who are likely to provide assistance when you need it.

CAREER FACTS

- ▶ <u>Nature of the Work:</u> Review the accounting information to make sure that everything is recorded correctly; organize the budget process; hire, train, and supervise accounting staff.
- ▶ <u>Training or Education Needed:</u> A bachelor's degree in accounting or finance, a master's degree in business administration, and at least five years of experience. Some companies require an accounting manager to have a CPA license.
- ▶ <u>Aptitudes, Abilities, and Skills:</u> Communication skills, technology skills, and analytical skills.
- ▶ <u>Salary Range:</u> $45,000 to $85,000 depending on location, level of responsibility, and company revenues.
- ▶ <u>Career Path:</u> Start by working as an accounting clerk, and then move into positions of increasing responsibility.

Thinking Critically   **Why is it important to be willing to ask for help?**

Key Concepts

1. A successful career begins with insight into your own personal skills, interests, goals, and lifestyle preferences. Get to know yourself. What you value plays a vital role in deciding what you want to pursue as a career.

Responsibility

Achievement

Relationships

Compassion

Courage

Recognition

As you decide on a career, consider lifestyle goals and personality traits.

Length of Work Week

Size of Paycheck

Work Environment

Growth Potential

Geographic Location

Work in Teams or Independently

Work with People or Things

Skill Strengths

Personality Traits

2. Researching career possibilities can include meeting with a guidance counselor, networking with friends and family, reading books and magazines, doing research on the Internet, and seeking information from professional organizations. Do your homework. Research jobs, salaries, geographic locations, work environments, and growth potentials. You want to know what you are getting into, don't you?

Library

Internet

Networking

Magazine

Work Experiences

Professional and
    Student Organizations

3. Use these strategies to set and accomplish career goals:

   - Map out a plan.
   - Consider the education required.
   - Find a part-time job to get some on-the-job training.
   - Check into internships available in your field of interest.

4. Accounting career opportunities vary from the entry-level accounting clerk to the accountant who handles a wide range of responsibilities. Some accountants work for public accounting firms and are certified public accountants. A *certified public accountant (CPA)* is licensed by the state to perform independent *audits* of corporations. Public accounting firms provide many job opportunities including

   - auditing,
   - financial planning,
   - preparing tax returns, and
   - forensic accounting.

5. Accountants work for almost any organization you can think of. Find a company you are interested in, and you can bet there is an accountant in the picture planning for next year's budget, chasing down an expense report from the owner, or advising managers on financial issues. For-profit businesses, not-for-profit organizations, and public accounting firms all hire accountants.

6. For-profit businesses operate to earn money for their owners. Not-for-profit organizations operate for other reasons such as charitable or educational purposes. Most not-for-profit organizations have the goal of balancing their income with expenses rather than earning a profit.

Key Terms

accountant	(p. 13)	not-for-profit organization	(p. 14)
accounting clerk	(p. 14)	personal interest tests	(p. 10)
audit	(p. 15)	personality	(p. 9)
certified public accountant (CPA)	(p. 15)	public accounting firm	(p. 15)
for-profit business	(p. 14)	skills	(p. 8)
lifestyle	(p. 9)	values	(p. 8)
networking	(p. 11)		

Check Your Understanding

1. **Personal Skills, Values, and Lifestyle Goals**
   a. Explain how your interests, skills, and values will affect your career choice.
   b. What are six common values that people have?

2. **Career Information**
   a. Describe at least three categories of career information resources.
   b. Describe how networking is beneficial to career planning.

3. **Career Goals**
   a. What is meant by mapping out a career plan?
   b. Describe five steps that are helpful in achieving career goals.

4. **Accounting Career Opportunities**
   a. What does an accountant do?
   b. Name "The Big Four" accounting firms from which you could likely obtain information about current career opportunities.

5. **Organizations That Hire Accountants**
   a. List and describe three types of organizations that offer accounting career opportunities.
   b. What task can be performed only by certified public accountants employed by public accounting firms?

6. **For-Profit Businesses and Not-for-Profit Organizations**
   a. What type of organization exists to earn money for the owners?
   b. Why would a not-for-profit organization need an accounting professional?

Apply Key Terms

Suppose you are preparing to interview a person who works in the accounting field. On a separate sheet of paper, write a list of questions that you will ask in the interview. Incorporate each of the following terms in your questions:

accountant	not-for-profit
accounting clerk	organization
audit	personal interest tests
certified public	personality
accountant (CPA)	public accounting
for-profit business	firm
lifestyle	skills
networking	values

Problem 1–7 Researching Careers in Your Library

It is never too early to begin researching careers.

Instructions Complete your research project using these steps.

1. Using a reference book (such as the *Occupational Outlook Handbook*), choose a career area that interests you.
2. Research the skills, education, and experience you would need to work in that career area. Your research can utilize any number of resources including books, magazines, and the Internet.
3. Write a brief profile of your chosen career, including a description of jobs in the field, education or training requirements, potential earnings, and working conditions.
4. Present your profile to the class.

Problem 1–8 Researching Careers in Your Local Newspaper

Instructions Follow these steps to organize employment information.

1. Review the employment ads in a local or regional newspaper.
2. Collect information on at least 10 job titles plus the skills and education required for each. Include at least two job titles related to the accounting field.
3. Present your information in table format. If you have access to a word processing program, use it to create and print your table.

Problem 1–9 Assessing Your Skills and Interests

Instructions Complete an assessment of your personal skills and interests by answering the questions in your working papers. Use the survey included in the working papers, or you can ask your guidance counselor to administer a personal interest test. Using the results of the test, find at least three careers that match your skills and interests.

Problem 1–10 Working with Others

Instructions As an accountant for a large business, you might be put in charge of training new hires in the accounting department. Or you might be asked to discuss project cost overruns with a department manager or to present operating results to senior managers. In these situations you need skills other than just your accounting knowledge. For each situation make a list of the skills needed; then decide whether you have those skills and, if not, how you plan to acquire them.

Problem 1–11 Summarizing Personal Traits

Instructions Sometimes you can learn about yourself by asking other people how they see you. Ask at least 10 people to name three words they think describe you. Ask them to give you descriptive words such as these:

- Dependable
- Fun
- Quick-thinking
- Decisive

Do not just choose friends. Ask teachers, co-workers, relatives, and others who are willing to give you an honest opinion. Make a list of each person's descriptions; then summarize your findings by identifying the five characteristics or traits that were mentioned most often. Do these descriptions match your self-perception? Why or why not?

Problem 1–12 Gathering Career Information

Instructions Arrange to interview someone who currently works in a career area that interests you. Before the interview prepare a list of the questions you want to ask. You may wish to cover the following topics:

- What are the major tasks that you perform?
- What do you enjoy most about your job?
- Is there much variety in your work?
- What specific skills are involved?

After the interview write two or three paragraphs describing your interview and the information you learned. Explain how this information will help you choose a career.

Problem 1–13 Exploring Careers in Accounting

Instructions Choose a local company that interests you, and find out who works as an accountant for the company. Call and ask whether you can observe the person at work for part of a day. Write a summary of your observations, and share the information with the class.

Problem 1–14 Exploring Global Careers

Instructions Many U.S. businesses operate in the global economy, which means they need accountants who understand international business. Find a local company that imports or exports products to or from one or more countries. Interview the accounting manager, and find out the skills, formal study, and personal traits he or she looks for in an accountant who works in international accounting. Write a short report about your findings.

Practice your test-taking skills! The questions on this page are reprinted with permission from national organizations:
- Future Business Leaders of America
- Business Professionals of America

Use a separate sheet of paper to record your answers.

Future Business Leaders of America

MULTIPLE CHOICE

1. Persons who plan, summarize, analyze, and interpret accounting information are called
    a. accountants.
    b. audit supervisors.
    c. bookkeepers.
    d. accounting clerks.
    e. none of these answers.

Business Professionals of America

MULTIPLE CHOICE

2. Solve: 2 3/8 − 1 1/2
   (Reduce to lowest terms.)
    a. 7/8
    b. 14/16
    c. 1 2/6
    d. 1 1/8

3. An employee earns $2,300 each pay period. He is paid on the first and fifteenth of each month. How much does he earn in one year?
    a. $55,200
    b. $59,800
    c. $27,600
    d. $55,220

4. Solve: 150% of $84
    a. $42
    b. $72
    c. $126
    d. $168

5. What is $580 increased by 1/5 of itself?
    a. $116
    b. $145
    c. $696
    d. $725

Need More Help?

Go to glencoeaccounting.glencoe.com and click on **Student Center**. Click on **Winning Competitive Events** and select **Chapter 1**.
- **Practice Questions and Test-Taking Tips**
- **Concept Capsules and Terminology**

Career Possibilities

1. What term describes the way you use your time, energy, and resources?
2. Compare and contrast the tasks of an accounting clerk and a certified public accountant. How are they similar? How are they different?
3. You have just graduated from high school and have found out about an opening for a summer job as an accounting clerk for a popular family-owned restaurant. Using the six components of personal values, predict whether this entry-level accounting job would be fulfilling.
4. What new issues would an accountant face in moving from a job at a for-profit business to a job at a not-for-profit organization?
5. A friend with an interest in an accounting career asked you for advice about the type of job to pursue. You know she has helped organize fund-raising events at school for diabetes research, and that she loves helping children. Recommend an accounting career that you think your friend would find fulfilling.
6. Make a list of the different ways discussed in this chapter to research careers. Create a table that compares advantages and disadvantages of each of these research options. Which one works best for you? Why?

Career Advice

Sean Smith is a senior in high school. He is taking an accounting course this year because he wants to be an accountant. Sean likes working with numbers, but he also likes working with people. He plans to go to college but doesn't know which ones offer accounting programs and what costs are involved.

INSTRUCTIONS

Take the role of Sean's career counselor. Write a one-page report advising Sean. Include the following in your report:
- Information on how to find the resources he needs to choose a college.
- Details on how to set education and career goals.
- Steps Sean needs to take over the next several months.
- A list of resources Sean might use to learn more about accounting careers, colleges, and financial help.

Padding a Résumé

Part of landing a great job is putting together a résumé that effectively represents your skills and background. Imagine that BMW has just opened a new regional headquarters in your area. You would like to work for BMW as a payroll clerk, but you're afraid you don't have the right qualifications. A friend suggests that you "change" your résumé to make yourself look better.

ETHICAL DECISION MAKING

1. What are the ethical issues?
2. What are the alternatives?
3. Who are the affected parties?
4. How do the alternatives affect the parties?
5. What would you do?

Writing an Article

Write a one-page article for a career newsletter. Describe the field of accounting and the types of businesses and organizations where accountants might work.

Acquiring and Evaluating Information

To make a decision, whether personal or business-related, you must be able to acquire and analyze information.

ON THE JOB
You have graduated and are ready for a job to match your skills and interests!

INSTRUCTIONS
1. List the businesses that advertise in a local or regional newspaper. You may want to use a Sunday issue since it is usually packed with ads.
2. Separate the businesses into for-profit and not-for-profit categories.
3. Write a summary of your findings, and describe the accounting career opportunities you think these businesses and organizations might offer.

An International Accounting Career

If you want to explore the world, the field of accounting can take you there. To land a job with an international accounting firm, knowledge of international trade laws and country-specific accounting standards will help. Experience with local business customs and a familiarity with the language is also a bonus.

INSTRUCTIONS Go to the global Web site of PricewaterhouseCoopers and list five countries in which the firm operates. In the Careers section, select a country from your list and name two career opportunities in that country.

Your Career

In this chapter you considered how interests, values, and lifestyle affect your career goals. You can learn more about what you want in a career from personal assessment tests. Meet with your guidance counselor or try an Internet search engine to learn more about these tests.

PERSONAL FINANCE ACTIVITY Imagine you have two job offers to work as an accountant. One is for a for-profit business. The work is not very exciting, but the company pays a high salary. The other job is at a not-for-profit organization dedicated to a cause that is important to you, but it pays about one-half as much. Based on what you discovered in your self-assessment, which job fits your goals? Why?

PERSONAL FINANCE ONLINE Log on to **glencoeaccounting.glencoe.com** and click on **Student Center.** Click on **Making It Personal** and select **Chapter 1.**

Be Your Own Boss

How would you like to be your own boss? Visit **glencoeaccounting .glencoe.com** and click on **Student Center.** Click on **WebQuest** and select **Unit 1** to continue your Internet project.

CHAPTER 2

The World of Business and Accounting

What You'll Learn

1. Describe profit, risk-taking, and entrepreneurs.

2. Describe service, merchandising, and manufacturing businesses.

3. Compare the sole proprietorship, partnership, and corporate forms of business.

4. List the advantages and disadvantages of each form of business organization.

5. Describe the purpose of accounting.

6. Explain financial and management accounting.

7. Describe three basic accounting assumptions.

8. Define the accounting terms introduced in this chapter.

Why It's Important

▶ The U.S. free enterprise system offers many different opportunities.

AVEDA
the art and science of pure flower and plant essences

Predict

1. What does the chapter title tell you?
2. What do you already know about this subject from personal experience?
3. What have you learned about this in the earlier chapters?
4. What gaps exist in your knowledge of this subject?

Exploring the *Real World* of Business

BECOMING AN ENTREPRENEUR

Aveda Corporation

Rosemary, peppermint, and almond bark—ingredients for a pot of tea? No, it's shampoo. **Aveda Corporation** founder Horst M. Rechelbacher believes that beauty begins with natural ingredients and treating the environment kindly.

At 14, Rechelbacher became an apprentice in the beauty and salon business in Europe. Interest in the powers of plants led him to launch **Aveda** in 1978 with one shampoo.

When creating products, the company considers the impact on the environment and on native communities. For example, **Aveda** stopped using an oil that could be poached from sacred trees in India. The company uses recyclable packaging in most of its products and does not test on animals.

Today, **Aveda** products are found in more than 10,000 salons and spas around the world.

What Do You Think?

What risks do you think Horst Rechelbacher faced when he launched the **Aveda** product line?

Working in the *Real World*

Entrepreneurs wear many business hats. They need to know how to sell products or services, what the competition is doing, how to provide good customer service, and how to manage a business as well as understand the finances of the business.

Personal Connection

1. At your workplace, or the workplace of family or friends, who owns the business?
2. If you owned this business, how would you use your accounting knowledge to manage the business?

Online Connection

Go to **glencoeaccounting.glencoe.com** and click on **Student Center.** Click on **Working in the Real World** and select **Chapter 2.**

Exploring the World of Business

BEFORE YOU READ

Main Idea
The United States has a free enterprise system with various kinds of businesses.

Read to Learn...
➤ about the environment of business. (p. 28)
➤ the three types of business operations. (p. 29)
➤ the three forms of business organization. (p. 29)

Key Terms
free enterprise system
profit
loss
entrepreneur
capital
service business
merchandising business
manufacturing business
sole proprietorship
partnership
corporation
charter

In this chapter you will learn about different types of businesses and how they are organized. All businesses need information that is generated by accounting systems in the form of reports. You will learn about the different types of accounting and accounting reports.

The Environment of Business
What Makes Up the Business Environment?

When you hear the word *business,* what do you think of? Nike, Microsoft, General Motors, IBM, Coca-Cola, or Tower Records? Large businesses like these are certainly players in the world of business today. Your neighborhood convenience store, clothing boutique, video rental store, and grocer are also important contributors in our free enterprise system. In a **free enterprise system**, people are free to produce the goods and services they choose. Individuals are free to use their money as they wish: spend it, invest it, save it, or donate it. Business owners in this system must compete to attract the customers they need to continue operating.

One measure of success in a business operation is the amount of profit it earns. The amount of money earned over and above the amount spent to keep the business operating is called **profit**. Businesses that spend more money than they earn operate at a **loss**. Whatever its size, a business must do two things to survive. It must operate at a profit, and it must attract and keep an individual willing to take the risk to run it.

The Need for Profit

Continued operation and success of a business require profit. Your local pizza parlor must pay for raw materials (flour, sauce, cheese, toppings), equipment (mixers, ovens, freezers), employees, utilities, and rent. The selling price of the pizza must be high enough to cover all costs. Once the owner pays these costs, the money left over is profit.

The Need for a Risk-Taker

In a business many people play different roles in daily operations, planning, and management. Inventors create ideas for new products or services. Investors provide money to help businesses get started. Employees supply the labor needed to operate the business. Managers supervise and plan.

Role of Entreprenuers. An **entrepreneur** is a person who transforms ideas for products or services into real-world businesses. Owning a business can offer flexible schedules, self-direction, and financial gain. Yet business ownership is not free from risk. See **Figure 2–1** for some pros and cons of entrepreneurship.

Pros	Cons
• You are your own boss.	• You probably need to work long hours.
• You create opportunities for earning money.	• You lose the security of steady wages and medical benefits an employer provides.
• You create and control your work schedule.	• You market your own services or products.
• You choose the people you serve.	• You pay for your own operating expenses.
• You select the people who work with you.	• You must be motivated and energetic each day.
• You benefit from the rewards of your own hard work.	• You face the possibility of losing money.
• You choose your own work hours.	

Figure 2–1
Entrepreneurship: Pros and Cons

Traits of Entrepreneurs. Most entrepreneurs share certain behaviors and attitudes. They are motivated self-starters willing to take necessary risks to create profitable and useful businesses. Strong organizational skills, marketing knowledge, and accounting skills are three areas of expertise that contribute to successful business ownership.

Entrepreneur—Who, Me? Have you ever considered owning a business? If so, you must first inventory your skills and interests. Do you have good writing and speaking skills? Are you creative? Mechanical? A self-starter? Do you have accounting or marketing skills? If you have vision, great energy, and imagination, you may have the makings of an entrepreneur! See **Figure 2–2** on pages 30–31 for the types of decisions entrepreneurs face.

Types and Forms of Businesses
What Do Businesses Do, and How Are They Organized?

Our free enterprise system allows an entrepreneur to choose the kind of business to operate as well as its organizational form.

Types of Business Operations

The three types of business operations are service, merchandising, and manufacturing. They are alike in many ways. Each sells products or services to customers and incurs expenses. They differ, however, in some basic ways. Each type needs money to begin and maintain operations; buy or make products; and cover operating costs like rent, utilities, and wages. Money that investors, banks, or business owners supply is called **capital** .

Service Businesses. A **service business** provides a needed service for a fee. Service businesses include travel agencies, salons like Fantastic Sam's, repair shops, real estate offices like Century 21, and medical centers.

Merchandising Businesses. A **merchandising business** buys finished products and resells them to individuals or other businesses. Examples are department stores, car dealers, supermarkets, drugstores, and hobby shops.

Manufacturing Businesses. A **manufacturing business** buys raw materials, uses labor and machinery to transform them into finished products, and sells the finished products to individuals or other businesses. Examples are shipbuilders, bakeries, and tire factories.

Forms of Business Organization

To start a business, a potential owner must have a sufficient amount of capital and must choose an appropriate form of business organization.

Connect to...
LANGUAGE ARTS

In accounting, *capital* refers to money used to start up or grow a new business. The term comes from the Latin word for head—*caput*. In ancient times nomadic herdsmen measured their wealth by the number of animals they had. They got this number by counting heads.

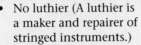
1. BEFORE

Entrepreneurs are aware of their environment.

- No luthier (A luthier is a maker and repairer of stringed instruments.)
- Does the community want one?

2. IN BETWEEN

Entrepreneurs evaluate alternatives.

- Customer preferences
- Accountant's guidance
- New tools are expensive. Use tools from home and buy new ones only when necessary.

Figure 2–2

With a few exceptions, U.S. businesses are organized in one of three basic ways: sole proprietorship, partnership, or corporation, illustrated in **Figure 2–3**. Notice that each of the different types of operations can use any form of organization.

Type of Business Operation	Form of Business Organization		
	Sole Proprietorship	Partnership	Corporation
Service	X	X	X
Merchandising	X	X	X
Manufacturing	X	X	X

Figure 2–3
Forms of Business Organization

Sole Proprietorship. *Sole* means "single" or "one." *Proprietor* means "owner." A **sole proprietorship**, therefore, is a business owned by one person. It is sometimes simply called a *proprietorship*. Being a sole proprietor does not mean working alone. Based on the operation's size and scope, a sole proprietorship may have many managers and employees. The oldest and most common form of business organization, the sole proprietorship is the easiest business form to start. Little or no legal paperwork (forms and documents) is required. The success or failure of the business depends heavily on the efforts and talent of the owner.

The advantages and disadvantages of organizing as a sole proprietorship are shown in **Figure 2–4**.

Advantages	Disadvantages
• Easy to set up • All profits go to owner • Owner has total control • Few regulations to follow	• Limited expertise • Hard to raise money • Owner has all the risks • Hard to attract talented employees

Figure 2–4
Advantages and Disadvantages of a Sole Proprietorship

Partnership. A **partnership** is a business owned by two or more persons, called *partners*, who agree to operate the business as co-owners. Business partners usually enter into a written, legal agreement. This agreement

Entrepreneurs seek the best solution.

- Find commercial space for rent near a music school and concert hall. Distribute fliers promoting business at classes and concerts.

3. AFTER

Entrepreneurs turn ideas into actions.

- Second Life Instrument Repair Shop quickly becomes the community's top option for making musical instruments sound their best.

specifies each partner's investment in money or property, responsibilities, and percent of profits and losses. Partnerships are often formed when a business needs more capital than one person can invest. Partnerships are not always small. For example, partnerships like the large accounting firm KPMG may have as many as 1,600 partners and more than 18,000 employees. **Figure 2–5** lists some partnership advantages and disadvantages.

Advantages	Disadvantages
• Easy startup • Pooled skills and talents • More money available	• Risk of partner conflict • Shared profits • Shared risks

Figure 2–5
Advantages and Disadvantages of a Partnership

Corporation. A **corporation** is a business recognized by law to have a life of its own. Unlike a sole proprietorship and a partnership, a corporation must get permission from the state to operate. This legal permission, called a **charter**, gives a corporation certain rights and privileges. It also spells out the rules under which the corporation is to operate.

Corporations often start as sole proprietorships or partnerships. The business owner(s) may "incorporate" to obtain money needed to expand. To raise this money, organizers sell shares of stock to hundreds or even thousands of people. These *shareholders,* or *stockholders,* are the corporation's legal owners. **Figure 2–6** outlines a few advantages and disadvantages of the corporate form of organization.

As You READ

In Your Own Words

Corporation
A corporation is recognized by law "to have a life of its own." What does this mean?

Advantages	Disadvantages
• Easier to raise money • Easy to expand • Easy to transfer ownership • Losses limited to investment	• More costs to start • More complex to organize • More regulations • Higher taxes

Figure 2–6
Advantages and Disadvantages of a Corporation

Regardless of their form as a sole proprietorship, partnership, or corporation, all businesses share common financial characteristics and methods for recording and reporting financial changes.

AFTER YOU READ

Reinforce the Main Idea

Use a diagram like this one to show details that support the following main idea: The United States has a free enterprise system with various kinds of businesses.

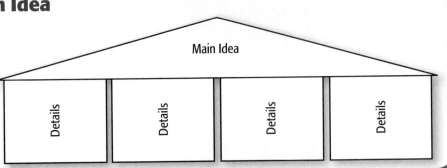

Main Idea

Details | Details | Details | Details

 ## Do the Math

Suppose that you bought 500 shares of Pinewood Dairy Corporation for $39 per share several months ago. Yesterday you sold 200 of the shares at the current price of $45 per share. How much money did you gain or lose on the shares that you sold? What was the gain or loss per share? Based on the price of $45 per share, what was the market value of your remaining shares yesterday?

 ## Problem 2–1 Assess Your Entrepreneurship Potential

Instructions The characteristics or traits needed to set up an owner-operated business and to run it successfully are listed below. Rank yourself, indicating whether this trait is most like you or least like you. Use the form provided in your working papers.

	Most Like Me				**Least Like Me**
Persistent	5	4	3	2	1
Creative	5	4	3	2	1
Responsible	5	4	3	2	1
Inquisitive	5	4	3	2	1
Goal-oriented	5	4	3	2	1
Independent	5	4	3	2	1
Demanding	5	4	3	2	1
Self-confident	5	4	3	2	1
Risk-taking	5	4	3	2	1
Restless	5	4	3	2	1

List the categories in which you ranked 3 or lower. Identify experiences, activities, and ways in which you could improve your entrepreneurial potential.

Accounting: The Universal Language of Business

Have you ever wondered how the band U2 determines which venues they will play, the cost of a tour, how profitable CD sales have been, or how much ticket prices should be? All these issues are probably tackled by the band's financial team: accountants, clerks, and financial advisors.

The Accounting System

What Does the Accounting System Do?

Whether you are the accountant for a band or the financial manager for a chain of mountain bike stores, accounting methods are universal. The **accounting system** is designed to collect, document, and report on financial transactions affecting the business. In a **manual accounting system**, the accounting information is processed by hand. In a **computerized accounting system**, the financial information is recorded by entering it into a computer. Owners and investors who risk their money depend on accountants to report the results of operations and the financial condition of the businesses in which they invest. **Figure 2–7** outlines the inputs, processes, and outputs of an accounting system.

All accountants follow the same set of rules to prepare financial reports. The Financial Accounting Standards Board (FASB) issues these rules. The rules are referred to as *generally accepted accounting principles* or **GAAP** (pronounced "gap").

Accounting principles provide a way to communicate financial information in a form understood by those interested in the operations and financial condition of a business.

Because it is so fundamental to the communication of financial information, accounting is often called the "language of business." **Financial reports** are summarized information about the financial status of a business.

BEFORE YOU READ

Main Idea
The accounting system produces information used to make decisions.

Read to Learn...
➤ how the accounting system works. (p. 33)
➤ how decision makers use accounting reports. (p. 34)
➤ three important accounting assumptions. (p. 35)

Key Terms
accounting system
manual accounting system
computerized accounting system
GAAP
financial reports
financial accounting
management accounting
business entity
accounting period
going concern

Inputs ➔	Processing ➔	Outputs
Source Documents	**Tasks**	**Financial and Management Accounting Reports**
• Checks	• Analyzing	• Financial condition
• Invoices	• Classifying	• Results of operations
• Sales Slips	• Recording	• Investments by and
• Receipts		distributions to owners

Figure 2–7 **How the Accounting System Works**

PROPERTY OF
DAVISON HIGH SCHOOL

As You READ

Instant Recall

Audits Many people outside a business depend on certified public accountants to audit the company's financial statements.

Using Accounting Reports for Making Business Decisions

Who Uses Accounting Reports?

The purpose of accounting is to provide financial information about a business or a not-for-profit organization. Individuals also need financial information in order to make decisions.

The information found in accounting reports has a wide audience. In general there are two groups that use accounting reports:

- individuals *outside* the business who have an interest in the business
- individuals *inside* the business

Financial Accounting

Financial accounting focuses on reporting information to *external* users. Financial accounting reports are prepared for individuals not directly involved in the day-to-day operations of the business.

Who uses financial accounting reports? The following examples describe just a few situations in which people use financial accounting reports.

- Suppose you wanted to invest in a business, such as Trek Mountain Bikes Inc. You would analyze financial accounting reports to estimate if an investment in the business would be profitable.
- Individuals or institutions, like banks that loan money to a business, use financial accounting reports to determine whether or not the business will be able to repay loans.
- Local, state, and federal governments review financial accounting reports. For example, the Internal Revenue Service may compare the tax return and financial reports of a business to determine whether the business is paying the proper amount of taxes.
- Workers, consumers, union leaders, and competitors are interested in the performance of businesses as presented in financial accounting reports.

As You READ

Compare and Contrast

Accounting Reports How is financial accounting similar to management accounting? How is it different?

Management Accounting

Management accounting, which focuses on reporting information to management, is often referred to as accounting for *internal* users of accounting information. Management accounting reports are prepared for managers involved in making the day-to-day operating decisions like purchasing, hiring, production, payments, sales, and collections.

Managers need accounting information so they can decide what to do, how to do it, when to do it, and whether or not the results match the plans for the future. **Figure 2–8** describes some of these decisions.

Accounting Assumptions

What Are Three Accounting Assumptions?

An assumption is something taken for granted as true. When you attend a movie, you assume the volume will be at a reasonable level, there will be a place to sit, and the film will be in focus. If these assumptions are wrong, the movie will be a disappointing experience.

Each business sets up an accounting system for its specific needs, but all businesses follow GAAP. These generally accepted accounting principles include three important assumptions:

- business entity
- accounting period
- going concern

Owners and managers use accounting reports to make decisions.

- Which flowers are the best sellers?
- Can we purchase a new delivery van?
- Should we hire more designers?
- Can we afford to attend floral conventions in Amsterdam?

Figure 2–8
Managerial Decisions

Recall that the corporation is the only form of business that is a separate *legal* entity. For *accounting* purposes, however, all businesses are separate entities from their owners. A **business entity** exists independently of its owner's personal holdings. The accounting records and reports are maintained separately and contain financial information related only to the business. The owner's personal financial activities or other investments are not included in the reports of the business.

For example, the personal residence of a flower shop owner, valued at $100,000, is not reported in the accounting records of the flower shop. Buildings owned by the business, however, are included in the financial records and reports of the flower shop.

For reporting purposes, the life of a business is divided into specific periods of time. An **accounting period** is a period of time covered by an accounting report. The accounting period can cover one month or three months (quarterly), but the most common period is one year. This assumption is necessary when accountants assign the cost of buildings and equipment over the estimated period of time they will be used. Comparison of reports from one period to the next also makes the accounting period concept necessary.

Unless there is evidence to the contrary, accountants assume that a business has the ability to survive and operate indefinitely. In other words a business is expected to continue as a **going concern**. Although many businesses fail within the first five years, the accountant assumes the business will continue to operate unless it is clear that it cannot survive.

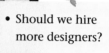 

As You READ

In Your Experience

Periodic Reports What kinds of reports have you used to make important decisions?

AFTER YOU READ

Reinforce the Main Idea

List at least three ways people use each type of accounting report. Use an organizer like the one shown here.

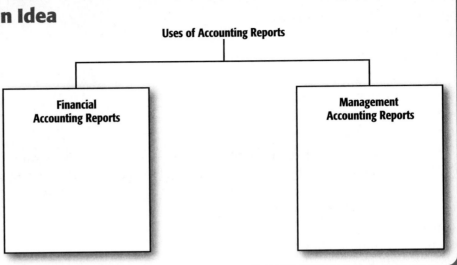

Uses of Accounting Reports

Financial Accounting Reports

Management Accounting Reports

Do the Math

Suppose that you are opening a 1,000-square-foot baseball card store in a shopping center. You have signed a lease that requires you to pay a monthly rent of $1.75 per square foot, plus 5 percent of your gross annual sales. What is the total amount of rent you will pay in one year if you have sales of $85,000?

Problem 2–2 Using Financial Information

Instructions Imagine that you are the manager of Valley Skateboard Shop. The accountant for the business has delivered the news that sales are down by 15 percent compared to last month. She also reports that the rent on the building will be increasing next month by $100. You believe the shop needs a more experienced salesperson and that the building needs new paint and awnings. How might the information delivered by the accountant affect your decisions and course of action?

Problem 2–3 Identifying Accounting Assumptions

Suppose you work for a company called Greenwood Sky Divers as a sky-diving instructor. Since you have your pilot's license, you also give flying lessons on the side. You and the owner of Greenwood Sky Divers both belong to a local club, the Greenwood Eagles, whose members get together for sky dives on weekends. Greenwood Sky Divers is a sole proprietorship that has been in business for six years. The owner of the company regularly reviews financial reports, and the company's accountant prepares end-of-the-year reports to compare results from one year to the next.

Instructions Decide what information in this paragraph is relevant to accounting for Greenwood Sky Divers. Identify the accounting assumptions for Greenwood, and give an example of each assumption from the information given here.

VICE PRESIDENT, FINANCE
3E Company, Carlsbad, California
Trish Lady

Q: What does 3E Company do?

A: We help businesses meet their environmental, health, and safety responsibilities.

Q: Why did you choose an accounting career?

A: I knew I had a strong aptitude in mathematics but I didn't know how to turn that into a career. Luckily, I had an algebra teacher in high school who steered me toward a practical application for my math skills: accounting.

Q: What are some factors that have been key to your success?

A: Being open to opportunities has definitely helped me. For example, I was working as a chief financial officer for a real estate firm. I then took a different career path to focus on business development, helping companies reach their long-term goals. The skills I learned from that experience gave me a better background to draw from in my current role.

Q: What do you like most about your job?

A: I like the variety of responsibilities and the intellectual challenge it presents.

Q: What skills are needed to become a vice president of finance?

A: You need a strong background in accounting. It's also important to know how to allocate time, money, and other resources. You must be able to shift your focus from day-to-day accounting procedures to ways you can help your company achieve its long-term goals.

Tips from . . .

 Robert Half International Inc.

On average, companies interview six candidates for each job opening. Distinguish yourself from the competition by rehearsing your answers to potential questions with a friend or family member. During the meeting you will come across as informed, prepared, and confident.

CAREER FACTS

▶ **Nature of the Work:** Ensure that the company follows state and federal laws, research and recommend investment opportunities, organize and manage the budget process.

▶ **Training or Education Needed:** A master's degree in finance or business administration; at least 10 years of experience in a public accounting firm or in finance. Many companies require a CPA license.

▶ **Aptitudes, Abilities, and Skills:** Long-term planning skills, negotiation skills, communication skills, and management skills. Management is the process of deciding how best to use the resources of a business.

▶ **Salary Range:** $70,000 and up, depending on experience, location, and company revenues.

▶ **Career Path:** Gain experience in a public accounting firm, and gradually assume roles of increasing responsibility.

Thinking Critically   What attributes can make a company exciting to work for?

Key Concepts

1. *Profit,* which is the money left after the owner pays all operating costs, is required so that a business can continue to operate and be successful. *Entrepreneurs* play an important role in business by taking ideas for products and services and turning them into actual businesses. Most entrepreneurs are willing to take risks, often by providing capital, to create profitable and useful businesses.

Money Earned > **Money Spent to** = **Profit**
from Sales   **Operate Business**

2. The three types of business operations follow:
   - *Service businesses* provide needed services, such as medical, legal, hair styling, and lawn mowing, for a fee.
   - *Merchandising businesses* buy products and resell them.
   - *Manufacturing businesses* use labor and machinery to transform raw materials into finished products.
3. The three forms of business organization follow:
   - A *sole proprietorship* is owned by one person.
   - A *partnership* is owned by two or more persons. Partners usually enter into a written, legal agreement.
   - A *corporation* is owned by its shareholders. It is recognized by law to have a life of its own.
4. Each of the three business forms has certain advantages and disadvantages as summarized here.

	Advantages	**Disadvantages**
Sole Proprietorship	• Easy to set up • All profits go to owner • Owner has total control • Few regulations to follow	• Limited expertise • Hard to raise money • Owner has all the risks • Hard to attract talented employees
Partnership	• Easy to start • Skills and talents are pooled • More money available	• Conflicts between partners • Profits must be shared • Owners share all risks

	Advantages	Disadvantages
Corporation	• Easy to raise money • Easy to expand • Easy to transfer ownership • Losses limited to investment	• Costs more to start • Complex to organize • More regulations • Higher taxes

5. Accounting provides financial information that is used to make decisions. To ensure that all financial information is presented in a consistent manner, accountants apply *generally accepted accounting principles (GAAP)*.

6. *Financial accounting* provides information to *external users,* people outside the business. *Management accounting* provides information to *internal users,* people inside the business.

7. Three basic accounting assumptions follow:
   - *Business entity* is the assumption that for accounting purposes, a business exists separately from the personal holdings of its owner. The owner's personal financial activities are not included in the reports of the business.
   - *Accounting period* is the assumption that the life of a business is divided into specific periods of time that are covered by accounting reports. Examples of accounting periods are a month, a quarter, and a year.
   - *Going concern* is the assumption that a business has the ability to survive and operate indefinitely unless evidence supports the fact that it cannot.

Key Terms

accounting period	(p. 35)	GAAP	(p. 33)
accounting system	(p. 33)	going concern	(p. 35)
business entity	(p. 35)	loss	(p. 28)
capital	(p. 29)	management accounting	(p. 34)
charter	(p. 31)	manual accounting system	(p. 33)
computerized accounting system	(p. 33)	manufacturing business	(p. 29)
corporation	(p. 31)	merchandising business	(p. 29)
entrepreneur	(p. 28)	partnership	(p. 30)
financial accounting	(p. 34)	profit	(p. 28)
financial reports	(p. 33)	service business	(p. 29)
free enterprise system	(p. 28)	sole proprietorship	(p. 30)

Check Your Understanding

1. **Profit, Risk-Taking, and Entrepreneurs**
   a. What is one measure of the success of a business?
   b. What is an entrepreneur? List two characteristics of an entrepreneur.

2. **Types of Business Operations**
   a. Name and describe the three types of business operations.
   b. What is the major difference between a merchandising business and a manufacturing business?

3. **Forms of Business Organization**
   a. Describe each of the three forms of business organization.
   b. What is the purpose of a partnership agreement?

4. **Advantages and Disadvantages of Forms of Business Organization**
   a. List two advantages and two disadvantages of each business form.
   b. What disadvantage do a sole proprietorship and partnership share?

5. **Purpose of Accounting**
   a. Describe the purpose of accounting.
   b. What does the accounting system do?

6. **Financial and Management Accounting**
   a. What is the major difference between financial accounting and management accounting?
   b. Explain how managers use the information in accounting reports.

7. **Basic Accounting Assumptions**
   a. What is meant by the term *assumption*?
   b. What are three important assumptions of accounting, and what does each mean?

Apply Key Terms

On a separate sheet of paper, write a brief definition for each of the following terms:

accounting period	going concern
accounting system	management
business entity	accounting
charter	manual accounting
computerized	system
accounting system	manufacturing
corporation	business
entrepreneur	merchandising
financial accounting	business
financial reports	partnership
free enterprise system	service business
GAAP	sole proprietorship

Problem 2–4 Identifying Types of Businesses

Instructions In your working papers, indicate whether each of the following businesses is a service business, a merchandising business, or a manufacturing business.

1. International Business Machines (IBM)
2. Gap
3. Glendale Memorial Hospital
4. Avis Rent A Car System
5. Ford Motor Company
6. Bank of America
7. Ace Hardware Stores
8. Michigan City Animal Hospital
9. Office Depot
10. Wal-Mart Stores
11. Allstate Insurance
12. U.S. Steel

Problem 2–5 Understanding Accounting Assumptions

Instructions In your working papers, indicate the assumption from the list below that best matches each numbered statement.

Accounting Period

Business Entity

Going Concern

1. Accounting reports may cover a month, a quarter, or a year.
2. Accountants expect a business to last indefinitely.
3. The personal property of a business owner is not included in the accounting records of the business.
4. The business has been in operation for several years and is expected to continue.
5. An owner's personal activities or properties are not mixed with the business activities or properties.
6. The accountant's report shows how much profit the business earned for one month.

Problem 2–6 Understanding Business Operations

Mary Torres owns and operates a bakery. During the past week, she sold 500 loaves of bread at $2.25 per loaf. The raw materials for each loaf cost Ms. Torres $1.80.

CONTINUE

Instructions In your working papers, write the answers to the following questions:

1. What type of business does Ms. Torres operate?
2. What was the profit on bread sales for the week?
3. Aside from the costs for raw materials, what other costs will Ms. Torres use to calculate her profit for the week?

Problem 2–7 Categorizing Forms of Business Organizations

Instructions Match the letter next to each form of business with the appropriate items in the following list of advantages and disadvantages. You may use a letter more than once. Use the form provided in your working papers.

A. Sole Proprietorship   B. Partnership   C. Corporation

1. Easier to raise money
2. Limited expertise
3. Higher start-up costs
4. Owner has total control
5. Shared profits
6. Higher taxes
7. Fewer regulations to follow
8. Easy transfer of ownership
9. Risk of conflict between owners
10. Easy to expand

 Problem 2–8 Working as an Entrepreneur

Instructions Using the form in your working papers, identify each of the following as an advantage or disadvantage of being an entrepreneur. For each item you label a disadvantage, decide what actions you would take to overcome that disadvantage. Analyze and describe how your actions might affect the profit your business earns.

1. Risking the loss of your savings
2. Deciding what you and everyone else needs to do each day
3. Lacking steady wages and employee benefits
4. Choosing when and where to work
5. Keeping the financial benefits of your hard work
6. Choosing the people you want to work with
7. Paying all the expenses of a new business

Practice your test-taking skills! The questions on this page are reprinted with permission from national organizations:

- Future Business Leaders of America
- Business Professionals of America

Use a separate sheet of paper to record your answers.

Future Business Leaders of America

MULTIPLE CHOICE

1. A business in which two or more persons combine their assets is called a(an)

    a. corporation.

    b. sole proprietorship.

    c. partnership.

    d. merchandising business.

    e. none of these answers.

2. An example of an accounting assumption is a(n)

    a. accounting system.

    b. accounting statement.

    c. going concern.

    d. computerized accounting.

3. A _____ buys raw materials and transforms them into finished products.

    a. merchandising business

    b. manufacturing business

4. The business entity concept means that

    a. a business exists.

    b. the business's and owner's personal records should not be mixed.

    c. a business is successful.

    d. none of the above.

Business Professionals of America

MULTIPLE CHOICE

5. A set of rules used by all accountants to provide a consistent form in which to provide financial information is referred to as

    a. American CPA Rules.

    b. GAAP.

    c. Financial Accounting.

    d. Management Accounting.

Need More Help?

Go to **glencoeaccounting.glencoe.com** and click on **Student Center.** Click on **Winning Competitive Events** and select **Chapter 2.**

- **Practice Questions and Test-Taking Tips**
- **Concept Capsules and Terminology**

Free Enterprise

1. Which accounting assumption separates the owner's personal finances from the financial activities of the business?
2. What is the difference between a sole proprietorship and a partnership?
3. Consider the businesses at your local mall. What type of business operation is the most popular? How do you think most of the businesses are organized?
4. Compare and contrast merchandising and manufacturing businesses.
5. Think of a business you would like to start. Describe the business operation and choose the best form of organization for your new business. Why did you choose this particular form of business organization?
6. Evaluate the going concern principle. Why should we use it if many businesses fail within the first five years?

Entrepreneurship

Interview two or three local entrepreneurs. If you need help finding entrepreneurs, contact your local chamber of commerce or other business organizations.

INSTRUCTIONS

1. Prepare questions such as these:
   * How did you get the idea for your business?
   * How did you finance the business?
   * What skills have helped you start and run the business?
   * What personal qualities have helped you be successful?
   * What has been your biggest challenge in starting a business?
   * What advice would you offer to other would-be entrepreneurs?
2. Conduct the interviews, and then write a general profile of the qualities and skills of a successful entrepreneur. Use information from all of your interviews.
3. After writing your profile, decide whether you are entrepreneurial material. Explain why or why not.

Becoming an Entrepreneur

Imagine that you work for a local day-care center. You attend a company meeting to discuss new services that would help the center stand out from its competition. You think you can use the services discussed to become an entrepreneur—by opening your own day-care center.

ETHICAL DECISION MAKING

1. What are the ethical issues?
2. What are the alternatives?
3. Who are the affected parties?
4. How do the alternatives affect the parties?
5. What would you do?

Summarizing Success

Locate and read a current magazine article featuring a successful entrepreneur. Try periodicals like *BusinessWeek, Forbes,* or *Inc.* Write a summary of the article, and explain why you think the person succeeded.

Individual Responsibility

High-performance workers exhibit perseverance and excellence in their job duties. Working well and showing a high level of concentration on any task indicates you can assume individual responsibility for your work.

ON THE JOB

As an accounting clerk for Prints-in-a-Minute, you prepare the financial statements for the owner, José Tirado. As you prepare for your year-end meeting with Mr. Tirado, you locate an error in the financial reports. What do you do?

INSTRUCTIONS

1. Mr. Tirado relies on you for accuracy. Write a memo to him explaining what has occurred and your plan for correcting the problem.
2. Mr. Tirado has read the memo and wants to talk with you. Pair up with another student and role-play the conversation, one of you as the accounting clerk, the other as Mr. Tirado. Discuss how you will fix the mistake.

International Accounting Standards

When two companies from different countries prepare financial statements, do you think they use the same accounting rules? If both companies use International Accounting Standards (IAS), the statements would be comparable and understandable. The International Accounting Standards Board (IASB) develops accounting rules so that investors can compare financial statements of publicly traded companies from any country. Since International Accounting Standards are not always the same as U.S. generally accepted accounting principles (GAAP), it is important to know which rules were used to prepare financial statements.

INSTRUCTIONS Explain why a U.S. company might choose to prepare its financial statements using both GAAP and IAS.

Making It Personal

Your Job Application

Almost all employers require you to fill out a job application as part of the hiring process. The quality of your job application can determine whether you "get in the door" for a job interview.

PERSONAL FINANCE ACTIVITY Suppose you are preparing for a job interview two weeks from now. What type of questions do you think you would have to answer on your job application form? Make a list of the parts of a job application you think you would have to fill out. Do you think you are well prepared? Why or why not?

PERSONAL FINANCE ONLINE Log on to **glencoeaccounting.glencoe.com** and click on **Student Center.** Click on **Making It Personal** and select **Chapter 2.**

Getting the Word Out

Does anybody really care about accounting information? Read all about it! Visit **glencoeaccounting .glencoe.com** and click on **Student Center.** Click on **WebQuest** and select **Unit 1** to continue your Internet project.

The Basic
Accounting Cycle

Personal Finance Q & A

Q: **Why do I need to know about the accounting cycle?**

A: In all aspects of your life, you will need to convert economic events into useful information.

Q: **What is an example of useful information?**

A: An example is a report showing how much money you earned, saved, and spent in a given period.

THINK IT OVER

What economic events occur in your life in a one-month period? How can you organize that information so that it is useful to you?

A Whole New Ball Game

Soccer is one of the world's most popular sports. However, in the United States, professional soccer has a history of losing money. That situation is changing as the U.S. fan base grows. In this project you will explore the business side of professional sports.

Log on to **glencoeaccounting.glencoe.com** and click on **Student Center.** Click on **WebQuest** and select **Unit 2.** Begin your WebQuest by reading the Task.

Continue working on your WebQuest as you study Unit 2.

Chapter	3	6	9	10	11
Page	75	161	247	275	303

BusinessWeek **THE BIG PICTURE**

WINNERS The world's largest sports franchises, based on revenue.

MILLIONS OF DOLLARS

MANCHESTER UNITED, English Premiership soccer	$303.4*
NEW YORK YANKEES, Major League Baseball	$294.2
JUVENTUS, Italian Serie A soccer	$263.4
A.C. MILAN, Italian Serie A soccer	$241.6
WASHINGTON REDSKINS, NFL	$238.6

Data: Deloitte   *Revenues converted from euros to dollars

Source: Reprinted by permission from *BusinessWeek.*

Business Transactions and the Accounting Equation

BEFORE YOU READ

Predict
1. What does the chapter title tell you?
2. What do you already know about this subject from personal experience?
3. What have you learned about this in the earlier chapters?
4. What gaps exist in your knowledge of this subject?

What You'll Learn

1. Describe the relationship between property and financial claims.

2. Explain the meaning of the term *equities* as it is used in accounting.

3. List and define each part of the accounting equation.

4. Demonstrate the effects of transactions on the accounting equation.

5. Check the balance of the accounting equation after a business transaction has been analyzed and recorded.

6. Define the accounting terms introduced in this chapter.

Why It's Important

To understand the financial condition of any business, you must first understand the accounting equation.

Exploring the *Real World* of Business

INVESTING CAPITAL

HARPO Productions, Inc.

Time magazine called her one of the "100 Most Influential People of the 20th Century," but millions of daytime television viewers know her as Oprah. Breaking records at every turn, Oprah Winfrey was the youngest person to anchor the news at Nashville's WTVF-TV. She was the first woman to own and produce her own talk show and the first African-American woman to become a billionaire.

In 1986, investing her own money, Winfrey created **HARPO Productions, Inc.**, the company that produces *The Oprah Winfrey Show.* Guests have included celebrities such as Gwyneth Paltrow and Denzel Washington. The talk show generates a tidy $104 million each year. **HARPO** also produces movies, videos, books, and *O: The Oprah Magazine.*

What Do You Think?

What kinds of assets do you think might have been purchased with the capital that Oprah Winfrey invested in **HARPO Productions, Inc.**?

Working in the *Real World*

APPLYING YOUR ACCOUNTING KNOWLEDGE

Every business has assets, liabilities, and owner's equity–the elements in the basic accounting equation that you will study in this chapter. A television studio's assets include cameras and computers. Its liabilities may include unpaid bills to videotape suppliers. The owner's equity of a business is what the business is worth.

Personal Connection

1. In your workplace what types of assets does the business have?

2. What types of debts or liabilities would you imagine the business to have?

Online Connection

Go to **glencoeaccounting.glencoe.com** and click on **Student Center.** Click on **Working in the Real World** and select **Chapter 3.**

Property and Financial Claims

BEFORE YOU READ

Main Idea
Any item of property has at least one financial claim against it.

Read to Learn...
➤ what it means to own property. (p. 50)
➤ the two types of financial claims to property. (p. 51)

Key Terms
property
financial claim
credit
creditor
assets
equities
owner's equity
liabilities
accounting equation

In Chapter 2 you learned that accounting is the language of business. In this chapter you will learn how to apply basic accounting concepts and terminology. You will also learn how the accounting equation expresses the relationship between property and the rights, or claims, to the property.

United Parcel Service (UPS), a corporation that provides global delivery services, uses accounting reports to communicate with its managers, employees, and investors. The UPS financial reports identify the property used in the business, such as airplanes, trucks, and computers. The reports also show how the company obtained the property, either from loans or from funds provided by investors.

Property
What Is Property?

The right to own property is basic to a free enterprise system. **Property** is anything of value that a person or business owns and therefore controls. When you own an item of property, you have a legal right to that item. For example, suppose you paid $600 for a mountain bike. As a result of the payment, you own the bike. If you had rented the bike for the weekend instead of buying it, you would pay a much smaller amount of money, but you would have the bike for only a limited time. You would have the right to use the bike for the weekend, but you would not own it.

Businesses also own property. One of the purposes of accounting is to provide financial information about property and financial claims to that property. A **financial claim** is a legal right to an item. In accounting, property and financial claims are measured in dollar amounts. Dollar amounts measure both the cost of the property and the financial claims to the property. In our mountain bike example, since you paid $600 cash to buy the bike, you have ownership and a financial claim of $600 to the bike. This relationship between property and financial claims is shown in the following equation.

Property (Cost)	=	Financial Claims
Bike	=	Your Claim to the Bike
$600	=	$600

When you buy property with cash, you acquire all of the financial claims to that property at the time of purchase. What happens to the financial claim, however, when you don't pay for the property right away?

When you buy something and agree to pay for it later, you are buying on **credit**. The business or person selling you the item on credit is called a **creditor**. A creditor can be any person or business to which you owe money. When you buy property on credit, you do not have the only financial claim to the property. You share the financial claim to that property with your creditor. For example, suppose you want to buy a $100 lock for the mountain bike, but you have only $60. You pay the store $60 and sign an agreement to pay the remaining $40 over the next two months. Since you owe the store (the creditor) $40, you share the financial claim to the lock with the creditor. The creditor's financial claim to the lock is $40 and your claim is $60. The combined claims equal the cost of the property. Your purchase of the lock can be expressed as an equation:

$$\text{PROPERTY} = \text{FINANCIAL CLAIMS}$$

Property	=	Financial Claims		
Bike Lock	=	Creditor's Financial Claim	+	Owner's Financial Claim
$100	=	$40	+	$60

As you can see, two (or more) people can have financial claims to the same property.

Only the property owner has control of the property. For example, suppose that you buy a used vehicle for $8,000. You pay $1,200 in cash and take out a loan from the credit union for the remaining $6,800.

Property	=	Financial Claims		
Vehicle	=	Creditor's Financial Claim	+	Owner's Financial Claim
$8,000	=	$6,800	+	$1,200

As the owner, you have control of the vehicle. However, if you don't make the payments to the credit union, the credit union can exercise its legal claim to the vehicle and you will lose ownership.

Financial Claims in Accounting
What Are the Two Types of Equities?

Property or items of value owned by a business are referred to as **assets**. Businesses can have various types of assets, such as:

- cash
- office equipment
- manufacturing equipment
- buildings
- land

The accounting term for the financial claims to these assets is **equities**. Let's explore the meaning of the term *equities* by introducing Maria Sanchez and her new business, Roadrunner Delivery Service, organized as a sole proprietorship.

Suppose Roadrunner Delivery Service purchases a delivery truck for $10,000. Roadrunner makes a cash down payment of $3,000 to the seller. A local bank loans Roadrunner the remaining $7,000. Both Roadrunner and the bank now have financial claims to the truck.

Property	=	Creditor's Financial Claim	+	Owner's Financial Claim
Truck $10,000	=	$7,000	+	$3,000

Over the years as Roadrunner repays the loan, its financial claim will increase. As less money is owed, the financial claim of the creditor (the bank) will decrease.

For example, after Roadrunner pays one-half of the loan ($7,000 × ½ = $3,500), the financial claims to the property will change as follows:

Property	=	Creditor's Financial Claim	+	Owner's Financial Claim
Truck $10,000	=	$3,500	+	$6,500

When the loan is completely repaid, the creditor's financial claim will be canceled. In other words the owner's financial claim will then equal the cost of the truck.

In accounting there are separate terms for owner's claims and creditor's claims. The owner's claims to the assets of the business are called **owner's equity**. Owner's equity is measured by the dollar amount of the owner's claims to the total assets of the business.

The creditor's claims to the assets of the business are called **liabilities**. Liabilities are the debts of a business. They are measured by the amount of money owed by a business to its creditors. The relationship between assets and the two types of equities (liabilities and owner's equity) is shown in the **accounting equation**:

ASSETS = LIABILITIES + OWNER'S EQUITY

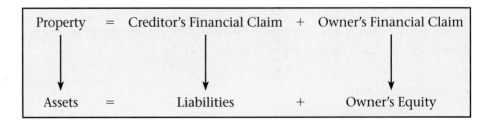

Reinforce the Main Idea

Use a diagram like this one to describe the financial claims of creditors and owners.

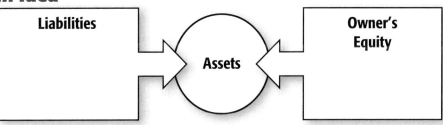

Do the Math

Owner's equity can be expressed as a fraction of the total equities. It can also be expressed as a decimal. Consider the following example:

$$\text{Assets} = \text{Liabilities} + \text{Owner's Equity}$$
$$\$10,000 = \$9,000 + \$1,000$$

Owner's equity is equal to 1/10, or 10 percent, of the total equities:

$$\begin{aligned} \text{Owner's Equity} &\div \text{Total Equities} \\ = \$1,000 &\div \quad \$10,000 \\ &= 1/10 \\ &= 0.10 \end{aligned}$$

Convert the following fractions into decimals.

1. $\frac{1}{2}$ **2.** $\frac{1}{5}$ **3.** $\frac{1}{3}$ **4.** $\frac{4}{5}$ **5.** $\frac{7}{8}$ **6.** $\frac{7}{10}$

Convert the following decimals into fractions.

7. 0.889   **8.** 0.60   **9.** 0.375   **10.** 0.25   **11.** 0.667   **12.** 0.75

Problem 3–1 Balancing the Accounting Equation

Instructions Determine the missing dollar amount indicated by the question mark in each equation. Write each missing amount in your working papers.

	ASSETS	=	LIABILITIES	+	OWNER'S EQUITY
1.	$17,000	=	$ 7,000	+	?
2.	?	=	$ 6,000	+	$20,000
3.	$10,000	=	?	+	$ 7,000
4.	?	=	$ 9,000	+	$17,000
5.	$ 8,000	=	$ 2,000	+	?
6.	$20,000	=	$ 7,000	+	?
7.	?	=	$12,000	+	$ 4,000
8.	$30,000	=	?	+	$22,000
9.	$22,000	=	$ 1,000	+	?
10.	$25,000	=	$ 5,000	+	?
11.	?	=	$10,000	+	$25,000
12.	$ 7,500	=	?	+	$ 3,000

Transactions That Affect Owner's Investment, Cash, and Credit

BEFORE YOU READ

Main Idea
Accounts are used to analyze business transactions.

Read to Learn...
➤ how businesses use accounts. (p. 54)
➤ the steps used to analyze a business transaction. (p. 55)

Key Terms
business transaction
account
accounts receivable
accounts payable
investment
on account

When you purchased a new sweater, bought popcorn at the movies, or put cash in your savings account, you were participating in business transactions. Business transactions involve the purchase, sale, or exchange of goods and services.

Business Transactions
How Are Accounts Used?

A **business transaction** is an economic event that causes a change—either an increase or a decrease—in assets, liabilities, or owner's equity. The change is reflected in the accounting system of the business.

When a business buys a computer with cash, its cash decreases, but its computer equipment increases. It records increases and decreases caused by business transactions in specific accounts. An **account** is a subdivision under assets, liabilities, or owner's equity. It shows the balance for a specific item and is a record of the increases or decreases for that item. Accounts represent things in the real world, such as money invested in a business or owed to a creditor. An account for office furniture represents the dollar cost of all office furniture the business owns.

Every business sets up its accounts and its accounting system to meet its needs. The number of accounts needed varies. Some businesses use only a few accounts, but others use hundreds. No matter how many accounts a business has, all of its accounts may be classified as either assets, liabilities, or owner's equity. Roadrunner Delivery Service uses these accounts:

Assets	=	Liabilities	+	Owner's Equity
Cash in Bank		Accounts Payable		Maria Sanchez, Capital
Accounts Receivable				
Computer Equipment				
Office Equipment				
Delivery Equipment				

As You READ

It's Not What It Seems

Accounts The word *accounts* might bring to mind checking accounts or credit card accounts. In an accounting system, *accounts* are subdivisions of the accounting equation.

The second asset account listed is **Accounts Receivable. Accounts receivable** is the total amount of money owed to a business—money to be received later because of the sale of goods or services on credit. The **Accounts Receivable** account is an asset because it represents a claim to the assets of other people or businesses. It represents a future value that eventually will bring cash into the business. When the business receives payment, it cancels the claim.

The liability account is **Accounts Payable.** **Accounts payable** is the amount owed, or payable, to the creditors of a business. The owner's equity account title is the owner's name, a comma, and then the word *Capital*.

Effects of Transactions on the Accounting Equation

What Happens to the Accounting Equation?

When a business transaction occurs, an accounting clerk analyzes the transaction to see how it affects each part of the accounting equation. Analyzing business transactions is simple. Use the following steps.

Business Transaction		
ANALYSIS *Identify*	1.	Identify the accounts affected.
Classify	2.	Classify the accounts affected.
+/−	3.	Determine the amount of increase or decrease for each account affected.
Balance	4.	Make sure the accounting equation remains in balance.

Most businesses have the following types of transactions: investments by the owner, cash transactions, credit transactions, revenue and expense transactions, and withdrawals by the owner.

Investments by the Owner

An **investment** is money or other property paid out in order to produce profit. Owner Maria Sanchez made two investments in her business, Roadrunner Delivery Service. The first was a cash investment; the second was a transfer of property.

Business Transaction 1		
Maria Sanchez took $25,000 from personal savings and deposited that amount to open a business checking account in the name of Roadrunner Delivery Service.		
ANALYSIS *Identify*	1.	Cash transactions are recorded in the account **Cash in Bank.** Maria Sanchez is investing personal funds in the business. Her investment in the business is recorded in the account called **Maria Sanchez, Capital.**
Classify	2.	**Cash in Bank** is an asset account. **Maria Sanchez, Capital** is an owner's equity account.
+/−	3.	**Cash in Bank** is increased by $25,000. **Maria Sanchez, Capital** is increased by $25,000.
Balance	4.	The accounting equation remains in balance.

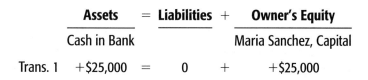

	Assets	=	**Liabilities**	+	**Owner's Equity**
	Cash in Bank				Maria Sanchez, Capital
Trans. 1	+$25,000	=	0	+	+$25,000

Maria Sanchez transferred two telephones valued at $200 each from her home to the business.

ANALYSIS	Identify	1. Maria Sanchez gave two telephones to the business. This affects the account **Office Equipment.** The investment of these assets affects the account **Maria Sanchez, Capital.**
	Classify	2. **Office Equipment** is an asset account. **Maria Sanchez, Capital** is an owner's equity account.
	+/−	3. **Office Equipment** is increased by $400. **Maria Sanchez, Capital** is increased by $400.
	Balance	4. The accounting equation remains in balance.

Instant Recall

Business Entity Assumption The financial activities and records of the owner are kept separate from those of the business.

	Assets		= Liabilities	+ Owner's Equity
	Cash in Bank	Office Equipment		Maria Sanchez, Capital
Prev. Bal.	$25,000	0	0	$25,000
Trans. 2		+$400		+400
Balance	$25,000 +	$400 =	0 +	$25,400

Cash Payment Transactions

Transaction 3 is the cash purchase of an asset. Any asset purchased for cash is recorded this way, but the account name of the asset purchased may vary. Transaction 3 affects only the assets side of the equation. Roadrunner exchanged one asset (cash) for another asset (computer equipment).

Roadrunner issued a $3,000 check to purchase a computer system.

ANALYSIS	Identify	1. Transactions involving any type of computer equipment are recorded in the **Computer Equipment** account. The business paid cash for the computer system, so the account **Cash in Bank** is affected. Check payments are treated as cash payments and are recorded in **Cash in Bank.**
	Classify	2. **Computer Equipment** and **Cash in Bank** are both asset accounts.
	+/−	3. **Computer Equipment** is increased by $3,000. **Cash in Bank** is decreased by $3,000.
	Balance	4. The accounting equation remains in balance.

	Assets			= Liabilities	+ Owner's Equity
	Cash in Bank	Computer Equipment	Office Equipment		Maria Sanchez, Capital
Prev. Bal.	$25,000	0	$400	0	$25,400
Trans. 3	−3,000	+$3,000			
Balance	$22,000 +	$3,000 +	$400 =	0 +	$25,400

Credit Transactions

Now that you have learned about cash transactions, let's look at how the use of credit affects the accounting equation. When a business buys an item on credit, it is buying **on account** . In the next four transactions, you will learn about a purchase on account, a sale on account, a payment made on account, and a payment received on account.

As You READ

In Your Experience

On Account Individuals as well as businesses buy things on account. What are some items that individuals buy on account?

Business Transaction 4

Roadrunner bought a used truck on account from North Shore Auto for $12,000.

ANALYSIS		
Identify	1.	Roadrunner purchased a truck to be used as a delivery vehicle, so the account **Delivery Equipment** is affected. The business promised to pay for the truck at a later time. The promise to pay is a liability; therefore, the **Accounts Payable** account is affected.
Classify	2.	**Delivery Equipment** is an asset account. **Accounts Payable** is a liability account.
+/−	3.	**Delivery Equipment** is increased by $12,000. **Accounts Payable** is also increased by $12,000.
Balance	4.	The accounting equation remains in balance.

	Assets				= Liabilities +	Owner's Equity
	Cash in Bank	Computer Equipment	Office Equipment	Delivery Equipment	Accounts Payable	Maria Sanchez, Capital
Prev. Bal.	$22,000	$3,000	$400	0	0	$25,400
Trans. 4				+$12,000	+$12,000	
Balance	$22,000 +	$3,000 +	$400 +	$12,000 =	$12,000 +	$25,400

Business Transaction 5

Roadrunner sold one telephone to Green Company for $200 on account.

ANALYSIS		
Identify	1.	Since Roadrunner has agreed to receive payment for the telephone at a later time, the **Accounts Receivable** account is affected. The business sold the telephone, so the account **Office Equipment** is also affected.
Classify	2.	Both **Accounts Receivable** and **Office Equipment** are asset accounts.
+/−	3.	**Accounts Receivable** is increased by $200. **Office Equipment** is decreased by $200.
Balance	4.	The accounting equation remains in balance.

	Assets					= Liabilities +	Owner's Equity
	Cash in Bank	Accounts Receivable	Computer Equipment	Office Equipment	Delivery Equipment	Accounts Payable	Maria Sanchez, Capital
Prev. Bal.	$22,000	0	$3,000	$400	$12,000	$12,000	$25,400
Trans. 5		+$200		−200			
Balance	$22,000 +	$200 +	$3,000 +	$200 +	$12,000 =	$12,000 +	$25,400

Business Transaction 6

Roadrunner issued a check for $350 in partial payment of the amount owed to its creditor, North Shore Auto.

ANALYSIS

Identify
1. The payment decreased the total amount owed to the creditor, so **Accounts Payable** is affected. Payment was made by check, so the account **Cash in Bank** is affected.

Classify
2. **Accounts Payable** is a liability account. **Cash in Bank** is an asset account.

+/−
3. **Accounts Payable** is decreased by $350. **Cash in Bank** is also decreased by $350.

Balance
4. The accounting equation remains in balance.

	Assets					= Liabilities +	Owner's Equity
	Cash in Bank	Accounts Receivable	Computer Equipment	Office Equipment	Delivery Equipment	Accounts Payable	Maria Sanchez, Capital
Prev. Bal.	$22,000	$200	$3,000	$200	$12,000	$12,000	$25,400
Trans. 6	−350					−350	
Balance	$21,650 +	$200 +	$3,000 +	$200 +	$12,000 =	$11,650 +	$25,400

Business Transaction 7

Roadrunner received and deposited a check for $200 from Green Co. The check received is full payment for the telephone sold on account in Transaction 5.

ANALYSIS

Identify
1. The check decreases the amount owed to Roadrunner, so **Accounts Receivable** is affected. A check is given in payment, so **Cash in Bank** is affected.

Classify
2. **Accounts Receivable** and **Cash in Bank** are asset accounts.

+/−
3. **Accounts Receivable** is decreased by $200. **Cash in Bank** is increased by $200.

Balance
4. The accounting equation remains in balance.

	Assets					= Liabilities +	Owner's Equity
	Cash in Bank	Accounts Receivable	Computer Equipment	Office Equipment	Delivery Equipment	Accounts Payable	Maria Sanchez, Capital
Prev. Bal.	$21,650	$200	$3,000	$200	$12,000	$11,650	$25,400
Trans. 7	+200	−200					
Balance	$21,850 +	$0 +	$3,000 +	$200 +	$12,000 =	$11,650 +	$25,400

As you can see, each business transaction causes a change in assets, liabilities, or owner's equity. Analyzing each transaction to see how it affects the accounting equation keeps everything in balance.

AFTER YOU READ

Reinforce the Main Idea

Create a diagram like the one shown here. For the boxes marked "?", fill in the correct labels and give one example of a related account for each category.

| **?** | = | **?** | + | **Owner's Equity** |

_____ _____ Leo Jones, Capital

Do the Math

The basic accounting equation is in the form of A = L + OE

1. What is the algebra equation to find L?
2. What is the algebra equation to find OE?

Using the rules of algebra, determine the missing dollar amount in each equation.

Assets	=	Liabilities	+	Owner's Equity
?		$9,000		$21,000
$25,000		?		$11,000
$10,000		$2,000		?

Problem 3–2 Determining the Effects of Transactions on the Accounting Equation

Instructions Use these accounts to analyze the business transactions of WordService.

Assets	=	Liabilities	+	Owner's Equity
Cash in Bank		Accounts Payable		Jan Swift, Capital
Accounts Receivable				
Computer Equipment				
Office Furniture				

On the form provided in your working papers, identify the accounts affected by each transaction and the amount of increase or decrease in each account. Make sure the accounting equation is in balance after each transaction.

1. Jan Swift, owner, deposited $30,000 in the business checking account.
2. The owner transferred to the business a desk and chair valued at $700.
3. WordService issued a check for $4,000 for the purchase of a computer.
4. The business bought office furniture on account for $5,000 from Eastern Furniture.
5. The desk and chair previously transferred to the business by the owner were sold on account for $700.
6. WordService wrote a check for $2,000 in partial payment of the amount owed to Eastern Furniture Company.

Transactions That Affect Revenue, Expense, and Withdrawals by the Owner

BEFORE YOU READ

Main Idea
Owner's equity is changed by revenue, expenses, investments, and withdrawals.

Read to Learn...
➤ how revenue and expenses affect owner's equity. (p. 60)
➤ how withdrawals affect owner's equity. (p. 61)

Key Terms
revenue
expense
withdrawal

United Parcel Service (UPS) has thousands of shareholders who expect a return on their investment in the business. The most common way for a business to provide a return is by selling goods or providing services. UPS earns revenue by providing a global delivery service. To provide the delivery service, UPS incurs expenses like salaries, transportation, and insurance. In this section you will learn about revenue and expense transactions as well as owner's withdrawals.

Revenue and Expense Transactions
What Are Revenue and Expenses?

Income earned from the sale of goods or services is called **revenue**. Examples of revenue are fees earned for services performed and cash received from the sale of merchandise. Revenue increases owner's equity because it increases the assets of the business.

Both revenues and investments by the owner increase owner's equity, but these represent very different transactions:

• Revenue is income from the sale of goods and services.
• Investment by the owner is the dollar amount contributed to the business by the owner.

To generate revenue most businesses must also incur expenses to buy goods, materials, and services. An **expense** is the cost of products or services used to operate a business. Examples of business expenses are

• rent,
• utilities, and
• advertising.

Expenses decrease owner's equity because they decrease the assets of the business or increase liabilities.

The effects of revenue and expenses are summarized as follows:

• Revenue increases assets and increases owner's equity.
• Expenses decrease assets and decrease owner's equity *or* increase liabilities and decrease owner's equity.

Business Transaction 8

Roadrunner received a check for $1,200 from a customer, Sims Corporation, for delivery services.

ANALYSIS	*Identify*	1.	Roadrunner received cash, so **Cash in Bank** is affected. The payment received is revenue. Revenue increases owner's equity, so **Maria Sanchez, Capital** is also affected.
	Classify	2.	**Cash in Bank** is an asset account. **Maria Sanchez, Capital** is an owner's equity account.
	+/−	3.	**Cash in Bank** is increased by $1,200. **Maria Sanchez, Capital** is also increased by $1,200.
	Balance	4.	The accounting equation remains in balance.

	Assets					= Liabilities +	Owner's Equity
	Cash in Bank	Accounts Receivable	Computer Equipment	Office Equipment	Delivery Equipment	Accounts Payable	Maria Sanchez, Capital
Prev. Bal.	$21,850	$0	$3,000	$200	$12,000	$11,650	$25,400
Trans. 8	+1,200						+1,200
Balance	$23,050 +	$0 +	$3,000 +	$200 +	$12,000 =	$11,650 +	$26,600

Business Transaction 9

Roadrunner wrote a check for $700 to pay the rent for the month.

ANALYSIS	*Identify*	1.	Roadrunner pays rent for use of building space. Rent is an expense. Expenses decrease owner's equity, so the account **Maria Sanchez, Capital** is affected. The business is paying cash for the use of the building, so **Cash in Bank** is affected.
	Classify	2.	**Maria Sanchez, Capital** is an owner's equity account. **Cash in Bank** is an asset account.
	+/−	3.	**Maria Sanchez, Capital** is decreased by $700. **Cash in Bank** is decreased by $700.
	Balance	4.	The accounting equation remains in balance.

	Assets					= Liabilities +	Owner's Equity
	Cash in Bank	Accounts Receivable	Computer Equipment	Office Equipment	Delivery Equipment	Accounts Payable	Maria Sanchez, Capital
Prev. Bal.	$23,050	$0	$3,000	$200	$12,000	$11,650	$26,600
Trans. 9	−700						−700
Balance	$22,350 +	$0 +	$3,000 +	$200 +	$12,000 =	$11,650 +	$25,900

Withdrawals by the Owner

What Is a Withdrawal?

If a business earns revenue, the owner will take cash or other assets from the business for personal use. This transaction is called a

As You READ

In Your Own Words

Withdrawal Explain how a withdrawal decreases owner's equity.

withdrawal . Withdrawals and investments have opposite effects. A withdrawal decreases both assets and owner's equity.

A withdrawal is not the same as an expense. Both decrease owner's equity, but each represents a different transaction. An expense is the price paid for goods and services used to operate a business. For example, a gardening service purchases fertilizer and lawncare supplies to conduct daily operations. Withdrawals by the owner are cash or other assets taken from the business for the owner's personal use. Transaction 10 illustrates the impact of a withdrawal on the accounting equation.

Business Transaction 10

Maria Sanchez withdrew $500 from the business for her personal use.

ANALYSIS		
Identify	1.	A withdrawal decreases the owner's claim to the assets of the business, so **Maria Sanchez, Capital** is affected. Cash is paid out, so the **Cash in Bank** account is affected.
Classify	2.	**Maria Sanchez, Capital** is an owner's equity account. **Cash in Bank** is an asset account.
+/−	3.	**Maria Sanchez, Capital** is decreased by $500. **Cash in Bank** is decreased by $500.
Balance	4.	The accounting equation remains in balance.

	Assets					**= Liabilities +**	**Owner's Equity**
	Cash in Bank	Accounts Receivable	Computer Equipment	Office Equipment	Delivery Equipment	Accounts Payable	Maria Sanchez, Capital
Prev. Bal.	$22,350	$0	$3,000	$200	$12,000	$11,650	$25,900
Trans. 10	−500						−500
Balance	$21,850 +	$0 +	$3,000 +	$200 +	$12,000 =	$11,650 +	$25,400

The following summarizes the transactions of this chapter. Can you describe what is happening in each line?

	Cash in Bank	Accounts Receivable	Computer Equipment	Office Equipment	Delivery Equipment =	Accounts Payable +	Owner's Equity
Prev. Bal.	0	0	0	0	0	0	0
Trans. 1	+25,000						+25,000
Trans. 2				+400			+400
Trans. 3	−3,000		+3,000				
Trans. 4					+12,000	+12,000	
Trans. 5		+200		−200			
Trans. 6	−350					−350	
Trans. 7	+200	−200					
Trans. 8	+1,200						+1,200
Trans. 9	−700						−700
Trans. 10	−500						−500
Balance	$21,850 +	$0 +	$3,000 +	$200 +	$12,000 =	$11,650 +	$25,400

Reinforce the Main Idea

Use a table like the one shown here to describe four transactions of a home decorating business. Indicate how each transaction affects owner's equity.

Type of Transaction	Transaction Description	Does Owner's Equity Increase or Decrease?
Revenue		
Expense		
Investment		
Withdrawal		

Do the Math

Determine the **Cash in Bank** balance for Wiemack Landscape Designs after the third transaction that follows. All three transactions occurred on the same day. The **Cash in Bank** balance before the first transaction was $10,000.

1. John Wiemack, the owner, withdrew $1,000 from personal savings and deposited that amount in the business checking account.
2. Purchased computer equipment for $5,000; issued a check for 20 percent of the price and agreed to pay the balance at a later date.
3. Issued a check for $100 to buy tools.

Problem 3–3 Determining the Effect of Transactions on the Accounting Equation

Instructions Use the accounts of WordService to analyze these business transactions. The beginning balance for each account is shown following the account name.

Assets	=	Liabilities	+	Owner's Equity
Cash in Bank, $24,000		Accounts Payable		Jan Swift, Capital
Accounts Receivable, $700		$3,000		$30,700
Computer Equipment, $4,000				
Office Equipment, $5,000				

On the form provided in your working papers, identify the accounts affected by each transaction and the amount of the increase or decrease for each account. Make sure the accounting equation is in balance after each transaction.

1. Paid $50 for advertising in the local newspaper.
2. Received $1,000 as payment for preparing a report.
3. Wrote a $600 check for the month's rent.
4. Jan Swift withdrew $800 for her personal use.
5. Received $200 on account from the person who had purchased the old office furniture.

Key Concepts

1. *Property* is anything of value that a person or business owns and therefore controls. Property is measured in dollars. In accounting, property appears in the records at the amount it cost the owner. Financial claims are the legal rights to property and are also measured in dollars. The relationship between property and financial claims is shown in the following equation:

PROPERTY = FINANCIAL CLAIMS

2. As it is used in accounting, the term *equities* refers to the financial claims on assets (property). The two types of equities in a business are

   - creditors' financial claims, called *liabilities,* and
   - the owner's financial claims, called *owner's equity.*

3. The accounting equation is ASSETS = LIABILITIES + OWNER'S EQUITY

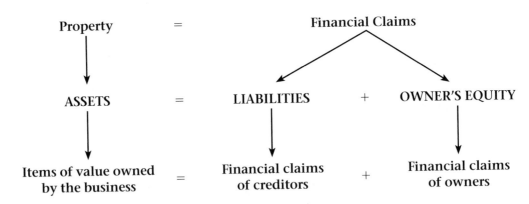

Property	=		Financial Claims	
↓				
ASSETS	=	LIABILITIES	+	OWNER'S EQUITY
↓		↓		↓
Items of value owned by the business	=	Financial claims of creditors	+	Financial claims of owners

4. A *business transaction* is an economic event that causes a change—either an increase or a decrease—in assets, liabilities, or owner's equity. The accounting equation remains in balance after each transaction:

	Assets			= Liabilities	+ Owner's Equity
	Cash in Bank	Computer Equipment	Office Equipment		Serge Toblek, Capital
Trans. 1	$15,000	0	0	0	$15,000
Trans. 2			+$600		+$600
Balance	$15,000 +	0 +	$600 =	0 +	$15,600
Trans. 3		+$3,000		+$3,000	
Balance	$15,000 +	$3,000 +	$600 =	$3,000 +	$15,600
		$18,600			$18,600

The following table shows the effects of typical business transactions on the parts of the accounting equation.

Transaction	Effects On:		
	Assets	Liabilities	Owner's Equity
Investment of cash by owner	+		+
Investment of property	+		+
Cash payment for office equipment	−,+		
Purchase of an asset on account	+	+	
Sale of office equipment on account	−,+		
Make a payment on account	−	−	
Record revenue from a cash sale	+		+
Record a cash payment for an expense	−		−
Record a cash withdrawal by the owner	−		−

5. Use the following steps to analyze a business transaction:

ANALYSIS	*Identify*	**1.**	Identify the accounts affected.
	Classify	**2.**	Classify the accounts affected.
	+/−	**3.**	Determine the amount of increase or decrease for each account affected.
	Balance	**4.**	Make sure the accounting equation remains in balance.

Key Terms

account	(p. 54)	expense	(p. 60)
accounting equation	(p. 52)	financial claim	(p. 50)
accounts payable	(p. 55)	investment	(p. 55)
accounts receivable	(p. 54)	liabilities	(p. 52)
assets	(p. 51)	on account	(p. 57)
business transaction	(p. 54)	owner's equity	(p. 52)
credit	(p. 51)	property	(p. 50)
creditor	(p. 51)	revenue	(p. 60)
equities	(p. 52)	withdrawal	(p. 62)

AFTER YOU READ

Check Your Understanding

1. **Property and Financial Claims**
   a. Define the terms *property* and *financial claim.*
   b. What is the relationship between property and financial claims?

2. **Equities**
   a. Describe the relationship between assets and equities.
   b. Name the two types of equities in a business, and give an example of an account that is used for each type.

3. **The Accounting Equation**
   a. What is the accounting equation?
   b. Give an example of an account for each part of the accounting equation.

4. **Effects of Transactions**
   a. What is a business transaction?
   b. How does each of the following transactions affect the three parts of the accounting equation?
      Trans. 1: Owner transferred cash from personal savings account to the business.
      Trans. 2: Owner withdrew cash from the business for personal use.
      Trans. 3: Purchased equipment for cash.
      Trans. 4: Purchased equipment on credit.
      Trans. 5: Issued a check for the first monthly payment for equipment purchased in Transaction 4.
      Trans. 6: Received payment on the date of service for design consulting.
      Trans. 7: Issued a check to pay the telephone bill.

5. **Accounting Equation in Balance**
   a. At least how many accounts must be affected by each business transaction? Why?
   b. Describe the four-step process described in this chapter used to analyze business transactions.

Apply Key Terms

Which of the following terms can be considered assets? Which terms relate to liabilities? Which terms do not fall easily into either category?

accounts payable	investment
accounts receivable	on account
credit	property
creditor	revenue
expense	withdrawal

Exploring Electronic Spreadsheets

Computer spreadsheets are important tools for organizing and analyzing data. A spreadsheet is made up of rows and columns. The columns are identified by letters and the rows are identified by numbers. As you create a spreadsheet, you will enter numbers, labels, and formulas into cells. Microsoft® Excel is the most commonly used spreadsheet application in the business world. The following is an example of a basic electronic spreadsheet:

	A	B	C	D	E	F	G	H	
1		Jan	Feb	March	April	May	June	July	▲
2	Sales	2,500	5,000	1,650	10,000	3,100	8,200	12,500	
3	Expenses	700	1,200	225	3,550	1,800	2,300	5,600	
4	Net income	1,800	3,800	1,425	6,450	1,300	5,900	6,900	
5									
6									▼

Before you create a computer spreadsheet, review the following spreadsheet terms.

	Spreadsheet Terms	Description
①	Row	Identified by numbers down the left side of the spreadsheet.
②	Column	Identified by letters along the top of the spreadsheet.
③	Cell address	Identified by a column letter and row number. For example, the cell address B4 indicates the cell where the number 1,800 is found.
④	Active cell	Indicated by a dark border.
⑤	Scroll arrows	Allows you to view other parts of the spreadsheet.
⑥	Labels	Text that identifies columns or rows of information; cannot be used for calculations.
⑦	Values	Numbers inserted in cells that can be used for calculations.
⑧	Formulas	Mathematical functions entered in a particular cell that tells the software to add, subtract, divide, or multiply values. For example, E2 − E3 represents 10,000 − 3,550, or 6,450

Problem 3–4 Classifying Accounts

All accounts belong in one of the following classifications: Asset, Liability, Owner's Equity.

Instructions In your working papers, indicate the classification for each of the following accounts.

1. John Jones, Capital
2. Cash in Bank
3. Accounts Receivable
4. Accounts Payable
5. Office Equipment
6. Delivery Equipment
7. Camping Equipment
8. Building
9. Land
10. Computer Equipment

Analyze Identify the accounts that represent financial claims to property.

Problem 3–5 Completing the Accounting Equation

A business owned and operated by Mike Murray uses these accounts.

Instructions Look at the following list of accounts, and determine the missing amount for each of the question marks.

Assets		=	Liabilities		+	Owner's Equity
Cash in Bank	$4,500		Accounts Payable			Mike Murray,
Accounts Receivable	1,350		?			Capital $9,250
Office Equipment	5,000					
	?					

Analyze Predict what would happen to owner's equity if this business paid all of its bills today.

Problem 3–6 Classifying Accounts Within the Accounting Equation

Listed here are the account names and balances for Wilderness Rentals.

Accounts Payable	$ 7,000	Cash in Bank	$ 5,000
Accounts Receivable	2,000	Office Equipment	3,000
Camping Equipment	12,000	Ronald Hicks, Capital	15,000

Instructions Using these account names and balances:

1. List and total the assets of the business.
2. Determine the amount owed by the business.
3. Give the amount of the owner's equity in the business.

Analyze Design a diagram that shows the accounting equation for Wilderness Rentals.

Problem 3–7 Determining Increases and Decreases in Accounts

Hot Suds Car Wash uses the following accounts:

Assets	=	Liabilities	+	Owner's Equity
Cash in Bank		Accounts Payable		Regina Delgado,
Accounts Receivable				Capital
Office Equipment				
Office Furniture				
Car Wash Equipment				

Instructions Use a form similar to the one that follows. For each transaction:

1. Identify the accounts affected.
2. Classify the accounts.
3. Determine the amount of the increase (+) or decrease (−) for each account affected.

The first transaction is completed as an example.

Trans.	Accounts Affected	Classification	Amount of Increase (+) or Decrease (−)
1.	Cash in Bank	Asset	+$25,000
	Regina Delgado, Capital	Owner's Equity	+$25,000

Date	Transactions
Jan. 1	1. Regina Delgado, the owner, invested $25,000 cash in the business.
4	2. Bought car wash equipment with cash for $12,000.
5	3. Purchased, on account, $2,500 of office equipment.
10	4. Wrote a check for the monthly rent, $800.
12	5. Received cash for services performed, $1,000.
15	6. The owner withdrew $600 cash from the business for personal use.
20	7. Purchased a desk for $1,000, paying $200 cash and agreeing to pay the balance of $800 in 30 days.
25	8. Provided services worth $600 on account.

Analyze Identify the transaction that affects the most accounts.

Problems

Problem 3–8 Determining the Effects of Transactions on the Accounting Equation

After graduating from college, Abe Shultz decided to start a pet grooming service called Kits & Pups Grooming.

Instructions Use a form similar to the one that follows. For each of the following transactions:

1. Identify the accounts affected, using the account names on the form.
2. Determine the amount of the increase or decrease for each account.
3. Write the amount of the increase (+) or decrease (−) in the space under each account affected.
4. On the following line, write the new balance for each account.
5. Transaction 1 is completed as an example.

	Assets				=	Liabilities	+	Owner's Equity
Trans.	Cash in Bank	Accts. Rec.	Office Equip.	Grooming Equip.	=	Accounts Payable	+	Abe Shultz, Capital
1	+$10,000							+$10,000

Date	Transactions
Jan. 2	1. Abe Shultz began the business by depositing $10,000 in a checking account at the Shoreline National Bank in the name of the business, Kits & Pups Grooming.
3	2. Bought grooming equipment for cash, $1,000.
8	3. Issued a check for $900 for the monthly rent.
9	4. Bought $6,000 worth of new office equipment on account for use in the business.
15	5. Received $700 cash for services performed for customers during the first week of business.
21	6. Issued a $2,000 check to the creditor as partial payment for the office equipment purchased on account.
29	7. Performed grooming services and agreed to be paid for them later, $500.

Analyze Explain the difference between Transaction 5 and Transaction 7.

Problem 3–9 Determining the Effects of Transactions on the Accounting Equation

Juanita Ortega is the owner of a professional guide service called Outback Guide Service.

Instructions Use a form similar to the one below. Complete these steps for each of the following transactions:

1. Identify the accounts affected.
2. Write the amount of the increase (+) or decrease (−) in the space provided on the form in your working papers.
3. Determine the new balance for each account.

	Assets					=	Liabilities	+	Owner's Equity
Trans.	Cash in Bank	Accts. Rec.	Hiking Equip.	Rafting Equip.	Office Equip.	=	Accounts Payable	+	Juanita Ortega, Capital

Date	Transactions
Jan. 3	1. Ms. Ortega, the owner, opened a checking account for the business by depositing $60,000 of her personal funds.
6	2. Paid by check the monthly rent of $3,000.
8	3. Bought hiking equipment for the business by writing a check for $3,000.
9	4. Purchased $24,000 of rafting equipment by writing a check.
11	5. Purchased office equipment on account for $4,000.
15	6. Received payment for guide services, $2,500.
18	7. Ms. Ortega contributed a desk valued at $450 to the business.
21	8. Withdrew $3,000 cash from the business for personal use.
26	9. Wrote a check to a creditor as partial payment on account, $1,500.
30	10. Took a group on a tour and agreed to accept payment later, $1,200.

Analyze Calculate the amount owed to creditors after Transaction 10.

SPREADSHEET SMART GUIDE

Step–by–Step Instructions: Problem 3–9

1. Select the spreadsheet template for Problem 3–9.
2. Enter your name and the date in the spaces provided on the template.
3. Complete the spreadsheet using the instructions in your working papers.
4. Print the spreadsheet and proof your work.
5. Complete the Analyze activity.
6. Save your work and exit the spreadsheet program.

Problem 3–10 Describing Business Transactions

Showbiz Video is a business owned by Greg Failla. The transactions that follow are shown as they would appear in the accounting equation.

Instructions In your working papers, describe what has happened in each transaction. Transaction 1 is completed as an example.

Example:
1. The owner invested $30,000 in the business.

CONTINUE

	Assets				=	Liabilities	+	Owner's Equity
Trans.	Cash in Bank	Accts. Rec.	Office Equip.	Video Equip.	=	Accounts Payable	+	Greg Failla, Capital
1	+$30,000							+$30,000
2	−$ 2,000		+$2,000					
3				+$8,000		+$8,000		
4	+$ 700							+$ 700
5		+$500						+$ 500
6			+$ 200					+$ 200
7	−$ 3,000					−$3,000		
8		+$200	−$ 200					
9	+$ 500	−$500						
10	−$ 1,000							−$ 1,000

Analyze Calculate the balance of the account, **Greg Failla, Capital.**

CHALLENGE PROBLEM ✓

Problem 3–11 Completing the Accounting Equation

The account names and balances for Job Connect are listed below.

Instructions Determine the missing amount for each of the question marks. Use the form in your working papers and write in the missing amounts.

	Assets			=	Liabilities	+	Owner's Equity
Trans.	Cash in Bank	Accounts Receivable	Business Equipment	=	Accounts Payable	+	Richard Tang, Capital
1	?	$ 2,000	$ 1,000		$ 500		$ 7,500
2	$ 3,000	$ 9,000	?		$2,000		$16,000
3	$ 8,000	$ 1,000	$10,000		?		$15,000
4	$ 4,000	?	$ 4,000		$1,000		$17,000
5	$ 9,000	$ 7,000	$ 6,000		$5,000		?
6	$10,000	$14,000	?		$6,000		$32,000
7	$ 6,000	$ 4,000	$10,000		?		$15,000
8	?	$ 5,000	$ 9,000		$1,000		?

Hint: In line 8, total assets are $18,000.

Analyze Explain the mathematical operations used to solve for the accounting equation.

Practice your test-taking skills! The questions on this page are reprinted with permission from national organizations:
- Future Business Leaders of America
- Business Professionals of America

Use a separate sheet of paper to record your answers.

Future Business Leaders of America

MULTIPLE CHOICE

1. Things of value a business uses to generate income are known as

    a. assets.
    c. expenses.
    b. capital.
    d. revenue.

Business Professionals of America

MULTIPLE CHOICE

2. If a customer sends in a payment on his account owed, which of the following statements is true?

    a. One asset increases and another asset decreases.
    b. One asset increases and one liability decreases.
    c. One liability decreases and owner's equity increases.
    d. One liability increases and owner's equity increases.

3. Use these account balances to complete the next two questions:

Cash in Bank	$3,200.00	Amy Smith, Capital	$6,200.00
Accounts Receivable	?	Amy Smith, Drawing	1,000.00
Office Supplies	300.00	Boarding Revenue	1,400.00
Office Furniture	1,200.00	Grooming Revenue	?
Office Equipment	1,800.00	Salaries Expense	300.00
Accounts Payable	?	Miscellaneous Expense	200.00

If the balance in Accounts Payable is $2,000.00 and Grooming Revenue is $400.00, what is the correct balance for the Accounts Receivable account?

    a. $800.00
    c. $2,000.00
    b. $1,500.00
    d. $2,500.00

4. Use the above table in #3 to answer this question.

If the Accounts Receivable balance is $800.00 and Grooming Revenue is $600.00, what is the balance in the Accounts Payable account?

    a. $600.00
    c. $1,200.00
    b. $800.00
    d. $2,000.00

5. If owner's equity is $25,500, and assets are $37,600, liabilities are

    a. $25,500.
    b. $37,600.
    c. $63,100.
    d. $12,100.

Need More Help?

Go to glencoeaccounting.glencoe.com and click on **Student Center**. Click on **Winning Competitive Events** and select **Chapter 3.**
- **Practice Questions and Test-Taking Tips**
- **Concept Capsules and Terminology**

The Accounting Equation

1. What term identifies the owner's claims to assets of the business?

2. Does owner's equity increase every time a business acquires a new asset? Explain your answer.

3. You are analyzing transactions when you have to answer the telephone. After you finish the conversation, how can you tell whether you completed the transaction you were working on when the phone rang?

4. How is an expense similar to a withdrawal? How is it different?

5. Describe a series of transactions that could result in negative owner's equity.

6. Assess the value of the four-step procedure for analyzing transactions.

Service Business: Health and Fitness

The Fitness Center, owned by Gail Chan, has been in business for two years. The business is successful with its expanded hours of operation.

You are a local business consultant and have worked with several other small businesses in the area. Ms. Chan has asked you about possible ways to obtain money for new equipment. She has already borrowed money from family members and cannot use them as a source of more funds.

INSTRUCTIONS

1. Evaluate possible sources of money for your client. Use the Internet and other sources to research alternatives with the Small Business Administration, the Chamber of Commerce, and local banks.

2. Make a list of alternatives. Include costs, interest rates, and advantages or disadvantages.

3. Make a recommendation to your client based on your list of alternatives.

4. Explain how the additional money will affect the accounting equation.

Company Property

Many companies provide office supplies for their employees' use while on the job. Imagine that you work for a large department store like JC Penney. Several of your co-workers take company supplies home for their personal use, such as pens, bags, hangers, and boxes. You need boxes to store some items at home, so you consider taking them from the supply room.

ETHICAL DECISION MAKING

1. What are the ethical issues?

2. What are the alternatives?

3. Who are the affected parties?

4. How do the alternatives affect the parties?

5. What would you do?

Writing a Tip Sheet

Using the four-step approach to transaction analysis, write a "tip sheet" to help a new employee remember the steps. Write a brief explanation and give an example of each step in the analysis. Create a business transaction to use in your explanation.

Applying Technology

Whether you work in a small or large business, technology is critical to efficiency in the workplace.

ON THE JOB

After graduating from college and working for a year as a junior accountant in a CPA firm, you decide to open an accounting business from your home. You'll need a computer, software, and office furniture to get started. Complete the activities below to help you select the right software for your needs.

INSTRUCTIONS

1. List the kinds of financial services you would like to provide.
2. Research three accounting software packages that would help you deliver the services you listed. List the name, price, system requirements, and features of each software package. Use the Internet and other sources.
3. Select the software package that best meets your anticipated needs. Write a paragraph explaining why you selected this product.

Money Around the World

If you were on vacation in Mexico, you would pay for your lunch in pesos. Just as different countries use different languages, they also use their own type of money or *currency*. Many countries in Europe use the euro. India uses the rupee, and China uses the yuan. If you were an accountant recording business transactions in Switzerland, you would use Swiss francs.

INSTRUCTIONS Find a Web site on the Internet that lists world currencies. What currency is used in Japan? In the United Kingdom?

Your Earning Power

Your future income will depend on various things including your career choice, your education, and the region where you live.

PERSONAL FINANCE ACTIVITY List three jobs that are in different fields and different regions of the United States. Use the Internet or your library to research their education requirements and their salary ranges. Create a table to organize the results of your research.

PERSONAL FINANCE ONLINE Log on to **glencoeaccounting.glencoe.com** and click on **Student Center.** Click on **Making It Personal** and select **Chapter 3.**

Sports Property

Like many industries, a professional sport can have assets that are unique to its type of business. Visit **glencoeaccounting .glencoe.com** and click on **Student Center.** Click on **WebQuest** and select **Unit 2** to continue your Internet project.

Transactions That Affect Assets, Liabilities, and Owner's Capital

What You'll Learn

1. Prepare a chart of accounts.

2. Explain the purpose of double-entry accounting.

3. Identify the normal balance of accounts.

4. Use T accounts to illustrate the rules of debit and credit for asset accounts, liability accounts, and the owner's capital account and to express the accounting equation.

5. Use T accounts to analyze transactions that affect assets, liabilities, and the owner's capital account.

6. Calculate the account balances after recording business transactions.

7. Define the accounting terms introduced in this chapter.

Why It's Important

In accounting you need to analyze transactions into debit and credit parts.

BEFORE YOU READ

Predict
1. What does the chapter title tell you?
2. What do you already know about this subject from personal experience?
3. What have you learned about this in the earlier chapters?
4. What gaps exist in your knowledge of this subject?

Exploring the *Real World* of Business

ANALYZING BUSINESS TRANSACTIONS

Panda Restaurant Group

When you think of a quick meal, do you think of Orange Flavored Chicken and Beef with Broccoli? These are two of the Chinese food entrées that Panda Express serves quickly and conveniently. Panda Express is part of the **Panda Restaurant Group**, owner of Panda Inn and Hibachi-San restaurants.

Andrew and Peggy Cherng opened their first Panda Inn in Pasadena, California, using recipes from Andrew's father, Master Chef Ming-Tsai Cherng. **Panda Restaurant Group** now has more than 700 stores in 36 states, Puerto Rico, and Japan.

The Cherngs are on a mission to reach a goal of 10,000 Panda Express restaurants. This means finding new locations and buying a lot of kitchen equipment and dining room furniture.

What Do You Think?

When **Panda Restaurant Group** opens a new store, how do you think its assets and liabilities are affected?

Working in the *Real World*

APPLYING YOUR ACCOUNTING KNOWLEDGE

Business transactions occur around us every day. A music store sells thousands of CDs. You may stop by for a meal at a local restaurant. A cruise ship line may buy new furniture for its dining cabins. Successful businesses have hundreds, even thousands, of transactions each day. Analyzing and recording these transactions are key duties of the accounting staff.

Personal Connection

1. What types of business transactions occur in your workplace or the workplace of your family or friends?
2. Who records these transactions into the accounting records?

Online Connection

Go to **glencoeaccounting.glencoe.com** and click on **Student Center.** Click on **Working in the Real World** and select **Chapter 4.**

Accounts and the Double-Entry Accounting System

BEFORE YOU READ

Main Idea
The double-entry accounting system uses debits and credits. *Debit* means "left side" and *credit* means "right side."

Read to Learn...
➤ about the chart of accounts. (p. 78)
➤ about the double-entry accounting system. (p. 78)

Key Terms
chart of accounts
ledger
double-entry accounting
debit
credit
T account
normal balance

In Chapter 3 you learned about the accounting equation. In this chapter you will learn how to keep it in balance using the double-entry accounting system. When The Coca-Cola Company records the dollar amount of a transaction in one account, it records an equal amount in another account. The same is true of a small barbershop. In this and following chapters, we discuss accounting for a sole proprietorship.

The Chart of Accounts
How Is the Chart of Accounts Organized?

A **chart of accounts** is a list of all accounts used by a business. A small business may require only 20 or 30 accounts, but a large one may have several thousand.

Recall that an account is a record of changes and balances of a specific asset, liability, or component of owner's equity. Accounts may have different physical forms, depending on the system. In a manual system, each account may be a separate page in a book or a separate card in a tray. In an electronic system, accounts are stored on disks or hard drives.

Whether a system is manual or electronic, accounts are grouped together in a **ledger** . The ledger is often referred to as the *general ledger*. "Keeping the books" refers to maintaining accounts in the ledger. Grouping accounts in a ledger makes information easy to find. Information is taken from the ledger and organized into financial statements.

A system for numbering accounts makes it easy to locate individual accounts in the ledger. Account numbers have two or more digits used for sorting information based on the kinds of reports the business needs. A small company may use a three-digit system. A very large corporation may use 35 or more digits. A typical numbering system used to prepare a chart of accounts is as follows:

- Asset accounts begin with 1.
- Liability accounts begin with 2.
- Owner's equity accounts begin with 3.
- Revenue accounts begin with 4.
- Expense accounts begin with 5.

Double-Entry Accounting
How Does Double-Entry Accounting Work?

In Chapter 3 you used the accounting equation for analyzing and recording changes in account balances. This approach works well if a business has only a few accounts. It becomes awkward, however, if a business has many accounts and many transactions to analyze.

Accountants use the **double-entry accounting** system to analyze and record a transaction. Double-entry accounting recognizes the different sides of business transactions as *debits* and *credits*. A **debit** is an entry on the left side of an account. A **credit** is an entry on the right side of an account. This system is more efficient than updating the accounting equation for each transaction.

T Accounts

An efficient tool for using double-entry accounting is a *T account*. The **T account**, so called because of its T shape, shows the dollar increase or decrease in an account that is caused by a transaction. T accounts help the accountant analyze the parts of a business transaction.

As in the illustration here, a T account has an account name, a left side, and a right side. The account name is at the top of the T. The left side of T accounts is *always* used for debit amounts. The right side of T accounts is *always* used for credit amounts. The words *debit* and *credit* are simply the accountant's terms for *left* and *right*. Accountants sometimes use **DR** for debit and **CR** for credit.

Account Name	
Left Side	Right Side
Debit Side	Credit Side
Debit	Credit

As You READ

In Your Experience

Chart of Accounts
A chart of accounts is organized as a table. What other tables have you worked with?

The Rules of Debit and Credit

Debits and credits are used to record the increase or decrease in each account affected by a business transaction. Under double-entry accounting, for each debit entry made in one account, a credit of an equal amount must be made in another account. Debit and credit rules vary according to whether an account is classified as an asset, a liability, or the owner's capital

Debit and Credit The terms *debit* and *credit* might remind you of debit cards and credit cards. In accounting *debit* simply means the left side of an account and *credit* means the right side.

account. Regardless of the type of account, however, the left side of an account is always the debit side and the right side is always the credit side.

Each account classification has a specific side that is its normal balance side. An account's **normal balance** is always on the side used to record increases to the account. The word *normal* used here means *usual.* Throughout this book, note that the normal balance side of each account is shaded.

Rules for Asset Accounts. Asset accounts follow three rules of debit and credit:

1. An asset account is *increased* (+) on the *debit* side (left side).
2. An asset account is *decreased* (−) on the *credit* side (right side).
3. The *normal balance* for an asset account is the *increase,* or the *debit* side. The normal balance side is shaded in the following T account.

Notice that assets appear on the left side of the accounting equation.

ASSETS = LIABILITIES + OWNER'S EQUITY

Asset Accounts

Debit	Credit
+	−
(1) Increase Side	(2) Decrease Side
(3) Normal Balance	

For asset accounts the *increase* side is the debit (left) side of the T account. The *decrease* side is the credit (right) side of the T account. Notice the (+) and (−) signs that are used to indicate the increase and decrease sides of the account. They do not mean the same thing as *debit* and *credit.*

Since the increase side of an asset account is always the debit side, asset accounts have a normal debit balance. For example, in the normal course of business, total increases to assets are larger than or exceed total decreases.

Cash in Bank

Debit	Credit
+	−
200	70
150	40
350	110
Bal. 240	

You would expect an asset account, then, to have a normal debit balance.

Let's apply these rules to an actual asset account. Look at the entries in the T account for **Cash in Bank** shown here. The increases in the account are recorded on the left, or debit, side. The decreases in the account are recorded on the right, or credit, side. Total debits equal $350 ($200 + $150). Total credits equal $110 ($70 + $40). To find the balance, subtract total credits from total debits ($350 − $110). The debit balance is $240.

Rules for Liability and Owner's Capital Accounts. The rules of debit and credit for liability and the owner's capital account are:

1. Liability and owner's capital accounts are *increased* on the *credit* (right) side.
2. Liability and owner's capital accounts are *decreased* on the *debit* (left) side.
3. The *normal balance* for liability and owner's capital accounts is the *increase,* or the *credit* side.

To illustrate these rules, let's look again at the accounting equation and the T accounts. Remember, the normal balance side is shaded.

Assets		=	Liabilities		+	Owner's Equity	
Debit + Increase Side	Credit − Decrease Side		Debit − (2) Decrease Side	Credit + (1) Increase Side		Debit − (2) Decrease Side	Credit + (1) Increase Side
Normal Balance				(3) Normal Balance			(3) Normal Balance

For all three types of accounts, the debit side is always the left side of the T account, and the credit side is always the right side. Notice, however, that the increase (+) and decrease (−) sides of the liability and owner's capital accounts are the opposite of those for assets. This difference exists because accounts classified as liabilities and owner's capital are on the opposite side of the accounting equation from accounts classified as assets. As a result, debit and credit rules on one side of the accounting equation—and the T accounts within it—are mirror images of those on the other side.

Let's apply these rules to actual accounts. First, look at the entries in the T account below for the liability account **Accounts Payable.** Increases are recorded on the right, or credit, side. The decreases are recorded on the left, or debit, side. Total credits equal $375 ($200 + $175); total debits equal $175 ($100 + $75). To find the balance, subtract the total debits from the total credits ($375 − $175). The credit balance is $200.

Accounts Payable

Debit −	Credit +
100	200
75	175
175	375
	Bal. 200

Now look at the entries in the T account for the owner's equity account **Maria Sanchez, Capital.** Remember that the rules of debit and credit for the capital account are the same as those for a liability account.

Increases to owner's capital are recorded on the right, or credit, side of the account. Decreases are recorded on the left, or debit, side. The capital account has a normal credit balance. If you subtract the total debits from the total credits ($4,000 − $550), you have a credit balance of $3,450.

Maria Sanchez, Capital

Debit −	Credit +
350	1,500
200	2,500
550	4,000
	Bal. 3,450

AFTER YOU **READ**

Reinforce the Main Idea

Create a chart like this one to summarize the rules of debit and credit. Fill in each blank box with the word *debit* or the word *credit*.

	Asset Accounts	Liability Accounts	Owner's Capital Account
Normal Balance			
Increase Side			
Decrease Side			

Do the Math

During the month of December, Poremba Pizza wrote checks totaling $4,800. Two-thirds of this amount was used to purchase a computer for cash. The remaining amount was used to pay an outstanding invoice for kitchen equipment purchased from Restaurant City.

1. List the account(s) debited and the debit amount(s).
2. List the account(s) credited and the credit amount(s).

Problem 4–1 Applying the Rules of Debit and Credit

Speedy Appliance Repair, owned by R. Lewis, uses the following accounts:

> **General Ledger**
> Cash in Bank
> Accounts Receivable
> Office Equipment
> Accounts Payable
> R. Lewis, Capital

Instructions In the form provided in your working papers:

1. Classify each account as an asset, liability, or owner's capital account.
2. Indicate whether the increase side is a debit or a credit.
3. Indicate whether the decrease side is a debit or credit.
4. Indicate whether the normal balance for the account is a debit or credit balance.

The **Cash in Bank** account is completed as an example.

Account Name	Account Classification	Increase Side	Decrease Side	Normal Balance
Cash in Bank	Asset	Debit	Credit	Debit

Applying the Rules of Debit and Credit

Now that you are familiar with the rules of debit and credit for asset, liability, and owner's capital accounts, you can use those rules to analyze business transactions.

Business Transaction Analysis

How Do You Analyze Transactions?

Whether a business is buying a new computer system, paying its utility bills, or receiving money for sales, the accountant must analyze how the transaction should be recorded. When analyzing business transactions, you should use the following step-by-step method:

BEFORE YOU READ

Main Idea
Use T accounts to analyze transactions.

Read to Learn...
➤ a step-by-step method for analyzing transactions. (p. 83)
➤ how to apply the method to asset, liability, and owner's capital transactions. (p. 83)

Business Transaction

BUSINESS TRANSACTION ANALYSIS: Steps to Success

ANALYSIS	*Identify* *Classify* +/−	1. Identify the accounts affected. 2. Classify the accounts affected. 3. Determine the amount of increase or decrease for each account affected.
DEBIT-CREDIT RULE		4. Which account is debited? For what amount? 5. Which account is credited? For what amount?
T ACCOUNTS		6. What is the complete entry in T-account form?

Account Name	Account Name

Asset and Equities Transactions

How Do You Use T Accounts for Assets and Equities?

The business transactions that follow are for Roadrunner Delivery Service. Throughout the next several pages, you will learn how to analyze each

Roadrunner transaction, apply the rules of debit and credit, and complete the entry in T-account form. The T accounts demonstrate the effects of transactions on the accounting equation. A debit in one account is offset by a credit in another account. Refer to the Roadrunner chart of accounts on page 79. These accounts will be used to analyze several business transactions.

Assets and Owner's Capital

Business Transactions 1 and 2 use T accounts to illustrate owner's investments in the business.

Business Transaction 1

On October 1 Maria Sanchez took $25,000 from personal savings and deposited that amount to open a business checking account in the name of Roadrunner Delivery Service.

ANALYSIS	*Identify* *Classify* +/−	1. The accounts **Cash in Bank** and **Maria Sanchez, Capital** are affected. 2. **Cash in Bank** is an asset account. **Maria Sanchez, Capital** is an owner's capital account. 3. **Cash in Bank** is increased by $25,000. **Maria Sanchez, Capital** is increased by $25,000.

DEBIT-CREDIT RULE	4. Increases in asset accounts are recorded as debits. Debit **Cash in Bank** for $25,000. 5. Increases in the owner's capital account are recorded as credits. Credit **Maria Sanchez, Capital** for $25,000.

T ACCOUNTS   6.

Cash in Bank		Maria Sanchez, Capital	
Debit + 25,000			Credit + 25,000

Business Transaction 2

On October 2 Maria Sanchez took two telephones valued at $200 each from her home and transferred them to the business as office equipment.

ANALYSIS	*Identify* *Classify* +/−	1. The accounts **Office Equipment** and **Maria Sanchez, Capital** are affected. 2. **Office Equipment** is an asset account. **Maria Sanchez, Capital** is an owner's capital account. 3. **Office Equipment** is increased by $400. **Maria Sanchez, Capital** is increased by $400.

| DEBIT-CREDIT RULE | 4. Increases in asset accounts are recorded as debits. Debit **Office Equipment** for $400. |
| | 5. Increases in owner's capital accounts are recorded as credits. Credit **Maria Sanchez, Capital** for $400. |

T ACCOUNTS	6.

Office Equipment	Maria Sanchez, Capital
Debit + 400	Credit + 400

Assets and Liabilities

The following examples show changes to assets and liabilities in T-account form:

- Business Transaction 3: increases an asset and decreases another asset
- Business Transaction 4: increases an asset and increases a liability
- Business Transaction 5: increases an asset and decreases another asset
- Business Transaction 6: decreases a liability and decreases an asset
- Business Transaction 7: increases an asset and decreases a liability

As You READ

Compare and Contrast

Transactions How are Business Transactions 2 and 3 similar? How are they different?

Business Transaction 3

On October 4 Roadrunner issued Check 101 for $3,000 to buy a computer system.

ANALYSIS	*Identify*	1. The accounts **Computer Equipment** and **Cash in Bank** are affected.
	Classify	2. **Computer Equipment** and **Cash in Bank** are asset accounts.
	+/−	3. **Computer Equipment** is increased by $3,000. **Cash in Bank** is decreased by $3,000.

| DEBIT-CREDIT RULE | 4. Increases in asset accounts are recorded as debits. Debit **Computer Equipment** for $3,000. |
| | 5. Decreases in asset accounts are recorded as credits. Credit **Cash in Bank** for $3,000. |

T ACCOUNTS	6.

Computer Equipment	Cash in Bank
Debit + 3,000	Credit − 3,000

Business Transaction 4

On October 9 Roadrunner bought a used truck on account from North Shore Auto for $12,000.

ANALYSIS

Identify
1. The accounts **Delivery Equipment** and **Accounts Payable–North Shore Auto** are affected.

Classify
2. **Delivery Equipment** is an asset account. **Accounts Payable–North Shore Auto** is a liability account.

+/–
3. **Delivery Equipment** is increased by $12,000. **Accounts Payable–North Shore Auto** is increased by $12,000.

DEBIT-CREDIT RULE
4. Increases in asset accounts are recorded as debits. Debit **Delivery Equipment** for $12,000.
5. Increases in liability accounts are recorded as credits. Credit **Accounts Payable–North Shore Auto** for $12,000.

T ACCOUNTS
6.

Delivery Equipment		Accounts Payable—North Shore Auto	
Debit + 12,000			Credit + 12,000

Business Transaction 5

On October 11 Roadrunner sold one phone on account to Green Company for $200.

ANALYSIS

Identify
1. The accounts **Accounts Receivable–Green Company** and **Office Equipment** are affected.

Classify
2. **Accounts Receivable–Green Company** is an asset account. **Office Equipment** is also an asset account.

+/–
3. **Accounts Receivable–Green Company** is increased by $200. **Office Equipment** is decreased by $200.

DEBIT-CREDIT RULE
4. Increases in asset accounts are recorded as debits. Debit **Accounts Receivable–Green Company** for $200.
5. Decreases in asset accounts are recorded as credits. Credit **Office Equipment** for $200.

T ACCOUNTS
6.

Accounts Receivable—Green Company		Office Equipment	
Debit + 200			Credit – 200

Business Transaction 6

On October 12 Roadrunner mailed Check 102 for $350 as the first installment payment on the truck purchased from North Shore Auto on October 9.

ANALYSIS

Identify
1. The accounts **Accounts Payable—North Shore Auto** and **Cash in Bank** are affected.

Classify
2. **Accounts Payable—North Shore Auto** is a liability account. **Cash in Bank** is an asset account.

+/−
3. **Accounts Payable—North Shore Auto** is decreased by $350. **Cash in Bank** is decreased by $350.

DEBIT-CREDIT RULE

4. Decreases in liability accounts are recorded as debits. Debit **Accounts Payable—North Shore Auto** for $350.
5. Decreases in asset accounts are recorded as credits. Credit **Cash in Bank** for $350.

T ACCOUNTS

6.

Accounts Payable—North Shore Auto		Cash in Bank	
Debit			Credit
−			−
350			350

Business Transaction 7

On October 14 Roadrunner received and deposited a check for $200 from Green Company. The check is full payment for the telephone sold on account to Green Company on October 11.

ANALYSIS

Identify
1. The accounts **Cash in Bank** and **Accounts Receivable—Green Company** are affected.

Classify
2. **Cash in Bank** is an asset account. **Accounts Receivable—Green Company** is an asset account.

+/−
3. **Cash in Bank** is increased by $200. **Accounts Receivable—Green Company** is decreased by $200.

DEBIT-CREDIT RULE

4. Increases in asset accounts are recorded as debits. Debit **Cash in Bank** for $200.
5. Decreases in asset accounts are recorded as credits. Credit **Accounts Receivable—Green Company** for $200.

T ACCOUNTS

6.

Cash in Bank		Accounts Receivable—Green Company	
Debit			Credit
+			−
200			200

AFTER YOU READ

Reinforce the Main Idea

Imagine that you have your own business. Write a description of a typical transaction your business would have. On a sheet of paper, express the same transaction in T-account form.

Do the Math

Diane Hendricks always dreamed of owning a recording studio. On February 1 Diane withdrew $10,000 from personal savings and deposited it in a new business checking account for Hendricks Sound. On February 2 Hendricks Sound made a $2,000 down payment on equipment that cost $8,000. The remaining balance will be paid at a later date. What is the accounting equation for Hendricks Sound after these transactions?

Problem 4–2 Identifying Increases and Decreases in Accounts

Alice Roberts uses the following accounts in her business:

> **General Ledger**
> Cash in Bank   Office Equipment
> Accounts Receivable   Accounts Payable
> Office Furniture   Alice Roberts, Capital

Instructions Analyze each of the following transactions. In your working papers, explain the debit and the credit. Use the format shown in the example.

Example:
On June 2 Alice Roberts invested $5,000 of her own money in a business called Roberts Employment Agency.

  a. The asset account **Cash in Bank** is increased. Increases in asset accounts are recorded as debits.

  b. The owner's capital account **Alice Roberts, Capital** is increased. Increases in the owner's capital account are recorded as credits.

Date	Transactions
June 3	1. Purchased a computer on account from Computer Inc. for $2,500.
9	2. Transferred a desk (Office Furniture) to the business. The desk is worth $750.
15	3. Made a partial payment on account of $1,000 to Computer Inc.

Accounting Careers in Focus

ACCOUNTING PROFESSOR
Francis Marion University, Florence, South Carolina
Tim Lowder

Q: Do you have other professional commitments besides teaching at the university?

A: Yes, I also work with Winthrop University Small Business Development Center and Florence-Darlington Technical College. I am also a management consultant.

Q: What factors have been key to your success?

A: I've realized that you can't put all your faith in the short term. To succeed, you must have a long-term vision and identify what steps you must take to achieve your goals.

Q: What do you like most about your job?

A: I like knowing that I've left a positive impact on students. As a consultant, I enjoy helping my clients improve their companies. Teaching and consulting are the most rewarding pursuits I've ever undertaken.

Q: What advice do you have for accounting students just beginning their careers?

A: Get as broad a background as possible. Accounting is integrated with all the other aspects of business, so you need to gain experience in things such as information systems, marketing, and financial management.

Q: What advice do you have for accounting students who are interested in pursuing your career path?

A: No matter what career you choose, you must do something because you love it. Start thinking early about the education and certifications you'll need.

Tips from . . .
RHI Robert Half International Inc.

If you'd like to learn more about a potential career path, arrange an informational interview with someone already working in that field. You can gain real-world insight and, if you make a good impression, you may even be considered for an entry-level position when one becomes available.

CAREER FACTS

▶ **Nature of the Work:** Create lesson plans and exams, teach classes, advise and motivate students.

▶ **Training or Education Needed:** A master's or doctoral degree in accounting or a related field. Relevant work experience and certifications can sometimes be substituted for an advanced degree. A CPA license is an example of a certification.

▶ **Aptitudes, Abilities, and Skills:** Time management skills, communication skills, and interpersonal skills.

▶ **Salary Range:** $35,000 to $90,000 depending on experience, size of educational institution, and location.

▶ **Career Path:** Pursue an advanced degree in accounting or a related field, or gain relevant work experience. Then become a graduate teaching assistant or part-time professor.

Thinking Critically **What do you think are the greatest challenges of teaching accounting?**

Key Concepts

1. A chart of accounts is a list of all accounts that a business uses. Each account is assigned a number, and the accounts are listed in numerical order.

2. Double-entry accounting is a system that recognizes the different sides of business transactions as debits and credits:

   - **debit:** an entry on the left side of an account
   - **credit:** an entry on the right side of an account

   This system is more efficient than updating the accounting equation after each transaction, as we did in Chapter 3.

3. An account's usual balance is called its *normal balance.*

   An asset has a normal debit balance:

   - The *increase* side is the *debit* (left) side.
   - The *decrease* side is the *credit* (right) side.

   Asset Rule:

Asset Accounts	
Debit Increase Side + Normal Balance	Credit Decrease Side −

   Both a liability account and the owner's capital account each have a normal credit balance:

   - The *increase* side is the *credit* (right) side.
   - The *decrease* side is the *debit* (left) side.

   Liability and Owner's Capital Rule:

Liability and Owner's Capital Accounts	
Debit Decrease Side −	Credit Increase Side + Normal Balance

4. Use debit and credit rules to record increases and decreases in accounts.

Assets		=	Liabilities		+	Owner's Equity	
Debit + Increase Side Normal Balance	Credit − Decrease Side		Debit − (2) Decrease Side	Credit + (1) Increase Side (3) Normal Balance		Debit − (2) Decrease Side	Credit + (1) Increase Side (3) Normal Balance

5. Use a six-step method to analyze a transaction:

Business Transaction		
BUSINESS TRANSACTION ANALYSIS: Steps to Success		
ANALYSIS	*Identify*	1. Identify the accounts affected.
	Classify	2. Classify the accounts affected.
	+/−	3. Determine the amount of increase or decrease for each account affected.
DEBIT-CREDIT RULE		4. Which account is debited? For what amount?
		5. Which account is credited? For what amount?
T ACCOUNTS		6. What is the complete entry in T-account form?

Account Name	Account Name

6. Account balances are calculated by following the rules of debit and credit:

Accounts Payable

Debit	Credit
−	+
100	200
75	175
175	375
	Bal. 200

Key Terms

chart of accounts	(p. 78)	ledger	(p. 78)
credit	(p. 79)	normal balance	(p. 80)
debit	(p. 79)	T account	(p. 79)
double-entry accounting	(p. 79)		

Check Your Understanding

1. **Chart of Accounts**
    a. What is a chart of accounts?
    b. Why are the accounts numbered?
2. **Double-Entry Accounting**
    a. What is double-entry accounting?
    b. Define the terms *debit* and *credit.*
3. **Normal Balances**
    a. What is meant by the term *normal balance?*
    b. What is the normal balance for asset accounts? For liability accounts? For the owner's capital account?
4. **T Accounts**
    a. What is the purpose of a T account?
    b. Name the three basic parts of a T account.
5. **Transaction Analysis**
    a. What are the six steps used to analyze a business transaction?
    b. Explain briefly what is meant by the following phrase:
        A debit of $100 to **Cash in Bank**
6. **Account Balances**
    a. How do you determine the balance of an account?
    b. The following information is for the **Cash in Bank** account on a single day. What is the balance of **Cash in Bank** at the end of the day?
        Beginning balance: $3,000 debit
        Transactions: $450 credit
                                      $1,275 credit
                                      $1,800 debit

Apply Key Terms

Your boss at Hillside Nurseries needs help understanding the double-entry accounting system. Using the key terms listed below, draft a list of definitions and illustrations that would help in your explanation.

chart of accounts	ledger
credit	normal balance
debit	T account
double-entry accounting	

Introduction to Computerized Accounting Systems
Making the Transition from a Manual to a Computerized System

Manual Methods	Computerized Methods
• Transactions are recorded into journals by hand. • The details of each transaction are then posted in the general ledger. • The accountant computes account balances and prepares a trial balance to verify that the accounting equation is still in balance. • Account names and balances are then transferred to the proper financial report and the report is summarized (totaled).	• Transactions are keyed to the appropriate screen in the accounting system. • Posting to the general ledger accounts occurs automatically. • The accounting system generates the trial balance. • Financial reports pull the appropriate accounts and their current balances from the general ledger computer files. The reports automatically summarize and can be printed when the user chooses.

Peachtree® Q & A

Peachtree Question	Answer
What types of transactions can be entered in Peachtree Complete® Accounting?	• General journal entries • Sales and cash receipts • Purchases and cash payments • Inventory adjustments • Payroll entries
What else will Peachtree do for the accountant?	• Reconciles bank statements • Prepares financial reports automatically • Prints checks and invoices • Closes the accounting period • Creates cash, collections, and payment management charts and graphs

QuickBooks® Q & A

QuickBooks Question	Answer
What types of transactions can be entered in QuickBooks® Pro?	• General journal entries • Sales and cash receipts • Purchases and cash payments • Inventory adjustments • Payroll entries
What else will QuickBooks® do for the accountant?	• Reconciles bank statements • Prepares financial reports automatically • Prints checks and invoices • Closes the accounting period • Creates sales, collections, and payables charts and graphs

For detailed instructions, see your Glencoe Accounting Chapter Study Guides and Working Papers.

Problems

Problem 4–3 Identifying Accounts Affected by Transactions

Ronald Hicks owns Wilderness Rentals and uses the following accounts in his business:

General Ledger
101 Cash in Bank	
105 Accounts Receivable— Helen Katz	201 Accounts Payable— Adventure Equipment Inc.
120 Office Equipment	301 Ronald Hicks, Capital
125 Camping Equipment	

Instructions For each of the following transactions:

1. Indicate the two accounts affected.
2. Indicate whether each account is debited or credited.

Date	Transactions
May 11	1. Sold on account to Helen Katz an unneeded office typewriter.
19	2. Purchased camping equipment on credit from Adventure Equipment Inc. Payment is due within 30 days.
22	3. Ronald Hicks brought a filing cabinet from home and transferred it to the business (**Office Equipment**).
23	4. Purchased tents and sleeping bags for cash.

Analyze Identify the transactions that affect the **Cash in Bank** account.

Problem 4–4 Using T Accounts to Analyze Transactions

Regina Delgado owns a business called Hot Suds Car Wash. She uses the following accounts:

General Ledger

101 Cash in Bank	201 Accounts Payable—
110 Accounts Receivable—	Allen Vacuum Systems
Valley Auto	301 Regina Delgado, Capital
125 Office Equipment	
130 Office Furniture	
135 Car Wash Equipment	

Instructions For each transaction:

1. Determine which accounts are affected.
2. Prepare T accounts for the accounts affected.
3. Enter the debit and credit amounts in the T accounts.

Date	Transactions
May 5	1. Regina Delgado invested an additional $40,000 cash in her business.
12	2. Bought another car wash system on account for $27,000 from Allen Vacuum Systems.
17	3. Regina Delgado transferred some of her personal office furniture, valued at $3,750, to her business.
24	4. Hot Suds Car Wash purchased additional office equipment for $7,500. Payment was made by check.
29	5. Hot Suds Car Wash sold some surplus car washing equipment on account to Valley Auto for $1,200.

Analyze Calculate the ending balance for the liability account Accounts Payable–Allen Vacuum Systems.

Problem 4–5 Analyzing Transactions into Debit and Credit Parts

Abe Shultz owns Kits & Pups Grooming and uses the following accounts:

General Ledger
101 Cash in Bank
115 Accounts Receivable—
    Martha Giles
125 Office Equipment
130 Office Furniture
140 Grooming Equipment

205 Accounts Payable—
    Dogs & Cats Inc.
301 Abe Shultz, Capital

Instructions For each transaction:

1. In your working papers, prepare a T account for each account listed.
2. Using the appropriate T accounts, analyze and record each of the following business transactions. Identify each transaction by number.
3. After recording all transactions, write the word *Balance* on the normal balance side of each T account. Then compute and record the balance for each account.

Date	Transactions
May 1	1. Abe Shultz invested an additional $45,000 cash in his business.
5	2. Bought grooming equipment on account from Dogs & Cats Inc. for $8,500.
10	3. Purchased an office lamp for $85, Check 150.
14	4. Abe Shultz transferred his personal typewriter, worth $200, to the business.
19	5. Made a $3,000 payment on the grooming equipment bought on account, Check 151.
22	6. Sold the typewriter on account to Martha Giles for $200.
29	7. Bought a photocopier for $1,500, Check 152.
31	8. Received a $100 payment for the typewriter sold on account.

Analyze Calculate the total cash spent in the month of May.

Problem 4–6 Analyzing Transactions into Debit and Credit Parts

Juanita Ortega runs Outback Guide Service. The accounts she uses to record and report business transactions are listed below.

SPREADSHEET SMART GUIDE

Step–by–Step Instructions: Problem 4–6

1. Select the spreadsheet template for Problem 4–6.
2. Enter your name and the date in the spaces provided on the template.
3. Complete the spreadsheet using the instructions in your working papers.
4. Print the spreadsheet and proof your work.
5. Complete the Analyze activity.
6. Save your work and exit the spreadsheet program.

General Ledger

101 Cash in Bank
105 Accounts Receivable—
    Mary Johnson
130 Office Equipment
140 Computer Equipment
145 Hiking Equipment
150 Rafting Equipment

205 Accounts Payable—
    Peak Equipment Inc.
207 Accounts Payable—
    Premier Processors
301 Juanita Ortega, Capital

Instructions For each transaction:

1. In your working papers, prepare a T account for each account.
2. Analyze and record each of the following business transactions in the appropriate T accounts. Identify each transaction by number.
3. After recording all transactions, compute and record the account balance on the normal balance side of each T account.
4. Add the balances of those accounts with normal debit balances.
5. Add the balances of those accounts with normal credit balances.
6. Compare the two totals. Are they the same?

Date	Transactions
May 2	1. Juanita Ortega transferred an additional $53,250 from her personal savings account into the business checking account.
6	2. Bought hiking equipment for $550, Check 367.
7	3. Bought rafting equipment on account from Peak Equipment Inc. for $2,675.
11	4. Juanita Ortega transferred her own computer, valued at $850, to the business.
16	5. Bought a cash register for the office on account from Premier Processors for $1,250.
19	6. Sold the computer on credit for $850 to Mary Johnson.
22	7. Paid $500 on account to Peak Equipment Inc., Check 368.
24	8. Purchased shelves for the office for $650, Check 369.
28	9. Paid $1,250 on account to Premier Processors, Check 370.
31	10. Bought rafting oars for $175, Check 371.

Analyze | Calculate the ending balance in the **Computer Equipment** account.

Problems

CHALLENGE PROBLEM

Problem 4–7 Analyzing Transactions Recorded in T Accounts

Richard Tang owns and operates a job placement service, Job Connect. The T accounts below summarize several business transactions for May.

Instructions Use a form similar to the one presented below. For each of the 10 transactions:

1. Identify the account debited, and record the account name in the appropriate column.
2. Indicate whether the account debited is being increased or decreased.
3. Identify the account credited, and write the account name in the appropriate column.
4. Indicate whether the account credited is being increased or decreased.
5. Write a short description of the transaction.

	(1)	(2)	(3)	(4)	(5)
Trans No.	Account Debited	Increase (I) or Decrease (D)	Account Credited	Increase (I) or Decrease (D)	Description
1	Cash in Bank	I	Richard Tang, Capital	I	Richard Tang invested $15,000 in the business.

Cash in Bank

Debit +	Credit −
(1) 15,000	(4) 1,225
(9) 225	(6) 900
	(7) 995
	(8) 2,000

Accounts Receivable

Debit +	Credit −
(5) 225	(9) 225

Office Equipment

Debit +	Credit −
(2) 225	(5) 225
(3) 8,000	
(4) 1,225	

Office Furniture

Debit +	Credit −
(6) 900	
(10) 145	

Computer Equipment

Debit +	Credit −
(7) 995	

Accounts Payable

Debit −	Credit +
(8) 2,000	(3) 8,000
	(10) 145

Richard Tang, Capital

Debit −	Credit +
	(1) 15,000
	(2) 225

Analyze Design a diagram that shows the accounting equation for Job Connect after all transactions have been completed.

Practice your test-taking skills! The questions on this page are reprinted with permission from national organizations:
- Future Business Leaders of America
- Business Professionals of America

Use a separate sheet of paper to record your answers.

Future Business Leaders of America

MULTIPLE CHOICE

1. If a business purchases a calculator on account, the accounts affected by this transaction are

    a. Cash in Bank and Accounts Payable.

    b. Office Equipment and Accounts Receivable.

    c. Office Equipment and Cash in Bank.

    d. Office Equipment and Accounts Payable.

2. A skeleton form of an account showing only the debit and credit columns is called a(n)

    a. accounting equation.

    b. T account.

    c. account balance.

    d. work sheet.

    e. none of these answers.

Business Professionals of America

ACCOUNT IDENTIFICATION

For each account name below, indicate its classification (**A = Asset, L = Liability, OE = Owner's Equity, R = Revenue, E = Expense**) by writing the correct capital letter(s) on the blank.

Then indicate its normal balance side (**DR = Debit, CR = Credit, N = Neither**).

Account Name	Classification	Normal Balance
3. Cash	_____	_____
4. Accounts Payable	_____	_____
5. Owner's Capital Account	_____	_____

Need More Help?

Go to glencoeaccounting.glencoe.com and click on **Student Center.** Click on **Winning Competitive Events** and select **Chapter 4.**
- **Practice Questions and Test-Taking Tips**
- **Concept Capsules and Terminology**

Double-Entry Accounting

1. Which side of an account is the debit side? Which is the credit side?
2. How is the term *credit* in Chapter 3 different from *credit* in Chapter 4?
3. For each of the following transactions, state whether **Cash in Bank** is debited, credited, or not changed: (a) the business paid cash for a desk; (b) the business bought a computer on account; (c) a customer paid an outstanding invoice.
4. What is the relationship of a T account to a ledger account?
5. Think of a business you would like to open. Create a chart of accounts for the business. Include at least 10 different accounts.
6. Evaluate the usefulness of double-entry accounting.

Service Business: Landscaping

While in school Martin Hamilton gained experience working for a large landscaping company. Martin plans to start a business called Landscapes and Beyond. He has made a list of everything he owns, with the estimated value for each category.

Lawn mowers	$1,500
Shovels and lawn-care tools	180
Truck	8,700
Stereo equipment	1,000
50 books on landscaping	400
Desk, chair, and file cabinet	700

Martin also borrowed $5,000 from his family and will repay the debt in one year.

INSTRUCTIONS Write the accounting equation for Martin's new business, listing each item in the appropriate part of the equation.

Software Piracy

Imagine that you are a bookkeeper for an attorney who likes to use state-of-the-art technology. The business just received the latest update on its Web site design software. You would like to use the software at home, so your assistant offers to make you a copy. Although you know that copyright laws protect software from unauthorized use, you figure that one little copy can't hurt a multimillion dollar software company; and besides, you are not doing the actual copying.

ETHICAL DECISION MAKING

1. What are the ethical issues?
2. What are the alternatives?
3. Who are the affected parties?
4. How do the alternatives affect the parties?
5. What would you do?

Demonstrating the Double-Entry System

Your supervisor asks you to teach some basic accounting to the other managers. Create a visual presentation to explain the double-entry accounting system. Use the purchase of a computer to show how transactions affect different accounts.

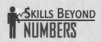

Teaching Others

Keeping up with technology and learning new skills are important in today's workplace. Learning from co-workers and supervisors is often the best way to increase your skills.

ON THE JOB

Assume that you work as the accountant for Westside Aquatics, a swim club in Florida. The club has 250 members. While some individuals pay cash on each visit, others are billed monthly for club use. A concession area featuring health foods and juices is a popular gathering place for members after swim lessons.

INSTRUCTIONS

List account names that would be used in a business like this. Describe to a classmate what kinds of transactions might affect each account. What is the normal balance side for each account?

Exchange Rates

Businesses use exchange rates to convert from one currency to another. Exchange rates change all the time and are found in newspapers, at banks, and on the Internet. Suppose that you want to convert U.S. dollars to Canadian dollars, and $1.00 (U.S.) is currently worth $1.25182 (Canadian). You would multiply the U.S. dollars by the exchange rate as follows:

U.S. dollars	×	exchange rate	=	Canadian dollars
$5.00	×	1.25182	=	$6.26

INSTRUCTIONS Using this exchange rate, analyze which company has the higher value of total assets:

Company A $150,000 (U.S.)
Company B $176,000 (Canadian)

Your Spending Plan

Cash is an asset. If you spend it, the asset decreases. A good way to safeguard your cash is to create a spending and savings plan, and then follow it.

PERSONAL FINANCE ACTIVITY Suppose you want to save $20.00 per month. You have kept track of your personal finances for several months and you see the following pattern:

Money coming in each month: allowance, $20.00; part-time job, $112.00

Money going out each month: lunches, $25.00; snacks, $8.50; bus fare, $8.00; CDs, $28.00; contributions to charity, $10.00; movie theatres, $22.00; pizza, $18.00; school supplies, $14.50

Using the above information, create a spending plan that allows you to save $20.00 per month.

PERSONAL FINANCE ONLINE Log on to **glencoeaccounting.glencoe.com** and click on **Student Center**. Click on **Making It Personal** and select **Chapter 4**.

Transactions That Affect Revenue, Expenses, and Withdrawals

What You'll Learn

1. Explain the difference between permanent accounts and temporary accounts.

2. List and apply the rules of debit and credit for revenue, expense, and withdrawals accounts.

3. Use the six-step method to analyze transactions affecting revenue, expense, and withdrawals accounts.

4. Test a series of transactions for equality of debits and credits.

5. Define the accounting terms introduced in this chapter.

Why It's Important

Temporary accounts show the changes in owner's equity during each accounting period.

SOUTHWEST®

BEFORE YOU READ

Predict

1. What does the chapter title tell you?
2. What do you already know about this subject from personal experience?
3. What have you learned about this in the earlier chapters?
4. What gaps exist in your knowledge of this subject?

Exploring the *Real World* of Business

ANALYZING REVENUE AND EXPENSES

Southwest Airlines

While other large airlines lost money after the 9/11 disaster, **Southwest Airlines** was flying high. The airline has posted more than 30 years of consecutive profits and become a model for newer airlines to follow.

Southwest carries more than 65 million passengers every year. Each one-way fare averaged over $88 per passenger.

Like any business, **Southwest** must consider expenses. Operating expenses include the cost of more than 1 billion gallons of jet fuel and payroll expenses for more than 32,000 employees. Don't forget the cost of snacks. **Southwest** serves 85 million bags of peanuts each year.

What Do You Think?

Aside from passenger fares, from what other sources do you think **Southwest Airlines** generates revenues?

Working in the *Real World*

APPLYING YOUR ACCOUNTING KNOWLEDGE

When you receive a paycheck, you probably think about the amount of money you have and the things you would like to buy. Businesses like Southwest Airlines also earn money and spend it on items used to operate the business. In this chapter you will learn to analyze transactions involving the revenue and expenses of a business.

Personal Connection

1. How does your workplace (or the workplace of family or friends) earn revenue?
2. What does the business buy with that revenue?
3. How do these revenue and expense transactions affect the profits of a business?

Online Connection

Go to **glencoeaccounting.glencoe.com** and click on **Student Center.** Click on **Working in the Real World** and select **Chapter 5.**

Relationship of Revenue, Expenses, and Withdrawals to Owner's Equity

BEFORE YOU READ

Main Idea
Revenues, expenses, and withdrawals are temporary accounts. They start each new accounting period with zero balances.

Read to Learn...
➤ how temporary account transactions change owner's equity. (p. 104)
➤ the rules of debit and credit for temporary accounts. (p. 106)

Key Terms
temporary accounts
permanent accounts

In Chapter 4 you learned to record transactions in asset, liability, and owner's capital accounts. In this chapter you will learn to record transactions in revenue, expense, and owner's withdrawals accounts. These accounts provide information about how the business is doing. A pilot for Southwest Airlines would never take off in a 737 equipped with only a speedometer and a gas gauge. These two instruments, although necessary, do not give a pilot all of the information needed to keep such a complex aircraft on course and operating smoothly. Operating a business is a bit like operating a 737. Owners need revenue and expense information to keep the business on course.

Temporary and Permanent Accounts
What Is the Difference Between Temporary Accounts and Permanent Accounts?

You learned earlier that the owner's capital account shows the amount of the owner's investment, or equity, in a business. Owner's equity is increased or decreased by transactions other than owner's investments. For example, the revenue, or income, earned by the business increases owner's equity. Both expenses and owner's withdrawals decrease owner's equity. (Remember that revenue is not the same as an owner's investment, and expense is not the same as an owner's withdrawal.)

Revenue, expenses, and withdrawals could be recorded as increases or decreases directly in the capital account. This method, however, makes classifying information about these transactions difficult. A more informative way to record transactions affecting revenue and expenses is to set up separate accounts for each type of revenue or expense. Such information helps the owner decide, for example, whether some expenses need to be reduced.

As you learned in Chapter 2, the life of a business is divided into periods of time called accounting periods. The activities for a given accounting period are summarized and then the period is closed. A new period starts, and transactions for the new period are entered into the accounting system. The process continues as long as the business exists.

Using Temporary Accounts. Revenue, expense, and withdrawals accounts are used to collect information for a single accounting period. These accounts are called **temporary accounts**. Temporary

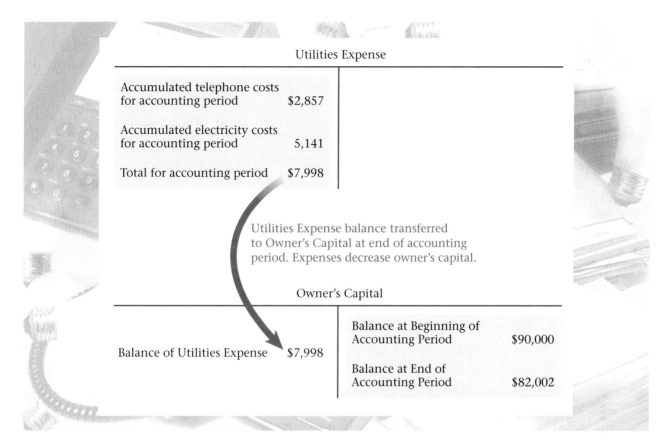

Utilities Expense

Accumulated telephone costs for accounting period	$2,857
Accumulated electricity costs for accounting period	5,141
Total for accounting period	$7,998

Utilities Expense balance transferred to Owner's Capital at end of accounting period. Expenses decrease owner's capital.

Owner's Capital

	Balance at Beginning of Accounting Period	$90,000
Balance of Utilities Expense $7,998	Balance at End of Accounting Period	$82,002

Figure 5–1 The Relationship of Temporary Accounts to the Owner's Capital Account

accounts start each new accounting period with zero balances. That is, the amounts in these accounts are not carried forward from one accounting period to the next. Temporary accounts are not temporary in the sense that they are used for a short time and then discarded. They continue to be used in the accounting system, but the amounts recorded in them accumulate for only one accounting period. At the end of that period, the balances in the temporary accounts are transferred to the owner's capital account. (The procedure for transferring these balances to owner's capital is explained in Chapter 10.)

Let's use **Utilities Expense,** a temporary account, as an example. During an accounting period, business transactions related to utilities such as electricity and telephones are recorded in **Utilities Expense.** By using this separate account, the owner can see at a glance how much money is being spent on this expense. The individual transaction amounts accumulate in the account as the accounting period progresses.

At the end of the period, the total spent is transferred to the owner's capital account and subtracted from the capital account balance. Remember, expenses decrease owner's capital. In **Figure 5–1,** the account, **Utilities Expense,** starts the next accounting period with a zero balance—ready for the transactions in the new period.

Using Permanent Accounts. In contrast to the temporary accounts, the owner's capital account is a permanent account. Asset and liability accounts are also permanent accounts. **Permanent accounts** are continuous from one accounting period to the next. In permanent accounts

As You READ

Instant Recall

Permanent Account Normal Balances

Assets → debit

Liabilities → credit

Owner's → credit
Capital

the dollar balances at the end of one accounting period become the dollar balances for the beginning of the next accounting period.

For example, if a business has furniture totaling $2,875 at the end of one accounting period, the business will start with $2,875 in furniture at the beginning of the next accounting period. The ending balances in permanent accounts are carried forward to the next accounting period as the beginning balances.

End of Accounting Period		Beginning of Next Accounting Period	
Furniture		Furniture	
Debit	Credit	Debit	Credit
End Bal. 2,875		Beg. Bal. 2,875	

The permanent accounts show balances on hand or amounts owed at any time. They also show the day-to-day changes in assets, liabilities, and owner's capital.

The Rules of Debit and Credit for Temporary Accounts

What Are the Normal Balances of Revenue, Expense, and Withdrawals Accounts?

In Chapter 4 you learned the rules of debit and credit for the asset, liability, and owner's capital accounts. In this chapter we will continue with the rules of debit and credit, this time for revenue, expense, and withdrawals accounts. Before looking at these rules, let's review quickly the T account showing the rules of debit and credit for the owner's capital account.

Owner's Capital Account	
Debit	Credit
−	+
Decrease Side	Increase Side Normal Balance

As you will see, the rules of debit and credit for accounts classified as revenue, expense, and withdrawals accounts are related to the rules for the owner's capital account.

Rules for Revenue Accounts

Accounts set up to record business income are classified as revenue accounts. The following rules of debit and credit apply to revenue accounts:

Rule 1: A revenue account is *increased* (+) on the *credit* side.

Rule 2: A revenue account is *decreased* (−) on the *debit* side.

Rule 3: The *normal balance* for a revenue account is the *increase* side, or the *credit* side. Revenue accounts normally have credit balances.

Revenue earned from selling goods or services increases owner's capital. The relationship of revenue accounts to the owner's capital account is shown by the T accounts in **Figure 5–2.** Can you explain why the T account for revenue is used to represent the credit (right) side of the capital account?

As You READ

It's Not What It Seems

Temporary The term *temporary* might make you think of something that lasts for a limited time. A *temporary* account, however, always stays in the ledger. Its balance is reduced to zero at the end of each accounting period.

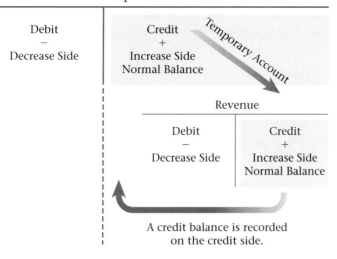

Permanent Account
Owner's Capital

As You READ

Key Point

Temporary Account Normal Balances
Revenue → credit
Expense → debit
Owner's → debit
Withdrawals

Figure 5–2 Rules of Debit and Credit for Revenue Accounts

Increases in owner's capital are shown on the credit side of that account. Revenue increases owner's capital, so the revenue account is used to represent the credit side of the owner's capital account.

We can summarize the rules of debit and credit for revenue accounts with a T account illustration.

Revenue Accounts	
Debit	Credit
–	+
(2) Decrease Side	(1) Increase Side
	(3) Normal Balance

Let's apply the rules of debit and credit to an actual revenue account. Look at the entries in the T account for the revenue account called **Fees.** The increases to the revenue account are recorded on the right, or credit, side of the T account. The decreases are recorded on the left, or debit, side. To find the balance, subtract total debits ($200) from total credits ($500 + $1,000 + $2,000 = $3,500). You get a balance of $3,300 on the credit side, the normal balance side for a revenue account.

Fees	
Debit	Credit
–	+
200	500
	1,000
	2,000
	Bal. 3,300

Rules for Expense Accounts

Accounts that record the costs of operating a business are expense accounts. These debit and credit rules apply to expense accounts:

Rule 1: An expense account is *increased* on the *debit* side.
Rule 2: An expense account is *decreased* on the *credit* side.
Rule 3: The *normal balance* for an expense account is the *increase* side, or the *debit* side. Expense accounts normally have debit balances.

As You READ

In Your Own Words

Temporary and Permanent Explain how the terms *temporary* and *permanent* apply to ledger accounts.

Expenses are the costs of doing business. Expenses decrease owner's capital. Revenues have the opposite impact; revenues increase owner's capital. Look at the T accounts in **Figure 5–3.** Can you explain why the T account for expenses is used to represent the debit (left) side of the capital account?

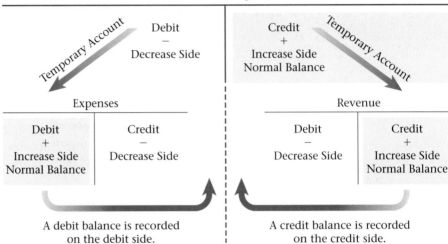

Figure 5–3 Rules of Debit and Credit for Expense Accounts

Decreases in owner's capital are shown on the debit side of that account. Since expenses decrease owner's capital, expense accounts are used to represent the debit side of the owner's capital account.

Let's use a T account to summarize the rules of debit and credit for expense accounts.

Expense Accounts	
Debit	Credit
+	−
(1) Increase Side	(2) Decrease Side
(3) Normal Balance	

Now look at the entries recorded in the T account called **Advertising Expense.** The increases to the expense account are recorded on the left, or debit, side of the T account. The decreases to the account are recorded on the right, or credit, side of the T account. When total credits ($125) are subtracted from total debits ($600), there is a balance of $475 on the debit side, which is the normal balance side for expense accounts.

Advertising Expense	
Debit	Credit
+	−
400	125
200	
Bal. 475	

Rules for the Withdrawals Account

A withdrawal is an amount of money or an asset the owner takes out of the business. The withdrawals account is classified as a temporary owner's equity account. Recall that the permanent owner's equity account is the owner's capital account. Withdrawals, like expenses, decrease capital, so the rules of debit and credit are the same as for expense accounts.

Withdrawals Account

Debit +	Credit −
(1) Increase Side (3) Normal Balance	(2) Decrease Side

W. Smith, Withdrawals

Debit +	Credit −
500	200
1,500	
Bal. 1,800	

Rule 1: The withdrawals account is *increased* on the *debit* side.

Rule 2: The withdrawals account is *decreased* on the *credit* side.

Rule 3: The *normal balance* for the withdrawals account is the *increase* side or *debit* side. The withdrawals account normally has a debit balance.

Review the entries in the T account **W. Smith, Withdrawals.** The increases are recorded on the left, or debit side, of the T account. The decreases are recorded on the right, or credit, side of the T account. When total credits ($200) are subtracted from total debits ($2,000), there is a balance of $1,800 on the debit side, which is the normal balance side for the withdrawals account.

As You READ

Compare and Contrast

Capital and Withdrawals Consider the owner's capital account and the owner's withdrawals account. How are they similar? How are they different?

Summary of the Rules of Debit and Credit for Temporary Accounts

Figure 5–4 summarizes the rules of debit and credit for the temporary accounts and the basic accounting relationships of these accounts to the owner's capital account.

Permanent Account
Owner's Capital

Debit − Decrease Side	Credit + Increase Side Normal Balance

Temporary Account

Expenses

Debit + Increase Side Normal Balance	Credit − Decrease Side

Revenue

Debit − Decrease Side	Credit + Increase Side Normal Balance

Withdrawals

Debit + Increase Side Normal Balance	Credit − Decrease Side

A debit balance is recorded on the debit side.

A credit balance is recorded on the credit side.

Figure 5–4 Rules of Debit and Credit for Temporary Accounts

Reinforce the Main Idea

Create a chart like this one to illustrate the different types of accounts. Fill in each blank box with one or more of the following terms: *assets, liabilities, owner's capital, revenue, expenses, owner's withdrawals.*

	Normal Debit Balance	**Normal Credit Balance**
Permanent Accounts		
Temporary Accounts		

Do the Math

A company had the following activity during the accounting period:

Made sales:	$5,000
Incurred advertising expenses:	500
Incurred salaries expenses:	3,000
Deposited a check from the owner's personal savings account:	1,200

Additionally, the owner removed a computer from the business for personal use. The business had paid $650 for the computer. What was the total effect on owner's equity?

Problem 5–1 Applying the Rules of Debit and Credit

Caroline Palmer uses the following accounts in her San Francisco–Los Angeles commuter shuttle service.

> **General Ledger**
> | | |
> |---|---|
> | Cash in Bank | Caroline Palmer, Capital |
> | Advertising Expense | Accounts Receivable |
> | Caroline Palmer, Withdrawals | Food Expense |
> | Airplanes | Flying Fees |
> | Fuel and Oil Expense | Accounts Payable |
> | Repairs Expense | |

Instructions In the form provided in your working papers, provide the following information for each account. The first account is completed as an example.

1. Classify the account as an asset, liability, owner's equity, revenue, or expense account.
2. Indicate whether the increase side is a debit or a credit.
3. Indicate whether the decrease side is a debit or a credit.
4. Indicate whether the account has a normal debit balance or a normal credit balance.

Account Name	Account Classification	Increase Side	Decrease Side	Normal Balance
Cash in Bank	Asset	Debit	Credit	Debit

Applying the Rules of Debit and Credit to Revenue, Expense, and Withdrawals Transactions

In Section 1 you learned the rules of debit and credit for revenue, expense, and withdrawals accounts. Learning to apply these rules to typical business transactions is our next task. In the course of a week, a business might receive money, pay rent, or pay utility bills. Let's look at more transactions for Roadrunner Delivery Service.

Analyzing Transactions

How Do You Analyze Transactions That Involve Temporary Accounts?

In Chapter 4 Roadrunner's transactions dealt with asset and liability accounts and with the permanent owner's equity account, **Maria Sanchez, Capital.** Using the rules of debit and credit, let's analyze several business transactions that affect revenue, expense, and owner's withdrawals accounts. Use the same six-step method you learned in Chapter 4. Refer to Roadrunner's chart of accounts on page 79 to analyze the following transactions.

BEFORE YOU READ

Main Idea
Double-entry accounting requires that total debits and total credits are always equal.

Read to Learn...
➤ how to analyze revenue, expense, and owner's withdrawals transactions. (p. 111)
➤ how to confirm that total debits and total credits are equal in the ledger. (p. 115)

Key Term
revenue recognition

Business Transaction 8

On October 15 Roadrunner provided delivery services for Sims Corporation. A check for $1,200 was received in full payment.

ANALYSIS	*Identify* *Classify*		
		1.	The accounts **Cash in Bank** and **Delivery Revenue** are affected.
		2.	**Cash in Bank** is an asset account. **Delivery Revenue** is a revenue account.
	+/−	3.	**Cash in Bank** is increased by $1,200. **Delivery Revenue** is increased by $1,200.

DEBIT-CREDIT RULE		
	4.	Increases in asset accounts are recorded as debits. Debit **Cash in Bank** for $1,200.
	5.	Increases in revenue accounts are recorded as credits. Credit **Delivery Revenue** for $1,200.

			T ACCOUNTS	**6.**	Cash in Bank		Delivery Revenue	

T ACCOUNTS   **6.**

Cash in Bank		Delivery Revenue	
Debit + 1,200	Credit −	Debit −	Credit + 1,200

Business Transaction 9

On October 16 Roadrunner mailed Check 103 for $700 to pay the month's rent.

ANALYSIS	*Identify* *Classify* +/−	1. The accounts **Rent Expense** and **Cash in Bank** are affected. 2. **Rent Expense** is an expense account. **Cash in Bank** is an asset account. 3. **Rent Expense** is increased by $700. **Cash in Bank** is decreased by $700.

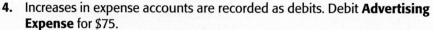

DEBIT-CREDIT RULE	4. Increases in expense accounts are recorded as debits. Debit **Rent Expense** for $700. 5. Decreases in asset accounts are recorded as credits. Credit **Cash in Bank** for $700.

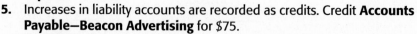

T ACCOUNTS   **6.**

Rent Expense		Cash in Bank	
Debit + 700	Credit −	Debit +	Credit − 700

Business Transaction 10

On October 18 Beacon Advertising prepared an advertisement for Roadrunner. Roadrunner will pay Beacon's $75 fee later.

ANALYSIS	*Identify* *Classify* +/−	1. The accounts **Advertising Expense** and **Accounts Payable—Beacon Advertising** are affected. 2. **Advertising Expense** is an expense account. **Accounts Payable—Beacon Advertising** is a liability account. 3. **Advertising Expense** is increased by $75. **Accounts Payable—Beacon Advertising** is increased by $75.

DEBIT-CREDIT RULE	4. Increases in expense accounts are recorded as debits. Debit **Advertising Expense** for $75. 5. Increases in liability accounts are recorded as credits. Credit **Accounts Payable—Beacon Advertising** for $75.

T ACCOUNTS	6.					
		Advertising Expense			Accounts Payable—Beacon Advertising	
		Debit + 75	Credit −		Debit −	Credit + 75

Business Transaction 11

On October 20 Roadrunner billed City News $1,450 for delivery services.

ANALYSIS	Identify	1.	The accounts **Accounts Receivable—City News** and **Delivery Revenue** are affected.
	Classify	2.	**Accounts Receivable—City News** is an asset account. **Delivery Revenue** is a revenue account.
	+/−	3.	**Accounts Receivable—City News** is increased by $1,450. **Delivery Revenue** is increased by $1,450.

DEBIT-CREDIT RULE	4.	Increases in asset accounts are recorded as debits. Debit **Accounts Receivable—City News** for $1,450.
	5.	Increases in revenue accounts are recorded as credits. Credit **Delivery Revenue** for $1,450.

T ACCOUNTS	6.				
		Accounts Receivable—City News		Delivery Revenue	
		Debit + 1,450	Credit −	Debit −	Credit + 1,450

In Transaction 11 Roadrunner recorded revenue for services provided, even though the money had not been collected. Following the GAAP principle of **revenue recognition**, revenue is recorded on the date earned, even if cash has not been received.

Business Transaction 12

On October 28 Roadrunner paid a $125 telephone bill with Check 104.

ANALYSIS	Identify Classify	1.	The accounts **Utilities Expense** and **Cash in Bank** are affected.
		2.	**Utilities Expense** is an expense account. **Cash in Bank** is an asset account.
	+/−	3.	**Utilities Expense** is increased by $125. **Cash in Bank** is decreased by $125.

DEBIT-CREDIT RULE	4.	Increases in expense accounts are recorded as debits. Debit **Utilities Expense** for $125.
	5.	Decreases in asset accounts are recorded as credits. Credit **Cash in Bank** for $125.

T ACCOUNTS	**6.**	Utilities Expense			Cash in Bank	
		Debit + 125	Credit −		Debit +	Credit − 125

Business Transaction 13

On October 29 Roadrunner wrote Check 105 for $600 to have the office repainted.

ANALYSIS	*Identify* *Classify* +/−	1. The accounts **Maintenance Expense** and **Cash in Bank** are affected. 2. **Maintenance Expense** is an expense account. **Cash in Bank** is an asset account. 3. **Maintenance Expense** is increased by $600. **Cash in Bank** is decreased by $600.

DEBIT-CREDIT RULE	4. Increases in expense accounts are recorded as debits. Debit **Maintenance Expense** for $600. 5. Decreases in asset accounts are recorded as credits. Credit **Cash in Bank** for $600.

T ACCOUNTS	**6.**	Maintenance Expense			Cash in Bank	
		Debit + 600	Credit −		Debit +	Credit − 600

Business Transaction 14

On October 31 Maria Sanchez wrote Check 106 to withdraw $500 cash for personal use.

ANALYSIS	*Identify* *Classify* +/−	1. The accounts **Maria Sanchez, Withdrawals** and **Cash in Bank** are affected. 2. **Maria Sanchez, Withdrawals** is an owner's equity account. **Cash in Bank** is an asset account. 3. **Maria Sanchez, Withdrawals** is increased by $500. **Cash in Bank** is decreased by $500.

DEBIT-CREDIT RULE	4. Increases in the owner's withdrawals account are recorded as debits. Debit **Maria Sanchez, Withdrawals** for $500. 5. Decreases in assets are recorded as credits. Credit **Cash in Bank** for $500.

6.

Maria Sanchez, Withdrawals		Cash in Bank	
Debit + 500	Credit –	Debit +	Credit – 500

Testing for the Equality of Debits and Credits

Why Should You Make Sure the Ledger Is in Balance?

In a double-entry accounting system, correct analysis and recording of business transactions should result in total debits being equal to total credits. Testing for the equality of debits and credits is one way of finding out whether you have made any errors in recording transaction amounts. To test for the equality of debits and credits, follow these steps:

Step 1. Make a list of the account names used by the business.
Step 2. To the right of each account name, list the balance of the account. Use two columns, one for debit balances and the other for credit balances.
Step 3. Add the amounts in each column.

If you have recorded all the amounts correctly, the total of the debit column will equal the total of the credit column. The test for equality of debits and credits for the transactions in Chapters 4 and 5 shows that total debits are equal to total credits, so the ledger is in balance.

ACCOUNT NAME	DEBIT BALANCES	CREDIT BALANCES
101 Cash in Bank	$ 21,125	
105 Accounts Receivable—City News	1,450	
110 Accounts Receivable—Green Company		
115 Computer Equipment	3,000	
120 Office Equipment	200	
125 Delivery Equipment	12,000	
201 Accounts Payable—Beacon Advertising		$ 75
205 Accounts Payable—North Shore Auto		11,650
301 Maria Sanchez, Capital		25,400
302 Maria Sanchez, Withdrawals	500	
303 Income Summary		
401 Delivery Revenue		2,650
501 Advertising Expense	75	
505 Maintenance Expense	600	
510 Rent Expense	700	
515 Utilities Expense	125	
	$ 39,775	$ 39,775

+/- MATH HINTS

Showing Cents When writing amounts of money, be consistent in showing cents. If one amount includes cents, show cents for all the amounts. Be sure to align the amounts on the decimal points.
Incorrect:
   $ 21,125
   1,450.77
Correct:
   $ 21,125.00
   1,450.77

AFTER YOU **READ**

Reinforce the Main Idea

Use a chart like this to organize the test for the equality of debits and credits. Write each of these terms in the appropriate box: *assets, liabilities, owner's capital, owner's withdrawals, revenue, expenses.* (Don't use the shaded boxes.)

Debit Balances	Credit Balances

Do the Math

This bar chart shows the first quarter's revenue and expense. In approximate amounts, what month had the most revenue and what was the amount? What month had the highest expense and what was the amount? Overall, did the business have a profit or loss? What was the amount?

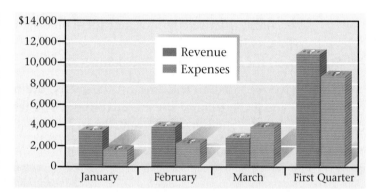

Problem 5–2 Identifying Accounts Affected by Transactions

John Albers uses the following accounts in his business.

General Ledger

Cash in Bank	John Albers, Capital	Advertising Expense
Accounts Receivable	John Albers, Withdrawals	Rent Expense
Office Equipment	Service Fees	Utilities Expense
Accounts Payable		

Instructions In your working papers:

1. Identify the two accounts affected by each of the following transactions.
2. Indicate whether each account is debited or credited.

Date		Transactions
July	1	1. Issued Check 543 to pay the electric bill for the month.
	3	2. Billed a customer for services provided on account.
	10	3. John Albers took cash from the business for his personal use.
	17	4. Issued Check 544 to pay for an advertisement.

EQUITY RESEARCH ASSOCIATE
Eaton Vance Management, Boston, Massachusetts
Rukma Raybardhan

Q: What does Eaton Vance Management do?

A: We manage portfolios, or groups of investments.

Q: What are your day-to-day responsibilities?

A: I conduct preliminary research for analysts who cover certain industries and build and maintain financial models. My job involves reviewing and summarizing financial statements and attending meetings.

Q: What do you find exciting about your job?

A: I love the fact that I get to see the results of my work by following the performance of our investments. I enjoy learning about various industries and companies, and I learn something new every day.

Q: What advice do you have for accounting students just beginning their careers?

A: Work hard and get good grades. Also, concentrate on finding internships. The internships I held worked in my favor when I was looking for my first job in finance. Try to network as much as possible. You never know who can help your career advancement and open doors for you.

Tips from . . .

RHI Robert Half International Inc.

When it comes to your job search, knowing the right person can make all the difference. Many job openings are filled by word of mouth or through referrals. Tell everyone you know about your job hunt, including your family, friends, neighbors, and teachers. You might be surprised by who is able to help you.

CAREER FACTS

▶ **Nature of Work:** Assist analysts with investment research.

▶ **Training or Education Needed:** A bachelor's degree with a concentration in accounting or finance.

▶ **Aptitudes, Abilities, and Skills:** An understanding of the stock market; strong analytical skills; attention to detail.

▶ **Salary Range:** $40,000 and up, depending on experience and employer.

▶ **Career Path:** Start in an entry-level position. As you gain experience and prepare to move into higher-level roles, consider obtaining a master's degree in business administration or becoming a chartered financial analyst (CFA). The CFA title is an important credential for people working in the investment field.

Thinking Critically What are some of the best ways to network with other accounting professionals?

Summary

Key Concepts

1. The accounts used by a business can be separated into permanent accounts and temporary accounts.

   Permanent accounts carry balances forward from one accounting period to the next. The following types of accounts are permanent accounts:

   - assets
   - liabilities
   - owner's capital

   Temporary accounts accumulate dollar amounts for only one accounting period and then start each new accounting period with a zero balance. The following types of accounts are temporary accounts:

   - revenue
   - expenses
   - owner's withdrawals

2. The rules of debit and credit for permanent accounts are summarized as follows:

ASSETS = LIABILITIES + OWNER'S EQUITY

Permanent Accounts

Asset Accounts		Liability Accounts		Owner's Capital Account	
Debit + Increase Side Normal Balance	Credit − Decrease Side	Debit − Decrease Side	Credit + Increase Side Normal Balance	Debit − Decrease Side	Credit + Increase Side Normal Balance

The rules of debit and credit for temporary accounts are summarized as follows:

Temporary Accounts

Revenue		Expenses		Withdrawals	
Debit − Decrease Side	Credit + Increase Side Normal Balance	Debit + Increase Side Normal Balance	Credit − Decrease Side	Debit + Increase Side Normal Balance	Credit − Decrease Side

Revenue Accounts

Rule 1: A revenue account is *increased* (+) on the *credit* side.

Rule 2: A revenue account is *decreased* (−) on the *debit* side.

Rule 3: The *normal balance* for a revenue account is the *increase* side, or the *credit* side. Revenue accounts normally have credit balances.

Expense Accounts

Rule 1: An expense account is *increased* on the *debit* side.

Rule 2: An expense account is *decreased* on the *credit* side.

Rule 3: The *normal balance* for an expense account is the *increase* side, or the *debit* side. Expense accounts normally have debit balances.

The Withdrawals Account

Rule 1: The withdrawals account is *increased* on the *debit* side.

Rule 2: The withdrawals account is *decreased* on the *credit* side.

Rule 3: The *normal balance* for the withdrawals account is the *increase* side or *debit* side. The withdrawals account normally has a debit balance.

3. Follow the six-step method you learned in Chapter 4 to analyze transactions affecting revenue, expense, and withdrawals.

Step 1: Identify the accounts affected.

Step 2: Classify the accounts affected.

Step 3: Determine the amount of increase or decrease for each account affected.

Step 4: Determine which account is debited and for what amount.

Step 5: Determine which account is credited and for what amount.

Step 6: Use T accounts to describe the entry.

4. In a double-entry accounting system, total debits should always equal total credits. Use these steps to test for the equality of debits and credits.

Step 1: List the account names the business uses.

Step 2: To the right of each account name, list its account balance. Use two columns, one for debit balances and the other for credit balances.

Step 3: Add the amounts in each column.

Key Terms

permanent accounts   (p. 105)

revenue recognition   (p. 113)

temporary accounts   (p. 104)

Check Your Understanding

1. **Permanent and Temporary Accounts**
   a. Why are temporary accounts used?
   b. What is the difference between a temporary account and a permanent account?

2. **Debit and Credit Rules**
   a. State briefly the rules of debit and credit for increasing and decreasing each of the following types of accounts:
      • assets
      • liabilities
      • owner's capital
   b. State briefly the rules of debit and credit for increasing and decreasing each of the following types of accounts:
      • revenue
      • expenses
      • owner's withdrawals

3. **Temporary Account Transactions**
   a. Which account classification contains both a permanent account and a temporary account?
   b. If one side of a transaction involves a revenue account, can the other side involve the owner's capital account? Why or why not?

4. **Tests of Equality**
   a. Why should you test for the equality of debits and credits?
   b. How would you test for the equality of debits and credits?

Apply Key Terms

You have been asked to make a presentation to your company's owners. For the owners to understand the difference in the accounts you manage, you must be able to explain the following key terms:

| permanent accounts | temporary accounts |
| revenue recognition | |

Create three examples that could be used as overhead transparencies. Each example (master) should show a term, a brief definition, and an illustration or example.

The Chart of Accounts

Making the Transition from a Manual to a Computerized System

Task	Manual Methods	Computerized Methods
Setting up the accounts in a general ledger	• Accounts are set up in the general ledger using general ledger account forms. • Accounts can be set up with or without beginning balances.	• Accounts are set up using defined account numbers and account types. • Accounts can be set up with or without beginning balances. • Accounting software programs offer hundreds of sample companies from which you can copy the chart of accounts instead of creating each account individually.

Chart of Accounts

Assets	Owner's Equity
Cash in Bank	Maria Sanchez, Capital
Accounts Receivable	Maria Sanchez, Withdrawals
Computer Equipment	
Office Equipment	**Revenue**
Delivery Equipment	Delivery Revenue
Liabilities	**Expenses**
Accounts Payable	Advertising Expense
	Maintenance Expense
	Rent Expense

 **Peachtree®** Q & A

Peachtree Question	Answer
How do I create general ledger accounts in Peachtree?	1. From the *Maintain* menu, select **Chart of Accounts.** 2. Enter the account number in the Account ID box. 3. Enter the account name in the Description box. 4. From the Account Type drop-down list, select the account type. 5. Click **Save.**

 **QuickBooks** Q & A

QuickBooks Question	Answer
How do I create general ledger accounts in QuickBooks?	1. From the *Lists* menu, select **Chart of Accounts.** 2. Click the Account pull-down menu and choose **New.** 3. From the Type drop-down list, select the account type. 4. Enter the account number in the *Number* field and account name in the *Name* field. 5. Click **OK.**

For detailed instructions, see your Glencoe Accounting Chapter Study Guides and Working Papers.

CHAPTER 5 | Problems

Complete problems using: **Manual** Glencoe Working Papers OR **Peachtree Complete Accounting** Software OR **Spreadsheet** Templates

Peachtree®

SMART GUIDE

Step–by–Step Instructions: Problem 5–3

1. Select the problem set for Wilderness Rentals (Prob. 5–3).
2. Rename the company and set the system date.
3. Print a Chart of Accounts using the **General Ledger** option in the **Reports** menu.
4. Review the Chart of Accounts.
5. Complete the Analyze activity manually.
6. End the session.

Problem 5–3 Identifying Increases and Decreases in Accounts

Ronald Hicks uses these accounts in his business, Wilderness Rentals.

General Ledger

101 Cash in Bank	301 Ronald Hicks, Capital
105 Accounts Receivable— Helen Katz	305 Ronald Hicks, Withdrawals
120 Office Equipment	401 Equipment Rental Revenue
125 Camping Equipment	505 Maintenance Expense
	525 Utilities Expense

Instructions Analyze each of the following transactions using the format shown in the example below. Record your answers in your working papers.

  a. Explain the debit.
  b. Explain the credit.
    Example:
    On Jan. 2 Ronald Hicks paid the bill for office cleaning, $100.
  a. The expense account **505 Maintenance Expense** is increased. Increases in expenses are recorded as debits.
  b. The asset account **101 Cash in Bank** is decreased. Decreases in assets are recorded as credits.

Date	Transactions
Jan. 3	1. Ronald Hicks withdrew $500 from his business for his own use, Check 225.
8	2. The business received $1,200 cash in rental fees from various customers.
12	3. The business paid a telephone bill of $85, Check 226.

Analyze | **Calculate the amount of increase or decrease in the Cash in Bank account.**

Peachtree®

SMART GUIDE

Step–by–Step Instructions: Problem 5–4

1. Select the problem set for Hot Suds Car Wash (Prob. 5–4).
2. Rename the company and set the system date.
3. Print a Chart of Accounts using the **General Ledger** option in the **Reports** menu.
4. Review the Chart of Accounts.
5. Complete the Analyze activity manually.
6. End the session.

TIP: You will learn how to enter transactions into the accounts in the next chapter.

Problem 5–4 Using T Accounts to Analyze Transactions

Regina Delgado, owner of Hot Suds Car Wash, uses these accounts:

General Ledger

101 Cash in Bank	401 Wash Revenue
125 Office Equipment	510 Maintenance Expense
205 Accounts Payable— O'Brian's Office Supply	520 Rent Expense
301 Regina Delgado, Capital	
305 Regina Delgado, Withdrawals	

CONTIN

Instructions In your working papers:

1. Determine which accounts are affected for each transaction.
2. Prepare T accounts for the accounts affected.
3. Enter the amount of the debit and the amount of the credit in the T accounts.

Date	Transactions
Jan. 7	1. Received a check for $1,675 for car wash services.
12	2. Paid the monthly rent of $450 by writing Check 212.
15	3. Regina Delgado withdrew $250 for her personal use, Check 213.
29	4. Had the computer repaired at O'Brian's Office Supply for $245 and was given until next month to pay.

Analyze Identify the transactions that affect expense accounts.

Problem 5–5 Analyzing Transactions into Debit and Credit Parts

Abe Shultz, owner of Kits & Pups Grooming, uses the following accounts to record transactions for the month.

General Ledger

101	Cash in Bank	401	Boarding Revenue
105	Accounts Receivable— Juan Alvarez	405	Grooming Revenue
140	Grooming Equipment	501	Advertising Expense
205	Accounts Payable— Dogs & Cats Inc.	505	Equipment Repair Expense
301	Abe Shultz, Capital	510	Maintenance Expense
305	Abe Shultz, Withdrawals	520	Rent Expense
		530	Utilities Expense

Instructions For each transaction:

1. Prepare a T account for each account listed.
2. Enter a balance of $15,000 in the **Cash in Bank** account; also enter a balance of $15,000 in the **Abe Shultz, Capital** account.
3. Analyze and record each of the following business transactions, using the appropriate T accounts. Identify each transaction by number.
4. After all the business transactions have been recorded, write the word *Balance* on the normal balance side of each account.
5. Compute and record the balance for each account.

Peachtree®

SMART GUIDE

Step–by–Step Instructions: Problem 5–5

1. Select the problem set for Kits & Pups Grooming (Prob. 5–5).
2. Rename the company and set the system date.
3. Add new general ledger accounts using the **Chart of Accounts** option in the *Maintain* menu.
4. Enter beginning balances using the **Chart of Accounts** option in the *Maintain* menu.
5. Print a Chart of Accounts using the **General Ledger** option in the *Reports* menu.
6. Proof your work.
7. Complete the Analyze activity manually.
8. End the session.

TIP: When a report list appears, double-click a report title to go directly to that report.

QuickBooks

PROBLEM GUIDE

Step–by–Step Instructions: Problem 5–5

1. Restore the Problem 5-5.QBB file.
2. Add new general ledger accounts using the **Chart of Accounts** option in the *Lists* menu.
3. Enter beginning balances using the **Chart of Accounts** option in the *Lists* menu.
4. Print a Chart of Accounts by selecting **Print List** in the *File* menu.
5. Proof your work.
6. Complete the Analyze activity manually.
7. Back up your work.

CONTINUE

Date	Transactions
Jan. 1	1. Purchased grooming equipment for $12,700, Check 283.
10	2. Wrote Check 284 for advertising, $125.
12	3. Received $1,850 cash for dog boarding services.
15	4. Paid $150 for equipment repair, Check 285.
17	5. Purchased a dog cage on account from Dogs & Cats Inc. for $75.
20	6. Abe Shultz withdrew $150 for personal use, Check 286.
22	7. Billed Juan Alvarez for $775 covering grooming services for all of the dogs boarded at the kennels he owns. Payment will be received later.
23	8. Paid the first two weeks' rent by writing Check 287 for $325.
25	9. Paid the electric bill at a cost of $115, Check 288.

Analyze   **Identify the transactions that affect owner's equity.**

Peachtree®

SMART GUIDE

**Step–by–Step Instructions:
Problem 5–6**

1. Select the problem set for Outback Guide Service (Prob. 5–6).
2. Rename the company and set the system date.
3. Add new general ledger accounts using the **Chart of Accounts** option in the **Maintain** menu.
4. Print a Chart of Accounts using the **General Ledger** option in the **Reports** menu.
5. Proof your work.
6. Complete the Analyze activity manually.
7. End the session.

TIP: You can use General Ledger Navigation Aid to access the Maintain Chart of Accounts window.

Problem 5–6   Analyzing Transactions into Debit and Credit Parts

Juanita Ortega operates Outback Guide Service. She uses the following accounts to record and summarize her business transactions.

General Ledger

101 Cash in Bank	301 Juanita Ortega, Capital
105 Accounts Receivable— Mary Johnson	302 Juanita Ortega, Withdrawals
	401 Guide Service Revenue
150 Rafting Equipment	505 Maintenance Expense
205 Accounts Payable— Peak Equipment Inc.	515 Rent Expense
	520 Utilities Expense

Instructions   For each transaction:

1. Prepare a T account for each account the business uses.
2. Analyze and record each of the following transactions using the appropriate T accounts. Identify each transaction by number.
3. After recording all transactions, compute and record the account balance on the normal balance side of each T account.
4. Test for the equality of debits and credits.

Date	Transactions
Jan. 2	1. Juanita Ortega invested $12,000 cash in her business.
7	2. Purchased two new whitewater rafts on account for $3,750 from Peak Equipment Inc.
10	3. Billed, but did not collect, $750 for guide services provided to Mary Johnson.

CONTINUE ▶

Date	Transactions (cont.)
12	**4.** Repaired a raft at a cost of $123, Check 411.
14	**5.** Wrote Check 412 to pay the electric bill of $95.
17	**6.** Received $225 for guide service fees.
21	**7.** Paid the $225 rent for the month, Check 413.
24	**8.** Paid $1,750 toward the rafts bought on account, Check 414.
27	**9.** Juanita Ortega withdrew $250 cash for personal use, Check 415.
29	**10.** Received guide service fees of $250.

Analyze   **Calculate the amount of revenue earned.**

Problem 5–7 Analyzing Transactions

Greg Failla owns Showbiz Video. He uses the following accounts to record business transactions.

General Ledger

101 Cash in Bank	205 Accounts Payable— Computer Horizons
105 Accounts Receivable— Gabriel Cohen	207 Accounts Payable— New Media Suppliers
110 Accounts Receivable— James Coletti	301 Greg Failla, Capital
140 Computer Equipment	305 Greg Failla, Withdrawals
145 Video Tapes	401 Video Rental Revenue
	405 VCR Rental Revenue
	505 Equipment Repair Expense
	520 Rent Expense
	530 Utilities Expense

Instructions For each transaction:

1. Prepare a T account for each account listed above.
2. Analyze and record each of the following transactions using the appropriate T accounts. Identify each transaction by number.
3. After recording all transactions, compute a balance for each account.
4. Test for the equality of debits and credits.

Date	Transactions
Jan. 1	**1.** Greg Failla invested $17,500 cash in Showbiz Video.
3	**2.** Purchased computer equipment on account from Computer Horizons for $2,400.
8	**3.** Purchased videos on account from New Media Suppliers for $375.
10	**4.** Paid monthly rent of $750, Check 1183.

CONTINUE →

Peachtree®

SMART GUIDE

Step–by–Step Instructions: Problem 5–7

1. Select the problem set for Showbiz Video (Prob. 5–7).
2. Rename the company and set the system date.
3. Add a new record for each of the general ledger accounts.
4. Print a Chart of Accounts.
5. Proof your work.
6. Complete the Analyze activity manually.
7. End the session.

TIP: Peachtree requires that you group accounts by type: asset, liability, equity, income, and expense.

Date	Transactions (cont.)
13	**5.** Wrote Check 1184 to pay for new videos, $265.
14	**6.** Sent a bill for $67 to Gabriel Cohen for a VCR rental.
16	**7.** Deposited the receipts from video rentals, $233.
19	**8.** Paid the gas and electric bill of $125, Check 1185.
21	**9.** Sent Check 1186 for $375 to New Media Suppliers as payment on account.
22	**10.** Greg Failla withdrew $150 for his personal use, Check 1187.
25	**11.** Paid $45 for VCR repair, Check 1188.
30	**12.** Deposited VCR rental receipts of $264 in the bank.

Analyze Identify the permanent accounts that have normal credit balances.

SPREADSHEET SMART GUIDE

Step–by–Step Instructions: Problem 5–8

1. Select the spreadsheet template for Problem 5–8.
2. Enter your name and the date in the spaces provided on the template.
3. Complete the spreadsheet using the instructions in your working papers.
4. Print the spreadsheet and proof your work.
5. Complete the Analyze activity manually.
6. Save your work and exit the spreadsheet program.

Problem 5–8 Completing the Accounting Equation

With the addition of temporary accounts, the basic accounting equation can be expressed as follows:

Owner's Equity

Assets = Liabilities + Owner's Capital − Withdrawals + Revenue − Expenses

Instructions Using the expanded equation shown above, determine the missing amounts for the following accounting equations. Use the form in your working papers. The first equation is completed as an example.

	Assets	= Liabilities +	Owner's Capital	− Withdrawals +	Revenue −	Expenses
1.	$64,400	$8,200	$56,300	$ 500	$10,000	$ 9,600
2.	$22,150	525	18,800	1,200	12,100	?
3.	17,500	75	21,650	?	4,115	3,250
4.	49,450	?	47,840	1,500	20,300	17,610
5.	21,900	1,150	20,005	950	?	16,570
6.	72,640	2,790	?	10,750	67,908	39,749
7.	?	1,988	41,194	6,196	52,210	42,597
8.	?	3,840	61,774	?	40,163	21,637

(Expenses plus withdrawals equal $27,749.)

9.	64,070	?	49,102	4,875	53,166	?

(Total owner's equity after adding revenue and subtracting expenses and withdrawals is $50,643.)

Analyze For equation 7, calculate the sum of owner's equity.

Practice your test-taking skills! The questions on this page are reprinted with permission from national organizations:
- Future Business Leaders of America
- Business Professionals of America

Use a separate sheet of paper to record your answers.

Future Business Leaders of America

MULTIPLE CHOICE

1. Which of the following statements is incorrect?
- a. The normal balance of the receivable account is a debit.
- b. The normal balance of the owner's personal account is a debit.
- c. The normal balance of an unearned revenues account is a credit.
- d. The normal balance of an expense account is a credit.
- e. All of the above statements are correct.

2. If Tim Jones, the owner of Jones Hardware proprietorship, uses cash of the business to purchase a family automobile, the business should record this use of cash with an entry to
- a. debit Salary Expense and credit Cash.
- b. debit Tim Jones, Salary and credit Cash.
- c. debit Cash and credit Tim Jones, Withdrawals.
- d. debit Tim Jones, Capital and credit Cash.
- e. none of the above.

Business Professionals of America

MULTIPLE CHOICE

3. Accounts that are continuous from one accounting period to the next and balances are carried forward are referred to as
- a. permanent accounts.
- b. fiscally continuous.
- c. post-closing assets.
- d. signature accounts.

4. Each of the following is a business expense except a payment for
- a. equipment
- b. advertising
- c. rent
- d. utility bills

5. If the owner of a company takes merchandise for personal use, what account is debited?
- a. Owner's capital
- b. Owner's withdrawals
- c. Purchases
- d. Cash

> **Need More Help?**
>
> ———————————
>
> Go to **glencoeaccounting.glencoe.com** and click on **Student Center**. Click on **Winning Competitive Events** and select **Chapter 5**.
> - **Practice Questions and Test-Taking Tips**
> - **Concept Capsules and Terminology**

Temporary and Permanent Accounts

1. What is the normal balance of the owner's withdrawals account?
2. What is the difference between *owner's equity* and the *owner's capital account?*
3. Your business receives a refund check from the utility company because it overcharged your business in the past. Which account is debited? Which account is credited?
4. Which temporary accounts affect profit or loss for an accounting period?
5. Write an equation for owner's equity at the end of an accounting period. Start the equation with "Beginning Owner's Capital" and end the equation with "Ending Owner's Equity."
6. Evaluate the practice of using temporary accounts for recording certain transactions, as opposed to using the owner's capital account.

Service Business: Web Site Design

Colleen Chapelli owns Web Design Source, a service that creates Web sites for local businesses. While Colleen is an expert with computers and software programming, her business finance expertise is limited. She has hired you as her accountant to organize her business information and suggest business accounts. Here are some of the items Colleen uses in the business:

- Computer
- Desk and chair
- Printer
- Bookcases
- Software
- Computer supplies

Colleen has been advertising in the local newspaper to find new clients. She manages the business from her home and has a separate telephone line for the business.

INSTRUCTIONS

1. Prepare a chart of accounts for Web Design Source.
2. Explain to Colleen why it is important to collect and organize the financial information resulting from business transactions.

Using a Toll-Free Number

Many businesses offer a toll-free telephone line for customers and business associates. Suppose you're an accountant for Procter & Gamble in Cincinnati, Ohio. Your friend Mike just moved to Houston and asks if your company has an 800 number he can use to call you. Your company does offer an 800 number, and you would like to hear from Mike. However, you also know that your company pays for each incoming call.

ETHICAL DECISION MAKING

1. What are the ethical issues?
2. What are the alternatives?
3. Who are the affected parties?
4. How do the alternatives affect the parties?
5. What would you do?

Promoting an Idea

As Southside Ballet Company's financial director, you think Southside should open a ballet supply and dancewear shop. Use word processing software to write a memo to the ballet director and owner, Jonathan Booth, asking him to consider it. Explain how you view the impact of additional revenue on his capital account. Use the rules for revenue accounts in your explanation.

Acquiring and Analyzing Data

To make a decision, whether business or personal, you must be able to acquire and analyze data (information).

ON THE JOB

You are a senior at Highland College, a small liberal arts college. Eighty percent of the students live in campus dorms or in apartments within one mile of the college. The student activities center closes at 9:00 p.m. during the school week, and students complain about the lack of food and beverage service for late night study sessions. You decide to analyze the market potential of a limited food and beverage delivery service.

INSTRUCTIONS

1. Develop a market survey of 5–10 questions related to the opening of an off-campus food and beverage delivery service.

2. Decide what type of food and beverage you can provide in a delivery service. How much investment would you need to begin? What do you anticipate your customer base to be?

Global E-Business

When you think about revenue and expenses for a company, consider how the Internet makes it faster and cheaper to do business. Business is conducted using Web sites, e-mail, and videoconferencing. Companies like Gap and K-Mart use Web sites to sell products at lower costs than store locations. Managers can communicate online with vendors or branch locations to avoid the high costs of travel.

INSTRUCTIONS If you owned a small business and wished to expand your market to a global audience, discuss how you might use the Internet.

Your Credit Card

Do you have a credit card? If you do not use a credit card yet, it is likely you will use one in the future. In either case, you need to know how to use your credit card wisely.

PERSONAL FINANCE ACTIVITY Suppose your friend used a credit card unwisely and lost the use of the card. You want to help your friend avoid future mistakes. Conduct research at the library, on the Internet, or at your local bank. Write some suggestions that will be helpful to your friend.

PERSONAL FINANCE ONLINE Log on to **glencoeaccounting.glencoe.com** and click on **Student Center**. Click on **Making It Personal** and select **Chapter 5**.

Recording Transactions in a General Journal

What You'll Learn

1. Explain the first three steps in the accounting cycle.

2. Give and describe several examples of source documents.

3. Explain the purpose of journalizing.

4. Apply information from source documents.

5. Describe the steps to make a general journal entry.

6. Make general journal entries.

7. Correct errors in general journal entries.

8. Define the accounting terms introduced in this chapter.

Why It's Important

▶ Every transaction you have with a business is documented in some way. Companies keep permanent records of transactions.

Predict

1. What does the chapter title tell you?
2. What do you already know about this subject from personal experience?
3. What have you learned about this in the earlier chapters?
4. What gaps exist in your knowledge of this subject?

Exploring the *Real World* of Business

RECORDING FINANCIAL INFORMATION

Google Inc.

Think about how often you look for information on the Internet, whether it is for school or just something you find interesting. There is a good chance your first stop is **Google**.

Larry Page and Sergey Brin were students at Stanford University when they met in 1995. During the next few years, they worked together on Web search technology. They developed a way to do searches using personal computers instead of big, expensive machines.

The company **Google Inc.** was started in a garage in 1998. The site performed about 10,000 searches a day. Within two and one-half years, that number grew to 100 million. Today **Google** is the top Internet search engine. The company takes in billions of dollars in advertising each year, keeping its team of accountants busy.

What Do You Think?

If you were just starting an Internet company, what types of financial information would you record?

Working in the *Real World*

APPLYING YOUR ACCOUNTING KNOWLEDGE

Have you ever kept a daily journal of the things that happen during your day? The general journal of a business is similar. The daily financial happenings are recorded there. A company like Google sells advertising, invests in computer equipment, and pays software engineers. You will learn how to record business transactions in a journal in this chapter.

Personal Connection

1. In your workplace, why is it important to keep accurate records of daily transactions?

2. List five business transactions that happen in your workplace.

Online Connection

Go to **glencoeaccounting.glencoe.com** and click on **Student Center.** Click on **Working in the Real World** and select **Chapter 6.**

The Accounting Cycle

Main Idea
The accounting cycle is a series of steps done in each accounting period to keep records in an orderly fashion.

Read to Learn...
➤ the steps in the accounting cycle. (p. 132)
➤ the different types of accounting periods. (p. 134)

Key Terms
accounting cycle
source document
invoice
receipt
memorandum
check stub
journal
journalizing
fiscal year
calendar year

In earlier chapters you learned to use the accounting equation and T accounts to analyze business transactions. In this chapter you will learn how to record business transactions in a journal.

The Steps of the Accounting Cycle
What Is the Accounting Cycle?

The accounting period of a business is separated into activities called the **accounting cycle**. These activities help the business keep its accounting records in an orderly fashion. Take a look at **Figure 6–1**, which describes accounting activities and their sequence.

In this chapter you will use Steps 1, 2, and 3 of the accounting cycle:

1. Collect and verify source documents.
2. Analyze each transaction.
3. Journalize each transaction.

After studying Chapters 3 through 10, you will have covered the entire accounting cycle for a service business organized as a sole proprietorship.

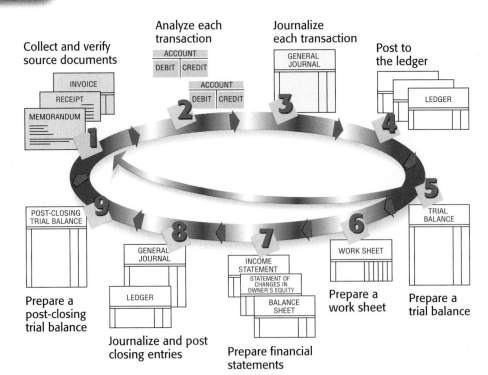

Figure 6–1 Steps in the Accounting Cycle with Steps 1, 2, 3 Highlighted

The First Step in the Accounting Cycle: Collecting and Verifying Source Documents

Most business transactions take place during the daily operations of a business. In the course of one day, a business may pay its rent, place an ad in a local newspaper, contract to have a Web site created, pay its employees, sell products, and purchase new equipment. When a business transaction occurs, a paper is prepared as evidence of that transaction. This paper is a **source document**.

There are several types of source documents that can be prepared by hand, by computer, or by a machine. The type of source document prepared depends on the nature of the transaction. **Figure 6–2** describes and illustrates commonly used source documents.

Invoice

Lists specific information about a business transaction involving the buying or selling of an item on account. The invoice contains the date of the transaction; the quantity, description, and cost of each item; and the payment terms.

KELLY'S OFFICE SUPPLIES		INVOICE NO. 479
354 Circle Drive. #150		
Santa Monica, CA 90405	DATE:	Dec. 1, 20--
	ORDER NO.:	150
TO Roadrunner Delivery Service	SHIPPED BY:	Truck
155 Gateway Blvd.	TERMS:	Payable in 30 days
Sacramento, CA 94230		

QTY.	ITEM	UNIT PRICE	TOTAL
3	Office Chairs	$ 99.00	$ 297.00

Receipt

A record of cash received by a business. It indicates the date the payment was received, the name of the person or business from whom the payment was received, and the amount of the payment.

Roadrunner Delivery Service
155 Gateway Blvd.
Sacramento, CA 94230

RECEIPT
No. 2

Nov. 26 20 --
RECEIVED FROM Greer's Market $ 200.00
Two hundred and no/100 ————————— DOLLARS
FOR Deliveries 11/26/20--
RECEIVED BY *Maria Sanchez*

Memorandum

A brief written message that describes a transaction that takes place within a business. A memorandum is often used if no other source document exists for the business transaction.

Roadrunner Delivery Service
155 Gateway Blvd.
Sacramento, CA 94230

MEMORANDUM 1

TO: Accounting Clerk
FROM: Maria Sanchez
DATE: October 1, 20--
SUBJECT: Contributed personal funds to the business

I have contributed $25,000 from my personal savings to be deposited to the business, Roadrunner Delivery Service.

Check Stub

The check stub lists the same information that appears on a check: the date written, the person or business to whom the check was written, and the amount of the check. The check stub also shows the balance in the checking account before and after each check is written.

$ 250.00		No. 110
Date November 2		20 --
To Info-Systems		
For fax/modem		

	Dollars	Cents
Balance brought forward	25,000	00
Add deposits		
Total	25,000	00
Less this check	250	00
Balance carried forward	24,750	00

Figure 6–2 Source Documents

The business owner, accountant, or accounting clerk (depending on the size of the business) uses source documents generated by business transactions to keep the records of the business. The accounting cycle starts by collecting and verifying the accuracy of source documents. One important activity is to check the arithmetic on each source document.

The Second Step in the Accounting Cycle: Analyzing Business Transactions

After collecting and verifying source documents, the second step in the accounting cycle can begin—analyzing information on the source documents to determine the debit and credit parts of each transaction.

You have already learned how to analyze business transactions using the rules of debit and credit. When you learned to analyze transactions, you were given a description of each transaction, such as: Roadrunner Delivery Service bought a computer system from Info-Systems Inc. for $3,000 and issued Check 101 in payment. On the job you will not get a description of the transaction. Instead, you must examine a source document to determine what occurred during a business transaction.

The Third Step in the Accounting Cycle: Recording Business Transactions in a Journal

You are now ready to apply information from source documents. The third step in the accounting cycle is to record the debit and credit parts of each business transaction in a journal. A **journal** is a record of the transactions of a business. Journals are kept in chronological order, that is, the order in which the transactions occur. The process of recording business transactions in a journal is called **journalizing**. Keeping a journal can be compared to keeping a diary in which all important events are written. A journal is the only place where complete details of a transaction, including both the debit and credit parts, are recorded. The journal is sometimes called the *book of original entry* because it is where transactions are first entered in the accounting system.

The Accounting Period
What Are the Different Types of Accounting Periods?

As discussed in Chapter 2, accounting records are summarized for a certain period of time, called an *accounting period*. An accounting period may be for any designated length of time, such as a month, a quarter, or a year. Most businesses use a year as their accounting period. An accounting period of 12 months is called a **fiscal year**. If the fiscal year for a business begins on January 1 and ends on December 31, it is called a **calendar year** accounting period. Many businesses start their accounting periods in months other than January. For example, department stores often have fiscal years that begin on February 1 and end on January 31 of the following year. School districts usually have fiscal years that begin on July 1 and end on June 30.

Reinforce the Main Idea

Create a table similar to this one to describe how the first three steps of the accounting cycle help organize the records of a business.

Step Number	Step Description	How This Step Helps Organize Business Records

Do the Math

Glen's Catering received an invoice from Conover Restaurant Suppliers for the following supplies:

- 6 cartons of napkins at $4.88 per carton
- 3 boxes of salt packets at $3.19 per box
- 3 boxes of paper plates at $7.28 per box
- 4 boxes of medium paper cups at $8.24 per box

Calculate the total for each item on the invoice. Then calculate the total for all items.

Problem 6–1 Analyzing a Source Document

Instructions Analyze the invoice shown below and answer the following questions.

JAYMAX OFFICE SUPPLY
554 Town Square
Fort Myers, FL 33902

INVOICE NO. 479

TO
Dario's Accounting Services
5821 Gulf Blvd.
Naples, FL 33940

DATE: Apr. 9, 20--
ORDER NO.:
SHIPPED BY: Truck
TERMS: Payable in 30 days

QTY.	ITEM	UNIT PRICE	TOTAL
1	Fax Machine	$ 299.00	$ 299.00

1. What is the name of the company providing the service or merchandise?
2. What is the name of the business receiving the service or merchandise?
3. What is the date of the invoice?
4. What is the invoice number?
5. What item was sold?
6. What is the price for this item?
7. What are the payment terms?

Recording Transactions in the General Journal

In Section 1 you learned about the first three steps in the accounting cycle. Let's apply these steps to business transactions for Roadrunner Delivery Service.

Recording a General Journal Entry

How Do You Record a General Journal Entry?

Many kinds of accounting journals are used in business. One of the most common is the general journal. As its name suggests, the **general journal** is an all-purpose journal in which all of the transactions of a business may be recorded. **Figure 6–3** shows the general journal you will be using throughout the accounting cycle for Roadrunner Delivery Service. The general journal has two amount columns. The first amount column, the amount column on the left, is used to record debit amounts. (Remember that debit means left.) The second amount column, the amount column on the right, is used to record credit amounts. (Remember that credit means right.) Look at **Figure 6–3** to find where each component of a general journal entry appears.

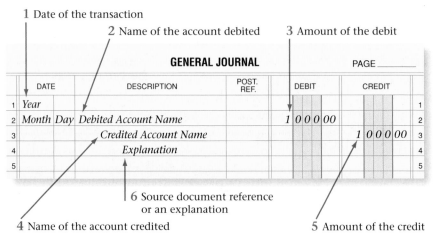

Figure 6–3 General Journal for Roadrunner Delivery Service

In Chapters 4 and 5, you learned a step-by-step method for analyzing business transactions. In this chapter you will learn to complete the journal entry for a business transaction in the same manner. Review the following steps before you continue.

Business Transaction

BUSINESS TRANSACTION ANALYSIS: *Steps to Success*

ANALYSIS	*Identify* *Classify* +/−	1. Identify the accounts affected. 2. Classify the accounts affected. 3. Determine the amount of increase or decrease for each account affected.
DEBIT-CREDIT RULE		4. Which account is debited? For what amount? 5. Which account is credited? For what amount?
T ACCOUNTS		6. What is the complete entry in T-account form?
JOURNAL ENTRY		7. What is the complete entry in general journal form?

Use these steps to determine the debit and credit parts of each journal entry. Remember, it is always helpful to use T accounts to analyze transactions. After analyzing many transactions, you will find that you need these tools less and less to determine the debit and credit parts of a journal entry. After the complete entry is recorded, verify that the total debits and total credits are equal.

Now, let's examine business transactions and their analysis for Roadrunner Delivery Service.

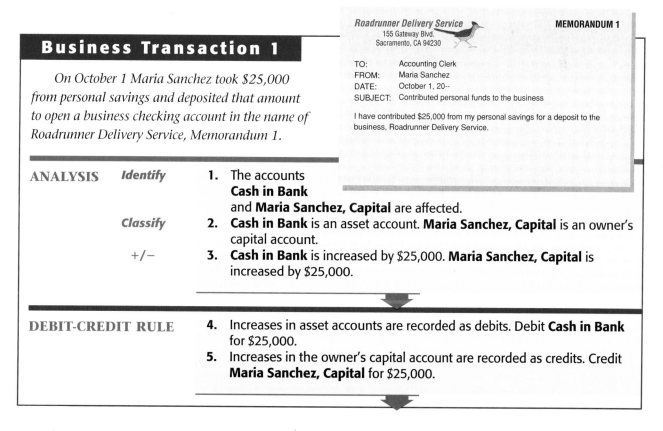

Business Transaction 1

On October 1 Maria Sanchez took $25,000 from personal savings and deposited that amount to open a business checking account in the name of Roadrunner Delivery Service, Memorandum 1.

Roadrunner Delivery Service
155 Gateway Blvd.
Sacramento, CA 94230

MEMORANDUM 1

TO: Accounting Clerk
FROM: Maria Sanchez
DATE: October 1, 20--
SUBJECT: Contributed personal funds to the business

I have contributed $25,000 from my personal savings for a deposit to the business, Roadrunner Delivery Service.

ANALYSIS	*Identify*	1. The accounts **Cash in Bank** and **Maria Sanchez, Capital** are affected.
	Classify	2. **Cash in Bank** is an asset account. **Maria Sanchez, Capital** is an owner's capital account.
	+/−	3. **Cash in Bank** is increased by $25,000. **Maria Sanchez, Capital** is increased by $25,000.
DEBIT-CREDIT RULE		4. Increases in asset accounts are recorded as debits. Debit **Cash in Bank** for $25,000. 5. Increases in the owner's capital account are recorded as credits. Credit **Maria Sanchez, Capital** for $25,000.

T ACCOUNTS

6.

Cash in Bank		Maria Sanchez, Capital	
Debit + 25,000	Credit −	Debit −	Credit + 25,000

JOURNAL ENTRY

7.

		GENERAL JOURNAL			PAGE _1_	
	DATE	DESCRIPTION	POST. REF.	DEBIT	CREDIT	
1	20--					1
2	Oct. 1	Cash in Bank		25 000 00		2
3		Maria Sanchez, Capital			25 000 00	3
4		Memorandum 1				4

Look again at the general journal entry shown above. Notice that in the upper right-hand corner there is a line for the page number. Journal pages are numbered in consecutive order; that is, 1, 2, 3, and so on. When you fill one page with journal entries, go on to the next page. Be sure to properly number each new page.

Business Transaction 2

On October 2 Maria Sanchez took two telephones valued at $200 each from her home and transferred them to the business as office equipment, Memorandum 2.

Roadrunner Delivery Service
155 Gateway Blvd.
Sacramento, CA 94230

MEMORANDUM 2

TO: Accounting Clerk
FROM: Maria Sanchez
DATE: October 2, 20--
SUBJECT: Contributed personal phones

I have contributed two telephones from my home to the business. The phones are valued at $200 each. Total contribution = $400.

ANALYSIS *Identify*
1. The accounts **Office Equipment** and **Maria Sanchez, Capital** are affected.

Classify
2. **Office Equipment** is an asset account. **Maria Sanchez, Capital** is an owner's capital account.

+/−
3. **Office Equipment** is increased by $400. **Maria Sanchez, Capital** is increased by $400.

DEBIT-CREDIT RULE
4. Increases in asset accounts are recorded as debits. Debit **Office Equipment** for $400.
5. Increases in owner's capital accounts are recorded as credits. Credit **Maria Sanchez, Capital** for $400.

T ACCOUNTS

6.

Office Equipment		Maria Sanchez, Capital	
Debit + 400	Credit −	Debit −	Credit + 400

7.

		GENERAL JOURNAL				PAGE ___1___	
	DATE	DESCRIPTION	POST. REF.	DEBIT	CREDIT		
5	Oct. 2	Office Equipment		400 00			5
6		Maria Sanchez, Capital			400 00		6
7		Memorandum 2					7
8							8

Business Transaction 3

On October 4 Roadrunner issued Check 101 for $3,000 to buy a computer system.

$	3,000.00		No. 101
Date	October 4		20 --
To	Info-Systems Inc.		
For	computer		

	Dollars	Cents
Balance brought forward	25,000	00
Add deposits		
Total	25,000	00
Less this check	3,000	00
Balance carried forward	22,000	00

ANALYSIS

Identify
1. The accounts **Computer Equipment** and **Cash in Bank** are affected.

Classify
2. **Computer Equipment** and **Cash in Bank** are asset accounts.

+/−
3. **Computer Equipment** is increased by $3,000. **Cash in Bank** is decreased by $3,000.

DEBIT-CREDIT RULE
4. Increases in asset accounts are recorded as debits. Debit **Computer Equipment** for $3,000.
5. Decreases in asset accounts are recorded as credits. Credit **Cash in Bank** for $3,000.

T ACCOUNTS

6.

Computer Equipment			Cash in Bank	
Debit +	Credit −		Debit +	Credit −
3,000				3,000

JOURNAL ENTRY

7.

		GENERAL JOURNAL				PAGE ___1___	
	DATE	DESCRIPTION	POST. REF.	DEBIT	CREDIT		
8	Oct. 4	Computer Equipment		3 000 00			8
9		Cash in Bank			3 000 00		9
10		Check 101					10
11							11

Business Transaction 4

On October 9 Roadrunner bought a used truck on account from North Shore Auto for $12,000, Invoice 200.

North Shore Auto
440 Lake Drive
Sacramento, CA 94230

INVOICE NO. 200

DATE: Oct. 9, 20--
ORDER NO.: 99674
SHIPPED BY: n/a
TERMS: Installment

TO Roadrunner Delivery Service
155 Gateway Blvd.
Sacramento, CA 94230

QTY.	ITEM	UNIT PRICE	TOTAL
1	Dodge Truck Used	$ 12,000.00	$ 12,000.00

ANALYSIS

Identify
1. The accounts **Delivery Equipment** and **Accounts Payable—North Shore Auto** are affected.

Classify
2. **Delivery Equipment** is an asset account. **Accounts Payable—North Shore Auto** is a liability account.

+/−
3. **Delivery Equipment** is increased by $12,000. **Accounts Payable—North Shore Auto** is increased by $12,000.

DEBIT-CREDIT RULE

4. Increases in asset accounts are recorded as debits. Debit **Delivery Equipment** for $12,000.
5. Increases in liability accounts are recorded as credits. Credit **Accounts Payable—North Shore Auto** for $12,000.

T ACCOUNTS

6.

Delivery Equipment		Accounts Payable—North Shore Auto	
Debit +	Credit −	Debit −	Credit +
12,000			12,000

JOURNAL ENTRY

7.

GENERAL JOURNAL   PAGE ___1___

	DATE		DESCRIPTION	POST. REF.	DEBIT	CREDIT	
11	Oct.	9	Delivery Equipment		12 000 00		11
12			Accts. Pay.—North Shore Auto			12 000 00	12
13			Invoice 200				13
14							14

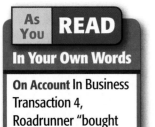

As You READ

In Your Own Words

On Account In Business Transaction 4, Roadrunner "bought a used truck on account…." What does this mean?

To separate the amounts to be paid to individual creditors, Roadrunner uses a different account name for each creditor. The account name consists of **Accounts Payable** followed by the name of the creditor. You may have to abbreviate the name to fit it on one line of the journal. An acceptable abbreviation in the preceding journal entry is **Accts. Pay.—North Shore Auto.**

Roadrunner uses the same naming system for the amounts to be paid by individual customers. The account name consists of **Accounts Receivable** followed by the customer's name.

Business Transaction 5

On October 11 Roadrunner sold one telephone on account to Green Company for $200, Memorandum 3.

Roadrunner Delivery Service
155 Gateway Blvd.
Sacramento, CA 94230

MEMORANDUM 3

TO: Accounting Clerk
FROM: Maria Sanchez
DATE: October 11, 20--
SUBJECT: Sold telephone

Sold one telephone on account to Green Company for $200.

ANALYSIS	*Identify*	**1.** The accounts **Accounts Receivable— Green Company** and **Office Equipment** are affected.
	Classify	**2.** Both accounts are asset accounts.
	+/−	**3.** **Accounts Receivable—Green Company** is increased by $200. **Office Equipment** is decreased by $200.

DEBIT-CREDIT RULE		**4.** Debit **Accounts Receivable—Green Company** for $200.
		5. Credit **Office Equipment** for $200.

T ACCOUNTS   **6.**

Accounts Receivable— Green Company		Office Equipment	
Debit + 200	Credit −	Debit +	Credit − 200

JOURNAL ENTRY   **7.**

GENERAL JOURNAL   PAGE ___1___

	DATE		DESCRIPTION	POST. REF.	DEBIT	CREDIT	
14	Oct.	11	Accts. Rec.—Green Company		200 00		14
15			Office Equipment			200 00	15
16			Memorandum 3				16
17							17

Business Transaction 6

On October 12 Roadrunner mailed Check 102 for $350 as the first installment on the truck purchased from North Shore Auto on October 9.

$	350.00		No. 102
Date	October 12		20 --
To	North Shore Auto		
For	installment on truck		

	Dollars	Cents
Balance brought forward	22,000	00
Add deposits		
Total	22,000	00
Less this check	350	00
Balance carried forward	21,650	00

ANALYSIS	*Identify*	**1.** The accounts **Accounts Payable— North Shore Auto** and **Cash in Bank** are affected.
	Classify	**2.** **Accounts Payable—North Shore Auto** is a liability account. **Cash in Bank** is an asset account.
	+/−	**3.** Both accounts are decreased by $350.

| DEBIT-CREDIT RULE | 4. Debit **Accounts Payable—North Shore Auto** for $350. |
| | 5. Credit **Cash in Bank** for $350. |

T ACCOUNTS

6.

Accounts Payable— North Shore Auto		Cash in Bank	
Debit –	Credit +	Debit +	Credit –
350			350

JOURNAL ENTRY

7.

GENERAL JOURNAL   PAGE ___1___

	DATE		DESCRIPTION	POST. REF.	DEBIT	CREDIT	
17	Oct.	12	Accts. Pay.—North Shore Auto		350 00		17
18			Cash in Bank			350 00	18
19			Check 102				19
20							20

Business Transaction 7

On October 14 Roadrunner received and deposited a check for $200 from Green Company, Receipt 1. The check is full payment for the telephone sold on account to Green on October 11.

Roadrunner Delivery Service
155 Gateway Blvd.
Sacramento, CA 94230

RECEIPT
No. 1

Oct. 14   20 --

RECEIVED FROM _Green Company_ $ _200.00_

Two hundred and $^{no}/_{100}$ ———————— DOLLARS

FOR _Telephone_

RECEIVED BY _Maria Sanchez_

ANALYSIS	*Identify*	1. The accounts **Cash in Bank** and **Accounts Receivable—Green Company** are affected.
	Classify	2. **Cash in Bank** is an asset account. **Accounts Receivable—Green Company** is an asset account.
	+/–	3. **Cash in Bank** is increased by $200. **Accounts Receivable—Green Company** is decreased by $200.

DEBIT-CREDIT RULE

4. Debit **Cash in Bank** for $200.
5. Credit **Accounts Receivable—Green Company** for $200.

T ACCOUNTS

6.

Cash in Bank		Accounts Receivable— Green Company	
Debit +	Credit –	Debit +	Credit –
200			200

JOURNAL ENTRY   **7.**

GENERAL JOURNAL   PAGE _____1_____

	DATE		DESCRIPTION	POST. REF.	DEBIT	CREDIT	
20	Oct.	14	Cash in Bank		200 00		20
21			Accts. Rec.—Green Company			200 00	21
22			Receipt 1				22
23							23

Business Transaction 8

On October 15 Roadrunner provided delivery services for Sims Corporation. A check for $1,200 was received in full payment, Receipt 2.

Roadrunner Delivery Service   **RECEIPT**
155 Gateway Blvd.
Sacramento, CA 94230   No. 2

Oct. 15   20 --
RECEIVED FROM __Sims Corporation__ $ __1,200.00__
One thousand two hundred and no/100 ——————— DOLLARS
FOR __Delivery services__
RECEIVED BY __Maria Sanchez__

ANALYSIS	*Identify*	**1.** The accounts **Cash in Bank** and **Delivery Revenue** are affected.
	Classify	**2.** **Cash in Bank** is an asset account. **Delivery Revenue** is a revenue account.
	+/−	**3.** **Cash in Bank** is increased by $1,200. **Delivery Revenue** is increased by $1,200.

DEBIT-CREDIT RULE

4. Increases in asset accounts are recorded as debits. Debit **Cash in Bank** for $1,200.

5. Increases in revenue accounts are recorded as credits. Credit **Delivery Revenue** for $1,200.

T ACCOUNTS   **6.**

Cash in Bank		Delivery Revenue	
Debit + 1,200	Credit −	Debit −	Credit + 1,200

JOURNAL ENTRY   **7.**

GENERAL JOURNAL   PAGE _____1_____

	DATE		DESCRIPTION	POST. REF.	DEBIT	CREDIT	
23	Oct.	15	Cash in Bank		1 200 00		23
24			Delivery Revenue			1 200 00	24
25			Receipt 2				25
26							26

Business Transaction 9

On October 16 Roadrunner mailed Check 103 for $700 to pay the month's rent.

	No. 103
$ 700.00	
Date October 16 20 --	
To Tooley & Co. Management	
For rent	

	Dollars	Cents
Balance brought forward	21,650	00
Add deposits 10/14	200	00
10/15	1,200	00
Total	23,050	00
Less this check	700	00
Balance carried forward	22,350	00

ANALYSIS

Identify

1. The accounts **Rent Expense** and **Cash in Bank** are affected.

Classify

2. **Rent Expense** is an expense. **Cash in Bank** is an asset.

+/−

3. **Rent Expense** is increased by $700. **Cash in Bank** is decreased by $700.

DEBIT-CREDIT RULE

4. Increases in expense accounts are recorded as debits. Debit **Rent Expense** for $700.
5. Decreases in asset accounts are recorded as credits. Credit **Cash in Bank** for $700.

T ACCOUNTS

6.

Rent Expense		Cash in Bank	
Debit +	Credit −	Debit +	Credit −
700			700

JOURNAL ENTRY

7.

GENERAL JOURNAL PAGE 1

DATE	DESCRIPTION	POST. REF.	DEBIT	CREDIT	
Oct. 16	Rent Expense		700 00		26
	Cash in Bank			700 00	27
	Check 103				28
					29

Business Transaction 10

On October 18 Beacon Advertising prepared an advertisement for Roadrunner. Roadrunner will pay Beacon's $75 fee later, Invoice 129.

BEACON Advertising
Beacon Advertising
10200 Prairie Parkway
Sacramento, CA 94206

INVOICE NO. 129

DATE: Oct. 18, 20--
ORDER NO.: 699
SHIPPED BY: n/a
TERMS: Payable in 30 days

TO Roadrunner Delivery Service
155 Gateway Blvd.
Sacramento, CA 94230

QTY.	ITEM	UNIT PRICE	TOTAL
1	Print Ad	$ 75.00	$ 75.00

ANALYSIS

Identify

1. The accounts **Advertising Expense** and **Accounts Payable—Beacon Advertising** are affected.

Classify

2. **Advertising Expense** is an expense account. **Accounts Payable—Beacon Advertising** is a liability account.

+/−

3. **Advertising Expense** is increased by $75. **Accounts Payable—Beacon Advertising** is increased by $75.

| DEBIT-CREDIT RULE | | 4. Increases in expense accounts are recorded as debits. Debit **Advertising Expense** for $75. |
| | | 5. Increases in liability accounts are recorded as credits. Credit **Accounts Payable—Beacon Advertising** for $75. |

T ACCOUNTS

6.

Advertising Expense		Accounts Payable—Beacon Advertising	
Debit	Credit	Debit	Credit
+	−	−	+
75			75

JOURNAL ENTRY

7.

GENERAL JOURNAL　　　　PAGE ___1___

	DATE		DESCRIPTION	POST. REF.	DEBIT	CREDIT	
29	Oct.	18	Advertising Expense		75 00		29
30			Accts. Pay.—Beacon Adv.			75 00	30
31			Invoice 129				31
32							32

Business Transaction 11

On October 20 Roadrunner provided delivery services for a customer, City News. Roadrunner billed City News $1,450, Sales Invoice 1.

Roadrunner Delivery Service
155 Gateway Blvd.
Sacramento, CA 94230

SALES INVOICE NO. 1
DATE: Oct. 20, 20--
ORDER NO.: 300
SHIPPED BY: n/a
TERMS: Payable in 30 days

TO　City News
10900 Main St.
Sacramento, CA 94230

QTY.	ITEM	UNIT PRICE	TOTAL
1	Delivery Services	$ 1,450.00	$ 1,450.00

ANALYSIS	*Identify*	1. The accounts **Accounts Receivable—City News** and **Delivery Revenue** are affected.
	Classify	2. **Accounts Receivable—City News** is an asset account. **Delivery Revenue** is a revenue account.
	+/−	3. **Accounts Receivable—City News** is increased by $1,450. **Delivery Revenue** is increased by $1,450.

| DEBIT-CREDIT RULE | 4. Increases in asset accounts are recorded as debits. Debit **Accounts Receivable—City News** for $1,450. |
| | 5. Increases in revenue accounts are recorded as credits. Credit **Delivery Revenue** for $1,450. |

T ACCOUNTS

6.

Accounts Receivable—City News		Delivery Revenue	
Debit	Credit	Debit	Credit
+	−	−	+
1,450			1,450

7.

GENERAL JOURNAL PAGE ___1___

	DATE		DESCRIPTION	POST. REF.	DEBIT	CREDIT	
32	Oct.	20	Accts. Rec.—City News		1 450 00		32
33			Delivery Revenue			1 450 00	33
34			Sales Invoice 1				34
35							35

Business Transaction 12

On October 28 Roadrunner paid a $125 telephone bill with Check 104.

$ ___125.00___ No. 104
Date ___October 28___ 20 --
To ___Pacific Bell Telephone___
For ___telephone bill___

	Dollars	Cents
Balance brought forward	22,350	00
Add deposits		
Total	22,350	00
Less this check	125	00
Balance carried forward	22,225	00

ANALYSIS

Identify

1. The accounts **Utilities Expense** and **Cash in Bank** are affected.

Classify

2. **Utilities Expense** is an expense account. **Cash in Bank** is an asset account.

+/−

3. **Utilities Expense** is increased by $125. **Cash in Bank** is decreased by $125.

DEBIT-CREDIT RULE

4. Increases in expense accounts are recorded as debits. Debit **Utilities Expense** for $125.
5. Decreases in asset accounts are recorded as credits. Credit **Cash in Bank** for $125.

T ACCOUNTS

6.

Utilities Expense		Cash in Bank	
Debit + 125	Credit −	Debit +	Credit − 125

JOURNAL ENTRY

7.

GENERAL JOURNAL PAGE ___1___

	DATE		DESCRIPTION	POST. REF.	DEBIT	CREDIT	
35	Oct.	28	Utilities Expense		1 25 00		35
36			Cash in Bank			1 25 00	36
37			Check 104				37
38							38

Business Transaction 13

On October 29 Roadrunner wrote Check 105 for $600 to have the office repainted.

$ 600.00			No. 105
Date October 29			20 --
To Rainbow Painting			
For office painted			

	Dollars	Cents
Balance brought forward	22,225	00
Add deposits		
Total	22,225	00
Less this check	600	00
Balance carried forward	21,625	00

ANALYSIS

Identify
1. The accounts **Maintenance Expense** and **Cash in Bank** are affected.

Classify
2. **Maintenance Expense** is an expense account. **Cash in Bank** is an asset account.

+/−
3. **Maintenance Expense** is increased by $600. **Cash in Bank** is decreased by $600.

DEBIT-CREDIT RULE
4. Increases in expense accounts are recorded as debits. Debit **Maintenance Expense** for $600.
5. Decreases in asset accounts are recorded as credits. Credit **Cash in Bank** for $600.

T ACCOUNTS

6.

Maintenance Expense		Cash in Bank	
Debit + 600	Credit −	Debit +	Credit − 600

JOURNAL ENTRY

7.

GENERAL JOURNAL　　　　PAGE 1

	DATE	DESCRIPTION	POST. REF.	DEBIT	CREDIT	
38	Oct. 29	Maintenance Expense		600 00		38
39		Cash in Bank			600 00	39
40		Check 105				40
41						41

Business Transaction 14

On October 31 Maria Sanchez wrote Check 106 to withdraw $500 cash for personal use.

$ 500.00			No. 106
Date October 31			20 --
To Maria Sanchez			
For withdrawal			

	Dollars	Cents
Balance brought forward	21,625	00
Add deposits		
Total	21,625	00
Less this check	500	00
Balance carried forward	21,125	00

ANALYSIS

Identify
1. The accounts **Maria Sanchez, Withdrawals** and **Cash in Bank** are affected.

Classify
2. **Maria Sanchez, Withdrawals** is an owner's withdrawals account. **Cash in Bank** is an asset account.

+/−
3. **Maria Sanchez, Withdrawals** is increased by $500. **Cash in Bank** is decreased by $500.

| DEBIT-CREDIT RULE | | 4. Increases in the owner's withdrawals account are recorded as debits. Debit **Maria Sanchez, Withdrawals** for $500. |
| | | 5. Decreases in asset accounts are recorded as credits. Credit **Cash in Bank** for $500. |

T ACCOUNTS

6.

Maria Sanchez, Withdrawals		Cash in Bank	
Debit + 500	Credit −	Debit +	Credit − 500

JOURNAL ENTRY

7.

GENERAL JOURNAL PAGE ___1___

	DATE		DESCRIPTION	POST. REF.	DEBIT	CREDIT	
41	Oct.	31	Maria Sanchez, Withdrawals		500 00		41
42			Cash in Bank			500 00	42
43			Check 106				43
44							44

Correcting the General Journal

How Do You Correct Errors in the General Journal?

Occasionally, errors occur when journalizing transactions. When an error is discovered, it must be corrected.

In a manual system, *an error should never be erased.* An erasure looks suspicious. It might be seen as an attempt to cover up a mistake or, worse, to change the accounting records illegally. To correct errors, use a pen and a ruler to draw a horizontal line through the entire incorrect item and write the correct information above the crossed-out error. A correction for an erroneous amount is shown in the general journal as follows:

GENERAL JOURNAL PAGE ___1___

	DATE		DESCRIPTION	POST. REF.	DEBIT	CREDIT	
1	20--						1
2	Oct.	1	Cash in Bank		25 000 00 ~~52 000 00~~		2
3			Maria Sanchez, Capital			25 000 00 ~~52 000 00~~	3
4			Memorandum 1				4

To correct for an erroneous account name, cross out the incorrect information and write the correct account name above.

GENERAL JOURNAL PAGE ___1___

	DATE		DESCRIPTION	POST. REF.	DEBIT	CREDIT	
1	20--						1
2	Oct.	1	Cash in Bank		25 000 00		2
3			Maria Sanchez, Capital ~~Delivery Revenue~~			25 000 00	3
4			Memorandum 1				4

As You READ

Compare and Contrast

Journal Errors What are the consequences of an error in an amount? In an account name? How are the consequences similar? How are they different?

AFTER YOU READ

Reinforce the Main Idea

Think of three different types of business transactions you might have in the next month. Use a table similar to this one to describe the general journal entry for each transaction.

Business Transaction	First Line of General Journal Entry	Second Line of General Journal Entry	Third Line of General Journal Entry

Do the Math

Hania Dance Company bought a computer system on account from Tech World. The regular price for the system is $3,000, but Tech World reduced the price by 20 percent for a storewide sale. Answer the following questions about the journal entry for this transaction.

1. Which account is debited and for what amount?
2. Which account is credited and for what amount?

Problem 6–2 Recording Business Transactions

Instructions The six steps for recording a business transaction in the general journal are shown below, out of order. In your working papers or on a blank sheet of paper, indicate the proper order of these steps.

A. Amount of the credit

B. Name of the account credited

C. Source document reference

D. Date of the transaction

E. Amount of the debit

F. Name of the account debited

Problem 6–3 Analyzing Transactions

Glenda Hohn recently started a day-care center. She uses the following accounts.

General Ledger

Cash in Bank

Accts. Rec.—Tiny Tots Nursery

Office Furniture

Passenger Van

Accts. Pay.—Acme Bus Service

Glenda Hohn, Capital

Glenda Hohn, Withdrawals

Day-Care Fees

Utilities Expense

Van Expense

Instructions In your working papers or on a separate sheet of paper, for each transaction: Determine which accounts are affected. Classify each account. Determine whether the accounts are being increased or decreased. Indicate which account is debited and which account is credited.

Transactions:

1. Bought a passenger van for cash.
2. Paid the telephone bill for the month.
3. Received cash from customers for day-care services.

Key Concepts

1. The accounting cycle is pictured below. The first three steps are highlighted:
   Step 1: Collect and verify source documents.
   Step 2: Analyze each transaction.
   Step 3: Journalize each transaction.

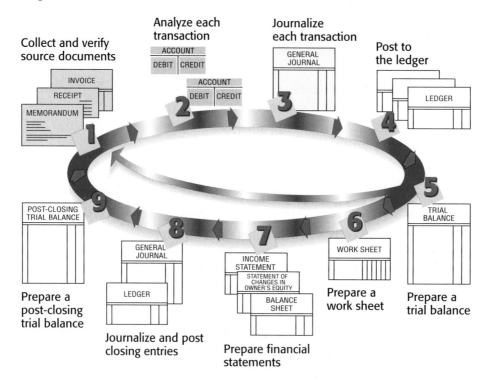

2. Source documents are evidence of business transactions. Four examples of source documents are listed below.

Invoice	➤	describes the buying or selling of an item on account
Receipt	➤	describes cash received by a business
Memorandum	➤	describes a transaction that takes place within a business
Check Stub	➤	describes a specific check and shows the checking account balance

3. Businesses use journals to keep records of transactions in the order they occur. The process of recording transactions in a journal is called *journalizing*.

4. Source documents contain the information needed for journalizing transactions. The check stub shown to the right is a source document. The highlighted information is used to make the journal entry.

$ 250.00		No. 110
Date November 2		20 --
To Info-Systems		
For fax/modem		

	Dollars	Cents
Balance brought forward	25,000	00
Add deposits		
Total	25,000	00
Less this check	250	00
Balance carried forward	24,750	00

5. Follow six steps to make a general journal entry:

GENERAL JOURNAL   PAGE _____

	DATE	DESCRIPTION	POST. REF.	DEBIT	CREDIT	
1	*(1) Date*	*(2) Account to Debit*		*(3) Debit Amt.*		1
2		*(4) Account to Credit*			*(5) Credit Amt.*	2
3		*(6) Source Document Reference*				3
4						4

6. Notice how information is applied from the source document (Check Stub 110) to the general journal.

GENERAL JOURNAL   PAGE _____1_____

	DATE		DESCRIPTION	POST. REF.	DEBIT	CREDIT	
1	*20--*						1
2	*Nov.*	*2*	*Office Equipment*		*2 5 0 00*		2
3			*Cash in Bank*			*2 5 0 00*	3
4			*Check 110*				4

7. In a manual system, never erase a general journal error. The procedure to correct an error is shown below.

GENERAL JOURNAL   PAGE _____1_____

	DATE		DESCRIPTION	POST. REF.	DEBIT	CREDIT	
1	*20--*						1
2	*Nov.*	*2*	*Office Equipment* ~~*Maintenance Expense*~~		*2 5 0 00*		2
3			*Cash in Bank*			*2 5 0 00*	3
4			*Check 110*				4

Key Terms

accounting cycle	(p. 132)	journal	(p. 134)
calendar year	(p. 134)	journalizing	(p. 134)
check stub	(p. 133)	memorandum	(p. 133)
fiscal year	(p. 134)	receipt	(p. 133)
general journal	(p. 136)	source document	(p. 133)
invoice	(p. 133)		

Check Your Understanding

1. **Accounting Cycle**
   a. List the first three steps of the accounting cycle.
   b. What would happen if you skipped Step 2?
2. **Source Documents**
   a. List four source documents and describe the contents of each.
   b. Explain when each source document is used.
3. **Journalizing**
   a. Why is a journal sometimes called the *book of original entry?*
   b. What is the purpose of recording transactions in a journal?
4. **Applying Information**
   a. Where do you get the information needed to make a journal entry?
   b. How do you determine the debit and credit parts of a journal entry?
5. **Steps to Make a General Journal Entry**
   a. What six types of information are included in each general journal entry?
   b. In what order do you record this information?
6. **Making General Journal Entries**
   a. How are the two amount columns of the general journal used to record dollar amounts?
   b. Describe the spacing of the information in the Description column.
7. **Correcting General Journal Errors**
   a. What procedure is used to correct a general journal entry error in a manual system?
   b. What are the possible consequences of erasing an error in the general journal?

Apply Key Terms

Assume you are an accountant who keeps financial records for small businesses. Write a one-page newsletter that you might send to potential clients describing the importance of accounting records. Use each of the terms below in your newsletter.

accounting cycle	journal
calendar year	journalizing
check stub	memorandum
fiscal year	receipt
general journal	source document
invoice	

General Journal Entries

Making the Transition from a Manual to a Computerized System

Task	Manual Methods	Computerized Methods
Recording general journal entries	• Analyze the source document to determine which accounts are affected. • Using a general journal form, enter the details of the transaction. • Check for equality of debits and credits.	• Analyze the source document to determine which accounts are affected. • Enter the transaction details in the general journal using the account numbers for each ledger account. • The software will calculate the equality of debits and credits.

Peachtree® Q & A

Peachtree Question	Answer
How do I enter general journal entries in Peachtree?	1. From the *Tasks* menu, select **General Journal Entry**. 2. Enter the date of the transaction. 3. Enter the source document reference. 4. Enter the account number to be debited. 5. Enter a brief description of the transaction. 6. Enter the debit amount. 7. Enter the account number to be credited. 8. Enter the credit amount. 9. Click **Save**.

QuickBooks Q & A

QuickBooks Question	Answer
How do I enter general journal entries in QuickBooks?	1. From the *Company* menu, select **Make General Journal Entries**. 2. Enter the date of the transaction. 3. Enter the account to be debited. 4. Enter the debit amount, source document reference, and description. 5. Enter the account to be credited. 6. Enter the credit amount, source document reference, and description. 7. Click **Save & Close**.

For detailed instructions, see your Glencoe Accounting Chapter Study Guides and Working Papers.

Problems

Peachtree®

SMART GUIDE

Step–by–Step Instructions: Problem 6–4

1. Select the problem set for Wilderness Rentals (Prob. 6–4).
2. Rename the company and set the system date.
3. Enter all of the general journal transactions using the **General Journal Entry** option in the **Tasks** menu.
4. Print a General Journal report.
5. Proof your work and make any needed corrections.
6. Complete the Analyze activity.
7. End the session.

QuickBooks

PROBLEM GUIDE

Step–by–Step Instructions: Problem 6–4

1. Restore the Problem 6-4.QBB file.
2. Enter all of the general journal transactions using the **Make General Journal Entries** option in the **Company** menu.
3. Print a Journal report.
4. Proof your work and make any needed corrections.
5. Complete the Analyze activity.
6. Back up your work.

Problem 6–4 Recording General Journal Transactions

Ronald Hicks owns and operates Wilderness Rentals. The following accounts are needed to journalize the month's transactions.

General Ledger

101	Cash in Bank	301	Ronald Hicks, Capital
105	Accts. Rec.—Helen Katz	305	Ronald Hicks, Withdrawals
110	Accts. Rec.—Polk and Co.	310	Income Summary
120	Office Equipment	401	Equipment Rental Revenue
125	Camping Equipment	501	Advertising Expense
201	Accts. Pay.—Adventure Equipment Inc.	505	Maintenance Expense
		515	Rent Expense
203	Accts. Pay.—Digital Tech Computers	520	Salaries Expense
		525	Utilities Expense
205	Accts. Pay.—Greg Mollaro		

Instructions: Record the following transactions on page 1 of the general journal in your working papers. For each transaction:

1. Enter the date. Use the current year.
2. Enter the name of the account debited.
3. Enter the amount of the debit.
4. Enter the name of the account credited.
5. Enter the amount of the credit.
6. Enter a source document reference.

Date	Transactions
Jan. 1	Wrote Check 310 for the part-time secretary's salary, $270.
3	Bought $2,000 of camping equipment on account from Adventure Equipment Inc., Invoice 320.
5	Received $500 from a client for equipment rental, Receipt 150.
7	Wrote Check 311 to pay the electricity bill of $110.
11	Billed a client, Polk and Co., $1,700 for rental equipment, Sales Invoice 262.
12	Ronald Hicks withdrew $800 for personal use, Check 312.
14	Bought a $300 scanner for the office computer from Digital Tech Computers, on account, Invoice 270.
16	Wrote Check 313 for $1,000 as an installment payment toward the amount owed to Adventure Equipment Inc.
25	Received $1,700 from Polk and Co. in payment on their account, Receipt 151.
30	Paid Digital Tech Computers $300 for the amount owed, Check 314.

Analyze   Calculate the amount of cash deducted from the **Cash in Bank** account in January.

Problem 6–5 Recording General Journal Transactions

Regina Delgado owns a business called Hot Suds Car Wash. She uses the following chart of accounts.

General Ledger

101	Cash in Bank	401	Wash Revenue
105	Accts. Rec.—Linda Brown	405	Wax Revenue
110	Accts. Rec.—Valley Auto	410	Interior Detailing Revenue
125	Office Equipment	501	Advertising Expense
130	Office Furniture	505	Equipment Rental Expense
135	Car Wash Equipment	510	Maintenance Expense
201	Accts. Pay.—Allen Vacuum Systems	520	Rent Expense
205	Accts. Pay.—O'Brian's Office Supply	525	Salaries Expense
301	Regina Delgado, Capital	530	Utilities Expense
305	Regina Delgado, Withdrawals		
310	Income Summary		

Instructions: Record the following transactions on page 1 of the general journal in your working papers.

Date	Transactions
Jan. 1	Regina Delgado invested $12,000 in the business, Memorandum 41.
5	Purchased $5,000 in desks, chairs, and cabinets from O'Brian's Office Supply on account, Invoice 1632.
8	Deposited $1,600 for income received from car washes for the week, Receipt 101.
10	Paid the *Village Bulletin* $75 for running an ad, Check 301.
13	Regina Delgado withdrew $900 for personal use, Check 302.
17	Billed Valley Auto $400 for interior detailing, Sales Invoice 102.
18	Paid O'Brian's Office Supply $2,500 as an installment payment on account, Check 303.
20	Regina Delgado transferred to the business an electronic calculator valued at $350, Memorandum 42.
22	Wrote Check 304 for $600 to Shadyside Realty for the office rent.
24	Purchased $1,500 in car wash equipment from Allen Vacuum Systems on account, Invoice 312.
26	Received a $400 check from Valley Auto in full payment of its account, Receipt 102.
30	Issued Check 305 for $2,500 to O'Brian's Office Supply for the balance due on account.

Analyze Identify the revenue account that was not used in the month of January.

Peachtree®

SMART GUIDE

Step–by–Step Instructions: Problem 6–5

1. Select the problem set for Hot Suds Car Wash (Prob. 6–5).
2. Rename the company and set the system date.
3. Enter all of the general journal transactions using the **General Journal Entry** option in the *Tasks* menu.
4. Print a General Journal report.
5. Proof your work and make any needed corrections.
6. Complete the Analyze activity.
7. End the session.

TIP: You can use General Ledger Navigation Aid as an alternative way to access the General Journal Entry window.

QuickBooks

PROBLEM GUIDE

Step–by–Step Instructions: Problem 6–5

1. Restore the Problem 6-5.QBB file.
2. Enter all of the general journal transactions using the **Make General Journal Entries** option in the *Company* menu.
3. Print a Journal report.
4. Proof your work and make any needed corrections.
5. Complete the Analyze activity.
6. Back up your work.

Problem 6–6 Recording General Journal Transactions

Abe Shultz owns and operates a pet grooming business called Kits & Pups Grooming. The following accounts are used to journalize transactions.

General Ledger

101 Cash in Bank	207 Accts. Pay.—Pet Gourmet
105 Accts. Rec.—Juan Alvarez	301 Abe Shultz, Capital
110 Accts. Rec.—N. Carlsbad	305 Abe Shultz, Withdrawals
115 Accts. Rec.—Martha Giles	310 Income Summary
125 Office Equipment	401 Boarding Revenue
130 Office Furniture	405 Grooming Revenue
135 Computer Equipment	501 Advertising Expense
140 Grooming Equipment	505 Equipment Repair Expense
145 Kennel Equipment	510 Maintenance Expense
201 Accts. Pay.—Able Store Equipment	520 Rent Expense
205 Accts. Pay.—Dogs & Cats Inc.	525 Salaries Expense
	530 Utilities Expense

Instructions: Record the following transactions on page 7 of the general journal in your working papers.

Date	Transactions
Jan. 1	Received $125 for boarding a client's dog for one week, Receipt 300.
3	Abe Shultz contributed to the business a computer valued at $2,500, Memorandum 33.
5	Billed a client, Juan Alvarez, $80 for grooming his pets, Sales Invoice 212.
9	Wrote Check 411 to Allegheny Power Co. for $150 in payment for the month's electricity bill.
11	Abe Shultz withdrew $700 for personal use, Check 412.
14	Purchased kennel equipment for $2,600 from Dogs & Cats Inc., on account, Invoice DC92.
16	Paid the part-time receptionist's salary of $400 by issuing Check 413.
18	Abe Shultz took from the business for his personal use a ten-key adding machine valued at $65, Memorandum 34.
23	Juan Alvarez sent a check for $80 in full payment of his account, Receipt 301.
28	Purchased on credit $250 in grooming equipment from the Pet Gourmet, Invoice PG333.
31	Issued Check 414 for $1,300 as an installment payment for the amount owed to Dogs & Cats Inc.

Analyze Calculate the total of the Accounts Receivable accounts as of January 31.

Problem 6–7 Recording General Journal Transactions

Juanita Ortega is the owner of Outback Guide Service. The following accounts are used to record the transactions of her business.

General Ledger

101 Cash in Bank	205 Accts. Pay.—Peak Equipment Inc.
105 Accts. Rec.—M. Johnson	207 Accts. Pay.—Premier Processors
110 Accts. Rec.—Feldman, Jones & Ritter	301 Juanita Ortega, Capital
	302 Juanita Ortega, Withdrawals
115 Accts. Rec.—Podaski Systems Inc.	310 Income Summary
	401 Guide Service Revenue
130 Office Equipment	501 Advertising Expense
135 Office Furniture	505 Maintenance Expense
140 Computer Equipment	515 Rent Expense
145 Hiking Equipment	520 Salaries Expense
150 Rafting Equipment	525 Utilities Expense
201 Accts. Pay.—A-1 Adventure Warehouse	

Instructions: Record the following transactions on page 1 of the general journal in your working papers.

Date	Transactions
Jan. 1	Juanita Ortega contributed the following assets to her business: cash, $1,500; hiking equipment, $2,000; rafting equipment, $2,500; and office furniture, $500; Memorandum 21.
2	Issued Check 515 to *Town News* for a $75 ad.
4	Purchased $3,000 in rafting equipment on account from A-1 Adventure Warehouse, Invoice AW45.
6	A group from Feldman, Jones & Ritter went on a hiking trip. The group was billed $4,800 for guide services, Sales Invoice 300.
10	Paid $300 to Dunn's Painting and Interior Co. for painting the office, Check 516.
13	Made a $1,000 payment to A-1 Adventure Warehouse toward the amount owed, Check 517.
15	Received a check for $4,800 from Feldman, Jones & Ritter in payment of their account, Receipt 252.
18	Juanita Ortega paid herself $600 by issuing Check 518.
22	Billed a client, Mary Johnson, $1,200 for completing guide services on a hiking expedition, Sales Invoice 301.
25	Paid the monthly telephone bill for $175 by issuing Check 519.
30	Purchased a $3,600 computer system from Premier Processors. Made a down payment for $1,800 and agreed to pay the balance within 30 days, Check 520 and Invoice 749.

Analyze Generalize about Outback's cash sales and credit sales.

Peachtree®

SMART GUIDE

Step–by–Step Instructions: Problem 6–7

1. Select the problem set for Outback Guide Service (Prob. 6–7).
2. Rename the company and set the system date.
3. Enter all of the general journal transactions.
4. Print a General Journal report.
5. Proof your work and make any needed corrections.
6. Complete the Analyze activity.
7. End the session.

TIP: Press **SHIFT+?** in an *Account No.* field to display an account list.

Problems

CHALLENGE PROBLEM

Problem 6–8 Recording General Journal Transactions

Greg Failla operates Showbiz Video. The following accounts are used to record business transactions.

SOURCE DOCUMENT PROBLEM

Problem 6–8

Use the source documents in your working papers to complete this problem.

Peachtree®

SMART GUIDE

Step–by–Step Instructions: Problem 6–8

1. Select the problem set for Showbiz Video (Prob. 6–8).
2. Rename the company and set the system date.
3. Enter all of the general journal transactions.
4. Print a General Journal report.
5. Proof your work and make any needed corrections.
6. Complete the Analyze activity.
7. End the session.

General Ledger

101 Cash in Bank	207 Accts. Pay.—New Media Suppliers
105 Accts. Rec.—G. Cohen	209 Accts. Pay.—Palace Films
110 Accts. Rec.—J. Coletti	301 Greg Failla, Capital
113 Accts. Rec.—S. Flannery	305 Greg Failla, Withdrawals
115 Accts. Rec.—Spring Branch School District	310 Income Summary
130 Office Equipment	401 Video Rental Revenue
135 Office Furniture	405 VCR Rental Revenue
140 Computer Equipment	501 Advertising Expense
145 Video Tapes	505 Equipment Repair Expense
150 Video Equipment	510 Maintenance Expense
201 Accts. Pay.—Broad Street Office Supply	520 Rent Expense
205 Accts. Pay.—Computer Horizons	525 Salaries Expense
	530 Utilities Expense

Instructions: Record the following transactions on page 5 of the general journal in your working papers.

Date	Transactions
Jan. 1	Deposited $3,400 in receipts. Of that amount, $1,900 was VCR rentals and $1,500 was video tape rentals, Receipt 435.
3	Wrote Check 1250 for $325 of equipment repairs.
5	Purchased $400 in video tapes from Palace Films on account, Invoice PF32.
7	Bought from New Media Suppliers $2,600 in video equipment. Made a down payment of $600 and agreed to pay the balance in two installments, Check 1251 and Invoice NM101.
10	Rented videos to Spring Branch School District. The school district agreed to pay $1,800 at a later date, Sales Invoice 1650.
12	Issued Check 1252 for $750 to Computer Horizons for the amount owed to them.
15	Deposited $5,600 in receipts. VCR rentals amounted to $4,400 and video tape rentals were $1,200, Receipt 436.
18	Paid Clear Vue Window Cleaners $100 for monthly window cleaning, Check 1253.
25	Made a $1,000 installment payment toward the amount owed to New Media Suppliers by issuing Check 1254.

Analyze Calculate the total expenses incurred in January.

Practice your test-taking skills! The questions on this page are reprinted with permission from national organizations:
- Future Business Leaders of America
- Business Professionals of America

Use a separate sheet of paper to record your answers.

Future Business Leaders of America

MULTIPLE CHOICE

1. Recording account information in chronological order is called

    a. posting.

    b. journalizing.

    c. analyzing.

    d. processing.

2. Every journal consists of four parts:

    a. account title, date, post reference, amount.

    b. date, debit, credit, source document.

    c. date, page number, debit, credit.

    d. date, post reference, debit, credit.

3. The amount of each asset in an opening entry is recorded in a journal in the

    a. General Debit column.

    b. General Credit column.

    c. both a and b.

    d. neither a nor b.

4. An example of a business document that indicates a transaction has occurred is

    a. a journal.

    b. a ledger.

    c. a memo.

    d. a balance sheet.

Business Professionals of America

MULTIPLE CHOICE

5. The source document used when a customer makes a payment on his/her account owed would be a

    a. sales invoice.

    b. check.

    c. receipt.

    d. memorandum.

Need More Help?

Go to **glencoeaccounting.glencoe.com** and click on **Student Center**. Click on **Winning Competitive Events** and select **Chapter 6**.
- **Practice Questions and Test-Taking Tips**
- **Concept Capsules and Terminology**

General Journal Entries

1. What term describes any accounting period of 12 months?
2. How is the general journal entry for a cash purchase different from the entry for a purchase on account?
3. It is your first day on a new job. Your task is to journalize transactions. You just sat at your desk, which is covered with papers. What do you do next?
4. Compare a general journal entry to a transaction recorded in T accounts. How is it similar? How is it different?
5. What items do you need to complete each of the first three steps of the accounting cycle? Include office supplies and forms as well as any information that will be needed.
6. What is the value of keeping the record of business transactions in chronological order?

Service Business: Exercise and Fitness

Elena Rodriguez started a business offering an exercise facility and personal physical training. Elena has hired you as a financial consultant to help her set up her accounting system. She has rented a space for her business, purchased several exercise machines, and hired a part-time exercise instructor. Elena's clients can either pay a fee for each visit or purchase a membership.

INSTRUCTIONS

1. Write a plan for Elena Rodriguez explaining the types of financial information she needs to record. Describe the source documents that might be a part of her business. For example, should Elena send invoices to her non-membership clients or ask them to pay at each visit? Describe why it is important for Elena to record both the cost of doing business and the income from the business.
2. Suggest a chart of accounts for Elena's business.

Gossip in the Workplace

Assume that you are an accounting clerk for a large insurance company like Farmers Insurance. Your boss introduces you to the newest hire, and you recognize her as a former classmate from high school named Sally. You remember that Sally had been suspended from school for a series of locker thefts. During lunch you consider telling other co-workers about Sally's history. You also wonder if your boss knows.

ETHICAL DECISION MAKING

1. What are the ethical issues?
2. What are the alternatives?
3. Who are the affected parties?
4. How do the alternatives affect the parties?
5. What would you do?

Describing Source Documents

Write a paragraph describing the content of invoices, check stubs, memorandums, and receipts. Explain how to verify and analyze these source documents before an entry is made in the journal.

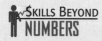

Creative Thinking

Congratulations! You have been chosen as the local Business Owner of the Year! Write a one-page press release describing your business and why you have been successful. Be sure to include a brief description of your business, the skills you use in running a successful business, and how you plan to continue being successful in the future.

Dating Documents

Source documents from different countries can have different date formats:

	United States	**Australia**
Date written out	July 6, 2010	6 July 2010
Abbreviation	7/6/10	6/7/10
Format	MM/DD/YY	DD/MM/YY

As you can see in this example, writing out the month prevents confusion. The International Organization for Standardization (ISO) promotes the worldwide use of a single format: YYYY-MM-DD.

INSTRUCTIONS Write the date *February 17, 2010,* using the ISO recommended format.

Your Personal Finance Records

Your day-to-day source documents are personal financial records. Personal financial records also include documents that are not related to everyday transactions. Vehicle titles, birth certificates, and tax returns are all personal financial documents. You can store your financial documents in home files, a home safe, or a safe-deposit box. You can also keep some financial records on a home computer.

PERSONAL FINANCE ACTIVITY Imagine a person your age who drives to a part-time job and has a credit card. Make a list of the types of records and documents such a person would probably have. Create a plan that describes which records and documents to store and where to store them.

PERSONAL FINANCE ONLINE Log on to **glencoeaccounting.glencoe.com** and click on **Student Center.** Click on **Making It Personal** and select **Chapter 6.**

Transactions in Sports

The general journal can be used to record all types of transactions. Visit **glencoeaccounting .glencoe.com** and click on **Student Center.** Click on **WebQuest** and select **Unit 2** to continue your Internet project.

CHAPTER 7

Posting Journal Entries to General Ledger Accounts

What You'll Learn

1. Describe the steps in the posting process.

2. Post general journal entries.

3. Prepare a trial balance.

4. Locate and correct trial balance errors.

5. Record correcting entries in the general journal.

6. Define the accounting terms introduced in this chapter.

Why It's Important

▶ Up-to-date account balances provide information for reports used by people both inside and outside the business.

Predict

1. What does the chapter title tell you?
2. What do you already know about this subject from personal experience?
3. What have you learned about this in the earlier chapters?
4. What gaps exist in your knowledge of this subject?

Exploring the *Real World* of Business

ACCOUNTS AND THE GENERAL LEDGER

Los Angeles Angels of Anaheim

In the big-money world of professional sports, it is hard to imagine the new owner of a major team actually *lowering* the prices of tickets, food, and souvenirs. That is exactly what Arturo "Arte" Moreno did when he bought baseball's **Los Angeles Angels of Anaheim** in 2003.

Moreno was a big hit with fans for his lower-price strategy. In his first year, the **Angels** attracted 750,000 more paying customers than in the previous season, when they won the World Series.

Moreno has been called "the people's owner" because he likes to meet fans and enjoys seeing families having a good time. "For baseball to exist as I've known it, the kids have to come to the park," he told *USA Today*.

What Do You Think?

What are some general ledger accounts that might be used by the **Angels?**

Working in the *Real World*

APPLYING YOUR ACCOUNTING KNOWLEDGE

In the last chapter, you learned how to record financial transactions in a journal. These journal entries show individual daily activities but do not show the total of all transactions. In this chapter you will learn that posting the journal entries is a means of organizing all transactions affecting the accounts of a business.

Personal Connection
What types of accounts would you imagine are used for accounting in your workplace?

Online Connection
Go to **glencoeaccounting.glencoe.com** and click on **Student Center.** Click on **Working in the Real World** and select **Chapter 7.**

The General Ledger

Before You READ

Main Idea
The general ledger is a permanent record organized by account number.

Read to Learn...
➤ how to set up the general ledger. (p. 164)
➤ how managers use journals and ledgers. (p. 166)

Key Terms
posting
general ledger
ledger account forms

In Chapter 6 you learned to analyze business transactions and enter those transactions in a general journal.

In this chapter you will learn to post journal entries to the general ledger and to prepare a trial balance (Steps 4 and 5 in the accounting cycle illustrated in **Figure 7–1**). **Posting** is the process of transferring information from the journal to individual general ledger accounts.

The Jeep dealer in your area records all business transactions in the journal and posts them to the general ledger. An up-to-date ledger allows the dealer's accountant to give management information such as sales of vehicles, service income, and salary and commission expense.

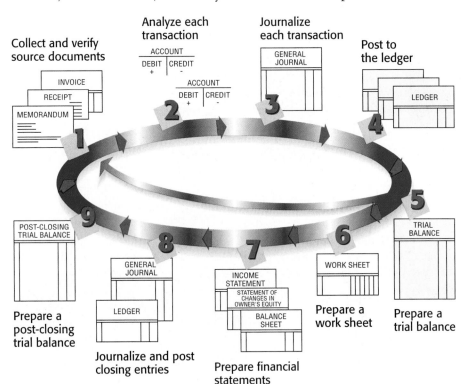

Figure 7–1 The Accounting Cycle with Steps 4 and 5 Highlighted

Setting Up the General Ledger
What Is a General Ledger?

Recall that the accounts used by a business are kept on separate pages or cards in a book or file called a ledger. In a computerized accounting system, the electronic files containing the accounts are still referred to as the ledger, or the ledger accounts. In either system the ledger is often called a general ledger. The **general ledger** is a permanent record organized by account number.

Posting journal entries to the ledger accounts creates a record of the impact of business transactions on each account used by a business. After journal entries have been posted, a business owner or manager can easily find the current balance of a specific account. If, for example, Maria Sanchez wants to know how much money Roadrunner Delivery Service has in its bank account, she can look at the balance of the **Cash in Bank** account.

The Four-Column Ledger Account Form

In a manual accounting system, information about specific accounts is recorded in **ledger account forms**. There are several common ledger account forms. These forms and other accounting stationery are usually described by the number of their amount columns. The number of columns refers only to those columns in which *dollar amounts* are recorded.

Roadrunner uses the four-column ledger account form shown in **Figure 7–2**. The four-column ledger account form has spaces to enter the account name, the account number, the date, a description of the entry, and the posting reference. It also has four columns in which to record dollar amounts: Debit, Credit, Debit Balance, and Credit Balance.

ACCOUNT						BALANCE	
						ACCOUNT NO.	
DATE	DESCRIPTION	POST. REF.	DEBIT	CREDIT		DEBIT	CREDIT

Figure 7–2 Four-Column Ledger Account Form

Debit and credit amounts are posted from journal entries to the first two amount columns. The new account balance is entered in one of the last two amount columns. The type of account (expense, revenue, asset, etc.) determines which balance column to use. For example, accounts with a normal debit balance—such as asset or expense accounts—use the Debit Balance column. Accounts with a normal credit balance—such as liability or revenue accounts—use the Credit Balance column.

Accounts in the Ledger

Before journal entries can be posted, a general ledger account is opened for each account listed on the chart of accounts.

Opening a General Ledger Account. Two steps are required:

1. Write the account name at the top of the ledger account form.
2. Write the account number on the ledger account form.

These two steps are performed each time a ledger page is needed for a new account. The accounts opened for the first three asset accounts on Roadrunner's chart of accounts (page 79) are shown in **Figure 7–3** on page 166.

The procedure in a computerized accounting system is similar. An account is opened by entering its name and number from the chart of accounts. Computerized accounting systems vary, but all require entering information such as the account numbers and names into the computer files.

CULTURAL Diversity

Business Etiquette
Americans shake hands with a firm grip to show confidence. In some cultures, however, a firm handshake can be considered a sign of aggression. In many countries the grip is limp and it can last up to 10 seconds. If you meet someone from a different culture, let him or her set the precedent.

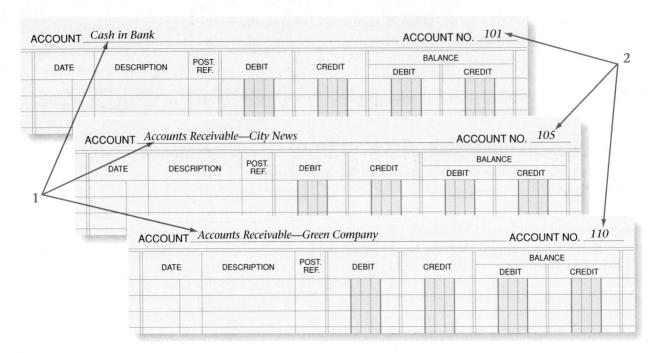

Figure 7–3 Opening General Ledger Accounts with Zero Balances

Starting a New Page for an Existing Account. When a ledger account page is filled, continue posting on the next page. Six steps are required to "open" a new page:

1. Write the account name at the top of the ledger account form.
2. Write the account number on the ledger account form.
3. Enter the complete date (year, month, and day) in the Date column.
4. Write the word *Balance* in the Description column.
5. Place a check mark (✓) in the Posting Reference column to show the amount entered on this line is not being posted from a journal.
6. Enter the balance in the appropriate Balance column. Usually asset, expense, and owner's withdrawals accounts have debit balances. Liability, owner's capital, and revenue accounts have credit balances.

Figure 7–4 shows an example of a new page opened for an account.

ACCOUNT _Cash in Bank_ 1   ACCOUNT NO. _101_ 2

	DATE		DESCRIPTION	POST. REF.	DEBIT	CREDIT	BALANCE DEBIT	BALANCE CREDIT
3	20--			5			6	
	Oct.	31	Balance 4	✓			21 1 2 5 00	

Figure 7–4 Starting a New Page for an Existing Account

The Usefulness of Journals and Ledgers
How Are These Records Useful to Managers?

Managers continually use the information from accounting records. To find information about a specific business transaction, a manager can refer to the journal entry. To learn the current balance of important accounts like **Accounts Receivable** and **Accounts Payable**, managers look at the general ledger. Managers use ledgers to obtain summarized information.

Reinforce the Main Idea

Use a chart like this one to compare and contrast a journal and a ledger. Add answer lines as needed.

Journal	Ledger
How are they alike?	
How are they different?	

Do the Math

The general ledger for Reese Delivery Service contains the following account balances:

Cash in Bank	$ 8,000
Supplies	$ 200
Delivery Equipment	?
Ed Reese, Capital	$16,200
Delivery Income	?

Using the following clues, determine the balances of the **Delivery Equipment** account and the **Delivery Income** account:

- Total debits equal $24,200.
- The balance of the **Delivery Income** account is one-half the balance of the **Delivery Equipment** account.

Problem 7–1 Opening Ledger Accounts

Instructions Use the step-by-step processes presented in this chapter for starting new ledger pages for the following accounts. Use the accounting stationery provided in your working papers. January 1 of the current year is the date.

Account Name	Account Number	Balance
Cash in Bank	101	$10,000
Accounts Receivable— Mark Cohen	104	2,000
Accounts Payable— Jenco Industries	203	1,000
Tom Torrie, Capital	301	35,000
Admissions Revenue	401	- 0 -

The Posting Process

BEFORE YOU READ

Main Idea
Posting is the process of transferring information from the journal to individual accounts in the ledger.

Read to Learn...
➤ how to post transactions to the general ledger. (p. 168)
➤ how to compute account balances. (p. 174)

AS YOU READ

Instant Recall

Journal The journal is sometimes called the *book of original entry*.

In the last section, you learned how to open accounts in the general ledger. In this section you will learn how to post general journal entries to the ledger. Recall that posting is the process of transferring information from the general journal to individual general ledger accounts. To provide current information to management, the accountant for the Jeep dealer in your area probably posts journal entries to the general ledger every day.

The Fourth Step in the Accounting Cycle: Posting
How Do You Post Transactions?

In Chapter 6 you learned that the general journal is a sort of business diary containing all of the transactions of a business. It is not easy to see the effect of changes in an account by looking at journal entries. To provide a clear picture of how a business transaction changes an account's balance, the information in a journal entry is posted to the general ledger. The purpose of posting, therefore, is to show the impact of business transactions on the individual accounts. The ledger is sometimes called the *book of final entry*.

The size of the business, the number of transactions, and whether the accounting system is manual or computerized all affect how often posting occurs. Ideally, businesses post daily to keep their accounts up-to-date. Regardless of how often posting is performed, the process remains the same.

As in journalizing a transaction, posting to a ledger account is completed from left to right. Let's look at a journal entry for Roadrunner that is ready to be posted to the ledger.

Posting to the Roadrunner General Ledger

Roadrunner's first transaction affects two accounts: **Cash in Bank** and **Maria Sanchez, Capital.** The information in the journal entry is transferred item by item from the journal to each of the accounts affected. As you read about each step in the posting process, refer to **Figure 7–5.**

Locate the account to be debited in the ledger; in this example, **Cash in Bank** is to be debited.

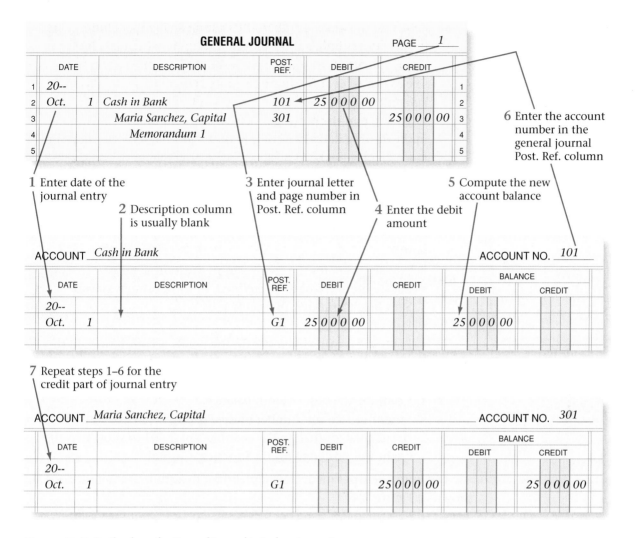

Figure 7–5 Posting from the General Journal to Ledger Accounts

1. Enter the date of the journal entry in the Date column of the account debited. Use the date of the journal entry, not the date on which the posting is done. Write the year and month in the left side of the Date column. It is not necessary to write the year and month for other postings to the same account on the same page unless the month or year changes. The day, however, is always entered.
2. The Description column on the ledger account is usually left blank. Some businesses use this space to write in the source document number.
3. In the ledger account Posting Reference (Post. Ref.) column, identify where the journal entry is recorded. Enter a letter for the specific journal and the journal page number. In this example the letter "G" represents the general journal and the "1" indicates page 1 of the general journal.
4. Enter the debit amount in the Debit column of the ledger account.
5. Compute and record the new account balance in the appropriate balance column. Every amount posted will either increase or decrease the balance of that account.

As You READ

Key Point

Posting to General Ledger Accounts For every journal entry, you will post to at least two ledger accounts.

6. Return to the journal and, in the Posting Reference column, enter the account number of the ledger account to which you just posted the debit part of the journal entry. Be sure it is entered on the same line as the debit entry. In this example enter 101 in the Posting Reference column on the line for **Cash in Bank.**

   This step in the posting process is very important. The notation in the Posting Reference column of the journal indicates that the journal entry has been posted. The posting reference also shows the account to which the entry was posted. If the posting process is interrupted, perhaps by a telephone call, the posting reference signals the point at which posting stopped. *Never* write an account number in the Posting Reference column until *after* you have posted.

7. Repeat steps 1–6 for the credit part of the journal entry.
   - Locate the account to be credited. In this example **Maria Sanchez, Capital**, is to be credited.
   - Enter the date.
   - Enter the posting reference on the ledger account form. In this example, G1 represents the first page of the general journal.
   - Enter the credit amount.
   - Compute the new account balance.
   - Enter the account number in the Posting Reference column of the general journal. In the example enter 301 to show that the credit was posted to **Maria Sanchez, Capital.**

The journal entries made in Chapter 6 for Roadrunner's transactions are shown in **Figure 7–6.**

The Importance of Posting

Posting organizes business transaction details into the proper accounts. As discussed earlier, transactions that are itemized in the general journal are helpful, but do not summarize similar transactions into the same location. Posting summarizes all business transactions so managers can see the cumulative effects on accounts like **Utilities Expense** or **Salaries Expense.**

GENERAL JOURNAL

	DATE		DESCRIPTION	POST. REF.	DEBIT	CREDIT	
1	20--						1
2	Oct.	1	Cash in Bank	101	25 0 0 0 00		2
3			Maria Sanchez, Capital	301		25 0 0 0 00	3
4			Memorandum 1				4
5		2	Office Equipment	120	4 0 0 00		5
6			Maria Sanchez, Capital	301		4 0 0 00	6
7			Memorandum 2				7
8		4	Computer Equipment	115	3 0 0 0 00		8
9			Cash in Bank	101		3 0 0 0 00	9
10			Check 101				10
11		9	Delivery Equipment	125	12 0 0 0 00		11
12			Accounts Payable—North Shore Auto	205		12 0 0 0 00	12
13			Invoice 200				13
14		11	Accounts Receivable—Green Co.	110	2 0 0 00		14
15			Office Equipment	120		2 0 0 00	15
16			Memorandum 3				16
17		12	Accounts Payable—North Shore Auto	205	3 5 0 00		17
18			Cash in Bank	101		3 5 0 00	18
19			Check 102				19
20		14	Cash in Bank	101	2 0 0 00		20
21			Accounts Receivable—Green Co.	110		2 0 0 00	21
22			Receipt 1				22
23		15	Cash in Bank	101	1 2 0 0 00		23
24			Delivery Revenue	401		1 2 0 0 00	24
25			Receipt 2				25
26		16	Rent Expense	510	7 0 0 00		26
27			Cash in Bank	101		7 0 0 00	27
28			Check 103				28
29		18	Advertising Expense	501	7 5 00		29
30			Accounts Payable—Beacon Advertising	201		7 5 00	30
31			Invoice 129				31
32		20	Accounts Receivable—City News	105	1 4 5 0 00		32
33			Delivery Revenue	401		1 4 5 0 00	33
34			Sales Invoice 1				34
35		28	Utilities Expense	515	1 2 5 00		35
36			Cash in Bank	101		1 2 5 00	36
37			Check 104				37
38		29	Maintenance Expense	505	6 0 0 00		38
39			Cash in Bank	101		6 0 0 00	39
40			Check 105				40
41		31	Maria Sanchez, Withdrawals	302	5 0 0 00		41
42			Cash in Bank	101		5 0 0 00	42
43			Check 106				43
44							44

Figure 7–6 General Journal Entries for October Business Transactions

The postings made to the general ledger accounts from these entries are shown in **Figure 7–7** on pages 172–173. Study these illustrations to check your understanding of the posting process.

ACCOUNT _Cash in Bank_ ACCOUNT NO. _101_

DATE	DESCRIPTION	POST. REF.	DEBIT	CREDIT	BALANCE DEBIT	BALANCE CREDIT
20--						
Oct. 1		G1	25 000 00		25 000 00	
4		G1		3 000 00	22 000 00	
12		G1		3 50 00	21 650 00	
14		G1	2 00 00		21 850 00	
15		G1	1 200 00		23 050 00	
16		G1		7 00 00	22 350 00	
28		G1		1 25 00	22 225 00	
29		G1		6 00 00	21 625 00	
31		G1		5 00 00	21 125 00	

ACCOUNT _Accounts Receivable—City News_ ACCOUNT NO. _105_

DATE	DESCRIPTION	POST. REF.	DEBIT	CREDIT	BALANCE DEBIT	BALANCE CREDIT
20--						
Oct. 20		G1	1 450 00		1 450 00	

ACCOUNT _Accounts Receivable—Green Company_ ACCOUNT NO. _110_

DATE	DESCRIPTION	POST. REF.	DEBIT	CREDIT	BALANCE DEBIT	BALANCE CREDIT
20--						
Oct. 11		G1	2 00 00		2 00 00	
14		G1		2 00 00	—	

ACCOUNT _Computer Equipment_ ACCOUNT NO. _115_

DATE	DESCRIPTION	POST. REF.	DEBIT	CREDIT	BALANCE DEBIT	BALANCE CREDIT
20--						
Oct. 4		G1	3 000 00		3 000 00	

ACCOUNT _Office Equipment_ ACCOUNT NO. _120_

DATE	DESCRIPTION	POST. REF.	DEBIT	CREDIT	BALANCE DEBIT	BALANCE CREDIT
20--						
Oct. 2		G1	4 00 00		4 00 00	
11		G1		2 00 00	2 00 00	

ACCOUNT _Delivery Equipment_ ACCOUNT NO. _125_

DATE	DESCRIPTION	POST. REF.	DEBIT	CREDIT	BALANCE DEBIT	BALANCE CREDIT
20--						
Oct. 9		G1	12 000 00		12 000 00	

ACCOUNT _Accounts Payable—Beacon Advertising_ ACCOUNT NO. _201_

DATE	DESCRIPTION	POST. REF.	DEBIT	CREDIT	BALANCE DEBIT	BALANCE CREDIT
20--						
Oct. 18		G1		75 00		75 00

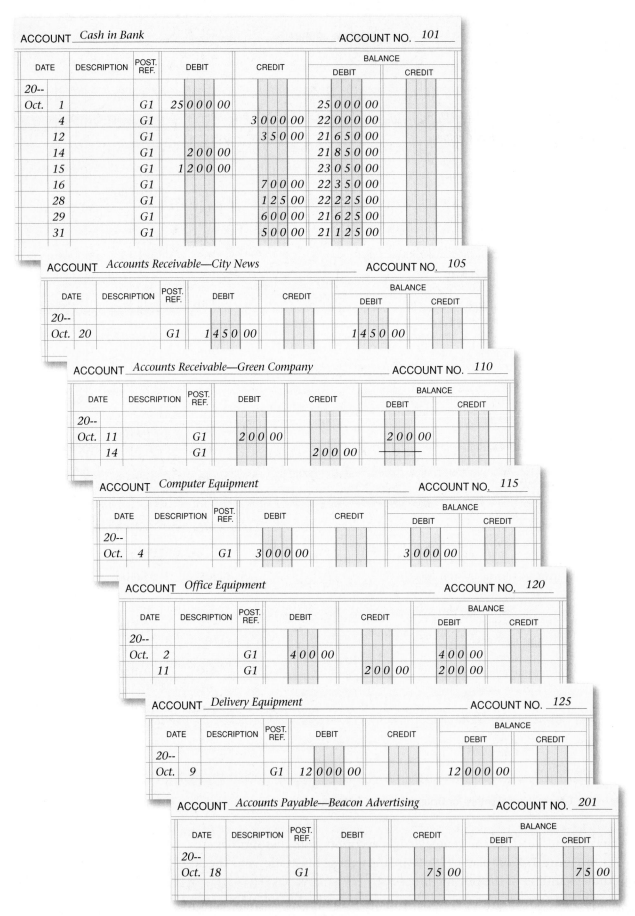

Figure 7–7 Postings to General Ledger Accounts for the Month of October

ACCOUNT _Accounts Payable—North Shore Auto_   **ACCOUNT NO.** _205_

DATE		DESCRIPTION	POST. REF.	DEBIT	CREDIT	BALANCE	
						DEBIT	CREDIT
20--							
Oct.	9		G1		12 0 0 0 00		12 0 0 0 00
	12		G1	3 5 0 00			11 6 5 0 00

ACCOUNT _Maria Sanchez, Capital_   **ACCOUNT NO.** _301_

DATE		DESCRIPTION	POST. REF.	DEBIT	CREDIT	BALANCE	
						DEBIT	CREDIT
20--							
Oct.	1		G1		25 0 0 0 00		25 0 0 0 00
	2		G1		4 0 0 00		25 4 0 0 00

ACCOUNT _Maria Sanchez, Withdrawals_   **ACCOUNT NO.** _302_

DATE	DESCRIPTION	POST. REF.	DEBIT	CREDIT	BALANCE	
					DEBIT	CREDIT
20--						
Oct. 31		G1	5 0 0 00		5 0 0 00	

ACCOUNT _Income Summary_   **ACCOUNT NO.** _303_

DATE	DESCRIPTION	POST. REF.	DEBIT	CREDIT	BALANCE	
					DEBIT	CREDIT

ACCOUNT _Delivery Revenue_   **ACCOUNT NO.** _401_

DATE		DESCRIPTION	POST. REF.	DEBIT	CREDIT	BALANCE	
						DEBIT	CREDIT
20--							
Oct.	15		G1		1 2 0 0 00		1 2 0 0 00
	20		G1		1 4 5 0 00		2 6 5 0 00

ACCOUNT _Advertising Expense_   **ACCOUNT NO.** _501_

DATE		DESCRIPTION	POST. REF.	DEBIT	CREDIT	BALANCE	
						DEBIT	CREDIT
20--							
Oct.	18		G1	7 5 00		7 5 00	

ACCOUNT _Maintenance Expense_   **ACCOUNT NO.** _505_

DATE		DESCRIPTION	POST. REF.	DEBIT	CREDIT	BALANCE	
						DEBIT	CREDIT
20--							
Oct.	29		G1	6 0 0 00		6 0 0 00	

ACCOUNT _Rent Expense_   **ACCOUNT NO.** _510_

DATE		DESCRIPTION	POST. REF.	DEBIT	CREDIT	BALANCE	
						DEBIT	CREDIT
20--							
Oct.	16		G1	7 0 0 00		7 0 0 00	

ACCOUNT _Utilities Expense_   **ACCOUNT NO.** _515_

DATE		DESCRIPTION	POST. REF.	DEBIT	CREDIT	BALANCE	
						DEBIT	CREDIT
20--							
Oct.	28		G1	1 2 5 00		1 2 5 00	

Figure 7–7 Postings to General Ledger Accounts for the Month of October (continued)

General Ledger Account Balances

How Do You Compute Account Balances?

On a four-column ledger account form, each time you post to an account, you also compute and show the new account balance.

Computing a New Account Balance

A rule of thumb for finding a new balance is that debits are added to debits, credits are added to credits, but debits and credits are subtracted. After you post to an account, compute the new account balance as follows:

When the existing account balance is a debit, and

- the amount posted is a debit, ADD the amounts.
- the amount posted is a credit, SUBTRACT the amounts.

When the existing account balance is a credit, and

- the amount posted is a debit, SUBTRACT the amounts.
- the amount posted is a credit, ADD the amounts.

A ledger account usually has space for several postings. Often, blank lines remain after the month's journal entries are posted. To save space the journal entries for more than one month are entered on the same ledger page. The new month and day are entered in the Date column, as in **Figure 7–8.**

ACCOUNT _Cash in Bank_   ACCOUNT NO. _101_

DATE		DESCRIPTION	POST. REF.	DEBIT	CREDIT	BALANCE DEBIT	BALANCE CREDIT
20--							
Oct.	1		G1	25 000 00		25 000 00	
	31		G2		500 00	24 500 00	
Nov.	1		G2		125 00	24 375 00	

Figure 7–8 A Ledger Account with Several Postings

Showing a Zero Balance in a Ledger Account

To show a zero balance after you post a transaction, draw a line across the center of the column—where the normal balance would appear. On October 11 Roadrunner sold a phone for $200 on account to Green Company and received full payment on October 14. When the October 14 journal entry is posted, **Accounts Receivable—Green Company** has a zero balance. The line across the Debit Balance column in **Figure 7–9** means that the account has a zero balance. The line is drawn in the Debit column because the normal balance for this account is a debit.

ACCOUNT _Accounts Receivable—Green Company_   ACCOUNT NO. _110_

DATE		DESCRIPTION	POST. REF.	DEBIT	CREDIT	BALANCE DEBIT	BALANCE CREDIT
20--							
Oct.	11		G1	200 00		200 00	
	14		G1		200 00	——	

Figure 7–9 Showing a Ledger Account with a Zero Balance

AFTER YOU **READ**

Reinforce the Main Idea

Create a diagram like this one to show how information is transferred between the journal and the ledger. For each line, draw an arrowhead to show the direction of the information transfer. The first line is provided as an example.

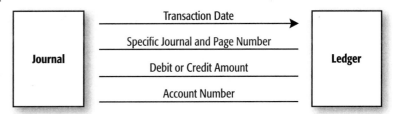

Journal	Transaction Date	Ledger
	Specific Journal and Page Number	
	Debit or Credit Amount	
	Account Number	

 ## Do the Math

As an employee of Always Fresh Bakery, you have been asked to analyze the impact that different sales levels have on the ultimate profit or loss of the business. After posting is completed, you prepare the following line graph to illustrate the sales figures for Always Fresh Bakery. Review the line graph and write a one-paragraph analysis of the impact of sales on the bakery's profit.

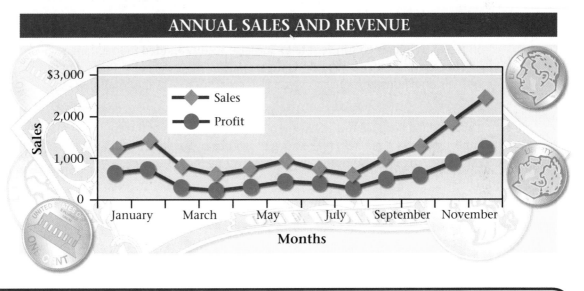

ANNUAL SALES AND REVENUE

Problem 7–2 Posting from the General Journal to the Ledger

Instructions David Serlo made the following cash investment in his business. Use the six-step process to post the entry to the ledger accounts in your working papers.

GENERAL JOURNAL   PAGE _____1_____

	DATE	DESCRIPTION	POST. REF.	DEBIT	CREDIT	
1	20--					1
2	May 1	Cash in Bank		10 0 0 0 00		2
3		David Serlo, Capital			10 0 0 0 00	3
4		Memorandum 101				4

Accounting Careers in Focus

COUNTY AUDITOR
Internal Audit Department,
Maricopa County, Arizona
Ross Tate

Q: What does the internal audit department do?

A: We audit and report on the county's operational and financial activities.

Q: What are your day-to-day responsibilities?

A: I serve as the county government's "eyes and ears" by forming teams to audit all county departments, and investigate financial inconsistencies and possible theft. I meet with managers of different audit teams, assign tasks, and make sure the work gets done.

Q: What are some of the factors that have been key to your success?

A: Continuing education has been key. Through continuing education, you stay on top of developments in your field. It is also recommended to maintain a CPA license and other certifications that can advance your career. Professional journals and industry associations are also great sources of information.

Q: What do you like most about your job?

A: It's rewarding because the government serves the people of the county in many important ways. I can help make a big difference by working in public service. The variety of tasks also makes my job interesting.

Q: What advice do you have for accounting students just beginning their careers?

A: Put in the extra time and effort whether it's asked for or not. This will help you to get ahead quickly and greatly improve the quality of your work.

Tips from . . .
RHI Robert Half International Inc.

Learning is a continuous process—even after you have graduated from school. Build your skills on the job by volunteering for projects beyond your immediate area of responsibility. You can also take courses and join industry associations to remain at the top of your field.

CAREER FACTS

▶ **Nature of the Work:** Supervise internal audits and communicate the results to management; always stay aware of new laws and rules.

▶ **Training or Education Needed:** A bachelor's degree in accounting or finance; a CPA or certified internal auditor (CIA) title.

▶ **Aptitudes, Abilities, and Skills:** Advanced knowledge of generally accepted accounting principles; critical thinking, communication, and technology skills.

▶ **Salary Range:** $35,000 to $120,000 depending on experience, level of responsibility, industry, and location.

▶ **Career Path:** Start by working as an entry-level internal auditor, and then gradually assume more responsibility as you gain knowledge and experience.

Thinking Critically | **In what ways could you demonstrate to an employer that you are a valuable employee?**

Preparing a Trial Balance

In the last section, you learned how to post to the ledger. In this section you will learn how to prepare a trial balance. Accountants use a trial balance to prove that the accounting system is in balance. Preparing a trial balance is the fifth step in the accounting cycle. Every time the accountant for the Jeep dealer in your area posts to the ledger, he or she prepares a trial balance. The trial balance provides assurance that the journal entries are posted properly.

The Fifth Step in the Accounting Cycle: The Trial Balance

What Is the Purpose of a Trial Balance?

After the journal entries have been posted to the accounts in the general ledger, the total of all of the debit balances should equal the total of all of the credit balances. Adding all the debit balances, then adding all the credit balances, and finally comparing the two totals to see whether they are equal is called **proving the ledger** .

A formal way to prove the ledger is to prepare a **trial balance** . A trial balance is a list of all the account names and their current balances. All of the debit balances are added. All of the credit balances are added. The totals are compared. If the totals are the same, the trial balance is in balance. If the totals are not equal, an error was made in journalizing, posting, or preparing the trial balance. You must find the error and correct it before continuing with the next step in the accounting cycle.

The equality of debits and credits does not, however, guarantee that the accounting records do not have errors. An amount might be posted to the wrong account. For example, suppose a credit sale for $500 was posted to the **Cash in Bank** account instead of **Accounts Receivable.** The trial balance remains in balance, but the company's cash is overstated by $500. What if a transaction did not get posted? Two accounts have wrong balances, but the total debits still equal the total credits.

The trial balance for Roadrunner Delivery Service for the month of October is shown in **Figure 7–10** on page 178. The trial balance was prepared on two-column accounting stationery. The account numbers are listed in the far left column. The account names are listed in the next column. All of the debit balances are entered in the first amount column, and all of the credit balances are entered in the second amount column. Trial balances do not have to be prepared on accounting stationery, however. They can be handwritten on plain paper, typed, or prepared on a computer.

BEFORE YOU READ

Main Idea
The trial balance is a proof that total debits equal total credits in the ledger.

Read to Learn...
➤ how to prepare a trial balance. (p. 177)
➤ how to find and correct errors in the trial balance. (p. 178)

Key Terms
proving the ledger
trial balance
transposition error
slide error
correcting entry

		Roadrunner Delivery Service		
		Trial Balance		
		October 31, 20--		
101	Cash in Bank		21 1 2 5 00	
105	Accounts Receivable—City News		1 4 5 0 00	
110	Accounts Receivable—Green Company			
115	Computer Equipment		3 0 0 0 00	
120	Office Equipment		2 0 0 00	
125	Delivery Equipment		12 0 0 0 00	
201	Accounts Payable—Beacon Advertising			7 5 00
205	Accounts Payable—North Shore Auto			11 6 5 0 00
301	Maria Sanchez, Capital			25 4 0 0 00
302	Maria Sanchez, Withdrawals		5 0 0 00	
303	Income Summary			
401	Delivery Revenue			2 6 5 0 00
501	Advertising Expense		7 5 00	
505	Maintenance Expense		6 0 0 00	
510	Rent Expense		7 0 0 00	
515	Utilities Expense		1 2 5 00	
	Totals		39 7 7 5 00	39 7 7 5 00

Figure 7–10 Trial Balance

Finding and Correcting Errors
What Do You Do if You Are Out of Balance?

Anyone who works in accounting understands the saying, "To err is human…" If the debits do not equal the credits, you need to find the errors and correct them.

Finding Errors

Most trial balance errors can be located easily and quickly. When total debits do not equal total credits, follow these steps:

1. Add the debit and credit columns again. You may have added one or both of the columns incorrectly.
2. Find the difference between the debit and credit columns. If this amount is 10, 100, 1,000, and so on, you probably made an addition error. Suppose, for example, you have total debits of $35,245 and total credits of $35,345. The difference is $100, which indicates an addition error is likely. Add the columns again to find the error.
3. Check if the amount you are out of balance is evenly divisible by 9. For example, suppose the difference between the debits and credits is $27. That amount is evenly divisible by 9 (27 ÷ 9 = 3). If the difference is evenly divisible by 9, you may have a transposition error or a slide error. A **transposition error** occurs when two digits within an amount are accidentally reversed, or transposed. For example, the amount $325 may have been written as $352.

A **slide error** occurs when a decimal point is moved by mistake. If you write $1,800 as either $180 or $18,000, you made a slide error.

To find a transposition error or a slide error, check the trial balance amounts against the general ledger account balances to make sure you copied the balances correctly.

As You READ

It's Not What It Seems

Slide When you think of the word *slide,* you might think of playground equipment. In accounting a *slide error* is a number with the decimal point in the wrong place.

4. Make sure that you included all general ledger accounts in the trial balance. Look in the general ledger for an account balance equal to the amount you are out of balance. For example, if the difference between total debits and credits is $725, look in the general ledger for an account with a balance of $725.

5. One of the account balances could have been recorded in the wrong column. That is, a debit was entered in the credit column or a credit was entered in the debit column. To find out if this happened, divide the out-of-balance amount by 2 and check whether the result matches the balance of an account. For example, suppose that the difference between the two columns is $300; $300 divided by 2 is $150. Look in the debit and credit columns for an account balance of $150. Then check to see if the $150 is entered in the wrong column.

6. If you still have not found the error, recompute the balance in each ledger account. You may have an addition or subtraction error on a ledger account form.

7. Finally, check the general ledger accounts to verify that the correct amounts are posted from the journal entries. Also, check to make sure that debit amounts are posted to the debit column and credit amounts are posted to the credit column.

Correcting Entries

When mistakes are made in accounting, one rule applies: *Never erase an error.* The method for correcting an error depends on when and where the error is found. There are three types of errors:

- Error in a journal entry that has not been posted.
- Error in posting to the ledger when the journal entry is correct.
- Error in a journal entry that has been posted.

In Chapter 6 you learned how to handle the first situation. When an error in a journal entry is discovered before posting, you draw a single line through the incorrect item in the journal and write the correction directly above it.

If the journal entry is correct but is posted incorrectly to the ledger, you draw a single line through the incorrect item in the ledger and write the correction directly above it.

When an error in a journal entry is discovered *after* posting, make a **correcting entry** to fix the error.

On November 15 the accountant for Roadrunner found an error in a journal entry made on November 2. A $100 check to pay the electricity bill was journalized and posted to the **Maintenance Expense** account by mistake. The original journal entry is shown in the following T accounts.

Maintenance Expense		Cash in Bank	
Debit	Credit	Debit	Credit
+	−	+	−
100			100

The following T accounts show how the transaction *should* have been recorded.

Utilities Expense		Cash in Bank	
Debit + 100	Credit –	Debit +	Credit – 100

As you can see, the $100 credit to **Cash in Bank** is correct. The error is in the debit part of the November 2 transaction. **Maintenance Expense** is incorrectly debited for $100. To correct the error, **Maintenance Expense** is credited for $100 and **Utilities Expense** is debited for $100.

The accountant wrote Memorandum 70 to notify the accounting clerk of the mistake. The correcting entry, recorded in the general journal, is shown in **Figure 7–11**.

GENERAL JOURNAL   PAGE ___3___

	DATE		DESCRIPTION	POST. REF.	DEBIT	CREDIT	
1	20--						1
2	Nov.	15	Utilities Expense		1 0 0 00		2
3			Maintenance Expense			1 0 0 00	3
4			Memorandum 70				4
5							5

Figure 7–11 Correcting Entry

Posting a correcting entry is similar to any other posting. In the Description column of the ledger accounts, however, the words *Correcting Entry* are written. **Figure 7–12** shows how the correcting entry is posted to the **Maintenance Expense** and **Utilities Expense** accounts.

ACCOUNT _Maintenance Expense_   ACCOUNT NO. _505_

DATE		DESCRIPTION	POST. REF.	DEBIT	CREDIT	BALANCE DEBIT	BALANCE CREDIT
20--							
Oct.	29		G1			6 0 0 00	
Nov.	2		G2	1 0 0 00		7 0 0 00	
	15	Correcting Entry	G3		1 0 0 00	6 0 0 00	

ACCOUNT _Utilities Expense_   ACCOUNT NO. _515_

DATE		DESCRIPTION	POST. REF.	DEBIT	CREDIT	BALANCE DEBIT	BALANCE CREDIT
20--							
Oct.	28		G1	1 2 5 00		1 2 5 00	
Nov.	15	Correcting Entry	G3	1 0 0 00		2 2 5 00	

Figure 7–12 Posting of Correcting Entry

AFTER YOU **READ**

Reinforce the Main Idea

Create a chart like this one to show how to correct errors in three situations.

Where Error Was Found	When Error Was Found	How to Correct the Error
Journal	Before Posting	
Ledger	After Posting	
Journal	After Posting	

Do the Math

1. Compare the numbers in Column 1 to those in Column 2. Find any transposition, slide, or omission errors. Identify the type of error for each line.

2. Using a calculator or adding machine, total Column 1. Correct any errors in Column 2, and then total Column 2. Do the totals of Columns 1 and 2 match?

Column 1	Column 2
$18.00	$180.00
$15,000	$1,500
$222.52	$222.25
$187,235,499.05	$187,235,499.50
$47,988	$47,988
$578,334.99	$5,778,334.99

Problem 7–3 Analyzing a Source Document

Instructions Analyze the transaction that is described in Memorandum 47, and then record and post the required correcting entry in your working papers.

FUNTIME MEMORANDUM 47
AMUSEMENT ARCADE

TO: Accounting Clerk
FROM: Dan Vonderhaar
DATE: May 20, 20--
SUBJECT: Correction of error

On May 10, we purchased an office copier for $1,500. I noticed in the general journal that the entry was recorded and posted to the Computer Equipment account. Please record the necessary entry to correct this error.

Problem 7–4 Recording and Posting a Correcting Entry

Instructions On July 7 Video Connection's accounting supervisor discovered that a July 3 transaction had been recorded incorrectly. The transaction, involving the purchase of advertising in the local newspaper with a $300 check, was incorrectly journalized and posted to the **Rent Expense** account. In your working papers, record and post the correcting entry using Memorandum 13 as the source document.

 VIDEO Connection MEMORANDUM 13

TO: Accounting Clerk
FROM: Accounting Manager
DATE: July 7, 20--
SUBJECT: Correction of error

On July 3, we paid $300 for advertising in the *Daily News Record* that was incorrectly journalized and posted to the Rent Expense account. Please record the necessary entry to correct this error.

Key Concepts

1. *Posting,* which is the fourth step in the accounting cycle, is the process of transferring information from a journal to specific ledger accounts. The *general ledger* is a permanent record organized by account number. In a manual accounting system, information about specific accounts is recorded in *ledger account forms.* In a computerized accounting system, information about accounts is kept in a group of electronic files.

   The purpose of posting is to show the impact of business transactions on the individual accounts. The steps for posting from the general journal to the general ledger are described in the following illustration.

2. Post general journal entries by following these steps:

GENERAL JOURNAL   PAGE ___1___

	DATE		DESCRIPTION	POST. REF.	DEBIT	CREDIT	
1	20--						1
2	Oct.	1	Cash in Bank	101	25 000 00		2
3			Maria Sanchez, Capital	301		25 000 00	3
4			Memorandum 1				4
5							5

1 Enter date of the journal entry

2 Description column is usually blank

3 Enter journal letter and page number in Post. Ref. column

4 Enter the debit amount

5 Compute the new account balance

6 Enter the account number in the general journal Post. Ref. column

ACCOUNT ___Cash in Bank___   ACCOUNT NO. ___101___

DATE		DESCRIPTION	POST. REF.	DEBIT	CREDIT	BALANCE DEBIT	BALANCE CREDIT
20--							
Oct.	1		G1	25 000 00		25 000 00	

7 Repeat steps 1–6 for the credit part of journal entry

ACCOUNT ___Maria Sanchez, Capital___   ACCOUNT NO. ___301___

DATE		DESCRIPTION	POST. REF.	DEBIT	CREDIT	BALANCE DEBIT	BALANCE CREDIT
20--							
Oct.	1		G1		25 000 00		25 000 00

3. After posting has been completed, a trial balance is prepared to prove the ledger. This is the fifth step in the accounting cycle. *Proving the ledger* is making sure that total debits equal total credits.

4. If total debits and total credits are not equal, you must locate and correct the errors. The following trial balance errors are the most common:

   - addition and subtraction errors
   - transpositions
   - slides
   - omissions
   - incorrect debiting or crediting

5. The method for correcting an error depends on when and where the error is found:

   - If the journal entry is wrong and has not yet been posted, draw a line through the incorrect item and write the correct information directly above it.
   - If the journal entry is correct but the error occurred in posting, draw a line through the incorrect item in the ledger and write the correct information directly above it.
   - If the journal entry is wrong and has already been posted, make a *correcting entry*. The correcting entry is posted to the general ledger. It is similar to any other posting except that it includes the words *Correcting Entry* in the Description column.

Key Terms

correcting entry	(p. 179)
general ledger	(p. 164)
ledger account forms	(p. 165)
posting	(p. 164)
proving the ledger	(p. 177)
slide error	(p. 178)
transposition error	(p. 178)
trial balance	(p. 177)

Check Your Understanding

1. **Steps in the Posting Process**
   a. What six steps are required to open a general ledger account?
   b. List the steps in the posting process.
2. **Posting General Journal Entries**
   a. What information is entered in the Posting Reference (Post. Ref.) column of the ledger account? Give an example.
   b. What information is entered in the Posting Reference (Post. Ref.) column of the general journal entry? Give an example.
3. **Trial Balance**
   a. What information does a trial balance contain?
   b. What is the purpose of a trial balance?
4. **Trial Balance Errors**
   a. What steps do you perform to locate trial balance errors?
   b. Distinguish between a slide error and a transposition error and give an example of each.
5. **Correcting Entries**
   a. What is the basic rule concerning mistakes in accounting?
   b. How do you correct an error in a journal entry that has already been posted?

Apply Key Terms

As a junior accounting clerk for Action Sports Outfitters, you are being evaluated for a raise. Your boss wants to see how well you understand basic accounting terminology. He asks you to write a sentence for each of the following terms, showing how you would use each term in connection with Action Sports Outfitters.

correcting entry	proving the ledger
general ledger	slide error
ledger account forms	transposition error
posting	trial balance

Posting to the General Ledger

Making the Transition from a Manual to a Computerized System

Task	Manual Methods	Computerized Methods
Posting to the General Ledger	• Transfer the details of each journal entry to individual ledger accounts. • Calculate the new account balance for each ledger account.	• After each journal entry is entered, amounts are posted automatically into the general ledger. • New account balances are calculated for you.

Peachtree® Q & A

Peachtree Question	Answer
How do I post general journal transactions?	• After entering a journal entry, click **Save**.
What if I find an error in my journal entry after it has been posted?	Changes to journal entries can be made before or after the entry has been posted. 1. From the General Journal Entry window, drop down the *Edit* menu. Select **Edit Record**. 2. Select the entry you want to change. 3. Make the correction. 4. Click **Save**, and then click **Close**.

QuickBooks Q & A

QuickBooks Question	Answer
How do I post general journal transactions?	• After entering a journal entry, click **Save & Close**.
What if I find an error in my journal entry after it has been posted?	Changes to journal entries can be made before or after the entry has been posted. 1. In the Make General Journal Entries window, click the **Previous** or **Next** buttons until you locate the entry to be changed. 2. Make the correction. 3. Click **Save & Close**.

For detailed instructions, see your Glencoe Accounting Chapter Study Guides and Working Papers.

Complete problems using: **Manual** Glencoe Working Papers OR **Peachtree Complete Accounting** Software OR **QuickBooks** Templates

Peachtree®

SMART GUIDE

Step–by–Step Instructions: Problem 7–5

1. Select the problem set for Wilderness Rentals (Prob. 7–5).
2. Rename the company and set the system date.
3. Print a General Ledger report.
4. Complete the Analyze activity.
5. End the session.

QuickBooks

PROBLEM GUIDE

Step–by–Step Instructions: Problem 7–5

1. Restore the Problem 7-5.QBB file.
2. Print a General Ledger report.
3. Complete the Analyze activity.
4. Back up your work.

Peachtree®

SMART GUIDE

Step–by–Step Instructions: Problem 7–6

1. Select the problem set for Hot Suds Car Wash (Prob. 7–6).
2. Rename the company and set the system date.
3. Print a General Ledger Trial Balance report.
4. Complete the Analyze activity.
5. End the session.

Problem 7–5 Posting General Journal Transactions

The accounts used by Wilderness Rentals have been opened and are included in the working papers accompanying this textbook. The general journal transactions for March of the current year are also included.

Instructions Post the transactions recorded on page 1 of the general journal to the accounts in the general ledger.

Analyze Identify the account with the highest debit balance.

Problem 7–6 Preparing a Trial Balance

The ledger accounts for Hot Suds Car Wash are shown in your working papers.

Instructions Prepare a trial balance as of March 31 of the current year.

Analyze Identify the account with the highest credit balance.

Problem 7–7 Journalizing and Posting Business Transactions

A partial chart of accounts for Kits & Pups Grooming follows.

General Ledger	
101 Cash in Bank	301 Abe Shultz, Capital
105 Accts. Rec.—J. Alvarez	305 Abe Shultz, Withdrawals
120 Grooming Supplies	401 Boarding Revenue
130 Office Furniture	405 Grooming Revenue
140 Grooming Equipment	525 Salaries Expense
205 Accts. Pay.—Dogs & Cats Inc.	

Instructions

1. In your working papers, open an account in the general ledger for each of these accounts.
2. Record the March transactions on page 1 of the general journal.
3. Post each journal entry to the appropriate ledger account.
4. Prove the ledger by preparing a trial balance.

Date	Transactions
Mar 1	Abe Shultz invested $5,000 in the business, Memorandum 51.
3	Abe Shultz transferred a desk and chairs valued at $1,200 to the business, Memorandum 52.

CONTINUE

Date		Transactions
Mar.	5	Issued Check 551 for $300 for grooming supplies.
	7	Bought grooming equipment on account for $1,800 from Dogs & Cats Inc., Invoice DC201.
	9	Groomed Juan Alvarez's show dogs on account, $400, Sales Invoice 350.
	12	Paid Dogs & Cats Inc. $900 on account, Check 552.
	15	Issued Check 553 for $500 to pay the office secretary's salary.
	18	Abe Shultz withdrew $1,000 cash from the business, Check 554.
	20	Deposited $1,400 received from clients for boarding their pets, Receipts 477–480.
	24	Wrote Check 555 for $900 to Dogs & Cats Inc. to apply on account.
	26	Received a check for $400 from Juan Alvarez on account, Receipt 481.

Analyze   **Identify the temporary accounts.**

Problem 7–8 Journalizing and Posting Business Transactions

The chart of accounts for Outback Guide Service follows.

General Ledger

101	Cash in Bank	301	Juanita Ortega, Capital
115	Accts. Rec.—Podaski Systems Inc.	302	Juanita Ortega, Withdrawals
140	Computer Equipment	401	Guide Service Revenue
145	Hiking Equipment	501	Advertising Expense
150	Rafting Equipment		
205	Accts. Pay.—Peak Equipment Inc.		
207	Accts. Pay.—Premier Processors		

Instructions

1. In your working papers, open an account in the general ledger for each account in the chart of accounts.
2. Record the following transactions on page 1 of the general journal.
3. Post each journal entry to the appropriate accounts in the ledger.
4. Prove the ledger by preparing a trial balance.

Date		Transactions
Mar.	1	Invested $20,000 in cash and transferred rafting equipment valued at $5,000 to the business, Memorandum 35.
	3	Purchased $600 in hiking equipment on account from Peak Equipment Inc., Invoice 101.

CONTINUE

QuickBooks

PROBLEM GUIDE

Step–by–Step Instructions: Problem 7–6

1. Restore the Problem 7-6.QBB file.
2. Print a Trial Balance report.
3. Complete the Analyze activity.
4. Back up your work.

Peachtree®

SMART GUIDE

Step–by–Step Instructions: Problem 7–7

1. Select the problem set for Kits & Pups Grooming (Prob. 7–7).
2. Rename the company and set the system date.
3. Enter all of the general journal transactions.
4. Print a General Journal report.
5. Proof your work.
6. Print a General Ledger report and a General Ledger Trial Balance report.
7. Complete the Analyze activity.
8. End the session.

QuickBooks

PROBLEM GUIDE

Step–by–Step Instructions: Problem 7–7

1. Restore the Problem 7-7.QBB file.
2. Enter all of the general journal transactions.
3. Print a Journal report.
4. Proof your work.
5. Print a General Ledger report and a Trial Balance report.
6. Complete the Analyze activity.
7. Back up your work.

Date	Transactions
Mar. 5	Bought a $2,800 computer from Premier Processors and agreed to pay for it within 60 days, Invoice 616.
7	Deposited $700 cash received from clients, Receipts 310–315.
9	Paid $400 to the *Daily Courier* for an ad, Check 652.
12	Sent a bill for $900 to Podaski Systems Inc. for conducting a group rafting trip for them, Sales Invoice 352.
15	Juanita Ortega wrote a check for $800 for personal use, Check 653.
18	Paid Premier Processors $1,400 to apply on account, Check 654.
22	Received $900 from Podaski Systems Inc. in full payment for the amount owed, Receipt 316.
27	Bought a $500 television ad with LIVE TV, Check 655.
28	Paid Peak Equipment Inc. $600 by writing Check 656.

Analyze | **Calculate the total change in accounts payable.**

SOURCE DOCUMENT PROBLEM

Problem 7–8

Use the source documents in your working papers to complete this problem.

Peachtree®

SMART GUIDE

Step–by–Step Instructions: Problem 7–8

1. Select the problem set for Outback Guide Service (Prob. 7–8).
2. Rename the company and set the system date.
3. Enter all of the general journal transactions.
4. Print a General Journal report.
5. Proof your work.
6. Print a General Ledger report and a General Ledger Trial Balance report.
7. Complete the Analyze activity.
8. End the session.

Peachtree®

SMART GUIDE

Step–by–Step Instructions: Problem 7–9

1. Select the problem set for Showbiz Video (Prob. 7–9).
2. Rename the company and set the system date.
3. Correct the general journal entries based on the auditor's report.
4. Print a General Journal report and a General Ledger report.
5. Proof your work.
6. Complete the Analyze activity.
7. End the session.

CHALLENGE PROBLEM
Problem 7–9 Recording and Posting Correcting Entries

An auditor reviewed the accounting records of Showbiz Video. The auditor wrote a list of transactions, outlined below, describing the errors discovered in the March records. The general journal for March and a portion of the general ledger are included in your working papers.

Instructions

1. Record correcting entries on general journal page 22. Use *March 31* as the date and *Memorandum 50* as the source document for all correcting entries.
2. Some errors will not require correcting entries but will require a general ledger correction. Make the appropriate general ledger corrections.
3. Post all correcting entries to the general ledger accounts.

Date	Transactions
Mar. 3	The $125 purchase was for office supplies.
7	A $200 payment to a creditor, Broad Street Office Supply, was not posted to the account.
13	Greg Failla withdrew $1,200 from the business for personal use.
17	Cash totaling $2,000 was received for video rentals.
19	A $75 receipt from Shannon Flannery was posted as $57.
27	Greg Failla invested an additional $3,000 in the business.
29	The revenue of $1,000 was for video rentals.

Analyze | **Compute the amount that Greg Failla, Capital was overstated or understated before the correcting entries were posted.**

Practice your test-taking skills! The questions on this page are reprinted with permission from national organizations:

- Future Business Leaders of America
- Business Professionals of America

Use a separate sheet of paper to record your answers.

Future Business Leaders of America

MULTIPLE CHOICE

1. An account balance is

    a. the total of the credit side of the account.

    b. the total of the debit side of the account.

    c. the difference between the increases and decreases recorded in the account.

    d. Assets = Liabilities + Owner's equity.

    e. unchanged by posting debits and credits to the account.

2. An error in posting may cause

    a. income to be overstated or understated on the income statement.

    b. a business to pay too much to a vendor.

    c. cash on hand to be less than the balance in the cash account.

    d. all of the above.

3. When preparing a trial balance, which of the following would not be considered a procedure?

    a. Check to see if both columns equal.

    b. Double rule both columns.

    c. Write the general ledger account names in the work sheet account name column.

    d. All of these are correct procedures.

    e. None of these answers.

Business Professionals of America

MULTIPLE CHOICE

4. When posting to the general ledger accounts, the information in the Post. Ref. Column of each ledger account refers to

    a. the transaction's source document.

    b. the account number.

    c. the journal and page number.

    d. the date.

5. The process of transferring information from the journal to the individual general ledger accounts is called

    a. journalizing

    b. carrying forward

    c. transferring

    d. posting

Need More Help?

Go to **glencoeaccounting.glencoe.com** and click on **Student Center**. Click on **Winning Competitive Events** and select **Chapter 7.**

- **Practice Questions and Test-Taking Tips**
- **Concept Capsules and Terminology**

The General Ledger and the Trial Balance

1. What is the purpose of each amount column in the four-column ledger account form?
2. Describe how correcting an error discovered after a transaction is posted is different from correcting an error before it is posted.
3. In your trial balance, the debits equal $18,000 and the credits equal $18,810. What are the most likely reasons for the difference?
4. Read the answer to "How do I post general journal transactions?" for Peachtree or QuickBooks on page 185. Identify the step(s) of the accounting cycle described in the answer.
5. Assume that you started a service business by depositing cash into a business checking account, purchasing various assets, and incurring a number of expenses. You have commitments from customers and you will start earning revenue next week. Develop a system for keeping accounting records.
6. What if your trial balance were out of balance by a small amount, for example by $8.39? Is it worthwhile to find the reason for differences? Why or why not?

Service Business: Accounting Services

Joel Rivlin studied accounting in college and then worked as an accountant for a local real estate company. After becoming a CPA, Joel decided to start his own company, Joel Rivlin, CPA.

Robert's Excavating Services came to Joel with a problem. The company's trial balance shows total debits of $76,240 and total credits of $75,090. The owner knows that clients paid for services worth at least $2,500 during the month, but the **Service Revenue** account balance is only $800. The owner also wrote a check for $550 for advertising, but the **Advertising Expense** account shows a zero balance.

INSTRUCTIONS

1. Describe what Joel should do to find the problems.
2. Suggest probable causes for the trial balance being out of balance.

Meeting a Deadline

Imagine that you are an accounting clerk for Ace Hardware. The store manager has asked you to prepare the trial balance. The totals on the trial balance are not equal and you cannot find the error. You realize that the trial balance is due at the end of the day. You are frustrated and consider changing one of the account balances just to get the trial balance to balance.

ETHICAL DECISION MAKING

1. What are the ethical issues?
2. What are the alternatives?
3. Who are the affected parties?
4. How do the alternatives affect the parties?
5. What would you do?

Teaching the Posting Process

You have been asked to teach new accounting clerks how to post business transactions. Create a written step-by-step guide to give to clerks on their first day on the job. Create an imaginary business transaction to illustrate the process.

Interpreting and Communicating Information

Every worker must learn how to interpret information and communicate effectively with co-workers, customers, and superiors.

ON THE JOB

As an accounting clerk for New Wave Inc., a surfboard manufacturer, one of your duties is to audit the accounting records and make the necessary corrections. Former employees did not always maintain the records accurately. The owner, Ron Lee, has asked you to provide written explanations for each error discovered in your audit.

INSTRUCTIONS

1. During an audit you discover a transposition error. An invoice for $510.00 payable to Marketing Pros was recorded and posted as $150.00. How do you correct this error?
2. Using word processing software, write a memo to Mr. Lee explaining how you corrected the error.

English: The Link Language

If business people from Sweden and Japan were conducting business, they would probably communicate in English—a language that both are likely to speak and understand. In international business, English is known as the link language. Although English is the third-most spoken native language in the world, it is the most widely learned second language. Approximately 375 million people speak English as a second language. The next time you turn on your computer, consider that more than 80 percent of the information stored in the world's computers is in English.

INSTRUCTIONS Justify why you think English is or is not a good choice for an international business "link" language.

Your Personal Balances

Knowing how to find accounting errors can help you in your personal life. Personal records that should be checked for accuracy include statements for bank accounts and credit cards; catalog invoices; and bills for medical services, insurance, and utilities. Verify all invoices before paying them.

PERSONAL FINANCE ACTIVITY Assume that you just received a statement from your credit card company. How would you go about checking its accuracy? List the items you would verify.

PERSONAL FINANCE ONLINE Log on to **glencoeaccounting.glencoe.com** and click on **Student Center.** Click on **Making It Personal** and select **Chapter 7.**

Setting Up Accounting Records for a Sole Proprietorship

Main Task

▶ Set up the accounting records and perform the daily activities for Canyon.com Web Sites.

Summary of Steps

▶ Open general ledger accounts.

▶ Analyze, journalize, and post transactions.

▶ Prepare a trial balance.

Why It's Important

▶ You could one day work with a sole proprietor as he or she starts a business from scratch. You might even open your own business!

Canyon.com Web Sites

Company Background: Whether you are interested in a Web site for your new hair salon or a corporate intranet site, Canyon .com Web Sites can provide design, hosting, and maintenance services for the small mom-and-pop business and the multinational corporation alike. Jack Hines, owner of Canyon, is known for his unique and dynamic presentations on the Web. His creativity and knowledge of Web culture makes him a success in electronic content delivery.

Organization: Canyon is organized as a sole proprietorship. The business is fully owned and operated by Jack Hines.

Your Job Responsibilities: As Canyon's accounting clerk, use the accounting stationery in your working papers for these tasks.

(1) Open a general ledger account for each account in the chart of accounts.
(2) Analyze each business transaction.
(3) Enter each business transaction in the general journal, page 1.
(4) Post each journal entry to the appropriate accounts in the general ledger.
(5) Prove the general ledger by preparing a trial balance.

CHART OF ACCOUNTS
Canyon.com Web Sites

ASSETS

101	Cash in Bank
105	Accts. Rec.–Andrew Hospital
110	Accts. Rec.–Indiana Trucking
115	Accts Rec.–Sunshine Products
130	Office Supplies
135	Office Equipment
140	Office Furniture
145	Web Server

LIABILITIES

205	Accts. Pay.–Computer Specialists Inc.
210	Accts. Pay.–Office Systems
215	Accts. Pay.–Service Plus Software Inc.

OWNER'S EQUITY

301	Jack Hines, Capital
305	Jack Hines, Withdrawals

REVENUE

401	Web Service Fees

EXPENSES

505	Membership Expense
506	Telecommunications Expense
507	Rent Expense
508	Utilities Expense

Canyon.com Web Sites (continued)

| Complete the project using: | **Manual** Glencoe Working Papers | OR | **Peachtree Complete Accounting** Software | OR | **QuickBooks** Templates |

Business Transactions: Jack Hines, owner of Canyon.com Web Sites, began business operations on May 1 of this year. During the month of May, the business completed the transactions that follow.

Date	Transactions
May 1	Jack Hines invested $50,000 in the business, Memorandum 1.
2	The owner, Jack Hines, invested a desktop computer and printer (Office Equipment) $3,500, Memorandum 2.
2	Issued Check 101 for $125 for the purchase of office supplies.
3	Bought office furniture for $2,700 on account from Office Systems, Invoice 457.
7	Bought a Web server from Computer Specialists Inc. on account for $35,000, Invoice WS4658421.
9	Received $1,000 from James Market for Web site services, Receipt 101.
11	Completed Web site design services for Andrew Hospital to be paid later, Invoice 101, $3,000.
12	Bought software for the Web server (Web Server) on account from Service Plus Software Inc., Invoice 876, $10,000.
14	Wrote Check 102 for $118 to pay the electric bill.
15	Jack Hines withdrew $2,500 for personal expenses, Check 103.
17	Completed Web site design on account for Sunshine Products, Invoice 102, $5,000.
18	Bought a filing cabinet (Office Furniture) for $275, Check 104.
19	Received a check for $4,000 as payment for Web site maintenance for one year to a client, Receipt 102.
20	Provided design services on account to Indiana Trucking, Invoice 103 for $2,000.
21	Prepared Receipt 103, $2,500, received on account, Sunshine Products.
22	Paid $4,900 for telecommunication services for the period May 1–May 31, Check 105.
22	Wrote check 106 for $3,333 to Service Plus Software Inc. as payment on account.
25	Sent Check 107 for $2,000 to Office Systems as payment on account.
26	Received $1,000 for two months of Web services, Receipt 104.
27	Paid the dues for membership in the All Inclusive Group for $7,000, Check 108.
30	Wrote Check 109 for the monthly rent $750.
30	Withdrew $2,500 for personal expenses, Check 110.
30	Sent Check 111 for $25,000 to Computer Specialists Inc., as payment on account.

Analyze **Compute the total of all the checks written during May.**

Peachtree®

SMART GUIDE

Step–by–Step Instructions:
1. Select the problem set for Canyon.com Web Sites (MP-1).
2. Rename the company and set the system date.
3. Record all of the business transactions using the **General Journal Entry** option.
4. Print a General Journal report.
5. Proof your work.
6. Print a General Ledger report.
7. Print a Trial Balance.
8. Complete the Analyze activity.
9. Complete the Audit Test.
10. End the session.

QuickBooks

PROBLEM GUIDE

Step–by–Step Instructions:
1. Restore the Problem Mini Practice 1.QBB file.
2. Record all of the business transactions using the **Make General Journal Entries** option.
3. Print a Journal report.
4. Proof your work.
5. Print a General Ledger report.
6. Print a Trial Balance.
7. Complete the Analyze activity.
8. Complete the Audit Test.
9. Back up your work.

The Six-Column Work Sheet

What You'll Learn

1. Explain the purpose of the work sheet.

2. Describe the parts of a six-column work sheet.

3. Prepare a six-column work sheet.

4. Calculate net income and net loss.

5. Define the accounting terms introduced in this chapter.

Why It's Important

The work sheet is the tool used to complete the final steps of the accounting cycle.

BEFORE YOU READ

Predict

1. What does the chapter title tell you?
2. What do you already know about this subject from personal experience?
3. What have you learned about this in the earlier chapters?
4. What gaps exist in your knowledge of this subject?

Exploring the *Real World* of Business

SUMMARIZING RESULTS

American Express Company

"Don't leave home without it." For decades, people and businesses worldwide have followed the ad slogan's advice and used their **American Express** card for purchases. The **American Express Company**, originally founded as a delivery service in 1850, is also the world's top travel agency.

American Express would not want to leave home without its chief executive officer, Kenneth Chenault. Described as a tough-minded yet warm person, this CEO gets results. His leadership during difficult times enabled the company to not only survive, but thrive.

The company's expenses include advertising, promotions, and salaries. Commissions from retailers provide large revenues. Accountants at **American Express** use tools like work sheets to summarize revenues and expenses.

What Do You Think?

Why do you think summarizing expenses and revenues might help manage a business like **American Express**?

Working in the *Real World*

APPLYING YOUR ACCOUNTING KNOWLEDGE

When you prepare to write a research paper, you probably use note cards, word processing software, or a database program to collect and organize information. You may also write a rough draft of your paper, further organizing the information. In accounting a work sheet is a tool used to collect and to organize financial information. You will learn how to create a work sheet in this chapter.

Personal Connection

1. How might your ability to organize information be valuable to your employer?
2. Why is it important for financial and other information to be organized in a certain way?

Online Connection

Go to **glencoeaccounting.glencoe.com** and click on **Student Center.** Click on **Working in the Real World** and select **Chapter 8** to learn more about the real-world workplace.

Preparing the Work Sheet

BEFORE YOU READ

Main Idea
The work sheet organizes general ledger account information for the financial statements.

Read to Learn...
➤ the purpose of a work sheet. (p. 197)
➤ the sections of a work sheet. (p. 197)

Key Terms
work sheet
ruling

As you learned in Chapter 6, the length of an accounting period can vary. The maximum period covered by the accounting cycle is one year. The first five steps of the accounting cycle are performed frequently during the cycle. The last four steps—preparing a work sheet, preparing financial statements, journalizing and posting closing entries, and preparing a post-closing trial balance—are performed at the end of the accounting period. Look at **Figure 8–1.** In this chapter you will learn how to prepare a work sheet, the sixth step of the accounting cycle. With this step, businesses like your local Midas Muffler shop or a Nike Outlet collect information from their ledger accounts and record this information on a single form.

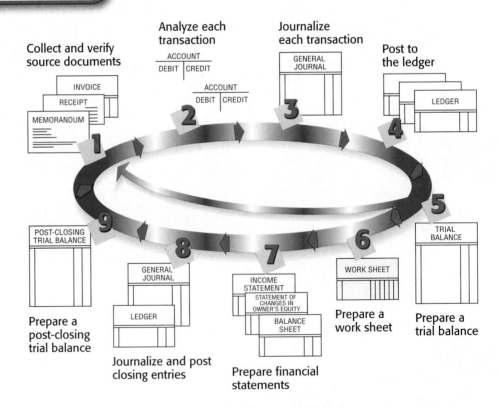

Figure 8–1 Steps in the Accounting Cycle with Step 6 Highlighted

The Sixth Step of the Accounting Cycle: The Work Sheet

What Is the Purpose of a Work Sheet?

A **work sheet** is just what its name implies—a working paper used to collect information from the ledger accounts in one place. Like the T account, the work sheet is a tool that the accountant uses. With the work sheet, an accountant gathers all of the information needed to prepare the financial statements and to complete the other end-of-period activities.

A work sheet may be prepared in pencil on standard multicolumn accounting paper. The paper comes in several sizes and is usually printed without column headings. Blank spaces for column headings allow the accountant to enter the headings needed by a particular business. The work sheet can also be prepared using computer spreadsheet software.

The Work Sheet Sections

How Is the Work Sheet Organized?

The Roadrunner Delivery Service work sheet, shown in **Figure 8–2**, has five sections:

1. the heading
2. the Account Name section
3. the Trial Balance section
4. the Income Statement section
5. the Balance Sheet section

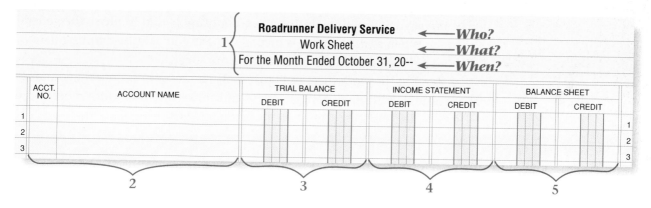

The Account Name section includes a column for the account number and a column for the account name. The Trial Balance, Income Statement, and Balance Sheet sections have Debit and Credit amount columns. The six amount columns give this work sheet its name: the six-column work sheet.

Figure 8–2 Six-Column Work Sheet

The Work Sheet Heading

The work sheet heading contains three kinds of information:

1. The name of the business *(Who?)*
2. The name of the accounting form *(What?)*
3. The period covered by the work sheet *(When?)*

Notice how these elements are positioned on the work sheet in **Figure 8–2.** Follow this format when preparing the heading of any work sheet.

Roadrunner Delivery Service

Work Sheet

For the Month Ended October 31, 20--

	ACCT. NO.	ACCOUNT NAME	TRIAL BALANCE DEBIT	TRIAL BALANCE CREDIT	INCOME STATEMENT DEBIT	INCOME STATEMENT CREDIT	BALANCE SHEET DEBIT	BALANCE SHEET CREDIT	
1	101	Cash in Bank	21125 00						1
2	105	Accts. Rec.—City News	1450 00						2
3	110	Accts. Rec.—Green Company	—						3
4	115	Computer Equipment	3000 00						4
5	120	Office Equipment	200 00						5
6	125	Delivery Equipment	12000 00						6
7	201	Accts. Pay.—Beacon Advertising		75 00					7
8	205	Accts. Pay.—North Shore Auto		11650 00					8
9	301	Maria Sanchez, Capital		25400 00					9
10	302	Maria Sanchez, Withdrawals	500 00						10
11	303	Income Summary	—	—					11
12	401	Delivery Revenue		2650 00					12
13	501	Advertising Expense	75 00						13
14	505	Maintenance Expense	600 00						14
15	510	Rent Expense	700 00						15
16	515	Utilities Expense	125 00						16
17									17

Figure 8–3 Work Sheet with Account Names and Trial Balance Amounts

The Account Name Section

Information for the Account Name and Trial Balance sections comes from the general ledger accounts. In Chapter 7 you prepared a trial balance by listing the account names and their final balances. A trial balance can be prepared at any time during the accounting period to prove the general ledger. When a trial balance is prepared at the end of an accounting period, though, it is prepared as a part of the work sheet.

Look at the work sheet in **Figure 8–3**. The account numbers and names are from Roadrunner's general ledger and are listed on the work sheet in the same order that they appear in the general ledger:

- Assets
- Liabilities
- Owner's Equity
- Revenue
- Expenses

All of the general ledger accounts are listed on the work sheet, even those that have a zero balance. Listing all of the accounts avoids accidentally omitting an account and ensures that the work sheet contains all accounts needed to prepare the financial reports.

The Trial Balance Section

The end-of-period balance in the general ledger for each account is entered in the appropriate amount column of the Trial Balance section. Accounts with debit balances are entered in the Trial Balance Debit column. Accounts with credit balances are entered in the Trial Balance Credit column.

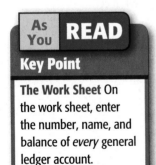

As You READ

Key Point

The Work Sheet On the work sheet, enter the number, name, and balance of *every* general ledger account.

If an account has a zero balance at the end of the period, a line is drawn in the normal balance column. Notice in **Figure 8–3** that a line was drawn in the Trial Balance Debit column for **Accounts Receivable—Green Company.** Lines were also recorded in the Trial Balance Debit and Credit columns for **Income Summary** since this account does not have a normal balance side. You will learn more about the **Income Summary** account in Chapter 10.

Ruling the Trial Balance Section. Ruling means "drawing a line." In accounting a single rule, or line, drawn under a column of amounts means that the entries above the rule are ready to be totaled. After all account names and balances have been entered on the work sheet, a single rule is drawn under the last entry and across both amount columns of the Trial Balance section as shown in **Figure 8–4.** The Debit and Credit columns are now ready for totaling.

Totaling the Trial Balance Section. If the ledger balances, the total debits will equal the total credits. Look at **Figure 8–4.** The totals match, with each column totaling $39,775. Since total debits equal total credits, a double rule is drawn across both amount columns just beneath the totals. This double rule means that the amounts just above it are totals and that no other entries will be made in the Trial Balance columns.

If the total debits do not equal the total credits, there is an error. Find and correct the error before completing the work sheet. Procedures for locating errors are discussed in Chapter 7.

Roadrunner Delivery Service

Work Sheet

For the Month Ended October 31, 20--

	ACCT. NO.	ACCOUNT NAME	TRIAL BALANCE		INCOME STATEMENT		BALANCE SHEET		
			DEBIT	CREDIT	DEBIT	CREDIT	DEBIT	CREDIT	
1	101	Cash in Bank	21125 00						1
2	105	Accts. Rec.—City News	1450 00						2
3	110	Accts. Rec.—Green Company	—						3
4	115	Computer Equipment	3000 00						4
5	120	Office Equipment	200 00						5
6	125	Delivery Equipment	12000 00						6
7	201	Accts. Pay.—Beacon Advertising		75 00					7
8	205	Accts. Pay.—North Shore Auto		11650 00					8
9	301	Maria Sanchez, Capital		25400 00					9
10	302	Maria Sanchez, Withdrawals	500 00						10
11	303	Income Summary	—	—					11
12	401	Delivery Revenue		2650 00					12
13	501	Advertising Expense	75 00						13
14	505	Maintenance Expense	600 00						14
15	510	Rent Expense	700 00						15
16	515	Utilities Expense	125 00						16
17			39775 00	39775 00					17
18									18

Figure 8–4 Work Sheet with Trial Balance Section Completed

AFTER YOU **READ**

Reinforce the Main Idea

Create a diagram similar to this one. List the information that is transferred from the general ledger to the worksheet. Add answer lines as needed.

Information Transferred

| General Ledger | → → → | Work Sheet |

 ## Do the Math

The columns in the Trial Balance section of the work sheet have different totals:

Debit total = $34,800   Credit total = $35,600

The accountant discovered that the balance for **Advertising Expense** had been entered in the Credit column instead of the Debit column. Calculate the balance for the **Advertising Expense** account that should have been entered in the Debit column. What is the new total of the Debit column and Credit column?

Problem 8–1 Entering Account Balances on the Work Sheet

The following accounts appear on the work sheet for Lee's Bike Shop.

Store Equipment	Scott Lee, Capital	Scott Lee, Withdrawals
Rent Expense	Advertising Expense	Maintenance Expense
Service Fees Revenue	Accts. Rec.—John Langer	Office Supplies
Accts. Pay.—Rubino Supply		

Instructions Use a form similar to the one below in your working papers. Classify each account and use an "X" to indicate whether the account balance is entered in the Debit or the Credit column of the Trial Balance section. The first account is completed as an example.

Account Name	Classification	Trial Balance	
		Debit	Credit
Store Equipment	Asset	X	

Problem 8–2 Analyzing a Source Document

Instructions Based on the invoice presented here, answer the following questions in your working papers.

1. Which company shipped the supplies?
2. Which company ordered the supplies?
3. On what date were the supplies received?
4. What does one box of file folders cost?
5. How many ring binders were ordered?
6. What is the invoice number?

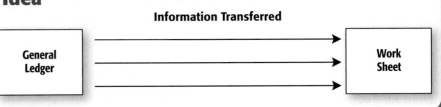

Completing the Work Sheet

In the previous section you learned how to set up the work sheet and prove the Trial Balance section. In this section you will learn how to extend the account balances and compute net income or net loss.

The Balance Sheet and Income Statement Sections

What Are the Balance Sheet and Income Statement?

The balance sheet and income statement are financial statements prepared at the end of the accounting period. The work sheet organizes the information for these reports.

The Balance Sheet Section

The Balance Sheet section of the work sheet contains the asset, liability, and owner's equity accounts. After proving the Trial Balance section, *extend,* or transfer, the appropriate amounts to the Balance Sheet section. To do this, copy the Trial Balance section amounts for the asset, liability, and owner's equity accounts to the appropriate Balance Sheet amount columns. Start with the first account and extend each account balance. Extend debit amounts to the Balance Sheet Debit column. Extend credit amounts to the Balance Sheet Credit column. **Figure 8–5** on page 202 shows the balances extended to the Balance Sheet section.

The Income Statement Section

The next step in completing the work sheet is to extend the appropriate account balances to the Income Statement section. The Income Statement section contains the revenue and expense accounts. After transferring the asset, liability, and owner's equity account balances to the Balance Sheet section, extend the revenue and expense account balances to the Income Statement section. Revenue accounts have a normal credit balance, so extend their balances to the Income Statement Credit column. Since expense accounts have a normal debit balance, extend expense account balances to the Debit column of the Income Statement section. **Figure 8–6** on page 202 shows the amounts in the Debit and Credit columns of the Income Statement section.

Totaling the Income Statement and Balance Sheet Sections

After all amounts have been extended to the Balance Sheet and Income Statement sections, these sections are totaled. A single rule drawn across

BEFORE YOU READ

Main Idea
After completing the work sheet, you will know the net income or net loss for the accounting period.

Read to Learn...
➤ how amounts are entered in the work sheet sections. (p. 201)
➤ how to calculate net income. (p. 203)
➤ how to enter totals. (p. 205)
➤ a summary of steps used to prepare a work sheet. (p. 206)

Key Terms
matching principle
net income
net loss

As You READ

Compare and Contrast

Income Statement and Balance Sheet Sections
How are the Income Statement and Balance Sheet sections similar? How are they different?

Roadrunner Delivery Service
Work Sheet
For the Month Ended October 31, 20--

ACCT. NO.	ACCOUNT NAME	TRIAL BALANCE DEBIT	TRIAL BALANCE CREDIT	INCOME STATEMENT DEBIT	INCOME STATEMENT CREDIT	BALANCE SHEET DEBIT	BALANCE SHEET CREDIT	
1	101 Cash in Bank	21 125 00				21 125 00		1
2	105 Accts. Rec.—City News	1 450 00				1 450 00		2
3	110 Accts. Rec.—Green Company							3
4	115 Computer Equipment	3 000 00				3 000 00		4
5	120 Office Equipment	200 00				200 00		5
6	125 Delivery Equipment	12 000 00				12 000 00		6
7	201 Accts. Pay.—Beacon Advertising		75 00				75 00	7
8	205 Accts. Pay.—North Shore Auto		11 650 00				11 650 00	8
9	301 Maria Sanchez, Capital		25 400 00				25 400 00	9
10	302 Maria Sanchez, Withdrawals	500 00				500 00		10
11	303 Income Summary							11
12	401 Delivery Revenue		2 650 00					12
13	501 Advertising Expense	75 00						13
14	505 Maintenance Expense	600 00						14
15	510 Rent Expense	700 00						15
16	515 Utilities Expense	125 00						16
17		39 775 00	39 775 00					17
18								18

Figure 8–5 Work Sheet with Trial Balance Amounts Extended to Balance Sheet Section

Roadrunner Delivery Service
Work Sheet
For the Month Ended October 31, 20--

ACCT. NO.	ACCOUNT NAME	TRIAL BALANCE DEBIT	TRIAL BALANCE CREDIT	INCOME STATEMENT DEBIT	INCOME STATEMENT CREDIT	BALANCE SHEET DEBIT	BALANCE SHEET CREDIT	
1	101 Cash in Bank	21 125 00				21 125 00		1
2	105 Accts. Rec.—City News	1 450 00				1 450 00		2
3	110 Accts. Rec.—Green Company							3
4	115 Computer Equipment	3 000 00				3 000 00		4
5	120 Office Equipment	200 00				200 00		5
6	125 Delivery Equipment	12 000 00				12 000 00		6
7	201 Accts. Pay.—Beacon Advertising		75 00				75 00	7
8	205 Accts. Pay.—North Shore Auto		11 650 00				11 650 00	8
9	301 Maria Sanchez, Capital		25 400 00				25 400 00	9
10	302 Maria Sanchez, Withdrawals	500 00				500 00		10
11	303 Income Summary							11
12	401 Delivery Revenue		2 650 00		2 650 00			12
13	501 Advertising Expense	75 00		75 00				13
14	505 Maintenance Expense	600 00		600 00				14
15	510 Rent Expense	700 00		700 00				15
16	515 Utilities Expense	125 00		125 00				16
17		39 775 00	39 775 00					17
18								18

Figure 8–6 Work Sheet with Trial Balance Amounts Extended to Income Statement Section

Roadrunner Delivery Service

Work Sheet

For the Month Ended October 31, 20--

	ACCT. NO.	ACCOUNT NAME	TRIAL BALANCE		INCOME STATEMENT		BALANCE SHEET		
			DEBIT	CREDIT	DEBIT	CREDIT	DEBIT	CREDIT	
1	101	Cash in Bank	21125 00				21125 00		1
2	105	Accts. Rec.—City News	1450 00				1450 00		2
3	110	Accts. Rec.—Green Company	—				—		3
4	115	Computer Equipment	3000 00				3000 00		4
5	120	Office Equipment	200 00				200 00		5
6	125	Delivery Equipment	12000 00				12000 00		6
7	201	Accts. Pay.—Beacon Advertising		75 00				75 00	7
8	205	Accts. Pay.—North Shore Auto		11650 00				11650 00	8
9	301	Maria Sanchez, Capital		25400 00				25400 00	9
10	302	Maria Sanchez, Withdrawals	500 00				500 00		10
11	303	Income Summary	—	—	—	—			11
12	401	Delivery Revenue		2650 00		2650 00			12
13	501	Advertising Expense	75 00		75 00				13
14	505	Maintenance Expense	600 00		600 00				14
15	510	Rent Expense	700 00		700 00				15
16	515	Utilities Expense	125 00		125 00				16
17			39775 00	39775 00	1500 00	2650 00	38275 00	37125 00	17
18									18

Figure 8–7 Work Sheet with Income Statement and Balance Sheet Sections Totaled

the four Debit and Credit columns indicates that the columns are ready to be added. Unlike the Trial Balance section debit and credit totals, the Debit and Credit column totals in these two sections will not be equal until the net income or net loss for the period is added. See **Figure 8–7**.

Showing Net Income or Net Loss on the Work Sheet

What Is Meant by Net Income or Net Loss?

The work sheet's Income Statement section shows the period's revenue and expenses. The GAAP **matching principle** requires matching expenses incurred in an accounting period with the revenue earned in the same period. Matching expenses with revenue gives a reliable measure of profit by showing the dollar value of resources used to produce the revenue. Owners and managers use this information to analyze results and make decisions.

Showing Net Income on the Work Sheet

After the Income Statement section columns have been totaled, total expenses (Debit column total) are subtracted from total revenue (Credit column total) to find net income. **Net income** is the amount of revenue that remains after expenses for the period have been subtracted. Net income is entered as a debit at the bottom of the Income Statement section of the work sheet. Look at **Figure 8–8** on page 204. Roadrunner's net income is $1,150.

1. Skip a line after the last account and write the words *Net Income* in the Account Name column. **A**

Connect to…
LANGUAGE ARTS

People often think of accounting as dull and mechanical. Johann von Goethe didn't. The Romantic author most famous for *Faust* described Luca Pacioli's system of accounting as "among the finest inventions of the human mind."

Roadrunner Delivery Service

Work Sheet

For the Month Ended October 31, 20--

	ACCT. NO.	ACCOUNT NAME	TRIAL BALANCE		INCOME STATEMENT		BALANCE SHEET		
			DEBIT	CREDIT	DEBIT	CREDIT	DEBIT	CREDIT	
1	101	Cash in Bank	21125 00				21125 00		1
2	105	Accts. Rec.—City News	1450 00				1450 00		2
3	110	Accts. Rec.—Green Company	—				—		3
4	115	Computer Equipment	3000 00				3000 00		4
5	120	Office Equipment	200 00				200 00		5
6	125	Delivery Equipment	12000 00				12000 00		6
7	201	Accts. Pay.—Beacon Advertising		75 00				75 00	7
8	205	Accts. Pay.—North Shore Auto		11650 00				11650 00	8
9	301	Maria Sanchez, Capital		25400 00				25400 00	9
10	302	Maria Sanchez, Withdrawals	500 00				500 00		10
11	303	Income Summary	—	—	—	—			11
12	401	Delivery Revenue		2650 00		2650 00			12
13	501	Advertising Expense	75 00		75 00				13
14	505	Maintenance Expense	600 00		600 00				14
15	510	Rent Expense	700 00		700 00				15
16	515	Utilities Expense	125 00		125 00				16
17			39775 00	39775 00	1500 00	2650 00	38275 00	37125 00	17
18		Net Income			1150 00			1150 00	18
19									19

A   B   C

Figure 8–8 Partial Work Sheet with Net Income

2. On the same line, enter the net income amount in the Income Statement Debit column. **B**
3. On the same line, enter the net income amount in the Balance Sheet Credit column. **C**

Why is the net income also shown in the Balance Sheet section of the work sheet? Remember, revenue and expense accounts are temporary accounts. As you can see in **Figure 8–9**, revenues increase capital, while

Figure 8–9 The Effects of Income or Loss on Capital

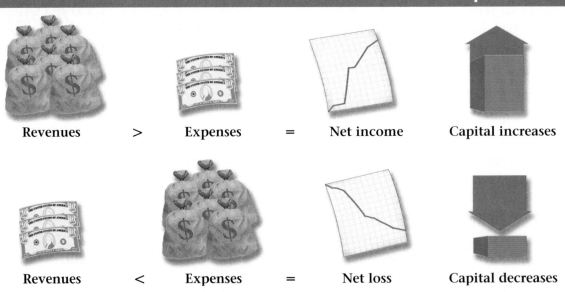

The Effects of Net Income or Net Loss on Capital

Revenues   >   Expenses   =   Net income   Capital increases

Revenues   <   Expenses   =   Net loss   Capital decreases

expenses decrease capital. Net income, therefore, increases capital since revenues exceed expenses.

During the accounting period, revenue and expense amounts are recorded in the temporary accounts (like **Delivery Revenue** and **Utilities Expense**). At the end of the period, net income will be transferred to the owner's capital account. Since the capital account is increased by credits, the amount of the net income is entered in the Credit column of the Balance Sheet section of the work sheet.

To check the accuracy of the net income amount in the Balance Sheet section, subtract the total of the Credit column from the total of the Debit column. If the result does not equal net income, there is an error. Before continuing, you must find and correct the error. To find the error, check that the amounts from the Trial Balance section are extended correctly and that the totals of all columns are added correctly.

Figure 8–10 Completed Work Sheet

Roadrunner Delivery Service
Work Sheet
For the Month Ended October 31, 20--

	ACCT. NO.	ACCOUNT NAME	TRIAL BALANCE DEBIT	TRIAL BALANCE CREDIT	INCOME STATEMENT DEBIT	INCOME STATEMENT CREDIT	BALANCE SHEET DEBIT	BALANCE SHEET CREDIT	
1	101	Cash in Bank	21125 00				21125 00		1
2	105	Accts. Receivable—City News	1450 00				1450 00		2
3	110	Accts. Receivable—Green Company	—				—		3
4	115	Computer Equipment	3000 00				3000 00		4
5	120	Office Equipment	200 00				200 00		5
6	125	Delivery Equipment	12000 00				12000 00		6
7	201	Accts. Payable—Beacon Advertising		75 00				75 00	7
8	205	Accounts Pay.—North Shore Auto		11650 00				11650 00	8
9	301	Maria Sanchez, Capital		25400 00				25400 00	9
10	302	Maria Sanchez, Withdrawals	500 00				500 00		10
11	303	Income Summary	—	—	—	—			11
12	401	Delivery Revenue		2650 00		2650 00			12
13	501	Advertising Expense	75 00		75 00				13
14	505	Maintenance Expense	600 00		600 00				14
15	510	Rent Expense	700 00		700 00				15
16	515	Utilities Expense	125 00		125 00				16
17			39775 00	39775 00	1500 00	2650 00	38275 00	37125 00	17
18		Net Income			1150 00			1150 00	18
19					2650 00	2650 00	38275 00	38275 00	19
20									20

A   B D   E   F   G C

Completing the Work Sheet

The completed work sheet for Roadrunner is shown in **Figure 8–10**. To complete the Income Statement and Balance Sheet sections, follow these steps:

1. On the line under the net income amount, draw a single rule across the four columns. **D**
2. In the Income Statement section Debit column, add the net income amount to the previous total and enter the new total. Bring down

the total of the Income Statement section Credit column. Total debits should equal total credits. **E**

3. In the Balance Sheet section Credit column, add net income to the previous total and enter the new total. Bring down the total of the Balance Sheet section Debit column. The total debit amount should equal the total credit amount. **F**

4. In the Balance Sheet and Income Statement sections, draw a double rule under the four column totals. The double rule indicates that the Debit and Credit columns are equal and that no more amounts are to be entered in these columns. **G**

Showing a Net Loss on the Work Sheet

What if total expenses are more than total revenue? When that happens, a **net loss** occurs. A net loss decreases owner's equity. This decrease will eventually be shown as a debit to the capital account. When a net loss occurs, the steps to complete the work sheet are the same as described for Net Income except that the words *Net Loss* are written in the Account Name column. The net loss amount is entered in the Credit column of the Income Statement section and in the Debit column of the Balance Sheet section. The partial work sheet in **Figure 8–11** shows a net loss. Expenses exceed revenue by $746.

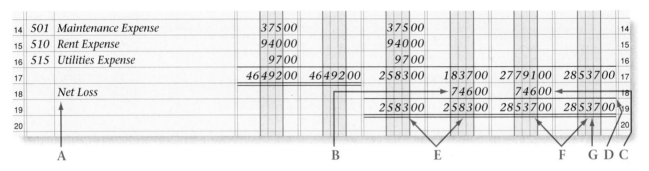

Figure 8–11 Partial Work Sheet Showing a Net Loss

A Review of the Steps in Preparing a Six-Column Work Sheet

How Do You Prepare a Work Sheet?

Follow these steps when preparing a six-column work sheet:

1. Write the heading on the work sheet.
2. In the Account Name and Trial Balance sections, enter the account numbers, names, and balances for all general ledger accounts.
3. Prove the equality of the Trial Balance total debits and total credits.
4. Extend the amounts of the Trial Balance section to the appropriate columns in the Balance Sheet and Income Statement sections.
5. Total the columns in the Income Statement and Balance Sheet sections.
6. Determine the amount of the net income or net loss for the period.
7. Enter the amount of the net income or net loss in the appropriate columns in the Income Statement and Balance Sheet sections.
8. Total and rule the Income Statement and Balance Sheet sections.

AFTER YOU **READ**

Reinforce the Main Idea

Create a chart like this one. Fill in the blanks to describe how net income and net loss are shown on the work sheet.

Situation	Is the result a net income or a net loss?	Extend to which column in the Income Statement section?	Extend to which column in the Balance Sheet section?
Revenue > Expenses			
Revenue < Expenses			

Do the Math

For Art's Sake is a sole proprietorship that sells artwork. The first two quarterly financial statements for this year have been grim. Using the revenue and expense information for the third quarter, calculate the net profit or loss. (Balances of the Accounts Receivable accounts represent third-quarter revenue.) Compare the third-quarter figure with the figures from the first and second quarters. What do you predict the future of For Art's Sake will be?

Third Quarter

Rent Expense	$2,000
Utilities Expense	800
Advertising Expense	3,000
Maintenance Expense	1,200
Accounts Receivable—Sammy Wong	500
Accounts Receivable—The Artist Collection	5,525
Accounts Receivable—Vera Samuels	3,200

Second Quarter Net Loss = $1,200

First Quarter Net Loss = $2,000

Problem 8–3 Extending Amounts Across the Work Sheet

The following accounts have balances and appear in the Account Name section of the work sheet for Lee's Bike Shop.

Store Equipment	Advertising Expense
Rent Expense	Accounts Receivable—John Langer
Service Fees Revenue	Scott Lee, Withdrawals
Accounts Payable—Rubino Supply	Maintenance Expense
Scott Lee, Capital	Office Supplies

Instructions Use a form similar to the one below in your working papers or on a separate sheet of paper. For the above accounts, enter an "X" in the column where the account balance is transferred. The first account has been completed as an example.

Account Name	Income Statement		Balance Sheet	
	Debit	Credit	Debit	Credit
Store Equipment			X	

Key Concepts

1. Preparing a work sheet is the sixth step in the accounting cycle. The purpose of the worksheet is to gather all the information needed to complete the end-of-period activities. Its heading contains the following information:

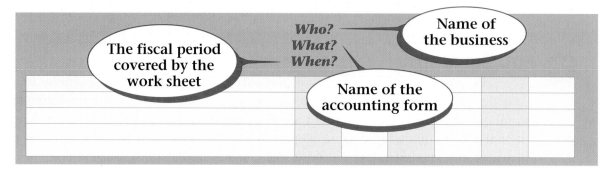

2. The six-column work sheet has five sections:
   (a) Heading
      • Who
      • What
      • When
   (b) Account Name section
      • Account number
      • Account name
      • List all accounts in general ledger order
   (c) Trial Balance section
   (d) Income Statement section
   (e) Balance Sheet section

   Three of these sections have amount columns. Each of the following sections has a Debit column and a Credit column:
   • Trial Balance section
   • Income Statement section
   • Balance Sheet section

3. Use the following steps to prepare a work sheet:
   (a) Create a heading.
   (b) In the Account Name and Trial Balance sections, enter account numbers, names, and balances.
   (c) Complete the Trial Balance section, making sure that total debits equal total credits.
   (d) Extend amounts from the Trial Balance section to the appropriate columns in the Balance Sheet and Income Statement sections.
   (e) Total the columns in the Income Statement and Balance Sheet columns.

(f) Calculate the net income or net loss for the period.

(g) Enter net income or net loss on the worksheet as follows:

Account Name	Income Statement		Balance Sheet	
	Debit	Credit	Debit	Credit
Net Income	X			X

Account Name	Income Statement		Balance Sheet	
	Debit	Credit	Debit	Credit
Net Loss		X	X	

(h) Total and rule the Income Statement and Balance Sheet sections.

4. The *matching principle* requires expenses incurred during an accounting period to be matched with revenues earned in the same period. The result is net income or net loss:

If revenue > expenses, then

$$\begin{array}{r} \text{Revenue} \\ -\ \text{Expenses} \\ \hline =\ \text{Net Income} \end{array}$$

If revenue < expenses, then

$$\begin{array}{r} \text{Expenses} \\ -\ \text{Revenue} \\ \hline =\ \text{Net Loss} \end{array}$$

Key Terms

matching principle (p. 203)

net income (p. 203)

net loss (p. 206)

ruling (p. 199)

work sheet (p. 197)

AFTER YOU READ

Check Your Understanding

1. **Purpose of a Work Sheet**
   a. Preparing the work sheet is which step of the accounting cycle?
   b. What is the purpose of the work sheet?

2. **Parts of a Six-Column Work Sheet**
   a. Name and briefly describe the five sections of a six-column worksheet.
   b. List the items that are included in the work sheet heading.

3. **Preparing a Six-Column Work Sheet**
   a. Which section of the work sheet should you complete first?
   b. Why are all accounts, including those with zero balances, listed on the work sheet?

4. **Net Income and Net Loss**
   a. Explain how to record net income or net loss on the work sheet.
   b. How does net income affect owner's equity? How does net loss affect owner's equity?

Apply Key Terms

You just finished the work sheet for the third quarter and it looks like your company will make a considerable profit. In the second quarter, the company had a net loss. On a separate sheet of paper, write a memo to your boss, Tonya Newman, asking her to review your trial balance and work sheet. Use the terms listed below in your memo.

matching principle	ruling
net income	work sheet
net loss	

The Trial Balance

Making the Transition from a Manual to a Computerized System

Task	Manual Methods	Computerized Methods
Preparing the trial balance	• After all journal entries have been posted and all general ledger balances have been updated, list account names and balances on two-column accounting stationery. • List debit balances in one column and credit balances in the other. • Add all debit balances. • Add all credit balances. • Compare the totals. If totals are not in balance, locate and correct any journalizing or posting errors. • The trial balance is correct when total debits equal total credits.	• Although the Trial Balance is not necessary to check the equality of debits and credits since out-of-balance entries cannot be posted, it is one of the most commonly used accounting statements. It provides a clear list format for reviewing accounts. You can view and print the Trial Balance from the *Reports* menu.

Peachtree® Q & A

Peachtree Question	Answer
How do I generate a trial balance in Peachtree?	1. From the *Reports* menu, select **General Ledger**. 2. From the Reports list, select **General Ledger Trial Balance**. 3. Click **Print**.

QuickBooks Q & A

QuickBooks Question	Answer
How do I generate a trial balance in QuickBooks?	1. From the *Reports* menu, select **Accountant & Taxes**. 2. From the Accountant & Taxes submenu, select **Trial Balance**. 3. Click **Print**.

For detailed instructions, see your Glencoe Accounting Chapter Study Guides and Working Papers.

Chapter 8   Computerized Accounting   **211**

Problems

Problem 8–4 Preparing a Six-Column Work Sheet

The ending balances in the general ledger accounts of Wilderness Rentals for the period ended May 31 follow.

SPREADSHEET SMART GUIDE

Step–by–Step Instructions: Problem 8–4

1. Select the spreadsheet template for Problem 8–4.
2. Enter your name and the date in the spaces provided on the template.
3. Complete the spreadsheet using the instructions in your working papers.
4. Print the spreadsheet and proof your work.
5. Complete the Analyze activity.
6. Save your work and exit the spreadsheet program.

		Debit Balances	Credit Balances
101	Cash in Bank	$5,814	
105	Accts. Rec.—Helen Katz	717	
110	Accts. Rec.—Polk and Co.	590	
115	Office Supplies	847	
120	Office Equipment	4,360	
125	Camping Equipment	6,130	
201	Accts. Pay.—Adventure Equipment Inc.		$ 1,680
203	Accts. Pay.—Digital Tech Computers		3,554
205	Accts. Pay.—Greg Mollaro		635
301	Ronald Hicks, Capital		12,760
305	Ronald Hicks, Withdrawals	1,200	
310	Income Summary	—	—
401	Equipment Rental Revenue		9,716
501	Advertising Expense	1,940	
505	Maintenance Expense	1,083	
515	Rent Expense	3,500	
525	Utilities Expense	2,164	

Instructions Prepare a work sheet for the period ended May 31.

1. Write the heading on the work sheet.
2. List all of the accounts in the Account Name and Trial Balance sections. For each account, include the account number, name, and balance.
3. Total and rule the Trial Balance section. Do total debits equal total credits? If not, find and correct the problem before continuing.
4. Extend the appropriate amounts to the Balance Sheet section.
5. Extend the appropriate amounts to the Income Statement section.
6. Total the amount columns in the Income Statement and Balance Sheet sections.
7. Enter the amount of net income or net loss in the appropriate columns in the Income Statement and Balance Sheet sections.
8. Total and rule the Income Statement and Balance Sheet sections.

Analyze Identify the permanent accounts on the work sheet that have normal debit balances.

Problem 8–5 Preparing a Six-Column Work Sheet

The general ledger for Hot Suds Car Wash shows the following account balances on May 31, the end of the period.

CONTI

101	Cash in Bank	$9,400
105	Accts. Rec.—Linda Brown	429
110	Accts. Rec.—Valley Auto	372
115	Detailing Supplies	694
120	Detergent Supplies	418
125	Office Equipment	15,195
130	Office Furniture	2,029
135	Car Wash Equipment	7,486
201	Accts. Pay.—Allen Vacuum Systems	4,346
205	Accts. Pay.—O'Brian's Office Supply	2,730
301	Regina Delgado, Capital	26,530
305	Regina Delgado, Withdrawals	2,500
310	Income Summary	
401	Wash Revenue	7,957
405	Wax Revenue	5,329
410	Interior Detailing Revenue	2,970
501	Advertising Expense	1,940
505	Equipment Rental Expense	3,836
510	Maintenance Expense	1,424
520	Rent Expense	3,500
530	Utilities Expense	639

Instructions Prepare a work sheet for Hot Suds Car Wash in your working papers.

Analyze Identify the temporary accounts on the work sheet that have normal credit balances.

Problem 8–6 Preparing a Six-Column Work Sheet

The account balances in the general ledger of Kits & Pups Grooming at the end of May are:

101	Cash in Bank	$11,194
105	Accts. Rec.—Juan Alvarez	357
110	Accts. Rec.—Nathan Carlsbad	547
115	Accts. Rec.—Martha Giles	1,450
120	Grooming Supplies	842
125	Office Equipment	4,147
130	Office Furniture	935
135	Computer Equipment	2,200
140	Grooming Equipment	1,948
145	Kennel Equipment	7,305
201	Accts. Pay.—Able Store Equipment	7,945
205	Accts. Pay.—Dogs & Cats Inc.	1,205
207	Accts. Pay.—Pet Gourmet	2,846
301	Abe Shultz, Capital	23,048
305	Abe Shultz, Withdrawals	2,500
310	Income Summary	—

CONTINUE

401	Boarding Revenue	11,596
405	Grooming Revenue	4,496
501	Advertising Expense	3,675
505	Equipment Repair Expense	932
510	Maintenance Expense	2,658
520	Rent Expense	7,500
530	Utilities Expense	2,946

Instructions Prepare a work sheet for the month ended May 31 for Kits & Pups Grooming in your working papers.

Analyze Compute the total liabilities for Kits & Pups.

Problem 8–7 Preparing a Six-Column Work Sheet

The general ledger account balances on May 31 for Outback Guide Service are:

101	Cash in Bank	$ 2,834
105	Accts. Rec.—Mary Johnson	384
125	Office Supplies	307
130	Office Equipment	5,902
135	Office Furniture	2,804
140	Computer Equipment	3,295
145	Hiking Equipment	922
150	Rafting Equipment	8,351
205	Accts. Pay.—Peak Equipment Inc.	1,204
301	Juanita Ortega, Capital	20,419
302	Juanita Ortega, Withdrawals	1,800
310	Income Summary	—
401	Guide Service Revenue	9,179
501	Advertising Expense	795
505	Maintenance Expense	125
515	Rent Expense	2,000
525	Utilities Expense	1,283

Instructions Prepare a work sheet for Outback Guide Service for the period ended May 31 in your working papers.

Analyze Compute the total assets for Outback.

CHALLENGE PROBLEM Problem 8–8 Completing the Work Sheet

The work sheet for Job Connect appears in your working papers. The amounts that have been entered are correct. Several amounts, however, are missing from various columns.

Instructions Calculate all missing amounts and complete the work sheet.

Analyze Calculate the owner's equity. (Hint: Be sure to include the temporary accounts.)

Practice your test-taking skills! The questions on this page are reprinted with permission from national organizations:
- Future Business Leaders of America
- Business Professionals of America

Use a separate sheet of paper to record your answers.

Future Business Leaders of America

MULTIPLE CHOICE

1. A(n) _____ results when revenue is larger than expenses.
- a. debit
- b. net income
- c. net loss
- d. credit

2. The asset, liability, and owner's equity accounts are extended to the _____ of the work sheet.
- a. Balance Sheet section
- b. Income Statement section
- c. Retained Earnings statement
- d. Trial Balance

3. Revenue and expense accounts are listed in the Trial Balance section of the work sheet and in the _____ of the work sheet.
- a. Retained Earnings statement
- b. Balance Sheet section
- c. Income Statement section
- d. Accounts Payable section

4. The amount of net income for the period is added to the Balance Sheet credit total because it increases the balance in the _____ account.
- a. accounts receivable
- b. accounts payable
- c. asset
- d. capital

Business Professionals of America

MULTIPLE CHOICE

5. A net loss will appear
- a. in the debit column of the Income Statement on the work sheet.
- b. in the credit column of the Income Statement on the work sheet.
- c. in the debit column of the Trial Balance.
- d. on the Post-Closing Trial Balance.

Need More Help?

Go to glencoeaccounting.glencoe.com and click on **Student Center**. Click on **Winning Competitive Events** and select **Chapter 8.**
- **Practice Questions and Test-Taking Tips**
- **Concept Capsules and Terminology**

The Six-Column Work Sheet

1. Name the types of accounts whose balances are extended to the Income Statement section of the work sheet.

2. Explain why the Trial Balance section is completed first.

3. What items do you need to complete the six-column work sheet? Include office supplies and forms as well as any information that will be needed.

4. Why is the net income amount entered in the Credit column of the Balance Sheet section? Why is net loss entered in the Debit column?

5. Predict what would happen if a revenue account balance were not extended to the Income Statement section of the work sheet.

6. What is the value of the matching principle?

Service Business: Advertising Agency

You work for Creative Advertising as an assistant to the company's accountant. You are preparing a work sheet for the month of July. The trial balance totals are $127,750, and you have extended the account balances to the amount columns in the Balance Sheet and Income Statement sections. After adding the Balance Sheet and Income Statement columns and calculating net income, you find that the totals do not balance.

INSTRUCTIONS

1. List the steps you would take to find the problem.

2. Provide a likely reason to explain why the net income amounts do not match.

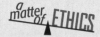

Padding Expense Accounts

Imagine that you are employed as an auditor for a public accounting firm like PricewaterhouseCoopers. You and a co-worker, Mark, have been sent to Chicago to perform an audit. You have an allowance of $200 a day to cover lodging, meals, and transportation. At the end of the trip, you are to turn in an expense account report detailing how you spent the allowance. Mark adds a few dollars to each of his expenses so he can have some extra cash. You figure that the firm will not miss a few dollars, so you consider doing the same.

ETHICAL DECISION MAKING

1. What are the ethical issues?

2. What are the alternatives?

3. Who are the affected parties?

4. How do the alternatives affect the parties?

5. What would you do?

Creating a Handout

Your accounting firm, AccountFast, volunteered to provide mentors to area schools for accounting and math programs. As a mentor, you are assigned to work with three accounting students. Your topic for this week is "Ruling and Totaling the Trial Balance." Create a handout to explain and illustrate this topic. Use any company, accounts, and account balances you wish. Remember, it is helpful to provide step-by-step instructions.

Understanding Organizational Systems

- Can you read and interpret a company's organizational chart?
- Can you identify who reports to whom?

If you can answer "yes" to these questions, then you can probably work and operate effectively within an organizational system.

ON THE JOB

Your employer, The Teen Scene, was just bought out by a large, national clothing chain—Natural Fibers. The buyout has created a huge reorganization.

INSTRUCTIONS

1. The change from a small clothing store to a national chain store has affected employee morale. What do you think would help build loyalty to Natural Fibers?

2. How would an organizational chart that depicts who reports to whom help with the transition?

Time Zones

What time is it now on your watch? What time is it in London or New York? Without knowledge of the world's time zones, the international businessperson may have difficulty contacting a person at the right place and the right time. There are 24 time zones in the world, each representing 15 degrees of longitude, or one hour intervals.

INSTRUCTIONS Imagine that your company has manufacturing locations in Dublin, Ireland and Denver, Colorado. Managers work from 8:00 a.m. to 3:30 p.m. at both locations. Dublin is 7 hours behind Denver. Schedule a telephone meeting so that both managers are present. What will you need to consider when scheduling the meeting?

Your Savings

A business needs to save for expansion and unexpected expenses. You also need to save to have money available when you want or need something. Without savings, both you and a business could have a difficult time.

PERSONAL FINANCE ACTIVITY List some typical cash expenditures a high school student might have in an average week. Include the amount spent on each item. Identify the items that could be easily eliminated or reduced. By reducing this spending, how much money would be saved in one year?

PERSONAL FINANCE ONLINE Go to **glencoeaccounting.glencoe.com** and click on **Student Center.** Click on **Making It Personal** and select **Chapter 8.**

CHAPTER 9

Financial Statements for a Sole Proprietorship

What You'll Learn

1. Explain the purpose of the income statement.

2. Prepare an income statement.

3. Explain the purpose of the statement of changes in owner's equity.

4. Prepare a statement of changes in owner's equity.

5. Explain the purpose of the balance sheet.

6. Prepare a balance sheet.

7. Explain the purpose of the statement of cash flows.

8. Explain ratio analysis and compute ratios.

9. Define the accounting terms introduced in this chapter.

Why It's Important

▶ Financial statements provide essential information for making sound decisions.

Predict

1. What does the chapter title tell you?
2. What do you already know about this subject from personal experience?
3. What have you learned about this in the earlier chapters?
4. What gaps exist in your knowledge of this subject?

Exploring the *Real World* of Business

PREPARING FINANCIAL STATEMENTS

Tapatío Hot Sauce Company

Not all businesses take off like wildfire. Some begin modestly, like **Tapatío Hot Sauce Company**. Jose-Luis Saavedra Sr. started it in 1971 in a tiny warehouse. He drove his own van for deliveries to stores and restaurants.

As **Tapatío** grew, Saavedra enlisted family to help meet the increased product demand. His son Jose-Luis Jr., a physician, became **Tapatío's** general manager. Daughter Dolores uses her law degree to handle the company's legal matters, and daughter Jacquie runs the office. Today the company owns a state-of-the-art facility with a fully automated production line.

Early on, **Tapatío's** revenues were small, and its financial statements were simple compared to those it prepares now to reflect the company's national and international distribution of its hot sauce.

What Do You Think?

What types of accounts do you think **Tapatío** used in 1971? What accounts do you think have been added?

Working in the *Real World*

APPLYING YOUR ACCOUNTING KNOWLEDGE

A sole proprietorship can be a small business with a few employees or a large business with thousands of employees. In a small business, one person may handle the accounting duties. A larger business might have several employees working in an accounting department. Whether large or small, the preparation of financial statements is an important task.

Personal Connection

1. In your work location, approximately how many people are employed?

2. If you were an accountant, do you think you would prefer to work for a large organization or a small one? Why?

Online Connection

Go to **glencoeaccounting.glencoe.com** and click on **Student Center**. Click on **Working in the Real World** and select **Chapter 9.**

The Income Statement

Main Idea
The income statement reports the net income or net loss for an accounting period.

Read to Learn...
➤ the four financial statements prepared for a business. (p. 220)
➤ how to prepare an income statement. (p. 221)

Key Terms
financial statements
income statement

To operate a business profitably, the owner needs to have current financial information. Businesses ranging from an oil company to a dairy farm must organize financial information to evaluate profits or losses. **Financial statements** summarize the changes resulting from business transactions that occur during an accounting period. As you can see in **Figure 9–1**, preparing financial statements is the seventh step in the accounting cycle.

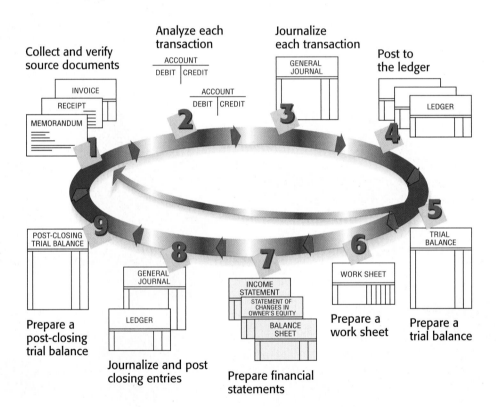

Figure 9–1 The Accounting Cycle with the Seventh Step Highlighted

Financial Statements
What Are the Four Financial Statements?

The primary financial statements prepared for a sole proprietorship are the income statement and the balance sheet. Two other statements, the statement of changes in owner's equity and the statement of cash flows, are also often prepared. The financial statements may be handwritten or typed but most often are prepared on a computer. With a computerized accounting system, the business owner can generate financial statements without first preparing a work sheet. Let's learn how to prepare financial statements for a service business such as Roadrunner Delivery Service.

The Income Statement

What Is the Purpose of the Income Statement?

The **income statement** reports the net income or net loss for a specific period of time. As you recall from Chapter 8, net income or net loss is the difference between total revenue and total expenses. For this reason the income statement is sometimes called a *profit-and-loss statement* or an *earnings statement*.

Income Statement Sections

The income statement contains the following sections:

- the heading
- the revenue for the period
- the expenses for the period
- the net income or net loss for the period

Heading. Like the work sheet heading, the heading of an income statement has three parts:

1. The name of the business *(Who?)*
2. The name of the report *(What?)*
3. The period covered *(When?)*

The heading for Roadrunner's income statement is shown in **Figure 9–2.** Each line of the heading is centered on the width of the statement.

When preparing an income statement heading, be sure to follow the wording and capitalization shown in **Figure 9–2.** The date line is especially important because the reporting period varies from business to business.

❶ *(Who?)*
❷ *(What?)*
❸ *(When?)*

Roadrunner Delivery Service ←
Income Statement ←
For the Month Ended October 31, 20-- ←

Figure 9–2 The Heading for an Income Statement

A business owner uses the same accounting periods year after year. This consistency allows the owner to compare the information from one period to the next.

Revenue Section. After the heading has been completed, enter the revenue earned for the period. Look at **Figure 9–3** on page 222. The information used to prepare the income statement comes from the Income Statement section of the work sheet.

Roadrunner's income statement is prepared on standard accounting stationery, which has a column for account names and two amount columns. The first amount column is used to enter the balances of the individual revenue and expense accounts. The second amount column is used to enter totals: total revenue, total expenses, and net income (or net loss).

Refer to **Figure 9–3** as you read the procedures for preparing an income statement:

1. Write *Revenue:* on the first line at the left side of the form. **A**
2. Enter the revenue account names beginning on the second line, indented about a half inch from the left edge of the form. **B**

Roadrunner Delivery Service
Work Sheet
For the Month Ended October 31, 20--

	ACCT. NO.	ACCOUNT NAME	TRIAL BALANCE DEBIT	TRIAL BALANCE CREDIT	INCOME STATEMENT DEBIT	INCOME STATEMENT CREDIT	BALANCE SHEET DEBIT	BALANCE SHEET CREDIT	
1	101	Cash in Bank	21 125 00				21 125 00		1
2	105	Accts. Rec.—City News	1 450 00				1 450 00		2
3	110	Accts. Rec.—Green Company	—				—		3
4	115	Computer Equipment	3 000 00				3 000 00		4
5	120	Office Equipment	200 00				200 00		5
6	125	Delivery Equipment	12 000 00				12 000 00		6
7	201	Accts. Pay.—Beacon Advertising		75 00				75 00	7
8	205	Accts. Pay.—North Shore Auto		11 650 00				11 650 00	8
9	301	Maria Sanchez, Capital		25 400 00				25 400 00	9
10	302	Maria Sanchez, Withdrawals	500 00				500 00		10
11	303	Income Summary	—	—					11
12	401	Delivery Revenue		2 650 00		2 650 00			12
13	501	Advertising Expense	75 00		75 00				13
14	505	Maintenance Expense	600 00		600 00				14
15	510	Rent Expense	700 00		700 00				15
16	515	Utilities Expense	125 00		125 00				16
17			39 775 00	39 775 00	1 500 00	2 650 00	38 275 00	37 125 00	17
18		Net Income			1 150 00			1 150 00	18
19					2 650 00	2 650 00	38 275 00	38 275 00	19
20									20

Roadrunner Delivery Service
Income Statement
For the Month Ended October 31, 20--

Revenue: A				
Delivery Revenue B			2 650 00	C
Expenses: D				
Advertising Expense		75 00		
Maintenance Expense	E	600 00	E	
Rent Expense		700 00		
Utilities Expense		125 00		
Total Expenses G	F		1 500 00	H
Net Income K			1 150 00	J I L

Figure 9–3 Preparing an Income Statement

3. Enter the balance of each revenue account. Since Roadrunner has only one revenue account, **Delivery Revenue**, total revenue is the same as the balance of the one revenue account. The balance is thus written in the second, or totals, column. C

Many businesses have more than one source of revenue and thus have a separate revenue account for each source. For example, a swim club might have accounts such as **Membership Fees** and **Pool Rental. Figure 9–4** illustrates the Revenue section of the income statement for a business with more than one revenue account. Notice that the words *Total Revenue* are indented about one inch from the left edge of the form.

Expenses Section.
The expenses incurred during the period are reported next. The expense account names and the balances in the Income Statement section of the work sheet are used to

Revenue:					
Rental Revenue	11 2 3 0 00				
Repair Revenue	4 8 5 0 00				
Total Revenue			16 0 8 0 00		

prepare the Expenses section of the income statement. Refer to **Figure 9–3** as you read the following instructions:

1. On the line following the revenue section, write *Expenses:* at the left side of the form. D
2. On the following lines, write the names of the expense accounts, indented half an inch, in the order that they appear on the work sheet. Since there are several expense accounts, enter the individual balances in the first amount column. E
3. Draw a single rule under the last expense account balance. F
4. Write the words *Total Expenses* on the line following the last expense account name, indented about one inch. G
5. Add the balances for all expense accounts. Write the total expenses amount in the second amount column, one line below the last expense account balance. H

Net Income Section. The next step is to enter net income. Net income, remember, occurs when total revenue is more than total expenses. Refer to **Figure 9–3** as you read the following instructions for the preparation of the Net Income section.

1. Draw a single rule under the total expenses amount. I
2. Subtract the total expenses from the total revenue to find net income. Enter the net income in the second amount column under the total expenses amount. J
3. On the same line, write *Net Income* at the left side of the form. K
4. If the amount of net income matches the amount on the work sheet, draw a double rule under the net income amount. L

As You READ

In Your Experience

Financial Reports What kinds of financial reports would a high school student be familiar with?

Reporting a Net Loss

If total expenses are more than total revenue, a net loss exists. To determine the amount of net loss, subtract total revenue from total expenses. Enter the net loss in the second amount column under the total expenses amount. Write the words *Net Loss* on the same line at the left side of the form. **Figure 9–5** illustrates how to report a net loss.

Revenue:					
Delivery Revenue			3 1 7 0 00		
Expenses:					
Advertising Expense	2 7 5 00				
Maintenance Expense	7 5 0 00				
Miscellaneous Expense	2 7 0 00				
Rent Expense	1 9 0 0 00				
Utilities Expense	3 2 5 00				
Total Expenses			3 5 2 0 00		
Net Loss			3 5 0 00		

Figure 9–5 Income Statement Showing a Net Loss

AFTER YOU READ

Reinforce the Main Idea

Using a diagram like this one, summarize the steps for creating an income statement. Add answer boxes for steps as needed.

Creating an Income Statement

```
┌──────────────────────────────────────┐
└──────────────────────────────────────┘
                    ↓
┌──────────────────────────────────────┐
└──────────────────────────────────────┘
                    ↓
┌──────────────────────────────────────┐
└──────────────────────────────────────┘
                    ↓
┌──────────────────────────────────────┐
└──────────────────────────────────────┘
```

Do the Math

Earth-Friendly Cleaning Service prepares monthly financial statements. The two revenue accounts show ending balances of $8,740.00 and $2,080.00. The following expense account balances also appear in the Income Statement section of this month's work sheet.

Advertising Expense	$3,690.00
Maintenance Expense	2,745.00
Miscellaneous Expense	605.00
Rent Expense	3,400.00
Utility Expense	985.00

Calculate the amount of net income or net loss for the month.

Problem 9–1 Analyzing a Source Document

Instructions Based on the receipt shown here, answer the following questions in your working papers.

1. What is the name of the business that received the money?
2. How much money was received?
3. Who paid the money?
4. Why was the money paid?
5. When was the payment made?
6. Who received the money and made out the receipt?
7. Where is the business that received the money located?

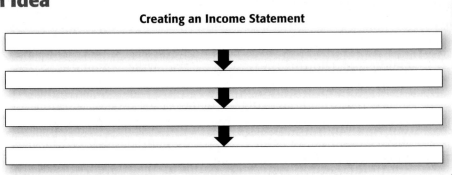

Stratford Learning Center — 243 Eastern Road, Roxbury, NY 14752

RECEIPT   No. 1834

Aug. 21   20 --

RECEIVED FROM   Sandra Miller $ 832.00

Eight hundred thirty-two and $^{no}/_{100}$ ———————— DOLLARS

FOR   On account

RECEIVED BY   Rose Hughes

The Statement of Changes in Owner's Equity

An important concern of a business owner is whether the owner's equity has increased or decreased during the period. An increase in owner's equity means the owner's claims to the assets of the business have grown. A decrease means the owner's claims to the assets of the business have been reduced.

The Statement of Changes in Owner's Equity

Where Do You Find the Information Needed to Prepare This Financial Statement?

The **statement of changes in owner's equity** summarizes changes in the owner's capital account as a result of business transactions that occur during the period. Eventually, the balances of revenues, expenses, and the owner's withdrawal account will be transferred to the owner's capital account. This statement is prepared at the end of the accounting period.

The heading of the statement of changes in owner's equity is set up in the same manner as the heading for the income statement.

1. The first line consists of the name of the business. *(Who?)*
2. The second line indicates the name of the statement. *(What?)*
3. The third line indicates the period covered. *(When?)*

Because the statement of changes in owner's equity and the income statement cover the same period, the third line of the heading of both statements will include the same wording and date.

The information to prepare this statement is found in three places:

- the work sheet
- the income statement
- the owner's capital account in the general ledger

Completing the Statement of Changes in Owner's Equity

How Do You Prepare This Financial Statement?

Look at **Figure 9–6** on page 226. It is the statement of changes in owner's equity for Roadrunner Delivery Service for the month ended October 31. The illustration shows the steps needed to complete this financial statement.

BEFORE YOU READ

Main Idea
The statement of changes in owner's equity shows how the owner's financial interest changed during the accounting period.

Read to Learn...
➤ the purpose of the statement of changes in owner's equity. (p. 225)
➤ how to prepare the statement of changes in owner's equity. (p. 225)

Key Terms
statement of changes in owner's equity

AS YOU READ

Key Point

Statement of Changes in Owner's Equity The statement of changes in owner's equity covers the same time period as the income statement.

Roadrunner Delivery Service					
Statement of Changes in Owner's Equity					
For the Month Ended October 31, 20--					
Beginning Capital, October 1, 20-- **A**				— **B**	
C Add: Investments by Owner	**D** 25 4 0 0 00				
Net Income	**E** 1 1 5 0 00				
Total Increase in Capital			26 5 5 0 00		**F**
Subtotal			26 5 5 0 00		**G**
Less: Withdrawals by Owner			5 0 0 00		**H**
Ending Capital, October 31, 20-- **I**			26 0 5 0 00		**J**

Figure 9–6 Statement of Changes in Owner's Equity

1. On the first line, write the words *Beginning Capital* followed by a comma and then by the first day of the period. For Roadrunner that date is October 1, 20--. **A**
2. In the second amount column, enter the balance of the capital account at the beginning of the period. The source of this information is the capital account in the general ledger. Since Roadrunner was formed after the beginning of the period, there is no beginning capital balance. Place a line in the second amount column. **B**
3. Next, enter the *increases* to the capital account:
   - investments by the owner
   - net income

   Investments made by the owner during the period are recorded in the capital account. Maria Sanchez, the owner of Roadrunner, invested a total of $25,400 during October. This includes $25,000 cash and two phones valued at $400. Write *Add: Investments by Owner.* **C** Enter the total investment in the first amount column. **D**

   On the next line, write the words *Net Income.* Indent so that *Net Income* aligns on the left with *Investments by Owner* in the line above. In the first amount column, enter the net income amount from the income statement. Draw a single rule under the net income amount. **E**
4. Write the words *Total Increase in Capital* on the next line at the left side of the form. Add the investments by owner and net income amounts and enter the total in the second amount column. Draw a single rule under the amount. **F**
5. Write *Subtotal* on the next line, at the left side of the form. Add the amounts for beginning capital and total increase in capital. Enter the result in the second amount column. **G**
6. The next section of the statement lists the *decreases* to the capital account:
   - withdrawals
   - net loss

   Since Roadrunner did not have a net loss for the period, write the words *Less: Withdrawals by Owner* at the left side of the form. Find

As You READ

Compare and Contrast

Income Statement and Statement of Changes in Owner's Equity
In what ways are the income statement and statement of changes in owner's equity similar? How are they different?

the withdrawals amount on the work sheet. Enter the withdrawals amount in the second amount column. Draw a single rule under the withdrawals amount. **H**

7. On the next line, at the left side of the form, write the words *Ending Capital* followed by a comma and the last day of the period. **I**

8. Subtract the withdrawals amount from the subtotal to determine the ending balance of the capital account. Finally, draw a double rule below the ending capital amount. **J**

Statement of Changes in Owner's Equity for an Ongoing Business

To prepare the statement of changes in owner's equity, you need to know the beginning balance of the owner's capital account. For an ongoing business, the balance entered on the work sheet for the capital account *may not* be the balance at the beginning of the period. If the owner made additional investments during the period, the investments would be recorded in the general journal, posted to the general ledger, and included in the amount shown on the work sheet.

For example, suppose the owner of Garo's Tree Service, James Garo, invested an additional $1,000 during the period. Look at **Figure 9–7**. The ledger account reflects the additional capital investment. The amount entered on the work sheet for **James Garo, Capital** includes the balance at the beginning of the period ($23,800) and the investment made during the period ($1,000).

ACCOUNT _James Garo, Capital_   ACCOUNT NO. _301_

DATE		DESCRIPTION	POST. REF.	DEBIT	CREDIT	BALANCE DEBIT	BALANCE CREDIT
20--							
Apr.	1	Balance	✓				23 800 00
	15		G1		1 000 00		24 800 00

Garo's Tree Service
Work Sheet
For the Month Ended April 30, 20--

	ACCT. NO.	ACCOUNT NAME	TRIAL BALANCE DEBIT	TRIAL BALANCE CREDIT	INCOME STATEMENT DEBIT	INCOME STATEMENT CREDIT	BALANCE SHEET DEBIT	BALANCE SHEET CREDIT	
12	301	James Garo, Capital		24 800 00				24 800 00	12
13	302	James Garo, Withdrawals	700 00				700 00		13
20	525	Utilities Expense	620 00		620 00				20
21			21 924 00	21 924 00	6 033 00	9 309 00	29 877 00	26 601 00	21
22		Net Income			3 276 00			3 276 00	22
23					9 309 00	9 309 00	29 877 00	29 877 00	23
24									24

Figure 9–7 Statement of Changes in Owner's Equity for an Ongoing Business

Garo's Tree Service												
Statement of Changes in Owner's Equity												
For the Month Ended April 30, 20--												
Beginning Capital, April 1, 20--									23	8 0 0	00
Add: Investments by Owner		1	0 0 0	00					
Net Income		3	2 7 6	00					
Total Increase in Capital								4	2 7 6	00
Subtotal								28	0 7 6	00
Less: Withdrawals by Owner									7 0 0	00
Ending Capital, April 30, 20--								27	3 7 6	00

Figure 9–7 Statement of Changes in Owner's Equity for an Ongoing Business (continued)

There are two ways to determine the owner's capital account balance at the beginning of the period:

- Look at the ledger.
- Subtract the additional investments from the account balance shown on the work sheet.

For **James Garo, Capital**, the $1,000 additional investment in Garo's Tree Service is subtracted from the $24,800 account balance shown on the work sheet to arrive at the beginning account balance of $23,800.

Figure 9–7 shows the statement of changes in owner's equity for an ongoing business.

Statement of Changes in Owner's Equity Showing a Net Loss

Figure 9–8 shows a statement of changes in owner's equity for an ongoing business with a net loss. Notice that since there is only one item that increases capital—investments by owner—the amount of the individual item is entered in the second amount column. Since there are two items that decrease capital—withdrawals by owner and net loss—the amounts of the individual items are entered in the first amount column. The total decrease in capital is entered in the second amount column.

Island Burgers												
Statement of Changes in Owner's Equity												
For the Month Ended April 30, 20--												
Beginning Capital, April 1, 20--									13	8 4 8	00
Add: Investments by Owner									1	5 0 0	00
Subtotal									15	3 4 8	00
Less: Withdrawals by Owner					9 0 0	00				
Net Loss					8 3 5	00				
Total Decrease in Capital								1	7 3 5	00
Ending Capital, April 30, 20--								13	6 1 3	00

Figure 9–8 Statement of Changes in Owner's Equity Showing a Net Loss

AFTER YOU **READ**

Reinforce the Main Idea

Using a diagram like this one, summarize the steps for creating a statement of changes in owner's equity. Add answer boxes for steps as needed.

Creating a Statement of Changes in Owner's Equity

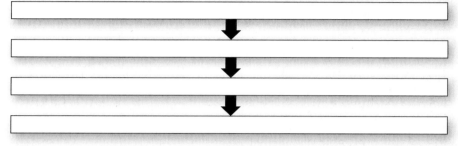

Do the Math

Tracy Murphy is a fashion designer who works from her home. She contributed her own funds and equipment to the business. She also continues to add new clients and increase her revenue. Tracy's investments in her business and the revenue she has earned over the past 10 months are shown below. Create a line graph, by date, comparing Tracy's investments to her revenue. What can you determine from this chart?

Investments			Revenue	
1/01/20--	Cash	$20,000	2/01/20--	$ 5,000
1/01/20--	Sewing machines	6,000	3/01/20--	6,000
1/01/20--	Mannequins	3,500	4/01/20--	12,000
1/01/20--	Material	25,000	5/01/20--	15,000
1/01/20--	Computer equipment	5,600	6/01/20--	17,500
1/01/20--	Business cards	500	7/01/20--	19,000
2/15/20--	Cash	12,000	8/01/20--	20,000
3/10/20--	Material	7,500	9/01/20--	26,000
Total Investments		$80,100	10/01/20--	20,000

Problem 9–2 Determining Ending Capital Balances

The financial transactions affecting the capital accounts of several different businesses are summarized below.

Instructions Use the form in your working papers. Determine the ending capital balance for each business.

	Beginning Capital	Investments	Revenue	Expenses	Withdrawals
1.	$60,000	$ 500	$ 5,100	$2,400	$ 700
2.	24,075	0	13,880	7,240	800
3.	28,800	1,000	6,450	6,780	0
4.	0	10,500	5,320	4,990	200
5.	6,415	0	4,520	3,175	700
6.	20,870	1,300	13,980	9,440	1,700

PARTNER

PricewaterhouseCoopers LLP, New York, New York

Alfred A. Peguero

Q: What is your main responsibility?

A: My job is to help the families and privately held corporations who are my clients. I look behind the numbers to show clients how to protect assets and pass them to the next generation. I always ask myself what needs to be done to ensure that client expectations are met. Being a partner is very much like owning your own business—with some constraints, of course.

Q: How did you become interested in accounting?

A: I was an economics major in college, but in my senior year I took two accounting classes that I really enjoyed. I realized this is where the opportunities are. Accounting as a general profession is very broad. The basic principles are the same but you can focus on areas and industries that really interest you—anything from technology to farming.

Q: Which skills are most important?

A: Analytical, reasoning, and communication skills are critical. Mathematical ability is also helpful.

Q: What do you enjoy most about your job?

A: I enjoy offering solutions to my clients. Helping real people solve their problems and achieve peace of mind over their financial matters is very rewarding.

Q: What advice do you have for accountants just beginning their careers?

A: Finding a good mentor is really important. Always follow through with what you say you're going to do and don't be afraid to ask questions.

Tips from . . .

RHI Robert Half International Inc.

A paycheck is not all a company can offer. Many firms also provide profit-sharing plans, tuition reimbursement, and training opportunities. Consider the benefits a prospective employer offers when deciding whether to accept a job offer.

CAREER FACTS

▶ **Nature of the Work:** Specialize in personal financial and business consulting; advise clients on complex accounting issues.

▶ **Training or Education Needed:** A bachelor's degree in business administration, accounting, or economics; a minor in communications and technology can be helpful; fulfill the requirements to become a CPA.

▶ **Aptitude, Abilities and Skills:** Communication, analytical, reasoning, and math skills.

▶ **Salary Range:** $150,000 and up depending on experience, level of responsibility, and firm performance.

▶ **Career Path:** Gather hands-on experience with a major accounting firm or reputable regional firm. Once you have a flavor for the areas that most appeal to you, consider getting a master's degree. It usually takes 10 to 15 years to become a partner at most firms.

Thinking Critically What qualities do you think employers look for when hiring?

The Balance Sheet and the Statement of Cash Flows

The third and fourth financial statements prepared at the end of the period are the balance sheet and the statement of cash flows. The balance sheet reflects the accounting equation at the end of the period. The statement of cash flows shows how the business acquired and spent cash during the period.

The Balance Sheet

What Is the Purpose of the Balance Sheet?

The **balance sheet** is a report of the balances in the permanent accounts at the end of the period. The main purpose of the balance sheet is to report the assets of the business and the claims against those assets *on a specific date.* In other words, the balance sheet states the financial position of a business at a specific point in time. The balance sheet summarizes the following information:

- what a business owns
- what a business owes
- what a business is worth

For this reason the balance sheet is sometimes called a *statement of financial position.*

The balance sheet is prepared from information in the Balance Sheet section of the work sheet and from the statement of changes in owner's equity. The balance sheet may be handwritten, typed, or, as in most cases, prepared by computer.

The Sections of the Balance Sheet

The balance sheet contains the following sections:

- the heading
- the assets section
- the liabilities and owner's equity sections

Heading. Like the heading of the income statement, the heading of the balance sheet answers the questions *who? what? when?* The balance sheet heading includes:

1. The name of the business *(Who?)*
2. The name of the financial statement *(What?)*
3. The date of the balance sheet *(When?)*

BEFORE YOU READ

Main Idea
The balance sheet reports the financial position at a specific point in time. The statement of cash flows reports the sources and uses of cash during the accounting period.

Read to Learn...
➤ how to prepare a balance sheet. (p. 231)
➤ the purpose of a statement of cash flows. (p. 234)
➤ how to perform ratio analysis. (p. 235)

Key Terms
balance sheet	current assets
report form	current
statement of	liabilities
cash flows	working capital
ratio analysis	liquidity ratio
profitability ratio	current ratio
return on sales	quick ratio

AS YOU READ

Install Recall

Permanent Accounts Permanent accounts are assets, liabilities, and the owner's capital account.

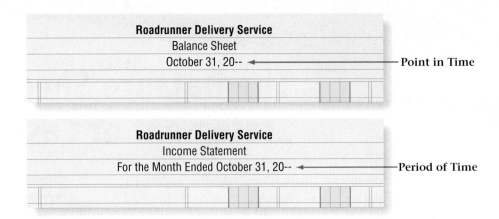

Roadrunner Delivery Service	
Balance Sheet	
October 31, 20-- ←	— Point in Time

Roadrunner Delivery Service	
Income Statement	
For the Month Ended October 31, 20-- ←	— Period of Time

Figure 9–9 Headings of Financial Statements

As You READ

Key Point

Balance Sheet The balance sheet is a "snapshot" of a business at a specific point in time.

Unlike the income statement, which covers the entire period, the balance sheet relates to a specific point in time. The amounts shown on the balance sheet are the general ledger balances in the accounts on the last day of the period. Notice the difference between the date lines on the balance sheet and on the income statement in **Figure 9–9.**

Assets Section. Refer to Roadrunner's balance sheet in **Figure 9–10** as you read how to prepare the balance sheet. Roadrunner's work sheet and statement of changes in owner's equity are also included to show the information sources used to prepare the balance sheet. Roadrunner's balance sheet is prepared in **report form** , listing the balance sheet sections one under the other.

The Assets section of the balance sheet is prepared as follows:

1. Write the word *Assets* on the first line in the center of the column containing the account names. **A**
2. On the following lines, list each asset account name and its balance in the same order as they appear in the Balance Sheet section of the work sheet. Enter the account balances in the first amount column. Draw a single rule under the last account balance. **B**
3. On the next line, write the words *Total Assets,* indented about half an inch. Add the individual asset balances and enter the total in the second amount column. **C**

Do *not* draw a double rule under the total yet. Enter it when the Liabilities and Owner's Equity sections are complete and equal to total assets.

Liabilities and Owner's Equity Sections. The information for the Liabilities and Owner's Equity sections is taken from the work sheet and from the statement of changes in owner's equity. Use the following steps to complete the Liabilities and Owner's Equity sections.

1. On the line after *Total Assets,* write the heading *Liabilities* in the center of the column containing the account names. **D**
2. On the following lines, list the liability account names and their balances in the same order as on the Balance Sheet section of the work sheet. Enter the account balances in the first amount column. Draw a single rule under the last account balance. **E**

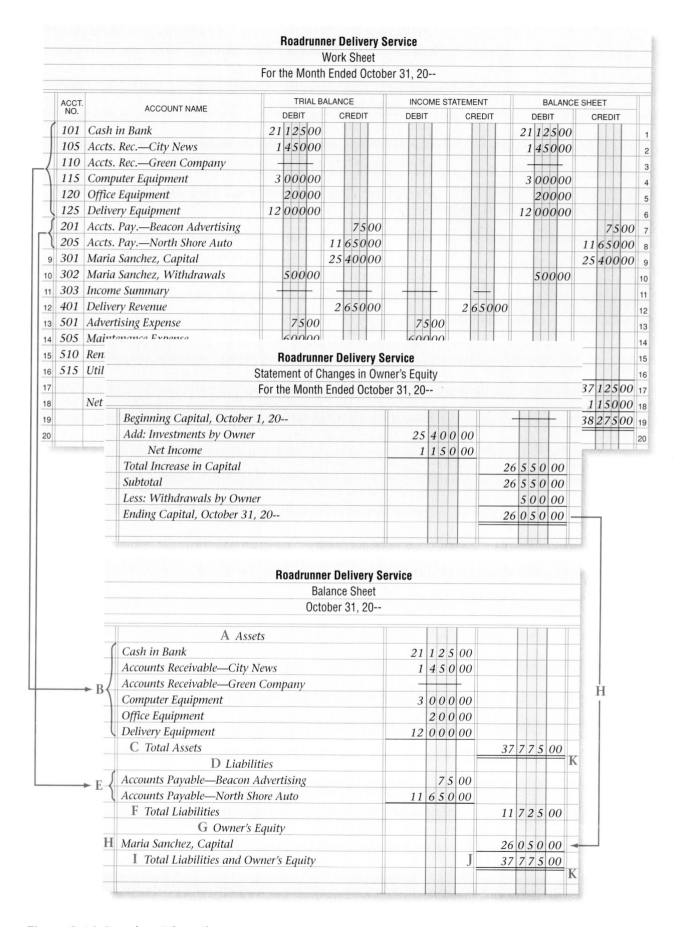

Roadrunner Delivery Service

Work Sheet

For the Month Ended October 31, 20--

ACCT. NO.	ACCOUNT NAME	TRIAL BALANCE DEBIT	TRIAL BALANCE CREDIT	INCOME STATEMENT DEBIT	INCOME STATEMENT CREDIT	BALANCE SHEET DEBIT	BALANCE SHEET CREDIT	
101	Cash in Bank	21 125 00				21 125 00		1
105	Accts. Rec.—City News	1 450 00				1 450 00		2
110	Accts. Rec.—Green Company	—				—		3
115	Computer Equipment	3 000 00				3 000 00		4
120	Office Equipment	200 00				200 00		5
125	Delivery Equipment	12 000 00				12 000 00		6
201	Accts. Pay.—Beacon Advertising		75 00				75 00	7
205	Accts. Pay.—North Shore Auto		11 650 00				11 650 00	8
301	Maria Sanchez, Capital		25 400 00				25 400 00	9
302	Maria Sanchez, Withdrawals	500 00				500 00		10
303	Income Summary	—	—	—	—			11
401	Delivery Revenue		2 650 00		2 650 00			12
501	Advertising Expense	75 00		75 00				13
505	Maintenance Expense	60 00		60 00				14
510	Ren							15
515	Util						37 125 00	17
	Net						1 150 00	18
							38 275 00	19
								20

Roadrunner Delivery Service

Statement of Changes in Owner's Equity

For the Month Ended October 31, 20--

Beginning Capital, October 1, 20--			
Add: Investments by Owner	25 400 00		
Net Income	1 150 00		
Total Increase in Capital		26 550 00	
Subtotal		26 550 00	
Less: Withdrawals by Owner		500 00	
Ending Capital, October 31, 20--		26 050 00	

Roadrunner Delivery Service

Balance Sheet

October 31, 20--

A Assets			
Cash in Bank	21 125 00		
Accounts Receivable—City News	1 450 00		
B Accounts Receivable—Green Company	—		
Computer Equipment	3 000 00		
Office Equipment	200 00		
Delivery Equipment	12 000 00		
C Total Assets		37 775 00	**K**
D Liabilities			
E Accounts Payable—Beacon Advertising	75 00		
Accounts Payable—North Shore Auto	11 650 00		
F Total Liabilities		11 725 00	
G Owner's Equity			
H Maria Sanchez, Capital		26 050 00	
I Total Liabilities and Owner's Equity	**J**	37 775 00	**K**

Figure 9–10 Preparing a Balance Sheet

3. On the next line, write the words *Total Liabilities,* indented about half an inch. Add the individual liability balances and enter the total in the second amount column. **F**

4. On the next line, enter the heading *Owner's Equity* in the center of the column containing the account names. **G**

5. On the next line, write the name of the capital account. In the second amount column, enter the ending balance of the capital account as shown on the statement of changes in owner's equity. **H**

Proving the Equality of the Balance Sheet

Recall that the basic accounting equation must always be in balance. The balance sheet represents the basic accounting equation, so the Assets section total must equal the total of the Liabilities and Owner's Equity sections.

Assets = Liabilities + Owner's Equity

To prove the equality of the balance sheet, follow these steps:

1. Draw a single rule under the balance of the capital account. On the next line, write the words *Total Liabilities and Owner's Equity,* indented about half an inch. **I**

2. Add the total liabilities amount and the ending capital balance. Enter the total in the second amount column. **J** This total must equal the total assets amount. If the totals are not equal, there is an error. Most errors occur when transferring amounts from the work sheet or from the statement of changes in owner's equity. Verify that each account balance has been transferred properly. Find and correct the error and then complete the balance sheet.

3. When total assets equal total liabilities and owner's equity, draw a double rule under the total assets amount *and* under the total liabilities and owner's equity amount. **K** The balance sheet is now complete.

Refer again to the amounts and their placement in **Figure 9–10.** As you can see, completion of the work sheet is the basis for preparing the three financial statements studied so far.

The Statement of Cash Flows

What Is the Purpose of the Statement of Cash Flows?

Cash flowing through a business is like blood flowing through your body. The flow of cash keeps a business alive. It is essential to have cash available for the daily operations of the business and for unexpected expenses.

The **statement of cash flows** summarizes the following information:

- the amount of cash the business took in
- the sources of cash
- the amount of cash the business paid out
- the uses of cash

Like the income statement, the statement of cash flows covers a single accounting period.

This information is essential for sound management and investment decisions. You will learn more about the statement of cash flows in Chapter 19.

Ratio Analysis

What Is Ratio Analysis?

Ratio analysis is the process of evaluating the relationship between various amounts in the financial statements. Owners and managers use ratio analysis to determine the financial strength, activity, and debt-paying ability of a business.

Profitability Ratios

Profitability ratios are used to evaluate the earnings performance of the business during the accounting period. The earning power of a business is an important measure of its ability to grow and continue to earn revenue.

One commonly used profitability ratio is return on sales. Business owners use the **return on sales** ratio to examine the portion of each sales dollar that represents profit. To calculate this ratio, divide net income by sales. For example, the return on sales for Roadrunner Delivery Service is calculated as follows:

$$\frac{\$1{,}150 \text{ net income}}{\$2{,}650 \text{ sales}} = 0.434 \text{ or } 43.4\%$$

This percentage indicates that each dollar of sales produced 43.4 cents of profit for Roadrunner. It can be compared to other accounting periods, to determine whether it is increasing or decreasing.

For example, if net income next year is $2,750 and sales are $5,000, the return on sales would be computed as follows:

$$\frac{\$2{,}750 \text{ net income}}{\$5{,}000 \text{ sales}} = 0.550 \text{ or } 55.0\%$$

As you can see, profit per sales dollar would increase by 11.6 cents.

Liquidity Measures

Liquidity refers to the ease with which an asset can be converted to cash. **Current assets** are those used up or converted to cash during the normal operating cycle of the business. These might include **Accounts Receivable**, **Cash in Bank**, and **Supplies**. **Current liabilities** are debts of the business that must be paid within the next accounting period. **Accounts Payable** is an example of a current liability.

The amount by which current assets exceed current liabilities is known as **working capital**. Because current liabilities are usually paid out of current assets, working capital represents the excess assets available to continue operations. The working capital for Roadrunner is calculated as follows:

Current Assets − Current Liabilities = Working Capital
$22,575   − $11,725   = $10,850

MATH HINTS

Calculating Ratios
When calculating ratios, be sure to use the correct figures for the *divisor* and the *dividend.*
For example, to calculate the ratio of net income to sales:
- the net income amount is the *dividend,*
- and the sales amount is the *divisor.*

A **liquidity ratio** is a measure of the ability of a business to pay its current debts as they become due and to provide for an unexpected need for cash. Two common ratios that are used to determine liquidity follow.

Current Ratio. The **current ratio** reflects the relationship between current assets and current liabilities. The current ratio is calculated by dividing the dollar amount of current assets by the dollar amount of current liabilities. The current ratio for Roadrunner based on the balance sheet in **Figure 9–10** is:

$$\frac{\text{Current Assets}}{\text{Current Liabilities}} = \text{Current Ratio} \qquad \frac{\$22{,}575}{\$11{,}725} = 1.92 \text{ or } 1.9{:}1$$

The current liabilities of a business must be paid within a year. These liabilities are paid from current assets.

A ratio of 2:1 or higher is considered favorable by creditors. It indicates that a business is able to pay its debts and that a business has twice as many current assets as current liabilities. A low ratio may indicate that a company could have trouble paying its debts.

Quick Ratio. A **quick ratio** is a measure of the relationship between short-term assets and current liabilities. Short-term liquid assets—those that can be quickly converted to cash—are cash and net receivables. The quick ratio is computed by dividing the total cash and receivables by total current liabilities.

The quick ratio for Roadrunner based on the Balance Sheet in **Figure 9–10** is:

$$\frac{\text{Cash and Receivables}}{\text{Current Liabilities}} = \text{Quick Ratio} \qquad \frac{\$22{,}575}{\$11{,}725} = 1.92{:}1$$

In some instances the current ratio and the quick ratio can be the same, as in the case in this example.

A quick ratio of 1:1 is considered adequate. This indicates that a business can pay its current debts with cash from incoming receivables. If a business has a quick ratio of 1:1 or higher, the business has $1.00 in liquid assets for each $1.00 of current liabilities.

Quick ratios may also be compared from one year to the next. For example, suppose that cash and receivables for the previous year were $48,653 and current liabilities were $53,245. That year's quick ratio would be computed as:

$$\frac{\$48{,}653}{\$53{,}245} = 0.91{:}1$$

As you can see, Roadrunner has improved its liquidity position in the current year. The $1.92 in liquid assets per $1.00 in current liabilities (current year) is stronger than $0.91 in liquid assets per $1.00 in current liabilities (previous year).

Reinforce the Main Idea

Using a diagram like this one, summarize the steps for creating a balance sheet. Add answer boxes for steps as needed.

Creating a Balance Sheet

```
┌──────────────────────────────────────┐
│                                      │
└──────────────────────────────────────┘
                  ↓
┌──────────────────────────────────────┐
│                                      │
└──────────────────────────────────────┘
                  ↓
┌──────────────────────────────────────┐
│                                      │
└──────────────────────────────────────┘
                  ↓
┌──────────────────────────────────────┐
│                                      │
└──────────────────────────────────────┘
```

Do the Math

Compute the four amounts that are missing from the balance sheet below. On a separate sheet of paper, write the description and the dollar value of the four missing amounts.

Interactive Communication		
Balance Sheet		
December 31, 20--		
Assets		
Cash in Bank	944 000 00	
Accounts Receivable—Chamber of Commerce	200 000 00	
Office Equipment	?	
Computer Equipment	1,000 000 00	
Total Assets		2,994 000 00
Liabilities		
Accounts Payable—Tip Top Advertising	275 500 00	
Interest Payable	?	
Salaries Payable	2 100 00	
Total Liabilities		?
Owner's Equity		
Chuck Thompson, Capital		2,715 100 00
Total Liabilities and Owner's Equity		?

Problem 9–3   Calculating Return on Sales

The Gawle Company is a family-owned and operated appliance rental and repair business. The income statement for the month ended August 31 includes the following:

Rental Revenue	$3,256	Rent Expense	$2,100
Repair Revenue	2,140	Utilities Expense	483
Advertising Expense	575	Net Income	1,108
Maintenance Expense	1,130		

Instructions Calculate the return on sales for the month for The Gawle Company.

Key Concepts

1. The *income statement* reports revenue earned and the expenses incurred for a specific period of time. It also reports the net income or net loss for the period.

2. Sections of the income statement:

Section	Information Presented
Heading	• Name of the business • Name of the report • Accounting period covered
Revenue	Balance of each revenue account for the period. The information comes from the Income Statement section of the work sheet.
Expenses	Balance of each expense account for the period. The information comes from the Income Statement section of the work sheet.
Net income	Total expenses subtracted from total revenue. The result is net income or net loss.

3. The *statement of changes in owner's equity* summarizes the impact that the period's business transactions had on the capital account.

4. Sections of the statement of changes in owner's equity:

Section	Information Presented
Heading	• Name of the business • Name of the report • Accounting period covered
Beginning Capital	The information comes from the owner's capital account in the general ledger.
Increases in Capital	• Investments by Owner • Net Income Information about investments by the owner comes from the owner's capital account in the general ledger. Information about net income comes from the income statement.
Decreases in Capital	• Withdrawals by Owner • Net Loss Information about withdrawals by the owner comes from the work sheet. Information about net loss comes from the income statement.
Ending Capital	Beginning Capital + Increases − Decreases

5. The *balance sheet* reports the balances in the permanent accounts at the end of the period. It states the financial position of a business *on a specific date*. Information comes from the Balance Sheet section of the work sheet and the statement of changes in owner's equity.

6. **Sections of the Balance Sheet:**

Section	Information Presented
Heading	• Name of the business • Name of the report • Date of the last day of the accounting period
Assets	Balance of each asset account. The information comes from the Balance Sheet section of the work sheet.
Liabilities	Balance of each liability account. The information comes from the Balance Sheet section of the work sheet.
Owner's Equity	The balance of the owner's capital account. The information comes from the statement of changes in owner's equity.

7. The *statement of cash flows* reports how much cash the business took in and paid out during the period and why the **Cash in Bank** account increased or decreased.

8. Ratio analysis evaluates the relationship between various financial statement amounts.

Profitability ratio	Earnings performance during the accounting period
Return on sales	Determines the percent of each sales dollar that is profit: Return on Sales = Net Income / Sales
Liquidity ratio	Ease with which an asset can be converted to cash
Current ratio	$\dfrac{\text{Current Assets}}{\text{Current Liabilities}}$
Quick ratio	$\dfrac{\text{Cash and Receivables}}{\text{Current Liabilities}}$

Key Terms

balance sheet	(p. 231)	**liquidity ratio**	(p. 236)	statement of cash flows	(p. 234)
current assets	(p. 235)	**profitability ratio**	(p. 235)		
current liabilities	(p. 235)	**quick ratio**	(p. 236)	statement of changes in owner's equity	(p. 225)
current ratio	(p. 236)	**ratio analysis**	(p. 235)		
financial statements	(p. 220)	**report form**	(p. 232)	working capital	(p. 235)
income statement	(p. 221)	**return on sales**	(p. 235)		

AFTER You READ

Check Your Understanding

1. **Income Statement**
   a. What is the purpose of the income statement?
   b. What is the source of information used to prepare the income statement?

2. **Preparing an Income Statement**
   a. List the sections of the income statement.
   b. How is net income or net loss calculated?

3. **Statement of Changes in Owner's Equity**
   a. What is the purpose of the statement of changes in owner's equity?
   b. What sources of information are used to prepare the statement of changes in owner's equity?

4. **Preparing a Statement of Changes in Owner's Equity**
   a. In a statement of changes in owner's equity, what items are totaled in the "Add" section?
   b. What items are subtracted from the subtotal?

5. **Balance Sheet**
   a. What is the purpose of the balance sheet?
   b. How does the date in a balance sheet heading differ from the other financial statements?

6. **Preparing a Balance Sheet**
   a. What sources of information are used to prepare the balance sheet?
   b. How are balance sheet account names shown using the report form?

7. **Statement of Cash Flows**
   a. What is the purpose of the statement of cash flows?
   b. Why does management need the information in the statement of cash flows?

8. **Ratio Analysis**
   a. What is the purpose of computing ratios from amounts on financial statements?
   b. Who might be interested in the profitability ratio of a business?

Apply Key Terms

As a game store owner, you want to develop an information sheet for the store manager. Explain the importance of financial statement preparation using these key terms.

balance sheet	quick ratio
current assets	ratio analysis
current liabilities	report form
current ratio	return on sales
financial statements	statement of cash flows
income statement	statement of changes in
liquidity ratio	owner's equity
profitability ratio	working capital

Preparing Financial Statements

Making the Transition from a Manual to a Computerized System

Task	Manual Methods	Computerized Methods
Preparing an income statement	• Transfer all revenue and expense accounts and their balances from the work sheet. • Subtract expenses from revenue to determine net income or net loss.	• From the *Reports* menu, select **Income Statement** or **Profit and Loss**, depending on the accounting software. • Click **Print**.
Preparing a statement of changes in owner's equity	• Transfer the beginning balance of the capital account from the work sheet. • Add additional investments and net income or loss. • Subtract withdrawals. • Calculate the ending balance for the capital account.	• Since the software automatically computes the ending balance of the capital account for you, it is not necessary to prepare this statement.
Preparing a balance sheet	• Transfer permanent accounts and their balances from the work sheet. • Transfer the ending capital account balance from the statement of changes in owner's equity. • Total all asset account balances. • Total all liabilities and owner's equity account balances. • Verify that assets equal liabilities and owner's equity.	• From the *Reports* menu, select **Balance Sheet**. • Click **Print**.

Peachtree® Q & A

Peachtree Question	Answer
How do I prepare financial statements in Peachtree?	1. From the *Reports* menu, select **Financial Statements**. 2. Choose the statement you wish to print from the Reports list. 3. Click **Print** when the statement appears on the screen.

QuickBooks Q & A

QuickBooks Question	Answer
How do I prepare financial statements in QuickBooks?	1. From the *Reports* menu, select **Company & Financial**. 2. Choose the report you wish to print from the list. 3. Click **Print**.

For detailed instructions, see your Glencoe Accounting Chapter Study Guides and Working Papers.

Complete problems using: **Manual** Glencoe Working Papers OR **Peachtree Complete Accounting** Software OR **QuickBooks** Templates OR **Spreadsheet** Templates

Peachtree®
SMART GUIDE

Step–by–Step Instructions: Problems 9–4, 9–5

1. Select the problem set for Wilderness Rentals (Prob. 9–4, 9–5).
2. Rename the company and set the system date.
3. Print a General Ledger Trial Balance, Income Statement, Statement of Changes in Owner's Equity, and Balance Sheet.
4. Complete the Analyze activity.
5. End the session.

Peachtree®
SMART GUIDE

Step–by–Step Instructions: Problem 9–6

1. Select the problem set for Hot Suds Car Wash (Prob. 9–6).
2. Rename the company and set the system date.
3. Print a General Ledger Trial Balance, Income Statement, Statement of Changes in Owner's Equity, and Balance Sheet.
4. Complete the Analyze activity.
5. End the session.

QuickBooks
PROBLEM GUIDE

Step–by–Step Instructions: Problem 9–6

1. Restore the Problem 9-6.QBB file.
2. Print a Trial Balance, Profit & Loss report, and Balance Sheet.
3. Complete the Analyze activity.
4. Back up your work.

Problem 9–4 Preparing an Income Statement

The work sheet for Wilderness Rentals for the month ended September 30, 20-- is in your working papers.

Instructions Using the work sheet, prepare an income statement for Wilderness Rentals.

Analyze Compute the return on sales for the period.

Problem 9–5 Preparing a Statement of Changes in Owner's Equity

Instructions Using the work sheet for Wilderness Rentals in your working papers and the income statement prepared in Problem 9–4, prepare a statement of changes in owner's equity and a balance sheet. Ronald Hicks made an additional investment in the business of $500 during the period.

Analyze Compute the current ratio for Wilderness Rentals as of September 30.

Problem 9–6 Preparing Financial Statements

The trial balance for the Hot Suds Car Wash is listed below and in your working papers.

Instructions

1. Complete the work sheet in your working papers.
2. Prepare an income statement for the quarter ended September 30, 20--.
3. Prepare a statement of changes in owner's equity. Regina Delgado made no additional investments during the period.
4. Prepare a balance sheet in report form.

Hot Suds Car Wash
Trial Balance
For the Quarter Ended September 30, 20--

		Debit	Credit
101	Cash in Bank	8 4 5 7 00	
105	Accts. Rec.—Linda Brown	5 8 4 00	
110	Accts. Rec.—Valley Auto	6 1 9 00	
115	Detailing Supplies	8 1 0 00	
120	Detergent Supplies	4 6 0 00	
125	Office Equipment	15 2 4 0 00	
130	Office Furniture	2 1 6 0 00	
135	Car Wash Equipment	7 5 2 2 00	
201	Accts. Pay.—Allen Vacuum Systems		3 5 2 8 00
205	Accts. Pay.—O'Brian's Office Supply		1 2 1 5 00
301	Regina Delgado, Capital		23 8 4 5 00
305	Regina Delgado, Withdrawals	1 5 0 0 00	
310	Income Summary		
401	Wash Revenue		9 6 2 3 00
405	Wax Revenue		8 0 1 9 00
410	Interior Detailing Revenue		2 6 2 8 00
501	Advertising Expense	1 9 6 3 00	
505	Equipment Rental Expense	4 1 3 7 00	
510	Maintenance Expense	1 1 8 6 00	
520	Rent Expense	3 5 0 0 00	
530	Utilities Expense	7 2 0 00	
		48 8 5 8 00	48 8 5 8 00

Analyze Calculate the return on sales for the period.

Problem 9–7 Preparing Financial Statements

The general ledger accounts and balances for Kits & Pups Grooming follow.

General Ledger

101	Cash in Bank	$ 4,296
105	Accts. Rec.—Juan Alvarez	1,528
110	Accts. Rec.—Nathan Carlsbad	904
115	Accts. Rec.—Martha Giles	1,219
120	Grooming Supplies	1,368
125	Office Equipment	8,467
130	Office Furniture	3,396
135	Computer Equipment	2,730
140	Grooming Equipment	1,974
145	Kennel Equipment	7,412
201	Accts. Pay.—Able Store Equipment	3,876
205	Accts. Pay.—Dogs & Cats Inc.	2,746
207	Accts. Pay.—Pet Gourmet	1,281
301	Abe Shultz, Capital	30,928
305	Abe Shultz, Withdrawals	1,900
310	Income Summary	—
401	Boarding Revenue	11,989
405	Grooming Revenue	4,420
501	Advertising Expense	3,934
505	Equipment Repair Expense	943
510	Maintenance Expense	2,483
520	Rent Expense	8,850
530	Utilities Expense	3,836

Instructions

1. Prepare a work sheet for the month ended September 30, 20--.
2. Prepare an income statement for the period.
3. Prepare a statement of changes in owner's equity. Abe Shultz made an additional investment of $2,500 during the period.
4. Prepare a balance sheet in report form.

Analyze Compute the quick ratio as of September 30.

Problem 9–8 Preparing a Statement of Changes in Owner's Equity

Instructions Use the balance sheet and income statement shown to prepare a statement of changes in owner's equity. (The owner made an additional investment of $4,000 and withdrew $1,500 during the period.)

CONTINUE

Peachtree®

SMART GUIDE

Step–by–Step Instructions: Problem 9–7

1. Select the problem set for Kits & Pups Grooming (Prob. 9–7).
2. Rename the company and set the system date.
3. Print a General Ledger Trial Balance, Income Statement, Statement of Changes in Owner's Equity, and Balance Sheet.
4. Complete the Analyze activity.
5. End the session.

QuickBooks

PROBLEM GUIDE

Step–by–Step Instructions: Problem 9–7

1. Restore the Problem 9-7.QBB file.
2. Print a Trial Balance, Profit & Loss report, and Balance Sheet.
3. Complete the Analyze activity.
4. Back up your work.

SPREADSHEET SMART GUIDE

Step–by–Step Instructions: Problem 9–8

1. Select the spreadsheet template for Problem 9–8.
2. Enter your name and the date in the spaces provided on the template.
3. Complete the spreadsheet using the instructions in your working papers.
4. Print the spreadsheet and proof your work.
5. Complete the Analyze activity.
6. Save your work and exit the spreadsheet program.

Outback Guide Service

Income Statement

For the Month Ended September 30, 20--

Revenue:		
Guide Service Revenue		8 9 1 3 00
Expenses:		
Advertising Expense	3 7 5 00	
Maintenance Expense	1 3 8 00	
Rent Expense	1 2 5 0 00	
Salaries Expense	1 5 0 0 00	
Utilities Expense	1 1 6 1 00	
Total Expenses		4 4 2 4 00
Net Income		4 4 8 9 00

Outback Guide Service

Balance Sheet

September 30, 20--

Assets		
Cash in Bank	3 1 1 7 00	
Accounts Receivable—Mary Johnson	4 2 3 00	
Accounts Receivable—Feldman, Jones & Ritter	4 4 3 00	
Accounts Receivable—Podaski Systems Inc.	1 0 0 8 00	
Hiking Supplies	1 5 3 00	
Office Supplies	3 3 8 00	
Office Equipment	6 4 9 2 00	
Office Furniture	3 0 8 4 00	
Computer Equipment	3 6 2 4 00	
Hiking Equipment	1 0 1 5 00	
Rafting Equipment	9 1 8 6 00	
Total Assets		28 8 8 3 00
Liabilities		
Accounts Payable—A-1 Adventure Warehouse	6 5 4 5 00	
Accounts Payable—Peak Equipment Inc.	1 3 2 5 00	
Accounts Payable—Premier Processors	6 4 2 00	
Total Liabilities		8 5 1 2 00
Owner's Equity		
Juanita Ortega, Capital		20 3 7 1 00
Total Liabilities and Owner's Equity		28 8 8 3 00

Analyze Identify the largest expense for this business during the period.

Practice your test-taking skills! The questions on this page are reprinted with permission from national organizations:

- Future Business Leaders of America
- Business Professionals of America

Use a separate sheet of paper to record your answers.

Future Business Leaders of America

MULTIPLE CHOICE

1. The balance sheet shows how a business is doing
  a. for a period of 12 months.
  b. on a specific date during the year.
  c. regarding its profit or loss.
  d. All of the above

2. Financial statements are prepared in the following order:
  a. income statement, balance sheet, owners' equity.
  b. income statement, statement of owners' equity, balance sheet.
  c. statement of owners' equity, balance sheet, income statement.
  d. balance sheet, income statement, statement of owners' equity.

3. The purpose of the Income Statement is to report
  a. all assets, liabilities, and owner's equity at a specified time.
  b. all the accounts used in journalizing a business's transactions.
  c. balances in the capital accounts in order to determine the net income or loss.
  d. the net income or loss for a fiscal period.

Business Professionals of America

MULTIPLE CHOICE

4. At the end of a fiscal period when a balance sheet is prepared, from which document may we find the ending owner's capital balance?
  a. Worksheet
  c. Trial Balance
  b. Income Statement
  d. Statement of Changes in Owner's Equity

5. During the month of February, Tom had the following transactions involving revenue and expenses:

  Paid $75 phone bill

  Provided services to clients for $1,200 cash

  Paid salaries of $650 to employees

  Paid $125 for computer maintenance

  Provided services on account totaling $2,000

  What was Tom's net income or net loss for the period?
  a. Net Income $350
  b. Net Loss $1,650
  c. Net Income $2,350
  d. Net Income $3,200

Need More Help?

Go to **glencoeaccounting.glencoe.com** and click on **Student Center**. Click on **Winning Competitive Events** and select **Chapter 9.**

- **Practice Questions and Test-Taking Tips**
- **Concept Capsules and Terminology**

Financial Statements

1. Name the one piece of information that is included on both the income statement and the statement of changes in owner's equity.
2. Explain why the date line on the balance sheet is different from the one on the other statements.
3. The net income computed on the income statement is different from the amount computed on the work sheet. How do you resolve this problem?
4. Explain why the **Withdrawals** account is reported on the statement of changes in owner's equity but is not reported on the income statement.
5. What items are needed to complete the first three financial statements? List office supplies, forms, and any information needed.
6. Assess the value of using the income statement, the statement of changes in owner's equity, and the balance sheet for making business decisions.

Service Business: Video Arcade

Taki Yamamoto owns a video arcade business called Arcadia. Taki has hired your accounting firm to record Arcadia's financial information. Taki hands you a folder containing these documents:

- Canceled checks with June dates: $800 for rent, $120 for electricity, $70 for telephone service, $180 for insurance, $250 for newspaper advertising, and $200 for a cleaning service.
- Invoice dated June 16 for a used video game sold on account for $2,000.
- Cash register tapes for June showing total cash sales of $5,890.

INSTRUCTIONS

1. Using the preceding information, make a list of accounts needed to record the transactions indicated by the financial documents Taki has given you.
2. Prepare an income statement for Arcadia for the month of June.

Financial Report or Repair?

Your favorite uncle, who owns a restaurant, has asked you to help with his bookkeeping. He desperately needs a bank loan and wants you to prepare the financial statements. After going over his accounting records, you do not believe a bank will give him a loan; but you notice that by leaving out an expense or two, your uncle's business could look more promising. After all, he does have some good ideas for improving the business.

ETHICAL DECISION MAKING

1. What are the ethical issues?
2. What are the alternatives?
3. Who are the affected parties?
4. How do the alternatives affect the parties?
5. What would you do?

Presenting the Balance Sheet

Team up with a classmate and give a brief presentation of the purpose and use of a balance sheet. Create a sample balance sheet for your presentation.

SKILLS BEYOND NUMBERS

Using Computers to Process Information

Being able to use computers and software is essential for most business tasks.

ON THE JOB

As the accounting clerk for Jewels and Treasures, you manually prepared the income statements in the past. This year you will use a spreadsheet program.

INSTRUCTIONS

Prepare a list of reasons why using a spreadsheet program is an improvement over manually preparing financial statements.

INTERNATIONAL ACCOUNTING

The Euro

Financial statements are generally prepared in the currency of the country in which the business operates. Many European countries use a single currency, the *euro*. Nations in the European Union began using the euro in 2002. Individuals and businesses both benefit by having a single currency. Travelers can use one currency in multiple countries. Businesses have a more stable business environment due to the elimination of exchange rate fluctuations.

INSTRUCTIONS Imagine that you own a business with locations in Italy and France. Describe how the adoption of the euro in both countries has changed your financial statement preparation.

Making It Personal

Your Business

Do you dream of having your own business? The experience of tracking your own finances can help you create the general ledger accounts for that business.

PERSONAL FINANCE ACTIVITY Create an income statement for a typical high school student. List revenue and expense accounts, and identify expenses that some, but not all, students would have.

PERSONAL FINANCE ONLINE Log on to **glencoeaccounting.glencoe.com** and click on **Student Center.** Click on **Making It Personal** and select **Chapter 9.**

Analyzing FINANCIAL Reports

Return on Sales

Business owners are especially interested in the *return on sales* (see page 235). This percentage shows how much of each revenue dollar becomes profit for the business.

INSTRUCTIONS Use Roadrunner's income statement on page 222 to calculate its return on sales. (Use $1,100 as net income instead of $1,150.) If total sales are about equal from month to month but return on sales decreases each month, what does this say about the business? What suggestions can you offer to improve the return on sales?

WebQuest

Financial Statements in Sports

Financial statements summarize results for owners, managers, and other interested parties. Visit **glencoeaccounting .glencoe.com** and click on **Student Center.** Click on **WebQuest** and select **Unit 2** to continue your Internet project.

Completing the Accounting Cycle for a Sole Proprietorship

What You'll Learn

1. Explain why it is necessary to update accounts through closing entries.

2. Explain the purpose of the Income Summary account.

3. Explain the relationship between the Income Summary account and the capital account.

4. Analyze and journalize the closing entries.

5. Post the closing entries to the general ledger.

6. Prepare a post-closing trial balance.

7. Define the accounting terms introduced in this chapter.

Why It's Important

▶ For accounting purposes the life of a business is divided into specific periods of time.

Predict

1. What does the chapter title tell you?
2. What do you already know about this subject from personal experience?
3. What have you learned about this in the earlier chapters?
4. What gaps exist in your knowledge of this subject?

Exploring the *Real World* of Business

LOOKING AT FISCAL YEAR-END ACTIVITIES

Radio Flyer

Many adults love to give children the same kinds of toys they enjoyed when they were young. A **Radio Flyer** wagon is that kind of toy. Antonio Pasin, an Italian immigrant living in Chicago, crafted and sold the first wooden red wagons in 1917.

The company has been passed down through the generations, just like the love of the toys it produces. Antonio's grandson, Robert Pasin, is now the chief executive officer of **Radio Flyer.** He has taken the company in new directions by adding tricycles, scooters, and other riding toys.

Radio Flyer's revenue comes from selling classic wagons and newer toys. At the end of each accounting period, the company closes its accounts and analyzes the revenues and expenses.

What Do You Think?

Why would **Radio Flyer** employees want to compare sales of different toys from one accounting period to another?

Working in the *Real World*

APPLYING YOUR ACCOUNTING KNOWLEDGE

Preparing financial statements can be a hectic time for the accounting staff of Radio Flyer. Professional accountants learn to manage stressful times using good organizational skills. Once the financial statements have been prepared, other tasks must be completed to close one accounting cycle and begin another. You will learn about these tasks to complete the accounting cycle in this chapter.

Personal Connection

1. In your workplace are there especially hectic times of the day or year?

2. How do you and your co-workers handle these busy times?

Online Connection

Go to **glencoeaccounting.glencoe.com** and click on **Student Center.** Click on **Working in the Real World** and select **Chapter 10.**

Preparing Closing Entries

Main Idea
Closing entries transfer the temporary account balances to the owner's capital account.

Read to Learn...
➤ the last two steps of the accounting cycle. (p. 250)
➤ the purpose of closing entries. (p. 250)
➤ the purpose of the **Income Summary** account. (p. 253)
➤ how to journalize the closing entries. (p. 253)

Key Terms
closing entries
Income Summary account
compound entry

Instant Recall

Accounting Period By dividing the life of a business into time periods, decision makers can see patterns and make comparisons.

In Chapter 9 you learned how to prepare three financial statements:

- The income statement reports revenue, expenses, and net income or net loss for the accounting period.
- The statement of changes in owner's equity summarizes the impact of the business transactions on the owner's capital account.
- The balance sheet reports the financial position of the business at the end of the period.

Accountants for a company like Mattel prepare financial statements and then journalize and post the closing entries. They prepare a post-closing trial balance to verify that the accounting records still balance.

Completing the Accounting Cycle
What Are the Last Two Steps of the Accounting Cycle?

During the accounting period, the accountant records transactions involving revenue, expenses, and withdrawals in temporary accounts. At the end of the period, the accountant transfers the balances in the temporary accounts to the owner's capital account to bring it up to date and to prepare the accounting records for the next period.

Closing entries are journal entries made to close, or reduce to zero, the balances in the temporary accounts and to transfer the net income or net loss for the period to the capital account.

After the closing entries have been journalized and posted, a trial balance is prepared to prove the equality of the general ledger after the closing process. The trial balance prepared after closing is called a *post-closing trial balance*. As you can see in **Figure 10–1**, the closing process and the post-closing trial balance complete the accounting cycle.

Starting the Eighth Step in the Accounting Cycle: Journalizing the Closing Entries
What Is the Purpose of Closing Entries?

Preparing financial records for the start of a new period is a little like keeping stats for a basketball team. For basketball stats, individual and team scores are recorded for every game, but each new game starts with a score of zero. Similarly, in keeping the stats or accounting for a business, entries are posted to the accounts during the accounting period (game), but the

Figure 10–1 The Accounting Cycle with Steps 8 and 9 Highlighted

Collect and verify source documents
INVOICE
RECEIPT
MEMORANDUM
1

Analyze each transaction
ACCOUNT
DEBIT | CREDIT
ACCOUNT
DEBIT | CREDIT
2

Journalize each transaction
GENERAL JOURNAL
3

Post to the ledger
LEDGER
4

Prepare a trial balance
TRIAL BALANCE
5

Prepare a work sheet
WORK SHEET
6

Prepare financial statements
INCOME STATEMENT
STATEMENT OF CHANGES IN OWNER'S EQUITY
BALANCE SHEET
7

Journalize and post closing entries
GENERAL JOURNAL
LEDGER
8

Prepare a post-closing trial balance
POST-CLOSING TRIAL BALANCE
9

temporary accounts (**Rent Expense, Maintenance Expense, Revenue**, etc.) start each new accounting period (game) with zero balances.

The income statement, you'll remember, reports the net income or net loss for *one accounting period.* The statement is prepared from information recorded and accumulated in the revenue and expense accounts. At the end of the period, the accountant records entries to close, or reduce to zero, the revenue and expense accounts because their balances also apply to only one accounting period. These closing entries also transfer the net income or net loss for the period to the capital account.

The closing process is shown in **Figure 10–2** on page 252.

- Prior to the closing process, you know that net income or net loss is calculated on the work sheet. **A**
- The net income or net loss amount then appears on the income statement. **B**
- On the statement of changes in owner's equity, the ending balance of the capital account includes net income or net loss. **C**
- The ending balance of the capital account then appears on the balance sheet. **D**
- At this point, however, the balance of the capital account in the general ledger does not equal the amount on the balance sheet because the closing entries need to be journalized and posted. **E**

For example, the balance on the work sheet for **Maria Sanchez, Capital** is $25,400, but on the balance sheet, it is $26,050. These two amounts differ because the withdrawals and the net income have not been recorded in the capital account in the general ledger. The closing process updates accounts through closing entries and brings the balance of the general ledger capital account up to date.

CULTURAL Diversity

Setting Deadlines
In international business be aware of cultural differences about time. Business is conducted at a faster pace in the United States than in some other cultures. Tight deadlines can cause problems overseas if workers resent being pressured to do things at a pace other than the one they are used to.

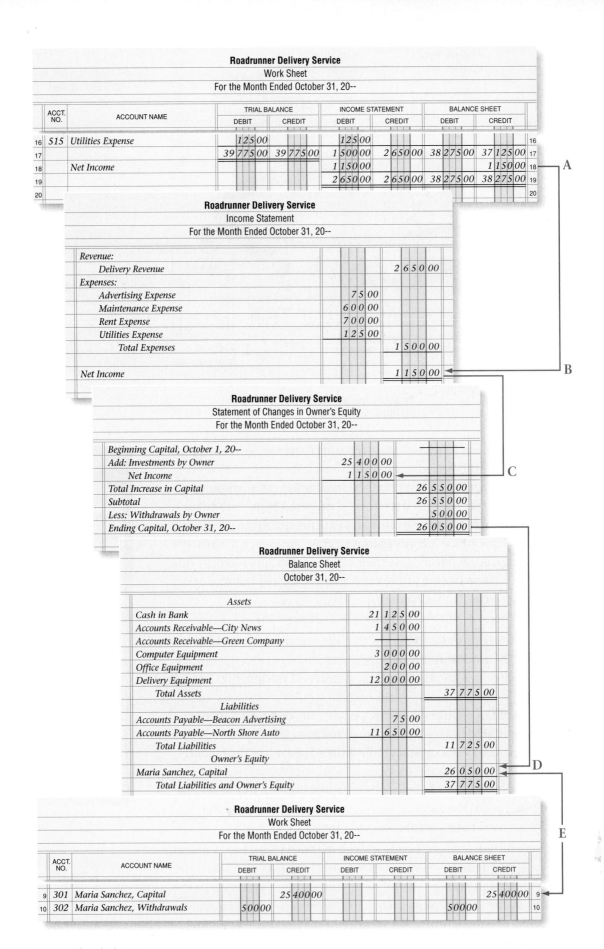

Figure 10–2 The Closing Process

The Income Summary Account

What Is the Purpose of the Income Summary Account?

Before the closing entries are journalized and posted, no single account in the general ledger shows all of the revenue and expenses for the period. This information is scattered among the individual revenue and expense accounts. There is, however, one general ledger account that, until this point, has not been used. That is the **Income Summary** account.

The **Income Summary account** is used to accumulate and summarize the revenue and expenses for the period. This account serves as a simple income statement in the ledger. Expenses, which have debit balances, are transferred as debits to **Income Summary**. Revenues, which have credit balances, are transferred as credits to **Income Summary**. The balance of the account equals the net income or net loss for the fiscal period.

Refer to the chart of accounts for Roadrunner Delivery Service on page 79. Notice that **Income Summary** is in the Owner's Equity section of the general ledger. It is located there because of its relationship to the owner's capital account. Remember that the revenue and expenses transferred to the **Income Summary** account actually represent increases and decreases to owner's equity. The balance of **Income Summary** (the net income or net loss for the period) is transferred to the capital account at the end of the closing process.

Like the withdrawals account, **Income Summary** is a temporary account. However, it is quite different from the other temporary accounts.

- **Income Summary** is used only at the end of the accounting period to summarize the balances from the revenue and expense accounts.
- **Income Summary** does not have a normal balance, which means that it does not have an increase or a decrease side. As shown in the following T account, the debit and credit sides of the account are simply used to summarize the period's revenue and expenses.
- The balance of the **Income Summary** account before and after the closing process is zero.
- The **Income Summary** account does not appear on any financial statement.

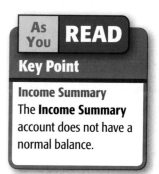

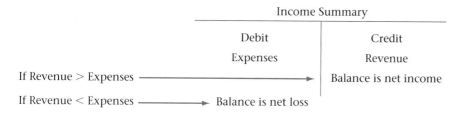

Preparing Closing Entries

How Do You Journalize Closing Entries?

Four journal entries are prepared to close the temporary accounts for Roadrunner:

1. Transfer the balances of all revenue accounts to the credit side of the **Income Summary** account.

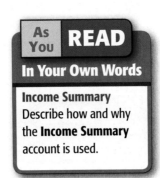

As You READ

In Your Own Words

Income Summary
Describe how and why the **Income Summary** account is used.

2. Transfer all expense account balances to the debit side of the **Income Summary** account.
3. Transfer the balance of the **Income Summary** account to the capital account (net income to the credit side; net loss to the debit side).
4. Transfer the balance of the withdrawals account to the debit side of the capital account.

Closing Revenue to Income Summary

The first step in the closing procedure is to transfer the balance of the revenue account to **Income Summary.** The balance for the revenue account is found in the Income Statement section of the work sheet. (Refer to the work sheet in **Figure 9–3** on page 222 when reading about closing entries.)

Closing Entry

First Closing Entry—Close Revenue to Income Summary

ANALYSIS   *Identify*   1. Roadrunner has only one revenue account, **Delivery Revenue.** The accounts affected are **Delivery Revenue** and **Income Summary.**

Classify   2. **Delivery Revenue** is a revenue account. **Income Summary** is a temporary owner's equity account.

+/−   3. The **Delivery Revenue** account balance is decreased by $2,650 to zero. That amount, $2,650, is transferred to the **Income Summary** account.

DEBIT-CREDIT RULE   4. Decreases in revenue accounts are recorded as debits. Debit **Delivery Revenue** for $2,650.

5. To transfer the revenue to the **Income Summary** account, credit **Income Summary** for $2,650.

T ACCOUNTS   6.

Delivery Revenue		Income Summary	
Debit	Credit	Debit	Credit
−	+		
Closing 2,650	Balance 2,650		Closing 2,650

JOURNAL ENTRY   7.

GENERAL JOURNAL   PAGE ___3___

	DATE		DESCRIPTION	POST. REF.	DEBIT	CREDIT	
1	20--		*Closing Entries*				1
2	Oct.	31	Delivery Revenue		2 650 00		2
3			Income Summary			2 650 00	3
4							4

To record closing entries in the general journal, follow these steps:

1. Enter *Closing Entries* in the center of the Description column.
2. Enter the date (the last day of the accounting period).
3. Enter the name(s) of the account(s) to be debited and the debit amount(s).
4. Enter the name of the account, **Income Summary**, to be credited and the amount to be credited.

Closing Expenses to Income Summary

The second closing entry transfers the balances of the expense accounts to **Income Summary.** The balances of the expense accounts are found in the Income Statement section of the work sheet.

Closing Entry

Second Closing Entry—Close Expenses to Income Summary

ANALYSIS   *Identify*

1. The accounts affected by the second closing entry are **Advertising Expense, Maintenance Expense, Rent Expense, Utilities Expense,** and **Income Summary.**

Classify

2. **Advertising Expense, Maintenance Expense, Rent Expense,** and **Utilities Expense** are expense accounts. **Income Summary** is a temporary owner's equity account.

+/−

3. The balances of the four expense accounts are decreased to zero; the total decrease is $1,500. The total amount, $1,500, is transferred to the **Income Summary** account.

DEBIT-CREDIT RULE

4. To transfer the expenses to the **Income Summary** account, debit **Income Summary** for $1,500.
5. Decreases in expense accounts are recorded as credits. Credit **Advertising Expense,** $75; **Maintenance Expense,** $600; **Rent Expense,** $700; **Utilities Expense,** $125.

T ACCOUNTS   6.

Income Summary	
Debit	Credit
Closing 1,500	

Advertising Expense	
Debit +	Credit −
Balance 75	Closing 75

Maintenance Expense	
Debit +	Credit −
Balance 600	Closing 600

Rent Expense	
Debit +	Credit −
Balance 700	Closing 700

Utilities Expense	
Debit +	Credit −
Balance 125	Closing 125

JOURNAL ENTRY   **7.**

	DATE		DESCRIPTION	POST. REF.	DEBIT	CREDIT	
			GENERAL JOURNAL		PAGE 3		
5	Oct.	31	Income Summary		1 500 00		5
6			Advertising Expense			75 00	6
7			Maintenance Expense			600 00	7
8			Rent Expense			700 00	8
9			Utilities Expense			125 00	9
10							10

It is not necessary to use a separate closing entry for each expense account. As you can see, Roadrunner's entry has one debit and four credits. A journal entry with two or more debits or two or more credits is called a compound entry . A compound entry saves both space and posting time. For example, each of Roadrunner's expense accounts could be closed to **Income Summary** separately. That, however, requires four entries and postings to the **Income Summary** account instead of one entry and posting.

Closing Income Summary to Capital

The third closing entry transfers the balance of the **Income Summary** account to the capital account. As shown in the T account, after closing Roadrunner's revenue and expense accounts, **Income Summary** has a credit balance of $1,150. A credit balance indicates net income for the period. It is the same amount that appears on the work sheet.

Income Summary		
2 Closing entry for expenses 1,500	1 Closing entry for revenue	2,650
	Balance	1,150

Closing Entry

Third Closing Entry—Close Income Summary to Capital

ANALYSIS	*Identify* *Classify*	1. The accounts **Income Summary** and **Maria Sanchez, Capital** are affected.
		2. **Income Summary** is a temporary owner's equity account. **Maria Sanchez, Capital** is an owner's capital account.
	+/−	3. The **Income Summary** account balance is reduced to zero by transferring $1,150, the net income amount, to the capital account. **Maria Sanchez, Capital** is increased by $1,150.

DEBIT-CREDIT RULE		4. To reduce the **Income Summary** balance to zero, debit **Income Summary** for $1,150.
		5. Net income is recorded as a credit to the owner's capital account. Credit **Maria Sanchez, Capital** for $1,150.

T ACCOUNTS   **6.**

	Income Summary			Maria Sanchez, Capital	
Debit		Credit	Debit		Credit
			−		+
Closing 1,150		Balance 1,150			Balance 25,400
					Closing 1,150

JOURNAL ENTRY   **7.**

		GENERAL JOURNAL				PAGE 3		
	DATE	DESCRIPTION	POST. REF.	DEBIT		CREDIT		
11	Oct. 31	Income Summary		1 150 00				11
12		Maria Sanchez, Capital				1 150 00		12
13								13

After the third closing entry has been posted, the **Income Summary** account appears in T-account form as follows.

Income Summary				
2 Closing entry for expenses	1,500	1 Closing entry for revenue	2,650
3 Closing balance to owner's capital account	1,150		

If a business has a net loss, **Income Summary** has a debit balance. In that case, the third closing entry debits the capital account and credits **Income Summary** for the amount of the net loss. **Figure 10–3** shows this general journal entry.

		GENERAL JOURNAL				PAGE 3		
	DATE	DESCRIPTION	POST. REF.	DEBIT		CREDIT		
1	20--	Closing Entries						1
2	Oct. 31	Maria Sanchez, Capital		7 00 00				2
3		Income Summary				7 00 00		3
4								4

Figure 10–3 Closing Income Summary for the Amount of Net Loss

Closing Withdrawals to Capital

The fourth and last closing entry transfers the balance of the withdrawals account to the capital account. As you recall, withdrawals decrease owner's equity. The balance of the withdrawals account is transferred to the capital account to reflect the decrease in owner's equity. The balance of the withdrawals account is found in the Balance Sheet section of the work sheet.

Closing Entry

Fourth Closing Entry—Close Withdrawals to Capital

ANALYSIS

Identify   1. The accounts affected by the fourth closing entry are **Maria Sanchez, Withdrawals** and **Maria Sanchez, Capital.**

Classify   2. **Maria Sanchez, Withdrawals** is a temporary owner's equity account. **Maria Sanchez, Capital** is an owner's capital account.

+/−   3. **Maria Sanchez, Withdrawals** is decreased by $500. **Maria Sanchez, Capital** is decreased by $500.

DEBIT-CREDIT RULE

4. Decreases in owner's capital accounts are recorded as debits. Debit **Maria Sanchez, Capital** for $500.
5. Decreases in owner's withdrawal accounts are recorded as credits. Credit **Maria Sanchez, Withdrawals** for $500.

T ACCOUNTS

6.

Maria Sanchez, Capital		Maria Sanchez, Withdrawals	
Debit −	Credit +	Debit +	Credit −
Closing 500	Balance 26,550	Balance 500	Closing 500

JOURNAL ENTRY

7.

		GENERAL JOURNAL			PAGE 3	
	DATE	DESCRIPTION	POST. REF.	DEBIT	CREDIT	
14	Oct. 31	Maria Sanchez, Capital		500 00		14
15		Maria Sanchez, Withdrawals			500 00	15

Figure 10–4 summarizes the closing entries for Roadrunner.

		GENERAL JOURNAL			PAGE 3	
	DATE	DESCRIPTION	POST. REF.	DEBIT	CREDIT	
1	20--	Closing Entries				1
2	Oct. 31	Delivery Revenue		2 650 00		2
3		Income Summary			2 650 00	3
4						4
5	31	Income Summary		1 500 00		5
6		Advertising Expense			75 00	6
7		Maintenance Expense			600 00	7
8		Rent Expense			700 00	8
9		Utilities Expense			125 00	9
10						10
11	31	Income Summary		1 150 00		11
12		Maria Sanchez, Capital			1 150 00	12
13						13
14	31	Maria Sanchez, Capital		500 00		14
15		Maria Sanchez, Withdrawals			500 00	15

Figure 10–4 Journalizing the Closing Entries

Reinforce the Main Idea

Use a table like this one to describe the closing entries that are made at the end of each accounting period.

General Journal Entry Description	Account Debited	Account Credited

Do the Math

Using these general ledger account balances, calculate the net income or net loss for the period. Then calculate the increase or decrease in owner's capital.

Anna Zarian, Capital	$25,000
Anna Zarian, Withdrawals	5,000
Accounting Fees Revenue	9,000
Advertising Expense	1,000
Miscellaneous Expense	2,000
Rent Expense	1,500
Utilities Expense	500

Problem 10–1 Preparing Closing Entries

Instructions Prepare closing entries for the following in your working papers.

1. A closing entry must be made for the account **Ticket Revenue**, which has a balance of $6,000.
2. A business has three expense accounts: **Gas and Oil Expense** (balance, $700), **Miscellaneous Expense** (balance, $600), and **Utilities Expense** (balance, $1,800). The end of the fiscal year is June 30.

Problem 10–2 Analyzing a Source Document

Instructions Using the source document:

1. Journalize the transaction in a general journal in your working papers.
2. Post the entry to the appropriate T accounts.
3. Assume it is the end of the accounting period. Record the closing entry for this account in the general journal.
4. Post the closing entry to the appropriate T accounts.

DEPARTMENT OF WATER & POWER
455 Main Street
Sarasota, FL 34230

ACCOUNT NO.: 00384843848-339
INVOICE NO.: 32004

TO   Gulfview Tropical Fish and Supplies
4524 West Palm Bay Avenue
Sarasota, FL 34222

DATES		USAGE	RATE	AMOUNT DUE
FROM	TO			
March 15, 20--	April 14, 20--	1,000 kWh	$.129 per kWh	$129.00

Posting Closing Entries and Preparing a Post-Closing Trial Balance

Main Idea
After the closing entries are posted, a post-closing trial balance is prepared to verify that debits equal credits.

Read to Learn...
➤ how to post the closing entries to the general ledger. (p. 260)
➤ how to prepare a post-closing trial balance. (p. 262)

Key Terms
post-closing trial balance

In Section 1 you learned how to journalize the closing entries. In this section you will complete the accounting cycle.

Completing the Eighth Step in the Accounting Cycle: Posting the Closing Entries to the General Ledger

What Is Special About Posting the Closing Entries?

The next step in the closing process is to post the closing entries to the general ledger accounts. The posting procedure is the same as for any other general journal entry, with one exception. The words *Closing Entries* are written in the Description column of the general ledger account. The posting of the closing entries for Roadrunner is shown in **Figure 10–5**. Note that *Closing Entries* can be abbreviated as *Clos. Ent.*

			GENERAL JOURNAL			PAGE	3
	DATE		DESCRIPTION	POST. REF.	DEBIT	CREDIT	
1	20--		*Closing Entries*				1
2	Oct.	31	Delivery Revenue	401	2 6 5 0 00		2
3			Income Summary	303		2 6 5 0 00	3
4							4
5		31	Income Summary	303	1 5 0 0 00		5
6			Advertising Expense	501		7 5 00	6
7			Maintenance Expense	505		6 0 0 00	7
8			Rent Expense	510		7 0 0 00	8
9			Utilities Expense	515		1 2 5 00	9
10							10
11		31	Income Summary	303	1 1 5 0 00		11
12			Maria Sanchez, Capital	301		1 1 5 0 00	12
13							13
14		31	Maria Sanchez, Capital	301	5 0 0 00		14
15			Maria Sanchez, Withdrawals	302		5 0 0 00	15
16							16

Figure 10–5 Closing Entries Posted to the General Ledger

ACCOUNT *Maria Sanchez, Capital*   **ACCOUNT NO.** _301_

DATE		DESCRIPTION	POST. REF.	DEBIT	CREDIT	BALANCE DEBIT	BALANCE CREDIT
20--							
Oct.	1		G1		25 000 00		25 000 00
	2		G1		400 00		25 400 00
	31	Clos. Ent.	G3		1 150 00		26 550 00
	31	Clos. Ent.	G3	500 00			26 050 00

ACCOUNT *Maria Sanchez, Withdrawals*   **ACCOUNT NO.** _302_

DATE		DESCRIPTION	POST. REF.	DEBIT	CREDIT	BALANCE DEBIT	BALANCE CREDIT
20--							
Oct.	31		G1	500 00		500 00	
	31	Clos. Ent.	G3		500 00	—	

ACCOUNT *Income Summary*   **ACCOUNT NO.** _303_

DATE		DESCRIPTION	POST. REF.	DEBIT	CREDIT	BALANCE DEBIT	BALANCE CREDIT
20--							
Oct.	31	Clos. Ent.	G3		2 650 00		2 650 00
	31	Clos. Ent.	G3	1 500 00			1 150 00
	31	Clos. Ent.	G3	1 150 00			—

ACCOUNT *Delivery Revenue*   **ACCOUNT NO.** _401_

DATE		DESCRIPTION	POST. REF.	DEBIT	CREDIT	BALANCE DEBIT	BALANCE CREDIT
20--							
Oct.	15		G1		1 200 00		1 200 00
	20		G1		1 450 00		2 650 00
	31	Clos. Ent.	G3	2 650 00			

ACCOUNT *Advertising Expense*   **ACCOUNT NO.** _501_

DATE		DESCRIPTION	POST. REF.	DEBIT	CREDIT	BALANCE DEBIT	BALANCE CREDIT
20--							
Oct.	18		G1	75 00		75 00	
	31	Clos. Ent.	G3		75 00	—	

ACCOUNT *Maintenance Expense*   **ACCOUNT NO.** _505_

DATE		DESCRIPTION	POST. REF.	DEBIT	CREDIT	BALANCE DEBIT	BALANCE CREDIT
20--							
Oct.	29		G1	600 00		600 00	
	31	Clos. Ent.	G3		600 00	—	

Figure 10–5 Closing Entries Posted to the General Ledger (continued)

ACCOUNT	Rent Expense						ACCOUNT NO. 510	
		POST.				BALANCE	
DATE	DESCRIPTION	REF.	DEBIT	CREDIT	DEBIT	CREDIT
20--						
Oct. 16		G1	7 0 0 00		7 0 0 00	
31	Clos. Ent.	G3		7 0 0 00	—	

ACCOUNT	Utilities Expense					ACCOUNT NO. 515	
		POST.				BALANCE	
DATE	DESCRIPTION	REF.	DEBIT	CREDIT	DEBIT	CREDIT
20--						
Oct. 28		G1	1 2 5 00		1 2 5 00	
31	Clos. Ent.	G3		1 2 5 00	—	

Figure 10–5 Closing Entries Posted to the General Ledger (continued)

As You READ

Compare and Contrast

Post-Closing Trial Balance How is the post-closing trial balance similar to the trial balance? How is it different?

The Ninth Step in the Accounting Cycle: Preparing a Post-Closing Trial Balance

If We Already Have a Trial Balance, Why Do We Need a Post-Closing Trial Balance?

The last step in the accounting cycle is to prepare a post-closing trial balance. The **post-closing trial balance** is prepared to make sure total debits equal total credits after the closing entries are posted. The post-closing trial balance for Roadrunner is shown in **Figure 10–6**.

Notice that only accounts with balances are listed on the post-closing trial balance. After the closing process, only permanent accounts have balances. Temporary accounts have zero balances, so there is no need to list those accounts on the post-closing trial balance.

Roadrunner Delivery Service		
Post-Closing Trial Balance		
October 31, 20--		
Cash in Bank	21 1 2 5 00	
Accounts Receivable—City News	1 4 5 0 00	
Computer Equipment	3 0 0 0 00	
Office Equipment	2 0 0 00	
Delivery Equipment	12 0 0 0 00	
Accounts Payable—Beacon Advertising		7 5 00
Accounts Payable—North Shore Auto		11 6 5 0 00
Maria Sanchez, Capital		26 0 5 0 00
Total	37 7 7 5 00	37 7 7 5 00

Figure 10–6 Post-Closing Trial Balance

AFTER YOU READ

Reinforce the Main Idea

Create a table like this one to list the general ledger account classifications. In the column titled "Appears on Post-Closing Trial Balance," place an X next to each account that carries a balance into the next accounting period.

Account Type	Appears on Post-Closing Trial Balance
Asset	
Liability	
Owner's Capital	
Owner's Withdrawals	
Revenue	
Expenses	

Do the Math

You work for a company with a large accounting department, and every accounting clerk has specific duties. Your co-worker responsible for preparing the post-closing trial balance is ill today. Your supervisor asked you to prepare the post-closing trial balance. Using your computer or lined paper, draft the post-closing trial balance using the following account balances: Cash, $27,800; Accounts Receivable, $33,000; Equipment, $81,000; Accounts Payable, $24,500; and Owner's Capital, $117,300.

Problem 10–3 Determining Accounts Affected by Closing Entries

The following list contains some of the accounts used by Living Well Health Spa.

General Ledger

Accts. Pay.—The Fitness Shop	Exercise Equipment	Rent Expense
Accts. Rec.—Linda Brown	Income Summary	Repair Tools
	Laundry Equipment	Ted Chapman, Capital
Advertising Expense	Maintenance Expense	Ted Chapman, Withdrawals
Cash in Bank	Membership Fees	Utilities Expense
Exercise Class Revenue	Miscellaneous Expense	
	Office Furniture	

Instructions Using the form in your working papers:

1. In the first column, indicate the financial statement where each account appears: balance sheet or income statement.
2. In the next column, indicate whether or not the account is affected by a closing entry.
3. In the last column, indicate whether or not the account appears on the post-closing trial balance.

The first account is shown as an example.

Account Name	Financial Statement	Is the account affected by a closing entry?	Does the account appear on the post-closing trial balance?
Accts. Pay.—The Fitness Shop	Balance Sheet	No	Yes

Key Concepts

1. The eighth step in the accounting cycle is to journalize and post the closing entries:
   - *Closing* is the process of transferring the balances in the temporary accounts to the owner's capital account.
   - The asset, liability, and owner's capital accounts are *never* closed.

2. The **Income Summary** account has two purposes:
   - to accumulate the revenue and expenses for an accounting period, and
   - to summarize the revenue and expenses for an accounting period.

3. **Income Summary** is a temporary owner's equity account used to record net income or net loss:
   - A credit balance (net income) in **Income Summary** increases capital.
   - A debit balance (net loss) decreases capital.
   - The **Income Summary** account does not have a normal balance. That is, it does not have an increase side or a decrease side.
   - The **Income Summary** account balance is zero before and after the closing process.
   - The **Income Summary** account does not appear on any financial statements.

4. Prepare four closing entries:
   a. Close the revenue account(s) to **Income Summary.**

1	20--											1
2	Dec.	31	Revenue Account			x x x xx						2
3			Income Summary					x x x xx				3

   b. Close the expense accounts to **Income Summary.**

4		31	Income Summary			x x x xx						4
5			Expense Account					x x x xx				5
6			Expense Account					x x x xx				6
7			Expense Account					x x x xx				7

   c. Close **Income Summary** to the owner's capital account.

8		31	Income Summary			x x x xx						8
9			Owner's Capital Account					x x x xx				9

   d. Close the owner's withdrawals account to the owner's capital account.

12		31	Owner's Capital Account			x x x xx						12
13			Withdrawals Account					x x x xx				13

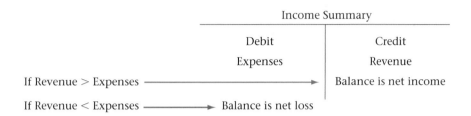

Income Summary

Debit	Credit
Expenses	Revenue

If Revenue > Expenses ⟶ Balance is net income

If Revenue < Expenses ⟶ Balance is net loss

5. After the closing entries have been journalized, follow this procedure:
   - Post them to the general ledger.
   - For each posted entry, enter the words *Closing Entry* in the Description column of the general ledger account.
6. The ninth step in the accounting cycle is to prepare a post-closing trial balance. Only the permanent accounts are listed on the post-closing trial balance.

Roadrunner Delivery Service
Post-Closing Trial Balance
December 31, 20--

Cash in Bank	21 1 2 5 00	
Accts. Rec.—City News	1 4 5 0 00	
Computer Equipment	3 0 0 0 00	
Office Equipment	2 0 0 00	
Delivery Equipment	12 0 0 0 00	
Accts. Pay.—Beacon Advertising		7 5 00
Accts. Pay.—North Shore Auto		11 6 5 0 00
Maria Sanchez, Capital		26 0 5 0 00
Totals	37 7 7 5 00	37 7 7 5 00

Key Terms

closing entries	(p. 250)
compound entry	(p. 256)
Income Summary account	(p. 253)
post-closing trial balance	(p. 262)

Check Your Understanding

1. **Closing Entries**
   a. Which accounts are considered temporary accounts?
   b. Why are temporary accounts closed at the end of the fiscal year?

2. **Income Summary Account**
   a. What is the purpose of the **Income Summary** account?
   b. How does the **Income Summary** account differ from the other temporary accounts?

3. **Income Summary and Capital Accounts**
   a. Explain the relationship between the **Income Summary** account and the capital account.
   b. Why doesn't the **Income Summary** account have a normal balance?

4. **Analyzing and Journalizing Closing Entries**
   a. What is the source of information for the closing entries?
   b. List the steps for journalizing the closing entries.

5. **Posting the Closing Entries**
   a. Classify the **Income Summary** account (asset, liability, owner's equity, revenue, or expense).
   b. How is the posting procedure for closing entries different from the posting procedure for other general journal entries?

6. **Post-Closing Trial Balance**
   a. What is the purpose of the post-closing trial balance?
   b. Why does the post-closing trial balance have balances of only permanent accounts?

Apply Key Terms

On a separate sheet of paper, write a brief definition for each of the following terms.

closing entries
compound entry
Income Summary account
post-closing trial balance

Closing the Accounting Period

Making the Transition from a Manual to a Computerized System

Task	Manual Methods	Computerized Methods
Closing Entries	• Using a general journal form, prepare closing entries for revenue, expense, income summary, and withdrawals accounts. Post the closing entries in the general ledger accounts.	• It is not necessary to journalize closing entries. Closing entries are performed by the computerized system.

Peachtree® Q & A

Peachtree Question	Answer
What is the difference between changing the accounting period and closing the fiscal year in Peachtree?	• In Peachtree the *accounting period* refers to the period used to record transactions. At the end of an accounting period (usually at month-end), you should change to the next accounting period. For example, at March 31, you would select the next accounting period, April 1, 20-- through April 30, 20--. • The fiscal year should be closed only when you are sure that all entries have been recorded and all reports have been printed for the year.
How do I close the fiscal year?	1. Post and print all journal entries before closing the fiscal year. Closing the fiscal year cannot be reversed. 2. From the *Tasks* menu, select **System**. 3. Select **Year-End Wizard**. 4. You will be prompted to complete Year-End closing procedures.

QuickBooks Q & A

QuickBooks Question	Answer
What is the difference between changing the accounting period and closing the fiscal year in QuickBooks?	• In QuickBooks the *accounting period* refers to the month used to record transactions. Changing the accounting period is as simple as entering the first day of the next month. The software does not require that you manually adjust accounting periods. • The fiscal year should be closed only when you are sure that all entries have been recorded and all reports have been printed for the year.
How do I close the fiscal year?	1. Record all journal entries before closing the fiscal year. 2. From the *Edit* menu, select **Preferences**. 3. Choose the **Accounting** preference and click the Company Preferences tab. 4. In the *Date* field, enter the closing date and click the **Set Password** button. 5. Enter and confirm the password, and click **OK**.

For detailed instructions, see your Glencoe Accounting Chapter Study Guides and Working Papers.

Complete problems using: **Manual** Glencoe Working Papers OR **Spreadsheet** Templates

Peachtree®

SMART GUIDE

Step–by–Step Instructions: Problem 10–4

1. Select the problem set for Wilderness Rentals (Prob. 10–4).
2. Rename the company and set the system date.
3. Select **System** from the **Tasks** menu and then choose **Year-End Wizard**.
4. Complete the Analyze activity.
5. End the session.

TIP: Print the General Ledger or General Ledger Trial Balance report to find an account balance.

Problem 10–4 Preparing Closing Entries

A portion of the work sheet for Wilderness Rentals for the period ended December 31 follows.

Instructions Using the information from the work sheet, prepare the journal entries to close the temporary accounts.

1. Record the closing entry for the revenue account.
2. Record the closing entry for the expense accounts.
3. Record the closing entry for the **Income Summary** account.
4. Record the closing entry for the withdrawals account.

Wilderness Rentals
Work Sheet
For the Period Ended December 31, 20--

	ACCT. NO.	ACCOUNT NAME	INCOME STATEMENT DEBIT	INCOME STATEMENT CREDIT	BALANCE SHEET DEBIT	BALANCE SHEET CREDIT	
1	101	Cash in Bank			7 000 00		1
2	105	Accts. Rec.—Helen Katz			2 000 00		2
3	110	Accts. Rec.—Polk and Co.			1 000 00		3
4	115	Office Supplies			900 00		4
5	120	Office Equipment			12 000 00		5
6	125	Camping Equipment			6 000 00		6
7	201	Accts. Pay.—Adventure Equip. Inc.				900 00	7
8	203	Accts. Pay.—Digital Tech Computers				400 00	8
9	205	Accts. Pay.—Greg Mollaro				500 00	9
10	301	Ronald Hicks, Capital				19 775 00	10
11	305	Ronald Hicks, Withdrawals			2 350 00		11
12	310	Income Summary					12
13	401	Equipment Rental Revenue		14 965 00			13
14	501	Advertising Expense	1 500 00				14
15	505	Maintenance Expense	1 560 00				15
16	515	Rent Expense	1 000 00				16
17	525	Utilities Expense	1 230 00				17
18			5 290 00	14 965 00	31 250 00	21 575 00	18
19		Net Income	9 675 00			9 675 00	19
20			14 965 00	14 965 00	31 250 00	31 250 00	20
21							21

Analyze Predict the balance of the capital account after the closing entries are posted.

Problem 10–5 Preparing a Post-Closing Trial Balance

Instructions Use the accounts shown on the next two pages to prepare a Dec. 31 post-closing trial balance for Hot Suds Car Wash.

Cash in Bank

Debit +	Credit −
Balance 8,000	

Accounts Receivable— Linda Brown

Debit +	Credit −
Balance 875	

Accounts Receivable— Valley Auto

Debit +	Credit −
Balance 5,050	

Office Equipment

Debit +	Credit −
Balance 6,000	

Office Furniture

Debit +	Credit −
Balance 9,000	

Car Wash Equipment

Debit +	Credit −
Balance 65,000	

Accounts Payable— Allen Vacuum Systems

Debit −	Credit +
	Balance 41,000

Accounts Payable— O'Brian's Office Supply

Debit −	Credit +
	Balance 2,500

Regina Delgado, Capital

Debit −	Credit +
Closing 1,500	35,925
	Closing 16,000

Regina Delgado, Withdrawals

Debit +	Credit
Balance 1,500	Closing 1,500

Income Summary

Debit	Credit
Closing 19,000	Closing 35,000
Closing 16,000	

Wash Revenue

Debit −	Credit +
Closing 15,000	Balance 15,000

Wax Revenue

Debit −	Credit +
Closing 8,000	Balance 8,000

Interior Detailing Revenue

Debit −	Credit +
Closing 12,000	Balance 12,000

Advertising Expense

Debit +	Credit −
Balance 2,500	Closing 2,500

Equipment Rental Expense

Debit +	Credit −
Balance 3,000	Closing 3,000

CONTINUE

Problems

Maintenance Expense			Rent Expense	
Debit +	Credit −		Debit +	Credit −
Balance 5,000	Closing 5,000		Balance 5,000	Closing 5,000

Utilities Expense	
Debit +	Credit −
Balance 3,500	Closing 3,500

Analyze Predict the balance of the temporary accounts after the closing entries are posted.

Peachtree®

SMART GUIDE

Step–by–Step Instructions: Problem 10–6

1. Select the problem set for Kits & Pups Grooming (Prob. 10–6).
2. Rename the company and set the system date.
3. Close the current fiscal year.
4. Complete the Analyze activity.
5. End the session.

Problem 10–6 Journalizing Closing Entries

The following account names and balances appear on the work sheet for Kits & Pups Grooming for the month ended December 31.

Kits & Pups Grooming
Work Sheet
For the Month Ended December 31, 20--

	ACCT. NO.	ACCOUNT NAME	INCOME STATEMENT DEBIT	INCOME STATEMENT CREDIT	BALANCE SHEET DEBIT	BALANCE SHEET CREDIT	
1		Cash in Bank			9 300 00		1
2		Accts. Rec.—Juan Alvarez			3 000 00		2
3		Accts. Rec.—Nathan Carlsbad			10 000 00		3
4		Accts. Rec.—Martha Giles			5 000 00		4
5		Office Equipment			8 000 00		5
6		Office Furniture			10 000 00		6
7		Computer Equipment			9 000 00		7
8		Grooming Equipment			15 000 00		8
9		Kennel Equipment			21 000 00		9
10		Accts. Pay.—Able Store Equip.				5 000 00	10
11		Accts. Pay.—Dogs & Cats Inc.				1 500 00	11
12		Accts. Pay.—Pet Gourmet				15 000 00	12
13		Abe Shultz, Capital				52 700 00	13
14		Abe Shultz, Withdrawals			7 000 00		14
15		Income Summary					15
16		Boarding Revenue		20 000 00			16
17		Grooming Revenue		8 000 00			17
18		Advertising Expense	700 00				18
19		Equipment Repair Expense	1 200 00				19
20		Maintenance Expense	500 00				20
21		Rent Expense	1 700 00				21
22		Utilities Expense	800 00				22

Instructions Using this information, record the closing entries for Kits & Pups Grooming. Use general journal page 11.

Analyze Calculate the change in the capital account for the period.

Problem 10–7 Posting Closing Entries and Preparing a Post-Closing Trial Balance

Period ending December 31 closing entries for Outback Guide Service are:

GENERAL JOURNAL   PAGE _1_

	DATE		DESCRIPTION	POST. REF.	DEBIT	CREDIT	
1	20--		Closing Entries				1
2	Dec.	31	Guide Service Revenue		16 3 0 0 00		2
3			Income Summary			16 3 0 0 00	3
4		31	Income Summary		10 0 0 0 00		4
5			Advertising Expense			3 0 0 0 00	5
6			Maintenance Expense			1 1 0 0 00	6
7			Rent Expense			4 0 0 0 00	7
8			Utilities Expense			1 9 0 0 00	8
9		31	Income Summary		6 3 0 0 00		9
10			Juanita Ortega, Capital			6 3 0 0 00	10
11		31	Juanita Ortega, Capital		4 0 0 0 00		11
12			Juanita Ortega, Withdrawals			4 0 0 0 00	12
13							13

Instructions Using your working papers, post the closing entries to the appropriate general ledger accounts and prepare a post-closing trial balance.

Analyze Calculate the balance of the capital account after closing.

Problem 10–8 Completing Period-End Activities

The general ledger for Showbiz Video shows the following at December 31:

General Ledger

101	Cash in Bank	12,000	207 Accts. Pay.—	
105	Accts. Rec.—G. Cohen	3,000	New Media Suppliers	3,000
110	Accts. Rec.—J. Coletti	900	209 Accts. Pay.—Palace Films	14,000
113	Accts. Rec.—S. Flannery	1,800	301 Greg Failla, Capital	33,775
115	Accts. Rec.—Spring		305 Greg Failla, Withdrawals	4,000
	Branch School District	1,500	310 Income Summary	—
130	Office Equipment	5,000	401 Video Rental Revenue	9,600
135	Office Furniture	8,000	405 VCR Rental Revenue	3,500
140	Computer Equipment	10,000	501 Advertising Expense	1,600
145	Video Tapes	20,000	505 Equipment Repair	
150	Video Equipment	9,000	Expense	1,200
201	Accts. Pay.—Broad Street		510 Maintenance Expense	400
	Office Supply	400	520 Rent Expense	1,000
205	Accts. Pay.—		530 Utilities Expense	375
	Computer Horizons	15,500		

CONTINUE

Peachtree®

SMART GUIDE

Step–by–Step Instructions:
Problem 10–7

1. Select the problem set for Outback Guide Service (Prob. 10–7).
2. Rename the company and set the system date.
3. Close the fiscal year.
4. Print a post-closing Trial Balance.
5. Complete the Analyze activity.
6. End the session.

Peachtree®

SMART GUIDE

Step–by–Step Instructions:
Problem 10–8

1. Select the problem set for Showbiz Video (Prob. 10–8).
2. Rename the company and set the system date.
3. Print a General Ledger Trial Balance.
4. Print an Income Statement, Balance Sheet, and Statement of Changes in Owner's Equity.
5. Close the fiscal year.
6. Print a post-closing Trial Balance.
7. Complete the Analyze activity.
8. End the session.

QuickBooks

PROBLEM GUIDE

Step–by–Step Instructions:
Problem 10–8

1. Restore the Problem 10-8.QBB file.
2. Print a Trial Balance, a Profit & Loss report, and a Balance Sheet.
3. Close the fiscal year and print a Trial Balance.
4. Complete the Analyze activity.
5. Back up your work.

Instructions Using the preceding account names and balances:

1. Prepare the six-column work sheet. The period covered is one month.
2. Prepare the financial statements. Greg Failla invested $10,000 during the month.
3. Record the closing entries on page 12 of the general journal.
4. Post the closing entries.
5. Prepare a post-closing trial balance.

Analyze Calculate the total amount of all the accounts receivable accounts on December 31.

SPREADSHEET SMART GUIDE

Step–by–Step Instructions: Problem 10–9

1. Select the spreadsheet template for Problem 10–9.
2. Enter your name and the date.
3. Complete the spreadsheet using the instructions in your working papers.
4. Print the spreadsheet and proof your work.
5. Complete the Analyze activity.
6. Save your work and exit the spreadsheet program.

CHALLENGE PROBLEM ✔

Problem 10–9 Completing End-of-Period Activities

At the end of December, the general ledger for Job Connect showed the following account balances:

General Ledger

101	Cash in Bank	6,000	207	Accts. Pay.—Wildwood	
105	Accts. Rec.—			Furniture Sales	2,000
	CompuRite Systems	1,000	301	Richard Tang, Capital	23,600
110	Accts. Rec.—		302	Richard Tang,	
	Marquez Manufact.	500		Withdrawals	3,000
113	Accts. Rec.—Roaring		303	Income Summary	—
	Rivers Water Park	600	401	Placement Fees Revenue	6,900
115	Accts. Rec.—M. Spencer	200	405	Technology Classes	
130	Office Equipment	7,000		Revenue	2,400
135	Office Furniture	5,000	501	Advertising Expense	3,000
140	Computer Equipment	8,500	505	Maintenance Expense	800
201	Accts. Pay.—Micro		510	Miscellaneous Expense	800
	Solutions Inc.	2,800	520	Rent Expense	2,000
205	Accts. Pay.—Vega		530	Utilities Expense	900
	Internet Services	1,600			

Instructions Using the preceding account names and balances:

1. Prepare the six-column work sheet. The period covered is one month.
2. Prepare the financial statements.
3. Record the closing entries on page 28 of the general journal.
4. Post the closing entries.
5. Prepare a post-closing trial balance.

Analyze Identify the largest expenditure for the period.

Practice your test-taking skills! The questions on this page are reprinted with permission from national organizations:

- Future Business Leaders of America
- Business Professionals of America

Use a separate sheet of paper to record your answers.

Future Business Leaders of America

MULTIPLE CHOICE

1. Which of the following accounts needs no closing entries?
- a. Capital
- b. Supplies Expense
- c. Fees Owed
- d. All of the above

2. After adjusting and closing entries have been posted, a
- a. balance sheet is prepared.
- b. trial balance is prepared.
- c. post-closing balance sheet is prepared.
- d. post-closing trial balance is prepared.

3. The Capital account balance minus the net loss minus the Drawing account balance equals
- a. net loss.
- b. total liabilities.
- c. the capital amount shown on a balance sheet.
- d. the capital amount shown on an income statement.

Business Professionals of America

MULTIPLE CHOICE

4. Which of the following *will not* appear on a post-closing trial balance?
- a. Accounts Payable
- b. Sales
- c. Owner's Capital
- d. Cash

5. At the end of the fiscal period, the income summary account shows a credit balance of $3,500. This income summary account balance will be closed out to which account?
- a. a debit to owner's capital
- b. a credit to owner's capital
- c. a debit to owner's revenue
- d. a credit to owner's withdrawals

> **Need More Help?**
>
> Go to **glencoeaccounting.glencoe.com** and click on **Student Center**. Click on **Winning Competitive Events** and select **Chapter 10**.
> - **Practice Questions and Test-Taking Tips**
> - **Concept Capsules and Terminology**

CRITICAL Thinking

Completing the Accounting Cycle

1. What is the last step of the accounting cycle?
2. Why are the temporary accounts closed to the owner's capital account at the end of the accounting period?
3. Make the closing entries for (a) a $5,000 net income for the year ending December 31 and (b) a $4,000 net loss for the quarter ending June 30.
4. Compare and contrast the closing entry for an expense account and the closing entry for the withdrawals account.
5. What items do you need to journalize the closing entries? Include office supplies and forms as well as any information that will be needed.
6. What is the value of preparing a post-closing trial balance?

CASE STUDY

Service Business: Computer Consulting

You note after preparing financial statements for Computer Works and completing the closing entries below that the owner's capital account balance is $34,400 in the general ledger but is $43,400 on the statement of changes in owner's equity. The capital account balance was $38,900 at the beginning of the month.

INSTRUCTIONS (1) Identify the mistakes in the closing entries and (2) calculate the correct capital account balance.

Date	Description	Debit	Credit
Aug. 31	Consulting Fee Revenue	9,240	
	Income Summary		9,240
Aug. 31	Income Summary	870	
	Advertising Expense		300
	Internet Access Expense		20
	Rent Expense		550
Aug. 31	Rex Moran, Capital	8,100	
	Income Summary		8,100

a matter of ETHICS

Computer Viruses

Computer viruses "reproduce" themselves in computer programs, slowing the system or destroying data. A friend gives you a computer game with a harmless virus. To add some fun at work, you load the game onto the company's network.

ETHICAL DECISION MAKING

1. What are the ethical issues?
2. What are the alternatives?
3. Who are the affected parties?
4. How do the alternatives affect the parties?
5. What would you do?

COMMUNICATING ACCOUNTING

Explaining Cause and Effect

Your boss left you a note questioning the decrease in his owner's capital account. You see that his withdrawals were the cause. List some points to explain the situation. Pick a classmate to listen to your explanation, which should prove that you understand that the withdrawals account is closed to the capital account.

Working in a Team

Imagine that you work in the accounting department for the multimedia division of MTV. The CD-ROM project manager wants to produce and sell a new CD-ROM with clips from the latest music videos. You and your co-workers have questions.

INSTRUCTIONS Form a team of five students and list the questions you may have. Compile your questions and opinions about the product (from a financial perspective) into a one-page report and present it to the class.

The World Trade Organization

The World Trade Organization (WTO) negotiates most trade agreements between nations. The organization is dedicated to resolving disputes, stimulating economic growth, and lowering trade barriers. It handles issues including tariffs, customs processes, professional services, e-commerce, and import licensing.

INSTRUCTIONS List the issues the WTO is reviewing this month. Locate the Web site for the WTO and click on the 'Events calendar' link.

Your Checking Account

Whether you are a business owner or a consumer, you will probably use a checking account. You are responsible for keeping track of your cash by recording deposits and withdrawals on the check stubs in the checkbook.

PERSONAL FINANCE ACTIVITY Assume that you opened a checking account by depositing $200 at the beginning of the month. During the month you wrote three checks: 101 for $25, 102 for $50, and 103 for $75. When and where should you record each deposit and check? Calculate the checking account balance.

PERSONAL FINANCE ONLINE Log on to **glencoeaccounting.glencoe.com** and click on **Student Center.** Click on **Making It Personal** and select **Chapter 10.**

Calculating Return on Owner's Equity

One measure of business success is the **return on owner's equity (ROE):**

$$\frac{\text{Net Income}}{\text{Beginning Owner's Equity} - \text{Withdrawals}} = \frac{\$3,600}{\$34,500 - \$2,500} = 11.25\%$$

The resulting percentage shows the amount earned during the period on each dollar invested by the owner.

INSTRUCTIONS Use Roadrunner's income statement (page 222) and statement of changes in owner's equity (page 226) to calculate October's ROE. How does this return compare with a bank savings account that pays 2 percent interest per year?

Closing Entries

The closing entries for professional sports teams are similar to those for other types of businesses. Go to **glencoeaccounting .glencoe.com** and click on **Student Center.** Click on **WebQuest** and select **Unit 2** to continue your Internet project.

Cash Control and Banking Activities

What You'll Learn

1. Describe the internal controls used to protect cash.

2. Describe the forms needed to open and use a checking account.

3. Record information on check stubs.

4. Prepare a check.

5. Prepare bank deposits.

6. Reconcile a bank statement.

7. Journalize and post entries relating to bank service charges.

8. Describe the uses of the electronic funds transfer system.

9. Define the terms introduced in this chapter.

Why It's Important

▶ Banking tasks are basic practices in business and in your personal life.

Predict

1. What does the chapter title tell you?
2. What do you already know about this subject from personal experience?
3. What have you learned about this in the earlier chapters?
4. What gaps exist in your knowledge of this subject?

Exploring the *Real World* of Business

CONTROLLING CASH

Jamba Juice

Snacking at school does not have to be about greasy chips, candy bars, and sugary sodas. Across the nation schools are getting healthier about snacks. In many places students can now choose from smoothies like the Tropical Awakening or the Strawberry Nirvana—both popular drinks from **Jamba Juice.** Made with 100 percent fruit juices, Jamba smoothies provide three to six of the daily recommended servings of fruit.

Founded in 1990, the company now operates more than 430 stores nationwide. You can imagine how important it is to control cash as customers buy smoothies, juice, and baked goods. Companies like **Jamba Juice** use cash registers and specific bank deposit procedures to be sure that cash is properly accounted for.

What Do You Think?

What do you think is the most common problem that occurs in **Jamba Juice** stores in regard to cash?

Working in the *Real World*

APPLYING YOUR ACCOUNTING KNOWLEDGE

You cash your paycheck, stuff the cash in your wallet or billfold, and before you know it, the cash is gone! It is easy to lose track of how you spend your money. Businesses also have to watch their money carefully. One way of safeguarding cash is to keep it in the bank and write checks to make payments. You will learn about a business checking account in this chapter.

Personal Connection

1. Do you handle cash, checks, or credit cards in your job?
2. What procedures help protect cash?

Online Connection

Go to **glencoeaccounting.glencoe.com** and click on **Student Center.** Click on **Working in the Real World** and select **Chapter 11.**

Banking Procedures

BEFORE YOU READ

Main Idea
Internal controls are steps taken to protect assets and keep reliable records.

Read to Learn…
➤ how a business protects cash. (p. 278)
➤ how to use a checking account. (p. 278)

Key Terms
internal controls
external controls
checking account
check
depositor
signature card
deposit slip
endorsement
blank endorsement
special endorsement
restrictive endorsement
payee
drawer
drawee
voiding a check

AS YOU READ

It's Not What It Seems

Cash is more than dollar bills. In accounting, *cash* also means checks and funds on deposit in a bank or credit union.

In any business, cash (currency, coins, and checks) is used in daily transactions. An important part of accounting for a business, therefore, involves tracking the cash received and paid out. For example, Jamba Juice has established procedures for processing the cash received from the sale of drinks and other items. Jamba Juice also has a system of monitoring and controlling cash paid out for wages, utilities, supplies, and numerous other expenses.

Protecting Cash
How Does a Business Protect Cash?

It is important to protect cash from loss, waste, theft, forgery, and embezzlement. Cash is protected through internal controls and external controls. **Internal controls** refer to procedures within the business that are designed to protect cash and other assets and to keep reliable records. Internal controls for cash include:

1. Limiting the number of persons handling cash.
2. Separating accounting tasks involving cash. For example, one person handles cash receipts, another handles cash payments, and a different person keeps the accounting records showing the amounts received or paid.
3. Bonding (insuring) employees who handle cash or cash records.
4. Using a cash register and a safe.
5. Depositing cash receipts in the bank daily.
6. Making all cash payments by check.
7. Reconciling the bank statement.

External controls are the measures and procedures provided outside the business to protect cash and other assets. For example, banks maintain controls to protect the funds their customers deposit. These controls include verifying the accuracy of signatures on checks and maintaining records of monetary transactions.

The Checking Account
How Do You Maintain a Checking Account?

A **checking account** allows a person or business to deposit cash in a bank and to write checks against the account balance. A **check** is a written order from a depositor telling the bank to pay a stated amount of cash to the person or business named on the check. A **depositor** is a person or business that has cash on deposit in a bank.

Opening a Checking Account

A checking account helps protect cash and provides a record of cash transactions.

The Signature Card. To open a checking account, a business owner fills out a **signature card** and deposits cash in the bank. A signature card contains the signature(s) of the person(s) authorized to write checks on the account. The bank keeps the signature card on file so that it can be matched against signed checks presented for payment. The use of a signature card protects both the account holder and the bank against checks with forged signatures. See **Figure 11–1** for the signature card used to open the checking account for Roadrunner Delivery Service.

The Checkbook. When a depositor opens a checking account, checks are printed for the depositor's use. Printed checks are packaged together in a *checkbook* like the one shown in **Figure 11–2**. Each page has several detachable checks attached to check stubs, and both are numbered in sequence. Using checks with preprinted numbers helps a business keep track of every check that it writes, an important internal control.

The ABA Number. In addition to having a preprinted check number, each check is printed with the account number and an *American Bankers Association (ABA) number*. The ABA number is the fractional number printed in the upper right corner of a check, just below the check number. The ABA number identifies the bank and speeds the hand sorting of checks.

Look at the ABA number on the check in **Figure 11–3** on page 280. The number above the line and to the left of the hyphen represents the city or state where the bank is located. The number to the right of the hyphen indicates the specific bank. The number below the line is the code for the Federal Reserve district where the bank is located.

The ABA number was developed to speed the sorting of checks by hand. An updated version of the ABA number is also printed on the bottom of each check for electronic sorting. The ABA number, the account number, and the check number are printed at the bottom of the check in a special ink and typeface. These specially printed numbers are called *MICR (magnetic ink character recognition) numbers.* Can you identify the MICR numbers on the check in **Figure 11–3**?

Figure 11–1 Checking Account Signature Card

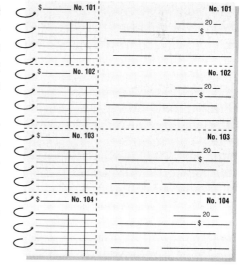

Figure 11–2 Checkbook

Making Deposits

A business makes regular deposits to protect the currency, coins, and checks it receives. Most businesses make daily deposits.

Deposits are accompanied by a **deposit slip**, a bank form listing the cash and checks to be deposited. The deposit slip, also called a *deposit ticket,*

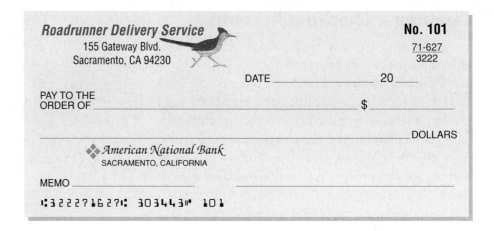

Figure 11–3 Printed Check

gives both the depositor and the bank a detailed record of the deposit. Most banks provide printed deposit slips with the depositor's name, address, and account number. A deposit slip for Roadrunner Delivery Service is shown in **Figure 11–4.**

To complete a deposit slip, follow these steps:

1. Write the date on the Date line.
2. On the Cash line, indicate the total amount of currency and coins.
3. List checks separately by their ABA numbers. Write only the number that appears above the line in the ABA number, including the hyphen. If there are many checks, list the checks by amount on a calculator tape and attach the tape to the deposit slip. On the first Checks line, write "See tape listing," followed by the total amount of the checks.
4. Add the amounts, and write the total amount on the Total line.

The checks are arranged in the order listed on the deposit slip. The deposit slip and the cash and checks are handed to a bank teller. The teller verifies the deposit and gives the depositor a receipt. The deposit receipt is usually a machine-printed form, although it may be a copy of the deposit slip stamped and initialed by the teller.

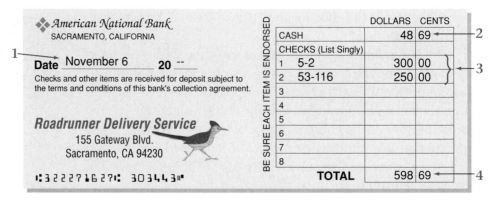

Figure 11–4 Deposit Slip

Endorsing Checks. A check is a form of property. When a business receives a check, it acquires the right to that check. To deposit the check in a checking account, the depositor endorses the check to transfer ownership to the bank. An **endorsement** is an authorized signature written or stamped on the back of a check that transfers ownership of the check.

A business can use three types of endorsements when transferring ownership of a check. The types of endorsements are shown in **Figure 11–5:**

- A **blank endorsement** includes only the signature or stamp of the depositor. It transfers ownership of the check, but it does not indicate who the new owner is. This is not a safe endorsement because the check can be cashed by anyone who presents it for payment.
- A **special endorsement** transfers ownership of the check to a specific individual or business.
- A **restrictive endorsement** transfers ownership to a specific owner and then limits, or restricts, how a check may be handled even after ownership is transferred. To protect checks from being cashed by anyone else, Roadrunner uses a restrictive endorsement that reads "For Deposit Only." Roadrunner stamps the endorsement on the back of each check as soon as it is received.

Recording Deposits. The check stubs in the checkbook are a record of the **Cash in Bank** account. That is, the completed stubs reflect all checking account transactions: payments, deposits, and bank service charges.

To see how to record a deposit in the checkbook, refer to **Figure 11–6** and follow these steps:

1. Enter the date of the deposit on the check stub for the next unused check. Use the Add deposits line.
2. Enter the total amount of the deposit on the same line in the Dollars and Cents (amount) columns.
3. Add the deposit amounts to the amount on the Balance brought forward line. Enter the result on the Total line. This total is the new checkbook balance.

Writing Checks

Writing a check is a simple procedure. You need to follow a few important rules, however, to ensure correct recordkeeping and proper handling of the money represented by the check.

- Write checks in ink, or prepare typewritten or computer-generated checks. Some businesses use a check-writing machine that perforates the amount of the check in words on the Dollars line. These perforations protect a check from alteration. Checks written in pencil are not acceptable because they can be easily altered.
- Complete the check stub *before* writing the check. This reduces the chance of forgetting to complete the stub.

Completing the Check Stub. Because the stub serves as a permanent record of the check, it must be complete and accurate. A check stub has two parts. The upper part summarizes the details of the cash payment transaction. The lower part is a record of how the transaction affects the checking account. To see how to complete the check stub, refer to **Figure 11–7** on page 282 and follow these steps:

1. In the upper part of the stub, enter the amount of the check, the date, the name of the payee (on the To line), and the purpose of the check (on the For line). A **payee** is the person or business to which a check is written.

Blank Endorsement

Special Endorsement

Restrictive Endorsement

Figure 11–5
Endorsements

$		No. 103
Date		20 --
To		
For		

	Dollars	Cents
Balance brought forward	21,650	00
Add deposits 1 10/14	200	00 2
10/15	1,200	00
Total	23,050	00 3
Less this check		
Balance carried forward		

Figure 11–6 Recording a Deposit in the Checkbook

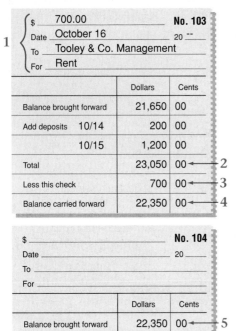

Figure 11-7 Filling Out the Check Stub

2. If it has not already been done, enter the balance on the Total line on the lower part of the stub.

3. Enter the amount of the check on the Less this check line. This amount is the same as the amount shown on the first line in the upper part of the stub.

4. Subtract the check amount from the total. Enter the new balance on the Balance carried forward line.

5. Enter the new balance on the first line of the bottom part of the *next* check stub, the Balance brought forward line.

Filling Out the Check. To see how to write a check, refer to **Figure 11-8** and follow these steps:

1. Write the date on which the check is being issued.

2. Write the payee's name on the Pay To The Order Of line. Start the payee's name as far left as possible.

3. Enter the amount of the check in numbers. Write clearly, and begin the first number as close to the printed dollar sign as possible.

4. On the next line, write the dollar amount of the check *in words*. Start at the left edge of the line. Write any cents as a fraction. For example, write 22 cents as 22/100. Draw a line from the cents fraction to the word *Dollars*.

5. Sign the check. Only an authorized person—one who has signed the signature card for the account—may sign the check. The person who signs a check is the **drawer**. The bank on which the check is written is the **drawee**.

The checkbook is now ready for the next transaction.

Voiding a Check. If an error is made while writing a check, the check is marked "Void" in large letters across the front (in ink). This is known as **voiding a check**. A new check is then prepared. When a check is voided, the stub is also voided.

Since a business needs to account for each check used, a voided check is never destroyed. Instead it is filed with the business records. A voided check may be placed in a special file, or it may simply be folded and stapled to the check stub.

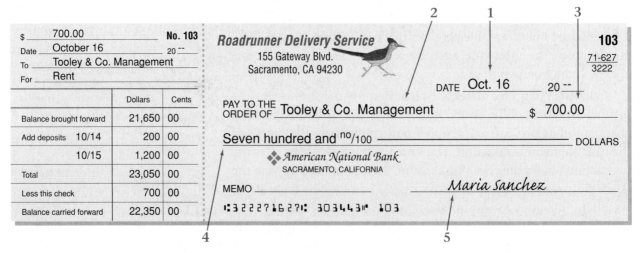

Figure 11-8 Completed Stub and Check

AFTER YOU READ

Reinforce the Main Idea

Create a chart like this one to list the activities involved in maintaining a checking account. Identify how each activity helps protect cash. Add more rows as needed.

Activity	How This Activity Protects Cash

Do the Math

Assume you work for a health food store that prepares two deposits each day. Using the following cash register summaries, determine how much cash should be deposited after the first shift ended at 3:00 p.m. and after the second shift ended at 9:00 p.m.

	First Shift (9:00 a.m. – 3:00 p.m.)			Second Shift (3:00 p.m. – 9:00 p.m.)		
	Cash Register			Cash Register		
	1	2	3	1	2	3
Coins	35.40	29.35	18.75	24.62	19.21	14.32
Currency	395.00	425.00	300.00	218.00	349.00	216.00
Checks	900.00	875.00	725.00	725.00	645.00	829.00

Problem 11–1 Preparing a Deposit Slip and Writing Checks

On August 14 Loretta Harper, owner of Peabody Cards and Gifts, deposited the following items in the checking account of the business.

Cash: $784.29

Checks: Charles Ling, drawn on American Bank of Commerce, ABA No. 32-7091; $39.44

Keith Lopez, drawn on People's Bank, ABA No. 84-268; $22.95

Marjorie Luke, drawn on Horizon Federal Savings and Loan, ABA No. 84-6249; $52.95

Mable Parker, drawn on Security National Bank, ABA No. 84-2242; $67.45

On August 15 Peabody received the July bill from Northeast Telephone for $214.80.

On August 17 Peabody received an advertising bill from the Bayside News for $275.00.

Instructions Using the forms provided in your working papers:

1. Complete a deposit slip.
2. Record the deposit on the check stub for Check 41.
3. Record the information for paying the telephone bill on Check Stub 41 and complete the check stub. Use August 16 as the date.
4. Prepare Check 41 to pay the telephone bill and sign your name as drawer.
5. Prepare the check stub and Check 42 to pay the bill for advertising. Use August 17 as the date and sign your name as drawer.

Reconciling the Bank Statement

Main Idea
The bank reconciliation is an important internal control.

Read to Learn...
➤ why businesses prove cash. (p. 284)
➤ how to read and reconcile a bank statement. (p. 284)
➤ about electronic funds transfer. (p. 290)

Key Terms
bank statement
canceled checks
imaged checks
reconciling the bank statement
outstanding checks
outstanding deposits
bank service charge
stop payment order
NSF check
Check 21
postdated check
electronic funds transfer system (EFTS)
bankcard
automated teller machine (ATM)

Instant Recall

Proving To *prove* something means to compare balances and make sure they are equal.

Have you ever been surprised to find that your bank account had less money than you thought because you forgot to record a withdrawal? If so, you realize the importance of reconciling (bringing into agreement) your checkbook with your bank statement. Business owners and their accountants also need to keep up-to-date records of cash.

Proving Cash
What Is Meant by Proving Cash?

The balance in the **Cash in Bank** account in the general ledger is regularly compared with the balance in the checkbook. If all cash receipts have been deposited, all cash payments have been made by check, and all transactions have been journalized and posted, the **Cash in Bank** account balance should agree with the checkbook balance. Comparing these two cash balances regularly is part of the internal control of cash. Some businesses prove cash daily or weekly, while others prove cash on a monthly basis.

If the **Cash in Bank** balance does not agree with the checkbook balance, and the trial balance has been proved, the error is probably in the checkbook. The following checkbook errors are the most common:

- faulty addition or subtraction
- failure to record a deposit or a check
- a mistake in copying the balance forward amount to the next check stub

If an error is made in the checkbook, the proper place to enter the correction is on the next unused check stub. For example, suppose Check 22 for $84.60 was recorded on the check stub as $48.60. The error is found when cash is proved. By this time several other checks have been written, so the next unused check stub is 31. In this case the amount of the error ($84.60 − $48.60 = $36.00) is subtracted from the balance brought forward on Check Stub 31 (see **Figure 11–9**). A note is made on Check Stub 22 to indicate that the error is corrected on Check Stub 31.

The Bank Statement
What Is a Bank Reconciliation?

A **bank statement** is an itemized record of all transactions in a depositor's account over a given period, usually a month. Typical bank statements include the following information:

1. the checking account balance at the beginning of the period
2. a list of all deposits made by the business during the period
3. a list of all checks paid by the bank
4. a list of any other deductions from the depositor's account
5. the checking account balance at the end of the period

Find each of these items on the bank statement for Roadrunner Delivery Service in **Figure 11–10.**

With the bank statement, a bank may include the **canceled checks** that it paid and deducted from the depositor's account. Instead of the actual checks, banks are increasingly sending images of the checks or simply a list of them. These **imaged checks** or *substitute checks* (copies of originals) or the list are used to verify the information on the bank statement. These checks and the bank statement should be kept in a file or storage box in case they are needed later as proof of payment or for other reasons.

Upon receipt, the bank statement is compared to the checkbook. The process of determining any differences between the bank statement and the checkbook is called **reconciling the bank statement** . It is also known as a *bank reconciliation.* The ending balance on the bank statement seldom agrees

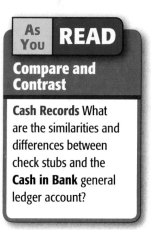

	No. 31
$ _____	
Date _____	20 --
To _____	
For _____	

	Dollars	Cents
Balance brought forward	4,750	00
Add deposits		
Less: Error corr. Ck. 22	36	00
Total	4,714	00
Less this check		
Balance carried forward		

Figure 11–9 Entering an Error Correction on the Check Stub

American National Bank
SACRAMENTO, CALIFORNIA

Roadrunner Delivery Service
155 Gateway Boulevard
Sacramento, CA 94230

Account Number: 303443

FDIC

Statement Date: 10/31/20--

Balance Last Statement	Deposits & Other Credits		Checks & Other Debits		Balance This Statement
	No.	Amount	No.	Amount	
1 00.00	3	26,400.00	5	4,183.00	5 22,217.00

Description	Checks & Other Debits	Deposits & Other Credits	Date	Balance
Balance Forward				00.00
Deposit		25,000.00	10/01	25,000.00
Check 101	3,000.00		10/04	22,000.00
Deposit		2 200.00	10/14	22,200.00
Check 102	3 350.00		10/15	21,850.00
Deposit		1,200.00	10/16	23,050.00
Check 103	700.00		10/20	22,350.00
Check 104	125.00		10/31	22,225.00
Service Charge	4 8.00		10/31	22,217.00

PLEASE EXAMINE YOUR STATEMENT AT ONCE. IF NO ERROR IS REPORTED IN 10 DAYS THE ACCOUNT WILL BE CONSIDERED CORRECT AND VOUCHERS GENUINE. ALL ITEMS ARE CREDITED SUBJECT TO FINAL PAYMENT.

The Bank for All Your Business Needs

Figure 11–10 Bank Statement

with the balance in the checkbook. There are three common reasons that the bank statement balance and the checkbook balance disagree:

- outstanding checks
- outstanding deposits
- bank charges

Outstanding Checks and Deposits

In banking terms the word *outstanding* simply means "not yet received." **Outstanding checks**, therefore, are checks that have been written but have not yet been presented to the bank for payment. It is not unusual for checks written in one statement period to reach the bank in a later period. **Outstanding deposits** are deposits that have been made and recorded in the checkbook but do not appear on the bank statement. A deposit made the same day the bank statement is prepared may not appear on the statement.

Bank Service Charges

The bank statement balance also reflects any service charges made by the bank during the statement period. Banks impose a **bank service charge**, which is a fee for maintaining bank records and processing bank statement items for the depositor. This charge varies from bank to bank. It is frequently based on either the number of checks and deposits handled during the statement period or the balance in the depositor's account. The bank subtracts the service charge from the depositor's account. The depositor usually does not know about the service charge, or other bank charges handled in the same manner, until the statement is received.

Before the bank statement is reconciled, the checkbook balance is adjusted by the amount of the bank service charge. As shown in **Figure 11–11**, the words *Less: Service Charge* are written on the next unused check stub on the line above the Total line. The amount of the service charge is entered in the amount column, preceded by a minus sign. The balance is recalculated and entered on the Total line.

$ _____	No. 107	
Date _____ 20 __		
To _____		
For _____		
	Dollars	Cents
Balance brought forward	21,125	00
Add deposits		
Less: Svc. Charge	−8	00
Total	21,117	00
Less this check		
Balance carried forward		

Figure 11–11 Entering a Bank Service Charge on the Check Stub

Interest Paid

Some banks pay interest on funds in a checking account. This is not a common practice, and the account must maintain a minimum balance to qualify. The interest appears on the bank statement. The amount of interest must be recorded in the checkbook, journalized, and posted. The journal entry for interest paid follows:

Debit **Cash in Bank**
   Credit **Interest Income**

The Bank Reconciliation

Promptly reconciling the bank statement is a good way to ensure orderly cash records and guard against cash losses. The bank expects to be notified immediately of any errors on the statement. Failure to do so may release the bank from responsibility for the errors.

Connect to...
ECONOMICS

In the early Middle Ages, Europe's economy used the barter system. Goods and services were paid for with other goods and services. As trade spread throughout Europe, the long distances made barter unwieldy. The use of currency, banks, and credit was far more convenient.

On the back of the bank statement is a form for reconciling the bank statement. This form documents the differences between the bank balance and the checkbook balance. Refer to **Figure 11–12** and follow these steps to reconcile a bank statement:

1. Arrange the canceled checks in numerical order. Compare the canceled checks with those listed on the statement and with the stubs. When you match a check and a stub, place a check mark beside the check amount on the bank statement and on the check stub. The stubs without check marks represent outstanding checks. List the outstanding check numbers and amounts on the bank reconciliation form.
2. Enter the ending balance shown on the bank statement.
3. Compare deposits listed on the bank statement to deposits listed in the checkbook. Enter the total of any outstanding deposits on the reconciliation form. Add this total to the bank statement balance and enter the result on the form.
4. Subtract the total of the outstanding checks from the amount calculated in Step 3. The result is the *adjusted bank balance.*
5. Compare the adjusted bank balance to the checkbook balance. When the balances match, the bank statement is reconciled.

Figure 11–13 illustrates a two-column account form.

If the adjusted bank balance does not match the checkbook balance, find and correct the error. Notify the bank immediately if it is a bank error. It is more likely, however, that the error is in the checkbook. Check the addition and subtraction on the check stubs and on the bank reconciliation form. Also look for any outstanding checks or deposits that have not been included in your calculations.

BANK RECONCILIATION FORM

PLEASE EXAMINE YOUR STATEMENT AT ONCE. ANY DISCREPANCY SHOULD BE REPORTED TO THE BANK IMMEDIATELY.

1. Record any transactions appearing on this statement but not listed in your checkbook.
2. List any checks still outstanding in the space provided to the right.
3. Enter the balance shown on this statement here.   2   22,217 | 00
4. Enter deposits recorded in your checkbook but not shown on this statement.   3 — | —
5. Total lines 3 and 4 and enter here.   22,217 | 00
6. Enter total checks outstanding here.   4   1,100 | 00
7. Subtract line 6 from line 5. This adjusted bank balance should agree with your checkbook balance.   5   21,117 | 00

CHECKS OUTSTANDING		
Number	Amount	
105	600	00
106	500	00
TOTAL	1,100	00

Figure 11–12 Bank Reconciliation Using a Bank Statement Form

Roadrunner Delivery Service
Bank Reconciliation Statement
October 31, 20--

Balance on bank statement			22 2 1 7 00
Additions:			
Deposits in transit		—	
			22 2 1 7 00
Deductions for outstanding checks:			
Check 105	6 0 0 00		
Check 106	5 0 0 00		
Total outstanding checks			1 1 0 0 00
Adjusted bank balance			21 1 1 7 00

Figure 11–13 Bank Account Reconciliation Using a Two-Column Account Form

Journalizing Bank Service Charges

Like any other business, banks charge fees for their services. A bank service charge is an expense that is recorded in the accounting records.

The bank deducted the service charge from Roadrunner's account, so it is not necessary to write a check for this expense. The bank statement is the source document for recording the bank service charge.

Business Transaction

On November 1 Roadrunner received the bank statement (Figure 11-10 on page 285). A bank service charge of $8 appeared on the statement.

ANALYSIS	*Identify*	**1.**	Bank service charges are often recorded in the **Miscellaneous Expense** account. Therefore, **Miscellaneous Expense** and **Cash in Bank** are affected.
	Classify	**2.**	**Miscellaneous Expense** is an expense account. **Cash in Bank** is an asset account.
	+/−	**3.**	**Miscellaneous Expense** is increased by $8. **Cash in Bank** is decreased by $8.

DEBIT-CREDIT RULE	**4.**	Increases in expense accounts are recorded as debits. Debit **Miscellaneous Expense** for $8.
	5.	Decreases in asset accounts are recorded as credits. Credit **Cash in Bank** for $8.

T ACCOUNTS   **6.**

Miscellaneous Expense		Cash in Bank	
Debit + 8	Credit −	Debit +	Credit − 8

JOURNAL ENTRY   **7.**

		GENERAL JOURNAL		PAGE 42		
	DATE	DESCRIPTION	POST. REF.	DEBIT	CREDIT	
1	20--					1
2	Nov. 1	Miscellaneous Expense		8 00		2
3		Cash in Bank			8 00	3
4						4

Special Banking Procedures

Checks are usually written or received and deposited without any problems. However, three problems may occur:

- A business does not want the bank to pay a check that was issued.
- A business receives and deposits a check from a customer whose account does not have enough money to cover the check.
- A customer presents a check that has a date in the future.

Stopping Payment on a Check. Occasionally, a drawer (Roadrunner) orders the drawee (bank) not to honor, or pay, a check. A **stop payment order** is a demand by the drawer, usually in writing, that the bank not honor a specific check. A stop payment order is often used when a check is lost. The bank must receive the stop payment order *before* the check is presented for payment. Otherwise, it is too late.

To record a stop payment order, the accountant writes the words *Stopped Payment* on the check stub for the stopped check. The accountant then adds the amount of the stopped check on the next unused check stub, illustrated in **Figure 11–14**. If appropriate, the accountant then issues a replacement check.

Most banks charge a fee for a stop payment order. The fee appears on the bank statement. A journal entry, similar to that made for the bank service charge, is prepared. Most businesses record the fee in **Miscellaneous Expense**. The source document for this entry is the bank statement.

Recording NSF Checks. An **NSF check** is a check returned to the depositor by the bank because the drawer's checking account does not have enough funds to cover the amount. *NSF* stands for *Not Sufficient Funds*. An NSF check is also known as a *dishonored check* or a *bounced check*.

Suppose that Burton Company (the drawer) wrote a check to Roadrunner (the payee) to pay for delivery services. What if Burton's account does not have sufficient funds to cover the amount of the check? American National Bank (the drawee) has already shown this check as being deposited to Roadrunner's account. When American National Bank finds out that Burton does not have enough funds to cover this check, it deducts the amount from Roadrunner's account. The bank also sends the check back to Roadrunner (not to Burton Company).

When the bank returns an NSF check, Roadrunner subtracts the amount of the dishonored check from the checkbook balance. Roadrunner also makes a journal entry to record the returned check. At this point Roadrunner has not yet been paid for the delivery services and must go back to Burton Company to collect payment. Burton can then deposit enough money in its own bank to cover the check or find another way to pay.

The *Check Clearing for the 21st Century Act,* known as **Check 21**, went into effect in 2004. It allows the conversion of a paper check to an electronic image that can be processed quickly. A bank can now pay a check on the day it is written, instead of several days later. However, Check 21 does not require banks to process deposits more quickly. As a result, the speed of check processing could cause an increase in the number of NSF checks.

Postdated Checks. A business might accept a check that has a future date instead of the actual date. This check is called a **postdated check**. It should not be deposited until the date on the check. Businesses sometimes accept postdated checks as a convenience to customers.

Check Stub for Stopped Check

$ 500.00		No. 633
Date January 12		20 --
To Smith Engineering		
For Electrical Work		

	Dollars	Cents
Balance brought forward	12,723	00
Add deposits		
Total		
Less this check	500	00
Balance carried forward	12,223	00

STOPPED PAYMENT

Next Unused Check Stub

$		No. 652
Date		20
To		
For		

	Dollars	Cents
Balance brought forward	10,452	00
Add deposits Stopped		
Payment on Ck 633	500	00
Total	10,952	00
Less this check		
Balance carried forward		

Figure 11–14 Recording a Stopped Check on the Check Stub

As You READ

Key Point

NSF Check A dishonored check "bounces" back to the depositor, not to the person who signed the check.

On November 15 a check for $450, written by Burton Company for payment on account and deposited by Roadrunner, was returned by the bank because of insufficient funds in Burton's account.

ANALYSIS *Identify*

1. **Accounts Receivable—Burton Company** and **Cash in Bank** are affected.

Classify

2. **Accounts Receivable—Burton Company** and **Cash in Bank** are both asset accounts.

+/−

3. **Accounts Receivable—Burton Company** is increased by the amount of the check returned by the bank, $450. **Cash in Bank** is decreased by $450.

DEBIT-CREDIT RULE

4. Increases in asset accounts are recorded as debits. Debit **Accounts Receivable—Burton Company** for $450.
5. Decreases in asset accounts are recorded as credits. Credit **Cash in Bank** for $450.

T ACCOUNTS

6.

Accounts Receivable—Burton Company		Cash in Bank	
Debit	Credit	Debit	Credit
+	−	+	−
450			450

JOURNAL ENTRY

7.

		GENERAL JOURNAL			PAGE 43	
	DATE	DESCRIPTION	POST. REF.	DEBIT	CREDIT	
1	20--					1
2	Nov. 15	Accts. Rec.—Burton Company		450 00		2
3		Cash in Bank			450 00	3
4						4

Electronic Funds Transfer System

What Is EFTS?

Look at **Figure 11–15.** It illustrates the route a check follows from the time it is written until the time it is returned with the bank statement.

Since millions of checks are written each day, the transfer of checks and funds is routine. This transfer of funds among banks is a huge job, however. Banks use the **electronic funds transfer system (EFTS)** to handle such a large volume of transfers. The EFTS allows banks to transfer funds among accounts quickly and accurately without the exchange of checks.

The EFTS has a tremendous impact on banking activities:

- **Direct payroll deposit.** Employers can electronically transfer employees' pay to each employee's bank account.

- **Automated bill paying.** A depositor can authorize the bank to transfer funds from his or her checking account to the creditor's bank account.
- **Bankcards.** A **bankcard**, also known as an *ATM card,* is a bank-issued card that can be used at an **automated teller machine (ATM)** to conduct banking activities. An ATM is a computer terminal outside a bank or at a different location entirely. When a bankcard can be used for transactions at other businesses besides the bank, it is called a *debit card.*
- **Bank-by-phone service.** Account holders can complete transactions with their banks' computer systems by telephone.
- **Online banking.** Using the Internet, an account holder can access the bank's Web site to conduct banking transactions.

When using any electronic banking procedure, be sure to record all transactions to avoid errors in the checking account.

Routing of Checks

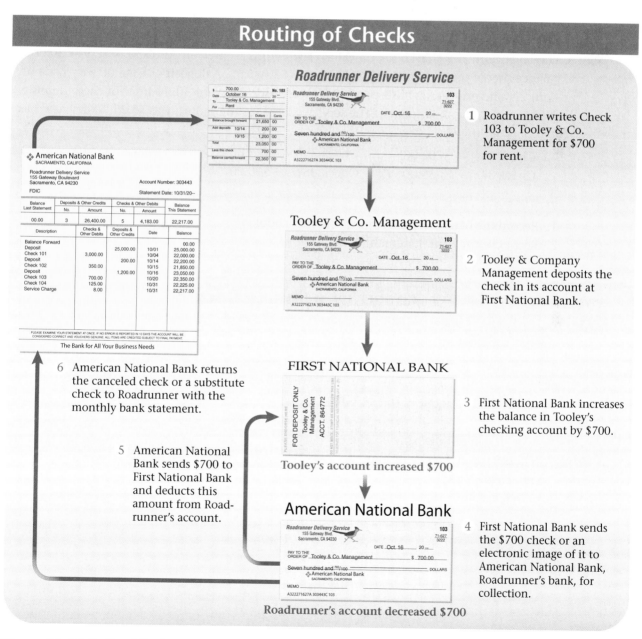

Figure 11–15 Routing of Checks

Reinforce the Main Idea

Create a chart like this one to list the adjustments that might be needed to reconcile the bank statement. Add answer rows as needed.

Reconciling the Bank Statement

Checkbook Balance Adjustments	Bank Statement Balance Adjustments

Do the Math

The balance in the checkbook of Valleyview Tennis Center on April 30 is $2,944.20. The balance shown on the April bank statement is $3,085.95. A deposit of $345.00 was made on April 29, and another deposit of $290.00 was made on April 30. Neither of these deposits appears on the bank statement. The service charge for the month was $5.25. Valleyview has four outstanding checks:

Check 344	$202.00	Check 350	$ 25.00
Check 346	55.00	Check 351	500.00

Instructions

1. Record the bank service charge in the checkbook.
2. Reconcile the bank statement.

Problem 11–2 Analyzing a Source Document

Instructions Review the Global Travel Agency bank statement and answer the following questions in your working papers.

1. What is the amount of the returned check?
2. How much did the bank charge Global Travel Agency for the returned check?
3. What account will be debited for the $12 bank service charge?

Security National Bank
155 Flower Street, Cambridge, MA 02138

STATEMENT

Global Travel Agency
200 Brattle Street
Cambridge, MA 02138

Account Number: 2649-84
Statement Date: 2/28/20--

FDIC

Balance Last Statement	Deposits & Other Credits		Checks & Other Debits		Balance This Statement
	No.	Amount	No.	Amount	
2,714.00	3	2,395.00	7	4,036.00	1,073.00

Checks & Other Debits	Deposits & Other Credits	Date	Balance
	1,250.00	2/05	3,964.00
700.00		2/10	3,264.00
900.00		2/10	2,364.00
	845.00	2/15	3,209.00
600.00		2/15	2,609.00
(R) 100.00		2/20	2,509.00
(S) 25.00		2/20	2,484.00
725.00		2/25	1,759.00
600.00		2/25	1,159.00
(S) 12.00		2/26	1,147.00
214.00		2/26	933.00
	300.00	2/27	1,233.00
160.00		2/27	1,073.00

PLEASE EXAMINE YOUR STATEMENT AT ONCE. IF NO ERROR IS REPORTED IN 10 DAYS THE ACCOUNT WILL BE CONSIDERED CORRECT AND VOUCHERS GENUINE. ALL ITEMS ARE CREDITED SUBJECT TO FINAL PAYMENT.

C=CERTIFIED CHECK T=DEBIT OR CREDIT S=SERVICE CHARGE L=LIST CR=OVERDRAFT R=RETURNED CHECK

Accounting Careers in Focus

RECRUITING MANAGER
Robert Half Finance & Accounting
Washington, D.C.
Raj Khanna

Q: What does Robert Half Finance & Accounting do?

A: We help companies locate highly skilled financial professionals for full-time positions.

Q: How did you become a recruiter?

A: I was a CPA for eight years, working in both public and private accounting environments, when my sister introduced me to a friend who owned a small recruiting firm. I had been there just a few months when the firm was acquired by Robert Half International. That's when things really started to happen for me. I had the opportunity to travel and attend key training workshops, which really gave my career momentum.

Q: What are some factors that have been key to your success?

A: Intense daily activity is critical. When it comes to providing customer service, thinking outside the box is important. These factors have helped me to establish longstanding relationships with my clients and candidates.

Q: Why do you think an accounting degree is valuable?

A: Accounting is one of the most solid business foundations out there. It is a discipline that transcends any industry and is relevant at any level throughout one's career.

> **Tips from . . .**
>
> **RHI Robert Half International Inc.**
>
> Being able to communicate your ideas is necessary for success in any work environment. Know the audience you are addressing, think before voicing your opinion, and keep your communication simple and brief to ensure your messages come through loud and clear.

CAREER FACTS

- ▶ <u>Nature of the Work:</u> Identify skilled candidates for available employment opportunities with client companies.
- ▶ <u>Training or Education Needed:</u> A bachelor's degree in accounting or related experience.
- ▶ <u>Aptitude, Abilities, and Skills:</u> Interpersonal and communication skills, aptitude for sales, familiarity with jobs in different industries.
- ▶ <u>Salary Range:</u> $50,000 and up depending on personal performance, company performance, and company size.
- ▶ <u>Career Path:</u> Work in a public accounting firm or corporate accounting department to gain experience and knowledge, and then transfer to a recruiting position with a firm that specializes in accounting and finance.

Thinking Critically | What do you think is meant by the term *company culture*? What might you look for in deciding whether or not a company's culture is right for you?

Key Concepts

1. The term *internal controls* refers to steps that a business takes to protect its cash and other assets, and to keep reliable records:
   - Limit the number of persons who handle cash.
   - Separate accounting tasks that involve cash.
   - Bond (insure) employees who handle cash or cash records.
   - Use a cash register and a safe.
   - Make daily deposits in the bank of cash received.
   - Make all cash payments by check.
   - Reconcile the bank statement promptly.

2. To open a checking account, a business owner fills out a signature card and deposits cash in the bank.
   The following forms are used to maintain a checking account:
   - deposit slip
   - check
   - checkbook in which deposits and checks are recorded on check stubs

3. All checks written and deposits made are recorded on the check stub, which serves as a permanent record of the check. The stub should be completed *before* writing a check.

4. Checks should be written in ink, or by typewriter, computer, or check-writing machine. Follow these steps: (a) Write the issue date; (b) write the payee's name on the Pay To The Order Of line starting as far left as possible; (c) write the amount of the check in numbers clearly, and begin the first number as close to the printed dollar sign as possible; (d) on the next line, write the dollar amount of the check in words starting at the left edge of the line, and write any cents as a fraction; (e) sign the check.

5. Checks are endorsed before they are deposited. Most businesses stamp a restrictive endorsement on a check as soon as it is received. A restrictive endorsement limits how checks are handled.

Blank Endorsement

Special Endorsement

Restrictive Endorsement

6. One way to *prove cash* is to reconcile the bank statement. Follow these steps to do a bank reconciliation: (a) Identify outstanding checks and list them on the bank reconciliation form, (b) enter the ending balance from the bank statement on the reconciliation form, (c) identify outstanding deposits and add them to the bank statement balance, (d) subtract outstanding checks from the bank statement balance, and (e) compare the adjusted bank statement balance with the checkbook balance. The bank statement is reconciled when the checkbook balance and the adjusted bank balance are equal.

7. A bank statement balance generally reflects any fees that a bank charged during the statement period. These service charges are for maintaining bank records and processing bank statement items. The depositor usually is not notified about the service charge or other bank fees until the statement arrives.

The bank statement is the source document for service charges. Write the bank service charge on the check stub. Also journalize and post the service charge:

	DATE	DESCRIPTION	POST. REF.	DEBIT	CREDIT	
GENERAL JOURNAL				PAGE ___1___		
1	20--					1
2	Date	Miscellaneous Expense		x x x x		2
3		Cash in Bank			x x x x	3
4		10/31/20—Bank Statement				4
5						5

8. The electronic funds transfer system (EFTS) allows banks to transfer funds without the exchange of checks. EFTS makes the following services available to individuals:
   - direct payroll deposit
   - automated bill paying
   - bankcards
   - bank-by-phone service
   - online banking

Key Terms

automated teller machine (ATM)	(p. 291)	endorsement	(p. 280)
bank service charge	(p. 286)	external controls	(p. 278)
bank statement	(p. 284)	imaged check	(p. 285)
bankcard	(p. 291)	internal controls	(p. 278)
blank endorsement	(p. 281)	NSF check	(p. 289)
canceled check	(p. 285)	outstanding checks	(p. 286)
check	(p. 278)	outstanding deposits	(p. 286)
Check 21	(p. 289)	payee	(p. 281)
checking account	(p. 278)	postdated check	(p. 289)
deposit slip	(p. 279)	reconciling the bank statement	(p. 285)
depositor	(p. 278)	restrictive endorsement	(p. 281)
drawee	(p. 282)	signature card	(p. 279)
drawer	(p. 282)	special endorsement	(p. 281)
electronic funds transfer system (EFTS)	(p. 290)	stop payment order	(p. 289)
		voiding a check	(p. 282)

Check Your Understanding

1. **Internal Controls**
   a. Why do businesses need internal controls?
   b. What internal controls can a business use to protect cash?

2. **Checking Account Forms**
   a. What is the purpose of a signature card?
   b. In addition to a signature card, what other forms are involved in using a checking account?

3. **Check Stubs**
   a. What is the purpose of a check stub?
   b. Why should you complete the check stub *before* writing the check?

4. **Writing a Check**
   a. How should the amount be written on the check?
   b. Why should checks be written in ink or by typewriter, computer, or check-writing machine?

5. **Bank Deposit**
   a. How often should a business deposit cash as part of its internal controls?
   b. What information should you include on a deposit slip?

6. **Bank Reconciliation**
   a. What information does a bank statement contain?
   b. List the steps to reconcile a bank statement.

7. **Bank Service Charges**
   a. What is a bank service charge?
   b. How does a business record bank service charges in its checkbook and in its accounting records?

8. **Electronic Funds Transfer System**
   a. How do banks use the electronic funds transfer system (EFTS)?
   b. What are some of the ways customers make electronic purchases?

Apply Key Terms

The manager of Valley View Bowling Center is concerned about cash control and banking procedures for the business. On a separate sheet of paper, write a memo explaining how the terms here relate to protecting cash.

automated teller machine (ATM)
bank service charge
bank statement
bankcard
blank endorsement
canceled check
check
Check 21
checking account
deposit slip
depositor

drawee
drawer
electronic funds transfer system (EFTS)
endorsement
external controls
imaged check
internal controls
NSF check
outstanding checks
outstanding deposits

payee
postdated check
reconciling the bank statement
restrictive endorsement
signature card
special endorsement
stop payment order
voiding a check

Reconciling the Bank Statement

Making the Transition from a Manual to a Computerized System

Task	Manual Methods	Computerized Methods
Reconciling the bank statement	• Using the form on the back of the bank statement or accounting stationery, follow the steps on page 287 to reconcile the bank statement.	• Before attempting to reconcile the bank statement, make sure all transactions for the month have been posted. • A computerized system will list all cash transactions and allow you to check off the appropriate cleared items. • You may enter adjustments such as bank fees. These will be posted to the general ledger.

Peachtree® Q & A

Peachtree Question	Answer
How do I reconcile the cash account in Peachtree?	1. Select **Account Reconciliation** from the *Tasks* menu. 2. Select the cash account to be reconciled. 3. Type the bank statement date. 4. Type the ending bank statement balance. 5. Click the Clear box for all items that appear on the bank statement. 6. When the unreconciled difference is $0.00, the account has been reconciled. 7. Click **OK** to save the reconciliation.

QuickBooks Q & A

QuickBooks Question	Answer
How do I reconcile the cash account in QuickBooks?	1. Choose **Reconcile** from the *Banking* menu. 2. Select the bank account in the *Account* field. 3. Type the bank statement date. 4. Type the ending balance and click **Continue**. 5. Click each line for each item that appears on the bank statement to mark it as cleared. 6. When the *Difference* field shows 0.00, the account has been reconciled. 7. Click **Reconcile Now** to save the reconciliation.

For detailed instructions, see your Glencoe Accounting Chapter Study Guides and Working Papers.

Peachtree®

SMART GUIDE

Step–by–Step Instructions: Problems 11–4

1. Select the problem set for Hot Suds Car Wash (Prob. 11–4).
2. Rename the company and set the system date.
3. Use the **Payments** option in the *Tasks* menu to record the checks issued.
4. Record the deposits using the **General Journal Entry** option.
5. Print an Account Register report using the **Account Reconciliation** option from the *Reports* menu.
6. Complete the Analyze activity.
7. End the session.

Peachtree®

SMART GUIDE

Step–by–Step Instructions: Problem 11–5

1. Select the problem set for Kits & Pups Grooming (Prob. 11–5).
2. Rename the company and set the system date.
3. Reconcile the bank statement.
4. Print the Account Reconciliation reports: Account Register, Account Reconciliation, Deposits in Transit, and Outstanding Checks.
5. Complete the Analyze activity.
6. End the session.

Problem 11–3 Handling Deposits

On October 4 the owner of Wilderness Rentals deposited the following in the business checking account at First National Bank. The beginning balance in the account is $3,306.54 before these transactions.

Cash: Currency, $374.00; Coins, $7.42

Checks: Bob Warner, drawn on Consumers Bank, ABA No. 63-706; $64.98

Joan Walkman, drawn on Mountain Bank, ABA No. 63-699; $349.81

Ernesto Garcia, drawn on Progressive Savings and Loan, ABA No. 63-710; $29.44

Instructions In your working papers:

1. Place a restrictive endorsement on each check. Use "Wilderness Rentals."
2. Fill out a deposit slip. Use the ABA number to identify each check.
3. Record the deposit in the checkbook on Check Stub 651.

Analyze Calculate the checkbook balance after the deposit is recorded on the check stub.

Problem 11–4 Maintaining the Checkbook

As the accounting clerk for Hot Suds Car Wash, you write checks and make deposits. The current checkbook balance is $3,486.29.

Instructions For each transaction:

1. Record the necessary information on the check stub. Determine the new balance and carry the balance forward.
2. Prepare the necessary checks and sign your name as drawer.

Date	Transactions
Oct. 3	Issued Check 504 for $868.45 to Custom Construction for construction supplies.
3	Deposited $601.35 in the checking account.
6	Issued Check 505 for $299.60 to CP Lumber for paint.
7	Issued Check 506 to Laverne Brothers for $1,000.00 for completing a painting job.
10	Deposited $342.80 in the checking account.
10	Issued Check 507 to Union Utilities for the September electricity bill of $175.50.

Analyze Calculate the balance brought forward amount on Check Stub 508.

Problem 11–5 Reconciling the Bank Statement

On October 31 George Flaum, the accountant for Kits & Pups Grooming, received the bank statement dated October 30. After comparing the company's checkbook with the bank statement, George found the following:

1. The checkbook balance on October 31 is $960.
2. The ending bank statement balance is $1,380.
3. The bank statement shows a service charge of $10.
4. A deposit of $405 was made on October 30, but does not appear on the bank statement.
5. Check 768 for $529 and Check 772 for $306 are outstanding.

Instructions In your working papers:

1. Record the bank service charge in the checkbook.
2. Reconcile the bank statement.
3. Journalize the bank service charge in the general journal, page 4.
4. Post the bank service charge journal entry to the appropriate general ledger accounts.

Analyze How many checks are outstanding? Identify the total amount that is outstanding.

Problem 11–6 Reconciling the Bank Statement

On October 31 Juanita Ortega, owner of Outback Guide Service, received a bank statement dated October 30. Juanita found the following:

1. The checkbook has a balance of $2,551.34.
2. The bank statement shows a balance of $2,272.36.
3. The statement shows a bank service charge of $20.00.
4. A check from Podaski Systems for $62.44, deposited on October 18, was returned by the bank. There is no fee for handling the NSF check.
5. A deposit of $672.48 made on October 30 does not appear on the bank statement.
6. These checks are outstanding:

| Check 872 for | $126.84 | Check 883 for | $192.80 |
| Check 881 for | 87.66 | Check 887 for | 68.64 |

Instructions Using the preceding information:

1. Record the service charge and the NSF check in the checkbook.
2. Reconcile the bank statement.
3. Record the service charge and NSF check on page 7 of the general journal.
4. Post the journal entries to the appropriate general ledger accounts.

Analyze Review the Miscellaneous Expense account found in your working papers. Identify the Miscellaneous Expense account balance after posting the October 31 entry.

QuickBooks

PROBLEM GUIDE

Step–by–Step Instructions: Problem 11–5

1. Restore the Problem 11-5.QBB file.
2. Reconcile the bank statement using the **Reconcile** option in the **Banking** menu.
3. Print a Detail reconciliation report and the Cash in Bank register.
4. Complete the Analyze activity.
5. Back up your work.

SPREADSHEET SMART GUIDE

Step–by–Step Instructions: Problem 11–6

1. Select the spreadsheet template for Problem 11–6.
2. Complete the spreadsheet using the instructions in your working papers.
3. Print the spreadsheet and proof your work.
4. Save your work and exit the spreadsheet program.

Peachtree®

SMART GUIDE

Step–by–Step Instructions: Problem 11–7

1. Select the problem set for Showbiz Video (Prob. 11–7).
2. Rename the company and set the system date.
3. Reconcile the bank statement using the **Account Reconciliation** option in the **Tasks** menu.
4. Print the Account Reconciliation reports.
5. Complete the Analyze activity.
6. End the session.

QuickBooks

PROBLEM GUIDE

Step–by–Step Instructions: Problem 11–7

1. Restore the Problem 11-7.QBB file.
2. Reconcile the bank statement.
3. Print a Detail reconciliation report and the Cash in Bank register.
4. Complete the Analyze activity.
5. Back up your work.

Problem 11–7 Reconciling the Bank Statement

On October 31 Showbiz Video received the bank statement dated October 30. The accountant reviewed it and found the following:

1. The checkbook balance on October 31 is $13,462.96.
2. The ending bank statement balance is $13,883.80.
3. The bank statement shows a service charge of $17.50.
4. Deposits of $675.00 on October 28 and $925.00 on October 29 do not appear on the bank statement.
5. The following checks are outstanding:

    Check 1766 $125.00   Check 1770 $1,462.19
    Check 1768   69.42   Check 1771   381.73

Instructions In your working papers:

1. Record the bank service charge in the checkbook in your working papers.
2. Reconcile the bank statement.
3. Record the entry for the bank service charge on general journal page 13.
4. Post the bank service charge journal entry to the proper ledger accounts.

Analyze Calculate the **Cash in Bank** balance after the October 31 posting. Does it agree with the adjusted checkbook balance?

SOURCE DOCUMENT PROBLEM

Problem 11–8
Use the source document in your working papers to complete this problem.

Peachtree®

SMART GUIDE

Step–by–Step Instructions: Problem 11–8

1. Select the problem set for Job Connect (Prob. 11–8).
2. Rename the company and set the system date.
3. Reconcile the bank statement.
4. Print the Account Reconciliation reports.
5. Complete the Analyze activity.
6. End the session.

CHALLENGE PROBLEM

Problem 11–8 Reconciling the Bank Statement Using the Account Form

On October 20 Job Connect received its bank statement dated October 18.

1. The checkbook balance on October 20 is $880.84.
2. The ending bank statement balance is $344.58.
3. A $14.00 service charge appears on the bank statement.
4. The following checks are outstanding:

    Check 864 $ 88.41   Check 871 $129.88
    Check 869   69.34   Check 873   14.25

5. A $68.42 check from Tom McCrary deposited on October 13 was returned by the bank for insufficient funds. The bank charged Job Connect's account $7.00 for the NSF check. No journal entry was made for the NSF check.
6. A $938.72 deposit on October 19 is not on the bank statement.
7. A check for $200.00 to Fontenot Inc. was lost in the mail and has not been deposited. A stop payment order, which cost $10.00, was issued on October 15. No new check was issued.

Instructions Reconcile the bank statement using the account form in your working papers.

Analyze Identify the account that will be debited for both the NSF check and the bank handling charge on the check.

Practice your test-taking skills! The questions on this page are reprinted with permission from national organizations:
- Future Business Leaders of America
- Business Professionals of America

Use a separate sheet of paper to record your answers.

Future Business Leaders of America

MULTIPLE CHOICE

Use the following choices for questions 1–3.

Indicate whether the following items in a bank reconciliation should be
- a. added to the checkbook balance.
- b. deducted from the checkbook balance.
- c. added to the bank statement balance.
- d. deducted from the bank statement balance.

1. Outstanding deposit of $1,200

2. An NSF check from customer Anne Campbell for $52

3. An outstanding check for $185 written to Cole Realty

4. The bank statement shows a checking account balance of $5,500. There are outstanding checks totaling $600, an outstanding deposit of $400, and a bank service charge of $15. The cash account balance should be
- a. $5,300.
- b. $5,700.
- c. $5,285.
- d. none of the above.

Business Professionals of America

MULTIPLE CHOICE

5. The first step in balancing a checkbook is
- a. subtracting fees on the bank statement from the checkbook balance.
- b. comparing checks in the check record with those on the statement.
- c. adding interest earned to the checkbook balance.
- d. adding recent deposits to the bank statement balance.

Need More Help?

Go to **glencoeaccounting.glencoe.com** and click on **Student Center**. Click on **Winning Competitive Events** and select **Chapter 11**.
- **Practice Questions and Test-Taking Tips**
- **Concept Capsules and Terminology**

Cash Control

1. Define *internal controls*.
2. Explain why the balance in the checkbook can differ from the balance on the bank statement.
3. Your bank sent you a dishonored check. What should you do?
4. Contrast check processing before Check 21 to check processing after Check 21. What are the differences?
5. Suppose you carry out all your transactions electronically. How do you reconcile your bank statement?
6. Assess the value of the electronic funds transfer system.

Service Business: Entertainment

Dexter Shuman owns a bowling alley called Ten Pin Alley. Each night, Dexter counts the cash in the two cash registers and makes a night deposit at the local bank. For the month of May, Dexter made deposits totaling $6,400. During May, Dexter wrote checks totaling $2,900. The last three checks he wrote were Check 1408 for $180; Check 1409 for $560; and Check 1410 for $212. The beginning cash balance for the month was $13,840, which is the amount shown as the beginning balance on the May bank statement. That statement also includes a $12 service charge and an $18 charge for printing new checks.

INSTRUCTIONS

1. Determine the ending bank statement balance if all checks written have cleared.
2. Determine the ending bank statement balance if Checks 1408, 1409, and 1410 are outstanding.
3. Calculate the balance of the **Cash in Bank** account.

Pocketing Differences

Imagine that you are a cashier at a grocery store like Ralphs. In a four-hour shift, you handle thousands of dollars. At the end of your shift, you total receipts and cash to see if they match. One day cash comes up short, and you report the discrepancy to the manager. A few weeks later, cash is over by $2. You know a couple of cashiers who pocket extra cash. You wonder who would miss $2.

ETHICAL DECISION MAKING

1. What are the ethical issues?
2. What are the alternatives?
3. Who are the affected parties?
4. How do the alternatives affect the parties?
5. What would you do?

Making the Case for Daily Deposits

Assume that you work for a sporting goods store that is open six days a week, 12 hours a day. A major promotion is resulting in record sales, and the manager has been too busy to make daily cash deposits. Discuss with your classmates and teacher the importance of taking time to make cash deposits every day.

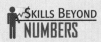

Customer Service

As a personal banker for Citizen's First National Bank, your duties include opening personal bank accounts, taking loan applications, and serving bank customers. Today Ms. Kelley wants to open a checking account. What items would you put in an information packet about opening her account? Pair up with another student and role-play teaching the new client to write a check and fill out a deposit slip. Model the customer service principles of thoroughness, courtesy, and respect.

Cash Management

Imagine how difficult it would be to control cash for hundreds of locations in the United States, Europe, and Asia. Many international companies select one large bank that can handle transactions in multiple currencies and countries.

INSTRUCTIONS Identify reasons why you would prefer to work with one bank if you were in charge of cash control for an international business.

Your Bank Statement

If you have a checking account, you know that the balances on the bank statement and in the checkbook seldom agree. You recognize the importance of reconciling the two balances so that you will know exactly how much money you have in the account.

PERSONAL FINANCE ACTIVITY Imagine that you just received your monthly bank statement. When comparing it to the checkbook, you found a $200.00 deposit that was not on the bank statement and two checks totaling $145.00 that were outstanding. The bank statement balance was $1,370.00 and the checkbook balance is $1,425.00. What is the reconciled balance?

PERSONAL FINANCE ONLINE Log on to **glencoeaccounting.glencoe.com** and click on **Student Center.** Click on **Making It Personal** and select **Chapter 11.**

Evaluating Working Capital

One measure of a company's ability to pay debts is its working capital.

Working Capital = Current Assets − Current Liabilities

Current assets are cash and assets that will be converted to cash within the next accounting period. *Current liabilities* are debts that must be paid within the next accounting period.

INSTRUCTIONS Refer to Roadrunner's balance sheet on page 233. If Maria Sanchez had made a $1,000 withdrawal, how would each of the following change?

1. Current assets
2. Current liabilities
3. Working capital

Bank Reconciliations

A big-name sports team must reconcile its bank statements just like your local batting cage business. Visit **glencoeaccounting .glencoe.com** and click on **Student Center.** Click on **WebQuest** and select **Unit 2** to continue your Internet project.

Completing the Accounting Cycle for a Sole Proprietorship

Main Task

▶ Set up the accounting records and complete the accounting cycle for Fast Track Tutoring Service.

Summary of Steps

▶ Open general ledger accounts.

▶ Analyze, journalize, and post transactions.

▶ Reconcile the bank statement.

▶ Journalize and post the bank service charge.

▶ Prepare a trial balance, a work sheet, and the financial statements.

▶ Journalize and post the closing entries.

▶ Prepare a post-closing trial balance.

Why It's Important

▶ This project pulls together all of the concepts and procedures you have learned.

Fast Track Tutoring Service

Company Background:
Fast Track Tutoring Service is owned and managed by Jennifer Rachael. It has been in business for one month. The business is organized as a sole proprietorship and provides tutoring services in a number of disciplines for students from pre-kindergarten through high school. The business earns revenue from tuition charged for one-on-one instruction and special classes.

Your Job Responsibilities: As the accounting clerk for this business, use the accounting stationery in your working papers to complete the following activities.

(1) Open a general ledger account for each account in the chart of accounts.

(2) Analyze each business transaction.

(3) Enter each business transaction in the general journal. Begin on journal page 1.

(4) Post each journal entry to the appropriate accounts in the general ledger.

(5) Reconcile the bank statement that was received on December 31. The statement is dated December 30. The checkbook has a current balance of $9,631. The bank statement shows a balance of $9,844. The bank service charge is $15. These checks are outstanding: Check 108, $183 and Check 109, $45. There are no outstanding deposits.

(6) Make any necessary adjustments to the checkbook balance.

(7) Journalize and post the entry for the bank service charge.

(8) Prepare a trial balance and complete the work sheet.

(9) Prepare an income statement, a statement of changes in owner's equity, and a balance sheet.

(10) Journalize and post the closing entries.

(11) Prepare a post-closing trial balance.

Business Transactions: Fast Track Tutoring Service began business operations on December 1 of this year.

Fast Track Tutoring Service (continued)

Complete the project using:	**Manual** Glencoe Working Papers	OR	**Peachtree Complete Accounting** Software	OR	**QuickBooks** Templates

CHART OF ACCOUNTS
Fast Track Tutoring Service

ASSETS

101 Cash in Bank
110 Accts. Rec.–Carla DiSario
120 Accts. Rec.–George McGarty
140 Office Supplies
150 Office Equipment
155 Instructional Equipment

LIABILITIES

210 Accts. Pay.–Educational Software
215 Accts. Pay.–T & N School Equip.

OWNER'S EQUITY

301 Jennifer Rachael, Capital

305 Jennifer Rachael, Withdrawals
310 Income Summary

REVENUE

401 Group Lessons Fees
405 Private Lessons Fees

EXPENSES

505 Maintenance Expense
510 Miscellaneous Expense
515 Rent Expense
525 Utilities Expense

SMART GUIDE

Step–by–Step Instructions:

1. Select the problem set for Fast Track Tutoring Service (MP–2).
2. Rename the company and set the system date.
3. Record all of the transactions.
4. Reconcile the bank statement.
5. Print a General Journal report and proof your work.
6. Print the Account Reconciliation reports.
7. Print a General Ledger and a Trial Balance.
8. Print the financial statements.
9. Close the fiscal year.
10. Print a post-closing trial balance.
11. Complete the Analyze activity and complete the Audit Test.
12. End the session.

QuickBooks

PROBLEM GUIDE

Step–by–Step Instructions:

1. Restore the Mini Practice Set 2.QBB file.
2. Record all of the transactions.
3. Reconcile the bank statement.
4. Print a Detail Reconciliation report.
5. Print a Journal report.
6. Print the register for the **Cash in Bank** account.
7. Print a General Ledger.
8. Print a Trial Balance.
9. Print a Profit and Loss report and Balance Sheet.
10. Close the fiscal year.
11. Print a post-closing Trial Balance.
12. Complete the Analyze activity and the Audit Test.
13. Back up your work.

Date	Transactions
Dec. 1	Jennifer Rachael invested $25,000 in the business, Memo 1.
2	Bought a cash register (**Office Equipment**) for $525, Check 101.
2	Purchased $73 in office supplies, Check 102.
5	Purchased instructional computers for $13,924, Check 103.
5	Received $950 for private instruction, Receipt 1.
6	Bought $8,494 of instructional materials, Invoice 395, from Educational Software on account.
8	Billed Carla DiSario for two group classes, $36, Invoice 101.
9	Wrote Check 104 for $850 for the December rent.
10	Billed George McGarty $275 for special group classes, Invoice 102.
10	Received Invoice 5495 for a $2,375 microcomputer system, for office use, bought on account from T & N School Equipment.
11	Prepared Receipt 2 for $695 for 20 private lessons given between December 1 and December 10.
13	Received $36 from Carla DiSario on account, Receipt 3.
14	Sent Check 105 for $200 to Educational Software on account.
15	Wrote Check 106 for $750 to repaint two classrooms.
18	Jennifer Rachael withdrew $500 for personal use, Check 107.
20	Sent Check 108 for the electric bill of $183.
24	Issued Check 109 for $45 for stamps (**Miscellaneous Expense**).

Analyze | **Identify the creditor to which Fast Track Tutoring Service owed the most money on December 31.**

Accounting for a Payroll System

Personal Finance Q & A

Q: **Why should I learn about payroll?**

A: Payroll is important to everyone. When you are paid at your job, you want to be sure the amounts are correct. The business also wants to be sure that all employees are paid in a legal and correct manner.

Q: **What is the minimum wage?**

A: The current federal minimum wage is $5.15 per hour. A business must also meet its state's minimum wage requirement, which is sometimes higher.

THINK IT OVER

Do you agree with the law requiring employees to pay taxes on their earnings? Why or why not?

 **WebQuest** **Internet Project**

You're the Boss

Employees have different goals and are motivated to work for a variety of reasons. You need to know how to pay your employees in a way that is appropriate and that motivates them to do the best job possible. In this online activity, you will learn different ways to pay and motivate your employees.

 Log on to **glencoeaccounting.glencoe.com** and click on **Student Center.** Click on **WebQuest** and select **Unit 3.** Begin your WebQuest by reading the Task.

Continue working on your WebQuest as you study Unit 3.

Chapter	12	13
Page	337	371

BusinessWeek **THE BIG PICTURE**

A CAUTIOUS BONUS BOOST Estimated bonus pay for the lucky workers expected to receive such a windfall, as a percentage of base salary:

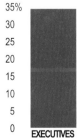

Data: Mercer Human Resources Consulting
Source: Reprinted by permission from *BusinessWeek.*

Payroll Accounting

What You'll Learn

1. Explain the importance of accurate payroll records.

2. Compute gross pay using different methods.

3. Explain and compute employee-paid withholdings.

4. Compute net pay.

5. Prepare payroll registers.

6. Explain the methods of distributing payroll funds.

7. Prepare an employee's earnings record.

8. Define the accounting terms introduced in this chapter.

Why It's Important

▶ Tax and labor laws protect the rights of both the employee and the employer.

Predict

1. What does the chapter title tell you?
2. What do you already know about this subject from personal experience?
3. What have you learned about this in the earlier chapters?
4. What gaps exist in your knowledge of this subject?

Exploring the *Real World* of Business

MOVING INTO THE WORKFORCE

Symantec Corporation

Since 1982 **Symantec Corporation** has designed programs to help users manage and protect their computer systems and files. Under John Thompson, CEO since 1999, **Symantec** has become a market leader with $1 billion in annual revenue.

Symantec believes in treating its employees right. It has one of the lowest employee loss rates in the United States. From software engineers to accountants, more than 5,000 employees deliver award-winning products and services.

CEO Thompson believes employees stay at **Symantec** because the work is challenging and morale is high. The long list of benefits—health-care plans, educational assistance, retirement plans, performance bonuses, and stock options—are just a few perks that keep employees happy.

What Do You Think?

Describe the kind of company culture and benefits that would make you happy in a job.

Working in the *Real World*

APPLYING YOUR ACCOUNTING KNOWLEDGE

When you get your paycheck, do you look at it carefully to see how much you have earned and what amounts have been deducted from the total? Employers are required to make certain deductions from your pay. You may also request voluntary deductions. You will learn about both types of deductions in this chapter.

Personal Connection

Look at your last pay stub. If money was deducted from your earnings, what do you think it was taken for?

Online Connection

Go to **glencoeaccounting.glencoe.com** and click on **Student Center.** Click on **Working in the Real World** and select **Chapter 12.**

Calculating Gross Earnings

BEFORE YOU READ

Main Idea
Gross earnings is the total amount an employee earns in a pay period.

Read to Learn...
➤ the two main functions of a payroll system. (p. 310)
➤ the different methods of computing gross pay. (p. 311)

Key Terms
payroll
pay period
payroll clerk
gross earnings
salary
wage
time card
electronic badge readers
commission
piece rate
overtime rate

In a private enterprise economy, people are free to work for any business they choose—as long as they meet the requirements for employment. Employers such as Ford Motor Company, Pier 1, and Symantec Corporation rely on their employees to operate the business and pay their employees for the services they perform. In paying their employees, businesses follow certain guidelines. For example, both federal and state laws require businesses to keep accurate payroll records and to report employees' earnings.

Most companies set up a payroll system to ensure that their employees are paid on time and that payroll checks are accurate. In this chapter you will learn about the payroll system.

Using a Payroll System
What Is a Payroll System?

A **payroll** is a list of the employees and the payments due to each employee for a specific pay period. A **pay period** is the amount of time over which an employee is paid. Most businesses use weekly, biweekly (every two weeks), semimonthly (twice a month), or monthly pay periods.

The payroll expense is a major expense for most companies. To compute salary expenses, most businesses set up a payroll system for recording and reporting employee earnings information. A well-designed payroll system achieves two goals:

1. The collection and processing of all information needed to prepare and issue payroll checks.
2. The generation of payroll records needed for accounting purposes and for reporting to government agencies, management, and others.

Businesses with many employees often hire a **payroll clerk**. The payroll clerk responsible for preparing the payroll

* makes sure employees are paid on time,
* makes sure each employee is paid the correct amount,
* completes payroll records,
* submits payroll reports, and
* pays payroll taxes.

All payroll systems have certain tasks in common, as shown in **Figure 12–1.**

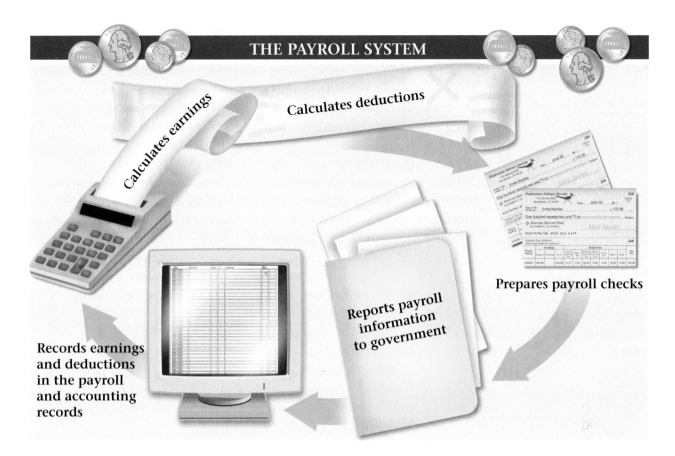

Calculates earnings

Calculates deductions

Prepares payroll checks

Reports payroll information to government

Records earnings and deductions in the payroll and accounting records

Figure 12–1 The Payroll System

Computing Gross Pay

How Do You Calculate Gross Earnings?

Most employees are paid for the specific amount of time they work during a pay period. The total amount of money an employee earns in a pay period is the employee's **gross earnings**, or *gross pay*. The gross earnings expense is sometimes called *salary expense*. The method used to compute gross pay depends on the basis on which an employee is paid. Employees can be grouped into different pay categories:

- salary
- hourly wage
- commission
- salary plus commission or bonus
- piece rate

Some employees are entitled to *overtime pay*. Let's look at each method of paying employees.

Salary

One common method of paying employees, especially those who are managers or supervisors, is by salary. A **salary** is a fixed amount of money paid to an employee for each pay period. In other words, an employee who is paid a salary earns the same amount regardless of the number of hours worked during the pay period. For example, Paula Ferguson, an adminis-trative assistant, is paid a salary of $2,000 a month. Her gross earnings are $2,000 for each monthly pay period. Paula may work 160 hours in one month and 170 hours in the next, but her gross earnings for each of the two months are the same—$2,000.

As You **READ**

It's Not What It Seems

Gross In accounting *gross* does not have a negative meaning. The term *gross* refers to an amount before anything is deducted or subtracted.

Hourly Wage

Another common way of paying employees is the hourly wage. A **wage** is an amount of money paid to an employee at a specified rate per hour worked. The number of hours worked multiplied by the hourly wage equals the gross earnings for the pay period. For example, Emily Kardos, a delivery driver for Roadrunner, is paid $6.75 per hour. During the last weekly pay period, she worked 36 hours. Emily's gross earnings are $243.00 (36 hours × $6.75).

Many employees are required to use time cards to accurately record their work hours during each pay period. A **time card** is a record of the times an employee arrives at work and leaves each day. The times may be recorded manually or by a time clock. The time card also shows the total hours worked each day. **Figure 12–2** shows a manual time card.

Many businesses divide an hour into four 15-minute quarters to measure employee work time. These quarter hours are determined as follows:

Quarter Hour	Example
On the hour	2:00 p.m.
15 minutes after the hour	2:15 p.m.
30 minutes after the hour	2:30 p.m.
45 minutes after the hour	2:45 p.m.

Employees seldom arrive and leave exactly on the quarter hour. As a result, some companies round arrival and departure times to the nearest quarter hour. Employees, therefore, are paid for working to the nearest quarter hour. Look at **Figure 12–2**. The times appearing on the time card for Emily Kardos for Monday will be rounded to the nearest quarter hour as follows:

Actual Time Recorded	Nearest Quarter Hour
7:58 a.m.	8:00 a.m.
12:25 p.m.	12:30 p.m.
1:32 p.m.	1:30 p.m.
4:18 p.m.	4:15 p.m.

Emily will be paid for working on Monday from 8:00 a.m. to 12:30 p.m. (4½ hours) and from 1:30 p.m. to 4:15 p.m. (2¾ hours) for a total of 7¼ hours.

Some businesses use computer technology to track employee arrival and departure times. One method uses **electronic badge readers** . The employee has an identification badge with a magnetic strip that contains employee information. The employee inserts the identification badge into a reader, which scans the magnetic strip and transfers the following information directly to the computer: the employee's name, the department or area where the employee works, and the arrival or departure time. This electronic equipment makes it fast and easy to prepare a daily printout of employee work hours.

Regardless of how employee work hours are recorded (manually, time clock, or electronic reader), business owners and supervisors check the accuracy of the hours reported and analyze the labor costs for every pay period.

NO. __11__

NAME __Emily Kardos__

SOC. SEC. NO. __201-XX-XXXX__

WEEK ENDING __6/30/20--__

DAY	IN	OUT	IN	OUT	IN	OUT	TOTAL
M	7:58	12:25	1:32	4:18			7¼
T	8:00	12:00	12:45	4:00			7¼
W	7:56	12:01	1:10	4:15			7
Th	8:01	11:55	1:02	4:16			7¼
F	7:45	12:02	1:05	3:58			7¼
S							
S							
					TOTAL HOURS		36

	HOURS	RATE	AMOUNT
REGULAR	36	$6.75	$243.00
OVERTIME	0		
		TOTAL EARNINGS	$243.00

SIGNATURE _Emily Kardos_ DATE _6/30/20--_

Figure 12–2 An Employee Time Card

Commission

A **commission** is an amount paid to an employee based on a percentage of the employee's sales. Sales employees are often paid a commission to encourage them to increase their sales. For example, Joyce Torrez is paid a 5% commission on all her sales. Last week Joyce's total sales were $8,254. Joyce's gross earnings for the week are $412.70 ($8,254 × .05).

Salary Plus Commission or Bonus

Some salespeople earn a base salary plus a commission or a bonus on the amount of their sales. For example, Juan Espito, who works at a car stereo shop, is paid a salary of $200 per week plus a commission of 3% of his sales. Juan's sales were $4,810 last week. His gross earnings are $344.30 [$200 + ($4,810 × .03)].

Piece Rate

Some manufacturing companies pay employees a specific amount of money for each item the employee produces. This method of payment is called **piece rate** . Businesses often pay a low hourly rate in addition to the piece rate.

Overtime Pay

State and federal laws regulate the number of hours some employees may work in a week. Generally, employers are required to pay overtime when employees covered by these laws work more than 40 hours per week. The **overtime rate** , set by the Fair Labor Standards Act of 1938, is 1½ (1.5) times the employee's regular hourly pay rate. For example, Jesse Dubow, a photo-lab clerk at Fast Photo, worked 43 hours last week. Jesse's hourly rate of pay is $6.60. His hourly overtime rate is $9.90 ($6.60 × 1.5). His gross earnings for the week are $293.70 determined as follows:

	Hours		Rate		
Regular	40	×	$6.60	=	$264.00
Overtime	3	×	$9.90	=	29.70
Total					$293.70

Some employees who are paid a salary are also entitled to overtime pay. If a salaried employee is paid overtime, the salary is converted to an hourly rate using a standard number of hours for the period covered by the salary. Then the hourly overtime rate is calculated. For example, Jim Halley's salary is $600 per week. His hourly rate is $15 assuming a standard 40-hour work week ($600 ÷ 40). His hourly overtime rate is $22.50 ($15 × 1.5). Jim's gross earnings for a 44-hour week are $690, determined as follows:

	Hours		Rate		
Regular				=	$600.00
Overtime	4	×	$22.50	=	90.00
Total					$690.00

As You **READ**

In Your Experience

Pay Categories If you or your friends have part-time jobs, what is the pay category?

Reinforce the Main Idea

Create a table similar to this one. For each category of employee, list the source of information for calculating gross earnings in a single pay period.

Method	Source of Information
Salary	
Hourly Wage	
Commission	
Salary plus Commission	

Do the Math

You have been interviewing with several financial consulting firms for entry-level management positions, and you received two job offers. One company, Bryson Consulting, offers you a starting salary of $30,000 with a 2% bonus (on salary) if you can bring 10 new clients into the firm. The other company, The Patterson Group, offers a salary of $25,000 plus a 3% commission on all new client billings. If you bring 10 new clients to Bryson, what would the amount of your bonus be? How much in new business would you have to bring to Patterson to equal the bonus from Bryson? Which offer seems to have the higher earnings potential? Why?

Problem 12–1 Calculating Gross Earnings

Cleary's Music Center has nine employees. The employees are paid weekly with overtime after 40 hours per week. The overtime rate is 1½ times the regular rate of pay. Payroll information for the week ending June 12 follows:

Employee	Pay Rate	Hours
David Clune	$6.95	33½
Richard Lang	$7.80	38
Jane Longas	$7.25	43
Betty Quinn	$8.30	44¼
John Sullivan	$8.30	39½
Kelly Talbert	$7.50	40
Gene Trimbell	$9.75	42½
Heidi Varney	$8.75	34¼
Kevin Wallace	$9.25	46

Instructions Prepare a form similar to the one that follows. Calculate regular earnings, overtime earnings, and gross earnings for each employee.

Employee	Total Hours	Pay Rate	Regular Earnings	Overtime Earnings	Gross Earnings
Clune, David	33½	$6.95	$232.83	– 0 –	$232.83

SECTION 2

Payroll Deductions

Whether you work at Target, McDonald's, or CompUSA, your earnings and deductions are determined in the same way. In this section you will compute the amounts withheld from an employee's earnings.

The first time you received a payroll check, you were probably surprised that its amount was less than you expected. Various amounts had been taken out of your gross earnings. An amount subtracted from gross earnings is a **deduction**. Deductions include those required by law and those an employee wishes to have withheld from earnings.

Deductions Required by Law
What Amounts Must Be Deducted from Earnings?

An employer is required by law to withhold payroll taxes. These taxes include the federal income tax and the social security tax. In addition, employers often must withhold city and state income tax.

Federal Income Tax

Most people pay the federal government a tax based on their annual income. To ensure that employees have the funds to pay their income taxes, employers are required to withhold a certain amount of money from each payroll check. The employer acts as a collection agent and sends the money withheld to the federal government.

The amount of income tax withheld is based on the estimated income tax the employee will actually owe. The exact income tax amount is determined when the employee prepares an income tax return. If too much money was withheld, the Internal Revenue Service (IRS) refunds the overpayment. If too little money was withheld, the employee pays the amount due when the income tax return is filed. To avoid penalties, an employee should have at least 90% of the actual tax liability deducted.

Form W-4. The federal income tax amount withheld depends on three factors: (1) the employee's marital status, (2) the number of allowances the employee claims, and (3) the employee's gross earnings. The first two items are found on Form W-4, the Employee's Withholding Allowance Certificate. Each employee fills out a Form W-4 when starting a job and files a revised Form W-4 if the marital status or number of allowances changes. Employers keep a current Form W-4 on file for each employee.

Figure 12–3 on page 316 shows the completed Form W-4 for Emily Kardos. The Form W-4 includes the employee's name, address, social security number, and marital status. The employee also lists the number of allowances claimed (refer to line 4). A **withholding allowance** reduces the amount of

BEFORE YOU READ

Main Idea
Payroll *deductions* are amounts withheld from an employee's gross earnings.

Read to Learn…
➤ the deductions required by law. (p. 315)
➤ the deductions an employee can choose. (p. 318)

Key Terms
deduction
withholding allowance
401(k) plan

Form **W-4**
Department of the Treasury
Internal Revenue Service

Employee's Withholding Allowance Certificate
► For Privacy Act and Paperwork Reduction Act Notice, see reverse.

OMB No. 1545-0010

20--

1 Type or print your first name and middle initial	Last Name	2 Your social security number
Emily M.	Kardos	201-XX-XXXX

Home address (number and street or rural route)
809 East Main Street

City or town, state, and ZIP code
Sacramento, CA 94230

3 Marital Status
☑ Single ☐ Married
☐ Married, but withhold at higher Single rate
Note: *If married, but legally separated, or spouse is a nonresident alien, check the Single box.*

4 Total number of allowances you are claiming (from line G above or from the Worksheets on back if they apply) . . . **4** 0

5 Additional amount, if any, you want deducted from each pay . . . . **5** $

6 I claim exemption from withholding and I certify that I meet **ALL** of the following conditions for exemption:
 • Last year I had a right to a refund of **ALL** federal income tax withheld because I had **NO** tax liability: **AND**
 • This year I expect a refund of **ALL** Federal income tax withheld because I expect to have **NO** tax liability; **AND**
 • This year if my income exceeds $500 and includes nonwage income, another person cannot claim me as a dependent.
 If you meet all of the above conditions, enter the year effective and "EXEMPT" here . . . . . ► **6**

7 Are you a full-time student? (**Note:** Full-time students are not automatically exempt.) . . . . **7** ☐ Yes ☑ No

Under penalty of perjury, I certify that I am entitled to the number of withholding allowances claimed on this certificate or entitled to claim exempt status.

Employee's signature ► *Emily M. Kardos*   Date ► *January 3*   20 --

8 Employer's name and address (**Employer:** Complete 8 and 10 only if sending to IRS)	9 Office code (optional)	10 Employee identification number
Roadrunner Delivery Service 155 Gateway Blvd. Sacramento, CA 94230		31-8042398

Figure 12–3 Employee's Withholding Allowance Certificate–Form W-4

income tax to be withheld. The more allowances a taxpayer claims, the lower the amount of income tax withheld from earnings. A taxpayer is usually allowed one personal allowance and one allowance for each person he or she supports (such as a child).

Some employees are *exempt* from federal income tax withholding. An employee is not required to have income tax withheld if he or she

- did not have a federal income tax liability in the previous year,
- expects no tax liability this year,
- has income of $700 or less including nonwage income such as savings account interest, and
- cannot be claimed as a dependent on someone else's tax return.

An exempt employee writes *EXEMPT* on Form W-4 so the employer will know not to withhold federal income tax.

Tax Tables. An employee's gross earnings affect the amount withheld for federal income taxes. Most employers use IRS tables to determine the amount of federal tax to withhold. See **Figure 12–4** for tables for single and married persons paid weekly. Other tax tables are available.

Let's use the tables to determine the tax withheld for Emily Kardos. She is single and claims no allowances. For the week ending June 30, she earned $243. This amount falls between $240 and $250 on the tax table for single persons. Reading across this line to the column for zero withholding allowances, you find that $29 is withheld from Emily's gross earnings.

Social Security Tax

Employers also collect social security taxes for the federal government. Established by the Federal Insurance Contributions Act (FICA) in 1935, social security taxes are often called *FICA taxes*. FICA taxes have two components: social security and Medicare. Each is listed separately on payroll records. The social security tax funds programs that provide income to certain individuals:

1. The *old-age* and *disability* insurance programs provide income to people who are retired or disabled and their dependent children.
2. The *survivors'* benefits program provides income to the spouse and dependent children of a deceased worker.

The Medicare tax finances health insurance benefits for people who are elderly or disabled.

SINGLE Persons—WEEKLY Payroll Period

If the wages are –		And the number of withholding allowances claimed is –										
At least	But less than	0	1	2	3	4	5	6	7	8	9	10
		The amount of income tax to be withheld is –										
$0	$55	0	0	0	0	0	0	0	0	0	0	0
55	60	1	0	0	0	0	0	0	0	0	0	0
60	65	2	0	0	0	0	0	0	0	0	0	0
65	70	2	0	0	0	0	0	0	0	0	0	0
70	75	3	0	0	0	0	0	0	0	0	0	0
75	80	4	0	0	0	0	0	0	0	0	0	0
80	85	5	0	0	0	0	0	0	0	0	0	0
85	90	5	0	0	0	0	0	0	0	0	0	0
90	95	6	0	0	0	0	0	0	0	0	0	0
95	100	7	0	0	0	0	0	0	0	0	0	0
100	105	8	0	0	0	0	0	0	0	0	0	0
105	110	8	1	0	0	0	0	0	0	0	0	0
110	115	9	2	0	0	0	0	0	0	0	0	0
115	120	10	2	0	0	0	0	0	0	0	0	0
120	125	11	3	0	0	0	0	0	0	0	0	0
125	130	11	4	0	0	0	0	0	0	0	0	0
130	135	12	5	0	0	0	0	0	0	0	0	0
135	140	13	5	0	0	0	0	0	0	0	0	0
140	145	14	6	0	0	0	0	0	0	0	0	0
145	150	14	7	0	0	0	0	0	0	0	0	0
150	155	15	8	0	0	0	0	0	0	0	0	0
155	160	16	8	1	0	0	0	0	0	0	0	0
160	165	17	9	1	0	0	0	0	0	0	0	0
165	170	17	10	2	0	0	0	0	0	0	0	0
170	175	18	11	3	0	0	0	0	0	0	0	0
175	180	19	11	4	0	0	0	0	0	0	0	0
180	185	20	12	4	0	0	0	0	0	0	0	0
185	190	20	13	5	0	0	0	0	0	0	0	0
190	195	21	14	6	0	0	0	0	0	0	0	0
195	200	22	14	7	0	0	0	0	0	0	0	0
200	210	23	15	8	0	0	0	0	0	0	0	0
210	220	25	17	9	2	0	0	0	0	0	0	0
220	230	26	18	11	3	0	0	0	0	0	0	0
230	240	28	20	12	5	0	0	0	0	0	0	0
240	250	29	21	14	6	0	0	0	0	0	0	0
250	260	31	23	15	8	0	0	0	0	0	0	0
260	270	32	24	17	9	2	0	0	0	0	0	0
270	280	34	26	18	11	3	0	0	0	0	0	0
280	290	35	27	20	12	5	0	0	0	0	0	0
290	300	37	29	21	14	6	0	0	0	0	0	0
300	310	38	30	23	15	8	0	0	0	0	0	0
310	320	40	32	24	17	9	1	0	0	0	0	0
320	330	41	33	26	18	11	3	0	0	0	0	0
330	340	43	35	27	20	12	4	0	0	0	0	0
340	350	44	36	29	21	14	6	0	0	0	0	0

MARRIED Persons—WEEKLY Payroll Period

If the wages are –		And the number of withholding allowances claimed is –										
At least	But less than	0	1	2	3	4	5	6	7	8	9	10
		The amount of income tax to be withheld is –										
$0	$125	0	0	0	0	0	0	0	0	0	0	0
125	130	1	0	0	0	0	0	0	0	0	0	0
130	135	1	0	0	0	0	0	0	0	0	0	0
135	140	2	0	0	0	0	0	0	0	0	0	0
140	145	3	0	0	0	0	0	0	0	0	0	0
145	150	4	0	0	0	0	0	0	0	0	0	0
150	155	4	0	0	0	0	0	0	0	0	0	0
155	160	5	0	0	0	0	0	0	0	0	0	0
160	165	6	0	0	0	0	0	0	0	0	0	0
165	170	7	0	0	0	0	0	0	0	0	0	0
170	175	7	0	0	0	0	0	0	0	0	0	0
175	180	8	0	0	0	0	0	0	0	0	0	0
180	185	9	1	0	0	0	0	0	0	0	0	0
185	190	10	2	0	0	0	0	0	0	0	0	0
190	195	10	3	0	0	0	0	0	0	0	0	0
195	200	11	3	0	0	0	0	0	0	0	0	0
200	210	12	5	0	0	0	0	0	0	0	0	0
210	220	14	6	0	0	0	0	0	0	0	0	0
220	230	15	8	0	0	0	0	0	0	0	0	0
230	240	17	9	1	0	0	0	0	0	0	0	0
240	250	18	11	3	0	0	0	0	0	0	0	0
250	260	20	12	4	0	0	0	0	0	0	0	0
260	270	21	14	6	0	0	0	0	0	0	0	0
270	280	23	15	7	0	0	0	0	0	0	0	0
280	290	24	17	9	1	0	0	0	0	0	0	0
290	300	26	18	10	3	0	0	0	0	0	0	0
300	310	27	20	12	4	0	0	0	0	0	0	0
310	320	29	21	13	6	0	0	0	0	0	0	0
320	330	30	23	15	7	0	0	0	0	0	0	0
330	340	32	24	16	9	1	0	0	0	0	0	0

Figure 12–4 Internal Revenue Service Tax Tables

The FICA taxes are exact taxes in that, unlike the federal income tax, they do not involve estimation and are not affected by allowances or marital status. Congress sets FICA tax rates and can change them at any time. Most employees are subject to FICA taxes, even those who are exempt from federal income taxes. The FICA tax rates are as follows:

Social security tax	6.20%
Medicare tax	1.45%
Total FICA taxes	7.65%

The social security tax is deducted from the employee's earnings until the maximum taxable earnings amount for the year is reached. This amount increases each year. For 2005, the maximum taxable earnings amount was $90,000. The maximum amount of social security tax that could be withheld from an employee in that year was $5,580.00 ($90,000 × .062). There is no maximum taxable earnings amount for the Medicare tax. For example, Lisa Gus earns $93,000 per year as a manager at a CPA firm. She has $6,928.50 in FICA taxes withheld from her earnings:

	Earnings Subject to Tax		Tax Rate		Tax
Social security tax	$90,000	×	.062	=	$5,580.00
Medicare tax	93,000	×	.0145	=	1,348.50
Total withheld					$6,928.50

State and Local Income Taxes

Most states and some cities tax the earnings of the people who live or work within their boundaries. Sometimes the withholdings are a percentage of gross earnings, like social security taxes. Amounts to be deducted also can be determined by tables similar to the ones for federal income tax.

Voluntary Deductions

What Deductions Can an Employee Choose?

Most employers agree to deduct other amounts from their employees' payroll check at the request of the employees. These deductions are withheld from each payroll check until the employee notifies the employer to stop. Voluntary employee deductions include union dues, health insurance payments, life insurance payments, pension and other retirement contributions, credit union deposits and payments, U.S. savings bonds, and charitable contributions.

The **401(k) plan** is a popular voluntary payroll deduction. The employee does not pay income tax on earnings contributed to the 401(k) plan until the money is withdrawn from the plan, usually after age 59½. In other words, taxable income is reduced by the amount of the contribution. Some employers make matching contributions to employees' 401(k) accounts.

Angelo Cappelli, a graphic artist, earns $644 each week and contributes $75 to his 401(k) account. Angelo will pay income tax on $569 ($644 − $75). He will not pay income tax on his $75 contribution until he withdraws it from his 401(k) account.

Reinforce the Main Idea

Use an organizer like this one to list one major advantage and one major disadvantage, from the employee's point of view, for each type of deduction. Add as many answer rows as needed.

Legally Required			Voluntary		
Type	Advantage	Disadvantage	Type	Advantage	Disadvantage

Do the Math

As the president of Creative Craft Memory Books, you have decided to add five new sales consultants to your sales force. You offer these sales consultants a gross salary of $23,000 each, but the consultants will not take home $23,000. Calculate the FICA taxes to be withheld from each consultant's gross pay. What remains of their gross pay after you deduct FICA taxes?

Problem 12–2 Determining Taxes on Gross Earnings

Information related to the just-completed pay period of MegaCom Computer Upgrades is provided in the following chart. Determine the amounts to be withheld from each employee's gross earnings for FICA and income taxes. It is a weekly pay period, so use the tables on page 317 to determine the amount of federal income tax to be withheld. The state income tax is 2% of gross earnings. The social security tax rate is 6.2%, and the Medicare tax rate is 1.45%. Use the format shown in your working papers.

Employee	Marital Status	Allowances	Gross Earnings
Cleary, Kevin	S	0	$155.60
Halley, James	S	1	184.10
Hong, Kim	S	0	204.65
Jackson, Marvin	M	1	216.40
Sell, Richard	M	2	196.81
Total			$957.56

Problem 12–3 Analyzing a Source Document

Examine the following partially completed payroll check stub. The employee, Melanie Galvin, is single and claims one allowance. What amount should be deducted for:

1. Medicare tax?
2. Social Security tax?
3. Federal Income tax?

Employee Pay Statement Detach and retain this statement.											260
	Earnings			Deductions							Net Pay
Period Ending	Regular	Overtime	Total	Social Security Tax	Med. Tax	Federal Income Tax	State Income Tax	Hosp. Ins.	Other	Total	
1/15/20--	315.00		315.00								

Payroll Records

In the previous sections you learned how to calculate gross earnings and deductions. Now you will learn how to compute net pay, prepare the payroll records for each period, and prepare payroll checks. Whether a business has many employees, like the Boeing Corporation, or a small staff, like a veterinarian's office, it is essential that the payroll be prepared on time and accurately.

Preparing the Payroll Register
What Is the Purpose of a Payroll Register?

Federal and state laws require businesses to keep accurate payroll records. To help meet these requirements, businesses use a payroll register. The **payroll register** is a form that summarizes information about employees' earnings for each pay period. Let's learn how to prepare payroll registers.

Figure 12–5 shows the payroll register for Roadrunner. As you can see, the payroll register lists each employee's I.D. number, name, marital status, and the number of allowances claimed. Refer to **Figure 12–5** as you read the descriptions of the payroll register.

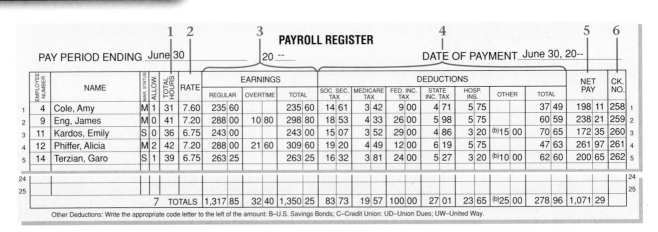

PAYROLL REGISTER

PAY PERIOD ENDING June 30   20 --   DATE OF PAYMENT June 30, 20--

	EMPLOYEE NUMBER	NAME	MAR STATUS	ALLOW	TOTAL HOURS	RATE	EARNINGS REGULAR	EARNINGS OVERTIME	EARNINGS TOTAL	SOC. SEC. TAX	MEDICARE TAX	FED. INC. TAX	STATE INC. TAX	HOSP. INS.	OTHER	TOTAL	NET PAY	CK. NO.	
1	4	Cole, Amy	M	1	31	7.60	235 60		235 60	14 61	3 42	9 00	4 71	5 75		37 49	198 11	258	1
2	9	Eng, James	M	0	41	7.20	288 00	10 80	298 80	18 53	4 33	26 00	5 98	5 75		60 59	238 21	259	2
3	11	Kardos, Emily	S	0	36	6.75	243 00		243 00	15 07	3 52	29 00	4 86	3 20	(b)15 00	70 65	172 35	260	3
4	12	Phiffer, Alicia	M	2	42	7.20	288 00	21 60	309 60	19 20	4 49	12 00	6 19	5 75		47 63	261 97	261	4
5	14	Terzian, Garo	S	1	39	6.75	263 25		263 25	16 32	3 81	24 00	5 27	3 20	(b)10 00	62 60	200 65	262	5
24																			24
25																			25
		7 TOTALS					1,317 85	32 40	1,350 25	83 73	19 57	100 00	27 01	23 65	(b)25 00	278 96	1,071 29		

Other Deductions: Write the appropriate code letter to the left of the amount: B–U.S. Savings Bonds; C–Credit Union: UD–Union Dues; UW–United Way.

Figure 12–5 Completed Payroll Register

1. *Total Hours Column.* Regular and overtime hours from the employee's time card are added together, and the total is entered in this column.
2. *Rate Column.* This column shows the employee's current rate of pay, found on the employee's earnings record.
3. *Earnings Section.* The earnings section is divided into three columns:

   - regular
   - overtime
   - total earnings

   To complete these columns, the payroll clerk multiplies the hours worked by the employee's regular hourly rate or, when applicable, overtime hourly rate.

Employee 4, Amy Cole, worked 31 hours. Her regular hourly rate is $7.60. Amy earned $235.60 (31 × $7.60) for the week. Since there are no overtime hours, regular and total earnings are the same.

Alicia Phiffer, employee 12, worked 2 overtime hours in addition to 40 regular hours. Her regular hourly rate is $7.20. Her overtime hourly rate is $10.80 ($7.20 × 1.5). Her regular earnings are $288.00 (40 × $7.20) and her overtime earnings are $21.60 (2 × $10.80). Her total earnings are $309.60 ($288.00 + $21.60).

4. *Deductions Section.* The illustrated payroll register has seven deduction columns. The number of deduction columns, however, varies among businesses depending on the specific needs of each business. In the illustration, columns are provided for the deductions required by law:

   - social security tax
   - Medicare tax
   - federal income tax
   - state income tax

   Columns are also provided for voluntary deductions. Certain voluntary deductions taken by many employees on a regular basis will usually have their own columns, such as the column shown in the illustration for hospital insurance. Deductions taken less frequently are often placed in a column titled *Other.* In the illustration these deductions include credit union, union dues, savings bonds, and charitable contributions. Finally, a column is provided for the total deductions of each employee.

Look at the deductions for Garo Terzian, employee 14. Garo's deductions include the taxes required by law. He also has two voluntary deductions, $3.20 for hospital insurance and $10.00, shown in the Other column, for U.S. Savings Bonds. The total deductions for Garo are $62.60 as shown in the *Total* column.

5. *Net Pay Column.* **Net pay** is the amount left after total deductions have been subtracted from gross earnings. The net pay for Garo Terzian is $200.65.

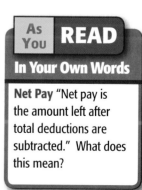

As You READ

In Your Own Words

Net Pay "Net pay is the amount left after total deductions are subtracted." What does this mean?

6. *Check Number Column.* Most employees are paid by check. The payroll check numbers are recorded in this column.

7. *Column Totals.* Each amount column is totaled, and the totals are entered on the last line of the payroll register. To ensure that there are no mathematical errors, subtract the Total Deductions column total from Total Earnings column total. The result should equal the Net Pay column total.

Paying Employees

How Are Employees Paid?

Once the accuracy of the payroll register has been verified, a payroll check is prepared for each employee. Most businesses pay their employees by check as a means of cash control. When a company has only a few employees, payroll checks are written from the company's regular checking account. Companies with many employees have a separate checking account for payroll.

When a separate payroll checking account is used, funds are transferred to this account each pay period. A check for the total net pay amount is written from the company's regular checking account and deposited in the payroll checking account. Then individual payroll checks are issued to employees from the payroll account.

The payroll register is the source of information for preparing the payroll checks. Along with a payroll check, each employee is given a written or printed explanation showing how the employee's net pay is calculated. This explanation is provided on a stub attached to the payroll check. **Figure 12–6** shows a typical payroll check and stub. Notice that for Emily Kardos, the amounts on the stub are the same as the amounts in the payroll register. After each payroll check has been written, the check number is recorded in the payroll register.

Roadrunner Delivery Service								260

155 Gateway Blvd.
Sacramento, CA 94230

63-947 / 670

Date __June 30__ 20 --

Pay to the Order of __Emily Kardos__ $ 172.35

One hundred seventy-two and 35/100 ————————— Dollars

❖ *American National Bank*
SACRAMENTO, CALIFORNIA

Maria Sanchez

⑆067009471⑆ 3939 043 417⑈ 260

- -

Employee Pay Statement
Detach and retain this statement.   **260**

Period Ending	Earnings			Deductions							Net Pay
	Regular	Overtime	Total	Social Security Tax	Med. Tax	Federal Income Tax	State Income Tax	Hosp. Ins.	Other	Total	
6/30/20--	243.00		243.00	15.07	3.52	29.00	4.86	3.20	15.00	70.65	172.35

Figure 12–6 Completed Payroll Check and Stub

Employees can be paid by check or by direct deposit. The employer makes a **direct deposit** of the net pay electronically in the employee's personal bank account. No payroll check is prepared. The employee does, however, receive a printed record of the payroll calculation. Direct deposits are made through electronic funds transfer. With this system the employer informs the employee's bank of the amount to be deposited.

The Employee's Earnings Record

What Is the Purpose of an Employee's Earnings Record?

In addition to the payroll register, an employer must also keep an **employee's earnings record** for each employee. This record contains all of the payroll information related to an employee. **Figure 12–7** on page 324 shows an example of an employee's earnings record. The earnings record and payroll register have the same amount columns:

- three earnings columns
- four columns for deductions required by law
- additional columns for voluntary deductions (in this case, two columns)
- the Total column
- the Net Pay column

An additional column for the employee's accumulated earnings is also provided. **Accumulated earnings** are the employee's *year-to-date* gross earnings. That is the amount of the employee's gross earnings from the beginning of the year through the end of the pay period just completed.

The accumulated earnings for Emily Kardos as of June 30 are computed by adding her gross earnings for the pay period just completed to her accumulated earnings for the previous pay period as follows:

Gross Earnings for Pay Period Just Completed		Accumulated Earnings for Previous Pay Period		Accumulated Earnings for Pay Period Just Completed
$243.00	+	$4,178.60	=	$4,421.60

Businesses keep employees' earnings records on a quarterly basis. This makes it easier to complete government reports that are required each quarter. At the end of a quarter, the amount columns on each employee's earnings record are totaled. The final amount in the Accumulated Earnings column is carried forward to the top of the employee's earnings record for the next quarter. **Figure 12–7** on page 324 illustrates how accumulated earnings amounts are carried forward.

As you can see from this chapter, preparing payroll is time consuming and detail oriented. A mistake that is not promptly detected and corrected can mean hours of rework. To reduce simple mathematical errors and to improve productivity, many businesses use computers and special software to prepare payroll. In a computerized system, the computer

- performs all payroll calculations,
- prepares and prints the payroll register,
- prints the payroll checks and stubs, and
- maintains the employees' earnings records.

This amount was carried forward from the previous quarter's record. —

EMPLOYEE'S EARNINGS RECORD FOR QUARTER ENDING June 30, 20--

Kardos   Emily   M
Last Name   First   Initial
809 East Main Street
Address
Sacramento, CA 94230

EMPLOYEE NO. 11   MARITAL STATUS S ALLOWANCES 0

POSITION Delivery Driver

RATE OF PAY 6.75   SOC. SEC. NO. 201-XX-XXXX

PAY PERIOD		EARNINGS			DEDUCTIONS							NET PAY	ACCUMULATED EARNINGS
NO.	ENDED	REGULAR	OVERTIME	TOTAL	SOC. SEC. TAX	MEDICARE TAX	FED. INC. TAX	STATE INC. TAX	HOSP. INS.	OTHER	TOTAL		1,490 39
1	4/07/--	199 13		199 13	12 35	2 89	22 00	3 98	3 20	(B) 15 00	59 42	139 71	1,689 52
2	4/14/--	205 88		205 88	12 76	2 99	23 00	4 12	3 20		46 07	159 81	1,895 40
3	4/21/--	270 00	30 38	300 38	18 62	4 36	38 00	6 01	3 20		70 19	230 19	2,195 78
4	4/28/--	222 75		222 75	13 81	3 23	26 00	4 46	3 20		50 70	172 05	2,418 53
5	5/05/--	229 50		229 50	14 23	3 33	26 00	4 59	3 20	(B) 15 00	66 35	163 15	2,648 03
6	5/12/--	162 00		162 00	10 04	2 35	17 00	3 24	3 20		35 83	126 17	2,810 03
7	5/19/--	256 50		256 50	15 90	3 72	31 00	5 13	3 20		58 95	197 55	3,066 53
8	5/26/--	270 00	20 25	290 25	18 00	4 21	37 00	5 81	3 20		68 22	222 03	3,356 78
9	6/02/--	204 19		204 19	12 66	2 96	23 00	4 08	3 20	(B) 15 00	60 90	143 29	3,560 97
10	6/09/--	212 63		212 63	13 18	3 08	25 00	4 25	3 20		48 71	163 92	3,773 60
11	6/16/--	189 00		189 00	11 72	2 74	20 00	3 78	3 20		41 44	147 56	3,962 60
12	6/23/--	216 00		216 00	13 39	3 13	25 00	4 32	3 20		49 04	166 96	4,178 60
13	6/30/--	243 00		243 00	15 07	3 52	29 00	4 86	3 20	(B) 15 00	70 65	172 35	4,421 60
QUARTERLY TOTALS		2,880 58	50 63	2,931 21	181 73	42 51	342 00	58 63	41 60	60 00	726 47	2,204 74	

Other Deductions: B—U.S. Savings Bonds; C—Credit Union; UD—Union Dues; UW—United Way.

Figure 12–7 Employee's Earnings Record

This amount will be carried forward to the next quarter's record. —

Managerial Implications for Payroll Accounting

How Do Managers Use Payroll Information?

Wages and salaries form a large part of a company's expenses. Accurate and timely payroll records will assist management in planning and controlling these expenses. This information can be used in the following ways:

- To determine whether overtime is justified or is a sign of possible inefficiency.
- To compare actual amounts to budgeted amounts to reveal any unplanned overtime and the reason for it.

This information helps managers investigate any amounts that were not expected or were unusual. After identifying any irregularities, managers can determine what caused them and how to resolve them.

Management should also put internal controls in place to prevent errors and fraud. For example, payroll records should be audited carefully and payroll procedures should be evaluated periodically.

Reinforce the Main Idea

Use a diagram like this one to show the similarities and differences between the payroll register and the employee's earnings record.

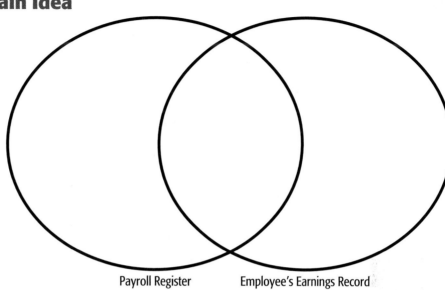

Payroll Register   Employee's Earnings Record

 ## Do the Math

While reviewing the payroll records from the past two years for Sports Junction, an athletic supply store, you notice that the increasing payroll cost could be holding down overall company profits. The company's payroll costs and revenue for the last eight quarters are provided. Use spreadsheet, accounting, or graphics software to create a line chart to compare the costs and revenue graphically. Analyze the chart, and make a recommendation to Sports Junction's management about the salary levels. Do you recommend downsizing to increase profit?

	Year 1				Year 2			
	Qtr 1	Qtr 2	Qtr 3	Qtr 4	Qtr 1	Qtr 2	Qtr 3	Qtr 4
Payroll	24,000	24,500	28,670	35,280	34,000	42,000	53,000	68,000
Revenue	136,700	151,200	183,500	234,000	143,000	142,500	143,000	138,500

 ## Problem 12–4 Preparing a Payroll Check

Use the information on the payroll register for Heather's Dance School and the form in the working papers to prepare a payroll check for Janice Burns for the week ending March 23, 20--.

PAYROLL REGISTER

PAY PERIOD ENDING March 23   20 --   DATE OF PAYMENT March 23, 20--

EMPLOYEE NUMBER	NAME	MAR. STATUS	ALLOW	TOTAL HOURS	RATE	EARNINGS			DEDUCTIONS							NET PAY	CK. NO.
						REGULAR	OVERTIME	TOTAL	SOC. SEC. TAX	MEDICARE TAX	FED. INC. TAX	STATE INC. TAX	HOSP. INS.	OTHER	TOTAL		
18	Burns, Janice	S	1	42	7.80	312 00	23 40	335 40	20 79	4 86	35 00	6 71	4 10	——	71 46	263 94	79

Key Concepts

1. Federal and state laws require employers to keep accurate records of all payroll information. Most employers use a payroll system to ensure that employees are paid on time and that their payroll checks and records are accurate. A well-designed payroll system achieves two goals:

   - To collect and process all information needed to prepare and issue payroll checks.
   - To generate payroll records needed for accounting purposes and for reporting to government agencies, management, and others.

   A computerized system does the following:

   - Performs all payroll calculations
   - Prepares and prints a payroll register
   - Prints the payroll checks and stubs
   - Maintains employee's earnings records

2. *Gross pay* is the amount an employee earns before deductions. It may be calculated by various methods including

   - salary,
   - hourly wage,
   - commission,
   - salary plus commission or bonus,
   - piece rate, or
   - a combination of these methods.

   Some employees who work more than 40 hours in a week are paid overtime. The *overtime rate* is usually 1½ times the regular rate of pay.

Regular Hourly Rate			Overtime Hourly Rate
$8.20	× 1.5	=	$12.30

3. Withholdings from gross earnings are called *deductions*. Some deductions are required by law. Other deductions are voluntary.

   Deductions Required By Law
   - federal income tax:
       determined by Form W-4 and tax tables
   - social security tax:
       6.2% of total gross earnings up to $90,000
   - Medicare tax:
       1.45% of total gross earnings
   - state or local tax:
       determined by the state or city

Voluntary Deductions

- union dues
- insurance payments
- charitable contributions
- 401(k) plans
- other retirement-related contributions

4. *Net pay* is the amount of money actually received by the employee.

Gross Pay − Total Payroll Deductions = Net Pay

5. A *payroll register* summarizes information for all employees in a single pay period. A *pay period* is the amount of time over which employees are paid (for example, once a week or twice a month). The payroll register includes

- total hours;
- rate of pay;
- regular earnings, overtime earnings, and total earnings;
- deductions;
- net pay;
- payroll check number; and
- totals.

6. Payroll funds can be distributed to employees by check or by direct deposit through electronic funds transfer.

7. The *employee's earnings record* contains all information for a single employee. This record is kept quarterly to make it easier for the business to complete reports and forms required by the government.

   The earnings record has the same amount columns that appear on the payroll register plus an additional column for *accumulated earnings*. These are the employee's earnings from the beginning of the year through the pay period just completed.

Key Terms

accumulated earnings	(p. 323)	pay period	(p. 310)
commission	(p. 313)	payroll	(p. 310)
deduction	(p. 315)	payroll clerk	(p. 310)
direct deposit	(p. 323)	payroll register	(p. 320)
electronic badge readers	(p. 312)	piece rate	(p. 313)
employee's earnings record	(p. 323)	salary	(p. 311)
401(k) plan	(p. 318)	time card	(p. 312)
gross earnings	(p. 311)	wage	(p. 312)
net pay	(p. 321)	withholding allowance	(p. 315)
overtime rate	(p. 313)		

Check Your Understanding

1. **Payroll Records**
   a. What are two goals of a payroll system?
   b. List five tasks that an effective payroll system performs.

2. **Gross Pay**
   a. List and describe five employee bases or categories used to compute gross pay.
   b. Define *overtime rate.*

3. **Withholdings**
   a. List the three federal taxes that businesses are required to withhold from employees' wages.
   b. What three factors determine the amount of federal income tax withheld from an employee's earnings each period?

4. **Net Pay**
   a. How is net pay calculated?
   b. Does an individual's net pay appear on the payroll register, the employee's earnings record, or both?

5. **Payroll Register**
   a. What information does the payroll register contain?
   b. Each page of the payroll register covers a period of time. What time period does it cover?

6. **Payroll Funds Distribution**
   a. Explain how direct deposit of earnings works.
   b. How does an employee who receives a payroll check know how the amount of net pay was determined?

7. **Employee's Earnings Record**
   a. What is the purpose of the employee's earnings record?
   b. What information does the Accumulated Earnings column on the employee's earnings record contain?

Apply Key Terms

You are the payroll clerk for Wild West Amusement Park. The new sales manager for the Western region, Will Klein, called and asked you to explain the items on his payroll check, dated January 31, 20--. He also asked you to explain any relevant company payroll procedures. Use these key terms in your written explanation. Use your imagination!

accumulated earnings	overtime rate
commission	pay period
deduction	payroll
direct deposit	payroll clerk
electronic badge readers	payroll register
employee's earnings	piece rate
record	salary
401(k) plan	time card
gross earnings	wage
net pay	withholding allowance

Preparing the Payroll

Making the Transition from a Manual to a Computerized System

Task	Manual Methods	Computerized Methods
Enter and maintain employee information; process payroll.	• Calculate employee gross earnings based on time cards or salary information. • Calculate required and voluntary deductions for each employee. • Complete the payroll register. • Prepare payroll checks. • Update employee earnings records. • Prepare journal entries. • Post journal entries to the general ledger.	• Set up information related to employee earnings and deductions in employees' records. • Based on rate, deduction, and withholding information for each employee, the software automatically calculates gross earnings and deductions. • The payroll checks, journal entries, and ledger postings are generated automatically.

Peachtree® Q & A

Peachtree Question	Answer
How do I process a payroll?	1. Select **Payroll Entry** from the *Tasks* menu. 2. Select the employee(s) to be paid. 3. Verify the pay amounts that are automatically entered for you. (These amounts are pulled from employee records stored in the system.) 4. Type the hours worked or the commission amounts. 5. Click **Save**. 6. To print payroll checks, click on **Open**, select checks to print and click **OK**. 7. Click **Print**.

QuickBooks Q & A

QuickBooks Question	Answer
How do I process a payroll?	1. Select **Pay Employees** from the *Employees* menu. 2. Set the date of payment and end of payroll period. 3. Select the employees to be paid and click **Create**. 4. Verify the pay amounts that are automatically entered for you. (These amounts are pulled from employee records stored in the system.) 5. Type the hours worked or the commission amounts. 6. Click **Create**. 7. To print payroll checks, click on *File*, select **Print Forms**, and then **Paychecks**. 8. Click **OK** and then **Print**.

For detailed instructions, see your Glencoe Accounting Chapter Study Guides and Working Papers.

Complete problems using: **Manual** Glencoe Working Papers OR **Peachtree Complete Accounting** Software OR **QuickBooks** Templates OR **Spreadsheet** Templates

Peachtree®

SMART GUIDE

Step–by–Step Instructions:
Problems 12–5

1. Select the problem set for Wilderness Rentals (Prob. 12–5).
2. Rename the company and set the system date.
3. Enter John Gilmartin's regular and overtime pay rates using the **Employees/Sales Reps** option in the *Maintain* menu.
4. Calculate the employees' gross pay using the **Payroll Entry** option.
5. Print a Payroll Register report.
6. Proof your work.
7. Complete the Analyze activity.
8. End the session.

QuickBooks

PROBLEM GUIDE

Step–by–Step Instructions:
Problem 12–5

1. Restore the Problem 12-5.QBB file.
2. Enter John Gilmartin's regular and overtime pay rates using the **Employee List** option in the *Employees* menu.
3. Calculate the employee's gross pay using the **Pay Employees** option in the *Employees* menu.
4. Print an Employee Earnings Summary report using the **Employees & Payroll** option in the *Reports* menu.
5. Proof your work.
6. Complete the Analyze activity.
7. Back up your work.

Problem 12–5 Calculating Gross Pay

Wilderness Rentals pays employees either an hourly wage or a salary plus commission based on rental revenue. Hourly wage employees can earn overtime. The overtime rate is 1½ times the regular hourly rate of pay for hours worked over 40 in a week.

Instructions For each of the following employees, determine the total gross pay for the pay period.

John Gilmartin
- Earns an hourly wage of $6.80.
- Worked 43 hours this week.

Arlene Stone
- Receives a salary of $250 per week plus a 3% commission on rental revenue.
- Had rental revenue of $760 this week.

Tom Driscoll
- Earns an hourly wage of $7.35.
- Worked 39 hours this week.

Ann Ryan
- Receives a salary of $185 per week plus 3% commission.
- Had rental revenue of $1,235 this week.

Analyze Identify the employee who had the lowest gross pay for the week.

Problem 12–6 Preparing a Payroll Register

Hot Suds Car Wash has four employees. They are paid on a weekly basis with overtime paid for all hours worked over 40 in a week. The overtime rate is 1½ times the regular rate of pay. The payroll information follows.

Employee	Employee Number	Rate per Hour	Marital Status	Allowances	Union Member
James Dumser	108	$6.40	Single	0	No
Gail Job	112	$7.22	Married	1	Yes
James Liptak	102	$6.70	Married	2	Yes
Bruce Stern	109	$7.80	Single	1	Yes

During the week ending October 9, Dumser worked 39 hours, Job worked 41 hours, and Liptak and Stern each worked 36 hours.

Instructions On the forms provided in your working papers:

1. Prepare a payroll register for the week ending October 9. The date of payment is also October 9. List employees in alphabetical order by *last* name. Use the tables on page 317 to determine the federal income tax withholding. The rate for the state income tax is 2%. Compute social security tax at 6.2% and Medicare tax at 1.45%. Union members pay weekly dues of $4.50. Both Gail Job and Bruce Stern had $6.75 deducted for health and hospital insurance.

2. Total the amount columns. Subtract total deductions from total earnings. Does the result equal the sum of the Net Pay column? If not, find and correct any error(s) on the payroll register.

Analyze Identify the employee who had the highest amount withheld for federal income tax for the week.

SPREADSHEET SMART GUIDE

Step–by–Step Instructions: Problem 12–6

1. Select the spreadsheet template for Problem 12–6.
2. Enter your name and the date in the spaces provided on the template.
3. Complete the spread-sheet using the instructions in your working papers.
4. Print the spreadsheet and proof your work.
5. Complete the Analyze activity.
6. Save your work and exit the spreadsheet program.

Problem 12–7 Preparing Payroll Checks and Employee's Earnings Records

The payroll register for Kits & Pups Grooming is presented here and also appears in your working papers.

PAYROLL REGISTER

PAY PERIOD ENDING October 17   20 --   DATE OF PAYMENT October 17, 20--

	EMPLOYEE NUMBER	NAME	MAR STATUS	ALLOW	TOTAL HOURS	RATE	EARNINGS REGULAR	EARNINGS OVERTIME	EARNINGS TOTAL	SOC. SEC. TAX	MEDICARE TAX	FED. INC. TAX	STATE INC. TAX	HOSP. INS.	OTHER	TOTAL	NET PAY	CK. NO.	
1	162	Hurd, Mildred	S	0	38	7.60	288 80		288 80	17 91	4 19	35 00	7 22		(B) 5 00	69 32	219 48		1
2	157	Montego, José	S	1	39	7.90	308 10		308 10	19 10	4 47	30 00	7 70	5 10		66 37	241 73		2
3	151	Pilly, Amanda	M	2	36	8.10	291 60		291 60	18 08	4 23	10 00	7 29	7 60	(B) 5 00	52 20	239 40		3
4	163	Steams, Margaret	S	0	41	7.60	304 00	11 40	315 40	19 55	4 57	40 00	7 89			72 01	243 39		4
24																			24
25																			25
						TOTALS	1,192 50	11 40	1,203 90	74 64	17 46	115 00	30 10	12 70	(B)10 00	259 90	944 00		

Other Deductions: Write the appropriate code letter to the left of the amount: B–U.S. Savings Bonds; C–Credit Union; UD–Union Dues; UW–United Way.

Instructions On the forms in your working papers:

1. Prepare a payroll check and stub for each employee. Where would you record the check numbers in the payroll register?
2. Record the payroll information in the employee's earnings records for José Montego and Amanda Pilly.

Analyze Identify the net pay for José Montego for this week.

Peachtree®

SMART GUIDE

Step–by–Step Instructions: Problem 12–7

1. Select the problem set for Kits & Pups Grooming (Prob. 12–7).
2. Rename the company and set the system date.
3. Print payroll checks using the **Payroll Entry** option.
4. Print a Payroll Register report and a Current Earnings report.
5. Complete the Analyze activity.
6. End the session.

Problem 12–8 Preparing the Payroll

Outback Guide Service has six employees and pays each week. Hourly employees are paid overtime for all hours worked over 40 in a week. The overtime rate is 1½ times the regular rate of pay. Outback pays its employees by hourly rate, salary, or salary plus a 5% commission on total amount of sales.

CONTINUE

Peachtree®

SMART GUIDE

Step–by–Step Instructions: Problem 12–8

1. Select the problem set for Outback Guide Service (Prob. 12–8).
2. Rename the company and set the system date.
3. Record the payroll and print a check for each employee using the **Payroll Entry** option.
4. Print a Payroll Register report and a Current Earnings report.
5. Proof your work and make any needed corrections.
6. Complete the Analyze activity.
7. End the session.

TIP: Use the Windows calculator accessory if you need to make a calculation (e.g., commission).

Method of Computing Earnings

Employee	Hourly Wage	Salary	Salary Plus Commission
Cummings, Carol		$270.00	
Dame, Ted	$6.95		
Lengyel, Tom			$160.00 plus 5%
Robinson, Jean			$140.00 plus 5%
Usdavin, James	$6.65		
Wong, Kim			$140.00 plus 5%

Employee deductions include federal income taxes (use the tables on page 317), FICA taxes at 6.2% for social security and 1.45% for Medicare, state income taxes of 1.5%, and hospital insurance premiums of $5.43 for single employees and $9.37 for married employees. Also, Kim Wong and Tom Lengyel have $10.00 withheld each week to purchase U.S. savings bonds.

During the pay period ending October 17, the sales were: Tom Lengyel $1,204.76, Jean Robinson $1,925.80, and Kim Wong $2,135.65.

The hourly employees filled in the following time cards.

NO. **73**

NAME **Ted Dame**

SOC. SEC. NO. **093-XX-XXXX**

WEEK ENDING **10/17/20--**

DAY	IN	OUT	IN	OUT	IN	OUT
M	8:58	12:03	12:55	5:09		
T	8:55	11:55	1:00	4:00		
W	9:30	12:10	1:04	3:30		
Th	8:57	12:03	12:59	6:00		
F	8:58	12:00	1:00	6:05		
S	9:00	12:00				
S						

TOTAL HOURS

	HOURS	RATE
REGULAR		
OVERTIME		

TOTAL EARNINGS

SIGNATURE_____ DATE_____

NO. **92**

NAME **James Usdavin**

SOC. SEC. NO. **087-XX-XXXX**

WEEK ENDING **10/17/20--**

DAY	IN	OUT	IN	OUT	IN	OUT	TOTAL
M	8:55	12:06	1:01	5:35			
T	7:58	11:01	12:03	6:38			
W	9:03	1:10	2:00	6:00			
Th	7:59	11:55	1:10	4:51			
F	9:01	12:06	1:05	3:47			
S	9:00	12:03					
S							

TOTAL HOURS

	HOURS	RATE	AMOUNT
REGULAR			
OVERTIME			

TOTAL EARNINGS

SIGNATURE_____ DATE_____

Instructions On the forms in your working papers:

1. Complete the time cards to the nearest quarter hour.
2. Prepare a payroll register for the week ending October 17. The date of payment is also October 17. Each employee's number, marital status, and number of allowances claimed are listed on her or his employee's earnings record.
3. Prepare a payroll check and stub for each employee.
4. Record the payroll information for each employee on her or his employee's earnings record.

Analyze **Calculate the total amount deducted from employees' gross pay for FICA taxes (social security and Medicare).**

Problem 12–9 Preparing the Payroll Register

Showbiz Video has six employees who are paid weekly. The hourly employees are paid overtime for hours worked over 40 in a week, at a rate 1½ times their regular rate of pay. Employee information follows:

Employee	Employee Number	Marital Status	Allowances
Mary Arcompora	105	Married	2
Barbara Fox	137	Married	1
John French	135	Single	1
Chris German	141	Married	4
David Izbecki	139	Single	0
Susan Tilbert	129	Married	1

Mary Arcompora, the store manager, is paid a salary of $300.00 per week plus 1% of all rental sales. Barbara Fox and John French, salespeople, are paid a salary of $200.00 per week plus a 6% commission on all rentals from the "Oldies but Goodies" section. Chris German and David Izbecki, office workers, are paid an hourly wage of $7.25. Susan Tilbert, a stock person, is paid $6.40 per hour.

The payroll deductions include federal income tax, social security tax of 6.2%, Medicare tax of 1.45%, and state income tax of 1.8%. Chris German and Susan Tilbert have $12.50 deducted each week for hospital insurance.

During the week ending October 24, "Oldies but Goodies" rentals were $484.90 for Barbara Fox and $641.70 for John French. Total rental revenue for the week was $3,917.30.

Peachtree®

SMART GUIDE

Step–by–Step Instructions: Problem 12–9

1. Select the problem set for Showbiz Video (Prob. 12–9).
2. Rename the company and set the system date.
3. Record the payroll for each employee.
4. Print a Payroll Register report.
5. Proof your work.
6. Complete the Analyze activity.
7. End the session.

NO. 141						
NAME	Chris German					
SOC. SEC. NO.	449-XX-XXXX					
WEEK ENDING	October 24, 20--					

DAY	IN	OUT	IN	OUT	IN	OUT	TOTAL
M	8:05	12:03	1:00	5:05			
T	8:00	12:05	1:10	5:00			
W	9:05	12:05	1:15	6:05			
Th	8:30	11:55	1:15	6:00			
F	8:00	12:00	1:00	6:15			
S							
S							
					TOTAL HOURS		

	HOURS	RATE	AMOUNT
REGULAR			
OVERTIME			
TOTAL EARNINGS			

CONTINUE

Instructions

Prepare a payroll register in your working papers for the week ending October 24. Complete time cards to the nearest quarter of an hour. Use the federal income tax tables provided in the chapter.

NO. __139__

NAME __David Izbecki__

SOC. SEC. NO. __461-XX-XXXX__

WEEK ENDING __October 24, 20--__

DAY	IN	OUT	IN	OUT	IN	OUT
M	8:00	12:05	1:00	5:00		
T	8:10	12:00	1:00	5:05		
W	8:05	12:30	1:30	5:00		
Th	8:00	12:00	1:00	5:10		
F	8:05	12:05	1:05	3:30		
S						
S						

TOTAL HOURS

	HOURS	RATE
REGULAR		
OVERTIME		

TOTAL EARNINGS

SIGNATURE _____ DATE _____

NO. __129__

NAME __Susan Tilbert__

SOC. SEC. NO. __401-XX-XXXX__

WEEK ENDING __October 24, 20--__

DAY	IN	OUT	IN	OUT	IN	OUT	TOTAL
M	8:05	12:00	1:00	5:00			
T	8:10	12:00	1:15	5:00			
W	8:30	12:00	1:00	6:00			
Th	9:00	12:00	12:45	5:00			
F	9:00	11:50					
S							
S							

TOTAL HOURS

	HOURS	RATE	AMOUNT
REGULAR			
OVERTIME			

TOTAL EARNINGS

SIGNATURE _____ DATE _____

Analyze Compute the total net pay of all employees for the pay period.

SOURCE DOCUMENT PROBLEM

Problem 12–10

Use the source documents in your working papers to complete this problem.

Peachtree®

SMART GUIDE

Step–by–Step Instructions: Problem 12–10

1. Select the problem set for Job Connect (Prob. 12–10).
2. Rename the company and set the system date.
3. Calculate the employees' gross pay using the **Payroll Entry** option.
4. Print a Payroll Register report.
5. Proof your work.
6. Complete the Analyze activity.
7. End the session.

CHALLENGE PROBLEM

Problem 12–10 Calculating Gross Earnings

Job Connect has seven employees, all of whom are paid weekly. For hourly wage employees, overtime is paid at 1½ times the regular rate of pay for hours worked over 40 in a week.

Barbara Miller, the office manager, is paid a salary of $375.00 per week plus a bonus of 3% of all revenue *over* $6,000 per week. Lynn Austin, an office assistant, is paid a salary of $250.00 per week plus 5% of all telephone sales made in the office. Charlene Womack, the office secretary, is paid a salary of $230.00 per week. Susan Dilloway and Doris Franco, placement workers, are paid an hourly wage of $8.95. Pam Darrah is also a placement worker but is paid a commission of $35.00 for every job placement that she completes. David Facini, a part-time maintenance worker, is paid $6.75 per hour.

For the week ending October 24, the office recorded the following payroll information.

- Total office sales for the week were $8,420.00.
- Susan Dilloway worked a total of 38½ hours.
- Doris Franco worked a total of 41¼ hours.
- Phone sales for the week were $1,375.00.
- Pam Darrah made seven job placements.
- David Facini worked a total of 23 hours.

Instructions Using the form provided in your working papers, calculate the gross earnings for the workers at Job Connect for the week ending October 24.

Analyze Identify the employee who had the highest gross earnings.

Practice your test-taking skills! The questions on this page are reprinted with permission from national organizations:

- Future Business Leaders of America
- Business Professionals of America

Use a separate sheet of paper to record your answers.

Future Business Leaders of America

MULTIPLE CHOICE

1. Which form is considered the Withholding Allowance Certificate?
    a. W-2
    b. W-4
    c. 1040
    d. 1099
    e. none of these answers

2. Julie earns $18.50 per hour. She is paid overtime (time and one-half) for hours worked on Sunday. The first Sunday in June she worked 6 hours, giving her 46 hours for the week. What were her gross wages if total taxes withheld equaled 18%?
    a. $851.00
    b. $1,069.67
    c. $743.33
    d. $906.50

Business Professionals of America

MULTIPLE CHOICE

3. The Accumulated Earnings column of the employee earnings record
    a. shows net pay for the year.
    b. is the total earnings since the first of the year.
    c. shows net pay for one quarter.
    d. is the gross earnings for one quarter.

4. The Medicare tax is calculated by
    a. multiplying total earnings by the tax rate.
    b. multiplying net earnings by the tax rate.
    c. using a tax table.
    d. none of these

5. Jacqueline earns 18% commission on sales. Her sales for three months were: $2,870, $3,150, and $3,940. What was her total commission for the three months?
    a. $9,960.00
    b. $1,792.08
    c. $1,792.80
    d. $1,792.81

Need More Help?

Go to glencoeaccounting.glencoe.com and click on Student Center. Click on Winning Competitive Events and select Chapter 12.

- **Practice Questions and Test-Taking Tips**
- **Concept Capsules and Terminology**

Payroll Accounting

1. Define *gross earnings*.
2. Compare and contrast gross earnings and net pay.
3. Classify the following deductions as voluntary or required by law: county income tax, dental insurance payment, federal income tax, Medicare insurance payment, United Way donation, vision insurance payment.
4. Refer to the payroll register on page 320 and look at the entry for Amy Cole. What documents were used to calculate Amy's net pay?
5. You need to create a new employee's earnings record for an employee whose record has been lost. What information will you need, and where will you find it?
6. Justify the fact that a business can have different pay categories for employees.

Payroll: Financial Planning

You are employed by Tallman Financial Advisors, owned by Marcy Tallman. Parker's Framing hired Tallman to design its payroll system. Parker's Framing will offer group health insurance to its employees and a retirement plan that will require contributions from both the employer and employees. Marcy has assigned the Parker's Framing payroll project to you.

INSTRUCTIONS

1. Draft a one-page report describing the payroll system you would design for Parker's Framing. Include information on payroll forms, how hours worked will be collected, and payroll deductions.
2. Proofread the draft. Make sure there is a supporting paragraph for each main point. Also check for correct spelling, grammar, and punctuation.
3. Prepare the final document.

Payroll Information

Payroll clerks have access to personal information about employees, such as rate of pay and marital status. Imagine that you are the payroll clerk for a clothing store like Gap. Your friend Janet, who also works at the store, is interested in one of the sales clerks. She wants you to find out how much money he makes and whether he is married.

ETHICAL DECISION MAKING

1. What are the ethical issues?
2. What are the alternatives?
3. Who are the affected parties?
4. How do the alternatives affect the parties?
5. What would you do?

Evaluating Direct Deposit

A new co-worker has the choice of receiving a paycheck or using direct deposit. She asks for your recommendation. Write a paragraph explaining direct deposit and recommending whether or not your co-worker should use it.

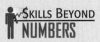
SKILLS BEYOND NUMBERS

Integrity

Employees who demonstrate integrity are able to make ethical decisions.

ON THE JOB As a payroll clerk for Fun 'n' Games Amusement Park, you have access to confidential information about employees. Your friend and co-worker, Mark Arnold, asked you to divulge payroll information about Melissa Porter, who has the same job title he has. Melissa just received a pay raise. Mark did not.

INSTRUCTIONS Write a few sentences explaining how you would respond to Mark's request.

INTERNATIONAL ACCOUNTING

Offshoring

Offshoring is the practice of U.S. companies using overseas providers for certain tasks. For example, technology companies like IBM and Microsoft have used programmers in India, mainly because overseas salaries are lower than U.S. salaries. Results have been mixed. Some companies report problems in employee turnover and communication. Others find that investors like the lower costs.

INSTRUCTIONS Define *offshoring* in your own words and discuss its potential advantages and disadvantages for a business.

Making It Personal

Your Part-Time Job

Students often seek part-time jobs to earn some spending money.

PERSONAL FINANCE ACTIVITY Ask your friends who have jobs how their hours worked are reported to the payroll accountant. Write a report discussing the different methods of reporting hours worked.

PERSONAL FINANCE ONLINE Log on to **glencoeaccounting.glencoe.com** and click on **Student Center.** Click on **Making It Personal** and select **Chapter 12.**

Analyzing FINANCIAL Reports

Analyzing Employee Productivity

One measure of productivity is the average sales dollars generated by each employee. For example, in a company with total revenue of $1,480,000 and 20 employees, sales per employee are $74,000, calculated as follows:

$$\frac{\text{Total Revenue}}{\text{Number of Employees}} = \text{Sales per Employee}$$

Calculating this measure from period to period or one part of a company to another can identify productivity changes. If sales per employee change greatly, the owner needs to learn why.

INSTRUCTIONS Answer these questions using Roadrunner's income statement on page 222.

1. If Roadrunner has two employees including the owner, what is the revenue per employee?

2. Suppose Roadrunner hires two more delivery people. The next month's revenue increases to $5,400. How has the productivity per employee changed?

Web Quest

Internet Project

How do people get paid? Visit **glencoeaccounting .glencoe.com** and click on **Student Center.** Click on **WebQuest** and select **Unit 3** to continue your Internet project.

Payroll Liabilities and Tax Records

What You'll Learn

1. Record payroll transactions in the general journal.

2. Describe the employer's payroll taxes.

3. Compute and complete payroll tax expense forms.

4. Record the payment of tax liabilities in the general journal.

5. Complete payroll tax reports.

6. Define the accounting terms introduced in this chapter.

Why It's Important

▶ Employers are legally required to make tax deposits on time and to report the earnings of each employee.

Predict

1. What does the chapter title tell you?
2. What do you already know about this subject from personal experience?
3. What have you learned about this in the earlier chapters?
4. What gaps exist in your knowledge of this subject?

Exploring the *Real World* of Business

EVALUATING PAYROLL COSTS

Verizon Wireless

Can you imagine the paperwork involved in preparing paychecks for 51,000 workers at **Verizon Wireless**? What if many of these workers are temporary or contract employees? Gathering all these time sheets and job assignments is a huge task. That's why **Verizon Wireless** decided to find a better way to automate the process for managing its contract work force.

The company now uses a Web-based payroll system called InSite. Requests and approvals for hiring contract employees, time sheets, and paychecks are handled online, faster and less costly than before. Now **Verizon Wireless** can spend more of its time and money fine-tuning new technologies like picture messaging, wireless Internet access, and 3-D games for its more than 43 million wireless phone customers.

What Do You Think?

Why do you think a company like **Verizon Wireless** chooses to hire temporary or contract employees rather than full-time employees?

Working in the *Real World*

APPLYING YOUR ACCOUNTING KNOWLEDGE

Almost everyone must pay taxes. You learned about the taxes you pay on your earnings in the last chapter. Your employer also pays taxes on what you earn. That money must be paid to the appropriate government agency within a certain amount of time. You will learn about the employer's payroll taxes in this chapter.

Personal Connection

1. Do you receive your paycheck in person, in the mail, or by direct deposit?
2. What do you imagine would happen if the accounting department failed to pay the taxes collected to the appropriate government agencies?

Online Connection

Go to **glencoeaccounting.glencoe.com** and click on **Student Center**. Click on **Working in the Real World** and select **Chapter 13**.

Journalizing and Posting the Payroll

BEFORE YOU READ

Main Idea
The release of cash for payroll is a transaction. It must be journalized and posted.

Read to Learn...
➤ how to analyze and journalize the payroll transaction. (p. 340)
➤ how to post the payroll transaction. (p. 343)

Key Terms
Salaries Expense

Employees, ranging from design engineers at Ford Motor Company to the waitresses at a neighborhood coffee shop, expect their payroll checks to arrive on time and to be accurate. You have learned that various amounts are withheld from employees' earnings for taxes and voluntary deductions. When the payroll register is complete, the payroll entry is journalized and the amounts are posted to the general ledger.

After the payroll has been prepared, a check is written to transfer the *total net pay* amount from the regular checking account of a business to its payroll checking account. The check is deposited in the payroll account, and all payroll checks for the period are written on the payroll account. The next step is to record the payment of the payroll in the accounting records.

Analyzing and Journalizing the Payroll
How Do You Journalize Payroll?

Let's analyze the effect of payroll on the employer's accounting system. Each pay period, the business pays out a certain amount of money to its employees in the form of wages and salaries. Employee earnings are a normal operating expense of a business. The expense account often used to record employees' earnings is called **Salaries Expense** . To increase the amount in **Salaries Expense**, the account is debited for the gross earnings for the pay period.

The business withholds various deductions, such as income and FICA taxes, from gross earnings each pay period. Employees also request voluntary withholdings such as premiums for insurance coverage. The employer retains the amounts withheld until it is time to pay the appropriate government agencies and businesses. The amounts withheld but not yet paid are liabilities of the business. Remember, a liability is an amount *owed* by a business.

As You READ

Instant Recall

Total Earnings
  Gross Pay
− Total Payroll Deductions
  Net Pay

Each type of payroll liability is recorded in a separate account.

Type of Deduction	Ledger Account
Federal income tax	**Employees' Federal Income Tax Payable**
Social security tax	**Social Security Tax Payable**
Medicare tax	**Medicare Tax Payable**
Hospital insurance premiums	**Hospital Insurance Premiums Payable**

As You READ

In Your Own Words

Salaries Expense
"Employee earnings are a normal operating expense of the business." What does this mean?

Depending on the business, it is possible that several different types of deductions are recorded in the Other Deductions column of the payroll register. If so, the total for each type of deduction is credited to the appropriate liability account. Refer to the Roadrunner Delivery Service payroll register shown in **Figure 12–5** on page 320. The deductions that may appear in the Other Deductions column each have an account in Roadrunner's general ledger:

- **U.S. Savings Bonds Payable**
- **Credit Union Payable**
- **Union Dues Payable**
- **United Way Payable**

The credit part of the payroll journal entry is made up of several items. The largest item is for net pay. Net pay is the amount actually paid out in cash by the employer to the employees. **Cash in Bank** is credited for total net pay.

The difference between gross earnings and net pay equals the employer's payroll liabilities. Each payroll liability account is separately credited for the total amount shown on the payroll register.

Business Transaction

*Roadrunner's payroll register in **Figure 12–5** on page 320 is the source document for the payroll journal entry.*

ANALYSIS		
	Identify	1. The accounts **Salaries Expense, Employees' Federal Income Tax Payable, Employees' State Income Tax Payable, Social Security Tax Payable, Medicare Tax Payable, Hospital Insurance Premiums Payable, U.S. Savings Bonds Payable,** and **Cash in Bank** are affected.
	Classify	2. **Salaries Expense** is an expense account. **Employees' Federal Income Tax Payable, Employees' State Income Tax Payable, Social Security Tax Payable, Medicare Tax Payable, Hospital Insurance Premiums Payable,** and **U.S. Savings Bonds Payable** are liability accounts. **Cash in Bank** is an asset account.
	+/−	3. **Salaries Expense** is increased by $1,350.25; **Employees' Federal Income Tax Payable** is increased by $100.00; **Employees' State Income Tax Payable** is increased by $27.01; **Social Security Tax Payable** is increased by $83.73; **Medicare Tax Payable** is increased by $19.57; **Hospital Insurance Premiums Payable** is increased by $23.65; **U.S. Savings Bonds Payable** is increased by $25.00; **Cash in Bank** is decreased by $1,071.29

| DEBIT-CREDIT RULE | 4. Increases in expense accounts are recorded as debits. Debit **Salaries Expense** for $1,350.25. |
| | 5. Decreases in asset accounts are recorded as credits. Credit **Cash in Bank** for $1,071.29. Increases in liability accounts are recorded as credits. Credit **Employees' Federal Income Tax Payable** for $100; **Employees' State Income Tax Payable** for $27.01; **Social Security Tax Payable** for $83.73; **Medicare Tax Payable** for $19.57; **Hospital Insurance Premiums Payable** for $23.65; **U.S. Savings Bonds Payable** for $25.00. |

T ACCOUNTS

6.

Salaries Expense			Employees' Federal Income Tax Payable	
Debit + 1,350.25	Credit −		Debit −	Credit + 100.00

Employees' State Income Tax Payable			Social Security Tax Payable	
Debit −	Credit + 27.01		Debit −	Credit + 83.73

Medicare Tax Payable			Hospital Insurance Premiums Payable	
Debit −	Credit + 19.57		Debit −	Credit + 23.65

U.S. Savings Bonds Payable			Cash in Bank	
Debit −	Credit + 25.00		Debit +	Credit − 1,071.29

JOURNAL ENTRY

7.

GENERAL JOURNAL PAGE 29

	DATE	DESCRIPTION	POST. REF.	DEBIT	CREDIT	
1	20--					1
2	June 30	Salaries Expense		1 3 5 0 25		2
3		Emplys' Fed. Inc. Tax Pay.			1 0 0 00	3
4		Emplys' State Inc. Tax Pay.			27 01	4
5		Social Sec. Tax Pay.			83 73	5
6		Medicare Tax Pay.			19 57	6
7		Hosp. Ins. Premiums Pay.			23 65	7
8		U.S. Savings Bonds Pay.			25 00	8
9		Cash in Bank			1 0 7 1 29	9
10		Pay. Reg. 6/30—Ck 186				10
11						11

The payroll expense is $1,350.25. The employees receive $1,071.29 in cash (net pay). Later the business will pay the federal government $203.30 ($100.00 federal income tax, $83.73 social security tax, and $19.57 Medicare tax). The business will also pay the state $27.01 for state income tax. A check for $23.65 will be written to the insurance company for hospital insurance premiums. Finally, a check for $25 will be sent to the federal government to purchase savings bonds.

These liabilities are the result of deductions that were taken from employees' earnings. In the next section, you will learn about the payroll tax liabilities of the employer.

Posting the Payroll Entry

How Do You Post the Payroll?

Figure 13–1 shows the general journal entry and the individual ledger accounts after posting.

GENERAL JOURNAL PAGE 29

	DATE		DESCRIPTION	POST. REF.	DEBIT	CREDIT	
1	20--						1
2	June	30	Salaries Expense	514	1 3 5 0 25		2
3			Employees' Fed. Inc. Tax Pay.	210		1 0 0 00	3
4			Employees' State Inc. Tax Pay.	215		27 01	4
5			Social Security Tax Pay.	220		83 73	5
6			Medicare Tax Pay.	225		19 57	6
7			Hosp. Ins. Premiums Pay.	230		23 65	7
8			U.S. Savings Bonds Pay.	235		25 00	8
9			Cash in Bank	101		1 0 7 1 29	9
10			Payroll Reg. 6/30—Ck. 186				10
11							11

ACCOUNT Salaries Expense ACCOUNT NO. 514

DATE		DESCRIPTION	POST. REF.	DEBIT	CREDIT	BALANCE DEBIT	BALANCE CREDIT
20--							
June	23	Balance	✓			34 6 8 3 10	
	30		G29	1 3 5 0 25		36 0 3 3 35	

ACCOUNT Employees' Federal Income Tax Payable ACCOUNT NO. 210

DATE		DESCRIPTION	POST. REF.	DEBIT	CREDIT	BALANCE DEBIT	BALANCE CREDIT
20--							
June	23	Balance	✓				2 9 3 18
	30		G29		1 0 0 00		3 9 3 18

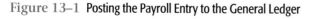

CONTINUE ▶

Figure 13–1 Posting the Payroll Entry to the General Ledger

ACCOUNT *Employees' State Income Tax Payable* **ACCOUNT NO.** _215_

DATE		DESCRIPTION	POST. REF.	DEBIT	CREDIT	BALANCE DEBIT	BALANCE CREDIT
20--							
June	23	Balance	✓				3 2 1 12
	30		G29		27 01		3 4 8 13

ACCOUNT *Social Security Tax Payable* **ACCOUNT NO.** _220_

DATE		DESCRIPTION	POST. REF.	DEBIT	CREDIT	BALANCE DEBIT	BALANCE CREDIT
20--							
June	23	Balance	✓				2 5 0 35
	30		G29		83 73		3 3 4 08

ACCOUNT *Medicare Tax Payable* **ACCOUNT NO.** _225_

DATE		DESCRIPTION	POST. REF.	DEBIT	CREDIT	BALANCE DEBIT	BALANCE CREDIT
20--							
June	23	Balance	✓				5 8 63
	30		G29		19 57		7 8 20

ACCOUNT *Hospital Insurance Premiums Payable* **ACCOUNT NO.** _230_

DATE		DESCRIPTION	POST. REF.	DEBIT	CREDIT	BALANCE DEBIT	BALANCE CREDIT
20--							
June	23	Balance	✓				4 73
	30		G29		23 65		2 8 38

ACCOUNT *U.S. Savings Bonds Payable* **ACCOUNT NO.** _235_

DATE		DESCRIPTION	POST. REF.	DEBIT	CREDIT	BALANCE DEBIT	BALANCE CREDIT
20--							
June	23	Balance	✓				7 5 00
	30		G29		25 00		1 0 0 00

ACCOUNT *Cash in Bank* **ACCOUNT NO.** _101_

DATE		DESCRIPTION	POST. REF.	DEBIT	CREDIT	BALANCE DEBIT	BALANCE CREDIT
20--							
June	23	Balance	✓			1 9 6 1 0 30	
	30		G29		1 0 7 1 29	1 8 5 3 9 01	

Figure 13–1 Posting the Payroll Entry to the General Ledger (continued)

AFTER YOU READ

Reinforce the Main Idea

Use an organizer like this one to express the payroll journal entry as an equation. Use broad account categories. (For example, use *liabilities* instead of listing all possible accounts.) Draw arrows (↑↓) in each box to show whether the account category increases or decreases.

 = 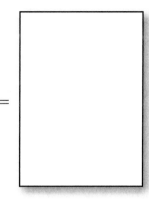 +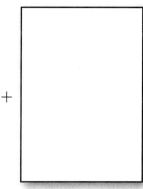

Do the Math

You are the payroll clerk for Queen City Motors. As you review the payroll records, you notice that two employees are nearing the $90,000 limit for social security tax. As commission-only sales employees, Marcie Laliberte and Kevin Hogan have earned $87,200 and $88,700, respectively.

1. How much more must Marcie and Kevin earn in commission to reach the social security tax limit?
2. If Marcie and Kevin are paid 7% commission on each sale, how much more in sales must each make to reach the social security tax limit?

Problem 13–1   Determining Payroll Amounts

SweepIt Cleaning Service reported the following amounts for the week ending November 4. The total amount earned by all employees is $2,193.40. The amount withheld for federal income tax is $263.00. Social security tax is $136.00, and Medicare tax is $31.80. Three of the employees each have $11.25 deducted for hospital insurance. The amount withheld for state income tax is $38.70.

Instructions Answer the following questions concerning the November 4 payroll for SweepIt Cleaning Service.

1. What amount is recorded in the **Salaries Expense** account?
2. What amount is recorded in the **Medicare Tax Payable** account?
3. What is the total amount of liabilities for the weekly payroll?
4. What amount is entered in the **Hospital Insurance Premiums Payable** account?
5. What amount is recorded as a credit for the **Cash in Bank** account?

Employer's Payroll Taxes

BEFORE YOU READ

Main Idea
Employers must pay taxes in addition to the amounts withheld from their employees. This is an expense for the business.

Read to Learn...
➤ how to compute payroll tax expense. (p. 346)
➤ how to journalize payroll tax expense. (p. 347)
➤ how to post payroll tax expense. (p. 349)

Key Terms
Federal Unemployment Tax Act (FUTA)
State Unemployment Tax Act (SUTA)
unemployment taxes
Payroll Tax Expense

In Section 1 you learned how to journalize and post the payroll entry. This entry, in part, records taxes that employees are required to pay on their earnings. Your local florist, employing designers, delivery workers, and sales clerks, must also pay taxes on these workers' earnings. These amounts need to be calculated, journalized, and posted.

Computing Payroll Tax Expenses
Which Payroll Taxes Are Paid by the Employer?

In addition to withholding taxes from employees' wages, the employer *pays* taxes on these wages. The employer's taxes, considered operating expenses of the business, consist of the employer's FICA taxes, the federal unemployment tax, and the state unemployment tax.

The Employer's FICA Taxes

Under the Federal Insurance Contributions Act, both the employee and the employer pay FICA taxes. As you recall, the employer withholds a percentage of gross earnings for social security and Medicare taxes. In addition, the employer pays FICA taxes using the same percentage of gross earnings. Recall that the current rates are 6.2% for social security tax and 1.45% for Medicare tax.

The employer and the employee pay social security tax on gross earnings up to the maximum taxable limit per employee ($90,000 in 2005). The employer and the employee pay Medicare tax on all gross earnings; there is no maximum taxable limit. The payroll clerk checks the accumulated earnings on each employee's earnings record to determine whether that employee has reached the maximum taxable amount. When an employee reaches the limit, the social security tax is no longer computed.

In determining social security tax and Medicare tax for both employee and employer, it makes no difference whether an employee is full-time, part-time, temporary, or permanent. A full-time adult employee and a student employed part-time only for the summer are subject to the same taxes.

At Roadrunner Delivery Service for the week ending June 30, the employees' total social security taxes are $83.73 and total Medicare taxes are $19.57. The employer's taxes on the total gross earnings are $83.72 (6.2% of $1,350.25) and $19.58 (1.45% of $1,350.25), respectively. Notice that the social security tax for the employees ($83.73) and the employer ($83.72) do

AS YOU READ

Key Point

FICA Taxes
Both employees and employers pay the same amount of FICA taxes.

not match. The same situation exists for the Medicare tax. This is because the employer's tax is calculated on the total gross earnings ($1,350.25). The employees' taxes are calculated on each employee's gross earnings and the individual tax amounts are totaled. This may result in small differences between the employees' and employer's taxes.

Federal and State Unemployment Taxes

Two unemployment laws, the **Federal Unemployment Tax Act (FUTA)** and the **State Unemployment Tax Act (SUTA)**, require employers to pay unemployment taxes. **Unemployment taxes** are collected to provide funds for workers who are temporarily unemployed. Unemployment taxes are based on a percentage of the employees' gross earnings.

The employer pays both federal and state unemployment taxes. The maximum federal unemployment tax is 6.2% on the first $7,000 of an employee's annual wages. State unemployment tax rates and maximum taxable amounts vary among states. Employers may deduct up to 5.4% of the state unemployment taxes from federal unemployment taxes. Most employers, therefore, pay a federal tax of .8% (6.2% − 5.4%) of taxable gross earnings.

In a few states, employees are also required to pay unemployment taxes. The percentage amount varies among these states.

For Roadrunner, since none of the employees has reached the maximum taxable amount, the federal unemployment tax for the week ended June 30 is $10.80 ($1,350.25 × .008, or .8%). The state unemployment tax is $72.91 ($1,350.25 × .054, or 5.4%).

Journalizing the Employer Payroll Taxes
How Do You Journalize Payroll Tax Expense?

The employer's payroll taxes are business expenses recorded in the **Payroll Tax Expense** account. Until paid, the employer's payroll taxes are liabilities of the business.

Use the **Social Security Tax Payable** and the **Medicare Tax Payable** accounts to record both the employees' and the employer's FICA taxes. Record the employer's unemployment taxes in the **Federal Unemployment Tax Payable** and **State Unemployment Tax Payable** accounts.

In the next business transaction, we will analyze the accounts affected when an employer pays its payroll taxes. This entry takes place in each payroll period.

As You READ

It's Not What It Seems

Unemployment Taxes
Unemployment taxes are not paid by the people who might become unemployed. These taxes are paid by employers.

*Roadrunner's payroll register in **Figure 12–5** on page 320 is the source document for the payroll tax journal entry.*

ANALYSIS	*Identify*	1.	The accounts **Payroll Tax Expense, Social Security Tax Payable, Medicare Tax Payable, State Unemployment Tax Payable,** and **Federal Unemployment Tax Payable** are affected.
	Classify	2.	**Payroll Tax Expense** is an expense account. **Social Security Tax Payable, Medicare Tax Payable, State Unemployment Tax Payable,** and **Federal Unemployment Tax Payable** are liability accounts.
	+/–	3.	**Payroll Tax Expense** is increased by $187.01; **Social Security Tax Payable** is increased by $83.72; **Medicare Tax Payable** is increased by $19.58; **State Unemployment Tax Payable** is increased by $72.91; **Federal Unemployment Tax Payable** is increased by $10.80.

DEBIT-CREDIT RULE	4.	Increases in expense accounts are recorded as debits. Debit **Payroll Tax Expense** for $187.01.
	5.	Increases in liability accounts are recorded as credits. Credit **Social Security Tax Payable** for $83.72; **Medicare Tax Payable** for $19.58; **State Unemployment Tax Payable** for $72.91; **Federal Unemployment Tax Payable** for $10.80.

T ACCOUNTS

6.

Payroll Tax Expense			Social Security Tax Payable	
Debit + 187.01	Credit –		Debit –	Credit + 83.72

Medicare Tax Payable			State Unemployment Tax Payable	
Debit –	Credit + 19.58		Debit –	Credit + 72.91

Federal Unemployment Tax Payable	
Debit –	Credit + 10.80

JOURNAL ENTRY

7.

	GENERAL JOURNAL		PAGE 30	
	DATE	DESCRIPTION	POST. REF.	DEBIT	CREDIT

	DATE		DESCRIPTION	POST. REF.	DEBIT	CREDIT	
1	20--						1
2	June	30	Payroll Tax Expense		187 01		2
3			Social Security Tax Pay.			83 72	3
4			Medicare Tax Pay.			19 58	4
5			State Unemplymnt. Tax Pay.			72 91	5
6			Fed. Unemplymnt. Tax Pay.			10 80	6
7			Payroll Reg. 6/30				7

Posting Payroll Taxes to the General Ledger

How Do You Post Payroll Tax Expense?

Figure 13–2 shows the individual ledger accounts after posting the payroll taxes entry.

Notice that the **Social Security Tax Payable** and the **Medicare Tax Payable** accounts have two entries for the June 30 payroll. The first entry is the amount of taxes withheld from the *employees'* earnings. The second entry is the amount of taxes paid by the *employer*.

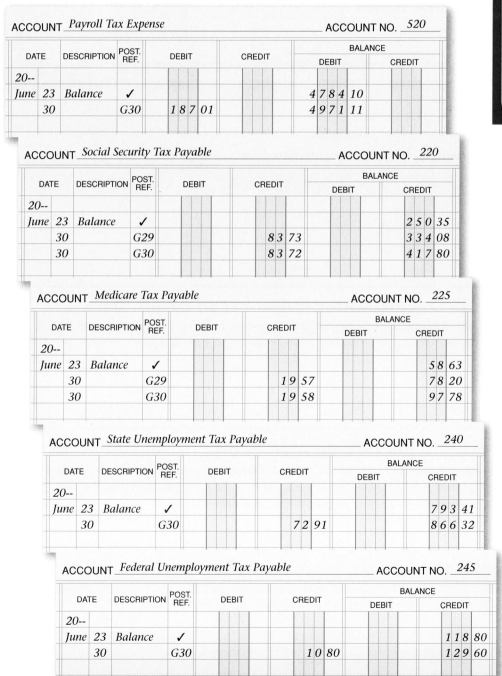

ACCOUNT *Payroll Tax Expense*   **ACCOUNT NO.** *520*

DATE		DESCRIPTION	POST. REF.	DEBIT	CREDIT	BALANCE DEBIT	BALANCE CREDIT
20--							
June	23	Balance	✓			4 7 8 4 10	
	30		G30	1 8 7 01		4 9 7 1 11	

ACCOUNT *Social Security Tax Payable*   **ACCOUNT NO.** *220*

DATE		DESCRIPTION	POST. REF.	DEBIT	CREDIT	BALANCE DEBIT	BALANCE CREDIT
20--							
June	23	Balance	✓				2 5 0 35
	30		G29		8 3 73		3 3 4 08
	30		G30		8 3 72		4 1 7 80

ACCOUNT *Medicare Tax Payable*   **ACCOUNT NO.** *225*

DATE		DESCRIPTION	POST. REF.	DEBIT	CREDIT	BALANCE DEBIT	BALANCE CREDIT
20--							
June	23	Balance	✓				5 8 63
	30		G29		1 9 57		7 8 20
	30		G30		1 9 58		9 7 78

ACCOUNT *State Unemployment Tax Payable*   **ACCOUNT NO.** *240*

DATE		DESCRIPTION	POST. REF.	DEBIT	CREDIT	BALANCE DEBIT	BALANCE CREDIT
20--							
June	23	Balance	✓				7 9 3 41
	30		G30		7 2 91		8 6 6 32

ACCOUNT *Federal Unemployment Tax Payable*   **ACCOUNT NO.** *245*

DATE		DESCRIPTION	POST. REF.	DEBIT	CREDIT	BALANCE DEBIT	BALANCE CREDIT
20--							
June	23	Balance	✓				1 1 8 80
	30		G30		1 0 80		1 2 9 60

Figure 13–2 General Ledger Accounts after Posting the Payroll Taxes Entry

AFTER YOU READ

Reinforce the Main Idea

Employer payroll taxes are paid at different rates. Use a chart like this one to show the rates of the employer payroll taxes.

	Employer Payroll Tax Rates	
Tax	**Percent of Total Earnings**	**Earnings Limit**
Social security		
Federal unemployment		
Medicare		
State unemployment		

Do the Math

Calculate the employer's federal unemployment tax rate for each of the following states:

State	State Unemployment Tax Rate
State A	1.5%
State B	3.0%
State C	4.5%
State D	5.4%
State E	6.0%

Problem 13–2 Calculating Employer's Payroll Taxes

For the week ending June 30, EZ Copy Center's payroll has total gross earnings of $4,836.60. Calculate the employer's payroll taxes. Use the following percentages:

Social security tax	6.2%	Federal unemployment tax	0.8%
Medicare tax	1.45%	State unemployment tax	5.4%

Problem 13–3 Identifying Entries for Payroll Liabilities

The following list includes several payroll-related items used in preparing the weekly payroll for Outdoor Adventures. These items are included in either the entry to record the payroll or the entry to record the employer's payroll taxes.

Employees' federal income tax	Employees' state income tax
Employer's social security tax	Union dues
U.S. savings bonds	Employees' social security tax
Employer's Medicare tax	State unemployment tax
Federal unemployment tax	Employees' Medicare tax

Instructions Use the form provided in your working papers. Place a check mark in the column that describes the entry in which the item is recorded:

- entry to record the payroll
- entry to record the employer's payroll taxes.

Tax Liability Payments and Tax Reports

After journalizing and posting the payroll entries, a business pays the amounts owed to government agencies and other institutions.

Paying the Payroll Tax Liabilities
How and When Do Employers Pay Their Liabilities?

Payroll liabilities are paid at regular intervals.

FICA and Federal Income Taxes

A business makes one payment combining (1) social security and Medicare taxes (for both employees and employer), and (2) employees' federal income taxes withheld. It makes the payment at an authorized financial institution or Federal Reserve Bank. Most small businesses, like Roadrunner, make this payment monthly. It is due by the 15th day of the month following the payroll month. Payment for the month ending June 30 is due by July 15. Larger businesses make the payment every two weeks.

Many small businesses prepare and send a **Form 8109** with the check. The Form 8109, or *Federal Tax Deposit Coupon,* identifies the type of tax and the tax period. Notice the ovals on the right side of Form 8109 in **Figure 13–3.** The 941 oval indicates FICA and federal income taxes. The 2nd Quarter oval indicates the period ending June 30.

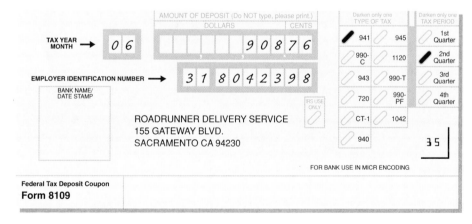

Figure 13–3 Federal Tax Deposit Coupon (Form 8109) for FICA and Federal Income Taxes

The **Electronic Federal Tax Payment System (EFTPS)** is used by larger businesses to make deposits. Eventually even small businesses will use EFTPS.

Business Transaction

*Roadrunner pays $908.76 payroll tax liabilities July 15 including $393.18 employees' federal income taxes, $417.80 social security taxes, and $97.78 Medicare taxes (refer to ledger accounts in **Figures 13–1** and **13–2**).*

ANALYSIS	Identify	1.	The accounts **Employees' Federal Income Tax Payable**, **Social Security Tax Payable**, **Medicare Tax Payable**, and **Cash in Bank** are affected.

ANALYSIS

Identify

Classify

+/−

1. The accounts **Employees' Federal Income Tax Payable**, **Social Security Tax Payable**, **Medicare Tax Payable**, and **Cash in Bank** are affected.
2. **Employees' Federal Income Tax Payable**, **Social Security Tax Payable**, and **Medicare Tax Payable** are liability accounts. **Cash in Bank** is an asset account.
3. **Employees' Federal Income Tax Payable** is decreased by $393.18; **Social Security Tax Payable** is decreased by $417.80; **Medicare Tax Payable** is decreased by $97.78; **Cash in Bank** is decreased by $908.76.

DEBIT-CREDIT RULE

4. Decreases in liability accounts are recorded as debits. Debit **Employees' Federal Income Tax Payable** for $393.18; **Social Security Tax Payable** for $417.80; **Medicare Tax Payable** for $97.78.
5. Decreases in asset accounts are recorded as credits. Credit **Cash in Bank** for $908.76.

T ACCOUNTS

6.

Employees' Federal Income Tax Payable	
Debit − 393.18	Credit +

Social Security Tax Payable	
Debit − 417.80	Credit +

Medicare Tax Payable	
Debit − 97.78	Credit +

Cash in Bank	
Debit +	Credit − 908.76

JOURNAL ENTRY

7.

	GENERAL JOURNAL				PAGE 31	
	DATE	DESCRIPTION	POST. REF.	DEBIT	CREDIT	
1	20--					1
2	July 15	Emplys' Fed. Inc. Tax Pay.		393 18		2
3		Social Security Tax Pay.		417 80		3
4		Medicare Tax Pay.		97 78		4
5		Cash in Bank			908 76	5
6		Check 208				6

State and Local Income Taxes

At regular intervals businesses pay the amounts withheld for state and local income taxes. Each state and local government determines how and when the payments are made and what reports are filed.

Business Transaction

*Roadrunner pays $348.13 to the state. This is the amount of state income tax withheld from employees' earnings, as indicated in the **Employees' State Income Tax Payable** account shown in **Figure 13–1**.*

ANALYSIS	Identify	1.	The accounts **Employees' State Income Tax Payable** and **Cash in Bank** are affected.
	Classify	2.	**Employees' State Income Tax Payable** is a liability account. **Cash in Bank** is an asset account.
	+/−	3.	**Employees' State Income Tax Payable** is decreased by $348.13. **Cash in Bank** is decreased by $348.13.

| DEBIT-CREDIT RULE | | 4. | Decreases in liabilities are debits. Debit **Employees' State Income Tax Payable** for $348.13. |
| | | 5. | Decreases in assets are credits. Credit **Cash in Bank** for $348.13. |

T ACCOUNTS

6.

Employees' State Income Tax Payable			Cash in Bank	
Debit −	Credit +		Debit +	Credit −
348.13				348.13

JOURNAL ENTRY

7.

	GENERAL JOURNAL			PAGE 32	
	DATE	DESCRIPTION	POST. REF.	DEBIT	CREDIT
1	20--				1
2	July 15	Emplys' State Inc. Tax Pay.		348 13	2
3		Cash in Bank			348 13	3
4		Check 209			4

Federal Unemployment Taxes

Most businesses pay the FUTA tax quarterly. If a business has accumulated FUTA taxes of less than $100, only one annual payment is necessary.

Business Transaction

*Roadrunner pays $129.60 for FUTA taxes. This is the balance of the **Federal Unemployment Tax Payable** account shown in **Figure 13–2**.*

ANALYSIS	Identify	1.	**Federal Unemployment Tax Payable** and **Cash in Bank** are affected.
	Classify	2.	**Federal Unemployment Tax Payable** is a liability account. **Cash in Bank** is an asset account.
	+/−	3.	**Federal Unemployment Tax Payable** is decreased by $129.60. **Cash in Bank** is decreased by $129.60.

| DEBIT-CREDIT RULE | | 4. | Decreases in liabilities are debits. Debit **Federal Unemployment Tax Payable** for $129.60. |
| | | 5. | Decreases in assets are credits. Credit **Cash in Bank** for $129.60. |

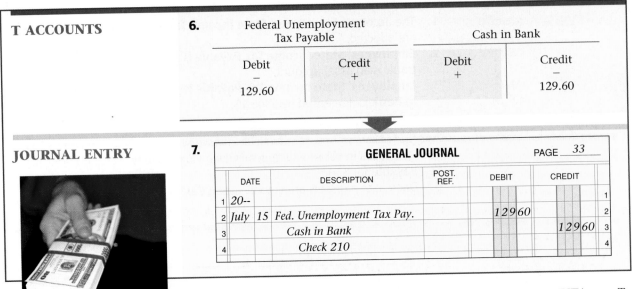

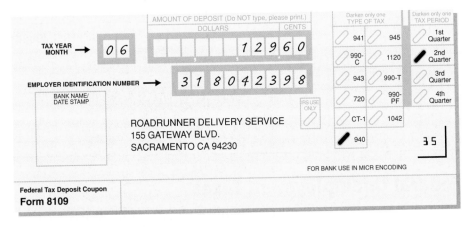

A Form 8109 is prepared and sent with the check for the FUTA tax. To indicate that FUTA taxes are being paid, the 940 oval is filled in. **Figure 13–4** shows the Form 8109 that Roadrunner sends with the FUTA payment.

Figure 13–4 Federal Tax Deposit Coupon (Form 8109) for Federal Unemployment Taxes

State Unemployment Taxes

State unemployment taxes are usually paid on a quarterly basis.

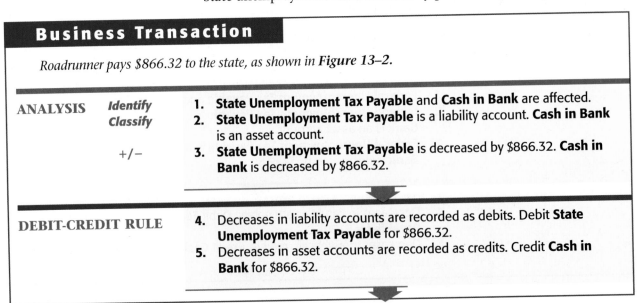

Business Transaction

Roadrunner pays $866.32 to the state, as shown in **Figure 13–2.**

ANALYSIS	*Identify* *Classify* +/−	1. **State Unemployment Tax Payable** and **Cash in Bank** are affected. 2. **State Unemployment Tax Payable** is a liability account. **Cash in Bank** is an asset account. 3. **State Unemployment Tax Payable** is decreased by $866.32. **Cash in Bank** is decreased by $866.32.
DEBIT-CREDIT RULE		4. Decreases in liability accounts are recorded as debits. Debit **State Unemployment Tax Payable** for $866.32. 5. Decreases in asset accounts are recorded as credits. Credit **Cash in Bank** for $866.32.

T ACCOUNTS	6.	State Unemployment Tax Payable		Cash in Bank	
		Debit –	Credit +	Debit +	Credit –
		866.32			866.32

JOURNAL ENTRY 7.

	GENERAL JOURNAL		PAGE 34		
	DATE	DESCRIPTION	POST. REF.	DEBIT	CREDIT
1	20--				1
2	July 15	State Unemployment Tax Pay.		866 32	2
3		Cash in Bank			866 32	3
4		Check 211			4

Other Payroll Liabilities

Employers also make payment for employees' voluntary deductions.

Business Transaction

*On July 15 Roadrunner pays $28.38 for hospital insurance premiums. (Refer to **Figure 13–1**.)*

ANALYSIS	*Identify*	1.	The accounts **Hospital Insurance Premiums Payable** and **Cash in Bank** are affected.
	Classify	2.	**Hospital Insurance Premiums Payable** is a liability account. **Cash in Bank** is an asset account.
	+/–	3.	**Hospital Insurance Premiums Payable** is decreased by $28.38. **Cash in Bank** is decreased by $28.38.

DEBIT-CREDIT RULE	4.	Decreases in liabilities are debits. Debit **Hospital Insurance Premiums Payable** for $28.38.
	5.	Decreases in assets are credits. Credit **Cash in Bank** for $28.38.

T ACCOUNTS	6.	Hospital Insurance Premiums Payable		Cash in Bank	
		Debit –	Credit +	Debit +	Credit –
		28.38			28.38

JOURNAL ENTRY 7.

	GENERAL JOURNAL		PAGE 35		
	DATE	DESCRIPTION	POST. REF.	DEBIT	CREDIT
1	20--				1
2	July 15	Hospital Ins. Premiums Pay.		28 38	2
3		Cash in Bank			28 38	3
4		Check 212			4

Posting the Payment of Payroll Liabilities

After the payments for the employer's payroll liabilities have been journalized, the entries are posted to the appropriate general ledger accounts. **Figure 13–5** shows Roadrunner's general ledger accounts after posting.

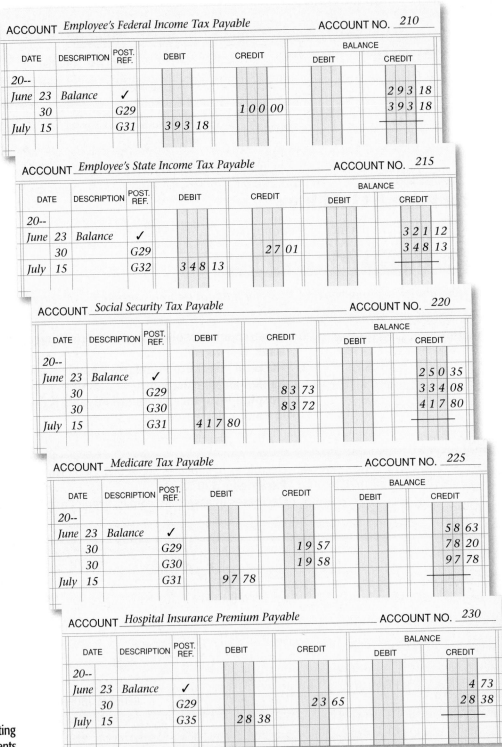

Figure 13–5 General Ledger Accounts after Posting of Payroll Liabilities Payments

ACCOUNT State Unemployment Tax Payable					ACCOUNT NO. 240	

DATE	DESCRIPTION	POST. REF.	DEBIT	CREDIT	BALANCE DEBIT	BALANCE CREDIT
20--						
June 23	Balance	✓				7 9 3 41
30		G30		72 91		8 6 6 32
July 15		G34	8 6 6 32			

ACCOUNT Federal Unemployment Tax Payable					ACCOUNT NO. 245	

DATE	DESCRIPTION	POST. REF.	DEBIT	CREDIT	BALANCE DEBIT	BALANCE CREDIT
20--						
June 23	Balance	✓				1 1 8 80
30		G30		10 80		1 2 9 60
July 15		G33	1 2 9 60			

Figure 13–5 General Ledger Accounts after Posting of Payroll Liabilities Payments (continued)

Preparing Payroll Tax Forms
How Does the Government Receive Payroll Information?

Employers must complete a variety of payroll-related tax forms.

Form	Name of Form	When Filed
W-2	Wage and Tax Statement	Annually
W-3	Transmittal of Wage and Tax Statements	Annually
941	Employer's Quarterly Federal Tax Return	Quarterly
940	Employer's Annual Federal Unemployment (FUTA) Tax Return	Annually

Forms W-2 and W-3

The Wage and Tax Statement, **Form W-2**, summarizes an employee's earnings and withholdings for the calendar year. Form W-2 reports (1) gross earnings, (2) federal income tax withheld, (3) FICA taxes withheld, and (4) state and local income taxes withheld.

Each employee receives a Form W-2 by January 31 of the following year. Employees use Form W-2 to prepare their individual income tax returns. **Figure 13–6** on page 358 shows the Form W-2 for Emily Kardos.

Employers prepare many copies of Form W-2. The employer sends Copy A to the IRS and gives Copies B and C to the employee. The employer keeps Copy D. Additional copies are sent to city or state government if necessary.

The employer files **Form W-3**, Transmittal of Wage and Tax Statements, with the federal government along with the Forms W-2. Form W-3 summarizes the information on the Forms W-2. Forms W-2 and W-3 are due by February 28. The federal government uses the Form W-2 information to check individual income tax returns. **Figure 13–7** on page 358 shows Roadrunner's Form W-3.

Form W-2 Wage and Tax Statement

a Control number		OMB No. 1545-0008	
b Employer's identification number 31-8042398		1 Wages, tips, other compensation 8,246.00	2 Federal income tax withheld 664.00
c Employer's name, address, and ZIP code Roadrunner Delivery Service 155 Gateway Blvd. Sacramento, CA 94230		3 Social security wages 8,246.00	4 Social security tax withheld 511.25
		5 Medicare wages and tips 8,246.00	6 Medicare tax withheld 119.57
		7 Social security tips	8 Allocated tips
d Employee's social security number 201-XX-XXXX		9 Advance EIC payment	10 Dependent care benefits
e Employee's name, address, and ZIP code Emily M. Kardos 809 East Main Street Sacramento, CA 94230		11 Nonqualified plans	12 Benefits included in box 1
		13	14 Other
		15 Statutory employee ☐ Deceased ☐ Pension plan ☐ Legal rep. ☐ Hshld. emp. ☐ Subtotal ☐ Deferred compensation ☐	

| 16 State CA | Employer's state I.D. no. 484972 | 17 State wages, tips, etc. 8,246.00 | 18 State income tax 128.74 | 19 Locality name | 20 Local wages, tips, etc. | 21 Local income tax |

Form **W-2** Wage and Tax Statement 20--   Department of the Treasury – Internal Revenue Service
Copy 1 For State, City, or Local Tax Department

Figure 13–6 Form W-2 Wage and Tax Statement

DO NOT STAPLE

a Control number 33333	For Official Use Only ▶ OMB No. 1545-0008	
b Kind of Payer 941 ☑ Military ☐ 943 ☐ CT-1 ☐ Hshld. emp. ☐ Medicare govt. emp. ☐	1 Wages, tips, other compensation 67,210.35	2 Federal income tax withheld 5,396.00
	3 Social security wages 67,210.35	4 Social security tax withheld 4,167.04
c Total number of Forms W-2 5	d Establishment number 7210	5 Medicare wages and tips 67,210.35	6 Medicare tax withheld 974.55
e Employer identification number 31-8042398	7 Social security tips	8 Allocated tips
f Employer's name Roadrunner Delivery Service	9 Advance EIC payments	10 Dependent care benefits
	11 Nonqualified plans	12 Deferred compensation
155 Gateway Blvd. Sacramento, CA 94230	13	
	14	
g Employer's address and ZIP code		
h Other EIN used this year	15 Income tax withheld by third-party payer	
i Employer's state I.D. No.		
Contact person	Telephone number ( )	Fax number ( )	E-mail address

Under penalties of perjury, I declare that I have examined this return and accompanying documents, and, to the best of my knowledge and belief, they are true, correct, and complete.

Signature ▶ *Maria Sanchez*   Title ▶ *Owner*   Date ▶ *1/29/20--*

Form **W-3** Transmittal of Wage and Tax Statements   Department of the Treasury Internal Revenue Service

Figure 13–7 Transmittal of Wage and Tax Statements

Forms 941 and 940

Form 941, illustrated in **Figure 13–8**, is the employer's quarterly federal tax return that reports accumulated amounts of FICA and federal income taxes withheld from employees' earnings, as well as FICA tax owed by the employer. The employer's federal unemployment tax is reported annually on **Form 940**.

Department of the Treasury
Internal Revenue Service

Employer's Quarterly Federal Tax Return

▶ See separate instructions for information on completing this return.
Please type or print.

Enter state code for state in which deposits were made ONLY if different from state in address to the right ▶ ⬚ (see page 3 of instructions).

Name (as distinguished from trade name)
Roadrunner Delivery Service
Trade name, if any

Address (number and street)
155 Gateway Blvd.

Date quarter ended
June 30, 20--

Employer identification number
31-8042398

City, state, and ZIP code
Sacramento, CA 94230

OMB No. 1545-0029

T	
FF	
FD	
FP	
I	
T	

If address is different from prior return, check here ▶ ⬚

IRS Use

```
1  1  1  1  1  1  1  1  1      2      3  3  3  3  3  3      4  4  4      5  5  5
   6     7     8  8  8  8  8  8  8     9  9  9  9    10 10 10 10 10 10 10 10 10 10
```

If you do not have to file returns in the future, check here ▶ ⬚ and enter date final wages paid ▶

If you are a seasonal employer, see **Seasonal employers** on page 1 of the instructions and check here ▶ ⬚

1	Number of employees in the pay period that includes March 12th . ▶	**1**		
2	Total wages and tips, plus other compensation	**2**	9,252	96
3	Total income tax withheld from wages, tips, and sick pay	**3**	747	64
4	Adjustment of withheld income tax for preceding quarters of calendar year	**4**	0	00
5	Adjusted total of income tax withheld (line 3 as adjusted by line 4—see instructions) . . .	**5**	773	55

6	Taxable social security wages	**6a**	9,252	96	× 12.4% (.124) =	**6b**	1,147	37
	Taxable social security tips	**6c**			× 12.4% (.124) =	**6d**	0	00
7	Taxable Medicare wages and tips . . .	**7a**	9,252	96	× 2.9% (.029) =	**7b**	268	33

8	Total social security and Medicare taxes (add lines 6b, 6d, and 7b). Check here if wages are not subject to social security and/or Medicare tax . . . . ▶ ⬚	**8**	1,415	70
9	Adjustment of social security and Medicare taxes (see instructions for required explanation) Sick Pay $ _____ ± Fractions of Cents $ _____ ± Other $ _____ =	**9**	0	00
10	Adjusted total of social security and Medicare taxes (line 8 as adjusted by line 9—see instructions) . .	**10**	1,415	70
11	**Total taxes** (add lines 5 and 10)	**11**	2,163	34
12	Advance earned income credit (EIC) payments made to employees	**12**	0	00
13	Net taxes (subtract line 12 from line 11). **This should equal line 17, column (d) below (or line D of Schedule B (Form 941))**	**13**	2,163	34
14	Total deposits for quarter, including overpayment applied from a prior quarter	**14**	2,163	34
15	**Balance due** (subtract line 14 from line 13). See instructions	**15**	0	00

16 Overpayment, if line 14 is more than line 13, enter excess here ▶ $ _____
and check if to be: ⬚ Applied to next return **OR** ⬚ Refunded.

- **All filers:** If line 13 is less than $500, you need not complete line 17 or Schedule B (Form 941).
- **Semiweekly schedule depositors:** Complete Schedule B (Form 941) and check here . . . . ▶ ⬚
- **Monthly schedule depositors:** Complete line 17, columns (a) through (d), and check here . . . . ▶ ⬚

17 **Monthly Summary of Federal Tax Liability.** Do not complete if you were a semiweekly schedule depositor.

(a) First month liability	**(b)** Second month liability	**(c)** Third month liability	**(d)** Total liability for quarter
627.29	627.29	908.76	2,163.34

Sign Here

Under penalties of perjury, I declare that I have examined this return, including accompanying schedules and statements, and to the best of my knowledge and belief, it is true, correct, and complete.

Signature ▶ *Maria Sanchez*
Print Your Name and Title ▶ Maria Sanchez, Owner
Date ▶ 6/30/20--

Figure 13–8 Form 941

AFTER YOU **READ**

Reinforce the Main Idea

Different payroll tax forms are used for different purposes. Using a chart like this one, indicate the purpose of each form.

FORM	PURPOSE
W-2	
W-3	
941	
940	

Do the Math

Small businesses (those that have revenues of less than $200,000 per year) pay their federal taxes by the 15th day of the month following the payroll month. Large businesses pay their taxes every two weeks. Review the graph, and answer the following questions.

1. Which businesses pay their taxes every two weeks?
2. What percent of businesses represented in the circle graph are large businesses?

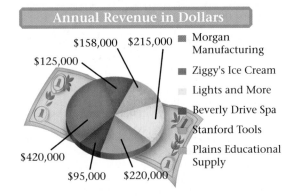

Annual Revenue in Dollars

$158,000 $215,000   ■ Morgan Manufacturing
$125,000
■ Ziggy's Ice Cream
□ Lights and More
■ Beverly Drive Spa
■ Stanford Tools
$420,000
■ Plains Educational Supply
$95,000 $220,000

Problem 13–4 Payment of Payroll Liabilities

The following account balances appear in the general ledger for Soap Box Laundry on April 30.

Instructions Record the payment of the four liability accounts on page 34 of the general journal. (Hint: Two checks are written.)

General Ledger	
Social Security Tax Payable	$318.55
State Income Tax Payable	205.60
Medicare Tax Payable	113.28
Employees' Federal Income Tax Payable	286.00

Problem 13–5 Analyzing a Source Document

PAYROLL REGISTER

PAY PERIOD ENDING May 19 _____ 20 -- ____   DATE OF PAYMENT May 19, 20--

EMPLOYEE NUMBER	NAME	MAR. STATUS	ALLOW.	TOTAL HOURS	RATE	EARNINGS			DEDUCTIONS							NET PAY	CK. NO.
						REGULAR	OVERTIME	TOTAL	SOC. SEC. TAX	MEDICARE TAX	FED. INC. TAX	STATE INC. TAX	HOSP. INS.	OTHER	TOTAL	
25																	25
	TOTALS					1,218 93	109 14	1,328 07	82 34	19 26	184 00	26 56	20 00	——	332 16	995 91

Other Deductions: Write the appropriate code letter to the left of the amount: B–U.S. Savings Bonds; C–Credit Union: UD–Union Dues; UW–United Way.

Instructions Based on this payroll register, record the appropriate journal entry in your working papers. Use page 14 in the general journal.

Accounting Careers in Focus

DIRECTOR OF SHARED SERVICES
Lear Corporation, Dearborn, Michigan
Bonnie Sims

Q: What does Lear Corporation do?

A: We manufacture parts for the interiors of automobiles.

Q: What are the responsibilities of your job?

A: I oversee a unit of our company that is called a shared service center. Shared service centers allow companies to centralize their financial, administrative, or customer support functions.

Q: Why did you choose an accounting career?

A: I was born into a family of accountants. Accounting was something in which I was always interested.

Q: What has helped you succeed?

A: My success is due in large part to hard work and dedication. I started my career as an accounts payable clerk, eventually became an accountant, and then worked in the shared services center at Lear. I'm now the director. Always keep your goals in mind and continually work toward them.

Q: What do you like most about your job?

A: I like that it involves accounting, finance, and project management. This mix provides me with many challenges.

Q: What types of challenges?

A: The biggest is dealing with periods like quarter-end. Things get extremely busy and hectic!

Tips from . . .

RHI Robert Half International Inc.

Your résumé should always be submitted along with a strong cover letter. The letter should expand upon the key points in your résumé, highlight your skills and experience that are most relevant to the job opening, and explain how you can benefit the prospective employer.

CAREER FACTS

- ▶ **Nature of the Work:** Oversee accounts payable, expense reporting, and payroll departments; hire, train, and manage accounting staff.
- ▶ **Training or Education Needed:** A bachelor's degree in accounting or finance; at least seven years' experience.
- ▶ **Aptitudes, Abilities, and Skills:** Strong communication, technology, analytical, and management skills.
- ▶ **Salary Range:** $45,000 to $115,000 depending on experience, company size, industry, and location.
- ▶ **Career Path:** Gain public accounting experience, and then move to a corporate environment. Gradually assume positions with increasing responsibility.

Thinking Critically Why is it important for managers to be able to see the big picture?

Key Concepts

1. Total gross earnings are often recorded in the **Salaries Expense** account. Amounts withheld from employees' earnings are liabilities of the business. The payroll register is the source document for paying the payroll. The payroll transaction is journalized here:

	DATE	DESCRIPTION	POST. REF.	DEBIT	CREDIT	
1	20--					1
2	Date	Salaries Expense		x x x x x		2
3		Emplys' Fed. Inc. Tax Pay.			x x x x x	3
4		Emplys' State Inc. Tax Pay.			x x x x x	4
5		Social Sec. Tax Pay.			x x x x x	5
6		Medicare Tax Pay.			x x x x x	6
7		Hosp. Ins. Premiums Pay.			x x x x x	7
8		U.S. Savings Bonds Pay.			x x x x x	8
9		Cash in Bank			x x x x x	9

GENERAL JOURNAL   PAGE ___9___

2. Employers pay taxes on employees' gross earnings. These taxes are in addition to the amounts withheld from earnings. The employer payroll taxes are an operating expense of the business. (Withheld taxes are not an expense. The business merely serves as the collection agent for the government.) Employers pay the following payroll taxes:

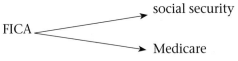

FICA → social security
FICA → Medicare

FUTA—federal unemployment insurance
SUTA—state unemployment insurance

3. The employer sends tax deposits to government agencies at regular intervals:

Tax Type	Tax Rate	Paid by Employee (Withholding)	Paid by Employer (Expense)	How Paid
Federal income tax	Based on W-4	✓		EFTPS or Form 8109 (941 oval)
Social security	6.2% of earnings up to $90,000 (2 × 6.2% = 12.4%)	✓	✓	EFTPS or Form 8109 (941 oval)
Medicare	1.45% of total earnings (2 × 1.45% = 2.9%)	✓	✓	EFTPS or Form 8109 (941 oval)
FUTA	6.2% *minus* SUTA rate up to 5.4% (usually 6.2% − 5.4% = .8%) of earnings up to $7,000		✓	EFTPS or Form 8109 (940 oval)

State Income Tax	Based on W-4	✓		Varies by state
SUTA	Varies by state		✓	Varies by state

4. The deposit for FICA and federal income tax is journalized here:

	DATE	DESCRIPTION	POST. REF.	DEBIT	CREDIT	
1	20--					1
2	Date	Emplys' Fed. Inc. Tax Pay.		x x x x x		2
3		Social Security Tax Pay.		x x x x x		3
4		Medicare Tax Pay.		x x x x x		4
5		Cash in Bank			x x x x x	5

GENERAL JOURNAL   PAGE _12_

5. A business is legally required to make various reports to different government agencies at specified time intervals. They report this information on various payroll-related tax forms:

1. Form W-2—Wage and Tax Statement—is filed *annually*. It summarizes each employee's calendar-year earnings and withholdings.
2. Form W-3—Transmittal of Wage and Tax Statements—is filed *annually*. It summarizes the information on the employees' Forms W-2 and is sent along with the Forms W-2.
3. Form 941—Employer's Quarterly Federal Tax Return—is filed *quarterly*. It reports the federal income tax and the FICA tax (for both employee and employer).
4. Form 940—Employer's Annual Federal Unemployment (FUTA) Tax Return—is filed *annually*. It reports the employer's federal unemployment taxes.

Key Terms

Electronic Federal Tax Payment
System (EFTPS)   (p. 351)

Federal Unemployment Tax Act
(FUTA)   (p. 347)

Form 8109   (p. 351)

Form 940   (p. 358)

Form 941   (p. 358)

Form W-2   (p. 357)

Form W-3   (p. 357)

Payroll Tax Expense   (p. 347)

Salaries Expense   (p. 340)

State Unemployment Tax Act
(SUTA)   (p. 347)

unemployment taxes   (p. 347)

Check Your Understanding

1. **Journalizing Payroll Transactions**
   a. In what expense account are employees' earnings often recorded?
   b. List the accounts in which the payroll liabilities for federal income tax and Medicare tax are recorded.

2. **Employer's Payroll Taxes**
   a. Which payroll taxes are expenses to the business?
   b. On what amount are the employer's FICA taxes computed?

3. **Computing Payroll Tax Expense**
   a. How is the employer's share of FICA tax calculated?
   b. The share of both the employer's and employee's FICA tax is calculated using the same percentages, but the amount for each can differ slightly. What causes this?

4. **Journalizing Tax Liabilities**
   a. What is the journal entry to record the FUTA tax expense?
   b. The amount of the FICA tax deposit is twice as much as the employer's FICA tax expense. Why?

5. **Payroll Tax Reports and Forms**
   a. What is the difference between Form 940 and Form 941?
   b. What information does Form W-3 contain?

Apply Key Terms

You are the owner of Accurate Financial Services. You have just been hired by Brad Justice, the owner of a new company called Snack Shack, to help establish a payroll system. As a new business owner, Brad understands the importance of complying with government requirements, but he is concerned that he may not be aware of all of the requirements related to payroll. Using the following key terms, prepare a presentation for Brad describing the government requirements for payroll.

Electronic Federal Tax Payment System (EFTPS)	Form W-2
	Form W-3
Federal Unemployment Tax Act (FUTA)	**Payroll Tax Expense**
	Salaries Expense
Form 8109	State Unemployment Tax Act (SUTA)
Form 940	
Form 941	unemployment taxes

Recording and Paying Payroll Tax Liabilities

Making the Transition from a Manual to a Computerized System

Task	Manual Methods	Computerized Methods
Record and post payroll entries; pay payroll tax liabilities	• Prepare the payroll journal entry based on the payroll register totals. • Post the payroll entries to the general ledger. • Prepare tax liability checks to pay federal, state, and local taxing authorities. • Prepare journal entries to record the payment of the liabilities.	• When the payroll checks are generated, the payroll tax journal entries are automatically prepared and posted.

Peachtree® Q & A

Peachtree Question	Answer
How do I journalize the employer's tax liabilities?	• When payroll checks are issued, Peachtree automatically journalizes the tax liabilities.
How do I pay the payroll tax liabilities?	1. Select **Payments** from the *Tasks* menu. 2. Select the taxing authority ID to be paid. 3. Enter the amount and cash account number. 4. Enter description and general ledger account (tax liability account). 5. Click **Print**.

QuickBooks Q & A

QuickBooks Question	Answer
How do I journalize the employer's tax liabilities?	• When payroll checks are issued, QuickBooks Payroll service automatically journalizes the liabilities.
How do I pay the payroll tax liabilities?	1. Select **Process Payroll Liabilities** from the *Employees* menu, and then select **Pay Payroll Liabilities**. 2. Enter the date range for the liabilities you want to pay, and click **OK**. 3. In the Pay by Check tab, enter the bank account and the check date, and then mark the items to be paid. 4. Click **Create**.

For detailed instructions, see your Glencoe Accounting Chapter Study Guides and Working Papers.

SPREADSHEET SMART GUIDE

Step–by–Step Instructions: Problem 13–6

1. Select the spreadsheet template for Problem 13–6.
2. Enter your name and the date in the spaces provided on the template.
3. Complete the spreadsheet using the instructions in your working papers.
4. Print the spreadsheet and proof your work.
5. Complete the Analyze activity.
6. Save your work and exit the spreadsheet program.

Peachtree®

SMART GUIDE

Step–by–Step Instructions: Problem 13–7

1. Select the problem set for Kits & Pups Grooming (Prob. 13–7).
2. Rename the company and set the system date.
3. Record the payroll entry using the **General Journal Entry** option.
4. Print a General Journal report and a General Ledger report.
5. Proof your work.
6. Complete the Analyze activity.
7. End the session.

Problem 13–6 Calculating Employer's Payroll Taxes

Instructions For each of the total gross earnings amounts recorded in the past five pay weeks for Hot Suds Car Wash, determine these taxes:

- employer's FICA taxes (social security 6.2%, Medicare 1.45%)
- federal unemployment tax (.8%)
- state unemployment tax (5.4%)

Use the form provided in the working papers. None of the employees has reached the taxable earnings limit.

Total gross earnings:

1. $914.80
2. $1,113.73
3. $2,201.38
4. $791.02
5. $1,245.75

Analyze Explain the relationship between federal and state unemployment tax rates.

Problem 13–7 Recording the Payment of the Payroll

The totals of the payroll register for Kits & Pups Grooming are shown in your working papers. On December 31 the owner, Abe Shultz, wrote Check 1400 to pay the payroll.

Instructions In your working papers:

1. Record the payroll entry in the general journal.
2. Post the entry to the general ledger accounts.

Analyze Identify the payroll liability account that has the largest credit entry.

Problem 13–8 Journalizing Payroll Transactions

The Outback Guide Service payroll register for the week ending Dec. 31 follows:

PAYROLL REGISTER

PAY PERIOD ENDING Dec. 31 _____ 20 -- _____   DATE OF PAYMENT Dec. 31, 20--

	EMPLOYEE NUMBER	NAME	MAR. STATUS	ALLOW.	TOTAL HOURS	RATE	EARNINGS REGULAR	EARNINGS OVERTIME	EARNINGS TOTAL	SOC. SEC. TAX	MEDICARE TAX	FED. INC. TAX	STATE INC. TAX	HOSP. INS.	OTHER	TOTAL	NET PAY	CK. NO.	
1	31	Coleman, Clarence	M	1	41	7.60	304 00	11 40	315 40	19 55	4 57	21 00	6 31			51 43	263 97		1
2	28	Lorman, Victoria	S	1	30	8.00	240 00		240 00	14 88	3 48	21 00	4 80		(UD)5 40	49 56	190 44		2
3	33	Peterson, Peg	S	1	38	7.25	275 50		275 50	17 08	3 99	26 00	5 51			52 58	222 92		3
4	35	Torrez, Joyce	M	2	36	7.25	261 00		261 00	16 18	3 78	6 00	5 22		(UD)5 40	36 58	224 42		4
24																			24
25																			25
		TOTALS					1,080 50	11 40	1,091 90	67 69	15 82	74 00	21 84	—	10 80	190 15	901 75		

Other Deductions: Write the appropriate code letter to the left of the amount: B–U.S. Savings Bonds; C–Credit Union; UD–Union Dues; UW–United Way.

Instructions In your working papers:

1. Record the entry for the payment of the payroll on page 15 of the general journal. (Check 1201, dated Dec. 31).
2. Use the information in the payroll register to compute the employer's payroll taxes:

   - FICA taxes (6.2% for social security, 1.45% for Medicare)
   - federal unemployment tax (0.8%)
   - state unemployment tax (5.4%)

   None of the employees has reached the taxable earnings limit.

3. Record the entry for the employer's payroll taxes on page 15 of the general journal.

Analyze Examine the entry recording the payment of payroll. Which account, **Social Security Tax Payable** or **Employees' Federal Income Tax Payable**, had the larger credit?

Problem 13–9 Recording and Posting Payroll Transactions

Showbiz Video completed the following payroll transactions during the first two weeks of December. Showbiz Video pays its employees on a biweekly basis (every two weeks).

Instructions In your working papers:

1. Record the December 13 transactions on page 38 in the general journal.
2. Post both payroll entries to the appropriate general ledger accounts.
3. Journalize and post the December 16 transactions.

Date	Transactions
Dec. 13	Wrote Check 2206 to pay the payroll of $3,840.58 (gross earnings) for the pay period ending December 13. The following amounts were withheld: FICA taxes, $238.12 for social security and $55.69 for Medicare; employees' federal income taxes, $639.00; employees' state income taxes, $96.02; insurance premium, $21.00; U.S. savings bonds, $20.00.
13	Recorded the employer's payroll taxes (FICA tax rates, 6.2% for social security and 1.45% for Medicare; federal unemployment tax rate, 0.8%; state unemployment tax rate, 5.4%). No employee has reached the maximum taxable amount.
16	Paid the amounts owed to the federal government for employees' federal income taxes and FICA taxes, Check 2215.
16	Purchased U.S. savings bonds for employees for $100.00, Check 2216.

CONTINUE

Peachtree®

SMART GUIDE

Step–by–Step Instructions: Problem 13–8

1. Select the problem set for Outback Guide Service (Prob. 13–8).
2. Rename the company and set the system date.
3. Record the payment of the payroll and the employer's payroll taxes.
4. Print a General Journal and a General Ledger report.
5. Proof your work.
6. Complete the Analyze activity.
7. End the session.

QuickBooks

PROBLEM GUIDE

Step–by–Step Instructions: Problem 13–8

1. Restore the Problem 13-8.QBB file.
2. Enter the payroll transactions using **Make General Journal Entries** and **Write Checks** options.
3. Print a Journal report and a General Ledger report.
4. Proof your work.
5. Complete the Analyze activity.
6. Back up your work.

SOURCE DOCUMENT PROBLEM

Problem 13–9

Use the source documents in your working papers to complete this problem.

Date	Transactions (cont.)
16	Paid $148.00 to American Insurance Company for employees' insurance, Check 2217.

Analyze **Identify the payroll accounts that have a balance after entries have been posted.**

Peachtree®

SMART GUIDE

Step–by–Step Instructions: Problem 13–9

1. Select the problem set for Showbiz Video (Prob. 13–9).
2. Rename the company and set the system date.
3. Record the transactions.
4. Print a General Journal report and a General Ledger report.
5. Proof your work.
6. Complete the Analyze activity.
7. End the session.

QuickBooks

PROBLEM GUIDE

Step–by–Step Instructions: Problem 13–9

1. Restore the Problem 13-9.QBB file.
2. Enter the payroll transactions.
3. Print a Journal and a General Ledger report.
4. Complete the Analyze activity.
5. Back up your work.

Peachtree®

SMART GUIDE

Step–by–Step Instructions: Problem 13–10

1. Select the problem set for Job Connect (Prob. 13–10).
2. Rename the company and set the system date.
3. Record all transactions.
4. Print a General Journal report and a General Ledger report.
5. Proof your work.
6. Manually prepare Form 8109.
7. Complete the Analyze activity.
8. End the session.

CHALLENGE PROBLEM

Problem 13–10 Recording and Posting Payroll Transactions

Job Connect pays its employees twice a month. Employee earnings and tax amounts for the pay period ending December 31 are:

Gross earnings	$12,543.40
Social security tax	777.69
Medicare tax	181.88
Employees' federal income tax	662.00
Employees' state income tax	250.87

Instructions In your working papers:

1. Prepare Check 1602 (payable to "Job Connect Payroll Account") to transfer the net pay amount to the payroll checking account.
2. On page 19 of the general journal, record the payment of the payroll.
3. Post the payroll transaction to the general ledger.
4. Compute payroll tax expense forms and journalize the entry to record employer's payroll taxes using these rates:

   - social security, 6.2%
   - state unemployment, 5.4%
   - Medicare, 1.45%
   - federal unemployment, 0.8%

   No employee has reached the taxable earnings limit.
5. Post the entry to the general journal.
6. Prepare checks dated December 31 to pay the following payroll liabilities:
   (a) Federal unemployment taxes, payable to First City Bank (Check 1603).
   (b) State unemployment taxes, payable to the State of North Carolina (Check 1604).
   (c) Employees' federal income taxes and FICA taxes, payable to First City Bank (Check 1605).
7. Journalize and post the entries for the payment of the payroll liabilities.
8. Complete payroll tax expense forms. Prepare a Form 8109 for each of the two federal tax deposits paid in Instruction 6, parts (a) and (c). The oval for FICA and federal income tax is 941. The oval for the federal unemployment tax is 940.

Analyze **Calculate the employer's total payroll-related expense for the pay period.**

Practice your test-taking skills! The questions on this page are reprinted with permission from national organizations:
- Future Business Leaders of America
- Business Professionals of America

Use a separate sheet of paper to record your answers.

Future Business Leaders of America

MULTIPLE CHOICE

1. When a semimonthly payroll is paid, the credit to Cash is equal to the
- a. total earnings of all employees.
- b. total deductions for income tax and social security tax.
- c. total deductions.
- d. net pay for all employees.

2. The form that accompanies the payment of taxes to the federal government is a
- a. Form W-2.
- b. Form 8109.
- c. Form 940.
- d. Form 941.

Business Professionals of America

MULTIPLE CHOICE

3. The account *payroll taxes expense* is used for
- a. recording employees' federal income taxes withheld.
- b. recording employees' social security and Medicare taxes.
- c. recording the employer's social security and Medicare taxes.
- d. recording the employer's social security, Medicare, FUTA, and SUTA taxes.

4. Until the amounts withheld from employee salaries are paid by the employer, they are recorded as
- a. assets.
- b. liabilities.
- c. salary expense.
- d. revenue.

5. The accounting document that provides a basis for recording payroll transactions is
- a. the payroll register.
- b. the employee earnings records.
- c. the general ledger.
- d. the general journal.

Need More Help?

Go to glencoeaccounting.glencoe.com and click on Student Center. Click on Winning Competitive Events and select Chapter 13.
- **Practice Questions and Test-Taking Tips**
- **Concept Capsules and Terminology**

CRITICAL Thinking

Payroll Records and Reports

1. When employees are paid, what amount is credited to **Cash in Bank**?
2. Why do employees' paycheck deductions become liabilities of the business?
3. Suppose that a business is located in a state that has an income tax. The business allows employees to take deductions for U.S. savings bonds. List the payroll liability accounts this business would have.
4. Predict what might happen to the **Social Security Tax Payable** account balance if the **Salaries Expense** entry was posted but the **Payroll Tax Expense** entry was never posted.
5. Design a diagram that shows FICA taxes from the payroll date through the tax deposit date.
6. Employers must deposit payroll taxes before they file the payroll tax returns. Do you agree with this practice? Why or why not?

CASE STUDY

Payroll: Warehousing Center

Morrison Distribution Center offers warehousing services. The company is considering adding a third shift with 12 new employees. Estimate the third shift payroll costs assuming: **(1)** The average warehouse employee earns $21,000 per year. **(2)** The state unemployment tax rate is 5.4% and the federal rate is 0.8% (both apply to the first $7,000 of earnings). **(3)** The employer's cost of health insurance averages 22% of an employee's earnings.

INSTRUCTIONS

1. Calculate the salary expense related to adding the 12 new employees.
2. Compute the additional payroll taxes Morrison will pay.
3. Determine the total cost to add the third shift.

a matter of ETHICS

Money Shuffling

Suppose that you are an accounting clerk at Cybercafé. The business owner wants you to use employees' 401(k) withholdings to pay off a pressing debt. She believes she can replace the funds within two months and that the employees will not lose very much by not having their money invested during that time.

ETHICAL DECISION MAKING

1. What are the ethical issues?
2. What are the alternatives?
3. Who are the affected parties?
4. How do the alternatives affect the parties?
5. What would you do?

COMMUNICATING ACCOUNTING

Public Speaking

As the senior payroll clerk for Fashion Square Gift Shop, you are to explain the deductions from employees' payroll checks at a new employee orientation.

1. Prepare an outline and visuals of the items you need to discuss.
2. Pair with a classmate and give your presentations to each other. Focus on both verbal and nonverbal communication skills (eye contact, gestures, and facial expressions). Give each other feedback and suggestions for improvements.

SKILLS BEYOND NUMBERS

Self-Management

People with self-management skills can set attainable goals and motivate themselves.

ON THE JOB

As a payroll clerk, you process all payroll and tax reports. It is December. What do you need to do now to make sure you process the payroll tax reports on time?

INSTRUCTIONS

Describe the reports you will need to file, and name the payroll records you will need to complete each one.

INTERNATIONAL ACCOUNTING

Cultural Values of Employees

Dutch sociologist Geert Hofstede interviewed thousands of employees worldwide to understand their cultures and values. One value dimension he studied was *individualism*—emphasis on the individual and individual achievement. He found that individualism is important in the United States, where workers prefer to work independently and do not expect organizations to take care of them. In Latin American countries like Mexico, employees value group experience, expect close supervision, and want their company to take care of their interests.

INSTRUCTIONS Discuss these differences found by Hofstede.

Making It **Personal**

Your Payroll Deductions

You may have wondered how your employer pays the taxes and other deductions from your paycheck.

PERSONAL FINANCE ACTIVITY Ask your friends what deductions are taken from their paychecks (categories, not amounts). Identify the forms related to the deductions and write a brief report about the deductions and forms.

PERSONAL FINANCE ONLINE Log on to **glencoeaccounting.glencoe.com** and click on **Student Center.** Click on **Making It Personal** and select **Chapter 13.**

Analyzing FINANCIAL Reports

Employee Costs

Employee benefits might include paid vacations and health insurance. Many employers calculate the cost of benefits as a percentage of total salaries.

INSTRUCTIONS Use the payroll register on page 320 and payroll tax information in this chapter to answer these questions.

1. If the employee benefits cost 24% of employee regular earnings, what is the benefits cost for this salary period?

2. If a new employee is to be hired for a 40-hour work week at wages of $8 an hour, what would be the total weekly cost for the new employee? (The company estimates its employee benefits cost at 22%.)

Tax Obligations

As you explore different ways of compensating employees, remember that taxes still apply. Visit **glencoeaccounting .glencoe.com** and click on **Student Center.** Click on **WebQuest** and select **Unit 3** to continue your Internet project.

Payroll Accounting

Main Task

▶ Prepare the weekly payroll for Green Thumb Plant Service.

Summary of Steps

▶ Calculate gross earnings, deductions, and net pay.

▶ Prepare the payroll register.

▶ Write paychecks for the employees.

▶ Enter information on employee's earnings records.

▶ Journalize and post the payroll transaction.

▶ Calculate, journalize, and post the employer's payroll tax liability.

▶ Make the payroll tax deposit.

▶ Journalize and post the payroll tax deposit.

▶ Pay the insurance premium, and journalize and post the entry.

Why It's Important

▶ Payroll is a basic cost of doing business.

Green Thumb Plant Service

Company Background: Green Thumb Plant Service is a plant maintenance company that is located in Kingsbury, Michigan. It is a service business that is organized as a sole proprietorship. It is owned and operated by Joanna Ecke. The company places and maintains plants, flowers, and small trees in offices and corporate buildings.

The business has been in operation for almost five years. During that time its revenue has increased each year, additional employees have been hired, and the business is now showing a good profit.

Payroll Information: The business presently employs eight people. A Form W-4 is on file for each employee. The list that follows summarizes the data on those documents.

Michael Alter	Single	claims 1 exemption
Christine Cuddy	Single	claims 0 exemptions
Jesse Dubow	Single	claims 0 exemptions
Joclyn Filley	Single	claims 1 exemption
Greg Millette	Married	claims 2 exemptions
Heather Repicky	Married	claims 3 exemptions
Daniel Ripp	Married	claims 2 exemptions
Yourself	Single	claims 1 exemption

The business pays its employees on a weekly basis. Overtime is paid at the rate of 1½ times the regular rate of pay for all hours worked over 40. The weekly pay period runs from Monday through Saturday, with employees being paid on Saturday for the week's work. Because most office buildings are closed on Sunday, the business is also closed.

The employees are paid by one of three methods: hourly rate, salary, or salary plus 10% commission on any new accounts they acquire for the company. The following table lists the employees, the method by which their wages are computed, and other pertinent information. Next, you will find the time cards for the employees who are paid on an hourly basis.

Green Thumb Plant Service (continued)

Complete the project using:	**Manual** Glencoe Working Papers	OR	**Peachtree Complete Accounting** Software	OR	**QuickBooks** Templates

Employee	Empl. No.	Position	Employee Status	Rate of Pay
Heather Repicky	010	Manager	Full-time	$725.00/weekly salary
Greg Millette	011	Salesperson	Full-time	$450.00/week plus 10% Commission
Jesse Dubow	012	Bookkeeper	Part-time	$250.00/week
Joclyn Filley	013	Supply clerk	Full-time	$7.40/hour
Daniel Ripp	016	Service	Full-time	$8.30/hour
Christine Cuddy	018	Service	Full-time	$8.30/hour
Michael Alter	019	Supply clerk	Part-time	$7.10/hour
Yourself	022	Accounting clerk	Part-time	$175.00/week

Peachtree®

SMART GUIDE

Step–by–Step Instructions:
1. Select the problem set for Green Thumb Plant Service (MP–3).
2. Rename the company and set the system date.
3. Enter your name for employee record 022.
4. Record the weekly payroll and print checks for all employees using the **Payroll Entry** option.
5. Print a Payroll Register for the current week and proof your work.
6. Print a Payroll Journal report.
7. Calculate and record the employer's payroll tax expense using the **General Journal Entry** option.
8. Record the deposit for the taxes owed to the federal government and enter the monthly insurance premium using the **General Journal Entry** option.
9. Manually complete Form 8109.
10. Print a General Journal report and proof your work.
11. Print a General Ledger report.
12. Print Quarterly Earnings reports for Michael Alter and Greg Millette.
13. Complete the Analyze activity and complete the Audit Test.
14. End the session.

The time cards for the hourly-rate employees are shown here.

NO. __019__
NAME __Michael Alter__
SOC. SEC. NO. __049-XX-XXXX__
WEEK ENDING __7/25/20--__

DAY	IN	OUT	IN	OUT	IN	OUT	TOTAL
M			2:00	5:00			
T			2:00	6:00			
W			3:00	5:00			
Th			2:00	6:00			
F			2:00	6:00			
S			9:00	2:00			
S							

NO. __018__
NAME __Christine Cuddy__
SOC. SEC. NO. __223-XX-XXXX__
WEEK ENDING __7/25/20--__

DAY	IN	OUT	IN	OUT	IN	OUT	TOTAL
M	9:00	12:00	12;30	5:00			
T	9:00	11:30	12:00	5:00			
W	9:00	1:00					
Th	9:00	12:00	12:30	4:00			
F	8:30	1:00	1:30	3:00			
S	9:00	1:30					
S							

NO. __013__
NAME __Joclyn Filley__
SOC. SEC. NO. __042-XX-XXXX__
WEEK ENDING __7/25/20--__

	DAY	IN	OUT	IN	OUT	IN	OUT	TOTAL
SIGN.	M	9:00	12:00	1:00	3:00			
	T	9:00	12:00	1:00	5:00			
	W	8:00	12:00	1:00	5:00			
	Th	9:00	12:00	1:00	3:30			
	F	9:00	12:00	1:00	4:00			
	S	9:00	12:00					
	S							

	HOURS	RATE	AMOUNT
TOTAL HOURS			
REGULAR			
OVERTIME			
TOTAL EARNINGS			

SIGNATURE_____ DATE_____

NO. __016__
NAME __Daniel Ripp__
SOC. SEC. NO. __011-XX-XXXX__
WEEK ENDING __7/25/20--__

	DAY	IN	OUT	IN	OUT	IN	OUT	TOTAL
SIGN.	M	9:00	12:00	12:30	5:00			
	T	9:00	12:30	1:00	6:00			
	W	9:00	12:00	1:00	4:30			
	Th	8:30	12:30	1:00	5:00			
	F	9:00	11:30	12:00	5:00			
	S	9:00	1:00					
	S							

	HOURS	RATE	AMOUNT
TOTAL HOURS			
REGULAR			
OVERTIME			
TOTAL EARNINGS			

SIGNATURE_____ DATE_____

Use the federal tax tables in the working papers to determine federal income tax withholding. These are the rates for other taxes: state income tax, 2%; FICA (employee and employer contributions) social security tax, 6.2% and Medicare tax, 1.45%; state unemployment tax, 5.4%; and federal unemployment tax, 0.8%.

QuickBooks

PROBLEM GUIDE

Step–by–Step Instructions:
1. Restore the Mini Practice Set 3.QBB file.
2. Enter your name in the Employee List.
3. Record the weekly payroll using the **Pay Employees** option and print the checks for all employees using the **Write Checks** option.
4. Print paychecks and an Employee Earnings Summary report.
5. Calculate and record the employer's payroll tax expense using the **Make General Journal Entries** option.
6. Record the deposit for the taxes owed to the federal government, and enter the monthly insurance premium using the **Write Checks** option.
7. Manually complete Form 8109.
8. Print a Journal report for July 21–25 and proof your work.
9. Print a General Ledger report.
10. Print a Payroll Summary report.
11. Complete the Analyze activity using the Profit & Loss Standard and Journal reports, and complete the Audit Test.
12. Back up your work.

YOUR JOB RESPONSIBILITIES
Green Thumb Plant Service

The business entered the third quarter of its fiscal year at the beginning of July. It is presently the last week of July. Jesse Dubow, the bookkeeper, is leaving on vacation. In his absence you are to prepare this week's payroll.

(1) Complete the timecards for the four hourly employees. Enter the total hours worked at the bottom of each card. Complete each timecard to the nearest quarter hour.

(2) Greg Millette recorded additional clients that brought in $925.00 in new business. Calculate his commission and add it to his salary to determine his gross earnings.

(3) Enter the payroll information for all employees in the payroll register. Each employee was recently assigned an employee number because the business is soon converting to an automated payroll preparation system. Since this payroll is being prepared manually, list the employees in the payroll register in alphabetical order by last name.

(4) Use the following information to complete the payroll register.
  (a) Use the federal tax chart to determine income tax amounts to be withheld.
  (b) Michael Alter, Christine Cuddy, Joclyn Filley, and Greg Millette each have $5.00 deducted for the purchase of U.S. savings bonds.

(c) Jesse Dubow, Heather Repicky, and Daniel Ripp each have $4.00 deducted for donations to the United Way.

(d) All employees pay an insurance premium each week. Married employees pay $9.00 and single employees pay $6.00.

(e) None of Green Thumb's employees has reached the maximum taxable amount for the social security tax.

(5) Calculate the net pay for each employee.

(6) Total all amount columns in the payroll register. Prove the accuracy of the totals.

(7) Write Check 972 for the amount of the total net pay on the regular checking account of the business. Make the check payable to the Green Thumb Plant Service—Payroll Account. In Jesse's absence Joanna Ecke will sign the check for you. Complete the deposit slip for the payroll account.

(8) Record the payroll transaction in the general journal, page 21. Use the information contained in the payroll register and Check 972 as the source documents. Post the transaction to the general ledger accounts.

(9) Write the paychecks for the employees. Use the information in the payroll register to complete the check stubs. After a check has been written for an employee, enter the check number in the payroll register.

Green Thumb Plant Service (continued)

(10) Enter this week's payroll information on the employee's earnings records for Michael Alter and Greg Millette only. Be sure to add the current gross earnings amount to the accumulated total.

(11) Calculate and record the employer's taxes for this pay period in the general journal. The source of information is the payroll register. Post the journal entry to the general ledger.

(12) Make a deposit for the taxes owed to the federal government. The total includes the amounts withheld for employees' federal income tax, social security tax, and Medicare tax. Complete Form 8109 by entering the amount owed. Write Check 973, payable to the First Federal Bank for the taxes.

(13) Enter the transaction in the general journal and post the entry to the general ledger.

(14) Pay the monthly insurance premium by writing Check 974 to the American Insurance Company for $228.00. Record the payment in the general journal and post the entry to the general ledger.

Analyze Identify the pay method that had the highest employee gross earnings this week.

The Accounting Cycle for a Merchandising Corporation

STANDARD &POOR'S

Personal Finance Q & A

Q: Why is learning about merchandising corporations important to me?

A: Most of the things you buy are probably purchased at merchandising corporations. Learning about these businesses can help you make wise consumer decisions.

Q: Where can I find financial information about these corporations?

A: The financial sections of newspapers and magazines often have information about well-known corporations.

THINK IT OVER

Name several large merchandising corporations. What are some of the most popular items sold at each company?

WebQuest Internet Project

Cyber-Shopping

Online shopping is a growing business with more than $100 million in annual sales. Consumers shop online for convenience and sometimes out of necessity. Because of their remote locations, people in Hawaii and Alaska make the most Internet purchases. In this project you will learn how to shop safely online.

Log on to **glencoeaccounting.glencoe.com** and click on **Student Center.** Click on **WebQuest** and select **Unit 4.** Begin your WebQuest by reading the Task.

Continue working on your WebQuest as you study Unit 4.

Chapter	14	16	18	20	21
Page	413	479	549	611	637

BusinessWeek THE BIG PICTURE

HAPPY HOL-E-DAYS Some 54% of Americans will use the Web to find holiday gifts. Here is what they will do online:

COMPARE PRICES	66%
BROWSE FOR GIFT IDEAS	62%
PURCHASE PRESENTS	57%
SEND CARDS OR PHOTOS	42%

Data: American Express Retail Index *Source:* Reprinted by permission from *BusinessWeek.*

Accounting for Sales and Cash Receipts

What You'll Learn

1. Explain the difference between a service business and a merchandising business.

2. Analyze transactions relating to the sale of merchandise.

3. Explain the difference between a retailer and a wholesaler.

4. Record a variety of sales and cash receipt transactions in a general journal.

5. Define the accounting terms introduced in this chapter.

Why It's Important

▶ As a consumer, you have frequent contact with merchandising businesses.

Predict

1. What does the chapter title tell you?
2. What do you already know about this subject from personal experience?
3. What have you learned about this in the earlier chapters?
4. What gaps exist in your knowledge of this subject?

Exploring the *Real World* of Business

ANALYZING SALES

Underground Station

If you are looking for the latest in urban-savvy footwear, **Underground Station** has you covered. From Puma to Fila, Phat Farm to GBX, this store has the brands that can take you from the basketball court to the dance floor.

Until recently **Underground Station** retail stores were found exclusively in malls. This changed with the grand opening of a large "street store" in the main shopping district in the heart of Brooklyn, New York. With the popularity of the brands it carries, **Underground Station** thinks the new sales strategy will be a good fit.

Underground Station wants to attract more women shoppers in the coming years. The company hopes that a new advertising campaign and more cutting-edge buyers in the shoe division will do the trick.

What Do You Think?

When shoppers purchase shoes at **Underground Station**, what general ledger accounts do you think are affected?

Working in the *Real World*

APPLYING YOUR ACCOUNTING KNOWLEDGE

Making sales is key to the financial success of a business. Sales dollars come from selling products or services to customers. Companies like Underground Station, Target, and Foot Locker buy merchandise and sell it to customers. Accurate tracking of sales transactions helps these businesses decide what merchandise to offer. Journalizing cash receipts is an essential part of recording sales revenue.

Personal Connection

1. Does your work or the work of friends or family involve selling merchandise?
2. What information from these sales do you think should be recorded in the accounting records?

Online Connection

Go to **glencoeaccounting.glencoe.com** and click on **Student Center.** Click on **Working in the Real World** and select **Chapter 14.**

Accounting for a Merchandising Business

Before You Read

Main Idea
A *wholesaler* sells to retailers, and a *retailer* sells to the final users.

Read to Learn...
➤ the operating cycle for a merchandising business. (p. 380)
➤ the accounts used in a merchandising business. (p. 382)
➤ issues relating to international sales. (p. 382)

Key Terms
retailer
wholesaler
merchandise
inventory
Sales

As you remember, a service business is one that provides a service to the public for a fee. In contrast a merchandising business buys goods (such as computers, clothing, and furniture) and then sells those goods to customers for a profit. You're probably familiar with merchandising businesses like Tower Records or Wal-Mart. Most merchandising businesses operate either as retailers or as wholesalers. Some merchandising businesses are both retailers and wholesalers. A **retailer** is a business that sells to the final user, that is, to you—the consumer. A **wholesaler** is a business that sells to retailers. In this chapter we will analyze transactions relating to the sale of merchandise for On Your Mark Athletic Wear, a retailer. Refer to the chart of accounts for On Your Mark Athletic Wear.

The Operating Cycle of a Merchandising Business

How Is the Operating Cycle Different from the Accounting Cycle?

Recall that the accounting cycle is a series of tasks performed in a single period to maintain records. The merchandising business *operating cycle* is a series of transactions, as illustrated in **Figure 14–1.**

The collection of cash from sales enables the business to purchase more items to sell, pay expenses, and make a profit. As long as the company is in business, this is a continuous, repeating sequence.

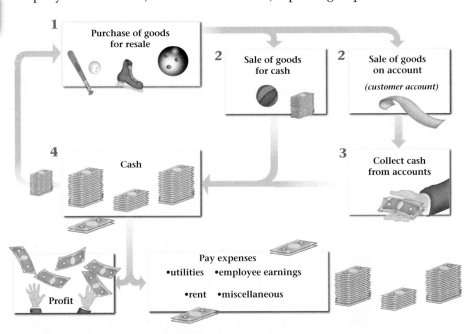

Figure 14–1 The Operating Cycle for a Merchandising Business

ON YOUR MARK
ATHLETIC WEAR
595 Leslie Street, Dallas, TX 75207

CHART OF ACCOUNTS

ASSETS

101 Cash in Bank
105 Change Fund
110 Petty Cash Fund
115 Accounts Receivable
117 Allowance for Uncollectible Accounts
118 Notes Receivable
120 Interest Receivable
125 Merchandise Inventory

130 Supplies
135 Prepaid Insurance
140 Delivery Equipment
142 Accumulated Depreciation—Delivery Equipment
145 Office Equipment
147 Accumulated Depreciation—Office Equipment
150 Store Equipment
152 Accumulated Depreciation—Store Equipment

LIABILITIES

201 Accounts Payable
202 Notes Payable
203 Discount on Notes Payable
204 Federal Corporate Income Tax Payable
205 Employees' Federal Income Tax Payable
211 Employees' State Income Tax Payable

212 Social Security Tax Payable
213 Medicare Tax Payable
214 Federal Unemployment Tax Payable
215 State Unemployment Tax Payable
220 Sales Tax Payable

STOCKHOLDERS' EQUITY

301 Capital Stock
305 Retained Earnings

310 Income Summary

REVENUE

401 Sales
405 Sales Discounts

410 Sales Returns and Allowances
415 Interest Income

COST OF MERCHANDISE

501 Purchases
505 Transportation In

510 Purchases Discounts
515 Purchases Returns and Allowances

EXPENSES

601 Advertising Expense
605 Bankcard Fees Expense
610 Cash Short and Over
612 Delivery Expense
615 Depreciation Expense—Delivery Equipment
620 Depreciation Expense—Office Equipment
625 Depreciation Expense—Store Equipment
630 Federal Corporate Income Tax Expense
635 Insurance Expense
640 Interest Expense

645 Loss/Gain on Disposal of Plant Assets
650 Maintenance Expense
655 Miscellaneous Expense
657 Payroll Tax Expense
660 Rent Expense
665 Salaries Expense
670 Supplies Expense
675 Uncollectible Accounts Expense
680 Utilities Expense

▶ Accounts Receivable Subsidiary Ledger		▶ Accounts Payable Subsidiary Ledger	
BRE	Break Point Sports Club	CHA	Champion Store Supply
DIM	Dimaio, Joe	COM	Computer Solutions
GAL	Galvin, Robert	DAR	Dara's Delivery Service
KLE	Klein, Casey	FAS	FastLane Athletics
MON	Montero, Anita	GEA	Geary Office Supply
RAH	Rahim, Shashi	PRO	Pro Runner Warehouse
RAM	Ramos, Gabriel	SLF	Sports Link Footwear
SOU	South Branch High School Athletics	SNS	Sports Nutrition Supply
SUL	Sullivan, Megan		
TAM	Tammy's Fitness Club		
WON	Wong, Kim		
YOU	Young, Lara		

As You READ

Compare and Contrast

Merchandise Inventory and Sales Accounts
How are the two accounts, **Merchandise Inventory** and **Sales**, similar? How are they different?

Accounts Used by a Merchandising Business

What Accounts Does a Merchandising Business Use?

A merchandising business buys goods from a wholesaler or a manufacturing business and then sells these goods to its customers. Goods bought for resale are called merchandise . The items of merchandise the business has in stock are referred to as inventory .

Merchandise Inventory Account

The inventory of a business is represented in the general ledger by the asset account **Merchandise Inventory.** Increases to **Merchandise Inventory** are recorded as debits, and decreases are recorded as credits. The normal balance of the **Merchandise Inventory** account is a debit. At the beginning of each period, the dollar amount of merchandise in stock is indicated by the debit balance in **Merchandise Inventory.**

During the operating cycle, the business sells merchandise that is in stock and purchases new items to replace the inventory sold. The sale of merchandise and the purchase of new merchandise are recorded in separate accounts.

Merchandise Inventory	
Debit + Increase Side Normal Balance	Credit − Decrease Side

Sales	
Debit − Decrease Side	Credit + Increase Side Normal Balance

Sales Account

When a retail merchandising business sells goods to a customer, the amount of the merchandise sold is recorded in the **Sales** account. **Sales** is a revenue account. Increases to the **Sales** account are recorded as credits, and decreases are recorded as debits. The normal balance of the **Sales** account is a credit. Both cash sales and sales on account are recorded as credits to the **Sales** account.

Sales on account affect the **Accounts Receivable** account, and cash sales affect the **Cash in Bank** account.

International Sales

What Challenges Face a Company That Has International Sales?

When companies have sales transactions on an international level, many complexities arise. The obligations and rights of each party to the sale extend across borders and into different sets of legal requirements.

The *United Nations Convention on Contracts for the International Sales of Goods (CISG)* was created to provide guidelines and laws governing the international sale of goods. While "The Convention" does not cover sales of all goods, it governs most business-to-business transactions.

International sales also introduce the challenge of multiple currencies. Which currency will be used for the transaction? How will currency exchange rates affect revenue? These are just a few considerations that must be examined when conducting international sales.

Assessment

Reinforce the Main Idea

Create a table similar to this one to describe service businesses and merchandising businesses.

Business Type	What is Sold?	Who is the Customer?
Service		
Retailer		
Wholesaler		

Do the Math

Alpine Outfitters estimates the annual cost of maintaining merchandise inventory to be 10% of the inventory value. Alpine's accountants are preparing a budget for the coming year, and they plan to maintain an inventory valued at $1.5 million. Answer the following questions:

1. What is the estimated cost of maintaining the inventory?
2. If the inventory was valued at $2 million, and the estimated rate of maintenance was 11%, what would be the estimated annual maintenance cost?

Problem 14–1 Recording Merchandising Transactions

Instructions Record the following transactions in T-account form in your working papers for Sharp Shot Camera Shop. A partial chart of accounts follows:

General Ledger
Cash in Bank
Accounts Receivable
Merchandise Inventory
Accounts Payable
Sales

Date	Transactions
Apr. 4	Sold 10 Canon cameras on account for $3,000, Sales Slip 224.
10	Sold 2 dozen photo albums for $150, cash, Sales Slip 225.
20	Sold 4 rolls of 35mm film for $24 cash, Sales Slip 226.
25	Sold a Canon camera to a customer for $380 cash, Sales Slip 227.

Analyzing Sales Transactions

BEFORE YOU READ

Main Idea
In addition to using the general ledger, a business keeps a subsidiary ledger of individual customer accounts.

Read to Learn...
➤ what a sale on account involves. (p. 384)
➤ the purpose of the accounts receivable subsidiary ledger. (p. 385)
➤ how to journalize sales on account. (p. 386)
➤ how to journalize and post sales returns and allowances. (p. 389)

Key Terms
sale on account
charge customer
credit cards
sales slip
sales tax
credit terms
accounts receivable
  subsidiary ledger
subsidiary ledger
controlling account
sales return
sales allowance
credit memorandum
contra account

In a merchandising business, the most frequent transaction is the sale of merchandise. Some businesses sell on a cash-only basis. Others sell only on credit. Most businesses handle both cash and credit sales.

Sales on Account
What Does a Sale on Account Involve?

The sale of merchandise that will be paid for at a later date is called a **sale on account**, a *charge sale,* or a *credit sale.* The sale on account is made to a **charge customer**; this credit option is also called a *charge account.*

Store Credit Card Sales

Charge customers use **credit cards** issued by a business such as Target to make their purchases. A store credit card, imprinted with the customer's name and account number, facilitates the sale on account.

Nonbank Credit Card Sales

In the next section, you will learn about bank credit cards. We consider nonbank credit cards here because they are similar to a store credit card. A *nonbank credit card* is a credit card issued by corporations such as American Express and Diners Club. Nonbank credit card sales are considered a form of credit sales because payment is collected at a later date.

Items Related to Sales on Account

A charge sale involves a sales slip, which shows the amount of tax charged and the credit terms.

The Sales Slip. A **sales slip** is a form that lists these details: date of the sale; customer account identification; and description, quantity, and price of the item(s) sold.

The description may include the physical details (such as "white athletic socks"), a stock number, or both. A sales slip is usually prepared in multiple copies. The customer receives the original as a receipt and as proof of purchase. The number of copies kept by the business varies with its needs. A copy is always used for accounting purposes as the source document for recording the journal entry.

Prenumbered sales slips help businesses keep track of all sales made on account. On Your Mark uses prenumbered sales slips printed with its name and address. On Your Mark's sales slip is shown in **Figure 14–2.**

Notice that the total amount on the sales slip includes cost of the items sold and *sales tax.*

Sales Tax. Most states and some cities tax the retail sale of goods and services with a **sales tax** . Items subject to sales tax and sales tax rates vary from state to state. The sales tax rate is usually stated as a percentage of the sale, such as 5%. Sales tax rates are determined by the proper taxing authority.

The sales tax is paid by the customer and collected by the business. The business acts as the collection agent for the state or city government. (In the future we will refer only to the state government.) At the time of the sale, the business adds the sales tax to the total selling price of the goods. Periodically, the business sends the collected sales tax to the state. Until the state is paid, however, the sales tax collected from customers represents a liability of the business. The business keeps a record of the sales tax owed to the state in a liability account called **Sales Tax Payable.** For **Sales Tax Payable**, the increase and balance side is a credit and the decrease side is a debit.

Sales Tax Payable	
Debit	Credit
−	+
Decrease Side	Increase Side
	Normal Balance

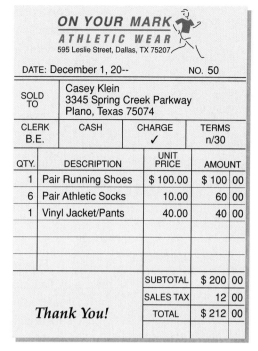

ON YOUR MARK				
ATHLETIC WEAR				
595 Leslie Street, Dallas, TX 75207				

DATE: December 1, 20--   NO. 50

SOLD TO	Casey Klein 3345 Spring Creek Parkway Plano, Texas 75074			
CLERK B.E.	CASH	CHARGE ✓	TERMS n/30	

QTY.	DESCRIPTION	UNIT PRICE	AMOUNT	
1	Pair Running Shoes	$ 100.00	$ 100	00
6	Pair Athletic Socks	10.00	60	00
1	Vinyl Jacket/Pants	40.00	40	00
		SUBTOTAL	$ 200	00
		SALES TAX	12	00
Thank You!		TOTAL	$ 212	00

Figure 14–2 On Your Mark Athletic Wear Sales Slip

To calculate the sales tax, multiply the merchandise subtotal by the sales tax rate (see **Figure 14–2**). Casey Klein bought $200 worth of merchandise. The sales tax rate is 6%. The sales clerk multiplied $200 by 6% (.06) to compute the $12 sales tax. The total transaction amount is $212.

Not all sales of retail merchandise are taxed. In most states, sales to tax-exempt organizations, such as schools, are not taxed. For example, South Branch High School purchased $1,500 worth of merchandise on account. Schools are tax exempt, so no sales tax is added to the amount of the sale.

Credit Terms. The sales slip in **Figure 14–2** has space to indicate the credit terms of the sale. **Credit terms** state the time allowed for payment. The credit terms for the sale to Casey Klein are n/30. The "n" stands for the *net,* or total, amount of the sale. The "30" stands for the number of days the customer has to pay for the merchandise. Casey Klein owes On Your Mark $212 (the net amount) by December 31 (30 days after December 1).

The Accounts Receivable Subsidiary Ledger

What Is a Subsidiary Ledger?

Businesses with few charge customers usually include an Accounts Receivable account for each customer in the general ledger. A large business, however, with many charge customers sets up a separate ledger that contains an account for each charge customer. This ledger is called the **accounts receivable subsidiary ledger** . A **subsidiary ledger** is a ledger, or book, that contains detailed data summarized to a controlling account in the general ledger. For example, the accounts receivable subsidiary ledger contains details of all the individuals and businesses that owe money to a company. Summary information about accounts receivable appears in the **Accounts Receivable** account in the general ledger. **Accounts Receivable** is a

MATH HINTS

Combining Math Functions When combining mathematical functions such as calculating and adding sales tax to a sale amount, keep the order of operations in mind: multiply first, then add.

Compute the transaction amount of a $184 sale of merchandise with a 6% sales tax:
- multiply first ($184.00 × 0.06) = $11.04
- then add ($184.00 + $11.04) = $195.04

controlling account because its balance equals the total of all account balances in the subsidiary ledger. The balance of **Accounts Receivable** thus serves as a control on the accuracy of the balances in the accounts receivable subsidiary ledger after all posting is complete.

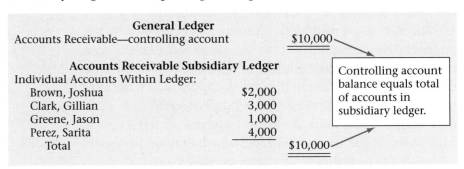

Figure 14–3 shows the accounts receivable subsidiary ledger form used by On Your Mark. The subsidiary ledger account form has lines at the top for the name and address of the customer. In a manual accounting system, subsidiary ledger accounts are arranged in alphabetical order. They are not usually numbered. In a computerized system, however, each charge customer is assigned a specific account number.

Notice that the subsidiary ledger account form has only three amount columns. The Debit and Credit columns are used to record increases and decreases to the customer's account. There is only one Balance column. Since **Accounts Receivable** is an asset account, the normal balance is a debit, so one balance amount is sufficient.

NAME						
ADDRESS						
DATE	DESCRIPTION	POST. REF.	DEBIT	CREDIT	BALANCE	

Figure 14–3 Subsidiary Ledger Account Form

Recording Sales on Account
How Are Sales on Account Recorded?

According to the revenue recognition principle, revenue for a sale on account is recognized and recorded at the time of the sale, when it is earned. Revenue must also be *realizable*, which means that it is expected to be converted to cash. Look at On Your Mark's sale on account to Casey Klein in the next business transaction.

Notice that the debit in the general journal entry is to "Accounts Receivable/Casey Klein." The slash indicates that two accounts are debited: **Accounts Receivable** (controlling) and **Accounts Receivable—Casey Klein** (subsidiary).

As mentioned earlier, when merchandise is sold to tax-exempt organizations, such as school districts, sales tax is not charged. An example of such a transaction follows on page 388.

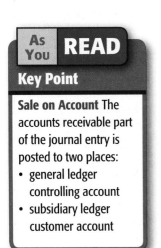

As You READ

Key Point

Sale on Account The accounts receivable part of the journal entry is posted to two places:
- general ledger controlling account
- subsidiary ledger customer account

Business Transaction

On December 1 On Your Mark sold merchandise on account to Casey Klein for $200 plus sales tax of $12, Sales Slip 50.

ON YOUR MARK
ATHLETIC WEAR
595 Leslie Street, Dallas, TX 75207

DATE: December 1, 20--   NO. 50

SOLD TO	Casey Klein 3345 Spring Creek Parkway Plano, Texas 75074		
CLERK B.E.	CASH	CHARGE ✓	TERMS n/30

QTY.	DESCRIPTION	UNIT PRICE	AMOUNT	
1	Pair Running Shoes	$ 100.00	$ 100	00
6	Pair Athletic Socks	10.00	60	00
1	Vinyl Jacket/Pants	40.00	40	00
		SUBTOTAL	$ 200	00
		SALES TAX	12	00
Thank You!		TOTAL	$ 212	00

ANALYSIS *Identify*

1. The accounts affected are **Accounts Receivable** (controlling), **Accounts Receivable–Casey Klein** (subsidiary), **Sales,** and **Sales Tax Payable.**

Classify

2. **Accounts Receivable** (controlling) and **Accounts Receivable–Casey Klein** (subsidiary) are asset accounts. **Sales** is a revenue account. **Sales Tax Payable** is a liability account.

+/−

3. **Accounts Receivable** (controlling) and **Accounts Receivable–Casey Klein** (subsidiary) are increased by the total amount, $212 (the dollar amount of merchandise sold plus sales tax). **Sales** is increased by the dollar amount of merchandise sold, $200. **Sales Tax Payable** is increased by the amount of sales tax charged, $12.

DEBIT-CREDIT RULE

4. Increases to asset accounts are recorded as debits. Debit **Accounts Receivable** (controlling) for $212. Also debit **Accounts Receivable–Casey Klein** (subsidiary) for $212.
5. Increases to revenue and liability accounts are recorded as credits. Credit **Sales** for $200 and **Sales Tax Payable** for $12.

T ACCOUNTS

6.

Accounts Receivable		Sales	
Debit + 212	Credit −	Debit −	Credit + 200

Accounts Receivable Subsidiary Ledger Casey Klein		Sales Tax Payable	
Debit + 212	Credit −	Debit −	Credit + 12

JOURNAL ENTRY

7.

GENERAL JOURNAL   PAGE ___20___

	DATE		DESCRIPTION	POST. REF.	DEBIT	CREDIT	
1	20--						1
2	Dec.	1	Accts. Rec./Casey Klein		212 00		2
3			Sales			200 00	3
4			Sales Tax Payable			12 00	4
5			Sales Slip 50				5

On December 3 On Your Mark sold merchandise on account to South Branch High School Athletics for $1,500, Sales Slip 51.

JOURNAL ENTRY

ON YOUR MARK
ATHLETIC WEAR
595 Leslie Street, Dallas, TX 75207

DATE: December 3, 20--   NO. 51

SOLD TO	South Branch High School Athletics 1750 Rutgers Dr. Dallas, TX 75207

CLERK B.E.	CASH	CHARGE ✓	TERMS 2/10, n/30

QTY.	DESCRIPTION	UNIT PRICE	AMOUNT
15	Baseball Uniforms	$ 40.00	$ 600 00
15	Baseball Caps	20.00	300 00
15	Baseball Mitts	35.00	525 00
2	Baseballs	15.00	30 00
3	Baseball Bats	15.00	45 00
		SUBTOTAL	$ 1,500 00
		SALES TAX	0 00
Thank You!		TOTAL	$ 1,500 00

GENERAL JOURNAL   PAGE 20

	DATE	DESCRIPTION	POST. REF.	DEBIT	CREDIT	
6	3	Accts. Rec./So. Branch H.S.		1 500 00		6
7		Sales			1 500 00	7
8		Sales Slip 51				8
9						9

This transaction is analyzed and recorded in the same manner as the December 1 entry for Casey Klein *except* there is no sales tax. On Your Mark's accountant debits **Accounts Receivable/South Branch High School Athletics** for $1,500 and credits the **Sales** account for $1,500.

Sales Returns and Allowances

All merchandising businesses expect that some customers will be dissatisfied with their purchases. The reasons for dissatisfaction vary. An item may be damaged or defective. The color or size may be incorrect. Whatever the reason, merchants usually allow dissatisfied customers to return merchandise. Any merchandise returned for credit or a cash refund is called a **sales return** .

Sometimes a customer discovers that merchandise is damaged or defective but still usable. When this happens, the merchant may reduce the sales price for the damaged merchandise. A price reduction granted for damaged goods kept by the customer is called a **sales allowance** .

The Credit Memorandum. If the sales return or allowance occurs on a charge sale, the business usually prepares a credit memorandum. A **credit memorandum** lists the details of a sales return or allowance. The charge customer's account is credited (decreased) for the amount of the return or allowance.

Figure 14–4 shows a credit memorandum, or credit memo, used by On Your Mark. The credit memo was prepared when Gabriel Ramos returned merchandise that he bought on account on November 29. Note that the credit memo includes a description of the returned item, the reasons for the return, and the amount to be credited to Gabriel Ramos' account.

On Your Mark's credit memo also includes spaces for the date and sales slip number of the original sale. Notice too that the total on the credit memo includes the sales tax charged on the original sale.

The same form is used if Gabriel Ramos is instead given a sales allowance. Of course, the amount credited to his account would be less. The credit granted for an allowance is the difference between the original sales price and the reduced price.

As You READ

In Your Experience

Sales Returns Have you ever tried to return something you bought? Why did you want to return it? What was the result?

On Your Mark's credit memos are prenumbered and prepared in duplicate. The original is given to the customer. The copy is kept by the business and is the source document used for the journal entry to record the transaction.

The Sales Returns and Allowances Account. Sales returns and allowances decrease the total revenue earned by a business. This decrease, however, is not recorded in the **Sales** account. Instead, a separate account called **Sales Returns and Allowances** is used. **Sales Returns and Allowances** summarizes the total returns and allowances for damaged, defective, or otherwise unsatisfactory merchandise. If the **Sales Returns and Allowances** account balance is large in proportion to the **Sales** account balance, there may be merchandising problems. The **Sales Returns and Allowances** account is carefully analyzed to detect any trouble.

The **Sales Returns and Allowances** account is a contra account. As a contra account, its balance decreases the balance of its related account. **Sales Returns and Allowances** is more specifically classified as a *contra revenue* account because it is related to a revenue account, **Sales**. Since the normal balance side of **Sales** is a credit, the normal balance side of **Sales Returns and Allowances** is a debit. This relationship is shown here:

Sales		Sales Returns and Allowances	
Debit	Credit	Debit	Credit
−	+	+	−
Decrease Side	Increase Side Normal Balance	Increase Side Normal Balance	Decrease Side

CREDIT MEMORANDUM

ON YOUR MARK ATHLETIC WEAR
595 Leslie Street, Dallas, TX 75207

NO. 124

ORIGINAL SALES DATE	ORIGINAL SALES SLIP	APPROVAL	
Nov. 29, 20--	No. 35	J.R.	X MDSE RET

DATE: December 4, 20--

NAME: Gabriel Ramos

ADDRESS: 278 Summit Avenue
Dallas, TX 75206

Gabriel Ramos
CUSTOMER SIGNATURE

QTY	DESCRIPTION	AMOUNT
1	Athletic Suit	$ 150 00

REASON FOR RETURN		
wrong color	SUB TOTAL	$ 150 00
THE TOTAL SHOWN AT THE RIGHT WILL BE CREDITED TO YOUR ACCOUNT.	SALES TAX	9 00
	TOTAL	$ 159 00

Figure 14–4
Credit Memorandum

As You READ

Key Point

Contra Accounts
The normal balance of a contra account is the opposite of its related account.

Cash Refunds

Sometimes a merchant will give a customer a cash refund instead of a credit. On Your Mark's store policy is to give a cash refund only if the original sale was a cash sale. For cash refunds the **Cash in Bank** account is credited instead of **Accounts Receivable**.

Posting to the Accounts Receivable Subsidiary Ledger

How Do You Post to the Accounts Receivable Subsidiary Ledger?

Refer to **Figure 14–5** on page 391. Look at the general journal entry. The credit is to **Accts Rec./Gabriel Ramos.** The slash indicates that both **Accounts Receivable** (controlling) and **Accounts Receivable—Gabriel Ramos** (subsidiary) are

Business Transaction

On December 4 On Your Mark issued Credit Memorandum 124 to Gabriel Ramos for the return of merchandise purchased on account, $150 plus $9 sales tax.

ON YOUR MARK ATHLETIC WEAR 595 Leslie Street, Dallas, TX 75207	CREDIT MEMORANDUM		NO. 124

ORIGINAL SALES DATE	ORIGINAL SALES SLIP	APPROVAL	
Nov. 29, 20--	No. 35	J.R.	☒ MDSE RET

DATE: December 4, 20--

NAME: Gabriel Ramos

ADDRESS: 278 Summit Avenue
Dallas, TX 75206

QTY	DESCRIPTION	AMOUNT
1	Athletic Suit	$ 150 00

Gabriel Ramos
CUSTOMER SIGNATURE

REASON FOR RETURN wrong color	SUB TOTAL	$ 150 00
THE TOTAL SHOWN AT THE RIGHT WILL BE CREDITED TO YOUR ACCOUNT.	SALES TAX	9 00
	TOTAL	$ 159 00

ANALYSIS

Identify

1. The accounts affected are **Accounts Receivable** (controlling), **Accounts Receivable—Gabriel Ramos** (subsidiary), **Sales Returns and Allowances,** and **Sales Tax Payable.**

Classify

2. **Accounts Receivable** (controlling) and **Accounts Receivable—Gabriel Ramos** (subsidiary) are asset accounts. **Sales Returns and Allowances** is a contra revenue account. **Sales Tax Payable** is a liability account.

+/−

3. **Sales Returns and Allowances** is increased by $150. **Sales Tax Payable** is decreased by $9. **Accounts Receivable** (controlling) and **Accounts Receivable—Gabriel Ramos** (subsidiary) are decreased by $159.

DEBIT-CREDIT RULE

4. Increases to a contra revenue account are recorded as debits. Debit **Sales Returns and Allowances** for $150. Decreases to liability accounts are recorded as debits. Debit **Sales Tax Payable** for $9.

5. Decreases to asset accounts are recorded as credits. Credit **Accounts Receivable** (controlling) for $159. Also credit **Accounts Receivable—Gabriel Ramos** (subsidiary) for $159.

T ACCOUNTS

6.

Accounts Receivable		Sales Returns and Allowances	
Debit +	Credit − 159	Debit + 150	Credit −

Accounts Receivable Subsidiary Ledger Gabriel Ramos		Sales Tax Payable	
Debit +	Credit − 159	Debit − 9	Credit +

JOURNAL ENTRY

7.

GENERAL JOURNAL   PAGE 20

	DATE	DESCRIPTION	POST. REF.	DEBIT	CREDIT	
9	4	Sales Returns and Allowances		150 00		9
10		Sales Tax Payable		9 00		10
11		Accts. Rec./Gabriel Ramos			159 00	11
12		Credit Memorandum 124				12
13						13

credited. Notice that a diagonal line is entered in the Post. Ref. column. This diagonal line indicates that the amount, $159, is posted in *two* places: *first* to the **Account Receivable** controlling account in the general ledger and *then* to the **Gabriel Ramos** account in the accounts receivable subsidiary ledger.

After the amount is posted to the Accounts Receivable controlling account, the account number (115) is entered to the *left* of the diagonal line in the Posting Reference column. After the amount is posted to the subsidiary ledger account, Gabriel Ramos, a check mark (✓) is entered to the *right* of the diagonal line.

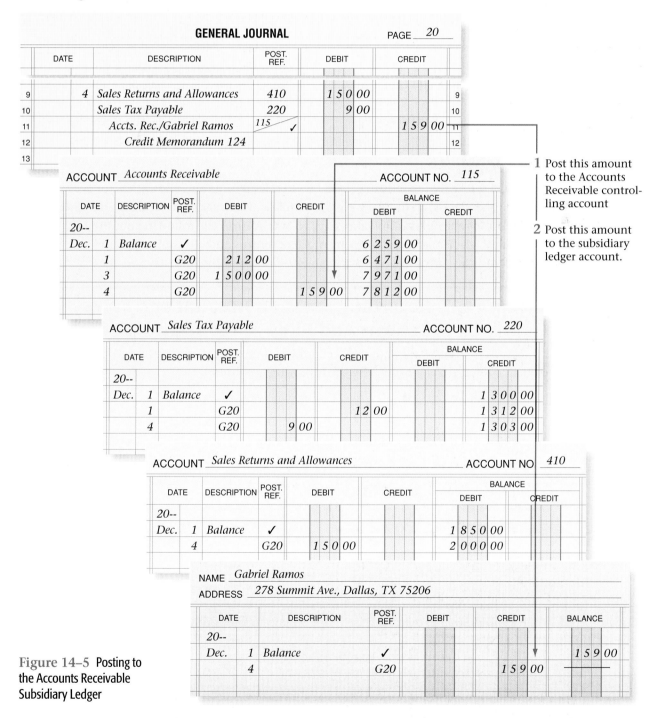

Figure 14–5 Posting to the Accounts Receivable Subsidiary Ledger

AFTER YOU READ

Reinforce the Main Idea

Create a flowchart like this one. Enter labels in the boxes and next to the arrows. Use these terms to create the labels: *general ledger, journal, posted to, recorded in, sales slip, subsidiary ledger*. Terms can be used more than once.

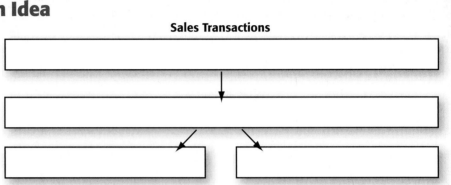

Sales Transactions

Do the Math

Assume the lighting fixture industry has $.065 in sales returns and allowances for every $1.00 in sales (in other words, an industry average of 6.5%). Last year Light House Gallery had sales of $900,000 and returns and allowances of $46,800. Answer the following questions:

1. What was Light House Gallery's percentage of returns and allowances to sales?
2. Is the percentage favorable or unfavorable compared to the industry average?

Problem 14–2 Recording Sales on Account and Sales Returns and Allowances Transactions

Instructions In your working papers, record the following transactions of Alpine Ski Shop on page 2 of the general journal. Use the following accounts:

General Ledger

Cash in Bank	Sales Tax Payable
Accounts Receivable	Accounts Payable
Merchandise Inventory	Sales
	Sales Returns and Allowances

Accounts Receivable Subsidiary Ledger
Palmer, James
Rodriguez, Anna

Date	Transactions
Sept. 1	Sold $300 in merchandise plus sales tax of $18 on account to James Palmer, Sales Slip 101.
4	Sold $600 in merchandise plus $36 sales tax to Anna Rodriguez on account, Sales Slip 102.
7	Issued Credit Memorandum 15 to James Palmer for the return of $300 in merchandise plus sales tax of $18.
19	Anna Rodriguez telephoned the manager of Alpine Ski Shop and said that the zipper on her ski jacket is broken. The manager agreed to give her a $40 credit on her purchase, plus a $2.40 sales tax credit, Credit Memorandum 16.

Analyzing Cash Receipt Transactions

Each business must account for the cash it receives. In this section you will explore cash sales, charge sales, bankcard sales, and cash discounts.

Cash Transactions

How Does Cash Come into a Business?

A transaction in which money is received by a business is called a **cash receipt**. The three most common sources of cash for a merchandising business are payments for cash sales, charge sales, and bankcard sales. Cash is also received, though much less frequently, from other types of transactions. Let's learn how to handle these four kinds of cash receipts.

Cash Sales

In a **cash sale** transaction, the business receives full payment for the merchandise sold *at the time of the sale*. The proof of sale and the source document generated by a cash sale transaction differ from those for a sale on account.

Most retailers use a cash register to record cash sales. Instead of using preprinted sales slips, cash sales are recorded on two rolls of paper tape inside the cash register. The details of a cash sale are printed on the two tapes at the same time. The portion of one tape that contains a record of the sale is torn off and given to the customer as a receipt. The other tape remains in the register.

A business totals and clears its cash register daily. The cash register tape lists the total cash sales and the total sales tax collected on these sales. The tape also shows the day's total charge sales. A proof is usually prepared to show that the amount of cash in the cash register equals the amount of cash sales and sales tax recorded on the cash register tape. The proof and the tape are sent to the accounting clerk, who uses the tape like the one in **Figure 14–6** as the source document for the journal entry to record the day's cash sales.

Charge Customer Payments

Businesses record cash received on account from charge customers by preparing receipts. A receipt, shown in **Figure 14–7** on page 394, is a form that serves as a record of cash received. Receipts are prenumbered and may be prepared in multiple copies. The receipt is a source document for the journal entry.

BEFORE YOU READ

Main Idea
Merchandising businesses receive cash from cash sales, payments on account, bankcard sales, and occasionally from other types of transactions.

Read to Learn…
➤ how and why businesses receive cash. (p. 393)
➤ how to calculate a cash discount. (p. 394)
➤ how to record cash receipts. (p. 395)

Key Terms
cash receipt
cash sale
cash discount
sales discount

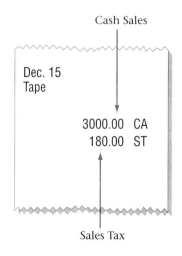

Figure 14–6
Cash Register Tape

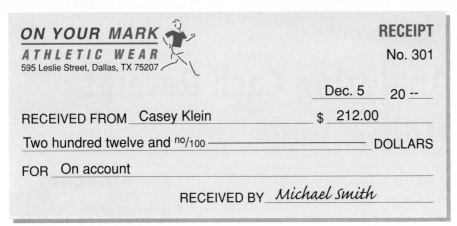

Figure 14–7 Receipt for Cash Received from a Charge Customer

As You READ

Key Point

Bankcard Account
The cardholder has an account with the bank, not with the store.

Bankcard Sales

Many businesses accept bankcards. Unlike a store credit card, which is issued by a business and is used only at that business, a bankcard is issued by a bank and honored by many businesses. The most widely used bank *credit cards* in North America are VISA, MasterCard, and Discover.

A debit card requires the entry of a personal identification number (PIN) on a keypad. The advantage of both cards to a store is that it does not have to wait to receive payment until the bank collects from the cardholder.

Both bank credit card and debit card transactions are usually recorded as though they are cash sales. However, some companies use a separate account for credit card sales.

Bankcard sales can be processed manually using multicopy bankcard slips or electronically. Either way, the total bankcard sales and related sales taxes are totaled and listed on the end-of-day cash register tape. **Figure 14–8** shows a cash register tape indicating the day's bankcard sales and related sales tax. The cash register tape is the source document to record bankcard sales. Bankcard sales are included on the daily cash proof.

In a manual system, the business uses a special deposit slip to deposit the bankcard and credit card slips in its checking account. There is often a three- or four-day delay before the amount is credited to the checking account. This is due to the time it takes the store's bank to collect the funds from the various banks that issued the customers' bankcards. In an electronic system, bankcard and credit cards are usually transmitted in daily batches, and the amount may be credited to the checking account of the business on the same or the next business day. Deposits of bankcard sales slips or electronic batch transmittal records are treated the same as cash deposits.

Other Cash Receipts

Merchants may also receive cash from infrequent transactions, such as a bank loan or the sale of assets other than merchandise. A receipt is prepared to indicate the source of the cash received.

Cash Discounts

Why Do Businesses Give Cash Discounts?

To encourage charge customers to pay promptly, some merchandisers offer a cash discount. A **cash discount**, or **sales discount**, is the amount a customer can deduct from the amount owed for purchased merchandise if payment is made within a certain time. A cash discount is an advantage to both the buyer, who receives merchandise at a reduced cost, and the seller, who receives cash quickly.

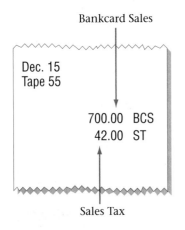

Figure 14–8 Bankcard Sales Tape

Businesses do not offer cash discounts to all customers. Some offer them only to business customers. On Your Mark offers a cash discount to charge customers who buy merchandise in large quantities. Its credit terms are *2/10, n/30.* These terms mean that the customer can deduct 2% of the merchandise cost if it pays within 10 days of the sale date. Otherwise, the full (net) amount is due within 30 days. A cash discount decreases the amount the business actually receives from the sale. Let's look at an example.

On December 3 On Your Mark sold $1,500 worth of merchandise on account to South Branch High School Athletics. It records the transaction as a credit to **Sales** and a debit to **Accounts Receivable** for $1,500. If South Branch pays within 10 days (by December 13), it will receive a cash discount. On Your Mark will receive $1,470, or the original price less the cash discount of $30.

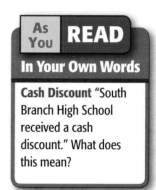

As You READ

In Your Own Words

Cash Discount "South Branch High School received a cash discount." What does this mean?

1. | Merchandise Sold | × | Discount Rate | = | Discount |
   |---|---|---|---|---|
   | $1,500 | × | .02 | = | $30 |

2. | Sales Slip Amount | − | Discount Amount | = | Amount Paid Within Discount Period |
   |---|---|---|---|---|
   | $1,500 | − | $30 | = | $1,470 |

Cash in Bank is debited for $1,470, the amount of cash actually received. **Accounts Receivable** is credited for the full $1,500 because the customer paid for the merchandise and does not owe any more on the purchase. The difference between $1,500 and $1,470, $30, is the discount amount. A cash discount is recorded only when the customer pays for the merchandise within the time stated. The discount is on the price of the merchandise *before* taxes.

A separate account is used to record cash discounts taken by customers. The $30 discount is entered in the contra revenue account **Sales Discounts**, which reduces the revenue earned from sales. The normal balance of the **Sales** account is a credit. The normal balance of the **Sales Discounts** account is a debit.

Sales		Sales Discounts	
Debit	Credit	Debit	Credit
−	+	+	−
Decrease Side	Increase Side Normal Balance	Increase Side Normal Balance	Decrease Side

Recording Cash Receipts
How Do Businesses Record the Receipt of Cash?

This section discusses recording cash from the four sources.

Charge Customer Payments

Let's look at a payment from a charge customer.

As You READ

It's Not What It Seems

Cash Receipt In a sales transaction, a *cash receipt* is not a source document. In this sense the term *receipt* means something that is received.

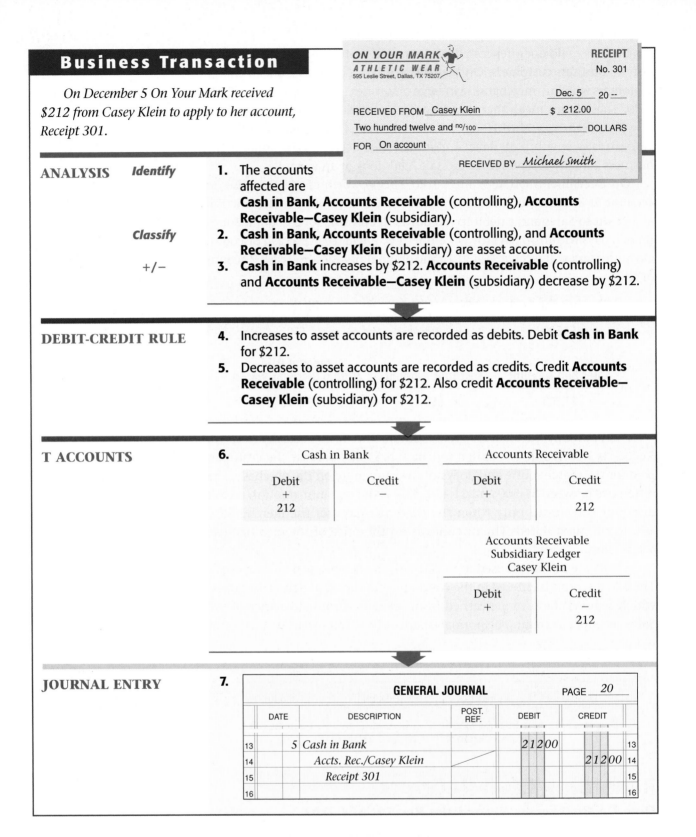

Business Transaction

On December 5 On Your Mark received $212 from Casey Klein to apply to her account, Receipt 301.

ON YOUR MARK
ATHLETIC WEAR
595 Leslie Street, Dallas, TX 75207

RECEIPT
No. 301

Dec. 5 20 --

RECEIVED FROM Casey Klein $ 212.00

Two hundred twelve and no/100 ———————— DOLLARS

FOR On account

RECEIVED BY *Michael Smith*

ANALYSIS

Identify

1. The accounts affected are **Cash in Bank, Accounts Receivable** (controlling), **Accounts Receivable—Casey Klein** (subsidiary).

Classify

2. **Cash in Bank, Accounts Receivable** (controlling), and **Accounts Receivable—Casey Klein** (subsidiary) are asset accounts.

+/−

3. **Cash in Bank** increases by $212. **Accounts Receivable** (controlling) and **Accounts Receivable—Casey Klein** (subsidiary) decrease by $212.

DEBIT-CREDIT RULE

4. Increases to asset accounts are recorded as debits. Debit **Cash in Bank** for $212.

5. Decreases to asset accounts are recorded as credits. Credit **Accounts Receivable** (controlling) for $212. Also credit **Accounts Receivable—Casey Klein** (subsidiary) for $212.

T ACCOUNTS

6.

Cash in Bank	
Debit +	Credit −
212	

Accounts Receivable	
Debit +	Credit −
	212

Accounts Receivable
Subsidiary Ledger
Casey Klein

Debit +	Credit −
	212

JOURNAL ENTRY

7.

	GENERAL JOURNAL			PAGE 20	
DATE	DESCRIPTION	POST. REF.	DEBIT	CREDIT	
5	Cash in Bank		212 00		13
	Accts. Rec./Casey Klein			212 00	14
	Receipt 301				15
					16

Cash Discount Payments

When a customer pays for a purchase on account within the discount period, the amount paid equals the invoice amount less the cash discount.

Business Transaction

On December 12 On Your Mark received $1,470 from South Branch High School Athletics in payment of Sales Slip 51 for $1,500 less the discount of $30, Receipt 302.

ON YOUR MARK	RECEIPT
ATHLETIC WEAR	No. 302
595 Leslie Street, Dallas, TX 75207	

Dec. 12 20 --

RECEIVED FROM South Branch H.S. Athletics $ 1,470.00

One thousand four hundred seventy and no/100 ———— DOLLARS

FOR On account

RECEIVED BY *Michael Smith*

ANALYSIS

Identify
1. The accounts affected are **Cash in Bank, Sales Discounts, Accounts Receivable** (controlling), and **Accounts Receivable—South Branch High School Athletics** (subsidiary).

Classify
2. **Cash in Bank, Accounts Receivable** (controlling), and **Accounts Receivable—South Branch High School Athletics** (subsidiary) are asset accounts. **Sales Discounts** is a contra revenue account.

+/−
3. **Cash in Bank** is increased by $1,470. **Sales Discounts** is increased by $30. **Accounts Receivable** (controlling), and **Accounts Receivable—South Branch High School Athletics** (subsidiary) are decreased by $1,500.

DEBIT-CREDIT RULE

4. Increases to asset accounts are recorded as debits. Debit **Cash in Bank** for $1,470. Increases to contra revenue accounts are recorded as debits. Debit **Sales Discounts** for $30.
5. Decreases to asset accounts are recorded as credits. Credit **Accounts Receivable** (controlling) for $1,500. Also credit **Accounts Receivable—South Branch High School Athletics** (subsidiary) for $1,500.

T ACCOUNTS

6.

Cash in Bank			Accounts Receivable	
Debit + 1,470	Credit −		Debit +	Credit − 1,500

Sales Discounts			Accounts Receivable Subsidiary Ledger South Branch High School Athletics	
Debit + 30	Credit −		Debit +	Credit − 1,500

JOURNAL ENTRY

7.

			GENERAL JOURNAL				PAGE 20		
	DATE		DESCRIPTION	POST. REF.	DEBIT		CREDIT		
16		12	*Cash in Bank*		1 47 0 00				16
17			*Sales Discounts*		30 00				17
18			*Accts. Rec./South Br. H.S.*				1 50 0 00		18
19			*Receipt 302*						19
20									20

Cash Sales

As a rule, businesses journalize cash sales and make cash deposits daily. Let's analyze transactions relating to sale of merchandise for cash on December 15.

Business Transaction

On December 15 On Your Mark had cash sales of $3,000 and collected $180 in sales taxes, Tape 55.

```
Dec. 15
Tape 55

        3000.00  CA
         180.00  ST
```

ANALYSIS   *Identify*   1. The accounts affected are **Cash in Bank, Sales,** and **Sales Taxes Payable.**

            Classify   2. **Cash in Bank** is an asset account. **Sales** is a revenue account. **Sales Tax Payable** is a liability account.

            +/−   3. **Cash in Bank** is increased by $3,180. **Sales** is increased by $3,000. **Sales Tax Payable** is increased by $180.

DEBIT-CREDIT RULE   4. Increases in asset accounts are recorded as debits. Debit **Cash in Bank** for $3,180.

       5. Increases in revenue and liability accounts are recorded as credits. Credit **Sales** for $3,000, and **Sales Tax Payable** for $180.

T ACCOUNTS   6.

Cash in Bank		Sales	
Debit + 3,180	Credit −	Debit −	Credit + 3,000

Sales Tax Payable	
Debit −	Credit + 180

JOURNAL ENTRY   7.

		GENERAL JOURNAL			PAGE 20	
	DATE	DESCRIPTION	POST. REF.	DEBIT	CREDIT	
20	15	Cash in Bank		3 180 00		20
21		Sales			3 000 00	21
22		Sales Tax Payable			180 00	22
23		Tape 55				23

Bankcard Sales

Let's record sales paid by bankcard. Note the similarity to cash sales.

Business Transaction

On Your Mark had bankcard sales of $700 and collected $42 in related sales taxes on December 15, Tape 55.

Dec. 15
Tape 55

700.00	BCS
42.00	ST

ANALYSIS   *Identify*   **1.** The accounts affected are **Cash in Bank, Sales,** and **Sales Tax Payable.**

Classify   **2.** **Cash in Bank** is an asset account. **Sales** is a revenue account. **Sales Tax Payable** is a liability account.

+/−   **3.** **Cash in Bank** is increased by $742. **Sales** is increased by $700. **Sales Tax Payable** is increased by $42.

DEBIT-CREDIT RULE   **4.** Increases in asset accounts are recorded as debits. Debit **Cash in Bank** for $742.

5. Increases in revenue and liability accounts are recorded as credits. Credit **Sales** for $700 and **Sales Tax Payable** for $42.

T ACCOUNTS   **6.**

Cash in Bank		Sales	
Debit + 742	Credit −	Debit −	Credit + 700

Sales Tax Payable	
Debit −	Credit + 42

JOURNAL ENTRY   **7.**

GENERAL JOURNAL   PAGE __20__

	DATE	DESCRIPTION	POST. REF.	DEBIT	CREDIT	
24	15	Cash in Bank		742 00		24
25		Sales			700 00	25
26		Sales Tax Payable			42 00	26
27		Tape 55				27

Other Cash Receipts

Occasionally a business receives cash from a transaction that does not involve the sale of merchandise. The **Sales** account is not used because the item is not a *merchandise* item.

Business Transaction

On December 16 On Your Mark received $30 from Mandy Harris, an office employee. She purchased a calculator that the business was no longer using, Receipt 303.

ON YOUR MARK
ATHLETIC WEAR
595 Leslie Street, Dallas, TX 75207

RECEIPT
No. 303

Dec. 16 20 --

RECEIVED FROM Mandy Harris $ 30.00

Thirty and no/100 ———————————————————— DOLLARS

FOR calculator

RECEIVED BY Michael Smith

JOURNAL ENTRY

	DATE	DESCRIPTION	POST. REF.	DEBIT	CREDIT	
28	16	Cash in Bank		30 00		28
29		Office Equipment			30 00	29
30		Receipt 303				30

GENERAL JOURNAL PAGE 20

Figure 14–9 shows the transactions discussed in this chapter.

GENERAL JOURNAL PAGE 20

	DATE		DESCRIPTION	POST. REF.	DEBIT	CREDIT	
1	20--						1
2	Dec.	1	Accts. Rec./Casey Klein		2 12 00		2
3			Sales			2 00 00	3
4			Sales Tax Payable			12 00	4
5			Sales Slip 50				5
6		3	Accts. Rec./South Branch H.S.		1 5 00 00		6
7			Sales			1 5 00 00	7
8			Sales Slip 51				8
9		4	Sales Returns and Allowances		1 50 00		9
10			Sales Tax Payable		9 00		10
11			Accts. Rec./Gabriel Ramos			1 59 00	11
12			Credit Memorandum 124				12
13		5	Cash in Bank		2 12 00		13
14			Accts. Rec./Casey Klein			2 12 00	14
15			Receipt 301				15
16		12	Cash in Bank		1 4 70 00		16
17			Sales Discounts		30 00		17
18			Accts. Rec./South Branch H.S.			1 5 00 00	18
19			Receipt 302				19
20		15	Cash in Bank		3 1 80 00		20
21			Sales			3 0 00 00	21
22			Sales Tax Payable			1 80 00	22
23			Tape 55				23
24		15	Cash in Bank		7 42 00		24
25			Sales			7 00 00	25
26			Sales Tax Payable			42 00	26
27			Tape 55				27
28		16	Cash in Bank		30 00		28
29			Office Equipment			30 00	29
30			Receipt 303				30

Figure 14–9 Sales and Cash Receipt Transactions

Reinforce the Main Idea

Create a table similar to this one to analyze four different types of cash receipt transactions, the debit and credit parts of each type, and the source document for each.

1. Cash Transaction	2. Account(s) Debited	3. Account(s) Credited	4. Source Document

Do the Math

This graph illustrates the sales of flowers throughout the year for Randy's Florist.

1. The sale of tulips was highest in which month?
2. Which type of flower sells at a steady rate, regardless of the month?

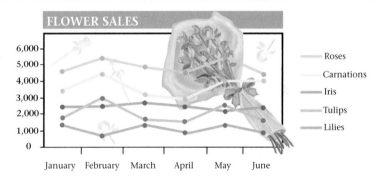

FLOWER SALES

Legend: Roses, Carnations, Iris, Tulips, Lilies

Months: January, February, March, April, May, June

Problem 14–3 Analyzing a Source Document

As the accounting clerk for Super Cycle Shop, you record the business transactions. The store's manager hands you the source document shown here.

Instructions Analyze the source document and record the necessary entries on page 17 of the general journal.

```
May 15
Tape 40

          1000.00  CA
            60.00  ST
           800.00  BCS
            48.00  ST
```

Problem 14–4 Recording Cash Receipts

Commerce Technology, a computer equipment retailer, had the following selected transactions in March.

Instructions Record each transaction on page 4 of the general journal in your working papers.

Date	Transactions
Mar. 1	Sold one modem for $130 plus $10.40 sales tax, Sales Slip 49.
5	Sold one computer monitor to Kelly Wilson on account for $300 plus $24 sales tax, Sales Slip 55.
17	Bankcard sales totaled $750 plus $60 sales tax, Tape 65.

Summary

Key Concepts

1. A service business provides a service to the public for a fee. In contrast a merchandising business buys goods and sells them to customers for a profit.

2. Accounts used by merchandising businesses include **Merchandise Inventory, Sales, Sales Tax Payable, Sales Returns and Allowances, Sales Discounts,** the **Accounts Receivable** controlling account, and individual customer accounts.

The **Merchandise Inventory** account is an asset account used to record the value of the merchandise in stock.

Merchandise Inventory	
Debit + Increase Side Normal Balance	Credit − Decrease Side

The **Sales** account is a revenue account used to record the sale of merchandise.

Sales	
Debit − Decrease Side	Credit + Increase Side Normal Balance

Most states and some cities tax the retail sale of goods. Businesses collect sales tax and record it as a liability in the **Sales Tax Payable** account. Later the business sends a check to the state or city for the sales tax collected.

Sales Tax Payable	
Debit − Decrease Side	Credit + Increase Side Normal Balance

The **Sales Returns and Allowances** account is used to record the cash refund or the credit granted to charge customers for returned or damaged merchandise.

Sales Returns and Allowances	
Debit + Increase Side Normal Balance	Credit − Decrease Side

The **Sales Discounts** account is used to record the amount of any cash discount taken by charge customers.

Sales Discounts	
Debit + Increase Side Normal Balance	Credit − Decrease Side

Accounts Receivable is a controlling account. Its balance must equal the sum of the customer account balances in the accounts receivable subsidiary ledger.

3. A *retailer* is a business that sells goods to the final user. A *wholesaler* sells goods to retailers.

4. The following summarizes the accounts involved in journalizing sales and cash receipts:

Cash sales:

Debit	Credit
Cash in Bank	**Sales**
	Sales Tax Payable

Sales on account:

Debit	Credit
Accounts Receivable—	**Sales**
Customer's Name	**Sales Tax Payable**

Payment for a sale on account:

Debit	Credit
Cash in Bank	**Accounts Receivable—Customer's Name**

Payment on account with a cash discount taken:

Debit	Credit
Cash in Bank	**Accounts Receivable—Customer's Name**
	Sales Discounts

Return of merchandise purchased on account:

Debit	Credit
Sales Returns and Allowances	**Accounts Receivable—Customer's Name**
Sales Tax Payable	

Return of merchandise purchased for cash:

Debit	Credit
Sales Returns and Allowances	**Cash in Bank**
Sales Tax Payable	

Key Terms

accounts receivable		**credit cards**	(p. 384)	**sales allowance**	(p. 388)
subsidiary ledger	(p. 385)	**credit memorandum**	(p. 388)	**sales discount**	(p. 394)
cash discount	(p. 394)	**credit terms**	(p. 385)	**sales return**	(p. 388)
cash receipt	(p. 393)	**inventory**	(p. 382)	**sales slip**	(p. 384)
cash sale	(p. 393)	**merchandise**	(p. 382)	**sales tax**	(p. 385)
charge customer	(p. 384)	**retailer**	(p. 380)	**subsidiary ledger**	(p. 385)
contra account	(p. 389)	**sale on account**	(p. 384)	**wholesaler**	(p. 380)
controlling account	(p. 386)	**Sales**	(p. 382)		

Check Your Understanding

1. **Service Business and Merchandising Business**
   a. Contrast a service business and a merchandising business.
   b. What are the two types of merchandising businesses?

2. **Sale of Merchandise**
   a. What accounts are posted for a sale on account?
   b. How does a merchandising business act as a collection agency for the state government?

3. **Retailer and Wholesaler**
   a. Which of the following businesses collects sales tax from customers: a wholesaler, a retailer, or both?
   b. What is the term for goods that a retailer buys from a wholesaler or a manufacturer to resell?

4. **Journalizing Sales and Cash Receipts**
   a. Classify the following accounts: **Merchandise Inventory, Sales, Sales Returns and Allowances, Sales Discounts,** and **Sales Tax Payable.**
   b. Which accounts are affected when a business receives a payment from a charge customer who has taken a cash discount?

Apply Key Terms

You have just hired Geoffrey Hillman to be the accounting clerk for the Hats Off Corporation, a merchandiser of hats, caps, and scarves. Geoffrey has worked as a payroll clerk, but not in sales or cash receipts jobs. To help him you have offered to make note cards with the definitions of the following terms. Provide an example of each term when possible.

accounts receivable subsidiary ledger	credit cards	sales allowance
cash discount	credit memorandum	sales discount
cash receipt	credit terms	sales return
cash sale	inventory	sales slip
charge customer	merchandise	sales tax
contra account	retailer	subsidiary ledger
controlling account	sale on account	wholesaler
	Sales	

Sales and Cash Receipts

Making the Transition from a Manual to a Computerized System

Task	Manual Methods	Computerized Methods
Recording sales transactions	• Prepare general journal entries based on a sales slip or an invoice. • Post journal entries to the appropriate general ledger accounts. • Calculate new account balances.	• Invoices can be created with the software and posted to the general ledger accounts at the same time. • New account balances are calculated for you.
Recording cash receipts transactions	• Prepare journal entries based on deposit slips, receipts, or cash register tapes. • Post journal entries to the appropriate general ledger accounts. • Calculate new account balances.	• Deposits are recorded and posted to the general ledger using the cash receipts task item. • General ledger accounts are updated automatically.

Peachtree® Q & A

Peachtree Question	Answer
How do I record a sale on account?	1. From the *Tasks* menu, select **Sales/Invoicing**. 2. Enter customer ID and invoice number. 3. Click on the Apply to Sales tab. 4. Enter details of the invoice and amount, and click **Save**.
How do I record a cash receipt from a customer on account?	1. From the *Tasks* menu, select **Receipts**. 2. In the Cash Account list, select the bank account in which the receipt is to be deposited. 3. Select the Apply to Invoices tab. Then select the invoices being paid. 4. Click **Save**.

QuickBooks Q & A

QuickBooks Question	Answer
How do I record a sale on account?	1. From the *Customers* menu, select **Create Invoices**. 2. Enter the customer's name, the date, and invoice number. 3. Enter the quantity and item code. QuickBooks will automatically fill in the description, price, and amount. 4. Click **Save & Close**.
How do I record a cash receipt from a customer on account?	1. From the *Customers* menu, select **Receive Payments**. 2. Enter the customer's name, the date, and the amount received. 3. In the Applied to section, select the invoices being paid. 4. Deposit the money either directly into a bank account or group with other undeposited funds to deposit at a later date, and click **Save & Close**.

For detailed instructions, see your Glencoe Accounting Chapter Study Guides and Working Papers.

Peachtree®

SMART GUIDE

Step–by–Step Instructions:
Problem 14–5

1. Select the problem set for Sunset Surfwear (Prob. 14–5).
2. Rename the company and set the system date.
3. Enter all sales on account transactions using the **Sales/Invoicing** option in the *Tasks* menu.
4. Process all credit memorandums using the **Credit Memos** option.
5. Record all cash receipts transactions using the **Receipts** option.
6. Print a Sales Journal report and a Cash Receipts Journal report.
7. Proof your work.
8. Complete the Analyze activity.
9. End the session.

QuickBooks

PROBLEM GUIDE

Step–by–Step Instructions:
Problem 14–5

1. Restore the Problem 14-5.QBB file.
2. Enter all sales on account using the **Create Invoice** options from the *Customers* menu.
3. Process all credit memorandums using the **Create Credit Memos/Refunds** option from the *Customers* menu.
4. Record all cash receipts using the **Receive Payments** option from the *Customers* menu.
5. Print a Journal report.
6. Proof your work.
7. Complete the Analyze activity.
8. Back up your work.

Problem 14–5 Recording Sales and Cash Receipts

Sunset Surfwear, a California-based merchandising store, had the following sales and cash receipt transactions for January. The partial chart of accounts for Sunset Surfwear follows.

General Ledger

101	Cash in Bank	401	Sales
115	Accounts Receivable	405	Sales Discounts
215	Sales Tax Payable	410	Sales Returns and Allowances

Accounts Receivable Subsidiary Ledger

ADA	Adams, Martha	**MOU**	Moulder, Nate
HAM	Hamilton, Alex	**WES**	Westwood High School Athletics
JUN1	Jun, Helen		

Instructions Record the following transactions on page 20 of the general journal.

Date	Transactions
Jan. 1	Sold $300 in merchandise plus a sales tax of $18 on account to Martha Adams, Sales Slip 777.
5	Sold $1,500 in merchandise on account to Westwood High School Athletics, Sales Slip 778.
7	Received $400 from Alex Hamilton on account, Receipt 345.
10	Issued Credit Memorandum 102 to Martha Adams for $318 covering $300 in returned merchandise plus $18 sales tax.
15	Recorded cash sales of $800 plus $48 in sales tax, Tape 39.
15	Recorded bankcard sales of $900 plus $54 in sales tax, Tape 39.
20	Received $1,500 from Westwood High School Athletics in payment of Sales Slip 778, Receipt 346.
25	Sold $1,200 in merchandise plus sales tax of $72 on account to Helen Jun, Sales Slip 779.
28	Granted a $106 sales allowance to Helen Jun, which includes $100 for damaged merchandise she kept and sales tax of $6, Credit Memorandum 103.
30	Received $500 from a charge customer, Nate Moulder, in payment of his $500 account, Receipt 347.

Analyze Calculate the sum of all the debits to the **Sales Returns and Allowances** account during January.

Problem 14–6 Posting Sales and Cash Receipts

The January transactions for InBeat CD Shop are recorded on page 15 of the general journal.

Instructions Post the transactions to the general ledger and subsidiary ledger in your working papers.

Peachtree®

SMART GUIDE

Step–by–Step Instructions: Problem 14–6

1. Select the problem set for InBeat CD Shop (Prob. 14–6).
2. Rename the company and set the system date.
3. Choose **General Ledger** from the **Reports** menu.
4. Print a General Ledger (GL) report.
5. Select the Accounts Receivable report area.
6. From the list on the right, select and print the Customer Ledgers report.
7. Compare each GL entry in your working papers to the GL report and Customer Ledgers report.
8. Use the GL report to complete the Analyze activity.
9. End the session.

GENERAL JOURNAL PAGE 15

	DATE		DESCRIPTION	POST. REF.	DEBIT	CREDIT	
1	20--						1
2	Jan.	1	Cash in Bank		3 88 00		2
3			Sales Discounts		12 00		3
4			Accts. Rec./Alicia Alvarez			4 00 00	4
5			Receipt 92				5
6		4	Accts. Rec./Dena Greenburg		7 35 00		6
7			Sales			7 00 00	7
8			Sales Tax Payable			35 00	8
9			Sales Slip 60				9
10		6	Cash in Bank		2 1 00 00		10
11			Sales			2 00 00 00	11
12			Sales Tax Payable			1 00 00	12
13			Tape 32				13
14		6	Cash in Bank		3 1 50 00		14
15			Sales			3 00 00 00	15
16			Sales Tax Payable			1 50 00	16
17			Tape 32				17
18		8	Sales Returns and Allowances		7 00 00		18
19			Sales Tax Payable		35 00		19
20			Accts. Rec./ Dena Greenburg			7 35 00	20
21			Credit Memorandum 15				21
22		10	Cash in Bank		1 3 58 00		22
23			Sales Discounts		42 00		23
24			Accts. Rec./Joe Montoya			1 4 00 00	24
25			Receipt 93				25
26		15	Accts. Rec./Alicia Alvarez		4 20 00		26
27			Sales			4 00 00	27
28			Sales Tax Payable			20 00	28
29			Sales Slip 61				29
30		27	Cash in Bank		1 3 65 00		30
31			Accts. Rec./Chelsea Wright			1 3 65 00	31
32			Receipt 94				32
33							33

Analyze Identify the customer with the highest balance at the end of January.

Problem 14–7 Recording Sales and Cash Receipts

Shutterbug Cameras had the following transactions during January. The partial chart of accounts for Shutterbug is shown here.

General Ledger

101 Cash in Bank	401 Sales
115 Accounts Receivable	405 Sales Discounts
130 Supplies	410 Sales Returns and Allowances
215 Sales Tax Payable	

Accounts Receivable Subsidiary Ledger

DIA Diaz, Arturo   **NAK** Nakata, Yoko
FAS FastForward Productions **SUL** Sullivan, Heather

Instructions Record the transactions on page 5 of the general journal in your working papers.

Date	Transactions
Jan. 1	Sold merchandise on account to Yoko Nakata for $250 plus a 4% sales tax of $10, Sales Slip 90.
3	Received $50 in cash from the sale of supplies to Betty's Boutique, Receipt 201.
7	Sold $300 in merchandise plus a sales tax of $12 to Arturo Diaz on account, Sales Slip 91.
12	Sold on account $1,500 in merchandise plus a sales tax of $60 to FastForward Productions, credit terms 2/10, n/30, Sales Slip 92.
13	Issued Credit Memorandum 20 for $312 to Arturo Diaz, which includes $300 in merchandise returned by him plus sales tax of $12.
14	Received a check for $260 from Yoko Nakata in full payment of his account, Receipt 202.
15	Cash sales amounted to $2,500 plus $100 in sales tax, Tape 75.
15	Bankcard sales were $3,000 plus $120 in sales tax, Tape 75.
21	Received a check for $1,530 from FastForward Productions in payment of their $1,560 account balance less a cash discount of $30, Receipt 203.
28	Granted Heather Sullivan a $104 allowance for damaged merchandise of $100 plus a 4% sales tax of $4, Credit Memorandum 21.

Analyze | Compute the net amount of sales tax for the month based on these transactions.

Problem 14–8 Recording Sales and Cash Receipt Transactions

Peachtree®

SMART GUIDE

Step–by–Step Instructions: Problem 14–8

1. Select the problem set for River's Edge (Prob. 14–8).
2. Rename the company and set the system date.
3. Enter all sales on account transactions using the **Sales/ Invoicing** option.
4. Process all credit memorandums using the **Credit Memos** option.
5. Record all cash receipts using the **Receipts** option.
6. Print a Sales Journal and Cash Receipts journal report.
7. Proof your work.
8. Print a GL report to complete the Analyze activity.
9. End the session.

River's Edge Canoe & Kayak is a merchandising business in Wyoming. The partial chart of accounts follows:

General Ledger

101 Cash in Bank	401 Sales
115 Accounts Receivable	405 Sales Discounts
135 Supplies	410 Sales Returns and Allowances
215 Sales Tax Payable	

Accounts Receivable Subsidiary Ledger

ADV Adventure River Tours	**WILD** Wildwood Resorts
DRA Drake, Paul	**WU** Wu, Kim

Instructions Record January transactions on page 10 of the general journal.

Date	Transactions
Jan. 1	Sold $2,000 in merchandise on account to Wildwood Resorts, a tax-exempt agency, credit terms 3/15, n/30, Sales Slip 103.
5	Granted Wildwood Resorts a $150 credit allowance for defective merchandise, Credit Memorandum 33.
8	Received $485 from Adventure River Tours for $500 in merchandise sold to it on Dec. 27 less a 3% cash discount of $15, Receipt 96.
10	Sold $500 in merchandise plus a 5% sales tax of $25 to Paul Drake on account, credit terms 3/15, n/30, Sales Slip 104.
12	Received a check for $1,794.50 from Wildwood Resorts on account ($1,850 less a 3% cash discount of $55.50), Receipt 97.
15	Cash sales were $3,500 plus sales tax of $175, Tape 22.
15	Bankcard sales amounted to $4,000 plus sales tax of $200, Tape 22.
20	Sold to Adventure River Tours $75 in supplies. Cash received recorded on Receipt 98.
22	Granted Kim Wu $63 credit for $60 in damaged merchandise sold to her last month and 5% sales tax of $3 on the merchandise, Credit Memorandum 34.
25	Paul Drake sent a check for $510 in payment of his account. The account balance was $525 ($500 in merchandise and $25 sales tax). He took a 3% cash discount of $15 on the merchandise, Receipt 99.

Analyze Compute the amount of cash that would have been collected in January if customers had not taken any cash discounts.

Problem 14–9 Recording and Posting Sales and Cash Receipts

Buzz Newsstand had the following transactions for the month of January.

General Ledger	
101 Cash in Bank	401 Sales
115 Accounts Receivable	405 Sales Discounts
135 Supplies	410 Sales Returns and Allowances
215 Sales Tax Payable	

Accounts Receivable Subsidiary Ledger

ADK Adkins, Lee	NAD Nadal, Saba
JAV Java Shops Inc.	ROL Rolling Hills Pharmacies

Instructions

1. Record the transactions on page 9 of the general journal.
2. Post each transaction to the appropriate general ledger and accounts receivable subsidiary ledger accounts. A partial general ledger and accounts receivable subsidiary ledger are included in the working papers. The current account balances are recorded in the accounts.

Date	Transactions
Jan. 1	Lee Adkins returned $200 in damaged merchandise purchased on account last month, issued Credit Memorandum 10 for $212 ($200 in merchandise plus 6% sales tax of $12).
3	Received a check from Rolling Hills Pharmacies for $2,256.62 in payment of its account of $2,300 less a 2% cash discount of $43.38, Receipt 75.
7	Gave credit to Saba Nadal for the return of $300 in merchandise sold to him on account, plus sales tax of $18. Issued Credit Memorandum 11 for $318.
10	Java Shops Inc. sent a check for $1471.70 in payment of its account of $1,500 less a 2% cash discount of $28.30, Receipt 76.
15	Cash sales were $2,500 plus $150 in sales tax, Tape 25.
15	Bankcard sales were $2,000 plus $120 in sales tax, Tape 25.
20	Janson Lee, a neighboring store, needed supplies urgently. Sold it $40 in supplies and received cash from the sale, Receipt 77.
25	Received a check for $636 from Lee Adkins on account, Receipt 78.
31	Sold $3,000 in merchandise plus sales tax of $180 on account to Rolling Hills Pharmacies, Sales Slip 114.

Analyze Calculate the net sales for January, which is **Sales** less **Sales Discounts** and **Sales Returns and Allowances.**

Practice your test-taking skills! The questions on this page are reprinted with permission from national organizations:
- Future Business Leaders of America
- Business Professionals of America

Use a separate sheet of paper to record your answers.

Future Business Leaders of America

MULTIPLE CHOICE

1. If the merchandise is purchased for $1,000 on August 1, with terms of sale of 2/10, n/30, the amount due to the vendor on August 9 is
   - a. $1,000.
   - b. $990.
   - c. $980.
   - d. $20.

2. The journal entry for a cash receipt on account is
   - a. debit Cash; credit Accounts Receivable.
   - b. debit Cash; credit Accounts Payable.
   - c. debit Accounts Payable; credit Cash.
   - d. debit Accounts Payable; credit Accounts Receivable.

3. When a customer is given a price reduction on an item (for example, a damaged item), the bookkeeper will use which one of the following accounts?
   - a. Purchase Allowance
   - b. Purchase Discount
   - c. Sales Discount
   - d. Sales Allowance

4. To decrease the Sales Returns and Allowances account, the bookkeeper will
   - a. credit the account.
   - b. debit the account.
   - c. both debit and credit the account.
   - d. use the Purchase Returns and Allowances account.

Business Professionals of America

MULTIPLE CHOICE

5. When bankcard sales are entered in the general journal, what account is debited?
   - a. Bankcard Sales
   - b. Cash
   - c. Bankcard Sales Expense
   - d. Sales

Need More Help?

Go to glencoeaccounting.glencoe.com and click on Student Center. Click on Winning Competitive Events and select Chapter 14.
- **Practice Questions and Test-Taking Tips**
- **Concept Capsules and Terminology**

Accounting for a Merchandising Business

1. Define *merchandising business*.
2. Explain how a purchase made with a store credit card is different from a purchase made with a bank credit card.
3. A sales slip shows that $1,500 in merchandise has been sold and the sales tax rate is 4%. Compute the cash receipt.
4. How are a bank credit card and a debit card similar? How are they different?
5. Your accounting supervisor has instructed you to verify the accuracy of the day's bank credit card sales and then deposit that amount into the business checking account. Summarize what you need to do.
6. Evaluate the practice of using a contra account to record sales returns and allowances.

Merchandising Business: Videos

Felix Andersen is a film buff. His business, Video Source, specializes in foreign titles and classic film collections. Video Source uses a manual accounting system. Sales are recorded from cash register tapes at the end of the day. Felix is thinking of updating to an electronic cash register that records sales information directly into a computerized accounting system.

INSTRUCTIONS

1. Describe the benefits of converting to an electronic system.
2. Explain how an analysis of sales would help when making decisions about what types of videos to stock.

Confidentiality

Imagine that you work as an accounting clerk for a fast-food franchise like Taco Bell. You have access to all of the accounting records for the business.

A friend of yours has promised to hire you as an accountant when he opens his own Mexican food restaurant. He has asked you to share information about Taco Bell's sales and expenses.

ETHICAL DECISION MAKING

1. What are the ethical issues?
2. What are the alternatives?
3. Who are the affected parties?
4. How do the alternatives affect the parties?
5. What would you do?

Presenting Your Case

You and your best friend, Inga Swenson, graduated from a prestigious art school. You have a degree in art history and business management; Inga has a degree in fine art. Inga is an award-winning weaver and creates wall hangings that are extremely popular in your community. Together you decide to form a business partnership. You want to open a retail store. Inga wants to sell directly to the customers at fairs and art shows. Draft a report to Inga that explains why selling art through a retail store is more profitable than seasonal shows and fairs.

Allocating Resources

When you operate a business, you must constantly evaluate the effective use of resources, including time, money, materials, space, and staff. You own Retro Café, a late-night spot for young professionals and college students, open 11 a.m. until midnight. Your review of the month's financial reports reveals that the café is showing a net loss for the third month in a row.

INSTRUCTIONS

Design a form to gather opinions on the menu, staffing, and operating hours. What are the staffing implications if most sales occur after 3 p.m.?

International Product Life Cycle

The *international product life cycle (IPLC)* theory explains how a product that is an export eventually becomes an import. At first sales are strong when a U.S. company sells to both U.S. and foreign consumers. Then foreign producers make the item at a lower cost, and U.S. exports decline. Finally foreign competitors undercut U.S. prices, and consumers buy the less expensive imported product.

INSTRUCTIONS Use a product such as a DVD player to illustrate the IPLC.

Your Budget

Businesses plan ahead, estimating their revenue and expenses. It is important for you to plan ahead and spend your money wisely. This is accomplished by developing a budget, which is a plan for spending money.

PERSONAL FINANCE ACTIVITY Develop a weekly budget for a person your age. Create two columns on a sheet of paper. Label one *Income* and the other *Expenses*. List all sources of income for the week in the first column and the planned spending in the second.

PERSONAL FINANCE ONLINE Log on to **glencoeaccounting.glencoe.com** and click on **Student Center.** Click on **Making It Personal** and select **Chapter 14.**

Dear Fellow Stockholders Letter

Public corporations publish annual reports giving financial and other information they want to make public. One item in most annual reports is a letter from the company's top executive officer.

INSTRUCTIONS

Use the PETsMART *Dear Fellow Stockholders* letter in the PETsMART annual report in Appendix F to answer these questions:

1. Name three measures of PETsMART's 2003 financial results.

2. Would this letter influence your decision to purchase PETsMART stock? Why or why not?

Safe and Secure

When buying online, always use an Internet-friendly credit card. Visit **glencoeaccounting .glencoe.com** and click on **Student Center.** Click on **WebQuest** and select **Unit 4** to continue your Internet project.

Accounting for Purchases and Cash Payments

BEFORE YOU **READ**

What You'll Learn

1. Explain the procedures for processing a purchase on account.

2. Describe the accounts used in the purchasing process.

3. Identify controls over cash.

4. Analyze transactions relating to the purchase of merchandise.

5. Record a variety of purchases and cash payment transactions.

6. Post to the accounts payable subsidiary ledger.

7. Define the accounting terms introduced in this chapter.

Why It's Important

The purchasing process results in a large outflow of cash.

SUNCOAST
The store for movie lovers.

Predict

1. What does the chapter title tell you?
2. What do you already know about this subject from personal experience?
3. What have you learned about this in the earlier chapters?
4. What gaps exist in your knowledge of this subject?

Exploring the *Real World* of Business

ANALYZING PURCHASES

Suncoast Motion Picture Company

If you were searching for *The Lord of the Rings: The Return of the King* DVD, would you care if it was new or used? In the DVD business, used is often as good as new. Sales of "previously viewed" DVDs have become a huge source of revenue for retailers like **Suncoast Motion Picture Company**, attracting customers by providing more choices.

Suncoast Motion Picture Company purchases used DVDs for resale. Customers either sell them to **Suncoast** for cash or trade in older titles for new or different ones.

Suncoast stores also offer movie memorabilia like posters, T-shirts, and books. Movie posters and T-shirts are purchased from various commercial printers.

What Do You Think?

If **Suncoast** purchased 5,000 posters from a commercial printer on credit, which accounts do you think would be affected?

Working in the *Real World*

APPLYING YOUR ACCOUNTING KNOWLEDGE

Have you ever gone shopping only to find that the store is out of the item you wanted? The store may have had a big sale and not yet received new merchandise. Stores order new items to replace the ones sold. In this chapter you will learn about the purchasing process and how to record purchases of merchandise and other items.

Personal Connection

1. If you work for a retail store, does it usually have most of its items in stock?
2. If it were up to you to decide on a new item to offer to your customers, what would it be?

Online Connection

Go to **glencoeaccounting.glencoe.com** and click on **Student Center.** Click on **Working in the Real World** and select **Chapter 15.**

Purchasing Items Needed by a Business

In Chapter 14 you learned that the primary source of income for a merchandising business is from the sale of its merchandise. However, to sell merchandise, a business must first buy the items. The items you find for sale at Wal-Mart—housewares, clothing, sporting goods, jewelry—are all purchased from wholesalers and suppliers. In this chapter you will learn how to analyze transactions relating to the purchase of merchandise.

The Purchasing Process
What Are the Four Stages of Purchasing?

All businesses, from the corner grocery store to a giant international corporation, are involved in the purchasing process. Retail businesses need shopping bags for customers, sales slips, and cash register tapes. They also need to purchase supplies, equipment, and merchandise.

The purchase of supplies, equipment, and merchandise is divided into four stages:

- requesting needed items
- ordering from a supplier
- verifying items received
- processing the supplier's invoice

Let's take a look at each of these stages.

Requesting Needed Items

In a small business, the owner does all the buying. In a large business, a separate purchasing department buys items for the entire company. When the company needs to buy equipment or supplies, or when the inventory of merchandise on hand is low, a purchase requisition is prepared.

A **purchase requisition** is a written request to order a specified item or items. Usually a purchase requisition is a prenumbered, multicopy form. The manager of the department requesting the item(s) approves the purchase requisition. Then the original copy of the purchase requisition goes to the purchasing department or the purchasing agent. The person making the request keeps a copy. **Figure 15–1** shows the purchase requisition form used by On Your Mark Athletic Wear.

Ordering from a Supplier

A **purchase order** is a written *offer* to a supplier to buy specified items. Much of the information on the purchase order comes directly

Before You READ

Main Idea
Merchandising businesses follow an orderly process for purchasing merchandise, supplies, and equipment.

Read to Learn...
➤ the four stages in purchasing items for a business and the processes and documents related to each stage. (p. 416)
➤ the purpose of the **Purchases** account. (p. 419)

Key Terms
purchase requisition
purchase order
packing slip
processing stamp
purchases discount
discount period
Purchases account
cost of merchandise

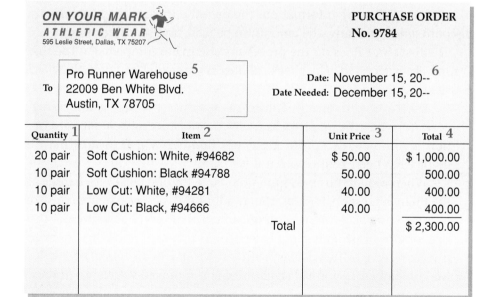

ON YOUR MARK ATHLETIC WEAR
PURCHASE REQUISITION

NO. 9421

FOR DEPARTMENT __Shoes__   DATE __Nov. 12, 20--__

NOTIFY __Vic Ventura__ ____ON DELIVERY   DATE WANTED __Dec. 15, 20--__

QUANTITY	DESCRIPTION	STOCK NO.
20 Pair	Soft Cushion, White	94682
10 Pair	Soft Cushion, Black	94788
10 Pair	Low Cut, White	94281
10 Pair	Low Cut, Black	94666

ORDER FROM __Pro Runner Warehouse__   APPROVED BY __Jennifer Mack__
                                                      SHOE DEPARTMENT MANAGER

Figure 15–1
Purchase Requisition

from the purchase requisition. Other information may be obtained from the supplier's catalog.

Look at the purchase order prepared by On Your Mark in **Figure 15–2**. The purchase order contains:

1. quantity
2. description
3. unit price
4. total cost
5. supplier's name and address
6. date needed
7. shipping method (optional)

The purchase order is a prenumbered multicopy form. The original of the purchase order goes to the supplier. One copy goes to the department requesting the items. The purchasing department keeps another copy.

As You READ

Key Point

Forms Used in Purchasing The purchase requisition stays *inside* the company. The purchase order goes *outside* the company.

As You READ

Compare and Contrast

Purchase Requisition and Purchase Order How are a purchase requisition and a purchase order similar? How are they different?

ON YOUR MARK
ATHLETIC WEAR
595 Leslie Street, Dallas, TX 75207

PURCHASE ORDER
No. 9784

To | Pro Runner Warehouse ⁵
22009 Ben White Blvd.
Austin, TX 78705

Date: November 15, 20-- ⁶
Date Needed: December 15, 20--

Quantity ¹	Item ²	Unit Price ³	Total ⁴
20 pair	Soft Cushion: White, #94682	$ 50.00	$ 1,000.00
10 pair	Soft Cushion: Black #94788	50.00	500.00
10 pair	Low Cut: White, #94281	40.00	400.00
10 pair	Low Cut: Black #94666	40.00	400.00
	Total		$ 2,300.00

Figure 15–2
Purchase Order

Verifying Items Received

Note that a purchase order is only an *offer* to buy items. Until the items are actually received, the buyer does not know whether or not the supplier has accepted the offer. A supplier may not be able to fill the purchase order

Estimate by Rounding

When you need an estimate of an answer to check for reasonableness, you can use rounding as shown:

$$4,682 \longrightarrow 5,000$$
$$+ \ 14,289 \longrightarrow + \ 14,000$$
$$18,971 \qquad 19,000$$

Round to the nearest thousand and add to get an estimate of 19,000. Because this is close to the calculated sum of 18,971, the answer is reasonable.

As You READ

Key Point

Purchase Order

A purchase order does not require a journal entry. It is only an *offer* to buy.

because an item is out of stock or has been discontinued. The mailing of a purchase order, therefore, does not require a journal entry. A supplier accepts a purchase order by shipping the items requested and billing the buyer for these items.

When a supplier ships to a buyer, the shipment includes a **packing slip**, which is a form that lists the items included in the shipment. When a shipment arrives, the buyer immediately unpacks and checks the contents against the quantities and items listed on the packing slip. If the shipment contents do not agree with those listed on the packing slip, a note about the differences is made on the packing slip. The packing slip is then sent to the accounting department to be checked against both the purchase order and the supplier's bill. A buyer does not have to pay for items that it did not receive, or that were damaged, or not ordered and returned to the supplier.

Processing the Supplier's Invoice

When it ships to a buyer, the supplier prepares a bill called an *invoice*. It lists the credit terms; the quantity, description, unit price, and total cost of the items shipped; the buyer's purchase order number; and the method of shipment.

The supplier sends the invoice directly to the buyer's accounting department, where it is date stamped to indicate when the invoice was received. The accounting clerk checks each detail (item, quantity, and price) on the invoice against the packing slip and the purchase order. This procedure verifies that the buyer is billed for the quantities and items actually ordered and received and that the prices are correct.

Once verified, the invoice is the source document for a journal entry. Before the invoice is recorded, a **processing stamp** is placed on the invoice to enter the following information: the date the invoice is to be paid, the discount amount, if any, the amount to be paid, and the check number.

The first three lines on the processing stamp are completed at the time the invoice is received. The check number is entered later, when the check is issued.

Look at the invoice in **Figure 15–3**. Notice the date stamp, which indicates when the invoice was received. The processing stamp information is complete except for the check number, which means that the invoice has been verified but not yet paid.

When a small business grows too large for one person to handle all the financial responsibilities, it may adopt the *voucher system* to provide internal control. A *voucher* is a document that serves as written authorization for a cash payment. The business prepares a voucher for every invoice received. The voucher, with invoice attached, is circulated within the company for approval signatures. The approved voucher is authorization to issue a check.

Purchases Discounts

Suppliers frequently offer charge customers a cash discount for early payment. For the buyer this discount is called a **purchases discount**. A purchases discount and cash discount are calculated in the same way.

Figure 15–3 Invoice

		INVOICE NO. 7894	

PRO RUNNER WAREHOUSE
22009 Ben White Blvd.
Austin, TX 78705

REC'D DEC. 14, 20--

DATE: Dec. 14, 20--
ORDER NO.:   9784
SHIPPED BY: Federal Trucking
TERMS: 2/10, n/30

TO   On Your Mark Athletic Wear
     595 Leslie Street
     Dallas, TX 75207

QTY.	ITEM	UNIT PRICE	TOTAL
20 pair	Soft Cushion: White, #94682	$ 50.00	$ 1,000.00
10 pair	Soft Cushion: Black, #94788	50.00	500.00
10 pair	Low Cut: White, #94281	40.00	400.00
10 pair	Low Cut: Black, #94666	40.00	400.00
	Total		$ 2,300.00

Due Date: _12/24_
Discount: _$ 46.00_
Net Amount: _$ 2,254.00_
Check No.: _____

For example, On Your Mark purchased $2,300 of merchandise on account from Pro Runner Warehouse. **Figure 15–3** shows the invoice dated December 14. The credit terms are 2/10, n/30. If On Your Mark pays for the merchandise on or before December 24, it may deduct 2% of the value of the merchandise. The 10 days, called the **discount period** , is the time within which an invoice must be paid if the discount is taken. If On Your Mark does not pay for the merchandise within the discount period, it pays the net, or total amount, within 30 days of the invoice date.

On Your Mark can save $46 if it pays the invoice within the 10-day discount period ending December 24. The end of the discount period can be determined by adding 10 days to the date of the invoice (December 14 + 10 days = December 24). The amount to be paid within the discount period is calculated as follows:

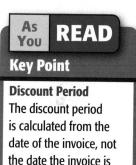

As You READ

Key Point

Discount Period
The discount period is calculated from the date of the invoice, not the date the invoice is received.

1.
$$\frac{\text{Merchandise Purchased}}{\$2,300} \times \frac{\text{Discount Rate}}{.02} = \frac{\text{Discount}}{\$46}$$

2.
$$\frac{\text{Invoice Amount}}{\$2,300} - \frac{\text{Discount Amount}}{\$46} = \frac{\text{Amount Paid Within Discount Period}}{\$2,254}$$

The Purchases Account

What Is the Purpose of the Purchases Account?

When a business buys merchandise to sell to customers, the cost of the merchandise is recorded in the **Purchases account** . The **Purchases** account is a temporary account, classified as a **cost of merchandise** account. Cost of merchandise accounts contain the actual cost to the business of the merchandise sold to customers.

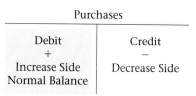

Purchases	
Debit	Credit
+	–
Increase Side	Decrease Side
Normal Balance	

Merchandise that is purchased for resale is a cost of doing business. Therefore, the **Purchases** account follows the rules of debit and credit for expense accounts. The **Purchases** account is increased by debits and decreased by credits. The normal balance of the **Purchases** account is a debit.

Reinforce the Main Idea

Create a table similar to this one to identify the four stages in the purchasing process, the activity involved in each stage, and the document used in that stage.

Stage	Stage Title	Activity	Document
1			
2			
3			
4			

Do the Math

As a new accountant for the South City School District, one of your primary duties involves preparing purchase requisitions. For each item ordered, you compute the extensions (quantity ordered multiplied by the cost per unit). On a separate sheet of paper, calculate the extensions for each of the following items ordered.

Quantity	Item Description	Unit Price
1	Box of copy paper	$34.00/box
5	Reams of art paper	$12/ream
2	Globes	$55/ea.
100	No. 2 pencils	$.12/ea.
4 doz.	Transparency markers	$6.50/doz.

Problem 15–1 Analyzing a Purchase Order

Instructions Analyze the purchase order shown here and answer the following questions in your working papers.

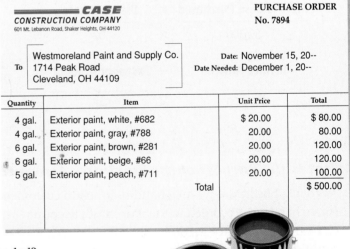

CASE
CONSTRUCTION COMPANY
601 Mt. Lebanon Road, Shaker Heights, OH 44120

PURCHASE ORDER
No. 7894

To
Westmoreland Paint and Supply Co.
1714 Peak Road
Cleveland, OH 44109

Date: November 15, 20--
Date Needed: December 1, 20--

Quantity	Item	Unit Price	Total
4 gal.	Exterior paint, white, #682	$ 20.00	$ 80.00
4 gal.	Exterior paint, gray, #788	20.00	80.00
6 gal.	Exterior paint, brown, #281	20.00	120.00
6 gal.	Exterior paint, beige, #66	20.00	120.00
5 gal.	Exterior paint, peach, #711	20.00	100.00
	Total		$ 500.00

1. What company ordered the merchandise?
2. What company was asked to supply the merchandise?
3. What is the purchase order number?
4. When was the purchase order prepared?
5. When is the merchandise needed?
6. How many gallons of paint were ordered?
7. How many different colors of paint were ordered?
8. What colors were ordered?
9. How much does each gallon of paint cost?
10. What is the total cost of the order?

Analyzing and Recording Purchases on Account

Small retailers may rely on a bookkeeper or part-time accountant to record purchase transactions. Large companies such as Kohl's Department Store can have thousands of suppliers. They need an entire accounts payable department to verify invoices and correct any discrepancies before recording purchases in the accounting records.

Purchases of Assets on Account

How Are the Purchases of Assets on Account Recorded?

Regardless of its type, size, or purpose, a retail business needs to buy supplies, equipment, and other assets. Most importantly, it buys merchandise to resell. Merchandise can be bought on a cash basis or on account. The business posts purchases on account in the accounts payable subsidiary ledger.

The Accounts Payable Subsidiary Ledger

In Chapter 14 you learned that when a business sells to many customers on credit, using an accounts receivable subsidiary ledger is efficient. Likewise, a business that purchases from many suppliers on account finds it efficient to set up an **accounts payable subsidiary ledger** with an account for each supplier or creditor. These individual accounts are summarized in the general ledger controlling account, **Accounts Payable.** The balance of the **Accounts Payable** controlling account and the total of all account balances in the accounts payable subsidiary ledger must agree after posting.

The Accounts Payable Subsidiary Ledger Form

The ledger account form in **Figure 15–4** on page 422 is used for both the accounts payable subsidiary ledger and the accounts receivable subsidiary ledger. The ledger account form has lines for the creditor's name and address. A manual accounting system arranges the accounts payable subsidiary ledger in alphabetical order with no account numbers. A computerized accounting

BEFORE YOU READ

Main Idea
Individual accounts payable transactions are posted to a subsidiary ledger.

Read to Learn...
➤ how to journalize purchases on account. (p. 421)
➤ how to journalize and post purchases returns and allowances. (p. 424)

Key Terms
accounts payable subsidiary ledger
tickler file
due date
purchases return
purchases allowance
debit memorandum

General Ledger	
Accounts Payable—controlling account	$4,500

Accounts Payable Subsidiary Ledger	
Individual Accounts Within Ledger:	
Sandals Etc.	$ 900
Shoe Warehouse	2,100
Shoe Wholesale Inc.	1,000
Store Supply Shop	500
Total	$4,500

Controlling account balance equals total of accounts in subsidiary ledger.

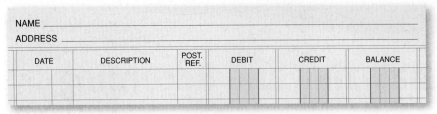

NAME _____					
ADDRESS _____					
DATE	DESCRIPTION	POST. REF.	DEBIT	CREDIT	BALANCE

Figure 15–4 Subsidiary Ledger Account Form

system assigns each creditor an account number.

The ledger account form has three amount columns. The normal balance of an Accounts Payable subsidiary account is a credit. The Debit column for payments to creditors records decreases to the account. The Credit column for purchases on account is for increases to it. The Balance column shows the amount owed to the creditor.

Merchandise Purchases on Account

On Your Mark's first purchase transaction in December involves a purchase of merchandise on account. When this entry is recorded in the journal, a diagonal line in the Posting Reference column indicates that the credit amount is posted in *two* places.

- *First* post to the **Accounts Payable** controlling account in the general ledger.
- *Then* post to the **Pro Runner Warehouse** account in the accounts payable subsidiary ledger.

After the invoice from Pro Runner Warehouse is journalized, it is put in a **tickler file**, which has a folder for each day of the month. Each invoice is placed in a folder according to its **due date**, the date it is to be paid. For example, an invoice due December 24 is placed in the "24" folder.

Business Transaction

On December 14 On Your Mark purchased $2,300 in merchandise on account from Pro Runner Warehouse, Invoice 7894.

PRO RUNNER WAREHOUSE
22009 Ben White Blvd.
Austin, TX 78705

INVOICE NO. 7894

REC'D DEC. 14, 20--

DATE: Dec. 14, 20--
ORDER NO.: 9784
SHIPPED BY: Federal Trucking
TERMS: 2/10, n/30

TO On Your Mark Athletic Wear
595 Leslie Street
Dallas, TX 75207

QTY.	ITEM	UNIT PRICE	TOTAL
20 pair	Soft Cushion: White, #94682	$ 50.00	$ 1,000.00
10 pair	Soft Cushion: Black, #94788	50.00	500.00
10 pair	Low Cut: White, #94281	40.00	400.00
10 pair	Low Cut: Black, #94666	40.00	400.00
		Total	$ 2,300.00

Due Date: _12/24_
Discount: _$ 46.00_
Net Amount: _$ 2,254.00_
Check No.:

ANALYSIS *Identify*
1. The accounts affected are **Purchases, Accounts Payable** (controlling), and **Accounts Payable—Pro Runner Warehouse** (subsidiary).

Classify
2. **Purchases** is a cost of merchandise account. **Accounts Payable** (controlling) and **Accounts Payable—Pro Runner Warehouse** (subsidiary) are liability accounts.

+/−
3. **Purchases** is increased by $2,300. This is the cost of the merchandise purchased. **Accounts Payable** (controlling) and **Accounts Payable—Pro Runner Warehouse** (subsidiary) are increased by $2,300.

DEBIT-CREDIT RULE
4. Increases to cost of merchandise accounts are recorded as debits. Debit **Purchases** for $2,300.
5. Increases to liability accounts are recorded as credits. Credit **Accounts Payable** (controlling) for $2,300. Also credit **Accounts Payable—Pro Runner Warehouse** (subsidiary) for $2,300.

T ACCOUNTS	6.	Purchases		Accounts Payable	
		Debit + 2,300	Credit −	Debit −	Credit + 2,300

Accounts Payable
Subsidiary Ledger
Pro Runner Warehouse

Debit −	Credit + 2,300

JOURNAL ENTRY 7.

		GENERAL JOURNAL			PAGE 21		
	DATE	DESCRIPTION	POST. REF.	DEBIT		CREDIT	
1	20--						1
2	Dec. 14	Purchases		2 300 00			2
3		Accts. Pay./Pro Runner Whs.				2 300 00	3
4		Invoice 7894					4

Other Purchases on Account

On Your Mark purchases assets other than merchandise, such as supplies, computer equipment, and store equipment. The following example illustrates the purchase of store equipment on account.

Business Transaction

On December 15 On Your Mark received Invoice 3417, dated December 13, from Champion Store Supply for store equipment bought on account for $1,200, terms n/30.

CHAMPION STORE SUPPLY
47249 Randall Parkway
Dallas, TX 75207

REC'D DEC. 15, 20--

INVOICE NO. 3417
DATE: Dec. 13, 20--
ORDER NO.: 9795
SHIPPED BY: Federal Trucking
TERMS: n/30

TO On Your Mark Athletic Wear
595 Leslie Street
Dallas, TX 75207

QTY.	ITEM	UNIT PRICE	TOTAL
3	Corner Shelf Units	$ 300.00	$ 900.00
1	Shirt Rack	300.00	300.00
	Total		$ 1,200.00

Due Date: 1/12
Discount: $0.00
Net Amount: $1,200.00
Check No.:

ANALYSIS

Identify
1. The accounts affected are **Store Equipment, Accounts Payable** (controlling), and **Accounts Payable—Champion Store Supply** (subsidiary).

Classify
2. **Store Equipment** is an asset account. **Accounts Payable** (controlling) and **Accounts Payable—Champion Store Supply** (subsidiary) are liability accounts.

+/−
3. **Store Equipment** is increased by $1,200. **Accounts Payable** (controlling) and **Accounts Payable—Champion Store Supply** (subsidiary) are increased by $1,200.

DEBIT-CREDIT RULE

4. Increases to asset accounts are recorded as debits. Debit **Store Equipment** for $1,200.
5. Increases to liability accounts are recorded as credits. Credit **Accounts Payable** (controlling) for $1,200. Also credit **Accounts Payable—Champion Store Supply** (subsidiary) for $1,200.

T ACCOUNTS

6.

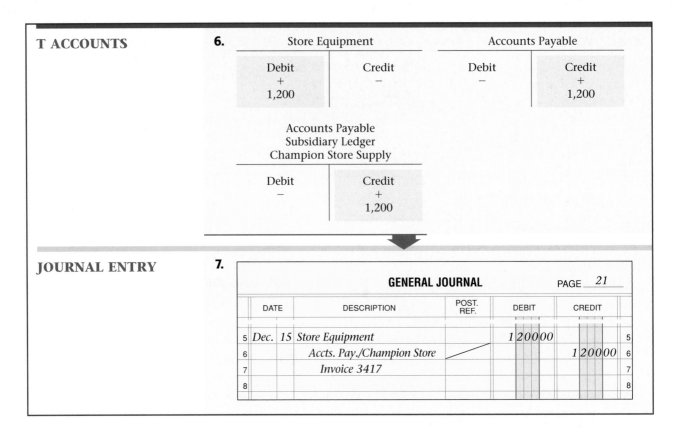

Store Equipment		Accounts Payable	
Debit + 1,200	Credit −	Debit −	Credit + 1,200

Accounts Payable
Subsidiary Ledger
Champion Store Supply

Debit −	Credit + 1,200

JOURNAL ENTRY

7.

		GENERAL JOURNAL				PAGE 21	
	DATE	DESCRIPTION	POST. REF.	DEBIT		CREDIT	
5	Dec. 15	Store Equipment		1 200 00			5
6		Accts. Pay./Champion Store				1 200 00	6
7		Invoice 3417					7
8							8

Purchases Returns and Allowances
How Are Purchases Returns and Allowances Recorded?

Occasionally, a business buys merchandise that, upon inspection, is unacceptable. A **purchases return** occurs when a business returns merchandise to the supplier for full credit. A **purchases allowance** occurs when a business keeps less than satisfactory merchandise and pays a reduced price.

A **debit memorandum**, or debit memo, is used to notify suppliers (creditors) of a return or to request an allowance. The "debit" in debit memorandum indicates that the creditor's account will be debited, or decreased.

Figure 15–5 shows a debit memorandum prepared by On Your Mark. As you can see, the debit memorandum is prenumbered and has spaces for the creditor's name and address and the invoice number. The original is sent to the creditor. The copy is the source document for the journal entry.

A debit memorandum always results in a debit (decrease) to the **Accounts Payable** controlling account in the general ledger and to the creditor's account in the subsidiary ledger. The account credited depends on whether the debit memorandum is for merchandise or another asset.

Figure 15–5
Debit Memorandum

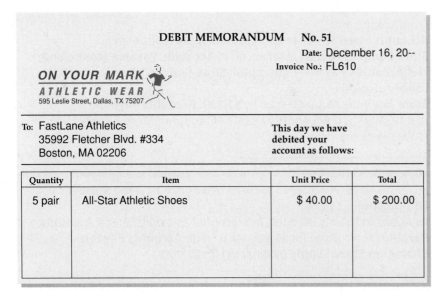

DEBIT MEMORANDUM   **No. 51**
Date: December 16, 20--
Invoice No.: FL610

ON YOUR MARK
ATHLETIC WEAR
595 Leslie Street, Dallas, TX 75207

To: FastLane Athletics
35992 Fletcher Blvd. #334
Boston, MA 02206

This day we have debited your account as follows:

Quantity	Item	Unit Price	Total
5 pair	All-Star Athletic Shoes	$ 40.00	$ 200.00

Purchases	
Debit + Increase Side Normal Balance	Credit − Decrease Side

Purchases Returns and Allowances	
Debit − Decrease Side	Credit + Increase Side Normal Balance

The **Purchases Returns and Allowances** account is used to record the return of merchandise to a supplier or to record an allowance. It is classified as a *contra cost of merchandise* account to the **Purchases** account. The normal balance of **Purchases** is a debit, so the normal balance of **Purchases Returns and Allowances** is a credit. This relationship is shown in these T accounts.

As You READ

Instant Recall

Contra Account A contra account is an account whose balance is a decrease to another related account.

Recording a Purchases Returns and Allowances Transaction

On Your Mark prepared and sent the debit memorandum shown in **Figure 15–5.**

DEBIT MEMORANDUM   No. 51
Date: December 16, 20--
Invoice No.: FL610

ON YOUR MARK
ATHLETIC WEAR
595 Leslie Street, Dallas, TX 75207

To: FastLane Athletics
35992 Fletcher Blvd. #334
Boston, MA 02206

This day we have debited your account as follows:

Quantity	Item	Unit Price	Total
5 pair	All-Star Athletic Shoes	$ 40.00	$ 200.00

Business Transaction

On December 16 On Your Mark issued Debit Memorandum 51 for the return of $200 in merchandise purchased on account from FastLane Athletics.

ANALYSIS   *Identify*
1. The accounts affected are **Accounts Payable** (controlling), **Accounts Payable—FastLane Athletics** (subsidiary), and **Purchases Returns and Allowances.**

Classify
2. **Accounts Payable** (controlling) and **Accounts Payable—FastLane Athletics** (subsidiary) are liability accounts. **Purchases Returns and Allowances** is a contra cost of merchandise account.

+/−
3. **Accounts Payable** (controlling) and **Accounts Payable—FastLane Athletics** (subsidiary) are decreased by $200. **Purchases Returns and Allowances** is increased by $200.

DEBIT-CREDIT RULE
4. Decreases to liability accounts are recorded as debits. Debit **Accounts Payable** (controlling) for $200. Also debit **Accounts Payable—FastLane Athletics** (subsidiary) for $200.
5. Increases to contra cost of merchandise accounts are recorded as credits. Credit **Purchases Returns and Allowances** for $200.

T ACCOUNTS
6.

Accounts Payable			Purchases Returns and Allowances	
Debit − 200	Credit +		Debit −	Credit + 200

Accounts Payable Subsidiary Ledger FastLane Athletics	
Debit − 200	Credit +

JOURNAL ENTRY 7.

	GENERAL JOURNAL				PAGE 21	
	DATE	DESCRIPTION	POST. REF.	DEBIT	CREDIT	
8	Dec. 16	Accts. Pay./FastLane Athletics		200 00		8
9		Purchases Returns and Allow.			200 00	9
10		Debit Memorandum 51				10
11						11

Posting to the Accounts Payable Subsidiary Ledger

In **Figure 15–6** note how the transaction is posted. The $200 debit is posted to two accounts—the **Accounts Payable** controlling account and the accounts payable subsidiary ledger account, **FastLane Athletics.** After it is posted to **Accounts Payable,** the account number *201* is entered to the *left* of the diagonal in the Posting Reference column. After the amount is posted to **FastLane Athletics,** a check mark (✓) is entered to the *right* of the diagonal line.

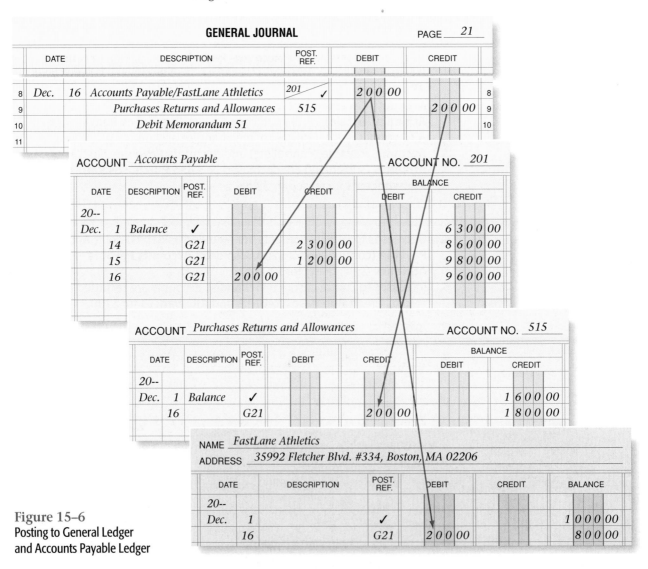

Figure 15–6
Posting to General Ledger
and Accounts Payable Ledger

426   **Chapter 15**   Accounting for Purchases and Cash Payments

Reinforce the Main Idea

Create a flowchart like this one and write the correct labels in the boxes and next to the arrows. Create the labels from these terms: *general ledger, invoice, journal, posted to, recorded in, subsidiary ledger.* Terms can be used more than once.

Do the Math

Alpha Enterprises received an invoice dated May 2 for the purchase of $3,000 of merchandise. Terms of sale are 2/10, n/30. Answer the following questions:

1. What is the due date of the invoice?
2. What is the amount of the cash discount?
3. What is the net amount to be paid?
4. If the discount period is missed, what is the last day the invoice is to be paid? How much would be paid?

Problem 15–2 Recording Purchases Transactions

Instructions Record the following purchases transactions on page 7 of the general journal in your working papers.

Date	Transactions
Sept. 2	Purchased $900 in merchandise on account from Sunrise Novelty Supply, Invoice SN110.
7	Issued Debit Memorandum 18 to Sunrise Novelty Supply for a $50 allowance granted on damaged merchandise.

Problem 15–3 Analyzing a Source Document

As an accounting intern for Kaleidoscope Comics, you perform a variety of accounting tasks. The accountant hands you this debit memo.

Instructions

1. Analyze the source document. Determine which accounts are to be debited or credited.
2. Record the entry on page 15 of the general journal in your working papers.

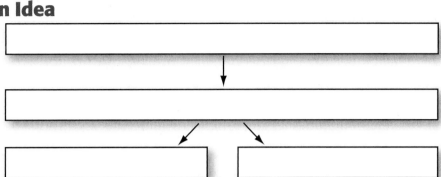

Accounting Careers in Focus

ANALYST
Morgan Stanley, Teaneck, New Jersey
Anwar Beatty

Q: What has helped you in your career?

A: Networking. I always try to get to know people in different positions and fields and learn what they do.

Q: What are your day-to-day responsibilities?

A: I help maintain the in-house computer systems for one of our business groups. I conduct systems checks, help resolve user issues, and carry through enhancements that allow for greater productivity and efficiency. In addition, I'm responsible for compiling a variety of reports and filing them with senior management and the Securities and Exchange Commission.

Q: What is the biggest challenge you face in your job?

A: Learning aspects of the finance industry that were not part of my coursework in school. Education should be ongoing—you must be able to pick up new things, digest them, and apply them the next day.

Q: What advice would you give students who are interested in becoming analysts?

A: Get involved with professional associations. They can help prepare you for your first job. They'll also help you build professional skills that you'll need in the business world. If you do your research, you'll find that there are a great deal more opportunities available in finance than you might realize. I never thought I would be involved in this aspect of the business, for example.

Tips from . . .
RHI Robert Half International Inc.

When reviewing a job candidate's resume, 53 percent of hiring managers say they look first for relevant experience. You can build your work history through volunteer opportunities, internships, and temporary assignments.

CAREER FACTS

▶ **Nature of the Work:** Work with stock traders to monitor stock positions and companies' earnings reports; interact with personnel from various financial institutions to resolve customer queries and problems concerning stock trades.

▶ **Training or Education Needed:** A bachelor's degree in accounting or finance is preferred.

▶ **Aptitudes, Abilities, and Skills:** Strong communication skills, organizational skills, and multitasking abilities.

▶ **Salary Range:** $30,000 to $50,000 depending on experience, level of responsibility, and firm size.

▶ **Career Path:** Start as an entry-level analyst, and then assume roles of increasing responsibility.

Thinking Critically How might you acquire the basic accounting experience you need for an entry-level position?

Analyzing and Recording Cash Payments

If cash is the lifeblood of a business, the accounting department is its heart. All cash entering or leaving a business is "pumped" through the accounting department at some time. If it is not, cash losses can occur.

Controls over Cash

How Does a Business Manage Cash Payments?

Earlier chapters explained ways to guard against losses of cash receipts. For example, businesses should deposit all cash receipts in a bank account. Businesses must also properly manage cash payments so that losses do not occur. The following are procedures to manage cash payments:

- Require proper authorization of all cash payments. Support each payment with an approved source document, such as an invoice.
- Write checks for all payments. Allow only authorized persons to sign checks.
- Use prenumbered checks.
- Retain and account for spoiled checks. Mark these checks "Void," and file them in sequence.

Cash Payment Transactions

How Does a Merchandising Business Make Cash Payments?

Businesses buy merchandise and other assets on account or by paying cash. On Your Mark makes all cash payments by check. When it makes a cash payment, the clerk records the details on the check stub. The check stub is the source document for the journal entry. Then the clerk prepares a check, which an authorized person signs. Let's look at how to record several types of cash payment transactions that occur frequently.

Recording Cash Purchase of Insurance

Businesses buy insurance to protect against losses from hazards such as theft, fire, and flood. Insurance policies cover varying time periods, such as six months or one year. The cost of insurance protection is called the **premium**. A premium is paid in advance at the beginning of the covered period. Insurance paid in advance is an asset because until the insurance protection expires, it represents a benefit to the company. The insurance premium is recorded in the asset account, **Prepaid Insurance.**

BEFORE YOU READ

Main Idea
The accounting department is responsible for making the cash payments for the business.

Read to Learn...
➤ the procedures for managing cash payments. (p. 429)
➤ how to record the different types of cash payment transactions. (p. 429)

Key Terms
premium
FOB destination
FOB shipping point
bankcard fee

AS YOU READ

Instant Recall

Internal Controls One of the key purposes of internal controls is to protect cash and other assets.

On December 17 On Your Mark paid $1,500 to Keystone Insurance Company for the premium on a six-month insurance policy, Check 1001.

ON YOUR MARK 1001
ATHLETIC WEAR 22-523
595 Leslie Street, Dallas, TX 75207 4210

DATE Dec. 17 20 --

PAY TO THE ORDER OF Keystone Insurance Company $ 1,500.00

One thousand five hundred and no/100 ———————————— DOLLARS

Security National Bank
DALLAS, TEXAS

MEMO _____ Michael Brown

⑁4210 22523⑁ 727596⑊ 1001

ANALYSIS *Identify*	1. The accounts affected are **Prepaid Insurance** and **Cash in Bank.**
Classify +/−	2. Both **Prepaid Insurance** and **Cash in Bank** are asset accounts.
	3. **Prepaid Insurance** is increased by $1,500. **Cash in Bank** is decreased by $1,500.
DEBIT-CREDIT RULE	4. Increases to asset accounts are recorded as debits. Debit **Prepaid Insurance** for $1,500.
	5. Decreases to asset accounts are recorded as credits. Credit **Cash in Bank** for $1,500.

T ACCOUNTS 6.

Prepaid Insurance			Cash in Bank	
Debit + 1,500	Credit −		Debit +	Credit − 1,500

JOURNAL ENTRY 7.

GENERAL JOURNAL PAGE 21

	DATE	DESCRIPTION	POST. REF.	DEBIT	CREDIT	
11	Dec. 17	Prepaid Insurance		1 50000		11
12		Cash in Bank			1 50000	12
13		Check 1001				13

Recording Cash Purchases of Merchandise

Usually businesses purchase merchandise on account. Sometimes a business buys merchandise for cash. Let's look at an example of a cash purchase of merchandise.

ON YOUR MARK 1002
ATHLETIC WEAR 22-523
595 Leslie Street, Dallas, TX 75207 4210

DATE Dec. 19 20 --

PAY TO THE ORDER OF FastLane Athletics $ 1,300.00

One thousand three hundred and no/100 ———————————— DOLLARS

Security National Bank
DALLAS, TEXAS

MEMO _____ Michael Brown

⑁4210 22523⑁ 727596⑊ 1002

On December 19 On Your Mark purchased merchandise from FastLane Athletics for $1,300, Check 1002.

ANALYSIS *Identify*	1. The accounts affected are **Purchases** and **Cash in Bank.**
Classify	2. **Purchases** is a cost of merchandise account. **Cash in Bank** is an asset account.
+/−	3. **Purchases** is increased by $1,300. **Cash in Bank** is decreased by $1,300.

| DEBIT-CREDIT RULE | **4.** Increases to cost of merchandise accounts are recorded as debits. Debit **Purchases** for $1,300. |
| | **5.** Decreases to asset accounts are recorded as credits. Credit **Cash in Bank** for $1,300. |

T ACCOUNTS   **6.**

Purchases		Cash in Bank	
Debit + 1,300	Credit −	Debit +	Credit − 1,300

JOURNAL ENTRY   **7.**

GENERAL JOURNAL   PAGE __21__

	DATE	DESCRIPTION	POST. REF.	DEBIT	CREDIT	
14	Dec. 19	Purchases		1 300 00		14
15		Cash in Bank			1 300 00	15
16		Check 1002				16
17						17

Recording Cash Payments for Items Purchased on Account

An invoice received by a business is verified for items, quantities, and prices, recorded in the journal, and filed by due date in a tickler file.

Each day, the invoices due for payment are removed from the tickler file. Checks are prepared, signed by an authorized person, and mailed to creditors.

The amount of the check in payment of an invoice depends on the credit terms and the payment date. For example, On Your Mark purchased $2,300 of merchandise on account from Pro Runner Warehouse. The invoice, dated December 14, listed credit terms of 2/10, n/30. If On Your Mark pays for the merchandise on or before December 24, it can take a discount of $46.

When it pays the invoice on December 24, On Your Mark debits **Accounts Payable** (controlling) and **Accounts Payable—Pro Runner Warehouse** for the full amount of the invoice, $2,300. On Your Mark is paying for all of the merchandise and doesn't owe any more money on this purchase.

Purchases	
Debit + Increase Side Normal Balance	Credit − Decrease Side

Purchases Discounts	
Debit − Decrease Side	Credit + Increase Side Normal Balance

Cash in Bank is credited for $2,254, the actual amount of the check. The difference between $2,300 and $2,254 is the cash discount, which is credited to the **Purchases Discounts** account.

The **Purchases Discounts** account tracks the cash discounts a business takes. **Purchases Discounts** is a contra cost of merchandise account. Its balance reduces the balance of the **Purchases** account. Its normal balance is therefore a credit.

Business Transaction

On December 24 On Your Mark paid $2,254 to Pro Runner Warehouse for merchandise purchased on account, $2,300 less a discount of $46, Check 1003.

ON YOUR MARK	1003
ATHLETIC WEAR	22-523
595 Leslie Street, Dallas, TX 75207	4210

DATE Dec. 24 20 --

PAY TO THE ORDER OF Pro Runner Warehouse $ 2,254.00

Two thousand two hundred fifty-four and no/100————————— DOLLARS

Security National Bank
DALLAS, TEXAS

MEMO _____   *Michael Brown*

⑆4210225230⑆ 727596⑆ 1003

ANALYSIS

Identify
1. The accounts affected are **Accounts Payable** (controlling), **Accounts Payable—Pro Runner Warehouse** (subsidiary), **Cash in Bank**, and **Purchases Discounts**.

Classify
2. **Accounts Payable** (controlling) and **Accounts Payable—Pro Runner Warehouse** (subsidiary) are liability accounts. **Cash in Bank** is an asset account. **Purchases Discounts** is a contra cost of merchandise account.

+/−
3. **Accounts Payable** (controlling) and **Accounts Payable—Pro Runner Warehouse** (subsidiary) are decreased by $2,300. **Cash in Bank** is decreased by $2,254. **Purchases Discounts** is increased by $46.

DEBIT-CREDIT RULE

4. Decreases to liability accounts are recorded as debits. Debit **Accounts Payable** (controlling) for $2,300. Also debit **Accounts Payable—Pro Runner Warehouse** (subsidiary) for $2,300.

5. Decreases to asset accounts are recorded as credits. Credit **Cash in Bank** for $2,254. Increases to contra cost of merchandise accounts are recorded as credits. Credit **Purchases Discounts** for $46.

T ACCOUNTS

6.

Accounts Payable			Cash in Bank	
Debit	Credit		Debit	Credit
−	+		+	−
2,300				2,254

Accounts Payable Subsidiary Ledger Pro Runner Warehouse			Purchases Discounts	
Debit	Credit		Debit	Credit
−	+		−	+
2,300				46

JOURNAL ENTRY

7.

		GENERAL JOURNAL			PAGE 21	
	DATE	DESCRIPTION	POST. REF.	DEBIT	CREDIT	
17	Dec. 24	Accts. Pay./Pro Runner Ware.		2 300 00		17
18		Cash in Bank			2 254 00	18
19		Purchases Discounts			46 00	19
20		Check 1003				20

Other Cash Payments

When a company buys merchandise from a supplier, there is often a charge for shipping the goods. The shipping terms determine whether the buyer or shipper will pay the shipping charges.

Shipping terms are stated as either FOB destination or FOB shipping point. "FOB" stands for "free on board." **FOB destination** means that the *supplier* pays the shipping cost to the buyer's destination or location. When merchandise is shipped **FOB shipping point**, the *buyer* pays the shipping charge from the supplier's shipping point.

As You READ

In Your Own Words

FOB Shipping Point In your own words, explain what the term *FOB shipping point* means.

Terms	Shipping Cost Paid By
FOB destination	Supplier
FOB shipping point	Buyer

A shipping charge is an additional cost of the merchandise. The account set up to handle shipping charges is **Transportation In**, which is a cost of merchandise account. **Transportation In** follows the rules of debit and credit for expense accounts. **Transportation In** is increased by debits and decreased by credits. The normal balance of **Transportation In** is a debit.

Transportation In	
Debit	Credit
+	−
Increase Side	Decrease Side
Normal Balance	

Here is an example of the payment of shipping charges.

Business Transaction

On December 24 On Your Mark issued Check 1004 for $275 to Dara's Delivery Service for shipping charges on merchandise purchased from Sports Link Footwear.

ON YOUR MARK ATHLETIC WEAR
595 Leslie Street, Dallas, TX 75207

1004
22-523
4210

DATE Dec. 24 20--

PAY TO THE ORDER OF Dara's Delivery Service $ 275.00

Two hundred seventy-five and no/100———— DOLLARS

Security National Bank
DALLAS, TEXAS

MEMO _____ *Michael Brown*

⑆4210 22523⑆ 727596⑈ 1004

JOURNAL ENTRY

		GENERAL JOURNAL			PAGE 21	
	DATE	DESCRIPTION	POST. REF.	DEBIT	CREDIT	
21	Dec. 24	Transportation In		275 00		21
22		Cash in Bank			275 00	22
23		Check 1004				23

Recording Bankcard Fees

On Your Mark makes the following entry to record the bankcard fee deducted from the business checking account. Banks charge a fee for handling bankcard sales slips. This **bankcard fee** is usually a percentage of the total of the amounts recorded on the bankcard sales slips processed.

Business Transaction

On December 31 On Your Mark records the bankcard fee of $75, December bank statement.

JOURNAL ENTRY

		GENERAL JOURNAL			PAGE 21	
	DATE	DESCRIPTION	POST. REF.	DEBIT	CREDIT	
24	Dec. 31	Bankcard Fees Expense		75 00		24
25		Cash in Bank			75 00	25
26		December Bank Statement				26

The journal entries for all of the transactions discussed and illustrated in this chapter are shown in **Figure 15–7**.

	DATE		DESCRIPTION	POST. REF.	DEBIT	CREDIT	
1	20--						1
2	Dec.	14	Purchases		2 3 0 0 00		2
3			Accounts Payable/Pro Runner Warehouse			2 3 0 0 00	3
4			Invoice 7894				4
5		15	Store Equipment		1 2 0 0 00		5
6			Accounts Payable/Champion Store Supply			1 2 0 0 00	6
7			Invoice 3417				7
8		16	Accounts Payable/FastLane Athletics		2 0 0 00		8
9			Purchases Returns & Allowances			2 0 0 00	9
10			Debit Memorandum 51				10
11		17	Prepaid Insurance		1 5 0 0 00		11
12			Cash in Bank			1 5 0 0 00	12
13			Check 1001				13
14		19	Purchases		1 3 0 0 00		14
15			Cash in Bank			1 3 0 0 00	15
16			Check 1002				16
17		24	Accounts Payable/Pro Runner Warehouse		2 3 0 0 00		17
18			Cash in Bank			2 2 5 4 00	18
19			Purchases Discounts			4 6 00	19
20			Check 1003				20
21		24	Transportation In		2 7 5 00		21
22			Cash in Bank			2 7 5 00	22
23			Check 1004				23
24		31	Bankcard Fees Expense		7 5 00		24
25			Cash in Bank			7 5 00	25
26			December Bank Statement				26
27							27

GENERAL JOURNAL   PAGE ___21___

Figure 15–7 Journal Entries for December Business Transactions

AFTER YOU READ

Reinforce the Main Idea

Create a chart similar to the one here to analyze each cash payment transaction for a merchandising business discussed in the chapter. Identify the accounts affected, the account(s) credited, and the account(s) debited.

Action	Accounts Affected	Account to Credit	Account to Debit

Do the Math

Clara's Designs is a crafts store with a large inventory of seasonal crafts items. As the inventory clerk, you are to create a chart or graph to compare the cost of the items purchased and the related shipping charges. Using the data provided, design a chart or graph that depicts both sets of data. What conclusions can you draw from your chart or graph?

	Cost of Item	Shipping Charges
Holiday decorator ribbon	$2,000	$200
Door wreaths and hangers	3,200	320
Potpourri	1,200	120
Styrofoam trees	4,350	435

Problem 15–4 Recording Cash Payment Transactions

Meadow Link Golf Club had the following cash payment transactions.

Instructions Record the following transactions on page 6 of the general journal in your working papers.

Date	Transactions
May 1	Purchased $10,500 in golf equipment (merchandise) from TopMax Golf Manufacturers, Check 1150.
5	Issued Check 1151 for $325 to Franco's Trucking for delivery charges on merchandise bought from TopMax Golf Manufacturers.
7	Paid Lone Star Insurance Company $2,500 for the annual premium on an insurance policy, Check 1152.

Key Concepts

1. Four documents are used in the purchasing process:
   - The *purchase requisition* is a request to order goods.
   - The *purchase order* is an offer to buy goods.
   - The *packing list* is a list of the goods shipped.
   - The *invoice* lists the credit terms; the quantity, description, unit price, and total cost of the items; the buyer's purchase order number; and the method of shipment.

2. The four accounts used in the purchasing process and their classifications are:

   Purchases—cost of merchandise

   Purchases Discounts—contra cost of merchandise

   Purchases Returns and Allowances—contra cost of merchandise

   Transportation In—cost of merchandise

3. Cash is the lifeblood of a business and must be protected from loss, waste, theft, forgery, and embezzlement. Good internal controls include the proper management of cash payments, requiring that they be authorized, made by check, and signed by an authorized person.

4. The **Purchases** account is used to record the cost of merchandise purchased during the period. The rules of debit and credit for **Purchases** are the same as those for expense accounts.

Purchases

Debit	Credit
+	−
Increase Side	Decrease Side
Normal Balance	

Suppliers may offer cash discounts to their credit customers to encourage prompt payment. Buyers who take a cash discount record it in the **Purchases Discounts** account.

Purchases Discounts

Debit	Credit
−	+
Decrease Side	Increase Side
	Normal Balance

When the buyer receives credit for returned or damaged merchandise, the amount is recorded in the **Purchases Returns and Allowances** account.

Purchases Returns and Allowances

Debit	Credit
−	+
Decrease Side	Increase Side
	Normal Balance

The shipping charges for merchandise purchased from suppliers are considered an additional cost of merchandise. Shipping charges are debited to the **Transportation In** account.

Transportation In

Debit	Credit
+	−
Increase Side	Decrease Side
Normal Balance	

5. The following summarizes the accounts involved in journalizing purchases and cash payments:

   Purchase of merchandise on account:

   > Debit: **Purchases**   Credit: **Accounts Payable—Creditor's Name**

   Other purchase on account (for example, store equipment):

   > Debit: **Store Equipment**   Credit: **Accounts Payable—Creditor's Name**

   Return or allowance for merchandise purchased on account:

   > Debit: **Accounts Payable—**   Credit: **Purchases Returns**
   >   **Creditor's Name**   **and Allowances**

   Cash purchase (for example, insurance coverage):

   > Debit: **Prepaid Insurance**   Credit: **Cash in Bank**

   Cash purchase of merchandise:

   > Debit: **Purchases**   Credit: **Cash in Bank**

   Payment for merchandise purchased on account (with a cash discount taken):

   > Debit: **Accounts Payable—**   Credit: **Cash in Bank**
   >   **Creditor's Name**   **Purchases Discounts**

   Cash payment for cost of shipping merchandise:

   > Debit: **Transportation In**   Credit: **Cash in Bank**

   Bankcard Fee

   > Debit: **Bankcard Fees Expense**   Credit: **Cash in Bank**

6. The *accounts payable subsidiary ledger* contains an account for each creditor. The total of the account balances in the subsidiary ledger must match the balance of the **Accounts Payable** controlling account in the general ledger. **Figure 15–6** on page 426 summarizes how to post purchases on account to the general ledger and the accounts payable subsidiary ledger.

Key Terms

accounts payable subsidiary ledger	(p. 421)	FOB destination	(p. 433)	Purchases account	(p. 419)
		FOB shipping point	(p. 433)	purchases allowance	(p. 424)
bankcard fee	(p. 433)	packing slip	(p. 418)	purchases discount	(p. 418)
cost of merchandise	(p. 419)	premium	(p. 429)	purchases return	(p. 424)
debit memorandum	(p. 424)	processing stamp	(p. 418)	tickler file	(p. 422)
discount period	(p. 419)	purchase order	(p. 416)		
due date	(p. 422)	purchase requisition	(p. 416)		

Check Your Understanding

1. **Processing a Purchase on Account**
   a. List the steps in making a purchase on account.
   b. Why is an invoice checked against both the purchase order and the packing slip?

2. **Accounts Used in Purchasing**
   a. What accounts are used when a business purchases merchandise on account?
   b. What type of account is **Transportation In?**

3. **Controls over Cash**
   a. Why must each payment be supported by an approved source document?
   b. List four procedures that a business should use to control its cash payments.

4. **Merchandise Purchases**
   a. Which accounts are debited and credited when merchandise is purchased for cash?
   b. Which accounts are debited and credited when merchandise is purchased on account?

5. **Recording Purchases and Cash Payments**
   a. What term is used to describe the payment for insurance coverage?
   b. What account is debited when insurance is purchased?

6. **Accounts Payable Subsidiary Ledger**
   a. What is the purpose of the accounts payable subsidiary ledger?
   b. Why do you post a purchase on account to two different ledgers?

Apply Key Terms

Work with a partner to pair these terms. Discuss the relationship between the terms. Is one the result of another? Are they opposite? Once you agree, write out your explanation for each pair.

accounts payable subsidiary ledger	premium
bankcard fee	processing stamp
cost of merchandise	purchase order
debit memorandum	purchase requisition
discount period	**Purchases** account
due date	purchases allowance
FOB destination	purchases discount
FOB shipping point	purchases return
packing slip	tickler file

Recording Purchases and Cash Payments

Making the Transition from a Manual to a Computerized System

Task	Manual Methods	Computerized Methods
Recording purchase transactions	• Prepare general journal entries and post them based on an invoice for merchandise purchased on account or for cash.	• The system automatically generates journal entries from the invoice information and posts them to the general ledger.
Recording cash payment transactions	• Write checks in payment of an invoice or memorandum. • Prepare journal entries to record the checks and post them to the general ledger. • Calculate new account balances.	• The system automatically generates journal entries as it prepares the check for payment. • The system posts journal entries and updates account balances.

 **Peachtree®** Q & A

Peachtree Question	Answer
How do I record the purchase of merchandise on account?	1. From the *Tasks* menu, select **Purchases/Receive Inventory.** 2. Enter Vendor ID, Invoice No., and Date. 3. Select the Apply to Purchases tab. 4. Enter quantity, description, general ledger account, and unit price for each item.
How do I record payments on account?	1. From the *Tasks* menu, select **Payments.** 2. Enter the Vendor ID, Check No., Date, and Cash account number. 3. Click the Apply to Invoices tab. 4. Select the invoice to be paid.

QuickBooks Q & A

QuickBooks Question	Answer
How do I record the purchase of merchandise on account?	1. From the *Vendors* menu, select **Enter Bills.** 2. Enter the vendor's name, date, purchase amount, reference number, and memo. 3. From the Items tab, select the item purchased. 4. Enter the quantity in the *Qty* field.
How do I record payments on account?	1. From the *Vendors* menu, select **Pay Bills.** 2. Select the **Due on or before** button, and enter the due date of the bills to pay. 3. Place a check mark to the left of the vendor to be paid, and set discounts or credits if applicable. 4. Select the **Assign check no.** radio button. 5. Enter the date of the transactions in the *Payment Date* field.

For detailed instructions, see your Glencoe Accounting Chapter Study Guides and Working Papers.

Problem 15–5 Determining Due Dates and Discount Amounts

Sunset Surfwear frequently purchases merchandise on account. When it receives invoices, a clerk puts a processing stamp on the invoice indicating the due date, the amount of any discount, and the amount to be paid. The following invoices were received during March.

	Invoice Number	Invoice Date	Credit Terms	Invoice Amount
1.	24574	March 5	2/10, n/30	$3,000.00
2.	530992	March 7	3/10, n/30	5,550.00
3.	211145	March 12	2/15, n/60	729.95
4.	45679	March 16	n/45	345.67
5.	34120	March 23	2/10, n/30	1,526.50
6.	00985	March 27	n/30	700.00

Instructions Prepare a form similar to the one that follows. The first invoice has been completed as an example. For each invoice do the following:

1. Determine the due date. Assume that Sunset Surfwear always pays invoices within the discount period.
2. Compute the discount amount, if any.
3. Compute the amount to be paid.

Invoice Number	Invoice Date	Credit Terms	Invoice Amount	Due Date	Discount Amount	Amout To Be Paid
24574	Mar. 5	2/10, n/30	$3,000.00	Mar. 15	$60.00	$2,940.00

Analyze Compute how much money Sunset Surfwear will save by taking all discounts.

SPREADSHEET SMART GUIDE

Step–by–Step Instructions: Problem 15–5

1. Select the spreadsheet template for Problem 15–5.
2. Enter your name and the date in the spaces provided on the template.
3. Complete the spreadsheet using the instructions in your working papers.
4. Print the spreadsheet and proof your work.
5. Complete the Analyze activity.
6. Save your work and exit the spreadsheet program.

Problem 15–6 Analyzing Purchases and Cash Payments

Peachtree®

SMART GUIDE

Step–by–Step Instructions: Problem 15–6

1. Select the problem set for InBeat CD Shop (Prob. 15–6).
2. Rename the company and set the system date.
3. Enter all of the purchases on account transactions using the **Purchases/Receive Inventory** option in the **Tasks** menu.
4. Process all debit memorandums using the **Vendor Credit Memos** option in the **Tasks** menu.
5. Record all cash payments using the **Payments** option.
6. Print a Purchases Journal report, a Cash Disbursements Journal, and a Vendor Ledgers report.
7. Proof your work.
8. Print a General Ledger report to complete the Analyze activity.
9. End the session.

TIP: To save time entering transactions, group them by type and then enter the transactions in batches.

InBeat CD Shop had the following transactions in March.

Instructions Use the T accounts in your working papers. For each transaction:

1. Determine which accounts are affected.
2. Enter the debit and credit amounts in the T accounts.

Date	Transactions
Mar. 2	Purchased merchandise on account from NightVision and Company, $2,000, Invoice NV-20, terms 2/10, n/30.
6	Issued Check 250 for $85 to Penn Trucking Company for delivering merchandise from NightVision and Company.
7	Purchased $300 in supplies on account from Temple Store Supply, Invoice 6011, terms n/30.
12	Issued Check 251 for $1,960 to NightVision and Company in payment of Invoice NV-20 for $2,000 less a cash discount of $40.
15	Paid Keystone Insurance Company $2,500 for the annual premium on business insurance, Check 252.
16	Purchased $3,000 in merchandise on account from NightVision and Company, Invoice NV-45, terms 2/10, n/30.
18	Issued Debit Memorandum 25 for $100 to NightVision and Company for the return of merchandise.
20	Purchased $900 in merchandise from Dandelion Records, Check 253.
22	Issued Check 254 to Temple Store Supplies for $300 for Invoice 6011.

Analyze Calculate the **Purchases** account balance at the end of March.

Problem 15–7 Recording Purchases Transactions

Shutterbug Cameras, a retail merchandising store, had the following purchases transactions in March.

Instructions In your working papers, record the transactions on page 31 of the general journal.

Date	Transactions
Mar. 3	Purchased $4,500 in merchandise on account from Photo Emporium, Invoice 1221, terms 2/10, n/30.
5	Bought $750 in supplies on account from State Street Office Supply, Invoice 873, terms n/30.

CONTINUE

Date	Transactions (cont.)
Mar. 9	Returned $225 in merchandise to Photo Emporium, issued Debit Memorandum 72.
10	Purchased $3,600 in merchandise on account from Video Optics Inc., Invoice VO94, terms 3/15, n/45.
15	State Street Office Supply granted a $60 credit for damaged supplies purchased on August 5, Debit Memorandum 73.
20	Bought $4,800 in store equipment from Digital Precision Equipment on account, Invoice 1288, terms n/30.
25	Issued Debit Memorandum 74 to Video Optics Inc. for the return of $120 in merchandise.
28	Purchased $1,800 in merchandise on account from U-Tech Products, Invoice UT66, terms n/30.
29	Bought $270 in supplies on account from ProStudio Supply, Invoice 4574, terms n/30.
30	Returned $150 in merchandise to U-Tech Products, Debit Memorandum 75.
31	Issued Debit Memorandum 76 to ProStudio Supply for the return of $35 in supplies bought on March 29.

Analyze Identify the total credit amount made to the **Purchases Returns and Allowances** account for the month.

Problem 15–8 Recording Cash Payment Transactions

Cycle Tech Bicycles had the following cash payment transactions in March.

Instructions In your working papers, record the transactions on page 19 of the general journal.

Date	Transactions
Mar. 1	Purchased $1,800 in merchandise from Summit Bicycles, Check 2111.
3	Issued Check 2112 for $2,450 to Spaulding Inc. in payment of the $2,500 account balance less a 2% cash discount of $50.
7	Issued Check 2113 for $3,100 to Desert Palms Insurance Company for the annual business insurance premium.
12	Paid $175 to Viking Express for delivery of merchandise purchased from Schwinn Inc., FOB shipping point, Check 2114.
17	Issued Check 2115 to Suspension Specialists for $3,880 in payment of Invoice 1492 for $4,000 less a 3% cash discount of $120.
20	Received the March bank statement and recorded bankcard fees of $275.

CONTINUE

Peachtree®

SMART GUIDE

Step–by–Step Instructions: Problem 15–7

1. Select the problem set for Shutterbug Cameras (Prob. 15–7).
2. Rename the company and set the system date.
3. Enter all of the purchases on account transactions using the **Purchases/Receive Inventory** option in the **Tasks** menu.
4. Process all debit memorandums using the **Vendor Credit Memos** option in the **Tasks** menu.
5. Print a Purchases Journal report and a Vendor Ledgers report.
6. Proof your work.
7. Print a general ledger report to complete the Analyze activity.
8. End the session.

QuickBooks

PROBLEM GUIDE

Step–by–Step Instructions: Problem 15–7

1. Restore the Problem 15-7.QBB file.
2. Enter all purchases on account transactions using the **Bill** option from the Enter Bills window in the **Vendors** menu.
3. Process all debit memorandums using the **Credit** option from the **Enter Bills** window.
4. Print a Journal report, a Vendor Balance Summary, and a General Ledger report.
5. Complete the Analyze activity.
6. Back up your work.

Date	Transactions (cont.)
Mar. 24	Paid All-Star News $130 to run an advertisement promoting the store, Check 2116.
28	Bought $100 in supplies and $700 in store equipment from Superior Store Equipment Inc., Check 2117 for $800.
31	Issued Check 2118 for $2,185.50 in payment of monthly wages of $3,000 less deductions for the following taxes: Employees' Federal Income Tax Payable, $480; Employees' State Income Tax Payable, $105; Social Security Tax Payable, $186; and Medicare Tax Payable, $43.50.

Analyze Determine the total decrease to the checking account for the month.

Problem 15–9 Recording Purchases and Cash Payment Transactions

River's Edge Canoe & Kayak had the following purchases and cash payment transactions for the month of March.

Instructions In your working papers, record the following transactions on page 16 of the general journal.

Date	Transactions
Mar. 1	Purchased $8,200 in merchandise on account from Trailhead Canoes, Invoice TC202, terms 2/10, n/30.
5	Issued Check 887 for $98 to Santini Trucking Company for delivery of merchandise purchased from Trailhead Canoes.
7	Bought $230 in supplies on account from StoreMart Supply, Invoice SM101, terms n/30.
9	Issued Check 888 to World-Wide Insurance Company for $2,500 in payment of business insurance premium.
11	Issued Check 889 to Trailhead Canoes for $8,036 in payment of Invoice TC202 for $8,200 less a 2% cash discount of $164.
15	Purchased $6,200 in merchandise on account from Mohican Falls Kayak Wholesalers, Invoice 45332, terms 3/15, n/45.
18	Issued Debit Memorandum 67 for $25 to StoreMart Supply for damaged supplies purchased on March 7.
21	Paid StoreMart Supply the balance due on their account, $205 ($230 less $25 credit), Check 890.
25	Returned $200 in merchandise to Mohican Falls Kayak Wholesalers, Debit Memorandum 68.
28	Rollins Plumbing Service completed $120 in repair work (**Maintenance Expense**) on account, Invoice RP432.

Analyze State the total debit amount to the **Purchases** account for the month.

Peachtree®

SMART GUIDE

Step–by–Step Instructions: Problem 15–8

1. Select the problem set for Cycle Tech (Prob. 15–8).
2. Rename the company and set the system date.
3. Record all cash payments.
4. Print a Cash Disbursements Journal and a General Journal report.
5. Complete the Analyze activity.
6. End the session.

QuickBooks

PROBLEM GUIDE

Step–by–Step Instructions: Problem 15–8

1. Restore the Problem 15-8.QBB file.
2. Record all cash payments.
3. Print a Journal report.
4. Complete the Analyze activity.
5. Back up your work.

Peachtree®

SMART GUIDE

Step–by–Step Instructions: Problem 15–9

1. Select the problem set for River's Edge (Prob. 15–9).
2. Rename the company and set the system date.
3. Enter all of the purchases on account.
4. Process all debit memorandums.
5. Record all cash payments.
6. Print a Purchases Journal, Cash Disbursements Journal, and a General Ledger.
7. Proof your work.
8. Complete the Analyze activity.
9. End the session.

Problems

CHALLENGE PROBLEM

Problem 15–10 Recording and Posting Purchases and Cash Payment Transactions

Buzz Newsstand's purchases and cash payment transactions for the month of March are described below.

Instructions In your working papers:

1. Record the transactions in the general journal, page 7.
2. Post the transactions to the ledger accounts.

Date	Transactions
Mar. 1	Purchased $5,600 in merchandise on account from ADC Publishing, Invoice 785, terms 3/15, n/45.
3	Issued Check 1400 for $735 to Pine Forest Publications in payment of Invoice PFP98 for $750 less a 2% cash discount of $15.
5	Issued Check 1401 for $275 to Rizzo's Trucking Company for transportation charges.
7	Issued Check 1402 for $588 to Delta Press in payment of Invoice DP166 for $600 less a 2% cash discount of $12.
9	American Trend Publishers granted a $100 allowance for damaged merchandise, Debit Memorandum 33.
11	Issued Check 1403 for $3,200 to Keystone Insurance Company for the annual premium for business insurance.
15	Issued Check 1404 for $5,432 to ADC Publishing in payment of Invoice 785 for $5,600 less a 3% cash discount of $168.
18	Bought $2,800 in merchandise on account from Delta Press, Invoice DP204, terms 2/10, n/30.
22	Issued Debit Memorandum 34 to Delta Press for the return of $300 in merchandise.
28	Paid American Trend Publishers the balance due on their account, $800, no discount, Check 1405.
30	Bought $120 in merchandise for cash from ADC Publishing, Check 1406.

Analyze Calculate how much Buzz Newsstand saved in March by taking cash discounts.

Practice your test-taking skills! The questions on this page are reprinted with permission from national organizations:
- Future Business Leaders of America
- Business Professionals of America

Use a separate sheet of paper to record your answers.

Future Business Leaders of America

MULTIPLE CHOICE

1. If bankcard fees are automatically deducted from the checking account of a business, how will the bookkeeper journalize the fee?
   a. Capital account is increased by the amount of the fee.
   b. Cash account is increased by the amount of the fee.
   c. Bank Card Fees Expense is increased by the amount of the fee and Cash is decreased.
   d. Cash account is increased by the amount of the fee and Bank Card Fees Expense is decreased.

2. A business transaction that involves a purchase on account is considered to be a(n)
   a. cash transaction.
   b. credit transaction.
   c. investment of the owner.
   d. expense transaction.

3. A liability resulting from the purchase of goods or services on credit is usually recorded as
   a. an account receivable.
   b. an account payable.
   c. a revenue.
   d. a reduction of equity.
   e. a net loss.

Business Professionals of America

MULTIPLE CHOICE

4. If an invoice dated September 9 and received on September 12 shows terms of 2/10 n/30, what is the last day that a discount may be taken?
   a. September 11
   b. September 19
   c. September 22
   d. October 9

5. A form prepared by the customer showing the price deducted taken by the customer for a return is a
   a. Purchases Discount.
   b. Sales Return.
   c. Credit Memorandum.
   d. Debit Memorandum.

> **Need More Help?**
>
> Go to **glencoeaccounting.glencoe.com** and click on **Student Center**. Click on **Winning Competitive Events** and select **Chapter 15**.
> - **Practice Questions and Test-Taking Tips**
> - **Concept Capsules and Terminology**

Processing Purchases

1. What is a purchases discount?
2. How do a purchase requisition and a purchase order differ?
3. In your job in the receiving department of a business, you are responsible for verifying the accuracy of a shipment. What do you do?
4. How are a purchases return and a purchases allowance similar? How are they different?
5. Explain the importance of using a purchase requisition, a purchase order, a packing slip, and a processing stamp in the purchasing process of a business.
6. Evaluate the usefulness of subsidiary ledgers.

Merchandising Business: Sportswear Store

The Sports Loft is a retail store that sells sports clothing, accessories, and equipment. Janet Loftis wants you to design a more automated system for ordering merchandise that will free her for other management duties.

INSTRUCTIONS

1. Identify issues involved in creating a new purchasing process. For example, how will it identify low stock?
2. Write a one-page report suggesting a purchasing system for The Sports Loft. Specify the information it should collect and how it would trigger new orders. Draw a diagram if necessary. Include a description of any forms needed.

Showing Favoritism

Manufacturers make purchases to conduct their business. Imagine that you work in the purchasing department of a large toy manufacturer like Mattel. Your job is to place orders for the parts used to make toy cars and trucks. One supplier, whose prices are only slightly higher than others, has indicated that it would send free tickets to a sports event if you order most of the parts from it.

ETHICAL DECISION MAKING

1. What are the ethical issues?
2. What are the alternatives?
3. Who are the affected parties?
4. How do the alternatives affect the parties?
5. What would you do?

A Plan for Quality

You were recently hired as an accounting clerk at The Writer's Desk. One of your tasks is to process the invoices to be paid. The previous clerk did not pay invoices within the discount period and often paid them late. Write out a plan to improve and maintain quality regarding accounts payable. Address how you will use a ticker file to implement the plan.

SKILLS BEYOND NUMBERS

Monitoring and Correcting Performance of Systems

Identifying trends, predicting changes, finding problems, and applying solutions are skills of a *systems thinker*.

ON THE JOB

Your town is hosting a big mountain bike competition. As an Action Athletics employee, you know the event offers a chance to increase cycling gear sales. You recommend adjusting and upgrading the cycling merchandise line for this event.

INSTRUCTIONS

1. Pair up with a student and role-play your "sales pitch" to persuade your employer to add to the current merchandise line.

2. Using a spreadsheet program, list 10 biking accessories to include in inventory. Make reasonable estimates for each item's price and its sales for the month of the bike event when about 200 cyclists will visit the store.

INTERNATIONAL ACCOUNTING

Utilizing E-Procurement

When Schlumberger Oilfield Services needed supplies for its global operations, it used an e-procurement system to connect buyers and suppliers via the Internet. Bidders around the world can compete online for contracts in different currencies and languages. The easy-to-use system saves Schlumberger nearly $400,000 a month in transaction costs and has decreased its order fulfillment time.

INSTRUCTIONS Imagine that your company has manufacturing plants in both the United States and Japan. Describe how an e-procurement system might be helpful.

Making It Personal

Applying for a Loan

You may soon apply for a loan from a financial institution to pay for your education or to buy a vehicle. When you borrow money, you must understand the loan's finance charges and what the application process involves.

PERSONAL FINANCE ACTIVITY Assume that you plan to borrow $6,000 from your bank to purchase a five-year-old automobile. What questions do you expect the bank to ask you? What questions will you ask?

PERSONAL FINANCE ONLINE Log on to **glencoeaccounting.glencoe.com** and click on **Student Center.** Click on **Making It Personal** and select **Chapter 15.**

Analyzing FINANCIAL Reports

Identifying Corporate Goals

The information in an annual report is directed to many audiences: existing and potential stockholders; financial analysts and advisors; government regulators, such as the Securities and Exchange Commission (SEC); employees; and creditors.

INSTRUCTIONS

Use the *Dear Fellow Stockholders* letter in PETsMART's annual report in Appendix F at the back of your textbook to complete the following.

1. List three of PETsMART's goals for 2004 and beyond that are measurable.

2. Name PETsMART's most powerful asset, and explain how PETsMART is investing in this asset.

Special Journals: Sales and Cash Receipts

What You'll Learn

1. Identify the special journals and explain how they are used in a merchandising business.

2. Record transactions in sales and cash receipts journals.

3. Post from the sales and cash receipts journals to customer accounts in the accounts receivable subsidiary ledger.

4. Foot, prove, total, and rule the sales and cash receipts journals.

5. Post column totals from the sales and cash receipts journals to general ledger accounts.

6. Prepare a schedule of accounts receivable.

7. Define the accounting terms introduced in this chapter.

Why It's Important

Using special journals instead of the general journal can save time and reduce errors.

THE SHARPER IMAGE®

Predict

1. What does the chapter title tell you?
2. What do you already know about this subject from personal experience?
3. What have you learned about this in the earlier chapters?
4. What gaps exist in your knowledge of this subject?

Exploring the *Real World* of Business

ANALYZING SALES GROWTH

The Sharper Image

The Sharper Image has everything you never thought you needed. How about a robotic massage chair? A heat sensitive foam pillow? Wireless outdoor speakers? **The Sharper Image** is known for its selection of innovative and fun lifestyle products.

Founded in 1977, the company sells products in more than 175 stores, through its primary Web site, and through a monthly catalog. **The Sharper Image** also sells close-out inventory through an online auction Web site.

Companies like **The Sharper Image** often track and try to identify customer shopping trends. For example, over a one year period, the company reported an increase of 22 percent in its Internet sales. Catalog sales in that period were also up by 20 percent. Meanwhile, in-store sales for the same time frame decreased by 1 percent.

What Do You Think?

How do you think data on customer shopping habits might be used to improve overall financial performance?

Working in the *Real World*

APPLYING YOUR ACCOUNTING KNOWLEDGE

In earlier chapters you learned about the cycle of buying and selling merchandise. Dollars from sales are used to buy merchandise, which is in turn sold to customers. Some sales dollars come from customers who pay cash, while others come from sales on credit. Both types are recorded in the accounting records. In this chapter you will see how special journals simplify the process of recording sales.

Personal Connection

1. In your job, do you handle cash and personal checks? Do you handle credit card sales?
2. If a business did not accept credit cards, how do you think this would affect overall sales?

Online Connection

Go to **glencoeaccounting.glencoe.com** and click on **Student Center**. Click on **Working in the Real World** and select **Chapter 16**.

The Sales Journal

Main Idea
The sales journal is used to record credit sales of merchandise.

Read to Learn...
➤ the purpose of special journals. (p. 450)
➤ how to use the sales journal. (p. 450)

Key Terms
special journals
sales journal
footing

You have learned how to record a variety of business transactions in a general journal. A merchandising business can record all of its transactions in a general journal. However, each transaction requires at least three journal lines—one line for the debit, one line for the credit, and one line for the explanation. Each debit and credit is posted separately to the general ledger. For merchandising businesses with many sales transactions, such as Crate & Barrel, this would be very time consuming. To improve efficiency many merchandising businesses use special journals. In this chapter and the next chapter, you will learn how to record transactions in special journals.

Using Special Journals
Why Are Special Journals Used?

Special journals have amount columns that are used to record debits and credits to specific general ledger accounts. Most transactions are recorded on one line. Special journals thus simplify the journalizing and posting process. The four most commonly used special journals and the type of transaction recorded in each journal are:

Journal	Transaction
Sales journal	sale of merchandise on account
Cash receipts journal	receipt of cash
Purchases journal	purchase of any asset on account
Cash payments journal	payment of cash, including payment by check

Businesses that use special journals still need the general journal to record transactions that cannot be entered in the special journals. Let's first look at the sales journal.

Journalizing and Posting to the Sales Journal
How Do You Use the Sales Journal?

The **sales journal** is a special journal used to record sales of merchandise on account. **Figure 16–1** shows a page from the sales journal used by On Your Mark Athletic Wear.

Like the general journal, the sales journal has a space for the page number and columns for the date and the posting reference. There is a separate column in which to record the sales slip number and a column

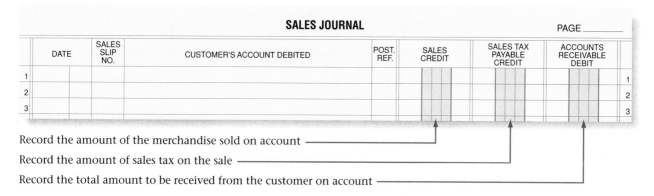

SALES JOURNAL   PAGE _____

	DATE	SALES SLIP NO.	CUSTOMER'S ACCOUNT DEBITED	POST. REF.	SALES CREDIT	SALES TAX PAYABLE CREDIT	ACCOUNTS RECEIVABLE DEBIT	
1								1
2								2
3								3

Record the amount of the merchandise sold on account ——————

Record the amount of sales tax on the sale ——————————

Record the total amount to be received from the customer on account ——————

Figure 16–1 Sales Journal

in which to record the name of the charge customer. There are also three special amount columns. **Figure 16–1** illustrates what is to be recorded in each column.

Recording Sales of Merchandise on Account

Are you ready to record a sale on account in the sales journal? It's simple. Let's look at the same transactions you analyzed in Chapter 14 for On Your Mark Athletic Wear. This time we will record transactions using the sales journal.

ON YOUR MARK
ATHLETIC WEAR
595 Leslie Street, Dallas, TX 75207

DATE: December 1, 20--   NO. 50

SOLD TO: Casey Klein
3345 Spring Creek Parkway
Plano, Texas 75094

CLERK B.E.	CASH	CHARGE ✓	TERMS n/30

QTY.	DESCRIPTION	UNIT PRICE	AMOUNT
1	Pair Running Shoes	$ 100.00	$ 100 00
6	Pair Athletic Socks	10.00	60 00
1	Vinyl Jacket/Pants	40.00	40 00
		SUBTOTAL	$ 200 00
		SALES TAX	12 00
Thank You!		TOTAL	$ 212 00

Business Transaction

On December 1 On Your Mark sold merchandise on account to Casey Klein for $200 plus $12 sales tax, Sales Slip 50.

JOURNAL ENTRY

SALES JOURNAL   PAGE ____12____

	DATE	SALES SLIP NO.	CUSTOMER'S ACCOUNT DEBITED	POST. REF.	SALES CREDIT	SALES TAX PAYABLE CREDIT	ACCOUNTS RECEIVABLE DEBIT	
1	20--							1
2	Dec. 1	50	Casey Klein		200 00	12 00	212 00	2
3	1	2	3		4	5	6	3

To record the transaction in the sales journal, journalize from left to right by following these steps.

1. Enter the date of the sales slip in the Date column.
2. Enter the sales slip number in the Sales Slip No. column.
3. Enter the name of the customer in the Customer's Account Debited column.
4. Enter the total of the merchandise sold in the Sales Credit column. (This is the amount shown in the subtotal box of the sales slip.)
5. Enter the amount of the sales tax in the Sales Tax Payable Credit column.
6. Enter the total amount to be received from the customer in the Accounts Receivable Debit column. (This is the amount shown in the total box of the sales slip.)

You learned in Chapter 14 that businesses do not impose sales tax on the sale of merchandise to tax-exempt organizations. The next business transaction involves a sale that On Your Mark makes to an organization that has tax-exempt status.

This transaction is analyzed in the same manner as the previous transac-

ON YOUR MARK
ATHLETIC WEAR
595 Leslie Street, Dallas, TX 75207

DATE: December 3, 20--		NO. 51

SOLD TO	South Branch High School Athletics 1750 Rutgers Dr. Dallas, TX 75207		

CLERK B.E.	CASH	CHARGE ✓	TERMS 2/10, n/30

QTY.	DESCRIPTION	UNIT PRICE	AMOUNT
15	Baseball Uniforms	$ 40.00	$ 600 00
15	Baseball Caps	20.00	300 00
15	Baseball Mitts	35.00	525 00
2	Baseballs	15.00	30 00
3	Baseball Bats	15.00	45 00
		SUBTOTAL	$ 1,500 00
		SALES TAX	0 00
	Thank You!	TOTAL	$ 1,500 00

Business Transaction

On December 3 On Your Mark sold merchandise on account to South Branch High School Athletics for $1,500, Sales Slip 51.

JOURNAL ENTRY

SALES JOURNAL   PAGE ___12___

	DATE	SALES SLIP NO.	CUSTOMER'S ACCOUNT DEBITED	POST. REF.	SALES CREDIT	SALES TAX PAYABLE CREDIT	ACCOUNTS RECEIVABLE DEBIT	
3	3	51	South Branch H.S. Ath.		1 500 00		1 500 00	3
4	1	2	3		4		5	4

tion—except there is no sales tax. Journalizing this transaction involves only five steps. The first four steps are the same. There is no sales tax so the fifth step is to enter the total amount to be received from the customer in the Accounts Receivable Debit column.

For sales that do not include a sales tax, amounts entered in the Sales Credit column and in the Accounts Receivable Debit column are the same.

Posting a Sales Journal Entry to the Accounts Receivable Subsidiary Ledger

In Chapter 14 you learned about posting to the accounts receivable subsidiary ledger. To keep the balances of the customer accounts current, sales journal transactions are posted daily to the accounts receivable subsidiary ledger. Whether you use the general journal or the sales journal when posting to the accounts receivable subsidiary ledger, the process is similar. Refer to **Figure 16–2** and follow these steps.

1. Enter the date of the transaction in the Date column of the subsidiary ledger account. Use the same date as the journal entry.
2. In the Posting Reference column of the subsidiary ledger account, enter the journal letter and the journal page number. Use the letter *S* for the sales journal.
3. In the Debit column of the subsidiary ledger account, enter the total amount to be received from the customer.
4. Compute the new balance and enter it in the Balance column. To find the new balance, add the amount in the Debit column to the previous balance amount.

As You READ

Key Point

Sales Journal Entry For each line of the sales journal, make sure that the credits (**Sales** and **Sales Tax Payable**) equal the debit (**Accounts Receivable**).

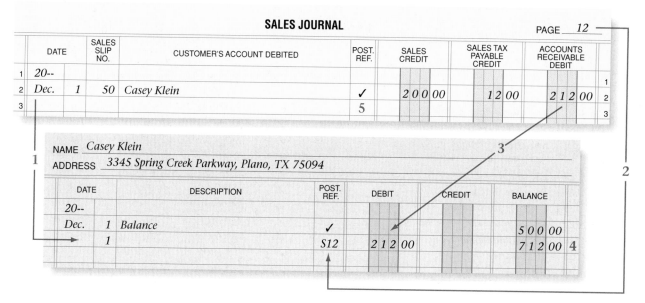

SALES JOURNAL

PAGE 12

	DATE	SALES SLIP NO.	CUSTOMER'S ACCOUNT DEBITED	POST. REF.	SALES CREDIT	SALES TAX PAYABLE CREDIT	ACCOUNTS RECEIVABLE DEBIT	
1	20--							1
2	Dec. 1	50	Casey Klein	✓	2 0 0 00	1 2 00	2 1 2 00	2
3				5				3

NAME *Casey Klein*

ADDRESS *3345 Spring Creek Parkway, Plano, TX 75094*

DATE	DESCRIPTION	POST. REF.	DEBIT	CREDIT	BALANCE	
20--						
Dec. 1	Balance	✓			5 0 0 00	
1		S12	2 1 2 00		7 1 2 00	4

5. Return to the sales journal and enter a check mark (✓) in the Posting Reference column. The check mark indicates that the transaction has been posted to the accounts receivable subsidiary ledger. In manual accounting systems, customer accounts are not numbered, so a check mark is used in the Posting Reference column.

Figure 16–2 Posting a Sales Journal Entry to the Accounts Receivable Subsidiary Ledger

Completing the Sales Journal

All special journals have amount columns used to record debits and credits to specific general ledger accounts. These amount columns simplify posting. Instead of posting each transaction separately to the general ledger, only the amount column totals are posted. For the sales journal, the column totals posted are the Sales Credit, the Sales Tax Payable Credit, and the Accounts Receivable Debit. Therefore, only three postings are made to the general ledger from the sales journal.

Footing, Proving, Totaling, and Ruling the Sales Journal

Before posting amounts to the general ledger, calculate and verify the column totals. Refer to **Figure 16–3** on page 454 for each step.

1. Draw a single rule across the three amount columns, just below the last transaction.
2. Foot the amount columns. A **footing** is a column total written in small penciled figures. A footing must be verified. It is written in pencil so that it can be erased if a mistake is discovered.
3. On a separate sheet of paper, test for the equality of debits and credits. The total of the debit column should equal the total of the two credit columns.

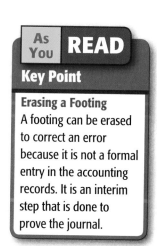

As You READ

Key Point

Erasing a Footing A footing can be erased to correct an error because it is not a formal entry in the accounting records. It is an interim step that is done to prove the journal.

Debit Column		**Credit Columns**	
Accounts Receivable	$11,305	Sales Tax Payable	$ 555
		Sales	10,750
Total	$11,305	Total	$11,305

	DATE		SALES SLIP NO.	CUSTOMER'S ACCOUNT DEBITED	POST. REF.	SALES CREDIT	SALES TAX PAYABLE CREDIT	ACCOUNTS RECEIVABLE DEBIT	
1	20--								1
2	Dec.	1	50	Casey Klein	✓	2 0 0 00	1 2 00	2 1 2 00	2
3		3	51	South Branch High School Athletics	✓	1 5 0 0 00		1 5 0 0 00	3
4		5	52	Break Point Sports Club	✓	3 5 0 0 00	2 1 0 00	3 7 1 0 00	4
5		9	53	Gabriel Ramos	✓	3 0 0 00	1 8 00	3 1 8 00	5
6		10	54	Kim Wong	✓	1 0 0 00	6 00	1 0 6 00	6
7		12	55	Robert Galvin	✓	2 5 0 00	1 5 00	2 6 5 00	7
8		18	56	Joe Dimaio	✓	4 0 0 00	2 4 00	4 2 4 00	8
9		20	57	Megan Sullivan	✓	5 0 0 00	3 0 00	5 3 0 00	9
10		24	58	Tammy's Fitness Club	✓	1 0 0 0 00	6 0 00	1 0 6 0 00	10
11		26	59	Anita Montero	✓	3 5 0 00	2 1 00	3 7 1 00	11
12		28	60	Shashi Rahim	✓	2 0 0 00	1 2 00	2 1 2 00	12
13		30	61	Lara Young	✓	2 4 5 0 00	1 4 7 00	2 5 9 7 00	13
14		31		Totals		10 7 5 0 00	5 5 5 00	11 3 0 5 00	14
15									15

4   5   3

1 2 6 7

Figure 16–3 Totaled and Ruled Sales Journal

4. In the Date column, on the line below the single rule, enter the date the journal is being totaled.
5. On the same line, in the Customer's Account Debited column, enter the word *Totals*.
6. Enter the column totals, in ink, just below the footings.
7. Double-rule the three amount columns. A double rule, as you know, indicates that the totals have been verified.

After the sales journal has been footed, proved, totaled, and ruled, the column totals are posted to the general ledger.

As You READ

Key Point

Posting from a Special Journal Post information from left to right across the ledger form. By following this procedure, you will post all information from the journal entry.

Posting the Total of the Sales Credit Column

Refer to **Figure 16–4** as you read the procedure for posting the total of the Sales Credit column to the **Sales** account in the general ledger.

1. In the Date column of the **Sales** account in the general ledger, enter the date from the Totals line of the sales journal.
2. Enter the sales journal letter and page number in the Posting Reference column. Remember that *S* is the letter for the sales journal.
3. In the Credit column, enter the total from the Sales Credit column of the sales journal.
4. Compute the new balance and enter it in the Credit Balance column. To determine the new balance, add the amount entered in the Credit column to the previous balance.
5. Return to the sales journal and enter the **Sales** account number, in parentheses, below the double rule in the Sales Credit column. The number written in parentheses indicates that the column total has been posted to the general ledger account.

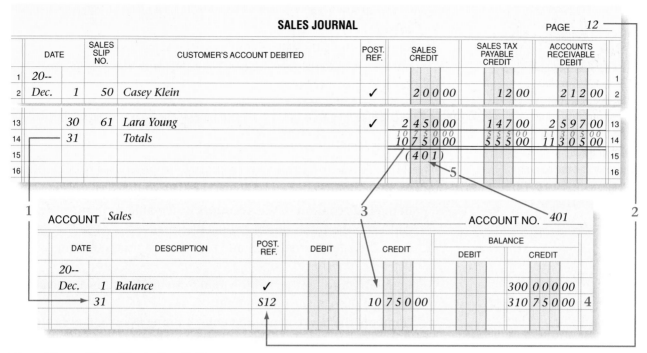

Figure 16–4 Posting the Sales Credit Total to the General Ledger Account

Posting the Total of the Sales Tax Payable Credit Column

The next amount to be posted is the Sales Tax Payable Credit column total. Refer to **Figure 16–5** as you read the following procedure.

1. In the Date column of the **Sales Tax Payable** account, enter the date from the Totals line of the sales journal.
2. Enter the sales journal letter and page number in the Posting Reference column.
3. In the Credit column, enter the total from the Sales Tax Payable Credit column of the sales journal.

Figure 16–5 Posting the Sales Tax Payable Credit Total to the General Ledger

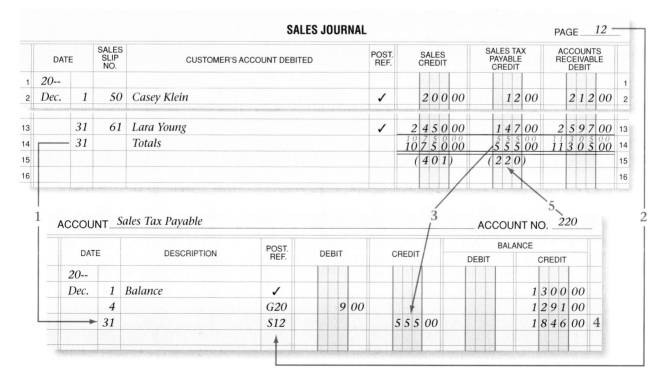

As You READ

Key Point

Posting a Special Journal Column Total
Entering an account number in parentheses under a column total means that the column total has been posted to the general ledger.

4. Compute the new balance and enter it in the Credit Balance column.
5. Return to the sales journal and enter the Sales Tax Payable account number, in parentheses, below the double rule in the Sales Tax Payable Credit column.

Posting the Total of the Accounts Receivable Debit Column

The last column of the sales journal to be posted is the Accounts Receivable Debit column. Refer to **Figure 16–6** as you read these steps.

1. In the Date column of the **Accounts Receivable** account, enter the date from the Totals line of the sales journal.
2. Enter the sales journal letter and page number in the Posting Reference column.
3. In the Debit column, enter the total from the Accounts Receivable Debit column of the sales journal.
4. Compute the new balance and enter it in the Debit Balance column.
5. Return to the sales journal and enter the **Accounts Receivable** account number, in parentheses, below the double rule in the Accounts Receivable Debit column.

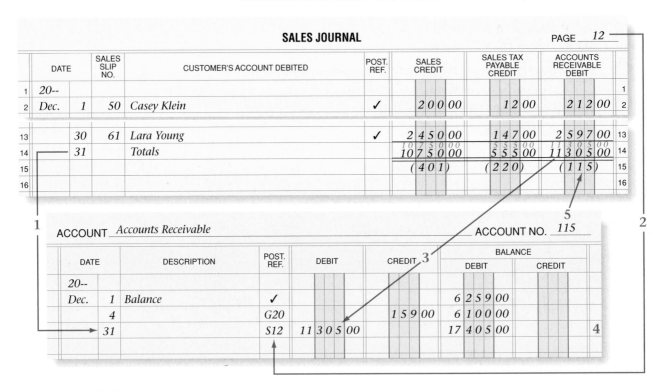

Figure 16–6 Posting Accounts Receivable Debit Total to the General Ledger

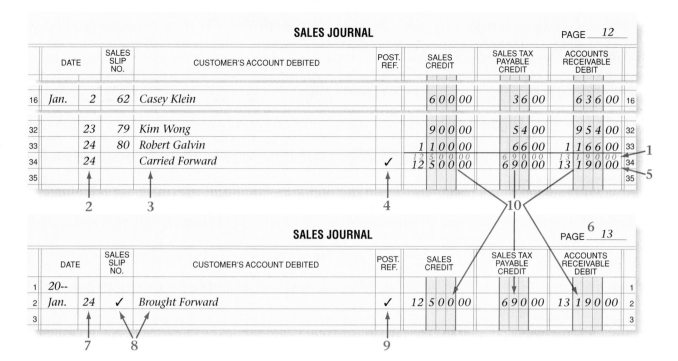

Figure 16-7 Starting a New Journal Page

Proving the Sales Journal at the End of a Page

All special journals are totaled and proved at the end of every month. Sometimes, however, a business has so many transactions in one month that it is impossible to fit them all on one journal page. When this occurs, the journal page is totaled and ruled before a new page is started.

Refer to **Figure 16–7** and follow these steps to record the totals and carry them forward to the next page.

1. Draw a single rule across the three amount columns below the last transaction. Foot the columns and prove the equality of debits and credits.

2. On the line following the last transaction, enter the date of the last transaction in the Date column.

3. In the Customer's Account Debited column, write *Carried Forward*.

4. Place a check mark (✓) in the Posting Reference column. This check mark indicates that these totals are not to be posted.

5. Enter the column totals in ink. *Do not* place a double rule under the columns.

6. On the next journal page, enter the new page number.

7. On lines 1 and 2, enter the complete date (year, month, and day) in the Date column. Use the same date as on the last line of the previous page.

8. Place a check mark (✓) in the Sales Slip No. column and write *Brought Forward* in the Customer's Account Debited column.

9. Place a check mark (✓) in the Posting Reference column.

10. Enter the column totals from the previous page on line 2.

The journal page is now ready for the recording of the next transaction.

As You READ

In Your Experience

Proving Accuracy
How have you proved the accuracy of your personal financial documents?

Reinforce the Main Idea

Create a table similar to this one to identify the four special journals and the kind of transaction recorded in each.

Special Journal	Kind of Transaction

Do the Math

Vijay Products had the following amounts entered in the Sales Credit Column of its October Sales Journal.

Oct.	2	$1,500
	10	3,400
	17	8,200
	30	7,600

Assume a 3% sales tax was imposed on each sale. Answer the following questions.

1. What amount should be entered in the Sales Tax Payable Credit Column for each sale?
2. What amount should be entered in the Accounts Receivable Debit Column for each sale?

Problem 16–1 Posting Column Totals from the Sales Journal

Instructions Here are the column totals of the sales journal for the month of April. In your working papers, post these totals to the appropriate general ledger accounts.

SALES JOURNAL   PAGE ___4___

	DATE	SALES SLIP NO.	CUSTOMER'S ACCOUNT DEBITED	POST. REF.	SALES CREDIT	SALES TAX PAYABLE CREDIT	ACCOUNTS RECEIVABLE DEBIT	
1	20--							1
2	Apr. 1	47	Amy Anderson	✓	800 00	48 00	848 00	2
32	30		Totals		12 000 00	720 00	12 720 00	32
33								33

Problem 16–2 Analyzing a Source Document

Metro Sports Distributors had this transaction that occurred on June 15.

Instructions

1. Analyze the sales slip shown. In your working papers, record the required entry on page 3 of the sales journal.
2. Post to the customer's account in the accounts receivable subsidiary ledger.

METRO
SPORTS DISTRIBUTORS
Kingston Mall, Williamsburg, Virginia 23185

DATE: June 15, 20--   NO. 113

SOLD TO: M&M Consultants
2816 Mt. Odin Drive
Williamsburg, VA 23185

CLERK RDP	CASH	CHARGE ✓	TERMS 3/15, n/45

QTY.	DESCRIPTION	UNIT PRICE	AMOUNT
10	Golf Bags	$ 50.00	$ 500 00
2 doz.	Ladies Golf Shirts	100.00/doz	200 00
20	Golf Caps	6.00	120 00
		SUBTOTAL	$ 820 00
		SALES TAX	41 00
	Thank You!	TOTAL	$ 861 00

The Cash Receipts Journal

In Chapter 14 you learned that the three most common sources of cash for a merchandising business are payments from charge customers, cash sales, and bankcard sales. These businesses also receive cash, but less frequently, from the sale of other business assets.

Can you imagine how many checks local cable television, electric, and telephone companies receive daily? They must have a streamlined cash receipts process to record checks efficiently. In this section you will learn to use a cash receipts journal as an efficient way to record cash receipts.

Journalizing and Posting to the Cash Receipts Journal

How Do You Use the Cash Receipts Journal?

The **cash receipts journal** is a special journal used to record all cash receipt transactions. It always has a Cash in Bank Debit column since every transaction in it debits the **Cash in Bank** account. The number of credit columns varies, depending on the company's needs. On Your Mark's cash receipts journal in **Figure 16–8** has six amount columns plus the date, source document, account name, and posting reference columns.

To keep the customer account balances current, the entries in the Accounts Receivable Credit column are posted daily to the accounts

BEFORE YOU READ

Main Idea
The cash receipts journal is used to record the cash a business receives.

Read to Learn...
➤ how to use the cash receipts journal. (p. 459)
➤ the purpose of the schedule of accounts receivable. (p. 466)
➤ about Internet sales. (p. 468)

Key Terms
cash receipts journal
schedule of accounts receivable

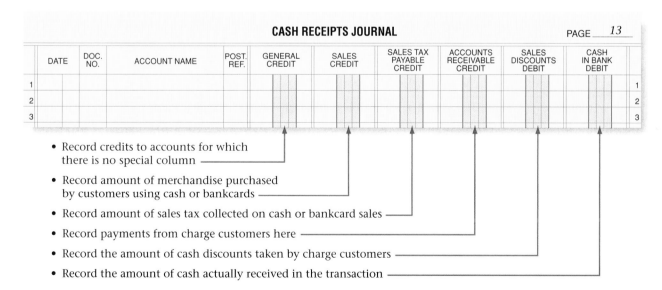

Figure 16–8 Cash Receipts Journal

receivable subsidiary ledger. The entries in the General Credit column are also posted daily to the individual general ledger accounts. At month-end all special amount column totals are posted to the general ledger accounts named in the column headings.

Recording Cash from Charge Customers

Follow these steps when journalizing cash receipts from charge customers. The source document for this transaction is the receipt.

1. Enter the date of the transaction in the Date column.
2. Enter the receipt number in the Document Number column. Write the letter *R* (for receipt) before the receipt number.
3. Enter the name of the customer in the Account Name column.
4. Enter the decrease in the amount owed by the customer in the Accounts Receivable Credit column.
5. Enter the amount of cash received in the Cash in Bank Debit column.

Business Transaction

On December 5 On Your Mark received $212 from Casey Klein to apply on account, Receipt 301.

ON YOUR MARK
ATHLETIC WEAR
595 Leslie Street, Dallas, TX 75207

RECEIPT
No. 301

Dec. 5   20 --

RECEIVED FROM Casey Klein $ 212.00

Two hundred twelve and no/100 —————————— DOLLARS

FOR On account

RECEIVED BY *Michael Smith*

JOURNAL ENTRY

CASH RECEIPTS JOURNAL   PAGE ___13___

	DATE	DOC. NO.	ACCOUNT NAME	POST. REF.	GENERAL CREDIT	SALES CREDIT	SALES TAX PAYABLE CREDIT	ACCOUNTS RECEIVABLE CREDIT	SALES DISCOUNTS DEBIT	CASH IN BANK DEBIT	
1	20--										1
2	Dec. 5	R301	Casey Klein					212 00		212 00	2
3	1	2	3					4		5	3

When this entry has been posted to the customer's account in the accounts receivable subsidiary ledger, enter a check mark (✓) in the Posting Reference column of the cash receipts journal.

Recording Cash Received on Account, Less a Cash Discount

Let's use these steps to record a cash receipt transaction with a cash discount.

1. Enter the date of the receipt in the Date column.
2. Enter the receipt number in the Document Number column. Remember to write the letter *R* before the receipt number.
3. Enter the name of the customer in the Account Name column.
4. In the Accounts Receivable Credit column, enter the amount of the original sales transaction (the amount that was debited in the sales journal) less any related sales returns or allowances.
5. Enter the cash discount amount in the Sales Discounts Debit column.
6. Enter the amount of cash received in the Cash in Bank Debit column.

Business Transaction

On December 12 On Your Mark received $1,470 from South Branch High School Athletics in payment of Sales Slip 51 for $1,500 less the discount of $30, Receipt 302.

ON YOUR MARK
ATHLETIC WEAR
595 Leslie Street, Dallas, TX 75207

RECEIPT
No. 302

Dec. 12 20 --

RECEIVED FROM South Branch H.S. Athletics $ 1,470.00

One thousand four hundred seventy and no/100 ———— DOLLARS

FOR On account

RECEIVED BY *Michael Smith*

JOURNAL ENTRY

CASH RECEIPTS JOURNAL   PAGE 13

	DATE	DOC. NO.	ACCOUNT NAME	POST. REF.	GENERAL CREDIT	SALES CREDIT	SALES TAX PAYABLE CREDIT	ACCOUNTS RECEIVABLE CREDIT	SALES DISCOUNTS DEBIT	CASH IN BANK DEBIT	
3	12	R302	South Branch H.S. Ath.					1 500 00	30 00	1 470 00	3
4	1	2	3					4	5	6	4

Recording Cash Sales

On Your Mark records cash sales every two weeks, but many businesses journalize cash sales and deposit cash daily. Follow these steps to enter cash sales in the cash receipts journal. The source document is the cash register tape.

1. Enter the date written on the cash register tape in the Date column.
2. Enter the number of the tape in the Document Number column. Write the letter *T* (for tape) before the tape number.
3. Enter the words *Cash Sales* in the Account Name column.
4. Enter a dash in the Posting Reference column to indicate that no entry has been posted individually to the general ledger accounts. Cash sales amounts are posted to the general ledger as part of the column totals at month-end.
5. Enter the amount of merchandise sold in the Sales Credit column.
6. Enter the amount of the sales taxes collected in the Sales Tax Payable Credit column.
7. Enter the total cash received in the Cash in Bank Debit column.

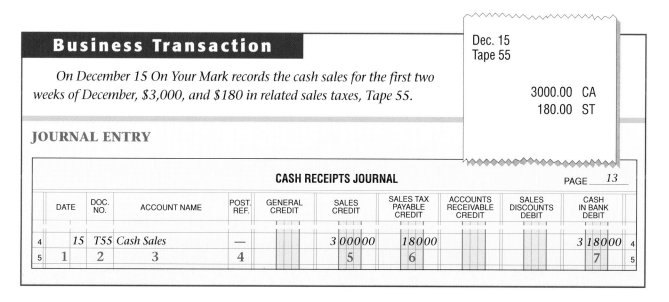

Business Transaction

On December 15 On Your Mark records the cash sales for the first two weeks of December, $3,000, and $180 in related sales taxes, Tape 55.

Dec. 15
Tape 55

3000.00 CA
180.00 ST

JOURNAL ENTRY

CASH RECEIPTS JOURNAL   PAGE 13

	DATE	DOC. NO.	ACCOUNT NAME	POST. REF.	GENERAL CREDIT	SALES CREDIT	SALES TAX PAYABLE CREDIT	ACCOUNTS RECEIVABLE CREDIT	SALES DISCOUNTS DEBIT	CASH IN BANK DEBIT	
4	15	T55	Cash Sales	—		3 000 00	180 00			3 180 00	4
5	1	2	3	4		5	6			7	5

Instant Recall

Normal Credit Balances
Sales
Sales Tax Payable

Recording Bankcard Sales

A business can record and deposit bankcard sales slips at any interval. On Your Mark processes them every two weeks. Follow these steps to enter bankcard sales in the cash receipts journal. Note the similarity to recording a cash sale. The entry's source document is the cash register tape.

1. Enter the date of the cash register tape in the Date column.
2. Enter the number of the tape in the Document Number column. Remember to write the letter *T* before the tape number.
3. Enter the words *Bankcard Sales* in the Account Name column.
4. Enter a dash in the Posting Reference column. The amounts recorded in the bankcard sales entry will be posted to the general ledger as part of the column totals at the end of the month.
5. Enter the amount of merchandise sold in the Sales Credit column.
6. Enter the sales taxes collected in the Sales Tax Payable Credit column.
7. Enter the total cash received in the Cash in Bank Debit column.

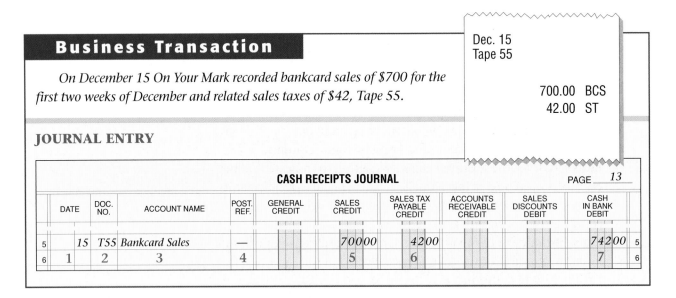

Business Transaction

On December 15 On Your Mark recorded bankcard sales of $700 for the first two weeks of December and related sales taxes of $42, Tape 55.

Dec. 15
Tape 55

700.00 BCS
42.00 ST

JOURNAL ENTRY

	DATE	DOC. NO.	ACCOUNT NAME	POST. REF.	GENERAL CREDIT	SALES CREDIT	SALES TAX PAYABLE CREDIT	ACCOUNTS RECEIVABLE CREDIT	SALES DISCOUNTS DEBIT	CASH IN BANK DEBIT	
5	15	T55	Bankcard Sales	—		700 00	42 00			742 00	5
6	1	2	3	4		5	6			7	6

CASH RECEIPTS JOURNAL PAGE ___13___

Recording Other Cash Receipts

Occasionally, a retail business receives cash from a transaction that does not involve the sale of merchandise. Since the business is receiving cash, it enters the transaction in the cash receipts journal. These are the steps to enter the next business transaction in the cash receipts journal:

1. Enter the date of the receipt in the Date column.
2. Enter an *R* and the receipt number in the Document Number column.
3. Enter *Office Equipment* in the Account Name column.
4. Enter the amount of the credit in the General Credit column. Use the General Credit column when the credit part of the entry is to an account that does not have a special amount column.
5. Enter the amount of cash received in the Cash in Bank Debit column.

Instant Recall

Normal Debit Balances
Accounts Receivable
Sales Discounts
Cash in Bank

Business Transaction

On December 16 On Your Mark received $30 from Mandy Harris, an office employee. She purchased a calculator that the business was no longer using, Receipt 303.

ON YOUR MARK ATHLETIC WEAR
595 Leslie Street, Dallas, TX 75207

RECEIPT
No. 303

Dec. 16 20 --

RECEIVED FROM Mandy Harris $ 30.00

Thirty and no/100 ———————————————— DOLLARS

FOR calculator

RECEIVED BY *Michael Smith*

JOURNAL ENTRY

	DATE	DOC. NO.	ACCOUNT NAME	POST. REF.	GENERAL CREDIT	SALES CREDIT	SALES TAX PAYABLE CREDIT	ACCOUNTS RECEIVABLE CREDIT	SALES DISCOUNTS DEBIT	CASH IN BANK DEBIT	
CASH RECEIPTS JOURNAL										PAGE 13	
6	16	R303	Office Equipment		30 00					30 00	6
7	1	2	3		4					5	7

Posting to the Accounts Receivable Subsidiary Ledger

A business posts daily from the Accounts Receivable Credit column to the accounts receivable subsidiary ledger so that customer accounts are always current. To post a cash receipt transaction to an account in the accounts receivable subsidiary ledger, follow these steps. Refer to **Figure 16–9**.

1. Enter the date of the transaction in the Date column of the subsidiary ledger account.
2. In the subsidiary ledger Posting Reference column, enter the journal letters and the page number. Use *CR* for the cash receipts journal.
3. In the subsidiary ledger Credit column, enter the amount from the Accounts Receivable Credit column of the cash receipts journal.
4. Compute and enter the new balance in the Balance column. If the account balance is zero, draw a line through the Balance column.

Figure 16–9 Posting from the Cash Receipts Journal to the Accounts Receivable Subsidiary Ledger

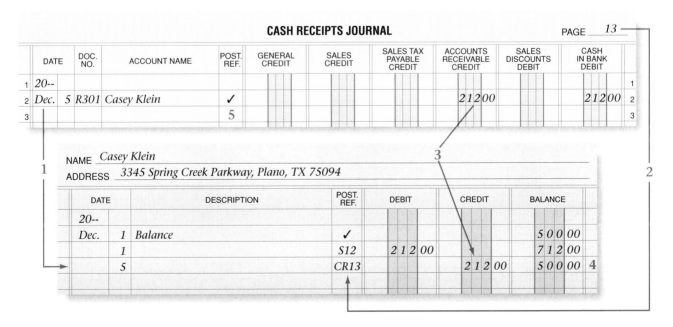

5. Return to the cash receipts journal and enter a check mark (✓) in the Posting Reference column.

Posting the General Credit Column

A business posts daily from the General Credit column of the cash receipts journal to the appropriate accounts in the general ledger. Refer to **Figure 16–10** as you read the steps for posting amounts from this column.

1. Enter the transaction date in the general ledger account Date column.
2. Enter the journal letters and page number in the Posting Reference column of the ledger account. Use *CR* for cash receipts journal.
3. In the Credit column of the ledger account, enter the amount from the General Credit column of the cash receipts journal.
4. Compute and enter the new account balance in the proper Balance column. For the **Office Equipment** account shown in **Figure 16–10**, use the Debit Balance column. If the account balance is zero, draw a line through the appropriate Balance column.
5. Return to the cash receipts journal and enter the general ledger account number in the Posting Reference column.

The cash receipts journal entry for the December 16 transaction is now posted. All transactions in the General Credit column are posted this way.

Footing, Proving, Totaling, and Ruling the Cash Receipts Journal

Follow these steps to complete the cash receipts journal. Refer to **Figure 16–11**.

1. Draw a single rule across the six amount columns, just below the last transaction.
2. Foot the columns.
3. Test for the equality of debits and credits as follows.

Figure 16–10 Posting from the General Credit Column of the Cash Receipts Journal

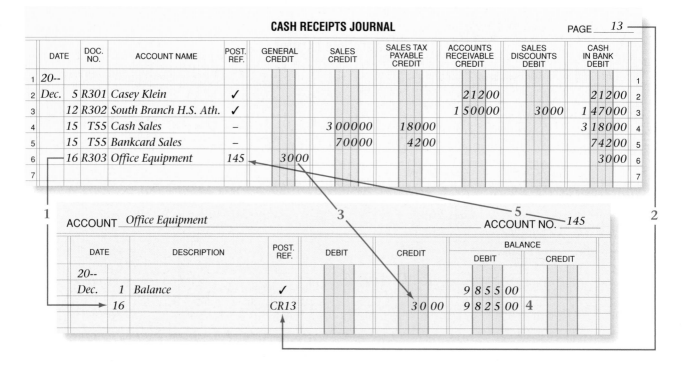

Debit Columns			Credit Columns	
Sales Discounts	$ 30		General	$ 30
Cash in Bank	17,283		Sales	9,700
			Sales Tax Payable	582
			Accounts Receivable	7,001
Total	$ 17,313		Total	$ 17,313

As You READ
In Your Own Words
What does it mean to "foot" the journal?

4. In the Date column, on the line below the single rule, enter the date the journal is being totaled.
5. On the same line in the Account Name column, enter the word *Totals*.
6. Enter the column totals, in ink, just below the footings.
7. Double-rule the amount columns.

Review the completed cash receipts journal. Consider time saved by using this special journal to record cash receipts in one location instead of on many general journal pages. After the cash receipts journal is footed, proved, totaled, and ruled, the column totals are posted to the general ledger.

Posting Column Totals to the General Ledger

On Your Mark uses a cash receipts journal with six amount columns. Only five of them are posted to the general ledger. The General Credit column total is *not* posted. The entries in this column have already been posted individually to the general ledger accounts. (See **Figure 16–10.**)

The total in each amount column is posted to the general ledger account named in the column heading. See **Figure 16–12** on page 467. The column heading indicates whether to post the amount to the ledger account's Debit or Credit column.

Figure 16–11 Totaled and Ruled Cash Receipts Journal

CASH RECEIPTS JOURNAL PAGE 13

	DATE	DOC. NO.	ACCOUNT NAME	POST. REF.	GENERAL CREDIT	SALES CREDIT	SALES TAX PAYABLE CREDIT	ACCOUNTS RECEIVABLE CREDIT	SALES DISCOUNTS DEBIT	CASH IN BANK DEBIT	
1	20--										1
2	Dec. 5	R301	Casey Klein	✓				212 00		212 00	2
3	12	R302	South Branch H.S. Ath.	✓				1 500 00	30 00	1 470 00	3
4	15	T55	Cash Sales	–		3 000 00	180 00			3 180 00	4
5	15	T55	Bankcard Sales	–		700 00	42 00			742 00	5
6	16	R303	Office Equipment	145	30 00					30 00	6
7	18	R304	Break Point Sports Club	✓				1 000 00		1 000 00	7
8	20	R305	Anita Montero	✓				100 00		100 00	8
9	22	R306	Gabriel Ramos	✓				500 00		500 00	9
10	23	R307	South Branch H.S. Ath.	✓				1 000 00		1 000 00	10
11	24	R308	Tammy's Fitness Club	✓				1 300 00		1 300 00	11
12	26	R309	Kim Wong	✓				300 00		300 00	12
13	27	R310	Lara Young	✓				200 00		200 00	13
14	27	R311	Robert Galvin	✓				465 00		465 00	14
15	28	R312	Joe Dimaio	✓				424 00		424 00	15
16	31	T56	Cash Sales	–		5 000 00	300 00			5 300 00	16
17	31	T56	Bankcard Sales	–		1 000 00	60 00			1 060 00	17
18	31		Totals		30 00	9 700 00	582 00	7 001 00	30 00	17 283 00	18
19					(✓)						19

Refer to **Figure 16–12** on page 467 and follow these steps to post column totals to the general ledger.

1. Place a check mark in parentheses under the General Credit column total to indicate that this total is not posted.
2. Post the **Sales** total to the **Sales** account Credit column.
3. Post the **Sales Tax Payable** total to the **Sales Tax Payable** account Credit column.
4. Post the **Accounts Receivable** total to the **Accounts Receivable** controlling account Credit column.
5. Post the **Sales Discounts** total to the **Sales Discounts** account Debit column.
6. Post the **Cash in Bank** total to the **Cash in Bank** account Debit column.
7. Compute new balances for each general ledger account.
8. Write each account number in parentheses below the double rule in the cash receipts journal.

Using the Schedule of Accounts Receivable

What Is a Schedule of Accounts Receivable?

Accountants prepare a schedule for each subsidiary ledger to determine whether the subsidiary ledger's sum equals the controlling account's ending balance.

Proving the Accounts Receivable Subsidiary Ledger

To prove the accounts receivable subsidiary ledger, accountants prepare a **schedule of accounts receivable** that lists each charge customer, the balance in the customer's account, and the total amount due from all customers. The **Accounts Receivable** account is the controlling account for the accounts receivable subsidiary ledger. That is, the controlling account is a summary of all customer accounts in the subsidiary ledger. At month-end after all posting is completed, the balance of **Accounts Receivable** (controlling) in the general ledger should equal the total of the balances of the individual accounts receivable subsidiary ledger accounts.

The schedule of accounts receivable may be prepared on plain paper, accounting stationery, or on a computer. The heading identifies the schedule type and the date. All customer accounts appear in alphabetical order, as they do in the accounts receivable subsidiary ledger. All accounts are included, even those with zero balances. This prevents omitting a customer by mistake. **Figure 16–13** on page 468 shows On Your Mark's schedule of accounts receivable for the end of December. Its total amount to be received from all customers is $10,404, which matches the balance of the **Accounts Receivable** account in the general ledger. This proves the accounts receivable subsidiary ledger.

CULTURAL Diversity

Misinterpreting Gestures Gestures that are common in the United States can be offensive to other cultures. For example, the okay symbol (the thumb and forefinger making a circle) is considered rude in parts of South America and Eastern Europe.

As You READ

It's Not What It Seems

Schedule You might think of a *schedule* as a timetable. In accounting, a *schedule* is a detailed list of the items that make up a general ledger account balance.

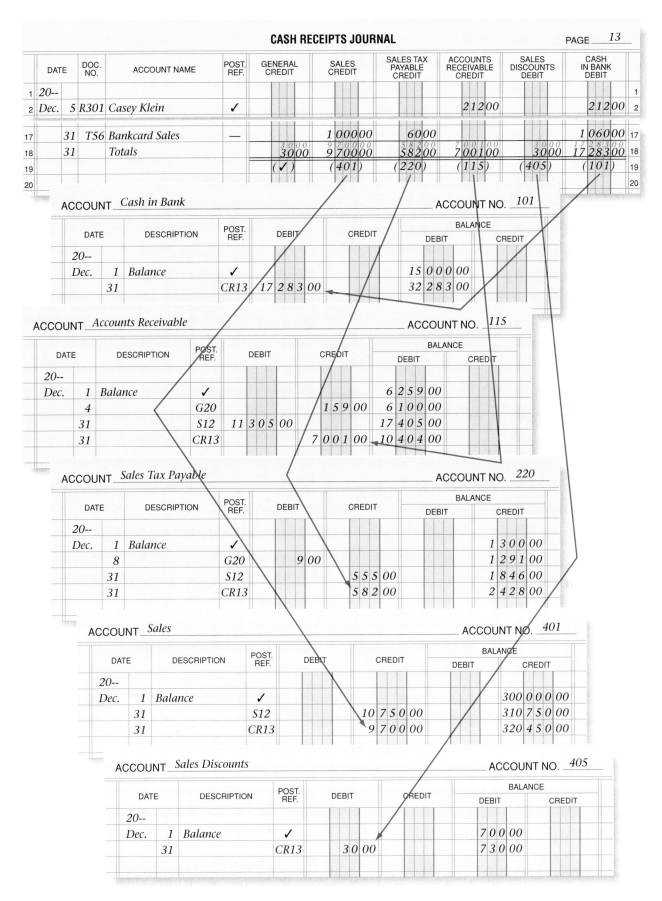

Figure 16–12 Posting Column Totals from the Cash Receipts Journal

DATE		DESCRIPTION	POST. REF.	DEBIT	CREDIT	BALANCE DEBIT	BALANCE CREDIT
20--							
Dec.	1	Balance	✓			6 2 5 9 00	
	4		G20		1 5 9 00	6 1 0 0 00	
	31		S12	11 3 0 5 00		17 4 0 5 00	
	31		CR13		7 0 0 1 00	10 4 0 4 00	

On Your Mark Athletic Wear
Schedule of Accounts Receivable
December 31, 20--

Break Point Sports Club	3 7 1 0 00	
Joe Dimaio	—	
Robert Galvin	—	
Casey Klein	5 0 0 00	
Anita Montero	3 7 1 00	
Shashi Rahim	2 1 2 00	
Gabriel Ramos	3 1 8 00	
South Branch High School Athletics	1 0 0 0 00	
Megan Sullivan	5 3 0 00	
Tammy's Fitness Club	1 0 6 0 00	
Kim Wong	1 0 6 00	
Lara Young	2 5 9 7 00	
Total Accounts Receivable		10 4 0 4 00

The balance of the **Accounts Receivable** account should equal the total of the schedule of accounts receivable.

Figure 16–13 Schedule of Accounts Receivable

Detecting Errors in the Subsidiary Ledger

Proving the accounts receivable subsidiary ledger with the controlling account verifies that the sum of the subsidiary ledger equals the controlling account's ending balance. This internal control procedure uncovers certain errors such as failing to post a transaction, or miscalculating an account balance. It does *not* ensure that transactions were posted to the correct customer account. The subsidiary ledger and the controlling account can balance even if an amount was posted to the wrong account. Often this type of error is discovered when a customer finds the error on a bill and reports it.

Internet Sales

How Do Internet Companies Receive Cash?

Companies can sell products with little expense and effort over the Internet, but they must have procedures and systems for processing online sales transactions. Companies can use an *Internet merchant account* for credit and debit card payments or an online payment service such as PayPal. Most Internet sales systems batch transactions daily to provide updated sales and inventory entries for the company's computer systems.

Online sales transactions must be secure. Businesses can use a card verification service to authenticate credit card security codes and personal identification data to protect against online fraud.

Reinforce the Main Idea

Create a table similar to this one to identify the journal to be used and the accounts to be debited and credited for each transaction.

Transaction	Journal	Account(s) Debited	Account(s) Credited
Bankcard Sales			
Sale of Merchandise on Account			
Sale of Asset for Cash			
Cash Sales			

Do the Math

You are hired to audit the books for a computer software retailer, Software Biz. As you review the books, you realize that the sales tax was not calculated on a sales slip. You also want to estimate cash receipts from a sale. On a separate sheet of paper, make the following calculations:

1. Accounts Receivable—Business World; Sales Slip 47: software for $550; sales tax at 6%. What is the total due?

2. Accounts Receivable—Cindy Caskey; Sales Slip 48:

Software	$46.53
Sales tax	2.79
Total	$49.32

   Terms: 1/10, n/30.

   How much will be received if it is paid within the discount period?

Problem 16–3 Completing the Cash Receipts Journal

The cash receipts journal for the month of January is provided in your working papers and illustrated here.

Instructions In your working papers, foot, prove, total, and rule the cash receipts journal.

CASH RECEIPTS JOURNAL PAGE ___10___

	DATE	DOC. NO.	ACCOUNT NAME	POST. REF.	GENERAL CREDIT	SALES CREDIT	SALES TAX PAYABLE CREDIT	ACCOUNTS RECEIVABLE CREDIT	SALES DISCOUNTS DEBIT	CASH IN BANK DEBIT	
1	20--										1
2	Jan.	3	R502 Jennifer Smith	✓				8000		8000	2
3		5	R503 Wilton High School	✓				3 10000	6200	3 03800	3
4		8	R504 Store Equipment	155	7500					7500	4
5		15	T42 Cash Sales	—		5 00000	30000			5 30000	5
6		15	T42 Bankcard Sales	—		1 20000	7200			1 27200	6
7		20	R505 Norwin High School	✓				2 40000	4800	2 35200	7
8		30	R506 Supplies	115	3000					3000	8
9											9

Key Concepts

1. Businesses that have many transactions use *special journals* to simplify the process of recording transactions. Special journals

   • have amount columns to record debits and credits to specific general ledger accounts
   • use one line to record most transactions

   Four special journals are commonly used in merchandising businesses:

   • sales journal
   • cash receipts journal
   • purchases journal
   • cash payments journal

2. A *sales journal* is used when two conditions are met:

   • merchandise is sold, and
   • the sale is on account instead of for cash

   The sales journal entry to record the sale of merchandise on account is illustrated here.

SALES JOURNAL PAGE ___1___

	DATE	SALES SLIP NO.	CUSTOMER'S ACCOUNT DEBITED	POST. REF.	SALES CREDIT	SALES TAX PAYABLE CREDIT	ACCOUNTS RECEIVABLE DEBIT	
1	*Date*	*Sales*	*Customer's Account Name*		x x x xx	x x xx	x x x xx	1
2		*Slip*						2
3		*No.*						3

The *cash receipts journal* is used to record all cash that a business receives. The following types of transactions are recorded in the cash receipts journal:

(a) cash received from a charge customer
(b) cash received from a charge customer less a cash discount
(c) cash sales
(d) bankcard sales
(e) cash received from the sale of other assets

CASH RECEIPTS JOURNAL PAGE ___1___

		DATE	DOC. NO.	ACCOUNT NAME	POST. REF.	GENERAL CREDIT	SALES CREDIT	SALES TAX PAYABLE CREDIT	ACCOUNTS RECEIVABLE CREDIT	SALES DISCOUNTS DEBIT	CASH IN BANK DEBIT	
(a)	1	*Date of Receipt*	*Receipt No.*	*Customer's Name*					x x x xx		x x x xx	1
(b)	2	*Date of Receipt*	*Receipt No.*	*Customer's Name*					x x x xx	x x xx	x x x xx	2
(c)	3	*Date of Tape*	*Tape No.*	*Cash Sales*			x x x xx	x x xx			x x x xx	3
(d)	4	*Date of Tape*	*Tape No.*	*Bankcard Sales*			x x x xx	x x xx			x x x xx	4
(e)	5	*Date of Receipt*	*Receipt No.*	*Account Affected*		x x x xx					x x x xx	5

3. Post these columns' individual amounts *daily:*

Journal	Individual Column Amounts		Are Posted To:
Sales Journal	Accounts Receivable Debit column	➤	Subsidiary ledger customer account
Cash Receipts Journal	Accounts Receivable Credit column	➤	Subsidiary ledger customer account
	General Credit column	➤	General ledger account

4. Complete seven steps before you post special journal column totals to the general ledger:
   (a) Rule the amount columns.
   (b) Foot the amount columns.
   (c) Prove the journal.
   (d) Under the last transaction, enter the date the journal is totaled in the Date column.
   (e) On the same line, enter the word *Totals* in the Customer's Account Debited column (sales journal) or the Account Name column (cash receipts journal).
   (f) Enter the column totals, in ink, just below the footings.
   (g) Double-rule the amount columns.

5. Post these column totals at *month-end:*

Journal	Column Total		Is Posted To:
Sales Journal	Sales Credit column	➤	**Sales** account
	Sales Tax Payable Credit column	➤	**Sales Tax Payable** account
	Accounts Receivable Debit column	➤	**Accounts Receivable** account
Cash Receipts Journal	Sales Credit column	➤	**Sales** account
	Sales Tax Payable Credit column	➤	**Sales Tax Payable** account
	Accounts Receivable Credit column	➤	**Accounts Receivable** account
	Sales Discounts Debit column	➤	**Sales Discounts** account
	Cash in Bank Debit column	➤	**Cash in Bank** account

6. To prove the accounts receivable subsidiary ledger, prepare a *schedule of accounts receivable,* which lists each charge customer, the balance in the customer's account, and the total amount due from all customers. **Accounts Receivable** is the controlling account for the accounts receivable subsidiary ledger. Review this relationship in **Figure 16–13** on page 468.

Key Terms

cash receipts journal (p. 459)
footing (p. 453)
sales journal (p. 450)
schedule of accounts receivable (p. 466)
special journals (p. 450)

AFTER YOU READ

Check Your Understanding

1. **Special Journals**
   a. When are special journals used in an accounting system?
   b. Name four commonly used special journals and describe the transactions entered in each.

2. **Sales Journal and Cash Receipts Journal**
   a. List the steps to record transactions in the sales journal.
   b. What are the source documents for transactions recorded in the cash receipts journal?

3. **Posting Single Transactions**
   a. When are sales transactions posted to the accounts receivable subsidiary ledger? Why?
   b. When are transactions in the cash receipts journal posted to the accounts receivable subsidiary ledger? Why?

4. **Footing, Proving, Totaling, and Ruling**
   a. What is a *footing*?
   b. Which columns in the sales journal are double-ruled? What does the double rule indicate?

5. **Posting Column Totals**
   a. Which sales journal column total is posted to the general ledger **Sales** account?
   b. When posting column totals from the cash receipts journal to the general ledger, which total is *not* posted?

6. **Schedule of Accounts Receivable**
   a. What is the purpose of a schedule of accounts receivable?
   b. The schedule of accounts receivable does *not* uncover what type of error?

Apply Key Terms

Imagine that you are the accounting manager for EarthWear Clothing. Recently you noticed that several sales associates are not keeping good records of sales transactions. Write an informational memorandum to the sales staff about the need for accurate, complete sales records. Use the following terms to describe a systematic method to track sales.

cash receipts journal	schedule of accounts
footing	receivable
sales journal	special journals

Mastering Sales and Cash Receipts

Making the Transition from a Manual to a Computerized System

Task	Manual Methods	Computerized Methods
Setting up customer records	• Ledger sheets or cards are prepared with customer account details such as customer name, address, and contact information. • Account activities are posted to the customer's subsidiary ledger account.	• Assign each customer an ID code. • Record details of customer accounts into customer records. • The customer's sales and payment history is maintained automatically.
Issuing and Recording a Credit Memorandum	• A credit memorandum is prepared. • A journal entry is prepared to record the credit memorandum. • The journal entry is posted to the customer's account and to the general ledger.	• The accounting software will create a credit memo and apply it to the appropriate outstanding customer invoice. • The credit memo is posted automatically to the customer account and to the general ledger.

 **Peachtree®** Q & A

Peachtree Question	Answer
How do I set up a new customer account?	1. From the *Maintain* menu, select **Customers/Prospects.** 2. Assign a Customer ID to the customer account. 3. Enter customer name and contact information. 4. Click on the Sales Defaults tab. 5. Verify or enter the appropriate sales default GL account number.
How do I issue and record a credit memorandum?	1. From the *Tasks* menu, select **Sales/Invoicing.** 2. Enter a customer ID and a reference number. 3. Click on the Apply to Sales tab and fill out the **Apply to Invoice.**

 QuickBooks Q & A

QuickBooks Question	Answer
How do I set up a new customer account?	1. From the *Lists* menu, select **Customer:Job List.** 2. Click the **Customer:Job** drop-down list and select **New.** 3. Enter customer name and contact information. 4. Click on the Additional Info tab and enter any additional customer data.
How do I issue and record a credit memorandum?	1. From the *Customers* menu, select **Create Credit Memos/Refunds.** 2. Enter customer name, date, and credit invoice number. 3. In the Item column, select the item returned. 4. Enter the number returned in the *Qty* field.

For detailed instructions, see your Glencoe Accounting Chapter Study Guides and Working Papers.

CHAPTER 16

Problems

| Complete problems using: | **Manual** Glencoe Working Papers | OR | **Peachtree Complete Accounting** Software | OR | **QuickBooks** Templates |

Peachtree®

SMART GUIDE

Step–by–Step Instructions: Problem 16–4

1. Select the problem set for Shutterbug Cameras (Prob. 16–4).
2. Rename the company and set the system date.
3. Enter all sales on account transactions using the **Sales/ Invoicing** option.
4. Record all cash sales using the **Receipts** option.
5. Print a Sales Journal report and a Cash Receipts Journal report.
6. Proof your work.
7. Print a General Ledger report and Customer Ledgers report.
8. Complete the Analyze activity.
9. End the session.

TIP: When you print a report, such as the General Ledger, you can use the filter options to customize the information that appears on the report.

Problem 16–4 Recording and Posting Sales Transactions

Shutterbug Cameras records its transactions in special journals. The accounts receivable subsidiary ledger and certain general ledger accounts are included in your working papers.

Instructions In your working papers:

1. Record each transaction on page 12 of the sales journal or on page 13 of the cash receipts journal.
2. Post to the customer accounts in the accounts receivable subsidiary ledger on a daily basis.
3. Foot, prove, total, and rule the sales journal.
4. Post the column totals from the sales journal and the cash receipts journal to the general ledger accounts named in the column headings.
5. Prepare a schedule of accounts receivable.

Date		Transactions
May	1	Sold merchandise on account to Yoko Nakata, $500 plus 4% sales tax of $20, Sales Slip 220.
	3	Cash sales totaled $1,500 plus $60 in sales tax, Tape 10.
	7	Cash sales totaled $200 plus $8 in sales tax, Tape 11.
	9	Sold merchandise on account to Heather Sullivan for $100 plus sales tax of $4, Sales Slip 223.
	12	Cash sales totaled $400 plus $16 in sales tax, Tape 12.
	15	Sold $3,000 in merchandise on account to FastForward Productions plus sales tax of $120, Sales Slip 225.
	18	Sold merchandise on account to Yoko Nakata, $200 plus sales tax of $8, Sales Slip 226.

Analyze Based on these transactions, calculate how much cash was collected for the month.

Problem 16–5 Recording and Posting Cash Receipts

River's Edge Canoe & Kayak uses special journals and an accounts receivable subsidiary ledger for recording business transactions. The accounts receivable subsidiary ledger accounts and certain general ledger accounts are included in your working papers. The current account balances are recorded in the accounts.

Instructions In your working papers:

1. Record the transactions on page 7 in the cash receipts journal.
2. Post the amounts from the Accounts Receivable Credit column to the customers' accounts in the accounts receivable subsidiary ledger. Post the individual amounts in the General Credit column to the general ledger accounts.
3. Foot, prove, total, and rule the cash receipts journal.
4. Post the column totals to the general ledger accounts named in the column headings.
5. Prepare a schedule of accounts receivable.

Date	Transactions
May 2	Received $400 from Paul Drake to apply on his account, Receipt 505.
5	Received $2,940 from Adventure River Tours in payment of its $3,000 account less a 2% cash discount of $60, Receipt 506.
7	Sold old shelving (**Store Equipment**) for $50, Receipt 507.
10	Wildwood Resorts sent us a check for $2,425 in payment of its account, $2,500 less a 3% cash discount of $75, Receipt 508.
15	Cash sales totaled $2,000 plus $100 in sales tax, Tape 20.
15	Bankcard sales were $3,000 plus $150 in sales tax, Tape 20.
18	Celeste Everett sent us a check for $150 to apply on her account, Receipt 509.
20	Isabel Rodriquez sent us $100 to apply on her account, Receipt 510.
30	Cash sales were $4,500 plus $225 sales tax, Tape 21. Bankcard sales totaled $3,800 plus sales tax of $190, Tape 21.

Analyze Identify the source document that would be used to record bankcard sales and cash sales.

Peachtree®

SMART GUIDE

Step–by–Step Instructions: Problem 16–5

1. Select the problem set for River's Edge Canoe & Kayak (Prob. 16–5).
2. Rename the company and set the system date.
3. Record all cash receipts using the **Receipts** option.
4. Print the following reports: Cash Receipts Journal, General Ledger, and Customer Ledgers.
5. Proof your work.
6. Complete the Analyze activity.
7. End the session.

TIP: You can apply a partial payment from a customer.

QuickBooks

PROBLEM GUIDE

Step–by–Step Instructions: Problem 16–5

1. Restore the Problem 16-5.QBB file.
2. Enter all cash receipts using the **Receive Payments** option.
3. Print a Journal report and a General Ledger.
4. Print a Customer Balance Summary.
5. Proof your work.
6. Complete the Analyze activity.
7. Back up your work.

CHALLENGE PROBLEM

Problem 16–6 Recording and Posting Sales and Cash Receipts

Buzz Newsstand had the following sales and cash receipt transactions for May. In your working papers, the accounts receivable subsidiary ledger and general ledger accounts have been opened with current balances.

Instructions

1. Record the sales and cash receipts for May on page 11 of the sales journal and page 11 of the cash receipts journal.
2. Post to the customer accounts in the accounts receivable subsidiary ledger on a daily basis.
3. Post from the General Credit column of the cash receipts journal on a daily basis.

SOURCE DOCUMENT PROBLEM

Problem 16–6

Use the source documents in your working papers to complete this problem.

CONTINUE ➡

Problems

4. Foot, prove, total, and rule both journals.
5. Post the column totals of the sales journal to the general ledger accounts named in the column headings.
6. Post the column totals from the cash receipts journal to the general ledger accounts named in the column headings.
7. Prepare a schedule of accounts receivable.

Peachtree®

SMART GUIDE

Step–by–Step Instructions: Problem 16–6

1. Select the problem set for Buzz Newsstand (Prob. 16–6).
2. Rename the company and set the system date.
3. Enter all sales on account transactions.
4. Record all cash receipts.
5. Print a Sales Journal report and a Cash Receipts Journal report.
6. Proof your work.
7. Print a General Ledger report and Customer Ledgers report.
8. Complete the Analyze activity.
9. End the session.

QuickBooks

PROBLEM GUIDE

Step–by–Step Instructions: Problem 16–6

1. Restore the Problem 16-6.QBB file.
2. Enter all sales on account transactions.
3. Record all cash receipts.
4. Print a Journal report and a General Ledger report.
5. Proof your work.
6. Print a Customer Balance Summary.
7. Complete the Analyze activity.
8. Back up your work.

Date		Transactions
May	1	Sold $300 in merchandise plus 6% sales tax of $18 on account to Ilya Bodonski, Sales Slip 170.
	3	Received $490 from Katz Properties in payment of its $500 account balance less a 2% discount of $10, Receipt 145.
	5	As a favor, sold $60 in supplies to Straka Stores, received cash, Receipt 146.
	7	Rothwell Management Inc. sent us a check for $294 in payment of its $300 account balance less a $6 cash discount, Receipt 147.
	9	Sold $100 in merchandise plus $6 sales tax on account to Saba Nadal, Sales Slip 171.
	10	Sold $600 in merchandise plus $36 sales tax on account to Java Shops Inc., terms 2/10, n/30, Sales Slip 172.
	12	Sold $50 in merchandise plus $3 sales tax on account to Lee Adkins, Sales Slip 173.
	15	Received a check for $196 from Rolling Hills Pharmacies in payment of its $200 account less a 2% cash discount of $4, Receipt 148.
	15	Cash sales were $2,400 plus $144 sales tax, Tape 33.
	15	Bankcard sales totaled $2,000 plus sales tax of $120, Tape 33.
	18	Sold $1,000 in merchandise plus sales tax of $60 on account to Katz Properties, terms 2/10, n/30, Sales Slip 174.
	20	Received $100 from Ilya Bodonski to apply on her account, Receipt 149.
	22	Sold $800 in merchandise plus $48 sales tax on account to Rothwell Management Inc., terms 2/10, n/30, Sales Slip 175.
	23	Lee Adkins sent us a check for $53 in payment of his account, Receipt 150.
	24	Received a $106 check from Saba Nadal to apply on account, Receipt 151.
	26	Java Shops Inc. sent us a check for $200 to apply on account, Receipt 152.
	27	Sold $200 in merchandise plus sales tax of $12 on account to Lee Adkins, Sales Slip 176.
	28	Received $75 from the sale of excess store equipment, Receipt 153.
	30	Cash sales totaled $2,600 plus $156 sales tax, Tape 34.
	30	Bankcard sales were $2,200 plus sales tax of $132, Tape 34.

Analyze | **Calculate the percent of sales discounts given in May to total May sales.**

Practice your test-taking skills! The questions on this page are reprinted with permission from national organizations:

- Future Business Leaders of America
- Business Professionals of America

Use a separate sheet of paper to record your answers.

Future Business Leaders of America

MULTIPLE CHOICE

1. ABC Corporation uses special journals to account for detailed transactions. Which of the following would not be considered a special journal?
   - a. purchases journal
   - b. cash payments journal
   - c. sales journal
   - d. general journal
   - e. none of these answers

2. Check marks are placed in parentheses below both General amount column totals in a journal to show that the column totals
   - a. are not posted.
   - b. have been posted.
   - c. balance.
   - d. none of the above

3. The Accounts Receivable controlling account in the general ledger
   - a. shows the total amount owed by all customers when posting is complete.
   - b. helps keep the general ledger a balancing ledger in which debits equal credits.
   - c. offers a means of testing the accuracy of the customer account balances.
   - d. does all of the foregoing.
   - e. does none of the foregoing.

4. A journal amount column that is not headed with an account name is called a
   - a. special amount column.
   - b. general amount column.
   - c. date column.
   - d. posting reference column.
   - e. none of these answers

Business Professionals of America

MULTIPLE CHOICE

5. A list of all customer accounts, account balances, and total amount due from all customers is a
   - a. Schedule of Accounts Payable.
   - b. Worksheet.
   - c. Schedule of Accounts Receivable.
   - d. none of the above

> **Need More Help?**
>
> Go to **glencoeaccounting.glencoe.com** and click on **Student Center**. Click on **Winning Competitive Events** and select **Chapter 16.**
> - **Practice Questions and Test-Taking Tips**
> - **Concept Capsules and Terminology**

Special Journals: Sales and Cash Receipts

1. Describe the purpose of a special journal.
2. How is the sales journal different from the cash receipts journal?
3. Your new job assignment is to prove the accounts receivable subsidiary ledger. All postings have been made. What do you do to prove the ledger?
4. Compare and contrast the receipt of cash from a charge customer with the receipt of cash at the time of the merchandise sale.
5. The schedule of accounts receivable total does not agree with the general ledger's **Accounts Receivable** balance. Develop a plan to locate the error(s).
6. What is the value of maintaining special journals?

Merchandising Business: Movie Theater

You work in the accounting department for Springdale Movie Theater. The owners are considering enlarging the concession area one and one-half times its current size to offer a wider variety of foods. No theater seats would be lost. The cost is estimated at $200,000. Sales figures for the past three years follow.

Year	Ticket Sales	Concession Sales
Year 1	$4,800,000	$1,800,000
Year 2	5,100,000	1,600,000
Year 3	5,400,000	1,480,000

INSTRUCTIONS

1. Use a spreadsheet program to analyze the sales and planned expansion. What percent of total sales are ticket sales and concession sales each year?
2. Assuming concession sales remain at $1,480,000, what percentage increase in concession revenue is needed to pay for the renovation costs in one year?

Working for a Competitor

Accounting clerks use sales journals to record sales on account, giving them direct access to the company's customer lists. As an accounting clerk at Haverty's Furniture Store, you work with Bob, a part-time accounting clerk. Recently Bob confided in you that during the mornings, he works at World Classic Furniture, a competitor of Haverty's.

ETHICAL DECISION MAKING

1. What are the ethical issues?
2. What are the alternatives?
3. Who are the affected parties?
4. How do the alternatives affect the parties?
5. What would you do?

Explaining a Transaction

You work for Equestrian Steps—Horse Boarding and Lessons. During an equestrian competition last weekend, you purchased grain on account from the local feed store for $85 plus 6% sales tax. On a separate sheet of paper, write a brief memo to the accounting clerk explaining the transaction so she can record it in the accounting records.

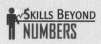

SKILLS BEYOND NUMBERS

Designing and Improving Systems

At Ice Cream Express, you keep the financial records and maintain inventory. You noticed that some ice cream flavors are popular only during certain seasons. For example peppermint ice cream is very popular during winter but not in the summer. You decide to get feedback about your customers' likes and dislikes.

INSTRUCTIONS Design a survey that will help identify your customers' preferences. Include questions to gather data about respondents' gender, age, and income level. What incentives will you offer to prompt customers to participate?

INTERNATIONAL ACCOUNTING

Tariffs and Duties

Thinking of boosting your company's sales by selling products in another country? Consider the impact of tariffs. A *tariff*, or *duty*, is a tax imposed on imports of specific products. For example if your U.S.-based company sells computer hardware in Venezuela, a 5 percent tariff will be charged on each item.

INSTRUCTIONS Assume that Venezuelan competitors sell Model AB computer monitors for $210. You typically charge $205. Will your price be competitive after considering the tariff? Why or why not?

Making It Personal

Examining Your Currency

You have learned that businesses have cash receipts in various forms including transactions with charge cards and bankcards; checks; and currency.

PERSONAL FINANCE ACTIVITY What do you know about the cash you use? Write a brief report about U.S. paper currency. Address what they are made of, the seven denominations in circulation today and the portrait appearing on each, the purpose of a security thread, and whether torn bills are acceptable.

PERSONAL FINANCE ONLINE Log on to **glencoeaccounting.glencoe.com** and click on **Student Center.** Click on **Making It Personal** and select **Chapter 16.**

Analyzing FINANCIAL Reports

Interpreting Sales

In addition to financial results, most annual reports contain management's analysis and interpretation of the financial data. For example if revenue has increased, the report might provide reasons for the increase and projections for the next fiscal period.

INSTRUCTIONS Use the *Fiscal 2003 Compared to Fiscal 2002* section of PETsMART's annual report in Appendix F to answer these questions.

1. Did store sales increase or decrease over the prior year? What reasons are given for this change?

2. Why would an analysis of sales be important to people reading an annual report?

Web Quest

Safe and Secure

Always research the company before buying something on the Internet. Beware of scams! Visit **glencoeaccounting.glencoe.com** and click on **Student Center.** Click on **WebQuest** and select **Unit 4** to continue your Internet project.

Special Journals: Purchases and Cash Payments

What You'll Learn

1. Explain the purpose of the purchases and cash payments journals.

2. Record transactions in the purchases and cash payments journals.

3. Record payroll transactions in the cash payments journal.

4. Post from the purchases and cash payments journals to the general ledger and the accounts payable subsidiary ledger.

5. Total, prove, and rule the purchases and cash payments journals.

6. Prepare a schedule of accounts payable.

7. Prove cash.

8. Define the accounting terms introduced in this chapter.

Why It's Important

Cash must be protected and accounted for.

BEFORE YOU READ

Predict

1. What does the chapter title tell you?
2. What do you already know about this subject from personal experience?
3. What have you learned about this in the earlier chapters?
4. What gaps exist in your knowledge of this subject?

Exploring the *Real World* of Business

LOOKING AT THE ROLE OF PURCHASES

Adler Planetarium & Astronomy Museum

Millions of people visit Chicago's **Adler Planetarium & Astronomy Museum** where the sky's the limit when it comes to finding new ways to view the cosmos. If you want to know more about our galaxy, the Adler has something for you. Visitors can observe a simulated night sky in action on the Sky Theater's 68-foot dome or build a solar system on a computer.

Operations like the **Adler** make many purchases. Its Galileo Café buys food and utensils. Exhibits might need giant models of planets or moons. The gift shop needs to stock puzzles, telescopes, and jewelry. The museum's accounting system documents each purchase.

What Do You Think?

When the **Adler Planetarium** gift shop purchases items for resale, what general ledger accounts are affected?

Working in the *Real World*

APPLYING YOUR ACCOUNTING KNOWLEDGE

Do you, or anyone you know, make regular payments to anyone—perhaps for car insurance or for a purchase you made on an installment plan? Businesses make many similar payments. Retail businesses buy the merchandise they sell to customers. They also buy many items used to operate the business, such as china and silverware for a restaurant. Businesses buy most items on credit and must keep track of when payments are due. You will learn how that is done in the accounting records as you study this chapter.

Personal Connection

1. What items might your employer buy on credit?

2. Do you have any ideas on how you might keep track of purchases and when payments are due on those items?

Online Connection

Go to **glencoeaccounting.glencoe.com** and click on **Student Center.** Click on **Working in the Real World** and select **Chapter 17.**

The Purchases Journal

In the last chapter, you learned that businesses use special journals to record transactions that are similar and occur frequently. If the accounting system were like a transit system, special journals would be like traffic police in helping avoid accounting traffic jams by channeling incoming data into appropriate "lanes." They also provide a shortcut for much of the data headed for the general ledger.

You also learned in the last chapter that the sales and cash receipts journals record the sale of merchandise and other assets. In this chapter you will learn how accountants use purchases and cash payments journals to record the purchase of merchandise and other assets. You will also learn about the accounts payable subsidiary ledger.

Businesses like Target purchase merchandise for resale from hundreds of suppliers. Target and other companies use purchases and cash payments journals to simplify the purchase and payment processes.

Using the Purchases Journal
What Is the Purpose of the Purchases Journal?

Accountants use the **purchases journal** as a special journal to record all purchases on account. **Figure 17–1** shows the purchases journal that On Your Mark Athletic Wear uses.

The purchases journal includes space for the page number, a column for the date, a column for the invoice number, a column for the name of the creditor, and a column for the posting reference. It also has three amount

Figure 17–1
Purchases Journal

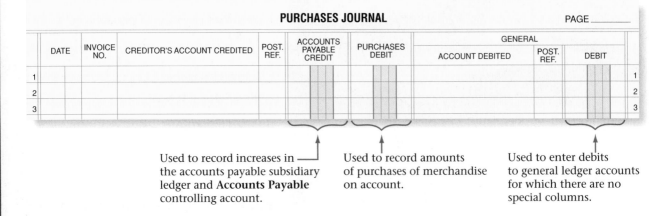

PURCHASES JOURNAL   PAGE_____

	DATE	INVOICE NO.	CREDITOR'S ACCOUNT CREDITED	POST. REF.	ACCOUNTS PAYABLE CREDIT	PURCHASES DEBIT	GENERAL			
							ACCOUNT DEBITED	POST. REF.	DEBIT	
1										1
2										2
3										3

Used to record increases in the accounts payable subsidiary ledger and **Accounts Payable** controlling account.

Used to record amounts of purchases of merchandise on account.

Used to enter debits to general ledger accounts for which there are no special columns.

columns. Refer to **Figure 17–1** for a description of what amounts should be recorded in each column.

Recording the Purchase of Merchandise on Account

After verifying an invoice, the accounting clerk records the purchase in the purchases journal. Refer to the purchases journal and follow these steps:

1. Enter the date in the Date column. Use the date the invoice was *received,* not the date the invoice was prepared.
2. Enter the invoice number in the Invoice Number column.
3. Enter the creditor's name in the Creditor's Account Credited column.
4. Enter the *total* of the invoice in the Accounts Payable Credit column.
5. For purchases of merchandise on account, enter the total amount of the invoice in the Purchases Debit column.

As You READ

Key Point

Purchasing Merchandise on Account
Debit   **Purchases**
Credit **Accounts Payable**

Business Transaction

On December 14 On Your Mark received Invoice 7894 from Pro Runner Warehouse for merchandise purchased on account, $2,300, terms 2/10, n/30.

PRO RUNNER WAREHOUSE
22009 Ben White Blvd.
Austin, TX 78705

REC'D DEC. 14, 20--

INVOICE NO. 7894
DATE: Dec. 14, 20--
ORDER NO.: 9784
SHIPPED BY: Federal Trucking
TERMS: 2/10, n/30

TO On Your Mark Athletic Wear
595 Leslie Street
Dallas, TX 75207

QTY.	ITEM	UNIT PRICE	TOTAL
20 pair	Soft Cushion: White, #94682	$ 50.00	$ 1,000.00
10 pair	Soft Cushion: Black, #94788	50.00	500.00
10 pair	Low Cut: White, #94281	40.00	400.00
10 pair	Low Cut: Black, #94666	40.00	400.00
		Total	$ 2,300.00

Due Date: _12/24_
Discount: _$ 46.00_
Net Amount: _$ 2,254.00_
Check No.:

JOURNAL ENTRY

	DATE	INVOICE NO.	CREDITOR'S ACCOUNT CREDITED	POST. REF.	ACCOUNTS PAYABLE CREDIT	PURCHASES DEBIT	GENERAL ACCOUNT DEBITED	POST. REF.	DEBIT	
6	14	7894	Pro Runner Warehouse		2 300 00	2 300 00				6
7	1	2	3		4	5				7

PURCHASES JOURNAL   PAGE _12_

After journalizing the invoice from Pro Runner Warehouse, the accounting clerk places it in a tickler file by due date. In this case it is filed in the December 24 folder. On Your Mark plans to take the discount, and December 24 is ten days after the invoice date.

Journalizing Other Purchases on Account

On Your Mark also purchases supplies and other assets on account. These purchases do not occur often enough to set up special columns in the purchases journal. When these purchases do occur, they are recorded in the General Debit column of the purchases journal.

Refer to the purchases journal on page 484 and follow these steps:

1. Enter the date the invoice was *received* in the Date column.
2. Enter the invoice number in the Invoice Number column.
3. Enter the creditor's name in the Creditor's Account Credited column.
4. Enter the *total* of the invoice in the Accounts Payable Credit column.

As You READ

Instant Recall

Merchandisers A merchandising business purchases merchandise from a supplier and resells it.

On December 15 On Your Mark received Invoice 3417, dated December 13, from Champion Store Supply for store equipment bought on account, $1,200, terms n/30.

CHAMPION STORE SUPPLY		INVOICE NO. 3417
47249 Randall Parkway		
Dallas, TX 75207	REC'D DEC. 15, 20--	DATE: Dec. 13, 20--
		ORDER NO.: 9795
On Your Mark Athletic Wear		SHIPPED BY: Federal Trucking
TO 595 Leslie Street		TERMS: n/30
Dallas, TX 75207		

QTY.	ITEM	UNIT PRICE	TOTAL
3	Corner Shelf Units	$ 300.00	$ 900.00
1	Shirt Rack	300.00	300.00
	Total		$ 1,200.00

Due Date: _1/12_
Discount: _$0.00_
Net Amount: _$1,200.00_
Check No.: _____

JOURNAL ENTRY

								GENERAL				
	DATE	INVOICE NO.	CREDITOR'S ACCOUNT CREDITED	POST. REF.	ACCOUNTS PAYABLE CREDIT	PURCHASES DEBIT		ACCOUNT DEBITED	POST. REF.	DEBIT		
7	15	3417	Champion Store Supply		1 200 00			Store Equipment		1 200 00		7
8	1	2	3		4			5		6		8

PURCHASES JOURNAL — PAGE _12_

5. Store equipment is not merchandise purchased for resale, so this transaction is not recorded in the Purchases Debit column. Instead, it is recorded in the General column. Write the name of the general ledger account being debited in the General Account Debited column.

6. Enter the total amount of the invoice in the General Debit column.

After journalizing the invoice, the accounting clerk places it in the tickler file. Because Champion Store Supply does not offer its credit customers a cash discount, the due date is January 12, 30 days after the date of the invoice. The invoice is filed in folder "12" to indicate this date.

Posting from the Purchases Journal
How Do You Post Entries from the Purchases Journal?

As you have learned, special journals save time in recording and posting business transactions. Each transaction in the purchases journal is a purchase on account. Therefore, each transaction is separately posted *daily* to the accounts payable subsidiary ledger to keep creditor accounts current.

Refer to **Figure 17–2** as you read about posting to the accounts payable subsidiary ledger.

1. In the Date column of the subsidiary ledger account, enter the date of the transaction.

2. In the Posting Reference column of the subsidiary ledger account, record the journal letter and the page number. *P* is the letter used for the purchases journal.

3. In the Credit column of the subsidiary ledger account, enter the amount owed to the creditor.

4. Compute the new account balance by adding the amount in the Credit column to the previous balance amount. Since there was no previous balance in Pro Runner's account, enter $2,300 in the Balance column.

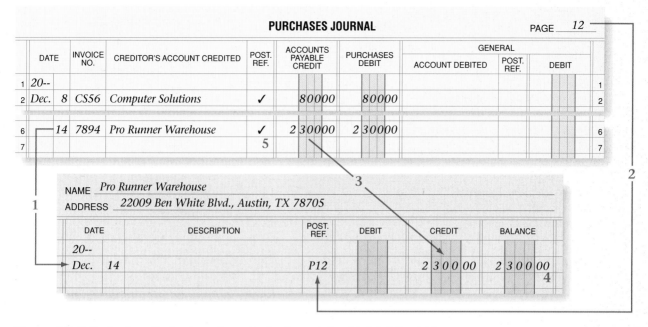

Figure 17–2 Posting from the Purchases Journal to the Accounts Payable Subsidiary Ledger

5. Return to the purchases journal and place a check mark (✓) in the *first* Posting Reference column (next to the Creditor's Account Credited column).

Posting from the General Debit Column

The clerk makes daily postings from the General Debit column of the purchases journal to the appropriate accounts in the general ledger. Refer to **Figure 17–3** on page 486 as you read the following steps:

1. Enter the date of the transaction in the Date column of the general ledger account.
2. In the Posting Reference column of the general ledger account, record the journal letter (*P* for purchases journal) and page number.
3. In the Debit column of the general ledger account, enter the amount recorded in the General Debit column of the purchases journal.
4. Compute and record the new balance in the Debit Balance column.
5. Return to the purchases journal and place the general ledger account number in the General Posting Reference column (following the General Account Debited column).

Totaling, Proving, and Ruling the Purchases Journal

To complete the purchases journal, refer to **Figure 17–4** on page 486 and follow these steps:

1. Draw a single rule across the three amount columns: Accounts Payable Credit, Purchases Debit, and General Debit.
2. Foot each amount column.

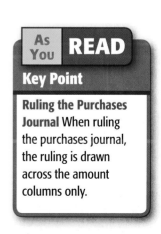

As You READ

Key Point

Ruling the Purchases Journal When ruling the purchases journal, the ruling is drawn across the amount columns only.

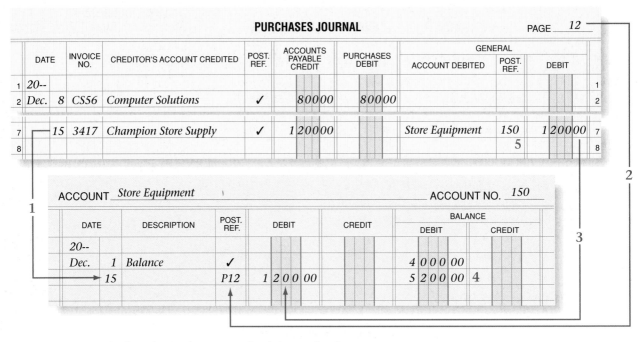

Figure 17–3 Posting from the Purchases Journal to the General Ledger

3. Test for the equality of debits and credits.

Debit Columns		Credit Column	
Purchases	$15,400	Accounts Payable	$16,850
General	1,450		
	$16,850		$16,850

4. In the Date column, on the line below the single rule, enter the date the journal is being totaled.
5. On the same line, write the word *Totals* in the Creditor's Account Credited column.
6. Enter the three column totals, in ink, just below the footings.
7. Draw a double rule across the three amount columns.

PURCHASES JOURNAL

PAGE 12

	DATE	INVOICE NO.	CREDITOR'S ACCOUNT CREDITED	POST. REF.	ACCOUNTS PAYABLE CREDIT	PURCHASES DEBIT	GENERAL			
							ACCOUNT DEBITED	POST. REF.	DEBIT	
1	20--									1
2	Dec. 8	CS56	Computer Solutions	✓	800 00	800 00				2
3	10	4692	Sports Link Footwear	✓	4 000 00	4 000 00				3
4	12	SN63	Sports Nutrition Supply	✓	600 00	600 00				4
5	14	2560	FastLane Athletics	✓	3 000 00	3 000 00				5
6	14	7894	Pro Runner Warehouse	✓	2 300 00	2 300 00				6
7	15	3417	Champion Store Supply	✓	1 200 00		Store Equipment	150	1 200 00	7
8	15	9881	Geary Office Supply	✓	250 00		Supplies	130	250 00	8
9	18	8560	FastLane Athletics	✓	2 000 00	2 000 00				9
10	20	6593	Computer Solutions	✓	1 200 00	1 200 00				10
11	27	5200	Sports Link Footwear	✓	1 500 00	1 500 00				11
12	31		Totals		16 850 00	15 400 00			1 450 00	12
13										13

Figure 17–4 The Completed Purchases Journal

The completed purchases journal is a quick reference tool for the accountant to review current transactions that affect the **Purchases** account and the **Accounts Payable** account. Miscellaneous purchases are also reflected in the purchases journal. If a general journal had been used, these transactions would have been mixed with other transactions (cash receipts, payments, and more) of the period.

What else can the accountant verify from the completed purchases journal? A quick review of the Post. Ref. column tells the accountant that amounts have been posted to the accounts payable subsidiary ledger.

Posting the Special Column Totals to the General Ledger

After totaling and ruling the purchases journal, the clerk posts the totals of the Accounts Payable Credit column and the Purchases Debit column to the general ledger accounts. Then the clerk calculates the new balance for each account, and enters the new balance in the appropriate Balance column. **Figure 17–5** shows the posting of these column totals.

After posting each column total, write the general ledger account number, in parentheses, in the column below the double rule as shown in **Figure 17–5**. The total of the General Debit column is not posted because the individual amounts were posted during the month. Place a check mark (✓) in parentheses below the double rule in the General Debit column to indicate that the total is not posted.

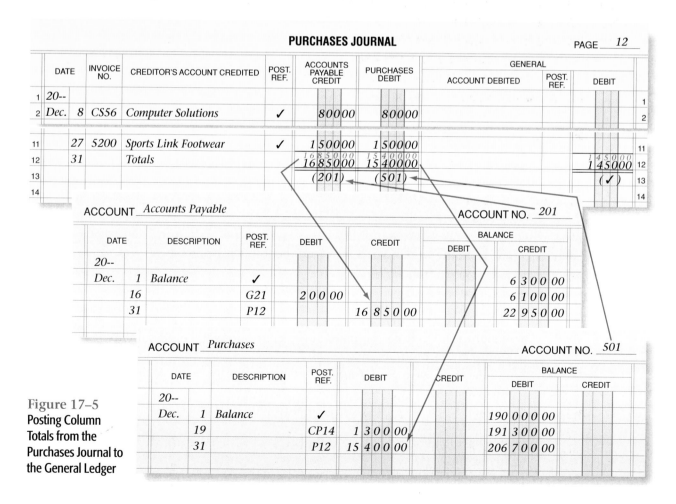

Figure 17–5
Posting Column Totals from the Purchases Journal to the General Ledger

Reinforce the Main Idea

Create a table similar to this one to describe how these three separate transactions would appear in the purchases journal.

Transaction	Account Debited	Account Credited	Amount Column Debited	Amount Column Credited
Purchased Merchandise on Account				
Purchased Store Equipment on Account				
Purchased Supplies on Account				

Do the Math

Dynamo Industries received an invoice from Santos Suppliers for merchandise purchased on July 5 for $12,000 with terms of 3/15, n/30. Answer the following questions:

1. What is the due date of the invoice?
2. What is the amount of cash discount?
3. What is the net amount to be paid?
4. What account is debited and for what amount?
5. What account is credited and for what amount?

Problem 17–1 Recording Transactions in the Purchases Journal

The Design Den, a retail merchandising business, uses special journals. On page 3 of the purchases journal in the working papers, record the following purchases:

Date	Transactions
Feb. 1	Purchased $1,400 in merchandise on account from Woodstock Furnishings, terms 3/15, n/30, Invoice WF39.
2	Bought $900 in store equipment on account from Holmes Equipment Company, terms n/30, Invoice 98.
4	Purchased $700 in merchandise from Fuller Fabrics, terms 3/10, n/30, Invoice 72.
7	Purchased computer speakers on account for $50 from Digital Solutions, terms 2/10, n/30, Invoice AB220.
10	Purchased fabric from Valley Upholstery for $1,500, terms 2/10, n/30, Invoice 947.

The Cash Payments Journal

You have learned about three special journals: the sales journal, the cash receipts journal, and the purchases journal. Now you will study the *cash payments journal*. For many businesses like grocers who must pay for the purchases of a wide variety of merchandise, frequent payments make the use of the *cash payments journal* necessary.

Using the Cash Payments Journal

How Do You Record Cash Payments?

The **cash payments journal** is used to record all transactions in which cash is paid out or decreased. These transactions include: payments to creditors for items bought on account, cash purchases of merchandise and other assets, payments for various expenses, payments for wages and salaries, and cash decreases for bank service charges and bankcard fees. The source documents for the journal entries are check stubs and the bank statement. The cash payments journal is also called the *cash disbursements journal*.

Figure 17–6 shows the cash payments journal that On Your Mark uses. Notice that it has five amount columns.

The seven transactions that follow are typical of those recorded in the cash payments journal. Note that each transaction in the cash payments journal results in a credit to the **Cash in Bank** account.

BEFORE YOU READ

Main Idea
The cash payments journal is used to record the cash a business pays out.

Read to Learn...
➤ how to record cash payment transactions. (p. 489)
➤ how to post from the cash payments journal. (p. 494)

Key Terms
cash payments journal
schedule of accounts payable
proving cash

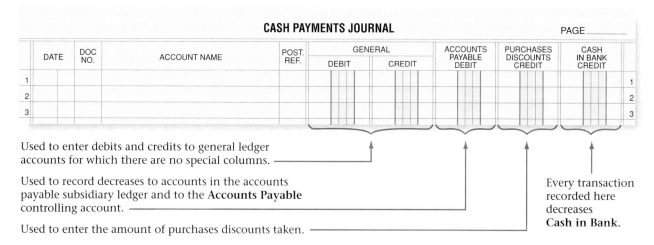

CASH PAYMENTS JOURNAL PAGE_____

	DATE	DOC NO.	ACCOUNT NAME	POST. REF.	GENERAL		ACCOUNTS PAYABLE DEBIT	PURCHASES DISCOUNTS CREDIT	CASH IN BANK CREDIT	
					DEBIT	CREDIT				
1										1
2										2
3										3

Used to enter debits and credits to general ledger accounts for which there are no special columns. ——

Used to record decreases to accounts in the accounts payable subsidiary ledger and to the **Accounts Payable** controlling account. ——

Used to enter the amount of purchases discounts taken. ——

Every transaction recorded here decreases **Cash in Bank.**

Figure 17–6 Cash Payments Journal

Recording the Cash Purchase of an Asset

Cash purchases of various assets are recorded in the cash payments journal. One asset commonly purchased for cash is insurance. Let's record a transaction involving a cash purchase of insurance.

Business Transaction

On December 17 On Your Mark paid $1,500 to Keystone Insurance Company for the premium on a six-month insurance policy, Check 1001.

Check 1001:

ON YOUR MARK
ATHLETIC WEAR
595 Leslie Street, Dallas, TX 75207

1001
22-523
4210

DATE Dec. 17 20 --

PAY TO THE ORDER OF Keystone Insurance Company $ 1,500.00

One thousand five hundred and no/100 ————— DOLLARS

Security National Bank
DALLAS, TEXAS

MEMO _____   Michael Brown

⑆421022523⑆ 727596⑈ 1001

JOURNAL ENTRY

	DATE	DOC NO.	ACCOUNT NAME	POST. REF.	GENERAL		ACCOUNTS PAYABLE DEBIT	PURCHASES DISCOUNTS CREDIT	CASH IN BANK CREDIT	
					DEBIT	CREDIT				
1	20--									1
2	Dec. 17	1001	Prepaid Insurance		1 500 00				1 500 00	2
3	1	2	3		4				5	3

CASH PAYMENTS JOURNAL   PAGE 14

As You READ

Compare and Contrast

Purchases and Cash Payments Journals
How are the purchases journal and the cash payments journal similar? How are they different?

Refer to the cash payments journal above and follow these steps:

1. Enter the date of the transaction in the Date column.
2. Enter the check number in the Document Number column.
3. Enter the name of the account debited in the Account Name column.
4. Because there is no special column for **Prepaid Insurance**, enter the amount of the debit in the General Debit column.
5. Enter the amount of the credit in the Cash in Bank Credit column.

After payment, the invoice for the insurance is filed.

Recording a Cash Purchase of Merchandise

Retail businesses are constantly purchasing merchandise for resale. While they make most purchases on account, many are for cash. Let's record a cash purchase of merchandise for resale.

Business Transaction

On December 19 On Your Mark purchased merchandise from FastLane Athletics for $1,300, Check 1002.

Check 1002:

ON YOUR MARK
ATHLETIC WEAR
595 Leslie Street, Dallas, TX 75207

1002
22-523
4210

DATE Dec. 19 20 --

PAY TO THE ORDER OF FastLane Athletics $ 1,300.00

One thousand three hundred and no/100 ————— DOLLARS

Security National Bank
DALLAS, TEXAS

MEMO _____   Michael Brown

⑆421022523⑆ 727596⑈ 1002

JOURNAL ENTRY

CASH PAYMENTS JOURNAL   PAGE 14

	DATE	DOC NO.	ACCOUNT NAME	POST. REF.	GENERAL		ACCOUNTS PAYABLE DEBIT	PURCHASES DISCOUNTS CREDIT	CASH IN BANK CREDIT	
					DEBIT	CREDIT				
3	19	1002	Purchases		1 300 00				1 300 00	3
4	1	2	3		4				5	4

Refer to On Your Mark's purchase from FastLane Athletics and the cash payments journal as you follow these steps:

1. Enter the date of the transaction in the Date column.
2. Enter the check number in the Document Number column.
3. Enter the name of the account debited in the Account Name column.
4. Because there is no special column for **Purchases**, enter the amount of the debit in the General Debit column.
5. Enter the amount of the check in the Cash in Bank Credit column.

After recording the transaction, the receipt for the cash purchase is filed.

As You READ

Key Point

The General Column
The General column of a special journal refers to the general ledger. The account named in the Account Name column is the general ledger account affected by the transaction.

Recording a Payment on Account

Now let's learn how to make a payment on account and take a purchase discount.

Business Transaction

On December 24 On Your Mark paid $2,254 to Pro Runner Warehouse for merchandise purchased on account, $2,300 less a discount of $46, Check 1003.

ON YOUR MARK ATHLETIC WEAR
595 Leslie Street, Dallas, TX 75207

1003
22-523
4210

DATE ___ Dec. 24 ___ 20 --

PAY TO THE ORDER OF ___ Pro Runner Warehouse ___ $ 2,254.00

Two thousand two hundred fifty-four and ⁿᵒ/₁₀₀——————— DOLLARS

Security National Bank
DALLAS, TEXAS

MEMO ___ *Michael Brown*

⑆4210 22523⑆ 727596⑈ 1003

JOURNAL ENTRY

CASH PAYMENTS JOURNAL   PAGE __ 14 __

	DATE	DOC NO.	ACCOUNT NAME	POST REF.	GENERAL DEBIT	GENERAL CREDIT	ACCOUNTS PAYABLE DEBIT	PURCHASES DISCOUNTS CREDIT	CASH IN BANK CREDIT	
4	24	1003	Pro Runner Warehouse				2 300 00	46 00	2 254 00	4
5	1	2	3				4	5	6	5

Refer to the purchases journal above and follow these steps:

1. Enter the date of the transaction in the Date column.
2. Enter the check number in the Document Number column.
3. Enter the creditor's name in the Account Name column.
4. Enter the amount of the original purchase in the Accounts Payable Debit column.
5. Enter the amount of the purchase discount in the Purchases Discounts Credit column.
6. Enter the amount of the check in the Cash in Bank Credit column.

Remember that a processing stamp is placed on each invoice when it is verified. After the cash payment has been journalized, the accounting clerk records the check number on the "Check No." line of the processing stamp. The paid invoice is then filed.

Companies offer no discount for some purchases. For others they offer a discount, but the business cannot pay within the discount period. In these cases the check is written for the full amount of the purchase.

Recording Other Cash Payments

Let's record a check written to pay for shipping charges when merchandise is sent FOB shipping point.

<table>
<tr><td>

Business Transaction

On December 24 On Your Mark issued Check 1004 for $275 to Dara's Delivery Service for shipping charges on merchandise purchased from Sports Link Footwear.

</td><td>

ON YOUR MARK | **1004**
ATHLETIC WEAR | 22-523
595 Leslie Street, Dallas, TX 75207 | 4210

DATE ___ Dec. 24 ___ 20 --

PAY TO THE ORDER OF Dara's Delivery Service ___ $ 275.00

Two hundred seventy-five and no/100———————— DOLLARS

Security National Bank
DALLAS, TEXAS

MEMO _____ *Michael Brown*

⑈4⑆⑈0⑈2⑈2⑈5⑈2⑈3⑈ 727596⑈ 1004

</td></tr>
</table>

JOURNAL ENTRY

	DATE	DOC NO.	ACCOUNT NAME	POST. REF.	GENERAL DEBIT	GENERAL CREDIT	ACCOUNTS PAYABLE DEBIT	PURCHASES DISCOUNTS CREDIT	CASH IN BANK CREDIT	
5	24	1004	Transportation In		275 00				275 00	5
6	1	2	3		4				5	6

CASH PAYMENTS JOURNAL   PAGE ___ 14 ___

Refer to the cash payments journal above and follow these steps:

1. Enter the date of the transaction in the Date column.
2. Enter the check number in the Document Number column.
3. Enter the name of the account debited in the Account Name column.
4. Because there is no special column for **Transportation In**, enter the amount in the General Debit column.
5. Enter the amount of the check in the Cash in Bank Credit column.

Recording Payment of Payroll

In an earlier chapter, you learned how to record the payroll entry in the general journal. When a business uses special journals, the entry for payment of the payroll is recorded in the cash payments journal. The information to record payroll transactions in journals is taken from the payroll register.

To record the payroll transaction, refer to the cash payments journal and follow these steps:

1. On the first line of the entry, enter the date of the transaction in the Date column.
2. Enter the check number in the Document Number column.
3. Enter the name of the account debited in the Account Name column.
4. Enter the amount of the payroll (gross pay) in the General Debit column.
5. Enter the net pay in the Cash in Bank Credit column.
6. On the next four lines, enter the names of the accounts credited in the Account Name column. Enter the amount of each liability in the General Credit column.

Connect to...
MATHEMATICS

A 1946 contest was held to determine whether a modern electric adding machine or an ancient abacus could calculate problems faster. The abacus won all rounds except multiplication.

On December 31 On Your Mark wrote Check 1012 for $2,974 to pay the payroll of $4,000 (gross earnings) for the pay period ended December 31. The following amounts were withheld: Employees' Federal Income Tax, $640; Employees' State Income Tax, $80; Social Security Tax, $248; and Medicare Tax, $58.

JOURNAL ENTRY

	DATE	DOC. NO.	ACCOUNT NAME	POST. REF.	GENERAL DEBIT	GENERAL CREDIT	ACCOUNTS PAYABLE DEBIT	PURCHASES DISCOUNTS CREDIT	CASH IN BANK CREDIT	
13	31	1012	Salaries Expense 3		4 000 00				5 2 974 00	13
14	1	2	Employees' Fed. Inc. Tax Pay.		4	640 00				14
15			Employees' State Inc. Tax Pay.	6		80 00				15
16			Social Security Tax Pay.			248 00				16
17			Medicare Tax Pay.			58 00				17
18										18

CASH PAYMENTS JOURNAL   PAGE 14

Recording Bank Service Charges

Bank service charges are automatically deducted from the checking account. Although no check is written to pay these charges, the transactions are recorded in the cash payments journal because the charges decrease the **Cash in Bank** account.

On December 31 On Your Mark recorded a bank service charge for $20 indicated on the bank statement.

JOURNAL ENTRY

	DATE	DOC. NO.	ACCOUNT NAME	POST. REF.	GENERAL DEBIT	GENERAL CREDIT	ACCOUNTS PAYABLE DEBIT	PURCHASES DISCOUNTS CREDIT	CASH IN BANK CREDIT	
18	31		Miscellaneous Expense		20 00				20 00	18
19										19

CASH PAYMENTS JOURNAL   PAGE 14

Recording Bankcard Fees

Most banks charge a fee for handling bankcard sales. This fee is automatically deducted from the business's checking account. For example, On Your Mark's bank deducted a bankcard fee of $75. The fee appeared on the bank statement as a deduction from the checking account balance. The accounting clerk recorded this decrease in cash in the cash payments journal.

As You READ

In Your Experience

Bank Service Charges
What bank service charges, if any, has your bank charged you?

On December 31 On Your Mark recorded the bankcard fee of $75 that appeared on the bank statement.

JOURNAL ENTRY

	DATE	DOC. NO.	ACCOUNT NAME	POST. REF.	GENERAL DEBIT	GENERAL CREDIT	ACCOUNTS PAYABLE DEBIT	PURCHASES DISCOUNTS CREDIT	CASH IN BANK CREDIT	
19		31	Bankcard Fees Expense		75 00				75 00	19
20										20

CASH PAYMENTS JOURNAL — PAGE 14

The clerk also enters the bank charges in the checkbook records. **Figure 17–7** illustrates one way to adjust the balance on the check stub. The deposit heading is crossed out, and the words *Bankcard Fees* are written in its place. A deduction of $75 is entered on the stub. On the next line, the words *Less Bank Service Charge* are written and an entry is made for the $20 deduction. Both amounts are subtracted from the balance brought forward.

Posting from the Cash Payments Journal

How Do You Post from the Cash Payments Journal?

Individual amounts in the Accounts Payable Debit column and the General Debit column are posted daily. Column totals are posted at the end of the month.

To keep creditors' accounts current, clerks make daily postings from the Accounts Payable Debit column to the accounts payable subsidiary ledger. Refer to **Figure 17–8** and follow these steps:

1. Enter the date of the transaction in the Date column of the subsidiary ledger account.
2. In the subsidiary ledger account's Posting Reference column, enter the journal letters (*CP* for the cash payments journal) and the page number.
3. In the Debit column of the subsidiary ledger account, enter the amount recorded in the Accounts Payable Debit column of the journal.
4. Compute the new account balance and enter it in the Balance column. If the account has a zero balance, draw a line through the Balance column.

	No. 1013
$ _____	
Date _____ 20 ____	
To _____	
For _____	

	Dollars	Cents
Balance brought forward	15,274	00
~~Add deposits~~ Bankcard Fees	−75	00
Less Bank Svc. Chg.	−20	00
Total	15,179	00
Less this check		
Balance carried forward		

Figure 17–7 Recording Bankcard Fees and Service Charges in the Checkbook

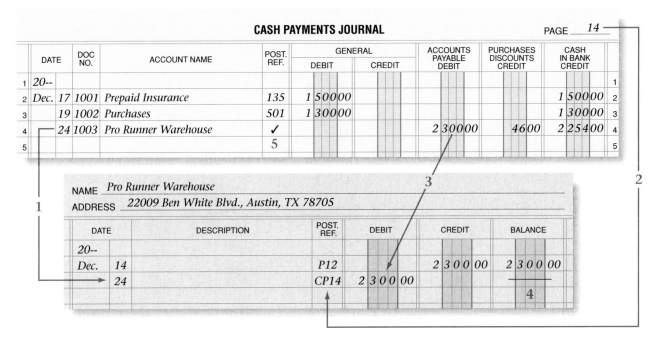

CASH PAYMENTS JOURNAL

PAGE _14_

	DATE	DOC NO.	ACCOUNT NAME	POST. REF.	GENERAL DEBIT	GENERAL CREDIT	ACCOUNTS PAYABLE DEBIT	PURCHASES DISCOUNTS CREDIT	CASH IN BANK CREDIT	
1	20--									1
2	Dec. 17	1001	Prepaid Insurance	135	1 500 00				1 500 00	2
3	19	1002	Purchases	501	1 300 00				1 300 00	3
4	24	1003	Pro Runner Warehouse	✓			2 300 00	46 00	2 254 00	4
5				5						5

NAME _Pro Runner Warehouse_

ADDRESS _22009 Ben White Blvd., Austin, TX 78705_

DATE	DESCRIPTION	POST. REF.	DEBIT	CREDIT	BALANCE
20--					
Dec. 14		P12		2 300 00	2 300 00
24		CP14	2 300 00		

Figure 17–8 Posting from the Cash Payments Journal to the Accounts Payable Subsidiary Ledger

5. Return to the cash payments journal and enter a check mark (✓) in the Posting Reference column.

Figure 17–9 shows On Your Mark's accounts payable subsidiary ledger after all postings have been made. Notice that the accounts contain entries from the purchases, cash payments, and general journals.

NAME _Champion Store Supply_

ADDRESS _99455 Williams Lane #334, Dallas, TX 75214_

DATE	DESCRIPTION	POST. REF.	DEBIT	CREDIT	BALANCE
20--					
Dec. 1	Balance	✓			1 000 00
15		P12		1 200 00	2 200 00
26		CP14	1 200 00		1 000 00

NAME _Computer Solutions_

ADDRESS _6990 Baker Circle, Dallas, TX 75219_

DATE	DESCRIPTION	POST. REF.	DEBIT	CREDIT	BALANCE
20--					
Dec. 1	Balance	✓			500 00
8		P12		800 00	1 300 00
20		P12		1 200 00	2 500 00
31		CP14	1 200 00		1 300 00

Figure 17–9 The Completed Accounts Payable Subsidiary Ledger

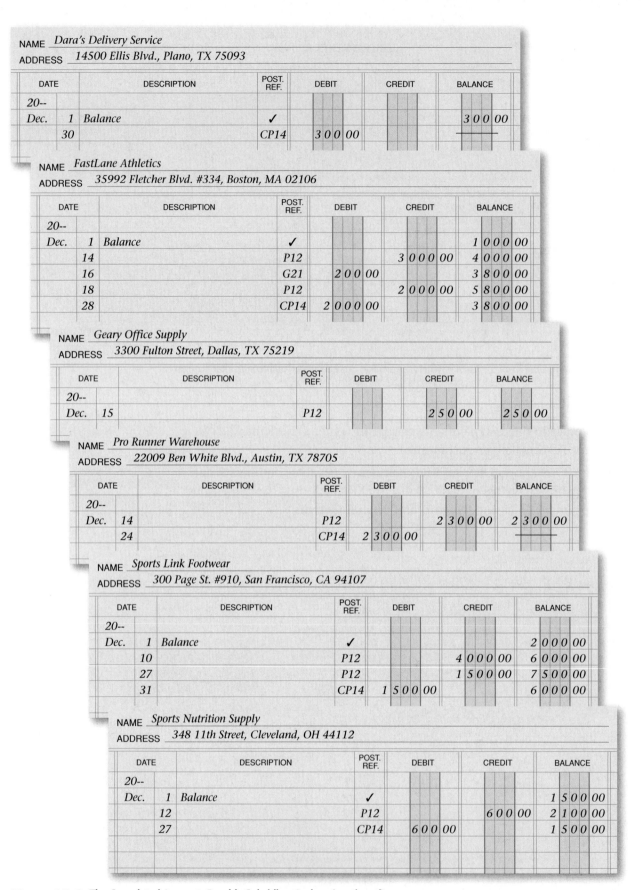

NAME Dara's Delivery Service

ADDRESS 14500 Ellis Blvd., Plano, TX 75093

DATE		DESCRIPTION	POST. REF.	DEBIT	CREDIT	BALANCE
20--						
Dec.	1	Balance	✓			3 0 0 00
	30		CP14	3 0 0 00		

NAME FastLane Athletics

ADDRESS 35992 Fletcher Blvd. #334, Boston, MA 02106

DATE		DESCRIPTION	POST. REF.	DEBIT	CREDIT	BALANCE
20--						
Dec.	1	Balance	✓			1 0 0 0 00
	14		P12		3 0 0 0 00	4 0 0 0 00
	16		G21	2 0 0 00		3 8 0 0 00
	18		P12		2 0 0 0 00	5 8 0 0 00
	28		CP14	2 0 0 0 00		3 8 0 0 00

NAME Geary Office Supply

ADDRESS 3300 Fulton Street, Dallas, TX 75219

DATE		DESCRIPTION	POST. REF.	DEBIT	CREDIT	BALANCE
20--						
Dec.	15		P12		2 5 0 00	2 5 0 00

NAME Pro Runner Warehouse

ADDRESS 22009 Ben White Blvd., Austin, TX 78705

DATE		DESCRIPTION	POST. REF.	DEBIT	CREDIT	BALANCE
20--						
Dec.	14		P12		2 3 0 0 00	2 3 0 0 00
	24		CP14	2 3 0 0 00		

NAME Sports Link Footwear

ADDRESS 300 Page St. #910, San Francisco, CA 94107

DATE		DESCRIPTION	POST. REF.	DEBIT	CREDIT	BALANCE
20--						
Dec.	1	Balance	✓			2 0 0 0 00
	10		P12		4 0 0 0 00	6 0 0 0 00
	27		P12		1 5 0 0 00	7 5 0 0 00
	31		CP14	1 5 0 0 00		6 0 0 0 00

NAME Sports Nutrition Supply

ADDRESS 348 11th Street, Cleveland, OH 44112

DATE		DESCRIPTION	POST. REF.	DEBIT	CREDIT	BALANCE
20--						
Dec.	1	Balance	✓			1 5 0 0 00
	12		P12		6 0 0 00	2 1 0 0 00
	27		CP14	6 0 0 00		1 5 0 0 00

Figure 17–9 The Completed Accounts Payable Subsidiary Ledger (continued)

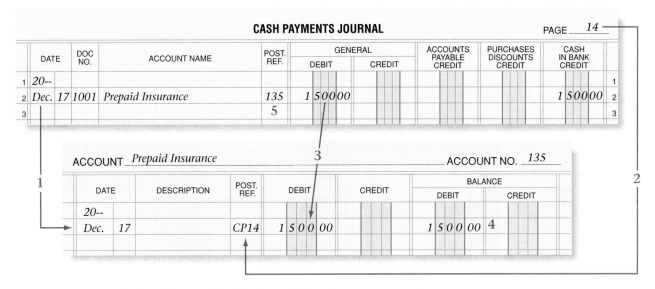

CASH PAYMENTS JOURNAL   PAGE ___14___

	DATE	DOC NO.	ACCOUNT NAME	POST. REF.	GENERAL DEBIT	GENERAL CREDIT	ACCOUNTS PAYABLE CREDIT	PURCHASES DISCOUNTS CREDIT	CASH IN BANK CREDIT	
1	20--									1
2	Dec. 17	1001	Prepaid Insurance	135	1 50000				1 50000	2
3				5						3

ACCOUNT _Prepaid Insurance_   3   ACCOUNT NO. _135_

DATE	DESCRIPTION	POST. REF.	DEBIT	CREDIT	BALANCE DEBIT	BALANCE CREDIT
20--						
Dec. 17		CP14	1 5 0 0 00		1 5 0 0 00 4	

Figure 17–10 Posting from the General Debit Column of the Cash Payments Journal

Posting from the General Debit Column

Accountants post daily from the General Debit column to the appropriate general ledger accounts. Refer to **Figure 17–10** as you read the following steps.

1. Enter the date of the transaction in the Date column of the general ledger account.
2. Enter the journal letters (*CP* for the cash payments journal) and the page number in the Posting Reference column of the general ledger account.
3. In the Debit column, enter the amount from the General Debit column of the cash payments journal.
4. Compute the new balance and enter it in the appropriate Balance column. (Because the example used here has no previous balance, the amount recorded in the Debit column is also entered in the Debit Balance column.)
5. Return to the cash payments journal and enter the account number in the Posting Reference column.

All the transactions in the General Debit column are posted to the general ledger accounts in the same way.

Accountants also post entries daily from the General Credit column to the appropriate general ledger accounts. This is done in the same way as shown for General Debit Column entries.

Totaling, Proving, and Ruling the Cash Payments Journal

Accountants total the cash payments journal following the same steps that they use for other special journals. Before they rule the journal, they prove the equality of debits and credits.

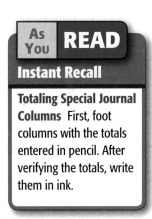

As You READ

Instant Recall

Totaling Special Journal Columns First, foot columns with the totals entered in pencil. After verifying the totals, write them in ink.

CASH PAYMENTS JOURNAL PAGE __14__

	DATE	DOC NO.	ACCOUNT NAME	POST. REF.	GENERAL DEBIT	GENERAL CREDIT	ACCOUNTS PAYABLE DEBIT	PURCHASES DISCOUNTS CREDIT	CASH IN BANK CREDIT	
1	20--									1
2	Dec. 17	1001	Prepaid Insurance	135	1 500 00				1 500 00	2
3	19	1002	Purchases	501	1 300 00				1 300 00	3
4	24	1003	Pro Runner Warehouse	✓			2 300 00	46 00	2 254 00	4
5	24	1004	Transportation In	505	275 00				275 00	5
6	26	1005	Champion Store Supply	✓			1 200 00		1 200 00	6
7	27	1006	Sports Nutrition Supply	✓			600 00		600 00	7
8	28	1007	FastLane Athletics	✓			2 000 00	40 00	1 960 00	8
9	30	1008	Dara's Delivery Service	✓			300 00		300 00	9
10	31	1009	Rent Expense	660	2 000 00				2 000 00	10
11	31	1010	Computer Solutions	✓			1 200 00	24 00	1 176 00	11
12	31	1011	Sports Link Footwear	✓			1 500 00	30 00	1 470 00	12
13	31	1012	Salaries Expense	665	4 000 00				2 974 00	13
14			Employee's Federal Inc. Tax Pay.	205		640 00				14
15			Employee's State Inc. Tax Pay.	211		80 00				15
16			Social Security Tax Payable	212		248 00				16
17			Medicare Tax Payable	213		58 00				17
18	31	—	Miscellaneous Expense	655	20 00				20 00	18
19	31	—	Bankcard Fees Expense	605	75 00				75 00	19
20	31		Totals		9 170 00	1 026 00	9 100 00	140 00	17 104 00	20
21										21

Figure 17–11 The Completed Cash Payments Journal

Debit Columns		Credit Columns	
General	$ 9,170	General	$ 1,026
Accounts Payable	9,100	Purchases Discounts	140
		Cash in Bank	17,104
	$18,270		$18,270

Since debits equal credits, the cash payments journal can be double-ruled, as shown in **Figure 17–11**.

Posting Column Totals to the General Ledger

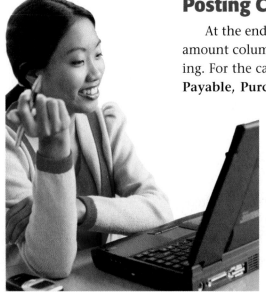

At the end of the month, the accountant posts the total of each special amount column to the general ledger account named in the column heading. For the cash payments journal, column totals are posted to **Accounts Payable, Purchases Discounts**, and **Cash in Bank. Figure 17–12** shows the posting of the three special column totals to the general ledger accounts. Note that the account numbers for the three general ledger accounts are written in parentheses below the double rule in the appropriate columns of the cash payments journal.

The totals of the General Debit and Credit columns are not posted. Each entry in those columns was posted individually to the general ledger accounts. A check mark (✓) is entered below the double rule in the General Debit and Credit columns.

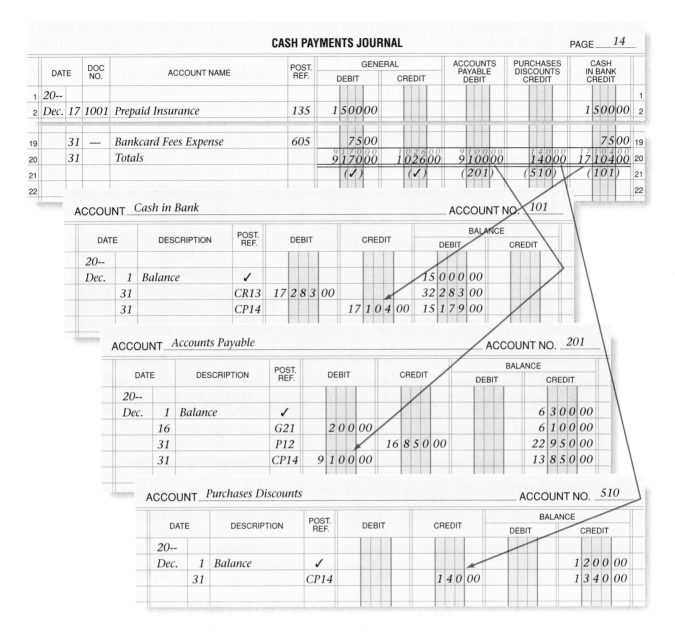

CASH PAYMENTS JOURNAL   PAGE __14__

	DATE	DOC NO.	ACCOUNT NAME	POST. REF.	GENERAL DEBIT	GENERAL CREDIT	ACCOUNTS PAYABLE DEBIT	PURCHASES DISCOUNTS CREDIT	CASH IN BANK CREDIT	
1	20--									1
2	Dec. 17	1001	Prepaid Insurance	135	1 50 00				1 50 00	2
19	31	—	Bankcard Fees Expense	605	75 00				75 00	19
20	31		Totals		9 170 00	1 026 00	9 100 00	140 00	17 104 00	20
21					(✓)	(✓)	(201)	(510)	(101)	21
22										22

ACCOUNT _Cash in Bank_   ACCOUNT NO. _101_

DATE	DESCRIPTION	POST. REF.	DEBIT	CREDIT	BALANCE DEBIT	BALANCE CREDIT
20--						
Dec. 1	Balance	✓			15 000 00	
31		CR13	17 283 00		32 283 00	
31		CP14		17 104 00	15 179 00	

ACCOUNT _Accounts Payable_   ACCOUNT NO. _201_

DATE	DESCRIPTION	POST. REF.	DEBIT	CREDIT	BALANCE DEBIT	BALANCE CREDIT
20--						
Dec. 1	Balance	✓				6 300 00
16		G21	200 00			6 100 00
31		P12		16 850 00		22 950 00
31		CP14	9 100 00			13 850 00

ACCOUNT _Purchases Discounts_   ACCOUNT NO. _510_

DATE	DESCRIPTION	POST. REF.	DEBIT	CREDIT	BALANCE DEBIT	BALANCE CREDIT
20--						
Dec. 1	Balance	✓				1 200 00
31		CP14		140 00		1 340 00

Figure 17–12 Posting Column Totals from the Cash Payments Journal

Proving the Accounts Payable Subsidiary Ledger

The accountant prepares a **schedule of accounts payable** after posting the column totals. This schedule lists all creditors in the accounts payable subsidiary ledger, the balance in each account, and the total amount owed to all creditors. The clerk proves the accounts payable subsidiary ledger when the total of the schedule of accounts payable agrees with the balance of the **Accounts Payable** (controlling) account in the general ledger.

Figure 17–13 on page 500 shows On Your Mark's schedule of accounts payable for December. The accounts are listed in alphabetical order. All creditors are listed, even those with zero balances. Notice that the total listed on the schedule ($13,850) agrees with the balance of the **Accounts Payable** (controlling) account.

						BALANCE			
ACCOUNT _Accounts Payable_								ACCOUNT NO. _201_	
DATE	DESCRIPTION	POST. REF.	DEBIT	CREDIT	DEBIT	CREDIT			
20--									
Dec. 1	Balance	✓				6 3 0 0 00			
16		G21	2 0 0 00			6 1 0 0 00			
31		P12		16 8 5 0 00		22 9 5 0 00			
31		CP14	9 1 0 0 00			13 8 5 0 00			

On Your Mark Athletic Wear
Schedule of Accounts Payable
December 31, 20--

Champion Store Supply	1 0 0 0 00		
Computer Solutions	1 3 0 0 00		
Dara's Delivery Service	—		
FastLane Athletics	3 8 0 0 00		
Geary Office Supply	2 5 0 00		
Pro Runner Warehouse	—		
Sports Link Footwear	6 0 0 0 00		
Sports Nutrition Supply	1 5 0 0 00		
Total Accounts Payable		13 8 5 0 00	

The balance of the Accounts Payable account should equal the total of the schedule of accounts payable.

Figure 17–13 Schedule of Accounts Payable

Proving Cash

Proving cash is the process of verifying that cash recorded in the accounting records agrees with the amount entered in the checkbook. Ideally businesses should prove cash each day. When a business uses special journals, however, it updates the **Cash in Bank** account in the general ledger at the end of the month. For many businesses, then, proving cash is done at the end of the month.

The cash proof may be prepared on plain paper, on accounting stationery, on a special cash proof form, or on a computer. The cash proof for On Your Mark, shown in **Figure 17–14**, is prepared on two-column accounting stationery. To prove cash, follow these steps:

1. On the first line, record the beginning balance of **Cash in Bank** according to the general ledger account.
2. On the next line, enter the total cash received during the month. This is the total of the Cash in Bank Debit column from the cash receipts journal.
3. Add the first and second lines.
4. From this subtotal subtract the cash payments for the month. This is the total of the Cash in Bank Credit column from the cash payments journal.
5. Compare this figure to the balance shown on the last check stub in the checkbook. If the ending balance of **Cash in Bank** and the balance on the check stub match, you have proved cash. In this example the ending balance of **Cash in Bank** is $15,179. The balance shown on the last check stub is also $15,179; therefore, cash is proved.

If the balances are not equal, you should look for errors. Recording a bank service charge or a bankcard fee in the checkbook but not in the general ledger can cause the cash proof to be out of balance. Next, you should verify that all disbursements and deposits were recorded in the accounting records. If cash is being proved at month-end, the accountant can then continue making month-end entries.

On Your Mark Athletic Wear				
Cash Proof				
December 31, 20--				
Beginning Cash in Bank Balance				15 0 0 0 00
Plus: Cash Receipts for the Month				17 2 8 3 00
Subtotal				32 2 8 3 00
Less: Cash Payments for the Month				17 1 0 4 00
Ending Cash in Bank Balance				15 1 7 9 00
Check Stub Balance				15 1 7 9 00

Figure 17–14 Cash Proof

Note that proving cash is different from reconciling a bank statement, which is taught in Chapter 11 (pages 284–287). Proving cash verifies that amounts recorded in the general ledger, cash receipts journal, and cash payments journal agree with the checking account balance. It does *not* confirm that the bank has processed all the deposits from the business or that all outstanding checks have cleared.

AFTER YOU **READ**

Reinforce the Main Idea

Create a table similar to the one here to identify the journal in which each of the following transactions should be recorded. Identify debit and credit parts for each transaction.

Transaction	Journal	Account(s) Debited	Account(s) Credited
1. Sold merchandise on account			
2. Purchased merchandise on account			
3. Paid a creditor			
4. Sold merchandise for cash			
5. Bankcard sales			
6. Paid the payroll			
7. Discovered that purchase of supplies was incorrectly debited to **Purchases**			

Do the Math

At Car Wash Palace, hourly wage earners are paid weekly. These employees earned $8,000 in total gross earnings this week.

1. Calculate each withholding amount.
2. What is the total net pay for this week?

Tax	Rate
Social Security	6.2%
Medicare	1.45%
Federal Unemployment	0.8%
State Unemployment	5.4%
State Income	4.0%

Problem 17–2 Preparing a Cash Proof

Apple Tree Boutique uses special journals. On September 30 the total of the Cash in Bank Debit column of the cash receipts journal is $18,750.12. The total of the Cash in Bank Credit column of the cash payments journal is $16,890.43. The checkbook balance on September 30 is $5,610.59.

Instructions Prepare a cash proof for September in your working papers. The balance of **Cash in Bank** on September 1 is $3,750.90.

Problem 17–3 Analyzing a Source Document

The Country Peddler, which is a retail merchandising business, had the following transaction that occurred on November 2.

Instructions Analyze Check Stub 104 that is shown here. In your working papers, make the necessary entry to record the transaction on page 11 of the cash payments journal.

$ 873.00		No. 104
Date November 2		20 --
To Colonial Products Inc.		
For Inv. 323 $900 less 3% disc. $27.00		

	Dollars	Cents
Balance brought forward	3,468	29
Add deposits		
Total	3,468	29
Less this check	873	00
Balance carried forward	2,595	29

Accounting Careers in Focus

DIRECTOR OF FINANCE
Leslie Karnauskas
Cobe Cardiovascular, Arvada, Colorado

Q: What does Cobe Cardiovascular do?

A: We identify and develop products that help treat cardiovascular disease.

Q: What are your day-to-day responsibilities?

A: I manage the general ledger, financial reporting, accounts payable, and cost accounting groups at three of our company's sites. I am part of a team responsible for budgeting and forecasting, internal and external audit, and financial analysis.

Q: What has been key to your success?

A: I have always set high standards for myself and those I manage. I continually look for new and better ways to get things done, not just in accounting but in all aspects of the business. I've also learned the importance of being proactive and taking initiative.

Q: What is most challenging about your job?

A: Finding the time and resources to meet our company's goals. I constantly reprioritize my tasks and manage several initiatives at once to make sure I meet all deadlines and still focus on growing the business.

Q: What advice do you have for accounting students?

A: Learn as much as you can about the company you join—its products, market, and strategy. Involve yourself in every aspect of the business. Join a professional organization and volunteer on a committee or its board to build leadership skills. Also, pursue interests outside of work to balance your life.

Tips from . . .
RHI Robert Half International Inc.

Before submitting your résumé, don't forget to proofread it. Reread the document several times and ask a friend to do the same. A single typo or grammatical mistake can cause a hiring manager to question your professionalism and attention to detail.

CAREER FACTS

▶ **Nature of the Work:** Maintain budgeting and forecasting models; assist with business-funding decisions; hire, train, and motivate finance staff.

▶ **Training or Education Needed:** At least 10 years of public accounting or finance experience. A master's degree in business administration, as well as a CPA or CMA designation is preferred.

▶ **Aptitudes, Abilities, and Skills:** Strong leadership abilities, technology skills, analytical skills, and communication skills.

▶ **Salary Range:** $80,000 to $180,000 depending on location, experience, and company size.

▶ **Career Path:** Obtain the required degrees and certifications. Gain job experience by either working for a public accounting firm or in management accounting. Once in a corporate environment, gradually take on increased responsibility and move into a management position.

Thinking Critically How can you improve your time-management skills and increase productivity?

Key Concepts

1. A *purchases journal* is used to record purchases made on credit instead of with cash. The Purchases Debit column is used for *merchandise* purchases only. Other purchases are recorded in the *General* column. The *cash payments journal* is used to record all decreases to cash.

2. The following illustrates the purchases journal entry to record the purchase of merchandise on account.

PURCHASES JOURNAL   PAGE ___12___

	DATE	INVOICE NO.	CREDITOR'S ACCOUNT CREDITED	POST. REF.	ACCOUNTS PAYABLE CREDIT	PURCHASES DEBIT	GENERAL ACCOUNT DEBITED	POST. REF.	DEBIT	
1	Date	Invoice No.	Creditor's Name		x x xx	x x xx				1
2										2
3										3

The following types of transactions are recorded in the cash payments journal:

   (a) merchandise purchased for cash

   (b) payment to a creditor

   (c) payment to a creditor with a cash discount taken

   (d) cash paid out but no check written (for example, a bank service charge)

CASH PAYMENTS JOURNAL   PAGE ___14___

		DATE	DOC NO.	ACCOUNT NAME	POST. REF.	GENERAL DEBIT	GENERAL CREDIT	ACCOUNTS PAYABLE DEBIT	PURCHASES DISCOUNTS CREDIT	CASH IN BANK CREDIT	
(a)	1	Date	Ck #	Purchases		x x xx				x x xx	1
(b)	2	Date	Ck #	Creditor's Account Name				x x xx		x x xx	2
(c)	3	Date	Ck #	Creditor's Account Name				x x xx	x x xx	x x xx	3
(d)	4	Date	---	Account Name to be Debited		x x xx				x x xx	4
	5										5

3. Follow these steps to record payroll transactions in the cash payments journal:

   (a) Enter the date of the transaction in the Date column.

   (b) Enter the check number in the Document Number column.

   (c) Enter the name of the account debited in the Account Name column.

   (d) Enter the amount of the payroll (gross pay) in the General Debit column.

   (e) Enter the net pay amount in the Cash in Bank Credit column.

   (f) On the next four lines, enter the names of the accounts credited in the Account Name column, and enter the amount of each liability in the General Credit column.

4. Post these columns' individual amounts *daily:*

Journal	Individual Column Amounts	Are Posted To:
Purchases Journal	Accounts Payable Credit column	➤ Subsidiary ledger creditor account
	General Debit column	➤ General ledger account

Journal	Individual Column Amounts		Are Posted To:
Cash Payments Journal	Accounts Payable Debit column	➤	Subsidiary ledger creditor account
	General Debit column	➤	General ledger account
	General Credit column	➤	General ledger account

Post these column totals at *month-end:*

Journal	Individual Column Amounts		Are Posted To:
Purchases Journal	Accounts Payable Credit column	➤	**Accounts Payable** account
	Purchases Debit column	➤	**Purchases** account
Cash Payments Journal	Accounts Payable Debit column	➤	**Accounts Payable** account
	Purchases Discounts Credit column	➤	**Purchases Discounts** account
	Cash in Bank Credit column	➤	**Cash in Bank** account

5. Complete seven steps before you post special journal column totals to the general ledger:
   (a) Rule the amount columns.
   (b) Foot the amount columns.
   (c) Prove the journal.
   (d) Under the last transaction, enter the date the journal is totaled in the Date column.
   (e) On the same line, enter the word *Totals*
      • in the purchases journal Creditors' Account Credited column
      • in the cash payments journal Account Name column
   (f) Enter the column totals, in ink, just below the footings.
   (g) Double-rule the amount columns.

6. To prove the accounts payable subsidiary ledger, accountants prepare a *schedule of accounts payable,* which is a list of each creditor, the balance in the creditor's account, and the total amount due to all creditors. The **Accounts Payable** account is the controlling account for the accounts payable subsidiary ledger. Review this relationship in **Figure 17–13** on page 500.

7. At the end of each month, prove cash by verifying that the cash recorded in the accounting records agrees with the amount shown in the checkbook.

Key Terms

cash payments journal   (p. 489)   **purchases journal**   (p. 482)

proving cash   (p. 500)   **schedule of accounts payable**   (p. 499)

Check Your Understanding

1. **Purchases and Cash Payments Journals**
   a. What are the source documents for the purchases journal?
   b. What are the source documents for the cash payments journal?

2. **Recording Transactions**
   a. List the steps to record transactions in the purchases journal.
   b. Bank service charges are automatically deducted from the bank account. Why are these charges recorded in the cash payments journal?

3. **Recording Payroll Payments**
   a. Where do you find the information for recording payroll transactions in the cash payments journal?
   b. In recording payroll, what four liabilities are entered in the General Credit column of the cash payments journal?

4. **Posting from Special Journals**
   a. When are purchases transactions posted to the accounts payable subsidiary ledger? Why?
   b. When are cash payments transactions posted to the accounts payable subsidiary ledger? Why?

5. **Totaling, Proving, and Ruling**
   a. When totaling, proving, and ruling the purchases journal, where are the double rules placed?
   b. What does the check mark (✓) in the first Posting Reference column indicate?

6. **Schedule of Accounts Payable**
   a. What information does the schedule of accounts payable include?
   b. With what account in the general ledger must the total of the schedule of accounts payable agree when proving the accounts payable subsidiary ledger?

7. **Proving Cash**
   a. When does a business that uses special journals update the **Cash in Bank** account in the general ledger?
   b. How does an accountant prove cash?

Apply Key Terms

You are an applicant for an accounting clerk position with PETCO and asked to write definitions for these terms. Make sure you connect your knowledge of these accounting terms to the financial activities you believe take place at PETCO.

cash payments journal
proving cash
purchases journal

schedule of accounts
payable

Mastering Purchases and Cash Payments

Making the Transition from a Manual to a Computerized System

Task	Manual Methods	Computerized Methods
Setting up vendor records	• Ledger sheet or card is prepared with vendor details such as name, address, and contact information. • Account activities are posted to the vendor subsidiary ledger accounts.	• Record details of vendor accounts into vendor records. • The software will access this information automatically each time the vendor ID code is used.
Recording a debit memorandum	• A journal entry is prepared to record the debit memorandum. • The journal entry is posted to the subsidiary account and to the general ledger.	• The accounting software creates a credit memo and applies it to the appropriate outstanding vendor invoice. • The accounting software automatically posts the credit memo to the vendor account and to the general ledger.

 **Peachtree®** Q & A

Peachtree Question	Answer
How do I set up a new vendor account?	1. From the *Maintain* menu, select **Vendors**. 2. Assign a Vendor ID to the new vendor. 3. Enter vendor name and contact information. 4. Click on the Purchases Defaults tab. 5. Verify or enter the appropriate purchase default GL account number.
How do I record a debit memorandum?	1. From the *Tasks* menu, select **Vendor Credit Memos**. 2. Select the appropriate vendor from the Vendor ID drop-down list. 3. Enter the Vendor Credit number in the *Credit Number* field. 4. Click on the Apply to Invoices tab, select the invoice to which the credit memo is applied, and enter the credit amount.

QuickBooks Q & A

QuickBooks Question	Answer
How do I set up a new vendor record?	1. From the *Lists* menu, select **Vendor List**. 2. Click the Vendor pull-down menu and choose **New**. 3. Enter vendor name and contact information. 4. Click on the Additional Info tab and enter any additional vendor information.
How do I issue and record a debit memorandum?	1. From the *Vendors* menu, select **Enter Bills**. 2. Click the **Credit** radio button and enter the vendor name. 3. Click on the Items tab and select the item to which the credit memo is applied. 4. Enter the quantity and select a customer from the *Customer:Job* field.

For detailed instructions, see your Glencoe Accounting Chapter Study Guides and Working Papers.

Peachtree®

SMART GUIDE

Step-by-Step Instructions: Problem 17–4

1. Select the problem set for Denardo's Country Store (Prob. 17–4).
2. Rename the company and set the system date.
3. Record the payment of the payroll using the **Payments** option.
4. Print a Cash Disbursements Journal report.
5. Proof your work.
6. Complete the Analyze activity.
7. End the session.

TIP: Remember to update the *G/L Account* field for each line of a multipart cash payment transaction.

Peachtree®

SMART GUIDE

Step-by-Step Instructions: Problem 17–5

1. Select the problem set for Sunset Surfwear (Prob. 17–5).
2. Rename the company and set the system date.
3. Record all purchases on account using the **Purchases/Receive Inventory** option.
4. Print a Purchases Journal report.
5. Proof your work.
6. Complete the Analyze activity.
7. End the session.

TIP: Remember to change the *G/L Account* field as needed for general purchases.

Problem 17–4 Recording Payment of the Payroll

Denardo's Country Store pays its employees on a biweekly basis. This week the payroll is $2,000. You issued Check 949 for $1,487 in payment of the payroll less the following amounts: Employees' Federal Income Tax, $320; Employees' State Income Tax, $40; Social Security Tax, $124; and Medicare Tax, $29.

Instructions In your working papers, record the July 15 payroll on page 4 of the cash payments journal.

Analyze Calculate the total deductions from employees' wages for federal, state, social security, and Medicare taxes. What percentage of gross payroll is this amount?

Problem 17–5 Recording Transactions in the Purchases Journal

Sunset Surfwear had the following purchases transactions for the month of July.

Instructions Use the purchases journal in your working papers.

1. Record each of the following transactions on page 4 of the purchases journal.
2. Foot, prove, total, and rule the purchases journal.

Date	Transactions
July 1	Purchased merchandise on account from Waverunner Designs for $1,200, Invoice WD121.
3	Received Invoice CA552 from Capital Accessories for the purchase of $1,600 in merchandise on account.
5	Purchased $2,000 in store equipment on account from Neilson Store Equipment, Invoice NS444.
9	Purchased $870 in merchandise on account from Kelley Apparel Inc., Invoice KA772.
12	Purchased $250 in supplies from Moore Paper & Office Supply Co., Invoice MPS266.
15	Purchased $1,800 in merchandise on account from AcaTan Products, Invoice ATP99.

CONTINUE ➡

Date	Transactions (cont.)
July 18	Purchased $500 in office equipment on account from Moore Paper & Office Supply Co., Invoice MPS275.
22	Received Invoice WD156 from Waverunner Designs for the purchase of $900 in merchandise on account.
25	Purchased $475 in merchandise on account from Capital Accessories, Invoice CA560.
28	Purchased from Kelley Apparel Inc. $390 in merchandise on account, Invoice KA800.
30	Received Invoice NS460 from Neilson Store Equipment for the purchase of $1,200 in store equipment on account.

Analyze Calculate the total purchases on account for the month.

Problem 17–6 Recording and Posting Purchases

Shutterbug Cameras, a retail merchandising business, had the following purchases on account for the month of July. In the working papers, the beginning balances in the accounts are opened for you.

Instructions In your working papers:

1. Record July's transactions on page 18 of the purchases journal.
2. Post to the accounts payable subsidiary ledger accounts daily.
3. Post amounts entered in the General Debit column daily.
4. Foot, prove, total, and rule the purchases journal at the end of the month.
5. Post the column totals at the end of the month to the account named in the column heading.
6. Prepare a schedule of accounts payable.

Date	Transactions
July 1	Purchased $1,200 in merchandise on account from U-Tech Products, Invoice UT220.
3	Purchased $140 in supplies on account from State Street Office Supply, Invoice 983, n/30.
6	Received Invoice 1338 from Photo Emporium for the purchase of $150 in merchandise on account, 2/10, n/30.
9	Invoice 445 for $90 was sent by Allen's Repair for plumbing repairs completed at the store (**Maintenance Expense**).
12	Purchased $800 in merchandise on account from Video Optics Inc., Invoice VO167, 3/15, n/45.
15	Received Invoice 1322 from Digital Precision Equipment for the purchase of $2,500 in store equipment on account, n/30.

QuickBooks

PROBLEM GUIDE

Step–by–Step Instructions: Problem 17–5

1. Restore the Problem 17-5.QBB file.
2. Enter all purchases on account using the **Enter Bills** option.
3. Print a Journal report.
4. Proof your work.
5. Print a Vendor Balance Summary.
6. Complete the Analyze activity.
7. Back up your work.

Peachtree®

SMART GUIDE

Step–by–Step Instructions: Problem 17–6

1. Select the problem set for Shutterbug Cameras (Prob. 17–6).
2. Rename the company and set the system date.
3. Record all purchases on account using the **Purchases/Receive Inventory** option.
4. Print a Purchases Journal report.
5. Proof your work.
6. Print a General Ledger report and a Vendor Ledgers report.
7. Complete the Analyze activity.
8. End the session.

TIP: Remember to change the G/L Account field for purchases other than merchandise.

CONTINUE

Date	Transactions (cont.)
July 18	Purchased $1,300 in merchandise on account from U-Tech Products, Invoice UT257.
20	Purchased $400 in supplies on account from ProStudio Supply, Invoice 4677.
23	Photo Emporium sent Invoice 1359 for the purchase of $600 of merchandise on account.
26	Received Invoice 478 for $120 from Allen's Repair for additional plumbing work completed at the store.
28	Purchased $200 in merchandise on account from Video Optics Inc., Invoice VO183.

Analyze Explain what problems would occur if the transaction of July 23 (Photo Emporium) was posted to the accounts payable subsidiary ledger as $60.

Peachtree®

SMART GUIDE

Step–by–Step Instructions: Problem 17–7

1. Select the problem set for River's Edge Canoe & Kayak (Prob. 17–7).
2. Rename the company and set the system date.
3. Record all cash payments using the **Payments** option.
4. Print a Cash Disbursements Journal report.
5. Proof your work.
6. Print a General Ledger report and a Vendor Ledgers report.
7. Complete the Analyze activity.
8. End the session.

TIP: Sometimes you may have to manually enter a cash discount when you record a cash payment.

Problem 17–7 Recording and Posting Cash Payments

River's Edge Canoe & Kayak is a retail merchandising business located in Jackson Hole, Wyoming. The beginning balances of the accounts needed to complete this problem are opened in your working papers.

Instructions In your working papers:

1. Record the transactions on page 19 of the cash payments journal.
2. Post the individual amounts in the Accounts Payable Credit column on a daily basis to the creditors' accounts.
3. Post the individual amounts in the General Debit and Credit columns on the date the transaction occurred.
4. Foot, prove, total, and rule the cash payments journal.
5. Post the column totals at the end of the month.
6. Prepare a schedule of accounts payable.
7. Prove cash at the end of the month. The beginning **Cash in Bank** balance was $8,000; cash receipts were $7,000; and the ending check stub balance is $8,402.

Date	Transactions
July 1	Issued Check 1405 for $1,372 to North American Waterways Suppliers in payment on account of $1,400 invoice less a 2% discount.
3	Received insurance premium statement from Rocky Mountain Insurance Company. Issued Check 1406 for $1,800.

CONTINUE

Date	Transactions (cont.)
July 5	Issued Check 1407 to Pacific Wholesalers for $500 to apply on account.
8	Received an invoice for $300 from Jackson News for advertising. Issued Check 1408.
12	Issued Check 1409 for $686 to Trailhead Canoes in payment on account of $700 invoice less a 2% discount.
15	Issued Check 1410 for $200 to Rollins Plumbing Service in full payment of the amount owed on account.
18	Issued Check 1411 for $75 to Ben Jacobs for completing odd jobs in the store (**Miscellaneous Expense**).
20	Purchased $90 in supplies from StoreMart Supply by issuing Check 1412.
22	Paid StoreMart Supply $400 to apply on account, Check 1413.
24	Issued Check 1414, $700 to Office Max, store equipment.
25	Paid Mohican Falls Kayak Wholesalers $200 to apply on account, Check 1415.
26	Issued Check 1416 to Office Max, $150 to apply on account.
28	Paid transportation charges of $125 to Stein's Trucking, Check 1417.

Analyze Identify the amount that River's Edge owes its creditors at month end.

Problem 17–8 Recording and Posting Purchases and Cash Payments

Buzz Newsstand had the following purchases and cash payment transactions for July. The balance in the accounts payable subsidiary ledger and general ledger accounts are opened in the working papers.

Instructions In your working papers:

1. Record the purchases and cash payment transactions on page 12 of the purchases journal and page 12 of the cash payments journal.
2. Post to the creditors' accounts in the accounts payable subsidiary ledger daily.
3. Post from the General Debit and Credit columns of the journals on the date the transaction occurred.
4. Foot, prove, total, and rule both journals.
5. Post the column totals of the purchases journal to the general ledger accounts named in the column headings.
6. Post the column totals of the cash payments journal to the general ledger accounts named in the column headings.
7. Prepare a schedule of accounts payable.

CONTINUE

Peachtree®

SMART GUIDE

Step–by–Step Instructions: Problem 17–8

1. Select the problem set for Buzz Newsstand (Prob. 17–8).
2. Rename the company and set the system date.
3. Enter the purchases on account.
4. Record all cash payments.
5. Print the following reports: Purchases Journal, Cash Disbursements Journal, and Vendor Ledgers.
6. Proof your work.
7. Print a General Ledger report.
8. Complete the Analyze activity.
9. End the session.

QuickBooks

PROBLEM GUIDE

Step–by–Step Instructions: Problem 17–8

1. Restore the Problem 17-8.QBB file.
2. Enter the purchases on account.
3. Record all cash payments.
4. Print a Journal report and a Vendor Balance Summary.
5. Proof your work.
6. Print a General Ledger report.
7. Complete the Analyze activity.
8. Back up your work.

SOURCE DOCUMENT PROBLEM

Problem 17–8

Use the source documents in your working papers to complete this problem.

Problems

8. Prepare a cash proof at the end of the month. The beginning **Cash in Bank** balance was $9,000. Cash receipts were $10,500. The check stub balance on July 31 is $10,178.

Date	Transactions
July 1	Issued Check 2455 for $1,552 to ADC Publishing in payment on account of $1,600 invoice less a 3% discount.
2	Purchased $400 in merchandise on account from Pine Forest Publications, Invoice PFP144, terms 2/10, n/30.
2	Paid Candlelight Software $1,358 in payment of $1,400 account less a 3% discount, Check 2456.
4	Issued Check 2457 to Nomad Computer Sales for $350 to apply on account.
5	Purchased $2,000 in store equipment on account from CorpTech Office Supply, Invoice CT67.
7	Issued Check 2458 for $125 to Wolfe Trucking for transportation charges.
9	Purchased $900 in merchandise on account from American Trend Publishers, Invoice ATP98.
12	Purchased $300 in supplies on account from CorpTech Office Supply, Invoice CT72.
14	Issued Check 2459 to Delta Press for $750 to apply on account.
15	Received insurance premium statement from SeaTac Insurance Co. for $1,600. Issued Check 2460.
16	Check 2461 was issued for $882 to American Trend Publishers in payment of $900 account less a 2% discount.
18	Purchased $500 in merchandise on account from Candlelight Software, Invoice CS101, terms n/30.
20	Purchased $200 in merchandise on account from Nomad Computer Sales, Invoice NC56, terms 2/10, n/30.
22	Paid Pine Forest Publications $100 to apply on account, Check 2462.
23	Issued Check 2463 for $2,000 to CorpTech Office Supply to apply on account.
25	Purchased $600 in merchandise on account from ADC Publishing, Invoice ADC70.
28	Issued Check 2464 for $450 to Nomad Computer Sales to apply on account.
30	Recorded the bank service charge of $25. Recorded the bankcard fees, $130. July bank statement.

Analyze Examine the purchases made during July and determine the dollar amount by which merchandise inventory increased.

Practice your test-taking skills! The questions on this page are reprinted with permission from national organizations:
- Future Business Leaders of America
- Business Professionals of America

Use a separate sheet of paper to record your answers.

Future Business Leaders of America

MULTIPLE CHOICE

1. A listing of vendor accounts, account balances, and total amount due all vendors is a

    a. schedule of accounts payable.

    b. schedule of accounts receivable.

    c. schedule of vendors.

    d. schedule of creditors.

Use the following choices for questions 2–4. Write the letter for the correct journal used to journalize each transaction.

    a. Purchases Journal

    b. Cash Receipts Journal

    c. Cash Payments Journal

    d. General Journal

    e. Sales Journal

2. Purchased merchandise for cash.

3. Paid cash on account.

4. Purchased merchandise on account.

Business Professionals of America

MULTIPLE CHOICE

5. Just for You Shoes purchased shoes for its two retail locations. The mall store ordered 20 pairs at $29.90/pair and 40 pairs at $18.50/pair. The downtown store ordered 35 pairs at $29.90/pair and 24 pairs at $18.50/pair. What was the total cost of the shoes for the two stores?

    a. $96.50

    b. $193.50

    c. $2,828.50

    d. $2,703.10

Need More Help?

Go to **glencoeaccounting.glencoe.com** and click on **Student Center**. Click on **Winning Competitive Events** and select **Chapter 17.**
- **Practice Questions and Test-Taking Tips**
- **Concept Capsules and Terminology**

Special Journals: Purchases and Cash Payments

1. Describe the purpose of the purchases and the cash payments journals.
2. Your test for the equality of debits and credits of the purchases journal does not balance. Explain how you would go about finding the error(s).
3. You are instructed to prepare a schedule of accounts payable and prove its accuracy. How do you perform the task?
4. Explain why the purchase of supplies is not recorded in the special columns of the purchases journal, store equipment is not recorded in the journal's Purchases Debit column, and the General Debit column of the purchases journal is not posted to the general ledger.
5. Your accounting supervisor asks you to prepare a cash proof for the month. What accounting documents do you need? What steps will you perform?
6. Explain why it is important to prove cash.

Merchandising Business: Books & More

Books & More sells hardcover and paperback books, music tapes, and CDs. It keeps a large stock of merchandise and orders new products often. The store may place an order for fast-selling items, such as a popular new CD, weekly.

You recently noticed two invoices for three dozen CDs ordered from the same music wholesaler. The CDs ordered and the amounts on both invoices are identical.

INSTRUCTIONS

1. Explain how you would determine whether the invoices are for two different orders or are duplicate invoices for one order.
2. Suggest steps to ensure that the company does not pay duplicate invoices.

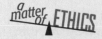

Insufficient Funds

As the owner of a sporting goods store, you manage the accounting records. Your delivery van has been in the shop for repairs and you need it back as soon as possible. The mechanic calls with the repair cost, which is much higher than you expected. Your checking account cannot cover the bill, but you authorize the work anyway. If you write a check for the repairs, you believe the account will have enough money when the mechanic cashes the check.

ETHICAL DECISION MAKING

1. What are the ethical issues?
2. What are the alternatives?
3. Who are the affected parties?
4. How do the alternatives affect the parties?
5. What would you do?

Requesting Information

Thomas Sampson is a purchasing agent for Complete Offices. He gave you an envelope full of receipts from a 10-day business trip without any explanations. Write a memo asking Thomas to identify which are cash purchases and which are purchases on account. Refer specifically to payment terms as you explain the information you need to analyze the transactions.

Selecting Equipment and Tools

Web Works is an online computer assistance service specializing in applications accessible through the Internet. In a recent staff meeting, Shelly Lazarus, your manager, asked you to assess online invoice payment.

INSTRUCTIONS

1. Use the Internet and read software reviews to explore different options for paying invoices online. Prepare a table showing the comparative data.
2. Draft a memorandum with your recommendations for the hardware and software Web Works will need to facilitate online invoice payment. Proofread the draft, make corrections as needed, and prepare the final memorandum.

International Competitive Advantage

If your company has resources, products, or skills that are valuable, unique, or difficult to imitate globally, it has an *international competitive advantage*. For example Wal-Mart has developed its inventory management and purchasing system into a powerful resource that has given it a sustained competitive advantage in the international retailing industry.

INSTRUCTIONS Brainstorm other resources or skills a company might use to gain international competitive advantage.

Your Federal Income Tax

If you are working, you know that your employer withholds federal income tax from your earnings each payday as required by law. You may also be required to file a federal tax return each year, either manually or electronically.

PERSONAL FINANCE ACTIVITY Assume you have a part-time job. List the information that you need to know about filing a federal income tax return.

PERSONAL FINANCE ONLINE Log on to **glencoeaccounting.glencoe.com** and click on **Student Center.** Click on **Making It Personal** and select **Chapter 17.**

Cost of Sales

To increase profits, corporations must increase sales or decrease costs. They share information about both in their annual reports. PETsMART's annual report has a section labeled *Management's Discussion and Analysis of Financial Condition and Results of Operations.* It includes a comparison of net sales and gross profit for the current year and previous year. Here is how gross profit is calculated:

$$\text{Sales} - \text{Cost of Sales} = \text{Gross Profit}$$

INSTRUCTIONS

Refer to the *Fiscal 2003 Compared to Fiscal 2002* section of PETsMART's annual report in Appendix F to answer these questions.

1. What items do you think would be included in PETsMART's cost of sales?
2. What factors contributed to a higher gross profit in 2003 versus 2002?

CHAPTER 18

Adjustments and the Ten-Column Work Sheet

BEFORE YOU **READ**

What You'll Learn

1. Describe the parts of a ten-column work sheet.

2. Generate trial balances and end-of-period adjustments.

3. Determine which general ledger accounts to adjust.

4. Calculate the adjustments.

5. Prepare a ten-column work sheet.

6. Journalize the adjustments.

7. Define the accounting terms introduced in this chapter.

Why It's Important

▶ Not all financial changes are caused by transactions with other businesses or individuals. Some financial changes occur within a business.

Predict

1. What does the chapter title tell you?
2. What do you already know about this subject from personal experience?
3. What have you learned about this in the earlier chapters?
4. What gaps exist in your knowledge of this subject?

Exploring the *Real World* of Business

ANALYZING ADJUSTMENTS

Plantronics, Inc.

"That's one small step for man, one giant leap for mankind." As Neil Armstrong stepped onto the moon's surface in 1969, his famous words were delivered via a **Plantronics** headset.

Since then, **Plantronics, Inc.** has taken giant steps in the lightweight communications headset industry. Some of its best sellers include wireless headsets for cell phones and iPods. U.S. soldiers, emergency response teams, and air traffic controllers also use the company's headsets.

Plantronics, like other companies, takes a physical count of inventory at the end of every fiscal period. Then it adjusts the accounting records so the **Merchandise Inventory** account matches the inventory it actually holds.

What Do You Think?

Can you think of other general ledger accounts like **Merchandise Inventory** that might need an adjustment?

Working in the *Real World*

APPLYING YOUR ACCOUNTING KNOWLEDGE

A merchandising business uses the work sheet for collecting and organizing financial information. In large businesses, several people might work on different parts of the work sheet. For example, one person might be responsible for accounts payable information and others for accounts receivable and payroll. The staff works as a team to prepare the work sheet. A team or project leader makes sure all team members complete their assigned sections.

Personal Connection

1. In your workplace are you asked to participate in group or team assignments?
2. How do team members work with each other?
3. What skills are needed to work well in a team?

Online Connection

Go to **glencoeaccounting.glencoe.com** and click on **Student Center.** Click on **Working in the Real World** and select **Chapter 18** to learn more about the real-world workplace.

Identifying Accounts to Be Adjusted and Adjusting Merchandise Inventory

BEFORE YOU READ

Main Idea
Adjustments transfer the cost of "used up" assets to expense accounts. Adjustments for changes in merchandise inventory are made directly to the **Income Summary** account.

Read to Learn...
➤ the purpose of the ten-column work sheet. (p. 518)
➤ how to use the ten-column work sheet for adjustments. (p. 518)

Key Terms
adjustment
beginning inventory
ending inventory
physical inventory

Recall that the work sheet is the basis for preparing end-of-period journal entries and financial statements. The purpose of all period-end reports is to provide essential information about a company's financial position.

Completing End-of-Period Work
What Is the Purpose of the Ten-Column Work Sheet?

The general ledger summarizes the effects of business transactions on individual accounts for an accounting period. Managers, stockholders, and creditors need more than account totals, however, to evaluate performance. They need to know net income and the value of stockholders' equity, which for a corporation is like owner's equity for a sole proprietorship. They need this information to make sound business decisions.

Earlier you worked with a six-column work sheet prepared for a service business organized as a sole proprietorship. In this chapter you will prepare a ten-column work sheet for a merchandising business organized as a corporation. This work sheet is the basis for preparing end-of-period financial statements, adjusting entries, and closing entries.

The Ten-Column Work Sheet
How Is the Ten-Column Work Sheet Different from the Six-Column Work Sheet?

The work sheet in Chapter 8 had six amount columns. The work sheet in this chapter, however, has ten amount columns. The additional columns are for the *Adjustments* and *Adjusted Trial Balance* sections.

Prepared in the same way as the six-column work sheet, the ten-column work sheet has five amount sections instead of three:

- Trial Balance
- Adjustments
- Adjusted Trial Balance
- Income Statement
- Balance Sheet

Completing the Trial Balance Section

A trial balance is prepared to prove the equality of debits and credits in the general ledger. **Figure 18–1** shows the end-of-period trial balance for On Your Mark Athletic Wear.

To prepare the trial balance, the number and name of each account in the general ledger are entered on the work sheet in the Account Number and Account Name columns. The accounts are listed in the order that they appear in the general ledger (Asset, Liability, Stockholders' Equity, Revenue, Cost of Merchandise, Expense). The balance of each account is entered in the appropriate Debit or Credit column of the Trial Balance section. Notice that every general ledger account is listed, even those with zero balances. After all balances are entered, the Trial Balance Debit and Credit columns are ruled, totaled, and proved. Then a double rule is drawn across both columns.

Calculating Adjustments

Not all changes in account balances result from daily business transactions. Some result from internal business operations or the passage of time.

	ACCT. NO.	ACCOUNT NAME	TRIAL BALANCE DEBIT	TRIAL BALANCE CREDIT
1	101	Cash in Bank	15 179 00	
2	115	Accounts Receivable	10 404 00	
3	125	Merchandise Inventory	84 921 00	
4	130	Supplies	5 549 00	
5	135	Prepaid Insurance	1 500 00	
6	140	Delivery Equipment	19 831 00	
7	145	Office Equipment	9 825 00	
8	150	Store Equipment	5 200 00	
9	201	Accounts Payable		13 850 00
10	204	Fed. Corp. Inc. Tax Payable		
11	205	Employees' Fed. Inc. Tax Pay.		640 00
12	211	Employees' State Inc. Tax Pay.		80 00
13	212	Social Security Tax Payable		248 00
14	213	Medicare Tax Payable		58 00
15	214	Fed. Unemployment Tax Payable		18 36
16	215	State Unemployment Tax Payable		114 73
17	220	Sales Tax Payable		2 428 00
18	301	Capital Stock		75 000 00
19	305	Retained Earnings		19 771 19
20	310	Income Summary		
21	401	Sales		320 450 00
22	405	Sales Discounts	730 00	
23	410	Sales Returns & Allowances	2 000 00	
24	501	Purchases	206 700 00	
25	505	Transportation In	4 036 18	
26	510	Purchases Discounts		1 340 00
27	515	Purchases Returns & Allowances		1 800 00
28	601	Advertising Expense	2 450 00	
29	605	Bankcard Fees Expense	4 199 27	
30	630	Fed. Corp. Income Tax Expense	9 840 00	
31	635	Insurance Expense		
32	650	Maintenance Expense	3 519 25	
33	655	Miscellaneous Expense	348 28	
34	657	Payroll Tax Expense	3 826 83	
35	660	Rent Expense	14 000 00	
36	665	Salaries Expense	29 374 60	
37	670	Supplies Expense		
38	680	Utilities Expense	2 364 87	
39			435 798 28	435 798 28
40				

Figure 18–1 The Trial Balance Section of the Work Sheet

For example, supplies such as paper, pens, shopping bags, and sales slips are bought for use by the business. They are recorded in an asset account called **Supplies.** These supplies are used gradually during the accounting period. Another example is insurance premiums, which cover a certain period of time. The premiums are recorded in an asset account called **Prepaid Insurance.** During the period some insurance is used up, or expires. At the end of the period, the balances in accounts such as **Supplies** and **Prepaid Insurance** are brought up to date.

To illustrate, suppose that supplies costing $500 were purchased during an accounting period and recorded in the **Supplies** account. At the end of the period, the **Supplies** account balance is $500; however, only $200 of supplies are still on hand. The account balance for **Supplies** is adjusted downward to show that the business used $300 of supplies.

Permanent Accounts and Temporary Accounts. Up to this point, the general ledger account balances have been changed by journal entries made to record transactions that are supported by source documents. There are no source documents, however, for the changes in account balances caused by the internal operations of a business or the passage of time. Such changes are recorded through adjustments made at the end of the period to the account balance. An **adjustment** is an amount that is added to or subtracted from an account balance to bring that balance up to date. Every adjustment affects at least one permanent account and one temporary account.

At the end of the period, adjustments are made to transfer the costs of the assets consumed from the asset accounts (permanent accounts) to the appropriate expense accounts (temporary accounts). Accountants say that these assets are "expensed" because the costs of consumed assets are expenses of doing business. Thus, when an adjustment is recorded, the expenses for a given period are matched with the revenue for that period.

The work sheet's Adjustments section is used to record the adjustments made at the period-end to bring various account balances up to date.

Determining the Adjustments Needed. How do you generate end-of-period adjustments? Review each account balance in the work sheet's Trial Balance section. If the balance for an account is not up to date *as of the last day of the fiscal period,* that account balance must be adjusted.

Refer to **Figure 18–1** on page 519. The first account listed is **Cash in Bank.** All cash received or paid out during the period was journalized and posted to the **Cash in Bank** account. This balance is up to date. The next account, **Accounts Receivable** (controlling), is also up to date since all amounts owed or paid by charge customers were journalized and posted.

The third account is **Merchandise Inventory,** used to report the cost of merchandise on hand. The balance reported in the Trial Balance section ($84,921) is the merchandise on hand at the *beginning* of the period.

The amount of merchandise on hand is constantly changing during the period. The changes are not recorded in the **Merchandise Inventory** account. During the period the cost of merchandise purchased is recorded in the **Purchases** account. As merchandise sales reduce inventory, the amount of each sale is recorded in the **Sales** account, not **Merchandise Inventory.**

As You READ

Instant Recall

Matching Principle
The matching principle requires revenue to be recorded in the same period as the expenses incurred to earn it.

At the end of the period, the balance in the **Merchandise Inventory** account does not reflect the amount of merchandise on hand. So the **Merchandise Inventory** account balance must be adjusted.

The other account balances on the work sheet are reviewed in the same manner. Additional adjustments are made as described later in this chapter.

Adjusting the Merchandise Inventory Account

Merchandise Inventory is an asset account used by merchandising businesses. **Beginning inventory** is the merchandise a business has on hand and available for sale at the *beginning* of a period. **Ending inventory** is the merchandise on hand at the *end* of a period. The ending inventory for one period becomes the beginning inventory for the next period.

The account balance of **Merchandise Inventory** does not change during the period. It is changed *only* when a physical inventory is taken. A **physical inventory** is an actual count of all merchandise on hand and available for sale. A physical inventory can be taken at any time. One is always taken at the end of a period.

For example, if a toy store counts inventory at the end of a period, it can calculate the cost of inventory. This is done by multiplying the quantity of each item by its unit cost.

At the end of each period, after the physical inventory has been taken and the cost of ending inventory has been calculated, the ending inventory amount replaces the beginning inventory amount recorded in **Merchandise Inventory**. This is accomplished by an adjustment to **Merchandise Inventory**.

Calculating the Adjustment for Merchandise Inventory. When calculating the adjustment for **Merchandise Inventory**, you need to know (1) the **Merchandise Inventory** account balance and (2) the physical inventory amount. For On Your Mark, this is:

Merchandise Inventory account balance	$84,921
Physical inventory	81,385

Adjustment

*To adjust the **Merchandise Inventory** account to reflect the physical inventory amount ($81,385), the following transaction is recorded.*

ANALYSIS	*Identify*	1.	The accounts **Merchandise Inventory** and **Income Summary** are affected.
	Classify	2.	**Merchandise Inventory** is an asset account (permanent). **Income Summary** is a stockholder's equity account.
	+/−	3.	**Merchandise Inventory** is decreased by $3,536. This amount is transferred to **Income Summary**.

DEBIT-CREDIT RULE		4.	To transfer the decrease in **Merchandise Inventory**, debit **Income Summary** for $3,536.
		5.	Decreases to asset accounts are recorded as credits. Credit **Merchandise Inventory** for $3,536.

6.

	Income Summary			Merchandise Inventory	
Debit		Credit		Debit +	Credit −
3,536					3,536

The effect of all the purchases and sales during the period is a decrease to **Merchandise Inventory** of $3,536 ($84,921 − $81,385). This reduction in inventory needs to be recorded as an adjustment in the accounting records. The two accounts affected by the inventory adjustment are **Merchandise Inventory** and **Income Summary**.

If the ending inventory amount is higher than beginning inventory, **Merchandise Inventory** is debited and **Income Summary** is credited. For example, suppose that the beginning inventory was $84,921 and the ending inventory is $88,226. Inventory increased by $3,305 ($88,226 − $84,921). The **Merchandise Inventory** account is debited for $3,305, and **Income Summary** is credited for $3,305.

Merchandise Inventory	
Debit + 3,305	Credit −

Income Summary	
Debit	Credit 3,305

Entering the Adjustment for Merchandise Inventory on the Work Sheet. Adjustments are entered in the Adjustments columns of the work sheet. The debit and credit parts of each adjustment are given a unique label. The label consists of a small letter in parentheses and is placed just above and to the left of the adjustment amounts. The adjustments are labeled as follows:

First adjustment	(a)
Second adjustment	(b)
Third adjustment	(c)

The number of adjustments varies depending on the business. Once the adjustments have been entered, the work sheet provides the information needed to make the adjusting journal entries.

Use the T accounts in step 6 of the preceding example as a guide to entering the inventory adjustment on the work sheet. Refer to **Figure 18–2**. To record the adjustment for **Merchandise Inventory**:

1. In the Adjustments Debit column, enter the debit amount of the adjustment on the Income Summary line. Label this amount *(a)*.
2. In the Adjustments Credit column, enter the credit amount of the adjustment on the Merchandise Inventory line. Label it *(a)* also.

Figure 18–2
Recording the Adjustment for Merchandise Inventory on the Work Sheet

	ACCT. NO.	ACCOUNT NAME	TRIAL BALANCE		ADJUSTMENTS	
			DEBIT	CREDIT	DEBIT	CREDIT
1	101	Cash in Bank	15 179 00			
2	115	Accounts Receivable	10 404 00			
3	125	Merchandise Inventory	84 921 00			(a) 3 536 00
20	310	Income Summary			(a) 3 536 00	
21						

Reinforce the Main Idea

Using a diagram like this one, summarize the steps for determining the **Merchandise Inventory** adjustment and entering it on the work sheet. Add answer boxes for steps as needed.

The Merchandise Inventory Adjustment

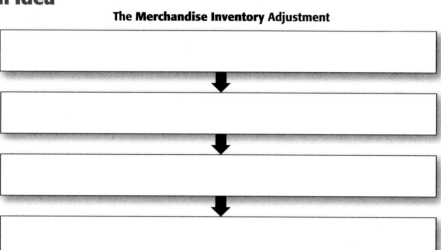

 ## Do the Math

Your company, Photo Shots, is looking to expand its merchandise, but the accounting manager wants to analyze inventory data for the last three years before recommending expansion. Using the data given, create a bar graph to depict the total amount of merchandise sold by year. Use the formula (Beginning Inventory + Purchases) – Ending Inventory = Cost of Merchandise Sold. Write a short paragraph summarizing your analysis of the results.

Merchandise Inventory in U.S.$

Year	Beginning	Ending	Purchases
Year 1	900	1,000	5,000
Year 2	1,000	2,000	8,000
Year 3	2,000	1,500	7,500

 ## Problem 18–1   Analyzing the Adjustment for Merchandise Inventory

Ely Corporation, a custom furniture manufacturer, has a general ledger account balance of $73,395 for **Merchandise Inventory** as of July 1. On the following June 30, the end of the fiscal period, Ely took a physical inventory and determined it had $74,928 in merchandise on hand. In your working papers, answer the following questions regarding the adjustment for **Merchandise Inventory**:

1. Is the value of the ending inventory more or less than the value of the beginning inventory?
2. What is the amount of the inventory adjustment?
3. Which account is debited?
4. Which account is credited?

Adjusting Supplies, Prepaid Insurance, and Federal Corporate Income Tax

Main Idea
Adjustments show the dollar amount of assets consumed during the period. They also recognize the corporation's income tax expense.

Read to Learn...
➤ how and why the **Supplies** account is adjusted. (p. 524)
➤ how and why the **Prepaid Insurance** account is adjusted. (p. 525)
➤ how and why the **Federal Corporate Income Tax Expense** account is adjusted. (p. 527)

Key Terms
prepaid expense

In Section 1 you learned that at the end of the period, the accountant must update the **Merchandise Inventory** account and adjust other accounts in the general ledger. For example insurance is a costly expense for high-risk businesses, such as building construction and demolition. Thus, the financial statements must reflect the proper insurance expenses each period. Supplies and federal corporate income taxes also represent significant expenses that must be reported accurately.

Adjusting the Supplies Account
Why Do You Make an Adjustment for Supplies?

A merchandising business buys various supplies for employees to use in the everyday operations of the business. Pencils, pens, computer paper, shopping bags, sales slips, price tags, and cash register tapes are purchased, and the cost is debited to the **Supplies** account.

Supplies are used daily. As they are consumed, they become expenses of the business. Keeping daily records of each item as it is used is inefficient, so the **Supplies** account is updated at the end of the period.

In the Trial Balance section of the work sheet in **Figure 18–1** on page 519, the balance of the **Supplies** account is $5,549. This amount is the cost of the supplies on hand on January 1 *plus* the cost of the additional supplies purchased during the period.

At the end of December, On Your Mark took a physical inventory. It found that $1,839 of supplies were on hand, meaning that it used $3,710 of supplies during the period ($5,549 − $1,839 = $3,710). The amount of supplies on hand decreased by $3,710. Therefore, **Supplies** (a permanent asset account) is credited for $3,710. **Supplies Expense** (a temporary account) is debited (increased) to record the cost of supplies used in the period.

Adjustment

Record the adjustment for supplies.

ANALYSIS	Identify Classify	1. The accounts affected are **Supplies** and **Supplies Expense**.
		2. **Supplies** is an asset account (permanent). **Supplies Expense** is an expense account (temporary).
	+/−	3. **Supplies** is decreased by $3,710. **Supplies Expense** is increased by $3,710.

| DEBIT-CREDIT RULE | 4. Increases to expense accounts are recorded as debits. Debit **Supplies Expense** for $3,710. |
| | 5. Decreases to asset accounts are recorded as credits. Credit **Supplies** for $3,710. |

6.

Supplies Expense			Supplies	
Debit + 3,710	Credit –		Debit +	Credit – 3,710

The adjustment for supplies is shown in **Figure 18–3** on page 526. To enter the adjustment on the work sheet, follow these steps:

1. In the Adjustments Debit column, enter the debit amount of the adjustment on the Supplies Expense line. Since this is the second adjustment, label it *(b)*.
2. In the Adjustments Credit column, enter the credit amount of the adjustment on the Supplies line. Label it *(b)* also.

Adjusting the Prepaid Insurance Account
Why Do You Make an Adjustment for Insurance?

On December 17 On Your Mark purchased an insurance policy for six months, mid-December through mid-May. The accounting clerk debited the premium of $1,500 ($250 per month) to the **Prepaid Insurance** account. This is an example of a **prepaid expense** , an expense paid in advance.

At the end of December, the **Prepaid Insurance** balance is $1,500 (see the work sheet's Trial Balance section in **Figure 18–1**). However, the coverage for half of a month, costing $125, has expired. The value of the unexpired portion of the coverage has decreased to $1,375 ($1,500 − $125), so the clerk adjusts **Prepaid Insurance** with a $125 credit to update its balance. The adjustment records the expired portion as a business expense.

As You READ

In Your Experience

Prepaid Have you heard the term *prepaid* before now? What type of product or service can be prepaid?

Adjustment

Record the adjustment for the expiration of one-half month's insurance coverage.

ANALYSIS	*Identify* *Classify* +/–	1. The accounts affected are **Insurance Expense** and **Prepaid Insurance**.
		2. **Insurance Expense** is an expense account (temporary). **Prepaid Insurance** is an asset account (permanent).
		3. **Insurance Expense** is increased by $125. **Prepaid Insurance** is decreased by $125.
DEBIT-CREDIT RULE		4. Increases to expense accounts are recorded as debits. Debit **Insurance Expense** for $125.
		5. Decreases to asset accounts are recorded as credits. Credit **Prepaid Insurance** for $125.

T ACCOUNTS

6.

Insurance Expense		Prepaid Insurance	
Debit +	Credit −	Debit +	Credit −
125			125

	ACCT. NO.	ACCOUNT NAME	TRIAL BALANCE DEBIT	CREDIT	ADJUSTMENTS DEBIT	CREDIT
1	101	Cash in Bank	15 179 00			
2	115	Accounts Receivable	10 404 00			
3	125	Merchandise Inventory	84 921 00			(a) 3 536 00
4	130	Supplies	5 549 00			(b) 3 710 00
5	135	Prepaid Insurance	1 500 00			(c) 125 00
6	140	Delivery Equipment	19 831 00			
7	145	Office Equipment	9 825 00			
8	150	Store Equipment	5 200 00			
9	201	Accounts Payable		13 850 00		
10	204	Fed. Corp. Inc. Tax Payable				(d) 155 00
11	205	Employees' Fed. Inc. Tax Pay.		640 00		
12	211	Employees' State Inc. Tax Pay.		80 00		
13	212	Social Security Tax Payable		248 00		
14	213	Medicare Tax Payable		58 00		
15	214	Fed. Unemployment Tax Payable		18 36		
16	215	State Unemployment Tax Payable		114 73		
17	220	Sales Tax Payable		2 428 00		
18	301	Capital Stock		75 000 00		
19	305	Retained Earnings		19 771 19		
20	310	Income Summary			(a) 3 536 00	
21	401	Sales		320 450 00		
22	405	Sales Discounts	730 00			
23	410	Sales Returns and Allowances	2 000 00			
24	501	Purchases	206 700 00			
25	505	Transportation In	4 036 18			
26	510	Purchases Discounts		1 340 00		
27	515	Purchases Returns and Allowances		1 800 00		
28	601	Advertising Expense	2 450 00			
29	605	Bankcard Fees Expense	4 199 27			
30	630	Fed. Corp. Income Tax Expense	9 840 00		(d) 155 00	
31	635	Insurance Expense			(c) 125 00	
32	650	Maintenance Expense	3 519 25			
33	655	Miscellaneous Expense	348 28			
34	657	Payroll Tax Expense	3 826 83			
35	660	Rent Expense	14 000 00			
36	665	Salaries Expense	29 374 60			
37	670	Supplies Expense			(b) 3 710 00	
38	680	Utilities Expense	2 364 87			
39			435 798 28	435 798 28	7 526 00	7 526 00
40						

Figure 18–3 Recording the Adjustments on the Work Sheet

The adjustment for **Prepaid Insurance** is shown in **Figure 18–3**. To enter the adjustment on the work sheet, follow these steps:

1. In the Adjustments Debit column, enter the debit amount of the adjustment on the Insurance Expense line. Since this is the third adjustment, label it *(c)*.

2. In the Adjustments Credit column, enter the credit amount of the adjustment on the Prepaid Insurance line. Label it *(c)* also.

Adjusting the Federal Corporate Income Tax Accounts

Why Does This Company Make an Adjustment for Income Tax?

On Your Mark is organized as a corporation. A corporation is considered to be a legal entity separate from its owners. On Your Mark owns assets, pays its own debts, and enters into legal contracts.

A corporation pays federal corporate income taxes on its net income. Many states and cities also tax corporate income. For now, we will discuss only federal corporate income taxes. A corporation's accountant estimates its federal corporate income taxes for the coming year and pays that amount to the federal government in quarterly installments. At the end of the year, the exact net income and the tax on that income are determined. If the corporation owes additional taxes, it pays them when it files its corporate income tax return.

At the beginning of the year, On Your Mark's accountant estimated that its federal corporate income taxes would be $9,840. The business made quarterly payments of $2,460 in March, June, September, and December. These payments were journalized as debits to **Federal Corporate Income Tax Expense** and credits to **Cash in Bank.**

At the end of the year, On Your Mark's accountant determined that the federal corporate income tax for the year is $9,995. On Your Mark has already paid $9,840 (2,460 × 4). Therefore the business owes an additional $155 ($9,995 − $9,840).

To bring the accounting records up to date, **Federal Corporate Income Tax Expense** and **Federal Corporate Income Tax Payable** must both be increased by $155. The following T accounts illustrate this adjustment.

Federal Corporate Income Tax Expense		Federal Corporate Income Tax Payable	
Debit +	Credit −	Debit −	Credit +
155			155

The adjustment for **Federal Corporate Income Tax Expense** is shown in **Figure 18–3.** Since this is the fourth adjustment, it is labeled *(d)*.

After all adjustments have been entered, the Adjustments section of the work sheet is totaled and ruled. Each adjustment has an equal debit and credit, so the totals of the Adjustments Debit and Credit columns should be the same. When the Adjustments section has been proved, a double rule is drawn under the totals and across both columns, as shown in **Figure 18–3.**

Reinforce the Main Idea

Use a chart like this one to describe three adjustments discussed in Section 2. List the accounts to be debited and credited for each adjustment.

Description of Adjustment	Account Debited	Account Credited

Do the Math

You own a personal-training franchise called Your Body. You want to provide health insurance for your 10 employees. As you review the alternative plans, you have to make a decision based not only on affordability, but also on total benefits. Determine the total annual premium of each plan and decide which plan best fits your needs.

Type of plan	Plan #1	Plan #2	Plan #3
Monthly cost per employee	$600	$500	$800
Co-pay for each employee	$10	$20	None

Problem 18–2 Analyzing Adjustments

Information related to accounts requiring adjustment on the work sheet for the year ended December 31 for Star City Resorts Corporation follows. Indicate in your working papers the amount of each adjustment, which account is debited, and which account is credited.

1. The Trial Balance section shows a balance of $3,347.45 for **Supplies.** The amount of supplies actually on hand is $892.75.
2. Star City paid an annual insurance premium of $4,440 on November 1.
3. Star City made quarterly federal corporate income tax payments of $945 each. Its actual tax, calculated at the end of the year, is $3,885.

Completing the Work Sheet and Journalizing and Posting the Adjusting Entries

After the adjustments have been entered in the Adjustments section of the work sheet, proving that the accounts are still in balance is important. This is done by completing an *adjusted trial balance*. After proving the Adjusted Trial Balance section, the accountant can complete the work sheet.

Extending Work Sheet Balances
What Does Extending Balances Involve?

At this point the amounts for each account must be *extended to,* or carried over to, the Adjusted Trial Balance, the Income Statement, and the Balance Sheet sections.

Completing the Adjusted Trial Balance Section

The next step after entering all adjustments is to finish the Adjusted Trial Balance section. This work sheet section shows the updated balances of all general ledger accounts. To complete this section, the accountant combines the balance of each account in the Trial Balance section with the adjustment, if any, in the Adjustments section. The new balance is then entered in the appropriate Adjusted Trial Balance column.

Note the way new balances are computed in **Figure 18–4** on page 530. If there is no adjustment, the account balance shown in the Trial Balance section is simply extended to the same column (Debit or Credit) in the Adjusted Trial Balance section. The first two accounts, **Cash in Bank** and **Accounts Receivable,** have no adjustments, so those balances are extended to the Adjusted Trial Balance Debit column.

If the account balance in the Trial Balance section has an adjustment, the accountant calculates a new balance. The amount of the adjustment (from the Adjustments section) is added to or subtracted from the amount in the Trial Balance section. Add debits to debits; add credits to credits; subtract debits and credits.

The first account in the Trial Balance section to have an adjustment is **Merchandise Inventory.** As you know from Section 1, **Merchandise Inventory** has an unadjusted debit balance of $84,921. Adjustment (a) is a credit of $3,536. To calculate the new balance, the accountant subtracts the credit adjustment from the debit balance. The adjusted balance of $81,385 ($84,921 − $3,536) is extended to the Adjusted Trial Balance Debit column.

Main Idea
Adjustments affect the amount of net income (or net loss).

Read to Learn…
➤ how to complete the ten-column work sheet. (p. 529)
➤ how to journalize and post the adjusting entries. (p. 531)

Key Terms
adjusting entries

ACCT. NO.	ACCOUNT NAME	TRIAL BALANCE DEBIT	TRIAL BALANCE CREDIT	ADJUSTMENTS DEBIT	ADJUSTMENTS CREDIT	ADJUSTED TRIAL BALANCE DEBIT	ADJUSTED TRIAL BALANCE CREDIT
1	101 Cash in Bank	15 179 00				15 179 00	
2	115 Accounts Receivable	10 404 00				10 404 00	
3	125 Merchandise Inventory	84 921 00			(a) 3 536 00	81 385 00	
4	130 Supplies	5 549 00			(b) 3 710 00	1 839 00	
5	135 Prepaid Insurance	1 500 00			(c) 125 00	1 375 00	
6	140 Delivery Equipment	19 831 00				19 831 00	
7	145 Office Equipment	9 825 00				9 825 00	
8	150 Store Equipment	5 200 00				5 200 00	
9	201 Accounts Payable		13 850 00				13 850 00
10	204 Fed. Corp. Inc. Tax Payable				(d) 155 00		155 00
11	205 Employees' Fed. Inc. Tax Pay.		640 00				640 00
12	211 Employees' State Inc. Tax Pay.		80 00				80 00
13	212 Social Security Tax Payable		248 00				248 00
14	213 Medicare Tax Payable		58 00				58 00
15	214 Fed. Unemployment Tax Payable		18 36				18 36
16	215 State Unemployment Tax Payable		114 73				114 73
17	220 Sales Tax Payable		2 428 00				2 428 00
18	301 Capital Stock		75 000 00				75 000 00
19	305 Retained Earnings		19 771 19				19 771 19
20	310 Income Summary			(a) 3 536 00		3 536 00	
21	401 Sales		320 450 00				320 450 00
22	405 Sales Discounts	730 00				730 00	
23	410 Sales Returns and Allowances	2 000 00				2 000 00	
24	501 Purchases	206 700 00				206 700 00	
25	505 Transportation In	4 036 18				4 036 18	
26	510 Purchases Discounts		1 340 00				1 340 00
27	515 Purchases Returns and Allowances		1 800 00				1 800 00
28	601 Advertising Expense	2 450 00				2 450 00	
29	605 Bankcard Fees Expense	4 199 27				4 199 27	
30	630 Fed. Corp. Income Tax Expense	9 840 00		(d) 155 00		9 995 00	
31	635 Insurance Expense			(c) 125 00		125 00	
32	650 Maintenance Expense	3 519 25				3 519 25	
33	655 Miscellaneous Expense	348 28				348 28	
34	657 Payroll Tax Expense	3 826 83				3 826 83	
35	660 Rent Expense	14 000 00				14 000 00	
36	665 Salaries Expense	29 374 60				29 374 60	
37	670 Supplies Expense			(b) 3 710 00		3 710 00	
38	680 Utilities Expense	2 364 87				2 364 87	
39		435 798 28	435 798 28	7 526 00	7 526 00	435 953 28	435 953 28
40							

Figure 18–4 Extending Balances to the Adjusted Trial Balance Section of the Work Sheet

The adjusted balances for **Supplies, Prepaid Insurance,** and **Federal Corporate Income Tax Expense** are calculated in the same way.

If an account has a zero balance in the Trial Balance section, the amount listed in the Adjustments section is extended to the Adjusted Trial Balance section. **Federal Corporate Income Tax Payable,** for example, has a zero balance in the Trial Balance section. Adjustment (d) is a credit of $155. This amount is extended to the Adjusted Trial Balance Credit column.

After extending all account balances to the Adjusted Trial Balance section, the accountant totals both columns. If total debits equal total credits, this section has been proved. The accountant then draws a double rule under the totals and across both columns. If total debits do not equal total credits, an error exists. To find it, re-add each column. If the error still exists, ensure that the Trial Balance and Adjustment amounts were extended properly to the Adjusted Trial Balance section.

Extending Amounts to the Balance Sheet and Income Statement Sections

Beginning with line 1, each account balance in the Adjusted Trial Balance section is extended to the appropriate column of either the Balance Sheet or the Income Statement section. See these extensions in **Figure 18–5** on pages 532 and 533.

The Income Statement section contains the balances of all temporary accounts. You will find the **Income Summary** and all revenue, cost of merchandise, and expense accounts in this section.

The Balance Sheet section contains the balances of all permanent accounts. In that section you will find all asset, liability, and capital accounts (**Capital Stock** and **Retained Earnings**).

Completing the Work Sheet

After all amounts have been extended to the Balance Sheet and Income Statement sections, the accountant draws a *single* rule across the columns in these sections and totals all four columns (see **Figure 18–5**). Notice that the words *Net Income* have been written in the Account Name column on the same line as the net income amount.

As you learned in Chapter 8, the totals of the debit and credit columns within the Balance Sheet and Income Statement sections are not equal at this point. The difference between the two column totals in each section is the amount of net income (or net loss) for the period. After the net income (or net loss) has been recorded, the columns in the Balance Sheet and Income Statement sections are ruled and totaled as shown in **Figure 18–5**.

If the totals of the two Income Statement columns are equal, and the totals of the two Balance Sheet columns are equal, a double rule is drawn across all four columns. The double rule indicates that these sections of the work sheet have been proved.

Journalizing and Posting Adjusting Entries

How Do You Journalize and Post Adjusting Entries?

The journal entries that update the general ledger accounts at the end of a period are called adjusting entries . The Adjustments section of the work sheet is the source of information for journalizing the adjusting entries. The accounts debited and credited in the Adjustments section are entered in the general journal.

Journalizing Adjustments

Before recording the first adjusting entry, the accountant writes the words *Adjusting Entries* in the Description column of the general journal.

	ACCT. NO.	ACCOUNT NAME	TRIAL BALANCE		ADJUSTMENTS	
			DEBIT	CREDIT	DEBIT	CREDIT
1	101	Cash in Bank	15 179 00			
2	115	Accounts Receivable	10 404 00			
3	125	Merchandise Inventory	84 921 00			(a) 3 536 00
4	130	Supplies	5 549 00			(b) 3 710 00
5	135	Prepaid Insurance	1 500 00			(c) 125 00
6	140	Delivery Equipment	19 831 00			
7	145	Office Equipment	9 825 00			
8	150	Store Equipment	5 200 00			
9	201	Accounts Payable		13 850 00		
10	204	Fed. Corp. Inc. Tax Payable				(d) 155 00
11	205	Employees' Fed. Inc. Tax Pay.		640 00		
12	211	Employees' State Inc. Tax Pay.		80 00		
13	212	Social Security Tax Payable		248 00		
14	213	Medicare Tax Payable		58 00		
15	214	Fed. Unemployment Tax Payable		18 36		
16	215	State Unemployment Tax Payable		114 73		
17	220	Sales Tax Payable		2 428 00		
18	301	Capital Stock		75 000 00		
19	305	Retained Earnings		19 771 19		
20	310	Income Summary			(a) 3 536 00	
21	401	Sales		320 450 00		
22	405	Sales Discounts	730 00			
23	410	Sales Returns and Allowances	2 000 00			
24	501	Purchases	206 700 00			
25	505	Transportation In	4 036 18			
26	510	Purchases Discounts		1 340 00		
27	515	Purchases Returns and Allowances		1 800 00		
28	601	Advertising Expense	2 450 00			
29	605	Bankcard Fees Expense	4 199 27			
30	630	Fed. Corp. Income Tax Expense	9 840 00		(d) 155 00	
31	635	Insurance Expense			(c) 125 00	
32	650	Maintenance Expense	3 519 25			
33	655	Miscellaneous Expense	348 28			
34	657	Payroll Tax Expense	3 826 83			
35	660	Rent Expense	14 000 00			
36	665	Salaries Expense	29 374 60			
37	670	Supplies Expense			(b) 3 710 00	
38	680	Utilities Expense	2 364 87			
39			435 798 28	435 798 28	7 526 00	7 526 00
40		Net Income				
41						
42						
43						

Figure 18–5 On Your Mark Athletic Wear Completed Work Sheet

Writing this heading eliminates the need for an explanation to be written after each adjusting entry.

The following entries are recorded in the Adjustments columns of the work sheet:

Athletic Wear

Sheet

December 31, 20--

| ADJUSTED TRIAL BALANCE | | INCOME STATEMENT | | BALANCE SHEET | | |
DEBIT	CREDIT	DEBIT	CREDIT	DEBIT	CREDIT	
15 179 00				15 179 00		1
10 404 00				10 404 00		2
81 385 00				81 385 00		3
1 839 00				1 839 00		4
1 375 00				1 375 00		5
19 831 00				19 831 00		6
9 825 00				9 825 00		7
5 200 00				5 200 00		8
	13 850 00				13 850 00	9
	155 00				155 00	10
	640 00				640 00	11
	80 00				80 00	12
	248 00				248 00	13
	58 00				58 00	14
	18 36				18 36	15
	114 73				114 73	16
	2 428 00				2 428 00	17
	75 000 00				75 000 00	18
	19 771 19				19 771 19	19
3 536 00		3 536 00				20
	320 450 00		320 450 00			21
730 00		730 00				22
2 000 00		2 000 00				23
206 700 00		206 700 00				24
4 036 18		4 036 18				25
	1 340 00		1 340 00			26
	1 800 00		1 800 00			27
2 450 00		2 450 00				28
4 199 27		4 199 27				29
9 995 00		9 995 00				30
125 00		125 00				31
3 519 25		3 519 25				32
348 28		348 28				33
3 826 83		3 826 83				34
14 000 00		14 000 00				35
29 374 60		29 374 60				36
3 710 00		3 710 00				37
2 364 87		2 364 87				38
435 953 28	435 953 28	290 915 28	323 590 00	145 038 00	112 363 28	39
		32 674 72			32 674 72	40
		323 590 00	323 590 00	145 038 00	145 038 00	41
						42
						43

Figure 18–5 On Your Mark Athletic Wear Completed Work Sheet (continued)

(a) adjusting merchandise inventory

(b) adjusting supplies

(c) adjusting insurance

(d) adjusting income tax

		GENERAL JOURNAL			PAGE	22	

	DATE		DESCRIPTION	POST. REF.	DEBIT	CREDIT	
1	20--		*Adjusting Entries*				1
2	Dec.	31	Income Summary		3 5 3 6 00		2
3			Merchandise Inventory			3 5 3 6 00	3
4		31	Supplies Expense		3 7 1 0 00		4
5			Supplies			3 7 1 0 00	5
6		31	Insurance Expense		1 2 5 00		6
7			Prepaid Insurance			1 2 5 00	7
8		31	Fed. Corporate Income Tax Exp.		1 5 5 00		8
9			Fed. Corp. Income Tax Pay.			1 5 5 00	9
10							10

Figure 18–6 Recording Adjusting Entries in the General Journal

The first adjustment, which was labeled *(a)* on the work sheet, is recorded in the general journal in **Figure 18–6** as a debit to **Income Summary** for $3,536 and a credit to **Merchandise Inventory** for $3,536. The label *(a)* is not recorded in the general journal.

Remaining adjustments are entered in the general journal in the same manner, with the debit part of the entry recorded first. The date for each adjusting entry is the last day of the period.

Posting Adjusting Entries to the General Ledger

After the adjusting entries have been recorded in the general journal, the accountant posts them to the general ledger accounts. Once the adjusting entries have been posted, the general ledger accounts are up to date. The balances in the general ledger accounts all agree with the amounts entered on the Income Statement and Balance Sheet sections of the work sheet.

Posting these entries accomplishes the following:

- The **Supplies Expense** account has been "charged" with the value of the supplies used in the period.
- The **Supplies** account reflects only the amount of items still remaining in inventory.
- The **Merchandise Inventory** account reflects the correct inventory value.
- The **Income Summary** account has been "charged" with the cost of goods sold for the period.
- The **Insurance Expense** account reflects the appropriate insurance expense for the period.
- The **Prepaid Insurance** account has been reduced by the amount of insurance expired.
- The **Federal Corporate Income Tax Payable** account has been increased to reflect the appropriate payable amount.
- The **Federal Corporate Income Tax Expense** account reflects the tax expense for the period.

Figure 18–7 shows the general journal and the general ledger accounts after the posting of the adjusting entries has been completed. Notice that the words *Adjusting Entry* have been written in the Description column of the general ledger accounts.

GENERAL JOURNAL   PAGE __22__

	DATE		DESCRIPTION	POST. REF.	DEBIT	CREDIT	
1	20--		*Adjusting Entries*				1
2	Dec.	31	Income Summary	310	3 5 3 6 00		2
3			Merchandise Inventory	125		3 5 3 6 00	3
4			Supplies Expense	670	3 7 1 0 00		4
5			Supplies	130		3 7 1 0 00	5
6			Insurance Expense	635	1 2 5 00		6
7			Prepaid Insurance	135		1 2 5 00	7
8			Fed. Corporate Income Tax Exp.	630	1 5 5 00		8
9			Fed. Corp. Income Tax Pay.	204		1 5 5 00	9
10							10
11							11

ACCOUNT _Merchandise Inventory_   ACCOUNT NO. _125_

DATE		DESCRIPTION	POST. REF.	DEBIT	CREDIT	BALANCE DEBIT	BALANCE CREDIT
20--							
Jan.	1	Balance	✓			84 9 2 1 00	
Dec.	31	Adjusting Entry	G22		3 5 3 6 00	81 3 8 5 00	

ACCOUNT _Supplies_   ACCOUNT NO. _130_

DATE		DESCRIPTION	POST. REF.	DEBIT	CREDIT	BALANCE DEBIT	BALANCE CREDIT
20--							
Dec.	1	Balance	✓			5 2 9 9 00	
	15		P12	2 5 0 00		5 5 4 9 00	
	31	Adjusting Entry	G22		3 7 1 0 00	1 8 3 9 00	

ACCOUNT _Prepaid Insurance_   ACCOUNT NO. _135_

DATE		DESCRIPTION	POST. REF.	DEBIT	CREDIT	BALANCE DEBIT	BALANCE CREDIT
20--							
Dec.	17		CP14	1 5 0 0 00		1 5 0 0 00	
	31	Adjusting Entry	G22		1 2 5 00	1 3 7 5 00	

Figure 18–7 Adjusting Entries Posted to the General Ledger

ACCOUNT *Federal Corporate Income Tax Payable*   **ACCOUNT NO.** _204_

DATE		DESCRIPTION	POST. REF.	DEBIT	CREDIT	BALANCE DEBIT	BALANCE CREDIT
20--							
Dec.	31	Adjusting Entry	G22		1 5 5 00		1 5 5 00

ACCOUNT *Income Summary*   **ACCOUNT NO.** _310_

DATE		DESCRIPTION	POST. REF.	DEBIT	CREDIT	BALANCE DEBIT	BALANCE CREDIT
20--							
Dec.	31	Adjusting Entry	G22	3 5 3 6 00		3 5 3 6 00	

ACCOUNT *Federal Corporate Income Tax Expense*   **ACCOUNT NO.** _630_

DATE		DESCRIPTION	POST. REF.	DEBIT	CREDIT	BALANCE DEBIT	BALANCE CREDIT
20--							
Dec.	1	Balance	✓			9 8 4 0 00	
	31	Adjusting Entry	G22	1 5 5 00		9 9 9 5 00	

ACCOUNT *Insurance Expense*   **ACCOUNT NO.** _635_

DATE		DESCRIPTION	POST. REF.	DEBIT	CREDIT	BALANCE DEBIT	BALANCE CREDIT
20--							
Dec.	31	Adjusting Entry	G22	1 2 5 00		1 2 5 00	

ACCOUNT *Supplies Expense*   **ACCOUNT NO.** _670_

DATE		DESCRIPTION	POST. REF.	DEBIT	CREDIT	BALANCE DEBIT	BALANCE CREDIT
20--							
Dec.	31	Adjusting Entry	G22	3 7 1 0 00		3 7 1 0 00	

Figure 18–7 Adjusting Entries Posted to the General Ledger (continued)

Reinforce the Main Idea

Use a diagram like this one to describe the process of updating the general ledger accounts.

Updating the General Ledger Accounts

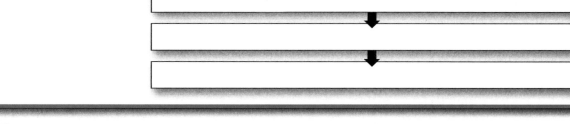

 ## Do the Math

The following column totals appear in the Balance Sheet section of the work sheet for Tonya's Toys on December 31.

Debit column	$317,290
Credit column	$323,730

Calculate the net income or net loss for the period.

 ## Problem 18–3 Analyzing the Work Sheet

Refer to **Figure 18–5** and answer the following questions in your working papers:

1. What amount is extended to the Income Statement section for **Federal Corporate Income Tax Expense**?
2. To which section of the work sheet is the balance of **Prepaid Insurance** extended?
3. What is the total amount of supplies consumed during the period?
4. What is the total amount still owed to the federal government for corporate income tax?

 ## Problem 18–4 Analyzing a Source Document

Answer these questions, based on the debit memorandum shown here.

1. Which company is returning the merchandise?
2. How many items are being returned?
3. What amount is entered in the journal entry?
4. Which account is debited?
5. Which account is credited?

DEBIT MEMORANDUM   No. 284

Date: May 4, 20--
Invoice No.: 378456

ROTARY SUPPLY CORPORATION
634 West Washington Avenue, Lincoln, SC 30856

To: K & L Electrical
845 Morgan Street
Plantsville, SC 30455

This day we have debited your account as follows:

Quantity	Item	Unit Price	Total
4	Locking Fixture #27304-78	$ 36.95	$ 147.80
2	Mirror/Reflectors #8935-231	11.24	22.48
	Subtotal		$ 170.28
	Tax		6.81
	Total		$ 177.09

Key Concepts

1. The ten-column work sheet contains Debit and Credit columns for these five sections:

   - Trial Balance—includes all general ledger accounts, even those with zero balances.
   - Adjustments—records the adjustments made at the end of the period to bring various account balances up to date.
   - Adjusted Trial Balance—shows the updated balances of all general ledger accounts.
   - Income Statement—contains the balances of all temporary accounts, including **Income Summary** and revenue, cost of merchandise, and expense accounts.
   - Balance Sheet—contains the balances of all permanent accounts, including assets, liabilities, and stockholders' equity.

2. To prepare the Trial Balance section, enter the number and name of each account in the general ledger in the appropriate columns in the order that they appear in the general ledger:

   - Asset
   - Liability
   - Stockholders' Equity
   - Revenue
   - Cost of Merchandise
   - Expense

   An *adjustment* is an amount that is added to or subtracted from an account balance to bring that balance up to date.

   - Adjustments reflect changes in account balances caused by the internal operations of the business or the passage of time.
   - Adjustments are made to match revenue with the expenses incurred to earn it.
   - Every adjustment affects one permanent and one temporary general ledger account.
   - Adjustments are recorded in the Adjustments section of the work sheet.

3. A general ledger account needs to be adjusted if the balance shown is not up to date *as of the last day of the period.*

4. Common adjusting entries and the information needed to calculate them:

Adjustment	Information Needed
Merchandise Inventory	• **Merchandise Inventory** account balance • Physical inventory amount
Supplies	• **Supplies** account balance • Cost of supplies on hand
Prepaid Insurance	• Expired portion of insurance coverage
Federal Corporate Income Tax	• **Federal Corporate Income Tax Expense** account balance (estimated quarterly payments) • Federal corporate income tax based on exact income

5. A work sheet is prepared

- to organize all of the data needed to update the accounts
- to prepare the financial statements
- to record end-of-period adjusting entries and closing entries

The completed work sheet lists all general ledger accounts and their updated balances and shows the net income (or net loss) for the period.

To prepare a ten-column work sheet:

- Complete the Trial Balance section. Enter the account numbers, names and balances for all general ledger accounts. Total, prove, and rule the section.
- Calculate the adjustments needed and enter them in the Adjustments section.
- Complete the Adjusted Trial Balance section. For each account, combine the Trial Balance section amount with the Adjustment section amount and enter the total in the Adjusted Trial Balance section.
  - Add debits to debits
  - Add credits to credits
  - Subtract debits and credits
- Total, prove, and rule the Adjustments and Adjusted Trial Balance sections.
- Extend the amounts in the Adjusted Trial Balance section to the appropriate columns in the Balance Sheet and Income Statement sections.
- Complete the work sheet. Calculate the net income (or net loss) and enter it in the appropriate columns in the Income Statement and Balance Sheet sections. Total, prove, and rule the Income Statement and Balance Sheet sections.

6. The adjustments entered on the work sheet must be recorded in the general journal. The source of information for journalizing adjustments is the Adjustments section of the work sheet. *Adjusting Entries* is written in the Description column immediately above the first adjusting entry, eliminating the need to write an explanation after each entry. The debit part of the entry is recorded first. The date for each adjusting entry is the last day of the period.

Key Terms

adjusting entries	(p. 531)	**ending inventory**	(p. 521)
adjustment	(p. 520)	**physical inventory**	(p. 521)
beginning inventory	(p. 521)	**prepaid expense**	(p. 525)

Check Your Understanding

1. **Components of the Ten-Column Work Sheet**
   a. What are the five sections of the ten-column work sheet?
   b. What sections does the ten-column work sheet contain that the six-column work sheet does not?

2. **Trial Balance and Period-End Adjustments**
   a. What is the purpose of preparing a trial balance?
   b. What is an adjustment?

3. **Adjusted General Ledger Accounts**
   a. Why must some general ledger accounts be updated at the end of the period?
   b. What is the step to follow after adjusting entries have been recorded in the general journal?

4. **Adjustment Calculation**
   a. How is the amount of merchandise on hand determined at the end of a period?
   b. After the physical inventory is taken, what happens to the **Merchandise Inventory** account?

5. **Completion of the Ten-Column Work Sheet**
   a. Which accounts are included on the Balance Sheet section of the work sheet?
   b. Which accounts are included on the Income Statement section of the work sheet?

6. **Adjustments**
   a. What is an *adjusting entry*?
   b. What is the source of information for journalizing adjusting entries?

Apply Key Terms

As the accounting manager for several Homemade Fresh Ice Cream stores in your region, you oversee the preparation of end-of-period financial statements. Before you complete your end-of-period reports, you need your staff to verify their work sheets and trial balances. Write a memorandum to the staff to remind them to verify their data, make adjustments where needed, give beginning and ending inventory figures, and complete a physical inventory. In the body of your memorandum, provide a brief definition of each term.

adjusting entries	ending inventory
adjustment	physical inventory
beginning inventory	prepaid expense

Adjusting Entries

Making the Transition from a Manual to a Computerized System

Task	Manual Methods	Computerized Methods
Recording adjusting entries	• From the general ledger, prepare a trial balance in the first two columns of a work sheet. • Record adjustments on the work sheet. • Calculate adjusted account balances in the Adjusted Trial Balance columns. • Extend account balances to Income Statement or Balance Sheet columns in the work sheet. • Calculate net income (loss) for the accounting period. • Record adjusting entries in the general journal. • Post adjusting entries to general ledger accounts.	• Print a Trial Balance. • Record the adjusting entries in the general journal. • General ledger accounts are automatically updated.

Peachtree® Q & A

Peachtree Question	Answer
How do I generate a trial balance for use in preparing adjustments?	1. From the *Reports* menu, select **General Ledger**. 2. From the Report list, select **Working Trial Balance**. 3. Click the **Print** button.
How do I journalize the adjusting entries?	1. List necessary adjustments on the Working Trial Balance form. 2. From the *Tasks* menu, select **General Journal Entry**. 3. Enter the adjusting entries. 4. Click **Save**.

QuickBooks Q & A

QuickBooks Question	Answer
How do I generate a trial balance for use in preparing adjustments?	1. From the *Reports* menu, select **Accountant & Taxes**. 2. From the **Accountant & Taxes** submenu, select **Trial Balance**. 3. Click the **Print** button.
How do I journalize the adjusting entries?	1. Use the Trial Balance to help you prepare the adjusting entries. 2. From the *Company* menu, select **Make General Journal Entries**. 3. Enter the adjusting entries. 4. Click **Save & Close**.

For detailed instructions, see your Glencoe Accounting Chapter Study Guides and Working Papers.

Complete problems using: **Manual** Glencoe   OR   **Peachtree Complete**   OR   **QuickBooks**   OR   **Spreadsheet**
                            Working Papers   **Accounting** Software   Templates   Templates

Problem 18–5 Completing a Ten-Column Work Sheet

The August 31 trial balance for InBeat CD Shop is entered on the work sheet in your working papers. Listed below is the data needed to make the adjustments.

Instructions In your working papers, complete the ten-column work sheet for InBeat CD Shop for the month ended August 31.

Data for Adjustments

Merchandise Inventory, August 31	$ 77,872
Supplies consumed during the period	2,171
Insurance premium expired during the period	489
Additional federal corporate income taxes owed	118

Analyze After the adjustments are entered on the work sheet, assess which expense account has the highest balance.

Problem 18–6 Completing a Ten-Column Work Sheet

The August 31 trial balance for Shutterbug Cameras is listed on the next page. Also listed is the data needed for the adjustments.

Instructions In your working papers, complete the ten-column work sheet for Shutterbug Cameras for the month ended August 31.

		Trial Balance	
		Debit	Credit
101	Cash in Bank	$13,873	
115	Accounts Receivable	5,382	
125	Merchandise Inventory	82,981	
130	Supplies	2,397	
135	Prepaid Insurance	1,350	
140	Store Equipment	30,769	
201	Accounts Payable		$ 8,481
207	Federal Corporate Income Tax Payable		—
210	Employees' Federal Income Tax Payable		194
211	Employees' State Income Tax Payable		48
212	Social Security Tax Payable		119
213	Medicare Tax Payable		25
215	Sales Tax Payable		381
216	Federal Unemployment Tax Payable		19
217	State Unemployment Tax Payable		92
301	Capital Stock		80,000
305	Retained Earnings		28,568
310	Income Summary	—	—
401	Sales		95,487
405	Sales Discounts	37	
410	Sales Returns and Allowances	945	
501	Purchases	39,491	
505	Transportation In	2,039	
510	Purchases Discounts		656
515	Purchases Returns and Allowances		219
601	Advertising Expense	128	
605	Bankcard Fees Expense	219	
620	Federal Corporate Income Tax Expense	1,580	
630	Insurance Expense	—	
640	Maintenance Expense	2,513	
645	Miscellaneous Expense	652	
647	Payroll Tax Expense	1,953	
650	Rent Expense	9,000	
655	Salaries Expense	18,631	
660	Supplies Expense	—	
670	Utilities Expense	349	

Data for Adjustments

Merchandise Inventory, August 31		$78,672
Supplies on hand, August 31		389
Insurance premium expired during the period		490
Additional federal income taxes owed		252

Analyze Identify which account in the Balance Sheet section, Accounts Payable or Accounts Receivable, has the higher balance.

Peachtree®

SMART GUIDE

Step–by–Step Instructions:
Problem 18–6

1. Select the problem set for Shutterbug Cameras (Prob. 18–6).
2. Rename the company and set the system date.
3. Print a Working Trial Balance and use it to help you prepare the adjustments.
4. Record the adjustments using the **General Journal Entry** option.
5. Print a General Journal report and proof your work.
6. Print a General Ledger Trial Balance report.
7. Complete the Analyze activity.
8. End the session.

TIP: Use the Inventory Adjustment account, not the Income Summary account, to record the adjustment for Merchandise Inventory.

Problem 18–7 Completing a Ten-Column Work Sheet

Peachtree®

SMART GUIDE

Step–by–Step Instructions: Problem 18–7

1. Select the problem set for Cycle Tech Bicycles (Prob. 18–7).
2. Rename the company and set the system date.
3. Print a Working Trial Balance and use it to help you prepare the adjustments.
4. Record the adjustments using the **General Journal Entry** option.
5. Print a General Journal report and proof your work.
6. Print a General Ledger Trial Balance report.
7. Complete the Analyze activity.
8. End the session.

QuickBooks

PROBLEM GUIDE

Step–by–Step Instructions: Problem 18–7

1. Restore the Problem 18-7.QBB file.
2. Print a Trial Balance and use it to help you prepare the adjustments.
3. Record the adjustments using the **Make General Journal Entries** option.
4. Print a Journal report and proof your work.
5. Print a Trial Balance.
6. Complete the Analyze activity.
7. Back up your work.

The balances of the general ledger accounts of Cycle Tech Bicycles, as of August 31, are listed below. Also listed is the data needed for the adjustments.

Instructions In your working papers:

Prepare a ten-column work sheet for Cycle Tech Bicycles for the month ended August 31.

101	Cash in Bank	$ 22,323
115	Accounts Receivable	1,737
125	Merchandise Inventory	23,654
130	Supplies	3,971
135	Prepaid Insurance	1,800
140	Store Equipment	25,395
145	Office Equipment	15,239
201	Accounts Payable	11,051
210	Federal Corporate Income Tax Payable	—
211	Employees' Federal Income Tax Payable	519
212	Employees' State Income Tax Payable	142
213	Social Security Tax Payable	408
214	Medicare Tax Payable	137
215	Sales Tax Payable	1,871
216	Federal Unemployment Tax Payable	51
217	State Unemployment Tax Payable	263
301	Capital Stock	40,000
305	Retained Earnings	14,908
310	Income Summary	—
401	Sales	128,231
405	Sales Discounts	214
410	Sales Returns and Allowances	1,289
501	Purchases	67,118
505	Transportation In	1,172
510	Purchases Discounts	810
515	Purchases Returns and Allowances	322
601	Advertising Expense	2,938
605	Bankcard Fees Expense	185
625	Federal Corporate Income Tax Expense	3,650
630	Insurance Expense	—
645	Maintenance Expense	2,450
650	Miscellaneous Expense	3,929
655	Payroll Tax Expense	834
657	Rent Expense	10,750
660	Salaries Expense	4,670
665	Supplies Expense	—
675	Utilities Expense	5,395

Peachtree®

Data for Adjustments

Ending merchandise inventory	$ 24,188
Ending supplies inventory	1,049
Insurance premium expired	675
Federal income tax expense for the month	3,827

Analyze Determine which section of the work sheet, the Trial Balance section or the Balance Sheet section, had the higher balance for **Merchandise Inventory**.

Problem 18–8 Completing a Ten-Column Work Sheet

The balances of the general ledger accounts of River's Edge Canoe & Kayak, as of August 31, are listed below.

Instructions In your working papers:

1. Prepare a ten-column work sheet for River's Edge Canoe & Kayak for the month ended August 31. The account names are entered on the work sheet. The data for the adjustments follows:
   (a) The cost of the ending merchandise inventory is $45,669.
   (b) The cost of the supplies on hand on August 31 is $619.
   (c) The one-year insurance premium of $1,680 was paid on April 1.
   (d) The total federal income taxes owed for the year are $2,635.
2. Enter the journal entries for the adjustments on page 31 of the general journal.
3. Post the journal entries to the general ledger accounts.

101	Cash in Bank	$ 15,387
115	Accounts Receivable	2,852
130	Merchandise Inventory	49,205
135	Supplies	3,027
140	Prepaid Insurance	1,680
145	Delivery Equipment	19,437
150	Store Equipment	29,504
201	Accounts Payable	13,339
204	Federal Corporate Income Tax Payable	—
210	Employees' Federal Income Tax Payable	632
211	Employees' State Income Tax Payable	117
212	Social Security Tax Payable	472
213	Medicare Tax Payable	108
215	Sales Tax Payable	2,931
216	Federal Unemployment Tax Payable	77
217	State Unemployment Tax Payable	315
219	U.S. Savings Bonds Payable	150
301	Capital Stock	50,000
305	Retained Earnings	25,425
310	Income Summary	—

CONTINUE

SMART GUIDE

Step–by–Step Instructions:
Problem 18–8

1. Select the problem set for River's Edge Canoe & Kayak (Prob. 18–8).
2. Rename the company and set the system date.
3. Print a Working Trial Balance and use it to help you prepare the adjustments.
4. Record the adjustments using the **General Journal Entry** option.
5. Print a General Journal report and proof your work.
6. Print a General Ledger report.
7. Print a General Ledger Trial Balance report.
8. Complete the Analyze activity.
9. End the session.

TIP: Enter the adjustments as one multipart entry to save time.

QuickBooks

PROBLEM GUIDE

Step–by–Step Instructions:
Problem 18–8

1. Restore the Problem 18-8.QBB file.
2. Print a Trial Balance and use it to help you prepare the adjustments.
3. Record the adjustments using the **Make General Journal Entries** option.
4. Print a Journal report and proof your work.
5. Print a General Ledger report.
6. Print a Trial Balance report.
7. Complete the Analyze activity.
8. Back up your work.

401	Sales	144,945
405	Sales Discounts	203
410	Sales Returns and Allowances	1,381
501	Purchases	79,310
505	Transportation In	1,192
510	Purchases Discounts	1,292
515	Purchases Returns and Allowances	576
601	Advertising Expense	3,151
605	Bankcard Fees Expense	288
625	Federal Corporate Income Tax Expense	2,480
635	Insurance Expense	—
650	Maintenance Expense	1,381
655	Miscellaneous Expense	3,772
658	Payroll Tax Expense	1,219
660	Rent Expense	10,350
665	Salaries Expense	11,965
670	Supplies Expense	—
680	Utilities Expense	2,595

Analyze   Calculate River's Edge net income (net loss) if it had *not* taken any purchases discounts for paying creditors within the discount period.

Problem 18–9 Locating Errors on the Work Sheet

The Trial Balance and adjustment sections for Buzz Newsstand have been prepared in your working papers. It is apparent from the totals on the work sheet that errors have been made in preparing these portions of the work sheet.

The accounting records show:

1. The merchandise on hand at the end of the month is valued at $12,950.
2. The supplies on hand on August 31 are valued at $529.
3. The insurance premium was paid on August 1. The premium was $980 and covers the period from August 1 to November 30.
4. The total federal income tax owed for the period is $249.

Instructions   In your working papers:

1. Find and correct the error(s) in the Trial Balance section.
2. On the line provided on the work sheet, write in the corrected totals for the Trial Balance section.
3. Find and correct the error(s) in the Adjustments section.
4. Write in the corrected totals for the Adjustments columns.

Analyze   Explain your calculations for the Merchandise Inventory adjustment.

Practice your test-taking skills! The questions on this page are reprinted with permission from national organizations:
- Future Business Leaders of America
- Business Professionals of America

Use a separate sheet of paper to record your answers.

Future Business Leaders of America

MULTIPLE CHOICE

1. Which of the following statements is incorrect concerning an adjusted trial balance?
- a. An adjusted trial balance lists account balances and their locations in the ledger.
- b. An adjusted trial balance shows proper balance sheet and income statement amounts.
- c. An adjusted trial balance is prepared before the adjusting entries have been journalized and posted.
- d. An adjusted trial balance can be used to prepare the financial statements.
- e. All of the above are true statements.

2. A store purchased a one-year insurance policy for $1,800 on September 1. Its fiscal period ended December 31. What is the amount of the adjustment and what accounts are debited and credited on December 31?
- a. $1,800; insurance expense and prepaid insurance
- b. $600; insurance expense and prepaid insurance
- c. $1,200; insurance expense and prepaid insurance
- d. $600; prepaid insurance and insurance expense

3. The Income Summary amount in a work sheet's Adjustments Debit column represents the
- a. decrease in Merchandise Inventory.
- b. increase in Merchandise Inventory.
- c. beginning Merchandise Inventory.
- d. ending Merchandise Inventory.

Business Professionals of America

MULTIPLE CHOICE

4. The ending balance of the Supplies account appears
- a. in the Trial Balance columns of the work sheet.
- b. in the Balance Sheet columns of the work sheet.
- c. in the Income Statement columns of the work sheet.
- d. on the statement of changes in owner's equity.

5. What entries are recorded at the end of the fiscal period to update general ledger accounts?
- a. Closing
- b. Adjusting
- c. Post-closing
- d. Reversing

Need More Help?

Go to glencoeaccounting.glencoe.com and click on **Student Center**. Click on **Winning Competitive Events** and select **Chapter 18**.
- **Practice Questions and Test-Taking Tips**
- **Concept Capsules and Terminology**

Adjustments and the Ten-Column Work Sheet

1. What is the term for the actual counting of merchandise on hand and available for sale at the end of the fiscal period?
2. Explain what *expensing an asset* means.
3. Compute the adjustment for **Supplies** if the business had $3,000 in supplies at the beginning of the period, bought $4,000 during the period, and estimated that it had used 60% of all supplies during the period.
4. Compare the **Federal Corporate Income Tax Expense** account with the **Federal Corporate Income Tax Payable** account. How are they different?
5. Explain where you could obtain the information needed to determine the amount of the insurance adjustment in the work sheet's Adjustments section.
6. Defend the concept that businesses cannot track supplies as they are used.

Merchandising Business: Training Videos

You are an accountant for EZ Training Systems. The company CEO has asked you to prepare financial statements without the appropriate adjusting entries.

INSTRUCTIONS Analyze this information for adjustments and complete the tasks.

	Beginning	Ending
Supplies	$5,000	$1,200
Prepaid Insurance	6,400	800

1. Net income before adjustments is $22,400. Calculate net income after the adjustments have been made.
2. Explain why the financial statements do not present an accurate picture of the company without considering the adjusting entries.

Out-of-Date Goods

The local bakery where you work as an accounting clerk does not sell its day-old baked goods but allows employees to have them. One day a mother with three children who cannot afford fresh donuts asks to buy some day-old ones. You consider giving her several that are about to be thrown away.

ETHICAL DECISION MAKING

1. What are the ethical issues?
2. What are the alternatives?
3. Who are the affected parties?
4. How do the alternatives affect the parties?
5. What would you do?

Training New Employees

You are preparing a presentation for the board of directors of Kids-n-Teens. As you review the quarterly financial statements, you see that the new clerk extended the account balances from the Adjusted Trial Balance section to the Balance Sheet section but not to the Income Statement section. Select a classmate and practice an explanation of how to extend to both sections.

SKILLS BEYOND NUMBERS

Leadership

You have just been promoted to Accounting Director for a national toy store chain. In reviewing the end-of-period financial reports, you see that net income was lower than in past periods. You believe a new line of toys could boost net income for the next period. Lee Rainwater, the Marketing Director, has been with the company for 25 years, and his decisions are rarely questioned.

INSTRUCTIONS Explain how you would approach Lee to discuss adding a new toy line.

INTERNATIONAL ACCOUNTING

Accounting for Inflation

If your money does not go as far as it used to, the cause is probably *inflation*. When there is a general increase in the cost of goods and services, inflation exists. Countries use different methods of accounting for inflation.

INSTRUCTIONS Explain why investors should know how inflation accounting is handled when reviewing financial statements.

Making It **Personal**

Your Household Supplies

Your family probably handles its kitchen supplies the way a business handles its supplies. That is, a family member buys them as needed. No one tracks them. When the supply gets low, someone decides to buy more.

PERSONAL FINANCE ACTIVITY List supplies a family might purchase weekly, monthly, and once or twice a year. Identify the group with the most items and methods to determine when to reorder items.

PERSONAL FINANCE ONLINE Log on to **glencoeaccounting.glencoe.com** and click on **Student Center.** Click on **Making It Personal** and select **Chapter 18.**

Analyzing FINANCIAL Reports

Classifying the Balance Sheet–Assets and Liabilities

Accounts on the balance sheet are *classified* or grouped into related categories. These classifications provide subtotals which can be used to compute ratios and do comparisons. For example any portion of a long-term liability that is due within the next year is classified as a current liability. This affects the company's liquidity ratios and working capital. (See pages 235–236 in Chapter 9.)

INSTRUCTIONS Use PETsMART's balance sheet in Appendix F to answer these questions.

1. What is the working capital as of February 1, 2004?
2. Obtain PETsMART's most recent annual report from the Internet or library. What is the working capital as of the balance sheet date?
3. Describe any change from the fiscal year ending February 1, 2004.

WebQuest

Online Business Transactions

Online transactions usually update general ledger accounts automatically. Visit **glencoeaccounting .glencoe.com** and click on **Student Center.** Click on **WebQuest** and select **Unit 4** to continue your Internet project.

Financial Statements for a Corporation

What You'll Learn

1. Explain how to record ownership of a corporation.

2. Explain the relationship between the work sheet and the financial statements for a merchandising corporation.

3. Explain how a corporation's financial statements differ from a sole proprietorship's.

4. Prepare an income statement, statement of retained earnings, and balance sheet, and describe the statement of cash flows for a merchandising corporation.

5. Analyze the financial data contained on the statements.

6. Define the accounting terms introduced in this chapter.

Why It's Important

▶ The corporate form of business and the merchandising operation both have unique financial reporting requirements.

Predict

1. What does the chapter title tell you?
2. What do you already know about this subject from personal experience?
3. What have you learned about this in the earlier chapters?
4. What gaps exist in your knowledge of this subject?

Exploring the *Real World* of Business

ANALYZING CORPORATE FINANCIAL STATEMENTS

99 Cents Only Stores

Do you think it is possible to buy a new 19-inch color TV for 99 cents? It was for the first nine customers at a recent grand opening of a **99 Cents Only Store.** Promoting its 223rd store, **99 Cents Only Stores** tempted customers with all kinds of bargains for 99 cents or less: name-brand and private-label foods, beverages, health and beauty products, toys, and household goods.

How can selling products at such a low price make the company a profit? This retailer focuses on close-out inventory and distressed products purchased at discount prices.

The financial condition and performance of **99 Cents Only Stores** can be examined using statements like the balance sheet and income statement and accompanying notes. Companies also publish growth trends, expansion plans, and financial milestones.

What Do You Think?

In purchasing stock in a company like **99 Cents Only Stores**, what would you review on its financial statements?

Working in the *Real World*

APPLYING YOUR ACCOUNTING KNOWLEDGE

Once the work sheet has been completed, the accounting staff is ready to prepare financial statements. Many corporations are required by law to disclose their financial information to the public. If you have listened to the evening news on television, you might remember an announcer reporting earnings increases or decreases for a large national corporation. This information is found in the financial statements or annual reports of the company.

Personal Connection

1. Is your employer a public corporation?
2. Are the financial statements available for you to review?
3. Can they be found on the Internet or in your local library?

Online Connection

Go to **glencoeaccounting.glencoe.com** and click on **Student Center.** Click on **Working in the Real World** and select **Chapter 19.**

The Ownership of a Corporation

BEFORE YOU READ

Main Idea
Owners' equity in a corporation is called *stockholders' equity.*

Read to Learn...
➤ the accounts used to record ownership of a corporation. (p. 552)
➤ the qualities expected in financial statements. (p. 554)
➤ the financial statements of a corporation. (p. 555)

Key Terms
Capital Stock
stockholders' equity
retained earnings
comparability
reliability
relevance
full disclosure
materiality

In Chapter 18 you learned that the work sheet organizes data for preparing financial statements and end-of-period journal entries. In this chapter you will use it to prepare financial statements for a merchandising corporation. This is an important task for all businesses.

Accounting for a Corporation

Who Owns a Corporation?

One person owns a sole proprietorship. A corporation may be owned by one person or by thousands of people. The ownership of a corporation is represented by shares of stock.

Recording the Ownership of a Corporation

As you recall, investments by the owner of a sole proprietorship are recorded in the owner's capital account. A $25,000 owner's investment in a sole proprietorship is recorded as shown in the T accounts. **Cash in Bank** is debited for $25,000, and **Maria Sanchez, Capital** is credited for $25,000.

Cash in Bank		Maria Sanchez, Capital	
Debit + 25,000	Credit −	Debit −	Credit + 25,000

Businesses organized as corporations have a **Capital Stock** account instead of the owner's capital account in a sole proprietorship. **Capital Stock** represents investments in the corporation by its stockholders (owners).

Capital Stock is classified as a stockholders' equity account. **Stockholders' equity** is the value of the stockholders' claims to the corporation. Like the owner's capital account in a sole proprietorship, increases to **Capital Stock** are recorded as credits and decreases are recorded as debits.

Reporting Stockholders' Equity in a Corporation

The form of business organization does not affect the amount of equity in the business. That is, one person may have an ownership interest in a

On January 1 stockholders invested $25,000 in exchange for shares of stock of the corporation, Receipt 997.

ANALYSIS	*Identify* *Classify* +/−	1. The accounts affected are **Cash in Bank** and **Capital Stock**. 2. **Cash in Bank** is an asset account. **Capital Stock** is a stockholders' equity account. 3. **Cash in Bank** is increased by $25,000. **Capital Stock** is increased by $25,000.
DEBIT-CREDIT RULE		4. Increases to asset accounts are recorded as debits. Debit **Cash in Bank** for $25,000. 5. Increases to stockholders' equity accounts are recorded as credits. Credit **Capital Stock** for $25,000.

T ACCOUNTS 6.

Cash in Bank		Capital Stock	
Debit + 25,000	Credit −	Debit −	Credit + 25,000

JOURNAL ENTRY 7.

		GENERAL JOURNAL			PAGE 1	
	DATE	DESCRIPTION	POST. REF.	DEBIT	CREDIT	
1	20--					1
2	Jan. 1	Cash in Bank		25 000 00		2
3		Capital Stock			25 000 00	3
4		Receipt 997				4

sole proprietorship worth $80,000, or 10 people may have shares of stock in a corporation worth a total of $80,000. The difference is in the way these two amounts are reported on the balance sheet.

A sole proprietorship reports the balance of the owner's capital account in the owner's equity section of the balance sheet. For a corporation the owner's equity section of the balance sheet is called stockholders' equity. The law requires that stockholders' equity be reported in two parts: (1) equity contributed by stockholders and (2) equity earned through business profits.

Equity Contributed by Stockholders

The first part of stockholders' equity is the amount of money invested by stockholders. This amount is comparable to the investments made by the owner in a sole proprietorship. In a corporation stockholders contribute to equity by buying shares of stock issued by the corporation. Stockholders' investments are recorded in the **Capital Stock** account.

Equity Earned Through Business Profits

The second part of stockholders' equity is the amount of accumulated net income earned and retained by the corporation. This amount is comparable to the amount of net income less any withdrawals by the owner in a sole proprietorship. In a corporation this amount, called **retained earnings**, represents the increase in stockholders' equity from the portion of net income not distributed to the stockholders.

Retained Earnings	
Debit	Credit
−	+
Decrease Side	Increase Side
	Normal Balance

Earnings retained by a corporation are recorded in the **Retained Earnings** account. **Retained Earnings** is classified as a stockholders' equity account. Like the **Capital Stock** account, it is increased by credits and decreased by debits. **Retained Earnings** has a normal credit balance.

In a sole proprietorship, net income increases owner's capital. This increase in owner's capital represents an increase in the assets of the business. In a corporation net income increases retained earnings, which represents the growth, or increase, in the assets of the corporation.

Balance Sheet Presentation

A comparison of the capital section of the balance sheet for a sole proprietorship and for a corporation follows:

Sole Proprietorship	Corporation
Owner's Equity:	Stockholders' Equity:
Owner's Capital	Capital Stock
	Retained Earnings

As You READ

Key Point

The Accounting Equation The basic accounting equation applies to any business regardless of the form of business organization:

Assets = Liabilities + Stockholders' Equity

Characteristics of Financial Information
What Qualities Are Required in Financial Statements?

At the end of a period, a business prepares various financial statements. These statements summarize the changes that have taken place during the period and report the financial condition of the business at the end of the period. Financial statements are used by many groups:

- Managers analyze financial statements to evaluate past performance and to make informed decisions and predictions for future operations.
- Stockholders are interested in the performance, potential future growth, and success of the business.
- Creditors want to know a company's ability to pay its debts in a timely manner and the amount of credit that should be extended to the company.
- Government agencies, employees, consumers, and the general public are also interested in the financial position of the business.

Comparability

For accounting information to be useful, it must be understandable and comparable. The data must be presented in a way that lets users recognize similarities, differences, and trends from one period to another. **Comparability** allows accounting information to be compared from one fiscal period to another. The same types of statements, therefore, are prepared at the end of each period for the same length of time (for example, one month or one year). By comparing financial statements in different periods of equal length, financial patterns and relationships can be identified and analyzed, and the information from the analysis can be used to make decisions regarding business operations. Comparability also allows the comparison of financial information between businesses.

Reliability

The users of accounting data assume that the data is reliable. **Reliability** refers to the confidence users have that the financial information is reasonably free from bias and error.

Relevance

Relevance is the requirement that all information that would affect the decisions of financial statement users be disclosed in the financial reports.

Full Disclosure

"To disclose" means "to uncover or to make known." **Full disclosure** means that financial reports include enough information to be complete.

Materiality

If something is "material," it is important. In accounting, **materiality** means that relevant information should be included in financial reports.

A Corporation's Financial Statements

What Financial Statements Does a Merchandising Corporation Prepare?

On Your Mark Athletic Wear, a merchandising corporation, prepares four financial statements: the income statement, the statement of retained earnings, the balance sheet, and the statement of cash flows. Three statements report the changes that have taken place over the period. One statement, the balance sheet, shows the financial position of the business on a specific date—the last day of the period. The work sheet provides most of the information needed to complete all four statements.

Today most businesses rely on automated equipment or computers to maintain the general and subsidiary ledgers and to prepare the end-of-period financial statements. Computers offer the advantages of speed and accuracy. The impact of a change in an estimate, operating procedure, or accounting method can be seen instantaneously. For example, electronic spreadsheets allow *what-if analysis,* which is when one or more variables are changed to see how the final outcome would be affected.

AFTER
YOU **READ**

Reinforce the Main Idea

Use a diagram like this one to describe the basic accounting equation for a corporation. Use three key terms from Section 1.

☐ = ☐ + ☐

| Account Name | Account Name |

Do the Math

Stock in Middlewood Corporation sells for $20 per share. The balance in the **Capital Stock** account at the beginning of the period was $72,400. The amount entered in the Balance Sheet section of the end-of-period work sheet is $83,100. How many shares of stock were sold during the fiscal period?

Problem 19–1 Analyzing Stockholders' Equity Accounts

1. An investment of $60,000 by Kevin Cleary in his sole proprietorship is recorded as a credit to which account?
2. The sale of 100 shares of stock for $8,500 by the Sims Corporation is recorded as a credit to which account?
3. Stockholders' equity consists of which two accounts?

Problem 19–2 Analyzing a Source Document

A sales slip for Cindy's Curtains is presented at right. The accountant noticed errors in the calculations.

Instructions Check all calculations and recalculate the sales tax using a rate of 4 percent.

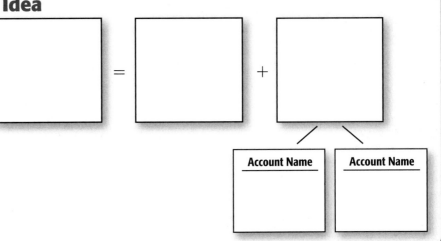

Cindy's Curtains
432 Meadowbrook Street
Wilcoxson, Georgia 30345-8417
404-555-2488

DATE: June 26, 20--   NO. 1441

| SOLD TO | Rachel C. Washington
59 Priscilla Drive
Park Ridge, IL 60068 | | |

| CLERK
K.C. | CASH
✓ | CHARGE | TERMS |

QTY.	DESCRIPTION	UNIT PRICE	AMOUNT
2	Curtain Rods #21847	$ 14.95	$ 29 09
4	Anchor Pieces #23104	6.75	27 00
15	Feet of ribbon per ft.	0.89	13 00
		SUBTOTAL	$ 69 09
		SALES TAX	2 76
	Thank You!	TOTAL	$ 71 85

The Income Statement

In Section 1 you learned that corporations prepare four financial statements at the end of each period. In this section you will learn how to prepare and analyze the income statement.

The Income Statement

How Is a Merchandising Business Income Statement Different from a Service Business Income Statement?

As you know, the income statement reports the net income or loss earned by a business. In Chapter 9 you prepared an income statement for Roadrunner Delivery Service, a service business organized as a sole proprietorship. You subtracted total expenses from revenue to find the period's net income or loss. When preparing the income statement, whether for a service or merchandising business, the *revenue realization* principle is applied. Revenue for a credit sale is recorded at the time of the sale because the account receivable is expected to be converted to cash. The matching principle is also applied when preparing the income statement. Expenses are matched with revenue earned during the same period.

Merchandising businesses have an additional cost—the cost of the merchandise that is purchased and then resold to customers. The income statement for a merchandising business is thus expanded to include the cost of merchandise sold.

An income statement for a merchandising business has five sections:

- Revenue
- Cost of Merchandise Sold
- Gross Profit on Sales
- Operating Expenses
- Net Income (or Loss)

A comparison of the income statements for a service business and for a merchandising business follows:

Service Business	Merchandising Business
Roadrunner Delivery Service	*On Your Mark Athletic Wear*
Revenue	Revenue
− Expenses	− Cost of Merchandise Sold
Net Income (Loss)	Gross Profit on Sales
	− Operating Expenses
	Net Income (Loss)

On Your Mark's income statement has four amount columns (see **Figure 19–1**). Totals are entered in the far right column. Balances that are added or subtracted are entered in the other columns. The format of a computer-generated income statement can vary from the format of an

On Your Mark Athletic Wear													
Income Statement													
For the Year Ended December 31, 20--													
Revenue:													
Sales								320	4 5 0	00			
Less: Sales Discounts					7 3 0	00							
Sales Returns and Allowances					2 0 0 0	00	2 7 3 0	00					
Net Sales										317 7 2 0	00		

Figure 19–1 The Heading and Revenue Section of the Income Statement

income statement prepared manually on accounting stationery. Regardless of how an income statement is prepared, the formats are very similar.

All information needed to prepare the income statement comes from the work sheet, particularly the Income Statement section. As with all other financial statements, the income statement begins with a three-line heading. The income statement for On Your Mark is prepared for the year ended December 31.

The Revenue Section

The first section on the income statement is the revenue section. This section reports the net sales for the period. The balances of the **Sales** revenue account and the **Sales Discounts** and **Sales Returns and Allowances** contra revenue accounts are reported in this section. Remember that contra revenue accounts *decrease* the revenue account. Therefore, **net sales** is the amount of sales for the period less any sales discounts, returns, and allowances. Refer to **Figure 19–1** as you learn how to complete the revenue section.

1. On the first line, enter the classification *Revenue:* at the left edge of the stationery.
2. On the second line, enter the name of the revenue account *Sales,* indented about half an inch. Enter the balance of the account in the *third* amount column.
3. On the next lines, enter the deductions from **Sales.** Write the word *Less:* followed by the names and balances of the two contra revenue accounts. (You may have to abbreviate the account names.) Enter the balances of the accounts in the *second* amount column.
4. Add the balances of the two contra revenue accounts. Write the total below the **Sales** balance on the fourth line, in the *third* amount column.
5. On the next line, enter the words *Net Sales,* indented about an inch. Subtract the total of the two contra accounts from the balance of the **Sales** account. Enter the amount in the *fourth* amount column. On Your Mark's net sales for the year are $317,720.

The Cost of Merchandise Sold Section

The cost of merchandise sold section follows the revenue section. As the words indicate, the *cost of merchandise sold* is the actual cost to the business of the merchandise it sold to customers during the period.

The cost of merchandise sold is calculated as follows:

Beginning Merchandise Inventory
+ Net Purchases During the Period
Cost of Merchandise Available for Sale
− Ending Merchandise Inventory
Cost of Merchandise Sold

Computing the cost of merchandise sold requires two steps:

1. Determine the cost of all merchandise available for sale.
2. Calculate the cost of merchandise sold.

Calculating Cost of Merchandise Available for Sale. To calculate the cost of merchandise available for sale, add net purchases to the beginning inventory amount. **Net purchases** represents all costs related to merchandise purchased during the period. To calculate net purchases, add the transportation charges for the period (**Transportation In**) to the **Purchases** balance and then subtract the balances of **Purchases Discounts** and **Purchases Returns and Allowances.**

Purchases
+ Transportation In
Cost of Delivered Merchandise
− Purchases Discounts
− Purchases Returns and Allowances
Net Purchases

Calculating Cost of Merchandise Sold. To calculate the cost of merchandise sold, subtract the ending merchandise inventory amount from the cost of merchandise available for sale. Refer to **Figure 19–2** on page 560 as you learn how to complete the cost of merchandise sold section.

1. On the line below net sales, enter the words *Cost of Merchandise Sold:* at the left edge.
2. Next, enter *Merchandise Inventory, January 1, 20—* indented about half an inch. Enter the amount of the beginning inventory in the *third* amount column. (The beginning inventory is found on the work sheet, in the Trial Balance section, on the Merchandise Inventory line.)
3. Next, enter *Purchases,* indented about half an inch, and place the **Purchases** account balance in the *first* amount column.
4. On the next line, enter *Plus: Transportation In* indented about half an inch. Enter the balance of **Transportation In** in the *first* amount column, below the **Purchases** amount. Draw a line across the *first* amount column under the **Transportation In** amount.
5. On the next line, write *Cost of Delivered Merchandise* indented about half an inch. Add the balances of **Purchases** and **Transportation In.** Enter the result in the *second* amount column.
6. On the next line, write *Less: Purchases Discounts,* indented about half an inch, and place the **Purchases Discounts** account balance in the *first* amount column.
7. On the next line, write *Purchases Returns and Allowances* so that it lines up with **Purchases Discounts** in the line above and place the

On Your Mark Athletic Wear

Income Statement

For the Year Ended December 31, 20--

Revenue:				
Sales			320 450 00	
Less: Sales Discounts		7 3 0 00		
Sales Returns and Allowances		2 0 0 0 00	2 7 3 0 00	
Net Sales				317 720 00
Cost of Merchandise Sold:				
Merchandise Inventory, January 1, 20--			84 9 2 1 00	
Purchases	206 7 0 0 00			
Plus: Transportation In	4 0 3 6 18			
Cost of Delivered Merchandise		210 7 3 6 18		
Less: Purchases Discounts	1 3 4 0 00			
Purchases Returns and Allowances	1 8 0 0 00	3 1 4 0 00		
Net Purchases			207 5 9 6 18	
Cost of Merchandise Available			292 5 1 7 18	
Merchandise Inventory, December 31, 20--			81 3 8 5 00	
Cost of Merchandise Sold				211 1 3 2 18
Gross Profit on Sales				106 5 8 7 82

Figure 19–2 Income Statement Through Gross Profit on Sales

Purchases Returns and Allowances account balance in the *first* amount column.

8. To find the total deduction from **Purchases**, add the balances of the **Purchases Discounts** and **Purchases Returns and Allowances** accounts. Enter the total on the Purchases Returns and Allowances line, in the *second* amount column. Draw a line across the *first* and *second* amount columns under this total.

9. On the next line, write *Net Purchases* indented about half an inch. Subtract the total of the **Purchases Discounts** and **Purchases Returns and Allowances** accounts from the cost of delivered merchandise. The difference is the amount of net purchases for the period. Enter the amount in the *third* amount column. Draw a line across the *third* amount column under this amount.

10. On the next line, write *Cost of Merchandise Available* indented about half an inch. Add the net purchases amount to the beginning inventory amount. The total is the cost of merchandise available for sale. Enter the total in the *third* amount column.

11. On the next line, write *Merchandise Inventory, December 31, 20—* indented about half an inch. Enter the amount of the ending inventory in the *third* amount column. (The ending inventory is found on the work sheet, in the Balance Sheet section, on the Merchandise Inventory line.) Draw a line across the *third* amount column under this amount.

12. On the next line, write *Cost of Merchandise Sold* indented about one inch. Subtract the ending inventory amount from the cost of merchandise available for sale. The difference is the cost of merchandise sold during the period. Enter the amount in the *fourth* amount column. Draw a line across the *fourth* amount column under this amount.

The Gross Profit on Sales Section

After the cost of merchandise sold has been calculated, the gross profit on sales can be determined. The **gross profit on sales** during the period is the profit made before operating expenses are deducted. Gross profit on sales is found by subtracting the cost of merchandise sold from net sales. *Gross Profit on Sales* is entered at the left edge, and the amount is placed in the *fourth* amount column. In **Figure 19–2** you can see that On Your Mark's gross profit on sales is $106,587.82.

As You READ

Instant Recall

Gross Recall that *gross* means the total amount before deductions or subtractions.

The Operating Expenses Section

The next section of the income statement shows the operating expenses for the period. **Operating expenses** are the costs of the goods and services used in the process of earning revenue for the business. Some businesses choose to further classify operating expenses into **selling expenses** (incurred to sell or market the merchandise sold) and **administrative expenses** (related to the management of the business). Look at **Figure 19–3** on page 562. *Operating Expenses* is entered at the left edge on the line following the gross profit on sales. On the following lines, the names and balances of all expense accounts except **Federal Corporate Income Tax Expense** are listed in the same order as on the work sheet. Federal corporate income tax is a normal expense for a corporation, but it is not considered to be an operating expense. Rather than a cost related to earning revenue, income tax represents a cost *resulting* from the revenue earned.

Notice that the balances of the expense accounts are entered in the *third* amount column. The balances are totaled. The total, $63,918.10, is entered in the *fourth* amount column.

The Net Income Section

The final section of the income statement reports the net income (or net loss) for the period, both before and after federal corporate income taxes. It is customary to present the federal corporate income tax amount *separately* on the income statement. This is done so that the income statement shows the amount of operating income. **Operating income** is the excess of gross profit over operating expenses. It is the amount of income earned before deducting federal corporate income taxes.

Look at **Figure 19–3** again. To calculate operating income, subtract the total operating expenses from the gross profit on sales. On Your Mark's operating income for the period is $42,669.72.

To calculate net income, follow these steps.

1. Enter *Less: Federal Corporate Income Tax Expense* on the next line, indented about half an inch.
2. Enter the amount of income taxes, $9,995, in the *fourth* amount column. Federal corporate income taxes appear in the Income Statement section of the work sheet. Draw a line across the *fourth* column under this amount.
3. Enter *Net Income* (or *Net Loss*) on the next line at the left edge.
4. Subtract the amount of federal corporate income taxes from the operating income. The result is net income or net loss.

As You READ

Compare and Contrast

Explain the difference between operating income and net income.

On Your Mark Athletic Wear							
Income Statement							
For the Year Ended December 31, 20--							

Revenue:					
Sales				320 4 5 0 00	
Less: Sales Discounts		7 3 0 00			
Sales Returns and Allowances		2 0 0 0 00	2 7 3 0 00		
Net Sales					317 7 2 0 00
Cost of Merchandise Sold:					
Merchandise Inventory, January 1, 20--			84 9 2 1 00		
Purchases	206 7 0 0 00				
Plus: Transportation In	4 0 3 6 18				
Cost of Delivered Merchandise		210 7 3 6 18			
Less: Purchases Discounts	1 3 4 0 00				
Purchases Returns and Allowances	1 8 0 0 00	3 1 4 0 00			
Net Purchases			207 5 9 6 18		
Cost of Merchandise Available			292 5 1 7 18		
Merchandise Inventory, December 31, 20--			81 3 8 5 00		
Cost of Merchandise Sold				211 1 3 2 18	
Gross Profit on Sales				106 5 8 7 82	
Operating Expenses:					
Advertising Expense			2 4 5 0 00		
Bank Card Fees Expense			4 1 9 9 27		
Insurance Expense			1 2 5 00		
Maintenance Expense			3 5 1 9 25		
Miscellaneous Expense			3 4 8 28		
Payroll Tax Expense			3 8 2 6 83		
Rent Expense			14 0 0 0 00		
Salaries Expense			29 3 7 4 60		
Supplies Expense			3 7 1 0 00		
Utilities Expense			2 3 6 4 87		
Total Operating Expenses				63 9 1 8 10	
Operating Income				42 6 6 9 72	
Less: Federal Corporate Income Tax Expense				9 9 9 5 00	
Net Income				32 6 7 4 72	

Figure 19–3 On Your Mark's Completed Income Statement

5. Enter the difference, $32,674.72, in the *fourth* amount column. Net income on the income statement must agree with the net income shown on the work sheet. If it does, draw a double rule under the amount to show that the income statement is proved and complete. If it does not, check the addition and subtraction on the income statement. Also check that all the accounts and balances in the Income Statement section of the work sheet appear correctly on the income statement.

Analyzing Amounts on the Income Statement

Why Do People Look at Percentages?

Managers use financial analysis to evaluate the company's financial performance. The information reported on the income statement and other financial statements is expressed in dollars. Dollar amounts are useful, but the analysis can be expanded and made more meaningful by expressing the dollar amounts as percentages. These percentages more clearly indicate the relationships among the items on the financial statements. They also enable financial statement users to compare the relationships within an accounting period and changes in these relationships between accounting periods.

One type of analysis is called **vertical analysis** . With vertical analysis, each dollar amount reported on a financial statement is also reported as a percentage of another amount, called a base amount, appearing on that same statement. For example, on the income statement, each amount is reported as a percentage of net sales. Current-period percentages can be compared with percentages from past periods or with percentages from other companies within the same industry.

Figure 19–4 shows a comparative income statement. As you can see, the net sales amount for each year is assigned a percentage of 100. Every other amount on the income statement is stated as a percentage of the net sales amount. Notice that net income was 14.68 percent of net sales in the previous year and only 10.28 percent of net sales for the current year. Managers would want to find the cause to *interpret* (explain) the decrease. Analysis like this helps managers make informed decisions about future operations.

On Your Mark Athletic Wear
Comparative Income Statement
For the Current and Previous Years Ended December 31

	Current Year		Previous Year	
	Dollars	**Percent**	**Dollars**	**Percent**
Revenue:				
Sales	$ 320,450.00	100.86 %	$ 296,350.00	100.79 %
Less: Sales Discounts	730.00	0.23	625.00	0.21
Sales Ret. and Allow.	2,000.00	0.63	1,700.00	0.58
Net Sales	$ 317,720.00	100.00 %	$ 294,025.00	100.00 %
Cost of Merchandise Sold:				
Merch. Inventory, Jan. 1	$ 84,921.00	26.73 %	$ 82,100.00	27.92 %
Net Purchases	207,596.18	65.34	186,836.56	63.54
Merch. Available for Sale	292,517.18	92.07 %	$ 268,936.56	91.47 %
Merch. Inventory, Dec. 31	81,385.00	25.62	84,921.00	28.88
Cost of Merchandise Sold	$ 211,132.18	66.45 %	$ 184,015.56	62.59 %
Gross Profit on Sales	$ 106,587.82	33.55 %	$ 110,009.44	37.41 %
Operating Expenses:				
Advertising Expense	$ 2,450.00	0.77 %	$ 1,779.00	0.61 %
Bankcard Fees Expense	4,199.27	1.32	3,569.37	1.21
Insurance Expense	125.00	0.04	0.00	0.00
Maintenance Expense	3,519.25	1.11	3,308.10	1.13
Miscellaneous Expense	348.28	0.11	742.00	0.25
Payroll Tax Expense	3,826.83	1.20	3,444.15	1.17
Rent Expense	14,000.00	4.41	13,200.00	4.49
Salaries Expense	29,374.60	9.25	26,437.14	8.99
Supplies Expense	3,710.00	1.17	2,968.00	1.01
Utilities Expense	2,364.87	0.74	2,305.75	0.78
Total Operating Expenses	$ 63,918.10	20.12 %	$ 57,753.51	19.64 %
Operating Income	$ 42,669.72	13.43 %	$ 52,255.93	17.77 %
Fed. Corp. Inc. Tax Exp.	9,995.00	3.15	9,085.00	3.09
Net Income	$ 32,674.72	10.28 %	$ 43,170.93	14.68 %

Figure 19–4 Comparative Income Statement Showing Vertical Analysis

Reinforce the Main Idea

Use a diagram like this one to describe the steps for preparing an income statement for a merchandising corporation.

Preparing an Income Statement for a Merchandising Corporation

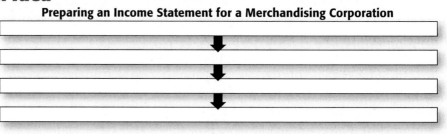

 ## Do the Math

Look at the comparative income statement provided here and answer the following questions using the vertical analysis of this financial statement.

1. What is the trend in sales?
2. How is that trend affecting the net income?
3. What expenses have decreased in the past year (as a percent of sales)?
4. Are there any significant changes in inventory?
5. What is the largest expense?
6. Would you invest your money in this business? Why or why not?

Comparative Income Statement
For the Current and Previous Years Ended December 31

	Current Year		Previous Year	
	Dollars	Percent	Dollars	Percent
Revenue:				
Sales	$ 1,500,000	100.13 %	$ 850,000	100.26 %
Less: Sales Ret. and Allow.	2,000	0.13	2,200	0.26
Net Sales	$ 1,498,000	100.00 %	$ 847,800	100.00 %
Cost of Merchandise Sold:				
Merch. Inventory, Jan. 1	$ 250,000	16.69 %	$ 100,000	11.80 %
Net Purchases	800,000	53.40	650,000	76.67
Merch. Available for Sale	$ 1,050,000	70.09 %	$ 750,000	88.46 %
Merch. Inventory, Dec. 31	60,000	4.01	250,000	29.49
Cost of Merchandise Sold	$ 990,000	66.09 %	$ 500,000	58.98 %
Gross Profit on Sales	$ 508,000	33.91 %	$ 347,800	41.02 %
Operating Expenses:				
Advertising Expense	$ 50,000	3.34 %	$ 25,000	2.95 %
Bankcard Fees Expense	10,000	0.67	8,000	0.94
Insurance Expense	5,300	0.35	5,300	0.63
Maintenance Expense	9,000	0.60	7,500	0.88
Payroll Tax Expense	6,200	0.41	3,200	0.38
Rent Expense	20,000	1.34	20,000	2.36
Salaries Expense	58,000	3.87	48,000	5.66
Supplies Expense	3,000	0.20	2,200	0.26
Utilities Expense	2,400	0.16	1,850	0.22
Total Operating Expenses	$ 163,900	10.94 %	$ 121,050	14.28 %
Operating Income	$ 344,100	22.97 %	$ 226,750	26.75 %
Fed. Corp. Inc. Tax Exp.	44,940	3.00	25,434	3.00
Net Income	$ 299,160	19.97 %	$ 201,316	23.75 %

 ## Problem 19–3 Calculating Amounts on the Income Statement

Instructions

For each group of figures that follows, determine the missing amount.

1. Beginning merchandise inventory $81,367
   Net purchases   15,139
   Cost of merchandise available for sale   ?
2. Net sales $52,935
   Cost of merchandise sold   36,232
   Gross profit on sales   ?
3. Purchases $26,472
   Transportation in   1,311
   Cost of delivered merchandise   ?
4. Cost of merchandise available for sale $49,769
   Ending merchandise inventory   32,621
   Cost of merchandise sold   ?

The Statement of Retained Earnings, Balance Sheet, and Statement of Cash Flows

In the previous section, you learned how to prepare and analyze the income statement, which reports the net income or loss for the period. In this section you will learn about a corporation's statement of retained earnings, balance sheet, and statement of cash flows.

The Statement of Retained Earnings

What Does This Statement Report?

A corporation has two stockholders' equity accounts, **Capital Stock** and **Retained Earnings**. The **Capital Stock** account represents the stockholders' investment in the corporation. Its balance changes only when the corporation issues additional shares of stock. The **Retained Earnings** account summarizes the accumulated profits of a corporation minus any amounts paid to stockholders as returns on their investments.

In Chapter 9 you learned about the statement of changes in owner's equity for a sole proprietorship. It shows the changes in the owner's capital account during the period. A corporation prepares a similar statement, the **statement of retained earnings**, that reports the changes in the **Retained Earnings** account during the period. These changes result from business operations and *dividends,* which are the distributions of earnings to stockholders.

The changes to **Retained Earnings** are summarized as follows:

Retained Earnings	
Debit	Credit
−	+
Decreased by net loss dividends	Increased by net income

The statement of retained earnings is prepared from information found on the work sheet. The statement of retained earnings is a supporting document for the balance sheet. The final balance of the **Retained Earnings** account, as calculated on the statement of retained earnings, is used when preparing the balance sheet.

Figure 19–5 shows the statement of retained earnings for On Your Mark. The first line shows the balance of the **Retained Earnings** account at the beginning of the period. This balance comes from the Balance

BEFORE YOU READ

Main Idea
In addition to the income statement, a corporation prepares the statement of retained earnings, the balance sheet, and the statement of cash flows.

Read to Learn...
➤ how and why a statement of retained earnings is prepared. (p. 565)
➤ how to prepare a balance sheet for a merchandising business organized as a corporation. (p. 566)
➤ how to apply horizontal analysis to a financial statement. (p. 568)
➤ about the statement of cash flows. (p. 569)

Key Terms
statement of retained earnings
horizontal analysis
base period
cash inflows
cash outflows
operating activities
investing activities
financing activities

Sheet section of the work sheet. The second line is the net income for the period. This is from the Income Statement columns of the work sheet. Add net income to the beginning balance of the **Retained Earnings** account. Since On Your Mark did not distribute any of its net income to stockholders during the period, there are no deductions from **Retained Earnings.** The new balance of the **Retained Earnings** account is $52,445.91.

On Your Mark Athletic Wear										
Statement of Retained Earnings										
For the Year Ended December 31, 20--										
Retained Earnings, January 1, 20--								19	7 7	1 19
Net Income								32	6 7	4 72
Retained Earnings, December 31, 20--								52	4 4	5 91

Figure 19–5 Statement of Retained Earnings

The Balance Sheet

How Is the Balance Sheet for a Corporation Different from the Balance Sheet for a Sole Proprietorship?

The balance sheet reports the balances of all asset, liability, and stockholders' equity accounts for a specific date. The balance sheet is prepared from the information in the Balance Sheet section of the work sheet and from the statement of retained earnings.

Figure 19–6 shows On Your Mark's balance sheet. This balance sheet is prepared in report form. In the report form, classifications (assets, liabilities, and stockholders' equity) are shown one under the other.

The assets are listed first. The classification *Assets* is centered on the first line. The account names are listed at the left edge in the same order as they appear on the work sheet. The individual balances are entered in the first amount column. *Total Assets* is entered on the line below the last account name, indented about half an inch. The total assets amount is entered in the second amount column. The double rule, however, is not drawn until the Liabilities and Stockholders' Equity sections are complete, and the total of these two sections equals the total of the Assets section.

The Liabilities section begins with *Liabilities* centered on the second line below total assets. As in the Assets section, the account names are listed at the left edge in the same order as they appear on the work sheet. The individual balances are entered in the first amount column. *Total Liabilities* follows on the line below the last account name, indented about half an inch. The total liabilities amount is then entered in the second amount column.

Next, the Stockholders' Equity section begins on the second line below total liabilities. *Stockholders' Equity,* which is centered on this line, consists of two accounts, **Capital Stock** and **Retained Earnings.** The **Capital Stock** account balance is from the work sheet's Balance Sheet section. The **Retained Earnings** account balance is from the statement of retained earnings. Again, the account names are listed at the left edge, and their individual balances are listed in the first amount column. *Total Stockholders' Equity* follows on the line below the last account name, indented about half an inch. The stockholders' equity total is entered in the second amount column.

On the line following total stockholders' equity, *Total Liabilities and Stockholders' Equity* is entered at the left edge. The total of the Liabilities section and the total of the Stockholders' Equity section are added. The total is entered in the second amount column. This total must agree with the total assets amount. If it does, double rule the balance sheet. If it does not, check the addition on the balance sheet. Also check that the accounts and amounts have been transferred from the work sheet accurately.

On Your Mark Athletic Wear		
Balance Sheet		
December 31, 20--		
Assets		
Cash in Bank	15 179 00	
Accounts Receivable	10 404 00	
Merchandise Inventory	81 385 00	
Supplies	1 839 00	
Prepaid Insurance	1 375 00	
Delivery Equipment	19 831 00	
Office Equipment	9 825 00	
Store Equipment	5 200 00	
Total Assets		145 038 00
Liabilities		
Accounts Payable	13 850 00	
Federal Corporate Income Tax Payable	155 00	
Employees' Federal Income Tax Payable	640 00	
Employees' State Income Tax Payable	80 00	
Social Security Tax Payable	248 00	
Medicare Tax Payable	58 00	
Federal Unemployment Tax Payable	18 36	
State Unemployment Tax Payable	114 73	
Sales Tax Payable	2 428 00	
Total Liabilities		17 592 09
Stockholders' Equity		
Capital Stock	75 000 00	
Retained Earnings	52 445 91	
Total Stockholders' Equity		127 445 91
Total Liabilities and Stockholders' Equity		145 038 00

Figure 19–6 On Your Mark's Balance Sheet

Analyzing Amounts on the Balance Sheet

How Can You Detect Trends?

When analyzing financial statements, you learned that while the dollar amounts provided on the statements are useful, the analysis can be expanded and made more meaningful by expressing the dollar amounts as percentages. Percentage amounts are used in vertical analysis and also in horizontal analysis. **Horizontal analysis** is the comparison of the same items on financial statements for two or more accounting periods or dates, and the determination of changes from one period or date to the next. In horizontal analysis, each amount on the current statement is compared with its corresponding amount on the previous statement. A **base period** is a period, usually a year, that is used for comparison.

Look at the example of a comparative balance sheet in **Figure 19–7.** By comparing the amounts for the two years, you can see that **Cash in Bank** increased by 49.76 percent and **Accounts Payable** decreased by 50.73 percent. The accountant might use this information to assess why cash has

On Your Mark Athletic Wear
Comparative Balance Sheet
December 31, Current Year and Previous Year

	Current Year	Previous Year	Increase (Decrease) Current over Previous — Dollars	Percent
Assets				
Cash in Bank	$ 15,179.00	$ 10,135.28	$ 5,043.72	49.76 %
Accounts Receivable	10,404.00	8,220.00	2,184.00	26.57
Merchandise Inventory	81,385.00	84,921.00	(3,536.00)	(4.16)
Supplies	1,839.00	1,587.00	252.00	15.88
Prepaid Insurance	1,375.00	0.00	1,375.00	—
Delivery Equipment	19,831.00	12,462.00	7,369.00	59.13
Office Equipment	9,825.00	5,854.00	3,971.00	67.83
Store Equipment	5,200.00	3,500.00	1,700.00	48.57
Total Assets	$ 145,038.00	$ 126,679.28	$ 18,358.72	14.49 %
Liabilities				
Accounts Payable	$ 13,850.00	$ 28,113.14	$ (14,263.14)	(50.73)%
Fed. Corp. Inc. Tax Payable	155.00	140.00	15.00	10.71
Employees' Fed. Inc. Tax Pay.	640.00	685.00	(45.00)	6.57
Employees' State Inc. Tax Pay.	80.00	72.00	8.00	11.11
Social Security Tax Payable	248.00	241.00	7.00	2.90
Medicare Tax Payable	58.00	56.35	1.65	2.93
Federal Unemployment Tax Pay.	18.36	16.50	1.86	11.27
State Unemployment Tax Pay.	114.73	103.10	11.63	11.14
Sales Tax Payable	2,428.00	2,481.00	(53.00)	2.14
Total Liabilities	$ 17,592.09	$ 31,908.09	$ (14,316.00)	(44.87)%
Stockholders' Equity				
Capital Stock	$ 75,000.00	$ 75,000.00	$ 0.00	0.00 %
Retained Earnings	52,445.91	19,771.19	32,674.72	165.26
Total Stockholders' Equity	$ 127,445.91	$ 94,771.19	$ 32,674.72	34.48 %
Total Liab. and Stockhldrs' Equity	$ 145,038.00	$ 126,679.28	$ 18,358.72	14.49 %

Figure 19–7 Comparative Balance Sheet Showing Horizontal Analysis

increased or why accounts payable have decreased. Perhaps the business is receiving more sales in cash instead of on account. The business may also be purchasing less inventory on account. These are trends that would be of interest to management.

The Statement of Cash Flows

What Does the Statement of Cash Flows Report?

As you learned in Chapter 9, the *statement of cash flows* reports how the activities of a business caused the cash balance to change during the accounting period. This information is vital for sound decision making. See **Figure 19–8** on page 570 for On Your Mark's statement of cash flows.

Most businesses consider cash to be a major asset, and they need a sufficient amount to operate efficiently. Maintaining a positive cash flow is a primary goal of financial management. An adequate amount of available cash allows a business to pay its debts in a timely manner, take advantage of discounts, purchase equipment, and fund expansion. Creditors and investors use the statement of cash flows to evaluate a company's ability to pay its debts and pay dividends.

Cash inflows (receipts of cash) come into and **cash outflows** (payments of cash) go out of a business from different activities. The statement of cash flows classifies these activities as *operating, investing,* or *financing.*

Cash Flows from Operating Activities

Operating activities include all transactions that occurred during the accounting period as part of normal business operations. The information needed to complete this section is taken from On Your Mark's income statement (**Figure 19–3**) and comparative balance sheet (**Figure 19–7**).

Recall that revenue is recorded when it is earned and expenses are recorded when they are incurred, regardless of when items are actually paid. This is called the *accrual basis of accounting.*

To determine operating cash inflows and outflows for the accounting period, the accountant must convert income statement and balance sheet amounts to the *cash basis of accounting,* which records revenues *only when cash is received* and

expenses *only when cash is paid out.* This is the reason that On Your Mark's net sales reported on the income statement is $317,720.00, but sales to customers reported on the statement of cash flows is $315,536.00.

Cash Flows from Investing Activities

Investing activities include loans the business makes, payments received for those loans, purchase and sale of plant assets, and investments. *Plant assets* are property that will be used in the business for more than one year.

During the current accounting period, On Your Mark purchased delivery equipment, office equipment, and store equipment for cash. When a plant asset is purchased for cash, the appropriate general ledger asset account is

On Your Mark Athletic Wear
Statement of Cash Flows
For the Year Ended December 31, 20--

Cash Flows from Operating Activities		
Cash Receipts from:		
Sales to Customers	$ 315,536.00	
Total Cash Receipts from Operating Activities		$ 315,536.00
Cash Payments for:		
Purchases	(221,859.32)	
Accrued Payables	(67.86)	
Operating Expenses	(65,545.10)	
Federal Corporate Income Tax Expense	(9,980.00)	
Total Cash Payments from Operating Activities		(297,452.28)
Net Cash Flows from Operating Activities		$ 18,083.72
Cash Flows from Investing Activities		
Purchase of Plant Assets	(13,040.00)	
Net Cash Flows from Investing Activities		(13,040.00)
Cash Flows from Financing Activities		-0-
Net Increase in Cash		$ 5,043.72

Figure 19–8 Statement of Cash Flows

debited and **Cash in Bank** is credited. Since the purchase of plant assets is a cash outflow, the $13,040.00 is placed in parentheses on the statement of cash flows.

Cash Flows from Financing Activities

Financing activities are the borrowing activities needed to finance the company operations and the repayment of these debts. On Your Mark had no financing activities during this accounting period.

The statement of cash flows indicates that cash increased by $5,043.72 during the period. This amount agrees with the increase in cash shown on the comparative balance sheet.

Typical cash inflows and outflows for the three activities of a business are shown here.

Activity	Cash Inflows (receipts)	Cash Outflows (payments)
Operating Activities	• Sales • Interest Income	• Merchandise Purchases • Operating Expenses • Interest Expense • Fed. Corp. Income Tax
Investing Activities	• Selling plant assets • Selling investments	• Purchasing plant assets • Purchasing investments
Financing Activities	• Long-term borrowing • Issuing stock	• Repaying loans (principal, not interest) • Paying dividends on stock

Reinforce the Main Idea

Use a chart like this one to describe how stockholders and creditors use each of the listed financial statements.

	Stockholders	Creditors
Statement of Retained Earnings		
Balance Sheet		
Statement of Cash Flows		

 ## Do the Math

Larry Campbell is the owner of Craftsman Furniture, a successful family-owned furniture store. As the accountant for Craftsman Furniture, it is your responsibility to run a vertical analysis on the income statement. Mr. Campbell asks you to prepare an Executive Summary of a three-year vertical analysis. Using the information provided, calculate the percentages for each year in your working papers and complete the columns of the draft report. Mr. Campbell will review the draft with you so he clearly understands the trends in sales for Craftsman Furniture.

	Year 1	Year 2	Year 3
Net Sales	$1,000,000	$1,500,000	$1,600,000
Gross Profit on Sales	600,000	750,000	780,000
Total Operating Expenses	25,000	21,000	23,000
Net Income	$ 575,000	$ 729,000	$ 757,000

 ## Problem 19–4 Analyzing a Balance Sheet

Use the comparative balance sheet for On Your Mark in **Figure 19–7** to answer the following questions.

1. Which asset account has the larger percentage of increase in the two years? Larger decrease?
2. Which liability account has the larger percentage increase in the two years?
3. Did the overall value (total assets) of the corporation increase or decrease in the two years? What is the dollar amount? What is the percentage?
4. What is the percentage increase in retained earnings in the two years?
5. What conclusions might you draw based on the change in Accounts Receivable? Accounts Payable?
6. Can you provide a possible explanation for the difference in the balance of the **Prepaid Insurance** account?

Key Concepts

1. Individuals become owners of a corporation by buying shares of stock. This ownership is known as *stockholders' equity*.

    Here is the entry to record ownership of a corporation:

	DATE		DESCRIPTION	POST. REF.	DEBIT	CREDIT	
1	20--						1
2	Date	1	Cash in Bank		X X XXX XX		2
3			Capital Stock			XX XXX XX	3
4							4

    GENERAL JOURNAL   PAGE ___1___

2. The work sheet is a tool that organizes all the accounting information needed to prepare the financial statements. Corporations prepare the income statement, the statement of retained earnings, the balance sheet, and the statement of cash flows.

    *   Most of the information needed to complete the *income statement* comes from the work sheet's Income Statement section.
    *   The *statement of retained earnings* reports the changes in the **Retained Earnings** account.
    *   The corporate *balance sheet* information comes from the work sheet's Balance Sheet section.
    *   Information for the *statement of cash flows* comes from the income statement and the comparative balance sheet.

3. The primary difference between financial statements for a sole proprietorship and a corporation involves how ownership is presented on the balance sheet.

	Sole Proprietor	**Corporation**
Balance Sheet Section	Owner's Equity	Stockholders' Equity
Account(s)	Owner's Capital—the owner's investment of cash and assets in the business	• Capital Stock—the investments by stockholders (owners) • Retained Earnings—earnings the corporation generated in past periods and retained instead of distributing to stockholders as dividends

4. For a merchandising business, the *income statement* contains the following elements:

    *   *Net sales* (total sales minus deductions for sales discounts, returns, and allowances).
    *   *Net purchases* (total cost of merchandise bought plus transportation charges minus deductions for purchases discounts, returns, and allowances).

- *Cost of merchandise sold* calculated as follows:

  　Beginning Merchandise Inventory
  <u>+ Net Purchases During the Period</u>
  　Cost of Merchandise Available for Sale
  <u>− Ending Merchandise Inventory</u>
  　Cost of Merchandise Sold

- *Gross profit on sales* (net sales minus cost of merchandise sold)
- Operating expenses
- Operating income
- *Federal income tax* paid by a corporation (listed separately)
- *Net income or net loss*

The *statement of retained earnings* reports the changes in the corporate **Retained Earnings** account that occurred during the period as a result of business operations and the distribution of earnings to stockholders through dividends.

The *balance sheet* reports asset, liability, and stockholders' equity accounts for a specific date and comes from the work sheet's Balance Sheet section.

The *statement of cash flows* reports how the activities of a business caused the cash balance to increase or decrease during the accounting period.

5. Vertical analysis helps the accountant determine the relationships among items on a financial statement and the changes in these relationships from one period to another.

Horizontal analysis compares amounts for the same item on a financial statement for two or more accounting periods.

Key Terms

administrative expenses	(p. 561)	net purchases	(p. 559)
base period	(p. 568)	net sales	(p. 558)
Capital Stock	(p. 552)	operating activities	(p. 569)
cash inflows	(p. 569)	operating expenses	(p. 561)
cash outflows	(p. 569)	operating income	(p. 561)
comparability	(p. 554)	relevance	(p. 555)
financing activities	(p. 570)	reliability	(p. 555)
full disclosure	(p. 555)	retained earnings	(p. 554)
gross profit on sales	(p. 561)	selling expenses	(p. 561)
horizontal analysis	(p. 568)	statement of retained earnings	(p. 565)
investing activities	(p. 569)	stockholders' equity	(p. 552)
materiality	(p. 555)	vertical analysis	(p. 563)

Check Your Understanding

1. **Ownership of a Corporation**
   a. How are stockholders' equity and owner's equity similar?
   b. What is retained earnings?

2. **Work Sheet and Financial Statements**
   a. What four financial statements are prepared by a corporation?
   b. How is the work sheet used to prepare financial statements?

3. **Financial Statement Differences**
   a. How does an income statement for a merchandising business differ from that for a service business?
   b. How does the stockholders' equity section of a balance sheet differ from the owner's equity section?

4. **Merchandising Corporation Financial Statements**
   a. What type of expense appears on the income statement of a corporation but not on those of a sole proprietorship or partnership?
   b. What is the difference between the cost of merchandise available for sale and the cost of merchandise sold?

5. **Financial Statement Analysis**
   a. Why would you analyze financial statement information using horizontal analysis?
   b. How is vertical analysis helpful?

Apply Key Terms

Your company, The Bookworm, was purchased several months ago by an international bookstore chain—The Best Seller. Your new boss, Gabriella Sitta, asks you to create the end-of-year financial statements. Gabriella is not native to the United States and does not understand all the English-language business terms. On a separate sheet of paper, write each term's definition and its relationship to the preparation of financial statements.

administrative expenses	gross profit on sales	relevance
base period	horizontal analysis	reliability
Capital Stock	investing activities	retained earnings
cash inflows	materiality	selling expenses
cash outflows	net purchases	statement of
comparability	net sales	retained earnings
financing activities	operating activities	stockholders' equity
full disclosure	operating expenses	vertical analysis
	operating income	

Preparing Financial Statements

Making the Transition from a Manual to a Computerized System

Task	Manual Methods	Computerized Methods
Preparing financial statements	• After all business transactions have been journalized and posted, prepare the trial balance. • Calculate, journalize, and post the adjusting entries. • Prepare the income statement, statement of retained earnings, and balance sheet.	• After all business transactions have been journalized and posted, print a working trial balance. • Journalize the adjusting entries. • Print the income statement, statement of retained earnings, and balance sheet.

Peachtree® Q & A

Peachtree Question	Answer
How do I print the Income Statement, Statement of Retained Earnings, and Balance Sheet?	1. From the *Reports* menu, select **Financial Statements**. 2. Select **Income Statement, Retained Earnings Statement,** or **Balance Sheet** from the Preview list. 3. Click the **Screen** icon to display the Options window. 4. Select a time frame for the information to be included in the report. Current period is the default. 5. Review the statement on the screen. 6. Click **Print**.

QuickBooks Q & A

QuickBooks Question	Answer
How do I print the Profit & Loss report and Balance Sheet?	1. From the *Reports* menu, select **Company & Financial**. 2. Select **Profit & Loss Standard** or **Balance Sheet Standard**. 3. Enter the correct dates for the statement. 4. Review the statement on the screen. 5. Click **Print**.

For detailed instructions, see your Glencoe Accounting Chapter Study Guides and Working Papers.

Complete problems using: **Manual** Glencoe Working Papers OR **Peachtree Complete Accounting** Software OR **QuickBooks** Templates OR **Spreadsheet** Templates

SPREADSHEET SMART GUIDE

Step–by–Step Instructions: Problem 19–5

1. Select the spreadsheet template for Problem 19–5.
2. Enter your name and the date in the spaces provided on the template.
3. Complete the spreadsheet using the instructions in your working papers.
4. Print the spreadsheet and proof your work.
5. Complete the Analyze activity.
6. Save your work and exit the spreadsheet program.

Peachtree®

SMART GUIDE

Step–by–Step Instructions: Problem 19–6

1. Select the problem set for Sunset Surfwear (Prob. 19–6).
2. Rename the company and set the system date.
3. Print a Statement of Retained Earnings and a Balance Sheet.
4. Complete the Analyze activity.
5. End the session.

QuickBooks

PROBLEM GUIDE

Step–by–Step Instructions: Problem 19–6

1. Restore the Problem 19-6. QBB file.
2. Print a Balance Sheet.
3. Complete the Analyze activity.
4. Back up your work.

Problem 19–5 Preparing an Income Statement

The work sheet for Sunset Surfwear for the year ended December 31 is shown in your working papers.

Instructions Prepare an income statement for Sunset Surfwear in your working papers. Refer to **Figure 19–3** for guidance in setting up the income statement.

Analyze Identify which general ledger account, **Purchases Discounts** or **Purchases Returns & Allowances**, had a higher amount this period.

Problem 19–6 Preparing a Statement of Retained Earnings and a Balance Sheet

Instructions Use the work sheet and the income statement from **Problem 19–5** to prepare a statement of retained earnings and a balance sheet for Sunset Surfwear. Use the accounting stationery provided in your working papers.

Analyze Calculate the ending balance of **Retained Earnings** assuming Sunset Surfwear had a net loss of $6,492 instead of a net income for the period.

Problem 19–7 Preparing Financial Statements

Instructions The partially completed work sheet for Shutterbug Cameras is included in your working papers.

1. Complete the work sheet.
2. Prepare an income statement.
3. Prepare a statement of retained earnings.
4. Prepare a balance sheet.

Analyze Identify the biggest asset account, the biggest liability account, and the highest expense account shown on the financial statements.

Problem 19–8 Completing a Work Sheet and Financial Statements

The trial balance for Cycle Tech Bicycles, prepared on a ten-column work sheet, is included in your working papers.

Instructions

1. Complete the work sheet for the year ended December 31. Use the following information to make the adjustments.

   Ending merchandise inventory $25,191

   Ending supplies inventory   1,221

   Expired insurance   825

   Total federal corporate income taxes for the year   3,472

2. Prepare an income statement.

3. Prepare a statement of retained earnings.

4. Prepare a balance sheet.

Cycle Tech Bicycles
Work Sheet
For the Year Ended December 31, 20--

	ACCT. NO.	ACCOUNT NAME	TRIAL BALANCE DEBIT	TRIAL BALANCE CREDIT
1	101	Cash in Bank	21 931 00	
2	115	Accounts Receivable	1 782 00	
3	125	Merchandise Inventory	24 028 00	
4	130	Supplies	4 159 00	
5	135	Prepaid Insurance	1 800 00	
6	140	Store Equipment	24 895 00	
7	145	Office Equipment	16 113 00	
8	201	Accounts Payable		11 224 00
9	210	Fed. Corp. Income Tax Payable		
10	211	Emplys' Fed. Inc. Tax Payable		522 00
11	212	Emplys' State Inc. Tax Payable		144 00
12	213	Social Security Tax Payable		413 00
13	214	Medicare Tax Payable		134 00
14	215	Sales Tax Payable		1 915 00
15	216	Fed. Unemployment Tax Payable		54 00
16	217	State Unemployment Tax Payable		271 00
17	301	Capital Stock		40 000 00
18	305	Retained Earnings		11 091 00
19	310	Income Summary		
20	401	Sales		127 151 00
21	405	Sales Discounts	246 00	
22	410	Sales Returns and Allowances	1 328 00	
23	501	Purchases	66 107 00	
24	505	Transportation In	983 00	
25	510	Purchases Discounts		822 00
26	515	Purchases Ret. and Allowances		376 00
27	601	Advertising Expense	2 380 00	
28	605	Bankcard Fees Expense	181 00	
29	625	Fed. Corp. Income Tax Expense	3 340 00	
30	630	Insurance Expense		
31	645	Maintenance Expense	1 950 00	
32	650	Miscellaneous Expense	1 831 00	
33	655	Payroll Tax Expense	834 00	
34	657	Rent Expense	10 800 00	
35	660	Salaries Expense	4 734 00	
36	665	Supplies Expense		
37	675	Utilities Expense	4 695 00	
38				
39			194 117 00	194 117 00
40		Net Income		
41				
42				

Analyze   Predict whether net income would be higher or lower if the ending value of **Merchandise Inventory** was actually $28,000.

Peachtree®

SMART GUIDE

Step–by–Step Instructions: Problem 19–7

1. Select the problem set for Shutterbug Cameras (Prob. 19–7).
2. Rename the company and set the system date.
3. Print the following reports: Adjusted Trial Balance, Balance Sheet, Income Statement, and Statement of Retained Earnings.
4. Complete the Analyze activity.
5. End the session.

Peachtree®

SMART GUIDE

Step–by–Step Instructions: Problem 19–8

1. Select the problem set for Cycle Tech Bicycles (Prob. 19–8).
2. Rename the company and set the system date.
3. Print a Working Trial Balance to help you prepare the adjustments.
4. Record the adjustments using the **General Journal Entry** option.
5. Print a General Journal report and proof your work.
6. Print the following reports: Adjusted Trial Balance, Income Statement, Statement of Retained Earnings, and Balance Sheet.
7. Complete the Analyze activity.
8. End the session.

Problems

QuickBooks

CHALLENGE PROBLEM

Problem 19–9 Evaluating the Effect of an Error on the Income Statement

The accounting clerk for River's Edge Canoe & Kayak prepared the income statement for the year ended December 31. The accounting supervisor at River's Edge noticed that the balance of the **Transportation In** account was erroneously omitted from this statement. **Transportation In** has a balance of $562.

Instructions Use the income statement shown in your working papers to answer the following questions.

1. In which section of the income statement is the account **Transportation In** entered?
2. How is net purchases affected by this omission (understated or overstated)? By what amount?
3. How does the omission of the **Transportation In** balance affect gross profit on sales? By what amount?
4. What is the correct amount for the cost of merchandise sold for the period?
5. What is the correct amount for net income?

Analyze Determine the effect that an overstatement of expenses would have on net income.

Practice your test-taking skills! The questions on this page are reprinted with permission from national organizations:
- Future Business Leaders of America
- Business Professionals of America

Use a separate sheet of paper to record your answers.

Future Business Leaders of America

MULTIPLE CHOICE

1. One way to increase gross profit on sales is to
    a. increase sales revenue.
    b. increase cost of merchandise sold.
    c. decrease sales revenue.
    d. decrease expenses.

2. The _____ account represents the increase in stockholders' equity from net income that is held by the corporation and not distributed to stockholders as a return on their investment.
    a. operating income
    b. retained earnings
    c. working capital
    d. net sales

3. When using _____, each dollar amount on a financial statement is also stated as a percentage of a base amount on the same statement.
    a. horizontal analysis
    b. vertical analysis
    c. statement of retained earnings
    d. comparability

4. You are given the following information: cost of merchandise sold, $404,000; operating expenses, $785,122; and net sales, $557,225. What is the company's gross profit on sales?
    a. $381,122
    b. $227,897
    c. $267,135
    d. $153,225

Business Professionals of America

MULTIPLE CHOICE

5. Beginning merchandise inventory plus net purchases minus ending inventory equals
    a. net income.
    b. gross profit on sales.
    c. total expenses.
    d. cost of goods sold.

Need More Help?

Go to glencoeaccounting.glencoe.com and click on Student Center. Click on Winning Competitive Events and select Chapter 19.
- **Practice Questions and Test-Taking Tips**
- **Concept Capsules and Terminology**

Financial Statements for a Corporation

1. Name the two parts of stockholders' equity.

2. Explain the difference between gross profit on sales and operating income.

3. Compare the statement of retained earnings and the statement of cash flows, and explain how they are similar.

4. Look at vertical and horizontal analysis of financial statements. Explain why the percentages on comparative income statements and balance sheets add vital information for analysis by owners and managers.

5. Write a statement to explain why financial statements are prepared in this order: income statement, statement of retained earnings, balance sheet, and statement of cash flows.

6. Support the statement that all four financial statements must be examined to obtain an accurate understanding of a corporation's financial condition.

Merchandising Business: Gourmet Food Gifts

Gourmet Express sells cookies, candies, food baskets, and other gourmet gift items in retail stores and catalogs. Prices increased recently for sugar and chocolate, causing net income to decrease. The manager, Tara, does not want to use lower-priced ingredients because they may lower the products' quality.

In preparation for the Valentine's Day rush, Tara has asked you to suggest some ideas for increasing net income.

INSTRUCTIONS

1. Identify the items that affect net income.

2. List some possible areas to cut costs.

Reporting a Mistake

You are an accounting clerk for a major league sports franchise. Your responsibilities do not include any end-of-period activities. You learn that a co-worker made a significant error on the work sheet. It will affect the financial statements. You wonder whether to report the error or assume that someone else will catch it.

ETHICAL DECISION MAKING

1. What are the ethical issues?

2. What are the alternatives?

3. Who are the affected parties?

4. How do the alternatives affect the parties?

5. What would you do?

Explaining Financial Statements

As the CEO of First Rate Products, you regularly present the financial results at stockholders' meetings. It is imperative that your recently hired accounting clerk, James Van, understands the importance of accurate financial statements. Write a clear, concise memo to him outlining each financial statement's purpose and its relationship to the company's overall performance.

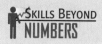

SKILLS BEYOND NUMBERS

Sociability

You work for Big League Sports—a professional-sports merchandising company. Your boss, Lily Chang, asks you to make a simple but colorful presentation about trends in professional sports at the annual stockholders' meeting and reception.

INSTRUCTIONS With several classmates, make an outline for the presentation. Decide on topics to cover and visuals to use. Practice presenting to one another. Brainstorm questions for the question-and-answer segment. Give feedback on each speaker's presentation—both verbal and nonverbal communication skills including eye contact, stance, gestures, facial expressions, and use of visual aids.

INTERNATIONAL ACCOUNTING

Financial Statement Formats

The format of financial statements can vary by country. An example is the balance sheet of the German car manufacturer, BMW. It presents noncurrent assets before current assets, and stockholders' equity before liabilities.

INSTRUCTIONS Illustrate how the BMW balance sheet differs from the balance sheet of most U.S. companies as taught in this book.

Making It Personal

Your Nest Egg

Social Security provides the only retirement funds for many people. Some analysts believe that it is in trouble and could become insolvent. You need to become educated about retirement funding and begin to plan early for it.

PERSONAL FINANCE ACTIVITY Use library resources or the Internet to research and compare the advantages and disadvantages of two retirement saving options.

PERSONAL FINANCE ONLINE Log on to **glencoeaccounting.glencoe.com** and click on **Student Center.** Click on **Making It Personal** and select **Chapter 19.**

Analyzing FINANCIAL Reports

Statement of Cash Flows

Look at PETsMART's statement of cash flows in Appendix F. It shows cash flows from operating activities, investing activities, and financing activities. It also shows the net cash provided (or used) by each activity. A company's *sources* of cash can be revealing. For long term success, a company's cash inflows must be from operating activities. If its main source of cash was investing activities, it may have sold some of its plant assets. If its main source of cash was financing activities, it may have issued stock or borrowed money. A firm that must sell its assets or borrow money to stay in business cannot do so indefinitely. A company's *use* of cash can also be revealing. A large use of cash for investing activities may indicate company expansion. A large use of cash for financing activities may mean that the company paid off its loans.

INSTRUCTIONS Use PETsMART's statements of cash flows in Appendix F to answer these questions.

1. For each of the three years shown, which activity *provided* the largest source of cash: operating, investing, or financing?

2. For each of the three years shown, which activity *used* the most cash: operating, investing, or financing?

Recording Business Transactions in Special Journals

In-Touch Electronics

Main Task

▸ Use special journals to complete the accounting tasks for In-Touch Electronics.

Summary of Steps

▸ Journalize and post transactions.

▸ Prove cash.

▸ Prepare a schedule of accounts receivable and a schedule of accounts payable.

▸ Prepare a trial balance.

Why It's Important

▸ Special journals are used more than the general journal for routine transactions.

Company Background: Pedro and Justina Cordova own and operate In-Touch Electronics, a merchandising business organized as a corporation. The retail business is a small electronics store providing a unique service to the local community. This husband and wife team has been operating successfully for 10 years.

Keeping the Accounting Records for In-Touch Electronics: Since In-Touch Electronics has a large volume of business transactions, the business uses special journals and a general journal. The chart of accounts for In-Touch Electronics appears on the next page. The previous accounting clerk, Manny Canseco, has journalized and posted the business transactions for May 1 through May 15. Those transactions are included in the accounting stationery in the working papers accompanying this textbook. The transactions that follow took place between May 16 and May 31.

Your Job Responsibilities: The forms for completing this activity are included in the working papers accompanying this textbook.

(1) Record the remaining May transactions in the sales journal (page 18), cash receipts journal (page 15), purchases journal (page 12), cash payments journal (page 14), and general journal (page 7).

(2) Post the individual amounts from the five journals to the accounts receivable and accounts payable subsidiary ledgers on a daily basis.

(3) Post the individual amounts from the General columns of the cash receipts, purchases, cash payments, and general journals on a daily basis.

(4) Foot, prove, total, and rule the special journals.

(5) Post the column totals of the special journals to the general ledger accounts. Use the following order for posting: sales journal, cash receipts journal, purchases journal, and cash payments journal.

In-Touch Electronics (continued)

(6) Prove cash. The balance shown on check stub 899 is $6,109.45.

(7) Prepare a schedule of accounts receivable and a schedule of accounts payable.

(8) Prepare a trial balance.

CHART OF ACCOUNTS
In-Touch Electronics

ASSETS

101	Cash in Bank
105	Accounts Receivable
110	Merchandise Inventory
115	Supplies
120	Prepaid Insurance
150	Store Equipment
155	Office Equipment

LIABILITIES

201	Accounts Payable
205	Sales Tax Payable
210	Employees' Federal Income Tax Payable
211	Employees' State Income Tax Payable
212	Social Security Tax Payable
213	Medicare Tax Payable
214	Federal Unemployment Tax Payable
215	State Unemployment Tax Payable

STOCKHOLDERS' EQUITY

301	Capital Stock
302	Retained Earnings
303	Income Summary

Accounts Receivable Subsidiary Ledger

LOR	Sam Lorenzo
MAR	Marianne Martino
MCC	Mark McCormick
SCO	Sue Ellen Scott
TRO	Tom Trout

REVENUE

401	Sales
405	Sales Discounts
410	Sales Returns and Allowances

COST OF MERCHANDISE

501	Purchases
505	Transportation In
510	Purchases Discounts
515	Purchases Returns and Allowances

EXPENSES

605	Advertising Expense
610	Bankcard Fees Expense
615	Miscellaneous Expense
620	Payroll Tax Expense
625	Rent Expense
630	Salaries Expense
635	Utilities Expense

Accounts Payable Subsidiary Ledger

COM	Computer Systems Inc.
DES	Desktop Wholesalers
HIT	Hi-Tech Electronics Outlet
LAS	Laser & Ink-Jet Products
OFF	Office Suppliers Inc.

Peachtree®

SMART GUIDE

Step–by–Step Instructions:

1. Select the problem set for In-Touch Electronics (MP–4).
2. Rename the company and set the system date.
3. Enter all sales on account using the **Sales/Invoicing** option.
4. Record and apply any sales returns using the **Credit Memos** option.
5. Process all cash receipts using the **Receipts** option.
6. Enter the purchases on account using the **Purchases/Receive Inventory** option.
7. Record and apply any purchases returns using the **Vendor Credit Memos** option.
8. Process all cash payments with the **Payments** option.
9. Use the **General Journal Entry** option to record the error discovered on May 26.
10. Record the employer's payroll taxes using the **General Journal Entry** option.
11. Print a General Journal, Purchases Journal, Cash Disbursements Journal, Sales Journal, and Cash Receipts Journal.
12. Proof your work.
13. Print the following reports: General Ledger, Vendor Ledgers, and Customer Ledgers.
14. Print a General Ledger Trial Balance.
15. Complete the Analyze activity and complete the Audit Test.
16. End the session.

TIP: Remember that you need to change the G/L Account in the Receipts window to enter a cash receipt for the sale of an asset (e.g., supplies, office equipment).

Business Transactions: In-Touch Electronics had the following transactions May 16 through May 31.

Date	Transactions
May 16	Sold $120.00 in merchandise plus 5% sales tax to Sam Lorenzo on account, Sales Slip 607.
17	Received $126.00 from Tom Trout to apply on his account, Receipt 356.
17	Issued Check 892 for $800.00 to Desktop Wholesalers in payment of our account balance.
18	Issued Debit Memo 38 to Laser & Ink Jet Products for our return of $75.00 in merchandise.
19	Wrote Check 893 for $1,200.00 to Computer Systems Inc. to apply on our account.
19	Paid Hi-Tech Electronics Outlet $1,750.00 in full payment of our account balance by issuing Check 894.
19	Issued Check 895 to Office Suppliers, Inc. for $770.00 in full payment of our account balance.
20	Sold $90.00 in office equipment for cash to an employee, Bob Bell, Receipt 357.
20	Purchased $1,200.00 in store equipment on account from Desktop Wholesalers, DW87, n/30.
20	Received $210.00 from Mark McCormick to apply on his account, Receipt 358.
20	Sue Ellen Scott sent us a check for $308.70 in payment of her $315.00 account less a 2% discount, Receipt 359.
21	Purchased $1,500.00 in merchandise on account from Hi-Tech Electronics Outlet, Invoice HT99, terms 2/10, n/30.
21	Marianne Martino sent us a $94.50 check to apply on her account, Receipt 360.
21	Sold $400.00 in merchandise plus 5% sales tax to Mark McCormick on account, Sales Slip 608, terms 2/10, n/30.
22	Issued Check 896 for $1,200.00 to Desktop Wholesalers, in payment of our account.
23	Sold $500.00 in merchandise to Sue Ellen Scott on account plus 5% sales tax, Sales Slip 609, terms 2/10, n/30.
24	Mark McCormick returned merchandise purchased on account, $100.00, plus 5% sales tax, Credit Memo 55.
25	Paid the annual insurance premium of $1,600.00 by issuing Check 897 to Surfside Insurance Co.
26	Discovered that **Transportation In** account should have been debited last month for $50.00 instead of the **Purchases** account. Recorded the correcting entry, Memorandum 26.
27	Bought $1,400.00 in merchandise on account from Computer Systems, Inc., CS75, terms 2/10, n/30.

CONTINUE

In-Touch Electronics (continued)

Date	Transactions (cont.)
May 28	Sold $200.00 in merchandise on account plus 5% sales tax to Marianne Martino, Sales Slip 610, terms 2/10, n/30.
29	Purchased $150.00 in supplies on account from Office Suppliers Inc., Invoice 9489.
30	Issued Check 898 for $1,500.00 in payment for the monthly rent.
31	Recorded cash sales of $1,200.00 plus 5% sales tax, Tape 22.
31	Recorded bankcard sales of $900.00 plus 5% sales tax, Tape 22.
31	Recorded bank service charge of $25.00 and bankcard fees of $100.00, May bank statement (record compound entry).
31	Wrote Check 899 to pay the payroll of $2,500.00 (gross earnings) for the pay period ended May 31. The following amounts were withheld: employees' federal income taxes, $400.00; employees' state income taxes, $50.00; FICA taxes: $155.00 for social security and $36.25 for Medicare.
31	Recorded the employer's payroll taxes for the May 31 payroll: FICA tax rate, 6.2% for social security and 1.45% for Medicare; federal unemployment tax rate, 0.8%; and state unemployment tax rate, 5.4%.

Analyze

1. Compute the amount by which the **Cash in Bank** account changed during the month.
2. Identify the two accounts that have the greatest impact on the trial balance total.
3. Calculate the total percentage of tax withholdings for the May 31 payroll.

QuickBooks

PROBLEM GUIDE

Step–by–Step Instructions:

1. Restore the Problem Mini Practice 4.QBB file.
2. Enter all sales on account using the **Create Invoices** option.
3. Record and apply any sales returns using the **Create Credit Memos/ Refunds** option.
4. Process all cash receipts.
5. Enter the purchases on account using the **Enter Bills** option.
6. Record and apply any purchase returns using the **Credit** option from the **Enter Bills** window in the **Vendors** menu.
7. Process all cash payments.
8. Use the **Make General Journal Entries** option to record the error discovered on May 26.
9. Record the employer's payroll taxes using the **Make General Journal Entries** option.
10. Print a Journal report.
11. Proof your work.
12. Print the following reports: General Ledger, Vendor Balance Summary, and Customer Balance Summary.
13. Print a Trial Balance.
14. Complete the Analyze activity and complete the Audit Test.
15. Back up your work.

Completing the Accounting Cycle for a Merchandising Corporation

What You'll Learn

1. Journalize closing entries for a merchandising corporation.

2. Post closing entries to the general ledger accounts.

3. Prepare a post-closing trial balance.

4. Describe the steps in the accounting cycle.

Why It's Important

▶ Like a sole proprietorship, a corporation "cleans the slate" to prepare for the next accounting period.

Exploring the *Real World* of Business

CLOSING THE BOOKS

PETsMART

Is your pet like a member of the family? The loyalty that leads to spoiling a cat with a heated cuddle bed or purchasing vitamins for a pet iguana is what contributes to making **PETsMART** the leader in the retail pet food and supply industry. A strong product mix, combined with pet services like grooming and boarding, have made the company a success. **PETsMART's** net income has risen to $68.1 million, more than double the earnings of its nearest competitor.

At the end of a fiscal period, companies like **PETsMART** prepare closing entries to transfer all temporary account balances to a permanent account. The general ledger is then ready for a new accounting period.

What Do You Think?

What might happen if temporary accounts were not closed before the next accounting period begins?

Working in the *Real World*

APPLYING YOUR ACCOUNTING KNOWLEDGE

You have almost completed another accounting cycle—this time for a merchandising company. After the financial statements have been prepared, closing entries are made to get the accounting records ready for the next fiscal period. Closing entries for a merchandising business are similar to those you learned about for a service business. There are just more of them.

Personal Connection

1. In your job are there duties that you perform at the end of a night or week that "wipe the slate clean" or "close out" the day's activities?

2. If you were preparing the closing entries for your workplace, what accounts do you imagine would be involved?

Online Connection

Go to **glencoeaccounting.glencoe.com** and click on **Student Center.** Click on **Working in the Real World** and select **Chapter 20.**

Journalizing Closing Entries

Main Idea

A corporation's net income (or net loss) is closed to **Retained Earnings.**

Read to Learn...

➤ how to journalize closing entries for a merchandising corporation. (p. 588)

➤ how to journalize a net loss. (p. 591)

In Chapter 10 you journalized and posted the closing entries for a sole proprietorship service business. In this chapter you will learn to journalize and post the closing entries for a merchandising corporation. The journalizing procedures are the same.

Steps for Closing the Ledger

How Are Closing Entries for a Corporation Different from Closing Entries for a Sole Proprietorship?

In Chapter 10 you made four entries to close the temporary general ledger accounts of a sole proprietorship:

1. Close the temporary accounts with credit balances to **Income Summary.**
2. Close the temporary accounts with debit balances to **Income Summary.**

On Your Mark
Work
For the Year Ended

	ACCT. NO.	ACCOUNT NAME	TRIAL BALANCE		ADJUSTMENTS	
			DEBIT	CREDIT	DEBIT	CREDIT
20	310	Income Summary			(a)3 536 00	
21	401	Sales		320 450 00		
22	405	Sales Discounts	730 00			
23	410	Sales Returns and Allowances	2 000 00			
24	501	Purchases	206 700 00			
25	505	Transportation In	4 036 18			
26	510	Purchases Discounts		1 340 00		
27	515	Purchases Returns and Allow.		1 800 00		
28	601	Advertising Expense	2 450 00			
29	605	Bankcard Fees Expense	4 199 27			
30	630	Fed. Corporate Income Tax Exp.	9 840 00		(d) 155 00	
31	635	Insurance Expense			(c) 125 00	
32	650	Maintenance Expense	3 519 25			
33	655	Miscellaneous Expense	348 28			
34	657	Payroll Tax Expense	3 826 83			
35	660	Rent Expense	14 000 00			
36	665	Salaries Expense	29 374 60			
37	670	Supplies Expense			(b)3 710 00	
38	680	Utilities Expense	2 364 87			
39			435 798 28	435 798 28	7 526 00	7 526 00
40		Net Income				
41						

Figure 20–1 Closing Entries Needed for a Corporation

3. Close the balance of **Income Summary** to capital.
4. Close the withdrawals account to capital.

Only the first three closing entries are made to close the temporary accounts for a merchandising business organized as a corporation. Since a corporation does not have a withdrawals account, the fourth closing entry is not needed.

The portion of On Your Mark's work sheet in **Figure 20–1** shows the account balances that are closed. Let's look closely at each closing entry.

1. Close the accounts with balances in the Credit column of the Income Statement section of the work sheet (revenue and contra cost of merchandise accounts) to **Income Summary.** After this closing entry has been journalized and posted, the **Sales, Purchases Discounts,** and **Purchases Returns and Allowances** accounts have zero balances.

Income Summary

Debit	Credit
Adj. 3,536.00	Clos. 323,590.00

Sales

Debit	Credit
–	+
Clos. 320,450.00	Bal. 320,450.00

Purchases Discounts

Debit	Credit
–	+
Clos. 1,340.00	Bal. 1,340.00

Purchases Returns and Allowances

Debit	Credit
–	+
Clos. 1,800.00	Bal. 1,800.00

GENERAL JOURNAL PAGE ___23___

	DATE	DESCRIPTION	POST. REF.	DEBIT	CREDIT	
1	20--	*Closing Entries*				1
2	Dec. 31	*Sales*		320 450 00		2
3		*Purchases Discounts*		1 340 00		3
4		*Purchases Returns and Allow.*		1 800 00		4
5		*Income Summary*			323 590 00	5

Athletic Wear

Sheet

December 31, 20--

ADJUSTED TRIAL BALANCE		INCOME STATEMENT		BALANCE SHEET		
DEBIT	CREDIT	DEBIT	CREDIT	DEBIT	CREDIT	
3 536 00		3 536 00				20
	320 450 00		320 450 00			21
730 00		730 00				22
2 000 00		2 000 00				23
206 700 00		206 700 00				24
4 036 18		4 036 18				25
	1 340 00		1 340 00			26
	1 800 00		1 800 00			27
2 450 00		2 450 00				28
4 199 27		4 199 27				29
9 995 00		9 995 00				30
125 00		125 00				31
3 519 25		3 519 25				32
348 28		348 28				33
3 826 83		3 826 83				34
14 000 00		14 000 00				35
29 374 60		29 374 60				36
3 710 00		3 710 00				37
2 364 87		2 364 87				38
435 953 28	435 953 28	290 915 28	323 590 00	145 038 00	112 363 28	39
		32 674 72			32 674 72	40
		323 590 00	323 590 00	145 038 00	145 038 00	41

1 Close temporary accounts with balances in the Income Statement Credit column to Income Summary.

2 Close temporary accounts with balances in the Income Statement Debit column to Income Summary.

3 Close Income Summary to Retained Earnings by the amount of the net income or loss.

Figure 20–1 Closing Entries Needed for a Corporation (continued)

Income Summary	
Debit	Credit
Adj. 3,536.00	Clos. 323,590.00
Clos. 287,379.28	

Sales Discounts	
Debit +	Credit −
Bal. 730.00	Clos. 730.00

Sales Returns and Allowances	
Debit +	Credit −
Bal. 2,000.00	Clos. 2,000.00

Purchases	
Debit +	Credit −
Bal. 206,700.00	Clos. 206,700.00

Transportation In	
Debit +	Credit −
Bal. 4,036.18	Clos. 4,036.18

Advertising Expense	
Debit +	Credit −
Bal. 2,450.00	Clos. 2,450.00

Bankcard Fees Expense	
Debit +	Credit −
Bal. 4,199.27	Clos. 4,199.27

Federal Corporate Income Tax Expense	
Debit +	Credit −
Bal. 9,995.00	Clos. 9,995.00

Insurance Expense	
Debit +	Credit −
Bal. 125.00	Clos. 125.00

Maintenance Expense	
Debit +	Credit −
Bal. 3,519.25	Clos. 3,519.25

Miscellaneous Expense	
Debit +	Credit −
Bal. 348.28	Clos. 348.28

Payroll Tax Expense	
Debit +	Credit −
Bal. 3,826.83	Clos. 3,826.83

Rent Expense	
Debit +	Credit −
Bal. 14,000.00	Clos. 14,000.00

Salaries Expense	
Debit +	Credit −
Bal. 29,374.60	Clos. 29,374.60

Supplies Expense	
Debit +	Credit −
Bal. 3,710.00	Clos. 3,710.00

Utilities Expense	
Debit +	Credit −
Bal. 2,364.87	Clos. 2,364.87

2. Close the accounts with balances in the Debit column of the Income Statement section of the work sheet (contra revenue, cost of merchandise, and expense accounts) to **Income Summary.** After this closing entry has been journalized and posted, the contra revenue, cost of merchandise, and expense accounts have zero balances.

Income Summary now has a credit balance of $32,674.72.

$ 323,590.00	closing credit
− 3,536.00	adjustment debit
− 287,379.28	closing debit
$ 32,674.72	credit balance

3. Close **Income Summary** to **Retained Earnings.**

Income Summary			Retained Earnings	
Debit	Credit	Debit −	Credit +	
Adj. 3,536.00	Clos. 323,590.00		Bal. 19,771.19	
Clos. 287,379.28			Clos. 32,674.72	
Clos. 32,674.72			Bal. 52,445.91	

After the entry to close **Income Summary** to **Retained Earnings** has been journalized and posted, **Income Summary** has a zero balance. The balance of **Retained Earnings** is increased to $52,445.91.

	DATE		DESCRIPTION	POST. REF.	DEBIT	CREDIT	
6	Dec.	31	Income Summary		287 379 28		6
7			Sales Discounts			7 30 00	7
8			Sales Returns and Allow.			2 000 00	8
9			Purchases			206 700 00	9
10			Transportation In			4 036 18	10
11			Advertising Expense			2 450 00	11
12			Bankcard Fees Expense			4 199 27	12
13			Fed. Corp. Inc. Tax Expense			9 995 00	13
14			Insurance Expense			1 25 00	14
15			Maintenance Expense			3 519 25	15
16			Miscellaneous Expense			3 48 28	16
17			Payroll Tax Expense			3 826 83	17
18			Rent Expense			14 000 00	18
19			Salaries Expense			29 374 60	19
20			Supplies Expense			3 710 00	20
21			Utilities Expense			2 364 87	21
22	Dec.	31	Income Summary		32 674 72		22
23			Retained Earnings			32 674 72	23
24							24

Closing Entry to Transfer a Net Loss
How Do You Close a Net Loss to Retained Earnings?

Sometimes businesses incur net losses. Suppose that after posting the first two entries closing the temporary accounts, the **Income Summary** account is as shown. Before it is closed, **Income Summary** has a debit balance of $5,000.00:

$$\begin{array}{rl}
\$\ 3,612.00 & \text{adjustment debit} \\
+\ 65,178.00 & \text{closing debit} \\
-\ 63,790.00 & \text{closing credit} \\
\hline
\$\ 5,000.00 & \text{debit balance}
\end{array}$$

Income Summary	
Debit	Credit
Adj. 3,612.00	Clos. 63,790.00
Clos. 65,178.00	

To close **Income Summary,** credit it for $5,000 and debit **Retained Earnings** for $5,000. The net loss amount *decreases* the earnings the business retains. This closing entry is recorded in the general journal as follows:

GENERAL JOURNAL   PAGE __23__

	DATE		DESCRIPTION	POST. REF.	DEBIT	CREDIT	
1			Closing Entries				1
22	Dec.	31	Retained Earnings		5 000 00		22
23			Income Summary			5 000 00	23
24							24

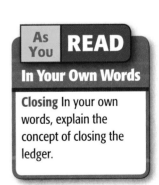

As You READ

In Your Own Words

Closing In your own words, explain the concept of closing the ledger.

AFTER YOU READ

Reinforce the Main Idea

Using a diagram like this one, describe the step-by-step process for journalizing a merchandising corporation's closing entries. Add or remove answer boxes as needed.

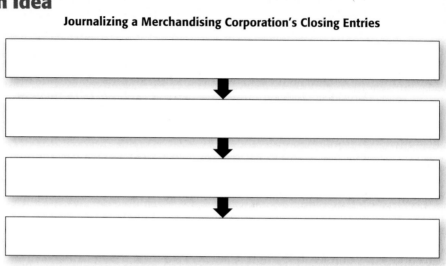

Journalizing a Merchandising Corporation's Closing Entries

Do the Math

The closing debit entry to the **Income Summary** account was $263,000, and the closing credit entry was $300,000. If the **Income Summary** account had a $42,000 credit balance after these entries, was the inventory adjustment a debit or credit? What was the amount?

Problem 20–1 Identifying Accounts Affected by Closing Entries

The following account names appear in the chart of accounts of Larkin's Department Store.

Accounts Receivable	Purchases
Bankcard Fees Expense	Purchases Discounts
Capital Stock	Purchases Returns and Allowances
Cash in Bank	Retained Earnings
Equipment	Sales
Fed. Corp. Income Tax Expense	Sales Discounts
Fed. Corp. Income Tax Payable	Sales Returns and Allowances
Income Summary	Sales Tax Payable
Insurance Expense	Supplies
Merchandise Inventory	Supplies Expense
Miscellaneous Expense	Transportation In
Prepaid Insurance	Utilities Expense

Instructions Use the form in your working papers to answer the following questions about each account. Assume that all accounts have normal balances.

1. Is the account affected by a closing entry?
2. During closing, is the account debited or credited?
3. During closing, is **Income Summary** debited or credited?

Posting Closing Entries

Closing entries recorded in the general journal are posted to the general ledger.

Closing the General Ledger
How Do You Close a Merchandising Corporation's General Ledger?

Figure 20–2 shows the portion of On Your Mark's general ledger affected by the closing process after the closing entries have been posted. Write the term *Closing Entry* (abbreviated *Clos. Ent.* here) for each posting in the Description column of the general ledger account.

ACCOUNT _Retained Earnings_   ACCOUNT NO. _305_

DATE	DESCRIPTION	POST. REF.	DEBIT	CREDIT	BALANCE DEBIT	BALANCE CREDIT
20--						
Dec. 1	Balance	✓				19 7 7 1 19
31	Clos. Ent.	G23		32 6 7 4 72		52 4 4 5 91

ACCOUNT _Income Summary_   ACCOUNT NO. _310_

DATE	DESCRIPTION	POST. REF.	DEBIT	CREDIT	BALANCE DEBIT	BALANCE CREDIT
20--						
Dec. 31	Adj. Ent	G22	3 5 3 6 00		3 5 3 6 00	
31	Clos. Ent.	G23		323 5 9 0 00		320 0 5 4 00
31	Clos. Ent.	G23	287 3 7 9 28			32 6 7 4 72
31	Clos. Ent.	G23	32 6 7 4 72			

ACCOUNT _Sales_   ACCOUNT NO. _401_

DATE	DESCRIPTION	POST. REF.	DEBIT	CREDIT	BALANCE DEBIT	BALANCE CREDIT
20--						
Dec. 1	Balance	✓				300 0 0 0 00
31		S12		10 7 5 0 00		310 7 5 0 00
31		CR13		9 7 0 0 00		320 4 5 0 00
31	Clos. Ent.	G23	320 4 5 0 00			

Figure 20–2 Partial General Ledger at the End of the Fiscal Period

BEFORE YOU READ

Main Idea
After posting the closing entries, prepare a post-closing trial balance.

Read to Learn…
➤ how to post the closing entries for a merchandising corporation. (p. 593)
➤ how to prepare a post-closing trial balance for a merchandising corporation. (p. 597)
➤ about a review of the accounting cycle for a merchandising business. (p. 598)

AS YOU READ

Instant Recall

Posting to the General Ledger Begin with the date, and continue posting by moving from the left to the right. Remember to enter the account number in the Posting Reference column of the general journal.

ACCOUNT Sales Discounts   ACCOUNT NO. 405

DATE	DESCRIPTION	POST. REF.	DEBIT	CREDIT	BALANCE DEBIT	BALANCE CREDIT
20--						
Dec. 1	Balance	✓			700 00	
31		CR13	30 00		730 00	
31	Clos. Ent.	G23		730 00		

ACCOUNT Sales Returns and Allowances   ACCOUNT NO. 410

DATE	DESCRIPTION	POST. REF.	DEBIT	CREDIT	BALANCE DEBIT	BALANCE CREDIT
20--						
Dec. 1	Balance	✓			1 850 00	
4		G20	150 00		2 000 00	
31	Clos. Ent.	G23		2 000 00		

ACCOUNT Purchases   ACCOUNT NO. 501

DATE	DESCRIPTION	POST. REF.	DEBIT	CREDIT	BALANCE DEBIT	BALANCE CREDIT
20--						
Dec. 1	Balance	✓			190 000 00	
19		CP14	1 300 00		191 300 00	
31		P12	15 400 00		206 700 00	
31	Clos. Ent.	G23		206 700 00		

ACCOUNT Transportation In   ACCOUNT NO. 505

DATE	DESCRIPTION	POST. REF.	DEBIT	CREDIT	BALANCE DEBIT	BALANCE CREDIT
20--						
Dec. 1	Balance	✓			3 761 18	
24		CP14	275 00		4 036 18	
31	Clos. Ent.	G23		4 036 18		

ACCOUNT Purchases Discounts   ACCOUNT NO. 510

DATE	DESCRIPTION	POST. REF.	DEBIT	CREDIT	BALANCE DEBIT	BALANCE CREDIT
20--						
Dec. 1	Balance	✓				1 200 00
31		CP14		140 00		1 340 00
31	Clos. Ent.	G23	1 340 00			

Figure 20–2 Partial General Ledger at the End of the Fiscal Period (continued)

ACCOUNT _Purchases Returns and Allowances_   **ACCOUNT NO.** _515_

DATE		DESCRIPTION	POST. REF.	DEBIT	CREDIT	BALANCE DEBIT	BALANCE CREDIT
20--							
Dec.	1	Balance	✓				1 6 0 0 00
	16		G21		2 0 0 00		1 8 0 0 00
	31	Clos. Ent.	G23	1 8 0 0 00			

ACCOUNT _Advertising Expense_   **ACCOUNT NO.** _601_

DATE		DESCRIPTION	POST. REF.	DEBIT	CREDIT	BALANCE DEBIT	BALANCE CREDIT
20--							
Dec.	1	Balance	✓			2 4 5 0 00	
	31	Clos. Ent.	G23		2 4 5 0 00		

ACCOUNT _Bankcard Fees Expense_   **ACCOUNT NO.** _605_

DATE		DESCRIPTION	POST. REF.	DEBIT	CREDIT	BALANCE DEBIT	BALANCE CREDIT
20--							
Dec.	1	Balance	✓			4 1 2 4 27	
	31		CP14	7 5 00		4 1 9 9 27	
	31	Clos. Ent.	G23		4 1 9 9 27		

ACCOUNT _Federal Corporate Income Tax Expense_   **ACCOUNT NO.** _630_

DATE		DESCRIPTION	POST. REF.	DEBIT	CREDIT	BALANCE DEBIT	BALANCE CREDIT
20--							
Dec.	1	Balance	✓			9 8 4 0 00	
	31	Adj. Ent.	G22	1 5 5 00		9 9 9 5 00	
	31	Clos. Ent.	G23		9 9 9 5 00		

ACCOUNT _Insurance Expense_   **ACCOUNT NO.** _635_

DATE		DESCRIPTION	POST. REF.	DEBIT	CREDIT	BALANCE DEBIT	BALANCE CREDIT
20--							
Dec.	31	Adj. Ent.	G22	1 2 5 00		1 2 5 00	
	31	Clos. Ent.	G23		1 2 5 00		

Figure 20–2 Partial General Ledger at the End of the Fiscal Period (continued)

ACCOUNT *Maintenance Expense*   **ACCOUNT NO.** *650*

DATE		DESCRIPTION	POST. REF.	DEBIT	CREDIT	BALANCE DEBIT	BALANCE CREDIT
20--							
Dec.	1	Balance	✓			3 5 1 9 25	
	31	Clos. Ent.	G23		3 5 1 9 25		

ACCOUNT *Miscellaneous Expense*   **ACCOUNT NO.** *655*

DATE		DESCRIPTION	POST. REF.	DEBIT	CREDIT	BALANCE DEBIT	BALANCE CREDIT
20--							
Dec.	1	Balance	✓			3 2 8 28	
	31		CP14	20 00		3 4 8 28	
	31	Clos. Ent.	G23		3 4 8 28		

ACCOUNT *Payroll Tax Expense*   **ACCOUNT NO.** *657*

DATE		DESCRIPTION	POST. REF.	DEBIT	CREDIT	BALANCE DEBIT	BALANCE CREDIT
20--							
Dec.	1	Balance	✓			3 8 2 6 83	
	31	Clos. Ent.	G23		3 8 2 6 83		

ACCOUNT *Rent Expense*   **ACCOUNT NO.** *660*

DATE		DESCRIPTION	POST. REF.	DEBIT	CREDIT	BALANCE DEBIT	BALANCE CREDIT
20--							
Dec.	1	Balance	✓			12 0 0 0 00	
	31		CP14	2 0 0 0 00		14 0 0 0 00	
	31	Clos. Ent.	G23		14 0 0 0 00		

ACCOUNT *Salaries Expense*   **ACCOUNT NO.** *665*

DATE		DESCRIPTION	POST. REF.	DEBIT	CREDIT	BALANCE DEBIT	BALANCE CREDIT
20--							
Dec.	1	Balance	✓			25 3 7 4 60	
	31		CP14	4 0 0 0 00		29 3 7 4 60	
	31	Clos. Ent.	G23		29 3 7 4 60		

Figure 20–2 Partial General Ledger at the End of the Fiscal Period (continued)

ACCOUNT: Supplies Expense ACCOUNT NO. 670

DATE	DESCRIPTION	POST. REF.	DEBIT	CREDIT	BALANCE DEBIT	BALANCE CREDIT
20--						
Dec. 31	Adj. Ent.	G22	3 7 1 0 00		3 7 1 0 00	
31	Clos. Ent.	G23		3 7 1 0 00		

ACCOUNT: Utilities Expense ACCOUNT NO. 680

DATE	DESCRIPTION	POST. REF.	DEBIT	CREDIT	BALANCE DEBIT	BALANCE CREDIT
20--						
Dec. 1	Balance	✓			2 3 6 4 87	
31	Clos. Ent.	G23		2 3 6 4 87		

Figure 20–2 Partial General Ledger at the End of the Fiscal Period (continued)

Preparing a Post-Closing Trial Balance
How Do You Prepare a Post-Closing Trial Balance?

A post-closing trial balance is prepared at the end of the accounting period to prove that the general ledger accounts are in balance after all adjusting and closing entries have been posted. **Figure 20–3** shows the post-closing trial balance for On Your Mark.

As You READ

Key Point

Post-Closing Trial Balance The post-closing trial balance and the balance sheet list the same account balances.

On Your Mark Athletic Wear		
Post-Closing Trial Balance		
December 31, 20--		
Cash in Bank	15 1 7 9 00	
Accounts Receivable	10 4 0 4 00	
Merchandise Inventory	81 3 8 5 00	
Supplies	1 8 3 9 00	
Prepaid Insurance	1 3 7 5 00	
Delivery Equipment	19 8 3 1 00	
Office Equipment	9 8 2 5 00	
Store Equipment	5 2 0 0 00	
Accounts Payable		13 8 5 0 00
Fed. Corp. Income Tax Payable		1 5 5 00
Employees' Fed. Income Tax Payable		6 4 0 00
Employees' State Income Tax Payable		8 0 00
Social Security Tax Payable		2 4 8 00
Medicare Tax Payable		5 8 00
Fed. Unemployment Tax Payable		1 8 36
State Unemployment Tax Payable		1 1 4 73
Sales Tax Payable		2 4 2 8 00
Capital Stock		75 0 0 0 00
Retained Earnings		52 4 4 5 91
Totals	145 0 3 8 00	145 0 3 8 00

Connect to... HISTORY

After the stock market crash in 1929 and the Great Depression that followed, Congress created the Securities and Exchange Commission (SEC) in 1934 to protect investors.

Figure 20–3 Post-Closing Trial Balance

As You READ

Compare and Contrast

Corporation and Sole Proprietorship How is closing the general ledger for these forms of businesses similar? How is it different?

Completing the Accounting Cycle for a Merchandising Business

What Is the Accounting Cycle for a Merchandising Business?

You have completed the study of the accounting cycle for a merchandising business organized as a corporation, which consists of the following steps:

1. Collect and verify source documents.
2. Analyze each business transaction.
3. Journalize each transaction.
4. Post to the general and subsidiary ledgers.
5. Prepare a trial balance.
6. Complete a work sheet.
7. Prepare the financial statements—income statement, statement of retained earnings, and balance sheet. Publicly held corporations also prepare a statement of cash flows.
8. Journalize and post the adjusting entries.
9. Journalize and post the closing entries.
10. Prepare a post-closing trial balance.

The accounting cycle for a service and a manufacturing business follows the same steps. Also, regardless of how a business is organized—sole proprietorship, partnership, or corporation—the basic steps of the accounting cycle are the same. **Figure 20–4** illustrates the accounting cycle.

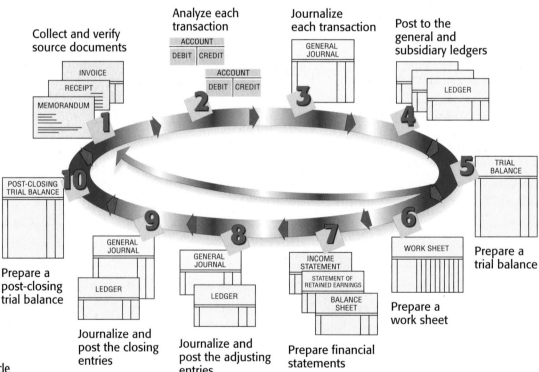

Figure 20–4
The Accounting Cycle

The accounting system used, whether manual or computerized, does not affect the steps in the accounting cycle. In a computerized accounting system, however, the computer performs many of the routine procedures such as posting.

AFTER YOU READ

Reinforce the Main Idea

Using a diagram like this one, describe the step-by-step process for posting a merchandising corporation's closing entries. Add or remove answer boxes as needed.

Posting a Merchandising Corporation's Closing Entries

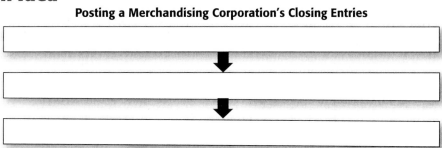

 ## Do the Math

Totals on the post-closing trial balance were assets, $156,000, and liabilities, $75,000. If the ending balance of **Retained Earnings** was $45,000, what was the capital stock account's ending balance?

Problem 20–2 Analyzing a Source Document

Instructions Review the source document and prepare the journal entry to record this transaction in your working papers. Your Backpack Inc. uses a cash payments journal to record disbursements.

Your Backpack Inc.
29000 White Road
Cold Springs, TX 77282-4513

MEMORANDUM
No. 42

TO: Robert Chan, Chief Accountant
FROM: James Perkins, President
DATE: July 12, 20--
SUBJECT: New Storage Facility Rent

Would you please make a check out to Warehouse Inc. for $750. The check is for the new storage facility we are renting. Please mail the check to:

Mr. James Skiller, Controller
Warehouse Inc.
7576 County Line Highway
Crossplains, TX 77361-8411

Problem 20–3 Organizing the Steps in the Accounting Cycle

Instructions List the following steps of the accounting cycle in their proper order. Use the form provided in your working papers or a separate sheet of paper.

Analyzing business transactions
Collecting and verifying source documents
Completing the work sheet
Journalizing business transactions
Journalizing and posting adjusting entries

Journalizing and posting closing entries
Posting journal entries to ledgers
Preparing financial statements
Preparing a post-closing trial balance
Preparing a trial balance

Key Concepts

1. The information for journalizing closing entries comes from the Income Statement section of the work sheet. Only three steps are necessary to close the temporary accounts of a corporate merchandising business.

   a. Close all temporary accounts with credit balances to **Income Summary.**

	DATE	DESCRIPTION	POST. REF.	DEBIT	CREDIT	
1	20--	*Closing Entries*				1
2	*Date*	Sales		xx xxx xx		2
3		Purchases Discounts		xx xxx xx		3
4		Purchases Returns and Allow.		xx xxx xx		4
5		Income Summary			xx xxx xx	5
6						6

   GENERAL JOURNAL PAGE __XX__

   b. Close all temporary accounts with debit balances to **Income Summary.**

   GENERAL JOURNAL PAGE __XX__

	DATE	DESCRIPTION	POST. REF.	DEBIT	CREDIT	
6	*Date*	Income Summary		xx xxx xx		6
7		Sales Discounts			x xxx xx	7
8		Sales Returns and Allow.			x xxx xx	8
9		Purchases			x xxx xx	9
10		Transportation In			x xxx xx	10
11		Expense Account			x xxx xx	11
12		Expense Account			x xxx xx	12
13		Expense Account			x xxx xx	13
14						14

   c. Close the balance of **Income Summary** to the **Retained Earnings** account.

   GENERAL JOURNAL PAGE __XX__

	DATE	DESCRIPTION	POST. REF.	DEBIT	CREDIT	
1		*Closing Entries*				1
22	*Date*	Income Summary		x xxx xx		22
23		Retained Earnings			x xxx xx	23
24						24

2. After you have recorded closing entries in the general journal, post them to the general ledger. Write *Closing Entry* in the Description column of the general ledger account. Refer to **Figure 20–2** on pages 593–597 to review a partial general ledger at the end of the accounting period.

3. A post-closing trial balance is prepared at the end of the accounting period to prove that the general ledger accounts are in balance, that is, their debits equal their credits. The following is an example of a post-closing trial balance.

On Your Mark Athletic Wear
Post-Closing Trial Balance
December 31, 20--

Account	Debit	Credit
Cash in Bank	15 1 7 9 00	
Accounts Receivable	10 4 0 4 00	
Merchandise Inventory	81 3 8 5 00	
Supplies	1 8 3 9 00	
Prepaid Insurance	1 3 7 5 00	
Delivery Equipment	19 8 3 1 00	
Office Equipment	9 8 2 5 00	
Store Equipment	5 2 0 0 00	
Accounts Payable		13 8 5 0 00
Fed. Corp. Income Tax Payable		1 5 5 00
Employees' Fed. Income Tax Payable		6 4 0 00
Employees' State Income Tax Payable		8 0 00
Social Security Tax Payable		2 4 8 00
Medicare Tax Payable		5 8 00
Fed. Unemployment Tax Payable		1 8 36
State Unemployment Tax Payable		1 1 4 73
Sales Tax Payable		2 4 2 8 00
Capital Stock		75 0 0 0 00
Retained Earnings		52 4 4 5 91
Totals	145 0 3 8 00	145 0 3 8 00

4. The basic accounting cycle is the same whether

- the business is a service provider or merchandiser
- the business is organized as a sole proprietorship, corporation, or partnership
- the business uses a manual or computerized accounting system

The following illustrates the complete accounting cycle.

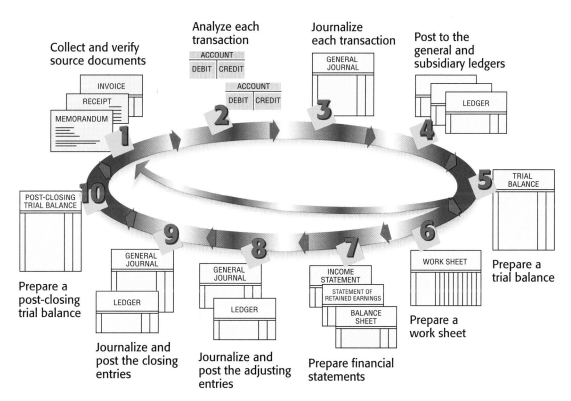

Check Your Understanding

1. **Journalizing the Closing Entries**
   a. Which account(s) are used to close temporary accounts with debit and credit balances?
   b. How are temporary accounts with debit balances closed?
2. **Posting the Closing Entries**
   a. What is written in the Description column of the general ledger account as the closing entries are posted?
   b. What is entered in the Posting Reference column of the general ledger account?
3. **Post-Closing Trial Balance**
   a. What is the purpose of preparing a post-closing trial balance?
   b. Does the **Income Summary** account appear on the post-closing trial balance? Why or why not?
4. **Accounting Cycle**
   a. Name the 10 steps in the accounting cycle.
   b. Which tasks in the accounting cycle are performed automatically in a computerized accounting system?

Apply Key Terms

The following key terms were introduced in Chapter 10. Let's review the terms as they relate to a merchandising corporation such as PETsMART. What differences exist between the closing entries for a sole proprietorship and the closing entries for a merchandising corporation? Use the following terms in your explanation.

closing entries	temporary accounts
permanent accounts	

Closing the Fiscal Year

Making the Transition from a Manual to a Computerized System

Task	Manual Methods	Computerized Methods
Closing a fiscal year	• Journalize the entries to close the revenue, expense, Income Summary, and Withdrawals accounts. • Post the closing entries.	• Closing the fiscal year is performed only if you want to clear income and expense accounts at the end of the fiscal year. • If you have selected the closing option, the software journalizes closing entries.
Preparing a post-closing trial balance	• After the closing entries have been posted to the ledger, prepare a trial balance to verify the equality of debits and credits. • All expense and revenue accounts should have zero balances.	• A post-closing trial balance can be printed to verify that all revenue and expense accounts have been closed.

Peachtree® Q & A

Peachtree Question	Answer
What tasks should I perform before closing a fiscal year?	1. Post and print all journal entries and reports before you close the fiscal year. 2. Back up all files before closing. Closing the fiscal year cannot be reversed.
How do I close the fiscal year?	1. From the *Tasks* menu, select **System**. 2. Choose **Year-End Wizard**. 3. You will be prompted if any procedures need to be completed before the system continues the closing process.

QuickBooks Q & A

QuickBooks Question	Answer
What tasks should I perform before closing a fiscal year?	1. Post and print all journal entries and reports before you close the fiscal year. 2. Back up the company file before closing.
How do I close the fiscal year?	1. From the *Company* menu, select **Set Up Users**. 2. Click **Closing Date**. 3. Enter the date on which you want to close your books and enter a password.

For detailed instructions, see your Glencoe Accounting Chapter Study Guides and Working Papers.

Complete problems using: | **Manual** Glencoe Working Papers | OR | **Peachtree Complete Accounting** Software | OR | **QuickBooks** Templates | OR | **Spreadsheet** Templates

Peachtree®

SMART GUIDE

Step–by–Step Instructions: Problem 20–4

1. Select the problem set for Sunset Surfwear (Prob. 20–4).
2. Rename the company and set the system date.
3. Choose **System** from the *Tasks* menu and then select **Year-End Wizard** to close the fiscal year.
4. Print a post-closing trial balance.
5. Complete the Analyze activity.
6. End the session.

TIP: Choose the General Ledger Trial Balance report whenever you are instructed to print a Post-Closing Trial Balance.

Problem 20–4 Journalizing Closing Entries

The following amounts appeared in the Income Statement section of Sunset Surfwear's work sheet.

Instructions In your working papers, record the closing entries for the year ended December 31. Start with general journal page 13.

	ACCT. NO.	ACCOUNT NAME	INCOME STATEMENT DEBIT	INCOME STATEMENT CREDIT
13	310	Income Summary		7 000 00
14	401	Sales		90 000 00
15	405	Sales Discounts	1 000 00	
16	410	Sales Returns and Allowances	2 400 00	
17	501	Purchases	25 000 00	
18	505	Transportation In	3 000 00	
19	510	Purchases Discounts		500 00
20	515	Purchases Returns and Allowances		1 500 00
21	625	Federal Corporate Income Tax Exp.	5 532 00	
22	635	Insurance Expense	300 00	
23	650	Miscellaneous Expense	600 00	
24	655	Rent Expense	12 000 00	
25	665	Supplies Expense	450 00	
26	675	Utilities Expense	14 000 00	
27			69 682 00	99 000 00
28		Net Income	29 318 00	
29			99 000 00	99 000 00
30				

Analyze Identify the effect of the closing entries on the Retained Earnings account.

Problem 20–5 Journalizing and Posting Closing Entries

The following account balances appeared in the Income Statement section of the work sheet of Shutterbug Cameras.

Instructions

1. Journalize the closing entries for the year ended December 31. Start with page 14 of a general journal (in your working papers).
2. Post the closing entries to the general ledger accounts, which are included in your working papers.

	ACCT. NO.	ACCOUNT NAME	INCOME STATEMENT	
			DEBIT	CREDIT
20	310	Income Summary	4 000 00	
21	401	Sales		150 000 00
22	410	Sales Returns and Allowances	5 000 00	
23	501	Purchases	90 000 00	
24	505	Transportation In	5 000 00	
25	510	Purchases Discounts		1 000 00
26	515	Purchases Returns and Allowances		1 500 00
27	620	Federal Corporate Income Tax Exp.	4 700 00	
28	645	Miscellaneous Expense	300 00	
29	650	Rent Expense	6 000 00	
30	660	Supplies Expense	1 630 00	
31	670	Utilities Expense	3 000 00	
32			119 630 00	152 500 00
33		Net Income	32 870 00	
34			152 500 00	152 500 00
35				

Analyze Describe what would happen if the accountant for Shutterbug Cameras made a mistake and did not close the Transportation In account.

Problem 20–6 Identifying Accounts for Closing Entries

A partial list of the accounts used by Cycle Tech Bicycles appears on page 606. All of the accounts have nonzero balances.

CONTINUE

Peachtree®

SMART GUIDE

Step–by–Step Instructions: Problem 20–5

1. Select the problem set for Shutterbug Cameras (Prob. 20–5).
2. Rename the company and set the system date.
3. Close the fiscal year.
4. Print a post-closing trial balance.
5. Complete the Analyze activity.
6. End the session.

QuickBooks

PROBLEM GUIDE

Step–by–Step Instructions: Problem 20–5

1. Restore the Problem 20-5.QBB file.
2. Enter the closing entries.
3. Print a post-closing trial balance.
4. Complete the Analyze activity.
5. Back up your work.

Peachtree®

SMART GUIDE

Step–by–Step Instructions:
Problem 20–6

1. Select the problem set for Cycle Tech Bicycles (Prob. 20–6).
2. Rename the company and set the system date.
3. Print a Chart of Accounts report.
4. List the accounts that will be debited and those that will be credited when closed.
5. Complete the Analyze activity.
6. End the session.

General Ledger

    101 Cash in Bank
    650 Miscellaneous Expense
    125 Merchandise Inventory
    665 Supplies Expense
    215 Sales Tax Payable
    505 Transportation In
    305 Retained Earnings
    401 Sales
    405 Sales Discounts
    310 Income Summary
    501 Purchases
    515 Purchases Returns and Allowances
    601 Advertising Expense
    625 Federal Corporate Income Tax Expense
    657 Rent Expense
    135 Prepaid Insurance

Instructions In your working papers, list all account numbers and names for accounts that will be debited when closed. Next, list all account numbers and names for accounts that will be credited when closed.

Analyze Examine your list. Determine whether it contains all of the accounts. If it does not, explain why.

SPREADSHEET SMART GUIDE

Step–by–Step Instructions:
Problem 20–7

1. Select the spreadsheet template for Problem 20–7.
2. Enter your name and the date in the spaces provided on the template.
3. Complete the spreadsheet using the instructions in your working papers.
4. Print the spreadsheet and proof your work.
5. Complete the Analyze activity.
6. Save your work and exit the spreadsheet

Problem 20–7 Completing End-of-Period Activities

The general ledger accounts for River's Edge Canoe & Kayak as of December 31, the end of the period, appear in the working papers.

Instructions In your working papers:

1. Prepare a trial balance on a ten-column work sheet.
2. Complete the work sheet. Use the following adjustment information.

Merchandise inventory, December 31	$20,000
Supplies inventory, December 31	900
Unexpired insurance, December 31	1,800
Total federal corporate income taxes for the year	2,965

3. Prepare an income statement from the work sheet information.
4. Prepare a statement of retained earnings.
5. Prepare a balance sheet.
6. Journalize and post the adjusting entries. Begin on general journal page 14.
7. Journalize and post the closing entries.
8. Prepare a post-closing trial balance.

Analyze Conclude whether the company made a profit for the year.

CHALLENGE PROBLEM

Problem 20–8 Preparing Adjusting and Closing Entries

In the middle of the end-of-period activities, the accountant for Buzz Newsstand was called away because of an illness in the family. Before leaving, the accountant prepared the work sheet and the financial statements. However, the business manager can locate only the trial balance shown here (before adjustments) and the income statement shown on page 608.

Instructions In your working papers:

1. Journalize the adjusting and closing entries on page 16 of the general journal.
2. Using the information provided, prepare a post-closing trial balance.

		Buzz Newsstand	
		Trial Balance, Before Adjustments	
		December 31, 20--	
101	Cash in Bank	12 035 00	
115	Accounts Receivable	6 106 00	
130	Merchandise Inventory	64 800 00	
135	Supplies	3 916 00	
140	Prepaid Insurance	5 400 00	
145	Delivery Truck	46 106 00	
201	Accounts Payable		4 690 00
204	Fed. Corp. Income Tax Pay.		
215	Sales Tax Payable		416 00
301	Capital Stock		40 000 00
305	Retained Earnings		24 603 00
310	Income Summary		
401	Sales		299 156 00
410	Sales Returns and Allowances	9 500 00	
501	Purchases	168 624 00	
505	Transportation In	8 236 00	
510	Purchases Discounts		2 950 00
515	Purchases Returns and Allowances		2 108 00
601	Advertising Expense	4 000 00	
625	Fed. Corp. Income Tax Expense	12 500 00	
635	Insurance Expense		
650	Miscellaneous Expense	1 600 00	
660	Salaries Expense	26 900 00	
665	Supplies Expense		
675	Utilities Expense	4 200 00	
	Totals	373 923 00	373 923 00

Peachtree®

SMART GUIDE

**Step–by–Step Instructions:
Problem 20–8**

1. Select the problem set for Buzz Newsstand (Prob. 20–8).
2. Rename the company and set the system date.
3. Print a Working Trial Balance to help you prepare the adjustments.
4. Record the adjustments using the **General Journal Entry** option.
5. Print a General Journal report and proof your work.
6. Complete the Analyze activity.
7. Close the fiscal year.
8. Print a post-closing trial balance.
9. End the session.

TIP: Peachtree automatically updates the general ledger accounts when you close the fiscal year.

QuickBooks

PROBLEM GUIDE

**Step–by–Step Instructions:
Problem 20–8**

1. Restore the Problem 20-8.QBB file.
2. Print a Trial Balance.
3. Record the adjustments.
4. Print a Journal report.
5. Complete the Analyze activity.
6. Enter the closing entries.
7. Print a post-closing trial balance.
8. Back up your work.

CONTINUE

Problems

Buzz Newsstand						
Income Statement						
For the Year Ended December 31, 20--						
Revenue:						
Sales				299 1 5 6 00		
Less: Sales Ret. and Allow.				9 5 0 0 00		
Net Sales					289 6 5 6 00	
Cost of Merch. Sold:						
Merch. Inv., Jan 1, 20--				64 8 0 0 00		
Purchases	168 6 2 4 00					
Plus: Transportation In	8 2 3 6 00					
Cost of Del. Merch.		176 8 6 0 00				
Less: Purch. Discounts	2 9 5 0 00					
Purch. Ret. and Allow.	2 1 0 8 00	5 0 5 8 00				
Net Purchases				171 8 0 2 00		
Cost of Merch. Avail.				236 6 0 2 00		
Merch. Inv., Dec. 31, 20--				60 4 0 0 00		
Cost of Merch. Sold					176 2 0 2 00	
Gross Profit on Sales					113 4 5 4 00	
Operating Expenses:						
Advertising Expense				4 0 0 0 00		
Insurance Expense				1 8 0 0 00		
Miscellaneous Expense				1 6 0 0 00		
Salaries Expense				26 9 0 0 00		
Supplies Expense				2 7 4 4 00		
Utilities Expense				4 2 0 0 00		
Total Oper. Expenses					41 2 4 4 00	
Operating Income					72 2 1 0 00	
Less: Fed. Inc. Tax Exp.					14 9 1 3 00	
Net Income					57 2 9 7 00	

Analyze Determine the impact of adjusting entries on net income.

Practice your test-taking skills! The questions on this page are reprinted with permission from national organizations:

- Future Business Leaders of America
- Business Professionals of America

Use a separate sheet of paper to record your answers.

Future Business Leaders of America

MULTIPLE CHOICE

1. Closing entries for a corporation are made from information in a work sheet's

    a. Trial Balance columns.

    b. Adjustments columns.

    c. Income Statement columns.

    d. Balance Sheet columns.

    e. none of these answers

2. The procedure for transferring information from a journal to ledger accounts is called

    a. journalizing.

    b. adjusting.

    c. file maintenance.

    d. posting.

    e. none of these answers

3. Proving the accuracy of the adjusting and closing entries is best defined as

    a. preparing a post-closing trial balance.

    b. preparing the statements.

    c. closing the temporary accounts.

    d. adjusting the ledger accounts.

    e. none of these answers

4. To close the Income Summary account of a corporation with a net loss, the balance is closed into the

    a. Retained Earnings account with a debit.

    b. Retained Earnings account with a credit.

    c. account which caused the net loss with a debit.

    d. none of the above

Business Professionals of America

MULTIPLE CHOICE

5. Which of the following accounts is closed at the end of a fiscal period?

    a. Membership Fees Income

    b. Accounts Receivable

    c. Delivery Equipment

    d. Retained Earnings

Need More Help?

Go to glencoeaccounting.glencoe.com and click on **Student Center.** Click on **Winning Competitive Events** and select **Chapter 20.**

- **Practice Questions and Test-Taking Tips**
- **Concept Capsules and Terminology**

Completing the Accounting Cycle

1. What is the source of information for journalizing the closing entries?

2. How are temporary accounts with credit balances closed?

3. Describe the journal entry to record a net loss.

4. Analyze the closing of the **Income Summary** and **Retained Earnings** accounts when the business has net income and when it has a net loss.

5. Create a memory device to help you remember all the closing entries for a corporation.

6. Justify the use of only three closing entries for a corporation although a sole proprietorship uses four.

Merchandising Business: Department Store

You work in the accounting department for Pearl's, a trendy department store. The accounting manager asked you to review the work of an accounting intern who completed the closing process. Some temporary accounts in the post-closing trial balance still have balances.

INSTRUCTIONS

1. Explain how to tell which accounts should have zero balances after closing.

2. Explain how to determine which accounts have and have not been closed.

3. Suggest ways to explain to the intern why temporary accounts have zero balances after closing.

4. List human-relations skills you might use in your explanation to the intern.

Handling Sales Returns

Most retail stores give employees specific instructions on how to process a sales return. For example, a cash refund can only be given if cash was paid. Imagine that you work for a large sporting goods store like The Sports Authority. Your friend, Martin, comes in to return a sweatshirt he purchased recently. You know he purchased the sweatshirt on sale, but he wants you to give him a full refund.

ETHICAL DECISION MAKING

1. What are the ethical issues?

2. What are the alternatives?

3. Who are the affected parties?

4. How do the alternatives affect the parties?

5. What would you do?

Explaining Results

As you are completing the closing entries for the fourth quarter, you realize that your company, Dynamic Sound, has a net loss. You know that management is not aware that the fourth quarter financial statements are so bleak. Select a partner from your class and role-play an explanation of how the **Income Summary** and **Retained Earnings** accounts are affected by the loss. In your explanation, model customer service principles of accuracy, thoroughness, and respect.

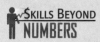
SKILLS BEYOND NUMBERS

Maintaining and Troubleshooting Technologies

In the accounting department of KidsWear Inc., you process the closing entries. This morning the printer will not print the ledgers or journals.

INSTRUCTIONS

List the steps you need to take to troubleshoot this problem. For each step indicate whom to call if the problem is not resolved.

INTERNATIONAL ACCOUNTING

Number Conventions

Many countries use decimal points instead of commas to separate thousands and use a comma instead of a decimal point as a decimal marker. For example the number 45,255.08 becomes 45.255,08.

INSTRUCTIONS Convert these numbers: (1) 121,309,411.98 (2) 74,520.229

Making It Personal

Your Stocks

Your future savings may include stock. Your stock investment becomes an asset for you and part of stockholders' equity for the company.

PERSONAL FINANCE ACTIVITY Choose a company to investigate as an investment. List how you could find the stock's current price.

PERSONAL FINANCE ONLINE Go to **glencoeaccounting.glencoe.com** and click on **Student Center.** Click on **Making It Personal** and select **Chapter 20.**

Analyzing FINANCIAL Reports

Calculating Return on Stockholders' Equity

One measure of a corporation's profitability is the return on stockholders' equity. It shows how much the business earned for each dollar invested by stockholders.

$$\frac{\text{Net Income}}{\text{Average Stockholders' Equity}} \quad \frac{\$20,990}{\$200,832} = 0.1045 \text{ or } 10.45\%$$

Average stockholders' equity = (beginning stockholders' equity + ending stockholders' equity) ÷ 2.

INSTRUCTIONS

Use PETsMART's financial statements in Appendix F to complete the following.

1. Calculate the return on stockholders' equity for the year ending February 1, 2004.
2. Explain why you think this calculation is important to potential buyers of a company's stock.

WebQuest

Closing the Books

How do business activities affect net income or net loss? Visit **glencoeaccounting .glencoe.com** and click on **Student Center.** Click on **WebQuest** and select **Unit 4** to continue your Internet project.

Accounting for Publicly Held Corporations

What You'll Learn

1. Describe the characteristics of the corporate form of business organization.

2. Prepare journal entries to record the issue of stock to investors.

3. Prepare journal entries to record the distribution of earnings to owners.

4. Prepare financial statements for publicly held corporations.

5. Define the accounting terms introduced in this chapter.

Why It's Important

▶ Many individuals and institutions buy the stock of publicly held corporations.

Predict

1. What does the chapter title tell you?
2. What do you already know about this subject from personal experience?
3. What have you learned about this in the earlier chapters?
4. What gaps exist in your knowledge of this subject?

Exploring the *Real World* of Business

ANALYZING CORPORATE STOCK

Hewlett-Packard

What do vitamins and network systems have in common? When Vitamin Shoppe, a high-quality vitamin retailer, decided to open 100 new stores in one month, **Hewlett-Packard (HP)** went to work. It designed and implemented standardized processes and equipment to connect all the new stores quickly. With **HP's** support, Vitamin Shoppe opened all its new stores on target.

You might think of your printer or computer when you hear **Hewlett-Packard's** name, but its information technology services department is one of the world's largest. Other satisfied clients include 7-11, Frontier Airlines, and Brandywine School District.

Investors like to hear success stories like these. They also like to see positive financial results, such as dividend payments to stockholders.

What Do You Think?

If you were considering purchasing stock in **Hewlett-Packard** or IBM, what factors would you investigate?

Working in the *Real World*

APPLYING YOUR ACCOUNTING KNOWLEDGE

Many people, both inside and outside the organization, review a corporation's financial reports. Some analyze the reports to decide whether to buy or sell stock in the company. Others evaluate the reports to decide whether to loan money to the company. Still others study the reports to plan for the future including staffing, purchasing, and budget plans. Because so many people make decisions based on financial reports, they must be prepared accurately.

Personal Connection

1. If your employer's financial statements are available, did it earn a profit last year?
2. If your employer's statements are not available, locate a public company's annual report on the Internet or in your library. Did it earn a profit or record a loss last year?

Online Connection

Go to **glencoeaccounting.glencoe.com** and click on **Student Center.** Click on **Working in the Real World** and select **Chapter 21.**

Publicly Held Corporations

BEFORE YOU READ

Main Idea
Investors from the general public purchase stock of publicly held corporations.

Read to Learn...
➤ the unique features of a corporation. (p. 614)
➤ how to account for the issue of stock. (p. 615)

Key Terms
closely held corporation
publicly held corporation
board of directors
authorized capital stock
par value
common stock
proxy
preferred stock
Paid-in Capital in Excess of Par

AS YOU READ

Key Point

Publicly Held and Closely Held Corporations A closely held corporation's stock is *not* sold to the public.

The United States has more sole proprietorships and partnerships than corporations. Corporations, however, account for more business activity than the other two forms of business combined. Many high profile companies like The Coca-Cola Company and General Motors are organized as corporations.

Characteristics of a Corporation

How Is a Corporation Different from Other Forms of Business Organization?

In Chapters 14 to 20 you learned to record business transactions for corporations. A **closely held corporation** is a corporation owned by a few persons or by a family. The stock of a closely held corporation is *not* sold to the general public.

In this chapter you will learn about transactions that apply specifically to *publicly held corporations*. A **publicly held corporation** is one whose stock is widely held, has a large market, and is usually traded on a stock exchange such as the New York Stock Exchange.

In previous chapters On Your Mark could have been either a closely held or publicly held corporation. In this chapter On Your Mark will illustrate transactions for a publicly held corporation.

The corporation has several unique features:

- **Legal Permission to Operate**—To operate a business as a corporation, its incorporators (organizers) file an application with state officials for permission to operate. When the application has been approved, it becomes the corporation's *charter*. The charter indicates the purpose of the business and spells out the rules under which the business is to operate. The charter also states the type and amount of stock a corporation is authorized to issue.

- **Separate Legal Entity**—A corporation is a separate legal entity that is created and exists only by law. A corporation may enter into contracts, borrow money, and conduct business in the same manner as a person. It may acquire, own, and sell property in its name. It can also sue and be sued in the courts.

- **Stockholders**—The ownership of a corporation is divided into units called *shares of stock*. The owners of a corporation are called *stockholders*. Each stockholder receives a *stock certificate* as proof of ownership. The stock certificate lists the name of the stockholder, the number of shares issued, and the date the shares were issued.

- **Professional Management**—Stockholders own the corporation, but they do not manage it. The stockholders elect a board of directors, who govern and are responsible for the affairs of the corporation.

Capital Stock

How Do You Measure Ownership of a Corporation?

Stockholders' equity is the value of the stockholders' claims to the corporation's assets. As you learned in Chapter 19, corporations report stockholders' equity in two parts:

- the equity paid into the corporation by stockholders
- the equity earned by the corporation and retained in the business

The maximum number of shares a corporation may issue is called its **authorized capital stock**. The authorized number of shares is usually much higher than the number of shares the corporation plans to sell right away. This allows the corporation to sell additional shares at a later time.

State laws may require that an amount or value be assigned to each share of stock before the corporation sells it to the public. The amount assigned to each share is referred to as **par value**, the per-share dollar amount printed on the stock certificates. The par value is used to determine the amount credited to the capital stock account. Par values of $1, $5, and $25 are common.

The corporate charter specifies the types of capital stock that a corporation may issue. The two main types of stock are *common* and *preferred*.

Common Stock

If the corporation issues only one class of capital stock, it is called **common stock**. The owners of common stock participate in the corporation as follows:

- Elect the board of directors and, through it, exercise control over the operations of the corporation. Stockholders are entitled to one vote for each share of stock they own. The election occurs at the stockholders' meeting, which is usually held once a year. If a stockholder cannot attend the meeting, he or she may send in a **proxy**, which gives the stockholder's voting rights to someone else.
- Share in the earnings of the corporation by receiving dividends declared by the board of directors.
- Are entitled to share in the assets of the corporation if it goes out of business.

Preferred Stock

To appeal to as many investors as possible, a corporation may also issue preferred stock. **Preferred stock** has certain privileges (or preferences) over common stock. Preferred stockholders participate as follows:

- Are entitled to receive dividends before common stockholders. The preferred stock dividend is stated in specific dollars, such as $6, or as a percentage of the stock's par value, such as 6 percent. The stock itself is then referred to as "preferred $6 stock" or "preferred 6% stock."

As You READ
In Your Own Words

Capital Stock In your own words, explain the meaning of *capital stock*.

As You READ
It's Not What It Seems

Par Value *Par value* is a fixed amount and is almost never the current value of a share of stock. A stock's current selling price on the stock market is called *market value*.

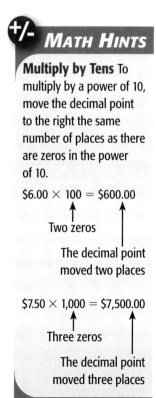

+/− MATH HINTS

Multiply by Tens To multiply by a power of 10, move the decimal point to the right the same number of places as there are zeros in the power of 10.

$6.00 × 100 = $600.00

Two zeros

The decimal point moved two places

$7.50 × 1,000 = $7,500.00

Three zeros

The decimal point moved three places

- Are given preference over common stockholders to distributions of the corporate assets should the company go out of business.

In return for these special privileges, the preferred stockholders give up two rights:

- to vote
- to participate in the control of the corporation.

Usually, investors buy preferred stock to receive the stated dividend.

Issuing Common Stock

When a corporation issues common stock, the **Common Stock** account is credited for the par value of the stock. Let's look at some examples.

Issuing Common Stock at Par Value. When On Your Mark was incorporated, it had the following transaction.

Business Transaction

On January 3 On Your Mark Athletic Wear issued 10,000 shares of $10 par common stock at $10 per share. On Your Mark received $100,000 for the shares, Memorandum 3.

JOURNAL ENTRY

	DATE		DESCRIPTION	POST. REF.	DEBIT	CREDIT	
1	20--						1
2	Jan.	3	Cash in Bank		100 000 00		2
3			Common Stock			100 000 00	3
4			Memorandum 3				4
5							5

GENERAL JOURNAL   PAGE 46

Issuing Common Stock in Excess of Par Value. Investors are often willing to pay more than par value for the stock of a corporation. When a corporation sells its stock at a price that is above par, the excess over par is credited to a separate stockholders' equity account called **Paid-in Capital in Excess of Par**. Paid-in Capital in Excess of Par appears in the chart of accounts immediately following the **Common Stock** account. The amounts recorded in this account are not profits to the corporation. Instead, they represent part of the stockholders' investment in the corporation. This account follows the same rules of debit and credit as other stockholders' equity accounts.

Paid-in Capital in Excess of Par	
Debit	Credit
−	+
Decrease Side	Increase Side
	Normal Balance

As You READ

Key Point

Recording the Issuance of Common Stock
When a corporation issues common stock, it credits
- **Common Stock** for the par value of the stock.
- **Paid-in Capital in Excess of Par** for any amount received in excess of par value.

One year after On Your Mark was incorporated, it had the following transaction.

Business Transaction

On January 5 On Your Mark issued 5,000 shares of $10 par common stock at $11.50 per share, Memorandum 147. On Your Mark received $57,500 for the shares.

Before recording the transaction, determine how much of the $57,500 is credited to **Common Stock** and how much is credited to **Paid-in Capital in Excess of Par.**

Credit to **Common Stock:**
    5,000 shares at $10 par value $50,000
Credit to **Paid-in Capital in Excess of Par:**
    5,000 shares at $1.50
    ($11.50 issue price − $10.00 par value) per share + 7,500
Total cash received $57,500

Remember, the amount credited to the **Common Stock** account is the par value of the shares issued.

JOURNAL ENTRY

	DATE		DESCRIPTION	POST. REF.	DEBIT	CREDIT	
1	20--						1
2	Jan.	5	Cash in Bank		57 500 00		2
3			Common Stock			50 000 00	3
4			Paid-in Cap. in Ex. of Par			7 500 00	4
5			Memorandum 147				5
6							6

GENERAL JOURNAL   PAGE __99__

Issuing Preferred Stock

When preferred stock is issued, a corporation credits the **Preferred Stock** account for the stock's par value. Preferred stock is almost always issued at its par value.

On Your Mark was incorporated on January 3. It was authorized to issue 1,000 shares of preferred stock with a par value of $100 and a stated dividend of $6. The next day the company had the following transaction.

Business Transaction

On January 4 On Your Mark issued 250 shares of preferred $6 stock, $100 par, at $100 per share. On Your Mark received $25,000 for the shares, Memorandum 5.

JOURNAL ENTRY

GENERAL JOURNAL   PAGE __47__

	DATE		DESCRIPTION	POST. REF.	DEBIT	CREDIT	
1	20--						1
2	Jan.	4	Cash in Bank		25 000 00		2
3			Preferred Stock			25 000 00	3
4			Memorandum 5				4
5							5

Reinforce the Main Idea

Create a chart like this one to compare common stock and preferred stock. Add answer rows as needed.

Characteristic	Common Stock	Preferred Stock

Do the Math

A corporation sells 3,000 shares of $25 par common stock and receives $97,500. How much did each share sell for? What was the per share amount of paid-in capital in excess of par?

Problem 21–1 Examining Capital Stock Transactions

Dublin Corporation was organized and authorized to issue 10,000 shares of $100 par, preferred 8% stock and 500,000 shares of $10 par common stock. The three transactions recorded in the following T accounts took place during the first month of operations.

Instructions In your working papers, describe each of the three transactions.

Cash in Bank		Preferred Stock	
Debit	Credit	Debit	Credit
+	–	–	+
(1) 300,000			(2) 200,000
(2) 200,000			
(3) 700,000			

Common Stock		Paid-in Capital in Excess of Par	
Debit	Credit	Debit	Credit
–	+	–	+
	(1) 300,000		(3) 200,000
	(3) 500,000		

Distribution of Corporate Earnings

In Section 1 you learned to record stock issue transactions for a corporation. In this section you will learn how corporations distribute earnings to the stockholders. Corporations like General Motors have a long history of distributing a portion of earnings to their stockholders every year, making their stock an attractive investment.

Dividend Accounts

What Are Corporate Dividends?

When an owner of a sole proprietorship or a partnership wishes to take money out of the business, a check is written on the checking account of the business. The amount of the check is recorded as a debit in the owner's withdrawals account, which reduces the owner's equity.

The owners (stockholders) of a publicly held corporation cannot withdraw cash whenever they want. Instead, they receive dividends. A **dividend** is a distribution of cash to stockholders. Dividends reduce retained earnings.

The corporation's board of directors *declares,* or authorizes, dividends. Before a dividend is declared, the corporation should have a sufficient amount of cash available to pay the dividend. In addition, since dividends decrease retained earnings, there must be an adequate balance in the **Retained Earnings** account. **Figure 21–1** on page 620 illustrates the important dates in the dividend process.

A separate account named **Dividends** is used to record dividends declared. The **Dividends** account is a contra-stockholders' equity account. At the end of the accounting period, the **Dividends** account is closed to the **Retained Earn-**

Dividends	
Debit + Increase Side Normal Balance	Credit – Decrease Side

ings account. The rules of debit and credit for **Dividends** are shown in this T account. Notice that they are the opposite of the rules for the stockholders' equity accounts.

Dividend amounts could be debited directly to the **Retained Earnings** account. Most corporations, however, prefer to use a separate account so that the dividend amounts can be easily determined.

A liability account, **Dividends Payable**, is used to record the amount of dividends that will be paid on the payment date. Like all liability accounts, **Dividends Payable** is increased by credits and decreased by debits. The normal balance of the **Dividends Payable** account is a credit balance.

BEFORE YOU READ

Main Idea
A corporation distributes a portion of its earnings to stockholders in the form of dividends.

Read to Learn...
➤ how to account for dividends. (p. 619)
➤ how to record dividend transactions. (p. 620)

Key Terms
dividend

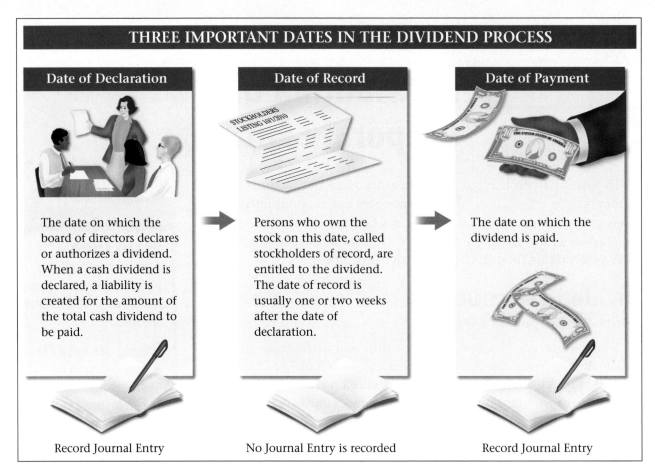

THREE IMPORTANT DATES IN THE DIVIDEND PROCESS

Date of Declaration	Date of Record	Date of Payment
The date on which the board of directors declares or authorizes a dividend. When a cash dividend is declared, a liability is created for the amount of the total cash dividend to be paid.	Persons who own the stock on this date, called stockholders of record, are entitled to the dividend. The date of record is usually one or two weeks after the date of declaration.	The date on which the dividend is paid.
Record Journal Entry	No Journal Entry is recorded	Record Journal Entry

Figure 21–1 Important Dates in the Dividend Process

Dividend Transactions
How Do You Journalize Dividend Transactions?

A corporation authorized to issue two types of stock uses separate dividend and dividend payable accounts for each type. On Your Mark uses these:

Dividends—Preferred	Dividends Payable—Preferred
Dividends—Common	Dividends Payable—Common

Let's look at the transactions involved when dividends are declared by the board of directors of On Your Mark during its second year of incorporation.

Dividends on Preferred Stock

As mentioned, preferred stockholders have certain preferences over common stockholders; one is the right to receive dividends before common stockholders. The preferred stock dividend amount is predetermined, or *stated*. The stated dividend indicates the amount to be paid to preferred stockholders per year. On Your Mark issued 250 shares of preferred $6 stock; that is, it will pay a $6 dividend for each share of preferred stock annually or in semiannual or quarterly installments:

Annually	$6.00	
Semiannually	$3.00	($6.00 ÷ 2)
Quarterly	$1.50	($6.00 ÷ 4)

Date of Declaration. A journal entry records the dividend on preferred stock on the *date of declaration,* the date the board declares it.

On November 15 On Your Mark's board of directors declared an annual cash dividend on the 250 shares of preferred $6 stock issued. It is payable to preferred stockholders of record on November 29 and will be paid on December 15. The total preferred dividends amount is $1,500 (250 shares × $6), Memorandum 215.

JOURNAL ENTRY

		GENERAL JOURNAL			PAGE 72	
	DATE	DESCRIPTION	POST. REF.	DEBIT	CREDIT	
1	20--					1
2	Nov. 15	Dividends—Preferred		1 500 00		2
3		Dividends Payable—Preferred			1 500 00	3
4		Memorandum 215				4

Date of Record. On November 29 the corporation checks its records and prepares a list of preferred stockholders entitled to receive the dividend. No journal entry is required on this date.

Date of Payment. On December 15 a check for $1,500, the total dividend payable on preferred stock, is written and deposited in a special dividends checking account. Separate checks written on this account are made payable to each preferred stockholder entitled to receive the dividend.

Business Transaction

On December 15 On Your Mark issued Check 1373 for $1,500 in payment of the dividend on preferred stock declared November 15.

JOURNAL ENTRY

		GENERAL JOURNAL			PAGE 81	
	DATE	DESCRIPTION	POST. REF.	DEBIT	CREDIT	
1	20--					1
2	Dec. 15	Dividends Payable—Preferred		1 500 00		2
3		Cash in Bank			1 500 00	3
4		Check 1373				4

Dividends on Common Stock

Dividends on common stock may be declared in one of two ways.

1. The board of directors may declare a dividend amount *per common share*. On Your Mark's board declared a 50¢ per common share dividend. It will pay a 50¢ dividend for each share of common stock.

2. The board may decide to declare the *total cash dividend* for both preferred and common stock. In this case the company first pays the preferred dividends and then divides the remainder equally among the common stockholders. For example, On Your Mark's board of directors declared a $3,000 total cash dividend. Preferred stockholders will receive $1,500 (250 shares × $6). It splits the remainder, $1,500 ($3,000 − $1,500), among the common stockholders. Each share of common stock receives a 10¢ dividend ($1,500 ÷ 15,000 shares).

Dividends on common stock, like preferred stock, can be paid annually, semiannually, or quarterly. Most publicly held corporations pay quarterly.

Reinforce the Main Idea

Create a diagram like this one to describe which accounts (if any) are debited and credited for each event.

Event	Account Debited	Account Credited
Dividend on common stock– date of declaration		
Dividend on common stock– date of record		
Dividend on common stock– date of payment		

Do the Math

On January 28 the board of directors for Jelly Bean Works declared an annual cash dividend on 200 shares of preferred $10 stock. What is the total amount of the dividend? How is this dividend accounted for in the company's books?

Problem 21–2 Distributing Corporate Earnings

During its first year of operation, Longhorn Corporation issued 17,500 shares of $10 par common stock. At the end of the year, the corporation had a net income of $350,000. The board of directors declared a cash dividend of $5 per share.

Instructions Answer these questions in your working papers. 1.) How much of the net income did Longhorn distribute to the stockholders? 2.) How much of the net income did the corporation retain?

Problem 21–3 Analyzing a Source Document

This memorandum contains data about the first quarter dividend on the common stock of Rob Williams Thrift Market Inc.

Instructions Prepare the journal entries to record the following in your working papers. Use general journal page 18.

- declaration of the dividend
- payment of the dividend, Check 221

> **Rob Williams Thrift Market Inc.**
> 2347 Eastern Parkway
> Orange, IA 50322-6922
>
> MEMORANDUM 37
>
> TO: Chief Financial Officer
> FROM: Albert MacFish, Chairman of the Board
> DATE: April 8, 20--
> SUBJECT: 1st quarter dividend
>
> On April 1, 20--, the board of directors declared a $1 per share dividend on the 5,679 shares of common stock issued. The date of record is April 15, 20--. The date of payment is April 30, 20--.

CONTROLLER

National Association of Black Accountants,
Inc. (NABA), Greenbelt, Maryland
Reginald Nance

Q: What does NABA do?

A: We work to expand the influence of minority professionals in the fields of accounting and finance.

Q: What are your day-to-day responsibilities?

A: I manage the overall finances of the organization. I make sure cash flow is where it should be and the financials are in order. Basically, I ensure that all revenue and expenses are accounted for properly. If it has to do with finance, it goes through me.

Q: What do you like most about your job?

A: I like that my job allows me to see the basis of the business. If you know how an organization is doing financially, you can determine where it is going. From a nonprofit standpoint, I enjoy the peace of mind of knowing that I'm working for something greater than just the bottom line—I'm helping the community at large.

Q: What is most challenging about your job?

A: The most challenging aspect is managing deadlines. An efficient time-management system is necessary to keep on top of things.

Q: What advice do you have for accounting students interested in becoming controllers?

A: Sit for the CPA exam as soon as possible. It is looked upon as a high achievement in the industry and will allow you to advance your career quickly. Also, identify a mentor; I've been fortunate to find several mentors in my career. And develop your written and oral communication skills as much as possible.

Tips from . . .

Robert Half International Inc.

You may have little idea what salary to expect when presented with your first job offer. Determine fair market compensation by conducting research on the Internet, reading industry publications, and contacting staffing firms like Robert Half International for annual salary publications.

CAREER FACTS

▶ **Nature of the Work:** Coordinate and prepare financial statements; design and implement internal control policies and procedures; hire, train, and retain accounting staff.

▶ **Training or Education Needed:** A bachelor's degree in accounting or finance; a master's degree in business administration; CPA or CMA designation is preferred; at least seven years of experience.

▶ **Aptitudes, Abilities and Skills:** Solid communication skills, technology skills, organizational skills, and management skills.

▶ **Salary Range:** $60,000 to $150,000 depending on location, level of responsibility and company revenues.

▶ **Career Path:** Gain public accounting experience, and then accept a position in a corporate environment, such as accounting manager, director of accounting, or assistant controller.

Thinking Critically | What kind of advice would you ask of a mentor?

Financial Reporting for a Publicly Held Corporation

BEFORE YOU **READ**

Main Idea
Corporate financial statements report stock issues and dividends.

Read to Learn...
➤ about a corporate income statement. (p. 624)
➤ how and why corporations prepare a statement of stockholders' equity (p. 624)
➤ about a corporate balance sheet. (p. 625)
➤ about a corporate statement of cash flows. (p. 626)

Key Terms
statement of stockholders' equity

Many corporations prepare a statement of stockholders' equity instead of a statement of retained earnings. This section examines the information reported on the statement of stockholders' equity, how this statement is prepared, and how stockholders' equity is reported on a corporation's balance sheet.

The Income Statement
Does a Publicly Held Corporation's Income Statement Differ from That of a Closely Held Corporation?

The income statement of a publicly held corporation is similar to that prepared by a closely held corporation. Remember, the federal corporate income taxes paid by a corporation are reported separately on the income statement.

The Statement of Stockholders' Equity
What Is a Statement of Stockholders' Equity?

In Chapter 19 you learned how to prepare a statement of retained earnings for a closely held corporation. That statement reports the changes in the **Retained Earnings** account during the period. It showed:

Retained Earnings, beginning balance
+ Net Income
Retained Earnings, ending balance

An increasing number of corporations prepare a statement of stockholders' equity rather than a statement of retained earnings. In contrast to the statement of retained earnings, the **statement of stockholders' equity** reports the changes in *all* stockholders' equity accounts during the period. It also provides information about the transactions affecting stockholders' equity during the period. The information reported on a statement of stockholders' equity includes

- the number of shares of each type of stock issued,
- the total amount received for those shares,
- the net income or net loss for the period, and
- dividends declared during the period.

Figure 21–2 shows the statement of stockholders' equity for On Your Mark at the end of its second year of incorporation. The information needed to prepare the statement comes from the work sheet and from the general ledger accounts. The statement is prepared as follows:

On Your Mark Athletic Wear Statement of Stockholders' Equity For the Year Ended December 31, 20--	$100 Par Preferred $6 Stock	$10 Par Common Stock	Paid-in Capital in Excess of Par	Retained Earnings	Totals	
1 Balance, January 1, 20--	25 000 00	100 000 00		27 600 00	152 600 00	1
2 Issuance of 5,000 shares of common stock		50 000 00	7 500 00		57 500 00	2
3 Net Income				13 525 00	13 525 00	3
4 Cash Dividends:						4
5 Preferred Stock				(1 500 00)	(1 500 00)	5
6 Common Stock				(7 500 00)	(7 500 00)	6
7 Balance, December 31, 20--	25 000 00	150 000 00	7 500 00	32 125 00	214 625 00	7
8						8

Figure 21–2 Statement of Stockholders' Equity

- The names of the four stockholders' equity accounts appear at the top of the amount columns. There is also a Totals column at the far right.
- The first line shows the balance of each account at the beginning of the period.
- The next lines describe various transactions affecting the stockholders' equity accounts, such as issuance of stock, net income, and dividends declared. The transactions are described in the left column. The increase or decrease amounts are recorded in the individual account columns and in the Totals column. For example, the second line on the statement indicates that the company issued 5,000 shares of common stock during the period. The issuance of the 5,000 shares increased the balance of the **Common Stock** account by $50,000. Since the shares were issued at a price above par value, the **Paid-in Capital in Excess of Par** account increased by $7,500.
- The final line shows the balance of each account at period-end.

As you review **Figure 21–2**, notice that the amounts that decrease account balances, like dividends declared, are enclosed in parentheses. The cash dividends declared are listed separately for preferred and common stock. Also notice that the Retained Earnings column of the statement of stockholders' equity contains the same information that is reported on a statement of retained earnings. Remember that net income increases retained earnings, and dividends declared decrease retained earnings. The statement of stockholders' equity is used to prepare the corporation's balance sheet.

The Balance Sheet

How Do You Prepare the Stockholders' Equity Section of the Balance Sheet?

The assets and liabilities sections of a balance sheet for a publicly held corporation are similar to those of a balance sheet for a closely held corporation. Notice in **Figure 21–3** on page 626 that the **Dividends Payable** accounts are reported in the liabilities section. Since On Your Mark paid the

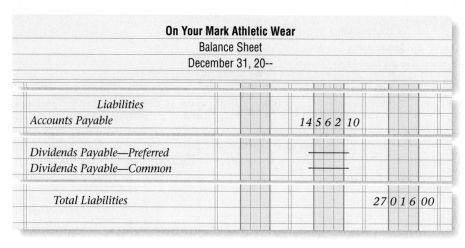

On Your Mark Athletic Wear

Balance Sheet

December 31, 20--

Liabilities				
Accounts Payable		14 5 6 2 10		
Dividends Payable—Preferred		—		
Dividends Payable—Common		—		
Total Liabilities			27 0 1 6 00	

Figure 21–3 Reporting the Balances of the Dividends Payable Accounts on the Balance Sheet

dividends before the end of the year, it reports zero balances in these liability accounts.

The stockholders' equity section of a publicly held corporation's balance sheet is more detailed than that of a closely held corporation. As you can see in **Figure 21–4**, each type of stock issued by On Your Mark is listed separately under the heading "Paid-in Capital." Preferred stock is listed before common stock. Each listing describes the following:

- the par value,
- the number of shares authorized, and
- the number of shares issued.

The **Dividends** accounts are not listed in the stockholders' equity section because they are closed to **Retained Earnings** at the end of the year. Thus, the retained earnings amount shown on the balance sheet has been reduced by the dividends declared during the period.

The Statement of Cash Flows
Where Are Stock Issues and Dividends Reported on This Statement?

The Financing Activities section of the statement of cash flows reflects activities related to ownership of the corporation. A stock issue results in a cash inflow from a financing activity. Payment of dividends is a cash outflow.

On Your Mark Athletic Wear

Balance Sheet

December 31, 20--

Stockholders' Equity					
Paid-in Capital:					
$6 Preferred Stock, $100 par, 1,000 shares authorized,					
250 shares issued	25 0 0 0 00				
Common stock, $10 par, 20,000 shares authorized,					
15,000 shares issued	150 0 0 0 00				
Paid-in Capital in Excess of Par	7 5 0 0 00				
Total Paid-in Capital			182 5 0 0 00		
Retained Earnings			32 1 2 5 00		
Total Stockholders' Equity				214 6 2 5 00	
Total Liabilities and Stockholders' Equity				241 6 4 1 00	

Figure 21–4 The Stockholders' Equity Section of the Balance Sheet

AFTER
YOU **READ**

Reinforce the Main Idea

Create a chart like this one to identify the financial statement on which each of the following appear: cash dividends, common stock, dividends payable, paid-in capital in excess of par, preferred stock, retained earnings. Add answer rows as needed.

Statement of Stockholders' Equity	Balance Sheet

Do the Math

Ron Kanai, president of Sunny Days, a Hawaiian-based sun care products manufacturer and retailer, is looking for a buyer. He believes an analysis of stock prices and dividends will appeal to potential corporate buyers. As the company's accounting manager, use spreadsheet, accounting, or graphics software to prepare the following information in a clustered column chart showing the stock price and dividends declared for the past two years. What does the chart say about Sunny Days' financial condition that could attract potential buyers?

	Year 1				Year 2			
	Q1	Q2	Q3	Q4	Q1	Q2	Q3	Q4
Stock Price	13.50	13.60	14.90	17.00	17.50	20.00	23.00	25.50
Dividend Declared	2.50	2.50	2.90	3.00	3.25	3.50	4.90	4.95

Problem 21–4 Examining the Statement of Stockholders' Equity

The following transactions of Victor Jewelry Corporation took place during the period.

Instructions Use the form in your working papers to indicate which of the transactions is reported on the statement of stockholders' equity.

Transactions:
1. Paid accounts payable of $50,000.
2. Issued 2,000 shares of $10 par common stock, receiving $15 per share.
3. The board of directors declared a cash dividend of $12,000 for all common stockholders.
4. Bought equipment on account at a total cost of $125,000.
5. Paid the cash dividend declared in Transaction 3.
6. Issued 500 shares of $100 par, $7 preferred stock.
7. Paid the federal income tax installment of $5,000.
8. Earned a net income of $150,000 for the period.

Key Concepts

1. The corporation has several unique characteristics:
   - legal permission from the state to operate
   - recognized as a separate legal entity
   - owned by stockholders
   - operated by professional managers hired by a board of directors that is elected by stockholders

   Two types of corporations are:
   - *closely held,* owned by a few persons or by a family
   - *publicly held,* whose stock is widely held, has a large market, and is usually traded on a stock exchange

2. Corporations may issue two types of stock, common and preferred. The T-account analysis of issuance of stock follows.

   a. Issuing preferred stock at par value:

Cash in Bank		Preferred Stock	
Debit	Credit	Debit	Credit
+	−	−	+
XXX			XXX

   b. Issuing common stock at par value:

Cash in Bank		Common Stock	
Debit	Credit	Debit	Credit
+	−	−	+
XXX			XXX

   c. Issuing common stock in excess of par (the issue of stock at a higher price than its par value):

Cash in Bank		Common Stock	
Debit	Credit	Debit	Credit
+	−	−	+
XXX			XXX

Paid-in Capital in Excess of Par	
Debit	Credit
−	+
	XXX
XXX	

3. Corporations may distribute part of their earnings to stockholders in the form of *dividends*. These are the journal entries required.

Event	Importance	Journal Entry Required
Dividend is declared	Corporation's board of directors votes to distribute earnings to owners.	Debit **Dividends** Credit **Dividends Payable**
Dividend date of record	The corporation makes a list to show who owns stock on the date of record.	No journal entry is made.
Dividend is paid	The corporation writes the dividend checks to owners.	Debit **Dividends Payable** Credit **Cash in Bank**
End of the year	The corporation closes the **Dividends** account.	Debit **Retained Earnings** Credit **Dividends**

4. Publicly held corporations prepare the following financial reports:

- income statement
- statement of stockholders' equity
- the balance sheet
- the statement of cash flows

The statement of stockholders' equity reports all changes in stockholders' equity accounts during the period. It usually replaces the statement of retained earnings. The statement of stockholders' equity includes information about

- the number of shares of each type of stock issued,
- the total amount received for those shares,
- net income (or loss) for the period, and
- the dividends declared during the period.

Refer to **Figure 21–2** on page 625 to review the statement of stockholders' equity.

Key Terms

authorized capital stock	(p. 615)	par value	(p. 615)
board of directors	(p. 615)	preferred stock	(p. 615)
closely held corporation	(p. 614)	proxy	(p. 615)
common stock	(p. 615)	publicly held corporation	(p. 614)
dividend	(p. 619)	statement of stockholders' equity	(p. 624)
Paid-in Capital in Excess of Par	(p. 616)		

AFTER YOU READ

Check Your Understanding

1. **Corporation Characteristics**
   a. Name three characteristics of a corporation.
   b. Explain the difference between a closely held corporation and a publicly held corporation.

2. **Record Stock Issue**
   a. When stock is sold at a price above its par value, what amount is credited to the capital stock account?
   b. What is the classification of the **Paid-in Capital in Excess of Par** account? What is its normal balance?

3. **Record Earnings Distribution**
   a. When a dividend is declared, which accounts are debited and which accounts are credited?
   b. Name and explain the three dates important to the dividend process.

4. **Corporate Financial Statements**
   a. What type of information is reported on the statement of stockholders' equity?
   b. Explain the difference between the statement of retained earnings and the statement of stockholders' equity.

Apply Key Terms

For each key term, give or find an example of the term in a newspaper, periodical, annual report, or on an Internet site. Then use the example in a sentence.

authorized capital stock	par value
board of directors	preferred stock
closely held corporation	proxy
common stock	publicly held corporation
dividend	statement of stockholders' equity
Paid-in Capital in Excess of Par	

Customizing Financial Statements

Making the Transition from a Manual to a Computerized System

Task	Manual Methods	Computerized Methods
Customizing financial statements	• Using accounting stationery, you may reorganize information or add details to financial statements.	• Accounting software gives you the option to select and sort data that appears on each financial statement. • You may also customize information on a report.

Peachtree® Q & A

Peachtree Question	Answer
How do I change the appearance or content of financial reports in Peachtree?	1. From the *Reports* menu, select **Financial Stmts.** 2. Select the report you wish to customize from the list. 3. Display it on the screen. 4. Select the **Design** icon above the report. 5. You can adjust the size of the columns, the types of information displayed in the report, the font style and size, and the report layout. 6. If you wish to save the report in the new format, rename the file, leaving the original files in their original form.
How do I filter information on preformatted reports?	1. After you have selected a report from the list, click **Preview** to display it on your screen. 2. At the **Filter** option, you may accept the current settings or make changes to the displayed fields. The information that can be filtered varies according to the report.

QuickBooks Q & A

QuickBooks Question	Answer
How do I change the appearance or content of financial reports in QuickBooks?	1. From the *Reports* menu, select **Company & Financial.** 2. Select the report you wish to customize. 3. Click the **Modify Report** button. You can adjust the size of columns, the types of information displayed in the report, the font style and size, and the report layout. 4. If you wish to save the report in the new format, click the **Memorize** button and give the report a new name.
How do I filter information on preformatted reports?	1. After you have selected a report, click the **Modify Report** button. 2. In the Filters tab, choose the item you wish to filter and enter the filter criteria. The information that can be filtered varies according to the report. 3. Click **OK**.

For detailed instructions, see your Glencoe Accounting Chapter Study Guides and Working Papers.

Complete problems using: **Manual** Glencoe Working Papers OR **Peachtree Complete Accounting** Software OR **QuickBooks** Templates OR **Spreadsheet** Templates

Peachtree®

SMART GUIDE

Step–by–Step Instructions: Problem 21–6

1. Select the problem set for InBeat CD Shop (Prob. 21–6).
2. Rename the company and set the system date.
3. Record all transactions using the **General Journal Entry** option.
4. Print a General Journal report and proof your work.
5. Complete the Analyze activity.
6. End the session.

QuickBooks

PROBLEM GUIDE

Step–by–Step Instructions: Problem 21–6

1. Restore the Problem 21-6.QBB file.
2. Record all transactions using the **Make General Journal Entries** option.
3. Print a Journal report and proof your work.
4. Complete the Analyze activity.
5. Back up your work.

Problem 21–5 Distributing Corporate Earnings

During the first year of operations, Sunset Surfwear issued 18,500 shares of $10 par common stock. At the end of the year, the corporation had net income of $380,000. The board of directors declared a $5 cash dividend per share of common stock.

Instructions Answer the following questions in your working papers:

1. How much of the net income earned for the year was paid to the common stockholders?
2. How much of the net income was retained by the corporation?

Analyze Compare the date of declaration and date of payment with the date of record. Explain what entry or action is required on each date.

Problem 21–6 Journalizing the Issue of Stock

On June 1 InBeat CD Shop was incorporated and authorized to issue 1,000 shares of $100 par, preferred 9% stock, and 10,000 shares of $25 par common stock.

Instructions In your working papers, record the following transactions on general journal page 1.

Date	Transactions
June 1	Issued 200 shares of preferred 9% stock at $100 per share, Memorandum 3.
2	Issued 3,000 shares of common stock at $25 per share, Memorandum 7.
6	Received $31 per share for 2,000 shares of common stock issued, Memorandum 10.
7	Issued 50 shares of preferred 9% stock at par, Memorandum 11.

Analyze Identify the stock issued at a price above par. Calculate the total amount of capital that InBeat CD Shop received in the first week of June.

Problem 21–7 Journalizing Common and Preferred Stock Dividend Transactions

Shutterbug Cameras issued 8,000 shares of $80 par, preferred 7% stock and 35,000 shares of $25 par common stock.

Instructions In your working papers:

1. Record the following transactions on general journal page 14.
2. Post the transactions to the general ledger accounts provided in your working papers. Net income was $296,490.

Date	Transactions
Oct. 15	The board of directors declared an annual cash dividend on the preferred 7% stock, payable on December 1, Memorandum 407.
Nov. 5	Declared an annual cash dividend of $1.25 on 35,000 shares of common stock, payable on December 17, Memorandum 415.
Dec. 1	Paid the dividend declared on October 15, Check 1163.
17	Paid the dividend declared on November 5, Check 1201.

Analyze Calculate the amount of dividends payable on common stock and dividends payable on preferred stock at the end of December.

SMART GUIDE

Step–by–Step Instructions: Problem 21–7

1. Select the problem set for Shutterbug Cameras (Prob. 21–7).
2. Rename the company and set the system date.
3. Record all transactions using the **General Journal Entry** option. Enter each transaction in the proper accounting period (month).
4. Print a General Journal report for the entire quarter and proof your work.
5. Print a General Ledger report.
6. Complete the Analyze activity.
7. End the session.

TIP: Set the date filter options to print a General Journal report that includes all of the entries for the quarter.

Problem 21–8 Preparing Corporate Financial Statements

River's Edge Canoe & Kayak is authorized to issue 10,000 shares of $100 par, preferred 9% stock and 500,000 shares of $5 par common stock. The following balances appeared in the Balance Sheet section of the company's work sheet for the year ended December 31.

Instructions

1. Prepare the statement of stockholders' equity.
   a. During the period the corporation issued 500 shares of 9% preferred stock at par and 25,000 shares of common stock at $9.
   b. The net income for the year was $425,000.
2. Prepare the balance sheet.

101 Cash in Bank	$506,010
115 Accounts Receivable	850,680
120 Notes Receivable	400,000
130 Merchandise Inventory	388,815
135 Prepaid Ins.	3,600
140 Supplies	10,500
145 Delivery Truck	139,298
150 Store Equipment	363,009
201 Accounts Payable	62,412
202 Dividends Payable—Preferred	22,500

SPREADSHEET SMART GUIDE

Step–by–Step Instructions: Problem 21–8

1. Select the spreadsheet template for Problem 21–8.
2. Enter your name and the date in the spaces provided on the template.
3. Complete the spreadsheet using the instructions in your working papers.
4. Print the spreadsheet and proof your work.
5. Complete the Analyze activity.
6. Save your work and exit the spreadsheet program.

CONTINUE

203 Dividends Payable—Common	$150,000
210 Fed. Corp. Income Tax Payable	20,000
215 Sales Tax Payable	4,500
301 Preferred Stock	500,000
303 Common Stock	750,000
304 Paid-in Capital in Excess of Par	300,000
305 Retained Earnings	735,000
307 Dividends—Common	262,500
308 Dividends—Preferred	45,000

Analyze **Identify the total stockholders' equity on December 31.**

Peachtree®

SMART GUIDE

Step–by–Step Instructions:
Problem 21–9

1. Select the problem set for Buzz Newsstand (Prob. 21–9).
2. Rename the company and set the system date.
3. Record all transactions. Enter each transaction in the proper accounting period (month).
4. Print a General Journal report and proof your work.
5. Print a Balance Sheet.
6. Complete the Analyze activity.
7. End the session.

SOURCE DOCUMENT PROBLEM

Problem 21–9

Use the source documents in your working papers to complete this problem.

QuickBooks

PROBLEM GUIDE

Step–by–Step Instructions:
Problem 21–9

1. Restore the Problem 21-9.QBB file.
2. Record all transactions.
3. Print a Journal report and proof your work.
4. Print a Balance Sheet.
5. Complete the Analyze activity.
6. Back up your work.

CHALLENGE PROBLEM

Problem 21–9 Recording Stockholders' Equity Transactions

Buzz Newsstand is authorized to issue 100,000 shares of $5 par common stock and 5,000 shares of $100 par, preferred 8% stock. On January 1, the beginning of the period, the stockholders' equity accounts had the following balances:

301 Preferred Stock	$150,000
302 Paid-in Capital in Excess of Par—Preferred	11,250
303 Common Stock	225,000
304 Paid-in Capital in Excess of Par—Common	112,500
305 Retained Earnings	366,800
307 Dividends—Preferred	0
308 Dividends—Common	0

Instructions In your working papers:

1. Record the following transactions on general journal page 42. Close the **Dividends** and **Retained Earnings** accounts.
2. Prepare the stockholders' equity section of the balance sheet.

Date	Transactions
Mar. 15	The board of directors approved a semiannual cash dividend of $62,250 for both preferred and common stockholders. The dividend is payable to stockholders of record as of April 15 with payment on May 1, Memorandum 635.
Apr. 19	Issued 500 shares of preferred stock at $108, Memorandum 651.
May 1	Paid the dividends declared on March 15, Check 1256.
Sept. 1	The board of directors approved a semiannual cash dividend of $79,250 for both preferred and common stockholders. The dividend is payable to stockholders of record as of October 1 with payment on November 1, Memorandum 828.
Nov. 1	Paid the dividend declared on September 1, Check 2451.

Analyze **Compare the December 31 Retained Earnings balance with the beginning balance of $366,800. Why did the balance change?**

Practice your test-taking skills! The questions on this page are reprinted with permission from national organizations:

- Future Business Leaders of America
- Business Professionals of America

Use a separate sheet of paper to record your answers.

Future Business Leaders of America

MULTIPLE CHOICE

1. Earnings distributed to stockholders are called
- a. retained earnings.
- b. revenue.
- c. capital gains.
- d. dividends.
- e. none of these answers

2. _____ stock is the type of stock issued by a corporation when only one class of stock is issued.
- a. Preferred
- b. Common
- c. Capital
- d. Dividend

3. When 10,000 shares of $10 par-value common stock are issued at $14 per share, Paid-In Capital in Excess of Par, Common Stock is credited for
- a. $140,000.
- b. $40,000.
- c. $100,000.
- d. none of the above

4. When a dividend is paid in cash, the accounts debited and credited are
- a. Dividends Received and Dividends Payable.
- b. Cash and Dividends Payable.
- c. Dividends Payable and Cash.
- d. Common Stock and Cash.

Business Professionals of America

MULTIPLE CHOICE

5. A legal form that asks stockholders to transfer their voting rights is called a
- a. security.
- b. proxy.
- c. preemptive right.
- d. stock split.

Need More Help?

Go to **glencoeaccounting.glencoe.com** and click on **Student Center.** Click on **Winning Competitive Events** and select **Chapter 21.**
- **Practice Questions and Test-Taking Tips**
- **Concept Capsules and Terminology**

CHAPTER 21 — Real-World Applications and Connections

Publicly Held Corporations

1. What is a publicly held corporation?
2. Describe the components of stockholders' equity.
3. Summarize the accounting entries when a corporation sells 200 shares of 9% preferred stock, with a par value of $100, for $125 per share.
4. Compare and contrast preferred and common stock.
5. Write a rule expressing when a dividend becomes a liability for a corporation. Explain the reason for the rule.
6. Justify the fact that corporations that sell their stock for an amount in excess of par cannot record the excess as profit.

Merchandising Business: Coffee Shop

Cyber Café is a retail store that sells a variety of coffees, gourmet pastries, and other snacks. The store also offers computer stations where customers can surf the Web.

Early success helped the owners of Cyber Café to incorporate and franchise the business. They now have franchises in 15 cities and want to raise additional money to open cafés in Japan.

INSTRUCTIONS

1. List at least three ways the business could raise money for the new franchises.
2. If you were considering investing in Cyber Café, describe the ratios and analyses you would calculate from its financial statements.
3. Explain how these calculations would help you make an investment decision.

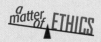

Using Insider Information

You are an accountant for a large shipping company, like United Parcel Service (UPS). Through your work, you learn that your company is planning to buy a company that makes shipping containers. It's a small company whose stock is traded on the stock exchange. You think about purchasing several thousand shares of this company's stock, expecting to make a profit when your company purchases it.

ETHICAL DECISION MAKING

1. What are the ethical issues?
2. What are the alternatives?
3. Who are the affected parties?
4. How do the alternatives affect the parties?
5. What would you do?

Describing Corporations

You work for a locally owned partnership that was just purchased by a corporation. You decide to share information about corporations with your co-workers. Create a one-page information sheet identifying the characteristics of a corporation. Write a paragraph explaining each characteristic.

Working in Teams

Annabelle Bradly owns Aussie Diners in Australia and North America. The corporation is considering going public and offering common stock on the New York Stock Exchange. She calls you to invite the North American executive management team to meet before she makes the final decision to go public.

INSTRUCTIONS

1. Describe how to get all executive management team members together quickly.
2. In groups of five, role-play holding an executive team meeting. Each student will be a manager: Marketing, Accounting, Personnel, Facilities, or Purchasing. List your department's concerns about going public.

World Federation of Exchanges

The World Federation of Exchanges (WFE) is the trade organization for regulated securities markets and organizations that serve the industry. Over 97 percent of the world's exchanges belong to the WFE, including the New York Stock Exchange and the Tokyo Stock Exchange. Enforcement, trading policies, business conduct, and self-regulation are a few of the issues that it studies.

INSTRUCTIONS Locate the WFE Web site and describe its general mission.

Your Investment Choices

In some ways your future depends on how well you plan for financial security. You can make wiser investment decisions when you know the choices available.

PERSONAL FINANCE ACTIVITY Use the library or Internet to find basic information about stock, bond, and real estate investments. Explain which investment most appeals to you and why.

PERSONAL FINANCE ONLINE Log on to **glencoeaccounting.glencoe.com** and click on **Student Center.** Click on **Making It Personal** and select **Chapter 21.**

Evaluating Stockholders' Equity

The statement of stockholders' equity provides details about changes in the stockholders' equity accounts during the period. This information helps investors and analysts better understand the company's capital. Successful companies earn money for future operations (reported as retained earnings) through sales and rely less on raising new capital through the issuance of stock.

INSTRUCTIONS Use PETsMART's statement of stockholders' equity in Appendix F to answer these questions.

1. Explain how retained earnings changed from a balance of $40,239,000 in 2003 to a balance of $174,053,000 in 2004.
2. How much did additional paid-in capital increase during this same time?

Why Invest?

Not all companies pay dividends. So, why invest? Visit **glencoeaccounting .glencoe.com** and click on **Student Center.** Click on **WebQuest** and select **Unit 4** to continue your Internet project.

Accounting for Special Procedures

STANDARD &POOR'S

Personal Finance Q & A

Q: I already know the accounting cycle; why do I need to learn special procedures?

A: A lot happens in Step 2 of the accounting cycle: *Analyze each transaction.* Many transactions are not as straightforward as those discussed so far.

Q: Can I continue to use the same method to analyze transactions?

A: Yes, and also use the basic accounting assumptions such as the matching principle, revenue recognition, and accounting period.

THINK IT OVER

Do you think individuals have special financial activities in their personal lives? Name some financial activities an individual or family might experience that are not everyday occurrences.

WebQuest Internet Project

The Magic of Matching

A company can pay millions of dollars for an office building. A small business might buy just a used truck and a computer, as Roadrunner Delivery Service did in Unit 2. In this project you will find out how to use the matching principle to assign asset costs to the revenue they generate.

Log on to **glencoeaccounting.glencoe.com** and click on **Student Center.** Click on **WebQuest** and select **Unit 5.** Begin your WebQuest by reading the Task.

Continue working on your WebQuest as you study Unit 5.

Chapter	23	24	25
Page	695	725	749

BusinessWeek THE BIG PICTURE

PRICEY PLACES Most expensive areas for commercial real estate.

CITY	RENT, PER SQUARE FOOT
LONDON, WEST END	$137.31
TOKYO	102.56
PARIS	89.28
NEW YORK, MIDTOWN	71.53
MOSCOW	67.73

Data: Cushman & Wakefield

Source: Reprinted by permission from *BusinessWeek.*

What You'll Learn

1. Record the entry to establish a change fund.

2. Prove the cash in the cash register drawers each business day.

3. Open and replenish a petty cash fund.

4. Journalize opening a petty cash fund.

5. Prepare a petty cash requisition to replenish the petty cash fund.

6. Use a petty cash register to record petty cash disbursements.

7. Journalize replenishing a petty cash fund.

8. Determine whether cash is short or over, and record the shortage or overage.

9. Define the accounting terms introduced in this chapter.

Why It's Important

▶ Cash is an asset, and it must be protected.

BEFORE YOU READ

Predict

1. What does the chapter title tell you?
2. What do you already know about this subject from personal experience?
3. What have you learned about this in the earlier chapters?
4. What gaps exist in your knowledge of this subject?

Exploring the *Real World* of Business

PROTECTING CASH

Applebee's International

Applebee's International owns restaurants with great food *and* work environments. Applebee's is a People Report™ "Heart of the Workplace Award" winner. This honor is given to companies that go the extra mile to care for employees and support their efforts to give back to the community.

The average guest spends about $10 on a meal at Applebee's, so you can imagine its daily cash inflow. Applebee's employees follow company rules for all financial transactions, including specific policies for cash control and record retention. Restaurants keep cash on hand to make change for customers and pay for small expenses like delivery fees or office supplies. Accounting for and protecting this cash is an important function in managing each restaurant.

What Do You Think?

What documentation should businesses like Applebee's International keep for small cash payments?

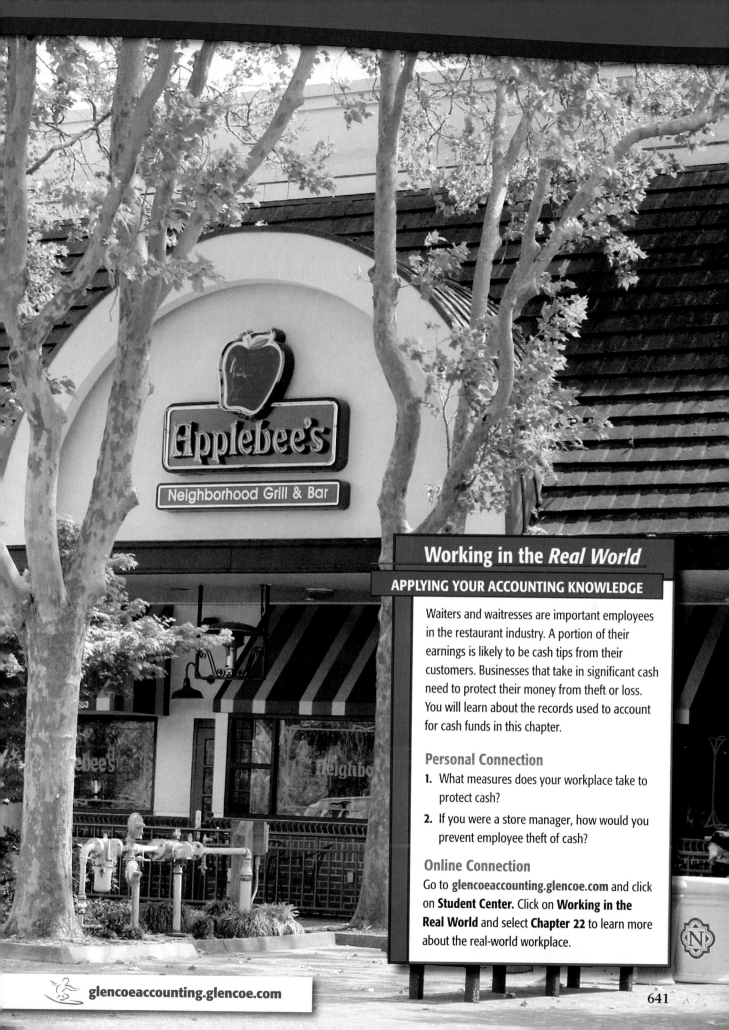

Working in the *Real World*

APPLYING YOUR ACCOUNTING KNOWLEDGE

Waiters and waitresses are important employees in the restaurant industry. A portion of their earnings is likely to be cash tips from their customers. Businesses that take in significant cash need to protect their money from theft or loss. You will learn about the records used to account for cash funds in this chapter.

Personal Connection

1. What measures does your workplace take to protect cash?
2. If you were a store manager, how would you prevent employee theft of cash?

Online Connection

Go to **glencoeaccounting.glencoe.com** and click on **Student Center.** Click on **Working in the Real World** and select **Chapter 22** to learn more about the real-world workplace.

The Change Fund

Main Idea
Some businesses keep cash on hand to make change for customers. The accounts used for this cash are **Change Fund** and **Cash Short & Over.**

Read to Learn...
➤ how and why to set up a change fund. (p. 642)
➤ how to use the change fund. (p. 643)
➤ how to record a discrepancy in the change fund. (p. 644)

Key Terms
change fund

In earlier chapters you learned that businesses use checking accounts for depositing cash receipts and making cash payments. Merchandising businesses, such as Sears or Blockbuster, keep some cash on hand so that they can make change for customers who pay for purchases with cash.

Establishing a Change Fund
What Is a Change Fund?

A change fund is an amount of money, consisting of varying denominations of bills and coins, that is used to make change in cash transactions. For example, a customer who pays for a $13.80 purchase with a $20 bill will receive $6.20 in change.

When a business first establishes a change fund, the amount needed for the fund is estimated. The size of the fund does not change unless the business finds that it needs more or less change than it had originally estimated. The change fund is established by writing a check for the amount of the fund. The check is made payable to the person in charge of the change fund. That person cashes the check and places the bills and coins in the cash register drawer. The transaction is recorded in an asset account called **Change Fund.** Let's look at On Your Mark's establishment of a change fund as an example.

Business Transaction

On May 1 the accountant for On Your Mark wrote Check 2150 for $100 to establish a change fund.

ANALYSIS	*Identify* *Classify* +/−	1. The accounts affected are **Change Fund** and **Cash in Bank.**
		2. Both **Change Fund** and **Cash in Bank** are asset accounts.
		3. **Change Fund** is increased by $100. **Cash in Bank** is decreased by $100.

DEBIT-CREDIT RULE	4. Increases to asset accounts are recorded as debits. Debit **Change Fund** for $100.
	5. Decreases to asset accounts are recorded as credits. Credit **Cash in Bank** for $100.

T ACCOUNTS

6.

Change Fund		Cash in Bank	
Debit + 100	Credit –	Debit +	Credit – 100

JOURNAL ENTRY

7.

GENERAL JOURNAL PAGE **32**

	DATE	DESCRIPTION	POST. REF.	DEBIT	CREDIT	
1	20--					1
2	May 1	Change Fund		100 00		2
3		Cash in Bank			100 00	3
4		Check 2150				4
5						5

If the business needs to increase the amount in the change fund, the accountant writes a check for the amount of the cash increase. For example, suppose that On Your Mark needs to increase the change fund from $100 to $125. The amount of the check is $25. The journal entry debits **Change Fund** for $25 and credits **Cash in Bank** for $25. This brings the **Change Fund** account balance to $125.

Using the Change Fund
How Do You Use the Change Fund?

The amount of cash in the change fund is put into the cash register drawer at the beginning of the day. When a cash sale occurs, the salesclerk rings the sale on the cash register. The sale is automatically recorded on the cash register tape. At the end of the day, the cash in the cash register drawer is counted. A cash proof is prepared to verify that the amount of cash in the drawer equals the total cash sales for the day plus the change fund. The amount of cash in the change fund is set aside for use as change for the next day. The balance of the cash from the drawer is deposited in the checking account.

Let's look at an example. Suppose On Your Mark has $470 in the cash register drawer at the end of the day on May 15. The cash register tape shows that cash sales, including sales tax, total $370. **Figure 22–1** on page 644 shows the cash proof. As you can see, the amount of cash in the drawer at the end of the day minus the amount of cash in the change fund equals the total sales shown on the cash register tape.

Most businesses require that salesclerks sign the cash proof to indicate that they have counted the cash in the drawer and verified its accuracy, both when they receive the drawer and turn it in. The supervisor also checks these amounts and signs the cash proof. The cash proof form is attached to the cash register tape, which is the source document for recording the cash sales for the day.

As You READ

In Your Experience

Change How do you verify that the change you receive from a clerk after a purchase is correct?

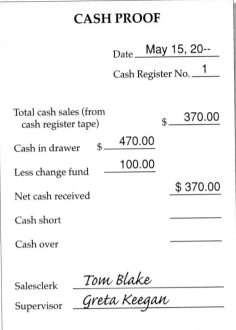

Figure 22–1 Cash Proof Form

Recording Cash Short and Over
What If Cash in the Drawer Does Not Match the Records?

Many cash transactions occur during each business day. Occasionally, a salesclerk makes an error and gives the incorrect amount of change to a customer. When this happens, the amount of cash in the cash register drawer, less the beginning change fund, does not agree with the cash sales amount recorded on the cash register tape. If the salesclerk gives a customer too much change, the amount of cash in the drawer at the end of the day is *short*, or less than it should be. If the salesclerk gives a customer too little change, the cash amount is *over*, or more than it should be.

The amount of cash either gained or lost because of errors is recorded in the **Cash Short & Over** account. **Cash Short & Over** is a temporary account. Because cash shortages are expenses to the business, they are recorded as debits to **Cash Short & Over.** Cash overages are revenue for the business; they are recorded as credits to the **Cash Short & Over** account. Note that the **Cash Short & Over** account does not have a normal balance.

Cash Short & Over	
Debit Cash Shortages	Credit Cash Overages

At the end of the accounting period, the balance of the **Cash Short & Over** account is closed to **Income Summary.** Let's look at an example of a shortage.

Business Transaction

On May 2 the cash register tape shows that cash sales are $520 and sales taxes are $26, for a total of $546. The actual cash in the cash register drawer, after subtracting the amount of the change fund, is $545.

T ACCOUNTS

Cash in Bank		Cash Short & Over	
Debit + 545	Credit −	Debit 1	Credit

Sales		Sales Tax Payable	
Debit −	Credit + 520	Debit −	Credit + 26

JOURNAL ENTRY

GENERAL JOURNAL PAGE _33_

	DATE	DESCRIPTION	POST. REF.	DEBIT	CREDIT	
1	20--					1
2	May 2	Cash in Bank		545 00		2
3		Cash Short & Over		1 00		3
4		Sales			520 00	4
5		Sales Tax Payable			26 00	5
6		Cash Proof—Cash reg. tape				6
7						7

The journal entry to record a cash overage is similar to that for a cash shortage. The only difference is that **Cash Short & Over** is *credited* for the amount of the overage.

In the previous example, suppose that the amount of cash in the drawer is $547 after the amount of the change fund is subtracted. The journal entry would debit **Cash in Bank** for $547 and credit **Cash Short & Over** for $1. The credits to **Sales** and **Sales Tax Payable** remain the same.

As You READ

Instant Recall

Debit-Credit Rules
Expenses are increased by debits. Revenue is increased by credits.

Reinforce the Main Idea

A business that uses a cash register prepares a cash proof each day. Create a diagram similar to this one to show the step-by-step method for proving cash and recording any discrepancy.

Proving Cash

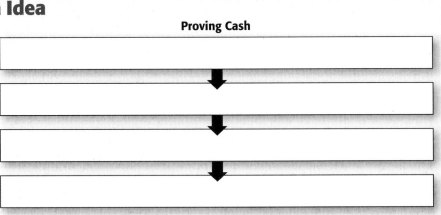

Do the Math

The Children's Consignment Shop operates primarily with cash transactions. One of your responsibilities is to prove cash register cash. The cash register tape showed cash received from sales and sales taxes collected to be $620.40. The count of cash in the drawer was: 16 $20 bills, 18 $10 bills, 26 $5 bills, 44 $1 bills, 66 quarters, 30 dimes, 52 nickels, and 130 pennies. The change fund is $75 dollars. What was the net cash received? Was cash short, over, or in balance? If the total sales tax Rate is 10%, what is the amount of cash sales and the sales tax payable?

Problem 22–1 Preparing a Cash Proof

The change fund for Messina's Grocery Store is $200 per cash register. On March 31 total cash sales from cash register 6 are $964 and sales taxes are $57.84. A count of cash shows $1,216.84 in the cash register drawer.

Mar 31
Tape 49

964.00 CA
57.84 ST

Instructions

1. Use the form in your working papers to prepare a cash proof. Sign your name as the salesclerk.
2. Record the March 31 cash sales on page 2 of a general journal.

Problem 22–2 Recording a Cash Overage

The change fund for Visions Hair Salon is $300 per register. On April 14, at the end of the business day, the manager counts the funds in the register. Cash sales total $1,496 and sales taxes amount to $89.77 in register 2. The cash drawer contains $1,895.77.

Instructions

1. Use the form in your working papers to prepare a cash proof. Sign your name as the salesclerk.
2. Record the April 14 cash sales and overage on page 4 of the general journal.

The Petty Cash Fund

Businesses often make small cash payments for delivery fees, postage stamps, supplies, and other similar purchases.

Establishing the Petty Cash Fund

What Is a Petty Cash Fund?

Small, incidental cash payments are made from the **petty cash fund** . The word *petty* indicates that only small amounts of cash are paid out of this fund. When setting up a petty cash fund, each business determines the maximum amount that will be paid out by a petty cash disbursement. A **petty cash disbursement** is any payment made from the petty cash fund. All payments over the maximum amount are paid by check. The person responsible for maintaining the petty cash fund and for making cash disbursements is called the **petty cashier** .

To establish a petty cash fund, a business estimates the amount of cash needed in the fund for a certain period of time, usually a month. This estimate is based on the company's past experiences.

On Your Mark decides to establish a petty cash fund. Crystal Casteel, an office clerk, is appointed petty cashier. The petty cash fund will contain $100. Any payments under $10 will be paid from the petty cash fund. Any payments over $10 will be paid by check. The company accountant, Greta Keegan, prepares a check for $100, payable to "Petty Cashier Crystal Casteel," to establish the fund. The transaction is recorded in an asset account called **Petty Cash Fund.** Crystal cashes the check and places the money, consisting of small denominations of bills and coins, in a petty cash box. For internal control purposes, the petty cash box is kept in an office safe or a locked desk drawer. Crystal is responsible for the $100 in the petty cash fund. When members of the staff need small amounts of cash for items like stamps or office supplies, Crystal will disburse the cash and store the receipts in the petty cash box. Let's learn how to journalize transactions to open a petty cash fund.

BEFORE YOU READ

Main Idea
Businesses use petty cash funds because writing checks for small amounts is impractical, costly, and time consuming.

Read to Learn…
➤ how and why to set up a petty cash fund. (p. 647)
➤ how to use the petty cash fund. (p. 648)
➤ how to record a discrepancy in the petty cash fund. (p. 653)

Key Terms
petty cash fund
petty cash disbursement
petty cashier
petty cash voucher
petty cash requisition
petty cash register

Business Transaction

On May 1 Check 2151 for $100 was issued to establish the petty cash fund.

ANALYSIS	*Identify*	1.	The accounts affected are **Petty Cash Fund** and **Cash in Bank**.
	Classify	2.	Both **Petty Cash Fund** and **Cash in Bank** are asset accounts.
	+/−	3.	**Petty Cash Fund** is increased by $100. **Cash in Bank** is decreased by $100.

| DEBIT-CREDIT RULE | **4.** Increases to asset accounts are recorded as debits. Debit **Petty Cash Fund** for $100. |
| | **5.** Decreases to asset accounts are recorded as credits. Credit **Cash in Bank** for $100. |

T ACCOUNTS

6.

Petty Cash Fund		Cash in Bank	
Debit + 100	Credit −	Debit +	Credit − 100

JOURNAL ENTRY

7.

GENERAL JOURNAL   PAGE ___32___

	DATE		DESCRIPTION	POST. REF.	DEBIT	CREDIT	
5	May	1	Petty Cash Fund		100 00		5
6			Cash in Bank			100 00	6
7			Check 2151				7
8							8

Sometimes petty cash disbursements occur more often than expected, and the petty cash fund is used up before the end of the specified time period. If this happens often, the company may decide to increase the fund's amount. To increase the petty cash fund, the accountant debits the **Petty Cash Fund** account and credits the **Cash in Bank** account for the amount of the increase.

Using the Petty Cash Fund

How Do You Use the Petty Cash Fund?

The petty cashier is responsible for making payments from the petty cash fund. Whenever a cash payment is made, a petty cash voucher is completed. A petty cash voucher is a proof of payment from the petty cash fund.

Figure 22–2 shows a petty cash voucher. These vouchers are usually prenumbered. If they are not, the petty cashier numbers them when issuing them.

The petty cash voucher includes the following information:

1. the date of the payment
2. the person or business to whom the payment is made
3. the amount of the payment
4. the reason for the payment
5. the account to be debited
6. the signature of the person approving the payment (usually the petty cashier)
7. the signature of the person receiving the payment

After the petty cash disbursement is made, the voucher is filed in the petty cash box until the fund is reimbursed.

PETTY CASH VOUCHER

No. 001   1 Date __May 2, 20--__

2 Paid to __Premier Office Supply Co.__   3 $ __7.10__

4 For __Printer paper__

5 Account __Supplies__

Approved by   Payment received by

6 *Crystal Casteel*   7 *John Marks*

Figure 22–2 Petty Cash Voucher

Replenishing the Petty Cash Fund

To *replenish* a petty cash fund means to restore the fund to its original cash balance. As the cashier makes payments from the fund, the amount of cash in the petty cash box decreases. Some businesses set a minimum amount that must be kept. When the amount of cash in the petty cash box reaches the minimum or a low amount, the accountant replenishes the petty cash fund.

On Your Mark replenishes its petty cash fund once a month, when the balance reaches the minimum amount, or at the end of the accounting period. Replenishing the petty cash fund affects the general ledger accounts that the petty cash disbursements impact (such as **Supplies** and **Delivery Fees**), which must be updated.

Replenishing the petty cash fund requires reconciling the cash balance in the fund and then preparing a petty cash requisition form.

Reconciling the Petty Cash Fund

The petty cashier reconciles the petty cash fund to determine whether it is in balance. To reconcile the petty cash fund, the petty cashier first adds all paid petty cash vouchers. This total is then subtracted from the original cash balance of the petty cash fund. The difference is the *reconciled petty cash balance,* or the amount of money that *should be* in the petty cash box. If the count of the cash in the petty cash box agrees with the reconciled balance, the petty cash fund is in balance. If the two amounts do not agree, the petty cash fund is either short or over.

On May 31 the total of all the petty cash vouchers for the month was $87.75. As you recall, the original petty cash balance was $100. The reconciled petty cash balance is:

Original balance	$100.00
Total of paid petty cash vouchers	− 87.75
Reconciled petty cash balance	$ 12.25

The amount of cash in the petty cash box that Crystal counted was $12.25. The petty cash fund, therefore, is in balance.

Preparing a Petty Cash Requisition Form

After reconciling the petty cash fund, the petty cashier prepares a **petty cash requisition**, which is a form requesting money to replenish the petty cash fund. **Figure 22–3** shows a typical petty cash requisition. This form serves as the source of information for the check written to replenish the petty cash fund. The check stub then serves as the source document for the entry recorded in the general journal.

To prepare the petty cash requisition, the petty cashier first sorts the paid petty cash vouchers by account and totals the vouchers for each account. The cashier records the account title and total amount to be debited to it on the petty cash requisition. Review **Figure 22–3** again. During May On Your Mark made petty cash disbursements affecting the general ledger accounts **Supplies**, **Delivery Expense**, **Miscellaneous Expense**, and **Advertising Expense**.

The total of all paid petty cash vouchers is the amount of cash needed to replenish the petty cash fund. After receiving the petty cash requisition from the petty cashier, the accountant writes a check for the total of the paid vouchers. The check is made payable to the petty cashier, who cashes the check and places the money in the petty cash box.

PETTY CASH REQUISITION

Accounts for which payments were made:	Amount
Supplies	$24.45
Delivery Expense	19.00
Miscellaneous Expense	29.50
Advertising Expense	14.80
TOTAL CASH NEEDED TO REPLENISH FUND	$87.75

Requested by: _Crystal Casteel_   Date _5/31/20--_

Approved by: _Greta Keegan_   Date _5/31/20--_

Check No. _2341_

Figure 22–3 Petty Cash Requisition

Using a Petty Cash Register

Some businesses use a **petty cash register** to record all disbursements made from the petty cash fund. The petty cash register is a supplemental record that summarizes the types of petty cash disbursements. It is not an accounting journal because amounts from it are not posted to general ledger accounts.

Recording Petty Cash Vouchers in a Petty Cash Register. Not all businesses that have a petty cash fund use a petty cash register. Those who do might use a form similar to that shown in **Figure 22–4.** This illustration shows a typical petty cash register with vouchers recorded. It shows the month's disbursements following the fund's establishment.

The establishment of the petty cash fund on May 1 is noted on line 2 of the register. On each line that follows, each petty cash payment is identified by date, voucher number, and a brief explanation. The amount of each disbursement is entered in the Payments column *and* in the appropriate Distribution of Payments column. The register has three special amount columns: Supplies, Delivery Expense, and Miscellaneous Expense. The General Amount column is used for petty cash payments that do not belong in one of the three special amount columns. This column has two subdivisions, one for the account name and the other for the amount.

Totaling and Proving the Petty Cash Register. Replenishing the petty cash fund requires totaling and proving the petty cash register. Refer to **Figure 22–4** as you read the following steps on totaling and proving a petty cash register:

1. Enter the date the fund is being replenished in the Date column. Also enter the word *Totals* in the Description column.

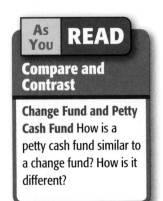

As You READ

Compare and Contrast

Change Fund and Petty Cash Fund How is a petty cash fund similar to a change fund? How is it different?

2. Single rule the amount columns.

3. Foot each amount column.

4. Verify that the total of the Payments column is equal to the total of the Distribution of Payments columns.

Payments		Distribution of Payments
	$24.45	Supplies
	19.00	Delivery Expense
	29.50	Miscellaneous Expense
	14.80	Advertising Expense
$87.75 =	$87.75	

Once verified, the totals are recorded below the footings.

5. Draw a double rule under the amount columns to show that the totals have been proved.

6. You will now enter the petty cash fund replenishment information. Skip one line, and then enter the reconciled petty cash balance (the amount of cash that *should be* in the petty cash box before it is replenished). For On Your Mark, that amount is $12.25.

7. On the next line, write the amount of the check written to replenish the petty cash fund.

8. Add the balance that *should be* in the petty cash fund and the amount of the check. The sum should equal the original amount of the petty cash fund.

PETTY CASH REGISTER　　　　　PAGE ___1___

	DATE	VOU. NO.	DESCRIPTION	PAYMENTS	DISTRIBUTION OF PAYMENTS			GENERAL		
					SUPPLIES	DELIVERY EXPENSE	MISC. EXPENSE	ACCOUNT NAME	AMOUNT	
1	20--									1
2	May 1	—	Est. Petty Cash ($100)							2
3	2	1	Printer paper	7 10	7 10					3
4	3	2	Postage on incoming mail	2 50			2 50			4
5	4	3	Newspaper Ad.	9 80				Adv. Expense	9 80	5
6	5	4	Gas & Parking	9 50			9 50			6
7	7	5	Daily newspaper	3 50			3 50			7
8	8	6	Collect telegram	1 25			1 25			8
9	10	7	Pens and pencils	2 50	2 50					9
10	12	8	Dara's Delivery Service	9 50		9 50				10
11	16	9	Daily newspaper	3 50			3 50			11
12	18	10	Memo pads	8 45	8 45					12
13	20	11	Postage stamps	1 00			1 00			13
14	22	12	Ad in H.S. yearbook	5 00				Adv. Expense	5 00	14
15	26	13	File folders	6 40	6 40					15
16	29	14	Dara's Delivery Service	9 50		9 50				16
17	30	15	Gas & tolls	8 25			8 25			17
18	31		Totals	87 75	24 45	19 00	29 50		14 80	18
19										19
20			Reconciled bal.	$ 12.25						20
21			Replen. check	+87.75						21
22			Total	$100.00						22
23										23

Figure 22–4 A Typical Petty Cash Register

As You READ

Key Point

Petty Cash Fund There are only two instances when the **Petty Cash Fund** account is debited.
- to initially establish the fund
- to increase the amount of money in it

As you can see, the petty cash register helps the petty cashier keep track of the petty cash disbursements by account. When the petty cash fund is replenished, the totals of the special columns and the amounts recorded in the General column are listed on the petty cash requisition form.

Using a Petty Cash Envelope

Small businesses sometimes use *petty cash envelopes* to record petty cash disbursements. A form very similar to the petty cash register is printed on the front of the petty cash envelope. Petty cash disbursements are recorded on the form on the envelope.

The paid petty cash vouchers are placed in the petty cash envelope. When the petty cash fund is replenished, the petty cash envelope, containing all paid vouchers for the period, is sealed and filed. A new envelope is used to record the next period's petty cash disbursements.

Journalizing the Check to Replenish the Petty Cash Fund

The check stub and the petty cash requisition are the source documents for recording the journal entry for a check written to replenish the petty cash fund. Let's learn how to journalize transactions to replenish a petty cash fund.

Notice that this transaction does not affect the **Petty Cash Fund** account. Replenishing petty cash requires crediting **Cash in Bank** and debiting the accounts for which petty cash payments were made.

Business Transaction

On May 31 Check 2341 is written to replenish the petty cash fund.

ANALYSIS	Identify	1. The accounts affected are **Supplies, Delivery Expense, Miscellaneous Expense, Advertising Expense,** and **Cash in Bank.**
	Classify	2. **Supplies** is an asset account. **Delivery Expense, Miscellaneous Expense,** and **Advertising Expense** are expense accounts. **Cash in Bank** is an asset account.
	+/−	3. **Supplies** is increased by $24.45. **Delivery Expense** is increased by $19. **Miscellaneous Expense** is increased by $29.50. **Advertising Expense** is increased by $14.80. **Cash in Bank** is decreased by $87.75.

DEBIT-CREDIT RULE	4. Increases in asset accounts are recorded as debits. Debit **Supplies** for $24.45. Increases in expense accounts are recorded as debits. Debit **Delivery Expense** for $19; and **Miscellaneous Expense** for $29.50. Debit **Advertising Expense** for $14.80.
	5. Decreases in asset accounts are recorded as credits. Credit **Cash in Bank** for $87.75.

T ACCOUNTS

6.

Supplies			Delivery Expense	
Debit + 24.45	Credit –		Debit + 19.00	Credit –

Miscellaneous Expense			Advertising Expense	
Debit + 29.50	Credit –		Debit + 14.80	Credit –

Cash in Bank	
Debit +	Credit – 87.75

JOURNAL ENTRY

7.

GENERAL JOURNAL PAGE __41__

	DATE	DESCRIPTION	POST. REF.	DEBIT	CREDIT	
1	20--					1
2	May 31	Supplies		24 45		2
3		Delivery Expense		19 00		3
4		Miscellaneous Expense		29 50		4
5		Advertising Expense		14 80		5
6		Cash in Bank			87 75	6
7		Check 2341				7
8						8

Handling Cash Short and Over in the Petty Cash Fund

How Do You Handle Shortages and Overages in the Petty Cash Fund?

The petty cashier could occasionally make an error when paying cash from the petty cash fund. This will cause the amount of cash in the petty cash box not to agree with the reconciled petty cash balance. Any amounts of cash *gained* or *lost* through errors made by the petty cashier are recorded in the **Cash Short & Over** account.

Let's look at an example. At the end of June, Crystal Casteel, On Your Mark's petty cashier, classified and totaled the petty cash vouchers. The accounts affected by the petty cash disbursements follow:

Supplies	$15.75
Delivery Expense	20.45
Miscellaneous Expense	21.80
Advertising Expense	25.00
	83.00

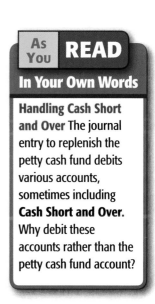

As You READ

In Your Own Words

Handling Cash Short and Over The journal entry to replenish the petty cash fund debits various accounts, sometimes including **Cash Short and Over.** Why debit these accounts rather than the petty cash fund account?

GENERAL JOURNAL   PAGE 43

	DATE		DESCRIPTION	POST. REF.	DEBIT	CREDIT	
1	20--						1
2	June	30	Supplies		15 75		2
3			Delivery Expense		20 45		3
4			Miscellaneous Expense		21 80		4
5			Advertising Expense		25 00		5
6			Cash Short & Over		1 50		6
7			Cash in Bank			84 50	7
8							8

Figure 22–5 Journal Entry to Replenish the Petty Cash Fund

The June petty cash disbursements totaled $83. Crystal then reconciled the petty cash fund.

Original balance	$100
Total of paid petty cash vouchers	− 83
Reconciled petty cash balance	$ 17

Crystal counted the cash in the petty cash box and found only $15.50—a shortage of $1.50 ($17.00 − 15.50). Bringing the petty cash fund up to the original $100.00 requires $84.50 ($83.00 + $1.50). The $1.50 cash shortage is an expense and is debited to the **Cash Short & Over** account.

When Crystal prepared the petty cash requisition form, she listed the accounts to be debited for the petty cash disbursements. She also indicated that the **Cash Short & Over** account is to be debited for $1.50. The journal entry to record the replenishment is shown in **Figure 22–5**.

A petty cash *overage* is recorded in a similar manner. If, for example, the cash in the petty cash box is $17.75, a cash overage of 75¢ exists. **Cash Short & Over** is credited for that amount in the journal entry. Instead of needing $83.00 to replenish the fund, only $82.25 is required.

The cash shortage or overage is also reported in the petty cash register if a business uses one. **Figure 22–6** shows how the June cash shortage of $1.50 is recorded in the petty cash register.

Figure 22–6 Recording a Cash Shortage in the Petty Cash Register

PETTY CASH REGISTER   PAGE 2

	DATE		VOU. NO.	DESCRIPTION	PAYMENTS	SUPPLIES	DELIVERY EXPENSE	MISC. EXPENSE	GENERAL ACCOUNT NAME	GENERAL AMOUNT	
1	20--										1
2	June	1	16	Postage stamps	5 00			5 00			2
14		30	29	Button	1 25				Adv. Expense	1 25	14
15		30		Totals	83 00 / 83 00	15 75	20 45	21 80		25 00 / 25 00	15
16											16
17				Reconciled bal. $ 17.00							17
18				Cash short (1.50)							18
19				Replen. check 84.50							19
20				Total $100.00							20
21											21

Reinforce the Main Idea

The journal entry to replenish the petty cash fund depends on whether the fund is in balance, over, or short. Use a diagram like this one to show the three possible journal entries using the accounts **Cash in Bank, Supplies, Delivery Expense, Miscellaneous Expense,** and **Cash Short and Over.**

Transaction Description	Account Debited	Account Credited

Do the Math

It is another busy day at Olde Time Swimming Hole, a private swimming facility for your neighborhood. You have a summer job running the concession stand, and you maintain the petty cash fund. To make your accounting easier, you record the cash sales and the petty cash transactions in one report at the end of the day. You always attach the cash register tape to prove the cash drawer. Using the following figures, determine the revenue and expenses for the day. How much money will remain in the cash drawer?

Opening cash drawer	$225
Petty cash fund	100
Cash sales	600
Pool supplies bought	55
Photocopy paper purchased	8

Problem 22–3 Analyzing a Source Document

The petty cash clerk for Riddle's Card Shop prepared the accompanying petty cash requisition.

Instructions Review the document and prepare Check 973 to replenish the petty cash fund in your working papers.

PETTY CASH REQUISITION

Accounts for which payments were made:	Amount
Office Supplies	$12.40
Postage Expense	12.00
Misc. Expense	16.00
Cash Short and Over	(.89)
TOTAL CASH NEEDED TO REPLENISH FUND	$39.51

Requested by: _Brent Roy_   Date _2/28/20--_

Approved by: _Hugh Morrison_   Date _____

Check No. _941_

Summary

Key Concepts

1. A *change fund* is the money used to make change for cash transactions. To establish a change fund, write a check for the fund amount payable to the person in charge of the fund. This person will cash it and place the money in the designated cash register drawer. Here is the entry to establish a change fund:

	DATE	DESCRIPTION	POST. REF.	DEBIT	CREDIT	
1	20--					1
2	Date	Change Fund		X X X XX		2
3		Cash in Bank			X X X XX	3
4						4

GENERAL JOURNAL   PAGE _____

2. At the end of each business day, a cash proof is prepared to reconcile the amount of cash in the register to the recorded cash sales. To prove cash, count the cash in the cash register drawer, subtract the change fund, and compare that amount with the amount of total cash sales, shown on the cash register tape.

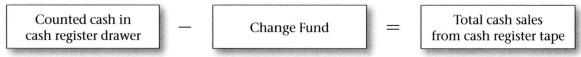

Counted cash in cash register drawer	−	Change Fund	=	Total cash sales from cash register tape

If the two amounts do not agree, the shortage or overage is recorded in the **Cash Short & Over** account.

Cash Short & Over

Debit	Credit
Cash	Cash
Shortages	Overages

3. A petty cash fund is the cash a business has on hand for making small, incidental cash payments. To open a petty cash fund:

- Estimate the amount of cash needed in the fund for a specific period.
- Write a check to the petty cashier, who is responsible for the cash.
- Record the transaction in the asset account **Petty Cash Fund.**

A petty cash fund is replenished by restoring the fund to its original amount. The cash balance in the fund must be reconciled with the petty cash vouchers and then a petty cash requisition form is prepared to replenish it.

4. Here is the entry to establish a petty cash fund:

	DATE	DESCRIPTION	POST. REF.	DEBIT	CREDIT	
1	20--					1
2	Date	Petty Cash Fund		X X X XX		2
3		Cash in Bank			X X X XX	3
4						4

GENERAL JOURNAL   PAGE _____

5. The petty cashier prepares a petty cash requisition form to request that the petty cash fund be replenished. The petty cash requisition includes this information:
   - Name and total of each account for which payments were made
   - Total amount of cash needed to replenish the fund

6. In some businesses, the petty cashier records petty cash disbursements in a petty cash register. The following is recorded for each petty cash payment:
   - date
   - voucher number
   - brief explanation for the payment
   - amount paid

7. The journal entry to replenish a petty cash fund depends on its balance.
   - If petty cash has no shortages or overages:

        Debit: **Various Assets and Expenses**   Credit: **Cash in Bank**

   - If petty cash has a shortage:

        Debit: **Various Assets and Expenses**   Credit: **Cash in Bank**
        Debit: **Cash Short & Over**

   - If petty cash has an overage:

        Debit: **Various Assets and Expenses**   Credit: **Cash in Bank**
        Credit: **Cash Short & Over**

8. At the end of each business day, a cash proof is prepared to reconcile the cash in the register to the recorded cash sales.
   - To record a cash shortage:

        Debit: **Cash in Bank**   Credit: **Sales**
        Debit: **Cash Short & Over**   Credit: **Sales Tax Payable**

   - To record a cash overage:

        Debit: **Cash in Bank**   Credit: **Sales**
                                      Credit: **Sales Tax Payable**
                                      Credit: **Cash Short & Over**

Key Terms

change fund	(p. 642)	petty cash requisition	(p. 650)
petty cash disbursement	(p. 647)	petty cash voucher	(p. 648)
petty cash fund	(p. 647)	petty cashier	(p. 647)
petty cash register	(p. 650)		

Check Your Understanding

1. **Change Fund**
   a. What is a change fund?
   b. Which accounts are debited and credited when a change fund is established?

2. **Cash Register Proof**
   a. When is the amount in the cash register proved?
   b. How is the cash register proof performed?

3. **Petty Cash Fund**
   a. Why would a business set up a petty cash fund?
   b. Explain the procedure for replenishing the petty cash fund.

4. **Opening a Petty Cash Fund**
   a. Which accounts are debited and credited to establish a petty cash fund?
   b. To whom is the check to establish a petty cash fund made payable?

5. **Petty Cash Requisition**
   a. What is a petty cash requisition?
   b. Explain how to prepare a petty cash requisition.

6. **Petty Cash Register**
   a. What information is included on each line of the petty cash register?
   b. Why is the petty cash register not considered a journal?

7. **Replenishing a Petty Cash Fund**
   a. What is meant by *reconciling the petty cash fund?*
   b. What accounts are debited when replenishing a petty cash fund?

8. **Cash Short and Over**
   a. When does a cash shortage occur?
   b. Explain why a cash shortage is treated like an expense.

Apply Key Terms

As the financial manager of The Tennis Center, you believe a petty cash fund should be established. Using these terms, prepare a one-page memorandum to convince your boss, Megan Long, to open a petty cash fund.

change fund	petty cash register
petty cash	petty cash requisition
disbursement	petty cash voucher
petty cash fund	petty cashier

Maintaining Cash Funds

Making the Transition from a Manual to a Computerized System

Task	Manual Methods	Computerized Methods
Maintaining the check register	• A check stub or deposit slip is the source document for journalizing cash payments. • Add deposits/deduct the checks to keep a running balance in the check register.	• Checks and deposits are automatically entered in the check register when transactions are journalized and posted. • The checking account balance is updated as each transaction is posted.
Reconciling the bank statement	• Compare the check register with the bank statement. • Add deposits in transit to the statement balance. Deduct outstanding checks. • Deduct bank charges from the check register. • Journalize and post bank charges.	• Enter the bank statement balance. • Verify outstanding checks and deposits not included on statement. • Record bank charges as a payment.

Peachtree® Q & A

Peachtree Question	Answer
How do I review the check register?	1. From the *Reports* menu, select **Accounts Payable**. 2. From the Reports list, select **Check Register** and click **Preview**. 3. At the Filter window, set the range of checks to be displayed.
How do I reconcile the bank statement?	1. From the *Tasks* menu, choose **Account Reconciliation**. 2. Select the account you wish to reconcile. 3. Enter the bank statement ending balance and date. 4. Mark the Clear box for each check and deposit listed on the statement. 5. Click **Adjust** to record the journal entry for the service charge. 6. If the unreconciled difference is $0.00, the reconciliation is complete.

QuickBooks Q & A

QuickBooks Question	Answer
How do I review the check register?	1. From the *Reports* menu, select **Banking**. 2. Select **Check Detail**, and enter the date range for this report.
How do I reconcile the bank statement?	1. From the *Banking* menu, select **Reconcile**. 2. Select the account you wish to reconcile. 3. Enter the bank statement date and ending balance, and click **Continue**. 4. Mark each check and deposit that have cleared. 5. If the unreconciled difference is 0.00, the reconciliation is complete. 6. Click **Reconcile Now** to save the reconciliation.

For detailed instructions, see your Glencoe Accounting Chapter Study Guides and Working Papers.

Complete problems using: **Manual** Glencoe Working Papers   OR   **Peachtree Complete Accounting** Software   OR   **QuickBooks** Templates

Peachtree®

SMART GUIDE

Step-by-Step Instructions: Problem 22–4

1. Select the problem set for Sunset Surfwear (Prob. 22–4).
2. Rename the company and set the system date.
3. Record the entry to establish the change fund using the **General Journal Entry** option.
4. Manually prepare a cash proof.
5. Record the cash sales using the **General Journal Entry** option.
6. Print a General Journal report and proof your work.
7. Complete the Analyze activity.
8. End the session.

Peachtree®

SMART GUIDE

Step-by-Step Instructions: Problem 22–5

1. Select the problem set for InBeat CD Shop (Prob. 22–5).
2. Rename the company and set the system date.
3. Record the entry to establish the petty cash fund.
4. Record the entry to replenish the petty cash fund.
5. Print a General Journal report and proof your work.
6. Complete the Analyze activity.
7. End the session.

TIP: Use the **General Journal Entry** option to record the petty cash fund transactions.

Problem 22–4 Establishing a Change Fund

On February 1 Sunset Surfwear issued Check 115 to establish a change fund of $150. At the end of the business day on February 2, the shop's cash register tape showed cash sales of $340 plus sales taxes of $17. An actual cash count of the money indicated that $505 was in the cash register drawer.

Instructions

1. Record the entry to establish the change fund on page 1 of the general journal.
2. Prepare a cash proof for Feb. 2. Sign your name on the Salesclerk line.
3. Record the cash sales for Feb. 2 on page 1 of the general journal.

Analyze | **Determine whether the shortage or overage represents revenue or expense to the business.**

Problem 22–5 Establishing and Replenishing a Petty Cash Fund

InBeat CD Shop established a petty cash fund for $100.

Instructions

1. In your working papers, record the entry to establish the petty cash fund on page 6 of a general journal.
2. Record the entry for replenishing the petty cash fund on page 10 of the general journal. There was $5 cash in the petty cash fund box on February 28.

Date		Transactions
Feb.	1	Issued Check 112 for $100 to establish the petty cash fund.
	28	Issued Check 146 to replenish the petty cash fund. Paid petty cash vouchers included Supplies, $40; Advertising Expense, $16; Maintenance Expense, $27; and Miscellaneous Expense, $12.

Analyze | **Conclude whether cash was short or over.**

Problem 22–6 Establishing and Replenishing a Petty Cash Fund

Shutterbug Cameras, a camera store, decided to establish a petty cash fund. On February 1 the accountant, Al Rosen, issued Check 1018 for $70 to establish the fund. The following disbursements were made.

Instructions

1. In your working papers, record the entry to establish the petty cash fund on page 9 of a general journal.
2. Make a list of the paid petty cash vouchers.
3. Classify the petty cash disbursements by account. Calculate the total amount paid out for each account.
4. Prepare a petty cash requisition, signing your name as the petty cashier. On February 28 there was $1.50 in the petty cash box.
5. Record the entry in the general journal (page 11) to replenish the petty cash fund on February 28. Use Check 1191.

Date	Transactions
Feb. 1	Purchased memo pads for the office, $2.75, Voucher 101 (**Supplies**).
3	Prepared Voucher 102 for a newspaper ad, $7.50 (**Advertising Expense**).
5	Prepared Voucher 103 for the postage on an outgoing package, $1.75 (**Miscellaneous Expense**).
8	Paid Dandy Delivery Service $5.65, Voucher 104 (**Delivery Expense**).
10	Prepared Voucher 105 for pens and pencils, $3.75 (**Supplies**).
12	Paid $2.20 for postage stamps, Voucher 106 (**Miscellaneous Expense**).
15	Paid Dandy Delivery Service $6.75, Voucher 107 (**Delivery Expense**).
20	Paid the news carrier $4.25 for delivery of the daily newspaper, Voucher 108 (**Miscellaneous Expense**).
22	Bought typing paper for $7.50, Voucher 109 (**Supplies**).
25	Paid $4.50 to Dandy Delivery Service, Voucher 110 (**Delivery Expense**).
27	Prepared Voucher 111 for an advertisement, $10 (**Advertising Expense**).
28	Paid $4.40 for postage stamps, Voucher 112 (**Miscellaneous Expense**).
28	Prepared Voucher 113 for an advertisement, $7.50 (**Advertising Expense**).

Analyze Calculate the total petty cash disbursements for **Delivery Expense** during February.

Peachtree®

SMART GUIDE

Step–by–Step Instructions: Problem 22–6

1. Select the problem set for Shutterbug Cameras (Prob. 22–6).
2. Rename the company and set the system date.
3. Record the entry to establish the petty cash fund.
4. List the petty cash vouchers and then manually prepare a petty cash requisition.
5. Record the entry to replenish the petty cash fund.
6. Print a General Journal report and proof your work.
7. Complete the Analyze activity.
8. End the session.

TIP: Use the **General Journal Entry** option to record the petty cash fund transactions.

QuickBooks

PROBLEM GUIDE

Step–by–Step Instructions: Problem 22–6

1. Restore the Problem 22-6.QBB file.
2. Record the entry to establish the petty cash fund using the **Write Checks** option.
3. Record the petty cash vouchers using the **Use Register** option.
4. Record the entry to replenish the petty cash fund using the **Write Checks** option.
5. Print a Journal report and proof your work.
6. Complete the Analyze activity.
7. Back up your work.

Problem 22–7 Using a Petty Cash Register

Cycle Tech Bicycles decided to establish a petty cash fund. On February 1 the accountant issued Check 3724 for $120 to establish the fund. The following disbursements were made.

Instructions

1. In your working papers, record the entry to establish the petty cash fund in a general journal, page 5.
2. Enter the information about the establishment of the petty cash fund on line 1 of a petty cash register, page 1.
3. Record the petty cash disbursements in the petty cash register.
4. Foot, total, and prove the petty cash register on February 28.
5. Record the petty cash fund replenishment information in the explanation column below the totals. On February 28 there was $4.35 in the petty cash box.
6. Prepare a petty cash requisition form. Use the form provided in your working papers and sign your name as petty cashier.
7. Record the issuance of Check 3875 to replenish the petty cash fund in the general journal, page 8.

Date		Transactions
Feb.	2	Prepared Voucher 1 for a $9.25 newspaper advertisement (**Advertising Expense**).
	5	Prepared Voucher 2 for pens and pencils, $5 (**Supplies**).
	9	Paid $12.50 for flowers for an employee's birthday, Voucher 3 (**Miscellaneous Expense**).
	12	Bought cash register tape for $3.95, Voucher 4 (**Supplies**).
	19	Prepared Voucher 5 for $15 to pay National Express for parts delivered (**Delivery Expense**).
	20	Paid $3.90 for postage stamps, Voucher 6 (**Miscellaneous Expense**).
	22	Paid $16 to have the show window cleaned, Voucher 7 (**Miscellaneous Expense**).
	24	Bought an $11 advertisement in the local newspaper, Voucher 8 (**Advertising Expense**).
	25	Bought stationery for $10, Voucher 9 (**Supplies**).
	26	Prepared Voucher 10 to National Express for packages delivered, $8.25 (**Delivery Expense**).
	27	Prepared Voucher 11 incorrectly and voided it.
	27	Purchased memo pads for the office for $3, Voucher 12 (**Supplies**).
	28	Paid the news carrier a $4 tip for the daily newspaper delivery, Voucher 13 (**Miscellaneous Expense**).

CONTINUE

Date	Transactions (cont.)
28	Paid $6.80 for postage stamps, Voucher 14 (**Miscellaneous Expense**).
28	Prepared Voucher 15 for a $10 newspaper advertisement (**Advertising Expense**).

Analyze | **Identify the number of payments that were made from the petty cash fund during the month of February.**

Problem 22–8 Handling a Petty Cash Fund

River's Edge Canoe & Kayak petty cash fund was established on February 1 for $100, by writing check 1763. The accounts for which petty cash disbursements are likely to be made include **Supplies**, **Gas Expense**, **Advertising Expense**, **Delivery Expense**, and **Miscellaneous Expense**.

Instructions

1. In your working papers, record the entry to establish the petty cash fund on page 12 of a general journal.
2. Record the establishment of the fund on the first line of the petty cash register, page 1.
3. Record each petty cash disbursement in the petty cash register.
4. Foot, prove, total, and rule the petty cash register on February 28.
5. Reconcile the petty cash fund. The amount in the petty cash box is $1.50.
6. Prepare a petty cash requisition. Sign your name as petty cashier.
7. Record the entry to replenish the petty cash fund by issuing Check 1798 in the general journal, page 15.
8. Record the replenishment information in the petty cash register.
9. The accountant believes the petty cash fund should be increased by $25. Record the issuance of Check 1799 on February 28.

Date	Transactions
Feb. 1	Bought an $8 advertisement in the local newspaper, Voucher 101.
2	Prepared Voucher 102 for $7.50 to pay Mercury Messenger for packages delivered.
3	Bought adding machine tape for 75¢, Voucher 103.
5	Paid $9.50 for flowers for an employee's birthday, Voucher 104.

CONTINUE

Peachtree®

SMART GUIDE

Step–by–Step Instructions: Problem 22–8

1. Select the problem set for River's Edge Canoe & Kayak (Prob. 22–8).
2. Rename the company and set the system date.
3. Record the entry to establish the petty cash fund.
4. Manually record the petty cash disbursements.
5. Reconcile the petty cash register and manually prepare a petty cash requisition.
6. Record the entry to replenish the petty cash fund.
7. Record the entry to increase the petty cash fund.
8. Print a General Journal report and proof your work.
9. Complete the Analyze activity.
10. End the session.

Date	Transactions (cont.)
7	Prepared Voucher 105 for $5.25 for a typewriter ribbon.
9	Paid $4.40 for postage stamps, Voucher 106.
12	Bought $9 worth of gasoline, Voucher 107.
15	Paid $8.50 to have the shop's windows washed, Voucher 108.
18	Bought memo pads, pencils, and pens for office use, $6.30, Voucher 109.
20	Prepared Voucher 110 for $7.50 to pay Mercury Messenger for packages delivered.
23	Prepared Voucher 111 incorrectly and voided it.
23	Bought stationery for $8, Voucher 112.
27	Paid the news carrier $4.75 for the daily newspaper, Voucher 113.
28	Prepared Voucher 114 for $7.50 to pay Mercury Messenger for packages delivered.
28	Bought gasoline, $5.80, Voucher 115.
28	Prepared Voucher 116 for a newspaper advertisement, $5.

Analyze List the petty cash disbursements that are charged to the Miscellaneous Expense account.

 CHALLENGE PROBLEM

Problem 22–9 Locating Errors in a Petty Cash Register

On February 1 a petty cash fund of $150 was established for Buzz Newsstand, Check 1198. The petty cashier writes a voucher for each petty cash disbursement. The vouchers are entered in a petty cash register, which is included in your working papers. When the petty cash register was totaled on February 28, the accounting clerk discovered that the footings of the Distribution of Payments columns did not equal the total of the Payments column.

Instructions

1. Compare the petty cash disbursement information in your working papers with the entries in the petty cash register.
2. Correct any errors you find in the petty cash register by drawing a line through the incorrect item and writing the correction above it.
3. Total all columns after the corrections are made.
4. Record the replenishment information on the register. The amount in the petty cash box on February 28 was $8.10.

Analyze Explain how you determined the amount of the check to replenish the petty cash fund on February 28.

Practice your test-taking skills! The questions on this page are reprinted with permission from national organizations:
- Future Business Leaders of America
- Business Professionals of America

Use a separate sheet of paper to record your answers.

Future Business Leaders of America

MULTIPLE CHOICE

1. An amount of cash kept on hand and used for making small payments is called
    a. revenue.
    b. cash.
    c. petty cash.
    d. prepaid interest.
    e. none of these answers

2. A form showing proof of a petty cash payment is a
    a. check.
    b. petty cash slip.
    c. petty cash check stub.
    d. journal.

3. A petty cash on hand amount that is more than a recorded amount is called
    a. cash over.
    b. cash short.
    c. cash credit.
    d. cash debit.

Business Professionals of America

MULTIPLE CHOICE

4. The entry to replenish the petty cash fund requires

	Debit	Credit
a.	Petty Cash Fund	Cash
b.	Petty Cash Expense	Petty Cash Fund
c.	Cash	Petty Cash Fund
d.	Various Expense accounts	Cash

5. Michelle is a cashier for The Pet Store. When she counted the cash in her register drawer at the end of the day, the total was $959.74. According to the electronic register, she should have had a balance of $969.85. Was Michelle short or over in her drawer and by how much?
    a. $10.11 short
    b. $10.11 over
    c. $10.38 short
    d. $10.38 over

Need More Help?

Go to glencoeaccounting.glencoe.com and click on Student Center. Click on Winning Competitive Events and select Chapter 22.
- **Practice Questions and Test-Taking Tips**
- **Concept Capsules and Terminology**

Cash Funds

1. What form is used to control payments from the petty cash fund?
2. What happens to cash in a cash register drawer at the end of a business day?
3. You are the petty cashier responsible for the petty cash fund. You counted the cash in the petty cash box and found that you will likely run out of petty cash soon. What would you do to restore the fund to its original cash balance?
4. How do you find out whether a petty cash fund amount is short or over?
5. Summarize the steps involved in replenishing the petty cash fund. What are the source document(s) for recording the journal entry, and which account(s) is (are) used to make the journal entry?
6. Which problem do you think is more serious in a change fund: cash short or cash over? Why?

Merchandising Business: Health Foods

The Healthy Alternative sells vitamins and natural health-care products. It has two electronic cash registers that track inventory and record sales directly to the computerized accounting system. The store owner is concerned because the actual cash on hand is usually short when it is compared to the sales records.

INSTRUCTIONS

1. You work for a local CPA firm that is auditing The Healthy Alternative's accounting records. What advice would you give the owner about cash controls and protection?
2. Explain to the owner why it is important for the cash records to match the accounting records.

Borrowing from Petty Cash

You are the petty cashier for a local theater group. Its petty cash fund pays for taxi fares to and from the airport for actors, directors, and set designers. Today you forgot to bring cash for your lunch. You consider borrowing $5 from the petty cash fund and leaving an IOU. After all, you will pay it back tomorrow.

ETHICAL DECISION MAKING

1. What are the ethical issues?
2. What are the alternatives?
3. Who are the affected parties?
4. How do the alternatives affect the parties?
5. What would you do?

Process to Increase the Change Fund

Retro Threads sells designer vintage clothing on consignment. The shop is open only on Fridays and Saturdays and does a brisk business. You maintain the accounting records for the shop. Dorothy Douglas, the owner, wants to increase the change fund from $100 to $200. Write her a note explaining the transaction. Remind her to notify the salesclerks that the change fund will increase by $100.

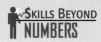

Integrity

Fun Farm is a hands-on, educational working farm where elementary students learn about planting crops and raising animals. In auditing its petty cash fund, you notice some unusual disbursements and cash shortages. You suspect an employee is taking funds from it and not preparing a voucher or falsifying one. Discuss with a partner how you should handle this situation.

International Monetary Fund

When Kenya suffered a severe drought in 2000, the International Monetary Fund (IMF) helped with a $52 million loan. The IMF helps promote a healthy world economy through exchange rate stability, the growth of international trade, and monitoring economic developments. Its members can get technical advice and training or financial assistance to correct underlying economic problems.

INSTRUCTIONS Summarize benefits available to IMF members.

Your Spending Records

You should track your cash daily to be aware of the cash you have at the start and end of each day. If the amounts differ, you should have receipts for expenses or estimate where the remainder went such as for cold drinks or snacks. If you cannot account for the difference, you should pay more attention to spending cash.

PERSONAL FINANCE ACTIVITY For three days, track your personal expenses like a petty cash fund. Record how much you spend on each item on an envelope or sheet of paper. At the end of each day, is your cash over or short?

PERSONAL FINANCE ONLINE Log on to **glencoeaccounting.glencoe.com** and click on **Student Center.** Click on **Making It Personal** and select **Chapter 22.**

Calculating Price-Earnings Ratio

To decide whether to buy stock, analysts and investors look at stock prices over time and calculate the price-earnings (PE) ratio. It compares a stock's current market value with its earnings per share. Suppose a company has a PE ratio of 10. At that price, investors are willing to pay $10 for every dollar of last year's earnings. Companies that are expected to grow will have a higher PE ratio than companies in decline. To calculate the PE ratio:

$$\text{Price-earnings ratio} = \frac{\text{Current market value per share}}{\text{Earnings per share}}$$

INSTRUCTIONS Use PETsMART's consolidated statements of operations in Appendix F to answer these questions. Use the "Basic" earnings per share figure, and round your answer to the nearest whole number.

1. For the fiscal year ended February 1, 2004, calculate the PE ratio assuming PETsMART stock is selling at (a) $32.50 per share and (b) $35.00 per share.

2. Describe how stock price affects the PE ratio. How would you use this ratio in deciding which stocks to buy?

Plant Assets and Depreciation

BEFORE YOU READ

What You'll Learn

1. Identify plant assets.

2. Explain the need to depreciate plant assets.

3. Calculate annual depreciation of plant assets.

4. Calculate partial-year depreciation of plant assets.

5. Determine the book value of a plant asset.

6. Record depreciation of plant assets.

7. Prepare depreciation schedules.

8. Define the accounting terms introduced in this chapter.

Why It's Important

▶ The matching principle requires expenses to be matched with revenues.

Predict

1. What does the chapter title tell you?
2. What do you already know about this subject from personal experience?
3. What have you learned about this in the earlier chapters?
4. What gaps exist in your knowledge of this subject?

Exploring the *Real World* of Business

DEPRECIATING ASSETS

Rush Trucking

If you owned a trucking company, would you get up at 3 a.m. to deliver shipments yourself? Andra Rush did when she started **Rush Trucking** in 1984. She also worked the phones as dispatcher, made sales calls, and repaired trucks.

Rush started her company with only three trucks purchased with her savings. "I believed that if we could get the business, we would do a good job and that would lead to repeat business and bigger contracts," Rush said about her business strategy. **Rush Trucking** now earns over $125 million annually and operates 2,000 tractors and 3,900 trailers.

Companies like **Rush Trucking** generate revenue with long-term assets. Depreciation allows them to match the cost of assets to revenue over several accounting periods.

What Do You Think?

What do you think **Rush Trucking** considers when it matches truck costs to revenue?

Working in the *Real World*

APPLYING YOUR ACCOUNTING KNOWLEDGE

All businesses have assets. Some of those assets become less useful because over time they wear out or become obsolete. Examples of these *depreciable* assets are company trucks and computers. You will learn how to identify depreciable assets, how to set up depreciation schedules, and how to make the adjusting entry for depreciation expense in this chapter.

Personal Connection

In your workplace are there assets that are wearing out or need to be replaced? What are they?

Online Connection

Go to **glencoeaccounting.glencoe.com** and click on **Student Center**. Click on **Working in the Real World** and select **Chapter 23.**

Plant Assets and Equipment

BEFORE YOU READ

Main Idea
A business uses plant assets for more than one accounting period, so it spreads the cost of these assets over a number of years.

Read to Learn...
➤ the difference between current assets and plant assets. (p. 670)
➤ four factors used to estimate the depreciation of plant assets. (p. 671)

Key Terms
plant assets
depreciation
disposal value
straight-line depreciation

As You READ

Key Point

Plant and Current Assets Current assets will be consumed or converted to cash in one accounting period. Plant assets will be used for more than one accounting period.

Businesses own many different types of assets. One category of asset requires special treatment in the accounting records. These assets, such as office equipment and buildings, have two things in common:

- They are expected to produce benefits for the business for more than one year.
- They are purchased for use in operating the business, not for resale.

Rush Trucking owns many assets in this category, including computer equipment, office equipment, and trucks. Let's explore how businesses account for these types of assets.

Current and Plant Assets

How Do You Match the Cost of Assets to the Revenue They Help Generate?

Throughout this textbook you have learned about various assets that a business uses in its operation. These assets can be classified as current assets or *plant assets*.

Current Assets	Plant Assets
Assets that are either consumed or converted to cash during the normal operating cycle of the business, usually one year. Examples are: • cash • accounts receivable (cash to be collected from customers within a short period of time) • merchandise (sold within a short period of time)	Long-lived assets that are used in the production or sale of other assets or services over several accounting periods. Examples are: • land • buildings • delivery equipment • store equipment • office equipment

In Chapter 18 you learned about assets such as supplies and prepaid insurance. As these assets are used, their costs are converted to expenses. This conforms to the *matching principle* of accounting, which states that during an accounting period, expenses must be matched with the revenue earned. Since current assets are consumed within one accounting period, the costs of current assets can be easily matched to the revenue for the period.

Estimating Depreciation of a Plant Asset

What Four Factors Are Used to Estimate Depreciation?

Plant assets are used over a number of accounting periods. To follow the matching principle, the cost of a plant asset is spread over, or allocated to, the periods in which the asset will be used to produce revenue.

Allocating, or spreading the cost of a plant asset over that asset's useful life is called **depreciation** . For accounting purposes businesses depreciate all plant assets except land. The cost of land is not depreciated because land is considered to have an unlimited useful life. In this chapter you will learn how to calculate and record the depreciation of plant assets.

For example, suppose that a plant asset costs $40,000 and has a useful life of 10 years. The cost of the asset is depreciated over 10 years. A portion of the $40,000 is transferred to an expense account each year. At the end of 10 years, the cost of this plant asset will have been recognized as an expense.

It is important to remember that depreciation is an *estimate*. No one can predict with certainty the useful life or the disposal value of an asset.

Four factors are used to calculate depreciation of a plant asset:

- its cost
- its estimated useful life
- its estimated disposal value
- the depreciation method used

Plant Asset Cost

The cost of a plant asset is the price the business paid to purchase it plus any sales taxes, delivery charges, and installation charges. The total cost is the amount debited to the plant asset account (for example, **Delivery Equipment**) at the time of purchase.

Estimated Useful Life of a Plant Asset

The *estimated useful life* of a plant asset is the number of years it is expected to be used before it wears out, becomes outdated, or is no longer needed by the business. The number of years a plant asset can be used varies from one asset to another. A delivery truck might have a useful life of six years. A building, on the other hand, might have a useful life of 30 years.

As You READ

Compare and Contrast

Current and Plant Assets How are current assets and plant assets similar and different?

As You READ

In Your Experience

What personal assets do individuals use for more than one year?

MATH HINTS

Rounding Cents
- Look at the digit to the *right* of the hundredths digit.
- If it is 5 or more, round up.
- If it is less than 5, do not change the hundredths digit.

Correct:
8.0347 ≈ 8.03 *4 is less than 5 so the hundredths digit does not change.*

Incorrect:
8.0347 ≈ 8.035 ≈ 8.04

In estimating useful life, the accountant considers past experiences with the same type of asset. The Internal Revenue Service (IRS) also publishes guidelines on the estimated useful lives for many types of assets.

Estimated Disposal Value of a Plant Asset

At some point a plant asset will be replaced or discarded. Usually this occurs while the asset still has some monetary value. For example, if a business buys a new delivery truck, the old delivery truck can often be traded in to reduce the price of the new truck.

The estimated amount that a plant asset will be worth at the time of its replacement is called the **disposal value**. The disposal value assigned to a plant asset is an estimate that is based on previous experience. The IRS also publishes guidelines on disposal values.

Depreciation Methods

Several methods for computing depreciation expense are acceptable. In this course you will learn a simple, widely used depreciation method called the *straight-line method*. **Straight-line depreciation** equally distributes the depreciation expense over the asset's estimated useful life. Other methods of computing depreciation include units-of-production and accelerated methods.

- *Units-of-production method* estimates useful life measured in units of *use* rather than units of *time*.
- *Accelerated depreciation methods* are based on the theory that an asset loses more value in the early years of its useful life than in the later years. Two types of accelerated depreciation are the *sum-of-the-years'-digits* method and the *declining-balance* method.

Depreciation for Tax Reporting

The federal income tax law has rules for depreciating assets. These rules include the accelerated cost recovery system (ACRS). It is called *accelerated* because it allows the business to recognize depreciation expense over a shorter period of time. The ACRS method does not take disposal value into consideration. Congress modified ACRS in 1986 resulting in *MACRS* (pronounced makers), the *modified accelerated cost recovery system*. This system is used for tax accounting purposes only. It is not used for business financial reports. It is intended to be an incentive for businesses to invest in plant assets. The higher depreciation expense results in a lower income tax liability.

AFTER YOU READ

Reinforce the Main Idea

Use a diagram like this one to show the four factors that are used to calculate a plant asset's depreciation.

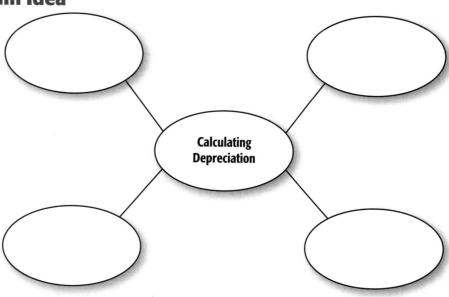

Calculating Depreciation

 ## Do the Math

You work for Island Tropics, a trendy clothing store. It recently purchased a computer system for $20,000. The computers have an estimated useful life of five years. The $20,000 cost can be depreciated over the useful life of the asset as an expense on the tax return of the business. What is the amount that can be deducted each year as an expense if the computer's estimated disposal value is $1,000 and the straight-line depreciation method is used?

 ## Problem 23–1 Classifying Asset Accounts

Listed here are the assets of New England Sports Equipment Inc.

Accounts Receivable	Office Equipment
Building	Office Furniture
Cash in Bank	Petty Cash Fund
Change Fund	Prepaid Insurance
Delivery Equipment	Store Equipment
Land	Supplies
Merchandise Inventory	

Instructions In your working papers, indicate whether each asset listed is a current asset or a plant asset by placing a check mark in the correct column. The first account is completed as an example.

Asset	Current Asset	Plant Asset
Accounts Receivable	✔	

Calculating Depreciation

BEFORE YOU READ

Main Idea
Businesses maintain a record of each plant asset and its related depreciation.

Read to Learn...
➤ how to calculate depreciation. (p. 674)
➤ how to determine book value. (p. 675)

Key Terms
accumulated depreciation
book value

On Your Mark Athletic Wear purchased a delivery truck on January 5 for $16,500 cash. The truck has an estimated disposal value of $1,500 and an estimated useful life of five years.

Calculating Depreciation
How Do You Calculate Plant Asset Depreciation?

To calculate depreciation you need to know the cost of the truck, its estimated useful life, and its estimated disposal value.

First calculate the amount to be depreciated:

Original Cost	−	Estimated Disposal Value	=	Amount to Be Depreciated
$16,500	−	$1,500	=	$15,000

The estimated disposal value represents the part of the asset's cost that the business expects to recover. Therefore, the estimated disposal value should not be treated as an expense.

Straight-Line Depreciation

Calculate the annual depreciation expense using the straight-line method:

Amount to Be Depreciated	÷	Estimated Useful Life	=	Annual Depreciation Expense
$15,000	÷	5	=	$3,000

The annual depreciation expense for the delivery truck is $3,000.

For straight-line depreciation, the depreciation rate is 1 divided by the years of useful life. In this example the depreciation rate is 20% per year (1 ÷ 5 years).

Note that the $3,000 depreciation expense is for a full year. Suppose that On Your Mark purchased the delivery truck on April 5 instead of January 5. During the first year, the delivery truck will be used for only nine months. Therefore, the depreciation expense is calculated for nine months.

Annual Depreciation Expense	×	Fraction of Year	=	Partial Year Depreciation Expense
$3,000	×	9/12	=	$2,250

Declining-Balance Depreciation

With the declining-balance method, the annual depreciation expense is the asset's book value multiplied by the declining-balance rate. The declining-balance rate can vary, but it is usually double the straight-line rate. For a five-year asset, the rate is 40% (2 × [1 ÷ 5]).

Disposal value is not used in the computation. However, after the last year of depreciation, the total depreciation expense "stops" at the asset's disposal value. The annual depreciation expense for the truck's first year is $6,600 ($16,500 × 40%).

Plant Asset Records

Where Do You Record Plant Asset Values?

Businesses maintain records for each plant asset and the depreciation taken for that asset. The record in **Figure 23–1** provides detailed information about the delivery truck, including:

1. the date of purchase
2. the original cost
3. the estimated useful life
4. annual depreciation
5. accumulated depreciation
6. book value at the end of each year

The lower part of the plant asset record contains the depreciation schedule. The amount of depreciation expense accumulates from one year to the next. **Accumulated depreciation** is the total amount of depreciation for a plant asset that has been recorded up to a specific point in time. The accumulated depreciation at the end of the third year is $9,000.

The far right column of the depreciation schedule shows the **book value** of the plant asset, the original cost less accumulated depreciation.

At the end of the third year, the book value of the delivery truck is $7,500 ($16,500 − $9,000). Note that the delivery truck's book value at the end of five years is $1,500. This is the truck's estimated disposal value. Under the straight-line method, it cannot be depreciated below its estimated disposal value.

PLANT ASSET RECORD

ITEM _Delivery Truck_   GENERAL LEDGER ACCOUNT _Delivery Equipment_

SERIAL NUMBER _2911-50041_   MANUFACTURER _VanPower_

PURCHASED FROM _Winding Creek Auto_   EST. DISPOSAL VALUE _$1,500.00_

ESTIMATED LIFE _5 years_ 3   LOCATION _Company Garage_

DEPRECIATION METHOD _Straight-line_   DEPRECIATION PER YEAR _$3,000.00_ 4

5

DATE	EXPLANATION	ASSET			ACCUMULATED DEPRECIATION			BOOK VALUE
		DEBIT	CREDIT	BALANCE	DEBIT	CREDIT	BALANCE	
1 1/5/2008	Purchased	16,500 2		16,500				6 16,500
12/31/2008						3,000	3,000	13,500
12/31/2009						3,000	6,000	10,500
12/31/2010						3,000	9,000	7,500
12/31/2011						3,000	12,000	4,500
12/31/2012						3,000	15,000	1,500

Figure 23–1 Plant Asset Record

Reinforce the Main Idea

Using a diagram like this one, show the step-by-step procedure to record the first year's depreciation using the straight-line method.

Steps to Record Depreciation

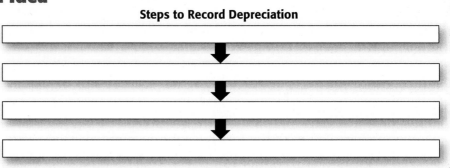

 ## Do the Math

Office furniture for Teen Counseling Center is estimated at a total value of $45,000 with a 10% disposal value. The estimated useful life is four years. Calculate the annual depreciation expense for the office furniture using the straight-line method.

 ## Problem 23–2 Calculating Depreciation Expense

Instructions

For each of the following plant assets:

1. calculate the amount to be depreciated,
2. calculate the annual depreciation expense using the straight-line method,
3. calculate the depreciation expense for the first year.

Use the form provided in your working papers.

	Plant Asset	Months Owned First Year	Original Cost	Estimated Disposal Value	Estimated Useful Life
1.	Cash register	8	$ 450	$ 30	7 years
2.	Computer	2	6,500	1,500	5 years
3.	Conference table	6	1,900	100	25 years
4.	Delivery truck	3	36,400	6,400	5 years
5.	Desk	11	3,180	300	20 years

 ## Problem 23–3 Completing a Plant Asset Record

Use the following information to complete the blank asset record found in your working papers. The company uses the straight-line method for depreciating all plant assets. Item Purchased: Xerox Copier—Serial No. X42599757, $12,500, from K&C Office Equipment.

Purchased: 10/1/2011
Estimated Life: 5 years
Location: Executive Offices
Estimated Disposal Value: $1,700

Accounting for Depreciation Expense at the End of a Year

After depreciation on plant assets has been calculated, adjustments are made to record depreciation for the period. These adjustments bring the general ledger into agreement with the plant asset records.

Adjusting for Depreciation Expense
How Do You Adjust for Depreciation Expense?

When a plant asset is purchased, the accountant sets up a depreciation schedule for the asset like the one in **Figure 23–1** on page 675. The amount of depreciation expense for each plant asset is recorded in the accounting records at the end of the year. The information to record the adjustments for depreciation comes from the plant asset records.

Many businesses prepare a summary of depreciation expense for each type of plant asset. For example, a business may have 10 delivery trucks. Each truck has its own plant asset record. At the end of the year, the depreciation expense for all 10 trucks is totaled. This total is entered on a summary form under the name of the asset account, in this case, **Delivery Equipment. Figure 23–2** shows On Your Mark's depreciation summary form for its plant assets.

On Your Mark's total depreciation expense for the year is $33,000. This amount includes the depreciation expense for all plant assets. The accumulated depreciation for all of On Your Mark's plant assets is $100,250.

Making the Depreciation Expense Adjustment

The adjustment for depreciation affects two accounts: **Depreciation Expense** and **Accumulated Depreciation**.

The Depreciation Expense Account. Depreciation Expense is an expense account. During the year the account has a zero balance because

BEFORE YOU READ

Main Idea
An end-of-period adjusting entry is made for depreciation expense.

Read to Learn...
➤ the accounts used to record depreciation. (p. 677)
➤ how to journalize adjusting and closing entries for depreciation expense. (p. 681)

2008 SUMMARY OF DEPRECIATION EXPENSE December 31, 2008			
Asset	Cost	Depreciation Expense	Depreciation to Date
Building	50,000	2,500	8,125
Delivery Equipment	16,500	3,000	9,000
Office Equipment	50,000	2,500	8,125
Store Equipment	250,000	25,000	75,000
Totals	366,500	33,000	100,250

Figure 23–2 Depreciation Summary Form

As You READ

Instant Recall

Adjusting Entries An adjusting entry affects one permanent account and one temporary account.

the adjustment for depreciation is recorded at the end of the period. **Depreciation Expense** is reported on the income statement. At the end of the year, **Depreciation Expense** is closed to **Income Summary**.

Businesses have a depreciation expense account for each type of plant asset. Some examples are:

- **Depreciation Expense—Delivery Equipment** (trucks, vans, automobiles)
- **Depreciation Expense—Office Furniture** (desks, chairs, filing cabinets)

The Accumulated Depreciation Account. The balance of **Accumulated Depreciation** represents the total amount of depreciation expensed since the business purchased the asset. Each type of plant asset has an accumulated depreciation account. Typical account names are:

- **Accumulated Depreciation—Delivery Equipment**
- **Accumulated Depreciation—Building**

Accumulated Depreciation is classified as a contra asset account. Recall that the balance of a contra account reduces the balance of its related account. In the case of an accumulated depreciation account, the related account is a plant asset account. For example, if the asset account is **Delivery Equipment**, the contra asset account is **Accumulated Depreciation—Delivery Equipment**.

Accumulated Depreciation	
Debit	Credit
−	+
Decrease Side	Increase Side Normal Balance Side

The debit and credit rules for an accumulated depreciation account are opposite those for an asset account. The balance of an accumulated depreciation account is reported on the balance sheet as a decrease to its related plant asset account.

Account Name

Asset	Expense	Contra Asset
Del. Equip.	Depr. Exp.—Del. Equip.	Accum. Depr.—Del. Equip.
Office Equip.	Depr. Exp.—Office Equip.	Accum. Depr.—Office Equip.
Store Equip.	Depr. Exp.—Store Equip.	Accum. Depr.—Store Equip.

The Adjustment. Let's learn how to record depreciation of plant assets. Look at On Your Mark's depreciation schedule in **Figure 23–1** on page 675. The delivery truck annual depreciation expense is $3,000.

Adjustment

On December 31 the accounting clerk for On Your Mark records the depreciation for the delivery truck.

ANALYSIS	Identify	1. The accounts affected are **Depreciation Expense—Delivery Equipment** and **Accumulated Depreciation—Delivery Equipment.**
	Classify	2. **Depreciation Expense—Delivery Equipment** is an expense account. **Accumulated Depreciation—Delivery Equipment** is a contra asset account.
	+/−	3. Both **Depreciation Expense—Delivery Equipment** and **Accumulated Depreciation—Delivery Equipment** are increased by $3,000.

| DEBIT-CREDIT RULE | 4. | Increases to expense accounts are recorded as debits. Debit **Depreciation Expense—Delivery Equipment** for $3,000. |
| | 5. | Increases to contra asset accounts are recorded as credits. Credit **Accumulated Depreciation—Delivery Equipment** for $3,000. |

T ACCOUNTS	6.	Depreciation Expense— Delivery Equipment		Accumulated Depreciation— Delivery Equipment	
		Debit + 3,000	Credit –	Debit –	Credit + 3,000

Accountants make similar adjustments to record depreciation for other plant assets, such as buildings and office equipment.

Analysis of the Accumulated Depreciation Account. Suppose this is the end of the third year of the estimated useful life of On Your Mark's delivery truck. For each year the same adjustment was made to record the depreciation of the delivery truck:

- a debit to **Depreciation Expense—Delivery Equipment**
- a credit to **Accumulated Depreciation—Delivery Equipment**

After the books have been closed each year, the **Depreciation Expense—Delivery Equipment** account has a zero balance. (Remember that expense accounts are closed at the end of each year.) In contrast the **Accumulated Depreciation—Delivery Equipment** account shows the total amount of depreciation expensed since the asset was purchased. At the end of the third year, the total is $9,000.

Accumulated Depreciation— Delivery Equipment	
Debit –	Credit +
	3,000 (first year depreciation)
	3,000 (second year depreciation)
	3,000 (third year depreciation)
	Bal. 9,000

Recording Depreciation Adjustments on a Work Sheet

After preparing the adjustment for depreciation, the accountant enters it in the Adjustments section of the work sheet.

Refer to **Figure 23–3** on pages 680 and 681. Locate the accumulated depreciation accounts in the Trial Balance Credit column ($6,000 and $5,625). Note that the depreciation expense accounts do not have balances in the Trial Balance section. Adjustments (e) and (f) are entered in the Adjustments section to show the depreciation adjustments for the year. Note that the depreciation expense accounts are debited and the accumulated depreciation accounts are credited. Also note that no adjustments are made to the asset accounts.

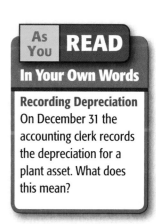

As You READ

In Your Own Words

Recording Depreciation On December 31 the accounting clerk records the depreciation for a plant asset. What does this mean?

	ACCT. NO.	ACCOUNT NAME	TRIAL BALANCE DEBIT	TRIAL BALANCE CREDIT	ADJUSTMENTS DEBIT	ADJUSTMENTS CREDIT
8	140	Delivery Equipment	16 500 00			
9	142	Accum. Depr.—Delivery Equip.		6 000 00		(e) 3 000 00
10	145	Office Equipment	50 000 00			
11	147	Accum. Depr.—Office Equipment		5 625 00		(f) 2 500 00
23	615	Depr. Expense—Delivery Equip.	—		(e) 3 000 00	
24	620	Depr. Expense—Office Equip.	—		(f) 2 500 00	
25						

Figure 23–3 Work Sheet with Depreciation Adjustments

Each amount is extended to the other work sheet columns.

Account	Column Extended to — Adjusted Trial Balance	Column Extended to — Financial Statement
Del. Equip.	Debit (unchanged)	Balance Sheet
Accum. Depr.—Del. Equip.	Credit (increased)	Balance Sheet
Office Equip.	Debit (unchanged)	Balance Sheet
Accum. Depr.—Office Equip.	Credit (increased)	Balance Sheet
Depr. Exp.—Del. Equip.	Debit (increased)	Income Statement
Depr. Exp.—Office Equip.	Debit (increased)	Income Statement

Reporting Depreciation Expense and Accumulated Depreciation on Financial Statements

Figure 23–4 shows placement of the depreciation expense accounts on the partial income statement of On Your Mark.

On Your Mark Athletic Wear				
Income Statement				
For the Year Ended December 31, 20--				
Operating Expenses				
Depreciation Expense—Delivery Equip.		3 000 00		
Depreciation Expense—Office Equip.		2 500 00		
Total Operating Expenses			94 351 00	
Operating Income			51 342 00	

Figure 23–4 Income Statement

Figure 23–5 shows placement of the plant asset and related accumulated depreciation accounts. Both types of accounts appear in the Assets section of the balance sheet. Notice that the accumulated depreciation account is listed immediately below the related plant asset account.

Athletic Wear

Sheet

December 31, 20--

	ADJUSTED TRIAL BALANCE		INCOME STATEMENT		BALANCE SHEET		
	DEBIT	CREDIT	DEBIT	CREDIT	DEBIT	CREDIT	
	16 500 00				16 500 00		8
		9 000 00				9 000 00	9
	50 000 00				50 000 00		10
		8 125 00				8 125 00	11
	3 000 00		3 000 00				23
	2 500 00		2 500 00				24
							25

Figure 23–3 Work Sheet with Depreciation Adjustments (continued)

For **Delivery Equipment:**

- The original cost is entered in the first amount column on the first line ($16,500).
- The accumulated depreciation is entered in the first amount column on the second line ($9,000).
- The difference between cost and accumulated depreciation is entered in the second amount column on the second line ($7,500).

The book value of the delivery equipment is $7,500. The book value of each plant asset reported on the balance sheet should be the same as that shown on the plant asset record.

On Your Mark Athletic Wear

Balance Sheet

December 31, 20--

Assets				
Delivery Equipment		16 500 00		
Less: Accum. Depr.—Delivery Equip.		9 000 00	7 500 00	
Office Equipment		50 000 00		
Less: Accum. Depr.—Office Equip.		8 125 00	41 875 00	

Figure 23–5 Balance Sheet

Adjusting and Closing Entries for Depreciation Expense

What Are the Adjusting and Closing Entries for Depreciation?

After the accountant has completed the work sheet and prepared the financial statements, the adjustments for depreciation expense are recorded in the general journal. The information for the journal entries is taken directly from the Adjustments section of the work sheet.

Record the December 31 adjusting journal entries for depreciation.

ANALYSIS	*Identify*	1.	The accounts affected are **Depreciation Expense—Delivery Equipment, Depreciation Expense—Office Equipment, Accumulated Depreciation—Delivery Equipment,** and **Accumulated Depreciation—Office Equipment.**
	Classify	2.	**Depreciation Expense—Delivery Equipment** and **Depreciation Expense—Office Equipment** are expense accounts. **Accumulated Depreciation—Delivery Equipment** and **Accumulated Depreciation—Office Equipment** are contra asset accounts.
	+/−	3.	**Depreciation Expense—Delivery Equipment** is increased by $3,000. **Depreciation Expense—Office Equipment** is increased by $2,500. **Accumulated Depreciation—Delivery Equipment** is increased by $3,000. **Accumulated Depreciation—Office Equipment** is increased by $2,500.

DEBIT-CREDIT RULE	4.	Increases in expense accounts are recorded as debits. Debit **Depreciation Expense—Delivery Equipment** for $3,000 and **Depreciation Expense—Office Equipment** for $2,500.
	5.	Increases in contra asset accounts are recorded as credits. Credit **Accumulated Depreciation—Delivery Equipment** for $3,000 and **Accumulated Depreciation—Office Equipment** for $2,500.

T ACCOUNTS

6.

Depreciation Expense— Delivery Equipment		Accumulated Depreciation— Delivery Equipment	
Debit + 3,000	Credit −	Debit −	Credit + 3,000

Depreciation Expense— Office Equipment		Accumulated Depreciation— Office Equipment	
Debit + 2,500	Credit −	Debit −	Credit + 2,500

JOURNAL ENTRY

7.

GENERAL JOURNAL PAGE __21__

	DATE		DESCRIPTION	POST. REF.	DEBIT	CREDIT	
1	20--						1
2	Dec.	31	Depr. Exp.—Del. Equip.		3 000 00		2
3			Accum. Depr.—Del. Equip.			3 000 00	3
4		31	Depr. Exp.—Office Equip.		2 500 00		4
5			Accum. Depr.—Office Equip.			2 500 00	5
6							6

After adjusting entries have been journalized and posted, the next step in the accounting cycle is to close the ledger. In the second closing entry, you'll remember, accounts with debit balances in the Income Statement Debit column of the work sheet are closed to **Income Summary**. This closing entry includes the depreciation expense accounts.

After this closing entry has been posted to the general ledger, the balances of the depreciation expense accounts are reduced to zero.

Closing

Second Closing Entry—Depreciation accounts only.

ON YOUR MARK
ATHLETIC WEAR
595 Leslie Street, Dallas, TX 75207

ANALYSIS	*Identify*	1. The accounts affected are **Depreciation Expense–Delivery Equipment, Depreciation Expense–Office Equipment,** and **Income Summary.**
	Classify	2. **Depreciation Expense–Delivery Equipment** and **Depreciation Expense–Office Equipment** are expense accounts. **Income Summary** is a temporary capital account.
	+/–	3. **Depreciation Expense–Delivery Equipment** is decreased by $3,000 and **Depreciation Expense–Office Equipment** is decreased by $2,500; the total decrease is $5,500. The $5,500 is transferred to the **Income Summary** account.

DEBIT-CREDIT RULE	4. To transfer the expenses to the **Income Summary** account, debit **Income Summary** for $5,500.
	5. Decreases in expense accounts are recorded as credits. Credit **Depreciation Expense–Delivery Equipment** for $3,000 and **Depreciation Expense–Office Equipment** for $2,500.

T ACCOUNTS   6.

Income Summary

Debit	Credit
5,500	

Depreciation Expense—Delivery Equipment

Debit +	Credit –
3,000	Clos. 3,000

Depreciation Expense—Office Equipment

Debit +	Credit –
2,500	Clos. 2,500

JOURNAL ENTRY   7.

GENERAL JOURNAL   PAGE 22

	DATE	DESCRIPTION	POST. REF.	DEBIT	CREDIT	
1	20--					1
2	Dec. 31	Income Summary		5 500 00		2
3		Depr. Exp.—Del. Equip.			3 000 00	3
4		Depr. Exp.—Office Equip.			2 500 00	4
5						5

AFTER YOU READ

Reinforce the Main Idea

Use a diagram like this one to show the last five steps of the accounting cycle as they relate to depreciation.

End-of-Period Accounting Cycle Steps	Step Number	How This Step Relates to Depreciation

Do the Math

You are preparing a depreciation schedule for a new piece of equipment you purchased for your business, Supreme T-Shirt Outfitters, for $5,000. It has a five-year estimated useful life and a $500 estimated disposal value. Calculate its annual depreciation using the straight-line method. Next calculate the accumulated depreciation and the equipment's book value at the end of each of the five years. Use a table like this one. Add rows for years 2 through 5.

End of	Purchase Price	Depreciation Expense	Accumulated Depreciation	Book Value
1ˢᵗ Year	5,000			

Problem 23–4 Analyzing a Source Document

Instructions In your working papers:

1. Record the purchase in the general journal, page 4.
2. Record the partial depreciation expense for the first year in the general journal, page 7.
    a. Disposal value—$200
    b. Estimated useful life—5 years
    c. Fiscal year end—December 31.
    d. Method—straight-line
3. Record the annual depreciation, one year later, in the general journal, page 13.

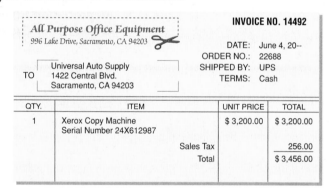

All Purpose Office Equipment
996 Lake Drive, Sacramento, CA 94203

INVOICE NO. 14492

TO Universal Auto Supply
1422 Central Blvd.
Sacramento, CA 94203

DATE: June 4, 20--
ORDER NO.: 22688
SHIPPED BY: UPS
TERMS: Cash

QTY.	ITEM	UNIT PRICE	TOTAL
1	Xerox Copy Machine Serial Number 24X612987	$ 3,200.00	$ 3,200.00
	Sales Tax		256.00
	Total		$ 3,456.00

Problem 23–5 Preparing a Depreciation Schedule and Journalizing the Depreciation Adjusting Entry

Quade Corporation bought a copy machine on January 7 of the current year for $2,360. It has an estimated useful life of five years and an estimated disposal value of $100.

Instructions In your working papers:

1. Prepare a depreciation schedule for the copy machine using the straight-line method of depreciation. (Use the form provided in your working papers.)
2. Journalize the adjustment for the copy machine's depreciation at the end of the first year.
3. Journalize the closing entry for the expense account affected by the adjusting entry.
4. What is the book value of the asset after five years? Is this the same as the disposal value?

Accounting Careers in Focus

U.S. OPERATIONS CONTROLLER
Viasystems, Mishawaka, Indiana
Brenda Engel

Q: What does Viasystems do?

A: We provide firms in a variety of industries with components for their manufacturing processes.

Q: How did you get into accounting?

A: I became interested in accounting at a young age when my mom let me help her with the bookkeeping for the family business.

Q: What is most challenging about your job?

A: Managing my time and attending to a variety of tasks. I'm responsible for overseeing the company's assets, as well as advising and training others in accounting software systems and overall business philosophy.

Q: What skills are needed for your job?

A: Strong analytical skills and patience are critical. It's equally important to have good communication and people skills. Being able to apply what you've learned in school to a work setting is also vital if you want to succeed in your job.

Q: What advice do you have for accounting students just beginning their careers?

A: Work in as many different settings and with as many different people as possible while you're in high school and college. You'll not only gain experience in different areas, but also meet other professionals who can guide you on an appropriate and exciting career path. In addition, make sure you learn and master software such as Microsoft Office. Computer skills are indispensable.

Tips from . . .
RHI Robert Half International Inc.

Learn to manage your time by planning ahead. Each morning, draft a quick "to do" list that includes all your short- and long-term projects. This document will help you determine the resources you need and allow you to prioritize your tasks.

CAREER FACTS

▶ **Nature of the Work:** Prepare and consolidate financial statements; manage all aspects of the general ledger; in some cases, supervise the accounts receivable, accounts payable, and general accounting departments.

▶ **Training or Education Needed:** A bachelor's degree in accounting or finance; a master's degree in business administration; CPA or CMA designation is preferred; at least five years of experience.

▶ **Aptitudes, Abilities, and Skills:** Strong analytical skills, technology skills, communication skills, and organizational skills.

▶ **Salary Range:** $45,000 to $115,000 depending on location, level of responsibility, and company revenues.

▶ **Career Path:** Start by working for a small company to learn a variety of skills, then gradually move into a management position.

Thinking Critically Why is it important for accounting professionals to have strong communication skills?

Key Concepts

1. The assets of a business can be classified as *current assets* or *plant assets*. Recall that current assets are either consumed or converted to cash during the normal operating cycle, usually one year. Examples are

   - cash
   - merchandise that will be sold shortly
   - supplies such as paper, pencils, and printer toner

   Plant assets are long-lived assets used in the production or sale of other assets or services over several accounting periods. Examples are

   - computers
   - copiers
   - cash registers
   - manufacturing equipment
   - office furniture
   - telephone systems
   - vehicles used in the business
   - the buildings that house the business

2. A plant asset is depreciated so that its cost is spread over its useful life. This spreads the cost over the periods that the asset will be used to generate revenue. This allows the business to conform to the matching principle of accounting, which requires that expenses be matched with the revenues the expenses helped to earn.

   Four factors used to calculate the depreciation of an asset are

   - its cost
   - its estimated useful life
   - its estimated disposal value
   - the depreciation method used

   The estimated useful life of a plant asset is the number of years it is expected to be used before it wears out. Depreciation is an estimate because no one can be certain how long an asset will last.

3. To match the cost of an asset with the revenue it is used to generate during a year, annual straight-line depreciation is calculated:

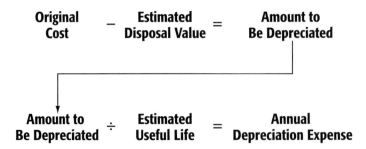

4. To calculate depreciation for part of a year:

$$\underset{\text{Depreciation Expense}}{\text{Annual}} \times \underset{\text{of Year}}{\text{Fraction}} = \underset{\text{Depreciation Expense}}{\text{Partial Year}}$$

5. An asset's book value is its original cost less its accumulated depreciation. To calculate book value:

$$\text{Original Cost} - \underset{\text{Depreciation}}{\text{Accumulated}} = \text{Book Value}$$

6. To record depreciation:

Depreciation Expense— Description of Asset		Accumulated Depreciation— Description of Asset	
Debit	Credit	Debit	Credit
+	–	–	+
XX			XX

7. When a business purchases a plant asset, it sets up a depreciation schedule for the asset. The amount of depreciation expense for each plant asset is recorded at the end of the year. The schedule typically has a column for each of the following:

- the date
- the asset's cost
- annual depreciation expense
- accumulated depreciation
- book value at the end of each year

Key Terms

accumulated depreciation	(p. 675)
book value	(p. 675)
depreciation	(p. 671)
disposal value	(p. 672)
plant assets	(p. 670)
straight-line depreciation	(p. 672)

Check Your Understanding

1. **Plant Assets**
   a. Explain the meaning of the term *plant asset.*
   b. Give four examples of plant assets.

2. **Plant Asset Depreciation**
   a. Depreciation is an application of what accounting principle?
   b. What distinguishes a plant asset from a current asset?

3. **Annual Depreciation**
   a. What four factors affect the depreciation calculation?
   b. How is the annual depreciation expense for a plant asset calculated under the straight-line method?

4. **Partial-Year Depreciation**
   a. Explain how depreciation for part of a year is calculated.
   b. What is meant by "allocating the cost" of a plant asset?

5. **Book Value of Plant Assets**
   a. What is accumulated depreciation?
   b. How is book value calculated?

6. **Record Depreciation**
   a. What is the classification of the **Accumulated Depreciation** account?
   b. Which two accounts are affected by an adjusting entry for depreciation?

7. **Prepare Depreciation Schedule**
   a. What is the purpose of a depreciation schedule?
   b. When is the depreciation of a plant asset recorded?

Apply Key Terms

You have just been hired as the plant accountant for Fast Runner, a large manufacturer of inline skates and skateboards. To do your job well, you must be able to understand and apply accounting procedures for plant assets and depreciation. Your immediate boss is the CEO for Fast Runner, Rob Myers. Rob wants you to define the following terms and give him some examples related to Fast Runner. Pair up with a colleague to discuss each term and find an example. Then write your ideas on a note pad for quick reference during your meeting with Rob. Good luck!

accumulated	depreciation	straight-line
depreciation	disposal value	depreciation
book value	plant assets	

Recording Depreciation

Making the Transition from a Manual to a Computerized System

Task	Manual Methods	Computerized Methods
Recording depreciation	• Estimated annual depreciation is calculated when a fixed asset is purchased. • Each accounting period, an adjusting entry is journalized and posted for each plant asset account in the general ledger. • Recording depreciation affects two accounts, **Accumulated Depreciation** and **Depreciation Expense**. • The **Depreciation Expense** account is closed at the end of the fiscal year.	• Estimated annual depreciation is calculated when a fixed asset is purchased. • A depreciation journal entry is recorded for the month's amount. The journal entry can be automatically posted each month as a recurring entry. • Amounts are posted to the **Depreciation Expense** and **Accumulated Depreciation** accounts. Their balances are automatically updated.

Peachtree® Q & A

Peachtree Question	Answer
How do I record depreciation for fixed assets in Peachtree?	1. From the *Tasks* menu, select **General Journal Entry**. 2. Enter the transaction to record the depreciation expense for the current period. 3. Select the **Recur** icon. 4. Select the number of times and how often you want this transaction to recur. (Each month? Each quarter? Each year?) 5. Click **OK**.

QuickBooks Q & A

QuickBooks Question	Answer
How do I record depreciation for fixed assets in QuickBooks?	1. From the *Company* menu, select **Make General Journal Entries**. 2. Enter the transaction to record the depreciation expense for the current period. 3. Memorize the recurring entry using **Memorize General Journal** from the *Edit* menu. 4. Set the number of times you want the entry to occur and click **OK**. 5. Click **Save & Close**.

For detailed instructions, see your Glencoe Accounting Chapter Study Guides and Working Papers.

Complete problems using: | **Manual** Glencoe Working Papers | OR | **Peachtree Complete Accounting** Software | OR | **QuickBooks** Templates

Peachtree®

SMART GUIDE

Step–by–Step Instructions: Problem 23–7

1. Select the problem set for InBeat CD Shop (Prob. 23–7).
2. Rename the company and set the system date.
3. Record the depreciation adjusting entries.
4. Print a General Journal report and proof your work.
5. Complete the Analyze activity.
6. End the session.

TIP: Use the **General Journal Entry** option to record adjusting entries.

Peachtree®

SMART GUIDE

Step–by–Step Instructions: Problem 23–8

1. Select the problem set for Shutterbug Cameras (Prob. 23–8).
2. Rename the company and set the system date.
3. Record the adjustments for depreciation using the **General Journal Entry** option.
4. Print a General Journal report and proof your work.
5. Print an Income Statement, a Statement of Retained Earnings, and a Balance Sheet.
6. Complete the Analyze activity.
7. End the session.

Problem 23–6 Opening a Plant Asset Record

On July 10 Sunset Surfwear purchased a scanner from Taunton Equipment for $1,500. Taunton Equipment charged Sunset Surfwear $200 to install the scanner. The scanner has an estimated useful life of four years and an estimated disposal value of $260.

Instructions Prepare a plant asset record, including the depreciation schedule for the new scanner. Use the form provided in your working papers.

> Serial number: TMC46312
> General ledger account: **Office Equipment**
> Location: Main Street store
> Depreciation method: Straight-line
> Manufacturer: Brothers Company

Analyze Describe how you determined the book value at the end of each period.

Problem 23–7 Recording Adjusting Entries for Depreciation

The following adjustments for depreciation were entered on the work sheet for InBeat CD Shop for the year ended December 31.

	Adjustments	
	Debit	Credit
Store Equipment		
Accumulated Depreciation—Store Equipment		(e) 3,800
Office Equipment		
Accumulated Depreciation—Office Equipment		(f) 1,400
Depreciation Expense—Store Equipment	(e) 3,800	
Depreciation Expense—Office Equipment	(f) 1,400	

Instructions Record the adjusting entries on general journal page 11.

Analyze Explain how the adjustment affects the book value of the store equipment.

Problem 23-8 Reporting Depreciation Expense on the Work Sheet and Financial Statements

The trial balance of Shutterbug Cameras appears on the work sheet included in your working papers. All adjustments, except those for depreciation, are already recorded on the work sheet.

Instructions

1. Record the following adjustments for depreciation expense on the work sheet.
   a. Depreciation for office equipment is $2,500.
   b. Depreciation for store equipment is $1,200.
2. Complete the work sheet.
3. Prepare an income statement, statement of retained earnings, and balance sheet for Shutterbug Cameras for the year ended December 31.

Analyze Calculate the total current assets.

Problem 23-9 Calculating and Recording Depreciation Expense

Cycle Tech Bicycles purchased manufacturing equipment on August 1 for $410,000. The equipment has an estimated useful life of 25 years and an estimated disposal value of $20,000. Cycle Tech uses the straight-line method of depreciation. The partial depreciation schedule found in your working papers is set up for the equipment.

Instructions

1. Calculate annual depreciation, accumulated depreciation, and book value for each of the first two years. The fiscal year ends December 31. Use the form provided in your working papers.
2. Calculate the depreciation adjustment to be entered on the work sheet at the end of the first year. Use T accounts to show the accounts debited and credited.
3. Journalize the adjustment for depreciation at the end of the first year, general journal page 21.

Analyze Determine the balance of the accumulated depreciation account at the end of the first and second years.

QuickBooks

PROBLEM GUIDE

Step–by–Step Instructions: Problem 23–8

1. Restore the Problem 23-8.QBB file.
2. Record the adjustments for depreciation using the **Make General Journal Entries** option.
3. Print a Journal report and proof your work.
4. Print a Profit & Loss report and Balance Sheet.
5. Complete the Analyze activity.
6. Back up your work.

Peachtree®

SMART GUIDE

Step–by–Step Instructions: Problem 23–9

1. Select the problem set for Cycle Tech Bicycles (Prob. 23–9).
2. Rename the company and set the system date.
3. Calculate the depreciation for the first two years.
4. Record the depreciation adjustment for the first year using the **General Journal Entry** option.
5. Print a General Journal report and a General Ledger report for the manufacturing equipment accounts and proof your work.
6. Complete the Analyze activity.
7. End the session.

Problems

SMART GUIDE

Step–by–Step Instructions: Problem 23–10

1. Select the problem set for River's Edge Canoe & Kayak (Prob. 23–10).
2. Rename the company and set the system date.
3. Calculate and record the end-of-period adjustments.
4. Print a General Journal report and proof your work.
5. Print an Income Statement and a Balance Sheet.
6. Close the fiscal year.
7. Print a Post-Closing Trial Balance.
8. Complete the Analyze activity.
9. End the session.

QuickBooks

PROBLEM GUIDE

Step–by–Step Instructions: Problem 23–10

1. Restore the Problem 23-10.QBB file.
2. Calculate and record the end-of-period adjustments.
3. Print a Journal report and proof your work.
4. Print a Profit & Loss report and Balance Sheet.
5. Enter the closing entries and print a Journal report.
6. Print a Post-Closing Trial Balance.
7. Complete the Analyze activity.

Problem 23–10 Calculating and Recording Adjustments

The December 31 trial balance of Rivers Edge Canoe & Kayak is included in your working papers.

Instructions

1. Calculate and record end-of-period adjustments on the work sheet.
   a. Ending **Merchandise Inventory** is $15,000.
   b. Supplies on hand total $1,450.
   c. The amount of the expired insurance premium is $5,000.
   d. Use the following information to calculate the estimated annual depreciation expense using the straight-line method.

Plant Asset	Cost	Estimated Disposal Value	Estimated Useful Life
Store Equipment	$ 13,000	$ 1,000	10 years
Delivery Truck	32,000	2,000	10 years
Building	160,000	10,000	25 years

   e. The total federal income tax expense for the year is $4,250.
2. Complete the work sheet.
3. Journalize and post the adjusting entries on page 16 of the general journal.
4. Journalize and post the closing entries on page 16 of the general journal.

Analyze   Calculate the total depreciation expense for the year.

Problem 23–11 Examining Depreciation Adjustments

On May 2 Buzz Newsstand purchased a new machine for $2,700. It has an estimated disposal value of $100 and an estimated useful life of eight years. Buzz uses the straight-line method.

On December 31 the adjustment for depreciation for the first year was entered: **Accumulated Depreciation—Store Equipment** was credited for $325, and **Depreciation Expense—Store Equipment** was debited for $325.

Instructions

Answer the following questions regarding this adjustment:

1. What is wrong with the adjustment for depreciation made on December 31? What is the correct entry?
2. One year from now, another adjustment for this machine will be entered on the work sheet. Assume the error from the previous year is not corrected. What amount should be entered in the Adjustments section for annual depreciation expense?

Analyze   Determine whether the current period net income will be too high or too low if the original error is not corrected.

Practice your test-taking skills! The questions on this page are reprinted with permission from national organizations:

- Future Business Leaders of America
- Business Professionals of America

Use a separate sheet of paper to record your answers.

Future Business Leaders of America

MULTIPLE CHOICE

1. A truck used in daily operations of a corporation would be considered a(n)

    a. long-term asset.

    b. plant asset.

    c. intangible asset.

    d. either A or B.

    e. none of these answers

2. A method that allocates an equal portion of the total depreciation for a plant asset (cost minus salvage) to each accounting period in its service life is

    a. accelerated depreciation.

    b. units-of-production.

    c. straight-line depreciation.

    d. sum-of-the-years'-digits depreciation.

    e. declining-balance depreciation.

3. The Crimson Cartage Company purchased a new truck at a cost of $42,000 on July 1. The truck is estimated to have a useful life of 6 years and a salvage value of $6,000. Using the straight-line method, how much depreciation expense will be recorded for the truck during the first year ended December 31?

    a. $3,000

    b. $3,500

    c. $4,000

    d. $6,000

    e. $7,000

4. The adjusting entry for the depreciation of a plant asset such as equipment involves a credit to

    a. equipment expense.

    b. accumulated equipment.

    c. depreciation expense.

    d. accumulated depreciation.

Business Professionals of America

MULTIPLE CHOICE

5. The entry to record depreciation for the fax machine at the end of the fiscal period

    a. Debit Accumulated Depreciation—Maintenance Equipment, credit Depreciation Expense—Maintenance Equipment

    b. Debit Depreciation Expense—Maintenance Equipment, credit Accumulated Depreciation—Maintenance Equipment

    c. Debit Accumulated Depreciation—Office Equipment, credit Depreciation Expense—Office Equipment

    d. Debit Depreciation Expense—Office Equipment, credit Accumulated Depreciation—Office Equipment

> **Need More Help?**
>
> **Go to glencoeaccounting.glencoe.com and click on Student Center. Click on Winning Competitive Events and select Chapter 23.**
> - **Practice Questions and Test-Taking Tips**
> - **Concept Capsules and Terminology**

Plant Assets

1. Name several plant assets that a business might use to sell merchandise.
2. Explain how current assets and plant assets differ.
3. A company purchased plant assets for $100,000. It expects to sell them in 4 years for 20 percent of the cost. What is the depreciation expense?
4. Classify these assets: land, building, cash, accounts receivable, computer equipment, merchandise inventory, supplies, and prepaid insurance into (a) plant assets or (b) current assets. Identify the assets to be depreciated.
5. Set up the formulas for calculating the amount to be depreciated, the annual depreciation expense, the accumulated depreciation, and book value.
6. Justify crediting the **Accumulated Depreciation** account rather than the **Plant Asset** account when recording depreciation expense.

Merchandising Business: Photography Studio

Karina Ludmiko is turning her photography hobby into a business called The Photo Studio. She asked you to set up the company's asset records.

INSTRUCTIONS

1. Assume that The Photo Studio's photography equipment cost $25,000, has a 10-year useful life, and no salvage value. Set up a depreciation schedule.
2. Explain to Karina how depreciation appears on the financial statements.

Whom Will They Believe?

After working for a year as payroll clerk for a small publishing company, you believe you have evidence of embezzlement—and suspect the department manager or senior accountant. Whom can you tell? Who would believe you?

ETHICAL DECISION MAKING

1. What are the ethical issues?
2. What are the alternatives?
3. Who are the affected parties?
4. How do the alternatives affect the parties?
5. What would you do?

Promoting Technology

As accountant for Playtime Preschool, you want to convince the owner to purchase computers for the children to use. Explain that the company can depreciate the $10,000 investment and deduct the depreciation on its tax return. With a classmate, brainstorm the four factors affecting the depreciation estimate. List your recommendations and practice presenting them to the owner.

Acquiring and Evaluating Information

As Westside Wholesale's newly hired manager, you plan for and control its plant assets. One standard you will be measured by is your budget and the controls you use to stay within that budget. Describe the information you will need to prepare a budget for equipment purchases and maintenance. List internal control procedures to help prevent asset loss and theft. Explain how the budget can be used to evaluate your performance.

Plant Assets

Global companies may use the *revaluation model* allowed by International Accounting Standard 16 to record plant assets. After initially recording an asset at cost, this model revalues an asset at its fair market value less subsequent depreciation, if fair market value can be measured reliably.

INSTRUCTIONS Define *fair market value*. How would revaluation affect the income statement?

Your Vehicle

A vehicle is a valuable asset. The vehicle declines in value each year, but if you keep it properly maintained, it will have a higher resale value when you sell it.

PERSONAL FINANCE ACTIVITY Determine the book value of your vehicle. It cost $20,000. Its value declined $6,000 in the first year, $4,000 in the second year, and $2,500 in the third year.

PERSONAL FINANCE ONLINE Log on to **glencoeaccounting.glencoe.com** and click on **Student Center.** Click on **Making It Personal** and select **Chapter 23.**

Vertical Analysis

Vertical analysis makes it easy to compare financial statements with industry standards, which are average percentages for companies in the same industry. Assume these partial vertical analyses of an income statement and balance sheet are for the pet food and pet supply industry.

Income Statement Vertical Analysis	
Net sales	100.0%
Cost of sales	68.9
Gross profit	31.1%

Balance Sheet Vertical Analysis	
Current assets	34.3%
Property & equipment	49.3
All other assets	16.4
Total assets	100.0%

INSTRUCTIONS Use PETsMART's financial statements in Appendix F for these tasks.

1. Complete a vertical analysis of PETsMART's cost of sales and gross profit for the year ended February 1, 2004. Compare them to the industry standards above.

2. Complete a vertical analysis of PETsMART's assets using the classifications above, as of February 1, 2004. Compare PETsMART's asset mix with the industry standard.

Depreciation

Proper procedures can save time in calculating depreciation. Visit **glencoeaccounting .glencoe.com** and click on **Student Center.** Click on **WebQuest** and select **Unit 5** to continue your Internet project.

CHAPTER 24

Uncollectible Accounts Receivable

What You'll Learn

1. Explain methods used to write off uncollectible accounts.

2. Determine uncollectible accounts receivable.

3. Use the direct write-off method for uncollectible accounts.

4. Calculate bad debts expense.

5. Make an adjusting entry for uncollectible accounts.

6. Use the allowance method to record uncollectible accounts.

7. Record the collection of an account previously written off.

8. Describe two methods to estimate uncollectible accounts expense.

9. Define the accounting terms introduced in this chapter.

Why It's Important

▶ When a business extends credit, it assumes the risk of uncollectible accounts.

BEFORE YOU READ

Predict

1. What does the chapter title tell you?
2. What do you already know about this subject from personal experience?
3. What have you learned about this in the earlier chapters?
4. What gaps exist in your knowledge of this subject?

Exploring the *Real World* of Business

ANALYZING CREDIT LOSSES

U.S. Government Accountability Office

Do you ever wonder who keeps watch on how your federal tax dollars are spent? The **Government Accountability Office (GAO)** has you covered. Independent and nonpartisan, the **GAO** recommends ways for government agencies to be more effective, audits federal expenditures, investigates fraudulent activities, and issues legal opinions.

You may hear news reports about budget deficits or social security shortfalls. Many Americans are worried about funding homeland security and health care. Business owners and farmers can secure government loans but may fail to repay them due to bad economic times. Elected officials express concern that the government is not collecting its outstanding loans and debts. In light of all these issues, the watchdog **GAO** is clearly the taxpayer's best friend.

What Do You Think?

Why is it important for the federal government to have good collection policies for the money it is owed?

Working in the *Real World*

APPLYING YOUR ACCOUNTING KNOWLEDGE

When people cannot pay their debts, businesses must decide what to do about these losses. Retailers and banks are examples of businesses that are likely to have customers who fail to pay what they owe. When a business cannot collect the amounts it is owed, it records them in the accounting records. In this chapter you will learn how to estimate and record uncollectible amounts.

Personal Connection

1. Does your workplace have customers who fail to pay what they owe?

2. How does the business handle amounts it cannot collect?

Online Connection

Go to **glencoeaccounting.glencoe.com** and click on **Student Center.** Click on **Working in the Real World** and select **Chapter 24.**

The Direct Write-Off Method

In previous chapters you learned that many businesses sell goods or services on account. Some charge customers cannot or will not pay the amounts they owe.

Extending Credit
Why Do Businesses Extend Credit?

Selling goods and services on credit is a standard practice for businesses of all sizes and types. They offer credit because they expect to sell more than they would by accepting only cash.

Retail stores typically ask customers seeking to purchase on account to complete a credit application. Before a business extends credit, it should check each prospective customer's credit rating to help determine the customer's ability to pay the amounts charged on account. Businesses get these credit ratings from the national consumer-credit-reporting companies Equifax, Experian, and TransUnion. Wholesalers and manufacturers use reports from wholesale credit bureaus and national credit-rating organizations such as Dun & Bradstreet.

An **uncollectible account**, or *bad debt,* is an account receivable that the business cannot collect. The business eventually removes the account receivable from its records, and the amount becomes an expense to the business. Businesses account for bad debts by using the *direct write-off method* or the *allowance method.*

The Direct Write-Off Method
What Is the Direct Write-Off Method?

The *direct write-off method* is used primarily by small businesses and those with few charge customers. Under the **direct write-off method**, when the business determines that the amount owed is not going to be paid, the uncollectible account is removed from the accounting records. **Uncollectible Accounts Expense** is debited and **Accounts Receivable** (both controlling and subsidiary) is credited. The direct write-off method is the only method a business can use for income tax purposes.

Writing Off an Uncollectible Account

On June 4 On Your Mark Athletic Wear sold football equipment on account to Robert Galvin for $250 plus $15 sales tax. It recorded the transaction as a $265 debit to **Accounts Receivable** (controlling) and the subsidiary account **Accounts Receivable—Robert Galvin** and as a credit to **Sales** for $250 and **Sales Tax Payable** for $15.

BEFORE YOU READ

Main Idea
A business using the direct write-off method converts an account receivable to an expense when it becomes clear the customer will not pay the bill.

Read to Learn...
➤ how and why businesses extend credit. (p. 698)
➤ how to write off an uncollectible account using the direct method. (p. 698)

Key Terms
uncollectible account
direct write-off method

As You READ

Key Point
Uncollectible Accounts Writing off an uncollectible account converts an asset to an expense.

For over a year, On Your Mark tried to collect this account. The length of time is one consideration used to determine uncollectible accounts receivable. It is now apparent that Robert Galvin is not going to pay the $265.

In effect, a business must decrease total assets and increase total expenses when a customer fails to pay a debt. On Your Mark must decrease its **Accounts Receivable** account and increase its expense related to uncollectible accounts.

Business Transaction

On August 25, 2011, On Your Mark wrote off as uncollectible Galvin's account for $265, Memorandum 170.

ANALYSIS	*Identify*	1.	The accounts affected are **Uncollectible Accounts Expense, Accounts Receivable** (controlling), and **Accounts Receivable–Robert Galvin** (subsidiary).
	Classify	2.	**Uncollectible Accounts Expense** is an expense account. **Accounts Receivable** (controlling) and **Accounts Receivable–Robert Galvin** (subsidiary) are asset accounts.
	+/–	3.	**Uncollectible Accounts Expense** is increased by $265. **Accounts Receivable** (controlling) and **Accounts Receivable–Robert Galvin** (subsidiary) are decreased by $265.

DEBIT-CREDIT RULE	4.	Increases to expense accounts are recorded as debits. Debit **Uncollectible Accounts Expense** for $265.
	5.	Decreases to asset accounts are recorded as credits. Credit **Accounts Receivable** (controlling) and **Accounts Receivable–Robert Galvin** (subsidiary) for $265.

T ACCOUNTS

6.

Uncollectible Accounts Expense		Accounts Receivable	
Debit + 265	Credit –	Debit +	Credit – 265

Accounts Receivable Subsidiary Ledger
Robert Galvin

Debit +	Credit – 265

JOURNAL ENTRY

7.

	GENERAL JOURNAL		PAGE 13	

	DATE	DESCRIPTION	POST. REF.	DEBIT	CREDIT	
1	2011					1
2	Aug. 25	Uncollectible Accounts Expense		265 00		2
3		Accts. Rec./Robert Galvin			265 00	3
4		Memorandum 170				4
5						5

Account: Accounts Receivable — Account No. 115

DATE		DESCRIPTION	POST. REF.	DEBIT	CREDIT	BALANCE DEBIT	BALANCE CREDIT
2011							
Aug.	1	Balance	✓			7 8 2 1 42	
	25	Write-off	G13		2 6 5 00	7 5 5 6 42	

Account: Uncollectible Accounts Expense — Account No. 675

DATE		DESCRIPTION	POST. REF.	DEBIT	CREDIT	BALANCE DEBIT	BALANCE CREDIT
2011							
Aug.	25		G13	2 6 5 00		2 6 5 00	

NAME Robert Galvin
ADDRESS 10223 Riggs Circle, Mesquite, TX 75181

DATE		DESCRIPTION	POST. REF.	DEBIT	CREDIT	BALANCE
2010						
June	4		S14	2 6 5 00		2 6 5 00
2011						
Aug.	25	Written off as uncollectible	G13		2 6 5 00	—

Figure 24–1 Ledger
Accounts After an
Uncollectible Write-Off

Figure 24–1 shows how this transaction is posted to the general ledger and the accounts receivable subsidiary ledger.

Notice the explanation entered in Robert Galvin's account. When an account is written off as uncollectible, it is important to note on the subsidiary ledger that the account was not paid off but was written off.

Collecting a Written-Off Account

Occasionally, a charge customer whose account was written off as uncollectible later pays the amount owed. When this happens:

- First, reinstate the customer's account, or reenter it in the accounting records.
- Second, record the cash receipt.

Business Transaction

On September 5 On Your Mark received $265 from Robert Galvin, whose account was written off as uncollectible on August 25, Memorandum 176 and Receipt 1109. First reinstate the account receivable.

ANALYSIS	Identify	1.	The accounts affected are **Accounts Receivable** (controlling), **Accounts Receivable—Robert Galvin** (subsidiary), and **Uncollectible Accounts Expense.**
	Classify	2.	**Accounts Receivable** (controlling) and **Accounts Receivable—Robert Galvin** (subsidiary) are asset accounts. **Uncollectible Accounts Expense** is an expense account.
	+/−	3.	**Accounts Receivable** (controlling) and **Accounts Receivable—Robert Galvin** (subsidiary) are increased by $265. **Uncollectible Accounts Expense** is decreased by $265.

| | | DEBIT-CREDIT RULE | **4.** Increases to asset accounts are recorded as debits. Debit **Accounts Receivable** (controlling) and **Accounts Receivable—Robert Galvin** (subsidiary) for $265. |
| | | | **5.** Decreases to expense accounts are recorded as credits. Credit **Uncollectible Accounts Expense** for $265. |

T ACCOUNTS

6.

Accounts Receivable		Uncollectible Accounts Expense	
Debit + 265	Credit –	Debit + 265	Credit – 265

Accounts Receivable Subsidiary Ledger
Robert Galvin

Debit + 265	Credit –

JOURNAL ENTRY

7.

	GENERAL JOURNAL			PAGE 14	
DATE	DESCRIPTION	POST. REF.	DEBIT	CREDIT	
1	2011					1
2	Sept. 5 Accts. Rec./Robert Galvin		265 00		2
3	Uncollectible Accts. Expense			265 00	3
4	Memorandum 176				4
5					5

After this transaction has been posted, the cash receipt is recorded as a debit to **Cash in Bank** for $265 and a credit to **Accounts Receivable** (controlling) for $265. Also, the subsidiary account **Accounts Receivable—Robert Galvin** is credited for $265. Receipt 1109 is the source document for this entry.

Robert Galvin's subsidiary ledger account in **Figure 24–2** contains data about the sale, write-off, reinstatement, and cash receipt.

NAME *Robert Galvin*
ADDRESS *10223 Riggs Circle, Mesquite, TX 75181*

DATE		DESCRIPTION	POST. REF.	DEBIT	CREDIT	BALANCE
2010						
June	4		S14	265 00		265 00
2011						
Aug.	25	Written off as uncollectible	G13		265 00	—
Sept.	5	Reinstated	G14	265 00		265 00
	5		G14		265 00	—

Figure 24–2 Robert Galvin Account

Reinforce the Main Idea

Create a diagram similar to the one here to show four journal entries related to the direct write-off method of accounting for uncollectible accounts receivable.

Transaction Description

Journal Entry

Do the Math

You are the accounts receivable clerk for Fast and Friendly Shipping. The balance of the **Accounts Receivable** account is $25,000. For six months you have been trying to collect the amounts owed by three companies: ABC Company, $450; XYZ Company, $500; and Nice Try Company, $350. These accounts are still unpaid. Your supervisor asked you to write off these accounts using the direct write-off method. What is the balance of **Accounts Receivable** after you write off these accounts as uncollectible?

Problem 24–1 Using the Direct Write-Off Method

The Parker Supply Company uses the direct write-off method of accounting for uncollectible accounts.

Instructions In your working papers:

1. Record the following transactions on page 21 of the general journal.
2. Post the transactions to the appropriate accounts.

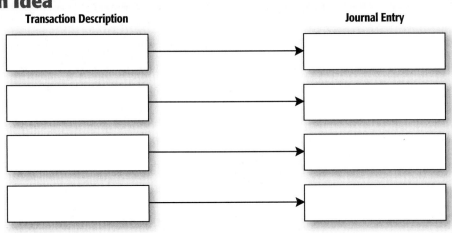

Parker Supply Company   MEMORANDUM 78

TO: Accounting Clerk
FROM: Jon Herbert, Collection Manager
DATE: November 30, 20--
SUBJECT: Account write-off

It has been determined by the collection department that Account No. 4698214, Sonya Dickson, in the amount of $630, is uncollectible. This memo is your authorization to write this amount off as uncollectible.
Thank you.

Date	Transactions
Apr. 10	Sold merchandise on account to Sonya Dickson, $600 plus $30 sales tax, Sales Slip 928.
Nov. 30	Wrote off Sonya Dickson's account as uncollectible, $630, Memorandum 78.
Dec. 30	Received $630 from Sonya Dickson in full payment of her account. This account was written off on November 30, Memorandum 89 and Receipt 277.

The Allowance Method

In Section 1 you learned that the direct write-off method is used by

- small businesses,
- businesses with few credit customers, and
- all businesses for tax purposes.

In contrast, businesses that have many credit customers use the allowance method of accounting for uncollectible accounts. This method allows businesses to match revenue with the expenses incurred to earn that revenue. In this section you will learn about the allowance method and continue to journalize transactions involving uncollectible accounts.

Matching Uncollectible Accounts Expense with Revenue

Why Do Businesses Use the Matching Principle to Report Uncollectible Accounts?

When the direct write-off method of accounting for uncollectible accounts is used, an unpaid account is written off when the business determines that it will not be paid. Under the direct write-off method, it often happens that the sale is recorded in one period, and the uncollectible accounts expense is recorded in the following period. This violates the matching principle.

One of the fundamental principles of accounting is that *revenue should be matched with the expenses incurred in generating that revenue.* This means that expenses incurred to earn revenue should be deducted in the same period that the revenue is recorded. The uncollectible accounts expense should be reported in the year in which the sale takes place. However, the uncollectible account expense is usually not determined with certainty until some future period. That is, a credit sale in the year 2010 may not be determined to be uncollectible until some time in 2011. In order to conform to the matching principle, the credit sales are recorded in the year 2010 and an *estimate* of the uncollectible accounts expense is also recorded in 2010.

Before You READ

Main Idea
A business using the allowance method estimates the bad debt expense and writes off that amount.

Read to Learn...
➤ why businesses apply the matching principle to accounts receivable. (p. 703)
➤ how businesses use the matching principle to recognize bad debt expense. (p. 704)

Key Terms
allowance method
book value of accounts receivable

The estimate of uncollectible accounts expense is recorded as an end-of-period adjustment. The adjusting entry meets two objectives:

1. **Accounts Receivable** is reduced to the amount the business can reasonably expect to receive.
2. The estimated uncollectible accounts expense is charged to the current period.

The Allowance Method

How Do You Use the Allowance Method to Report Uncollectible Accounts Expense?

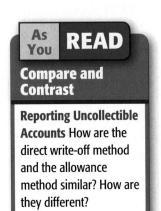

As You READ

Compare and Contrast

Reporting Uncollectible Accounts How are the direct write-off method and the allowance method similar? How are they different?

The **allowance method** of accounting for uncollectible accounts matches the estimated uncollectible accounts expense with sales made during the same period. At the end of the period, the accountant must calculate the uncollectible accounts expense that will result from the sales made during the period. The estimated uncollectible accounts expense is recorded as an adjustment on the work sheet. The two accounts affected by this adjustment are **Uncollectible Accounts Expense** and **Allowance for Uncollectible Accounts.**

When the adjustment is made, the business does not know exactly which charge customers will not pay the amounts they owe. Therefore, the estimated uncollectible amount cannot be credited to **Accounts Receivable** (neither the controlling nor the subsidiary). Since the **Accounts Receivable** account cannot be used to record the estimated uncollectible amount, another account is opened. This account is **Allowance for Uncollectible Accounts.**

Allowance for Uncollectible Accounts is used to summarize the *estimated* uncollectible accounts receivable of the business. It is classified as a contra asset account.

Allowance for
Uncollectible Accounts

Debit	Credit
−	+
Decrease Side	Increase Side
	Normal Balance

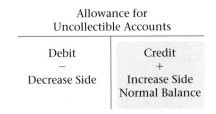

On Your Mark
Work
For the Year Ended

	ACCT. NO.	ACCOUNT NAME	TRIAL BALANCE		ADJUSTMENTS	
			DEBIT	CREDIT	DEBIT	CREDIT
1	101	Cash in Bank	12 650 00			
2	115	Accounts Receivable	44 893 00			
3	117	Allowance for Uncollectible Accts.		125 00		(b)1 350 00
23	670	Supplies Expense	600 00			
24	675	Uncollectible Accounts Expense			(b)1 350 00	
25						

Figure 24–3 Recording the Adjustment for Uncollectible Accounts on the Work Sheet

Adjustment

On December 31 On Your Mark estimates its uncollectible accounts expense for the year ended December 31 to be $1,350. (Various methods are used to estimate uncollectible accounts expense. You will learn about two of these methods later in this chapter.)

ANALYSIS — *Identify*
1. The accounts affected are **Uncollectible Accounts Expense** and **Allowance for Uncollectible Accounts.**

Classify
2. **Uncollectible Accounts Expense** is an expense account. **Allowance for Uncollectible Accounts** is a contra asset account.

+/−
3. **Uncollectible Accounts Expense** is increased by $1,350. **Allowance for Uncollectible Accounts** is increased by $1,350.

DEBIT-CREDIT RULE
4. Increases to expense accounts are recorded as debits. Debit **Uncollectible Accounts Expense** for $1,350.
5. Increases to contra asset accounts are recorded as credits. Credit **Allowance for Uncollectible Accounts** for $1,350.

T ACCOUNTS
6.

Uncollectible Accounts Expense		Allowance for Uncollectible Accounts	
Debit + 1,350	Credit −	Debit −	Credit + 1,350

JOURNAL ENTRY
7.

GENERAL JOURNAL PAGE 15

	DATE		DESCRIPTION	POST. REF.	DEBIT	CREDIT	
1	20--		*Adjusting Entries*				1
2	Dec.	31	Uncollectible Accts. Expense		1 350 00		2
3			Allow. for Uncollectible Accts.			1 350 00	3
4							4
5							5

Athletic Wear

Sheet

December 31, 20--

ADJUSTED TRIAL BALANCE		INCOME STATEMENT		BALANCE SHEET		
DEBIT	CREDIT	DEBIT	CREDIT	DEBIT	CREDIT	
12 650 00				12 650 00		1
44 893 00				44 893 00		2
	1 475 00				1 475 00	3
600 00		600 00				23
1 350 00		1 350 00				24
						25

Figure 24–3 Recording the Adjustment for Uncollectible Accounts on the Work Sheet (continued)

Book Value *Book value* of a plant asset is the initial cost minus accumulated depreciation. *Book value* of accounts receivable is the controlling account balance minus the allowance for uncollectible accounts.

Allowance for Uncollectible Accounts appears on the balance sheet as a deduction from **Accounts Receivable**. By using **Allowance for Uncollectible Accounts**:

- The balance of **Accounts Receivable** still equals the total of the customer accounts in the subsidiary ledger.
- The balance of **Allowance for Uncollectible Accounts** represents the amount the business *estimates* to be uncollectible.
- The difference between **Accounts Receivable** and **Allowance for Uncollectible Accounts** represents the book value of accounts receivable.

The **book value of accounts receivable** is the amount the business can reasonably expect to collect from its accounts receivable. **Figure 24–3** on pages 704 and 705 illustrates how this adjustment is recorded and extended on the work sheet.

Notice that **Allowance for Uncollectible Accounts** has a $125 balance in the Trial Balance Credit column. This balance is carried over from previous years. If the previous years' uncollectible accounts exactly equaled the estimate, **Allowance for Uncollectible Accounts** would have a zero balance. This seldom happens.

Also notice that the new balance is extended first to the Adjusted Trial Balance Credit column and then to the Balance Sheet Credit column.

Reporting Estimated Uncollectible Amounts on the Financial Statements

The **Uncollectible Accounts Expense** account appears on On Your Mark's income statement as an expense. See **Figure 24–4** for the placement of the **Uncollectible Accounts Expense** account in its partial income statement.

Figure 24–4 Reporting Uncollectible Accounts on the Income Statement

On Your Mark Athletic Wear						
Income Statement						
For the Year Ended December 31, 20--						
Operating Expenses						
Supplies Expense				6 0 0 00		
Uncollectible Accounts Expense			1 3 5 0 00			
Total Operating Expenses					38 3 4 5 00	
Operating Income					24 6 9 8 00	

Figure 24–5 Reporting Allowance for Uncollectible Accounts on the Balance Sheet

On Your Mark Athletic Wear				
Balance Sheet				
December 31, 20--				
Assets				
Cash in Bank				12 6 5 0 00
Accounts Receivable		44 8 9 3 00		
Less: Allowance for		1 4 7 5 00	43 4 1 8 00	
Uncollectible Accounts				

On the balance sheet, **Allowance for Uncollectible Accounts** is listed immediately below **Accounts Receivable** in the Assets section. See On Your Mark's partial balance sheet in **Figure 24–5.**

Notice that the balances of **Accounts Receivable** and **Allowance for Uncollectible Accounts** are entered in the first amount column. The difference between the two balances—the book value of accounts receivable—is entered in the second amount column.

Journalizing the Adjusting Entry for Uncollectible Accounts

After the work sheet has been completed and the financial statements have been prepared, the adjusting entries are journalized. The information for the adjusting entries is found in the Adjustments section of the work sheet as shown in **Figure 24–3** on pages 704 and 705.

As You READ

Instant Recall

Adjusting Entry An adjusting entry affects one *temporary* account and one *permanent* account.

GENERAL JOURNAL   PAGE 14

	DATE		DESCRIPTION	POST. REF.	DEBIT	CREDIT	
1	20--		*Adjusting Entries*				1
2	Dec.	31	Uncollectible Accounts Expense	675	1 3 5 0 00		2
3			Allowance for Uncollectible Accounts	117		1 3 5 0 00	3
4							4

ACCOUNT *Allowance for Uncollectible Accounts*   ACCOUNT NO. 117

DATE		DESCRIPTION	POST. REF.	DEBIT	CREDIT	BALANCE DEBIT	BALANCE CREDIT
20--							
Dec.	1	Balance	✓				1 2 5 00
	31	Adjusting Entry	G14		1 3 5 0 00		1 4 7 5 00

ACCOUNT *Uncollectible Accounts Expense*   ACCOUNT NO. 675

DATE		DESCRIPTION	POST. REF.	DEBIT	CREDIT	BALANCE DEBIT	BALANCE CREDIT
20--							
Dec.	31	Adjusting Entry	G14	1 3 5 0 00		1 3 5 0 00	

See **Figure 24–6** for the way the adjusting entry for the estimated uncollectible accounts expense is recorded in the general journal and posted to the appropriate general ledger accounts.

At the end of the period, the balance of the **Uncollectible Accounts Expense** account is closed, along with the balances of the other expense accounts, to **Income Summary. Uncollectible Accounts Expense** has a zero balance at the beginning of the next period. The balance of **Allowance for Uncollectible Accounts** is not affected by the closing entries. It is a permanent account, and its balance at the beginning of the next period remains $1,475.

Figure 24–6 Journalizing and Posting the Adjusting Entry for Uncollectible Accounts

Writing Off Uncollectible Accounts Receivable

When it becomes clear that a charge customer is not going to pay the amount owed, the accountant removes the uncollectible account from the accounting records.

Allowance for Uncollectible Accounts acts as a reservoir; that is, at the end of the period, the adjusting entry "fills it up." The account balance is saved until it is needed some time in the future. When a charge customer's account finally proves uncollectible, the business dips into that reservoir to write off the account. In other words **Allowance for Uncollectible Accounts** is reduced when a specific account is written off. Let's look at an example.

Business Transaction

On April 18, after many attempts to collect the amount owed, On Your Mark decides to write off the account of Megan Sullivan for $150, Memorandum 236.

ANALYSIS	*Identify*	1. The accounts affected are **Allowance for Uncollectible Accounts, Accounts Receivable** (controlling), and **Accounts Receivable—Megan Sullivan** (subsidiary).
	Classify	2. **Allowance for Uncollectible Accounts** is a contra asset account. **Accounts Receivable** (controlling) and **Accounts Receivable—Megan Sullivan** (subsidiary) are asset accounts.
	+/−	3. **Allowance for Uncollectible Accounts** is decreased by $150. **Accounts Receivable** (controlling) and **Accounts Receivable—Megan Sullivan** (subsidiary) are decreased by $150.

DEBIT-CREDIT RULE	4. Decreases to contra asset accounts are recorded as debits. Debit **Allowance for Uncollectible Accounts** for $150.
	5. Decreases to asset accounts are recorded as credits. Credit **Accounts Receivable** (controlling) and **Accounts Receivable—Megan Sullivan** (subsidiary) for $150.

T ACCOUNTS

6.

Allowance for Uncollectible Accounts	
Debit −	Credit +
150	

Accounts Receivable	
Debit +	Credit −
	150

Accounts Receivable Subsidiary Ledger
Megan Sullivan

Debit +	Credit −
	150

JOURNAL ENTRY

7.

			GENERAL JOURNAL			PAGE 16
	DATE	DESCRIPTION	POST. REF.	DEBIT	CREDIT	
1	20--					1
2	Apr. 18	Allow. for Uncollectible Accts.		150 00		2
3		Accts. Rec./Megan Sullivan			150 00	3
4		Memorandum 236				4
5						5

Under the allowance method, the write-off of a specific account does not affect an expense account. Recall that the expense was already recorded as an adjusting entry.

The adjusting entry recorded the entire estimated expense for the period, not just this one customer's bad debt.

Collecting an Account Written Off by the Allowance Method

A charge customer whose account was written off as uncollectible might later pay the amount owed. When this happens:

- First, reinstate the customer's account.
- Second, record the cash receipt.

As You READ

In Your Own Words

Reinstatement What does it mean to *reinstate* an account receivable?

Business Transaction

On November 19 On Your Mark received a check for $150 from Megan Sullivan, whose account was written off April 18, Memorandum 294 and Receipt 2243.

ANALYSIS	*Identify*	1. The accounts affected are **Accounts Receivable** (controlling), **Accounts Receivable—Megan Sullivan** (subsidiary), and **Allowance for Uncollectible Accounts.**
	Classify	2. **Accounts Receivable** (controlling) and **Accounts Receivable—Megan Sullivan** (subsidiary) are asset accounts. **Allowance for Uncollectible Accounts** is a contra asset account.
	+/−	3. **Accounts Receivable** (controlling) and **Accounts Receivable—Megan Sullivan** (subsidiary) are increased by $150. **Allowance for Uncollectible Accounts** is increased by $150.

DEBIT-CREDIT RULE	4. Increases to asset accounts are recorded as debits. Debit **Accounts Receivable** (controlling) and **Accounts Receivable—Megan Sullivan** (subsidiary) for $150.
	5. Increases to contra asset accounts are recorded as credits. Credit **Allowance for Uncollectible Accounts** for $150.

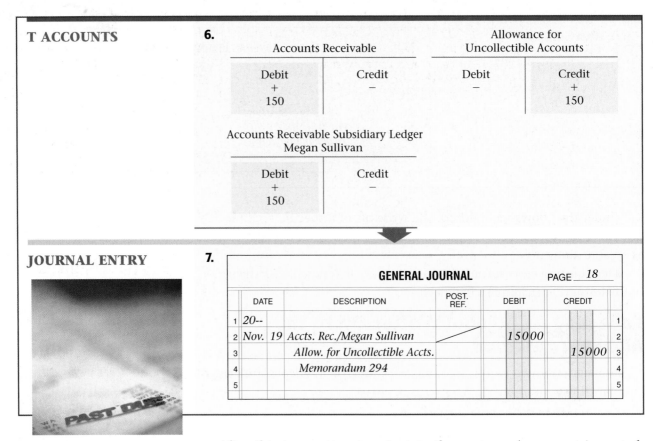

T ACCOUNTS

6.

Accounts Receivable		Allowance for Uncollectible Accounts	
Debit + 150	Credit −	Debit −	Credit + 150

Accounts Receivable Subsidiary Ledger
Megan Sullivan

Debit + 150	Credit −

JOURNAL ENTRY

7.

		GENERAL JOURNAL			PAGE 18	
	DATE	DESCRIPTION	POST. REF.	DEBIT	CREDIT	
1	20--					1
2	Nov. 19	Accts. Rec./Megan Sullivan		150 00		2
3		Allow. for Uncollectible Accts.			150 00	3
4		Memorandum 294				4
5						5

After this transaction to reinstate the customer's account is posted, the cash receipt transaction is journalized and posted. **Figure 24–7** shows Megan Sullivan's account after the cash receipt transaction is posted. The account shows that:

1. The account had been declared uncollectible and was written off.
2. The account was reinstated.
3. The account was collected in full.

NAME _Megan Sullivan_
ADDRESS _883 Bisbee Drive, Dallas, TX 75211_

DATE		DESCRIPTION	POST. REF.	DEBIT	CREDIT	BALANCE
20--						
Jan.	1	Balance	✓			150 00
Apr.	18	Written off as uncollectible	G16		150 00	—
Nov.	19	Reinstated	G18	150 00		150 00
	19		G18		150 00	—

Figure 24–7 Megan Sullivan Account

Reinforce the Main Idea

Use a diagram like the one shown here to describe what happens when payment is received for an account receivable that had been written off.

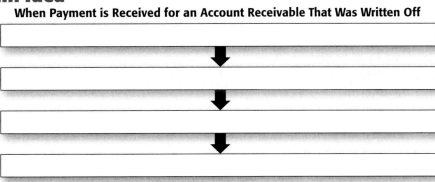

When Payment is Received for an Account Receivable That Was Written Off

Do the Math

A review of the accounting records for Mary Sawyer's business, Secret Garden, revealed a disturbing trend. Her uncollectible accounts continue to increase. You suspect that Mary is far too nice about extending "in store" credit. You strongly recommend that she change her credit policies and collect on the outstanding accounts for this year. However Mary does not seem to understand the big picture, and she requested an illustration. Use a line graph to chart the uncollectibles for the past five years using the following figures.

Year 1 $1,500   Year 4 $2,422
Year 2 $1,875   Year 5 $2,800
Year 3 $2,300

Problem 24–2   Writing Off Accounts Using the Allowance Method

Taylor Furniture Company Inc. uses the allowance method to account for uncollectible accounts.

Instructions   In your working papers:

1. Record the following transactions in the general journal on page 24.
2. Post the transactions to the appropriate accounts.
3. Prepare the Assets section of the balance sheet for Taylor Furniture Company Inc. using the partial general ledger in your working papers. The balance of other asset accounts are **Merchandise Inventory**, $42,000; **Supplies**, $1,500; and **Prepaid Insurance**, $1,200.

Date	Transactions
May 4	Using the allowance method, wrote off the account of Jack Bowers for $1,050 as uncollectible, Memorandum 241.
Nov. 18	Received $1,050 from Jack Bowers in full payment of his account, which was written off May 4, Memorandum 321 and Receipt 1078.
Dec. 31	The adjusting entry for the estimated uncollectible accounts expense for the year ended December 31 was $1,850.

Estimating Uncollectible Accounts Receivable

Main Idea
Different methods can be used to estimate the allowance for uncollectible accounts. Two methods are *percentage of net sales* and *aging of accounts receivable.*

Read to Learn...
➤ how to use the percentage of net sales method. (p. 712)
➤ how to use the aging of accounts receivable method. (p. 713)

Key Terms
percentage of net sales method
aging of accounts receivable method

As you learned in the previous section, businesses estimate the uncollectible accounts expense at the end of the period using the allowance method. In this section you will learn about the percentage of net sales and the aging of accounts receivable methods. These two ways to estimate uncollectible accounts expenses are based on judgment and past experience.

Percentage of Net Sales Method
How Do You Use Net Sales to Compute Uncollectible Amounts?

When using the **percentage of net sales method** for estimating uncollectible accounts expense, the business assumes that a certain percentage of each year's net sales will be uncollectible. To find the adjustment for uncollectible accounts expense:

1. Determine the percentage.
2. Calculate net sales.
3. Multiply net sales by the percentage.
4. Enter the amount calculated above on the work sheet.

Let's see how this method works. First, the percentage is determined. As you can see, in recent years On Your Mark's actual uncollectible accounts have been approximately 2 percent of net sales. On this basis, On Your Mark's accountant believes that the 2 percent figure should be used to estimate uncollectible accounts expense.

Year	Net Sales	Uncollectible Accounts	Percentage
2008	$ 59,000	$1,062	(1.8%)
2009	65,000	1,430	(2.2%)
2010	67,000	1,273	(1.9%)
Totals	$191,000	$3,765	(2.0%)

Second, the amount of net sales is calculated. Remember that net sales equals sales minus sales discounts and sales returns and allowances.

As shown, net sales for On Your Mark is $67,500.

Sales		$74,500
Less: Sales Discounts	$3,000	
Sales Returns and Allowances	4,000	− 7,000
Net Sales		$67,500

Third, the uncollectible accounts expense for the current year is determined by multiplying net sales by the percentage. On Your Mark's uncollectible accounts expense for the period is estimated to be $1,350 ($67,500 × .02).

Under this method the amount calculated is recorded as the adjustment on the work sheet and later is entered into the accounting records by journalizing the adjusting entry. At the beginning of the next period, **Allowance for Uncollectible Accounts** will have a credit balance of $1,475 ($1,350 adjustment plus $125 existing balance in the account).

Aging of Accounts Receivable Method
How Do You Use Accounts Receivable to Compute Uncollectible Amounts?

The **aging of accounts receivable method** classifies the accounts receivables according to the number of days each account is past due. This method assumes that the longer an account is overdue, the less likely it is to be collected. Use these steps to find the adjustment for uncollectible accounts expense:

1. *Age,* or classify and group, each account according to the number of days it is past due.
2. Use past experience to determine the percentage of each group that will be uncollectible.
3. Multiply the uncollectible amount for each group by the percentage for that group.
4. Add the results for all groups.
5. Enter on the work sheet the total estimated uncollectible amount (calculated above) adjusted by any balance in **Allowance for Uncollectible Accounts.**

Let's look at an example. First, each customer account is *aged,* or classified and grouped according to the number of days it is overdue. The computer printout in **Figure 24–8** is a schedule of On Your Mark's aged accounts receivable that has grouped each customer account.

On Your Mark Athletic Wear
ANALYSIS OF ACCOUNTS RECEIVABLE
December 31, 20--

Account ID	Customer's Name	Total Amount Owed	Not Yet Due	Days Past Due			
				1–30	31–60	61–90	Over 90
DIM	Joe Dimaio	$ 300.00	$ 300.00				
GAL	Robert Galvin	50.00		$ 50.00			
KLE	Casey Klein	800.00					$ 800.00
MON	Anita Montero	200.00	200.00				
RAH	Shashi Rahim	175.00			$ 175.00		
RAM	Gabriel Ramos	1,000.00	1,000.00				
SUL	Megan Sullivan	40.00				$ 40.00	
TAM	Tammy's Fitness	225.00	225.00				
WON	Kim Wong	306.50		306.50			
YOU	Lara Young	750.00	750.00				
	TOTALS	$ 3,846.50	$ 2,475.00	$ 356.50	$ 175.00	$ 40.00	$ 800.00

Figure 24–8 Computer-Generated Analysis of Accounts Receivable

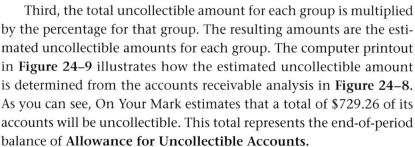

On Your Mark Athletic Wear
AGING OF ACCOUNTS RECEIVABLE
Estimated Uncollectible Amount
December 31, 20--

Age Group	Amount	Estimated Percentage Uncollectible	Estimated Uncollectible Amount
Not yet due	$ 2,475.00	2%	$ 49.50
1–30 days past due	356.50	4%	14.26
31–60 days past due	175.00	10%	17.50
61–90 days past due	40.00	20%	8.00
Over 90 days past due	800.00	80%	640.00
Total	$ 3,846.50		$ 729.26

Figure 24–9 Accounts Receivable Aging Schedule

Next, On Your Mark's accountant estimates what percentage of each group will be uncollectible based on past experience. The percentages range from 2 to 80 percent.

Third, the total uncollectible amount for each group is multiplied by the percentage for that group. The resulting amounts are the estimated uncollectible amounts for each group. The computer printout in **Figure 24–9** illustrates how the estimated uncollectible amount is determined from the accounts receivable analysis in **Figure 24–8**. As you can see, On Your Mark estimates that a total of $729.26 of its accounts will be uncollectible. This total represents the end-of-period balance of **Allowance for Uncollectible Accounts.**

Finally, an adjustment is entered on the work sheet. This adjustment will bring the balance of **Allowance for Uncollectible Accounts** to $729.26, the estimated amount.

Suppose the balance of **Allowance for Uncollectible Accounts** reported in the Trial Balance Credit column is $49.80. To determine the adjustment, subtract the balance of **Allowance for Uncollectible Accounts** from the total estimated uncollectible amount. The adjustment amount is $679.46 ($729.26 − $49.80).

After the adjusting entry has been journalized and posted, the balance of **Allowance for Uncollectible Accounts** is $729.26 (the balance as determined by the aging schedule).

Uncollectible Accounts Expense		Allowance for Uncollectible Accounts	
Debit	Credit	Debit	Credit
+	−	−	+
Adj. 679.46			Bal. 49.80
			Adj. 679.46
			Bal. 729.26

AFTER YOU **READ**

Reinforce the Main Idea

Use a diagram like this one to compare and contrast the two methods for estimating uncollectible accounts discussed in Section 3.

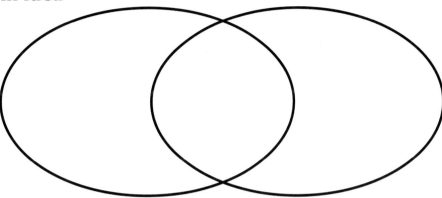

Do the Math

Hernando's Card Shop is planning to expand. Before it expands, the owner wants to review the uncollectible accounts. Hernando asks you to calculate the percentage of uncollectible accounts per year.

	Net Sales	Uncollectible Accounts
Year 1	$23,000	$ 800
Year 2	28,750	1,200
Year 3	46,000	1,345
Year 4	52,000	1,150

Problem 24–3 Estimating Uncollectible Accounts Expense Using the Percentage of Net Sales Method

Following are the end-of-period account balances for several stationery and office supply companies. Each company uses the percentage of net sales method to estimate its uncollectible accounts expense. The percentage used by each company is also listed.

Instructions Using the form provided in your working papers:

1. Calculate the amount of the adjustment for uncollectible accounts expense using the percentage of net sales method.
2. Record the adjusting entry for the estimated uncollectible accounts expense for Davis Inc.

	Sales	Sales Discounts	Sales Returns and Allowances	Percentage of Net Sales Uncollectible
Andrews Co.	$142,360	$1,423	$ 936	2
The Book Nook	209,100	3,180	1,139	1
Cable Inc.	173,270	1,730	1,540	1½
Davis Inc.	65,460	650	690	2
Ever-Sharp Co.	95,085	900	1,035	1¼

Key Concepts

1. Customer accounts that are uncollectible are expenses to the business. When it is apparent that a customer account is uncollectible, it is written off using either the *direct write-off method* or the *allowance method*. The allowance method enables the business to match sales revenue and uncollectible accounts expense in the same period.

2. An *uncollectible account,* or *bad debt,* is created when a customer fails to pay the amount due on account. **Allowance for Uncollectible Accounts** is used to summarize the *estimated* uncollectible accounts receivable of a business. The estimate is based on judgment and past experience.

Allowance for Uncollectible Accounts	
Debit	Credit
–	+
Decrease Side	Increase Side Normal Balance

3. Write off a specific uncollectible account using the direct write-off method:

Uncollectible Accounts Expense		Accounts Receivable (controlling/subsidiary)	
Debit	Credit	Debit	Credit
+	–	+	–
XXX		XXX	XXX

4. At the end of the fiscal period, the accountant calculates the amount of *bad debt expense* that will result from sales during the period. This estimated uncollectible account expense appears as an adjustment on the work sheet.

5. Record the adjusting entry using the allowance method:

Uncollectible Accounts Expense		Allowance for Uncollectible Accounts	
Debit	Credit	Debit	Credit
+	–	–	+
XXX			XXX

6. Write off a specific account using the allowance method:

Allowance for Uncollectible Accounts		Accounts Receivable (controlling/subsidiary)	
Debit	Credit	Debit	Credit
–	+	+	–
XXX			XXX

7. When a charge customer whose account was previously written off pays the amount owed,

   a. reinstate the customer's account, and
   b. record the cash receipt.

   Collection of an account that was written off using the direct write-off method.

   a. Reinstate the customer's account.

Accounts Receivable (controlling/subsidiary)		Uncollectible Accounts Expense	
Debit	Credit	Debit	Credit
+	–	+	–
XXX			XXX

b. Record the cash receipt by debiting **Cash in Bank** and crediting **Accounts Receivable** (controlling and subsidiary).

Collection of an account that was written off using the allowance method.

a. Reinstate the customer's account.

Accounts Receivable (controlling/subsidiary)		Allowance for Uncollectible Accounts	
Debit + XXX	Credit −	Debit −	Credit + XXX

b. Record the cash receipt by debiting **Cash in Bank** and crediting **Accounts Receivable** (controlling and subsidiary).

8. Two common methods used to estimate uncollectible Accounts Receivable are the *percentage of net sales method* and the *aging of accounts receivable method*.

Percentage of net sales method:

Net Sales × Percentage of Net Sales Estimated Uncollectible = Uncollectible Accounts Expense

Aging of accounts receivable method:

Age Group	Amount	×	Estimated Percentage Uncollectible	=	Estimated Uncollectible Amount
Not yet due	XXXXX		XX		XXXX
1–30 days past due	XXXXX		XX		XXXX
31–60 days past due	XXXXX		XX		XXXX
61–90 days past due	XXXXX		XX		XXXX
91–180 days past due	XXXXX		XX		XXXX
Over 180 days past due	XXXXX		XX		XXXX
Total					**XXXX**

Allowance for Uncollectible Accounts, end of period

Key Terms

aging of accounts receivable
 method (p. 713)

allowance method (p. 704)

book value of accounts receivable (p. 706)

direct write-off method (p. 698)

percentage of net sales method (p. 712)

uncollectible account (p. 698)

Check Your Understanding

1. **Accounting for Uncollectible Accounts**
   a. Explain the difference between the direct write-off method and the allowance method.
   b. Which method is likely to be used by a business with many charge customers? Which is likely to be used by a business that sells mainly on a cash basis?

2. **Determining Uncollectible Accounts Receivable**
   a. How does the direct write-off method identify the uncollectible accounts expense amount?
   b. What factors does the allowance method consider in determining bad debt expense?

3. **Direct Write-Off Method**
   a. Which accounting principle does the direct write-off method violate?
   b. In the direct write-off method of recording an uncollectible account receivable, which accounts are debited and credited?

4. **Bad Debts Expense**
   a. What is another term for *bad debts expense?*
   b. What can businesses do to prevent bad debts?

5. **Adjusting Entry**
   a. What accounts are debited and credited in the adjusting entry to record uncollectible accounts using the allowance method?
   b. What is the account classification of **Allowance for Uncollectible Accounts?**

6. **Allowance Method**
   a. When does the allowance method recognize the bad debt expense for a year's sales?
   b. When a specific account receivable is written off using the allowance method, which accounts are debited and credited?

7. **Collecting a Written-Off Account**
   a. What is the first journal entry made when a customer pays an amount that was previously written off? Name the accounts debited and credited for both methods.
   b. In the second journal entry, which accounts are debited and credited?

8. **Estimating Uncollectible Accounts Expense**
   a. Describe the percentage of net sales method.
   b. Describe the aging of accounts receivable method.

Apply Key Terms

As a quick review of uncollectible accounts, define each of the following key terms and explain its relationship to **Accounts Receivable.**

aging of accounts receivable method	book value of accounts receivable	percentage of net sales method
allowance method	direct write-off method	uncollectible account

Writing Off Uncollectible Accounts Receivable

Making the Transition from a Manual to a Computerized System

Task	Manual Methods	Computerized Methods
Preparing an aged accounts receivable report	• Examine each customer account and organize it based on its due date. • Using accounting stationery, list each customer's account in the appropriate past due columns.	• A preformatted report feature allows the accountant to generate an aging schedule. The software pulls data from information stored in the accounts receivable ledgers.
Writing off an uncollectible account	• Determine the method to be used to write off uncollectible accounts. • Record a general journal entry to record the write-off and post it to the general ledger and subsidiary ledger. • Calculate new balances.	• Determine the method to be used to write off uncollectible accounts. • Outstanding invoices due are tied to the customer's ID and assigned to the account, **Allowance for Uncollectible Accounts.**

Peachtree® Q & A

Peachtree Question	Answer
How do I set up defaults for the aging of Accounts Receivable ledgers in Peachtree?	1. From the *Maintain* menu, select **Default** Information. 2. Select **Customers** to set or to change default information. (In Peachtree, Accounts Receivable ledgers are referred to as *customer accounts*.) 3. Click on the Account Aging tab, and set the account defaults.
How do I write off an uncollectible account in Peachtree?	1. From the *Tasks* menu, select **Receipts** and enter the Customer ID. 2. In the *Cash Account* field, select **Allowance for Uncollectible Accounts.** 3. Click the Apply to Invoices tab. 4. Select the Pay box next to the invoices you wish to write off.

QuickBooks Q & A

QuickBooks Question	Answer
How do I set up defaults for the aging of Accounts Receivable ledgers in QuickBooks?	1. From the *Edit* menu, select **Preferences** and click on **Reports & Graphs.** 2. Click the Company Preferences tab. 3. Choose either the **Age from due date** or **Age from transaction** radio button to set how Accounts Receivable are aged.
How do I write off an uncollectible account in QuickBooks?	1. From the *Company* menu, select **Make General Journal Entries.** 2. Enter the date and reference, the debit amount, the description, and **Uncollectible Accounts Expense** as the account to be debited. 3. Enter the credit amount, the description, the customer name, and **Accounts Receivable** as the account to be credited.

For detailed instructions, see your Glencoe Accounting Chapter Study Guides and Working Papers.

Peachtree®

SMART GUIDE

Step–by–Step Instructions: Problem 24–4

1. Select the problem set for Sunset Surfwear.
2. Rename the company and set the system date.
3. Record the transactions to write off bad debts and reinstate Alex Hamilton's account.
4. Print a Cash Receipts Journal, Sales Journal, Customer Ledgers, and General Ledger.
5. Complete the Analyze activity.
6. End the session.

Step–by–Step Instructions: Problem 24–5

1. Select the problem set for InBeat CD Shop.
2. Rename the company and set the system date.
3. Record the uncollectible accounts adjustment.
4. Print the General Journal and General Ledger.
5. Complete the Analyze activity.
6. End the session.

QuickBooks

PROBLEM GUIDE

Step–by–Step Instructions: Problem 24–4

1. Restore the Problem 24-4.QBB file.
2. Record the transactions to write off bad debts and reinstate Alex Hamilton's account.
3. Print a Journal, General Ledger report, and Customer Balance Summary report.
4. Complete the Analyze activity.
5. Back up your work.

Problem 24–4 Using the Direct Write-Off Method

Sunset Surfwear uses the direct write-off method of accounting for uncollectible accounts.

Instructions

1. In your working papers, record the following transactions on page 14 in the general journal.
2. Post the transactions to the appropriate accounts.

Date	Transactions
June 1	Wrote off the $288.75 account of Alex Hamilton as uncollectible, Memorandum 223.
4	Wrote off the $243.60 account of Helen Jun as uncollectible, Memorandum 249.
14	Wrote off the $57.75 account of Nate Moulder as uncollectible, Memorandum 255.
22	Received $288.75 from Alex Hamilton in full payment of his account, Memorandum 298 and Receipt 944.
29	Wrote off the $100.80 account of Martha Adams as uncollectible, Memorandum 329.

Analyze Describe the impact on **Accounts Receivable** and **Uncollectible Accounts Expense** when an account is written off.

Problem 24–5 Calculating and Recording Estimated Uncollectible Accounts Expense

InBeat CD Shop uses the percentage of net sales method of accounting for uncollectible accounts. At the end of the period, the following account balances appeared on InBeat's trial balance:

Accts. Rec.	$110,000	Allow. for Uncoll. Accts.	$ 4,000
Sales	900,000	Sales Ret. and Allow.	50,000
Sales Disc.	10,000	Uncoll. Accts. Expense	—

Instructions

1. In your working papers, calculate the amount of the adjustment for uncollectible accounts for the period ended June 30. Management estimates that uncollectible accounts will be 1 percent of net sales.
2. Journalize the adjusting entry on page 8 in the general journal.
3. Post the adjusting entry to the general ledger accounts.

Analyze Determine the book value of accounts receivable.

Problem 24–6 Writing Off Accounts Under the Allowance Method

Shutterbug Cameras uses the allowance method of accounting for uncollectible accounts.

Instructions

1. In your working papers, record the following transactions on page 9 in the general journal.
2. Post the transactions to the appropriate accounts.
3. Prepare the Assets section of the balance sheet for Shutterbug Cameras using the partial general ledger in the working papers. The balances of other asset accounts are **Merchandise Inventory**, $33,000; **Supplies**, $2,000; and **Prepaid Insurance**, $1,200.

Date	Transactions
June 2	Wrote off the $593.25 account of Kalla Booth as uncollectible, Memorandum 329.
9	Wrote off the $840 account of Click Studios as uncollectible, Memorandum 343.
10	Received $131.25 from Jimmy Thompson in full payment of his account, which was written off on November 10, Memorandum 349 and Receipt 210.
12	Wrote off the $945 account of FastForward Productions as uncollectible, Memorandum 474.
30	Recorded the adjusting entry for estimated uncollectible accounts for the period. The uncollectible accounts expense estimate is based on 2 percent of the net sales of $150,000.
30	Recorded the closing entry for **Uncollectible Accounts Expense.**

Analyze Calculate the book value of the accounts receivable after the closing entries have been posted.

Problem 24–7 Estimating Uncollectible Accounts Expense

Cycle Tech Bicycles uses the allowance method of accounting for uncollectible accounts. The company estimates the uncollectible amount by aging its accounts receivable accounts.

Instructions

1. Complete the analysis of accounts receivable that is included in your working papers.
2. Calculate the estimated uncollectible amount. Use the form provided in your working papers.

CONTINUE

3. Journalize the June 30 adjusting entry for uncollectible accounts expense on page 11 of the general journal. Before the adjusting entry, **Allowance for Uncollectible Accounts** had a credit balance of $142.
4. Post the adjusting entry to the general ledger accounts.

Analyze | Calculate the book value of accounts receivable.

Problem 24–8 Reporting Uncollectible Amounts on the Financial Statements

The work sheet for River's Edge Canoe & Kayak is included in your working papers. The trial balance is complete, and all of the adjustments except the one required for uncollectible accounts have been entered.

Instructions

1. Record the adjustment for uncollectible accounts expense in the Adjustments section of the work sheet. Uncollectible accounts are estimated to be 1.5 percent of net sales. Label the adjustment (a).
2. Complete the work sheet.
3. Prepare an income statement, a statement of retained earnings, and a balance sheet.
4. Record the adjusting entries on page 18 of the general journal.
5. Post the adjusting entries. Record and post the closing entries.

Analyze | Compute the balance of **Allowance for Uncollectible Accounts** before and after the adjusting entry.

 CHALLENGE PROBLEM

Problem 24–9 Using the Allowance Method for Write-Offs

Buzz Newsstand uses the allowance method for uncollectible accounts.

Instructions

In your working papers, journalize the following transactions on page 13 in the general journal. Post the transactions to the account of Lee Adkins.

Date	Transactions
Jan. 14	Wrote off the $194.50 account of Lee Adkins as uncollectible, Memorandum 498.
June 25	Received a check for $30 from Lee Adkins on account, Memorandum 767 and Receipt 98.
Dec. 10	Received notice that Lee Adkins declared bankruptcy. Received 40 percent of the balance not paid, Receipt 288 and Memorandum 941.

Analyze | Conclude which account you would debit when writing off an account using the direct write-off method instead of the allowance method.

Practice your test-taking skills! The questions on this page are reprinted with permission from national organizations:
- Future Business Leaders of America
- Business Professionals of America

Use a separate sheet of paper to record your answers.

Future Business Leaders of America

MULTIPLE CHOICE

1. The _____ of accounting for uncollectible accounts matches potential bad debts expense with the sales from the same period.
   a. direct write-off method
   b. matching principle
   c. aging of accounts receivable method
   d. allowance method

2. Under the allowance method, the entry to record the estimated bad debts expense
   a. has no effect on net income.   c. has no effect on total assets.
   b. increases net income.   d. reduces total assets.

3. Cameron Corporation ages accounts receivable to estimate uncollectibles. The aging schedule estimates $2,340 of uncollectible accounts. Prior to adjustment, allowance for uncollectible accounts has a debit balance of $300. The expense reported on the income statement for uncollectibles will be
   a. $2,640.   c. $2,340.
   b. $2,040.   d. $300.

4. Vasquez Construction uses the percentage of sales method to estimate uncollectibles. Net credit sales for the current year amount to $500,000 and management estimates 2% will be uncollectible. Allowance for doubtful accounts prior to adjustment has a debit balance of $890. The amount of expense reported on the income statement will be
   a. $10,000.   c. $9,110.
   b. $10,890.   d. $890.

Business Professionals of America

MULTIPLE CHOICE

5. SPH, Inc. uses the direct write-off method for uncollectible accounts. The entry to record the $64 invoice that Dave Case did not pay is
   a. debit Accounts Receivable/Dave Case, credit Uncollectible Accounts Expense.
   b. debit Allowance for Uncollectible Accounts, credit Accounts Receivable/Dave Case.
   c. debit Uncollectible Accounts Expense, credit Accounts Receivable/Dave Case.
   d. debit Uncollectible Accounts Expense, credit Cash.

> **Need More Help?**
>
> **Go to glencoeaccounting.glencoe.com** and click on **Student Center.** Click on **Winning Competitive Events** and select **Chapter 24.**
> - **Practice Questions and Test-Taking Tips**
> - **Concept Capsules and Terminology**

Uncollectible Accounts Receivable

1. Before a business extends credit, it should determine whether potential credit customers are likely to pay their bills. Explain why this is important.
2. Contrast the direct write-off method and the allowance method.
3. Prepare the journal entry to write off an uncollectible account using (a) the direct write-off method and (b) the allowance method.
4. Compare the journal entries to reinstate a customer account that had been written off using (a) the direct write-off method and (b) the allowance method.
5. To determine the amount of the adjustment for uncollectible accounts expense, develop (a) a formula for the percentage of net sales method and (b) a step-by-step procedure for the aging of accounts receivable method.
6. Evaluate (a) the direct write-off method and (b) the allowance method.

Merchandising Business: Formal Wear

The Black Tie rents formal attire. It accepts cash, debit cards, credit cards, and personal checks. To reserve an outfit requires a down payment. The balance, due 10 days after the return, is recorded as an account receivable. Lately the store has had problems collecting accounts receivable. Customers say they do not receive an invoice for the balance until it is past due.

INSTRUCTIONS

1. Develop a plan for quality that will reduce uncollectible accounts. Your plan must be attainable and measurable.
2. Determine how to implement your plan. Will you need to change procedures, modify the accounts receivable system, hire another clerk, or retrain personnel?

Early Write-Off

Suppose you are an accounts receivable clerk for an advertising agency. Your friend, Hector, owns a deli and has hired your agency to create an ad for a local magazine. Hector's business is having financial difficulties, and he asks you to write off his account although it should not be considered uncollectible yet.

ETHICAL DECISION MAKING

1. What are the ethical issues?
2. What are the alternatives?
3. Who are the affected parties?
4. How do the alternatives affect the parties?
5. What would you do?

Collecting an Outstanding Account

At The Music Connection, you handle accounts receivable and uncollectible accounts. Six months ago a new dance club bought an expensive, state-of-the-art music system on account. It is still unpaid. Write the customer a letter requesting payment. State that if payment is not received within 30 days, you will turn the account over to a collection agency.

Communicating Information

The Clothes Horse, a well-known retailer of men's apparel, is closing. Before it does it wants to collect all its accounts receivable.

INSTRUCTIONS Write a collection letter to send to all customers with outstanding balances now and a second letter to send in four weeks.

Transaction Risks

International companies strive to collect accounts receivable as quickly as possible. A firm that expects to receive payment in a foreign currency faces a *transaction risk* that currency values will change to its disadvantage between the time the contract is entered and the time payment is made.

INSTRUCTIONS Assume that British Airways purchases airplanes from Boeing, a U.S. manufacturer. Boeing agrees to accept British pounds for the purchase. British Airways takes three months to pay. Describe the transaction risk involved.

Credit Check

To obtain credit, you must complete a credit application. The business will check your income, banking record, current debt amount, debt payment record, age, employment history, current employer, address, and so on.

PERSONAL FINANCE ACTIVITY Imagine that you just graduated from high school, have a part-time job, and plan to work your way through college. What are some steps you can take to establish a good credit rating?

PERSONAL FINANCE ONLINE Log on to **glencoeaccounting.glencoe.com** and click on **Student Center.** Click on **Making It Personal** and select **Chapter 24.**

Horizontal Analysis

Horizontal analysis compares the same items on a financial statement for two or more accounting periods. For example you might compare the change in accounts receivable from one year to the next. Look at PETsMART's balance sheet in Appendix F on page A-46. To complete a horizontal analysis, subtract the item's base year amount (2003) from the current year amount (2004). Then calculate the result as a percentage of the base year amount. The result is the increase or decrease over the base year.

INSTRUCTIONS Use PETsMART's balance sheet in Appendix F to complete the following.

1. Calculate the amount and percentage that total assets and total stockholders' equity changed from 2003 to 2004.

2. How does horizontal analysis provide useful information to a reader of a financial statement?

Write It Off

All types of companies can experience uncollectible accounts receivable. Visit **glencoeaccounting .glencoe.com** and click on **Student Center.** Click on **WebQuest** and select **Unit 5** to continue your Internet project.

CHAPTER 25 Inventories

What You'll Learn

1. Explain the importance of maintaining accurate inventory records.

2. Explain the difference between a periodic and a perpetual inventory system.

3. Take a physical inventory count and record inventories.

4. Determine the cost of merchandise inventory using the specific identification; first-in, first-out; last-in, first-out; and weighted average cost methods.

5. Assign a value to merchandise inventory using the lower-of-cost-or-market rule.

6. Explain the accounting principles of consistency and conservatism.

7. Define the accounting terms introduced in this chapter.

Why It's Important

Merchandise inventory is typically the largest current asset of a business.

www.rei.com

BEFORE YOU READ

Predict

1. What does the chapter title tell you?
2. What do you already know about this subject from personal experience?
3. What have you learned about this in the earlier chapters?
4. What gaps exist in your knowledge of this subject?

Exploring the *Real World* of Business

TRACKING INVENTORIES

REI, Inc.

Grill some French toast on a camp stove, practice your climbing skills on a 30-foot wall, and then take a spin on a mountain bike. Does this sound like the great outdoors? You can do all this at your local **REI** retail store. From cycling shoes to skis, sleeping bags to windbreakers, **REI** stocks everything you will need for outdoor adventures.

How does a retail store like **REI** keep track of the inventory at its stores? **REI's** computerized software program analyzes which products are selling at specific stores on a day-to-day basis. The system also tracks what is on order and what is in stock at the distribution center. With this data on hand, **REI** employees ensure that the right products are purchased and available to customers at the right stores at the right time.

What Do You Think?

What might happen if a company like **REI** could not effectively evaluate which products it should carry in inventory?

Working in the *Real World*

APPLYING YOUR ACCOUNTING KNOWLEDGE

Have you ever noticed a sign on a store that says "Closed for Inventory"? Or gotten a great deal from a special "Pre-Inventory Sale"? At the end of a fiscal period, many businesses physically count items of merchandise they have in stock. Seasonal businesses often perform physical inventory counts after their peak season, when stock on hand tends to be lowest. In this chapter you will learn about several ways to track inventory and assign a value to it at the end of a fiscal period.

Personal Connection

1. What kinds of inventory does your workplace carry?
2. How often does your employer take an inventory?
3. Who counts the items?

Online Connection

Go to **glencoeaccounting.glencoe.com** and click on **Student Center.** Click on **Working in the Real World** and select **Chapter 25.**

Determining the Quantity of Inventories

BEFORE YOU READ

Main Idea
Two methods of tracking merchandise are the perpetual inventory system and the periodic inventory system.

Read to Learn...
➤ how businesses use inventory control information. (p. 728)
➤ how businesses keep track of inventory. (p. 728)

Key Terms
perpetual inventory system
point-of-sale terminal (POS)
online
periodic inventory system

Maintaining control over inventory is essential. To maintain this control, a business establishes a system of inventory-tracking procedures. A manufacturer controls inventories of raw materials, work in process, and finished goods. Wholesalers and retailers maintain control over merchandise inventory. Can you imagine the problems that a store like Wal-Mart would encounter if it did not have an inventory control system?

Merchandise Inventory
How Is Tracking Merchandise Helpful?

Earlier you learned that *merchandise* refers to goods a business purchases for resale to customers. The **Merchandise Inventory** account shows the cost of goods purchased for resale. By tracking merchandise, a business knows how much merchandise is sold and which items are selling well. **Merchandise Inventory** is the only account reported on both the balance sheet (as a current asset) and the income statement (to calculate the cost of merchandise sold).

Methods of Tracking Inventory
How Do You Keep Track of Inventory?

Businesses can choose between two methods to track merchandise: the *perpetual inventory system* and the *periodic inventory system.*

Perpetual Inventory System

Most large businesses and smaller ones with automated accounting systems use the **perpetual inventory system**, which keeps a constant, up-to-date record of merchandise on hand at any point in time. When a business uses a perpetual inventory system, management can obtain the quantity on hand and cost of any item at any point in time. The business can use the information to determine when to reorder items. This avoids loss of sales due to inadequate inventory. **Figure 25–1** shows an example of a computer printout for a perpetual inventory system.

The perpetual inventory system records an entry in the **Merchandise Inventory** account every time a

Figure 25–1 Computer Printout from a Perpetual Inventory System

Wilton Outdoor Center					
DAILY INVENTORY REPORT					
Department 47					
October 13, 20--					
Stock No.	Item	Unit	Quantity	Unit Cost	Total Value
7651	Kilmer Rods	Each	8	$ 31.80	$ 254.40
7560	Tyon Rods	Each	12	36.40	436.80
7762	Peterson Rods	Each	11	29.75	327.25
7785	K & R Rods	Each	6	26.30	157.80
7208	Weber Reels	Each	5	35.20	176.00
7338	Pro Reels	Each	8	41.40	331.20
7193	Artcraft Reels	Each	4	47.10	188.40
7525	#7 Fishing Hook	Box	26	4.86	126.36
7937	#9 Fishing Hook	Box	31	5.24	162.44
	Total				$ 2,160.65

purchase or sale occurs. After each sale the system also enters the cost of merchandise sold in the accounting records. The perpetual inventory system uses a **Cost of Merchandise Sold** account.

Computers update a perpetual inventory system through electronic cash registers, or **point-of-sale terminals (POS)**, that are **online** (linked to a central computer system). Such machines read bar codes that identify the item being sold. The computer records the sale and automatically updates the inventory information. Merchandise purchases are also entered into the computer to update the inventory records.

Businesses that have not yet automated their operations can also use a perpetual inventory system. They use stock cards or sheets like the one in **Figure 25–2** to record the amount of increase or decrease for every purchase and sale. For example, a business records the quantity of merchandise purchased in the stock card's *In* column and the quantity of sold items in the *Out* column.

Periodic Inventory System

In the **periodic inventory system**, inventory records are updated only after a physical count of merchandise on hand is made. This system does not adjust inventory records for every purchase and sale. Instead, an adjusting entry is made at the end of the accounting period. See Chapter 18, pages 521–522 for a review of how to calculate the inventory adjustment. Small businesses that maintain manual accounting records generally use this system.

Physical Inventory Count

In either inventory tracking system, a business takes a physical count of its merchandise at least once a year. This is called *taking inventory* and is part of the system of internal controls. Businesses using the periodic inventory system must use the physical count to update their accounting records.

The process of identifying and counting all items of merchandise for businesses with many items in inventory is very time consuming. Therefore, inventory is usually counted when it is at its lowest level. Seasonal businesses take physical counts and record inventories at the end of the peak selling period after they have sold most of the merchandise. A ski shop, for instance, probably takes inventory in May or June.

The total number of a particular item on hand is recorded on an inventory card or an inventory sheet. **Figure 25–3** shows a typical inventory sheet. It lists each item's stock number, description, quantity on hand, unit cost, and the total cost of its inventory on hand.

STOCK CARD

STOCK NO.	ITEM
C 1297	Altmore Disc Player

SUPPLIER	SUPPLIER'S CATALOGUE NO.
Star Electric	91246

UNIT	MINIMUM	MAXIMUM
Each	15	60

DATE	EXPLANATION	IN	OUT	BALANCE
7/1/20--	Balance on Hand			48
7/8/20--	Shipping Order 21928		6	42
7/12/20--	Shipping Order 22201		10	32
7/20/20--	Shipping Order 22456		8	24
7/24/20--	Shipping Order 22719		12	12
7/24/20--	Purchase Req. 19426			
7/31/20--	Receiving Report 21563	48		60

Figure 25–2 Stock Card Used in a Perpetual Inventory System

As You READ

In Your Experience

Give an example of a store that gave you information regarding an inventory item. Did it use a manual or computer system to obtain the information?

Figure 25–3 Inventory Sheet

INVENTORY SHEET

DATE Jan. 5, 20--   CLERK Arlene Stone   PAGE 8

STOCK NO.	ITEM	UNIT	QUANTITY	UNIT COST		TOTAL VALUE	
1901	Needles	Pkg	24	1	14	27	36
2132	Thread	Spool	12		65	7	80
2136	Thread	Spool	18		55	9	90
3245	Zipper	Each	18	1	50	27	00
1917	Pins	Box	24		79	18	96
4971	Buttons	Pkg	12		89	10	68
4993	Tape Measure	Each	15	1	49	22	35
				TOTAL FOR THIS SHEET		789	14

AFTER YOU READ

Reinforce the Main Idea

Identify three facts about each inventory tracking system covered in this section. Create a chart similar to this one.

Tracking System	Fact #1	Fact #2	Fact #3

Do the Math

Katie's Ceramic Emporium received 9 dozen ceramic elephants for a total cost of $306.72. The invoice also includes 17 dozen songbird figurines in various colors, with a cost of $822.12. Based on the information on the invoice, calculate the unit cost of the elephants and the songbirds.

Problem 25–1 Preparing Inventory Reports

In your working papers, complete the manual inventory sheet for Carole's Gift Shop. Use today's date and your name as the clerk.

Stock No.	Item	Unit	Quantity	Unit Cost
1790	Greeting Cards	Doz.	32	6.00
2217	Plush Toys	Each	20	2.50
1900	Balloons	Doz.	12	.50
1201	Wrapping Paper	Each	30	1.12
1205	Ribbon	Spool	25	.75
3495	Novelty Buttons	Doz.	12	2.50
2722	Music Boxes	Doz.	6	60.00
4200	Party Supplies	Doz.	10	6.50
1907	Gift Boxes	Doz.	5	2.75
1742	Vases	Doz.	2	12.50

Determining the Cost of Inventories

Once a business determines the quantity of merchandise it has on hand, it calculates the cost of that merchandise. There are four inventory costing methods used to assign costs to merchandise.

Inventory Costs
Why Is It Difficult to Determine Inventory Costs?

When merchandise is purchased, it is recorded in the accounting records at cost. However, assigning a cost to each item in inventory can be complicated. A business may purchase the same item many times within a single inventory period, and the cost may change from one purchase to the next. The challenge is to decide which cost applies to each item.

Methods of Assigning Costs to Inventories
How Do You Set the Cost of Inventory?

Businesses use one of four methods to determine inventory cost:

- specific identification
- first-in, first-out (FIFO)
- last-in, first-out (LIFO)
- weighted average cost

The Specific Identification Costing Method

Under the **specific identification method**, the exact cost of each item is determined and assigned to that item. The actual cost of each item is obtained from the invoice.

Businesses that sell a small number of items with high unit prices most often use the specific identification method. Appliance stores, automobile dealerships, and furniture stores often use this method.

The Entertainment Store uses the periodic inventory system. It started the year with a beginning inventory of 15 DVD players. During the period the store purchased an additional 50 players. When a physical inventory count was taken on May 31, there were 12 players still on hand. The cost of the players was calculated as shown on page 732.

Date	Description	Units	Cost		Total
June 1	Beginning inventory	15	$250	=	$ 3,750
Aug. 4	Purchase	20	250	=	5,000
Dec. 8	Purchase	10	253	=	2,530
Feb. 27	Purchase	10	258	=	2,580
May 1	Purchase	10	260	=	2,600
	Total	65			$16,460

Using the specific identification method, the accountant checks the invoices to find the actual cost of each of the 12 players still on hand at the end of May. The accountant found the following:

4	purchased @ $253 each	=	$1,012
5	purchased @ $258 each	=	1,290
3	purchased @ $260 each	=	780
12	players (ending inventory)		$3,082

The cost of ending inventory is $3,082. Once the cost of ending inventory has been calculated, the cost of merchandise sold can be computed:

Purchases available for sale
− Cost of ending inventory
Cost of merchandise sold

In this example the cost of merchandise sold using the specific identification method is $13,378:

	Units	Cost
Cost of players available for sale	65	$16,460
Less ending inventory	12	3,082
Cost of merchandise sold	53	$13,378

The First-In, First-Out Costing Method

The **first-in, first-out method (FIFO)** of assigning cost assumes that the first items purchased (first in) are the first items sold (first out). The FIFO method assumes that the items purchased most recently are the ones on hand at the end of the period. The physical flow of most merchandise is first-in, first-out. For example, think about milk that is stocked by a supermarket. Since milk is perishable, the supermarket stocks the shelves with the milk it purchased first. As that milk is sold, later purchases of milk are added at the back of the shelves.

Let's apply the FIFO costing method to our DVD player example.

Date	Description	Units	Cost		Total
June 1	Beginning inventory	15	$250	=	$ 3,750
Aug. 4	Purchase	20	250	=	5,000
Dec. 8	Purchase	10	253	=	2,530
Feb. 27	Purchase	10	258	=	2,580
May 1	Purchase	10	260	=	2,600
	Total	65			$16,460

As You READ

In Your Own Words

Specific Identification Costing Explain why all businesses do not use the specific identification costing method.

Under the FIFO method, the items purchased first are assumed to be the items sold first. In other words the 53 players sold are assumed to be as follows:

	Units
Beginning inventory	15
Aug. 4	20
Dec. 8	10
Feb. 27	8
Total sold	53

The items remaining in inventory are:

	Units
Feb. 27 (10 bought − 8 sold)	2
May 1	10
Total	12

The cost of the ending inventory using the FIFO method is:

10 units @ $260 each	=	$2,600
2 units @ $258 each	=	516
12 units		$3,116

The cost of merchandise sold using the FIFO method is $13,344:

	Units	
Cost of players available for sale	65	$16,460
Less ending inventory	12	3,116
Cost of merchandise sold	53	$13,344

The Last-In, First-Out Costing Method

The **last-in, first-out method (LIFO)** of assigning inventory cost assumes that the last items purchased (last in) are the first items sold (first out). The LIFO method assumes that the items purchased first are still on hand at the end of the period. The earliest costs, therefore, are the ones used to assign a cost to the inventory. The physical flow of a stone and gravel company is last-in, first-out. When new gravel is purchased and delivered, it is deposited on top of the existing gravel. As gravel is taken from the top of the pile, the first gravel used is the last gravel delivered.

Let's return to the DVD player example and apply the LIFO costing method.

As You READ

Compare and Contrast

Cost Flow Assumptions How are FIFO and LIFO similar? How are they different?

Date	Description	Units	Cost		Total
June 1	Beginning inventory	15	$250	=	$ 3,750
Aug. 4	Purchase	20	250	=	5,000
Dec. 8	Purchase	10	253	=	2,530
Feb. 27	Purchase	10	258	=	2,580
May 1	Purchase	10	260	=	2,600
	Total	65			$16,460

Using the LIFO method, the 12 players remaining in stock are from the beginning inventory of 15 units. The cost of the ending inventory is $3,000 (12 units @ $250 each).

The cost of merchandise sold using the LIFO method is $13,460:

	Units	
Cost of players available for sale	65	$16,460
Less ending inventory	12	3,000
Cost of merchandise sold	53	$13,460

The Weighted Average Cost Method

A fourth method of assigning inventory costs is the weighted average cost method. The **weighted average cost method** assigns the average cost to each unit in inventory. The average cost is calculated by:

- adding the number of units on hand at the beginning of the period and the number of units purchased
- adding the cost of the units on hand at the beginning of the period and the cost of the units purchased
- dividing the total cost by the total number of units

The average cost per unit is used to determine the cost of the ending inventory. Again, we will use the The Entertainment Store example to apply the weighted average cost method.

Date	Description	Units	Cost		Total
June 1	Beginning inventory	15	$250	=	$ 3,750
Aug. 4	Purchase	20	250	=	5,000
Dec. 8	Purchase	10	253	=	2,530
Feb. 27	Purchase	10	258	=	2,580
May 1	Purchase	10	260	=	2,600
	Total	65			$16,460

The average cost per player is $253.23 ($16,460 ÷ 65 units).

The cost of the ending merchandise inventory using the weighted average cost method is $3,038.76 (12 units × $253.23).

The cost of merchandise sold using the weighted average cost method is $13,421.24:

	Units	
Cost of players available for sale	65	$16,460.00
Less ending inventory	12	3,038.76
Cost of merchandise sold	53	$13,421.24

The following table illustrates the different inventory costing methods for The Entertainment Store's inventory of DVD players. After the company selects an inventory costing method, it is applied consistently as you will see in the next section.

Method	Cost of Players Sold	Ending Inventory
Specific identification	$13,378.00	$3,082.00
FIFO	13,344.00	3,116.00
LIFO	13,460.00	3,000.00
Weighted average	13,421.24	3,038.76

AFTER YOU **READ**

Reinforce the Main Idea

Identify two facts about each inventory costing method covered in this section. Create a chart similar to this one.

Costing Method	Fact #1	Fact #2

Do the Math

Foxfire Golf Club Pro Shop uses the first-in, first-out method for inventory costing. At the beginning of the year, Foxfire had 30 golf club sets on hand. The golf club sets were purchased for $800 each. An additional 12 golf club sets were purchased during the year at $875 each. When inventory was taken at the end of the season, 5 golf sets were still on hand. Using the FIFO method of inventory valuation, what was the total cost of merchandise sold?

Problem 25–2 Determining Inventory Costs

The following items were purchased by Kudos Leather Goods during the month of April:

April 2	34 wallets @ $12.95 each
April 8	24 wallets @ $13.10 each
April 18	15 wallets @ $13.25 each
April 26	20 wallets @ $13.27 each

On April 1 the business had in inventory 19 wallets valued at $12.90 each. On April 30 the business had 36 wallets in inventory; of these wallets, 8 were purchased on April 2, 15 were purchased on April 8, 3 were purchased on April 18, and 10 were purchased on April 26.

Instructions In your working papers, calculate the cost of the ending inventory using:

a. the specific identification method
b. the FIFO method
c. the LIFO method
d. the weighted average method

Accounting Careers in Focus

CHIEF FINANCIAL OFFICER
Water Replenishment District of Southern California, Cerritos, California
Scott M. Ota

Q: Why is accounting appealing to you?

A: Accounting is like learning a different language. Some people think because you are an accountant, you must be good at math. That is true, but the key is actually knowing how to balance accounts and understanding their relationships.

Q: What key factors are necessary for success?

A: As you move up the corporate ladder, your success will depend a great deal on how effectively you communicate and relate to others. When working with nonaccountants, know your audience and bring the conversation to their level of understanding.

Q: Do you have any advice for accounting students?

A: Don't get discouraged. If accounting were easy, everyone would do it. Stay on target and make definite, attainable goals and stick to them. There are so many different careers in accounting—the options are limitless.

Q: What advice would you offer those interested in a career track leading to a chief financial officer position?

A: Talk to people in the industry. Investigate the requirements for becoming a CFO to determine whether you are willing to put in the time and effort. The background and experience that you develop over the early part of your career is very important. It will lay the foundation for things to come.

Tips from . . .
RHI Robert Half International Inc.

When looking for a job, consider your ideal work environment. Do you want to work for a large or small company? Which is more important, pay or advancement opportunity? You can learn more about prospective employers through research conducted on the Internet or at your library or career center.

CAREER FACTS

- **Nature of the Work:** Direct the company's accounting policies, procedures, and finance functions; ensure the integrity of the company's financial information; identify and manage business risks and insurance requirements.
- **Training or Education Needed:** At least 10 years of experience, including public accounting experience and a minimum of five years in a management role; a master's degree in business administration. Many companies require a CPA license.
- **Aptitudes, Abilities, and Skills:** This is an executive-level position. Strong analytical skills, long-term planning skills, and communication skills are required. CFOs work directly with a company's chief executive officer, board members, and other senior executives.
- **Salary Range:** $85,000 to $350,000 depending on experience, location, and company revenue.
- **Career Path:** Gain experience in a public accounting firm and then accept positions of increasing responsibility in a corporate environment, such as director of finance, director of accounting, or controller.

Thinking Critically | **What qualities do you think are important to be a good manager?**

Choosing an Inventory Costing Method

A business may use any one of the four inventory costing methods. Careful consideration is given to this choice because it affects the gross profit reported by the business.

Consistency and Inventory Costing
How Do You Apply the Consistency Principle?

When a business applies the same accounting methods in the same way from one period to the next, the business is applying the GAAP **consistency principle**. Once a business chooses an inventory costing method, the business must use it consistently. This helps owners and creditors compare financial reports from one period to another.

Businesses are permitted to change costing methods but must declare the reasons for changing and how the change will affect the financial statements. In addition the business must get permission for the change from the Internal Revenue Service.

Comparison of the Four Inventory Costing Methods
How Does the Inventory Costing Method Affect the Reported Gross Profit?

When deciding which inventory costing method to use, the owner or manager compares the four methods and selects the one that is likely to be the most beneficial to the company. The owner or manager considers the present economic conditions and the future economic outlook. He or she will also consider whether prices and demand for the product will remain stable, increase, or decrease.

The cost of ending inventory affects the cost of merchandise sold, which in turn affects the income or loss reported on the income statement. The following table compares The Entertainment Store's gross profit on sales using the four inventory costing methods. The company sold all of the DVD players for $320 each. Total sales are $16,960 (53 units $\times$ $320).

	Specific Identification	First-In, First-Out	Last-In, First-Out	Weighted Average
Sales	$16,960.00	$16,960.00	$16,960.00	$16,960.00
Less: Cost of merchandise sold	13,378.00	13,344.00	13,460.00	13,421.24
Gross profit on sales	$ 3,582.00	$ 3,616.00	$ 3,500.00	$ 3,538.76

BEFORE YOU READ

Main Idea
Apply consistency and conservatism when reporting merchandise inventory on the financial statements.

Read to Learn...
➤ about the consistency principle and inventory costing methods. (p. 737)
➤ how the inventory costing method affects the reported gross profit. (p. 737)
➤ about the conservatism principle and the lower-of-cost-or-market rule. (p. 738)

Key Terms
consistency principle
lower-of-cost-or-market rule
market value
conservatism principle

AS YOU READ

Instant Recall

Income Statement
    Sales
− Cost of merchandise sold
    Gross profit on sales
− Operating expenses
    Net income (loss)

As You **READ**

Key Point

The Effect of Inventory Costing on Net Income
A company's gross profit on sales and net income are affected by the inventory costing method used.

Over the year, the price that The Entertainment Store paid to purchase each player increased from $250 to $260. As the table on page 737 shows, in a period of rising prices, the LIFO method results in the lowest gross profit on sales. The FIFO method results in the highest gross profit on sales.

Businesses pay income taxes on income earned. As this example indicates, the inventory costing method used by a business can increase or decrease its taxes.

Conservatism and the Lower-of-Cost-or-Market Rule
How Do You Apply the Conservatism Principle?

Merchandise inventory appears the income statement and the balance sheet. Cost is the most common basis for reporting inventory. However, inventory might be worth less than its cost. For example, some merchandise items may deteriorate or become obsolete. If their value becomes less than the recorded cost, the difference is a loss to the business.

The **lower-of-cost-or-market rule** requires that the cost of the ending inventory that appears on the financial statements is the lower of its cost (calculated using one of the four inventory methods) or its *market value.* **Market value** of an item is the current price that is charged for a similar item of merchandise in the market. That is, it is the price that a retailer like The Entertainment Store would pay a wholesaler or manufacturer for a specific item. Market value is the cost at which the inventory item could be replaced at the date of the financial statements.

Let's look at an example. Assume that The Entertainment Store determines that the current market value of the DVD players is $248 each. At market the players are worth $2,976 ($248 × 12 units). Assume also that The Entertainment Store uses the FIFO inventory costing method. Under this method the cost of the ending inventory was $3,116.

Following the lower-of-cost-or-market rule, The Entertainment Store will report inventory at $2,976.

As You **READ**

It's Not What It Seems

Market Value For inventory purposes, *market value* is not the retail price you pay at the store for an item. It is the wholesale price a store would pay a supplier to replace that item.

Lower of	
Cost (FIFO)	$3,116
or	
Market	2,976

The GAAP **conservatism principle** of accounting states that it is best to present amounts that are least likely to result in an overstatement of income or assets. To be conservative is to take the safe route. The lower-of-cost-or-market rule is conservative for two reasons:

1. Decreases in inventory value (losses) are recognized when they occur, but increases in inventory value are not recorded.
2. Inventory as reported on the balance sheet is never more, but may be less, than the actual cost of the inventory.

Reinforce the Main Idea

Create a chart like this one to describe the two accounting principles covered in this section. Also describe how each principle applies to merchandise inventory.

Accounting Principle	Description	Application to Inventory

Do the Math

The management of Baby Steps Children's Store wants to report the largest gross profit on sales. Using the graph, compare the gross profit on sales for the four inventory costing methods. Which method results in the largest gross profit on sales?

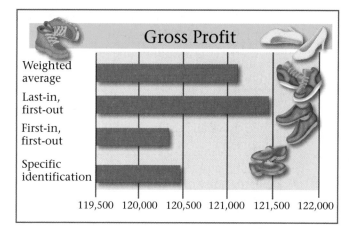

Gross Profit

Weighted average

Last-in, first-out

First-in, first-out

Specific identification

119,500 120,000 120,500 121,000 121,500 122,000

Problem 25–3 Analyzing a Source Document

Read the following memorandum and complete the assigned task.

Toys & Things

MEMORANDUM

TO: Accounting Clerk
FROM: Accounting Manager
DATE: June 30, 20--
SUBJECT: Change in Inventory Method

We have received approval to change from the LIFO to the FIFO method of determining our inventory costs. Please calculate the cost of the Walk-A-Long Dolls using the FIFO method. There are 36 dolls in inventory.

Walk-A-Long Dolls	Beginning inventory	8@ $15.45
	Purchases 6/11	12@ $15.95
	6/17	10@ $16.25
	6/22	6@ $16.40

Instructions

1. What is the new value of the ending inventory?
2. Assume that all 36 dolls were sold for $21.95. What is the gross profit for this item?

Key Concepts

1. Merchandise inventory is often the largest current asset of a business. **Merchandise Inventory** is the only account that appears on both the balance sheet and the income statement:

   - as a current asset on the balance sheet
   - as part of the calculation for cost of merchandise sold on the income statement

   To control its merchandise, a merchandising business establishes a system of inventory procedures that identifies:

   - how much of its merchandise has been sold
   - which items are selling well
   - which items should not be replaced after they are sold

2. Differences between a periodic and perpetual inventory system:

Periodic Inventory System	Perpetual Inventory System
Used by small businesses with manual accounting records.	Used by most large businesses and smaller ones with automated accounting systems.
Requires a physical count of the merchandise on hand to update inventory records.	Provides current inventory records at any point in time.
How inventory accounting records are updated: • An adjusting entry is made to the **Merchandise Inventory** account at the end of the accounting period. (To review this, see Chapter 18, pages 521–522.) • The cost of merchandise sold is calculated at the end of the accounting period (To review this, see Chapter 19, page 559.)	How inventory accounting records are updated: • When a sale is made, the decrease to inventory is handled electronically using point of sale terminals that scan in the product's bar code. • When merchandise is purchased, the increase to inventory is entered directly into the inventory system.

3. At least once a year, a business *takes inventory* by physically counting its merchandise. This is a good practice for all merchandisers, regardless of the inventory tracking system used. The count is usually made when inventory is at its lowest level, generally after a company's peak selling period.

   An inventory card or inventory sheet is used to record the following information about each item at a particular date:

   - stock number
   - item name
   - unit description
   - quantity on hand
   - unit cost

4. Businesses choose one of four methods to assign costs to the merchandise that it has on hand. A company's gross profit on sales and net income are affected by the inventory costing method it uses.

Inventory Costing Methods:

Specific identification method	Tracks the exact cost of each item.
First-in, first-out method (FIFO)	Assumes that the first items purchased are the first items sold.
Last-in, first-out method (LIFO)	Assumes that the last items purchased are the first items sold.
Weighted average cost method	Uses an average cost for each inventory item.

5. The lower-of-cost-or-market rule applies the conservatism principle to reporting inventory on financial statements. It requires a business to report its ending inventory using whichever of these two is *lower:*

   • the inventory's cost as calculated using the costing method selected by the company (specific identification method, FIFO, LIFO, or weighted average method)
   • the inventory's *market value,* which is the wholesale cost to replace the inventory at the date of the financial statements

6. In reporting its inventory, a business must follow two accounting principles:

   • **Consistency** This principle requires that once a business chooses an inventory costing method, it must use that method consistently. If it changes methods, it must obtain permission from the Internal Revenue Service and then report the reasons for the change and how it affects the financial statements.
   • **Conservatism** This accounting principle requires that when they can choose among procedures, accountants must choose the safer, or more conservative, route by presenting amounts that are least likely to result in an overstatement of income or assets.

Key Terms

conservatism principle	(p. 738)	online	(p. 729)
consistency principle	(p. 737)	periodic inventory system	(p. 729)
first-in, first-out method (FIFO)	(p. 732)	perpetual inventory system	(p. 728)
last-in, first-out method (LIFO)	(p. 733)	point-of-sale terminal (POS)	(p. 729)
lower-of-cost-or-market rule	(p. 738)	specific identification method	(p. 731)
market value	(p. 738)	weighted average cost method	(p. 734)

Check Your Understanding

1. **Inventory Records**
   a. Why does a company need a control system for its merchandise inventory?
   b. What information does tracking inventory provide to a business?

2. **Inventory Tracking Systems**
   a. What is the difference between a periodic and a perpetual inventory system?
   b. What is the advantage to using a perpetual inventory system? Why is it difficult for some businesses to use it?

3. **Physical Inventory Count**
   a. When is the best time for a business to take a physical inventory?
   b. Which tracking system requires a physical inventory count for financial reporting purposes?

4. **Inventory Costing Methods**
   a. What is meant by the phrase "with the FIFO method, the inventory cost is based on the most recent costs"?
   b. Why does the inventory costing method used affect gross profit on sales and net income?

5. **Lower-of-Cost-or-Market Rule**
   a. In this rule, what is meant by the term *cost?* By the term *market?*
   b. State the lower-of-cost-or-market rule using your definitions of *cost* and *market.*

6. **Consistency and Conservatism**
   a. How does the consistency principle help the owners, creditors, and the general public?
   b. What approach to presenting income does the conservatism principle require?

Apply Key Terms

Grandma's Toy Attic is changing from a manual to an automated inventory control system. As the owner, you plan to hire an inventory supervisor who understands accounting principles, inventory control, and business economics as well as computer applications. Use the following terms to write a job description for this position. Then write a newspaper advertisement to attract the most qualified individual. Suggest some layout ideas for the advertisement.

conservatism principle
consistency principle
first-in, first-out method
   (FIFO)
last-in, first-out method
   (LIFO)
lower-of-cost-or-market rule

market value
online
periodic inventory system
perpetual inventory system
point-of-sale terminal (POS)
specific identification method
weighted average cost method

Inventory Costing

Making the Transition from a Manual to a Computerized System

Task	Manual Methods	Computerized Methods
Determining the cost of inventories in a perpetual inventory system	• Enter purchases of merchandise onto stock cards. • Enter sales of items onto stock cards. • At period end, calculate the number and value of remaining inventory items.	• When the accounting system is set up, the costing method must be determined. • Purchases of merchandise update not only the general ledger but also update the inventory records. • As sales are made, the system updates the inventory records. • Inventory quantities and values are available when needed.

Peachtree® Q & A

Peachtree Question	Answer
How is inventory set up and tracked in Peachtree?	1. From the *Maintain* menu, select **Default Information**. 2. Select **Inventory Items**. 3. Click the GL Accts/Costing tab and enter the GL account numbers for sales and purchases. 4. Click the Taxes/Shipping tab and enter a (✓) if sales taxes are to be collected on items sold. Click **OK**. 5. From the *Maintain* menu, select **Inventory Items**. 6. Enter Item ID codes, descriptions, price, and cost method (FIFO, LIFO, or Average) for all inventory items. 7. When recording sales or purchases of inventory items, use the established item codes. With each transaction, the system will update the inventory records.

QuickBooks Q & A

QuickBooks Question	Answer
How is inventory set up and tracked in QuickBooks?	1. From the *Lists* menu, select **Item List**. 2. Click the Item drop-down menu, and choose **New**. 3. From the *Type* field, choose **Inventory Part**. 4. Complete the Purchase, Sales, and Inventory Information sections. 5. Click **OK**. 6. When recording sales, purchases, or returns of inventory, use the established item codes. QuickBooks will automatically update the inventory records.

For detailed instructions, see your Glencoe Accounting Chapter Study Guides and Working Papers.

Complete problems using: **Manual** Glencoe Working Papers OR **Peachtree Complete Accounting** Software OR **QuickBooks** Templates OR **Spreadsheet** Templates

Peachtree®

SMART GUIDE

Step–by–Step Instructions: Problem 25–4

1. Select the problem set for Sunset Surfwear.
2. Rename the company and set the system date.
3. Print an Inventory Valuation Report, Cost of Goods Sold Journal, and Item Costing Report.
4. Complete the Analyze activity.
5. End the session.

QuickBooks

PROBLEM GUIDE

Step–by–Step Instructions: Problem 25–4

1. Restore the Problem 25-4.QBB file.
2. Print an Inventory Valuation Detail report.
3. Complete the Analyze activity.
4. Back up your work.

SPREADSHEET SMART GUIDE

Step–by–Step Instructions: Problem 25–6

1. Select the spreadsheet template for Problem 25–6.
2. Enter your name and the date in the spaces provided on the template.
3. Complete the spreadsheet using the instructions in your working papers.
4. Print the spreadsheet and proof your work.
5. Complete the Analyze activity.
6. Save your work and exit the spreadsheet program.

Problem 25–4 Calculating the Cost of Ending Inventory

Sunset Surfwear sells wet suits. On January 2 there were 21 wet suits at a total cost of $4,809 in inventory.

Date	Description	Wet Suits	Cost	Total
Jan. 2	Beginning inventory	21	$229	$ 4,809
Jan. 3	Purchase	10	235	2,350
Mar. 17	Purchase	6	238	1,428
July 27	Purchase	12	240	2,880
Sept. 27	Purchase	10	241	2,410
Nov. 29	Purchase	6	244	1,464
	Total	65		$15,341

At the end of the year, there were 17 wet suits in ending inventory. Of these, 1 was purchased on July 27, 10 were purchased on September 27, and 6 were purchased on November 29.

Instructions Assign a cost to the ending inventory using the following:

  a. the specific identification method
  b. the FIFO method
  c. the LIFO method
  d. the weighted average cost method

Analyze | Determine which inventory method resulted in the lowest cost of ending inventory.

Problem 25–5 Completing an Inventory Sheet

InBeat CD Shop assigns a cost to its inventory using the lower-of-cost-or-market rule. In your working papers, there is a partial inventory record. As an example, the first line of the inventory record has been completed.

INVENTORY RECORD						
Item No.	Item	Ending Inventory	Cost per Unit	Current Market Value	Price to be Used	Total Cost
0247	Blank CDs	24	2.67	2.88	2.67	64.08

Instructions Complete the inventory record. Do the following:

1. Select the lower-of-cost-or-market value. Enter that amount in the Price to be Used column.
2. Calculate the total cost of each item by multiplying the units in ending inventory by the Price to be Used column.
3. Add the amounts in the Total Cost column to determine the total cost of the ending inventory.

Analyze | Identify how many items used market value rather than actual cost.

Problem 25–6 Calculating Gross Profit on Sales

Using the four inventory costing methods, Shutterbug Cameras summarized the cost of its ending inventory as follows:

Specific Identification	First-In, First-Out	Last-In, First-Out	Weighted Average Cost
$21,476.00	$21,581.40	$21,410.93	$21,447.36

Shutterbug Cameras also reported the following amounts:

Net sales $53,874.92

Purchases available for sale 57,621.31

Instructions Using the preceding information, determine the cost of merchandise sold and the gross profit on sales for each of the inventory costing methods.

Analyze | Conclude which method resulted in the largest gross profit on sales.

Problem 25–7 Reporting Ending Inventory on the Income Statement

Cycle Tech Bicycles operates on a fiscal year beginning January 1. At the beginning of the year, the shop had in stock six Model #8274, 10-speed bicycles, valued at $2,364 (6 bicycles @ $394 each). During the year the business made the following purchases:

Date	Bicycles	Cost		Total
Jan. 20	4	$399	=	$ 1,596
Mar. 5	5	415	=	2,075
Apr. 23	7	419	=	2,933
Aug. 14	4	423	=	1,692
Oct. 3	6	430	=	2,580
Nov. 17	3	435	=	1,305
Total Purchases	29			$12,181

There were seven bicycles in inventory at the end of the period. During the year the bicycles sold for $675 each.

Peachtree®

SMART GUIDE

Step–by–Step Instructions: Problem 25–7

1. Select the problem set for Cycle Tech Bicycles.
2. Rename the company and set the system date.
3. Print an Inventory Valuation Report, Cost of Goods Sold Journal, and Item Costing Report.
4. Print an Income Statement and a Balance Sheet.
5. Complete the Analyze activity.
6. End the session.

Peachtree®

SMART GUIDE

Step–by–Step Instructions: Problem 25–8

1. Select the problem set for Buzz Newsstand.
2. Rename the company and set the system date.
3. Record all purchases transactions using the **Purchases/Receive Inventory** option.
4. Record the transportation charges using the **Payments** option.
5. Record the camera sales using the **Receipts** option.
6. Print a Purchases Journal, Cash Disbursements Journal, and a Cash Receipts Journal to proof your work.
7. Print an Inventory Valuation Report, Cost of Goods Sold Journal, and Item Costing Report.
8. Print an Income Statement.
9. Complete the Analyze activity.
10. End the session.

CONTINUE

Instructions

1. Calculate the cost of the ending inventory using the FIFO, LIFO, and weighted average cost methods.
2. Using the costs calculated in (1), determine the cost of merchandise sold for each inventory costing method.
3. Prepare a partial income statement for each inventory costing method showing sales and the calculation of gross profit on sales. Assume that the sales and purchases are net amounts.

Analyze | Identify the method that resulted in the lowest cost of merchandise sold.

CHALLENGE PROBLEM

Problem 25–8 Calculating Cost of Merchandise Sold and Gross Profit on Sales

Buzz Newsstand started the month of May with the following inventory of disposable cameras:

Stock No.	Brand	Units on Hand	Unit Cost	Selling Price
3845	Lenox	4	$9.60	$ 17.95
4931	Lancaster	6	8.40	17.29
9265	Paterson	3	8.10	16.88
4850	McMahon	5	7.60	15.95

Buzz Newsstand uses the FIFO method to calculate the cost of its merchandise inventory. The May 31 physical inventory count indicated:

Lenox	4 cameras	Paterson	7 cameras
Lancaster	5 cameras	McMahon	5 cameras

Instructions

1. How many units of each of the four cameras were sold during May?
2. Using the chart provided in your working papers, calculate the gross profit on sales for each type of camera.

Date	Transactions
May 2	Purchased 10 Lancaster cameras at $8.45 each.
4	Purchased 5 McMahon cameras at $7.80 each.
9	Purchased 6 Lenox cameras at $9.95 each plus a $4 transportation charge.
14	Purchased 5 Paterson cameras at $8.25 each.
17	Purchased 8 Lancaster cameras at $8.60 each.
19	Purchased 4 Lenox cameras at $10.10 each plus a $5 transportation charge.
27	Purchased 8 Paterson cameras at $8.30 each.
29	Purchased 4 Lancaster cameras at $8.85 each.

Analyze | Conclude which camera sold the most number of units.

Practice your test-taking skills! The questions on this page are reprinted with permission from national organizations:
- Future Business Leaders of America
- Business Professionals of America

Use a separate sheet of paper to record your answers.

Future Business Leaders of America

MULTIPLE CHOICE

1. The inventory system in which a constant, up-to-date record of merchandise on hand is maintained is called the

a. first-in, first-out system.
c. perpetual inventory system.
b. last-in, first-out system.
d. periodic inventory system.

Use the following information to answer questions 2–4.

Johnson, Inc. had the following inventory data: Inventory item T25 had 1,600 units at a unit price of $14 in inventory on January 1. The first purchase during the year was for 1,000 units at $15. The second purchase was for 1,000 units at $18. The December 31 inventory consisted of 1,200 units. The market price is $15.

2. The total cost of the ending inventory using FIFO is

a. $16,800.
c. $18,468.
b. $18,000.
d. $21,000.

3. The weighted average unit price is

a. $14.50.
c. $15.67.
b. $15.39.
d. $16.00.

4. Assume the weighted average cost method is used. Calculate the ending inventory using the lower-of-cost-or-market rule.

a. $16,000
c. $18,468
b. $18,000
d. $21,000

Business Professionals of America

MULTIPLE CHOICE

5. FIFO

a. Assumes that old goods are sold first and that goods which are on hand are valued at current prices.
b. Assumes that new goods are sold first and inventory is valued at old prices.
c. Assumes that the cost of current inventory at the conclusion of a period and the cost of goods sold is the overall representation of all the costs that were incurred during this period.
d. Assumes that amounts charged as expenses are actual cost of goods sold.

> **Need More Help?**
>
> **Go to glencoeaccounting.glencoe.com and click on Student Center. Click on Winning Competitive Events and select Chapter 25.**
> - **Practice Questions and Test-Taking Tips**
> - **Concept Capsules and Terminology**

Inventories

1. Name and describe the two systems used to determine the quantity of merchandise on hand.

2. Explain what is meant by an inventory system that is *online*.

3. Compute the cost of merchandise sold if the cost of the ending inventory is $35,280 and the cost of the merchandise available for sale is $97,200.

4. Explain why the specific identification costing method is the most accurate in determining inventory cost.

5. Explain why an ice cream stand would not use the LIFO method of inventory costing.

6. Defend the practice of most businesses to estimate the cost of their inventory using a method other than specific identification, which is the most accurate.

Merchandising Business: Home Building and Supply

Remodeling a kitchen? Adding a deck to your home? Home Helper is a building supply store that sells everything from lightbulbs to lumber, cabinet fixtures to appliances. Because it stocks many sizes and varieties of building products, the store has a huge inventory.

You work for a local CPA firm hired to evaluate the store's inventory procedures. The store manager wants to make sure the store is using the most appropriate inventory costing method.

INSTRUCTIONS

Think about the types of products stocked by such a store. Of the four inventory costing methods you studied in this chapter, recommend the best method for Home Helper. Assume that costs are expected to remain stable over the next few years. Explain the reasons for your recommendation.

Keeping Promotional Items

Imagine that you work in the cosmetics department of a large department store like Macy's. You have access to free samples—shampoo, moisturizer, lipstick, and nail polish—offered by manufacturers to get customers to try their products. This is great! You will never have to buy these products again. You figure that by using them, you are helping to promote them.

ETHICAL DECISION MAKING

1. What are the ethical issues?

2. What are the alternatives?

3. Who are the affected parties?

4. How do the alternatives affect the parties?

5. What would you do?

Inventory Systems

Natural Wonder offers products organically grown or made from organic materials. Its products include clothing, jewelry, gardening materials, and hair and body care products. The store is interested in a system that will keep an accurate count of inventory. Discuss the different inventory systems and explain how frequently each system is updated.

SKILLS BEYOND NUMBERS

Selecting Equipment and Tools

Your manager, Richard Smythe, is considering switching from a manual inventory system to an automated perpetual system. Write a proposal to Mr. Smythe that emphasizes the benefits of a perpetual inventory system. Specifically address time savings and revenue possibilities.

INTERNATIONAL ACCOUNTING

Inventory Measurement

Many countries use International Accounting Standards (IAS) as their national GAAP. IAS No. 2 allows inventory valuation using the specific identification, FIFO, and weighted average methods. It does not allow the LIFO method although countries such as the United States, Japan, and Mexico permit its use.

INSTRUCTIONS Explain why you think IAS do not permit the use of LIFO.

Making It Personal

Inventory Value

When shopping for a vehicle, you probably want a wide selection from which to choose. For this reason dealers try to have a large inventory, yet not so large it becomes impossible to track and control.

PERSONAL FINANCE ACTIVITY Businesses often cannot estimate the cost of their inventory merely by looking. To understand why, choose a room at your school and estimate the cost of its entire contents. Next, individually list all the large items in the room and estimate the cost of each, then total them. How do the two estimates compare?

PERSONAL FINANCE ONLINE Log on to **glencoeaccounting.glencoe.com** and click on **Student Center.** Click on **Making It Personal** and select **Chapter 25.**

Analyzing FINANCIAL Reports

Inventory Levels

Knowing how much inventory is on hand helps managers make decisions about how much merchandise to purchase. Too much inventory means the business has not sold what it purchased and its money is tied up in inventory. A business that holds too little inventory may run out often and need to make frequent purchases which increases costs. It also can lose business when customers go to a competitor to purchase an out-of-stock item. Higher costs and out-of-stock situations mean lower profits.

INSTRUCTIONS Use PETsMART's balance sheet and *Dear Fellow Stockholders* letter in Appendix F to answer the following questions.

1. How did PETsMART's merchandise inventory change from 2003 to 2004?
2. What could have caused this change?

Web Quest

Tracking and Costing

Some businesses store inventory in warehouses. Visit **glencoeaccounting .glencoe.com** and click on **Student Center.** Click on **WebQuest** and select **Unit 5** to continue your Internet project.

What You'll Learn

1. Explain how businesses use promissory notes.

2. Calculate and record notes payable and notes receivable.

3. Explain the difference between interest-bearing and non-interest-bearing notes.

4. Journalize transactions involving notes payable.

5. Journalize transactions involving notes receivable.

6. Define the accounting terms introduced in this chapter.

Why It's Important

▶ Businesses often borrow and lend money.

BEFORE YOU READ

Predict

1. What does the chapter title tell you?
2. What do you already know about this subject from personal experience?
3. What have you learned about this in the earlier chapters?
4. What gaps exist in your knowledge of this subject?

Exploring the *Real World* of Business

EVALUATING NOTES

Advanced Micro Devices

When Hector Ruiz took over as Chief Executive Officer of **Advanced Micro Devices (AMD)**, his work was cut out for him. Competition from Intel was fierce, and sales were down. From his start in a research lab at Texas Instruments to president of Motorola's Semiconductor Products Sector, Ruiz was known for profitable operations in the ever-changing semiconductor industry.

Believing the time was right for expansion, Ruiz began building **AMD's** newest "fab" (manufacturing facility) in Dresden, Germany. Fab 36 was expected to cost $2.4 billion over four years.

Companies like **AMD** often issue notes for cash needs. Fab 36's funding is from bank loans, grants from the Federal Republic of Germany, and company equity.

What Do You Think?

When a bank loans money to a company like **Advanced Micro Devices**, what factors do you think it considers?

Working in the *Real World*

APPLYING YOUR ACCOUNTING KNOWLEDGE

Have you or your parents ever bought a new or used car? Chances are you made a down payment and then signed a note payable for the rest of the purchase price. When businesses buy costly items, such as manufacturing equipment or even an office building, they also sign a note payable. In this chapter you will learn how to calculate the interest on a business note and record the total amount payable.

Personal Connection

Have you noticed any items that your employer purchased that required signing a note payable? This could include purchases like equipment, buildings, vehicles, or land.

Online Connection

Go to **glencoeaccounting.glencoe.com** and click on **Student Center.** Click on **Working in the Real World** and select **Chapter 26.**

Promissory Notes

BEFORE YOU READ

Main Idea
The formula for calculating interest is
Principal × Interest Rate × Time.

Read to Learn...
➤ how promissory notes are used. (p. 752)
➤ how to calculate the interest on a note (p. 754)

Key Terms
promissory note
note payable
note receivable
principal
face value
term
issue date

payee
interest rate
maturity date
maker
interest
maturity value

Many people sign a note to pay for the purchase of a vehicle over a certain period of time. The note may be with a company like Ford Motor Credit or a financial institution. In this chapter you will learn about notes payable and notes receivable.

A Promise to Pay
What Is a Promissory Note?

A **promissory note**, often shortened to *note,* is a written promise to pay a certain amount of money at a specific time. Promissory notes are formal documents that are evidence of credit granted or received. Laws require a promissory note to contain certain information as shown in **Figure 26–1**.

Notes Payable and Notes Receivable

A **note payable** is a promissory note that a business issues to a creditor when it borrows or buys on credit. A **note receivable** is a promissory note that a business accepts from a credit customer.

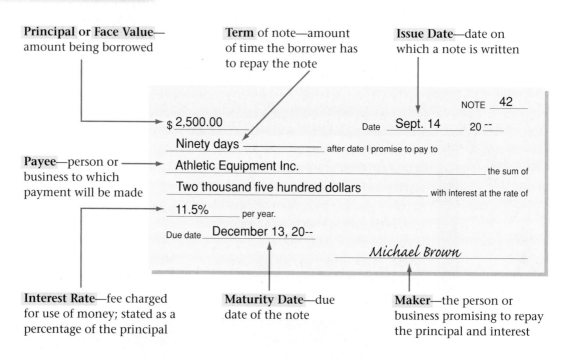

Principal or Face Value—amount being borrowed

Term of note—amount of time the borrower has to repay the note

Issue Date—date on which a note is written

NOTE __42__

$ 2,500.00   Date __Sept. 14__ 20 --

Ninety days _____ after date I promise to pay to

Payee—person or business to which payment will be made

Athletic Equipment Inc. _____ the sum of

Two thousand five hundred dollars _____ with interest at the rate of

11.5% _____ per year.

Due date __December 13, 20--__

Michael Brown

Interest Rate—fee charged for use of money; stated as a percentage of the principal

Maturity Date—due date of the note

Maker—the person or business promising to repay the principal and interest

Figure 26–1 Promissory Note

The Maturity Date of a Note

When a note is signed, the maker of the note agrees to repay the amount of the note within a certain period of time, usually stated in days, months, or years. This time period is the **term** of the note. Both the term and the **issue date** (date on which the note is signed) are needed to determine the **maturity date** (due date) of a note.

In the note in **Figure 26–1**, Michael Brown, manager of On Your Mark Athletic Wear, agreed to pay Athletic Equipment Inc. the principal plus interest 90 days from September 14. To determine the maturity date:

<table>
</table>

1. Determine the number of days remaining in the month in which the note is issued. No interest is charged for the issue date, so subtract the date of the note from the number of days in the month.

    30 days   in September
   −14 days issue date is September 14
    16 days

2. Determine the number of days remaining after the first month. To do this subtract the number of days calculated in Step 1 from the term of the note.

    90 days   term of note
   −16 days in September
    74 days   remaining

3. Subtract the number of days in the next month (October) from the number of days remaining after Step 2.

    74 days
   −31 days in October
    43 days   remaining

4. Subtract the number of days in the next month (November) from the days remaining after Step 3.

    43 days
   −30 days in November
    13 days   remaining

5. Since there are only 13 days remaining, the due date is 13 days into the next month (December).

The due date for this note is December 13.

As You READ

Key Point

Number of Days in Months January, March, May, July, August, October, and December have 31 days.

April, June, September, and November have 30 days.

February has 28 days (29 days in a leap year).

As You READ

In Your Own Words

Maker and Payee Explain who the maker and the payee of a note are.

Some businesses and banks use time calendars to calculate a note's maturity date. **Figure 26–2** on page 754 shows an example of a time calendar. The time calendar has two sets of days: (1) the day of the month (left and right columns), and (2) the day of the year, by month (middle column).

To calculate a maturity date using the time calendar, follow these steps:

1. Locate the issue date of the note (for example, 14) in the Day of month column. Move across the month columns to the issue month (September). In our example September 14 is the 257th day of the year.

2. Add the number of days in the term of the note (90) to the day of the year. The sum of the two numbers is 347 (257 + 90).

3. Find the number 347 in the month columns. The 347th day of the year is in December. The maturity month is December. Move across to the Day of month column. The 347th day of the year corresponds to the 13th day of the month. The due date of the note is December 13.

Day of month	Jan.	Feb.	Mar.	Apr.	May	June	July	Aug.	Sept.	Oct.	Nov.	Dec.	Day of month
1	1	32	60	91	121	152	182	213	244	274	305	335	1
2	2	33	61	92	122	153	183	214	245	275	306	336	2
3	3	34	62	93	123	154	184	215	246	276	307	337	3
4	4	35	63	94	124	155	185	216	247	277	308	338	4
5	5	36	64	95	125	156	186	217	248	278	309	339	5
6	6	37	65	96	126	157	187	218	249	279	310	340	6
7	7	38	66	97	127	158	188	219	250	280	311	341	7
8	8	39	67	98	128	159	189	220	251	281	312	342	8
9	9	40	68	99	129	160	190	221	252	282	313	343	9
10	10	41	69	100	130	161	191	222	253	283	314	344	10
11	11	42	70	101	131	162	192	223	254	284	315	345	11
12	12	43	71	102	132	163	193	224	255	285	316	346	12
13	13	44	72	103	133	164	194	225	256	286	317	347	13
14	14	45	73	104	134	165	195	226	257	287	318	348	14
15	15	46	74	105	135	166	196	227	258	288	319	349	15
16	16	47	75	106	136	167	197	228	259	289	320	350	16
17	17	48	76	107	137	168	198	229	260	290	321	351	17
18	18	49	77	108	138	169	199	230	261	291	322	352	18
19	19	50	78	109	139	170	200	231	262	292	323	353	19
20	20	51	79	110	140	171	201	232	263	293	324	354	20
21	21	52	80	111	141	172	202	233	264	294	325	355	21
22	22	53	81	112	142	173	203	234	265	295	326	356	22
23	23	54	82	113	143	174	204	235	266	296	327	357	23
24	24	55	83	114	144	175	205	236	267	297	328	358	24
25	25	56	84	115	145	176	206	237	268	298	329	359	25
26	26	57	85	116	146	177	207	238	269	299	330	360	26
27	27	58	86	117	147	178	208	239	270	300	331	361	27
28	28	59	87	118	148	179	209	240	271	301	332	362	28
29	29	...	88	119	149	180	210	241	272	302	333	363	29
30	30	...	89	120	150	181	211	242	273	303	334	364	30
31	31	...	90	...	151	...	212	243	...	304	...	365	31

NOTE: For leap years, after February 28, the number of the day is one greater than that given in the table.

Figure 26–2 Time Calendar

Calculation of Interest on a Note

How Do You Calculate Interest on a Note?

Interest is the fee charged for the use of money. The **interest rate** is the interest stated as a percentage of the principal. The interest on a promissory note is based on three factors: *principal, interest rate,* and *term of the note.*

Calculating Interest Using a Formula

The formula used to calculate interest follows:

Interest = Principal × Interest Rate × Time

Interest rates are usually stated on an annual basis, that is, on a borrowing period of one year. To find the interest on a one-year promissory note, multiply the principal by the interest rate. The interest on an 11.5%, one-year $2,500 promissory note is $287.50 ($2,500 × .115 = $287.50).

If the term of a promissory note is less than one year, the time in the calculation is expressed as a fraction of one year. The fraction may be stated in days or months. For example, on September 14 On Your Mark signed a note for $2,500 at 11.5% interest for 90 days. Since the term

of the note is expressed in days, 365 days is used as the denominator of the time fraction. The interest is calculated as follows:

Principal × Interest Rate × Time = Interest
$2,500 × .115 × 90/365 = $70.89

As You READ

Key Point

Interest Rates Interest rates are stated for a period of one year. To calculate interest on a note signed for a period of less than one year, express the term of the note as a fraction of one year.

The interest on the note shown in **Figure 26–1** on page 752 is $70.89.

On the maturity date, On Your Mark will repay the maturity value of the note. **Maturity value** is the amount due at the due date. In our example the maturity value is $2,570.89 ($2,500.00 + $70.89).

If the term of this note had been three months instead of 90 days, the denominator of the time fraction would be 12. The interest would be calculated as follows:

Principal × Interest Rate × Time = Interest
$2,500 × .115 × 3/12 = $71.88

The maturity value would be $2,571.88 ($2,500.00 + $71.88).

Calculating Interest Using an Interest Table

To calculate interest, businesses and banks often use an interest table similar to the one in **Figure 26–3**. We use On Your Mark's note to illustrate.

- Find the term of the note in the Day column, 90.
- Follow the row across until you reach the column for the interest rate, 11.5%. Where the Day row and the Interest column meet is a factor, 2.835616. The factor is based on a principal amount of $100.
- Divide the principal of the note by 100. The result is 25 ($2,500 ÷ 100).
- Multiply the result by the factor to find the interest. The interest is $70.89 (25 × 2.835616).

In this example the interest calculated using both the equation and the interest table are the same. Sometimes small differences occur due to rounding.

SIMPLE INTEREST ON $100 (365 DAY BASIS)

	11.50 %		11.75 %		12.00 %		12.25 %		12.50 %		12.75 %
DAY	**INTEREST**	**DAY**	**INTEREST**	**DAY**	**INTEREST**	**DAY**	**INTEREST**	**DAY**	**INTEREST**	**DAY**	**INTEREST**
30	0.945205	30	0.965753	30	0.986301	30	1.006849	30	1.027397	30	1.047945
60	1.890411	60	1.931507	60	1.972603	60	2.013699	60	2.054795	60	2.095890
90	2.835616	90	2.897260	90	2.958904	90	3.020548	90	3.082192	90	3.143836
120	3.780822	120	3.863014	120	3.945205	120	4.027397	120	4.109589	120	4.191781
150	4.726027	150	4.828767	150	4.931507	150	5.034247	150	5.136986	150	5.239726
180	5.671233	180	5.794521	180	5.917808	180	6.041096	180	6.164384	180	6.287671
210	6.616438	210	6.760274	210	6.904110	210	7.047945	210	7.191781	210	7.335616
240	7.561644	240	7.726027	240	7.890411	240	8.054795	240	8.219178	240	8.383562
270	8.506849	270	8.691781	270	8.876712	270	9.061644	270	9.246575	270	9.431507
300	9.452055	300	9.657534	300	9.863014	300	10.068493	300	10.273973	300	10.479452
330	10.397260	330	10.623288	330	10.849315	330	11.075342	330	11.301370	330	11.527397
360	11.342466	360	11.589041	360	11.835616	360	12.082192	360	12.328767	360	12.575342
365	11.500000	365	11.750000	365	12.000000	365	12.250000	365	12.500000	365	12.750000
366	11.531507	366	11.782192	366	12.032877	366	12.283562	366	12.534247	366	12.784932

Figure 26–3 Interest Table

Reinforce the Main Idea

Using a chart like this, describe the step-by-step procedure for determining the maturity value of a promissory note.

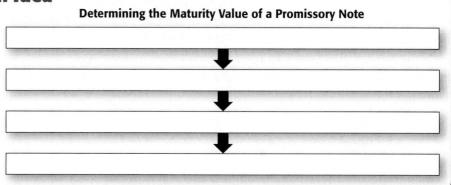

Determining the Maturity Value of a Promissory Note

 ## Do the Math

Marty Herick is the owner of CyberAction, a new computer-game store. Marty has just signed a promissory note with Excelsior Bank. He plans to use the loan to purchase and update his computer-game inventory. Using the formula, what is the interest on the $20,000, 90-day note with a 10.5% interest rate? What is the maturity value?

 ## Problem 26–1 Calculating Interest and Finding Maturity Values

Instructions Using the formula, compute the interest and maturity values for each of the following notes. Record your answers in your working papers. Use the interest table to check your computations.

	Principal	Interest Rate	Term
1.	$ 4,000	11.5%	60 days
2.	10,000	11.75%	90 days
3.	6,500	12.75%	60 days
4.	900	12.25%	120 days

 ## Problem 26–2 Calculating Interest

Instructions Calculate the interest for each of the following notes. Record your answers in your working papers.

	Principal	Interest Rate	Term
1.	$ 600	15%	90 days
2.	3,500	12%	60 days
3.	9,600	9%	4 months
4.	2,500	10%	180 days

Notes Payable

In this section you will journalize transactions involving notes payable. Recall that a note payable is a promissory note issued to a creditor. For example, a business may issue a note payable to borrow money from a bank. Notes that a business issues are recorded in the **Notes Payable** account. **Notes Payable** is a liability account; its normal balance is a credit. When the due date of a note extends beyond one year, the note is classified as a *long-term liability*. **Long-term liabilities** are debts that become due after one year.

Businesses frequently issue two types of notes: interest-bearing notes and non-interest-bearing notes. We consider both types of notes in this section.

Interest-Bearing Notes Payable
What Is an Interest-Bearing Note Payable?

A note that requires the principal plus interest to be paid on the maturity date is called an **interest-bearing note payable**. The note issued by On Your Mark (in Section 1) is an interest-bearing note. Its maturity value is $2,570.89 ($2,500.00 principal + $70.89 interest).

Recording the Issuance of an Interest-Bearing Note Payable

Let's record On Your Mark's interest-bearing note payable as an example.

> **BEFORE YOU READ**
>
> ## Main Idea
> Businesses issue and accept two types of notes: interest-bearing notes and non-interest-bearing notes.
>
> ## Read to Learn...
> ➤ what an interest-bearing promissory note is. (p. 757)
> ➤ why a "non-interest-bearing" note does have interest expense. (p. 759)
>
> ## Key Terms
> long-term liabilities
> interest-bearing note payable
> non-interest-bearing note payable
> bank discount
> proceeds
> other expense

Business Transaction

On April 3 On Your Mark borrowed $7,000 from State Street Bank and issued a 90-day, 12% note payable to the bank, Note 6.

ANALYSIS	*Identify* *Classify* +/−	
		1. The accounts affected are **Cash in Bank** and **Notes Payable.**
		2. **Cash in Bank** is an asset account. **Notes Payable** is a liability account.
		3. **Cash in Bank** is increased by $7,000. **Notes Payable** is increased by $7,000.

DEBIT-CREDIT RULE	**4.** Increases to asset accounts are recorded as debits. Debit **Cash in Bank** for $7,000.
	5. Increases to liability accounts are recorded as credits. Credit **Notes Payable** for $7,000.

T ACCOUNTS	**6.**

Cash in Bank		Notes Payable	
Debit + 7,000	Credit −	Debit −	Credit + 7,000

JOURNAL ENTRY

7.

GENERAL JOURNAL PAGE __12__

	DATE		DESCRIPTION	POST. REF.	DEBIT	CREDIT	
1	20--						1
2	Apr.	3	Cash in Bank		7 000 00		2
3			Notes Payable			7 000 00	3
4			Note 6				4
5							5

Recording the Payment of an Interest-Bearing Note Payable

The maturity date of On Your Mark's note payable to State Street Bank is July 2. You can verify this by using the time calendar in **Figure 26–2** on page 754. The interest is $207.12, calculated as follows:

Principal	×	Interest Rate	×	Time	=	Interest
$7,000	×	.12	×	90/365	=	$207.12

The maturity value of the note is $7,207.12 ($7,000.00 principal + $207.12 interest).

Business Transaction

On July 2 On Your Mark issued Check 3892 for $7,207.12 payable to State Street Bank in payment of the note payable issued April 3.

ANALYSIS	Identify	**1.** The accounts affected are **Notes Payable, Interest Expense,** and **Cash in Bank.**
	Classify	**2.** **Notes Payable** is a liability account. **Interest Expense** is an expense account. **Cash in Bank** is an asset account.
	+/−	**3.** **Notes Payable** is decreased by $7,000. **Interest Expense** is increased by $207.12. **Cash in Bank** is decreased by $7,207.12.

| DEBIT-CREDIT RULE | 4. Decreases to liability accounts are recorded as debits. Debit **Notes Payable** for $7,000. Increases to expense accounts are recorded as debits. Debit **Interest Expense** for $207.12. |
| | 5. Decreases to asset accounts are recorded as credits. Credit **Cash in Bank** for $7,207.12. |

T ACCOUNTS

6.

Notes Payable		Cash in Bank	
Debit	Credit	Debit	Credit
–	+	+	–
7,000			7,207.12

Interest Expense	
Debit	Credit
+	–
207.12	

JOURNAL ENTRY

7.

		GENERAL JOURNAL			PAGE 22	
	DATE	DESCRIPTION	POST. REF.	DEBIT	CREDIT	
1	20--					1
2	July 2	Notes Payable		7 000 00		2
3		Interest Expense		207 12		3
4		Cash in Bank			7 207 12	4
5		Check 3892				5

Non-Interest-Bearing Notes Payable
How Is Interest Paid on a Non-Interest-Bearing Note?

Sometimes a bank requires a borrower to pay the interest on a note in advance. On the issue date, the bank deducts the interest from the face

value of the note. This reduces the amount of money the borrower receives. When interest is deducted in advance from the face value of the note, the note is called a **non-interest-bearing note payable**. The note is "non-interest-bearing" because no interest rate is stated on the note. The interest deducted in advance is called the **bank discount**. The interest rate used to calculate the bank discount is called the *discount rate*. The cash received by the borrower is called the **proceeds**. The proceeds equal the face value of the note minus the bank discount.

For a non-interest-bearing note payable, the maturity value is the same as the face value. This is because the interest is deducted from the face value on the issue date. **Figure 26–4** on page 760 shows an example of a non-interest-bearing note payable.

NOTE ___13___

$ _1,500.00_____ Date __June 12____ 20 _--_

___Ninety days_____ after date I promise to pay to

___First Federal Bank_____ the sum of

___One thousand five hundred_____ dollars.

Due date __September 10, 20--__

Michael Brown

Figure 26–4 Non-Interest-Bearing Note Payable

Calculating Non-Interest-Bearing Notes Payable

Let's calculate the proceeds of the non-interest-bearing note payable shown in **Figure 26–4.** The note was discounted at a rate of 12% by First Federal Bank, Note 13.

The first step in calculating the proceeds on a non-interest-bearing note is to calculate the bank discount. This is the interest on the note. (Notice that the formula is similar to the one used to compute interest on an interest-bearing note.)

Face Value	×	Discount Rate	×	Time	=	Bank Discount
$1,500	×	.12	×	90/365	=	$44.38

The bank discount is subtracted from the face value of the note to determine the proceeds. The proceeds are $1,455.62 ($1,500.00 − $44.38).

Recording the Issuance of a Non-Interest-Bearing Note Payable

The bank discount is recorded in a contra liability account called **Discount on Notes Payable.** The normal balance of **Discount on Notes Payable** is a debit. The bank discount is the future interest expense on the note. However, the bank discount is not recorded in an expense account until the note matures and the interest expense has been incurred.

Now that we calculated the discount, let's record the issuance of the non-interest-bearing note for On Your Mark.

Business Transaction

On June 12 On Your Mark signed a $1,500, 90-day non-interest-bearing note payable that First Federal Bank discounted at a rate of 12%, Note 13.

ANALYSIS	Identify	1.	The accounts affected are **Cash in Bank, Discount on Notes Payable,** and **Notes Payable.**
	Classify	2.	**Cash in Bank** is an asset account. **Discount on Notes Payable** is a contra liability account. **Notes Payable** is a liability account.
	+/−	3.	**Cash in Bank** is increased by $1,455.62. **Discount on Notes Payable** is increased by $44.38. **Notes Payable** is increased by $1,500.00.

| DEBIT-CREDIT RULE | **4.** Increases to asset accounts are recorded as debits. Debit **Cash in Bank** for $1,455.62. Increases to contra liability accounts are recorded as debits. Debit **Discount on Notes Payable** for $44.38. |
| | **5.** Increases to liability accounts are recorded as credits. Credit **Notes Payable** for $1,500.00. |

T ACCOUNTS

6.

Cash in Bank		Notes Payable	
Debit + 1,455.62	Credit −	Debit −	Credit + 1,500.00

Discount on Notes Payable	
Debit + 44.38	Credit −

JOURNAL ENTRY

7.

GENERAL JOURNAL   PAGE _20_

	DATE		DESCRIPTION	POST. REF.	DEBIT	CREDIT	
1	20--						1
2	June	12	Cash in Bank		1 455 62		2
3			Discount on Notes Payable		44 38		3
4			Notes Payable			1 500 00	4
5			Note 13				5
6							6

Businesses report the **Discount on Notes Payable** account on the balance sheet as a deduction from **Notes Payable**. The difference between the **Notes Payable** account and the **Discount on Notes Payable** account is the book value of notes payable. **Figure 26–5** shows the Liabilities section of the balance sheet for On Your Mark on June 30. It shows that the book value of notes payable is $1,455.62 ($1,500 − $44.38).

On Your Mark Athletic Wear
Balance Sheet
June 30, 20--

Liabilities			
Notes Payable		1 500 00	
Less: Discount on Notes Payable		44 38	1 455 62

Figure 26–5 Reporting Non-Interest-Bearing Notes Payable on the Balance Sheet

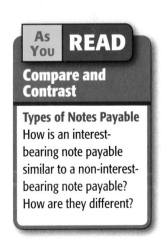

As You READ

Compare and Contrast

Types of Notes Payable
How is an interest-bearing note payable similar to a non-interest-bearing note payable? How are they different?

Recording the Payment of a Non-Interest-Bearing Note Payable

When the non-interest-bearing note payable matures and is due, On Your Mark will

- pay First Federal Bank $1,500, the face value of the note, and
- record the interest expense by transferring the bank discount to interest expense.

We will look at each of these individually and as a compound journal entry.

Business Transaction

On September 10 On Your Mark issued Check 4241 for $1,500 to First Federal Bank in payment of the June 12 non-interest-bearing note payable.

ANALYSIS   *Identify*   *Classify*

    +/−

1. The accounts affected are **Notes Payable** and **Cash in Bank.**
2. **Notes Payable** is a liability account. **Cash in Bank** is an asset account.
3. **Notes Payable** is decreased by $1,500. **Cash in Bank** is decreased by $1,500.

DEBIT-CREDIT RULE

4. Decreases to liability accounts are recorded as debits. Debit **Notes Payable** for $1,500.
5. Decreases to asset accounts are recorded as credits. Credit **Cash in Bank** for $1,500.

T ACCOUNTS   6.

Notes Payable		Cash in Bank	
Debit −	Credit +	Debit +	Credit −
1,500			1,500

JOURNAL ENTRY   7.

		GENERAL JOURNAL		PAGE 42		
	DATE	DESCRIPTION	POST. REF.	DEBIT	CREDIT	
1	20--					1
2	Sept. 10	Notes Payable		1 500 00		2
3		Cash in Bank			1 500 00	3
4		Check 4241				4
5						5

When a non-interest-bearing note payable matures, the amount of the bank discount is recognized as an expense. The bank discount is transferred from the **Discount on Notes Payable** account to the **Interest Expense** account. As the following T accounts demonstrate, **Interest Expense** is debited for $44.38 and **Discount on Notes Payable** is credited for $44.38. When this transaction is recorded, the balance of the **Discount on Notes Payable** account is reduced to zero.

Interest Expense		Discount on Notes Payable	
Debit + 9/10 44.38	Credit –	Debit + 6/12 44.38	Credit – 9/10 44.38

You could record two separate journal entries:

1. the payment of the non-interest-bearing note payable (in the cash payments journal), then
2. the interest expense (in the general journal)

It is simpler, however, to prepare one compound entry in the general journal as shown.

	DATE		DESCRIPTION	POST. REF.	DEBIT	CREDIT	
1	20--						1
2	Sept.	10	Notes Payable		1 500 00		2
3			Interest Expense		44 38		3
4			Cash in Bank			1 500 00	4
5			Discount on Notes Payable			44 38	5
6			Check 4241				6
7							7

GENERAL JOURNAL PAGE 43

The **Interest Expense** account is classified as an other expense account. An **other expense** is a nonoperating expense. This means that the expense does not result from the normal operations of the business. Other expenses appear in a separate section on the income statement, as deductions from operating income.

AFTER YOU **READ**

Reinforce the Main Idea

Create a table similar to this one to list three facts about the types of notes covered in this section.

Type of Note	Fact #1	Fact #2	Fact #3

Do the Math

Franklin Enterprises can borrow $10,000 for 30 days at 5% at the Jefferson City Bank or $10,000 for 45 days at 4.5% at Lincoln National Bank. Answer the following questions.

1. Which bank note results in the least amount of interest expense?
2. How much in interest expense can be saved?

Problem 26–3 Recording the Issuance of an Interest-Bearing Note Payable

On June 12 Frank's Lobster Pound issued a $9,000, 120-day, 12% note payable to American Bank of Commerce.

1. Which account is debited? What is the debit amount?
2. Which account is credited? What is the credit amount?
3. What is the classification of each account?
4. What is the maturity value of the note?

Problem 26–4 Recording the Issuance of a Non-Interest-Bearing Note Payable

On October 14 Canton Car Care Center issued a $10,000, 60-day, 12% non-interest-bearing note payable to Canton National Bank.

1. Which accounts are debited and which are credited? What are the debit and credit amounts?
2. Compute the bank discount. What is the amount of the proceeds?

Notes Receivable

In this section you will journalize transactions involving notes receivable. If you have ever loaned someone money and asked the person to repay the loan by a specific date, you understand the basic concept of a note receivable. Sometimes such a loan includes payment of a specified amount of interest; other times no interest is expected.

Recording the Receipt of a Note Receivable

How Do You Convert an Account Receivable to a Note Receivable?

When a customer needs additional time to pay an account receivable, he or she may be asked to sign a promissory note. The note replaces the account receivable. Promissory notes that a business accepts from customers are called *notes receivable.*

Notes Receivable is an asset account, and its normal balance is a debit. A note receivable is due on a specific date and carries an interest charge for the term of the note.

The interest earned on a note receivable is recorded in the **Interest Income** account. **Interest Income** is an other revenue account. **Other revenue**, also known as *nonoperating revenue* accounts, track revenue that a business receives from activities other than its normal operations. Other revenue appears in a separate section on the income statement, as an increase to operating income.

BEFORE YOU READ

Main Idea
Businesses record the receipt of a note receivable as well as the payment of the note.

Read to Learn...
➤ how to record a note receivable. (p. 765)
➤ how to record the payment of a note receivable. (p. 766)

Key Terms
other revenue

Business Transaction

On March 1 On Your Mark sold $1,750 of merchandise on account to Joe Dimaio. That transaction was recorded in On Your Mark's sales journal. Joe cannot pay his account by the due date. On April 8 On Your Mark received a 60-day, 12.5% note dated April 6 for $1,750 from Joe Dimaio to settle the account receivable, Note 4.

ANALYSIS	*Identify*	1.	The accounts affected are **Notes Receivable, Accounts Receivable** (controlling), and **Accounts Receivable—Joe Dimaio** (subsidiary).
	Classify	2.	**Notes Receivable, Accounts Receivable** (controlling), and **Accounts Receivable—Joe Dimaio** (subsidiary) are asset accounts.
	+/−	3.	**Notes Receivable** is increased by $1,750. **Accounts Receivable** (controlling) and **Accounts Receivable—Joe Dimaio** (subsidiary) are decreased by $1,750.

| DEBIT-CREDIT RULE | **4.** Increases to asset accounts are recorded as debits. Debit **Notes Receivable** for $1,750. |
| | **5.** Decreases to asset accounts are recorded as credits. Credit **Accounts Receivable** (controlling) for $1,750. Also credit **Accounts Receivable— Joe Dimaio** (subsidiary) for $1,750. |

T ACCOUNTS

6.

Notes Receivable			Accounts Receivable	
Debit	Credit		Debit	Credit
+	−		+	−
1,750				1,750

Accounts Receivable Subsidiary Ledger
Accounts Receivable—Joe Dimaio

Debit	Credit
+	−
	1,750

JOURNAL ENTRY

7.

GENERAL JOURNAL PAGE 13

	DATE		DESCRIPTION	POST. REF.	DEBIT	CREDIT	
1	20--						1
2	Apr.	8	Notes Receivable		1 750 00		2
3			Accts. Rec./Joe Dimaio			1 750 00	3
4			Note 4				4

Recording the Payment of a Note Receivable

How Do You Record Payment of a Note?

The note from Joe Dimaio is due on June 5. The maturity value of the note is $1,785.96 ($1,750.00 principal + $35.96 interest).

Principal	×	**Interest Rate**	×	**Time**	=	**Interest**
$1,750	×	.125	×	60/365	=	$35.96

Business Transaction

On June 7 On Your Mark received a check dated June 5 for $1,785.96 from Joe Dimaio in payment of the $1,750 note of April 6 plus interest of $35.96, Receipt 996.

JOURNAL ENTRY

GENERAL JOURNAL PAGE 18

	DATE		DESCRIPTION	POST. REF.	DEBIT	CREDIT	
1	20--						1
2	June	7	Cash in Bank		1 785 96		2
3			Notes Receivable			1 750 00	3
4			Interest Income			35 96	4
5			Receipt 996				5

AFTER
YOU   **READ**

Reinforce the Main Idea

Create a table similar to the one here to determine which accounts to debit and credit for each transaction. Choose from these accounts and write the account title in the proper column: **Accounts Receivable/Customer; Cash in Bank; Interest Income; Sales; Sales Tax Payable;** and **Notes Receivable.**

Transaction	Account(s) Debited	Account(s) Credited
Sold merchandise on account to a charge customer plus sales tax		
Received an interest-bearing note in payment of the account receivable		
Received payment for the note		

Do the Math

Your accounting manager has just finished a graph illustrating the possible interest-bearing notes available from the region's banks. Review the graph and give your boss your recommendation of which bank will provide the best loan value.

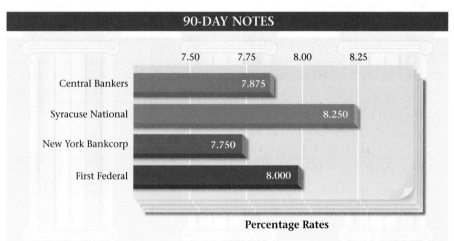

90-DAY NOTES

	7.50	7.75	8.00	8.25
Central Bankers		7.875		
Syracuse National				8.250
New York Bankcorp	7.750			
First Federal			8.000	

Percentage Rates

Problem 26–5 Analyzing a Source Document

Instructions Examine the note illustrated here. In your working papers, make the appropriate journal entry on page 14 of the general journal for Eli's Catering Company. The note was discounted at a rate of 12% by First Federal Bank.

NOTE ___55___

$ 2,500.00 _____   Date ___June 12___ 20 -- ___

___Ninety days___ —————— after date I promise to pay to

___First Federal Bank___ _____ the sum of

___Two thousand five hundred and no/100___ —————— dollars.

Due date ___September 10, 20--___

___Owner, Eli's Catering Co.___

Key Concepts

1. A *promissory note*, often just called a *note,* is a written promise to pay an amount of money by a specific future date. It allows businesses to make purchases and pay for them at a later date.

2. A *note payable* is a promissory note that a business issues to a creditor or to a bank to obtain a loan. A *note receivable* is a promissory note that a business accepts from a credit customer. Laws require a promissory note to contain certain information:

   - *maker:* person or business signing a note and promising to repay the principle and interest
   - *payee:* person or business the payment will be made to
   - *principal* or *face value:* amount borrowed
   - *interest rate:* fee charged for use of money; stated as a percentage of the principal
   - *term:* amount of time the borrower has to repay the note
   - *issue date:* date on which a note is written
   - *maturity date:* due date of the note

   The formula used to calculate interest is:

   Interest = Principal × Interest Rate × Time

3. Here is a comparison of interest-bearing and non-interest-bearing notes payable:

	Interest-Bearing Note Payable	**Non-Interest-Bearing Note Payable**
Distinction	Interest rate is stated on note.	No interest rate is stated on the note.
Interest	Interest is paid at maturity date.	Interest is called bank discount. It is deducted from the face value on the note's issue date.
Example	Interest rate = 6% Face value = $1,000 Term = 3 months	Bank discount = 6% Face value = $1,000 Term = 3 months

Calculation	Interest = Principal × Interest
	    Rate × Time
	Interest = $1,000 × 0.06 × 3/12
	Interest = $15
		Bank Discount = Face Value × Discount
		    Rate × Time
		Bank Discount = $1,000 × 0.06 × 3/12
		Bank Discount = $15

Proceeds	Proceeds = Face Value Proceeds = $1,000	Proceeds = Face Value − Bank Discount Proceeds = $1,000 − $15 = $985

Issuance of Note	Cash in Bank 1,000
	    Notes Payable 1,000
		Cash in Bank 985
		Discount on Notes Payable 15
		    Notes Payable 1,000

Payment of Note	Notes Payable 1,000
	Interest Expense 15
	    Cash in Bank 1,015
		Notes Payable 1,000
		Interest Expense 15
		    Cash in Bank 1,000
		    Discount on Notes Payable 15

4. To record the *issuance* of an interest-bearing note payable:

Cash in Bank		Notes Payable	
Debit + xxx	Credit −	Debit −	Credit + xxx

To record the *payment* of an interest-bearing note payable:

Notes Payable		Interest Expense		Cash in Bank	
Debit	Credit	Debit	Credit	Debit	Credit
−	+	+	−	+	−
xxx		xxx			xxx

To record the *issuance* of a non-interest-bearing note payable:

Cash in Bank		Discount on Notes Payable		Notes Payable	
Debit	Credit	Debit	Credit	Debit	Credit
+	−	+	−	−	+
xxx		xxx			xxx

To record the *payment* of a non-interest-bearing note payable:

Notes Payable		Interest Expense		Cash in Bank		Discount on Notes Payable	
Debit	Credit	Debit	Credit	Debit	Credit	Debit	Credit
−	+	+	−	+	−	+	−
xxx		xxx			xxx		xxx

5. To record the *receipt* of a note receivable converted from an account receivable:

Notes Receivable		Accounts Receivable (controlling/subsidiary)	
Debit	Credit	Debit	Credit
+	−	+	−
xxx			xxx

To record the *payment* of a note receivable:

Cash in Bank		Notes Receivable		Interest Income	
Debit	Credit	Debit	Credit	Debit	Credit
+	−	+	−	−	+
xxx			xxx		xxx

Key Terms

bank discount	(p. 759)	maker	(p. 752)	other revenue	(p. 765)
face value	(p. 752)	maturity date	(p. 752)	payee	(p. 752)
interest	(p. 754)	maturity value	(p. 755)	principal	(p. 752)
interest-bearing note payable	(p. 757)	non-interest-bearing note payable	(p. 759)	proceeds	(p. 759)
interest rate	(p. 752)	note payable	(p. 752)	promissory note	(p. 752)
issue date	(p. 752)	note receivable	(p. 752)	term	(p. 752)
long-term liabilities	(p. 757)	other expense	(p. 763)		

Check Your Understanding

1. **Promissory Notes**
   a. Name the two parties to a promissory note. Which party issues the note? Which party receives the note?
   b. Describe a situation in which a business might (a) receive a promissory note and (b) issue a promissory note.

2. **Notes Payable and Notes Receivable**
   a. What type of account is **Notes Payable,** and what is its normal balance?
   b. What type of account is **Notes Receivable,** and what is its normal balance?

3. **Interest-Bearing and Non-Interest-Bearing Notes**
   a. What is the difference between interest-bearing and non-interest-bearing notes?
   b. What is the difference between interest and a bank discount?

4. **Notes Payable**
   a. What accounts are affected by the *issuance* of an interest-bearing note payable, and how are they affected?
   b. What accounts are affected by the *payment* of an interest-bearing note payable, and how are they affected?

5. **Journalizing Notes Receivable**
   a. What accounts are affected by the *receipt* of a note receivable, and how are they affected?
   b. What accounts are affected by the *payment* of a note receivable, and how are they affected?

Apply Key Terms

As a staff accountant for Advanced Micro Devices, you have been asked to discuss the company's notes payable and receivable with the accounting clerks. Prepare note cards containing the terms below. Arrange these terms in meaningful groups. Explain why you have grouped terms together. Are they related? Are they part of the same thing? Is one the result of another? Are they opposites?

bank discount	maker	other revenue
face value	maturity date	payee
interest	maturity value	principal
interest-bearing note payable	non-interest-bearing note payable	proceeds
interest rate		promissory note
issue date	note payable	term
long-term liabilities	note receivable	
	other expense	

Notes Receivable and Payable

Making the Transition from a Manual to a Computerized System

Task	Manual Methods	Computerized Methods
Recording notes receivable and payable transactions	• Using the general journal, record the receipt or issuance of the note. • Post the entry to the appropriate accounts in the general ledger and subsidiary ledgers. • Journalize and post the entry to record the receipt or payment of cash and interest. • Calculate new balances for all accounts affected.	• Using the general journal, record the receipt or issuance of the note. The entry is automatically posted to the appropriate accounts. • Record receipts or payment of notes.

Peachtree® Q & A

Peachtree Question	Answer
How do I record the issuance of a note payable?	1. From the *Tasks* menu, select **Receipts**. 2. Accept the **Cash in Bank** account number as the Cash account. 3. Enter a Reference number, usually the note number. 4. Click on the Apply to Revenues tab. 5. Enter the **Notes Payable** account number and the note amount.
How do I record the receipt of a note receivable payment?	1. From the *Tasks* menu, select **Receipts**. 2. Accept the **Cash in Bank** account number as the Cash account. 3. Enter a Reference number, usually the note number. 4. Enter the **Notes Receivable** account number and the note amount. 5. Enter the **Interest Income** account number and amount.

QuickBooks Q & A

QuickBooks Question	Answer
How do I record the issuance of a note payable?	1. From the *Banking* menu, select **Make Deposits**. 2. Accept **Cash in Bank** in the *Deposit To* field and enter the date. 3. Enter the name of the payee. 4. Enter **Notes Payable** as the account, an explanation, and the note amount.
How do I record the receipt of a note receivable payment?	1. From the *Customers* menu, select **Make General Journal Entries**. 2. Enter the date and reference. 3. Debit the Cash account for the total amount received. 4. Credit **Notes Receivable** for the note portion of the amount received. 5. Credit **Interest Income** for the interest portion of the amount received.

For detailed instructions, see your Glencoe Accounting Chapter Study Guides and Working Papers.

Peachtree®

SMART GUIDE

Step–by–Step Instructions: Problem 26–6

1. Select the problem set for Sunset Surfwear (Prob. 26–6).
2. Rename the company and set the system date.
3. Record the transactions using the **Receipts** and **Payments** options. Enter each transaction in the proper accounting period (month).
4. Print a Cash Receipts Journal and a Cash Disbursements Journal to proof your work.
5. Complete the Analyze activity.
6. End the session.

TIP: Set the date range on the journal reports to print the transactions for all of the periods.

QuickBooks

PROBLEM GUIDE

Step–by–Step Instructions: Problem 26–6

1. Restore the Problem 26-6.QBB file.
2. Record the transactions using the **Make Deposits** and **Write Checks** options. Enter each transaction in the proper accounting period (month).
3. Print a Journal report.
4. Complete the Analyze activity.
5. Back up your work.

Problem 26–6   Recording Transactions for Interest-Bearing Notes Payable

Instructions In your working papers, record the following transactions in a cash receipts journal (page 22) and a cash payments journal (page 26).

Date	Transactions
Jan. 14	Sunset Surfwear borrowed $1,500 from First One Bank by issuing a 90-day, 12% interest-bearing note payable, Note 78.
Apr. 14	Issued Check 168 for $1,544.38 to First One Bank in payment of the $1,500 note issued on January 14, plus interest of $44.38.
May 31	Borrowed $12,400 from Merchant's Bank and Trust by issuing a 90-day, 12.5% interest-bearing note, Note 79.
Aug. 29	Paid Merchant's Bank and Trust the maturity value of the note issued on May 31, $12,782.19, Check 284.

Analyze   Calculate the amount of interest paid on notes in January.

Problem 26–7   Recording Transactions for Non-Interest-Bearing Notes Payable

Instructions In your working papers, record the following transactions in a cash receipts journal (page 14) and a cash payments journal (page 16).

Date	Transactions
June 10	InBeat CD Shop borrowed $6,000 from BankOne by issuing a 60-day, non-interest-bearing note payable (proceeds, $5,901.37) that the bank discounted at 10%, Note 67.
Aug. 9	Issued Check 205 for $6,000 in payment of the note issued June 10 and recorded the interest expense.
30	Borrowed $16,000 from Citizens Bank by issuing a 120-day, non-interest-bearing note payable less the 10.5% bank discount of $552.33, Note 68.
Dec. 28	Issued Check 398 in payment of the note issued on August 30 and recorded the interest expense.

Analyze   Explain why the account **Discount on Notes Payable** is used.

Peachtree®

SMART GUIDE

Step–by–Step Instructions: Problem 26–7

1. Select the problem set for InBeat CD Shop.
2. Rename the company and set the system date.
3. Record the transactions.
4. Print a Cash Receipts Journal and a Cash Disbursements Journal to proof your work.
5. Complete the Analyze activity.
6. End the session.

Step–by–Step Instructions: Problem 26–8

1. Select the problem set for Cycle Tech Bicycles.
2. Rename the company and set the system date.
3. Record the transactions.
4. Print a Cash Receipts Journal and a Cash Disbursements Journal to proof your work.
5. Complete the Analyze activity.
6. End the session.

Step–by–Step Instructions: Problem 26–9

1. Select the problem set for River's Edge Canoe & Kayak.
2. Rename the company and set the system date.
3. Record the transactions.
4. Print a Cash Receipts Journal and a Cash Disbursements Journal to proof your work.
5. Complete the Analyze activity.
6. End the session.

Problem 26–8 Recording Notes Payable and Notes Receivable

Instructions In your working papers, record the following transactions in a cash receipts journal (page 47), cash payments journal (page 56), and general journal (page 19) for Cycle Tech Bicycles.

Date	Transactions
Mar. 19	Borrowed $9,000 from Desert Palms Savings and Loan by issuing a 90-day, 12% interest-bearing note payable, Note 87.
June 4	Received a 120-day, 13% note receivable for $1,900 from Greg Kellogg as a time extension on his account receivable, Note 6.
17	Paid Desert Palms Savings and Loan the maturity value of the note issued on March 19, Check 2784.
Sept. 29	Received a check from Greg Kellogg for the maturity value of the note dated June 1, Receipt 628.
Oct. 6	Borrowed $2,700 from Jonesboro Bank and Trust by issuing a 60-day, non-interest-bearing note payable discounted at 11.5%, Note 88.
Dec. 5	Prepared a check for the note issued on October 6 and recorded the interest expense, Check 3954.

Analyze Compute the amount of interest Cycle Tech Bicycles will earn on Greg Kellogg's June 4 note.

Problem 26–9 Recording Notes Payable and Notes Receivable

The following is a partial list of accounts used by River's Edge Canoe & Kayak.

101	Cash in Bank	205	Notes Payable
115	Accounts Receivable	207	Discount on Notes Payable
120	Notes Receivable	415	Interest Income
201	Accounts Payable	640	Interest Expense

Instructions In your working papers, record the following transactions in a cash receipts journal (page 67), cash payments journal (page 73), and general journal (page 27).

CONTINUE

Date	Transactions (cont.)
May 7	Borrowed $4,000 from Union Bank by issuing a 60-day, 9.5% non-interest-bearing note, Note 284.
15	Issued a $3,000, 90-day, 9% interest-bearing note to Trailhead Canoes in place of the amount owed on account, Note 285.
21	Received a 120-day, 10% note for $1,200 from Cathy Wilcox for an extension of time on her account, Note 94.
July 6	Issued Check 4711 in payment of the non-interest-bearing note given to Union Bank on May 7.
Aug. 13	Issued Check 5044 for the maturity value of the note issued to Trailhead Canoes on May 15.
Sept. 18	Received a check from Cathy Wilcox for the maturity value of the note dated May 21, Receipt 5921.

Analyze   Compare Notes 284 and 285. Which of the two notes was most advantageous to River's Edge Canoe & Kayak?

Peachtree®

SMART GUIDE

Step–by–Step Instructions:
Problem 26–10

1. Select the problem set for Buzz Newsstand.
2. Rename the company and set the system date.
3. Record the transactions in the correct period.
4. Print a Sales Journal, Cash Receipts Journal, and a General Journal.
5. Complete the Analyze activity.
6. End the session.

QuickBooks

PROBLEM GUIDE

Step–by–Step Instructions:
Problem 26–10

1. Restore the Problem 26-10.QBB file.
2. Record the transactions in the correct period.
3. Print a Journal report.
4. Complete the Analyze activity.
5. Back up your work.

SOURCE DOCUMENT PROBLEM

Problem 26–10

Use the source documents in your working papers to record the transactions for this problem.

CHALLENGE PROBLEM

Problem 26–10 Renewing a Note Receivable

Occasionally, on the maturity date, a note may be renewed instead of being paid. When this occurs, (1) the interest on the first note is paid, (2) the first note is canceled, and (3) a new note for the same principal amount is issued, usually at a higher interest rate. Buzz Newsstand had the following transactions.

Instructions In your working papers, record the following transactions on general journal page 24.

Date	Transactions
Mar. 14	Sold merchandise on account to Saba Nadal for $1,800, plus sales tax of $108.00, terms 30 days, Sales Slip 388.
Apr. 13	Accepted a 60-day, 9% note for $1,908.00 from Saba Nadal in place of the account receivable, Note 416.
June 12	Received the interest due from Saba Nadal for the note dated April 13 and agreed to renew the note at 10% for 90 days, Receipt 1387 and Note 417.
Sept. 10	Received a check from Saba Nadal for the maturity value of the note issued June 12, Receipt 1555.

Analyze   Calculate the total amount of interest earned in March.

Practice your test-taking skills! The questions on this page are reprinted with permission from national organizations:
- • Future Business Leaders of America
- • Business Professionals of America

Use a separate sheet of paper to record your answers.

Future Business Leaders of America

MULTIPLE CHOICE

1. Signed a 90-day, 10% note
- a. Debit Cash, credit Notes Receivable
- b. Debit Cash, credit Notes Payable
- c. Debit Accounts Receivable, credit Cash
- d. Debit Cash, credit Accounts Receivable

Use the following information for questions 2 & 3.

October 15, Morton Co. accepts a 60-day, 11% note from Anderson Imports for an extension of time on its account, $990.00 Notes Receivable No. 5.

2. The credit for this transaction would be made to
- a. Accounts Payable.
- b. Accounts Receivable.
- c. Notes Payable.
- d. Notes Receivable.

3. The effect of this transaction on the customer's account in the accounts receivable ledger is
- a. to decrease the account balance.
- b. to increase the account balance.
- c. no change in the account balance.
- d. not known.

4. Find the interest and maturity value for a 60-day note with principal of $1,500 and interest at 8 percent.
- a. $120.00 interest; $1,620.00 maturity value
- b. $32.88 interest; $1,532.88 maturity value
- c. $3.29 interest; $1,503.29 maturity value
- d. $19.74 interest; $1,519.74 maturity value

Business Professionals of America

MULTIPLE CHOICE

5. Qupre, Inc. signed a 90-day, 9.75% note with First State Bank for $1,200 on August 1. The maturity date for the note is
- a. October 30.
- b. November 1.
- c. October 28.
- d. November 2.

> **Need More Help?**
>
> Go to **glencoeaccounting.glencoe.com** and click on **Student Center**. Click on **Winning Competitive Events** and select **Chapter 26.**
> - • **Practice Questions and Test-Taking Tips**
> - • **Concept Capsules and Terminology**

Notes Payable and Receivable

1. Explain what a promissory note is and distinguish between the two types, notes payable and notes receivable.

2. Explain how an interest-bearing note and a non-interest-bearing note differ.

3. Calculate the amount of interest to be charged on a $12,000, 8.5%, 90-day interest-bearing note.

4. Explain the difference between interest expense and interest income.

5. You need to borrow $10,000 for six months. Interest rates are expected to drop from 7% to 5.5% within the next week. How much would you save by waiting an additional week to obtain your loan?

6. Consider a $5,000, 6%, 180-day interest-bearing note and a non-interest-bearing note for the same amount and time period with a bank discount of 6%. From the borrower's point of view, which is the better loan and why?

Merchandising Business: Restaurant/Retail Shop

Moreno's Italian Oven is open seven days a week for lunch and dinner. The restaurant seats 60 patrons in a day and averages 90 percent capacity. It is considering expanding into the space adjacent to the restaurant. The cost to remodel the area and buy additional kitchen and restaurant equipment is estimated at $200,000. The rent on the additional space is $1,200 a month.

INSTRUCTIONS

1. If Moreno's could double the number of customers served weekly, calculate how many it could serve per week.

2. If each customer spends an average of $12 per meal, calculate the additional revenue the restaurant would earn per day if it expands and maintains 90 percent capacity.

Is the Boss Always Right?

You work for a large property management company. Your boss, Joan, is the senior accountant; and her boss, Frank, is vice president. For the past several months, Joan has been coming to work late, taking long lunches, and leaving early. When Frank calls, she has asked you to tell him that she is "away from her desk." You think Frank is getting suspicious, and you are starting to feel guilty about lying.

ETHICAL DECISION MAKING

1. What are the ethical issues?

2. What are the alternatives?

3. Who are the affected parties?

4. How do the alternatives affect the parties?

5. What would you do?

Promote Your Project

You write the copy for and design brochures to highlight New South Bank's many financial products. Today you were asked to prepare a brochure explaining the value of non-interest-bearing notes. Write the copy for this brochure. Design it by hand or on a computer.

SKILLS BEYOND NUMBERS

Allocating Time and Money

Good Times Amusement Park has offered you a full-time job. Before you can accept it, you must arrange for transportation.

INSTRUCTIONS List estimated costs of owning a car compared to using other transportation. How would each impact the use of your time and your budget?

INTERNATIONAL ACCOUNTING

Long-Term International Loans

The International Finance Corporation (IFC) helps finance projects in developing countries to reduce poverty and improve people's lives. Projects must be profitable and benefit the host country's economy. For instance, it has provided loans of about $44 million to build a hospital and clinic in Mexico City. Other recipient sectors include transportation, education, and tourism.

INSTRUCTIONS Describe how IFC affects people in developing countries.

Your Vehicle Loan

If you want to buy a vehicle but cannot pay cash, you need to borrow from a financial institution. To do so, you will be required to sign a legally binding note to make monthly payments for a required period of time.

PERSONAL FINANCE ACTIVITY Assume you want to buy a preowned vehicle but do not have all of the cash needed, and prefer not to ask your parents for it. Write a plan considering all aspects of the purchase.

PERSONAL FINANCE ONLINE Log on to **glencoeaccounting.glencoe.com** and click on **Student Center.** Click on **Making It Personal** and select **Chapter 26.**

Analyzing FINANCIAL Reports

Evaluating Long-Term Debt

When considering a borrower's long-term debt, lenders often consider the debt to equity ratio. This ratio compares the resources the lender will provide to the borrower's resources. It is calculated by dividing total liabilities by total stockholders' equity. Here's an example:

$$\frac{\text{Total liabilities}}{\text{Total stockholder's equity}} = \frac{\$125,670}{\$103,680} = 1.21$$

This debt to equity ratio of 1.21 to 1 means that lenders would provide more resources than the borrower has. The higher the ratio, the higher is the lender's claims on the applicant's assets. A heavy reliance on creditors increases the risk that a business may not be able to meet its financial obligations during a business downturn.

INSTRUCTIONS

Obtain **PETsMART's** most recent balance sheet from the Internet or a public library. Use this and the February 2004 balance sheet in Appendix F for the following tasks.

1. Calculate **PETsMART's** debt to equity ratio for both years.

2. Compare how the ratio has changed. As a creditor, how would you interpret this change?

Completing the Accounting Cycle for a Merchandising Corporation

Main Task

▶ Complete the accounting cycle within an assigned time frame.

Summary of Steps

▶ Record transactions in various journals.

▶ Post individual transactions to various ledgers.

▶ Prove the special journals and post the column totals.

▶ Prove cash.

▶ Prepare schedules of accounts receivable and accounts payable.

▶ Complete the work sheet.

▶ Prepare financial statements.

▶ Journalize and post the adjusting and closing entries.

▶ Prepare a post-closing trial balance.

Why It's Important

▶ Whether you are taking a test or working at a job, you will have time constraints.

Kite Loft Inc.

Company Background: The Ramspart family owns and operates a wholesale-retail merchandising business organized as a corporation. The business, called Kite Loft Inc., sells a variety of kites and paper airplanes to regional and local toy store businesses.

Your teacher will assign a due date for this project. Working with Kite Loft Inc. will give you an opportunity to complete the accounting cycle within an assigned time frame.

Keeping the Accounting Records for Kite Loft Inc.: Kite Loft Inc. uses special journals and a general journal to record its business activity.

Max Martin, Kite Loft's previous accounting clerk, has already journalized and posted the transactions for December 1 through December 15. The transactions recorded thus far are included in the accounting stationery in your working papers. The transactions for December 16 through December 31 are shown on the following pages.

Your Job Responsibilities: The forms for completing this activity are included in the working papers. As the accountant for Kite Loft, you are to complete these tasks:

(1) Record the remaining December transactions in the sales, cash receipts, purchases, cash payments, and general journals.

(2) Post the individual amounts from the five journals to the accounts receivable and accounts payable subsidiary ledgers daily.

(3) Post the individual amounts from the General columns of the cash receipts, purchases, cash payments, and general journal daily.

(4) Foot, prove, total, and rule the special journals at the end of the month.

(5) Post the column totals of the special journals to the general ledger. Use this order for posting: sales, cash receipts, purchases, and cash payments.

(6) Prove cash. The balance shown on check stub 619 is $22,752.83.

(7) Prepare a schedule of accounts receivable and a schedule of accounts payable.

(8) Prepare a trial balance on a ten-column work sheet for the year ended December 31.

Kite Loft Inc. (continued)

(9) Complete the work sheet. Use this December 31 adjustment information:

Merchandise Inventory	$24,850.43
Supplies inventory	120.00
Unexpired insurance	660.00
Total federal income taxes	4,500.00

(10) Prepare the income statement from the work sheet information.

(11) Prepare a statement of retained earnings.

(12) Prepare a balance sheet.

(13) Journalize and post the adjusting entries.

(14) Journalize and post the closing entries.

(15) Prepare a post-closing trial balance.

CHART OF ACCOUNTS
Kite Loft Inc.

ASSETS

101	Cash in Bank
105	Accounts Receivable
110	Merchandise Inventory
115	Supplies
120	Prepaid Insurance
125	Office Equipment
130	Store Equipment

LIABILITIES

201	Accounts Payable
205	Federal Corp. Income Tax Payable
210	Sales Tax Payable

STOCKHOLDERS' EQUITY

301	Capital Stock
305	Retained Earnings
310	Income Summary

REVENUE

401	Sales
405	Sales Discounts
410	Sales Returns and Allowances

COST OF MERCHANDISE

501	Purchases
505	Transportation In
510	Purchases Discounts
515	Purchases Returns and Allowances

EXPENSES

605	Advertising Expense
610	Bankcard Fees Expense
615	Insurance Expense
620	Miscellaneous Expense
625	Rent Expense
630	Salaries Expense
635	Supplies Expense
640	Utilities Expense
650	Federal Corp. Income Tax Expense

Accounts Receivable Subsidiary Ledger

BES	Best Toys
LAR	Lars' Specialties
SER	Serendipity Shop
SMA	Small Town Toys
TOY	The Toy Store

Accounts Payable Subsidiary Ledger

BRA	Brad's Kites Ltd.
CRE	Creative Kites Inc.
EAS	Easy Glide Co.
RED	Reddi-Bright Manufacturing
STA	Stars Kites Outlet
TAY	Taylor Office Suppliers

Peachtree®

SMART GUIDE

Step–by–Step Instructions:

1. Select the problem set for Kite Loft Inc. (MP–5).
2. Rename the company and set the system date.
3. Enter all of the sales on account using the **Sales/Invoicing** option.
4. Record and apply any sales returns using the **Credit Memos** option.
5. Process the cash receipts using the **Receipts** option.
6. Enter the purchases on account using the **Purchases/Receive Inventory** option.
7. Record and apply any purchases returns using the **Vendor Credit Memos** option.
8. Process all of the cash payments with the **Payments** option.
9. Record the adjusting entries.
10. Print the following reports: General Journal, Purchases Journal, Cash Disbursements Journal, Sales Journal, and Cash Receipts Journal.
11. Proof your work.
12. Print the following reports: General Ledger, Vendor Ledgers, and Customer Ledgers.
13. Print a General Ledger Trial Balance.
14. Print an Income Statement.
15. Print a Statement of Retained Earnings.
16. Print a Balance Sheet.
17. Close the fiscal year.
18. Print a post-closing trial balance.
19. Complete the Analyze activity and the Audit Test.
20. End the session.

TIP: You should back up your Peachtree files before you perform the year-end closing.

Business Transactions: Kite Loft Inc. had the following transactions December 16 through December 31.

Date	Transactions
Dec. 16	Received Invoice 410 from Reddi-Bright Manufacturing for merchandise purchased on account, $1,475.00.
16	Paid the quarterly federal income tax installment of $1,050.00, Check 610.
16	Issued Check 611 for $2,548.00 to Brad's Kites Ltd. in payment of Invoice 112 for $2,600.00 less discount of $52.00.
17	Paid the monthly salaries by issuing Check 612 for $4,750.00.
17	Purchased $80.00 of supplies from Taylor Office Suppliers on account, Invoice 830.
17	Received a check for $1,965.60 from Best Toys in payment of Sales Slip 479 for $2,003.40 less a cash discount of $37.80, Receipt 358.
19	Sold merchandise on account to Best Toys, $2,600.00 plus $156.00 sales tax, Sales Slip 484.
19	Prepared Receipt 359 for a $1,716.00 check received from Lars' Specialties in payment of Sales Slip 480 for $1,749.00 less a $33.00 cash discount.
20	Purchased merchandise on account from Brad's Kites Ltd., Invoice 215, $1,560.00.
20	Wrote Check 613 to Creative Kites Inc. to apply on account, $375.00.
21	Prepared Credit Memorandum 44 for $106.00 for the return of $100.00 in merchandise by Best Toys, plus sales tax of $6.00.
23	Sold merchandise to Lars' Specialties on account, $1,580.00 plus sales tax of $94.80, Sales Slip 485.
23	Received a check from Serendipity Shop to apply on account, Receipt 360 for $300.00.
23	Paid Easy Glide Co. for Invoice 326 for $1,890.00 less a $37.80 discount, Check 614 for $1,852.20.
26	Received from The Toy Store a check for $1,102.40 in payment of Sales Slip 483 for $1,123.60 less a cash discount of $21.20, Receipt 361.
26	Returned defective merchandise purchased on account from Brad's Kites Ltd., $150.00, Debit Memorandum 28.
26	Received Invoice 335 from Easy Glide Co. for merchandise purchased on account totaling $1,630.00.
28	Wrote Check 615 for $120.00 to the *Daily Examiner* for a monthly advertisement.
28	Small Town Toys sent a check for $450.00 to apply on account, Receipt 362.
29	Paid Stars Kites Outlet $1,625.00 on account, Check 616.

CONTINUE

Kite Loft Inc. (continued)

Date	Transactions (cont.)
29	Sold to The Toy Store $1,990.00 of merchandise on account, plus $119.40 sales tax, Sales Slip 486.
30	Issued Check 617 to Reddi-Bright Manufacturing for $700.00 to apply on account.
30	Sold merchandise totaling $560.00 plus $33.60 sales tax to the Serendipity Shop on account, Sales Slip 487.
31	Recorded the bank service charge of $10.00 and the bankcard fee of $150.00, from December bank statement.
31	Paid transportation charges of $51.60 for merchandise shipped from Easy Glide Co., Check 618.
31	Recorded cash sales of $3,995.10 plus $239.71 in sales tax, Tape 41.
31	Recorded bankcard sales of $1,736.27 plus sales tax of $104.18, Tape 41.

Analyze
1. **Identify where Kite Loft's outstanding customer balances are kept, and report which customer has the largest balance outstanding and the amount owed.**
2. **Locate the cash receipts journal, and identify the amount of cash to be debited to the general ledger Cash in Bank account.**
3. **Calculate Kite Loft's working capital at December 31.**

QuickBooks

PROBLEM GUIDE

Step–by–Step Instructions:
1. Restore the Problem Mini Practice 5.QBB file.
2. Enter all sales on account using the **Create Invoices** option.
3. Record and apply any sales returns using the **Create Credit Memos/ Refunds** option.
4. Process all cash receipts.
5. Enter the purchases on account using the **Enter Bills** option.
6. Record and apply any purchase returns using the **Credit** option from the **Enter Bills** window in the *Vendors* menu.
7. Process all cash payments.
8. Record the adjusting entries.
9. Print a Journal report.
10. Proof your work.
11. Print the following reports: General Ledger, Vendor Balance Summary, and Customer Balance Summary.
12. Print a Trial Balance.
13. Print a Profit & Loss report.
14. Print a Balance Sheet.
15. Close the fiscal year.
16. Print a post-closing Trial Balance.
17. Complete the Analyze activity and the Audit Test.
18. Back up your work.

Additional Accounting Topics

STANDARD &POOR'S

Personal Finance Q & A

Q: Why do I need to know about partnerships?

A: Partnership accounting is different from accounting for corporations and sole proprietorships.

Q: What does ethics have to do with accounting?

A: Everything. Accountants are held to high ethical standards because they are the keepers and communicators of important information. People rely on accountants.

THINK IT OVER

Since partnerships are a common form of business enterprise, would you consider having a partner in your business? Give several reasons that you would or would not be in favor of this idea.

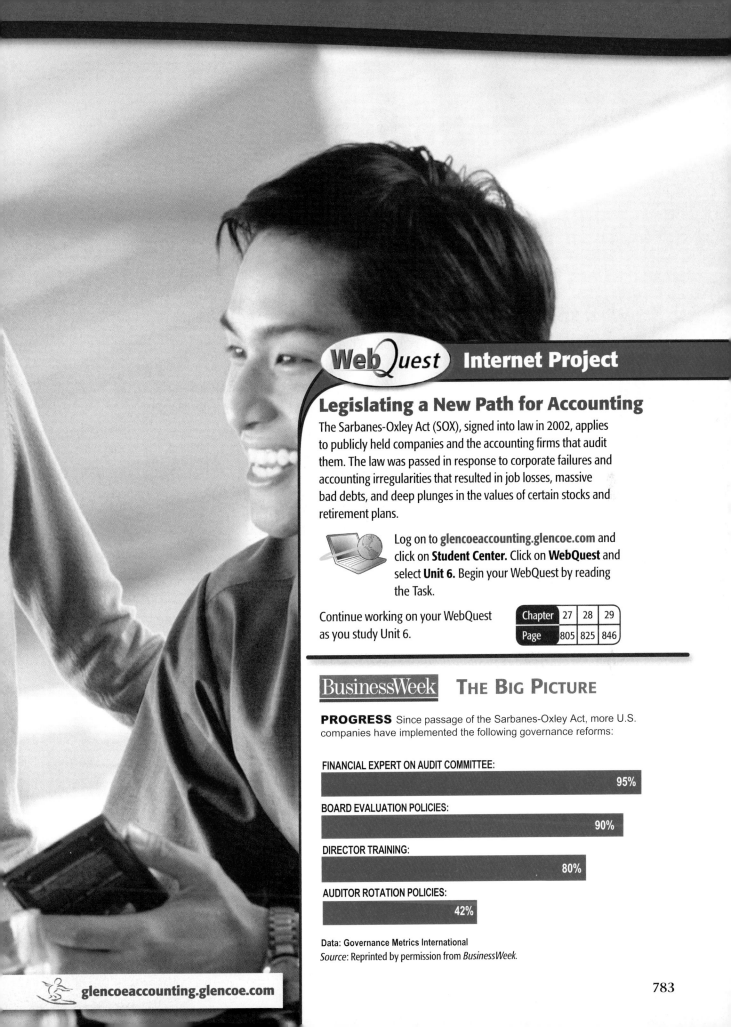

WebQuest · Internet Project

Legislating a New Path for Accounting

The Sarbanes-Oxley Act (SOX), signed into law in 2002, applies to publicly held companies and the accounting firms that audit them. The law was passed in response to corporate failures and accounting irregularities that resulted in job losses, massive bad debts, and deep plunges in the values of certain stocks and retirement plans.

Log on to **glencoeaccounting.glencoe.com** and click on **Student Center.** Click on **WebQuest** and select **Unit 6.** Begin your WebQuest by reading the Task.

Continue working on your WebQuest as you study Unit 6.

Chapter	27	28	29
Page	805	825	846

BusinessWeek — THE BIG PICTURE

PROGRESS Since passage of the Sarbanes-Oxley Act, more U.S. companies have implemented the following governance reforms:

FINANCIAL EXPERT ON AUDIT COMMITTEE:
95%

BOARD EVALUATION POLICIES:
90%

DIRECTOR TRAINING:
80%

AUDITOR ROTATION POLICIES:
42%

Data: Governance Metrics International
Source: Reprinted by permission from *BusinessWeek*.

Introduction to Partnerships

What You'll Learn

1. Identify the characteristics of a partnership.

2. Identify the various accounting functions involved with a partnership.

3. Account for investments in a partnership.

4. Account for partners' withdrawals.

5. Allocate profits and losses to the partners by different methods.

6. Define the accounting terms introduced in this chapter.

Why It's Important

▶ Many businesses are organized as partnerships.

MOSS-ADAMS LLP

Predict

1. What does the chapter title tell you?
2. What do you already know about this subject from personal experience?
3. What have you learned about this in the earlier chapters?
4. What gaps exist in your knowledge of this subject?

Exploring the *Real World* of Business

LOOKING AT PARTNERSHIPS

Moss Adams LLP

Moss Adams LLP claims its spot as the 11th largest accounting and consulting firm in the United States. Its staff of 1,400 offers audit and tax services, business consulting, risk management services, and asset valuations.

When this accounting partnership began in 1913, it primarily served local forest product businesses in the Seattle, Washington area. The firm now earns approximately $180 million per year with clients in a variety of industries.

Moss Adams attributes its success to a decision to become the dominant accounting service provider in selected industries. The firm's partners and accountants have skills specific to industries like auto sales, apparel, forestry, construction, and health care.

What Do You Think?

If you were looking for an accounting firm to handle your audit, why would it be important to you that the firm have specialized experience in your industry?

Working in the *Real World*

APPLYING YOUR ACCOUNTING KNOWLEDGE

Going into business with someone can be smart when two or more people have complementary business skills and resources that can help a business succeed. Business partners should agree about each person's role in the business and how to share profits and losses. In this chapter you will learn how a partnership agreement helps avoid conflict and contributes to the smooth operation of the business.

Personal Connection

1. What are some rules in your workplace?
2. How do these rules help you and your co-workers avoid conflict?
3. If conflicts occur, how are they resolved?

Online Connection

Go to **glencoeaccounting.glencoe.com** and click on **Student Center.** Click on **Working in the Real World** and select **Chapter 27.**

Partnership Characteristics and Partners' Equity

BEFORE YOU READ

Main Idea
The partnership form of business organization has unique features.

Read to Learn...
➤ the characteristics of a partnership. (p. 786)
➤ how to account for equity in a partnership. (p. 787)

Key Terms
partnership agreement
mutual agency

As you learned in Chapter 2, a *partnership* is an association of two or more persons as co-owners to operate a business for profit. Any type of business may be organized as a partnership, but it is more common for those providing professional services such as accounting and legal firms.

Characteristics of a Partnership
What Are the Characteristics of a Partnership?

The partnership organizational form has certain unique features.

Ease of Formation

No special legal requirements must be met to form a partnership.

A Voluntary Arrangement. A partnership is formed when two or more persons agree to operate as partners. No one can be forced into a partnership or required to continue as a partner.

The Partnership Agreement. A partnership may be formed when two or more individuals verbally agree to operate a business as co-owners. However, it is advisable to have a **partnership agreement** in writing that states the terms under which the partnership will operate. It should include (1) each partner's name and address; (2) the name, location, and nature of the partnership; (3) the agreement date and the length of time the partnership is to exist; (4) each partner's investment; (5) each partner's duties, rights, and responsibilities; (6) the amount of withdrawals allowed each partner; (7) the procedure for sharing profits and losses; and (8) the procedures to follow when the partnership ceases to exist. Each partner should sign the agreement.

Unlimited Liability

Each partner is *personally* liable for the partnership's debts. This means that if the assets of the partnership cannot pay its creditors, the partners' personal assets may be used to pay those debts.

Limited Life

A partnership may end for a number of reasons, including any partner's death, withdrawal, bankruptcy, or incapacity. It may also end upon the completion of the project for which the partnership was formed, or at the expiration of the time set by the partners. For example, two architects may agree to combine their talents to design and oversee the construction of a building. When the building is completed, the partnership is dissolved.

As You READ

Instant Recall

Other Forms of Organization A sole proprietorship is owned by one person. A corporation is owned by any number of people and is a separate entity for legal purposes.

Mutual Agency

Each partner is an agent of the partnership. In other words any partner has the legal right, in the name of the firm, to enter into agreements that are binding on all other partners. This is known as **mutual agency**.

Co-ownership of Partnership Property

When a partner invests assets in the partnership, he or she gives up all personal rights of ownership. The partners co-own all partnership assets.

Advantages and Disadvantages of a Partnership

A partnership combines the abilities, experiences, and resources of two or more individuals. It is easy to form and requires only the partners' agreement. Partners can usually make decisions without meeting formally. A partnership must have a legal purpose but has few other restrictions. Finally, it does not pay federal or state income taxes because each partner pays personal income taxes on his or her share of the net income of the business.

Of course, a partnership has disadvantages. It has a limited life, each partner is personally liable for the partnership's debts, and all partners may be held responsible for one partner's decisions. A partner cannot transfer his or her partnership interest without the other partners' consent. The partners need to be able to work together without major disagreements.

Accounting for Partners' Equity

How Do You Account for a Partnership?

Accounting for owner's equity for a partnership is basically the same as for a sole proprietorship. A sole proprietorship has only one capital account, but a partnership has two or more capital accounts. A separate capital account is set up for each partner to record that partner's investment in the business. Each partner also has a separate withdrawals account.

Recording Partner Investments

When a partnership is formed, the value of cash and other assets invested by each partner is listed in the partnership agreement. Separate entries then record each partner's investment in the business. Let's look at an example.

On January 1 Molly Gill and Don Putman agree to form a partnership to operate a business. The name of the partnership is Surfside Bike & Skate Rentals. Each partner agrees to invest the following assets in the new business.

	Gill	Putman
Cash		$12,000
Office supplies		1,000
Office equipment (market value)		12,000
Building (market value)	$30,000	
Land	15,000	
Total assets invested	$45,000	$25,000

When assets other than cash are invested in a partnership, the asset accounts are debited for the market value of the assets.

On January 1 Molly Gill and Don Putman contributed cash and other assets to form a partnership, Memorandum 1.

JOURNAL ENTRY

	DATE		DESCRIPTION	POST. REF.	DEBIT	CREDIT	
1	20--						1
2	Jan.	1	Building		30 000 00		2
3			Land		15 000 00		3
4			Molly Gill, Capital			45 000 00	4
5			Memorandum 1				5
6		1	Cash in Bank		12 000 00		6
7			Office Supplies		1 000 00		7
8			Office Equipment		12 000 00		8
9			Don Putman, Capital			25 000 00	9
10			Memorandum 1				10
11							11

GENERAL JOURNAL   PAGE ___1___

As You READ

Key Point

Partnership Investments A partner's investment of noncash assets is recorded at the market value of the assets.

Recording Additional Partner Investments

Any additional investments by the partners are recorded in a similar manner. For example, in April each partner agreed to invest $5,000 cash in the business. **Cash in Bank** is debited for $10,000 and the two partners' capital accounts are credited for $5,000 each.

Recording Partner Withdrawals

Because partners do not receive a salary, they may withdraw cash or other assets for personal use during the year. The withdrawal amounts must follow the terms of the partnership agreement. The amount is debited to the partner's withdrawals account and is credited to the appropriate asset account.

On May 12 Molly Gill withdrew $1,800 cash for personal use, Check 123, and Don Putman withdrew $1,200 cash for personal use, Check 124.

JOURNAL ENTRY

GENERAL JOURNAL   PAGE ___36___

	DATE		DESCRIPTION	POST. REF.	DEBIT	CREDIT	
1	20--						1
2	May	12	Molly Gill, Withdrawals		1 800 00		2
3			Cash in Bank			1 800 00	3
4			Check 123				4
5			Don Putman, Withdrawals		1 200 00		5
6			Cash in Bank			1 200 00	6
7			Check 124				7

Reinforce the Main Idea

The partnership form of business organization is different from the other forms you have studied. Make a chart like this one and fill in the blanks with a short definition of each partnership characteristic.

CHARACTERISTICS OF A PARTNERSHIP

Ease of Formation	
Unlimited Liability	
Limited Life	
Mutual Agency	
Co-ownership of Partnership Property	

Do the Math

A partnership has two partners. Assume that assets total $123,400, liabilities are $18,700, and partner A has a capital balance of $63,234. What is the capital balance of partner B?

Problem 27–1 Recording Partners' Investments

On June 1 Matthew Deck and Jennifer Rusk agree to combine their sole proprietorships into a new business, Dreamscapes Catering, organized as a partnership. The partnership will take over all assets of the two proprietorships. The assets invested by Deck and Rusk follow.

Instructions Prepare the journal entries required to record the investment by each partner. Use page 1 of the general journal in your working papers. The source document is Memorandum 1.

Investments	Deck	Rusk
Cash	$ 1,200	$ 2,300
Accounts receivable	2,000	7,000
Merchandise	8,000	5,000
Equipment	5,000	12,000
Van	12,000	—
Office Furniture	1,000	500

Division of Income and Loss

Main Idea
Partners divide profits and losses in several different ways.

Read to Learn...
➤ how to divide net income and net loss equally. (p. 790)
➤ how to divide net income and net loss on a fractional basis. (p. 791)
➤ how to divide net income and net loss based on capital investments. (p. 793)

BEFORE YOU READ

At the end of each accounting period, the net income or net loss from partnership operations is divided among the partners. Partners may divide the income or loss among themselves in any way they choose. The specific method should be defined in the partnership agreement. If it is not, the law provides that net income or net loss be divided equally among the partners.

There are many ways for partners to divide profits and losses. The division of profits and losses is generally based on the services and capital contributed by the partners to the partnership. For example, if the partners share equally in the work of the business, but one partner has invested more capital, it seems only fair that the one who has invested more should profit more.

When the profits of the accounting period are divided, each partner's capital account is increased. If the business incurs a net loss for the accounting period, the capital account of each partner is decreased.

A number of methods can be used to distribute partnership profits or losses. We consider three of these methods:

- equal basis
- fractional share basis
- capital investment basis

We will look at two examples for Surfside Bike & Skate Rentals for each method: a net income of $24,000 and a net loss of $12,000.

Dividing Profits and Losses Equally

What Is the Journal Entry to Divide Income or Loss Equally?

The easiest way to divide a partnership's net income or net loss is on an equal basis. This method is often used when all partners invest equal amounts of capital and share equally in the work of the business.

The partnership agreement for Surfside Bike & Skate Rentals states that the profits or losses are to be divided between the two partners equally. During the first year of operation, the partnership earned a net income of $24,000. Each partner's share is $12,000 ($24,000 ÷ 2).

Remember that the balance of the **Income Summary** account is the net income or net loss for the period. In the third closing entry, **Income Summary** is closed to capital. On December 31 the balance of **Income Summary**, a $24,000 credit, is divided equally between the two partners.

As You READ

Key Point

Distribution of Net Income or Net Loss
If the partnership agreement does not explain how net income or net loss is to be distributed, it is divided equally among the partners.

GENERAL JOURNAL   PAGE ___66___

	DATE	DESCRIPTION	POST. REF.	DEBIT	CREDIT	
1	20--	*Closing Entries*				1
2	Dec. 31	Income Summary		24 000 00		2
3		Molly Gill, Capital			12 000 00	3
4		Don Putman, Capital			12 000 00	4

After the journal entry has been posted, the balance of Molly Gill's capital account is $62,000 and the balance of Don Putman's capital account is $42,000.

Molly Gill, Capital			Don Putman, Capital	
Debit	Credit		Debit	Credit
−	+		−	+
	Bal. 50,000			Bal. 30,000
	Clos. 12,000			Clos. 12,000
	Bal. 62,000			Bal. 42,000

If the partnership incurs a net loss of $12,000 for the period, each partner's share of the net loss is $6,000 ($12,000 ÷ 2).

On December 31 the balance of **Income Summary**, a $12,000 debit, is divided equally between the two partners.

GENERAL JOURNAL   PAGE ___66___

	DATE	DESCRIPTION	POST. REF.	DEBIT	CREDIT	
1	20--	*Closing Entries*				1
2	Dec. 31	Molly Gill, Capital		6 000 00		2
3		Don Putman, Capital		6 000 00		3
4		Income Summary			12 000 00	4

After the journal entry has been posted, the balance of Molly Gill's capital account is $44,000 and the balance of Don Putman's capital account is $24,000.

Molly Gill, Capital			Don Putman, Capital	
Debit	Credit		Debit	Credit
−	+		−	+
Clos. 6,000	Bal. 50,000		Clos. 6,000	Bal. 30,000
	Bal. 44,000			Bal. 24,000

As You READ

In Your Experience

Partnership Have you, a friend, or a family member ever done business with a partnership?

Dividing Profits and Losses on a Fractional Share Basis

How Do You Compute and Record Profit or Loss Based on Fractions?

Another way to divide net income or net loss is to assign each partner a stated fraction of the total. The size of the fraction usually depends on (1) the amount of each partner's investment and (2) the value of each partner's services to the business.

Suppose that the Surfside Bike & Skate Rentals partnership agreement states that the net income or net loss is to be divided between the two partners on the following basis:

- Gill, two-thirds
- Putman, one-third

When partners agree to share net income or net loss on a fractional share basis, that basis is often stated as a ratio. For example, Molly Gill's two-thirds share and Don Putman's one-third share could be expressed as a 2:1 ratio (2 to 1). To turn a ratio into a fraction, add the figures and use the total as the denominator of the fraction. In this particular example, the ratio is converted to fractions as follows:

$$2{:}1 \ = \ (2 + 1 = 3) \ = \ \text{⅔ and ⅓}$$

The division of the $24,000 net income based on a 2:1 ratio is calculated as follows:

Gill's share:	$24,000 × ⅔ =	$16,000
Putman's share:	$24,000 × ⅓ =	$8,000

The December 31 closing entry follows:

GENERAL JOURNAL				PAGE	_66_

	DATE		DESCRIPTION	POST. REF.	DEBIT	CREDIT	
1	20--		*Closing Entries*				1
2	*Dec.*	*31*	*Income Summary*		24 000 00		2
3			*Molly Gill, Capital*			16 000 00	3
4			*Don Putman, Capital*			8 000 00	4

After the journal entry has been posted, the balance of Molly Gill's capital account is $66,000 and the balance of Don Putman's capital account is $38,000. Refer to the following T account for each of the partners.

Molly Gill, Capital			Don Putman, Capital	
Debit	Credit		Debit	Credit
–	+		–	+
	Bal. 50,000			Bal. 30,000
	Clos. 16,000			Clos. 8,000
	Bal. 66,000			Bal. 38,000

If the partnership incurs a net loss of $12,000 for the period, the December 31 distribution to the partners based on a 2:1 ratio is calculated as follows:

Gill's share:	($12,000) × ⅔ =	($8,000)
Putman's share:	($12,000) × ⅓ =	($4,000)

On December 31 the partnership makes the following closing entry:

	DATE	DESCRIPTION	POST. REF.	DEBIT	CREDIT	
1	20--	*Closing Entries*				1
2	Dec. 31	Molly Gill, Capital		8 000 00		2
3		Don Putman, Capital		4 000 00		3
4		Income Summary			12 000 00	4

GENERAL JOURNAL   PAGE _66_

Molly Gill, Capital				Don Putman, Capital	
Debit	Credit			Debit	Credit
–	+			–	+
Clos. 8,000	Bal. 50,000			Clos. 4,000	Bal. 30,000
	Bal. 42,000				Bal. 26,000

MATH HINTS

Fractions, Decimals, and Percents
- To change a fraction to a decimal, divide the numerator by the denominator.
  $3/8 = 0.375$
- To change a decimal to a percent, move the decimal point two places to the *right* and add the percent symbol.
  $0.375 = 37.5\%$
- To change a percent to a fraction, replace the percent symbol with $1/100$.
  $37.5\% = 37.5(1/100) = 37.5/100$

After the journal entry has been posted, the balance of Molly Gill's capital account is $42,000 and the balance of Don Putman's capital account is $26,000.

Dividing Profits and Losses Based on Capital Investments

How Do You Use Capital Investment to Divide Profit or Loss?

Net income and net loss can also be divided on the basis of the amount of capital contributed by the individual partners. To do this, compute the percentage of each partner's capital investment as follows:

$$\frac{\text{Individual Partner's Investment}}{\text{Total Partnership Investment}} = \text{Partner's Percentage}$$

Then multiply the net income or net loss by each partner's percentage.

Molly Gill and Don Putman made the following capital investments:

Molly Gill	$50,000
Don Putman	$30,000
Total investment	$80,000

Gill's Percentage	Putman's Percentage
$\dfrac{50,000}{80,000} = 62.5\%$	$\dfrac{30,000}{80,000} = 37.5\%$

The share of the $24,000 net income for each partner is calculated as follows:

Gill's share	$24,000	×	.625	=	$15,000
Putman's share	$24,000	×	.375	=	$9,000

On December 31 the partnership makes the following closing entry:

	DATE		DESCRIPTION	POST. REF.	DEBIT	CREDIT	
			GENERAL JOURNAL			PAGE _66_	
1	20--		*Closing Entries*				1
2	Dec.	31	Income Summary		24 000 00		2
3			*Molly Gill, Capital*			15 000 00	3
4			*Don Putman, Capital*			9 000 00	4
5							5

Molly Gill, Capital			Don Putman, Capital		
Debit –	Credit +		Debit –	Credit +	
	Bal. 50,000			Bal. 30,000	
	Clos. 15,000			Clos. 9,000	
	Bal. 65,000			Bal. 39,000	

After the journal entry has been posted, the balance of Molly Gill's capital account is $65,000 and the balance of Don Putman's capital account is $39,000.

If the partnership incurs a net loss of $12,000 for the period, the December 31 distribution is calculated as follows:

Gill's share   ($12,000) × .625 = ($7,500)
Putman's share   ($12,000) × .375 = ($4,500)

On December 31 the closing entry is as follows:

	DATE		DESCRIPTION	POST. REF.	DEBIT	CREDIT	
			GENERAL JOURNAL			PAGE _66_	
1	20--		*Closing Entries*				1
2	Dec.	31	Molly Gill, Capital		7 500 00		2
3			*Don Putman, Capital*		4 500 00		3
4			*Income Summary*			12 000 00	4
5							5

After the journal entry has been posted, the balance of Molly Gill's capital account is $42,500, and the balance of Don Putman's capital account is $25,500.

Molly Gill, Capital			Don Putman, Capital		
Debit –	Credit +		Debit –	Credit +	
Clos. 7,500	Bal. 50,000		Clos. 4,500	Bal. 30,000	
	Bal. 42,500			Bal. 25,500	

AFTER You READ

Reinforce the Main Idea

Identify two facts about the methods of dividing partnership profits and losses covered in this section. Use a chart like this one to organize the information.

Method of Dividing Profits and Losses	Fact #1	Fact #2

Do the Math

You and your best friend, Mary Jo Perry, operate an ice cream kiosk at the local outdoor shopping mall. You agree to divide profits and losses based on the capital investments made by each partner. Calculate the share of profit and loss due to each partner.

Your investment	$15,000
Mary Jo Perry's investment	25,000
Net income	32,000

1. What is the percentage of investment by each partner?
2. What is your share of the profit?
3. If there is a loss, which partner will have the largest share of the loss?

Problem 27–2 Determining Partners' Fractional Shares

Following are the ratios used by several partnerships to divide net income or net loss.

Instructions Determine the fractions that are used to calculate each partner's share of net income or net loss. Use the form provided in your working papers.

1. 3:1   4. 2:1:1
2. 5:3:1   5. 2:1
3. 3:2:2:1

Problem 27–3 Analyzing a Source Document

The deposit slips for Mr. Walter's and Ms. Yount's investments in the partnership of Walter and Yount Tax Service are presented here.

Instructions Prepare a journal entry to record the investments by the partners. Use the journal provided in your working papers.

Nations National Bank of U.S.A.
Auburn, Alabama 36831

Date November 13   20 --
Checks and other items are received for deposit subject to the terms and conditions of this bank's collection agreement.

Walter & Yount Tax Service
200 Market Square
Rockford, Alabama 35136

⑈0⑈⑈00653456⑈ 45098 7⑈

	DOLLARS	CENTS
CASH		
CHECKS (List Singly)		
1 234/67	8,000	00
2 Walter		
3		
4		
5		
6		
7		
8		
TOTAL	8,000	00

BE SURE EACH ITEM IS ENDORSED

Nations National Bank of U.S.A.
Auburn, Alabama 36831

Date November 13   20 --
Checks and other items are received for deposit subject to the terms and conditions of this bank's collection agreement.

Walter & Yount Tax Service
200 Market Square
Rockford, Alabama 35136

⑈0⑈⑈00653456⑈ 45098 7⑈

	DOLLARS	CENTS
CASH		
CHECKS (List Singly)		
1 234/89	12,000	00
2 Yount		
3		
4		
5		
6		
7		
8		
TOTAL	12,000	00

BE SURE EACH ITEM IS ENDORSED

Key Concepts

1. A partnership is an association of two or more persons to operate, as co-owners, a business for profit. The actions of one partner acting on behalf of the partnership are binding on all partners. Partnership characteristics include:

   - the ease of formation
   - unlimited liability for the partnership's debts
   - limited life
   - mutual agency
   - co-ownership of partnership property

   Advantages include:

   - brings together abilities, experiences, and resources of two or more individuals
   - requires only the partners' agreement to form
   - allows one or more partners to make decisions without a formal meeting of all partners
   - does not pay federal or state income taxes; each partner pays taxes on his or her share of the net income of the business

   Disadvantages include:

   - limited life
   - personal liability for partnership debts
   - responsibility for actions of other partners
   - restriction of transfer of a partner's interest without permission of other partners
   - potential for disagreements between partners

   It is advisable to have a partnership agreement signed by each partner that states the following in writing:

   - each partner's name and address
   - the name, location, and nature of the partnership
   - the agreement date and the length of time the partnership is to exist
   - each partner's investment
   - each partner's duties, rights, and responsibilities
   - the amount of withdrawals allowed each partner
   - the procedure for sharing profits and losses
   - the procedures to follow when the partnership ceases to exist

2. Accounting for a partnership involves recording partners' original and subsequent investments in separate capital accounts and recording partners' withdrawals in separate withdrawals accounts.

Partner 1, Capital		Partner 1, Withdrawals		Partner 2, Capital		Partner 2, Withdrawals	
Debit	Credit	Debit	Credit	Debit	Credit	Debit	Credit
−	+	+	−	−	+	+	−
	XXX	XXX			XXX	XXX	

3. The formation of a partnership involves recording the value of cash and other assets that each partner invests. To record a partner's *investment* in a partnership:

Cash in Bank (or other asset)			Individual Partner's Capital	
Debit	Credit		Debit	Credit
+	−		−	+
XXX				XXX

4. The terms of a partnership agreement should determine how partners may withdraw cash or assets from the business. To record a partner's cash *withdrawal* from the partnership:

Individual Partner's Withdrawals			Cash in Bank	
Debit	Credit		Debit	Credit
+	−		+	−
XXX				XXX

5. The net income or net loss of a partnership is divided among the partners according to the terms set forth in the partnership agreement. The division is usually based on the contribution of services and capital by the partners.

The division may be determined

- on an equal basis
- on a fractional share basis
- on the basis of investment

Dividing profits among partners:

Individual Partner's Capital			Income Summary	
Debit	Credit		Debit	Credit
−	+		XXX	
	XXX			

Dividing losses among partners:

Individual Partner's Capital			Income Summary	
Debit	Credit		Debit	Credit
−	+			
XXX				XXX

Key Terms

mutual agency   (p. 787)
partnership agreement   (p. 786)

Check Your Understanding

1. **Partnership Form of Organization**
   a. List five characteristics of a partnership.
   b. List three advantages and three disadvantages of the partnership form of business.

2. **Partnership Accounting**
   a. What information is usually included in a partnership agreement?
   b. How does accounting for a partnership differ from that for a sole proprietorship?

3. **Partnership Investments**
   a. When assets other than cash are invested in a partnership, at what amount are the assets recorded?
   b. What is the journal entry to record a partner's investment of cash?

4. **Partnership Withdrawals**
   a. What accounts are affected when a partner withdraws cash for personal use?
   b. What determines the amount of cash or other assets a partner may withdraw from the business for personal use?

5. **Allocation of Profits and Losses**
   a. What factors do partners usually consider when deciding on how the profits and losses of the partnership will be divided?
   b. Name three methods partners might use to divide profits and losses.

Apply Key Terms

You and your friend Marianne Shelton have discussed forming a partnership to provide desktop publishing and layout services to local businesses. You have chosen a business name: The Perfect Paper. You are ready to launch your business idea, but you need Marianne to agree so that you can obtain a business loan. Using the terms listed here, write a letter to Marianne and formally invite her to join you in this venture.

mutual agency
partnership agreement

Starting a New Company

Making the Transition from a Manual to a Computerized System

Task	Manual Methods	Computerized Methods
Starting a new company	• Determine the form of business ownership. • Create a chart of accounts. • Open a general ledger account for each account. • Record the journal entry for the initial investment by the owner(s). • Post the opening entry to the appropriate ledger accounts.	• Use the new company setup guide offered with most computerized accounting systems. • Follow the steps that will prompt you to enter general information about the business, as well as specific information about the accounting records.

Peachtree® Q & A

Peachtree Question	Answer
What information will I enter in the New Company Setup wizard?	• Company information • Chart of accounts • Accounting method • Posting method • Accounting periods • Defaults • Beginning balances

QuickBooks Q & A

QuickBooks Question	Answer
What information will I enter in the new company EasyStep Interview?	• Company information • Fiscal year start date • Company preferences • Chart of accounts • Opening balances

For detailed instructions, see your Glencoe Accounting Chapter Study Guides and Working Papers.

Complete problems using: | **Manual** Glencoe Working Papers | OR | **Peachtree Complete Accounting** Software | OR | **QuickBooks** Templates | OR | **Spreadsheet** Templates

SPREADSHEET SMART GUIDE

Step–by–Step Instructions: Problem 27–5

1. Select the spreadsheet template for Problem 27–5.
2. Enter your name and the date in the spaces provided on the template.
3. Complete the spreadsheet using the instructions in your working papers.
4. Print the spreadsheet and proof your work.
5. Complete the Analyze activity.
6. Save your work and exit the spreadsheet program.

Peachtree®

SMART GUIDE

Step–by–Step Instructions: Problem 27–6

1. Select the problem set for JR Landscaping (Prob. 27–6).
2. Rename the company, change the accounting period to May 1– May 31, 2010 and set the system date.
3. Enter the transactions to record the investment by each partner using the **General Journal Entry** option.
4. Print a General Journal report and proof your work.
5. Complete the Analyze activity.
6. End the session.

Problem 27–4 Dividing Partnership Earnings

Listed here are the net income and the method of dividing net income or net loss for several partnerships.

Instructions Use the form provided in your working papers to determine each partner's share of the net income.

	Net Income	Method of Dividing Partnership Earnings
1.	$45,000	Equally: 2 partners
2.	$89,700	Fractional share: 2/3, 1/3
3.	$22,000	Fractional share: 3:1
4.	$32,000	Fractional share: 2/5, 2/5, 1/5
5.	$92,700	Equally: 3 partners

Analyze Identify the accounts affected when net income is distributed to the partners.

Problem 27–5 Calculating the Percentage of a Partner's Capital Investment

Listed here are an individual partner's investments for several partnerships.

Instructions Using the form provided in your working papers, calculate Partner A's percentage ownership in each partnership.

Partnership	Partner A's Investment	Total Partnership Investment
1.	$60,000	$180,000
2.	25,000	125,000
3.	11,250	28,125
4.	30,000	40,000

Analyze Calculate the percentage of ownership for the other partner(s) in partnerships 1 and 4.

Problem 27–6 Recording Investments of Partners

On May 1 Jason Pua and Roy Nelson formed the partnership called JR Landscaping. Jason contributed $8,100 cash and all of his landscaping equipment. Jason had purchased the equipment for $2,500 last year. The market value of this equipment is now $1,800. Roy contributed $1,000 cash and his truck to the partnership. The truck currently has a market value of $5,600.

Instructions Prepare the journal entries required to record the investment that each partner contributed in creating the partnership. Use page 1 of the general journal in your working papers. The source document for this assignment is Memorandum 1.

> **Analyze** Compare the balance of Jason Pua's capital account with the capital account of Roy Nelson.

Problem 27–7 Sharing Losses Based on Capital Balances

Mariela DeJesus and Natasha Faircloth started the partnership In Shape Fitness. Mariela contributed a capital balance of $35,000. Natasha's capital contribution totaled $45,000. Their partnership agreement specified sharing net profits and net losses on the basis of their capital balances. The net loss for their first year of operation for In Shape Fitness was $28,500.

Instructions Prepare the journal entry required to divide the net loss between the partners. Use the journal in your working papers to record your entry.

> **Analyze** If Mariela took a $1,500 withdrawal, what was her capital account balance on December 31 after the closing entries were posted?

Problem 27–8 Partners' Withdrawals

Toni Graff, Ahmad Nu, and Lindsay Pane are partners in Travel Essentials. Their partnership agreement stated that withdrawals would be 10 percent for each partner based on the partnership's net profits or net losses recorded for the year. In the first year of operation, the partnership reported $25,000 in net profit.

Instructions Prepare the entry to record the withdrawals of Graff, Nu, and Pane based on the partnership agreement. Use the journal paper provided in your working papers.

> **Analyze** Explain how the $25,000 in profit would be shared among Graff, Nu, and Pane.

Peachtree®

SMART GUIDE

Step–by–Step Instructions: Problem 27–7

1. Select the problem set for In Shape Fitness (Prob. 27–7).
2. Rename the company and set the system date.
3. Record the entry to divide the loss between the two partners using the **General Journal Entry** option.
4. Print a General Journal.
5. Complete the Analyze activity.
6. End the session.

QuickBooks

PROBLEM GUIDE

Step–by–Step Instructions: Problem 27–7

1. Restore the Problem 27-7.QBB file.
2. Record the entry to divide the loss between the two partners using the **Make General Journal Entries** option.
3. Print a Journal report.
4. Complete the Analyze activity.
5. Back up your work.

Peachtree®

SMART GUIDE

Step–by–Step Instructions: Problem 27–8

1. Select the problem set for Travel Essentials (Prob. 27–8).
2. Rename the company and set the system date.
3. Enter the transactions to record the partners' withdrawals.
4. Print a General Journal.
5. Complete the Analyze activity.
6. End the session.

Problem 27–9 Preparing Closing Entries for a Partnership

Barbara Scott and Martin Towers are partners in the firm of Ten Column Accounting Services. Their partnership agreement states that Scott and Towers share net income or net loss in a 3:2 ratio.

At the end of the period, December 31, the business had a net loss of $9,700. During the period Scott withdrew $6,600 and Towers withdrew $5,400.

Instructions In your working papers, do the following:

1. Journalize the closing entries to divide the net loss between the partners and to close the withdrawals accounts. Use general journal page 14.
2. Post the closing entries to the general ledger accounts.

Analyze Calculate the reductions in the Scott and Towers capital accounts.

QuickBooks

PROBLEM GUIDE

Step–by–Step Instructions: Problem 27–8

1. Restore the Problem 27-8.QBB file.
2. Enter the transaction to record the partners' withdrawals using the **Make General Journal Entries** option.
3. Print a Journal report.
4. Complete the Analyze activity.
5. Back up your work.

Peachtree®

SMART GUIDE

Step–by–Step Instructions: Problem 27–9

1. Select the problem set for Ten Column Accounting Services (Prob. 27–9).
2. Rename the company and set the system date.
3. Record the entry to divide net loss between partners using **General Journal Entry** option.
4. Print a General Journal report and proof your work.
5. Complete the Analyze activity.
6. End the session.

 CHALLENGE PROBLEM

Problem 27–10 Evaluating Methods of Dividing Partnership Earnings

Jo Garrity, Maureen O'Riley, and David White decided to form a partnership called OnTime Copy Shop. The partners will invest the following assets in the business:

	Garrity	O'Riley	White
Cash	0	$22,000	$40,000
Supplies	0	5,000	2,000
Equipment	0	7,500	4,000
Building	$50,000	0	0
Land	15,000	0	0

They are considering the following plans for the division of net income or net loss:

1. Equally
2. Garrity, 20%; O'Riley, 40%; White, 40%
3. In the same ratio as the beginning balances of their capital accounts

Instructions Assume that the business had a net income of $17,500 in its first year of operations. Calculate the division of net income under each of the three plans.

Analyze Identify which method O'Riley would prefer and why.

Practice your test-taking skills! The questions on this page are reprinted with permission from national organizations:
- Future Business Leaders of America
- Business Professionals of America

Use a separate sheet of paper to record your answers.

Future Business Leaders of America

MULTIPLE CHOICE

1. The drawing account shows each partner's
  a. withdrawal of cash only.
  b. withdrawal of all assets.
  c. additional investments.
  d. all of the above.
  e. none of these answers

2. The right of all partners to contract for a partnership is called
  a. mutual agency.
  b. a partnership.
  c. a partner's agreement.
  d. voting rights.
  e. none of these answers

3. Assume that Bernard's Novelty is a partnership. Which transaction would occur if Partner A withdraws cash for personal use to purchase an automobile?
  a. Debit Salary Expense and credit Cash
  b. Debit Cash and credit Partner A, Withdrawal
  c. Debit Partner A, Withdrawal and credit Cash
  d. Debit Capital and credit Cash

4. If a partner invests a noncash asset in the partnership, the amount to be debited and credited would be
  a. the asset's cost.
  b. the asset's book value.
  c. the asset's current market value.
  d. an amount determined by the investing partner.

Business Professionals of America

MULTIPLE CHOICE

5. Rewrite: 3/5 as a decimal.
  a. 1.67
  b. .4
  c. .6
  d. .0167

Need More Help?

Go to glencoeaccounting.glencoe.com and click on **Student Center.** Click on **Winning Competitive Events** and select **Chapter 27.**
- **Practice Questions and Test-Taking Tips**
- **Concept Capsules and Terminology**

CRITICAL Thinking

Introduction to Partnerships

1. Name three methods partners can use to divide net income and net loss.

2. Explain what *mutual agency* means in terms of a partnership.

3. Three people form a partnership. A invests $10,000; B, $25,000; and C, $35,000. If they share net income of $100,000 based on their original investments, what is the profit sharing ratio, and how much would each partner receive?

4. Explain the purpose of withdrawals accounts for a partnership.

5. Analyze what you believe to be the most important advantage and disadvantage of the partnership form of organization.

6. Defend the statement that a partnership agreement is advisable.

Partnership: Dentists

Arturo Garcia and Marcela Melendez are partners in Family Dental Center. They share equally the income and the costs of office rent, utilities, insurance, and salaries for the four people who work for them.

You just graduated from dental school. Arturo and Marcela offer you a partnership in their practice. Since you lack their years of experience, they offer you a 20 percent interest in return for a $40,000 investment.

INSTRUCTIONS

1. Assume that the revenue for the dental practice averages $10,000 a week. If you become a partner, you could generate additional revenue of $3,500 a week. Compute your 20 percent share of the income.

2. Compute your share of the expenses if total weekly expenses are $6,000.

3. Do you think that the 20% interest return in the partnership is a good deal? Would you negotiate a different arrangement? Explain.

Partner Loyalty

You and your best friend Harold have started a jewelry business. He manages the business while you make the jewelry. Your designs are very successful, but because of Harold's mismanagement, the business is not making any money. He suggests "doctoring" the financial statements and using them to raise capital from other investors. You are afraid that the business will not grow as long as Harold is running it, but he is a good friend and has some good ideas.

ETHICAL DECISION MAKING

1. What are the ethical issues?

2. What are the alternatives?

3. Who are the affected parties?

4. How do the alternatives affect the parties?

5. What would you do?

Creating a Partnership Agreement

Choose a classmate and discuss a partnership for a business the two of you might like to own and operate. Use your creativity. Prepare a partnership agreement that spells out the details. Include information about what each partner will contribute to the business. Be sure to sign the agreement to make it legal and binding.

Negotiating

Two of your friends own The Gold Medal, a sports restaurant. They may have to close it because, as partners, they disagree about expanding.

INSTRUCTIONS

1. Acting as a mediator, role-play the partners' conflict with two classmates. Have them discuss their expansion disagreement.
2. Write down all the problems they mention and possible solutions for each.
3. Present your solutions, and help the partners decide whether to expand.

Joint Ventures

One way a company can increase sales is to enter a foreign market in a *joint venture* with a local firm. The two companies share capital, technology, risks, rewards, and control. The local company offers cultural knowledge and business contacts. Joint ventures require a lower investment than other entry methods, but control is diluted and they can be difficult to manage.

INSTRUCTIONS Brainstorm factors to consider before forming a joint venture.

Your Entrepreneurial Traits

Entrepreneurs recognize and meet the needs of the business world. They must organize, manage, and assume risks. If you plan to be a sole proprietor, partner, or corporate executive, you will need the same traits.

PERSONAL FINANCE ACTIVITY Microsoft's Bill Gates and TV executive and personality Oprah Winfrey are two well-known entrepreneurs. List the characteristics you think made them successful.

PERSONAL FINANCE ONLINE Log on to **glencoeaccounting.glencoe.com** and click on **Student Center.** Click on **Making It Personal** and select **Chapter 27.**

Analyzing Partners' Equity

The net income or net loss from a partnership represents a return on the equity the partners invested in the business. Return on equity states a company's net profit or net loss as a percentage of equity. To compute it, divide net income by equity. Partners may invest different amounts of equity, so each partner's return may be different.

INSTRUCTIONS Use the beginning balances in the T accounts for Putman and Gill on page 792 to complete these tasks.

1. If total net income is $24,000, calculate the return on total partnership equity.
2. Using an equal split of net income, calculate the return on each partner's equity.
3. Which partner earned the better return? Explain why. Why is this percentage different than the return on total equity?

Evolution of a Business

Some large corporations started as partnerships. Visit **glencoeaccounting .glencoe.com** and click on **Student Center.** Click on **WebQuest** and select **Unit 6** to continue your Internet project.

CHAPTER 28

Financial Statements and Liquidation of a Partnership

What You'll Learn

1. Prepare an income statement for a partnership.

2. Prepare a statement of changes in partners' equity.

3. Prepare the Partners' Equity section of a balance sheet.

4. Account for partnership liquidation losses.

5. Account for partnership liquidation gains.

6. Prepare the final entry to liquidate a partnership.

7. Define the accounting terms introduced in this chapter.

Why It's Important

▶ Partners' equity receives specific treatment on financial statements and at the termination of a business.

King&King Architects LLP

BEFORE YOU READ

Predict

1. What does the chapter title tell you?
2. What do you already know about this subject from personal experience?
3. What have you learned about this in the earlier chapters?
4. What gaps exist in your knowledge of this subject?

Exploring the *Real World* of Business

EVALUATING PARTNERSHIP FINANCIAL STATEMENTS

King & King, Architects, LLP

How can a 19th century business express itself in the 21st century? Founded in 1868 by Archimedes Russell, **King & King Architects, LLP**, is the oldest architectural firm in New York state. Specializing in highly technical spaces like labs, media centers, and intensive care units, **King & King** also designs hospitals, schools, and shopping centers.

When a partnership like **King & King** begins a new project, it evaluates the costs and decides how much to charge for its services. Aging buildings and an increase in enrollment make school projects a significant portion of the firm's business. Since 1990, **King & King** has grown from a staff of 25 to more than 65, and seen a comparable increase in revenues.

What Do You Think?

How do you think income is allocated among partners in a company like **King & King**?

Working in the *Real World*

APPLYING YOUR ACCOUNTING KNOWLEDGE

In previous chapters you have learned how to prepare financial statements for a sole proprietorship and for a corporation. Preparing financial statements for a partnership is similar. In this chapter you will learn how to use partnership capital accounts in the preparation of financial statements and when a partnership business ceases its operations.

Personal Connection

1. If your workplace went out of business, what do you think would happen to the assets of the business?

2. What would happen to the debts?

Online Connection

Go to **glencoeaccounting.glencoe.com** and click on **Student Center.** Click on **Working in the Real World** and select **Chapter 28.**

Financial Statements for a Partnership

At the end of the year, Deloitte & Touche LLP, one of The Big Four accounting firms, prepares its financial statements including an income statement, a statement of changes in partners' equity, and a balance sheet. You will learn about these statements in this section.

The Income Statement
What Does a Partnership Income Statement Report?

A partnership's income statement is prepared in the same way as that for any business. If the partnership is a service business, expenses are subtracted from revenue to determine the net income or loss. It is not required, but the division of net income or net loss among the partners may be shown on the income statement.

The partnership agreement of Surfside Bike & Skate Rentals states that net income or net loss will be divided equally between the partners. At the end of the year, the firm had a net income of $24,000. Each partner's share is $12,000. **Figure 28–1** illustrates how to report the division of net income on the income statement.

Surfside Bike & Skate Rentals		
Income Statement		
For the Year Ended December 31, 20--		
Net Income		24 0 0 0 00
Division of Net Income:		
Molly Gill	12 0 0 0 00	
Don Putman	12 0 0 0 00	
Net Income		24 0 0 0 00

Figure 28–1 Reporting the Division of Net Income on the Income Statement

Surfside Bike & Skate Rentals						
Statement of Changes in Partners' Equity						
For the Year Ended December 31, 20--						
		Gill		Putman		Totals
Beginning Capital, Jan. 1, 20--						
Add: Investments		50 000 00		30 000 00		80 000 00
Net Income		12 000 00		12 000 00		24 000 00
Subtotal		62 000 00		42 000 00		104 000 00
Less: Withdrawals		5 000 00		3 000 00		8 000 00
Ending Capital, Dec. 31, 20--		57 000 00		39 000 00		96 000 00

Figure 28–2 Statement of Changes in Partners' Equity

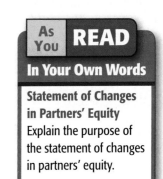

As You READ

In Your Own Words

Statement of Changes in Partners' Equity
Explain the purpose of the statement of changes in partners' equity.

The Statement of Changes in Partners' Equity

What Is Unique About Reporting Equity in a Partnership?

The **statement of changes in partners' equity** reports the change in each partner's capital account resulting from business operations, investments, and withdrawals. It is similar to the statement of changes in owner's equity for a sole proprietorship, except it has a separate column for each partner. See the statement of changes in partners' equity for Surfside Bike & Skate Rentals in **Figure 28–2.** Notice that the net income is divided between the partners.

The Balance Sheet

What Does a Partnership Balance Sheet Report?

The owners' equity section of the balance sheet for a partnership is called the *Partners' Equity* section. This section lists each partner's capital account separately. (See **Figure 28–3.**) The capital account amounts on the balance sheet are the ending capital amounts from the statement of changes in partners' equity.

Surfside Bike & Skate Rentals			
Balance Sheet			
December 31, 20--			
Partners' Equity			
Molly Gill, Capital		57 000 00	
Don Putman, Capital		39 000 00	
Total Partners' Equity			96 000 00
Total Liabilities and Partners' Equity			126 000 00

Figure 28–3 The Partners' Equity Section of the Balance Sheet

As You READ

Instant Recall

Characteristics of a Partnership The characteristics include ease of formation, unlimited liability, limited life, mutual agency, and co-ownership of partnership property.

AFTER YOU **READ**

Reinforce the Main Idea

The financial statements for a partnership are the same as those for other forms of business except for items related to owners' equity. Make a chart like this one to describe how partnership financial statements are different from those of a sole proprietorship.

Differences in Partnership Financial Statements	
STATEMENT	DIFFERENCE
Income Statement	
Statement of Changes in Partners' Equity	
Balance Sheet	

Do the Math

On January 1 Don had a capital balance of $23,000 and Ruth's capital balance was $34,000. Compute each partner's capital balance on December 31 given the following:

- Net income of $28,000 is divided equally between the two partners.
- Don withdrew $3,600.
- Ruth withdrew $4,000.

Problem 28–1 Preparing the Income Statement and Balance Sheet for a Partnership

Information related to the operations of the Goldman and Jones partnership follows.

Instructions In your working papers, prepare the Division of Net Income section of the income statement and the Partners' Equity section of the balance sheet.

1. Goldman and Jones share profits in the ratio of 2:3.
2. Net income for the year ended December 31, 20--, was $35,000.
3. The January 1 capital balance for Goldman was $23,000.
4. The January 1 capital balance for Jones was $47,000.

Problem 28–2 Analyzing a Source Document

Instructions In your working papers or on a separate sheet of paper, determine each partner's share of the gain.

N *Buie Norman & Company*
CERTIFIED PUBLIC ACCOUNTANTS

Minutes of the Partners' Meeting
January 12, 20--

The partnership sold equipment for a gain of $26,400. The partners agreed to share the gain as follows:

Larry Bass, CPA	6/22
John Buie, CPA	6/22
Teri Anderson, CPA	3/22
Robert Norman, CPA	3/22
Paula Dunham, CPA	2/22
John Ruppe, CPA	2/22

Liquidation of a Partnership

A partnership does not have an unlimsited life. Partnerships end because of death or incapacity of a partner, upon the completion of a project, or at the end of a specified time period. In this section you will learn about the procedures followed to end a partnership.

Ending a Partnership

What Is the Difference Between Dissolving and Liquidating?

A partnership can be either *dissolved* or *liquidated.* Both are legal terminations of the partnership. A **dissolution** occurs when the partners change, but the partnership continues operations. For example, when a new partner is admitted, the partnership dissolves and a new partnership begins.

A **liquidation** occurs when the business ceases to exist. The liquidation converts all partnership assets to cash and pays all partnership debts. The individual partners then are paid any remaining cash. The process involves four steps:

1. Sell all noncash assets for cash.
2. Add all gains (or deduct all losses) resulting from the sale of noncash assets to or from the capital accounts of the partners based on the partnership agreement.
3. Pay all partnership creditors.
4. After the creditors have been paid, distribute any cash remaining to the partners based on the final balance in their capital accounts.

Liquidating Surfside Bike & Skate Rentals

How Do You Liquidate a Partnership?

Let's explore the liquidation of the Surfside Bike & Skate Rentals partnership. **Figure 28–4** on page 812 shows the balance sheet on the date the partners decided to end Surfside Bike & Skate Rentals.

Molly Gill and Don Putman share profits and losses equally and agree to end the partnership based on the April 15 balance sheet. The liquidation requires converting all partnership assets to cash, paying all debts, and distributing the remaining cash to the partners. Ending the partnership required five transactions over a period of weeks.

BEFORE YOU READ

Main Idea
In a liquidation the assets are sold, creditors are paid, and any remaining cash is distributed to the partners.

Read to Learn...
➤ two types of legal termination of a partnership. (p. 811)
➤ how to liquidate a partnership. (p. 811)

Key Terms
dissolution
liquidation

Liquidation of a Business Have you ever attended a "going-out-of-business" sale? Explain how this sale uses a type of liquidation.

Surfside Bike & Skate Rentals							
Balance Sheet							
April 15, 20--							
Assets							
Cash in Bank				18 000 00			
Accounts Receivable				33 000 00			
Merchandise Inventory				35 000 00			
Equipment	48 000 00						
Less: Accumulated Depreciation	(8 000 00)						
				40 000 00			
Total Assets						126 000 00	
Liabilities							
Note Payable				10 000 00			
Accounts Payable				20 000 00			
Total Liabilities						30 000 00	
Partners' Equity							
Molly Gill, Capital				57 000 00			
Don Putman, Capital				39 000 00			
Total Partners' Equity						96 000 00	
Total Liabilities and Partners' Equity						126 000 00	

Figure 28–4 Surfside Bike & Skate Rentals Balance Sheet

Sale of Partnership Accounts Receivable at a Loss

On April 20 Surfside sold its $33,000 in accounts receivable to a finance broker for $29,000. The receivables sale resulted in a $4,000 ($29,000 − $33,000) loss to the partnership. Gill and Putman divided the loss equally. The following entry records the company's sale of the receivables and loss distribution:

	GENERAL JOURNAL		PAGE 109	
DATE	DESCRIPTION	POST. REF.	DEBIT	CREDIT
20--				
Apr. 20	Cash in Bank		29 000 00	
	Molly Gill, Capital		2 000 00	
	Don Putman, Capital		2 000 00	
	Accounts Receivable			33 000 00
	Receipt 341			

The individual balances in the accounts receivable subsidiary ledger are credited for a total of $33,000.

Sale of Partnership Merchandise at a Loss

On April 29 Surfside sold its merchandise inventory, which cost $35,000, for $32,000 to a discounter. The sale resulted in a $3,000 ($32,000 − $35,000) loss to the partnership. The partners divided the loss equally. The following entry records the sale of the inventory and the distribution of the loss to the partners:

		GENERAL JOURNAL				PAGE _110_	
	DATE	DESCRIPTION	POST. REF.	DEBIT		CREDIT	
1	20--						1
2	Apr. 29	Cash in Bank		32 000 00			2
3		Molly Gill, Capital		1 500 00			3
4		Don Putman, Capital		1 500 00			4
5		Merchandise Inventory				35 000 00	5
6		Receipt 363					6
7							7

Sale of Partnership Equipment at a Gain

The partnership owns equipment that cost $48,000 and has accumulated depreciation of $8,000. The book value of the equipment is $40,000 ($48,000 − $8,000).

On May 5 Surfside sold the equipment to a dealer for $42,000 resulting in a gain of $2,000 ($42,000 − $40,000). The gain was divided equally between the partners. The entry to record the sale of the equipment and distribution of the gain is as follows:

		GENERAL JOURNAL				PAGE _111_	
	DATE	DESCRIPTION	POST. REF.	DEBIT		CREDIT	
1	20--						1
2	May 5	Accum. Depr.—Equipment		8 000 00			2
3		Cash in Bank		42 000 00			3
4		Molly Gill, Capital				1 000 00	4
5		Don Putman, Capital				1 000 00	5
6		Equipment				48 000 00	6
7		Receipt 371					7
8							8

Payment of Partnership Liabilities

On May 11 the partnership mailed Check 234 to pay the bank note and Checks 235 through 238 to pay the accounts payable balances. The entry to record the transactions follows.

GENERAL JOURNAL　　　　PAGE _112_

	DATE		DESCRIPTION	POST. REF.	DEBIT	CREDIT	
1	20--						1
2	May	11	Notes Payable		10 000 00		2
3			Accounts Payable		20 000 00		3
4			Cash in Bank			30 000 00	4
5			Checks 234–238				5
6							6

The individual balances in the accounts payable subsidiary ledger are debited for a total of $20,000. This entry brings the **Accounts Payable** account to zero.

Only three accounts remain in the ledger after all noncash assets have been sold and the debts of the partnership have been paid: **Cash in Bank; Molly Gill, Capital;** and **Don Putman, Capital.**

Cash in Bank			Molly Gill, Capital	
Debit	Credit		Debit	Credit
Bal. 18,000	30,000		2,000	Bal. 57,000
29,000			1,500	1,000
32,000				
42,000				
Bal. 91,000				Bal. 54,500

Don Putman, Capital	
Debit	Credit
2,000	Bal. 39,000
1,500	1,000
	Bal. 36,500

Now cash can be distributed to the partners based on the final balances in their capital accounts: Gill, $54,500 and Putman, $36,500.

Final Distribution of Cash

On May 15 the partnership is ended by distributing the balance of **Cash in Bank** to Gill and Putman. The final transaction to end the partnership is recorded as follows:

GENERAL JOURNAL　　　　PAGE _113_

	DATE		DESCRIPTION	POST. REF.	DEBIT	CREDIT	
1	20--						1
2	May	15	Molly Gill, Capital		54 500 00		2
3			Don Putman, Capital		36 500 00		3
4			Cash in Bank			91 000 00	4
5			Checks 239 and 240 to				5
6			liquidate the partnership				6
7							7

AFTER YOU **READ**

Reinforce the Main Idea

Use a diagram like this one to describe the actions needed to liquidate a partnership. Add answer boxes as needed.

Liquidating a Partnership

Do the Math

Max & Tex novelty store, a partnership, is ending. You are to help liquidate the partnership. Listed below are the remaining assets and liabilities of the business. Max & Tex share profits and losses equally.

Assets		Liabilities	
Cash in Bank	$20,000	Accounts Payable	$15,500
Accounts Receivable	$12,000	**Partners' Equity**	
Merchandise Inventory	$42,000	Marilyn Max, Capital	$59,250
Equipment	$60,000	Tom Tex, Capital	$59,250

Liquidation Transactions:

1. Customers will pay their accounts in full before the liquidation date.
2. Merchandise inventory was sold for $40,000 resulting in a $2,000 loss to the partnership.
3. Equipment was sold to a local retailer for $70,000 resulting in a gain of $10,000.
4. Accounts payable will be paid in full.

Instructions How much cash will each partner receive at final liquidation?

Problem 28–3 Recording a Loss and a Gain on the Sale of Noncash Assets by a Partnership

Partners Gunther and Pertee share profits equally. In the process of ending the business, they sell all of the partnership's noncash assets. The transactions for the sales follow.

Instructions Record the transactions in general journal form in your working papers. Use general journal page 275.

Date	Transactions
Sept. 4	The merchandise inventory, which cost $45,000, was sold for $38,000.
15	The office equipment, with a book value of $27,000, was sold for $29,000.

Key Concepts

1. The income statement of a partnership may have a special section showing the division of profits or losses among partners.

ABC Partnership
Income Statement
For the Year Ended July 31, 20--

Net Income		56 000 00
Division of Net Income:		
Partner A	14 000 00	
Partner B	14 000 00	
Partner C	28 000 00	
Net Income		56 000 00

2. A partnership prepares a *statement of changes in partners' equity*. This statement reflects beginning balances, investments, and withdrawals by each partner.

ABC Partnership
Statement of Changes in Partners' Equity
For the Year Ended July 31, 20--

	A	B	C	Totals
Beginning Capital, Aug 1, 20--				
Add: Investments	7 500 00	7 500 00	15 000 00	30 000 00
Net Income	14 000 00	14 000 00	28 000 00	56 000 00
Subtotal	21 500 00	21 500 00	43 000 00	86 000 00
Less: Withdrawals	8 000 00	12 500 00	18 000 00	38 500 00
Ending Capital, July 31, 20--	13 500 00	9 000 00	25 000 00	47 500 00

3. The balance sheet of a partnership contains a capital section titled Partners' Equity:

ABC Partnership
Balance Sheet
July 31, 20--

Partners' Equity		
Partner A, Capital	13 500 00	
Partner B, Capital	9 000 00	
Partner C, Capital	25 000 00	
Total Partners' Equity		47 500 00
Total Liabilities and Partners'		60 500 00
Equity		

4. *Dissolution* refers to the legal termination of a partnership due to a change in partners. Business operations continue, and a new partnership is formed.

   Liquidation refers to the legal termination of a partnership due to the termination of its business operations. It is the process of settling the partnership's business affairs when it ends.

Liquidation involves the following four steps:

a. Sell all noncash partnership assets for cash.

b. Add all gains from the sale of the assets to the capital accounts based on the partnership agreement. If the asset sales result in a loss, deduct the amount from the capital accounts based on the partnership agreement.

c. Pay all partnership liabilities.

d. Distribute any remaining cash to the partners based on the final balance in the partners' capital accounts.

For example, the sale of accounts receivable at a loss is recorded as follows, with the loss divided and debited to each partner according to the partnership agreement:

Debit **Cash in Bank.**

Debit the capital account of each partner.

Credit **Accounts Receivable.**

Sale of merchandise at a loss is recorded as follows:

Debit **Cash in Bank.**

Debit the capital account of each partner.

Credit **Merchandise Inventory.**

When plant equipment is sold, its book value is zeroed out by crediting the asset and debiting the related **Accumulated Depreciation** account. If the equipment is sold at a loss, the loss is divided and debited to each partner according to the partnership agreement:

Debit **Accumulated Depreciation—Equipment.**

Debit **Cash in Bank.**

Debit the capital account of each partner.

Credit **Equipment.**

5. If sale of an asset results in a gain, the gain is divided and credited to each partner according to the partnership agreement:

Debit **Cash in Bank.**

Credit the capital account of each partner.

Credit the asset.

6. After all noncash assets have been sold and the partnership liabilities have been paid, the only accounts that remain in the ledger are:

• **Cash in Bank**

• the capital account for each partner

The final transaction to liquidate a partnership is to distribute the cash to the partners based on the ending balances in their capital accounts:

Debit the capital account of each partner.

Credit **Cash in Bank.**

Key Terms

dissolution	(p. 811)	statement of changes	
liquidation	(p. 811)	in partners' equity	(p. 809)

Check Your Understanding

1. **Partnership Income Statement**
   a. What does a partnership income statement report?
   b. How may the income statement for a partnership differ from that of a sole proprietorship?

2. **Statement of Changes in Partners' Equity**
   a. Explain what a statement of partners' equity shows.
   b. How does a statement of changes in partners' equity differ from a statement of changes in owner's equity?

3. **Partnership Balance Sheet**
   a. What does a partnership balance sheet report?
   b. How does the balance sheet for a partnership differ from that of a sole proprietorship and a corporation?

4. **Liquidation Losses**
   a. When selling partnership accounts receivable at a loss, what accounts are affected?
   b. What happens to the partners' capital accounts when noncash assets are sold at a loss?

5. **Liquidation Gains**
   a. What happens to the partners' capital accounts when noncash assets are sold at a gain?
   b. What basis is used to distribute gains and losses from the sale of noncash assets?

6. **Final Liquidation Entry**
   a. Which accounts remain on the ledger after all noncash assets have been sold and the partnership liabilities have been paid?
   b. When liquidating a partnership, what is the final transaction?

Apply Key Terms

Imagine that you have been asked to explain the following terms and how they might relate to a timber company organized as a partnership.

dissolution
liquidation
statement of changes
   in partners' equity

Setting Up the General Ledger

Making the Transition from a Manual to a Computerized System

Task	Manual Methods	Computerized Methods
Setting up general ledger accounts with balances	• Using accounting stationery, open general ledger accounts based on the expected transactions of the business. • Record the balance of each account. Ideally, end-of-period balances should be used. This ensures that the accounting records were in balance when they were transferred.	• Create a chart of accounts, selecting from predefined charts offered, or by entering select accounts based on the expected transactions for the business. • Enter the beginning balance for each account.

Peachtree® Q & A

Peachtree Question	Answer
How do I convert a manual accounting general ledger system into Peachtree?	1. Create a general ledger account in Peachtree for each account in the manual system. From the *Maintain* menu, select **Chart of Accounts.** 2. Enter the account number, name, and account type for all accounts. 3. Click the arrow for **Beginning Balances.** 4. Select the period from which the balance was taken. 5. Enter the beginning balance for each account. 6. Click **OK** when all balances have been entered and the Trial Balance Difference at the bottom of the screen is 0.00. 7. Click **Save.**

QuickBooks Q & A

QuickBooks Question	Answer
How do I convert a manual accounting general ledger system into QuickBooks?	1. Create a general ledger account in QuickBooks for each account in the manual system. From the *Lists* menu, select **Chart of Accounts.** 2. Click the Account drop-down list, and select **New.** 3. Enter the account type, number, name, and description. 4. Enter the beginning balance in the *Opening Balance* field and the date. 5. Click **Next** to enter additional accounts. 6. Click **OK** when you have finished.

For detailed instructions, see your Glencoe Accounting Chapter Study Guides and Working Papers.

SPREADSHEET SMART GUIDE

Step–by–Step Instructions: Problem 28–4

1. Select the spreadsheet template for Problem 28–4.
2. Enter your name and the date in the spaces provided on the template.
3. Complete the spreadsheet using the instructions in your working papers.
4. Print the spreadsheet and proof your work.
5. Complete the Analyze activity.
6. Save your work and exit the spreadsheet program.

Peachtree®

SMART GUIDE

Step–by–Step Instructions: Problem 28–5

1. Select the problem set Problem 28–5.
2. Rename the company and set the system date.
3. Record the transactions to liquidate the partnership using the **General Journal Entry** option.
4. Print a General Journal report and proof your work.
5. Complete the Analyze activity.
6. End the session.

Problem 28–4 Preparing an Income Statement and Balance Sheet for a Partnership

Joy Webster and Diana Ruiz have been in business since the beginning of the year. Now at the end of the year, they would like to know how the partnership has done in its first year of operation. Joy and Diana stated in the partnership agreement that they will share profits equally. The net income for the year was $5,780. The January 1 capital balances for both partners were $0. Joy invested $6,000 cash in the partnership throughout the year and withdrew $1,800. Diana invested $5,500 cash in the partnership and withdrew $1,200.

Instructions In your working papers, prepare the Division of Net Income section of the income statement and the Partners' Equity section of the balance sheet for the partnership.

Analyze   **Identify the ending balances in the partners' capital accounts.**

Problem 28–5 Liquidating the Partnership with Losses on the Sale of Noncash Assets

Guice and Ward decide to end their partnership on September 21. They share profits and losses equally. The account balances of the partnership as of that date follow.

Cash	$6,500
Inventory	8,800
Equipment (book value)	2,700
Accounts Payable	4,000
Guice, Capital	6,800
Ward, Capital	7,200

The partnership sold the inventory for $5,000 and the equipment for $2,000. All of the accounts payable will be paid in full with the cash.

Instructions In your working papers, prepare the journal entries to record the liquidation of this partnership. Use general journal page 85.

Analyze   **Conclude whether the partners' capital accounts increased or decreased as a result of the liquidation (before the final distribution). Explain why.**

Problem 28–6 Recording a Gain or a Loss on the Sale of Noncash Assets by a Partnership

Hudson and Franklin are in the process of liquidating their partnership. They share profits and losses in a 3:1 ratio. They have sold all of the partnership's noncash assets. The transactions for the sales follow.

Date	Transactions
May 29	The equipment, with a book value of $14,500, was sold for $12,775.
June 2	The $7,800 in accounts receivable was sold to a finance broker for $6,900.
4	The merchandise inventory, which cost $2,800, was sold for $1,900.

Instructions In your working papers, record the journal entries for the sale of noncash assets. Use general journal page 120.

Analyze Explain why losses are distributed to the partners' capital accounts before any cash is paid out to the partners.

Problem 28–7 Preparing a Statement of Changes in Partners' Equity

On January 1 Carol Farmer and Jim Romans formed a partnership, Research Consultants. Each partner invested $50,000 in cash on that date. The partnership agreement stated that the partners would share net income or loss equally.

During the year Farmer invested an additional $2,000 and withdrew $7,500 for personal use. Romans invested an additional $1,500 and withdrew $8,500. Net income for the first year was $33,176.

Instructions In your working papers, prepare a statement of changes in partners' equity for the year ended December 31.

Analyze Identify the amount of partners' equity for Carol Farmer that will appear on the December 31 balance sheet.

Peachtree®

SMART GUIDE

Step–by–Step Instructions: Problem 28–8

1. Select the problem set Problem 28–8.
2. Rename the company and set the system date.
3. Record the transactions to liquidate the partnership.
4. Print a General Journal report. Proof your work.
5. Complete the Analyze activity.
6. End the session.

QuickBooks

PROBLEM GUIDE

Step–by–Step Instructions: Problem 28–8

1. Restore the Problem 28-8.QBB file.
2. Record the transactions to liquidate the partnership.
3. Print a Journal report and proof your work.
4. Complete the Analyze activity.
5. Back up your work.

SPREADSHEET SMART GUIDE

Step–by–Step Instructions: Problem 28–9

1. Select the template for Problem 28–9.
2. Enter your name and the date in the spaces provided.
3. Complete the spreadsheet using the instructions in your working papers.
4. Print the spreadsheet and proof your work.
5. Complete the Analyze activity.
6. Save your work and exit the program.

Problem 28–8 Liquidating the Partnership

On October 15 Martinez and Royka decide to end their partnership. Their assets consist of $10,000 in cash and inventory that cost $105,000 and was sold for $95,000. Their only liability is a note payable for $10,000 that will be paid in full. Their capital balances are Martinez, $60,000 and Royka, $45,000. They share profits and losses equally.

Instructions In your working papers, prepare the journal entries to record the liquidation of the partnership.

Analyze Calculate how much cash each partner would receive at the liquidation if the inventory was sold for $80,000.

 CHALLENGE PROBLEM

Problem 28–9 Completing End-of-Period Activities for a Partnership

Richard Smooth and Carrie Overhill are partners in the firm of R&C Roofing. They agreed to divide net income or loss on the following basis: Smooth, ¾; Overhill, ¼.

The completed work sheet for R&C Roofing for the year ended December 31 appears in your working papers.

Instructions In your working papers:

1. Prepare an income statement for the partnership.
2. Prepare a statement of changes in partners' equity.
3. Prepare a balance sheet.
4. Journalize the adjusting and closing entries, beginning on page 27 of the general journal.

Analyze Calculate the total year-end partners' equity if neither Smooth nor Overhill had withdrawn any cash from the business.

Practice your test-taking skills! The questions on this page are reprinted with permission from national organizations:
- Future Business Leaders of America
- Business Professionals of America

Use a separate sheet of paper to record your answers.

Future Business Leaders of America

MULTIPLE CHOICE

1. When there is a net loss, the
- a. Capital account is increased by the amount of the net loss.
- b. Drawing (Withdrawals) account is increased by the amount of the net loss.
- c. Capital account is decreased by the amount of the net loss.
- d. Drawing (Withdrawals) account is decreased by the amount of the net loss.

2. A partnership may be terminated by the
- a. partners' mutual agreement.
- b. death of a partner.
- c. admission of a new partner.
- d. all of the above.
- e. none of these answers

3. A partnership's capital accounts are changed if
- a. net income or net loss is recorded.
- b. partners invest additional cash in the business.
- c. partners withdraw cash from the business.
- d. all of the above.
- e. none of these answers

4. When both a partnership and the partnership business end, this is called a
- a. mutual understanding.
- b. dissolution.
- c. termination.
- d. liquidation.

Business Professionals of America

MULTIPLE CHOICE

5. The _____ shows the picture of a firm's financial position at a point in time.
- a. income statement
- b. balance sheet
- c. distribution of net income
- d. none of the above

Need More Help?

Go to **glencoeaccounting.glencoe.com** and click on **Student Center.** Click on **Winning Competitive Events** and select **Chapter 28.**
- **Practice Questions and Test-Taking Tips**
- **Concept Capsules and Terminology**

Partnerships

1. What happens when a partnership dissolves?
2. How is dissolution different from liquidation?
3. For each of the following transactions, state whether partners' capital is debited or credited.
    a. Sold an asset at a loss.
    b. Sold an asset at a gain.
    c. Sold an asset at book value.
4. Why does the final partnership liquidation entry involve just one asset account?
5. After selling all partnership assets and paying all creditors, the capital account balance of partner A is a $10,000 credit and of partner B is a $2,000 debit. What is the **Cash in Bank** balance? What entries would close the books?
6. Defend the requirement that creditors must be paid before partners can distribute remaining cash in a liquidation process.

Partnership: Building and Design

Barnes Construction is a homebuilder that wants to expand into commercial real estate. It has a client who owns 10 acres of land on which she wants to build an apartment complex. Barnes is looking for a partner to help design and build it.

Slater Architectural Design is looking for new projects. Barnes and Slater form a partnership to design and build the complex for $10,400,000. Based on estimated costs, the project should earn net profits of 18 percent.

INSTRUCTIONS

1. If Barnes and Slater agree to share revenue and expenses equally, how much profit will each partner earn?
2. To limit each partner's liability to this project only, list the information that should be in the partnership agreement.

Using Another Person's Idea

You are an accounting clerk for two dentists who are partners. The partners recently began a program to give a bonus to employees for making suggestions that are implemented and result in cost savings. You submitted a suggestion for which you received a $1,000 bonus. A co-worker had originally mentioned the idea.

ETHICAL DECISION MAKING

1. What are the ethical issues?
2. What are the alternatives?
3. Who are the affected parties?
4. How do the alternatives affect the parties?
5. What would you do?

Presenting Your Case

Maurice Lance and Terry Klaus are partners in M&T Computer Solutions. Maurice wants to contribute more money to the partnership, but Terry is satisfied with his initial investment. Choose a classmate for a role-play situation involving partners. Discuss the pros and cons of making additional investments.

Decision to Liquidate

You and a partner operate a small sports center. A large national sports complex recently opened in a nearby mall, causing your business to drop sharply. You have decided to close the center and liquidate the assets.

INSTRUCTIONS List all of the pros and cons of liquidating a business. List and prioritize the tasks necessary to complete the liquidation.

Organization of Petroleum Exporting Countries (OPEC)

OPEC is an alliance of 11 oil producing nations. It seeks to stabilize oil prices and help producers achieve a reasonable rate of return. OPEC members discuss oil production levels, pricing, demand, and environmental issues. OPEC can increase its oil production in order to prevent price increases or reduce oil production to hedge against falling prices.

INSTRUCTIONS List the ways in which OPEC impacts the oil market.

Your Understanding of Accounting

You have been studying accounting for almost a year and have some ideas about what it takes to be an accountant. In the last two decades, computer technology has changed the profession from one providing number-crunching services to one that provides knowledge-based services.

PERSONAL FINANCE ACTIVITY Based on what you know about accounting, make a list of the qualities and skills a person would need to be a successful accountant.

PERSONAL FINANCE ONLINE Log on to **glencoeaccounting.glencoe.com** and click on **Student Center.** Click on **Making It Personal** and select **Chapter 28.**

Evaluating Partnership Operating Results

You learned earlier how to use ratio analysis to evaluate the financial health of a business. Partnerships are also interested in these measures of financial health. Return on sales is a measure of how much profit the business is earning for each dollar of total revenue. The current ratio and quick ratio show a company's ability to repay its debts.

INSTRUCTIONS Review the ratios on pages 235–236, then use the balance sheet on page 812 for the following tasks.

1. Calculate the return on sales for Surfside Bike & Skate Rentals, assuming a revenue of $192,000 and net income of $24,000 for the fiscal period just ended.

2. Analyze Surfside's liquidity based on the current ratio and the quick ratio.

3. Write one to two paragraphs describing Surfside's financial health based on your analysis of its financial information.

Liquidation

A liquidation is a busy time for accountants. Visit **glencoeaccounting .glencoe.com** and click on **Student Center.** Click on **WebQuest** and select **Unit 6** to continue your Internet project.

Completing the Accounting Cycle for a Partnership

Main Task

▶ Complete the accounting cycle for Fine Finishes for its first month of business.

Summary of Steps

▶ Set up new general ledger accounts.

▶ Analyze the transactions.

▶ Journalize and post the transactions.

▶ Prepare a trial balance and a work sheet.

▶ Prepare the financial statements.

▶ Journalize and post the closing entries.

▶ Prepare a post-closing trial balance.

Why It's Important

▶ You might work for a partnership someday. Maybe you will even open your own business with some partners. While you create the best product or service, you also need to know what is happening with your company's finances.

Fine Finishes

Company Background:

Fine Finishes is an interior and exterior painting company organized as a partnership. The partners are Laura Andersen, Sean Woo, and David Ingram. The business earns revenue from consultation and painting fees. The partnership divides income and losses as follows: Laura and Sean each receive 33 percent, and David receives 34 percent.

Fine Finishes (continued)

Your Job Responsibilities: As the accountant for Fine Finishes, use the accounting stationery in your working papers to complete the following activities.

(1) Open a general ledger account for each account in the chart of accounts.

(2) Analyze each business transaction.

(3) Enter each business transaction in the general journal. Begin on journal page 1.

(4) Post each journal entry to the appropriate accounts in the general ledger.

(5) Prepare a trial balance and then complete the work sheet.

(6) Prepare an income statement.

(7) Prepare a statement of partners' equity.

(8) Prepare a balance sheet.

(9) Journalize and post the closing entries.

(10) Prepare a post-closing trial balance.

CHART OF ACCOUNTS
Fine Finishes

ASSETS

101   Cash in Bank
105   Accts. Rec.—Mountain View City
        School District
120   Computer Equipment
130   Office Supplies
135   Office Equipment
140   Painting Supplies
145   Painting Equipment

LIABILITIES

205   Accts. Pay.—Custom Color
210   Accts. Pay.—J & J Hardware and
        Lumber
215   Accts. Pay.—Paint Palace

PARTNERS' EQUITY

301   Laura Andersen, Capital
302   Laura Andersen, Withdrawals
303   David Ingram, Capital
304   David Ingram, Withdrawals
305   Sean Woo, Capital
306   Sean Woo, Withdrawals
310   Income Summary

REVENUE

401   Painting Fees
405   Consultation Fees

EXPENSES

505   Advertising Expense
510   Miscellaneous Expense
515   Rent Expense
520   Utilities Expense

Business Transactions: Fine Finishes began business operations on February 1 of this year. During the month of February, the business completed the transactions that follow.

Peachtree®

SMART GUIDE

Step–by–Step Instructions:

1. Select the problem set for Fine Finishes (MP–6).
2. Rename the company and set the system date.
3. Record all of the business transactions using the **General Journal Entry** option.
4. Print a General Journal report and proof your work.
5. Print a General Ledger report.
6. Print a General Ledger Trial Balance.
7. Print an Income statement and a Balance Sheet.
8. Click the **Save Pre-Closing Balances** button in the Glencoe Smart Guide window.
9. Record the closing entries using the **General Journal Entry** option.
10. Print a general journal report and proof your work.
11. Print a Post-Closing Trial Balance.
12. Complete the Analyze activity and the Audit Test.
13. End the session.

TIP: Peachtree can only close a fiscal year. To close a monthly fiscal period, enter the closing entries using the **General Journal Entry** option.

Date		Transactions
Feb.	1	Laura Andersen, David Ingram, and Sean Woo agreed to form a partnership and invest the following assets, Memorandum 1:

Contributed Assets	Andersen	Ingram	Woo
Cash	$1,500	$1,000	$1,200
Computer Equipment	——	2,800	——
Office Equipment	100	——	——
Painting Supplies	150	——	225
Painting Equipment	1,375	——	1,675
Total assets invested	$3,125	$3,800	$3,100

Date		Transactions
	1	Signed a one-year rental agreement for a warehouse and small office at $1500 per month. The first month's rent was paid, Check 1101.
	1	Put an ad in the Call an Expert circular for $25, Check 1102.
	1	Paid $100 to the utility company to start electric service, Check 1103.
	1	Paid telephone company $175 to begin phone service and run dedicated line for computer, Check 1104.
	2	Awarded a contract to paint a kitchen and family room for the McGuires. Collected $250 deposit, Receipt 1.
	2	Bought paint and border stencils from Custom Color for $200 on account, Invoice 742.
	2	Issued check 1105 for $55 for a business license to operate in the city of Mountain View, Alabama (Miscellaneous Expense).
	4	Purchased $115 in office supplies, Check 1106.
	5	Finished painting the kitchen and family room for the McGuires. Collected final payment of $450, Receipt 2.
	6	Joined Mountain View Chamber of Commerce by purchasing membership of $45 (Miscellaneous Expense), Check 1107.
	8	Bought painting equipment on account for $375 from Paint Palace, Invoice 1162.
	10	Received $60 for color and painting consultation, Receipt 3.

CONTINUE

Fine Finishes (continued)

Date	Transactions (cont.)
12	Finished painting the cafeteria at the elementary school. Issued Invoice 101 to Mountain View City School District for $835.
14	Sent Check 1108 for $200 to Custom Color on account.
15	Andersen, Ingram, and Woo each made a withdrawal of $650 for personal use, Checks 1109, 1110, and 1111, respectively.
15	Awarded a contract to paint exterior of the Wicker and Hartel law office building. Received deposit of $1,000, Receipt 4.
16	Spent $135 for new paint brushes (Painting Supplies), Check 1112.
16	Bought paint from Custom Color for $395 on account, Invoice 750.
17	Received and paid Invoice 303 from Mountain View Realtors for ad in real estate brochure for $77, Check 1113.
18	Received $125 for painting consultation, Receipt 5.
19	Wrote Check 1114 for $85 to repair computer printer (Miscellaneous Expense).
21	Paid Paint Palace $375 on account, Check 1115.
22	Finished painting the Wicker and Hartel law office building. Collected final payment of $2,000, Receipt 6.
24	Bought $90 of lumber (Painting Supplies) on account from J & J Hardware and Lumber, Invoice 207.
25	Received $575 for painting and making minor repairs to a garage, Receipt 7.
28	Andersen, Ingram, and Woo each made a withdrawal of $650 for personal use, Checks 1116, 1117, and 1118, respectively.

QuickBooks

PROBLEM GUIDE

Step–by–Step Instructions:

1. Restore the Mini Practice 6.QBB file.
2. Enter all of the business transactions using the **Make General Journal Entries** option in the **Company** menu.
3. Print a Journal report, a General Ledger report, a Trial Balance, an Income Statement, and a Balance Sheet.
4. Enter the closing entries using the **Make General Journal Entries** option in the Company menu.
5. Print a Journal report displaying only the closing entries.
6. Print a Post-Closing Trial Balance.
7. Proof your work and make any needed corrections.
8. Complete the Analyze activity and the Audit Test.
9. Back up your work.

Analyze For each partner, calculate the rate of return on equity for February, the first month of operations. Use the Partners' original investments of equity in the formula: Return on Equity = Net Income ÷ Equity. How does each partner's return compare to the overall return for the partnership?

What You'll Learn

1. Explain the meaning of ethics.

2. Describe the components of business ethics.

3. Identify the role of the accountant in business ethics.

4. Discuss how ethical behavior benefits individuals, businesses, and society.

5. Explain the key principles an accountant is expected to follow.

6. Identify the accounting organizations that establish codes of ethics for the profession.

7. Describe the Sarbanes-Oxley Act.

8. Define the accounting terms introduced in this chapter.

Why It's Important

▶ The business community and the public place their trust in the accounting profession.

The Institute of Internal Auditors

BEFORE YOU READ

Predict

1. What does the chapter title tell you?
2. What do you already know about this subject from personal experience?
3. What have you learned about this in the earlier chapters?
4. What gaps exist in your knowledge of this subject?

Exploring the *Real World* of Business

ASSURING RESPONSIBLE GOVERNANCE

The Institute of Internal Auditors

The success or failure of business depends on ethical corporate governance and accounting practices. The term *governance* refers to the exercise of authority, administration, and decision making for an organization. **The Institute of Internal Auditors,** an international professional organization, believes that the internal auditor must play a strong and visible role in governance.

Internal auditors work independently within a business to review and improve the company's operations and internal control processes. They use strict standards to make sure that the business sticks to its agreements with suppliers, government, and customers. In addition, the internal auditor designs plans to protect assets and to make the best use of the company's resources.

What Do You Think?

Internal auditors evaluate procedures used to safeguard the resources of a business. What are some of these resources?

Working in the *Real World*

APPLYING YOUR ACCOUNTING KNOWLEDGE

Do you, or anyone you know, work for a fast-food restaurant? Whether selling burgers, tacos, or salads, these restaurants must ensure that the food they sell is safe for consumption. They must also provide a safe and sanitary place for their customers to eat. Companies establish controls to ensure that their quality standards are met. In this chapter we will look at ethical standards that accountants are expected to follow.

Personal Connection

1. What risks do you think a fast-food restaurant faces in regard to customer health?
2. What kinds of controls would you suggest to guard against these risks?

Online Connection

Go to **glencoeaccounting.glencoe.com** and click on **Student Center.** Click on **Working in the Real World** and select **Chapter 29.**

The Nature of Ethics

BEFORE YOU READ

Main Idea
All elements of society benefit from ethical behavior.

Read to Learn...
➤ what is meant by the term *ethics.* (p. 832)
➤ who benefits from ethical behavior. (p. 834)

Key Terms
ethics
business ethics
code of ethics
ethics officer

Have you ever had to make a difficult decision about a particular course of action or behavior? Did you consider how you would feel about the action or how others would view your choice? Did you consider how your behavior would affect others? If so, you have probably encountered an ethical dilemma.

Ethics

What Is Meant by Ethics?

Ethics is the study of our notions of right and wrong. In its broadest sense, ethics deals with human conduct in relation to what is morally good and bad. The term *ethics* often refers to a set of basic principles. Life is complex and individuals must face a variety of situations. A person's ethics, or basic principles, can provide guidelines for action when facing ethical dilemmas.

The basic values found in a system of personal ethics exist in systems of *business ethics* as well. Business ethics are not very different from ethics in general.

How Are Business Ethics Determined?

Business ethics refers to the policies and practices that reflect a company's core values such as honesty, trust, respect, and fairness. The ethics of a business can be seen by the way it treats employees and customers and how it attends to shareholder value, community service, supplier relationships, and regulatory law. Review the following components to understand how a business ethics program can be established.

The Law As a Guide. A discussion of ethical performance should consider the relationship between law and ethics. While law and ethics both define proper and improper behavior, law attempts to formally define the general public's ideas about what makes something right or wrong. The law describes a minimum acceptable level of correct behavior.

In contrast, ethical concepts have more subtle implications and are more complex than written rules of law. For example, although a business may be well within the law to advertise certain products to teenagers, it may not be the "right" or "ethical" thing to do. A business may use law as a guide, but it must consider ethical principles and standards as well.

Statements of Company Values. If you have heard the phrase, "actions speak louder than words," then you already know one of the best methods of maintaining a strong business ethics program. A person learns standards and values by observing what others do, *not* by what they say.

As You READ

Key Point

Modeling Behavior
Employees learn ethical standards of an organization by watching the behaviors of their employers and managers.

In addition to having management and employees set good examples of ethical behavior, a business must state a well-defined framework of ethical concerns and core values. A **code of ethics** is a formal policy of rules and guidelines that describes the standards of conduct that a company expects from all its employees. The following topics are often addressed within a code of ethics:

- Conflicts of interest
- Product quality and testing
- Customer relations
- Employee relations
- Suppliers and consultants
- Expense reports
- Security

- Political contributions
- Environmental actions
- International business
- Workplace safety
- Technology
- Whistle-blowing

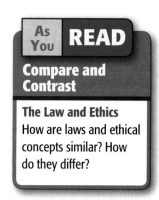

As You READ

Compare and Contrast

The Law and Ethics How are laws and ethical concepts similar? How do they differ?

Training and Outreach. After a code of ethics has been created, it is important to communicate that policy properly. Distribution of the written code, along with formal training, helps employees understand the importance of these policies and gives them realistic and concrete examples of what to do when they face an ethical dilemma.

Ethics Committees. Ethics committees and *ethics officers* play an important role in developing and enforcing ethical processes. An **ethics officer** is the employee directly responsible for creating business conduct programs, evaluating performance, and enforcing standards of conduct. As ethical dilemmas surface, these officials help settle disputed issues and resolve problems. Once a hearing has been held and all issues have been resolved, an enforcement phase may follow.

Enforcement. Effective enforcement is necessary to achieve an ethical work environment. A company's code of ethics might contain penalties for violations that include performance appraisal notes, probation, suspension, demotion, and termination.

What Is the Accountant's Role?

Accountants play a major role in the operation, management, and development of business. In this role, they can face many ethical dilemmas. For example, if an accountant's manager gives instructions to record the physical inventory at its original costs when it is obvious that the inventory's value has decreased, what should the accountant do? If an auditor finds questionable accounting practices within a client's financial reporting, but knows the client is a major source of revenue for his or her firm, what action should he or she take?

As you can see, the actions and behaviors of accountants play a critical role in the maintenance of public trust in the business community. The accountant's opinions, practices, and behaviors directly impact how the company is viewed and how the profession, in turn, is assessed.

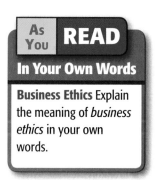

As You READ

In Your Own Words

Business Ethics Explain the meaning of *business ethics* in your own words.

In general, the accountant should focus on the following goals:

- Avoid harm to stockholders.
- Optimize the interests of the public.
- Adhere to universal standards of what is right.
- Respect the human rights of all people.

Specific responsibilities of the accounting profession are expressed in the various codes of ethics created by major organizations. These codes of ethics are addressed in Section 2 of this chapter.

Ethical Behavior
What Are the Benefits of Acting Ethically?

While it may seem obvious that ethical behavior naturally benefits individuals, business, and society, the following discussion addresses specific benefits to each group.

Individuals

Acting ethically produces benefits that can affect the course of your life and the lives of others. These benefits include increased self-esteem, contentment, and self-respect. Ethical behavior also paves the way for achieving life goals. Your honesty, trustworthiness, and integrity will allow you to find a satisfying career with the type of organization that shares your core values.

As you act ethically, you will also enjoy the benefit of acceptance in a society that rewards and honors appropriate behavior. As you focus more on the common good rather than selfish interests, you will earn trust and respect from friends, co-workers, employers, and society in general. Finally, ethical behavior will dramatically improve the quality of your decisions.

Businesses

A DePaul University study found that companies that made commitments to an ethics code provided more than twice the value to shareholders than those that did not. A study by Walker Information, a shareholder research firm, supports this finding, reporting that "good corporate behavior" leads to positive business outcomes.

Society

Society can be viewed as the sum of all social relationships between humans. Therefore, it is easy to understand why our individual actions contribute to the overall nature of our society. We cannot expect our society to become more ethical unless individuals and businesses commit to ethical behaviors.

As businesses act in ethical ways, new wealth for society is created. In the realm of ethical financial reporting, the public can be confident in the data provided and make informed investment decisions. In turn, greater capital funding is available for growth and productivity, yielding strong and healthy economies.

Connect to...
MATHEMATICS

Cost/benefit analysis is a decision model for comparing alternatives. To use it you subtract each alternative's costs from its financial benefits. Not all costs and benefits can be measured in dollars, though. You should also consider the potential impact each alternative would have on other people.

AFTER YOU READ

Reinforce the Main Idea

Identify five components of a business ethics program that were discussed in this section. Use a chart like this one to list two examples of each component.

Component of a Business Ethics Program	Example #1	Example #2

Do the Math

Assume that you are the chief financial officer for a major manufacturer of infant car seats. The lead product designer has informed management that the installation of a new latch system would improve product safety by 25 percent. The new latch system will add $4 to production costs per car seat. Current production costs are $52.50 per seat, and the product sells for $69.50. Management wants to compare the effect on net income if the product price increases by (a) $1, (b) $2, or (c) $5.

1. If the company sells 8,000 car seats in a year, what is the effect on net income for each proposed price increase scenario? Assume fixed operating costs are $115,000 annually.
2. As an officer of the company, what factors (other than pricing) do you think should be considered when making product design changes?

Problem 29–1 Reporting Ethics Violations

Instructions Results from Walker Information's study on business integrity state that 65 percent of employees who know about an ethical violation choose not to report it. What weaknesses in a company's ethical environment might be responsible for such a finding? Discuss the components of a strong business ethics plan that management could apply to resolve this situation.

Problem 29–2 Exploring the Difference Between Ethics and Law

Instructions Adhering to legal regulations is the first step in behaving ethically. Explain why ethical behavior extends beyond the law. Describe one situation in which a company might act within the boundaries of the law yet still engage in an unethical act.

Ethics in the Accounting Profession

Main Idea
The accounting profession requires its members to follow a code of ethics.

Read to Learn...
➤ the key principles an accountant is expected to observe. (p. 836)
➤ the guidelines that accounting organizations provide for decision making. (p. 838)
➤ the impact of the Sarbanes-Oxley Act on the accounting profession. (p. 838)

Key Terms
integrity
objectivity
independence
competence
confidentiality

BEFORE YOU READ

As YOU READ

Key Point

Public Trust
The practices of the accountant directly reflect the credibility of a business and the trust the public has in the accounting profession.

Professional organizations are often separated from other organizations by a code of conduct or a code of ethics. To build public trust, most accountants voluntarily join a professional organization and accept the standards of conduct expected by the organization.

However, ethical behavior requires commitment beyond abiding by a few rules of conduct. No ethics code or written rules can apply to all situations that might arise on the job. Day-to-day job experiences often test an individual's personal judgment and personal ethics.

Written codes of ethics are generally designed to encourage ideal behavior. However, the codes must be both realistic and enforceable. Professional organizations are charged with enforcing the rules of conduct outlined in their codes.

Key Principles
What Is the Foundation for Ethics in Accounting?

Certain principles provide the framework for rules of conduct that an accountant is expected to follow. These principles include *integrity, objectivity, independence, competence,* and *confidentiality.*

Integrity

The principle of **integrity** requires that accountants choose what is right and just over what is wrong. Guidance for behaving with integrity suggests that the accountant ask the following questions: Is this what a person of integrity would do? Have I made a right and just decision? Have I maintained the spirit of ethical conduct?

How do you explain the concept of integrity as related to the accounting profession? Making false or misleading entries in a client's books violates the accounting principle of integrity. Failing to correct false and misleading financial statements also violates integrity. Integrity helps accountants establish the trust necessary for others to rely on their professional judgment.

Objectivity

Every year publicly traded corporations must submit financial statements to the Securities and Exchange Commission. Certified public accountants (CPAs) audit these financial statements.

CPAs who perform audits are known as *independent auditors*. They do not work for the companies they audit. For example, suppose that Paul Corporation needs to give audited financial statements to the SEC. Paul

Corporation hires Findlay & Partners, a public accounting firm. Five CPAs who work for Findlay & Partners go to the offices of Paul Corporation and perform the audit. Paul Corporation is the *client* and Findlay & Partners is the *independent auditor*. The work of the independent auditor is critical. Many different users of financial information depend on audited financial statements when making decisions.

The principle of **objectivity** requires that accountants be impartial, honest, and free of conflicts of interest. When forming professional judgments, accountants should not be influenced by personal interests or relationships with others or behave in a way that would give even the *appearance* of improper behavior.

As You READ

Key Point

The Sum of the Parts The behavior of individuals and businesses contributes to the overall ethical performance of society.

Independence

CPAs who audit public companies must maintain a position of *independence*. **Independence** in this sense means that the CPA does not have a financial interest in or a loan from the company he or she is auditing. An investment in the company or a loan from the company would interfere with the independence required of an auditor. Serving as a director, officer, or employee of the company would also demonstrate a lack of independence.

An accountant must act in such a way that maintains the general public's confidence in the services provided by the profession. Even if the accountant's financial interest is minor, the relationship could be suspect, and the accountant would be considered to lack independence. Even non-CPA employees in a public accounting firm may not accept more than token gifts from clients.

Competence

Competence refers to the knowledge, skills, and experience needed to complete a task. Accountants must perform only those services that they are competent to provide. Accountants are expected to maintain an appropriate level of competence through continuing education and to continually improve the quality of professional services. Services should be rendered promptly, carefully, thoroughly, and in accordance with appropriate technical and ethical standards. Accountants must be committed to learning and professional improvement throughout their professional lives.

Confidentiality

Accountants learn about everything from individual salaries to the business strategies of their clients. **Confidentiality** as related to the accounting profession is the requirement that accountants who acquire information in the course of work protect it and not disclose it without the appropriate legal or professional responsibility to do so. Above all, information should not be used for personal gain.

Codes of Ethics

What Accounting Organizations Provide Guidelines?

Several accounting organizations provide guidelines to assist in ethical decision making.

American Institute of Certified Public Accountants

AICPA is the national organization of certified public accountants. The preamble to the AICPA Principles of Professional Conduct states that membership is voluntary and by accepting membership, a CPA assumes an obligation of self-discipline above and beyond the requirements of laws and regulations.

The AICPA Code also expresses the profession's recognition of its responsibilities to the public, to clients, and to colleagues. It calls for an unswerving commitment to honorable behavior, even at the sacrifice of personal advantage.

Institute of Management Accountants

The IMA is the leading professional organization devoted exclusively to management accountants and financial managers. Members of the IMA have a responsibility to maintain professional competence, uphold professional standards of confidentiality, avoid conflicts of interest, and communicate information fairly and objectively.

Institute of Internal Auditors

The IIA expects its members to demonstrate competence and to follow the principles of integrity, objectivity, and confidentiality. The IIA's code of ethics is necessary and appropriate because of the public trust placed in internal auditors.

Sarbanes-Oxley Act

How Does Federal Legislation Affect Accounting?

In recent years, the need for stricter accounting regulations to protect investors arose from several corporate financial scandals. Certain major corporations were accused of misrepresenting their financial position. Public accounting firms that audited them failed to identify and prevent it.

Congress decided that the accounting profession and publicly held corporations needed to abide by legal standards of conduct. The most significant changes to corporate governance and accounting practice since the 1930s were implemented when the Sarbanes-Oxley (SOX) Act was signed into law in 2002. SOX requires that CEOs, financial officers, accountants, and auditing firms comply with the new regulations and procedures. It also established an accounting board to oversee and investigate the audits and auditors of public companies.

AFTER YOU READ

Reinforce the Main Idea

Identify five key principles for accountants that were discussed in this section. Use a chart like this one to describe two situations in which the accountant would need to apply each principle.

Principle	Situation #1	Situation #2

Do the Math

Assume that the cost per CPA employee to maintain professional competence is as follows: continuing professional education course, $900; travel, $350; lodging, $135; meals, $75; and lost work time, $480. If the firm has 37 CPA employees, what is the total cost of the commitment to quality work? What is the cost per employee? What is the possible cost of *not* maintaining professional competence?

Problem 29–3 Promoting Principles of Conduct

Instructions Read the following scenario. Identify and discuss behaviors that you believe might violate the key principles of conduct for accountants.

In your new position as accounting manager with Triple B Markets, you supervise three staff accountants: Jennifer, Marcus, and Ing. You become aware of the following situations:

- Jennifer, a new employee, has never worked as an accountant but scored high marks in her college math classes.
- Marcus often records payments of utilities as assets instead of expenses because he wants to show a higher net income for the business.
- You overheard Ing talking with a friend on the phone about the payroll details of the company.

Key Concepts

1. *Ethics* is the study of our notions of right and wrong. The word *ethics* also refers to a set of basic principles.

2. *Business ethics* are the policies and practices that reflect a company's core values such as honesty, trust, respect, and fairness. A business ethics program can be established with the following components:

   - adherence to written law
   - statement of company values
   - training and outreach
   - ethics committees
   - enforcement

   A business code of ethics often addresses these topics:

   - Conflicts of interest
   - Product quality and testing
   - Customer relations
   - Employee relations
   - Suppliers and consultants
   - Expense reports
   - Security
   - Political contributions
   - Environmental actions
   - International business
   - Workplace safety
   - Technology
   - Whistle-blowing

3. The behaviors and practices of the accountant are critical to public trust in the business as well as the integrity of the accounting profession. An accountant should focus on the following goals:

   - avoiding harm to stockholders
   - optimizing the interests of the public
   - adhering to the universal standards of what is right
   - respecting the human rights of all people

4. Ethical behavior benefits these groups:

Individuals	• increases one's self-esteem, contentment, and self-respect • earns the trust and respect of one's friends, co-workers, employers, and society
Businesses	• improves business outcomes and shareholder value • increases employee loyalty • enhances company reputation
Society at large	• provides confidence in financial data which leads to informed investor decisions • informed investors provide capital funding for growth and productivity, which yields a strong and healthy economy

5. Accountants are expected to follow these key principles:

Integrity	Choosing what is right and just over what is wrong
Objectivity	Being impartial, honest, and free from conflicts of interest, including personal interests or relationships that could influence professional judgment
Independence	Having no financial interest in the company being audited
Competence	Possessing the knowledge, skills and experience to perform assigned duties
Confidentiality	Protecting information gained during the course of work, not disclosing that information without the appropriate legal or professional responsibility to do so, and not using that information for personal gain

6. Professional accountants are distinguished by their willingness to accept a high degree of responsibility to the public. Several professional accounting organizations have created guidelines for making ethical decisions. The primary organizations and major ethical principles follow.

- American Institute of Certified Public Accountants (AICPA) is a national professional organization of certified public accountants. The preamble to the AICPA Principles of Professional Conduct states that by accepting membership, a CPA assumes an obligation of self-discipline. It also expresses the profession's recognition of its responsibilities to the public, clients, and colleagues, and calls for an unswerving commitment to honorable behavior.
- Institute of Management Accountants (IMA) serves management accountants and financial managers. Its members have the responsibility to maintain professional competence, uphold professional standards of confidentiality, avoid conflicts of interest, and communicate information fairly and objectively.
- Institute of Internal Auditors (IIA) is a global professional group specializing in internal auditing. Its members are expected to demonstrate competence and follow the principles of integrity, objectivity, and confidentiality.

7. The Sarbanes-Oxley Act (SOX) was signed into law in 2002 to implement new regulations of corporate governance and accounting practice when some major companies were accused of misrepresenting their financial position.

Key Terms

business ethics	(p. 832)	ethics officer	(p. 833)
code of ethics	(p. 833)	independence	(p. 837)
competence	(p. 837)	integrity	(p. 836)
confidentiality	(p. 837)	objectivity	(p. 837)
ethics	(p. 832)		

Check Your Understanding

1. **Ethics**
   a. What does *ethics* mean?
   b. How can personal ethics help an individual face the dilemmas that are part of life's complexities?

2. **Ethics in Business**
   a. How can a company communicate a code of ethics to its employees?
   b. Name five topics often addressed in a code of ethics.

3. **Ethics in Accounting**
   a. List four goals of an ethically trained accountant.
   b. What role does the accountant play in maintaining public trust in the business community?

4. **Benefits of Ethical Behavior**
   a. How does acting ethically benefit an individual?
   b. How does a business benefit from acting ethically?

5. **Key Principles**
   a. Explain the concepts of integrity, objectivity, and independence as related to the accounting profession.
   b. Explain the concepts of competence and confidentiality as related to the accounting profession.

6. **Codes of Ethics**
   a. What is the purpose of a code of ethics for a professional organization?
   b. Name three professional accounting organizations that have codes of ethics for their members.

Apply Key Terms

As the new training director for a public accounting firm, you are to design and present a program to employees on the importance of ethical behavior. A list of terms, which you are to use in your program, follows. Write a complete definition for each term, and write one or two sentences describing the importance of each term to the success of the firm.

business ethics	ethics officer
code of ethics	independence
competence	integrity
confidentiality	objectivity
ethics	

Problem 29–4 Researching Ethics in the News

Instructions Use the library, newspaper, or Internet to find three recent examples of businesses accused of engaging in unethical practices. For each example describe the company's practices, any legal charges involved, and why you think the business chose this course of action.

Problem 29–5 Creating a Business Ethics Program

Instructions As the ethics officer for a national chain of coffeehouses, you must prepare a one- or two-page outline for a business ethics plan that covers the main issues you think are relevant to the company's operations. Include outline headings for a code of ethics, enforcement measures, and how you will communicate the ethics plan to the company's employees and managers.

Problem 29–6 Making Ethical Decisions

Instructions Sean McGee works as a graphics designer for a large design firm. In his job he utilizes dozens of expensive software programs that the company purchased for its employees to use to complete client projects. Because Sean often takes work home to meet deadlines, he copied all software programs and installed them on his personal home computer. In addition to the work he does for his employer, he takes freelance jobs for extra cash. What are the ethical issues? Who are the affected parties? Do you think Sean has made an ethically correct decision? Why or why not? What would you have done?

Problem 29–7 Making Ethical Decisions

Instructions Randy Simpson and Kyung Won worked as recruiters for a national job placement company. The company provided them a database of potential companies that might use a placement service as well as qualified applicants seeking jobs. After working together for several years, Randy and Kyung decided to open their own recruiting agency. When they worked for the national job placement company, both had signed an agreement not to take any company property with them if they left.

When Randy and Kyung were setting up their new offices, Kyung noticed Randy downloading files from a CD-ROM to his computer. When questioned, Randy said he had copied his list of clients in addition to names of potential new clients and qualified applicants. Kyung was worried that this act violated the agreement they had signed. Randy maintained that he had built solid relationships with his clients, and that he was entitled to

CONTINUE

take their contact information. As for the names of applicants, he argued, "These people need jobs. If I can help make that happen, I should." What are the ethical issues? What would you do if you were Kyung?

Problem 29–8 Examining the Impact of Unethical Decisions

Instructions Assume that the accountant for a drug manufacturing company made the decision to record the company's ending drug inventory at an amount higher than its actual worth. How does this decision affect gross profit and net income for that accounting period? In what ways might this decision affect shareholder value? How might this affect confidence in the company's financial statements in the future?

Problem 29–9 Finding Out What Ethical Principles Mean to Your Classmates

Instructions Make a list of the five ethical principles discussed in this chapter. Ask your friends how they think the principles might influence their everyday life. Report your results in class.

Problem 29–10 Finding Out What Ethical Principles Mean to Adults

Instructions Ask adults how they think the five principles of ethics influence professional behavior. Share your results in class.

Problem 29–11 Applying a Code of Ethics to Personal Behavior

Instructions Write a code of ethics to guide student behavior in school organizations. Interview students outside your class to get ideas.

Problem 29–12 Analyzing the Preamble to the Principles Section of the AICPA Code of Professional Conduct

Instructions Review the AICPA Preamble in the text. List two key points covered in each of the two paragraphs. Are the points important to your everyday behavior? Why or why not?

Ethics

1. Define *business ethics*.
2. What is the purpose of a code of ethics?
3. If you were on a committee to establish a student code of ethics for your school, what would you include in it?
4. Compare and contrast ethics and the law.
5. If accountants had no code of conduct, what behavioral guide should be used?
6. The Sarbanes-Oxley Act of 2002 requires that independent auditors report to the client's audit committee, not to the client's management. The audit committee is independent of the management. Defend this requirement.

CPA Firm: Audits

Chris Snyder is an audit supervisor for an accounting firm. She and her staff are scheduled to audit Gemma Industries. Gemma's CEO invites Chris and her staff to arrive one day before the audit for a round of golf and dinner at an exclusive country club.

INSTRUCTIONS

1. Determine whether Chris and the audit staff should accept the invitation.
2. If not, explain how Chris could decline the invitation without offending the CEO and possibly losing a client.
3. What ethical issue could arise if Chris accepts the invitation?

Working Conditions

You are a stockholder of a corporation that manufactures sports apparel. The company recently moved its operations to a developing country where labor is cheaper. Employees work more than 16 hours per day and the factory conditions are far below those in the United States. While not comparable to U.S. standards, the conditions are better than those found in other local factories, and the rate of pay is nearly double what local workers earned in the past. The company has offered to pay for any work-related injuries. As a stockholder do you agree with this manufacturing strategy?

ETHICAL DECISION MAKING

1. What are the ethical issues?
2. What are the alternatives?
3. Who are the affected parties?
4. How do the alternatives affect the parties?
5. What would you do?

Writing E-mail

Your friend Samantha recently graduated with a degree in accounting. As a member of the American Institute of Certified Public Accountants, you encourage her to become a CPA and join the organization. Draft an e-mail message to Samantha that includes reasons you think she should join the AICPA and how she will benefit from the membership. Use the Internet or your library to learn more about the AICPA.

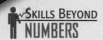

Working with Diverse Cultures

Your ability to work with a variety of ethnic, social, educational, and gender groups indicates your acceptance of cultural diversity.

ON THE JOB As the owner of Say it Right, an interpreting service, you hire employees from many cultures. You decide to offer your employees workshops on cultural acceptance techniques.

INSTRUCTIONS List 10 items to discuss in these workshops. Include issues that deal with cultural awareness and gender issues in the workplace.

The Decade of Education for Sustainable Development (DESD)

Global ethics include concern for the future of humankind, respect for the planet, and recognition of diverse cultures. Such values are being addressed during the Decade of Education for Sustainable Development (DESD), established by the United Nations for 2005 through 2014. DESD initiatives will address education, corporate citizenship, and network building for a sustainable future.

INSTRUCTIONS Outline how the DESD might impact future trade policies. Consider the effect of trade policies on the environment and human rights.

Your Ethics

Some decisions you will face have no clear-cut answers and require choosing between actions that could hurt someone close to you.

PERSONAL FINANCE ACTIVITY Review the five key principles discussed on pages 836–837. Write a report describing situations in which a high school student would need to apply the principles. Provide one situation for each principle.

PERSONAL FINANCE ONLINE Log on to **glencoeaccounting.glencoe.com** and click on **Student Center.** Click on **Making It Personal** and select **Chapter 29.**

Corporate Responsibility

An ethical corporation makes a commitment to manage its roles in society—as a producer, employer, customer, and citizen—in a responsible manner. Implementing policies and practices in these areas is generally considered sound management. Many companies publish their commitment to corporate responsibility in their annual reports.

INSTRUCTIONS Use PETsMART's statement of corporate responsibility in Appendix F for these activities.

1. Explain why it is crucial for a board of directors to be independent from management.
2. Identify any key principles of conduct discussed on pages 836–837 that this statement of responsibility addresses.
3. In what areas does management want its financial statement users to have confidence?

Fallen Giants

Many people are affected by accounting scandals and corporate failures. Go to **glencoeaccounting .glencoe.com** and click on **Student Center.** Click on **WebQuest** and select **Unit 6** to continue your Internet project.

APPENDIXES

Adjustments for a Service Business Using a Ten-Column Work Sheet

BEFORE YOU **READ**

Main Idea
Some general ledger accounts must be adjusted to bring their balances up to date.

Read to Learn...
➤ how to make adjusting entries. (p. A–2)
➤ how to complete the ten-column work sheet. (p. A–6)
➤ how to journalize and post adjusting entries. (p. A–7)
➤ about the additional step in the ten-step accounting cycle. (p. A–8)

Key Terms
adjustment
premium

In Chapter 8 you prepared a six-column work sheet for a service business. If you completed Chapter 18, you prepared a ten-column work sheet for a merchandising business. The ten-column work sheet has the same additional columns whether it is used for a service or merchandising business. The additional columns are for the Adjustments and Adjusted Trial Balance sections.

Information for the Account Name and Trial Balance sections comes from the general ledger accounts. Each account's end-of-period balance is entered in the appropriate amount column of the Trial Balance section. In Chapter 8 you entered the final account balances and completed the Trial Balance section by totaling and ruling the columns.

Adjusting Entries
How Do You Make Adjusting Entries?

To this point the general ledger account balances have been changed by journal entries that record transactions supported by source documents. Changes in account balances caused by the internal operations of a business or the passage of time, however, have no source documents. Such changes are recorded by making adjustments to the account balances at the end of the period. An **adjustment** is an amount that is added to or subtracted from an account balance to bring that balance up to date. If an account balance is not up to date *as of the last day of the accounting period,* then that account must be updated. Adjustments help match expenses and revenue for a given accounting period.

In this appendix you will learn how to calculate end-of-period adjustments for a service business, Maximum Delivery Service. Every adjustment affects at least one permanent account and one temporary account. Two examples of general ledger accounts that need adjusting at the end of the accounting period are **Supplies** and **Prepaid Insurance**.

Adjusting the Supplies Account

All businesses purchase supplies such as paper, ink cartridges, and staples in order to operate. When businesses purchase supplies, the asset account **Supplies** is debited (increased). Supplies may be purchased by paying cash or by charging them on account.

Recording the Purchase of Supplies. When a business purchases supplies for cash, the asset account **Supplies** is increased, so it is debited for the amount of the purchase. **Cash in Bank** is also an asset account, and it is decreased (credited). On February 14 Maximum Delivery Service purchased supplies for $300, Check 229.

		GENERAL JOURNAL					PAGE __11__		
	DATE	DESCRIPTION	POST. REF.	DEBIT		CREDIT		
1	20--							1
2	Feb. 14	Supplies		3 0 0 00				2
3		Cash in Bank				3 0 0 00		3
4		Check 229						4
5								5

When supplies are purchased on account, the **Supplies** account is again debited. Since additional money is owed to a creditor, the liability account **Accounts Payable** is credited. On August 21 Maximum Delivery Service purchased $400 worth of supplies on account from Shade Supply Company, Invoice 28714.

		GENERAL JOURNAL					PAGE __14__		
	DATE	DESCRIPTION	POST. REF.	DEBIT		CREDIT		
1	20--							1
2	Aug. 21	Supplies		4 0 0 00				2
3		Accts. Pay./Shade Supply Co.				4 0 0 00		3
4		Invoice 28714						4
5								5

Calculating the Adjustment for Supplies. Each time Maximum Delivery Service purchases supplies, its **Supplies** account must be debited for the amount of the purchase. For example, Maximum Delivery Service had $100 in supplies on hand at the beginning of the period. During the period the company made two purchases of supplies for $300 and $400. The final balance in the **Supplies** account in the general ledger on December 31 is $800 ($100 + $300 + $400). However, some of these supplies were used or consumed during the period. Although businesses use supplies every day, it is inefficient to update the records of all supplies used on a daily basis.

At the end of the period, Maximum Delivery Service does not have all $800 worth of supplies because most of them have been used. By examining the remaining supplies, Maximum determines that only $200 worth of the supplies are still on hand. This means that $600 of supplies have been used or consumed during the period ($800 − $200 = $600). The **Supplies**

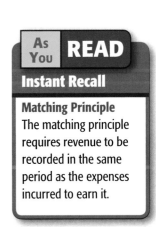

As You READ

Instant Recall

Matching Principle
The matching principle requires revenue to be recorded in the same period as the expenses incurred to earn it.

account balance must be adjusted to report a final balance of $200. The account balance must be reduced by $600.

As supplies are used, they become expenses of the business. At the end of the period, adjustments are made to transfer the costs of the assets consumed from the asset accounts (permanent accounts) to the appropriate expense accounts (temporary accounts).

Entering the Supplies Adjustment on the Work Sheet. The Adjustments section of the work sheet is used to enter the necessary adjustments for the period. Since $600 worth of supplies were used during the period, the **Supplies** account is decreased, or credited, for this amount. The account **Supplies Expense** is increased, or debited, for $600.

Adjustment

ANALYSIS	*Identify* *Classify*	1. The accounts affected are **Supplies** and **Supplies Expense**.
		2. **Supplies** is an asset account (permanent). **Supplies Expense** is an expense account (temporary).
	$+/-$	3. **Supplies** is decreased by $600. **Supplies Expense** is increased by $600.

| **DEBIT-CREDIT RULE** | 4. Increases to expense accounts are recorded as debits. Debit **Supplies Expense** for $600. |
| | 5. Decreases to asset accounts are recorded as credits. Credit **Supplies** for $600. |

T ACCOUNTS   **6.**

Supplies Expense			Supplies	
Debit	Credit		Debit	Credit
+	−		+	−
600				600

The adjustment for **Supplies** in the Adjustments section of the work sheet is shown in **Figure A–1.** To enter the adjustment on the work sheet, follow these steps:

1. In the Adjustments Debit column, enter the debit amount of the adjustment ($600) on the Supplies Expense line.
2. In the Adjustments Credit column, enter the credit amount of the adjustment ($600) on the Supplies line.

On the work sheet, the debit and credit parts of each adjustment are given a unique label. The label consists of a small letter in parentheses. It is placed just above and to the left of the adjustment amounts. The supplies adjustment is the first adjustment, so it is labeled (*a*). The next adjustment will be labeled (*b*), then (*c*), and so on.

As You READ

Key Point

Labeling Adjustments On the work sheet, an adjustment's debit and credit parts are labeled with a lower case letter in parentheses, such as (*a*).

	ACCT. NO.	ACCOUNT NAME	TRIAL BALANCE		ADJUSTMENTS		ADJUSTED TRIAL BALANCE	
			DEBIT	CREDIT	DEBIT	CREDIT	DEBIT	CREDIT
1	101	Cash in Bank	7 264 00				7 264 00	
2	105	Accts. Rec.—Wein Corp.	336 00				336 00	
3	110	Accts. Rec.—Mike Cassidy	917 00				917 00	
4	115	Supplies	800 00			(a) 600 00	200 00	
5	120	Prepaid Insurance	750 00			(b) 250 00	500 00	
6	125	Office Equipment	11 364 00				11 364 00	
7	130	Delivery Equipment	14 600 00				14 600 00	
8	201	Accts. Pay.—Gillespie Co.		1 774 00				1 774 00
9	205	Accts. Pay.—Shade Supply Co.		200 00				200 00
10	210	Accts. Pay.—Trip Travel		2 632 00				2 632 00
11	301	Kevin Chan, Capital		16 734 00				16 734 00
12	302	Kevin Chan, Withdrawals	2 500 00				2 500 00	
13	303	Income Summary						
14	401	Delivery Revenue		28 724 00				28 724 00
15	501	Advertising Expense	3 083 00				3 083 00	
16	505	Insurance Expense			(b) 250 00		250 00	
17	510	Maintenance Expense	710 00				710 00	
18	515	Rent Expense	6 500 00				6 500 00	
19	520	Supplies Expense			(a) 600 00		600 00	
20	525	Utilities Expense	1 240 00				1 240 00	
21		Totals	50 064 00	50 064 00	850 00	850 00	50 064 00	50 064 00
22								

Figure A–1 Ten-Column Work Sheet (Partial) Showing the Adjusted Trial Balance

Adjusting the Prepaid Insurance Account

Businesses buy insurance to protect against losses from hazards such as theft, fire, and flood. Insurance policies cover varying time periods, such as six months or one year. The cost of insurance protection is called the **premium** . A premium is paid in advance at the beginning of the covered period. Insurance paid in advance is an asset because, until the insurance protection expires, it represents a benefit to the business. The insurance premium is recorded in the asset account **Prepaid Insurance.**

On November 1 Maximum Delivery Service paid a six-month insurance premium of $750, Check 314.

GENERAL JOURNAL PAGE __19__

	DATE		DESCRIPTION	POST. REF.	DEBIT	CREDIT	
1	20--						1
2	Nov.	1	Prepaid Insurance		7 5 0 00		2
3			Cash in Bank			7 5 0 00	3
4			Check 314				4
5							5

At the end of December, the balance in the **Prepaid Insurance** account is still $750. However, two months of the six months of coverage have expired.

Nov. 1–Dec. 31		Jan. 1–Apr. 30		
Expired		Not Expired		
$250	+	$500	=	$750

The monthly cost of the insurance is $125 ($750 ÷ 6 = $125). Since the coverage for November and December has expired, $250 ($125 × 2) of the $750 in the premium has been used. The asset account **Prepaid Insurance** must be decreased (credited) for $250. The amount of insurance expired is charged to the expense account **Insurance Expense.** In this adjustment **Insurance Expense** is debited for $250.

Adjustment

ANALYSIS	*Identify* *Classify*	1. The accounts affected are **Prepaid Insurance** and **Insurance Expense.**
		2. **Prepaid Insurance** is an asset account (permanent). **Insurance Expense** is an expense account (temporary).
	+/−	3. **Prepaid Insurance** is decreased by $250. **Insurance Expense** is increased by $250.

DEBIT-CREDIT RULE	4. Increases to expense accounts are recorded as debits. Debit **Insurance Expense** for $250.
	5. Decreases to asset accounts are recorded as credits. Credit **Prepaid Insurance** for $250.

T ACCOUNTS	6.	Insurance Expense		Prepaid Insurance	
		Debit + 250	Credit −	Debit +	Credit − 250

To enter the adjustment on the work sheet, follow these steps:

1. In the Adjustments Debit column, enter the debit amount of the adjustment ($250) on the Insurance Expense line. Since this is the second adjustment, label it (*b*).
2. In the Adjustments Credit column, enter the credit amount of the adjustment ($250) on the Prepaid Insurance line. Label it (*b*) also.

Completing the Work Sheet

How Do You Complete the Ten-Column Work Sheet?

After the adjustments have been entered on the work sheet, the Adjusted Trial Balance section can be completed. This section of the work sheet shows the updated balances of all general ledger accounts.

Completing the Adjusted Trial Balance Section

To complete this section, the balance of each account in the Trial Balance section is combined with the adjustment, if any, in the Adjustments section. The new balance is then entered in the appropriate Adjusted Trial Balance column.

Refer to **Figure A–2** on pages A–8 and A–9 and look at how new balances are computed. If there is no adjustment, the account balance shown on the Trial Balance section is simply extended to the same column (Debit or Credit) in the Adjusted Trial Balance section. After all account balances have been extended to the Adjusted Trial Balance section, both columns are totaled. If total debits equal total credits, this section is proved. A double rule is drawn under the totals and across both columns.

Extending Amounts to the Balance Sheet and Income Statement Sections

Beginning with line 1, each account balance in the Adjusted Trial Balance section is extended to the appropriate column of either the Balance Sheet section or the Income Statement section. Remember that the Balance Sheet section includes the asset, liability, and owner's equity accounts. The Income Statement section includes the revenue and expense accounts.

Showing Net Income on the Work Sheet

The Income Statement and Balance Sheet sections of the work sheet are totaled. The net income (or net loss) is entered on the work sheet as shown in **Figure A–2**.

Journalizing and Posting the Adjusting Entries
How Do You Record and Post Adjustments?

The journal entries that update the general ledger accounts at the end of a period are called *adjusting entries*. The source of information for journalizing the adjusting entries is the Adjustments section of the work sheet. The accounts debited and credited in the Adjustments section are entered in the general journal.

Before recording the first adjusting entry, the words *Adjusting Entries* are written in the Description column of the general journal. This heading eliminates the need to write an explanation after each adjusting entry.

The first adjustment, labeled (*a*) on the work sheet, is recorded in the general journal as a debit to **Supplies Expense** for $600 and a credit to **Supplies** for $600. The second adjustment is a debit to **Insurance Expense** for $250 and a credit to **Prepaid Insurance** for $250.

After the adjusting entries have been recorded in the general journal, they are posted to the general ledger accounts. Once the adjusting entries have been posted, the general ledger accounts are up to date. Refer to **Figure A–3** on page A–10 to see how to record end-of-period adjustments and update accounts through adjusting entries.

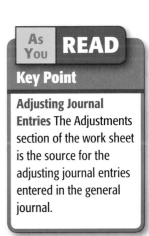

As You READ

Key Point

Adjusting Journal Entries The Adjustments section of the work sheet is the source for the adjusting journal entries entered in the general journal.

The Steps in the Accounting Cycle
What Is the Additional Step in the Ten-Step Accounting Cycle?

There are additional general ledger accounts that need to be adjusted at the end of the period. The reasons and procedures for adjusting other accounts are presented throughout this textbook.

Figure A–2 Work Sheet Showing Ending Adjusted Balances and Net Income

Maximum
Work
For Year Ended

	ACCT. NO.	ACCOUNT NAME	TRIAL BALANCE DEBIT	TRIAL BALANCE CREDIT	ADJUSTMENTS DEBIT	ADJUSTMENTS CREDIT
1	101	Cash in Bank	7 264 00			
2	105	Accts. Rec.—Wein Corp.	336 00			
3	110	Accts. Rec.—Mike Cassidy	917 00			
4	115	Supplies	800 00			(a) 600 00
5	120	Prepaid Insurance	750 00			(b) 250 00
6	125	Office Equipment	11 364 00			
7	130	Delivery Equipment	14 600 00			
8	201	Accts. Pay.—Gillespie Co.		1 774 00		
9	205	Accts. Pay.—Shade Supply Co.		200 00		
10	210	Accts. Pay.—Trip Travel		2 632 00		
11	301	Kevin Chan, Capital		16 734 00		
12	302	Kevin Chan, Withdrawals	2 500 00			
13	303	Income Summary				
14	401	Delivery Revenue		28 724 00		
15	501	Advertising Expense	3 083 00			
16	505	Insurance Expense			(b) 250 00	
17	510	Maintenance Expense	710 00			
18	515	Rent Expense	6 500 00			
19	520	Supplies Expense			(a) 600 00	
20	525	Utilities Expense	1 240 00			
21			50 064 00	50 064 00	850 00	850 00
22		Net Income				
23						
24						
25						
26						
27						
28						
29						
30						
31						
32						
33						
34						
35						
36						
37						
38						
39						
40						
41						

When adjustments are made at the end of the period, this procedure becomes an additional step in the accounting cycle. After Step 7, *Prepare financial statements*, Step 8 is *Journalize and post the adjusting entries*. The final two steps in the cycle remain the same. We now have a ten-step cycle instead of a nine-step cycle.

Delivery Service
Sheet
December 31, 20--

ADJUSTED TRIAL BALANCE DEBIT	ADJUSTED TRIAL BALANCE CREDIT	INCOME STATEMENT DEBIT	INCOME STATEMENT CREDIT	BALANCE SHEET DEBIT	BALANCE SHEET CREDIT	
7 264 00				7 264 00		1
336 00				336 00		2
917 00				917 00		3
200 00				200 00		4
500 00				500 00		5
11 364 00				11 364 00		6
14 600 00				14 600 00		7
	1 774 00				1 774 00	8
	200 00				200 00	9
	2 632 00				2 632 00	10
	16 734 00				16 734 00	11
2 500 00				2 500 00		12
						13
	28 724 00		28 724 00			14
3 083 00		3 083 00				15
250 00		250 00				16
710 00		710 00				17
6 500 00		6 500 00				18
600 00		600 00				19
1 240 00		1 240 00				20
50 064 00	50 064 00	12 383 00	28 724 00	37 681 00	21 340 00	21
		16 341 00			16 341 00	22
		28 724 00	28 724 00	37 681 00	37 681 00	23
						24
						25
						26
						27
						28
						29
						30
						31
						32
						33
						34
						35
						36
						37
						38
						39
						40
						41

Figure A–2 Work Sheet Showing Ending Adjusted Balances and Net Income (continued)

As You READ

Key Point

Step 8 Journalizing and posting the adjusting entries is the 8th step in the accounting cycle. It is done after preparing the financial statements (step 7) and before journalizing and posting the closing entries (step 9).

GENERAL JOURNAL

	DATE		DESCRIPTION	POST. REF.	DEBIT	CREDIT	
1	20--		*Adjusting Entires*				1
2	Dec.	31	Supplies Expense	520	6 0 0 00		2
3			Supplies	115		6 0 0 00	3
4		31	Insurance Expense	505	2 5 0 00		4
5			Prepaid Insurance	120		2 5 0 00	5
6							6

ACCOUNT _Supplies_   ACCOUNT NO. _115_

DATE		DESCRIPTION	POST. REF.	DEBIT	CREDIT	BALANCE DEBIT	BALANCE CREDIT
20--							
Jan.	1	Balance				1 0 0 00	
Feb.	14		G11	3 0 0 00		4 0 0 00	
Aug.	21		G14	4 0 0 00		8 0 0 00	
Dec.	31	Adjusting Entry	G22		6 0 0 00	2 0 0 00	

ACCOUNT _Prepaid Insurance_   ACCOUNT NO. _120_

DATE		DESCRIPTION	POST. REF.	DEBIT	CREDIT	BALANCE DEBIT	BALANCE CREDIT
20--							
Nov.	1		G19	7 5 0 00		7 5 0 00	
Dec.	31	Adjusting Entry	G22		2 5 0 00	5 0 0 00	

ACCOUNT _Insurance Expense_   ACCOUNT NO. _505_

DATE		DESCRIPTION	POST. REF.	DEBIT	CREDIT	BALANCE DEBIT	BALANCE CREDIT
20--							
Dec.	31	Adjusting Entry	G22	2 5 0 00		2 5 0 00	

ACCOUNT _Supplies Expense_   ACCOUNT NO. _520_

DATE		DESCRIPTION	POST. REF.	DEBIT	CREDIT	BALANCE DEBIT	BALANCE CREDIT
20--							
Dec.	31	Adjusting Entry	G22	6 0 0 00		6 0 0 00	

Figure A–3 Adjusting Entries Posted to the General Ledger

Problem A–1 Analyzing Adjustments

Information related to accounts requiring adjustments on the work sheet for the year ended December 31 for Magner's Advertising Center follows.

Instructions In your working papers, identify the amount of each adjustment, which account is debited, and which account is credited.

1. The Trial Balance section shows a balance of $4,239.80 for **Supplies.** The amount of supplies actually on hand at the end of the period is $912.15.
2. Magner's paid an annual insurance premium of $4,920.00 on October 1.

Problem A–2 Analyzing Adjustments

Ace Advertising Agency has the following information regarding supplies. The beginning balance in the general ledger account **Supplies** on August 1 was $214.00. On August 13 the agency purchased $302.00 worth of supplies. On August 26 it purchased additional supplies for $176.00. At the end of August, Ace counted the supplies and determined that supplies worth $273.00 were still on hand.

Instructions Analyze the preceding information and then answer the following questions regarding the **Supplies** account.

1. What amount should be entered in the Trial Balance section of the work sheet for **Supplies**? Which column should be used?
2. What amount should be entered in the Adjustments section of the work sheet for **Supplies**? Which column should be used?
3. Should any other amount be entered in the Adjustments section? If yes, answer these questions:
   a. Which account?
   b. Which column?
   c. What amount?
4. What amounts should be entered in the Adjusted Trial Balance section? For each amount list the name of the account and specify which column should be used (Debit or Credit).

Problems

Problem A–3 Entering Adjustments and Preparing an Adjusted Trial Balance

The general ledger for Schellhorn's Water Slide shows the following account balances on December 31, the end of the fiscal period.

Instructions In your working papers:

1. Prepare the Trial Balance section of the work sheet. The account names are entered on the work sheet.
2. Enter the adjustments for **Office Supplies** and **Prepaid Insurance** in the Adjustments section. The data for the adjustments is as follows:
   a. The amount of supplies on hand on December 31 is $492.
   b. The insurance premium expired is $860.
3. Extend the amounts and complete the Adjusted Trial Balance section.

101	Cash in Bank	$10,230
105	Accts. Rec.—Chiara Adin	519
110	Accts. Rec.—Miguel Hendrickson	207
115	Office Supplies	1,820
120	Prepaid Insurance	1,290
125	Office Equipment	3,117
130	Water Slide Equipment	14,204
201	Accts. Pay.—Northern Slide Co.	6,281
205	Accts. Pay.—Advertising World	1,559
210	Accts. Pay.—Merit Cleaning	332
301	Phil Schellhorn, Capital	12,641
302	Phil Schellhorn, Withdrawals	1,400
303	Income Summary	—
401	Slide Revenue	29,209
501	Advertising Expense	1,350
505	Insurance Expense	—
510	Maintenance Expense	719
515	Rent Expense	12,800
520	Office Supplies Expense	—
525	Utilities Expense	2,366

Problem A–4 Preparing a Ten-Column Work Sheet

The general ledger for Ryan's Canoe Rentals shows the following account balances on December 31, the end of the fiscal period.

Instructions In your working papers:

1. Prepare the Trial Balance section of the work sheet. The account names are entered on the work sheet.
2. Enter the adjustments for **Office Supplies** and **Prepaid Insurance** in the Adjustments section. The data for the adjustments is as follows:
   a. Ryan's determines that 20 percent of the supplies purchased are still on hand on December 31.
   b. The insurance premium expired is $1,337.
3. Extend the amounts and complete the Adjusted Trial Balance section.
4. Extend the appropriate amounts to the Balance Sheet and Income Statement sections and determine the net income or net loss for the period.

101	Cash in Bank	$13,826
105	Accts. Rec.—Nancy Burrows	803
110	Accts. Rec.—Patrick Chang	519
115	Supplies	2,880
120	Prepaid Insurance	2,292
125	Office Equipment	3,117
130	Rental Equipment	14,204
135	Canoes	20,182
201	Accts. Pay.—South Canoe Co.	6,991
205	Accts. Pay.—H & T Advertising	2,046
210	Accts. Pay.—Cassidy's Equipment	855
301	Ryan Gillespie, Capital	38,619
305	Ryan Gillespie, Withdrawals	3,700
310	Income Summary	—
401	Rental Revenue	31,624
402	Lesson Revenue	3,475
501	Advertising Expense	2,730
505	Insurance Expense	—
510	Maintenance Expense	1,664
515	Rent Expense	14,900
520	Supplies Expense	—
525	Utilities Expense	2,793

Using the Numeric Keypad

Electronic calculators and computer keyboards have ten-key numeric keypads. When you key numerical data, your ability to use the numeric keypad by touch will make your task easier and faster.

Locating Keys

How Are Keys Arranged on a Numeric Keypad?

The ten-key numeric keypad is usually arranged in four rows of three keys. The locations of the 1 to 9 keys are the same on all equipment. The locations of the 0 (zero), decimal, Enter, and other function keys vary. Some typical arrangements are illustrated here.

On the ten-key numeric keypad, the 4-5-6 keys are called the **home keys**. These keys are the "starting point" from which you operate the other number keys. The index finger of your right hand should rest on the 4 key, your middle finger on the 5 key, and your ring finger on the 6 key. Most

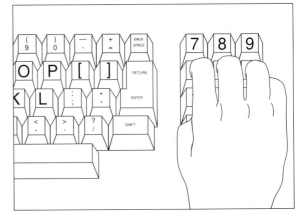

keypads have a special "help" on the home keys so you can easily locate them: the 5 key may have a raised dot or the surfaces of the 4-5-6 keys may be concave (indented).

From the home keys, you reach up or down to tap other keys. The index finger is also used for the 7 and 1 keys. The middle finger is used for the 8 and 2 keys. The ring finger is used for the 9 and 3 keys.

The fingers used for the 0 (zero), decimal, and Enter keys depend on the keypad's arrangement. On some keypads, the thumb taps the 0 (zero) key and the ring finger taps the decimal key. Depending on its location, the Enter key on a computer may be operated by the little finger or the thumb.

On an electronic calculator, numbers are entered by using function keys: plus (+), minus (−), multiply (×), divide (÷), and so on. A computer keypad has different function keys for multiply (*) and divide (/). On an electronic calculator, the asterisk (*) is used for the total.

The fingers used to operate these keys depend on the keys' location on the keyboard. Locate these keys on your keypad and determine the correct fingers to use to operate them.

Entering Numbers by Touch
How Do You Use the Keys by Touch?

Throughout the remaining pages of this appendix, you will demonstrate use of the numeric keypad by touch. That is, you will enter numbers on the keypad without looking at your fingers.

Your practice consists of adding columns of numbers. If you are using an electronic calculator, tap the plus (+) key after you have entered a number in a column. After entering all the numbers in a column, tap the total (*) key. If you are using a computer spreadsheet program, tap the Enter key after you have entered a number in a column. This will force a line break; each time you strike the Enter key, the cursor will move to the next line. After entering all the numbers in a column, use the software function or formula to add the numbers.

Using the 4-5-6 Keys

1. Demonstrate use of the numeric keypad by touch. Locate the 4-5-6 keys (the home keys) on your keypad. Also locate the Enter key if you are using a computer or the plus key if you are using a calculator.
2. Place your index finger on the 4 key, your middle finger on the 5 key, and your ring finger on the 6 key.
3. To enter a number, tap the number keys, one at a time, in the same order as you read the digits from left to right. Always keep your fingers on the home keys.
4. When you have entered the last digit, tap the Enter key (computer) or the plus key (calculator).
5. Using the following problems, practice entering columns of numbers at a comfortable pace until you feel confident about each key's location.
6. After entering all of the numbers in a column, add the numbers using the software (computer) or tap the total key once (calculator).

1.	2.	3.	4.	5.	6.
444	555	666	456	554	664
555	666	454	654	445	445
666	444	545	465	564	566
456	654	446	556	664	645
564	546	646	656	565	465
646	465	546	465	655	654

Using the 1, 7 and 0 Keys

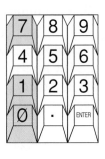

1. Demonstrate use of the numeric keypad by touch. Locate the 1, 7 and 0 (zero) keys on your keypad.
2. Place your fingers on the home keys.
3. Practice the reach from the home keys to each new key. Reach down to the 1 key and up to the 7 key with your index finger. Be sure to return your finger to the home keys after tapping the 1 and 7 keys. Strike the 0 (zero) key with your thumb.
4. Using the following problems, practice adding columns of numbers containing the new keys. Practice at a comfortable pace until you feel confident about each key's location. Be sure to keep your fingers in home-key position.

1.	2.	3.	4.	5.	6.
444	014	140	107	011	141
471	107	701	074	170	117
174	740	701	104	710	417
741	101	704	007	004	047
710	114	471	411	471	104
407	441	117	047	174	114

Using the 3 and 9 Keys

1. Locate the 3 and 9 keys on your keypad.
2. Place your fingers on the home keys.
3. Practice the reach from the home keys to each new key. Reach down to the 3 key and up to the 9 key with your ring finger. Be sure to return your finger to the home keys after tapping the 3 and 9 keys.
4. Using the following problems, practice adding columns of numbers containing the new keys. Practice at a comfortable pace until you feel confident about each key's location. Be sure to keep your fingers in home-key position.

1.	2.	3.	4.	5.	6.
666	669	339	966	939	699
999	663	363	393	363	936
333	936	336	966	393	939
963	396	936	633	639	336
639	936	636	393	369	696
399	363	996	993	369	939

Using the 2 and 8 Keys

1. Locate the 2 and 8 keys on your keypad.
2. Place your fingers on the home keys.
3. Practice the reach from the home keys to each new key. Reach down to the 2 key and up to the 8 key with your middle finger. Be sure to return your finger to the home keys after tapping the 2 and 8 keys.

4. Using the following problems, practice adding columns of numbers containing the new keys. Practice at a comfortable pace until you feel confident about each key's location. Be sure to keep your fingers in home-key position.

1.	2.	3.	4.	5.	6.
555	228	885	285	582	828
888	852	285	258	558	825
222	522	825	525	582	852
582	252	588	858	825	258
822	528	258	582	525	885
522	855	852	825	582	282

Using the Decimal Key

1. Locate the decimal key on your keypad.
2. Place your fingers on the home keys.
3. Depending on the arrangement of keys on your numeric keypad, you may use your thumb, your middle finger, or your ring finger to tap the decimal key. Practice the reach from the home keys to the decimal key. Be sure to return your finger to the home keys after tapping the decimal key.

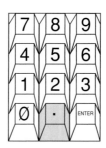

4. Using the following problems, practice adding columns of numbers containing the decimal key. Practice at a comfortable pace until you feel confident about the key's location. Be sure to keep your fingers in home-key position.

1.	2.	3.	4.	5.	6.
.777	.978	.998	8.78	7.88	8.79
.888	.987	.879	8.89	7.87	7.98
.999	.878	.787	8.87	8.97	9.89
.789	.987	.878	7.88	9.77	9.87
.897	.789	.797	9.87	7.97	7.89
.978	.797	.899	7.98	8.79	9.78

7.	8.	9.	10.	11.	12.
468.	48.2	.8	284.0	41.87	154.88
.489	2,537.	5,827.	100.	4,057.4	888.
214.2	852.	.024	8.45	89.45	.0082
7.12	3.978	18.73	56.0	2.25	200.08
6,394.4	257.0	85.00	23.00	20.0	632.48
.58	.2684	1.045	.89	36.248	64.1

13.	14.	15.	16.	17.	18.
267.50	425.21	1.25	467.54	65.27	9.78
4.19	414.50	0.18	95.14	102.38	5.94
87.64	1,684.84	585.56	6,926.95	8,216.58	652.25
654.84	49.95	7.50	35.00	1,852.84	3,782.70
1,750.67	720.65	11.60	7.13	4.60	39.25
141.82	77.61	23.55	154.95	79.15	36.87

Recording Transactions in the Combination Journal

BEFORE YOU READ

Main Idea
Small businesses often use a multicolumn combination journal that combines the features of the general journal and the special journals into one book of original entry.

Read to Learn...
➤ how to use the combination journal. (p. A–18)
➤ posting the journal's columns. (p. A–19)

Key Terms
combination journal

Businesses with a large volume of financial transactions use special journals to record those transactions. If you completed Chapters 16 and 17, you learned that special journals are designed for recording a specific type of business transaction. For example the sales journal is used to record the sale of merchandise on account.

Although the use of special journals is ideal for large businesses, they are not practical for small service and retail businesses that usually have only one accounting clerk. It is impractical for one clerk to record transactions in five different journals. At the same time, using only a general journal is very time consuming. Many small businesses use one journal—a combination journal.

Using the Combination Journal
How Do You Use a Combination Journal?

As its name implies, a **combination journal** is a multicolumn journal that combines the features of the general journal and the special journals into one book of original entry. Like special journals, the combination journal has special amount columns to record transactions that occur frequently. It also has General Debit and Credit columns for recording transactions for which there are no special amount columns. Therefore all the transactions of a business can be recorded in a single, multicolumn journal.

A business designs its combination journal to fit its own special needs. The number of columns and the selection and arrangement of the special columns depend on the type of business and the transactions that occur. Most combination journals have between 10 and 13 columns.

The arrangement of the columns varies from one business to another. The columns should be arranged to make recording and posting easy and accurate. For example, look at On Your Mark Athletic Wear's combination journal in **Figure C–1.** The Date, Account Name, Document Number, and Posting Reference columns are located at the far left. These columns are followed by the General Debit and Credit columns.

Figure C–1 The Combination Journal

	DATE	ACCOUNT NAME	DOC. NO.	POST. REF.	GENERAL DEBIT	GENERAL CREDIT	ACCOUNTS RECEIVABLE DEBIT	ACCOUNTS RECEIVABLE CREDIT
1								
2								
3								

COMBINATION

The General columns are followed by the special amount columns for **Accounts Receivable, Sales, Sales Tax Payable, Accounts Payable, Purchases,** and **Cash in Bank.**

Notice that the line numbers appear to the left and right sides of each page of the journal. These line numbers help the accounting clerk avoid writing amounts on the wrong lines.

A properly designed combination journal can be used efficiently for recording every possible business transaction.

- Receipts of cash are recorded in the Cash in Bank Debit column.
- Cash payments are entered in the Cash in Bank Credit column.
- The purchase of merchandise, for cash or on account, is recorded in the Purchases Debit column.
- Transactions affecting creditor accounts are written in the Accounts Payable Debit and Credit columns.
- The sale of merchandise is recorded in the Sales Credit and Sales Tax Payable Credit columns.
- Transactions affecting charge customer accounts are entered in the Accounts Receivable Debit and Credit columns.
- General ledger accounts for which there are no special columns are recorded in the General Debit and Credit columns. Adjusting and closing entries, for example, would be recorded in the General Debit and Credit columns.

On Your Mark Athletic Wear's business transactions for the month of June are recorded in the combination journal shown in **Figure C–2.**

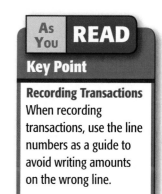

As You READ

Key Point

Recording Transactions
When recording transactions, use the line numbers as a guide to avoid writing amounts on the wrong line.

As You READ

Key Point

Recording Transactions
The General columns are used to record any amount for which no special columns are provided.

Proving and Posting the Journal
What Columns Are Posted Daily? Monthly?

Like special journals, an important feature of the combination journal is that it saves time in both recording and posting transactions. The amounts entered in the General columns are posted on a daily basis to the appropriate general ledger accounts. Amounts entered in the Accounts Receivable and Accounts Payable columns are also posted on a daily basis to the appropriate charge customer or creditor accounts in the accounts receivable and accounts payable subsidiary ledgers. At the end of the month, the combination journal is footed, proved, totaled, and ruled. Totals of the special amount columns of the combination journal are then posted to the general ledger accounts named in the column headings. **Figure C–2** shows how the combination journal will look at the end of the month after all postings have been made.

JOURNAL   PAGE _____

| SALES CREDIT | SALES TAX PAYABLE CREDIT | ACCOUNTS PAYABLE | | PURCHASES DEBIT | CASH IN BANK | | |
		DEBIT	CREDIT		DEBIT	CREDIT	
							1
							2
							3

	DATE	ACCOUNT NAME	DOC. NO.	POST. REF.	GENERAL DEBIT	GENERAL CREDIT	ACCOUNTS RECEIVABLE DEBIT	ACCOUNTS RECEIVABLE CREDIT
1	20--							
2	June 6	Cash Sales	T61	—				
3	8	Sales Discounts	R62	405	8 00			
4		Casey Klein		✓				424 00
5	10	Tammy's Fitness Club	S75	✓			530 00	
6	13	Office Equipment	I011	145	650 00			
7		Geary Office Supply		✓				
8	14	Sales Returns and Allowances	CM5	410	90 00			
9		Sales Tax Payable		220	5 40			
10		Lara Young		✓				95 40
11	15	Gabriel Ramos	M12	✓			80 00	
12		Shashi Rahim		✓				80 00
13	16	Computer Solutions	I008	✓				
14	18	Supplies	I214	130	100 00			
15		Geary Office Supplies		✓				
16	21	FastLane Athletics	CK350	✓				
17		Purchases Discounts		510		6 00		
18	23	Utilities Expense	CK351	680	175 00			
19	24	Purchases	CK352	—				
20	26	Salaries Expense	CK353	665	3 200 00			
21		Social Security Tax Payable		212		198 40		
22		Medicare Tax Payable		213		46 40		
23		Employees' Federal Income Tax Payable		205		480 00		
24		Employees' State Income Tax Payable		206		70 40		
25	26	Payroll Tax Expense	P.Reg.	657	456 00			
26		Social Security Tax Payable		212		198 40		
27		Medicare Tax Payable		213		46 40		
28		Federal Unemployment Tax Payable		214		25 60		
29		State Unemployment Tax Payable		215		185 60		
30	27	Supplies	CK354	130	500 00			
31	28	Champion Store Supply	DM10	✓				
32		Purchases Returns and Allowances		515		90 00		
33	29	Supplies	M13	130	125 00			
34	30	Purchases		501		125 00		
35	30	Totals			5 309 40	1 472 20	610 00	599 40
36					(✓)	(✓)	(115)	(115)
37								

Daily
Post each individual amount in the General columns to the general ledger. Put the general ledger account number in the Post. Ref. column to indicate that posting has been completed.

Daily
Post each individual amount in the Accounts Receivable columns to the accounts receivable subsidiary ledger. Put a check mark in the Post. Ref. column to indicate that posting has been completed.

Daily
Post each individual amount in the Accounts Payable columns to the accounts payable subsidiary ledger. Put a check mark in the Post. Ref. column to indicate that posting has been completed.

Figure C–2 Recording Transactions in a Combination Journal

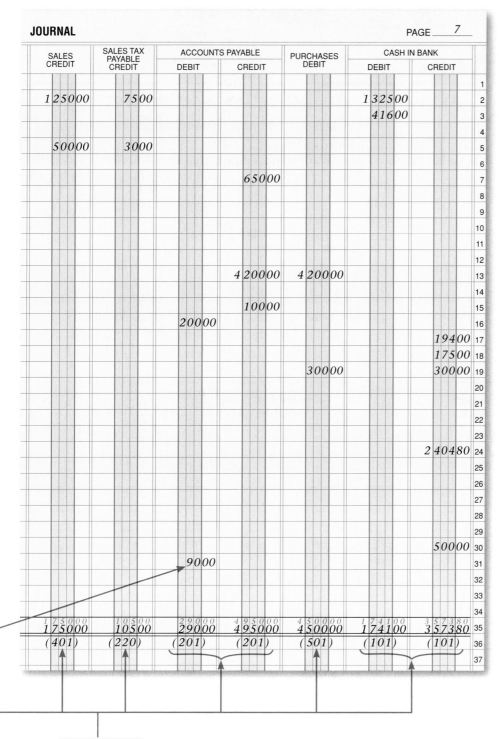

SALES CREDIT	SALES TAX PAYABLE CREDIT	ACCOUNTS PAYABLE		PURCHASES DEBIT	CASH IN BANK		
		DEBIT	CREDIT		DEBIT	CREDIT	
							1
1 250 00	75 00				1 325 00		2
					416 00		3
							4
500 00	30 00						5
							6
			650 00				7
							8
							9
							10
							11
							12
		4 200 00	4 200 00				13
							14
			100 00				15
		200 00					16
						194 00	17
						175 00	18
				300 00		300 00	19
							20
							21
							22
							23
						2 404 80	24
							25
							26
							27
							28
							29
						50 00	30
		90 00					31
							32
							33
							34
1750 00	105 00	290 00	4 950 00	4 500 00	1 741 00	3 573 80	35
(401)	(220)	(201)	(201)	(501)	(101)	(101)	36
							37

End of Month
Post the column totals for Accounts Receivable, Sales, Sales Tax Payable, Accounts Payable, Purchases, and Cash in Bank to the general ledger. The General column totals are not posted. Put the general ledger account numbers in parentheses below the column totals to indicate that posting has been completed.

Figure C–2 Recording Transactions in a Combination Journal (continued)

Problem C–1 Analyzing Transactions for Combination Journal Entries

John Dunn owns The Country Store, a small retail store. He uses a combination journal with the following columns.

General Debit   Accounts Payable Debit

General Credit   Accounts Payable Credit

Accounts Receivable Debit   Purchases Debit

Accounts Receivable Credit   Cash in Bank Debit

Sales Credit   Cash in Bank Credit

Sales Tax Payable Credit

Instructions Use the form provided in your working papers. For each of the following selected transactions, indicate in which column(s) of the combination journal the debit and credit parts of the entry would be recorded. The first transaction has been completed as an example.

Date	Trans.	General Dr.	General Cr.	Accounts Receivable Dr.	Accounts Receivable Cr.	Sales Cr.	Sales Tax Payable Cr.	Accounts Payable Dr.	Accounts Payable Cr.	Purchases Dr.	Cash in Bank Dr.	Cash in Bank Cr.
Dec. 1	Debit	✓										
	Credit								✓			

Date		Transactions
Dec.	1	Purchased a computer on account from King's Computer Outlet.
	2	John Dunn withdrew cash for personal use.
	5	Sold merchandise on account to Bernard Peterson, plus sales tax.
	10	Issued Credit memo 14 to Tom Tray, a charge customer, for the return of merchandise sold on account plus sales tax.
	13	Issued Debit Memo 20 to Cory Distributors for the return of merchandise purchased from them on account.
	15	Received a check from Bernard Peterson in full payment of his account.
	18	Issued a check to Cory Distributors in payment of our account less the purchases return and less a purchases discount.
	22	John Dunn invested a calculator in the business.
	25	Issued a check for the monthly payroll less deductions for FICA.
	25	Recorded the employer's payroll tax liabilities for FICA taxes, federal unemployment tax, and state unemployment tax.
	30	Recorded cash sales plus sales tax.
	31	Recorded the adjusting entry for the office supplies consumed during the period.

Problem C–2 Recording Transactions, Totaling, Proving, and Ruling the Combination Journal

Craig Glasser is a physician who operates a family medical practice, Glasser Family Medical Center. He uses the combination journal found in your working papers.

Instructions

1. Record the following transactions on page 17 of the combination journal.
2. Total, prove, and rule the combination journal.

Date		Transactions
Oct.	1	Received $2,100 in medical fees from patients, Receipt 90.
	2	Issued Check 414 for the cash purchase of $120 of office supplies.
	4	Purchased medical supplies on account from Wharton Laboratories, Invoice 14006 for $1,950, terms n/60.
	6	Craig Glasser invested medical equipment valued at $750 in the medical practice, Memorandum 30.
	8	Billed a patient, Daniel O'Connell, $150 for his annual physical, Statement 40.
	9	Completed lab services for Carl Fisher and billed him $160, Statement 41.
	11	Purchased a new examination table (medical equipment) on account from Medical Suppliers, Invoice L163 for $1,452.50, terms n/45.
	13	Billed Patricia Vallano $300 for medical services, Statement 42.
	15	Issued Check 415 for $2,004.81 for the monthly salaries expense of $2,500.00 less deductions: social security tax, $155.00; Medicare tax, $36.25; employees' federal income taxes, $209.00; employees' state income taxes, $94.94.
	15	Recorded the employer's payroll tax liabilities: social security tax, $155; Medicare tax, $36.25; federal unemployment taxes, $20; state unemployment taxes, $145; payroll register.
	18	Issued Debit memo 16 to Wharton Laboratories for $200 for the return of medical supplies purchased on account.
	20	Paid the telephone bill, Check 416 for $110.
	22	A check for $110 was received from John Marshall to apply on his account, Receipt 91.

CONTINUE

Date	Transactions (cont.)
25	Craig Glasser withdrew $1,250 cash from the business, Check 417.
28	Received $75 from Daniel O'Connell to apply on his account, Receipt 92.
31	Completed lab services for Donna Gordon and billed her $95, Statement 43.
31	Issued Check 418 for the November rent of $900.

Problem C–3 Recording Transactions, Totaling, Proving, and Ruling the Combination Journal

Sunset Surfwear is a small merchandise business specializing in a variety of surfwear items. Sunset Surfwear uses a combination journal with these amount columns.

General Debit   Accounts Payable Debit
General Credit   Accounts Payable Credit
Accounts Receivable Debit   Purchases Debit
Accounts Receivable Credit   Cash in Bank Debit
Sales Credit   Cash in Bank Credit
Sales Tax Payable Credit

Instructions In your working papers:

1. Record these transactions on page 12 of the combination journal.
2. Total, prove, and rule the combination journal.

Date	Transactions
Dec. 1	Issued Check 151 for $700 to Pine Valley Realty for the monthly rent.
2	Received a check for $204.82 from Martha Adams in payment of her account of $209 less a discount of $4.18, Receipt 303.
3	Purchased $400 of merchandise on account from Kelley Apparel, Invoice 479 dated December 2, terms 2/10, n/30.
4	Issued Check 152 for $75 to The Knight Crier for advertisements.
5	Issued Check 153 for $230.30 to Neilson Store Equipment in payment of its invoice for $235.
6	Sent Credit Memo 35 to Alex Hamilton for damaged merchandise returned, $50 plus $2.25 sales tax.
8	Sold merchandise on account to Nate Moulder, $100 plus sales tax of $4.50, Sales Slip 205.

CONTINUE

Date	Transactions (cont.)
10	Discovered that $95 received on account from Helen Jan on November 16 had been journalized and posted to Harriett Junell's account, Memorandum 16.
11	Recorded the monthly salaries of $2,100 less deductions: social security tax, $130.20; Medicare tax, $30.45; employees' federal income taxes, $326; and employees' state income taxes, $48.09; Check 154 for $1,565.26.
11	Recorded the employer's payroll tax liabilities: social security tax, $130.20; Medicare tax, $30.45; federal unemployment tax, $16.80; state unemployment tax, $121.80; payroll register.
12	Sent Check 155 for $392 to Kelley Apparel in payment of Invoice 479 less a discount of $8.
15	Received $150 from Martha Adams to apply on her account, Receipt 304.
18	Issued Debit Memorandum 20 to Waverunner Designs for $25 for the return of merchandise purchased on account.
24	Sold $200 in merchandise on account to Westwood High School Athletics plus sales tax of $9, Sales Slip 206.
26	Purchased $300 of merchandise on account from Capital Accessories, Invoice 601.
28	Purchased store equipment on account from Neilson Store Equipment, $200, Invoice 609.
29	Paid a $150 electric bill for the month by issuing Check 156 to Dukane Power Company.
31	Recorded cash sales of $3,000, plus $135 sales taxes, Tape 52.

Problem C–4 Recording Adjusting and Closing Entries in a Combination Journal

A partial work sheet for December 31 for In Beat CD Shop is shown in your working papers.

Instructions

1. Record the adjusting entries in the combination journal. Then total, prove, and rule the General columns of the journal.
2. Record the closing entries in the combination journal. Then total, prove, and rule the General columns of the journal.

The Accrual Basis of Accounting

BEFORE YOU READ

Main Idea
Accrual accounting recognizes when revenue and expenses are earned and incurred rather than when they are collected and paid.

Read to Learn...
➤ how to record accrual entries. (p. A–26)
➤ how to record deferral entries. (p. A–30)
➤ how to use reversing entries. (p. A–32)

Key Terms
cash basis of accounting
accrual basis of accounting
accruals
accrued revenue
accrued expense
deferrals
unearned revenue
prepaid expense
reversing entry

Some small businesses keep their financial records on a cash basis. The **cash basis of accounting** recognizes and records revenues when cash is received and expenses only when cash is paid out. Often, however, cash is received and payments are made in an accounting period other than the period in which the original transaction took place. For example, a landscaping service performs work for a client in December, but the customer may not be required to pay until January of the next year. However, if the revenue is not recorded for the service performed in December, the financial statements may not present fairly the business earnings for the year just ended. To overcome this, the accounting profession requires that most businesses use what is called the **accrual basis of accounting**. In accrual accounting, revenues are recognized and recorded when earned, and expenses are recognized and recorded when they are actually incurred. The system for accrual accounting focuses on when earned and incurred rather than on when collected and paid.

The accrual basis of accounting requires that accountants recognize revenue when the business makes a sale or performs a service, regardless of when the company receives the cash. Expenses are recognized as incurred, whether or not the business has paid out the cash. To accrue revenue means to record an amount in anticipation of future receipts and to accrue an expense means to record an amount in anticipation of a future payment. Accrual accounting involves two types of revenue and expenses: accruals and deferrals.

Accruals
How Do You Record Accruals?

Accruals relate to *transactions which have not yet been recorded* in the accounts. The word *accrue* means to accumulate or amass. Accruals for unrecorded revenue and expenses are required when:

1. *A revenue has been earned but not yet received.* For example, interest earned on a note receivable in one accounting period but not collected until the next accounting period.
2. *An expense has been incurred but not yet paid.* For example, you may earn wages from April 27 to April 30, but your employer may not pay your check to you until May 5.

Accruals are revenues or expenses that are gradually earned or incurred over time. In order to report a company's financial position fairly, accruals should be recognized in the accounting period in which they belong.

Accrued Revenue

Accrued revenue is revenue that has been earned but not received or recorded. Examples of unrecorded accrued revenues include unpaid fees for services completed and rent earned but not yet received. The accrued revenue example that follows is for unpaid interest earned on a note receivable.

Adjustment

On December 5, 2010, Rapid Growth Co. accepted a $5,000, 90-day, 9% note receivable from a charge customer, Janie Pippa. Pippa issued the note as an extension on her charge account. Rapid Growth Co. recorded the transaction as a debit of $5,000 to **Notes Receivable** and a credit of $5,000 to **Accounts Receivable** and Janie Pippa's account in the subsidiary ledger. On December 31, 26 days of interest had been earned (accrued) on the note receivable: $5,000 \times .09 \times 26/365 = 32.05. An adjusting entry is required on December 31 to record the amount of interest income earned from December 5 to December 31.

ANALYSIS

Identify
1. For the adjusting entry, the accounts **Interest Receivable** and **Interest Income** are affected.

Classify
2. **Interest Receivable** is an asset account. **Interest Income** is a revenue account.

+/−
3. **Interest Receivable** is increased and **Interest Income** is increased.

DEBIT-CREDIT RULE
4. Increases to assets are recorded as debits. Debit **Interest Receivable** for $32.05.
5. Increases to revenues are recorded as credits. Credit **Interest Income** for $32.05.

T ACCOUNTS

6.

Interest Receivable		Interest Income	
Debit +	Credit −	Debit −	Credit +
Adj. 32.05			Adj. 32.05

JOURNAL ENTRY

7.

GENERAL JOURNAL PAGE 18

	DATE		DESCRIPTION	POST. REF.	DEBIT	CREDIT	
1	2010		*Adjusting Entries*				1
2	Dec.	31	Interest Receivable		32 05		2
3			Interest Income			32 05	3
4							4

As You READ

Key Point

Adjusting Entries
Adjusting entries must be recorded when (1) there are unrecorded revenues and expenses at the end of the accounting period, and (2) there are recorded revenues and expenses that must be allocated over two or more accounting periods.

On March 5, 2011, Rapid received a check from Janie Pippa for $5,110.96, the maturity value of the note ($5,000.00 principle + $110.96 interest). Of the total interest, $32.05 had been earned and recorded in the previous accounting period. The remaining $78.91 should be recorded as income earned in the *current* fiscal year.

In the entry for the receipt of Janie's payment, **Cash in Bank** is debited for $5,110.96, the total amount of cash received. **Notes Receivable** is credited for $5,000.00. **Interest Receivable** is credited for $32.05 since the amount owed has now been received. **Interest Income** is credited for $78.91, the amount of the interest earned that applies to the current accounting period. The entry for this transaction is shown below.

GENERAL JOURNAL　　　　PAGE ___7___

	DATE		DESCRIPTION	POST. REF.	DEBIT	CREDIT	
1	2011						1
2	Mar.	5	Cash in Bank		5 1 1 0 96		2
3			Notes Receivable			5 0 0 0 00	3
4			Interest Receivable			3 2 05	4
5			Interest Income			7 8 91	5
6			Receipt 416				6
7							7

Accrued Expenses

Most expenses are recorded when they are paid or when a liability is incurred. There are, however, some business expenses that have not been paid—but accrue daily—and are not recorded until an adjusting entry is made at the end of the fiscal period. Some examples of these **accrued expenses** are salaries or wages earned by working employees but not yet paid to them, property taxes owed but not yet paid, and interest accrued on unpaid notes payable. The example that follows shows how to calculate interest due and payable.

Adjustment

On November 1, 2010, Rapid Growth Co. signed a $2,000, 90-day, 12% note payable for the purchase of equipment from Taylor Equipment. Rapid Growth Co. recorded the transaction as a debit of $2,000 to **Equipment** and a credit of $2,000 to **Notes Payable**. On December 31, 60 days of interest was owed (accrued) on the note payable: $2,000 × .12 × 60/365 = $39.45. An adjusting entry is required on December 31 to record the amount of interest expense incurred from November 1 to December 31.

ANALYSIS	*Identify*	1.	For the adjusting entry, the accounts **Interest Expense** and **Interest Payable** are affected.
	Classify	2.	**Interest Expense** is an expense account. **Interest Payable** is a liability account.
	+/−	3.	**Interest Expense** is increased and **Interest Payable** is increased.

4. Increases to expenses are recorded as debits. Debit **Interest Expense** for $39.45.
5. Increases to liabilities are recorded as credits. Credit **Interest Payable** for $39.45.

T ACCOUNTS

6.

Interest Expense		Interest Payable	
Debit + Adj. 39.45	Credit −	Debit −	Credit + Adj. 39.45

JOURNAL ENTRY

7.

			GENERAL JOURNAL			PAGE 18	
	DATE		DESCRIPTION	POST. REF.	DEBIT	CREDIT	
4	Dec.	31	Interest Expense		39 45		4
5			Interest Payable			39 45	5
6							6

On March 5 Rapid sent a check to Taylor Equipment for $2,059.18, the maturity value of the note ($2,000.00 principal + $59.18 interest). Of the total interest expense, $39.45 was already owed as of December 31. That amount was recorded as an adjusting entry in the previous accounting period. The remaining $19.73 should be recorded as an expense for the *current* accounting period.

In the entry for the payment of the note, **Notes Payable** is debited for $2,000.00. **Interest Expense** is debited for $19.73, the amount of interest expense incurred that applies to the current accounting period. **Interest Payable** is debited for $39.45 since the amount that was accrued has now been paid. **Cash in Bank** is credited for $2,059.18, the total amount of cash paid. The entry for this transaction is shown below.

			GENERAL JOURNAL			PAGE 7	
	DATE		DESCRIPTION	POST. REF.	DEBIT	CREDIT	
7	Mar.	5	Notes Payable		2 0 0 0 00		7
8			Interest Expense		1 9 73		8
9			Interest Payable		3 9 45		9
10			Cash in Bank			2 0 5 9 18	10
11			Check # 1597				11

To acquire cash with which to provide services, communities impose a tax on real property. Property taxes are usually paid twice a year, with each payment covering a six-month period or one-half the annual tax.

Underwood Merchandisers operates in a building on its own land. The value of the real property is $300,000. The total annual property taxes are $7,800. Underwood is located in a state where property taxes must be paid in May and November. The May payment covers the first six months of the calendar year, and the November payment covers the last six months of the calendar year.

Underwood's fiscal period ends on April 30. As a result, at the end of its fiscal period, Underwood owes property taxes of $2,600 ($7,800 × 4/12 or $3,900 × 4/6) for the months of January, February, March and April. These taxes, however, are not due to be paid until May.

On April 30 Underwood makes the following adjustment to the accounting records to reflect the correct amount of property tax for the period.

GENERAL JOURNAL   PAGE ___26___

	DATE		DESCRIPTION	POST. REF.	DEBIT	CREDIT	
1	20--		*Adjusting Entries*				1
2	Apr.	30	Property Tax Expense		2 6 0 0 00		2
3			Property Tax Payable			2 6 0 0 00	3
4							4

On May 15 Underwood wrote a check for the semiannual property tax payment of $3,900. Of this amount, $2,600 is an expense that was already charged to the prior fiscal period, and $1,300 is an expense charged to the current accounting period. The entry in May to record this payment is shown in the general journal below.

GENERAL JOURNAL   PAGE ___3___

	DATE		DESCRIPTION	POST. REF.	DEBIT	CREDIT	
1	20--						1
2	May	15	Property Tax Expense		1 3 0 0 00		2
3			Property Tax Payable		2 6 0 0 00		3
4			Cash in Bank			3 9 0 0 00	4
5			Check 401				5

Deferrals

How Do You Record Deferrals?

Deferrals are for *transactions that have been recorded* in the accounts. The word *defer* means to wait or delay. Deferrals are for receipts that are not yet earned and for payments that are not yet expenses.

1. *Cash may have been received but not yet earned.* For example, rent received in advance when some of the rental time is in one accounting period and the balance is in the next accounting period.
2. *Cash may have been paid but the expenses not incurred.* For example, when premiums on insurance are paid covering part of one accounting period and the balance covers the next accounting period.

Adjusting entries are required to: (1) recognize unrecorded accrued revenues and expenses or (2) allocate recorded deferred revenues and expenses to the appropriate accounting period.

Unearned Revenue

Unearned revenue is revenue received before it is actually earned. Examples include cash received in advance for rental properties, for season tickets to various events, for insurance premiums, and for work to be performed in the future. Because the business has an obligation to deliver the merchandise or perform the service for which it has already received payment, unearned revenue represents a current liability for the business.

Boyce Real Estate rents space in its building to a tax accountant. On November 1 the accountant paid Boyce $1,200 in advance for rent covering the months of November through April. The entry to record this transaction is shown below.

GENERAL JOURNAL PAGE 55

	DATE		DESCRIPTION	POST. REF.	DEBIT	CREDIT	
1	20--						1
2	Nov.	1	Cash in Bank		1 2 0 0 00		2
3			Unearned Rental Income			1 2 0 0 00	3
4			Receipt 181				4

As the business delivers the merchandise or performs the service, it earns a part of the advance payment. The earned portion must be transferred from the liability account to a revenue account through an adjusting entry made at the end of the period.

When Boyce's fiscal period ends on December 31, the company will have earned rental income of $400 for two of the six months paid in advance ($1,200 × ⅓). The adjusting entry to record the rental income is shown below.

GENERAL JOURNAL PAGE 65

	DATE		DESCRIPTION	POST. REF.	DEBIT	CREDIT	
1	20--		Adjusting Entries				1
2	Dec.	31	Unearned Rental Income		4 0 0 00		2
3			Rental Income			4 0 0 00	3
4							4

Prepaid Expenses

A **prepaid expense** is an expense paid in advance. Examples include the purchase of office supplies, premiums paid on insurance policies, rent paid in advance on the use of property or equipment, and bank discounts on non-interest-bearing notes payable. Examples of adjustments for prepaid expenses appear in Chapter 18 of this textbook.

As You READ

Key Point

Unearned Revenue Revenue received in advance is usually recorded in a liability account. That account must be adjusted at the end of the fiscal period to recognize the amount of revenue earned during the period.

Reversing Entries

What Are Reversing Entries?

After the financial statements have been prepared and the books are closed, many accountants find it helpful to reverse some of the adjusting entries before starting to record routine transactions for the new accounting period. A **reversing entry** is an optional general journal entry that is the exact opposite of a specific adjusting entry. Reversing entries are made on the first day of the new accounting period and simplify the recordkeeping in the new period.

We will use the note receivable accrual on page A–27 to see how reversing entries work. But first, we will review it *without* using reversing entries. The adjusting entry recorded accrued revenue of $32.05 in 2010 as a debit to **Interest Receivable** and a credit to **Interest Income:**

Interest Receivable		Interest Income	
Debit	Credit	Debit	Credit
+	−	−	+
Adj. 32.05			Adj. 32.05

Refer to the general journal entry on page A–28. When Janie paid the note on March 5, 2011, the total amount of interest received was $110.96. Since the interest owed was received, the accountant credited **Interest Receivable** for $32.05. The remaining interest of $78.91 ($110.96 − $32.05) was recorded as interest income. Notice that the accountant had to allocate the total interest to **Interest Receivable** and **Interest Income** based on the adjusting entry made in the prior period. These two accounts appear as follows after posting:

Interest Receivable		Interest Income	
Debit	Credit	Debit	Credit
+	−	−	+
Adj. 32.05	3/5 32.05		3/5 78.91
Bal. 0			Bal. 78.91

Now let's use a reversing entry instead. The adjusting entry is recorded the same way whether reversing entries are used or not:

	DATE		DESCRIPTION	POST. REF.	DEBIT	CREDIT	
GENERAL JOURNAL						PAGE 18	
1	2010		*Adjusting Entries*				1
2	Dec.	31	Interest Receivable		32 05		2
3			*Interest Income*			32 05	3
4							4

The accountant records the following reversing entry on January 1, 2011. Note that it is the exact opposite of the December 31 adjusting entry.

GENERAL JOURNAL					PAGE 1	
DATE	DESCRIPTION	POST. REF.	DEBIT	CREDIT		
1	2011	*Reversing Entries*				1
2	Jan. 1	Interest Income		32 05		2
3		Interest Receivable			32 05	3

The accountant writes the words *Reversing Entries* in the Description column of the General Journal before recording the first reversing entry. This heading eliminates the need for an explanation to be written after each reversing entry. The date of each reversing entry is the first day of the new accounting period. After recording reversing entries, the accountant posts them to the general ledger accounts.

The **Interest Income** account is a temporary account that is closed at the end of each accounting period. It begins the new period with a zero balance. After the reversing entry is posted in the new period, **Interest Income** has a $32.05 debit balance. This is not the normal balance for this account. As you recall, income accounts have a normal credit balance. Here are the accounts after the reversing entry is posted:

Interest Income			Interest Receivable	
Debit	Credit		Debit	Credit
−	+		+	−
Rev. 32.05			Adj. 32.05	Rev. 32.05
Bal. 32.05			Bal. 0	

When the note is paid, the accountant records it in the normal manner:

GENERAL JOURNAL					PAGE 7	
DATE	DESCRIPTION	POST. REF.	DEBIT	CREDIT		
1	2011					1
2	Mar. 5	Cash in Bank		5 110 96		2
3		Notes Receivable			5 000 00	3
4		Interest Income			110 96	4
5		Receipt 416				5

Notice that the accountant does *not* need to allocate the interest between the receivable and income accounts based on the adjusting entry. Instead, all interest is credited to **Interest Income**. Here is **Interest Income** after posting:

Interest Income	
Debit	Credit
−	+
Rev. 32.05	3/5 110.96
	Bal. 78.91

The Interest Income account balance is $78.91, the same as it would have been if reversing entries had not been used. The reversing entry simplifies the entry *made in the new period* to record the note's interest. Reversing entries save time and help prevent errors in the new period.

Problems

Problem D–1 Identifying Accruals and Deferrals

Instructions Use the form in your working papers that is similar to the one below. For each item listed below, indicate by placing a check mark in the correct column whether the item is a prepaid expense, unearned revenue, an accrued expense, or accrued revenue. The first item has been completed as an example.

1. Rent received in advance for a two-year rental of a computer.
2. A two-year premium paid on a fire insurance policy.
3. Advance tuition collected by a university.
4. Interest on an interest-bearing note payable due next year.
5. Cash received for a three-year subscription to a magazine.
6. Fees due for the completed designs for three of five buildings.
7. Property taxes incurred for the last three months of the fiscal period.
8. Salaries owed but not yet paid.
9. Interest on an interest-bearing note receivable that matures in the next accounting period.
10. Office supplies purchased.
11. Cash received for season tickets for home football games.

Item	Prepaid Expense	Unearned Revenue	Accrued Expense	Accrued Revenue
1.		✓		

Problem D–2 Recording Adjusting Entries

The Gore Paper Company uses the accrual basis of accounting. Its fiscal period ends on June 30. The following account balances appear in the company's general ledger as of year-end.

Cash in Bank	$34,616	Office Supplies Expense	$0
Interest Receivable	0	Salaries Expense	75,000
Office Supplies	8,335	Rental Income	0
Salaries Payable	0	Interest Income	0
Unearned Rental Income	1,000		

Instructions Record the adjusting entries on general journal page 14 in your working papers.

1. The office supplies on hand as of June 30 are valued at $935.
2. Gore's 5-day weekly payroll totals $1,500. Salaries have been earned but not yet paid or recorded for June 28–30.
3. On June 30, 30 days of interest had accrued on an $8,000, 90-day, 9% note receivable from a charge customer.
4. Of the $1,000 recorded in the **Unearned Rental Revenue** account, $250 had been earned as of June 30.

Problem D–3 Recording Transactions for Notes Payable

The Villareal Corporation uses the accrual basis of accounting. Its fiscal period ends on December 31. On November 15, the Villareal Corporation borrowed $9,500 from the Second National Bank by issuing a 120-day, 9.5% interest-bearing note payable.

Instructions Record the following transactions on general journal page 41.

1. The issuance of the note payable (Note 7).
2. The adjusting entry to record the amount of accrued interest payable at year-end.
3. The payment of the note on the maturity date (Check 411).

Problem D–4 Recording Accrued Expenses

The Cassenada Dance Company uses the accrual basis of accounting. Located in Seattle, Washington, the company's fiscal year-end is July 31. Property taxes are paid in June and December. Total annual property taxes on the studio and parking lot are $12,000.

Instructions

1. Record the payment made on June 30 for the first six months' property tax in the general journal, page 22.
2. Record the adjusting entry necessary at the fiscal year-end, July 31.

Federal Personal Income Tax

BEFORE YOU READ

Main Idea
Every income-earning individual must file an income tax return to report taxable income and to calculate income tax owed.

Read to Learn...
➤ how the federal tax system was created. (p. A–36)
➤ the purpose of some common federal tax forms.(p. A–36)
➤ how a federal income tax return is prepared. (p. A–37)
➤ how to file a return online. (p. A–38)

Key Terms
voluntary compliance
Form W-4
Form 1099
Form 1040EZ
adjusted gross income
taxable income
e-file

In order to become an informed and contributing member of society, every individual should have a basic knowledge of the federal income tax system. For the system to work fairly and efficiently, everyone must pay their fair share in an accurate and timely manner.

Creation of the Federal Income Tax System

How Was the Federal Tax System Created?

At its founding in 1776, this country did not have a federal personal income tax system. Individual states taxed their residents to raise revenue for needed expenditures. The first personal income tax was created in 1862 to finance the Civil War. A commission levied taxes on a small percentage of people to generate needed revenue. However, this tax was abolished in 1872, soon after the war ended. A federal personal income tax was again proposed in 1895 but was declared unconstitutional.

In 1913 Congress ratified the 16th Amendment to the Constitution allowing the federal government to levy a tax on individuals based on personal income. The income tax system was established under the principle of **voluntary compliance** . This means that all individual taxpayers are responsible for filing their tax return. All taxpayers must report their taxable income, accurately calculate the income tax owed, and file the necessary forms on time.

The Internal Revenue Service (IRS) also has responsibilities under our present tax system. The IRS must administer the tax laws fairly and process tax returns in an efficient manner.

Tax Forms and Procedures

What Are Three Common Tax-Related Forms?

For the federal tax system to run efficiently, all income-earning individuals must prepare and file certain tax forms. For personal income tax, the earning period is from January 1 through December 31. Every individual has from January 1 until April 15 each year to file a tax return and pay the government any taxes owed on income earned in the previous year.

For most taxpayers the most common and largest form of income is the gross earnings paid to them by employers. Other common forms of taxable income include interest earned on savings accounts and investments, stock dividends, rental income, and profits from business operations run as sole proprietorships or partnerships.

Federal Withholding Tax Estimation

As you have learned, the employer withholds a certain amount from each employee's paycheck for taxes. This system of "pay as you earn" was enacted during the early 1940s.

Since the exact amount earned for the year will not be determined until the end of December, the amount of taxes withheld from each employee's paycheck is an *estimate* of the amount the employee will owe at the end of the year. As you learned in Chapter 12, all employees fill out a **Form W-4** when they begin work. This indicates to the employer how much to withhold for federal income tax from each paycheck. For more information on completing Form W-4, refer back to Chapter 12, pages 315–316.

Earned Income

Individual taxpayers receive two common federal forms to report income for the year. The first is Form W-2. This form is prepared by employers and reports to employees and the federal government the total gross wages for the year and the amount withheld from employees' wages to pay the federal income tax. This form is given to the employees in the month of January so the information is available for employees to complete their individual tax returns. To review the Form W-2, refer to Chapter 13, page 358.

Interest Income

The other common form used to report income is **Form 1099** . This form reports interest earned in savings accounts and is prepared by banks or other institutions. Interest from all 1099 forms is added together and the total interest earned for the year is reported on your federal tax return.

The Federal Income Tax Return

What Tax Form Do Most Students File?

The most common tax return prepared by students is Form 1040EZ.

Preparing Form 1040EZ

To file **Form 1040EZ** , several requirements must be met including:

1. Taxable income from wages and tips must be less than $100,000.
2. Taxable interest cannot be more than $1,500.

A completed Form 1040EZ is presented in **Figure E–1** on pages A–39 and A–40. To complete this form, follow these steps:

1. Enter your name, address, and social security number.
2. Check the box on the next line if you want $3 to go to the Presidential Election Campaign Fund.
3. Add the amount(s) in box 1 of your Form(s) W-2 and put that amount on line 1 of the form. This should be the total gross earnings from **all** of your jobs this year.
4. Add the total interest received, as reported on Form(s) 1099, and enter the total amount of interest on line 2.
5. Add lines 1 and 2 and put the total on line 4. This is your total income for the year, called **adjusted gross income** .

As You READ

Key Point

Completing Your Tax Form You must receive all of your W-2 and 1099 forms before you complete your tax return.

6. Since you are a student, you are probably claimed as a dependent by your parents or guardians. On line 5, check YES.
7. Go to the worksheet for dependents on the back of the form and complete A through G. Enter the amount from G on line 5 on the front of the form.
8. Subtract line 5 from line 4 and enter the amount on line 6. This is your **taxable income**, the amount of income that is taxed.
9. Add the amounts in box 2 of your Form(s) W-2 and enter the amount on line 7. This is the amount *already* deducted from your wages to pay your federal tax liability.
10. Enter the amount from line 7 on line 9.
11. Take the amount entered on line 6, and look up the amount of your actual tax liability on the tax table in your working papers. Enter this amount on line 10.
12. If line 9 is greater than line 10, then you have paid in more than you owe and are entitled to a **refund.** Enter the amount of the overpayment on line 11a.
13. If line 10 is greater than line 9, then you owe the federal government more money. Enter the amount you owe on line 12.

If you owe additional money, you must include a check for the entire amount when you file the tax return. Sign the return and enter the date and your occupation on the designated lines.

Before your file your tax return, Form 1040EZ, make sure you:

1. Check all calculations.
2. Attach Copy B (one copy) of each of your W-2s, which are supplied to you by your employer(s).
3. File the return by April 15.

Filing a Tax Return Electronically
How Do I File My Return Online?

Most taxpayers are eligible to file their tax returns online. The Internal Revenue Service (IRS) offers the *e-file* option as a quick, easy, and accurate way to file tax returns. Detailed information about *e-file* is available on the IRS Web site.

Paid income tax preparers can use *e-file* if they are an Authorized IRS *e-file* Provider. If you prepare your own tax return, you can use *e-file* with a personal computer connected to the Internet. In most states, you can also file your state return at the same time.

You have several options to prepare and *e-file* your own tax return:

- purchase commercially available software,
- download software from an Internet site, or
- prepare and file your return online.

The IRS does not provide *e-file* software or offer online filing. A number of companies, tested and approved by the IRS, offer it. Some charge a fee and others do not. The IRS Web site provides additional information. Like any product or service, you must shop around and choose the product that is right for you.

After you transmit your return, you are notified whether it has been accepted or rejected. If it is not accepted, you are provided with customer support to correct the return and resubmit it.

If you owe money, you can authorize an electronic funds withdrawal from your bank account or use a credit card. If you are due to receive a refund,

Form **1040EZ**	Department of the Treasury—Internal Revenue Service **Income Tax Return for Single and Joint Filers With No Dependents** (99) **20--**		OMB No. 1545-0675

Label (See page 11.) **Use the IRS label.** Otherwise, please print or type.

L A B E L   H E R E

Your first name and initial — Joan J.
Last name — Bustelos
Your social security number — 031 XX XXXX

If a joint return, spouse's first name and initial
Last name
Spouse's social security number

Home address (number and street). If you have a P.O. box, see page 11. — 84 Elm Street
Apt. no.

City, town or post office, state, and ZIP code. If you have a foreign address, see page 11. — Norwalk, VA 23514

▲ **Important!** ▲
You **must** enter your SSN(s) above.

Presidential Election Campaign (page 11) ▶

Note. Checking "Yes" will not change your tax or reduce your refund.
Do you, or your spouse if a joint return, want $3 to go to this fund? . . . . . . ▶

You ✔Yes ☐No   Spouse ☐Yes ☐No

Income

Attach Form(s) W-2 here. Enclose, but do not attach, any payment.

1	Wages, salaries, and tips. This should be shown in box 1 of your Form(s) W-2. Attach your Form(s) W-2.	1	5954	00
2	Taxable interest. If the total is over $1,500, you cannot use Form 1040EZ.	2	167	00
3	Unemployment compensation and Alaska Permanent Fund dividends (see page 13).	3		
4	Add lines 1, 2, and 3. This is your **adjusted gross income.**	4	6121	00

Note. You **must** check Yes or No.

| 5 | Can your parents (or someone else) claim you on their return? **Yes.** ✔ Enter amount from worksheet on back. **No.** ☐ If **single,** enter $7,950. If **married filing jointly,** enter $15,900. See back for explanation. | 5 | 4850 | 00 |
| 6 | Subtract line 5 from line 4. If line 5 is larger than line 4, enter -0-. This is your **taxable income.** ▶ | 6 | 1271 | 00 |

Payments and tax

7	Federal income tax withheld from box 2 of your Form(s) W-2.	7	204	00
8a	**Earned income credit (EIC).**	8a		
b	Nontaxable combat pay election. 8b		204	00
9	Add lines 7 and 8a. These are your **total payments.** ▶	9	204	00
10	**Tax.** Use the amount on **line 6 above** to find your tax in the tax table on pages 24–32 of the booklet. Then, enter the tax from the table on this line.	10	126	00

Refund
Have it directly deposited! See page 18 and fill in 11b, 11c, and 11d.

| 11a | If line 9 is larger than line 10, subtract line 10 from line 9. This is your **refund.** ▶ | 11a | 78 | 00 |

▶ b Routing number [ ][ ][ ][ ][ ][ ][ ][ ][ ]   ▶ c Type: ☐ Checking ☐ Savings

▶ d Account number [ ][ ][ ][ ][ ][ ][ ][ ][ ][ ][ ][ ][ ][ ][ ][ ][ ]

Amount you owe

| 12 | If line 10 is larger than line 9, subtract line 9 from line 10. This is the **amount you owe.** For details on how to pay, see page 19. ▶ | 12 | | |

Third party designee

Do you want to allow another person to discuss this return with the IRS (see page 19)? ☐ **Yes.** Complete the following. ☐ **No**

Designee's name ▶
Phone no. ▶ ( )
Personal identification number (PIN) [ ][ ][ ][ ][ ]

Sign here
Joint return? See page 11. Keep a copy for your records.

Under penalties of perjury, I declare that I have examined this return, and to the best of my knowledge and belief, it is true, correct, and accurately lists all amounts and sources of income I received during the tax year. Declaration of preparer (other than the taxpayer) is based on all information of which the preparer has any knowledge.

Your signature — Joan J. Bustelos
Date — 3/19/20--
Your occupation — clerk
Daytime phone number — (123)555-2000

Spouse's signature. If a joint return, **both** must sign.
Date
Spouse's occupation

Paid preparer's use only

Preparer's signature ▶
Date
Check if self-employed ☐
Preparer's SSN or PTIN

Firm's name (or yours if self-employed), address, and ZIP code ▶
EIN
Phone no. ( )

For Disclosure, Privacy Act, and Paperwork Reduction Act Notice, see page 23.
Cat. No. 11329W
Form **1040EZ** (20--)

Figure E–1 Completed Form 1040EZ

it can be deposited directly into your bank account. Refunds are received much faster using this system compared to mailing your tax return.

The IRS also offers a service called *Tele-Tax*. You can call the IRS 24 hours a day and hear recorded messages on over 150 common tax topics. These topics can also be accessed on the IRS Web site.

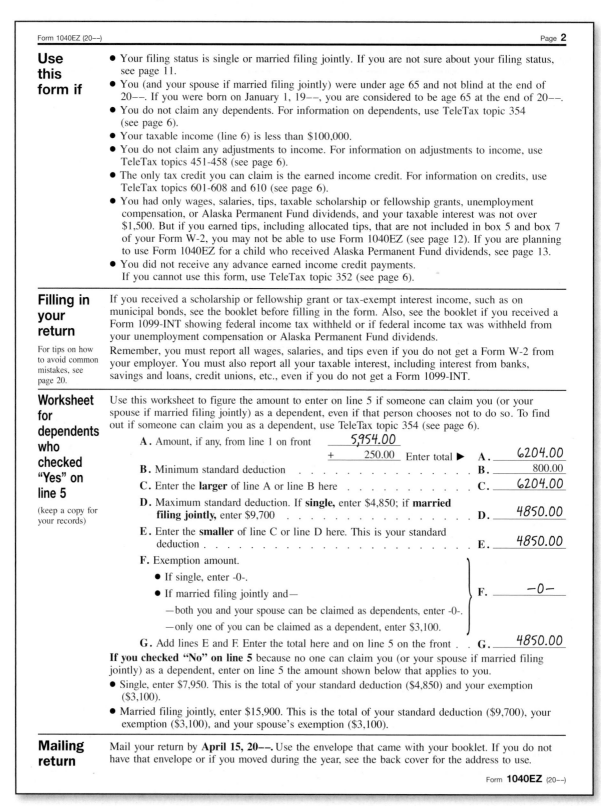

Figure E–1 Completed Form 1040EZ (continued)

Problem E–1 Preparing Form 1040EZ

Michael Feld is a junior at Lewiston High School. He lives with his parents at 274 West Polomia Drive in Hanksville, Ohio, 03856. Mike's social security number is 036-23-8825. Mike wants to contribute $3 to the Presidential Election Campaign Fund.

Mike worked full-time last summer at Harriet's Sub Shop as a counter clerk. He received a Form W-2, which stated that he had total gross wages of $6,201.00 and $192.00 was deducted for federal income tax.

Mike also had a savings account. The Kingsman National Bank sent him Form 1099, which stated he had earned interest of $113.00 on his account.

Mike lives at home with his parents and is claimed as a dependent on their tax return.

Instructions Using this information, prepare Form 1040EZ for Mike Feld. A blank Form 1040EZ is provided in your working papers. Use the tax chart in your working papers to calculate the federal income tax.

Problem E–2 Preparing Form 1040EZ

Alicia DeSantis is a senior at Georgetown High School. She lives at 825 Patterson Street in Montville, Texas, 09436. Her social security number is 043-73-8217. She worked part-time during the school year at Hilltop Deli and full-time during the summer as a lifeguard and swimming instructor at Montville's town pool.

Alicia wants to contribute $3 to the Presidential Election Campaign Fund. Alicia lives with her mother and is claimed as a dependent on her mother's tax return.

Her Form W-2 from the deli reported that she earned $2,143.60 during the year and $112.00 was deducted for federal income tax. The town of Montville sent her a W-2 that reported she earned $4,815.00 during the summer and $206.00 was deducted for federal income tax.

Alicia opened a savings account at the local bank that sent her a Form 1099 that stated she earned $118.50 in interest last year. She also had another savings account set up for college that paid her $201.70 in interest.

Instructions Prepare Form 1040EZ for Alicia. A blank Form 1040EZ is provided in your working papers. Use the tax charts in your working papers to calculate the tax owed.

Building a Powerful Brand

Excerpts from the PETsMART, Inc. 2003 Annual Report

Intended for Use in Chapters 14–26, 29

In this appendix, we present excerpts from the 2003 Annual Report of PETsMART, a publicly held corporation. These excerpts were selected to illustrate many of the concepts discussed in this textbook. Not all of the terminology and policies appearing in this report are consistent with our text discussions. This illustrates some of the diversity that exists in financial reporting. For the complete annual report, visit the PETsMART Web site.

April 26, 2004

Dear Fellow Stockholders:

In 2003, we made strides in our quest to drive strong, sustainable results, and we set the foundation for the next phase of our evolution—building a powerful brand.

For the year, PETsMART earned $0.95 per share, compared to $0.63 per share in 2002. Topline sales grew 11.2 percent year over year, and comparable store sales increased 7.0 percent. Our pet services business continued to surpass expectations, growing at 25.4 percent for the year. And, we generated $246.4 million in cash from operations, further strengthening our balance sheet and our ability to finance new growth initiatives.

We ended the year with 60 net new stores, giving us a presence in nearly all of North America's top 60 markets. In 2004, we will open 90 net new stores, adding up to annual square footage growth of about 12 percent.

We completed reformats of virtually every store in the chain, changing the shopping experience in ways that matter to our customer, driving returns

and further differentiating PETsMART from the competition. The format is flexible and gives us the ability to easily adapt to an ever-changing marketplace. In 2004, we're building on that format. By the fourth quarter, each of our stores will have new in-store signage that's designed to improve our communications with customers.

"Once pet parents discover our services, they do not leave us."

And, we're testing other in-store enhancements to make our stores easier to shop and to build long-term relationships with our customers.

Pet services continue to be an engine of profitable growth and give us the opportunity to create and enhance our relationships with our customers. And, once pet parents discover our services, they do not leave us. Our pet services are three times more profitable than the core store and have consistently grown at or above our target of 20 percent. We expect these growth rates to continue for at least the next two years. Our customers trust us, and by providing high-quality grooming and training services, we've earned the right to move into new service adjacencies.

During the year, we expanded the test of the PETsMART PETsHOTEL℠, a unique boarding and day care concept. We opened six additional locations inside our larger PETsMART stores and incorporated one hotel into the construction of a new store. Based on the results of our small initial test, we believe the PETsHOTEL concept is working and we're expanding the test to an additional 14 or so hotels in 2004.

"When it comes to customer relationships, our associates are our most powerful asset."

When it comes to customer relationships, our associates are our most powerful asset. That's why we're continuing to make investments in associate education. We've enhanced our hiring and training programs to bring in and keep the highest quality candidates in our stores. In 2004 and beyond, we're dedicated to ensuring our associates have the tools they need to provide our customers with superior service and solutions.

Over the next two years, we'll rollout a customer relationship marketing program to better meet our customers' unique needs. These concepts have the potential to increase business and reinforce PETsMART's position as the destination for the Total Lifetime Care for pets.

In addition to all we've accomplished and all that's ahead, I'd like to point out the lives saved through PETsMART Charities® Adoption Centers. Taking care of pets is who we are and we're committed to making a difference in the communities we serve. In 2003, more than 311,000 homeless pets found families through our in-store adoption centers—and I'm very proud of that.

Our accomplishments in 2003 were many, and we're bullish about PETsMART's ability to build long-term relationships with our customers—relationships that translate into continued profitability and returns for our shareholders.

Sincerely,

Philip L. Francis

Philip L. Francis
Chairman and Chief Executive Officer

Statement of Corporate Responsibility

The management of PETsMART is dedicated to ensuring our high standards of corporate governance are maintained, including compliance with our established financial accounting policies and for reporting our results with objectivity and the highest degree of integrity. The culture at PETsMART demands integrity and we have the highest confidence in our people and our underlying systems of internal controls. Management fully embraces and understands its responsibility for the integrity and accuracy of our financial statements.

Here we share a few of the various aspects of our corporate governance:

• Our Board of Directors has adopted and posted on our Web site our Corporate Governance Guidelines and related information.

• Eight of the nine members of the Board of Directors are independent of PETsMART and our management.

• The Lead Director and all members of the board committees—the Audit Committee, the Compensation Committee, and the Corporate Governance Committee—are independent.

• The independent board members regularly meet without management present.

• The charters for these board committees clearly establish committee member roles and responsibilities.

• PETsMART has a clear code of business ethics and policies.

• PETsMART has complaint procedures in place for both associates and others.

• The internal audit department of PETsMART reviews key areas of our business and financial processes and controls, and reports directly to the Audit Committee.

We are committed to improving stockholder value and fully understand and embrace our oversight responsibilities. It is a PETsMART tenet that investors and other users of our financial statements have confidence the financial information we provide is timely, complete, relevant, fair, and accurate. We will continue to strive to strengthen your confidence by our actions.

Philip L. Francis

Philip L. Francis
Chairman and Chief Executive Officer

Timothy E. Kullman

Timothy E. Kullman
Senior Vice President, Chief Financial Officer

Management's Discussion and Analysis of Financial Condition and Results of Operations

Except for the historical information contained herein, the following discussion contains forward-looking statements that involve risks and uncertainties. Our actual results could materially differ from those discussed here.

Overview

Based on our 2003 sales of $3.0 billion, we are the leading provider of products, services, and solutions for the lifetime needs of pets in North America. As of February 1, 2004, we operated 643 retail stores in North America, typically ranging in size from 19,000 to 27,000 square feet. We also reach customers through our direct marketing channels, including PETsMART.com, the internet's most popular pet e-commerce site, a separate web-site dedicated to equine products, and two major branded catalogs.

We complement our extensive product assortment with a wide selection of value-added pet services, including grooming and pet training. Virtually all our stores offer complete pet training services and feature pet styling salons that provide high quality grooming services. In addition, through our strategic relationship with Banfield, The Pet Hospital, full-service veterinary care is available in approximately 350 of our stores.

During 2003, we opened 60 net new stores, and remodeled the final group of approximately 145 stores under a new store format. The new store format eliminates most of the high-steel shelving, organizes consumable and hard good products by pet species, and also places a stronger visual emphasis on in-store services like pet training, grooming, adoptions, and veterinary care. We continue to invest in training for our approximately 26,500 associates as part of our on-going cultural shift with an emphasis on customer service and providing pet solutions. In 2004, we expect to open approximately 90 new stores, net of store closures.

Fiscal 2003 Compared to Fiscal 2002

Net Sales

Net sales increased $300.9 million, or 11.2%, to $2,996.1 million for 2003, from 2002 sales of $2,695.2 million. Store sales increased by $310.6 million as a result of 60 additional net new stores and a 7.0% increase in comparable store sales. Included in store sale, services sales increased by 25.4%, or $39.2 million. The increase in services revenue, which includes grooming, training, and PETsHOTEL operations, was due primarily to higher volume. The increases were partially offset by a decrease in direct marketing channel sales of $9.7 million. As of February 1, 2004, we operated 643 stores, compared with 583 stores as of February 2, 2003.

Gross Profit

Gross profit increased as a percentage of net sales to 30.4% for 2003, from 29.2% for 2002. The increase primarily reflected lower product cost of goods sold and increased sales of higher margin products during 2003, compared with 2002. We also continued to leverage expenses in 2003 through lower inventory shrinkage and occupancy costs as a percentage of sales, compared with 2002.

PETsMART, INC. AND SUBSIDIARIES
CONSOLIDATED BALANCE SHEETS

	February 1, 2004	February 2, 2003
	(In thousands, except par value)	
ASSETS		
Cash and cash equivalents	$ 327,810	$ 253,936
Receivables, net	16,628	9,657
Merchandise inventories	309,140	257,090
Deferred income taxes	2,876	8,809
Prepaid expenses and other current assets	31,198	31,656
Total current assets	687,652	561,148
Property and equipment, net	577,182	489,947
Investments	33,694	33,694
Deferred income taxes	47,463	46,061
Goodwill, net	14,422	14,422
Intangible assets, net	2,621	2,838
Other assets	13,661	10,746
Total assets	$1,376,695	$1,158,856
LIABILITIES AND STOCKHOLDERS' EQUITY		
Accounts payable and bank overdraft	$ 128,303	$ 102,169
Accrued payroll, bonus, and employee benefits	73,058	70,256
Accrued occupancy expenses	27,971	24,285
Current maturities of capital lease obligations	4,964	7,564
Other current liabilities	105,518	84,190
Total current liabilities	339,814	288,464
Capital lease obligations	165,738	159,443
Deferred rents and other noncurrent liabilities	31,988	29,750
Total liabilities	537,540	477,657
Commitments and contingencies Stockholders' Equity:		
Preferred stock; $.0001 par value; 10,000 shares authorized, none issued and outstanding	—	—
Common stock; $.0001 par value; 250,000 shares authorized, 144,813 and 139,914 shares issued	14	14
Additional paid-in capital	705,265	642,767
Deferred compensation	(6,658)	(19)
Retained earnings	174,053	40,239
Accumulated other comprehensive income (loss)	1,458	(1,802)
Less: treasury stock, at cost, 1,406 and 0 shares	(34,977)	—
Total stockholders' equity	839,155	681,199
Total liabilities and stockholders' equity	$1,376,695	$1,158,856

The accompanying notes are an integral part of these consolidated financial statements.

[Note to the student: For the complete accompanying notes, refer to the 2003 Annual Report on the PETsMART Web site.]

Assets = Liabilities + Stockholders' Equity
Feb. 1, 2004: $1,376,695 = $537,540 + $839,155

PETsMART, INC. AND SUBSIDIARIES

CONSOLIDATED STATEMENTS OF OPERATIONS

	Fiscal Year Ended		
	February 1, 2004	February 2, 2003	February 3, 2002
	(In thousands, except per share data)		
Net sales	$2,996,051	$2,695,184	$2,501,012
Cost of sales	2,086,117	1,907,144	1,827,527
Gross profit	909,934	788,040	673,485
Operating expenses	551,388	498,343	483,657
General and administrative expenses	114,618	117,851	119,156
Operating income	243,928	171,846	70,672
Interest income	3,358	2,803	2,007
Interest expense	(19,454)	(20,836)	(27,436)
Income before income tax expense, and minority interest	227,832	153,813	45,243
Income tax expense	88,283	64,958	7,972
Income before minority interest	139,549	88,855	37,271
Minority interest in subsidiary loss	—	—	2,296
Net income	139,549	88,855	39,567
Other comprehensive income (loss), net of income tax expense (benefit):			
Foreign currency translation adjustments	3,260	1,003	(357)
Comprehensive income	$ 142,809	$ 89,858	$ 39,210
Basic earnings per share	$ 0.99	$ 0.66	$ 0.35
Diluted earnings per share	$ 0.95	$ 0.63	$ 0.35

The accompanying notes are an integral part of these consolidated financial statements.

[Note to the student: For the complete accompanying notes, refer to the 2003 Annual Report on the PETsMART Web site.]

Statement of Operations

- **Net sales.** Total sales of the company minus the value of products discounted or returned.
- **Cost of sales.** Actual cost the business incurred for the merchandise sold and services provided to customers during the accounting period.
- **Gross profit.** Net sales minus cost of sales.
- **Operating expenses.**
- **General and administrative expenses.**
- **Operating income.** Income earned from normal business activities.
- **Income tax expense.** Federal and state income taxes based on the company's taxable income.
- **Minority interest in subsidiary loss.** This refers to the loss from PETsMART.com, which sells PETsMART products through its Web site. In the fiscal year ending February 3, 2002, PETsMART owned less than 100 percent of PETsMART.com's stock.
- **Net income.** The "bottom line," or final income after taxes and minority interest.
- **Foreign currency translation adjustments.** PETsMART has stores that use Canadian currency. This line reports the adjustments to convert Canadian financial statements into U.S. dollars.
- **Comprehensive income.** Comprehensive income includes items that businesses must disclose but report separately from net income. PETsMART's only comprehensive income item is the foreign currency translation adjustments.

PETsMART, INC. AND SUBSIDIARIES
CONSOLIDATED STATEMENTS OF STOCKHOLDERS' EQUITY

Amounts (In thousands, except per share data)

	Shares Common Stock	Shares Treasury Stock	Common Stock	Additional Paid-In Capital	Deferred Compensation	Retained Earnings/ Accumulate Deficit	Accumulated Other Comprehensive Income (Loss)	Notes Receivable from Officers	Treasury Stock	Total
BALANCE AT JANUARY 28, 2001	117,753	(6,350)	12	403,758	(663)	(88,183)	(2,448)	(4,319)	(27,578)	280,579
Tax benefit from exercise of stock options				172						172
Issuance of common stock under stock incentive plans	1,231			5,909						5,909
Amortization of deferred compensation, net of award reacquisitions and adjustments	(25)			(263)	367					104
Other comprehensive loss, net of income tax:										
Foreign currency translation adjustments							(357)			(357)
Accrued interest on notes receivable issued to officers								(511)		(511)
Repayments of notes receivable issued to officers								343		343
Retirement of treasury stock	(6,350)	6,350	(1)	(27,577)					27,578	—
Net income						39,567				39,567
BALANCE AT FEBRUARY 3, 2002	112,609	—	11	381,999	(296)	(48,616)	(2,805)	(4,487)	—	325,806
Tax benefit from exercise of stock options				14,112						14,112
Issuance of common stock under stock incentive plans	4,037		1	27,188						27,189
Issuance of common stock under an offering	3,492			43,925						43,925
Conversion of 6¾% Subordinated Convertible Notes to common stock	19,797		2	174,730						174,732
Amortization of deferred compensation, net of award reacquisitions and adjustments	(21)			(351)	277					(74)
Compensation expense related to options held by non-employees				1,164						1,164
Other comprehensive income, net of income tax:										
Foreign currency translation adjustments							1,003			1,003
Accrued interest on notes receivable issued to officers and notes issued to officers								(717)		(717)
Repayments of notes receivable issued to officers								5,204		5,204
Net income						88,855				88,855

PETsMART, INC. AND SUBSIDIARIES
CONSOLIDATED STATEMENTS OF STOCKHOLDERS' EQUITY (continued)

| | Shares | | Amounts (In thousands, except per share data) | | | | | | | |
	Common Stock	Treasury Stock	Common Stock	Additional Paid-In Capital	Deferred Compen- sation	Retained Earnings/ (Accumulate Deficit)	Accumulated Other Comprehensive Income (Loss)	Notes Receivable from Officers	Treasury Stock	Total
BALANCE AT FEBRUARY 2, 2003	139,914	—	14	642,767	(19)	40,239	(1,802)	—	—	681,199
Tax benefit from exercise of stock options				17,743						17,743
Issuance of common stock under stock incentive plans	4,344			36,007						36,007
Amortization of deferred compensation, net of award reacquisitions and adjustments	555			8,748	(6,639)					2,109
Cash Dividends ($0.02 per share)						(5,735)				(5,735)
Other comprehensive income, net of income tax:										
Foreign currency translation adjustments							3,260			3,260
Purchase of treasury stock, at cost		(1,406)							(34,977)	(34,977)
Net income						139,549				139,549
BALANCE AT FEBRUARY 1, 2004	144,813	(1,406)	$14	$705,265	$(6,658)	$174,053	$1,458	$ —	$(34,977)	$839,155

The accompanying notes are an integral part of these consolidated financial statements.

[Note to the student: For the complete accompanying notes, refer to the 2003 Annual Report on the PETsMART Web site.]

Stockholders' Equity

This is called the book value of the owners' stake in the company. It includes proceeds that the company received from the initial and subsequent sales of stock to the public, plus accumulated profits, called retained earnings.

Book value is not the same as the stock's value on the public stock market, called market value. The stock market determines in its own ways whether the company is worth more than the book value of what it owns minus what it owes. For example, a company's stock price changes regularly without regard to the value of the assets and liabilities it uses to run the company.

PETsMART, INC. AND SUBSIDIARIES

CONSOLIDATED STATEMENTS OF CASH FLOWS

	Fiscal Year Ended		
	February 1, 2004	February 2, 2003	February 3, 2002
	(In thousands)		
CASH FLOWS FROM OPERATING ACTIVITIES:			
Net income	$ 139,549	$ 88,855	$ 39,567
Adjustments to reconcile net income to net cash provided by operating activities —			
Depreciation and amortization	95,948	77,268	58,709
Loss on disposal of property and equipment	4,655	4,377	5,796
Elimination of goodwill in PETsMART.com	—	—	8,575
Impairment charge and write-down of subsidiary assets	—	—	9,747
Minority interest in subsidiary	—	—	(2,296)
Capital assets received through vendor settlement	(1,288)	(3,442)	—
Gain on early extinguishment of debt	—	—	(1,190)
Compensation expense related to non-employee options	—	1,164	—
Tax benefit from exercise of stock options	17,743	14,112	172
Deferred income taxes	4,532	(15,941)	(26,556)
Changes in assets and liabilities:			
Receivables, net	(6,646)	13,654	13,525
Merchandise inventories	(50,504)	14,609	48,651
Prepaid expenses and other current assets	1,021	(2,250)	(12,134)
Other noncurrent assets	(2,977)	1,844	(242)
Accounts payable	16,400	5,299	(37,651)
Accrued payroll, bonus, and employee benefits	2,858	18,433	26,251
Accrued occupancy expenses	3,723	(2,584)	6,643
Other current liabilities	17,305	7,052	48,397
Deferred rents and other noncurrent liabilities	4,114	320	4,030
Net cash provided by operating activities	246,433	222,770	189,994
CASH FLOWS FROM INVESTING ACTIVITIES:			
Purchases of property and equipment	(172,227)	(163,698)	(105,104)
Investment in equity holdings	—	(9,500)	(741)
Proceeds from sales of property and equipment	315	674	28,481
Net cash used in investing activities	(171,912)	(172,524)	(77,364)

Statement of Cash Flows

Purpose. This financial statement explains the difference between the company's beginning and ending balances of cash during the accounting period.

Definition. The term *cash flows* includes both cash and cash equivalents. PETsMART considers any liquid investments with a maturity of three months or less to be cash equivalents.

Method. Companies can use either the direct or indirect method to report cash flows from operating activities. The results are the same. PETsMART uses the indirect method. This method starts with net income and adjusts noncash items (such as depreciation) to arrive at the net cash flows provided by operating activities.

The direct method reports all cash receipts and cash payments from operating activities.

PETsMART, INC. AND SUBSIDIARIES

CONSOLIDATED STATEMENTS OF CASH FLOWS (continued)

	Fiscal Year Ended		
	February 1, 2004	February 2, 2003	February 3, 2002
	(In thousands)		
CASH FLOWS FROM FINANCING ACTIVITIES:			
Proceeds from issuance of common stock	36,007	71,114	5,909
Net repayments (issuances) of notes receivable from officers....	—	4,487	(168)
Purchase of treasury stock	(34,977)	—	—
Borrowings from bank credit facility........................	—	—	171,200
Repayments of bank credit facility	—	—	(171,200)
Purchases of subordinated convertible notes	—	(275)	(6,382)
Payments on capital lease obligations.......................	(7,892)	(12,304)	(12,733)
Increase (decrease) in bank overdraft	9,716	3,397	(3,806)
Payments of deferred financing fees	(464)	—	(2,280)
Cash dividends paid to stockholders	(2,871)	—	—
Net cash (used in) provided by financing activities	(481)	66,419	(19,460)
EFFECT OF EXCHANGE RATE CHANGES ON CASH	(166)	160	114
INCREASE IN CASH AND CASH EQUIVALENTS.........	73,874	116,825	93,284
CASH AND CASH EQUIVALENTS AT BEGINNING OF YEAR	253,936	137,111	43,827
CASH AND CASH EQUIVALENTS AT END OF YEAR.....	$ 327,810	$ 253,936	$ 137,111

The accompanying notes are an integral part of these consolidated financial statements.

[Note to the student: For the complete accompanying notes, refer to the 2003 Annual Report on the PETsMART Web site.]

Cash Flows from Operating Activities. Include transactions and events that are the result of actual business operations.

Cash Flows from Investing Activities Include transactions and events that involve plant assets and investment assets except those classified as cash equivalents.

Cash Flows from Financing Activities Include transactions and events that affect long-term liabilities and stockholders' equity accounts.

Additional Reinforcement Problems

Complete appendix problems using: **Manual** Glencoe Working Papers   OR   **Spreadsheet** Templates

SPREADSHEET SMART GUIDE

Step–by–Step Instructions: Problem 3A

1. Select the spreadsheet template for Problem 3A.
2. Enter your name and the date in the spaces provided on the template.
3. Complete the spreadsheet using the instructions in your working papers.
4. Print the spreadsheet and proof your work.
5. Complete the Analyze activity.
6. Save your work and exit the spreadsheet program.

Chapter 3, Problem 3A   Determining the Effects of Business Transactions on the Accounting Equation

Pamela Wong started her own business called Thunder Graphics Desktop Publishing.

Instructions Use the form provided in your working papers. For each of the following transactions:

1. Identify the accounts affected.
2. Write the amount of the increase (+) or decrease (−) in the space provided on the form.
3. Determine the new balance for each account.

Trans. No.	Transactions
1	Pamela Wong, the owner, opened a checking account for the business by depositing $48,000 of her personal funds.
2	Paid the monthly rent of $1,500.
3	Bought office furniture on account for $1,000.
4	Pamela Wong invested $3,000 of office equipment in the business.
5	Paid cash for a new computer for the business, $5,000.
6	Paid for an advertisement in the local newspaper, $200.
7	Completed graphic desktop publishing services for a client and sent a bill for $800.
8	Paid $700 on account for the office furniture bought earlier.
9	Received $500 on account from a client.
10	Pamela Wong withdrew $1,000 for personal use.
11	Received $400 cash for desktop publishing services completed for a client.

Analyze   After analyzing all of the transactions, complete the following tasks.
(a) Compute the amount of total equipment assets.
(b) Compute the amount of total assets.
(c) Compute the total liabilities and owner's equity.
(d) Conclude whether the accounting equation is in balance.

Chapter 4, Problem 4A   Analyzing Transactions Affecting Assets, Liabilities, and Owner's Equity

Thunder Graphics Desktop Publishing had the following transactions. A partial list of the accounts used to record and report business transactions appear below.

101 Cash in Bank	201 Accounts Payable—
110 Accounts Receivable—	Computer Warehouse, Inc.
Roger McFall	205 Accounts Payable—
125 Office Equipment	Pro Computer Company
130 Office Furniture	301 Pamela Wong, Capital
135 Computer Equipment	

Instructions On the forms provided in your working papers:

1. Prepare a T account for each account listed above.
2. Analyze and record each of the following business transactions in the appropriate T accounts. Identify each transaction by number.
3. After recording all transactions, compute and record the account balance and identify the normal side of each T account.
4. Add the balances of those accounts with normal debit balances.
5. Add the balances of those accounts with normal credit balances.

Trans. No.	Transactions
1	Pamela Wong invested $30,000 into the business.
2	Invested office equipment, valued at $650, into the business.
3	Bought a computer on account from Computer Warehouse, Inc. for $9,360.
4	Bought new office equipment for $1,550, Check 100.
5	Bought new office furniture on account from Computer Warehouse, Inc. for $1,250.
6	Sold the older office equipment on account to Roger McFall for $650.
7	Paid $3,000 on account to Computer Warehouse Inc., Check 101.
8	Received $400 on account from Roger McFall.
9	Paid $3,500 on account to Computer Warehouse Inc., Check 102.
10	Bought computer on account from Pro Computer Company for $775.

Analyze Appraise whether the accounting equation is in balance.

Chapter 5, Problem 5A   Analyzing Transactions Affecting Revenue, Expenses, and Withdrawals

Pamela Wong owns and operates Thunder Graphics Desktop Publishing. A partial list of the chart of accounts appears in your working papers.

Instructions On the forms provided in your working papers:

1. Prepare a T account for each account listed.
2. Analyze and record each of the following business transactions in the appropriate T accounts. Identify each transaction by number.
3. After recording all transactions, compute a balance for each account.
4. Test for the equality of debits and credits.

CONTINUE

Trans. No.	Transactions
1	Pamela Wong invested $25,000 in the business.
2	Bought a new computer on account from Computer Warehouse, Inc. for $1,400.
3	Ms. Wong invested office equipment, valued at $650, in the business.
4	Paid the rent for the month, $750, Check 207.
5	Wrote Check 208 for $145 for minor repairs to the equipment.
6	Completed graphics design work on account for Adams, Bell, and Cox, Inc., $850.
7	Paid the $175 utility bill, Check 209.
8	Deposited the daily design receipts in the bank, $1,200.
9	Sent Check 210 for $700 to Computer Warehouse, Inc. as payment on account.
10	Received $425 from Adams, Bell, and Cox, Inc.
11	Ms. Wong withdrew $150 for personal needs.
12	Paid the $85 telephone bill, Check 211.

Analyze Calculate the total expenses the business recorded in the above transactions.

Chapter 6, Problem 6A   Recording General Journal Transactions

Instructions On the form provided in your working papers, record the following transactions for the month of January on page 7 of the general journal for Thunder Graphics Desktop Publishing.

Date	Transactions
Jan. 1	Received $900 for completion of design work for Designers Boutique, Receipt 545.
3	Purchased a desk, chairs, and table valued at $2,400 from Computer Warehouse, Inc. Made a down payment of $400 and agreed to pay the balance within 60 days, Check 801/Invoice CW402.
7	Ran a $300 special feature ad in Solutions Software's monthly magazine on account, Invoice SS60.
10	Completed a $3,500 print production job for Adams, Bell, and Cox, Inc. Received a down payment of $500 and agreed to receive the balance within 30 days, Receipt 546/ Invoice TG90.
15	Pamela Wong withdrew $1,500 from the business for personal use, Check 802.
17	Paid a carpenter $175 to install a new office door, Check 803.
20	Purchased a $4,000 computer system from Pro Computer Company on account, Invoice 783.
27	Paid Computer Warehouse, Inc. $1,000 to apply on our account, Check 804.
29	Wrote Check 805 for $300 to Solutions Software in payment of an ad purchased on July 7.
31	Pamela Wong invested a $200 file cabinet in the business, Memo 40.

Analyze Calculate the total cash the business received during January.

Chapter 7, Journalizing and
Problem 7A Posting Transactions

The balances in the general ledger accounts of Thunder Graphics are shown below.

101	Cash in Bank	$ 10,000
110	Accounts Receivable—Roger McFall	—
125	Office Equipment	2,500
135	Computer Equipment	3,000
201	Accts. Pay.—Computer Warehouse, Inc.	—
301	Pamela Wong, Capital	8,000
302	Pamela Wong, Withdrawals	4,000
401	Design Revenue	9,000
405	Print Production Revenue	4,000
505	Maintenance Expense	1,200
510	Miscellaneous Expense	300

Instructions On the forms provided in your working papers:

1. Open the accounts in the general ledger with their beginning balances as of March 1 of the current year.
2. Record March transactions on page 15 of the general journal.
3. Post each journal entry to the appropriate accounts in the ledger.
4. Prove the ledger by preparing a trial balance.

Date	Transactions
Mar. 1	Pamela Wong invested additional assets in the business: cash, $3,000, and office equipment, $500, Memorandum 75.
5	Paid $600 to Premier Painters for painting the office, Check 912.
7	Discovered that $1,500 in design revenue was incorrectly journalized and posted to the **Print Production Revenue** account last month, Memorandum 76.
9	Purchased $3,600 computer system from Computer Warehouse, Inc. on account, Invoice CW204.
12	Deposited $4,000 into the checking account. $3,000 was earned from design revenue and $1,000 from print production revenue, Receipts 300–310.
15	Completed print production for Roger McFall. Sent him a bill for $600, Invoice TG601.
20	Discovered that $50 in miscellaneous expense was incorrectly journalized and posted to the **Maintenance Expense** account, Memorandum 77.
25	Pamela Wong withdrew $2,000 from the business, Check 913.
28	Received $300 from Roger McFall to apply to his account, Receipt 311.
31	Issued Check 914 for $1,800 to Computer Warehouse, Inc. to apply on our account.

Analyze Compute the change in the cash account for March.

Problems

Chapter 8, Preparing a Six-Column
Problem 8A Work Sheet

The final balances in the general ledger of Thunder Graphics Desktop Publishing at the end of May are listed below.

101	Cash in Bank	$16,095
105	Accts. Rec.—Adams, Bell, and Cox Inc.	1,729
110	Accts. Rec.—Roger McFall	281
113	Accts. Rec.—Designers Boutique	—
115	Accts. Rec.—Pat Cooper	714
120	Office Supplies	228
125	Office Equipment	5,027
130	Office Furniture	2,940
135	Computer Equipment	8,200
201	Accts. Pay.—Computer Warehouse, Inc.	4,027
205	Accts. Pay.—Pro Computer Company	2,441
207	Accts. Pay.—Solutions Software	—
301	Pamela Wong, Capital	24,927
305	Pamela Wong, Withdrawals	2,400
310	Income Summary	—
401	Design Revenue	8,116
405	Print Production Revenue	4,050
501	Advertising Expense	735
505	Maintenance Expense	1,335
510	Miscellaneous Expense	285
520	Rent Expense	3,100
530	Utilities Expense	492

Instructions Use the form in your working papers to prepare a work sheet for the month ended May 30.

Analyze Identify the net income or net loss for the month of May, and explain its effect on the **Pamela Wong, Capital** account.

Chapter 9, Interpreting Financial Information
Problem 9A

You are applying for a job with Thunder Graphics Desktop Publishing. The job includes preparing financial statements. In order to determine your ability to do the job, the owner, Pamela Wong, has given you the following information. At the beginning of the last fiscal period, the **Pamela Wong, Capital** account had a balance of $46,295. At the end of the period, the account showed a balance of $49,152. During the period, Ms. Wong made an additional investment of $2,000 and had withdrawals of $600. The revenue for the period was $12,948.

Analyze Use the form provided in your working papers to compute the total expenses for the period.

Chapter 10, Preparing Closing Entries
Problem 10A

The work sheet of Thunder Graphics Desktop Publishing for the year ended December 31 is presented in your working papers.

Instructions Using the information in the work sheet, prepare the four journal entries to close the temporary capital accounts. Use general journal page 21 provided in your working papers.

Analyze Compute the balance in the **Pamela Wong, Capital** account after the closing entries.

Chapter 11, Recording Deposits in
Problem 11A the Checkbook

On October 20, Pamela Wong, owner of Thunder Graphics Desktop Publishing, deposited the following in the checking account of the business.

Cash: $800
Checks: Boyden Company; drawn on National Bank of Commerce; Monroe; ABA No 45-1204; $50.29.
Gail's Supplies; drawn on Regent Bank; Rayville; ABA No 49-3401; $255.48.
Clinton Co.; drawn on Sun Federal Savings and Loan; Bastrop; ABA No 52-6429; $788.40.

On October 21, Pamela Wong received the electricity bill from Central Utilities for $314.69 for September 17 to October 18 service.

The October bank statement for Thunder Graphics listed a bank service charge of $21.80, dated October 23.

Instructions On the forms provided in your working papers:

1. Complete a deposit slip using the October 20 information.
2. Record the deposit on check stub 1068 using $2,468.14 as the balance brought forward.
3. Complete check stub 1068 and prepare Check 1068 to Central Utilities. Use October 22 as the date and sign your name as drawer.
4. Record this service charge in the checkbook on check stub 1069.
5. Journalize the entry for the bank service charge in the general journal. Use October 25 as the date.
6. Answer the following questions.
   a. What was the amount carried forward from check stub 1067?
   b. What was the checkbook balance before writing Check 1068?
   c. What was the total amount deposited on October 20?
   d. Identify the payee of Check 1068.
   e. What was the balance brought forward on check stub 1069?

Analyze Assess the effect on net income if the bank service charge was not journalized.

Chapter 12, Preparing a Payroll Register
Problem 12A

Thunder Graphics Desktop Publishing has four employees. They are paid on a weekly basis with overtime paid for all hours worked over 40. The overtime rate is 1½ times the regular hourly rate of pay. The names of the employees and other information needed to prepare the payroll are as follows.

Employee No.	Employee	Status	Exemptions	Rate/Hour	Union
173	Don Hoffman	M	1	$6.95	No
168	Manual Gongas	S	0	7.10	Yes
167	Riley Sullivan	M	2	7.40	Yes
175	Marcy Jackson	S	1	6.95	Yes

During the week ended Oct. 15, Gongas worked 41 hours, Sullivan worked 39¼ hours, Jackson worked 42½ hours, and Hoffman worked 38¾ hours.

Instructions On the form provided in your working papers:

1. Prepare a payroll register. The date of payment is October 15. List employees in alphabetical order by last name.
   a. Compute FICA taxes at 6.2% for social security and 1.45% for Medicare.
   b. Use the tax table in Chapter 12 to determine federal income taxes. The state income tax is 1.5% of gross earnings.
   c. All employees have a deduction for hospital insurance that is $4.75 for single employees and $7.85 for married employees.
   d. Union members pay weekly dues of $3.25.
2. After the payroll information is entered in the payroll register, total the columns and check the accuracy of the totals.

Analyze Identify the employee with the highest gross pay and the employee with the highest net pay.

Chapter 13, Recording Payroll Transactions
Problem 13A

Thunder Graphics Desktop Publishing pays its employees each week. The payroll register for the week ended December 17 is shown in your working papers.

Instructions On the general journal form provided in your working papers:

1. Record the December 17 payment of the payroll on page 34, Check 831.
2. Compute the employer's payroll taxes (FICA tax rates, 6.2% social security, 1.45% Medicare; state unemployment tax rate, 5.4%; federal unemployment tax rate, 0.8%).
3. Record the journal entry for the employer's payroll taxes.
4. Record the payment of all FICA and employees' federal income taxes, Check 832. The previous account balances were: **Employees' Federal Income Tax Payable**, $189, **Social Security Tax Payable**, $191.48, and **Medicare Tax Payable**, $44.92.
5. Record the income tax payment to the state, Check 833. The balance in the **Employees' State Income Tax Payable** account before the December 17 payroll was $178.40.

Analyze Calculate the company's total FICA liability for the week ended December 17.

Chapter 14, Recording and Posting Sales and
Problem 14A Cash Receipt Transactions

On January 1, T-Shirt Trends, a merchandising business, had the following balances in its general ledger and accounts receivable subsidiary ledger.

General Ledger	
101 Cash In Bank	$ 7,500
115 Accounts Receivable	10,920
215 Sales Tax Payable	1,500
401 Sales	18,620
405 Sales Discounts	1,400
410 Sales Returns and Allowances	300

Accounts Receivable Subsidiary Ledger	
MOR Morales, Gabriela	$ 420
ROU Roundabout Fashions	3,150
SAM Samstead Fashions	5,250
SAN Sandpiper Sports Club	2,100

Instructions On the forms provided in your working papers:

1. Open the general ledger accounts and record the January 1 balances.
2. Open the customer accounts in the accounts receivable subsidiary ledger and record the January 1 balances.
3. Record the January transactions. Use page 12 in the general journal.
4. Post the transactions to the general ledger and accounts receivable subsidiary ledger accounts.

Date	Transactions
Jan. 1	Received a check for $3,087 from Roundabout Fashions payment of their $3,150 account less a 2% cash discount of $63, Receipt 82.
4	Gabriela Morales notified us that $40 in T-shirts were defective. Issued Credit Memorandum 20 for $42, which includes a 5% sales tax of $2.
9	Sold $1,000 in merchandise plus a sales tax of $50 to Roundabout Fashions on account, Sales Slip 90.
15	Sandpiper Sports Club sent us a check in payment of their $2,100 account less a 2% cash discount, Receipt 83.
17	Granted Samstead Fashions $252 credit for the return of $240 in merchandise plus a $12 sales tax, Credit Memorandum 21.
20	Received a check from Roundabout Fashions in payment of their $1050 account balance less a cash discount of $21, Receipt 84.
25	Samstead Fashions sent us a check for $2,000 to apply on their account, Receipt 85.
31	Cash sales for the month were $5,000 plus $250 in sales tax, Tape 44.
31	Bankcard transactions for the month were $6,000 plus $300 in sales tax, Tape 44.

Analyze Break down January's sales into cash sales (including bankcard) and sales on account.

Chapter 15,   Recording Purchases and Cash
Problem 15A   Payment Transactions

Business transactions for the month of March for T-Shirt Trends are presented below. A partial general ledger appears in your working papers.

Instructions On the form provided in your working papers, record March transactions on page 11 of the general journal.

Date	Transactions
Mar. 2	Issued Check 5500 for $6,790 to Dancing Wind Clothing Manufacturers in payment of their $7,000 invoice less a 3% cash discount.
4	Purchased $2,800 in merchandise on account from Wilmington Shirt Factory, Invoice WSF123, terms 2/10, n/30.
6	Wrote Check 5501 for $180 to Mario's Trucking for delivery of merchandise shipped from Wilmington Shirt Factory, FOB shipping point.
8	Received a credit allowance of $300 from Wilmington Shirt Factory for damaged merchandise, issued Debit Memo 44.
10	Received a premium notice from Keystone Insurance Company for $3,400, issued Check 5502.
12	Bought $175 in supplies from Carter Office Supply on account, Invoice 97, terms n/30.
14	Paid Wilmington Shirt Factory the $2,500 balance owed less a 2% cash discount, Check 5503.
19	Returned $50 in supplies to Carter Office Supply, issued Debit Memorandum 45.
25	Paid employees gross earnings of $4,000. Rates for taxes withheld are: Employees' Federal Income Tax, 15%; State Income Tax, 6%; Social Security Tax, 6.2%; and Medicare Tax, 1.45%. Issued Check 5504 for the net amount.
30	Wrote Check 5505 to Carter Office Supply for the amount due on our account.

Analyze   Determine the number of postings to the accounts payable subsidiary ledger based on the transactions provided.

Chapter 16,   Recording and Posting Sales,
Problem 16A   Cash Receipts, and General
Journal Transactions

T-Shirt Trends, a retail merchandising store, uses special journals for recording its business transactions. On May 1, the store had the following balances in its general ledger and accounts receivable subsidiary ledger accounts.

Problems

General Ledger

101	Cash in Bank	$ 4,700
115	Accounts Receivable	7,250
135	Supplies	300
215	Sales Tax Payable	600
401	Sales	40,000
405	Sales Discounts	1,500
410	Sales Returns and Allowances	500

Accounts Receivable Subsidiary Ledger

HAL	Hal's Fitness Studios	$ 1,500
HIO	Dave Hioki	200
MOR	Gabriela Morales	100
ROU	Roundabout Fashions	2,000
SAM	Samstead Fashions	2,500
SAN	Sandpiper Sports Club	900
WIL	Virginia Williams	50

Instructions On the forms provided in your working papers:

1. Open the accounts and enter beginning balances in T-Shirt Trends' general ledger.
2. Open the customer accounts in the accounts receivable subsidiary ledger and record the beginning balances.
3. Record the following transactions in the sales journal (page 9), the cash receipts journal (page 10), and the general journal (page 2).
4. Post to the customer accounts daily from the journals.
5. Post the entries in the General Credit column of the cash receipts journal daily.
6. Post general journal entries daily.
7. Foot, prove, total, and rule the sales and cash receipts journals.
8. Post the column totals from the special journals.
9. Prepare a schedule of accounts receivable.

Date	Transactions
May 1	Received a check for $50 from Virginia Williams in payment of her account, Receipt 202.
3	Sandpiper Sports Club sent a check for $882 in payment of their $900 account less 2% cash discount, Receipt 203.
5	Sold Virginia Williams $300 in merchandise plus 5% sales tax of $15, Sales Slip 404.
7	Received a check for $1,470 from Hal's Fitness Studios in payment of their $1,500 account balance less 2% cash discount, Receipt 204.
9	Virginia Williams returned $100 in merchandise plus sales tax of $5, issued Credit Memo 50.
11	Sold $700 in merchandise on account to Sandpiper Sports Club plus sales tax of $35, terms, 2/10, n/30, Sales Slip 405.
13	Dave Hioki sent a check for $100 to apply on his account, Receipt 205.
14	Received $25 from the sale of supplies to Hanson's Market, Receipt 206.
15	Cash sales amounted to $2,000 plus sales tax of $100, Tape 27.
15	Bankcard sales were $1,500 plus sales tax of $75, Tape 27.
18	Issued Credit Memo 51 to Roundabout Fashions for $210, which included $200 in defective merchandise and a sales tax of $10. **CONTINUE**

Date	Transactions (cont.)
22	Sold $3,000 in merchandise on account to Hal's Fitness Studios plus 5% sales tax of $150, Sales Slip 406.
23	Samstead Fashions sent us a check for $1,250 to apply to their account, Receipt 207.
24	Received a check for $100 from Gabriela Morales in payment of her account, Receipt 208.
27	Sold Gabriela Morales $200 in merchandise plus 5% sales tax of $10, Sales Slip 407.
28	Roundabout Fashions sent us a check for $900 to apply on their account, Receipt 209.

Analyze **Calculate the percentage of sales on account to total sales in May.**

Chapter 17, Recording Special Journal and Problem 17A General Journal Transactions

T-Shirt Trends, a retail merchandising business, uses special journals to record its business transactions.

Instructions On the forms provided in your working papers:

1. Record the July transactions in the sales journal (page 15), cash receipts journal (page 16), purchases journal (page 15), cash payments journal (page 16), and general journal (page 3).
2. Foot, prove, total, and rule the special journals.
3. Prove cash. The beginning cash in bank balance is $7,500. The check stub balance at the end of the month is $13,409.

Date	Transactions
July 2	Sold $500 in merchandise on account to Dave Hioki plus 5% sales tax, Sales Slip 333.
2	Purchased $1,400 in merchandise on account from Cherokee Productions, Inc., Invoice 7001, terms 2/10, n/30.
3	Issued Check 535 for $1,960 in payment of Dancing Wind Clothing Manufacturers $2,000 invoice less a 2% discount.
4	Received $1,764 from Hal's Fitness Studios in payment of our $1,800 invoice less a 2% discount, Receipt 200.
5	Issued Credit Memo 27 to Gabriela Morales for the return of $100 in merchandise plus $5 sales tax.
6	Purchased $2,000 in store equipment on account from Carter Office Supply, Invoice CO123, terms n/30.
6	Received $2,450 from Sandpiper Sports Club in payment of our $2,500 invoice less a 2% discount, Receipt 201.
7	Sold $1,000 in merchandise on account plus 5% sales tax to Virginia Williams, Sales Slip 334.

CONTINUE

Date	Transactions (cont.)
7	Issued Debit Memo 14 for $300 to Wilmington Shirt Factory for credit taken on damaged merchandise.
8	Wrote Check 536 to Chapel Hills Realtors in payment of monthly rent of $900.
8	Sold old office equipment for $75 cash to Ann Martin, an employee, Receipt 202.
9	Purchased $3,000 in merchandise on account from CompuRite Solutions, Invoice CR79, terms 2/10, n/30.
10	Sold $3,500 in merchandise plus 5% sales tax on account to Roundabout Fashions, Sales Slip 335.
12	Bought $150 in supplies from Palace Party Supplies, on account, Invoice 876.
13	Issued Check 537 for $1,600 to Academy Insurance Company for annual business insurance premium.
14	Wrote Check 538 to CompuRite Solutions for $2,940 in payment of Invoice CR79 for $3,000 less 2% discount.
15	Cash sales amounted to $3,000 plus 5% sales tax, Tape 29.
15	Bankcard sales were $5,000 plus 5% sales tax, Tape 29.
18	Purchased $1,100 in merchandise on account from Sullivan Screen Printers, Invoice 423, terms 2/10, n/30.
20	Purchased $750 in merchandise for cash from Cherokee Productions, Inc., Check 539.
22	Paid the monthly utility bill, $150, Check 540.
23	Purchased $4,500 in merchandise on account from Dancing Wind Clothing Manufacturers, Invoice 777, terms, 2/10, n/30.
24	Received $525 from Dave Hioki to apply on his account, Receipt 203.
24	Wrote Check 541 to Sullivan Screen Printers for $1,078 in payment of Invoice 423 for $1,100 less a 2% discount.
26	Issued Debit Memo 15 for $200 to Dancing Wind Clothing Manufacturers for the return of merchandise.
31	Cash sales amounted to $2,200 plus $110 sales tax, Tape 30.
31	Bank card sales amounted to $1,500 plus $75.00 sales tax, Tape 30.
31	Wrote Check 542 to pay the payroll of $2,000 (Gross Earnings) for the pay period ended July 31. The following amounts were withheld: employees' federal income taxes, $300; FICA taxes, $124 for social security and $29 for Medicare; employees' state income taxes, $60.
31	Recorded the employer's payroll taxes (FICA tax rate, 6.2% for social security, and 1.45% for Medicare; federal unemployment tax rate, 0.8%; and state unemployment rate, 5.4%).

Analyze Identify any transactions recorded in the purchases journal that were *not* for merchandise to resell.

Chapter 18, Problem 18A   Calculating Adjustments and Preparing the Ten-Column Work Sheet

A partially completed work sheet for T-Shirt Trends is shown in your working papers. Adjustments need to be made to the following items at year-end.

Data for Adjustments

Merchandise Inventory, December 31	$47,394
Supplies on hand, December 31	678
Insurance premium expired during the period	1,260
Additional federal corporate income tax owed	168

Instructions On the form provided in your working papers, complete the December 31 work sheet including adjustments for T-Shirt Trends.

> **Analyze** Identify which asset accounts are affected by adjustments.

Chapter 19, Problem 19A   Preparing Financial Statements

The completed work sheet for T-Shirt Trends for the year ended December 31 appears in your working papers.

Instructions On the forms provided in your working papers, prepare the following financial statements:

1. The income statement for the fiscal year ended December 31.
2. A statement of retained earnings.
3. A balance sheet.

> **Analyze** Identify the change in the **Retained Earnings** account during the year.

Chapter 20, Problem 20A   Journalizing Closing Entries

The account balances for T-Shirt Trends appear in your working papers as of December 31.

Instructions On the form provided in your working papers, journalize all the closing entries on page 17 in the general journal.

> **Analyze** Identify the balance in the **Income Summary** account before it was closed to **Retained Earnings**.

Chapter 21, Problem 21A   Recording Stockholders' Equity Transactions

T-Shirt Trends was organized as a publicly held corporation on September 1 and authorized to issue 10,000 shares of $100 par, $8 preferred stock, and 25,000 shares of $50 par common stock.

Instructions On the form provided in your working papers, record the following transactions on page 1 of the general journal.

Date	Transactions
2010	
Sept. 1	Issued 4,000 shares of $8 preferred stock at $100 per share, Receipt 101.
12	Issued 12,000 shares of common stock at $50 per share, Receipt 102.
Nov. 15	Received $52.50 per share for 2,500 shares of common stock issued, Receipt 215.
Dec. 16	Received $5,000 for 50 shares of $8 preferred stock issued, Receipt 298.
2011	
Mar. 24	Issued 1,000 shares of common stock at $55 per share, Receipt 389.
Aug. 15	Declared a dividend of $32,400 on 4,050 shares of $8 preferred stock outstanding, payable on September 15 to stockholders of record on September 1, Memorandum 316.
15	Declared cash dividend of 25¢ per share on 15,500 shares of common stock outstanding, payable on September 30 to stockholders of record on September 1, Memorandum 317.
Sept. 15	Paid preferred stock dividend declared August 15, Check 1763.
30	Paid common stock dividend declared August 15, Check 1802.
Dec. 31	Prepared the closing entries in the general journal to close **Income Summary** for the net income of $102,600 and to close the two Dividends accounts.

Analyze Identify the effect on **Retained Earnings** of the dividends declared on August 15.

Chapter 22, Maintaining a Petty Cash Register
Problem 22A

Maureen Miller operates T-Shirt Trends, a T-shirt specialty business. She established a petty cash fund on February 1 by writing Check 336 for $100. She also records all petty cash disbursements in a petty cash register. Petty cash disbursements are usually made for expenses such as office supplies, delivery expense, miscellaneous expenses, and advertising expense.

Instructions On the forms provided in your working papers:

1. Record the establishment of the petty cash fund on the first line of the petty cash register, page 1.
2. Record each of the following petty cash disbursements in the petty cash register.
3. Foot, prove, total, and rule the petty cash register at the end of the month.
4. Reconcile the petty cash fund. An actual cash count of the fund shows a balance of $5.68.
5. Check 362 was issued to replenish the petty cash fund. Record the replenishment information in the petty cash register.

CONTINUE

Date	Transactions
Feb. 1	Paid $1.20 for postage due on a letter, Voucher 101.
3	Purchased a $9 ad in the *Towne Sentinel* paper, Voucher 102.
5	Bought a ream of typing paper for $4.75, issued Voucher 103.
6	Paid $6 for a mailgram, Voucher 104.
8	Issued Voucher 105 for $9.90 to Express Couriers in payment for the delivery of packages.
10	Paid the newscarrier $4.10 for daily newspapers and issued Voucher 106.
13	Bought pens, pencils, and memo pads for $6.60, Voucher 107.
15	Purchased a $9.50 advertisement in a local trade journal, Voucher 108.
19	Issued Voucher 109 for $8.70 for office supplies.
22	Express Couriers delivered financial data from a client, $9.90, Voucher 110.
26	Issued Voucher 111 for $2.12 for additional postage due on mail.
27	Bought an ad in the *Towne Sentinel* for $8.70 and issued Voucher 112.
28	Purchased a typewriter ribbon for $5.50, issuing Voucher 113.
28	Voided Voucher 114 due to an error.
28	Issued Voucher 115 for $4.10 to the newscarrier.

Analyze At the end of February, conclude whether cash was short or over, by what amount, and whether this should be recorded as a revenue or an expense.

SPREADSHEET SMART GUIDE

Step–by–Step Instructions: Problem 23A

1. Select the spreadsheet template for Problem 23A.
2. Enter your name and the date in the spaces provided on the template.
3. Complete the spreadsheet using the instructions in your working papers.
4. Print the spreadsheet and proof your work.
5. Complete the Analyze activity.
6. Save your work and exit the spreadsheet program.

Chapter 23, Problem 23A Calculating and Recording Depreciation Expense

The T-Shirt Trends Company purchased a delivery truck on October 12, 2009, at a cost of $78,900. The delivery truck has an estimated useful life of three years and an estimated disposal value of $900.

Instructions On the forms provided in your working papers:

1. Prepare a depreciation schedule for the delivery truck using the straight-line method.
2. Record the following transactions on general journal page 41. Post the transactions to the ledger accounts provided.
3. Answer the following questions.
   a. How did you determine the depreciation from October 12 to December 31?
   b. What was the book value of the truck on December 31, 2009?
   c. What was the book value of the truck on December 31, 2010?
   d. How did you determine the annual depreciation on December 31, 2012?

Date	Transactions
2009 Dec. 31	Recorded the adjusting entry for the year's depreciation expense on the delivery truck.
2010 Dec. 31	Recorded the adjusting entry for the year's depreciation expense on the delivery truck.

Analyze Identify how much depreciation expense will be recorded over the useful life of the asset. Identify which account will show the depreciation recorded over the asset's useful life.

Chapter 24, Calculating and Recording
Problem 24A Uncollectible Accounts Expense

T-Shirt Trends uses the allowance method of accounting for uncollectible accounts. At the end of the fiscal period, the following accounts appeared on T-Shirt's trial balance.

Accounts Receivable	$ 18,647.25
Allowance for Uncollectible Accounts	1,060.50
Sales	452,612.00
Sales Discounts	5,431.35
Sales Returns and Allowances	13,578.36
Uncollectible Accounts Expense	0.00

Instructions On the forms provided in your working papers:

1. Determine the amount of the adjustment for uncollectible accounts for the fiscal period ended December 31. Management estimates that uncollectible accounts will be 1.25% of net sales.
2. Journalize the adjusting entry in the general journal, page 10.
3. Post the adjusting entry to the general ledger accounts.
4. Determine the book value of accounts receivable.

Analyze When an account is written off in the next fiscal period, identify the account to be debited.

Chapter 25, Accounting for Inventories
Problem 25A

The Shoooot-It Camera Shop uses a one-year fiscal period beginning January 1. At the beginning of the fiscal period, the shop had a beginning inventory of film valued at $867.90 (526 rolls at $1.65 per roll). During the year, the shop made the following purchases:

January 13	400 rolls of film @ $1.67 =	$ 668
March 2	600 rolls of film @ $1.73 =	1,038
April 14	300 rolls of film @ $1.76 =	528
July 8	700 rolls of film @ $1.79 =	1,253
September 3	200 rolls of film @ $1.81 =	362
November 19	300 rolls of film @ $1.83 =	549
Totals	2,500 rolls	$4,398

There were 621 rolls of film in inventory at the end of the fiscal year.

Instructions On the form provided in your working papers, calculate the cost of the ending inventory using the specific identification, FIFO, LIFO, and weighted average cost methods. For the specific identification method, 165 of the rolls were purchased on September 3 and 456 were purchased on July 8.

Analyze Conclude which inventory valuation method gives the highest value to Shoooot-It's ending inventory.

Chapter 26, Problem 26A — Calculating Current and Future Interest

Frequently, notes that are issued or received in one fiscal period do not mature until the next fiscal period. As a result, the interest expense paid or the interest income received applies to two different fiscal periods. Listed below is the information for 10 different notes.

Instructions On the form provided in your working papers, determine the following for each note.

1. Determine the maturity date. Assume February has 28 days.
2. Determine what portion of the interest applies to the current year and what portion of the interest applies to the following year. December 31 is the end of the fiscal period.

	Amount	Issue Date	Interest Rate	Term	
1.	$ 1,100	December 10	9%	30	days
2.	700	November 21	12%	60	days
3.	17,100	October 10	10%	90	days
4.	4,000	December 5	15%	60	days
5.	15,000	November 10	6.5%	120	days
6.	3,000	September 8	7%	180	days
7.	6,600	November 17	10%	70	days
8.	840	October 1	9.5%	6	months
9.	1,200	December 1	10%	3	months
10.	2,700	August 1	8%	9	months

Analyze Identify which notes will have more interest expense for the following year as compared to the current year.

Chapter 26, Problem 26B — Recording Non-Interest-Bearing Notes Payable

Your company, National Paper Supplies, frequently borrows money for short periods from First Bank by issuing promissory notes.

Instructions In your working papers, record the following transactions on page 6 of the general journal.

Date	Transactions
Jan. 15	Borrowed $12,000 from First Bank by issuing a 90-day, non-interest-bearing note payable that the bank discounted at 12%, Note 45.
Apr. 15	Issued Check 2561 for $12,000 in payment of the note issued Jan.15 and recorded the interest expense.
Oct. 31	Borrowed $18,000 from First Bank by issuing a 120-day, non-interest-bearing note payable that the bank discounted at 13%, Note 46.
Dec. 31	Made an adjusting entry to record the accrued interest expense for Note 46 at year-end.

Analyze Calculate the amount of interest expense incurred in the current year for Notes 45 and 46.

Chapter 27, Recording Partners' Investments
Problem 27A

On June 15, Walter Cohen and Janice Connor agreed to combine their individual sole proprietorships into one firm organized as a partnership called Cohen & Connor Legal Services. The partners were to invest all the assets of their two former businesses. Those assets are listed below.

	Cohen	Connor
Cash	$247,000	$517,500
Accounts Receivable	78,000	
Merchandise Inventory	123,000	
Equipment	154,500	

Instructions Prepare the general journal entries (page 1) required to record the partners' investments. The source document is Memorandum 1.

Analyze Calculate the total of all the assets contributed to the new partnership.

Chapter 28, Liquidation of a Partnership
Problem 28A

The partnership of Joyce, Jane, and Jill is liquidating. The partnership account balances as of November 30 are:

Cash	$ 8,000	Accounts Payable	$ 8,000
Accounts Receivable	16,000	Joyce, Capital	10,800
Inventory	8,000	Jane, Capital	13,200
Equipment	3,000	Jill, Capital	3,000

Profits and losses are shared 4:5:1 to Joyce, Jane, and Jill respectively.

Date	Transactions
Dec. 1	The accounts receivable are sold for $15,000.
8	The inventory is sold for $7,000.
15	The equipment is sold for $5,000.
23	The accounts payable are paid in full.
24	The balance of cash is distributed to the partners.

Instructions Prepare the entries required to liquidate the partnership. Start with general journal page 213.

Analyze Calculate the gain or loss on each asset that was sold.

Answers to Section Assessment Problems

Chapter 1

Problem 1-1
Perform an honest analysis of likes and dislikes. Use the chart on page 7 to help identify skills and traits you possess.

Problem 1-2
Use the personal career profile form (Figure 1-1) as a reference for the types of information. List personal information (values, interests, skills, etc.) and then select three possible careers.

Problem 1-3
The possibility for individuals with accounting degrees vary but include careers as: tax accountants, auditors, management accountants, controllers, or chief financial officers.

Problem 1-4
For the accountants mentioned in the section:
> Drew Taylor – Interested in working with numbers and music.
> Maya Cruz – Involved in environmental causes, studied accounting.
> Jana Passeno – Interested in serving the public; good at decision making.

Problem 1-5
Answers will vary.

Problem 1-6
Answers will vary.

Chapter 2

Problem 2-1
Perform an honest analysis of personal traits. Try to relate the answers to personal activities and experiences that correspond with entrepreneurship.

Problem 2-2
The situations such as these have opposing viewpoints. The drop in sales could signal that a new salesperson is needed or some improvements are in order. Some owners, though, may be reluctant to invest more money in a business where sales are down. You might ask for new paint and awnings in return for the higher rent.

Problem 2-3
Greenwood Sky Divers is the name of the business entity. It has been in business for six years, and is a "going concern." The accounting period for Greenwood Sky Divers is one year.

Chapter 3

Problem 3-1
1. $10,000
2. $26,000
3. $3,000
4. $26,000
5. $6,000
6. $13,000
7. $16,000
8. $8,000
9. $21,000
10. $20,000
11. $35,000
12. $4,500

Problem 3-2
1. Cash in Bank increased $30,000. Jan Swift, Capital increased $30,000.
2. Office Furniture increased $700. Jan Swift, Capital increased $700.
3. Cash in Bank decreased $4,000. Computer Equipment increased $4,000.
4. Office Furniture increased $5,000. Accounts Payable increased $5,000.
5. Accounts Receivable increased by $700. Office Furniture decreased $700.
6. Cash in Bank decreased $2,000. Accounts Payable decreased $2,000.

Problem 3-3
1. Cash in Bank decreased by $50. Jan Swift, Capital decreased by $50.

2. Cash in Bank increased by $1,000. Jan Swift, Capital increased by $1,000.
3. Cash in Bank decreased by $600. Jan Swift, Capital decreased by $600.
4. Cash in Bank decreased by $800. Jan Swift, Capital decreased by $800.
5. Cash in Bank increased by $200. Accounts Receivable decreased by $200.

Chapter 4

Problem 4-1
Accounts Receivable – asset, debit, credit, debit
R. Lewis, Capital – owner's equity, credit, debit, credit
Office Equipment – asset, debit, credit, debit
Accounts Payable – liability, credit, debit, credit

Problem 4-2
1a. The asset Office Equipment is increased. Increases in assets are recorded as debits.
 b. The liability Accounts Payable is increased. Increases in liabilities are recorded as credits.
2a. The asset Office Furniture is increased. Increases in assets are recorded as debits.
 b. The owner's capital account Alice Roberts, Capital is increased. Increases in the owner's capital account are recorded as credits.
3a. The liability Accounts Payable is decreased. Decreases in liabilities are recorded as debits.
 b. The asset Cash in Bank is decreased. Decreases in assets are recorded as credits.

Chapter 5

Problem 5-1
Cash in Bank—asset, debit, credit, debit
Accounts Receivable—asset, debit, credit, debit
Airplanes—asset, debit, credit, debit
Accounts Payable—liability, credit, debit, credit
Caroline Palmer, Capital—owner's equity, credit, debit, credit
Caroline Palmer, Withdrawals—owner's equity, debit, credit, debit
Flying Fees—revenue, credit, debit, credit
Advertising Expense—expense, debit, credit, debit
Food Expense—expense, debit, credit, debit
Fuel and Oil Expense—expense, debit, credit, debit
Repairs Expense—expense, debit, credit, debit

Problem 5-2
1. Dr. Utilities Expense; Cr. Cash in Bank
2. Dr. Accounts Receivable; Cr. Service Fees
3. Dr. John Albers, Withdrawals; Cr. Cash in Bank
4. Dr. Advertising Expense; Cr. Cash in Bank

Chapter 6

Problem 6-1
1. JayMax Office Supply
2. Dario's Accounting Services
3. April 9, 20--
4. 479
5. Fax Machine
6. $299
7. Payable in 30 days

Problem 6-2
Step 1 D
Step 2 F
Step 3 E
Step 4 B
Step 5 A
Step 6 C

Problem 6-3
1. Passenger Van, asset, increase, debit; Cash in Bank, asset, decrease, credit
2. Utilities Expense, expense, increase, debit; Cash in Bank, asset, decrease, credit
3. Cash in Bank, asset, increase, debit; Day Care Fees, revenue, increase, credit

Chapter 7

Problem 7-1
Cash in Bank $10,000 Dr.
Accounts Receivable – Mark Cohen $2,000 Dr.
Accounts Payable – Jenco Industries $1,000 Cr.
Tom Torrie, Capital $35,000 Cr.
Admissions Revenue $0

Problem 7-2
Account Balances:
Cash in Bank $10,000 (Dr.)
David Serlo, Capital $10,000 (Cr.)

Problem 7-3
May 20: Dr. Office Equip. $1,500;
Cr. Computer Equip. $1,500; Memorandum 47

Problem 7-4
July 7: Dr. Advertising Expense $300;
Cr. Rent Expense $300; Memoradum 13

Chapter 8

Problem 8-1
Store Equipment, asset, debit
Rent Expense, expense, debit
Service Fees Revenue, revenue, credit
Accounts Payable–Rubino Supply, liability, credit
Scott Lee, Capital, owner's equity, credit

APPENDIX H Answers

Advertising Expense, expense, debit
Accounts Receivable–John Langer, asset, debit
Scott Lee, Withdrawals, owner's equity, debit
Maintenance Expense, expense, debit
Office Supplies, asset, debit

Problem 8-2
1. Hailey Office Supply
2. Garmot Electrical Co.
3. June 15
4. $6.23
5. Two
6. The invoice number is 220

Problem 8-3
Store Equipment, Balance Sheet, debit
Rent Expense, Income Statement, debit
Service Fees Revenue, Income Statement, credit
Accounts Payable–Rubino Supply, Balance Sheet, credit
Scott Lee, Capital, Balance Sheet, credit
Advertising Expense, Income Statement, debit
Accounts Receivable–John Langer, Balance Sheet, debit
Scott Lee, Withdrawals, Balance Sheet, debit
Maintenance Expense, Income Statement, debit
Office Supplies, Balance Sheet, debit

Chapter 9

Problem 9-1
1. Stratford Learning Ctr.
2. $832
3. Sandra Miller
4. Payment on account
5. August 21
6. Rose Hughes
7. Roxbury, N.Y.

Problem 9-2
1. $62,500
2. $29,915
3. $29,470
4. $10,630
5. $7,060
6. $25,010

Problem 9-3
Return on Sales = 20.53%

Chapter 10

Problem 10-1
1. Dr. Ticket Revenue $6,000; Cr. Income Summary $6,000
2. Dr. Income Summary $3,100; Cr. Gas and Oil Expense $700, Miscellaneous Expense $600, Utilities Expense $1,800

Problem 10-2
1.,2. Dr. Utilities Expense $129; Cr. Cash in Bank $129
3.,4. Dr. Income Summary $129; Cr. Utilities Exp. $129

Problem 10-3
Accts. Rec.–Linda Brown, Balance Sheet, No, Yes
Advertising Expense, Income Statement, Yes, No
Cash in Bank, Balance Sheet, No, Yes
Exercise Class Revenue, Income Statement, Yes, No
Exercise Equipment, Balance Sheet, No, Yes
Income Summary, N/A, Yes, No
Laundry Equipment, Balance Sheet, No, Yes
Maintenance Expense, Income Statement, Yes, No
Membership fees, Income Statement, Yes, No
Miscellaneous Expense, Income Statement, Yes, No
Office Furniture, Balance Sheet, No, Yes
Rent Expense, Income Statement, Yes, No
Repair Tools, Balance Sheet, No, Yes
Ted Chapman, Capital, Balance Sheet, Yes, Yes
Ted Chapman, Withdrawals, Balance Sheet, Yes, No
Utilities Expense, Income Statement, Yes, No

Chapter 11

Problem 11-1
1.,2. Total Deposit $967.08
3. Balance $2,394.24
4. Balance $2,394.24
5. Balance $2,119.24

Problem 11-2
1. $100
2. $25
3. Miscellaneous Expense

Chapter 12

Problem 12-1
Lang, Richard: 38, $7.80, $296.40, $0, $296.40
Longas, Jane: 43, $7.25, $290, $32.63, $322.63
Quinn, Betty: 44 1/4, $8.30, $332.00, $52.91, $384.91
Sullivan, John: 39 1/2, $8.30, $327.85, $0, $327.85
Talbert, Kelly: 40, $7.50, $300.00, $0, $300.00
Trimbell, Gene: 42 1/2, $9.75, $390.00, $36.56, $426.56
Varney, Heidi: 34 1/4, $8.75, $299.69, $0, $299.69
Wallace, Kevin: 46, $9.25, $370.00, $83.25, $453.25

Problem 12-2
Cleary, Kevin: S, 0, $155.60, $9.65, $2.26, $16, $3.11, $31.02, $124.58
Halley, James: S, 1, $184.10, $11.41, $2.67, $12, $3.68, $29.76, $154.34
Hong, Kim: S, 0, $204.65, $12.69, $2.97, $23, $4.09, $42.75, $161.90
Jackson, Marvin: M, 1, $216.40, $13.42, $3.14, $6, $4.33, $26.89, $189.51
Sell, Richard: M, 2, $196.81, $12.20, $2.85, $0, $3.94, $18.99, $177.82
Totals: $957.56, $59.37, $13.89, $57, $19.15, $149.41, $808.15

Problem 12-3

Medicare $4.57

Social Security $19.53

Federal Income Tax $32.00

Problem 12-4

Check number 79, net pay $263.94

Chapter 13

Problem 13-1

1. $2,193.40	4. $33.75
2. $31.80	5. $1,690.15
3. $503.25	

Problem 13-2

Social Security Tax Payable $299.87

Medicare Tax Payable $70.13

Federal Unemployment Tax Payable $38.69

State Unemployment Tax Payable $261.18

Problem 13-3

Employees' federal income tax, payroll entry

Employer's social security tax, payroll tax entry

U.S. savings bonds, payroll entry

Employer's Medicare tax, payroll tax entry

Federal unemployment tax, payroll tax entry

Employees' state income tax, payroll entry

Union dues, payroll entry

Employees' social security tax, payroll entry

State unemployment tax, payroll tax entry

Employees' Medicare tax, payroll entry

Problem 13-4

April 30: Dr. Social Security Tax Payable $318.55, Medicare Tax Payable $113.28, Employees' Federal Income Tax Payable $286; Cr. Cash in Bank $717.83

April 30: Dr. State Income Tax Payable $205.60; Cr. Cash in Bank $205.60

Problem 13-5

Dr. Salaries Exp. $1,328.07, Cr. Soc. Sec. Tax Pay. $82.34, Cr. Medicare Tax Payable $19.26, Cr. Fed. Inc. Tax Pay. $184.00, Cr. State Inc. Tax. Pay. $26.56, Cr. Hosp. Ins. Prem. Pay. $20.00, Cr. Cash in Bank $995.91

Chapter 14

Problem 14-1

Ending account balances:

Cash in Bank $554

Accounts Receivable $3,000

Sales $3,554

Problem 14-2

Sept. 1: Dr. Accts. Rec./James Palmer $318; Cr. Sales $300, Sales Tax Pay. $18; Sales Slip 101

Sept. 4: Dr. Accts. Rec./Anna Rodriguez $636; Cr. Sales $600, Sales Tax Pay. $36; Sales Slip 102

Sept. 7: Dr. Sales Ret. + Allow. $300, Sales Tax Pay. $18;

Cr. Accts. Rec./James Palmer $318; Credit Memo. 15

Sept. 19: Dr. Sales Ret. + Allow. $40, Sales Tax Pay. $2.40; Cr. Accts. Rec./Anna Rodriguez $42.40; Credit Memo. 16

Problem 14-3

May 15: Dr. Cash in Bank $1908; Cr. Sales $1800, Sales Tax Payable $108; Tape 40

Problem 14-4

Mar. 1: Dr. Cash in Bank $140.40; Cr. Sales $130, Sales Tax Payable $10.40; Sales Slip 49

Mar. 5: Dr. Accts. Rec./Kelly Wilson $324; Cr. Sales $300, Sales Tax Payable $24; Sales Slip 55

Mar. 17: Dr. Cash in Bank $810; Cr. Sales $750, Sales Tax Payable $60; Tape 65

Chapter 15

Problem 15-1

1. Case Construction Company
2. Westmoreland Paint and Supply Company
3. 7894
4. November 15, 20--
5. December 1, 20--
6. 25 gallons
7. 5
8. White, gray, brown, beige and peach.
9. $20.00
10. $500.00

Problem 15-2

Sept. 2: Dr. Purchases $900; Cr. Accts. Pay./Sunrise Novelty Supply $900; Invoice SN110

Sept 7: Dr. Accts. Pay./Sunrise Novelty Supply $50; Cr. Purchases Returns and Allowances $50; Debit Memorandum 18

Problem 15-3

Nov. 12: Dr. Accts. Pay./Randall's Café and Bookstore $16.00; Cr. Purchases Ret. and Allow. $16.00; Debit Memo 559

Problem 15-4

May 1: Dr. Purchases $10,500; Cr. Cash in Bank $10,500; Check 1150

May 5: Dr. Transportation In $325; Cr. Cash in Bank $325; Check 1151

May 7: Dr. Prepaid Insurance $2,500; Cr. Cash in Bank $2,500; Check 1152

Chapter 16

Problem 16-1

Ending debit balance:

Accounts Receivable $27,720

Ending credit balances:

Sales Tax Payable $2,020

Sales $37,000

Problem 16-2

1. Sales credit $820, Sales Tax Payable credit $41, Accounts Receivable debit $861
2. Ending Balance $1,161

Problem 16-3

Totals:

General credit $105

Sales credit $6,200

Sales Tax Payable credit $372

Accounts Receivable credit $5,580

Sales Discounts debit $110

Cash in Bank debit $12,147

Total debits/credits $12,257

Chapter 17

Problem 17-1

Column totals:

Accounts Payable $4,550

Purchases $3,600

General $950

Problem 17-2

Ending Cash in Bank balance $5,610.59

Problem 17-3

Nov. 2: Dr. Accts. Pay./Colonial Products Inc. $900; Cr. Purchases Discounts $27, Cash in Bank $873; Check 104

Chapter 18

Problem 18-1

1. More
2. $1,533
3. Merchandise Inventory
4. Income Summary

Problem 18-2

1. Amount $2,454.70
   Account debited, Supplies Expense
   Account credited, Supplies
2. Amount $740
   Account debited, Insurance Expense
   Account credited, Prepaid Insurance
3. Amount $105
   Account debited, Federal Corporate Income Tax Expense
   Account credited, Federal Corporate Income Tax Payable

Problem 18-3

1. $9,995
2. Balance Sheet

3. $3,710
4. $155

Problem 18-4

1. Rotary Supply Corporation
2. 6
3. $177.09
4. Accounts Payable—K & L Electrical
5. Purchases Returns and Allowances

Chapter 19

Problem 19-1

1. Kevin Cleary, Capital
2. Capital Stock
3. Capital Stock and Retained Earnings

Problem 19-2

Subtotal $70.25, sales tax $2.81

Total $73.06

Problem 19-3

1. $96,506
2. $16,703
3. $27,783
4. $17,148

Problem 19-4

1. Office Equipment, Merchandise Inventory.
2. Federal Unemployment Tax Payable.
3. It increased by $18,358.72, or 14.49%.
4. 165.26%
5. The increase in Accounts Receivable indicates that either the company is selling more product or is less efficient at collecting payments. The decrease in Accounts Payable indicates that the company is paying bills earlier. In order to see the whole picture, one would need to analyze the data in relation to the other financial statements.
6. The company prepaid for a new insurance contract.

Chapter 20

Problem 20-1

Accounts Receivable, no

Bankcard Fees Expense, yes, credited, debited

Capital Stock, no

Cash in Bank, no

Equipment, no

Fed. Corp. Income Tax Expense, yes, credited, debited

Fed Corp. Income Tax Payable, no

Income Summary, yes, depends (loss = credit), depends (loss = credit)

Insurance Expense, yes, credited, debited

Merchandise Inventory, no

Miscellaneous Expense, yes, credited, debited

Prepaid Insurance, no

Purchases, yes, credited, debited

Purchases Discounts, yes, debited, credited

Purchases Returns and Allowances, yes, debited, credited

Retained Earnings, yes, depends (loss = debit), depends (loss = credit)

Sales, yes, debited, credited

Sales Discounts, yes, credited, debited

Sales Returns and Allowances, yes, credited, debited

Sales Tax Payable, no

Supplies, no

Supplies Expense, yes, credited, debited

Transportation In, yes, credited, debited

Utilities Expense, yes, credited, debited

Problem 20-2

July 12: Dr. Rent Exp. $750; Cr. Cash in Bank $750

Problem 20-3

Collecting and verifying source documents

Analyzing business transactions

Journalizing business transactions

Posting journal entries to ledgers

Preparing a trial balance

Completing the work sheet

Preparing financial statements

Journalizing and posting adjusting entries

Journalizing and posting closing entries

Preparing a post-closing trial balance

Chapter 21

Problem 21-1

1. 30,000 shares of common stock were issued at par, $10 per share in cash.
2. 2,000 shares of preferred stock were issued at par, $100 per share in cash.
3. 50,000 shares of common stock, par $10, were issued at $14 per share.

Problem 21-2

1. $87,500
2. $262,500

Problem 21-3

Apr. 1: Dr. Dividends—Common $5,679; Cr. Dividends Payable—Common $5,679; Memorandum 37

Apr. 30: Dr. Dividends Payable—Common $5,679; Cr. Cash in Bank $5,679; Check 221

Problem 21-4

The transactions that are reported on the statement of stockholders' equity are 2, 3, 6, and 8.

Chapter 22

Problem 22-1

1. Net cash $1,016.84
   Cash short $5

2. Mar 31: Dr. Cash in Bank $1,016.84, Cash Short and Over $5; Cr. Sales $964, Sales Tax Payable $57.84

Problem 22-2

1. Net cash $1,595.77
   Cash over $10
2. Apr. 14: Dr. Cash in Bank $1,595.77; Cr. Sales 1,496, Sales Tax Pay. $89.77, Cash Short and Over $10

Problem 22-3

Check $39.51; new check stub balance $77,393.35

Chapter 23

Problem 23-1

Accounts Receivable, current

Building, plant

Cash in Bank, current

Change Fund, current

Delivery Equipment, plant

Land, plant

Merchandise Inventory, current

Office Equipment, plant

Office Furniture, plant

Petty Cash Fund, current

Prepaid Insurance, current

Store Equipment, plant

Supplies, current

Problem 23-2

Cash register $420, $60, $40

Computer $5,000, $1,000, $166.67

Conference table $1,800, $72, $36

Delivery truck $30,000, $6,000, $1,500

Desk $2,880, $144, $132

Problem 23-3

Book Value:

10/01/2011, $12,500

12/31/2011, $11,960

12/31/2012, $9,800

12/31/2013, $7,640

12/31/2014, $5,480

12/31/2015, $3,320

09/31/2016, $1,700

Problem 23-4

1. June 4: Dr. Office Equipment $3,456; Cr. Cash in Bank $3,456; Invoice 14492
2. Dec. 31: Dr. Depreciation Expense $379.87; Cr. Accumulated Depreciation $379.87
3. Dec. 31: Dr. Depreciation Expense $651.20; Cr. Accumulated Depreciation $651.20

Problem 23-5

1. Book Value:
   Jan. 7, $2,360
   First year, $1,908

Second year, $1,456
Third year, $1,004
Fourth year, $552
Fifth year, $100

2. Dec. 31: Dr. Depr. Exp.—Office Equip. $452; Cr. Accum. Depr.—Office Equip. $452
3. Dec. 31: Dr. Income Summary $452; Cr. Depr. Exp.—Office Equip. $452
4. $100, Yes

Chapter 24

Problem 24-1
Journal Entries

Apr. 10: Dr. Accts. Rec./Sonya Dickson $630; Cr. Sales $600, Sales Tax Pay. $30; Sales Slip 928

Nov. 30: Dr. Uncollectible Accounts Expense $630; Cr. Accts. Rec./Sonya Dickson $630; Memorandum 78

Dec. 30: Dr. Accts. Rec./Sonya Dickson $630; Cr. Uncollectible Accounts Expense $630; Memorandum 89

Dec. 30: Dr. Cash in Bank $630; Cr. Accts. Rec./Sonya Dickson $630; Receipt 277

Ledger Balances
Ending debit balances:
Cash in Bank $10,058
Accounts Receivable $7,290
Uncollectible Accounts Expense $928
Accts. Rec.—Sonya Dickson $0
Ending credit balances:
Sales Tax Pay. $278
Sales $24,760

Problem 24-2
Journal Entries

May 4: Dr. Allowance for Uncollectible Accounts $1,050; Cr. Accts. Rec./Jack Bowers $1,050; Memorandum 241

Nov. 18: Dr. Accts. Rec./Jack Bowers $1,050; Cr. Allowance for Uncollectible Accounts $1,050; Memorandum 321

Nov. 18: Dr. Cash in Bank $1,050; Cr. Accts. Rec./Jack Bowers $1,050; Receipt 1078

Dec. 31: Dr. Uncollectible Accounts Expense $1,850; Cr. Allowance for Uncollectible Accounts $1,850

Ledger Balances
Ending debit balances:
Cash in Bank $10,470

Accounts Receivable $19,350
Uncollectible Account Expense $1,850
Accts. Rec.—Jack Bowers $0
Ending credit balances:
Allowance for Uncollectible Accounts $3,050

Problem 24-3
(1) Uncollectible Accounts Expense:
   Andrews Co. $2,800.02
   The Book Nook $2,047.81
   Cable Inc. $2,550.00
   Davis Inc. $1,282.40
   Ever-Sharp Co. $1,164.38
(2) Dec. 31: Dr. Uncollectible Accounts Expense $1,282.40; Cr. Allowance for Uncollectible Accounts $1,282.40

Chapter 25

Problem 25-1
Preparing Inventory Reports
Total value of inventory $794.10

Problem 25-2
Determining Inventory Costs
   a. $472.55
   b. $477.25
   c. $465.25
   d. $470.52

Problem 25-3
1. Ending inventory $575.90
2. Gross profit $214.30

Chapter 26

Problem 26-1
1. Interest $75.62, Maturity value $4,075.62
2. Interest $289.73, Maturity value $10,289.73
3. Interest $136.23, Maturity value $6,636.23
4. Interest $36.25, Maturity value $936.25

Problem 26-2
1. Interest $22.19
2. Interest $69.04
3. Interest $288.00
4. Interest $123.29

Problem 26-3
1. Cash in Bank $9,000
2. Notes Payable $9,000
3. Cash in Bank, asset; Notes Payable, liability
4. $9,355.07

Problem 26-4
1. Cash in Bank is debited for $9,802.74; Discount on Notes Payable is debited for $197.26; Notes Payable is credited for $10,000.
2. Discount $197.26, Proceeds $9,802.74

Problem 26-5
June 12: Dr. Cash in Bank $2,426.03, Discount on Notes Payable $73.97; Cr. Notes Payable $2,500; Note 55

Chapter 27
Problem 27-1
June 1: Dr. Cash in Bank $1,200, Accts. Rec. $2,000, Merchandise Inventory $8,000, Equiment $5,000, Van $12,000, Office Furniture $1,000; Cr. Matthew Deck, Capital $29,200; Memorandum 1

June 1: Dr. Cash in Bank $2,300, Accts. Rec. $7,000, Merchandise Inventory $5,000, Equipment $12,000, Office Furniture $500; Cr. Jennifer Rusk, Capital $26,800; Memorandum 1

Problem 27-2
1. 3/4, 1/4
2. 5/9, 3/9, 1/9
3. 3/8, 2/8, 2/8, 1/8
4. 2/4, 1/4, 1/4
5. 2/3, 1/3

Problem 27-3
Nov. 13: Dr. Cash in Bank $20,000; Cr. Walter, Capital $8,000, Yount, Capital $12,000

Chapter 28
Problem 28-1
Division of Net Income:
Goldman $14,000
Jones $21,000
Partners' Equity:
Goldman $37,000
Jones $68,000

Problem 28-2
Shares of gain:
Bass $7,200
Buie $7,200
Anderson $3,600
Norman $3,600
Dunham $2,400
Ruppe $2,400

Problem 28-3
Sept. 4: Dr. Cash in Bank $38,000, Gunther, Capital $3,500, Pertee, Capital $3,500; Cr. Merchandise Inventory $45,000

Sept. 15: Dr. Cash in Bank $29,000; Cr. Gunther, Capital $1,000, Pertee, Capital $1,000, Office Equipment $27,000

Chapter 29
Problem 29-1
Weaknesses might include ethics programs that do not provide clear guidelines for action when faced with various situations. Some employees might not report violations out of fear of retribution. A business ethics plan that includes well-communicated methods for reporting violations (like a Web site, an ethics office, or ethics seminars) could help remedy this problem.

Problem 29-2
The law covers most major ideas about the public's definition of proper and improper behavior, but it does not offer guidance on every dilemma. Ethical concepts cover more subtle instances, where the proper course of action might not be so clear-cut. Use the following resources to find an example in which the actions of a business were legal but might be considered unethical: *BusinessWeek* Online, *The Wall Street Journal*, local newspapers, and business magazines.

Problem 29-3
The following behaviors are possible violations of principles of professional conduct. Marcus appears to be recording transactions in a misleading manner in order to increase the amount of profit reported for the business. This violates the accounting principle of integrity. Jennifer has not been appropriately trained and educated for accounting work. This violates the principle of competence. Ing's behavior violates confidentiality when he shares confidential financial information with anyone not approved to receive it.

GLOSSARY

A

account A subdivision under assets, liabilities, or owner's equity that summarizes the changes and shows the balance for a specific item.

accountant A person who handles a broad range of responsibilities, makes business decisions, and prepares and interprets financial reports.

accounting clerk An entry-level job that can vary from specializing in one part of the system to doing a wide range of tasks.

accounting cycle Activities performed in an accounting period that help the business keep its records in an orderly fashion.

accounting equation The accounting relationship between assets and the two types of equities. Assets = liabilities + owner's equity.

accounting period The period of time covered by an accounting report.

accounting system A system designed to collect, document, and report on business transactions.

accounts payable The amount of money owed, or payable, to the creditors of a business.

accounts payable subsidiary ledger A separate ledger that contains accounts for all creditors; it is summarized in the **Accounts Payable** controlling account in the general ledger.

accounts receivable The amount of money owed to a business by its credit customers.

accounts receivable subsidiary ledger A separate ledger that contains accounts for each charge customer; it is summarized in the **Accounts Receivable** controlling account in the general ledger.

accrual basis of accounting A system that recognizes and records revenues and expenses when they are earned and incurred rather than when cash is collected and paid.

accruals Transactions that *have not yet been recorded* in the accounts because a revenue has been earned but not yet received or an expense has been incurred but not yet paid.

accrued expense A business expense that has been incurred but not paid or recorded.

accrued revenue Business revenue that has been earned but not received or recorded.

accumulated depreciation The total amount of depreciation for a plant asset that has been recorded up to a specific point in time.

accumulated earnings The employee's year-to-date gross earnings.

adjusted gross income The total income for the year after adjustments on a federal income tax return.

adjusting entries Journal entries that update the general ledger accounts at the end of a period.

adjustment An amount that is added to or subtracted from an account balance to bring that balance up to date.

administrative expenses Costs related to the management of a business (for example, office expenses).

aging of accounts receivable method A method of estimating the uncollectible accounts expense in which each customer's account is classified by age; the age classifications are multiplied by certain percentages; and the total estimated uncollectible amounts are added to determine the end-of-period balance of **Allowance for Uncollectible Accounts.**

allowance method A procedure for uncollectible accounts receivable; the business matches the estimated uncollectible accounts expense with the sales made during the same period.

assets Property or items of value owned by a business.

audit The review of a company's accounting systems and financial statements to confirm that they follow generally accepted accounting principles.

authorized capital stock The maximum number of shares of stock a corporation may issue.

automated teller machine (ATM) Computer terminal where account holders can conduct various banking activities.

B

balance sheet A report of the balances in the permanent accounts on a specific date.

bank discount The interest charge deducted in advance on a non-interest-bearing note payable.

bank service charge A fee the bank charges for maintaining bank records and processing bank statement items for the depositor.

bank statement An itemized record of all the transactions in a depositor's account over a given period, usually a month.

bankcard A bank-issued card honored by many businesses that can be used to withdraw cash and to make payments for goods and services at many businesses instead of writing checks; also called a *debit card, ATM card,* or *check card.*

bankcard fee A fee charged for handling bankcard sales slips; usually based on the total amounts recorded on the sales slips processed.

base period A period that is used for comparison in financial statements analysis.

beginning inventory The merchandise a business has on hand at the beginning of a period.

blank endorsement A check endorsement that includes only the signature or stamp of the depositor. It does not specify the new owner of the check.

board of directors A group of people, elected by the stockholders, who govern and are responsible for the affairs of a corporation.

book value The original cost of a plant asset minus accumulated depreciation.

book value of accounts receivable The amount the business can reasonably expect to collect from its accounts receivable.

business entity The accounting assumption that a business exists independently of its owner's personal holdings. The accounting records and reports are maintained separately and contain financial information related only to the business.

business ethics The policies and practices that reflect a company's core values such as honesty, trust, respect, and fairness.

business transaction An economic event that causes a change—either an increase or a decrease—in assets, liabilities, or owner's equity.

C

calendar year Accounting period that begins on January 1 and ends on December 31.

canceled check A check paid by the bank, deducted from the depositor's account, and returned with the bank statement to the account holder.

capital Money supplied by investors, banks, or owners of a business.

Capital Stock The account that represents the total amount of investment in the corporation by its stockholders (owners).

cash basis of accounting A system that recognizes and records revenue only when cash is received and expenses only when cash is paid out.

cash discount The amount a customer can deduct from the total owed for purchased merchandise if payment is made within a certain time; also called *sales discount.*

cash inflows Receipts of cash.

cash outflows Payments of cash.

cash payments journal A special journal used to record all transactions in which cash is paid out or decreased.

cash receipt The cash received by a business in a single transaction.

cash receipts journal A special journal used to record all transactions in which cash is received.

cash sale A transaction in which the business receives full payment for the merchandise sold at the time of the sale.

certified public accountant (CPA) A licensed professional who has met certain education and experience requirements and passed a national test.

change fund An amount of money, consisting of varying denominations of bills and coins, that is used to make change in cash transactions.

charge customer A customer to whom a sale on account is made.

chart of accounts A list of all accounts used by a business.

charter The legal permission, granted by a state, that gives a corporation certain rights and privileges and spells out the rules under which the corporation is to operate.

check A written order from a depositor telling the bank to pay a stated amount of cash to the person or business named on the check.

Check 21 The Check Clearing for the 21st Century Act; it allows the conversion of a paper check to an electronic image that can be quickly processed between banks.

check stub A source document that lists the same information that appears on a check and shows the balance in the checking account before and after each check is written.

checking account An account that allows a person or business to deposit cash in a bank and then write checks and make ATM withdrawals and purchases against the account balance.

closely held corporation A corporation, often owned by a few people or by a family, that does not offer its stock for sale to the general public.

closing entries Journal entries made to close, or reduce to zero, the balances in the temporary accounts and to transfer the net income or net loss for the period to the capital account.

code of ethics A formal policy of rules and guidelines that describes the standards of conduct that a company expects from all its employees.

combination journal A multicolumn journal that combines the features of the general journal and the special journals into one book of original entry.

commission An amount paid to an employee based on a percentage of the employee's sales.

common stock The stock issued by a corporation when it issues only one class of stock.

comparability Accounting characteristic that allows the financial information to be compared from one period to another period; also allows the comparison of financial information between businesses.

competence The principle that requires accountants to have the knowledge, skills, and experience needed to complete a task.

compound entry A journal entry with two or more debits or two or more credits.

computerized accounting system A type of accounting system in which information is recorded by entering it into a computer.

confidentiality The principle that requires accountants to protect and not disclose information acquired in the course of work unless they have the appropriate legal or professional responsibility to do so.

conservatism principle Accounting principle requiring that when there is a choice, accountants choose the safer or more conservative method that is least likely to result in an overstatement of income or assets.

consistency principle Accounting principle requiring a business to apply the same accounting methods in the same way from one period to the next.

contra account An account whose balance is a decrease to its related account.

controlling account An account that serves as a control on the accuracy of the account balances in the subsidiary ledger; its balance must equal the total of all account balances in the subsidiary ledger.

corporation A business organization recognized by law to have a life of its own.

correcting entry An entry made to correct an error in a journal entry discovered *after* posting.

cost of merchandise The actual cost to the business of the merchandise sold to customers.

credit An agreement to pay for a purchase at a later time; an entry on the right side of an account.

credit card A card, issued by a business and bearing a customer's name and account number, which facilitates the sale on account.

credit memorandum A form that lists the details of a sales return or sales allowance.

credit terms Terms that state the time allowed for payment for a sale on account.

creditor A business or person to whom money is owed.

current assets The assets that are either used up or converted to cash during the normal operating cycle of the business.

current liabilities The debts of the business that must be paid within the next accounting period.

current ratio The relationship between current assets and current liabilities; calculated by dividing current assets by current liabilities.

D

debit An entry on the left side of an account.

debit memorandum The form a business uses to notify its suppliers (creditors) of a return or to request an allowance.

deduction An amount that is subtracted from an employee's gross earnings.

deferrals Transactions that *have been recorded* in the accounts because cash has been received but not yet earned or cash has been paid but the expenses not yet incurred.

deposit slip A bank form used to list the cash and checks to be deposited.

depositor A person or business that has cash on deposit in a bank.

depreciation Allocating a plant asset's cost over its useful life.

direct deposit Depositing net pay directly into an employee's personal bank account through electronic funds transfer.

direct write-off method A procedure for uncollectible accounts receivable; the business removes the uncollectible account from its accounting records when it determines the amount is not going to be paid.

discount period The period of time within which an invoice must be paid if a discount is to be taken.

disposal value The estimated value of a plant asset at its replacement time; also called *salvage value*.

dissolution A legal change to the partnership such as a change in partners that does not generally affect the operations of the business.

dividend A distribution of cash to stockholders of a corporation; reduces the corporation's retained earnings.

double-entry accounting A system that recognizes the different sides of business transactions as *debits* and *credits*.

drawee The bank on which a check is written.

drawer The person who signs a check.

due date The date by which an invoice must be paid.

E

e-file A system for filing tax returns with the IRS using a computer connected to the Internet.

electronic badge reader An electronic device that scans the magnetic strip containing employee information on an employee's identification badge and then transfers the information directly to a computer.

Electronic Federal Tax Payment System (EFTPS) System used by large businesses to deposit federal tax payments by electronic funds transfer.

electronic funds transfer system (EFTS) A system that allows banks to transfer funds among accounts quickly and accurately without the exchange of checks.

employee's earnings record A record prepared for each employee that contains all payroll information related to the employee; it is kept on a quarterly basis.

ending inventory The merchandise a business has on hand at the end of a period.

endorsement An authorized signature written or stamped on the back of a check that transfers ownership of the check.

entrepreneur A person who transforms ideas for products or services into real-world businesses.

equities The total financial claims to the assets of a business.

ethics The study of our notions of right and wrong; a set of basic principles.

ethics officer The employee directly responsible for creating business conduct programs, evaluating performance, and enforcing standards of conduct.

expense The cost of goods or services used to operate a business.

external controls Measures and procedures provided outside the business to protect cash and other assets.

F

face value The amount written on the face of a promissory note; also called *principal*.

Federal Unemployment Tax Act (FUTA) Law that requires employers to pay unemployment taxes to the federal government.

financial accounting The type of accounting that focuses on reporting information to *external* users.

financial claim Legal right to an item.

financial reports Documents that present summarized information about the financial status of a business.

financial statements Reports prepared to summarize the changes resulting from business transactions that occur during an accounting period.

financing activities Business activities involving debt and equity transactions.

first-in, first-out method (FIFO) An inventory costing method that assumes that the first items purchased (first in) were the first items sold (first out).

fiscal year An accounting period of twelve months.

FOB destination Shipping term specifying that the supplier pays the shipping cost to the buyer's destination.

FOB shipping point Shipping term specifying that the buyer pays the shipping charge from the supplier's shipping point.

footing A column total written in small pencil figures.

Form 940 Form that reports the employer's federal unemployment taxes.

Form 941 Employer's Quarterly Federal Tax Return; form used to report accumulated amounts of FICA and federal income tax withheld from employees' earnings for the quarter, as well as FICA tax owed by the employer.

Form 1040EZ Federal income tax return; most students file this return.

Form 1099 Form used by banks and other institutions to report interest earned on savings accounts and other income.

Form 8109 Federal Deposit Tax Coupon; form sent with payment for FICA and federal income taxes or federal unemployment taxes.

Form W-2 Wage and Tax Statement; form that summarizes an employee's earnings and amounts withheld for federal, state, and local taxes.

Form W-3 Transmittal of Wage and Tax Statements; summarizes the information contained on the employees' Forms W-2 and accompanies the Forms W-2 sent to the federal government.

Form W-4 A form employees complete when they begin work; it indicates to the employer how much to withhold for federal income tax from each paycheck.

for-profit business A business that operates to earn money for its owners.

401(k) plan A voluntary payroll deduction from gross earnings; the employee does not pay income tax on the amount contributed until the money is withdrawn from the plan, usually after age 59½.

free enterprise system A system in which individuals are free to produce the goods and services they choose.

full disclosure Accounting principle requiring a financial report to include enough information so that it is complete.

G

general journal An all-purpose journal in which all the transactions of a business may be recorded.

general ledger A permanent record organized by account number.

generally accepted accounting principles (GAAP) The set of rules that all accountants use to prepare financial reports.

going concern The accounting assumption that a business is expected to operate indefinitely.

gross earnings The total amount of money an employee earns in a pay period; also called *gross pay*.

gross profit on sales The amount of profit made during the fiscal period before expenses are deducted; it is found by subtracting the cost of merchandise sold from net sales.

H

home keys The 4, 5, 6 keys on a numeric keypad.

horizontal analysis The comparison of the same item(s) on financial statements for two or more accounting periods or dates; used to determine changes from one period to another.

I

imaged check A copy of a canceled check; it is sent with the bank statement in place of the original canceled check.

income statement A report of the net income or net loss for a specific period; sometimes called a *profit-and-loss statement* or *earnings statement*.

Income Summary account The general ledger account used to summarize the revenue and expenses for the period.

independence The principle that requires accountants to have no financial interest in the company being audited.

integrity The principle that requires accountants to choose what is right and just over what is wrong.

interest The fee charged for the use of money.

interest rate The fee charged for the use of money stated as a percentage of the principal.

interest-bearing note payable A note that requires the face value plus interest to be paid on the maturity date.

internal controls Procedures within the business that are designed to protect cash and other assets and to keep reliable records.

inventory The items of merchandise a business has in stock.

investing activities Business activities involving investments and plant assets.

investment Money or other property provided for the purpose of making a profit.

invoice A source document that lists the quantity, description, unit price, and total cost of the items sold and shipped to a buyer.

issue date The date on which a promissory note is written.

J

journal A chronological record of the transactions of a business.

journalizing The process of recording business transactions in a journal.

L

last-in, first-out method (LIFO) An inventory costing method that assumes that the last items purchased (last in) are the first items sold (first out).

ledger A group of accounts; also referred to as a *general ledger.*

ledger account form The accounting stationery used to record financial information about specific accounts.

liabilities Amounts owed to creditors; the claims of creditors to the assets of a business.

lifestyle The way a person uses time, energy, and resources.

liquidation When the business ceases to exist and dissolution is complete, all partnership assets are converted to cash, all debts are paid, and any remaining cash is distributed to the individual partners.

liquidity ratio The measure of a business's ability to pay its current debts as they become due and to provide for an unexpected need for cash.

long-term liabilities Debts that are not required to be paid within the next accounting period.

loss The result when a business spends more money than it earns.

lower-of-cost-or-market The requirement that ending merchandise inventory be stated at the lesser of cost (calculated using one of the four inventory costing methods) or market value.

M

maker The person or business promising to repay the principal and interest when a loan is made.

management accounting The type of accounting that focuses on reporting information to management; often referred to as accounting for *internal* users of accounting information.

manual accounting system A type of accounting system in which information is processed by hand.

manufacturing business A business that buys raw materials and transforms them into finished products by using labor and machinery.

market value The current price that is charged for a similar item of merchandise in the market.

matching principle Principle requiring that the expenses incurred in an accounting period are matched with revenue earned in the same period.

materiality An accounting guideline stating that information considered important (relative to the other information) should be included in financial reports.

maturity date The due date of a promissory note; the date on which the principal and interest must be paid.

maturity value The principal plus interest that must be paid on a promissory note's due date.

memorandum A brief written message that describes a transaction that takes place within a business.

merchandise Goods bought to resell to customers.

merchandising business A business that buys finished goods and resells them to individuals or other businesses.

mutual agency The legal right of any partner to enter into agreements for the business that are binding on all other partners.

N

net income The amount by which total revenue exceeds total expenses for the accounting period.

net loss The amount by which total expenses exceed total revenue for the accounting period.

net pay The amount left after total deductions have been subtracted from gross earnings.

net purchases The total cost of all merchandise purchased during a period, less any purchases discounts, returns, and allowances.

net sales The amount of sales for the period less any sales discounts, returns, and allowances.

networking Making contacts with people to share information and advice.

non-interest-bearing note payable A note from which the interest is deducted in advance from the face value of the note; no interest rate is stated on the note.

normal balance The increase side of an account. The word *normal* here means usual.

note payable A promissory note issued to a creditor.

note receivable A promissory note that a business accepts from a customer.

not-for-profit organization An organization that operates for purposes other than making a profit.

NSF check A check returned to the depositor by the bank because the drawer's checking account does not have sufficient funds to cover the amount; also called *dishonored check.*

O

objectivity The principle that requires accountants to be impartial, honest, and free of conflicts of interest.

on account The purchase of an item on credit.

online The link of a terminal or cash register to a centralized computer system.

operating activities Business activities involving normal business operations.

operating expenses The cash spent or assets consumed to earn revenue for a business; operating expenses do not include federal income tax expense.

operating income The excess of gross profit over operating expenses; taxable income.

other expense A nonoperating expense; an expense that does not result from the normal operations of the business.

other revenue Nonoperating revenue that a business receives from activities other than its normal operations.

outstanding check A check that has been written but has not yet been presented to the bank for payment.

outstanding deposit A deposit that has been made and recorded in the checkbook but does not yet appear on the bank statement.

overtime rate Pay rate employers are required to pay certain employees covered by state and federal laws; the Fair Labor Standards Act of 1938 sets the rate at 1½ times the regular hourly rate after 40 hours per week.

owner's equity The owner's claims to the assets of the business.

P

packing slip A form that lists the items included in the shipment.

Paid-in Capital in Excess of Par The account that represents the amount of cash received by a corporation over the stock's par value.

par value The dollar amount assigned to each share of stock before it is sold to the public; used to determine the amount credited to the capital stock account.

partnership A business owned by two or more persons, called *partners,* who agree to operate the business as co-owners.

partnership agreement A written agreement that states the terms under which the partnership will operate.

pay period The amount of time over which an employee is paid.

payee The person or business to which a check is written or a note is payable.

payroll A list of the employees and the payments due to each employee for a specific pay period.

payroll clerk An employee responsible for preparing the payroll.

payroll register A form that summarizes information about employees' earnings for each pay period.

Payroll Tax Expense The expense account used to record the employer's payroll taxes (FICA, FUTA, SUTA).

percentage of net sales method A method of estimating uncollectible accounts expense in which a business assumes that a certain percentage of each year's net sales will be uncollectible.

periodic inventory system An inventory system which requires a physical count of the merchandise on hand to update inventory records.

permanent accounts Accounts that are continuous from one accounting period to the next; balances are carried forward to the next period (for example, assets, liabilities, and the owner's capital account).

perpetual inventory system An inventory system that keeps a constant, up-to-date record of the amount of merchandise on hand.

personal interest tests Tests that help individuals to identify their preferences and to match interests to potential careers.

personality A set of unique qualities that makes a person different from all other people.

petty cash disbursement Any payment made from the petty cash fund.

petty cash fund Cash kept on hand for making small, incidental cash payments.

petty cash register A record of all disbursements made from the petty cash fund.

petty cash requisition A form requesting money to replenish the petty cash fund.

petty cash voucher A form that provides proof of payment from the petty cash fund.

petty cashier The person responsible for maintaining the petty cash fund and for making petty cash disbursements.

physical inventory An actual count of all merchandise on hand and available for sale.

piece rate A rate of pay based on the number of items produced.

plant assets Long-lived assets that are used in the production or sale of other assets or services over several accounting periods.

point-of-sale terminal (POS) An electronic cash register.

post-closing trial balance A list of the permanent general ledger account balances; it is prepared to prove the ledger after the closing entries are posted.

postdated check A check that has a future date instead of the actual date; it should not be deposited until the date on the check.

posting The process of transferring information from the journal to individual general ledger accounts.

preferred stock Stock whose owners have certain privileges over common stockholders.

premium The amount paid for insurance.

prepaid expense An expense paid in advance.

principal The amount of money borrowed on a promissory note.

proceeds The cash actually received by the borrower on a non-interest-bearing note payable.

processing stamp A stamp placed on a creditor's invoice that outlines the steps to be followed in processing the invoice for payment.

profit The amount earned above the amount of expense incurred to keep the business operating.

profitability ratio A ratio used to evaluate the earnings performance of a business during the accounting period.

promissory note A written promise to pay a certain amount of money at a specific time.

property Anything of value that a business or person owns and therefore controls.

proving cash The process of verifying that cash recorded in the accounting records agrees with the amount entered in the checkbook.

proving the ledger Adding all debit balances and all credit balances of ledger accounts, and then comparing the two totals to see whether they are equal.

proxy A document that transfers a stockholder's voting rights to someone else.

public accounting firm A business that provides a variety of accounting services including the independent audit.

publicly held corporation A corporation whose stock is widely held, has a large market, and is usually traded on a stock exchange.

purchase order A written *offer* to a supplier to buy specified items.

purchase requisition A written request that a specified item or items be ordered.

Purchases account The account used to record the cost of merchandise purchased during a period.

purchases allowance A price reduction given when a business keeps unsatisfactory merchandise it has bought.

purchases discount The buyer's cash discount for early payment of an invoice on account.

purchases journal A special journal used to record all transactions in which items are bought on account.

purchases return The return of merchandise bought on account to the supplier for full credit.

Q

quick ratio A measure of the relationship between short-term assets and current liabilities; calculated by dividing the total cash and receivables by the current liabilities.

R

ratio analysis The process of evaluating the relationship between various amounts in the financial statements.

receipt A source document that serves as a record of cash received.

reconciling the bank statement The process of determining any differences between a bank statement balance and a checkbook balance.

relevance An accounting characteristic requiring that all information that would affect the decisions of financial statement users be disclosed in the financial reports.

reliability A characteristic requiring that accounting information be reasonably free of bias and error.

report form A balance sheet format that lists classifications one under another.

restrictive endorsement A check endorsement that transfers ownership to a specific owner *and* limits how the check may be handled (for example, *For Deposit Only*).

retailer A business that sells to the final user, the consumer.

retained earnings A corporation's accumulated net income that is not distributed to stockholders.

return on sales A ratio that examines the portion of each sales dollar that represents profit; calculated by dividing net income by sales.

revenue Income earned from the sale of goods and services.

revenue recognition The GAAP principle that revenue is recorded on the date it is earned even if cash has not been received.

reversing entry An optional general journal entry recorded on the first day of the new period that is the exact opposite of a specific adjusting entry made in the previous period; it simplifies the recordkeeping in the new period.

ruling Drawing a line; a single *rule* (line) drawn under a column of figures indicates that the entries above the rule are to be added or subtracted. If an amount is a total and no further processing is needed, a double rule is drawn under it.

S

Salaries Expense The expense account used to record employees' earnings.

salary A fixed amount of money paid to an employee for each pay period.

sale on account The sale of merchandise that will be paid for at a later date.

Sales A revenue account to record the amount of the merchandise sold.

sales allowance A price reduction granted for damaged goods kept by the customer.

sales discount See *cash discount*.

sales journal A special journal used to record only the sale of merchandise on account.

sales return Any merchandise returned for credit or a cash refund.

sales slip A form that lists the details of a sale.

sales tax A tax levied by a city or state on the retail sale of goods and services.

schedule of accounts payable A list of all creditors in the accounts payable ledger, the balance in each account, and the total amount owed to all creditors.

schedule of accounts receivable A list of each charge customer, the balance in the customer's account, and the total amount due from all customers.

selling expenses Expenses a business incurs to sell or market its merchandise or services.

service business A business that provides a needed service for a fee.

signature card A bank form containing the signature(s) of the person(s) authorized to write checks on a checking account.

skills The activities that a person does well.

slide error Error that occurs when a decimal point is moved by mistake.

sole proprietorship A business owned by one person.

source document A paper prepared as evidence that a transaction occurred.

special endorsement A check endorsement that transfers ownership of the check to a specific individual or business.

special journals Journals that have amount columns for recording debits and credits to specific general ledger accounts.

specific identification method An inventory costing method in which the exact cost of each item in inventory is determined and assigned; used most often by businesses that have a low unit volume of merchandise with high unit prices.

State Unemployment Tax Act (SUTA) Law that requires employers to pay unemployment taxes to individual states.

statement of cash flows A financial statement that summarizes the cash receipts and cash payments resulting from business activities during a period.

statement of changes in owner's equity A financial statement that summarizes changes in the owner's capital account as a result of business transactions during the period.

statement of changes in partners' equity A financial statement that reports the change in each partner's capital account resulting from business operations, investments, and withdrawals.

statement of retained earnings A financial statement that reports the changes in the **Retained Earnings** account during the period.

statement of stockholders' equity A financial statement that reports the changes that have taken place in all of the stockholders' equity accounts during the period.

stockholders' equity The value of the stockholders' claims to the corporation.

stop payment order A demand by the drawer, usually in writing, that the bank not honor a specific check.

straight-line depreciation A method that equally distributes the depreciation expense over an asset's estimated useful life.

subsidiary ledger A ledger with detailed data that is summarized in a controlling account in the general ledger.

T

T account A visual representation of a ledger account. The T account is a tool used to analyze transactions.

taxable income The amount of income that is taxed on a federal income tax return.

temporary accounts Accounts used to collect information that will be transferred to a permanent capital account at the end of the accounting period (for example, revenue, expense, and the owner's withdrawals account).

term The length of time the borrower has to repay a promissory note.

tickler file A file that contains a folder for each day of the month into which invoices are placed according to their due dates.

time card A record of the time an employee arrives at work, leaves work, and the total number of hours worked each day.

transposition error Error that occurs when two digits within an amount are accidentally reversed, or transposed.

trial balance A list of all the general ledger account names and balances; it is prepared to prove the ledger.

U

uncollectible account An account receivable that the business cannot collect; also called a *bad debt*.

unearned revenue Revenue that is received before it is actually earned.

unemployment taxes Taxes collected to provide funds for workers who are temporarily out of work; usually paid only by the employer (FUTA and SUTA).

V

values The principles a person lives by and the beliefs that are important to the person.

vertical analysis A method of analysis that expresses financial statement items as percentages of a base amount.

voiding a check Making a check unusable by writing the word *Void* in ink across the front of the check.

voluntary compliance The principle that all taxpayers are responsible for filing their tax returns accurately and on time.

W

wage An amount of money paid to an employee at a specified rate per hour worked.

weighted average cost method An inventory costing method in which all purchases of an item are added to the beginning inventory of that item; the total cost is then divided by the total units to obtain the average cost per unit.

wholesaler A business that sells to retailers.

withdrawal The removal of cash or another asset from the business by the owner for personal use.

withholding allowance An allowance an individual claims on a Form W-4; it is used to calculate the amount of income tax withheld from an employee's paycheck.

work sheet A working paper used to collect information from the ledger accounts for use in completing end-of-period activities.

working capital The amount by which current assets exceed current liabilities.

Index

Index

Real-World Applications and Connections

Real-World Applications and Connections

Real-World Applications and Connections

Real-World Applications and Connections

Real-World Applications and Connections

Cover photography by: Royalty-free/CORBIS **CV(tr)**; Jordan Miller Photography **CV(center)**; Winfried Wisniewski/Age Fotostock **CV(b)**; Ariel Skelley/CORBIS **CV(br)**.

Phil Banko/Getty Images **142**; Paul Barton/CORBIS **55, 828–829(b)**; Peter Beck/ CORBIS **35**; Bettman/CORBIS **x, 162**; Robert Brenner/PhotoEdit **31(tl)**; Keith Brofsky/ Photodisc Blue/Getty Images **500**; Frak Chmura/ImageState **770**; Ralph A. Clevenger/ CORBIS **555(br)**; CoverSpot/Alamy Images **x, 194**; Francisco Cruz/SuperStock **92**; Kayte M. Deioma/PhotoEdit **xii, 276**; Doris DeWitt/Getty Images **481**; Steve Dunwell/Index Stock **26**; Gary Edwards/Zefa/Getty Images **798**; Macduff Everton/CORBIS **94**; Chris Farina/CORBIS **49**; Najlah Feanny/CORBIS **751**; Jon Feingersh/Masterfile **785**; Sandy Felsenthal/CORBIS **xv, 480**; Fisher/Thatcher/Getty Images **219**; Tom Fox/Dallas Morning News/CORBIS **103**; Graham French/Masterfile **6**; Bob Gelberg/Masterfile **658**; Getty Images **xvi, xix, 550, 750**; Kim Gloding/Getty Images **382**; Rick Gomez/Masterfile **339**; Spencer Grant/PhotoEdit **645**; Jeff Greenberg/PhotoEdit **7,18(c), 347**; Charles Gupton/CORBIS **120, 842**; R.W. Hapke/ CORBIS **140**; Walter Hodges/CORBIS **782–783, 831**; Image Source/SuperStock **617**; Sean Justice/Photonica/Getty Images **742**; Wolfgang Kaehler/CORBIS **778**; Zigy Kaluzny/Getty Images **40**; Bonnie Kamin/PhotoEdit **641**; Ray Katchatorian/Stocn/Getty Images **708**; Ronnie Kaufman/CORBIS **587**; Michael Keller/CORBIS **236**; Shuji Kobayashi/Getty Images **34**; Kim Kulish/CORBIS **ix, 130, 131**; Owaki-Kulla/CORBIS **30(tl)**; Javier Larrea/Age Fotostock America, Inc. **434, 506**; Boden/Ledingham/Masterfile **30(tr)**; Stephen Lengnick/Plum Street Studio **669**; Rob Lewine/CORBIS **317(br)**; R. Ian Loyd/Masterfile **731**; Dennis MacDonald/ Age Fotostock **66**; Tim Mantoani/Masterfile **2–3, 808**; Simon Marcus/CORBIS **xv, 516, 517**; Stephanie Maze/CORBIS **697**; Tom & Dee Ann McCarthy/CORBIS **163**; Jordan Miller Photography **638–639**; Zoran Milich/Masterfile **18(t)**; Warren Morgan/CORBIS **793**; MTPA Stock/Masterfile **317(tr)**; David Muir/Masterfile **31(tr)**; Michael Newman/PhotoEdit **112, 559, 807**; Andrew Olney/Masterfile **18(b)**; Scott Olsen/Getty Images **482**; Gregory Pace/ CORBIS **viii, 48**; Panda Express **77**; Jose Louis Pelaez, Inc./CORBIS **415, 472**; Courtesy of Petsmart **A-42, A-43, A-45**; Photographer's Choice/Getty Images **192**; Photonica **379**; PM Images/Getty Images **14**; Posing Productions/Photonica **727**; John Prince/ImageState **833**; Alec Pytlowany/Masterfile **818**; Jose Fuste Raga/Zefta/CORBIS **555(tr)**; Patrick Ramsey/ ImageState **630**; Roger Ressmeyer/CORBIS **375, 449**; Reuters/CORBIS **438**; Jon Riley/Getty Images **320**; Rommel/Masterfile **688**; Royalty-free/BananaStock/Alamy Images **304**; Royalty-free/BananaStock/Imagestate **582**; Royalty-free/Blue Moon Stock/Alamy Images **240**; Royalty-free/Brand X Pictures/Getty Images **210**; Royalty Free/CORBIS(Royalty-free) **xiii, 46–47, 51, 134, 139, 146, 149, 277, 306–307, 313, 364, 378, 625, 703, 826(b)**; Royalty-free/Digital Vision/Getty Images **309, 520, 552**; Royalty-Free/Getty Images(Royalty-free) **xii, 308, 759**; Royalty-free/Image Source/CORBIS **132**; Royalty-free/Image Source/SuperStock **551**; Royalty-free/iStockphoto **144**; Royalty-Free/Masterfile **376-377**; Royalty-free/Photodisc/Getty Images **286, 540**; Royalty-free/PictureArts/CORBIS **17**; Royalty-free/SuperStock **574**; Alan Schein Photography/CORBIS **671**; Michael Segal/SuperStock **xi, 248, 249**; Juan Manuel Silva/Age Fotostock America Inc. **168**; Ariel Skelley/CORBIS **781, 826(tr)**; Adam Smith/Getty Images **152**; Lee Snider/Photo Images/CORBIS **372**; Justin Sullivan/Getty Images **xviii, 612**; SuperStock, Inc./SuperStock **179**; Mario Tama/Getty Images **195**; LWA-Dann Tardif/CORBIS **266**; Anton Vengo/SuperStock **649**; Paul Viant/Getty Images **404**; Karl Wheatherly/CORBIS **321**; David Williams/Alamy Images **232**; Winfried Wisniewski/Age Fotostock America Inc. **5**; David Young-Wolff/PhotoEdit **20, 613**; Kwame Zikomo/SuperStock **418, 604**.

Glencoe's
Business Transaction Analysis Model

Business Transaction

On October 1 Maria Sanchez took $25,000 from personal savings and deposited that amount to open a business checking account in the name of Roadrunner Delivery Service, Memorandum 1.

ANALYSIS

Identify

1. The accounts **Cash in Bank** and **Maria Sanchez, Capital** are affected.

Classify

2. **Cash in Bank** is an asset account. **Maria Sanchez, Capital** is an owner's capital account.

+/−

3. **Cash in Bank** is increased by $25,000. **Maria Sanchez, Capital** is increased by $25,000.

DEBIT-CREDIT RULE

4. Increases in asset accounts are recorded as debits. Debit **Cash in Bank** for $25,000.
5. Increases in the owner's capital account are recorded as credits. Credit **Maria Sanchez, Capital** for $25,000.

T ACCOUNTS

6.

Cash in Bank		Maria Sanchez, Capital	
Debit + 25,000	Credit −	Debit −	Credit + 25,000

JOURNAL ENTRY

7.

GENERAL JOURNAL   PAGE ___1___

	DATE		DESCRIPTION	POST. REF.	DEBIT	CREDIT	
1	20--						1
2	Oct.	1	Cash in Bank		25 000 00		2
3			Maria Sanchez, Capital			25 000 00	3
4			Memorandum 1				4
5							5